Managerial Finance

J Fred Weston
Professor of Managerial Economics and Finance
University of California, Los Angeles

Eugene F Brigham
Professor of Finance
University of Florida

Managerial Finance

First British edition adapted from the sixth American edition by

John Boyle
Senior Lecturer in Finance
Polytechnic of the South Bank, London

Robin J Limmack
Lecturer in Accountancy and Finance
University of Stirling

Holt, Rinehart and Winston

London · New York · Sydney · Toronto

Holt, Rinehart and Winston Ltd: 1 St Anne's Road
Eastbourne, East Sussex BN21 3UN

Typeset in India by the Macmillan Company of India Ltd.
Printed in Great Britain by J W Arrowsmith Ltd, Bristol.

This edition is an adaptation of *Managerial Finance*, Sixth Edition, © 1978 The Dryden Press, a division of Holt, Rinehart and Winston, New York.

ISBN 0–03–910197–5

Last digit is print number: 9 8 7 6 5 4 3 2

Preface

In the United Kingdom in recent years, academics and business practitioners alike have shown a growing awareness of the importance of the study of managerial finance. The major accountancy bodies have reflected this awareness by including the study of finance in their examination schemes. Additionally, an increasing number of universities and polytechnics have introduced courses, at the undergraduate, postgraduate and post-experience levels, which involve the study of finance. The popularity of courses such as the Certified Diploma in Accounting and Finance is evidence of the demand for this by business practitioners.

We have been engaged for several years in the teaching of finance on various courses and have become increasingly concerned by the scarcity of comprehensive textbooks which include a study of the theoretical concepts of finance within the framework of the United Kingdom financial environment. While there have been some excellent textbooks produced for this subject, very few have related specifically to the United Kingdom or have taken students from a study of the basic concepts of finance through to the major recent developments.

In creating this British version of *Managerial Finance* we have attempted to fulfil the need for such a text by appropriately adapting a highly successful and well-proven United States book. Thus we have made maximum use of the vast academic and business experience embodied in the sixth edition of *Managerial Finance* but have reset it in the context of the United Kingdom environment. Wherever possible, original material has been retained although chapters relating to the institutional framework and sources of finance have been completely rewritten, as have several end-of-chapter problems. References have been supplemented by more recent British publications, and terminology has been revised in an attempt to overcome the traditional reluctance of British students to use textbooks with American terminology. The major areas of change can be summarized as follows:

1. We have up-dated all material that may change over time and wherever possible we have used British rather than American examples.
2. Chapters 2 to 5 have been recast to conform with British practices of financial reporting. An appendix which examines limitations of financial statements in an inflationary environment has been added to Chapter 2.

3. Chapter 6 has been revised to take account of the special features of the market for short-term funds in Britain. These special features have influenced the approach to current asset management dealt with in Chapter 7. The sources of short-term funds for British industry have been outlined in Chapter 8 with particular reference to bank finance, trade credit and bills of exchange.
4. Chapters 12, 13 and 14 have been completely rewritten to take account of the British financial environment. At the same time, the new material has been added with the intention of retaining the spirit and, wherever possible, the form of the original. Problems and questions relevant to British experience have been added to these chapters.
5. The Appendix to Chapter 16 on the Option Pricing Model has been up-dated to include developments in the recently opened traded options market in London.
6. Chapter 21 has been extensively revised to incorporate the relationship between long-term and short-term interest rates which operate in the London market. The implications of these relationships for investment timing have been discussed.
7. The chapters on mergers, reconstructions and small businesses have been revised and new material, appropriate to Britain, has been added.

Treatment of some topics has had to be kept to a minimum in order to maintain the philosophy of the original text. For example, Appendix A to Chapter 2 has been included to make students aware of the limitations of financial statements for analytical purposes, and not to provide a detailed study of the problems of accounting for inflation. In one case – Chapter 24 – no alteration has been made to the subject matter of the chapter, because by its very nature it has an international flavour.

We believe that this textbook offers sufficient flexibility to form the foundation for courses in finance at various levels. The book may be used as a first course in finance at the undergraduate and professional levels by omitting selected chapters and appendices. More advanced courses would include the more advanced chapters, together with various appendices and cases, supplemented by journal articles.

In our work of adaptation we benefited enormously from constructive criticism from a number of sources. In particular we should like to thank for their help the following: A. F. Fox (Stirling), A. J. Mason (London), H. Lipman (London), Dr D. Garbutt (Dundee), A. V. Pizzey (Nottingham), Dr R. Spencer (London), S. J. Curry (Birmingham) and R. H. Berry (Coventry).

We would also like to express our appreciation to all of the Holt, Rinehart and Winston editorial staff, and in particular David Inglis and Patricia Terry, for their discipline in keeping us to deadlines and ensuring a timely publication.

Polytechnic of the South Bank — John Boyle
University of Stirling — Robin J. Limmack
1979

Preface to Sixth American Edition

Financial management has undergone many changes in recent years. Strong inflationary pressures have pushed interest rates to unprecedented heights, and the resulting high cost of capital has led to profound changes in corporate financial policies and practices. Academic researchers have made significant advances, especially in the areas of capital budgeting and the cost of capital. At the same time, business practitioners are making increasing use of financial theory, and feedback from the 'real world' has led to revisions in financial theory. To a large extent, these trends dictated the revisions made in this Sixth Edition of *Managerial Finance*.

The changes in the Sixth Edition of *Managerial Finance* continue the basic philosophy of previous editions. This is to provide users with coverage of all important areas of managerial finance and financial management, while providing flexibility in the use of the materials. At present, the major theoretical chapters on the cost of capital and valuation are near the end of the book in order to work up to the most difficult material as an increasing challenge to the reader. However, some users tell us they start with these chapters so they can use the concepts in their treatment of the materials in the earlier chapters. Different sequencing patterns have been reported by other professors. Still others use different combinations of the materials in the first, second or subsequent courses in a finance sequence. Since faculty, students and curriculum needs and personalities vary among different schools, we believe this flexibility is an important strength of *Managerial Finance* – and it is no accident; we have planned for it.

This flexibility objective has guided the placement of some new materials in the Sixth Edition. Three important recent developments in finance are the Capital Asset Pricing Model (CAPM), the Options Pricing Model (OPM) and the State-Preference Model (SPM). The Capital Asset Pricing Model is discussed in Appendix D to Chapter 11 and in Appendix C to Chapter 19. The Option Pricing Model has been set forth in Appendix A to Chapter 16. We utilize the State-Preference Model to provide a wrap-up of the discussion of financial leverage in Appendix D to Chapter 19. These and other materials continue the up-to-date coverage of *Managerial Finance* while providing flexibility in the sequence and in the courses in which the topics are treated.

In addition to containing new materials, the revision reflects our experience, and that of others, in teaching business finance. Organizational changes have been made to provide for smoother flow and greater continuity; points that proved troublesome to students have been clarified; a few outright errors have been corrected; and, of course, descriptive materials have been updated. Moreover, the end-of-chapter questions, problems, and references have been clarified and strengthened.

Much of the specific content of the book is the result of our experience in executive development programs over a number of years. This experience, in addition to our consulting with business firms on financial problems and policies, has helped us to identify the most significant responsibilities of financial managers, the most fundamental problems facing firms, and the most feasible approaches to practical decision-making. Some topics are conceptually difficult, but so are the issues faced by financial managers. Business managers must be prepared to handle complex problems, and finding solutions to these problems necessarily involves the use of advanced tools and techniques.

We have not sought to avoid the many unresolved areas of business financial theory and practice. Although we could have simplified the text in many places by avoiding the difficult issues, we preferred to provide a basic framework based on the 'received doctrine', then to go on (often in appendixes) to present materials on a number of important but controversial issues. It is hoped that our presentation, along with the additional references provided at the end of each chapter, will stimulate the reader to further inquiry.

We acknowledge that the level and difficulty of the material is uneven. Certain sections are simply descriptions of the institutional features of the financial environment and, as such, are not difficult to understand. Other parts – notably the material on capital budgeting, uncertainty, and the cost of capital – are by nature rather abstract, and, as such, are difficult for those not used to thinking in abstract terms. In some of the more complex sections, we have simply outlined procedures in the main body of the text, then justified the procedures in the chapter appendixes.

The appendixes permit great flexibility in the use of *Managerial Finance*. The book can be used in a basic course by omitting selected appendix topics. If instructors wish to cover selected topics from the appendixes, they may do so, and the more interested or mature student may also choose to select appendix topics for independent study. Alternatively, the book may be used in a two-semester course, supplemented, as the instructor sees fit, with outside readings or cases, or both. At both UCLA and Florida we use the basic chapters plus a very few appendixes in the introductory course, then cover selected appendixes plus cases and some articles in the advanced course. In fact, some of the appendixes were written specifically to help bridge the gap between basic texts and journal literature.

Changes in the sixth edition

The Sixth Edition of *Managerial Finance* differs from the Fifth in several key respects.

1. We have updated all materials that have a time aspect.
2. A listing of 'Frequently Used Symbols' in *Managerial Finance* has been developed which relates and makes consistent all symbols used in the capital budgeting, cost of capital, uncertainty, valuation and other basic conceptual themes that run through the book. The symbols used seek to reflect the widest usage found in the journal literature. This has a number of advantages. The reader has the assurance that on the central conceptual materials one set of symbols is consistently used. Furthermore, this will help the reader increase his familiarity with the symbols used in the general literature. It will thereby facilitate the access of the reader to the journal literature. Another benefit of the list of 'Frequently Used Symbols' is that it provides a perspective which allows some simplification and reduction in the number of symbols employed in *Managerial Finance*.

3. Chapter 1 has been rewritten to focus more directly and fully on the nature of the finance function and to discuss the goals of the firm in a broader perspective.
4. We have added an appendix to Chapter 2 to discuss accounting under inflation and its implications for financial ratio analysis.
5. We have added a section to Chapter 10 for comparing mutually exclusive projects with unequal lives.
6. An appendix has been developed for Chapter 10, utilizing the Capital Asset Pricing Model for measuring the required risk adjusted return for new investment projects.
7. Another appendix to Chapter 10 describes the adjustments required for capital budgeting under inflation.
8. The section on leasing has been reworked to reflect the important development in the recent new articles on the subject.
9. Chapter 17 uses the market price of risk relationships to show how the risk premium in the returns to investments and to securities can be measured.
10. The new and complex formulas for option pricing are shown to use a combination of materials already covered in *Managerial Finance*; simple, clear applications of the Black and Scholes formulas are made to pricing options as well as to other corporate securities. This is placed as an appendix to Chapter 16.
11. Some recent work on state-preference theory is applied in discussing the determination of optimal financial leverage. Again the material is presented in clear, easy-to-follow examples, and its use in a managerial finance decision-framework is demonstrated in an appendix to Chapter 19.
12. Capital investment decisions are explicitly integrated with the valuation of the firm.
13. The materials on capital budgeting are further developed and clarified.
14. A correct conceptualization of multi-period stock valuation models is presented in Chapter 17.
15. New institutional materials are added to continue up-to-date coverage related to real world developments.
16. We have added new problems to round out the coverage of concepts as well as to provide appropriate emphasis to areas of central importance.

Several reviewers suggested that it might be desirable to reduce the total length of the book. The idea was appealing, but we did not follow their suggestion for several reasons. We want the book to cover the entire field of business finance and to deal with all the functions of the financial manager. Eliminating institutional material and concentrating on theory and technique would give the student an unrealistic, sterile view of finance. Some of the more advanced theory and techniques could have been eliminated on the ground that they probably would not be covered in basic courses, but it is useful to show where this material fits into the scheme of things and to provide the student with a bridge to the journal literature. Finally, our verbosity results, to a large extent, from a deliberate addition of statements, examples, and other materials to clarify points that our students have found difficult; eliminating these would have reduced the clarity of the book. These factors, *together with the fact that the book is structured so that instructors do not have to assign all the material*, caused us to forego a marked reduction in the book's length.

Ancillary materials

Several items are available to supplement *Managerial Finance*. First, there are two casebooks, *Cases in Managerial Finance*, 3rd Edition, and *Decisions in Financial Management: Cases*, by Eugene F. Brigham et al. Second, there are a number of readings books which can be used to supplement the text. One book in particular, *Issues in Managerial Finance*, edited by E. F. Brigham and R. E. Johnson, is a useful supplement to *Managerial Finance*. Finally, many students will find the *Study Guide* useful. The *Study*

Guide highlights the key points in the text and presents a comprehensive set of problems similar to those at the end of each chapter. Each problem is solved in detail, so a student who has difficulty working the end-of-chapter problems can be aided by reviewing the *Study Guide*.

Acknowledgments

In its several revisions, the book has been worked on and critically reviewed by numerous individuals, and we have received many detailed comments and suggestions from instructors (and students) using the book in our own schools and elsewhere. All this help has improved the quality of the book, and we are deeply indebted to the following individuals, and others, for their help: M. Adler, E. Altman, J. Andrews, R. Aubey, P. Bacon, W. Beranek, V. Brewer, W. Brueggeman, R. Carleson, S. Choudhury, P. Cooley, C. Cox, D. Fischer, R. Gray, J. Griggs, R. Haugen, S. Hawk, R. Hehre, J. Henry, A. Herrmann, G. Hettenhouse, R. Himes, C. Johnson, R. Jones, D. Kaplan, M. Kaufman, D. Knight, H. Krogh, R. LeClair, W. Lee, D. Longmore, J. Longstreet, H. Magee, P. Malone, R. Moore, T. Morton, T. Nantell, R. Nelson, R. Norgaard, J. Pappas, R. Pettit, R. Pettway, J. Pinkerton, G. Pogue, W. Regan, F. Reilly, R. Rentz, R. Richards, C. Rini, R. Roenfeldt, W. Sharpe, K. Smith, P. Smith, R. Smith, D. Sorenson, M. Tysseland, P. Vanderheiden, D. Woods, J. Yeakel, and D. Ziegenbein for their careful reviews of this and previous editions.

We owe special thanks to V. Apilado, J. Dran, M. Ertell, G. Laber, G. Hettenhouse, J. Longstreet, R. Melicher, and G. Pinches for providing us with detailed reviews of the manuscript of this edition. Particularly helpful in the present revision was the assistance of L. Dann, H. DeAngelo, J. Kiholm, M. McElroy, P. Scharf, and I. Woodward. We would like to thank C. Barngrover, S. Manshinghka, W. Eckardt, H. Rollins, H. Alwan, D. Wort, and J. Zumwalt for their assistance in helping us to develop the acetate program; we would also like to express our appreciation to Bob LeClair and to The American College for their help in preparing the transparencies, available from The Dryden Press. (Note to instructors: a set of additional problems with solutions developed with the assistance of Professors Roger Bey, Keith Johnson and Ramon Johnson will be made available to adoptors by The Dryden Press.)

The Universities of California and Florida, and our colleagues on these campuses, provided us with intellectual support in bringing the book to completion. Finally, we are indebted to the Dryden Press staff – principally Garret White, Paul R. Jones, Jo-Anne Naples, and Ray Ashton – for their special efforts in getting the manuscript into production and for following through to the bound book.

The field of finance will continue to experience significant changes. It is stimulating to participate in these exciting developments, and we sincerely hope that *Managerial Finance* will contribute to a better understanding of the theory and practice of finance.

Los Angeles, California
Gainesville, Florida
December 1977

J. Fred Weston
Eugene F. Brigham

Contents

PART 1

OVERVIEW OF FINANCE: ANALYSIS, PLANNING AND CONTROL

Part 1 consists of five chapters. The first describes the scope and nature of managerial finance and serves as an introduction to the book. In Chapter 2 we examine the construction and use of the basic ratios of financial analysis; through ratio analysis, the firm's strengths and weaknesses can be pinpointed. Chapter 3 explains two key tools used in financial planning: break-even analysis and the sources and uses of funds statement. In Chapter 4 we take up financial forecasting: given a projected increase in sales, how much money must the financial manager raise to support this level of sales? Finally, in Chapter 5, we consider the budget system through which management controls and coordinates the firm.

Finance deals, in the main, with very specific questions: Should we lease or buy the new machine? Should we expand capacity at the Hartford plant? Should we raise capital this year by long-term or short-term debt or by selling shares? Should we go along with the marketing department, which wants to expand stocks, or with the production department, which wants to reduce them? Specific questions such as these, which are typical of the types of decisions facing the financial manager, are considered in the remainder of the book. But here in Part 1 we take an *overview* of the firm. Because all specific decisions are made within the context of the firm's overall position, this overview is critical to an understanding of any specific proposal.

Chapter 1

Scope and Nature of Managerial Finance

What is managerial finance? What is the finance function in the firm? What specific tasks are assigned to the financial manager? What tools and techniques are available to him, and how does one go about measuring his performance? On a broader scale, what is the role of finance in the British economy, and how can managerial finance be used to further national goals? Providing at least tentative answers to these questions is the principal purpose of this book.

THE FINANCE FUNCTION

Financial management is defined by the functions and areas of responsibilities of financial managers. While the specifics vary among individual organizations, some finance tasks are basic. Funds are raised from external financial sources. Funds are allocated among different uses. The flows of funds involved in the operations of the enterprise are managed. Benefits are returned to sources of financing in the form of returns, repayments or products and services. These key financial functions must be performed in any organization whether it be a large company such as Courtaulds, a nationalized industry, a charity such as Shelter, or even a local amateur dramatic society.

In Figure 1–1, the functions of financial managers are shown to link the financing of an organization to its financing sources via the financial markets. The major parts of Figure 1–1 will be explained in the remaining sections of this discussion of the finance function. Funds for conducting the operations of organizations are obtained from a wide range of financial institutions. The funds are obtained in the form of debentures, ordinary shares, etc. The financial manager has primary responsibilities for acquiring funds and participates in the allocation of the funds among alternative projects and to specific forms such as stocks, plant, and equipment. The cash flow cycle must be managed. Payments are made for labour, materials, and capital goods purchased from the external markets. Products and services are created which generate fund inflows. In managing cash inflows and cash outflows, some cash is recycled and some returned to financing sources.

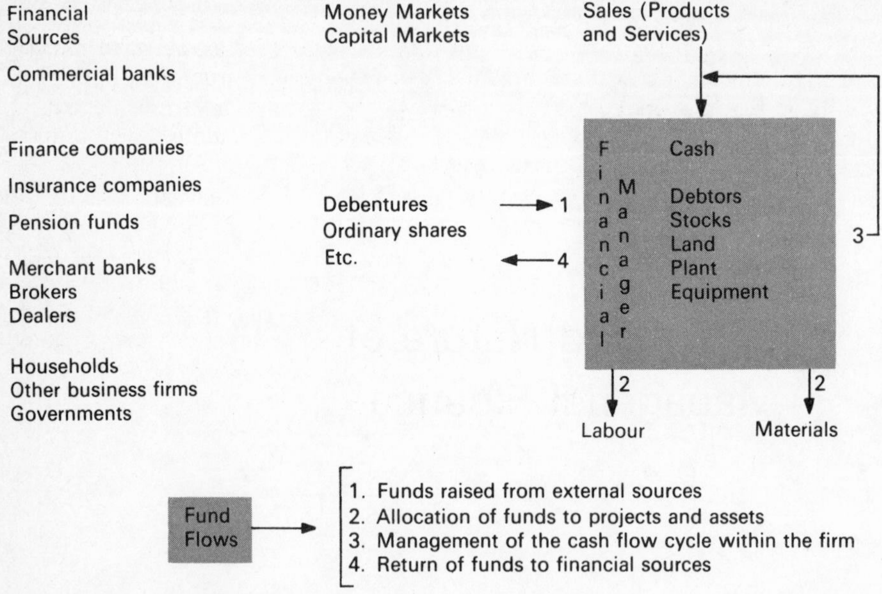

Figure 1–1 *Financial Markets, the Financial Manager, and the Firm.*

Financial markets

The financial manager functions in a complex financial network because the savings and investment functions in a modern economy are performed by different economic agents. For savings surplus units, savings exceed their investment in real assets and they own financial assets. For savings deficit units, current savings are less than investment in real assets so they issue financial liabilities. The savings deficit units issue a wide variety of financial claims such as promissory notes, debentures and ordinary shares.

The transfer of funds from a savings surplus unit or the acquisition of funds by a savings deficit unit involves the creation of a financial asset *and* a financial liability. For example, when a person places funds in a savings account in a bank or building society, his deposit represents a financial asset in his personal balance sheet along with real assets such as a motor car or household goods. The savings deposit is a liability account of the financial institution and represents a financial liability. When the funds are loaned to aid another person in the purchase of a home, for example, the loan by the building society represents a financial asset on its balance sheet. The borrower has incurred a financial liability represented by the loan owed to the financial institution. Consider another example. When a person buys goods on credit from a department store, this adds to 'trade debtors' on the books of the department store. The amounts payable by the person who has purchased goods on credit represent a financial liability that he has incurred.

A financial transaction results in the creation simultaneously of a financial asset and a financial liability. The creation and transfer of financial assets and financial liabilities constitute *financial markets*. The nature of financial markets can be further analysed by analogy to an actual market such as the market for motor cars. The motor car market is defined by all transactions in motor cars. Some cars are bought at a dealer's showroom, some at motor car auctions and some by private deals as a result of advertisements in local newspapers. These constitute the motor car market because all the transactions make up a part of the total demand and supply curves for motor cars.

Similarly, financial markets are comprised of all trades that result in the creation of financial assets and financial liabilities. Some trades may be made through organized institutions such as the London Stock Exchange or various provincial stock exchanges. Our own individual transactions with department stores, savings banks, or other financial institutions also create financial assets and financial liabilities as we have illustrated above. Thus financial markets are not just specific physical structures, nor are they remote – all of us are involved in them in one way or another in various degrees.

Continuing the motor car analogy, just as a distinction is made between a new car market and a used car market because somewhat different demand and supply influences are operating in each segment, different segments of the financial markets have been placed into categories and given names. When the financial claims and financial obligations bought and sold have a maturity of less than one year, such transactions constitute *money markets*. When the maturities of the instruments traded are more than one year, the markets are referred to as *capital markets*. The latter term is somewhat confusing because real capital in an economy is represented by such things as plant, machinery, and equipment. But long-term financial instruments are regarded as ultimately representing claims on the real resources in an economy and for that reason the markets in which long-term financial instruments are traded are referred to as capital markets.

Financial sources and financial intermediation

The financial markets, composed of money markets and capital markets, provide a mechanism through which the financial manager obtains funds from a wide range of financing sources. The nature of each of these financing sources is now briefly described.

Commercial banks offer both current and deposit account facilities to their customers. It is this ability to offer cheque facilities to their customers that distinguishes them from other financial institutions. These cheques represent a widely accepted medium of exchange and account for a large part of all financial transactions. Building societies receive funds from depositors and use these funds to lend to other individuals who wish to buy property. Finance houses make loans to firms and private individuals through the medium of hire-purchase agreements. Life insurance companies sell protection against the loss of income from premature death or disability. The insurance policies they sell typically have a savings element in them. Pension funds collect contributions from employees and or employers to make periodic payments on the employees' retirement. Investment and unit trusts sell shares or units to investors and use the proceeds to purchase already existing ordinary shares.

Merchant banks are responsible for issuing new shares to the public. Sometimes they act as agents for issuing these shares (e.g. public issue by prospectus) and at other times they buy shares from companies and then re-issue them to the public. Stockbrokers act as agents to link prospective buyers and sellers of shares. They use the jobbing mechanism of the Stock Exchange to carry out this function. These deals which involve the transfer of shares take place either within the new issue market or, in the case of the transfer of secondhand shares, within the stock market.

Finally, on the left hand side of Figure1 – 1, other sources of funds are households, other business firms, and governments. At any point in time some of these will be borrowers and others will be lenders.

Financial intermediation is accomplished through the transactions in the financial markets, which bring the savings surplus units together with the savings deficit units so that savings can be redistributed into their most productive uses. The specialized business firms whose activities include the creation of financial assets and financial liabilities are called financial intermediaries. Without financial intermediaries and the processes of financial intermediation described above, the allocation of savings into real investment would be limited by whatever the distribution of savings happened to be. With financial intermediation, savings are transferred to economic units that have opportunities for profitable investment of the savings. In the process real resources are allocated more effectively and real output for the economy as a whole is increased.

Financial managers have important responsibilities in the financial intermediation process described. They are part of the process by which funds are allocated to their most productive uses.

We can, therefore, now re-state the functions of financial managers in the perspective of this broader social framework. In the aggregate, business firms are savings deficit units that obtain funds to make investments to increase the supply of goods and services. Financial managers utilize financial markets to obtain external funds. How shall the funds be acquired efficiently? What is the most economical mix of financing to be obtained? From what alternative sources and in what specific forms should the funds be raised? What should be the timing and forms of returns and repayments to financing sources?

Since funds are acquired as a part of the process by which resources are allocated to their most productive uses, financial managers have responsibilities for the effective use of funds. To what projects and products should the funds be allocated? What assets and resources should the organization acquire in order to produce its products and services? What standards and controls should be employed to monitor the effective utilization of funds allocated among the segments of operating activities? How should the planning and control of funds be managed so that the organization will produce and sell its products and services most efficiently?

In summary, the main functions of financial managers are to plan for, acquire, and utilize funds to make the maximum contribution to the efficient operation of an organization. This requires knowledge of the financial markets from which funds are drawn. It requires a knowledge of how to make sound investment decisions and to stimulate efficient operations in the organization. A large number of alternative sources and uses of funds will have to be considered. There are always alternative choices involved in financial decisions. The choices include the use of internal versus external funds, long-term projects versus short-term projects, long-term fund sources versus short-term fund sources, a higher rate of growth versus a lower rate of growth, etc.

Up to this point, much of our discussion of the finance function applies to all types of organizations. What is unique about business organizations is that they are directly and measurably subject to the discipline of the financial markets. The financial markets are continuously making determinations of the valuations of the securities of business firms, which provide measures of the performance of business firms.[1] As a consequence of the continuous reassessment of the managerial performance of business firms by the capital markets, the relative valuation levels of business firms will change. Changes in valuations signal changes in performance. Valuations, therefore, provide a stimulus to the efficiency of business firms and provide incentives to business managers to improve their performance. It is difficult to formulate tests of the efficiency and performance of organizations other than business firms because of the lack of financial markets for continuously placing valuations on these other organizations and thereby providing a continuous assessment of their performance. This leads to a consideration of financial goals.

1. The financial markets provide continuous valuations of firms whose shares are traded. The relationships established between returns and risk provide the basis for the valuation as well of private companies.

GOALS OF THE FIRM

It is in the context of the valuation processes of the financial markets in evaluating business firms that the objectives of financial management have been formulated. The goal of financial management is to maximize shareholder wealth. By formulating the firm's objectives in terms of the shareholder's interest, the discipline of the financial markets is implemented. This means that firms with better performance will have higher share prices. Additional funds can be raised under more favourable terms. If funds go to firms with favourable share price trends, the economy's resources are being directed to their efficient allocation and use. Hence, throughout this book we operate on the assumption that management's primary goal is to maximize the wealth of its shareholders.

Just how good is this assumption – does management really try to maximize shareholder wealth, or is it equally interested in profits, in sales, in survival, in the personal satisfaction of the managers themselves, in employees' welfare, or in the good of the community and society at large? Further, does management really try to *maximize*? Or does it 'satisfice'; that is, does it seek satisfactory rather than optimal results?

Profit versus wealth maximization

Let us consider the question of profits versus wealth. Suppose management is interested primarily in shareholders, making its decisions so as to maximize their welfare. Will profit maximization be best for shareholders?

Total profits

In answering this question, we must consider first the matter of total corporate profits versus earnings per share. Suppose a firm raises capital by selling shares and then invests the proceeds in government stock. Total profits will rise, but more shares will be outstanding. Earnings per share would probably decline, pulling down the value of each share and, hence, the existing shareholders' wealth. Thus, to the extent that profits are important, management should concentrate on earnings per share rather than on total corporate profits.

Earnings per share

Will maximization of earnings per share maximize shareholder welfare, or should other factors be considered? Consider the timing of the earnings. Suppose one project will cause earnings per share to rise by 20 pence per year for five years, or £1.00 in total, while another project has no effect on earnings for four years but increases earnings by £1.25 in the fifth year. Which project is better? The answer depends upon which project adds the most to the value of the shares, and this in turn depends upon the time value of money to investors. In any event, timing is an important reason to concentrate upon wealth as measured by the price of the shares rather than upon earnings alone.

Risk

Still another issue relates to risk. Suppose one project is expected to increase earnings per share by £1.00, while another is expected to raise earnings by £1.20 per share. The first project is not very risky; if it is undertaken, earnings will almost certainly rise by about £1.00 per share. The other project is quite risky, so while our best guess is that earnings will rise by £1.20 per share, we must recognize the possibility that there may be no increase whatever. Depending upon how averse shareholders are to risk, the first project may be preferable to the second.

Recognizing all those factors, managers interested in maximizing shareholder welfare seek to maximize the value of the firm's ordinary shares. The price of the shares reflects the market's evaluation of the firm's prospective earnings stream over time, the riskiness of this stream, and a host of other factors. The higher the price of the shares, the better is management's performance from the standpoint of the shareholders; thus, market price provides a performance index by which management can be judged.[2]

Maximizing shareholder wealth versus other goals

In theory, shareholders own the firm and elect the management team; management, in turn, is supposed to operate in the best interests of the shareholders.

Might not managements pursue goals other than maximizing shareholder wealth? Some alternative goals are examined in this section.

Maximizing versus 'satisficing'

First, consider the question of *maximizing*, which involves seeking the best possible outcome, versus 'satisficing', which involves a willingness to settle for something less.[3] A firm that is on the brink of bankruptcy may be forced to operate as efficiently as possible. But some argue that the management of a large, well-entrenched company could work to keep shareholder returns at a fair or 'reasonable' level and then devote part of its efforts and resources to public service activities, to employee benefits, to higher management salaries, or to golf.

Similarly, an entrenched management could avoid risky ventures, even when the possible gains to shareholders are high enough to warrant taking the gamble. The theory behind that argument is that shareholders are generally well-diversified, holding portfolios of many different shares, so if one company takes a chance and loses, the shareholders lose only a small part of their wealth. Managers, on the other hand, are not diversified, so setbacks affect them more seriously. Accordingly, some argue that the managers of widely held firms tend to play it safe rather than aggressively seek to maximize the prices of their firms' shares.

It is extremely difficult to determine whether a particular management team is trying to maximize shareholder wealth or is merely attempting to satisfice on this factor while pursuing other goals. Are relatively high management salaries really necessary to attract and retain excellent managers who, in turn, will keep the firm ahead of its competition? When a risky venture is turned down, does this reflect management conservatism or a correct judgement that the risks of the venture outweigh the potential rewards?

It is impossible to give definitive answers to these questions – several studies have suggested that managers are not completely shareholder-oriented, but the evidence is

---

2. A firm's share price might, of course, decline because of factors beyond management's control. Accordingly, it is useful to look at comparative statistics; even though a firm's share price declines by ten per cent, management will have performed well if other firms in the industry decline by 20 per cent.

3. J. Fred Weston, *The Scope and Methodology of Finance* (Englewood Cliffs, N.J.: Prentice-Hall, 1966), chap. 2; Herbert A. Simon, Theories of decision making in economics and behavioral science, *American Economic Review*, June 1959, pp. 253–283.

cloudy.[4] It is true that more and more firms are tying management's compensation to the company's performance, and research suggests that this motivates management to operate in a manner consistent with share price maximization.[5] Finally, a firm operating in a competitive market, or almost any firm during an economic downswing, will be forced to undertake actions that are reasonably consistent with shareholder wealth maximization. Thus, while managers may not seek only to maximize shareholder wealth, there are reasons to view this as a dominant goal for most firms. And even though a management group may pursue other goals, shareholder wealth is bound to be of considerable importance. Often the same types of actions that could maximize wealth are also necessary to keep it at a satisfactory level; it may therefore be difficult, in practice, to determine which goal is dominant.

Maximizing wealth versus utility

In many formulations, the objective is stated in terms of utility – the satisfactions enjoyed by individuals that result in a set of preferences. But the utility patterns or utility functions of individuals vary greatly. For example, some individuals receive positive gratification from the excitement of exposure to risks; for other individuals even moderate risks may cause nervousness and even illness. Who is to determine or to interpret the risk attitudes of individual investors? What would the financial manager do if shareholders have widely divergent utility preferences?

Again the capital markets come to the rescue. Whatever the individual attitudes that may be held towards risk, the market returns in relation to various measures of risk establish that investors on the average exhibit risk aversion – the bearing of risk is considered a 'bad' rather than a 'good'. Furthermore, capital market relationships make it possible to quantify the relationships between required returns and measures of risk. From the returns-to-risks relationships methods of valuation are provided.

Thus the maximization of shareholder wealth as an objective can be made a usable or operational guide to financial decisions. But since it is utility maximization that is ultimately involved, the formal statement of the firm's objective may be expressed in the form of a utility function to be maximized. From such formal statements of the firm's objective, analytical solutions may be reached and theorems or propositions set forth. Such results may lead to development of theories that may in turn be useful for decisions by financial managers. While such theoretical formulations provide the basis for some of the concepts utilized in this book, our emphasis is on practical financial decision making. We find that the decision criteria and decision rules for financial management are more operational and usable when the analysis is formulated in terms of the objective of shareholder wealth maximization rather than utility maximization.

Social responsibility

Another viewpoint that deserves consideration is *responsibility*: should business operate strictly in shareholders' best interests, or are they also partly responsible for the welfare of

---

4. W. J. Baumol, *Business Behavior, Value, and Growth* (New York: Macmillan, 1959), argues that firms may seek to maximize sales subject to a minimum profit constraint. J. W. Elliott, Control, size, growth, and financial performance in the firm, *Journal of Financial and Quantitative Analysis*, January 1972, concludes that firms managed by the owners hold fewer liquid assets; this suggests a greater propensity to take risks. On the other hand W. G. Lewellen, in Management and ownership in the large firm, *Journal of Finance*, May 1969, concluded that top managers of large firms have most of their wealth tied to their firms' fortunes, hence they behave more like owners than earlier literature would suggest.

5. See R. T. Masson, Executive motivations, earnings, and consequent equity performance, *Journal of Political Economy*, November 1971.

society at large? This is a complex issue with no easy answers. As economic agents whose actions have considerable impact, business firms should take into account the effects of their policies and actions on society as a whole. No one and especially large firms can ignore obligations for responsible citizenship. Furthermore, it may even be good for wealth maximization in the long run to develop goodwill by being viewed as a 'good citizen' that has made substantial contributions to social welfare. Even more fundamentally, some amount of social responsibility by business firms may be required for the survival of a private enterprise system in which business firms can operate.

But many different views of what is best for society are held by different people. By what authority do businessmen have the right to allocate funds in terms of their own views of the social good? In addition, if some firms attempt to be socially responsible and their costs thereby increase substantially, they will be at a disadvantage if their competitors do not incur the same additions to costs. Because of these considerations, an argument can be made that social programmes should be formulated through the processes of representative government in our democracy. This implies that most cost-increasing programmes would be enacted by the government and put on a mandatory rather than voluntary basis, at least initially, to ensure that the burden of such action falls uniformly across all businesses. It is critical that industry and government cooperate in establishing the rules of corporate behaviour and that firms follow the spirit as well as the letter of the law in their actions. Thus, the rules of the game become constraints, and firms should strive to maximize shareholder wealth subject to these constraints. Throughout the book, we shall assume that managements operate in this manner.

CHANGING ROLE OF FINANCIAL MANAGEMENT

The development of finance as a study separate from accountancy and economics has been slower in Britain than in the United States. This is possibly because capitalism developed earlier in Britain. The industrial revolution coincided with the 'heroic' age of capitalist entrepreneurship. After the introduction of limited liability in a series of Acts between 1856 and 1862 the emphasis of the literature of the subject was on the problems of raising new finance by the issue of securities.

After the First World War business failures became more common and finance focused on areas such as bankruptcy, working capital management and the problems of company liquidity. Finance was still a descriptive, legalistic subject but the emphasis shifted to survival rather than expansion. During the 1940s and 1950s finance continued to be taught as a descriptive institutional subject viewed from the outside rather than from within a firm's management.

The developments in asset analysis which took place in the United States during the late 1950s led to an increasing awareness of the subject of finance amongst British academics. Mathematical models became more common. Increasingly the focus of finance shifted from the outsider's to the insider's point of view as financial decisions within a firm were recognized to be the critical issues in corporate finance. Descriptive, institutional materials on capital markets were still studied, but these topics were considered within the context of the internal financial decision of companies.

The emphasis on decision making has continued in recent years, with the increasing belief that sound capital budgeting procedures require accurate measurements of the cost of capital. Accordingly ways of quantifying the cost of capital now play a key role in finance. Secondly, capital has been in short supply, rekindling the old interest in ways of raising funds. Thirdly, there has been a renewed interest in merger activity with an increase in the process of conglomeration. Fourthly, accelerated progress in transportation and communications has brought the countries of the world closer together: this in turn has stimulated interest in international finance. Fifthly, inflation is now recognized as a critical problem as so much of the financial manager's time is now devoted to coping with high wages, prices and interest rates. Finally, the increasing blurring of the distinction between the private sector and the public sector has stimulated an interest in the financial problems of nationalized industries and public sector finance in general.

The impact of inflation on financial management

During the 1950s and 1960s, prices rose at an average rate of between 1 and 5 per cent per year, but in the 1970s the rate of inflation in some years has been more than 10 per cent. This 'double figure inflation' has had a tremendous impact on business firms, especially on their financial operations. As a result, many established financial policies and practices are undergoing dramatic changes, some of which are outlined below.

1. *Interest rates.* The rate of interest on British government securities (called the default-free rate) consists of a 'real rate of interest' of 1 to 3 per cent plus an 'inflation premium' that reflects the expected long-run rate of inflation. Accordingly, an increase in the rate of inflation is quickly translated into higher default-free interest rates.

   The cost of money to firms is the default-free rate plus a risk premium, so inflation-induced increases in the default-free rate are also reflected in business borrowing rates.
2. *Planning difficulties.* Businesses operate on the basis of long-run plans. For example, a firm builds a plant only after making a thorough analysis of expected costs and revenues over the life of the plant. Reaching such estimates is not easy under the best of conditions, but during rapid inflation, when labour and materials costs are changing dramatically, accurate forecasts are especially important yet exceedingly hard to make. Efforts are, of course, being made to improve forecasting techniques, and financial planning must include more flexibility to reflect the increased level of uncertainty in the economy. Incidentally, the increased uncertainty in many industries tends to raise the risk premiums for firms in those industries, driving their costs of capital still higher.
3. *Demand for capital.* Inflation increases the amount of capital required to conduct a given volume of business. When stocks are sold, they must be replaced with more expensive goods. The costs of expanding or replacing plants are also greater, while workers demand higher wages. All of these things put pressure on financial managers to raise additional capital. At the same time, in an effort to hold down the rate of inflation, the authorities tend to restrict the supply of loanable funds.[6] The ensuing scramble for limited funds drives interest rates still higher.
4. *Bond price declines.* Long-term bond prices fall as interest rates rise, so, in an effort to protect themselves against such capital losses, lenders are beginning (a) to put more funds into short-term than into long-term debt, and (b) to insist upon bonds whose interest rates vary with 'the general level of interest rates' as measured by an index of interest rates. Brazil and other inflation-plagued South American countries have used such index bonds for years. Unless inflation in Britain is controlled, their use is likely to develop in this country.
5. *Accounting problems.* With high rates of inflation, reported profits are distorted. The sale of low-cost stocks results in higher reported profits, but cash flows are held down as firms restock with higher-cost stocks. Similarly, depreciation charges are inadequate, as they do not reflect the new costs of replacing plant and equipment. If a firm is unaware of the 'shakiness' of profits that reflect stock valuation and inadequate

---

6. The 'authorities' are the Bank of England and the Treasury working in conjunction in order to operate Government economic policy.

depreciation charges, and if it plans dividends and capital expenditures on the basis of such figures, then it could develop serious financial problems.

High levels of inflation are a disturbing problem for financial managers. Although no one knows what the full impact of continued inflation will be, one thing is clear: if double figure inflation does continue, many financial policies and practices will have to be modified to meet this new situation.

Increased importance of financial management

Those evolutionary changes have greatly increased the importance of financial management. In earlier times, the marketing manager would project sales; the engineering and production staffs would determine the assets necessary to meet these demands; and the financial manager would simply raise the money necessary to purchase the plant, equipment, and stocks. This mode of operation is no longer prevalent: today decisions are made in a much more coordinated manner, with the financial manager directly responsible for the control process.

FINANCIAL DECISIONS: RISK-RETURN TRADE-OFF

Financial decisions affect the value of a firm's shares by influencing both the size of the earnings stream, or profitability, and the riskiness of the firm. These relationships are shown in Figure 1–2. Policy decisions, which are made subject to government constraints, affect both profitability and risk; these two factors jointly determine the value of the firm.

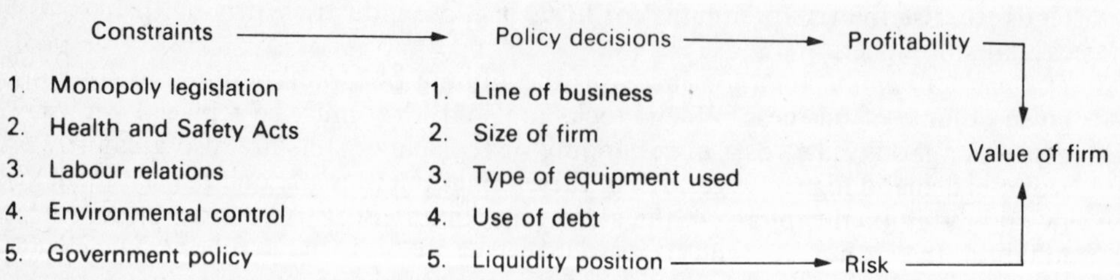

Figure 1–2 *Valuation as the Central Focus of the Finance Function.*

The primary policy decision is that of choosing the industry in which to operate – the product-market mix of the firm. When this choice has been made, both profitability and risk are determined by decisions relating to the size of the firm, the types of equipment used, the extent to which debt is employed, the firm's liquidity position, and so on. Such decisions generally affect both risk and profitability. An increase in the cash position, for instance, reduces risk; however, since cash is not an earning asset, converting other assets to cash also reduces profitability. Similarly, the use of additional debt raises the rate of return, or the profitability, on the shareholders' net worth; at the same time, more debt means more risk. The financial manager seeks to strike the particular balance between risk and profitability that will maximize the wealth of the firm's shareholders. That is called a *risk-return trade-off*, and most financial decisions involve such trade-offs between risk and return.

ORGANIZATION AND STRUCTURE OF THIS BOOK

The optimal structure for a finance text, if one exists, is most elusive. On the one hand, it is desirable to set out a theoretical structure first, then use the theory in later sections to explain behaviour and to attack real-world decision problems. On the other hand, it is easier to understand the theoretical concepts of finance if one has a working knowledge of certain institutional details. Given this conflict, what should come first, theory or institutional background? We have wrestled with this problem, experimenting with both approaches in our own classes, and the following outline of the six parts of the book reflects our own experience and that of others who shared their ideas and preferences with us.

1. Overview of finance: financial analysis, planning, and control
2. Working capital management
3. Decisions involving long-term assets
4. Sources and forms of long-term financing
5. Financial structure, the cost of capital, and dividend policy
6. Integrated topics in financial management

The contents of each part are next discussed briefly to provide an overview of both the book and the field of managerial finance.

Part 1. Overview of finance: financial analysis, planning, and control

Part 1, which consists of Chapters 1 to 5, develops certain key concepts and commonly used tools of financial analysis. Included are such topics as ratio analysis, operating gearing, sources and uses of funds analysis, financial forecasting, and financial control techniques. The material provides a useful overview of finance, and the ideas and terminology developed facilitate an understanding of all the other parts of the book.

Part 2. Working capital management

Financial management involves the acquisition and use of assets, and to a large extent these actions are reflected in the firm's balance sheet. Accordingly, to a degree, the book is organized in a balance sheet sequence, with Part 2 focusing on the bottom section of the balance sheet, or the 'working capital' section. Working capital refers to the firm's short-term, or current, assets and liabilities, and the emphasis is placed on determining optimal levels for these items. Chapter 6 is on the theory of working capital, Chapter 7 concerns current assets, and Chapter 8 discusses current liabilities. The theory chapter sets forth a rational framework within which to consider decisions affecting the specific balance sheet items that make up working capital. Firms make two kinds of working capital decisions: (a) *strategic* decisions relating to target working capital levels, and (b) *tactical* decisions that relate to day-to-day operations. The strategic decisions are fundamentally related to the trade-off between risk and return we discussed earlier, to alternative sources of capital, to management's view of the term structure of interest rates, to the effectiveness of internal control procedures (that is, stock control), to credit policy decisions, and so forth. The tactical operating decisions involve short-run adjustments in current assets and current liabilities to meet temporary conditions. The most obvious short-run adjustment relates to changing sales levels – fixed assets and long-term liabilities are inflexible in the short run, so changes in market demand must be met by working capital adjustments. Working capital is also adjusted from the target levels to reflect changes in long- and short-run interest rates and other changes in the availability of, and the need for, funds.

In Chapter 7 we discuss some factors bearing on (a) target levels of each kind of current asset and (b) methods for economizing on the investment in each kind of current asset. For example, the target stock level is determined jointly by costs of stock-outs, costs of carrying and ordering stocks, order lead times and usage rates, and the probability distributions of each of those factors. With this in mind, we base our discussion of stock levels on the standard economic order quantity (EOQ)-plus-safety-stock model. Then, in Chapter 8, we examine the sources and forms of short-term credit.

Part 3. Decisions involving long-term assets

In Part 3 we move into the upper part of the right-hand side of the balance sheet, examining the decisions involved in fixed-asset acquisitions. After a discussion of compound interest in Chapter 9, we take up capital budgeting techniques, explaining in some detail the mechanics of capital budgeting in Chapter 10. Next, in Chapter 11, we expand the discussion to include uncertainty, covering the basic concepts of probability distributions, the trade-off between risk and rate of return, decision trees, and simulation.

Part 4. Sources and forms of long-term financing

In Part 4 we move to the upper left-hand side of the balance sheet, examining the various kinds of long-term capital available to finance long-term investments. Chapter 12 presents an overview of the capital markets, explaining briefly certain institutional material without which no basic finance course is complete. Chapter 13 analyses the financial characteristics of ordinary shares, Chapter 14 examines debentures and preference shares, Chapter 15 analyses the lease or buy decision, and Chapter 16 discusses the nature and use of warrants and convertibles.

Part 5. Financial structure, the cost of capital, and dividend policy

In Part 5 we pull together the threads developed in earlier chapters. We show how (a) financial structure affects both risk and expected returns; (b) risk and return interact to determine the optimal capital structure; (c) the cost of capital, which is required when making fixed-asset decisions, is calculated; and (d) investment opportunities and cost of capital considerations interact to determine the way the firm should distribute its profits between dividends and retained earnings.

Part 6. Integrated topics in financial management

In the final five chapters we take up important but somewhat specialized topics that draw upon the concepts developed in the earlier sections. In Chapter 21 we introduce dynamics into the decision process, showing how financial managers react to changing conditions in the capital markets. We next discuss the external growth of firms through mergers and holding companies, as well as the factors affecting this development, in Chapter 22. Throughout most of the text we deal with growing and successful firms; however, many firms face financial difficulties, so the causes and possible remedies to these difficulties are discussed in Chapter 23. Chapter 24 deals with an increasingly important aspect of financial management – the finance function in a multinational company. Finally, in Chapter 25, we discuss the financial situation facing the small business firm and show how the tools of financial analysis may be applied to such a company.

QUESTIONS

1–1. What activities of financial managers are depicted by Figure 1–1?

1–2. What are financial intermediaries and what economic functions do they perform?

1–3. What are the main functions of financial managers?

1–4. Why is wealth maximization a better operating goal than profit maximization?

1–5. What role does utility maximization perform in finance theory?

1–6. What have been the major developmental periods in the field of finance and what circumstances led to the evolution of the emphasis in each period?

1–7. What is the nature of the risk-return trade-off faced in financial decision making?

SELECTED REFERENCES

Anthony, Robert N. The trouble with profit maximization. *Harvard Business Review* 38 (November–December 1960): 126–34.

Branch, Ben. Corporate objectives and market performance. *Financial Management* 2 (Summer 1973): 24–29.

Brigham, Eugene F. and Pappas, James L. *Managerial Economics*. Hinsdale, Ill.: Dryden Press, 1972, chap. 1.

Davis, Keith. Social responsibility is inevitable. *California Management Review* 19 (Fall 1976): 14–20.

Donaldson, Gordon. Financial goals: management versus stockholders. *Harvard Business Review* 41 (May–June 1963): 116–129.

Donaldson, Gordon. Financial management in an affluent society. *Financial Executive* 35 (April 1967): 52–56, 58–60.

Elliott, J. W. Control, size, growth, and financial performance in the firm. *Journal of Financial and Quantitative Analysis* 7 (January 1972): 1309–1320.

Findlay, Chapman M. and Whitmore, G. A. Beyond shareholder wealth maximization. *Financial Management* 3 (Winter 1974): 25–35.

Glautier, M. E. Is social responsibility accounting an accounting responsibility? *Accountants Review* (December 1975): 248–261.

Gordon, Myron J. A portfolio theory of the social discount rate and the public debt. *Journal of Finance* 31 (May 1976): 199–214.

Grabowski, Henry G. and Mueller, Dennis C. Managerial and stockholder welfare models of firm expenditures. *Review of Economics and Statistics* 54 (February 1972): 9–24.

Haley, Charles W. and Schall, Lawrence D. *The Theory of Financial Decisions*. New York: McGraw-Hill, 1973, chap. 5.

Harkins, Edwin P. *Organizing and Managing the Corporate Financial Function*. Studies in Business Policy, no. 129. New York: National Industrial Conference Board, Inc., 1969.

Hill, Lawrence W. The growth of the corporate finance function. *Financial Executive* 44 (July 1976): 38–43.

Lewellen, Wilbur G. Management and ownership in the large firm. *Journal of Finance* 24 (May 1969): 299–322.

Masson, Robert Tempest. Executive motivations, earnings, and consequent equity performance. *Journal of Political Economy* 79 (November–December 1971): 1278–1292.

Merton, Robert C. Distinguished speaker series. *Journal of Financial and Quantitative Analysis* 10. (November 1975): 659–674.

Moag, Joseph S., Carleton, Willard T. and Lerner, Eugene M. Defining the finance function: a model-systems approach. *Journal of Finance* 22 (December 1967): 543–556.

Scanlon, John J. Bell system financial policies. *Financial Management* 1 (Summer 1972): 16–26.

Simkowitz, Michael A. and Jones, Charles P. A note on the simultaneous nature of finance methodology. *Journal of Finance* 27 (March 1972): 103–108.

Solomon, Ezra. *The Theory of Financial Management*. New York: Columbia University Press, 1963.

Weston, J. Fred. New themes in finance. *Journal of Finance* 24 (March 1974): 237–243.

Weston, J. Fred. *The Scope and Methodology of Finance*. Englewood Cliffs, N. J.: Prentice-Hall, 1966.

Weston, J. Fred. Towards theories of financial policy. *Journal of Finance* 10 (May 1955): 130–143.

Zettergren, L. Financial issues in strategic planning. *Long Range Planning* (June 1975): 23–33.

Chapter 2

Ratio Analysis

Planning is the key to the financial manager's success. Financial plans may take many forms, but any good plan must be related to the firm's existing strengths and weaknesses. The strengths must be understood if they are to be used to proper advantage, and the weaknesses must be recognized if corrective action is to be taken. For example, are stocks adequate to support the projected level of sales? Does the firm have too much funds invested in trade debtors, and does this condition reflect a lax collection policy? The financial manager can plan his future financial requirements in accordance with the forecasting and budgeting procedures we will present in succeeding chapters, but his plan must begin with the type of financial analysis developed in this chapter.

BASIC FINANCIAL STATEMENTS

Because ratio analysis employs financial data taken from the firm's balance sheet and profit and loss account (i.e. income statement), it is useful to begin this chapter with a review of these accounting reports. For illustrative purposes, we shall use data taken from the Walker-Wilson Manufacturing Company, a producer of specialized machinery used in the motor car repair business. Formed in 1961, when Charles Walker and Ben Wilson set up a small factory to produce certain tools they had developed while in the army, Walker-Wilson grew steadily and earned the reputation of being one of the best small firms in its line of business. In December 1976, both Walker and Wilson were killed in a crash of their private plane, and for the next two years the firm was managed by Walker-Wilson's accountant.

In 1978 the widows, who are the principal shareholders in Walker-Wilson, acting on the advice of the firm's bankers and solicitors, engaged David Thompson as managing director. Although Thompson is experienced in the machinery business, especially in production and sales, he does not have a detailed knowledge of his new company, so he has decided to conduct a careful appraisal of the firm's position and, on the basis of this position, to draw up a plan for future operations.

Table 2–1 *Walker-Wilson Company Ltd, Illustrative Balance Sheet (£000).*

	31 Dec. 1977		31 Dec. 1978			31 Dec. 1977		31 Dec. 1978	
		£		£			£		£
Ordinary share capital:					Fixed assets:				
600 000 £1 ordinary shares		600		600	Plant and equipment, at cost		1610		1800
Revenue reserve		380		400	less depreciation		400		500
Net worth		980		1000			1210		1300
Debenture stock					Current assets:				
8% First mortgage stock		520		500					
10% Unsecured loan stock		200		200	Stocks	355		300	
					Debtors	250		200	
		1700		1700	Quoted investments	175		150	
Current liabilities:					Cash	52		50	
Creditors and accruals	97		70				832		700
Short-term loans	110		100						
Corporation tax	135		130						
		342		300					
Total liabilities		£2042		£2000	Total assets		£2042		£2000

Balance sheet

Walker-Wilson's balance sheet, given in Table 2–1, shows the value of the firm's assets, and of the liabilities, at two particular points in time, 31 December 1977, and 31 December 1978. The assets are arranged from top to bottom in order of increasing liquidity; that is, assets towards the bottom of the column will be converted to cash sooner than those towards the top of the column. The bottom group of assets – cash, quoted investments, trade debtors and stock, which are expected to be converted into cash within one year – is defined as *current assets.* Assets in the top part of the statement – plant and equipment – are not expected to be converted to cash within one year; these are defined as *fixed assets.*

The left side of the balance sheet is arranged similarly. Those items at the bottom of the liabilities column mature, and must be paid off, relatively soon; those towards the top of the column are due in the more distant future. Current liabilities must be paid within one year; because the firm never has to repay ordinary shareholders, ordinary share capital and reserves represent 'permanent' capital.

Profit and loss account

Walker-Wilson's profit and loss account statement is shown in Table 2–2. Sales are shown at the top of the statement; various costs, including corporation tax, deducted to arrive at the net income available to ordinary shareholders. The figure on the last line represents earnings per share (EPS), calculated as net income divided by number of shares outstanding.

Table 2–2 *Walker-Wilson Company Ltd, Illustrative Profit and Loss Account for Year Ended 31 December 1978.*

	£000	£000
Sales (net)		3000
Cost of goods sold		2555
Gross profit		445
Less: operating expenses		
Selling	22	
General and administrative	40	
Lease payment on office building	28	90
Gross operating income		355
Depreciation		100
Net operating income		255
Add other income		15
		270
Less other expenses		
Interest on short-term loan	10	
Interest on debenture mortgage	40	
Interest on unsecured loan	20	70
Profit before tax		200
Corporation tax		80
Net profit after tax, available to ordinary shareholders		£120
Earnings per share		£0.20

Statement of retained earnings

Earnings may be paid out to shareholders as dividends or retained and reinvested in the business. Shareholders like to receive dividends, of course, but if earnings are ploughed back into the business, the value of the shareholders' position in the company increases. Later in the book we shall consider the pros and cons of retaining earnings versus paying them out in dividends, but for now we are simply interested in the effects of dividends and retained earnings on the balance sheet. For this purpose we may use the statement of retained earnings, illustrated for Walker-Wilson in Table 2–3. Walker-Wilson earned £120 000 during the year, paid £100 000 in dividends to shareholders, and ploughed £20 000 back into the business. Thus the retained earnings at the end of 1978, as shown both on the balance sheet and on the statement of retained earnings, is £400 000, which is £20 000 larger than the year-end 1977 figure.

Table 2–3 *Walker-Wilson Company Ltd, Statement of Retained Earnings for Year Ended 31 December 1978.*

	£000
Balance of retained earnings, 31 December 1977	380
Add net profit, 1978	120
	500
Less dividends to ordinary shareholders	100
Balance of retained earnings, 31 December 1978	£400

Relationship among the three statements

It is important to recognize that the balance sheet is a statement of the firm's financial position *at a point in time*, whereas the profit and loss account shows the results of operations *during an interval of time*. Thus, the balance sheet represents a snapshot of the firm's position on a given date, while the profit and loss account is based on a flow concept, showing what occurred between two points in time.

The statement of retained earnings indicates how the revenue reserves account on the balance sheet is adjusted between balance sheet dates. Since its inception, Walker-Wilson had retained a total of £380 000 by 31 December 1977. In 1978 it earned £120 000, and £20 000 of this amount was retained. Thus, the retained earnings shown on the balance sheet for 31 December 1978 is £400 000.

When a firm retains earnings, it generally does so to expand the business; that is, to finance the purchase of assets such as plant, equipment, and stocks. As a result of operations in 1978, Walker-Wilson has £20 000 available for that purpose. Sometimes retained earnings will be used to build up the cash balance, but retained earnings as shown on the balance sheet are *not* cash. Through the years they have been invested in bricks and mortar and other assets, so retained earnings as shown on the balance sheet are not 'available' for anything. The earnings *for the current year* may be available for investment, but the *past retained earnings* have already been employed.

Stated another way, the balance sheet item 'retained earnings' simply shows how much of their earnings the shareholders, through the years, have elected to retain in the business. Thus, the retained earnings account shows the additional investment the shareholders as a group have made in the business, over and above their initial investment at the inception of the company and through any subsequent issues of shares.

BASIC TYPES OF FINANCIAL RATIOS

Each type of analysis has a purpose or use that determines the different relationships emphasized in the analysis. The analyst may, for example, be a banker considering whether or not to grant a short-term loan to a firm. He is primarily interested in the firm's short-term, or liquidity, position, so he stresses ratios that measure liquidity. In contrast, long-term creditors place far more emphasis on earnings capacity and on operating efficiency. They know that unprofitable operations will erode asset values and that a strong current position is no guarantee that funds will be available to repay a 20-year debenture issue. Equity investors are similarly interested in long-term profitability and efficiency. Management is, of course, concerned with all those aspects of financial analysis – it must be able to repay its debts to long- and short-term creditors as well as earn profits for shareholders.

It is useful to classify ratios into four fundamental types:

1. *Liquidity ratios*, which measure the firm's ability to meet its maturing short-term obligations.
2. *Gearing ratios*, which measure the extent to which the firm has been financed by debt.
3. *Activity ratios*, which measure how effectively the firm is using its resources.
4. *Profitability ratios*, which measure management's overall effectiveness as shown by the returns generated on sales and capital employed.

Specific examples of each ratio are given in the following sections, where the Walker-Wilson case history is used to illustrate their calculation and use.

Liquidity ratios

Generally, the first concern of the financial analyst is liquidity: is the firm able to meet its current liabilities? Walker-Wilson has debts totalling £300 000 that must be paid within the coming year. Can these liabilities be met? Although a full liquidity analysis requires the use of cash budgets (described in Chapter 5), ratio analysis, by relating the amount of cash and other current assets to the current liabilities, provides a quick and easy-to-use measure of liquidity. Two commonly used liquidity ratios are presented below.

Current ratio

The current ratio is computed by dividing current assets by current liabilities. Current assets normally include cash, quoted investments, trade debtors, and stocks; current liabilities consist of trade creditors, short-term loans, maturing long-term liabilities, corporation tax due, and other accrued expenses (principally wages). The current ratio is the most commonly used measure of short-term solvency, since it indicates the extent to which the claims of short-term creditors are covered by assets that are expected to be converted to cash in a period roughly corresponding to the maturity of the claims.

The calculation of the current ratio for Walker-Wilson at year-end 1975 is shown below.

$$\text{Current ratio} = \frac{\text{current assets}}{\text{current liabilities}} = \frac{£700\,000}{£300\,000} = 2.3 \text{ times.}$$

Industry average = 2.5 times.

The current ratio is slightly below the average for the industry, 2.5, but not low enough to cause concern. It appears that Walker-Wilson is about in line with most other firms in this particular line of business. Since current assets are relatively liquid, it is highly probable that they could be realized at close to book value. With a current ratio of 2.3, Walker-Wilson could dispose of current assets at only 43 per cent of book value and still pay off current liabilities in full.[1]

Although industry average figures are discussed later in the chapter, it should be stated at this point that the industry average is not a magic number that all firms should strive to maintain. In fact, some very well managed firms will be above it, and other good firms will be below it. However, if a firm's ratios are very far removed from the average for its industry, the analyst must be concerned about why this variance occurs; that is, a deviation from the industry average should signal the analyst to check further.

Quick ratio or acid test

The quick ratio is calculated by deducting stocks from current assets and dividing the remainder by current liabilities. Stocks are typically the least liquid of a firm's current assets and the assets on which losses are most likely to occur in the event of disposal. Therefore, this measure of the firm's ability to pay off current liabilities without relying on the sale of stocks is important.

$$\text{Quick, or acid test, ratio} = \frac{\text{current assets} - \text{stocks}}{\text{current liabilities}} = \frac{£400\,000}{£300\,000}$$

$$= 1.3 \text{ times.}$$

$$\text{Industry average} = 1.0 \text{ times.}$$

The industry average quick ratio is 1, so Walker-Wilson's 1.3 ratio compares favourably with other firms in the industry. Thompson knows that if the quoted securities can be sold at book value and if he can collect the amounts outstanding on trade debtors, he can pay off his current liabilities without selling any stock.

Gearing ratios

Gearing ratios, which measure the funds supplied by owners as compared with the financing provided by the firm's creditors, have a number of implications. First, creditors look to the equity, or owner-supplied funds, to provide a margin of safety. If owners have provided only a small proportion of total financing, the risks of the enterprise are borne mainly by the creditors. Second, by raising funds through debt, the owners gain the benefits of maintaining control of the firm with a limited investment. Third, if the firm earns more on the borrowed funds than it pays in interest, the return to the owners is magnified. For example, if assets earn 10 per cent and debt costs only 8 per cent, there is a 2 per cent differential accruing to the shareholders. Gearing cuts both ways, however; if the return on assets falls to 3 per cent, the differential between that figure and the cost of debt must be made up from equity's share of total profits. In the first instance, where assets earn more than the cost of debt, gearing is favourable; in the second, it is unfavourable.

Firms with low gearing ratios have less risk of loss when the economy is in a *recession*, but they also have lower expected returns when the economy booms. Conversely, firms with high gearing ratios run the risk of large losses but also have a chance of gaining high profits. The prospects of high returns are desirable, but investors are averse to risk. Decisions about the use of gearing, then, must balance higher expected returns against increased risk.[2]

---

1. (1/2.3) = 0.43, or 43 per cent. Note that (0.43) (£700 000) ≈ £300 000, the amount of current liabilities.
2. The problem of determining optimum gearing for a firm with given risk characteristics is examined extensively in Chapters 17, 18, and 19.

In practice, gearing is approached in two ways. One approach examines balance sheet ratios and determines the extent to which borrowed funds have been used to finance the firm. The other approach measures the risks of debt by income statement ratios designed to determine the number of times fixed charges are covered by operating profits. These sets of ratios are complementary, and most analysts examine both gearing ratios.

Total debt to total assets

The ratio of total debt to total assets, generally called the *debt ratio*, measures the percentage of total funds provided by creditors. Debt includes current liabilities and all loans. Creditors prefer moderate debt ratios, since the lower the ratio, the greater the cushion against creditors' losses in the event of liquidation. In contrast to the creditors' preference for a low debt ratio, the owners may seek high gearing either (a) to magnify earnings or (b) because raising new equity means giving up some degree of control. If the debt ratio is too high, there is a danger of encouraging irresponsibility on the part of the owners. The stake of the owners can become so small that speculative activity, if it is successful, will yield a substantial percentage return to the owners. If the venture is unsuccessful, however, only a moderate loss is incurred by the owners because their investment is small.

$$\text{Debt ratio} = \frac{\text{total debt}}{\text{total assets}} = \frac{£1\,000\,000}{£2\,000\,000} = 50\,\%.$$

$$\text{Industry average} = 33\,\%.$$

Walker-Wilson's debt ratio is 50 per cent; this means that creditors have supplied half the firm's total financing. Since the average debt ratio for this industry – and for manufacturing generally – is about 33 per cent, Walker-Wilson would find it difficult to borrow additional funds without first raising more equity capital. Creditors would be reluctant to lend the firm more money, and Thompson would probably be subjecting the shareholders to undue dangers if he sought to increase the debt ratio still more by borrowing.[3]

Times interest earned

The times-interest-earned ratio is determined by dividing earnings before interest and taxes (gross income in Table 2–2) by the interest charges. The times-interest-earned ratio measures the extent to which earnings can decline without resultant financial embarrassment to the firm because of inability to meet annual interest costs. Failure to meet this obligation can bring legal action by the creditors, possibly resulting in *bankruptcy*. Note that the before-tax profit figure is used in the numerator. Because corporation tax is computed after interest expense is deducted, the ability to pay current interest is not affected by corporation tax.

---

3. The ratio of debt to equity is also used in financial analysis. The debt to assets (D/A) and debt to equity (D/E) ratios are simply transformations of one another:

$$D/E = \frac{D/A}{1 - D/A} \text{ and } D/A = \frac{D/E}{1 + D/E}.$$

Both ratios increase as a firm of a given size (total assets) uses a greater proportion of debt, but D/A rises linearly and approaches a limit of 100 per cent while D/E rises exponentially and approaches infinity.

$$\text{Times interest earned} = \frac{\text{gross income}}{\text{interest charges}} = \frac{\text{profit before taxes} + \text{interest charges}}{\text{interest charges}}$$

$$= \frac{£270\,000}{£70\,000} = 3.9 \text{ times.}$$

$$\text{Industry average} = 8.0 \text{ times.}$$

Walker-Wilson's interest charges consist of three payments totalling £70 000 (see Table 2–2). The firm's gross income available for servicing these charges is £270 000, so the interest is covered 3.9 times. Since the industry average is 8 times, the company is covering its interest charges by a minimum margin of safety and deserves only a fair rating. This ratio reinforces the conclusion based on the debt ratio that the company is likely to face some difficulties if it attempts to borrow additional funds.

Fixed charge coverage

This ratio is similar to the times-interest-earned ratio, but it is somewhat more inclusive in that it recognizes that many firms lease assets and incur long-term obligations under lease contracts. As we show in Chapter 15, leasing has become quite widespread in recent years, making this ratio preferable to the times-interest-earned ratio for most financial analyses. 'Fixed charges' are defined as interest plus annual long-term lease obligations, and the fixed charge coverage ratio is defined as

$$\text{Fixed charge coverage} = \frac{\begin{matrix}\text{profit} \\ \text{before taxes}\end{matrix} + \begin{matrix}\text{interest} \\ \text{charges}\end{matrix} + \begin{matrix}\text{lease} \\ \text{obligations}\end{matrix}}{\text{interest charges} + \text{lease obligations}}$$

$$= \frac{£200\,000 + £70\,000 + £28\,000}{£70\,000 + £28\,000}$$

$$= 3.04 \text{ times.}$$

$$\text{Industry average} = 5.5 \text{ times.}$$

Walker-Wilson's fixed charges are covered 3.04 times, as opposed to an industry average of 5.5 times. Again, this indicates that the firm is somewhat weaker than creditors would prefer it to be, and it further points up the difficulties Thompson would be likely to encounter if he should attempt additional borrowing.

Activity ratios

Activity ratios measure how effectively the firm employs the resources at its command. These ratios all involve comparisons between the level of sales and the investment in various asset accounts. The activity ratios presume that a 'proper' balance should exist between sales and the various asset accounts – stocks, trade debtors, fixed assets, and others. As we shall see in the following chapters, this is generally a good assumption.

Stock turnover

The stock turnover is defined as sales divided by stocks.

$$\text{Stock turnover} = \frac{\text{sales}}{\text{stocks}} = \frac{£3\,000\,000}{£300\,000} = 10 \text{ times.}$$

Industry average = 9 times.

Walker-Wilson's turnover of 10 compares favourably with an industry average of 9 times. This suggests that the company does not hold excessive stocks; excess stocks are, of course, unproductive and represent an investment with a low or nil rate of return. This high stock turnover also reinforces Thompson's faith in the current ratio. If the turnover was low – say 3 or 4 times – Thompson would wonder whether the firm was holding damaged or obsolete materials not actually worth their stated value.

Two problems arise in calculating and analysing the stock turnover ratio. First, sales are at market prices; if stocks are carried at cost, as they generally are, it would be more appropriate to use cost of goods sold in place of sales in the numerator of the formula. As this information is rarely made available to external analysts, it is necessary to measure stock turnover with sales in the numerator, as shown above.

The second problem lies in the fact that sales occur over the entire year, whereas the stock figure is for one point in time. This makes it better to use an average stock, computed by adding beginning and ending stocks and dividing by 2. If it is determined that the firm's business is highly seasonal, or if there has been a strong upward or downward sales trend during the year, it becomes essential to make some such adjustment. Neither of these conditions holds for Walker-Wilson; to maintain comparability with industry averages, Thompson did not use the average stock figure.

Average collection period

The average collection period, which is a measure of the debtors turnover, is computed in two steps: (a) annual sales are divided by 360 to get the average daily sales;[4] (b) daily sales are divided into trade debtors to find the number of days' sales tied up in debtors. This is defined as the average collection period, because it represents the average length of time that the firm must wait after making a sale before receiving cash. The calculations for Walker-Wilson show an average collection period of 24 days, slightly above the 20-day industry average.

$$\text{Sales per day} = \frac{£3\,000\,000}{360} = £8333. \qquad (1\text{–}1)$$

$$\text{Average collection period} = \frac{\text{debtors}}{\text{sales per day}} = \frac{£200\,000}{£8333} = 24 \text{ days.} \qquad (2\text{–}2)$$

Industry average = 20 days.

This ratio can also be evaluated by comparison with the terms on which the firm sells its goods. For example, Walker-Wilson's sales terms call for payment within 20 days, so the 24-day collection period indicates that customers, on the average, are not paying their accounts on time. If the trend in the collection period over the past few years had been rising while the credit policy has not changed, this would be even stronger evidence that steps should be taken to expedite the collection of debtors' accounts.

One non-ratio financial tool should be mentioned in connection with debtor analysis – the *debtors profile*, which breaks down trade debtors according to how long they have been outstanding. The debtors profile for Walker-Wilson is given below:

4. Because information on credit sales is generally unavailable, total sales must be used. Since all firms do not have the same percentage of credit sales, there is a good chance that the average collection period will be somewhat in error. Also, note that for convenience the financial community generally uses 360 rather than 365 as the number of days in the year for purposes such as these.

Age of debt (days)	Percent of total value of trade debtors
0–20	50
21–30	20
31–45	15
46–60	3
over 60	12
Total	100

The 24-day collection period looked bad by comparison with the 20-day terms, and the debtors profile shows that the firm is having especially serious collection problems with some of its accounts. Fifty percent are overdue, many for over a month. Others pay quite promptly, bringing the average down to only 24 days, but the debtors profile shows this average to be somewhat misleading.

Fixed asset turnover

The ratio of sales to fixed assets measures the turnover of plant and equipment.

$$\text{Fixed assets turnover} = \frac{\text{sales}}{\text{net fixed assets}} = \frac{£3\,000\,000}{£1\,300\,000} = 2.3 \text{ times.}$$

Industry average = 5.0 times.

Walker-Wilson's turnover of 2.3 times compares poorly with the industry average of 5 times, indicating that the firm is not using its fixed assets to as high a percentage of capacity as are the other firms in the industry. Thompson should bear this fact in mind when his production people request funds for new capital investments.

Total assets turnover

The final activity ratio measures the turnover of all the firm's assets. It is calculated by dividing sales by total assets.

$$\text{Total assets turnover} = \frac{\text{sales}}{\text{total assets}} = \frac{£3\,000\,000}{£2\,000\,000} = 1.5 \text{ times.}$$

Industry average = 2.0 times.

Walker-Wilson's turnover of total assets is well below the industry average. The company is simply not generating a sufficient volume of business for the size of its asset investment. Sales should be increased, or some assets should be disposed of, or both steps should be taken.

Profitability ratios

Profitability is the net result of a large number of policies and decisions. The ratios examined thus far reveal some interesting things about the way the firm is operating, but the profitability ratios give final answers about how effectively the firm is being managed.

Profit margin on sales

The profit margin on sales, computed by dividing net income after taxes by sales, gives the profit per £1 of sales.

$$\text{Profit margin} = \frac{\text{net profit after taxes}}{\text{sales}} = \frac{£120\,000}{£3\,000\,000} = 4\%.$$

$$\text{Industry average} = 5\%.$$

Walker-Wilson's profit margin is somewhat below the industry average of 5 per cent, indicating that the firm's sales prices are relatively low or that its costs are relatively high or both.

Return on total assets

The ratio of net profit to total assets measures the return on total investment in the firm, or the ROI, as it is frequently called.[5]

$$\text{Return on total assets} = \frac{\text{net profit after taxes}}{\text{total assets}} = \frac{£120\,000}{£2\,000\,000} = 6\%.$$

$$\text{Industry average} = 10\%.$$

Walker-Wilson's 6 per cent return is well below the 10 per cent average for the industry. This low rate results from the low profit margin on sales and from the low turnover of total assets.

Return on net worth

The ratio of net profit after taxes to net worth measures the rate of return on the shareholders' investment.

$$\text{Return on net worth} = \frac{\text{net profit after taxes}}{\text{net worth}} = \frac{£120\,000}{£1\,000\,000} = 12\%.$$

$$\text{Industry average} = 15\%.$$

Walker-Wilson's 12 per cent return is below the 15 per cent industry average but not as far below as the return on total assets. In a later section of this chapter, where the du Pont method of analysis is applied to the Walker-Wilson case, we will see why this is so.

Summary of the ratios

The individual ratios, which are summarized in Table 2–4, give Thompson a reasonably good idea of Walker-Wilson's main strengths and weaknesses. First, the company's liquidity position is reasonably good; its current and quick ratios appear to be satisfactory

5. In calculating the return on total assets, it is sometimes desirable to add interest to net profits after taxes to form the numerator of the ratio. The theory here is that since assets are financed by both shareholders and creditors, the ratio should measure the productivity of assets in providing returns to both classes of investors. We have not done so at this point because the published averages we use for comparative purposes exclude interest. Later in this book, however, when we deal with gearing decisions, we do add back interest. This addition has a material bearing on the value of the ratio for companies which have large amounts of fixed assets financed by debt.

Table 2–4 *Summary of Financial Ratio Analysis.*

Ratio	Formula for calculation	Calculation	Industry average	Evaluation
Liquidity				
Current	$\frac{\text{current assets}}{\text{current liabilities}}$	$\frac{£\ 700\,000}{£\ 300\,000} = 2.3$ times	2.5 times	Satisfactory
Quick, or acid test	$\frac{\text{current assets} - \text{stocks}}{\text{current liabilities}}$	$\frac{£\ 400\,000}{£\ 300\,000} = 1.3$ times	1.0 times	Good
Gearing				
Debt to total assets	$\frac{\text{total debt}}{\text{total assets}}$	$\frac{£1\,000\,000}{£2\,000\,000} = 50$ per cent	33 per cent	Poor
Times interest earned	$\frac{\text{profit before taxes plus interest charges}}{\text{interest charges}}$	$\frac{£\ 270\,000}{£\ 70\,000} = 3.9$ times	8.0 times	Poor
Fixed charge coverage	$\frac{\text{income available for meeting fixed charges}}{\text{fixed charges}}$	$\frac{£\ 298\,000}{£\ 98\,000} = 3.04$ times	5.5 times	Poor
Activity				
Stock turnover	$\frac{\text{sales}}{\text{stocks}}$	$\frac{£3\,000\,000}{£\ 300\,000} = 10$ times	9 times	Satisfactory
Average collection period	$\frac{\text{trade debtors}}{\text{sales per day}}$	$\frac{£\ 200\,000}{£\ 8\,333} = 24$ days	20 days	Satisfactory
Fixed assets turnover	$\frac{\text{sales}}{\text{fixed assets}}$	$\frac{£3\,000\,000}{£1\,300\,000} = 2.3$ times	5.0 times	Poor
Total assets turnover	$\frac{\text{sales}}{\text{total assets}}$	$\frac{£3\,000\,000}{£2\,000\,000} = 1.5$ times	2 times	Poor
Profitability				
Profit margin on sales	$\frac{\text{net profit after taxes}}{\text{sales}}$	$\frac{£\ 120\,000}{£3\,000\,000} = 4$ per cent	5 per cent	Poor
Return on total assets	$\frac{\text{net profit after taxes}}{\text{total assets}}$	$\frac{£\ 120\,000}{£2\,000\,000} = 6.0$ per cent	10 per cent	Poor
Return on net worth	$\frac{\text{net profit after taxes}}{\text{net worth}}$	$\frac{£\ 120\,000}{£1\,000\,000} = 12.0$ per cent	15 per cent	Poor

by comparison with the industry averages. Second, the gearing ratios suggest that the company is rather heavily indebted. With a debt ratio substantially higher than the industry average, and with coverage ratios well below the industry averages, it is doubtful that Walker-Wilson could do much additional debt financing except on relatively unfavourable terms. Even if Thompson could borrow more, to do so would be subjecting the company to the danger of default and liquidation in the event of a business downswing.

Turning to the activity ratios, the stock turnover and average collection period both indicate that the company's current assets are pretty well in balance, but the low fixed asset turnover suggests that there has been too heavy an investment in fixed assets. This low fixed asset turnover means, in effect, that the company probably could have operated with a smaller investment in fixed assets. Had the excessive fixed asset investment not been made, the company could have avoided some of its debt financing and would now have lower interest payments. This, in turn, would have led to improved gearing and coverage ratios.

The profit margin on sales is low, indicating that costs are too high or that prices are too low or both. In this particular case, the sales prices are in line with other firms; high costs are, in fact, the cause of the low margin. Further, the high costs can be traced to (a) high depreciation charges and (b) high interest expenses. Both these costs are, in turn, attributable to the excessive investment in fixed assets.

Returns on both total investment and net worth are also below the industry averages. These relatively poor results are directly attributable to the low profit margin on sales, which lowers the numerators of the ratios, and to the excessive investment, which raises the denominators.

Trend analysis

While the preceding ratio analysis gives a reasonably good picture of Walker-Wilson's operation, it is incomplete in one important respect – it ignores the time dimension. The ratios are snapshots of the picture at one point in time, but there may be trends in motion that are in the process of rapidly eroding a relatively good present position. Conversely, an analysis of the ratios over the past few years may suggest that a relatively weak position is being improved at a rapid rate.

The method of trend analysis is illustrated in Figure 2–1, which shows graphs of Walker-Wilson's sales, current ratio, debt ratio, fixed assets turnover, and return on net worth. The figures are compared with industry averages; industry sales have been rising steadily over the entire period, and the industry average ratios have been relatively stable throughout. Thus, any trends in the company's ratios are due to its own internal conditions, not to environmental influences affecting all firms. In addition, Walker-Wilson's deterioration since the death of the two principal directors is quite apparent. Prior to 1976, Walker-Wilson was growing more rapidly than the average firm in the industry; during the following two years, however, sales actually declined.

Walker-Wilson's liquidity position as measured by its current ratio has also gone downhill in the past two years. Although the ratio is only slightly below the industry average at the present time, the trend suggests that a real liquidity crisis may develop during the next year or two unless corrective action is taken immediately.

The debt ratio trend line shows that Walker-Wilson followed industry practices closely until 1975, when the ratio jumped to a full 10 percentage points above the industry average. Similarly, the fixed assets turnover declined during 1975, even though sales were still rising. The records reveal that the company borrowed heavily during 1975 to finance a major expansion of plant and equipment. Walker and Wilson had intended to use this additional capacity to generate a still higher volume of sales and to redeem the debt out of expected high profits. Their untimely death, however, led to a decrease in sales rather than an increase, and the expected high profits that were to be used to redeem the debt did not

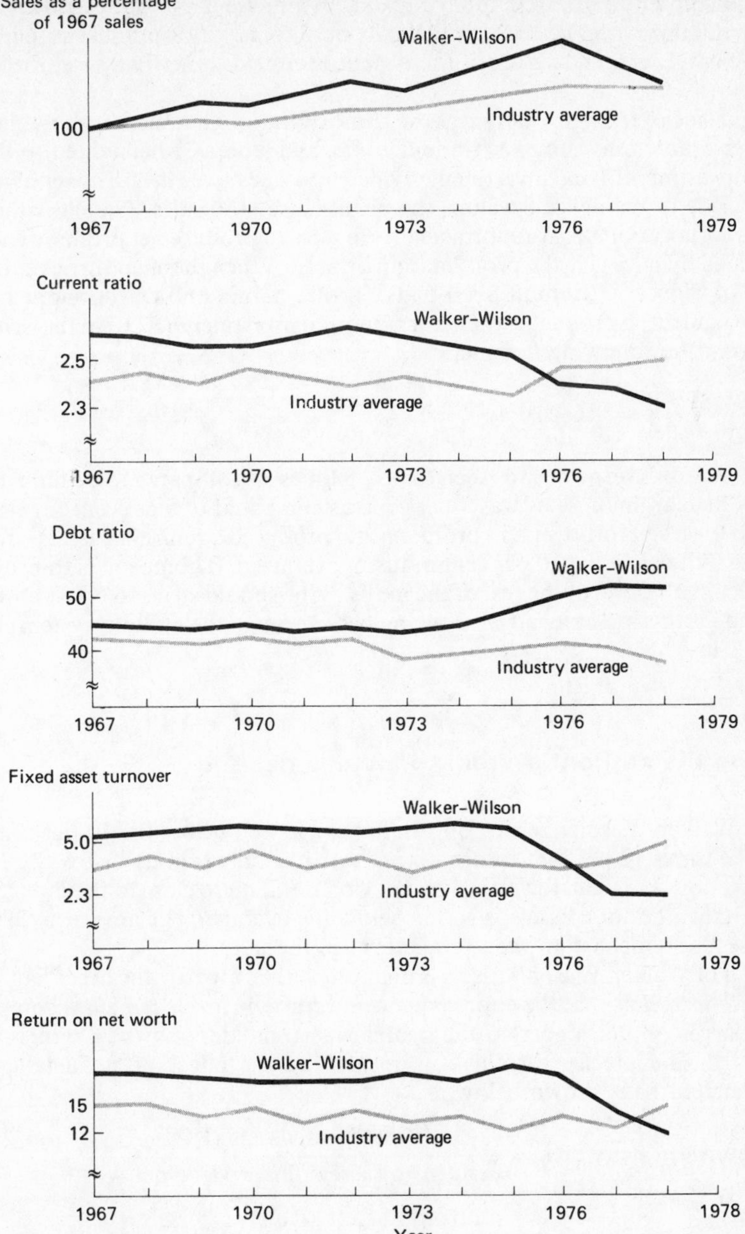

Figure 2–1 *Illustration of Trend Analysis.*

materialize. The analysis suggests that the bankers were correct when they advised Mrs Walker and Mrs Wilson of the need for a change in management.

du Pont system of financial analysis

The du Pont system of financial analysis has achieved wide recognition in American industry, and could usefully be applied to UK companies. It brings together the activity ratios and profit margin on sales and shows how these ratios interact to determine the profitability of assets. The nature of the system, modified somewhat, is set forth in Figure 2–2.

The right side of the figure develops the turnover ratio. That section shows how current assets (cash, quoted investments, trade debtors, and stocks), when added to fixed assets, give total investment. Total investment divided into sales gives the turnover of investment.

The left side of the figure develops the profit margin on sales. The individual expense items plus corporation tax are subtracted from sales to produce net profits after taxes. Net profit divided by sales give the profit margin on sales. When the asset turnover ratio on the right side of Figure 2–2 is multiplied by the profit margin on sales developed on the left side of the figure, the product is the return on total investment (ROI) in the firm. This can be seen from the following formula:

$$\frac{\text{sales}}{\text{investment}} \times \frac{\text{profit}}{\text{sales}} = \text{ROI}.$$

Walker-Wilson's turnover was seen to be 1.5 times, as compared to an industry average of 2 times; its margin on sales was 4 per cent, as compared to 5 per cent for the industry. Multiplied together, turnover and profit margin produced a return on assets equal to 6 per cent, a rate well below the 10 per cent industry average. If Thompson is to bring Walker-Wilson back to the level of the rest of the industry, he should strive to boost both his profit margin and his total asset turnover. Tracing back through the du Pont system should help him in this task.

Extending the du Pont system to include gearing

Although Walker-Wilson's return on total assets is well below the 10 per cent industry average, the firm's 12 per cent return on net worth is only slightly below the 15 per cent industry average. How can the return on net worth end up so close to the industry average when the return on total assets is so far below the average? The answer is that Walker-Wilson uses more debt than the average firm in the industry.

Only half of Walker-Wilson's assets is financed with net worth; the other half is financed with debt. This means that the entire 6 per cent return on assets (which is computed after interest charges on debt) goes to the ordinary shareholders, so their return is boosted substantially. The precise formula for measuring the effect of financial gearing on stockholder returns is shown below.

$$\text{Rate of return on net worth} = \frac{\text{return on assets (ROI)}}{\text{per cent of assets financed by net worth}}$$

$$= \frac{\text{return on assets (ROI)}}{1.0 - \text{debt ratio}}.$$

Calculation for Walker-Wilson:

$$\text{Return on net worth} = \frac{6\%}{1.0 - 0.50} = \frac{6\%}{0.5} = 12\%.$$

Calculation for the industry average:

$$\text{Return on net worth} = \frac{10\%}{1.0 - 0.33} = \frac{10\%}{0.67} = 15\%.$$

This formula is useful for showing how financial gearing can be used to increase the rate

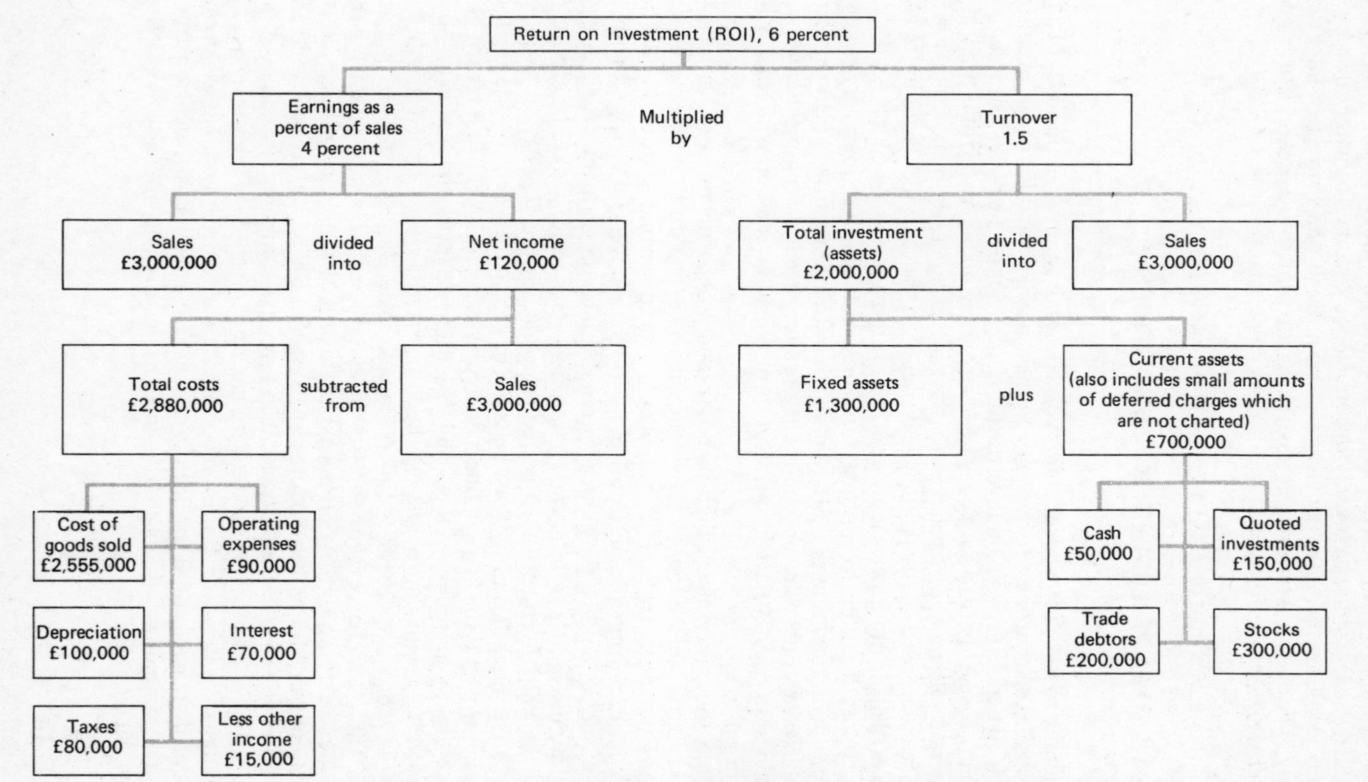

Figure 2–2 *Modified du Pont System of Financial Control Applied to Walker-Wilson.*

of return on net worth.[6] But increasing returns on net worth by using more and more gearing causes the gearing ratios to rise higher and higher above the industry norms. Creditors resist this tendency, so there are limitations to the practice. Moreover, greater gearing increases the risk of insolvency and thus endangers the firm's shareholders. Since widows Walker and Wilson are entirely dependent on income from the firm for their support, they would be in a particularly bad position if the firm goes into default. Consequently, Thompson would be ill-advised to attempt to use gearing to boost the return on net worth much further.

RATES OF RETURN IN DIFFERENT INDUSTRIES

Would it be better to have a 5 per cent margin on sales and a total asset turnover of 2 times, or a 2 per cent sales margin and a turnover of 5 times? It makes no difference – in either case the firm has a 10 per cent return on investment. Actually, most firms are not free to make the kind of choice posed in the above question. Depending on the nature of its industry, the firm *must* operate with more or fewer assets, and it will experience a turnover that depends on the characteristics of its particular line of business. In the case of a dealer in fresh fruits and vegetables, fish, or other perishable items, the turnover should be high – every day or two would be most desirable. In contrast, some lines of business require very heavy fixed investment or long production periods. A haulage contractor requires a heavy investment in motor vehicles; a shipbuilder or an aircraft producer needs a long production period. Such companies necessarily have a low asset turnover rate but a correspondingly higher profit margin on sales.

If a discount warehouse has a high turnover, and a department store, with its heavy investment in fixed assets, a low turnover, would you expect to find differences in their profit margins on sales? In general, you would – the department store should have a considerably higher profit margin to offset its lower turnover. Otherwise, the discount warehouse business would be much more profitable than department stores, investment would flow into discount warehousing, and profits in this sector would be eroded to the point where the rate of return was about equal to that in the department store sector.

We know, however, that gearing must be taken into account when considering the rate of return on net worth. If the firms in one industry have a somewhat lower return on total assets but use slightly more financial gearing than do those in another industry, both sets of firms may end up with approximately the same rate of return on net worth.[7]

These points, which are necessary for a complete understanding of ratio analysis, are illustrated in Table 2–5. There we see how turnover and profit margins interact with each other to produce varying returns on assets, and also how financial gearing affects the return on shareholders funds. Tesco Stores Ltd, Imperial Chemical Industries Ltd and the average for all manufacturing and distribution firms are compared. Imperial Chemicals with a very heavy investment in fixed assets has a relatively low sales turnover; Tesco Stores has a high sales turnover. Both end up with similar return on total assets because of the different profit margins on sales. Both companies have profit ratios well above average for all quoted companies and both use financial gearing to increase the return on shareholders' funds.

6. There are limitations on this statement – specifically, the return on net worth increases with gearing only i the return on assets exceeds the rate of interest on debt, after considering the tax deductibility of interes payments. This whole concept is explored in detail in Chapter 18, which is devoted entirely to financial gearing
7. The factors that make it possible for firms to use more gearing are taken up in Chapters 14 and 18. It may b stated now, however, that the primary factor favouring gearing is sales stability.

Table 2–5 *Turnover, Profit Margins and Returns on Net Worth.*

	Sales to total assets (times)	×	Profit[a] to sales (per cent)	=	Total debt to total assets (per cent)	Profit[a] to total assets (per cent)	Profit to shareholders' funds[b] (per cent)
All manufacturing and distribution firms	1.34		6.12		8.2	52	17.1
Imperial Chemical Industries Ltd	0.94		17.5		16.5	45	29.9
Tesco Stores Ltd	3.08		5.79		17.8	44	31.7

[a] Profit defined as net profit after interest and depreciation but before tax.
[b] The figures in this column may be found as

$$\text{Profit to shareholders' funds} = \frac{\text{profit to total assets}}{1 - \text{total debt to total assets}}$$

Sources: Business Monitor Series and Company Accounts for 1974.

SOURCES OF COMPARATIVE RATIOS

There are several sources of information on individual companies in the United Kingdom apart from published accounts. Sources of information for construction of industry average ratios are, however, less easy to find. Some of the more accessible of these sources are listed below.

Government publications

Probably the most common sources of industry average ratios are government publications such as the Business Monitor series entitled *Company Finance*, which sets out the results of a regular analysis of companies' published accounts. As long delays exist before the information for a particular year is published much of its usefulness is negated. Sample ratios extracted from the ninth issue of *Company Finance*[8] are shown in Table 2–6.

Centre for Inter-firm Comparisons

The Centre for Inter-firm Comparison is a body which was formed by the British Institute of Management to provide ratios to participating firms. The ratios are prepared from information provided by subscribers in a standardized form and often include information which would not be available in published accounts.

Extel Statistical Services Ltd

This is a subscription service which distributes, in a summarized form, publicly available corporate financial information on about 8000 companies. The cards include not only financial figures but also information relating to the type of business, basic financial history of the company, and details relating to the directors.

Trade associations

Many trade associations provide average ratios to their members in return for information relating to the subscribers' own financial affairs. When available, this source is often the most useful as it would probably be the most up-to-date information available to the firm.

Financial Times

This publishes information for broad industry groups quarterly.

USE OF FINANCIAL RATIOS IN CREDIT ANALYSIS

In this chapter we have discussed a rather long list of ratios and have learned what each ratio is designed to measure. Sometimes it will be unnecessary to go beyond a few

---

8. Business Monitor, M3, *Company Finance*, published annually by the Economics and Statistics Division of the Department of Industry.

Table 2–6 *Ratios for Selected Industries (Based on Provisional Figures for 1976, Listed Companies Only).*

Industry classification[a]	Current assets to current liabilities (times)	Net income[b] to net sales (per cent)	Net income[b] to shareholders' funds (per cent)	Net income[b] to net working capital (per cent)	Net sales to shareholders' funds (times)	Net sales to net working capital (times)	Average collection period (days)
Food	1.41	6.08	32.37	65.59	5.32	10.78	42
Drink	1.80	10.87	23.49	54.20	2.16	4.98	42
Tobacco	1.73	6.21	24.93	34.63	4.01	5.58	40
Chemical and allied industries	1.88	11.42	31.21	44.41	2.73	3.89	72
Metal manufacture	1.61	6.13	22.92	31.80	3.74	5.19	79
Non-electrical engineering	1.68	7.62	24.96	32.94	3.27	4.32	87
Electrical engineering	1.80	10.31	30.37	39.64	2.94	3.84	80
Shipbuilding and[c] marine engineering	2.00	4.08	14.63	18.22	3.58	4.46	81

Industry classification[a]	Net sales to stocks (times)	Fixed assets to total assets (per cent)	Current liabilities to total assets (per cent)	Total debt to total assets (per cent)	Stocks to net working capital (per cent)	Current debt to stocks (per cent)	Net sales to total assets (times)
Food	6.6	37.7	46.3	51.6	163.3	147.6	1.97
Drink	4.3	51.7	26.9	39.5	115.6	108.6	1.07
Tobacco	4.7	32.7	38.8	53.2	118.3	115.4	1.59
Chemical and allied industries	4.9	41.4	31.2	48.7	79.1	143.5	1.07
Metal manufacture	3.9	33.7	41.3	52.2	133.1	123.9	1.30
Non-electrical engineering	4.0	24.5	45.0	52.0	107.3	137.4	1.32
Electrical engineering	4.6	28.5	39.7	49.6	83.7	149.1	1.22
Shipbuilding and[c] marine engineering	4.8	26.7	36.7	42.3	92.9	107.3	1.63

[a] Standard Industrial Classification categories.
[b] Net income = profit after interest and depreciation but before tax.
[c] Low coverage because accounts for Swan Hunter were not available.

Source: Business Monitor, M3, *Company Finance* (1978, ninth issue: Department of Industry, Business Statistic Office).

calculations to determine that a firm is in very good or very bad condition, but often the analysis is equivalent to a detective-story investigation; what one ratio will not indicate, another may. Also, a relation vaguely suggested by one ratio may be corroborated by another. For these reasons, it is often useful to calculate a number of different ratios.

In numerous situations, however, a few ratios will tell the story. For example, a credit controller who has a great many invoices flowing across his desk each day may limit himself to three ratios as evidence of whether the prospective buyer of his goods will pay promptly: (a) He may use either the current or the quick ratio to determine how burdened the prospective buyer is with current liabilities; (b) he may use the debt to total assets ratio to determine how much of the prospective buyer's own funds are invested in the business; (c) he may use any one of the profitability ratios to determine whether or not the firm has favourable prospects. If the profit margin is high enough, it may justify the risk of dealing with a slow-paying customer; profitable companies are likely to grow and thus to become better customers in the future. However, if the profit margin is low in relation to other firms in the industry, if the current ratio is low, and if the debt ratio is high, a credit controller probably will not approve a sale involving an extension of credit.[9]

Of necessity, the credit controller is more than a calculator and a reader of financial ratios. Qualitative factors may override quantitative analysis. For instance, clothes manufacturers, in selling to new retailers, often find that the financial ratios are adverse and that if they based their decisions solely on financial ratios, they would not make sales. Or, to take another example, profits may have been low for a period, but if the customer understands why profits have been low and can remove the cause of the difficulty, a credit controller may be willing to approve a sale to him. The credit controller's decision is also influenced by his own firm's profit margin. If the selling firm is making a large profit on sales, it is in a better position to take credit risks than if its own margin is low. Ultimately, the credit controller must judge a customer with regard to his character and management ability, and intelligent credit decisions must be based on careful consideration of conditions in the selling firm as well as in the buying firm.

USE OF FINANCIAL RATIOS IN SECURITY ANALYSIS

We have emphasized the use of financial analysis by the financial manager and by outside credit analysts. However, this type of analysis is also useful in security analysis, that is, in the analysis of the investment merits of shares and debentures. When the emphasis is on security analysis, the principal focus is on judging the long-run profit potential of the firm. Profitability is dependent in large part on the efficiency with which the firm is run; because financial analysis provides insights into this factor, it is useful to the security analyst.

SOME LIMITATIONS OF RATIO ANALYSIS

Although ratios are exceptionally useful tools, they do have limitations and must be used with caution. Ratios are constructed from accounting data, and accounting data are

9. Statistical techniques have been developed to improve the use of ratios in credit analysis. One such development is the discriminant analysis model reported by Edward I. Altman (Financial ratios, discriminant analysis, and the prediction of corporate bankruptcy, *Journal of Finance* 23 [September 1968]). In his model, Altman combines a number of liquidity, leverage, activity, and profitability ratios to form an index of a firm's probability of going bankrupt. His model has predicted bankruptcy quite well one or two years in the future. See also Altman, Haldeman, and Narayanan, ZETA analysis: a new model to identify bankruptcy risk of corporations, *Journal of Banking and Finance* 1 (June 1977), pp. 29–54.

subject to different interpretations and even to manipulation. For example, two firms may use different depreciation methods or stock valuation methods; depending on the procedures followed, reported profits can be raised or lowered. Similar differences can be encountered in the treatment of research and development expenditures, pension fund costs, mergers, and bad-debt provisions. Further, if firms use different fiscal years, and if seasonal factors are important, this can influence the comparative ratios. Thus, if the ratios of two firms are to be compared, it is important to analyse the basic accounting data upon which the ratios were based and to reconcile any major differences.[10]

A financial manager must also be cautious when judging whether a particular ratio is 'good' or 'bad' and in forming a composite judgement about a firm on the basis of a set of ratios. For example, a high stock turnover ratio could indicate efficient stock control, but it could also indicate a serious shortage of stocks and suggest the likelihood of stock-outs. Further, there is nothing sacred about the industry average figures; after all, any management worth its salt will try to be better than average.

Ratios, then, are extremely useful tools. But as with other analytical methods, they must be used with judgement and caution, not in an unthinking, mechanical manner.

SUMMARY

Ratio analysis, which relates balance sheet and profit and loss statement items to one another, permits the charting of a firm's history and the evaluation of its present position. Such analysis also allows the financial manager to anticipate reactions of investors and creditors and thus gives him a good insight into how his attempts to acquire funds are likely to be received.

Basic Types of ratios

Ratios are classified into four basic types: (a) liquidity, (b) gearing, (c) activity, and (d) profitability. Data from the Walker-Wilson Manufacturing Company were used to compute each type of ratio and to show how a financial analysis is made in practice. An almost unlimited number of ratios may be calculated, but in practice a limited number of each type is sufficient. We have discussed in this chapter what are probably the 12 most common ratios.

Use of ratios

A ratio is not a meaningful number in and of itself; it must be compared with something before it becomes useful. The two basic kinds of comparative analysis are (a) trend analysis, which involves computing the ratios of a particular firm for several years and comparing the ratios over time to see if the firm is improving or deteriorating, and (b) comparisons with other firms in the same industry. These two comparisons are often combined in the graphic analysis illustrated in Figure 2–1.

du Pont system

The du Pont system shows how the return on investment is dependent upon asset turnover

10. Recent attempts to reduce some of these differences have included the establishment of the Accounting Standards Committee in 1971 by the Consultative Committee of Accountancy Bodies.

and the profit margin. The system is generally expressed in the form of the following equation:

$$\frac{\text{sales}}{\text{investment}} \times \frac{\text{profit}}{\text{sales}} = \text{ROI}.$$

The first term, investment turnover, times the profit margin equals the rate of return on investment. The kinds of actions we discussed in this chapter can be used to effect needed changes in turnover and the profit margin and thus improve the return on investment.

The du Pont system can be extended to encompass financial gearing and to examine the manner in which turnover, sales margins, and gearing all combine to determine the rate of return on net worth. The following equation is used to show this relationship:

$$\text{Rate of return on net worth} = \frac{\text{return on assets (ROI)}}{1.0 - \text{debt ratio}}.$$

Rates of return in different industries

The extended du Pont system shows why firms in different industries – even though they have widely different turnovers, profit margins, and debt ratios – may end up with very similar rates of return on net worth. In general, firms dealing with relatively perishable products are expected to have high turnovers but low profit margins; firms whose production processes require heavy investments in fixed assets are expected to have low turnover ratios but high profit margins.

QUESTIONS

2–1. 'A uniform system of accounts, including identical forms for balance sheets and income statements, would be a most reasonable requirement for the Stock Exchange to impose on all quoted companies.' Discuss.

2–2. We have divided financial ratios into four groups: liquidity, gearing, activity, and profitability. We could also consider financial analysis as being conducted by four groups of analysts: management, equity investors, long-term creditors, and short-term creditors.
(a) Explain the nature of each type of ratio.
(b) Explain the emphasis of each type of analyst.

2–3. Why can norms with relatively well-defined limits be stated in advance for some financial ratios but not for others?

2–4. How does trend analysis supplement the basic financial ratio calculations and their interpretation?

2–5. Why would you expect the stock turnover figure to be more important to a grocery store than to a shoe repair store?

2–6. How can a firm have a high current ratio and still be unable to pay its debts?

2–7. 'The higher the rate of return on investment (ROI), the better the firm's management.' Is this statement true for all firms? Explain. If you disagree with the statement, give examples of instances in which it might not be true.

2–8. What factors would you, as a financial manager, want to examine if a firm's rate of return (a) on assets or (b) on net worth is too low?

2–9. Profit margins and turnover rates vary from industry to industry. What industry characteristics account for these variations? Give some contrasting examples to illustrate your answer.

2–10. Which relation would you as a financial manager prefer:
(a) a profit margin of 10 per cent and a capital turnover of 2, or
(b) a profit margin of 20 per cent and a capital turnover of 1?
Can you think of any firm with a relation similar to (b)?

PROBLEMS

2–1. The following data were taken from the financial statements of the Geordie Company for the calendar year 1977. Industry average ratios are given below.
(a) Fill in the ratios for Geordie.
(b) Indicate by comparison with industry averages the possible errors in management policies reflected in these financial statements.

Geordie Company Balance Sheet 31 December 1977.

Ordinary share capital		£100 000	Net fixed assets		£150 000
Reserves		200 000	Current assets		
Long-term debentures (6%)		55 000	Stocks	£200 000	
Current liabilities			Debtors	70 000	
Short-term loan	£55 000		Cash	55 000	
Creditors and accruals	65 000	120 000			325 000
		£475 000			£475 000

Geordie Company Profit and Loss Account for Year Ended 31 December 1977.

Sales		£690 000
Cost of goods sold		
Materials	£260 000	
Labour	165 000	
Heat, light and power	25 000	
Indirect labour	40 000	
Depreciation	15 000	505 000
Gross profit		185 000
Selling expenses	£ 70 000	
General and administrative expenses	80 000	150 000
Operating profit		35 000
Less: interest expense		6 050
Net profit before taxes		28 950
Less: corporation tax (assumed at 50%)		14 475
Net profit		£ 14 475

Ratio	Ratios: Geordie	Ratios: Industry averages
current assets / current liabilities	______	2.5 times
debt / total assets	______	35%
times interest earned	______	7 times
sales / stocks	______	9.9 times
average collection period	______	33 days
sales / total assets	______	1.2 times
net profit / sales	______	3.2%
net profit / total assets	______	3.8%
net profit / net worth	______	10.7%

2–2. Griffin Supply Company, a small manufacturer of surgical supplies and equipment, has been plagued with relatively low profitability in recent years. As a result, the board of directors replaced the managing director of the firm. The new managing director, Pat Roffman, asks you to make an analysis of the firm's financial position using the du Pont system. The most recent financial statements are reproduced below.
(a) Calculate some ratios which you feel would be useful in this case.
(b) Construct a du Pont chart of analysis for Griffin similar to the one in Figure 2–2.
(c) Do the balance sheet items or the profit and loss figures seem to be primarily responsible for the low profits?
(d) Which specific accounts seem to be most out of line in relation to other firms in the industry?

	Industry average ratios
Current ratio	2/1
Quick ratio	1/1
Debt to total assets	30%
Times interest earned	7 times
Fixed charge coverage	5 times
Stock turnover	10 times
Average collection period	15 days
Fixed assets turnover	6 times
Total assets turnover	3 times
Net profit on sales	3%
Return on total assets	9%
Return on net worth	12.8%

Griffin Supply Company Balance Sheet 31 December 1978.

	£000	£000		£000	£000
Ordinary share capital		1140	Fixed assets		2250
Retained earnings		2010	*Less*: depreciation		780
Total shareholders' funds		3150			1470
Long-term debentures (5%)		240	Current assets:		
		3390	Stocks	1590	
Current liabilities:			Debtors (net)	660	
Short-term loan (5%)	450		Quoted investments	330	
Trade creditors	450		Cash	450	
Other creditors	210	1110			3030
		£4500			£4500

Griffin Supply Company Profit and Loss Account for year ended 31 December 1978.

	£000	£000
Sales (net)		7950
Cost of goods sold		6600
Gross profit		1350
Operating expenses	735	
Depreciation expense	120	
Interest expense	45	
Total expenses		900
Net profit before tax		450
Corporation tax (at 50%)		225
Net profit after tax		£ 225

2-3. Indicate the effect of the transactions listed below on each of the following: total current assets, working capital, current ratio, and net profit. Use + to indicate an increase, − to indicate a decrease, and 0 to indicate no effect. State necessary assumptions and assume an initial current ratio of more than 1 to 1.

	Total current assets	Net working capital[a]	Current ratio	Net profit
1. Cash is acquired through issue of additional ordinary shares.	____	____	____	____
2. Stocks of finished goods are sold for cash.	____	____	____	____
3. Corporation tax is paid.	____	____	____	____
4. A fixed asset is sold for less than book value.	____	____	____	____
5. A fixed asset is sold for more than book value.	____	____	____	____
6. Goods are sold on account.	____	____	____	____
7. Payment is made to trade creditors for previous purchases.	____	____	____	____
8. A cash dividend is declared and paid.	____	____	____	____
9. Cash is obtained through bank loans.	____	____	____	____
10. A short-term loan is obtained.	____	____	____	____
11. Previously issued share options are exercised by company shareholders.	____	____	____	____
12. A profitable firm increases its fixed asset depreciation charge.	____	____	____	____
13. Quoted investments are sold below cost.	____	____	____	____
14. Bad debts are written off against bad debts provision.	____	____	____	____
15. Loans are made to employees.	____	____	____	____
16. Current operating expenses are paid.	____	____	____	____
17. Short-term promissory notes are issued to trade creditors for prior purchase.	____	____	____	____
18. A ten-year loan is raised to pay off trade creditors.	____	____	____	____

Table (*contd.*)

	Total current assets	Net working capital[a]	Current ratio	Net profit
19. A fully depreciated asset is disposed of.	____	____	____	____
20. A cash sinking fund for the redemption of debentures is created.	____	____	____	____
21. Debentures are redeemed by the use of the sinking fund.	____	____	____	____
22. Trade debtors are collected.	____	____	____	____
23. A capital dividend is declared and paid.	____	____	____	____
24. Equipment is purchased with a short-term loan.	____	____	____	____
25. The allowance for doubtful debts is increased.	____	____	____	____
26. Goods are purchased on account.	____	____	____	____
27. Controlling interest in another firm is acquired by the issue of additional ordinary shares.	____	____	____	____
28. An associated company pays the firm a cash dividend from current earnings.	____	____	____	____
29. The estimate for corporation tax liability is increased.	____	____	____	____
30. A transfer is made from earnings to provide for increased replacement cost of fixed assets.	____	____	____	____

[a] Net working capital is defined as current assets minus current liabilities.

2–4.[1] Jeff Jones, vice-president and loan officer of the First National Bank of Kansas City, was recently alerted to the deteriorating financial position of one of his clients, Midwest Cannery, by his bank's newly instituted computer loan analysis programme. The bank requires quarterly financial statements – balance sheets and income statements – from each of its major loan customers. This information is punched on cards and fed into the computer, which then calculates the key ratios for each customer, charts trends in these ratios, and compares the statistics on each company with the average ratios and trends of other firms in the same industry. If any ratio of any company is significantly poorer than the industry average, the computer output makes note of this fact. Moreover, if the terms of a loan require that certain ratios be maintained at specified minimum levels, and if these minimums are not being met by a company, the computer output notes the deficiency.

When an analysis was run on Midwest three months earlier, Jones saw that certain of Midwest's ratios were showing downward trends and were dipping below the averages for the canning industry. Jones sent John Herndon, president of Midwest, a copy of the computer output, together with a note voicing his concern. Although Herndon acknowledged receipt of the material, he took no action to correct the situation.

While problems appeared to be developing in the financial analysis three months ago, no ratio was below the level specified in the loan agreement between the bank and Midwest. However, the latest analysis, which was based on the data given in Tables 2P–1, 2P–2 and 2P–3, showed that the current ratio was below the 2.0 times specified in the loan agreement. Legally, according to the loan agreement, the Kansas City Bank could call upon Midwest for immediate payment of the entire bank loan and, if payment was not forthcoming within ten days, the bank could force the company into bankruptcy. Jones had no intention of enforcing the contract to the full extent that he legally could, but he did intend to use the loan agreement provision to prompt Midwest to take some decisive action to improve its financial picture.

Midwest is a medium-sized cannery whose products – canned fruits, vegetables and juices – are sold to distributors throughout the midwestern states. Seasonal working capital needs have been financed primarily by loans from the Kansas City Bank, and the current line of credit permits the cannery to borrow up to $360 000. In accordance with standard banking practices, however, the loan agreement requires that the bank loan be repaid in full at some time during the year, in this case by February 1979.

A limitation on prices of canned goods, coupled with higher costs, caused a decline in Midwest's profit margin and net income during the last half of 1977 as well as during most of 1978. Sales increased during both these years, however, because of the cannery's aggressive marketing programme.

When Herndon received a copy of Jones' latest computer analysis and his blunt statement that the bank would insist on immediate repayment of the entire loan unless Midwest presented a report showing how its poor current financial picture could be improved, Herndon tried to determine what could be done. He rapidly concluded that the present level of sales could not be continued without an *increase* in the bank

1 . This problem was adapted from E. F. Brigham, R. L. Crum, T. J. Nantell, R. T. Aubey and R. H. Pettway, *Cases in Managerial Finance* (New York: Holt, Rinehart and Winston, Second edition).

Table 2P–1 *Midwest Cannery Balance Sheets.*

	31 December			
	1970	1976	1977	1978
Land and buildings	$76 500	$61 200	$163 200	$153 000
Machinery	102 000	188 700	147 900	127 500
Other fixed assets	61 200	35 700	10 200	7 600
	239 700	285 600	321 300	288 100
Stocks	255 000	382 500	637 500	1 032 800
Debtors	204 000	306 000	346 800	484 500
Cash	51 000	76 500	35 700	25 500
	$749 700	$1 050 600	$1 341 300	$1 830 900
Ordinary share capital	$459 000	$459 000	$459 000	$459 000
Retained earnings	51 000	351 900	438 600	489 600
	510 000	810 900	897 600	948 600
Mortgage debenture	76 500	56 100	51 000	45 900
	586 500	867 000	948 600	994 500
Bank loan	—	—	127 500	357 000
Trade creditors	112 200	122 400	193 800	382 500
Accruals	51 000	61 200	71 400	96 900
	$749 700	$1 050 600	$1 341 300	$1 830 900

Table 2P–2 *Midwest Cannery Income Statements.*

	Year ended 31 December		
	1976	1977	1978
Net sales	$3 315 000	$3 442 500	$3 570 000
Cost of goods sold	2 652 000	2 754 000	2 856 000
Gross operating profit	$663 000	$688 500	$714 000
General administration and selling	255 000	280 500	306 000
Depreciation	102 000	127 500	153 000
Miscellaneous	51 000	107 100	153 000
Net income before taxes	$255 000	$173 400	$102 000
Corporation tax (50%)	127 500	86 700	51 000
Net income	$127 500	$86 700	$51 000

Table 2P–3

	Canning industry ratios (1978)[a]
Quick ratio	1.0
Current ratio	2.7
Stock turnover[b]	7 times
Average collection period	32 days
Fixed asset turnover[b]	13.0 times
Total asset turnover[b]	2.6 times
Return on total assets	9%
Return on net worth	18%
Debt ratio	50%
Profit margin on sales	3.5%

[a] Industry average ratios have been constant for the past three years.
[b] Based on year-end balance sheet figures.

loan from $360 000 to $510 000 since payments of $150 000 for construction of a plant addition would have to be made in January 1979. Although the cannery had been a good customer of the Kansas City Bank for over 50 years, Herndon was concerned whether the bank would continue to supply the present line of credit, let alone increase the outstanding loan. Herndon was especially troubled in view of the fact that the Federal Reserve had recently tightened bank credit considerably, forcing the Kansas City Bank to ration credit even to its best customers.

(a) Calculate the key financial ratios for Midwest and plot trends in the firm's ratios against the industry averages.
(b) What strengths and weaknesses are revealed by the ratio analysis?

Questions to be answered at the option of the tutor:

(c) What sources of *internal* funds would be available for the retirement of the loan? If the bank grants additional credit and extends the increased loan from a due date of 1 February 1979 to 30 June 1979 would the company be able to repay the loan on 30 June 1979? *Hint:* To answer this question, consider profits and depreciation, as well as the amount of stocks and debtors that would be carried if Midwest's stock turnover and average collection period were at industry average levels, that is, how much funds would be released if Midwest's current assets were at industry average levels?
(d) In 1978, Midwest's return on equity was 5.38 per cent versus 18 per cent for the industry. Use the du Pont equation to pinpoint the factors causing Midwest to fall so far below the industry average.
(e) On the basis of your financial analysis, do you believe that the bank should grant the additional loan and extend the entire line of credit to 30 June 1979?
(f) If the credit extension is not made, what alternatives are open to Midwest?
(g) Under what circumstances is the validity of comparative ratio analysis questionable?

SELECTED REFERENCES

Altman, Edward I. Financial ratios, discriminant analysis and the prediction of corporate bankruptcy. *Journal of Finance* 23 (September 1968): 589–609.

Altman, Edward I. Railroad bankruptcy propensity. *Journal of Finance* 26 (May 1971): 1971): 333–345.

Altman, Edward I. Haldeman, R. G. and Narayanan, P. ZETA analysis: a new model to identify bankruptcy risk of corporations. *Journal of Banking and Finance* 1 (June 1977): 29–54.

Beaver, William H. Financial ratios as predictors of failure. *Empirical Research in Accountancy: Selected Studies* in *Journal of Accounting Research* (1966): 71–111.

Benishay, Haskel. Economic information on financial ratio analysis. *Accounting and Business Research* 2 (Spring 1971): 174–179.

Bierman, Harold, Jr. Measuring financial liquidity. *Accounting Review* 35 (October 1960): 628–632.

Brinkman, Donald R. and Prentiss, Paul H. Replacement cost and current-value measurement: how to do it. *Financial Executive* 43 (October 1975): 20–26.

Carsberg, B. and Hope, T., eds. *Current Issues in Accounting.* Oxford: Philip Alan, 1977.

Cutler, R. S. and Westwick, C. A. The impact of inflation accounting on the stock market. *Accounting* (March 1973): 15–24.

Davidson, S. and Weil, R. L. Predicting inflation-adjusted results. *Financial Analysts Journal* 31 (January–February 1975): 27–31.

Davidson, S. and Weil, R. L. Inflation accounting and 1974 earnings. *Financial Analysts Journal* 31 (September–October 1975): 42–54.

Davidson, S. and Weil, R. L. Replacement cost disclosure. *Financial Analysts Journal* 32 (March–April 1976): 57–66.

Donaldson, Gordon. New framework for corporate debt capacity. *Harvard Business Review* 40 (March–April 1962).

Drury, J. C. Financial analysis of UK industry. *Management Accounting* (November 1976).

Edey, H. C. Accounting principles and business reality. In *Modern Financial Management*, B. V. Carsberg and H. C. Edey, eds. London: Penguin, 1969, pp. 21–49.

Edmister, Robert O. An empirical test of financial ratio analysis for small business failure predictions. *Journal of Financial and Quantitative Analysis* 7 (March 1972): 1477–1493.

Gibbs, Martin. The Hyde gearing adjustment. *Accountancy* (February 1978): 87–90.

Gibbs, M., Percy, K. and Saville, R. Inflation accounting: Sandilands – the effect on dividends. *Accountancy* (August 1976): 62–66.

Grinyer, John R. and Lewis, Richard W. Valuation and meaningful accounts. *Accounting and Business Research* (Autumn 1972): 275–283.

Helfert, Erich A. *Techniques of Financial Analysis.* 3rd ed. Homewood, Ill.: Irwin, 1972.

Horrigan, James C. A short history of financial ratio analysis. *Accounting Review* 43 (April 1968): 284–294.

Horrigan, James C. The determination of long-term credit standing with financial ratios. *Empirical Research in Accounting: Selected Studies* in *Journal of Accounting Research* (1966): 44–62.

Johnson, Craig C. Ratio analysis and the prediction of firm failure. *Journal of Finance* 25 (December 1970): 1116–1168. See also Edward I. Altman. Reply. *ibid.*: 1169–1172.

Lee, T. A. *Income and Value Measurement: Theory and Practice*. London: Nelson, 1974.

Sterling, R. R. Decision oriented financial accounting. *Accounting and Business Research* (Summer 1972): 198–208.

Terborgh, George. Inflation and profits. *Financial Analysts Journal* 30 (May–June 1974): 19–23.

Theil, Henri. On the use of information theory concepts in the analysis of financial statements. *Management Science* 15 (May 1969) 459–480.

Weston, Frank T. Adjust your accounting for inflation. *Harvard Business Review* 53 (January–February 1975): 22–29.

Weston, J. Fred and Goudzwaard, Maurice B. Financial policies in an inflationary environment. In *The Treasurer's Handbook*, J. Fred Weston and Maurice B. Goudzwaard, eds. Homewood, Illinois: Dow Jones-Irwin, 1976, pp. 20–42.

Westwick, C. *How to Use Management Ratios*. London: Gower Press, 1973.

Appendix A to Chapter 2:

Implications of Changes in Price Levels

Immediately after the Second World War with the removal of price controls that had held prices to arbitrary levels, there was a burst of inflation. Annual price increases thereafter were contained mainly in the range of 1 to 5 per cent per annum until the late 1960s when inflation again began to accelerate in the United Kingdom.

Double-figure inflation as measured by the Consumer Price Index has been a reality or threat in the United Kingdom since 1971. As a result proposals have been made to modify accounting procedures to recognize that the traditional postulate of a stable measuring unit is no longer valid. In 1971, the Accounting Standard Committee produced a discussion paper on inflation accounting. This was followed on 17 January 1973 by an exposure draft of a proposed statement entitled 'Accounting for changes in the purchasing power of money'.[1] Finally, in May 1974 a provisional statement of standard accounting practice[2] was issued, based on the earlier exposure draft. The provisional nature of this statement was explained in the formation by the Government in January 1974 of an independent Committee of Enquiry, under the chairmanship of Sir Francis Sandilands, to consider the various methods of adjusting company accounts for changes in costs and prices, having regard to the proposals put forward by the Accounting Standards Steering Committee and to take into account the wider implications of inflation accounting.

The report published by the Sandilands Committee in September 1975[3] effectively rejected the preparation of accounts based on historic costs, with adjustments for changes in the general purchasing power of money. They recommended instead preparation of accounts based on a current cost system. The accounting profession gave guarded support to the recommendations of the committee and, following a Government request, set up a Steering Group to produce an accounting system based on the recommendations of the Sandilands Committee. An exposure draft[4] was subsequently issued in November 1976 but was withdrawn after rejection of its proposal for a compulsory system of current cost accounting by a meeting of the Institute of Chartered Accountants in England and Wales, in June 1977. Following from this, a special subcommittee of the Accounting Standards Committee produced in December 1977 an interim report, known as the Hyde Proposals,[5] which recommended that quoted companies should produce a supplementary profit and loss account showing the effects of the main current cost accounting adjustments. These latest proposals have been supported by the Council of the Stock Exchange as a welcome interim recommendation.

If any lesson can be drawn from the above history of reports dealing with the problems of inflation accounting it is the lack of agreement as to how best the problem should be tackled. Two different methods have emerged:

---

1 Accounting Standards Committee, Accounting for changes in the purchasing power of money. Exposure Draft No. 8, London 1973.

2. Accounting Standards Committee, Accounting for changes in purchasing power of money. Provisional statement of standard accounting practice, No. 7, May 1974.

3. Report of the Inflation Accounting Committee, HMSO Cmnd paper 6225, 1975.

4. Accounting Standards Committee, Exposure Draft No. 18, London 1976.

5. Inflation accounting – an interim recommendation, Accounting Standards Committee, London 1977.

one is based on general purchasing power adjustments to historic cost accounts and the other on specific adjustment through a current cost accounting system. As the two approaches have implications for financial statement analysis, they will both be reviewed in this appendix.

It has been pointed out that in a period of inflation distortions will result from the use of the historic cost postulate. Assets are recorded at cost, but revenue and other expense flows are in units of different purchasing power. The depreciation of fixed costs does not reflect the current cost of these assets.[6] Furthermore, net income during periods when assets are held do not reflect the effects of management's decision to hold the assets rather than sell them. Assets are not stated on the balance sheet at their current values, so that the firm's financial position cannot be accurately evaluated. And when assets are sold, gains or losses are reported during that period even though these results reflect decisions in prior periods to hold the assets.[7]

PROCEDURES IN CURRENT COST ACCOUNTING

In current cost accounting, two major categories of problems must be solved. One is to decide upon a measure of the current value to the business of the assets held. A second is to measure income after the first problem is solved. Each is considered in turn.

The current value of the assets of an entity is defined as the loss which the entity would suffer if deprived of the use of these assets.

Three methods of measuring the current value of assets have been identified:

1. Current replacement costs.
2. Net realizable value.
3. Present value of future cash flows.

Recent proposals by accountancy bodies have favoured the use of current replacement cost as a measure of current values. Current replacement cost is by nature an entry value to the business and, as the name implies, is the current cost of an identical asset or an asset equivalent in capacity and service. For the majority of valuation circumstances current replacement cost will correctly represent the value to the business.

However, if a company were to be liquidated by selling off its assets, the relevant measure of value is the net realizable values of the individual assets. But in applying this approach, the only assets for which current market values are quoted are those continuously traded such as quoted investments. Consequently, exit values are hardly relevant for a going concern for which liquidation is not contemplated.

The present values of future cash flows or the discounted cash flows are considered by many to represent economic values. Their practical implementation requires dependable forecasts and the selection of the applicable discount rates. For most companies new investments continue to be made, seeking to add to the earning power of existing assets. Hence it becomes difficult to segregate the future cash of the firm between the firm's existing assets and its new investments. Thus the discounted cash flow method, while widely and effectively used in evaluating individual investment projects, is more difficult to apply in placing values upon the physical assets of the firm as a whole.

It has been stated that in judging the ability of a business to do the same kinds of things in the future as in the past and to pay dividends or to finance expansion without requiring new external financing, 'replacement costs are perhaps the most useful measure of current value.'[8] It might also be argued that the discounted cash flow method, soundly applied, yields results consistent with current replacement values.

In some situations current replacement cost will be higher than both net realizable value and present value. In these cases it would be inappropriate to consider replacement cost as a measure of the deprival value of the assets as replacement cost would presumably not be considered. Instead, current cost should be taken as the higher of net realizable value and present value.

Postulating that a measure of replacement costs has been achieved, the second task, that of measuring income and financial position, is considered. Several concepts of income are involved. The simplified illustration presented by Falkenstein and Weil is utilized here. Their illustration and three concepts of income are reproduced in Table 2A–1.

Pretax *distributable income* is defined as revenues less expenses based on replacement costs. It is a measure of income that can be distributed as taxes and returns to owners without impairing the firm's physical capacity to remain in business at current levels.

---

6. W. T. Baxter, *Accounting Values and Inflation* (London: McGraw-Hill, 1975), pp. 13–16.
7. Davidson et al, *Financial Accounting* (Hindsale, III.: Dryden Press, 1975), p. 441.
8. A. Falkenstein and R. L. Weil, Replacement cost accounting, *Financial Analysts Journal* 33 (January–February 1977), pp. 47–48. An earlier and perhaps more comprehensive study of this area may be found in E. O. Edwards and P. W. Bell's *The Theory and Measurement of Business Income* (California: University of California Press, 1961), pp. 33–69.

Table 2A–1 *Replacement Cost Income Statement. Simple Illustration.*

Assumed data		(Historical) Acquisition cost	Replacement cost
Opening stock, 1/1/76		£ 900	£1100
Closing stock, 31/12/76		1200	1550
Cost of goods sold for 1976		4000	4500
Sales for 1976	£5200		
Income statement for 1976			
Sales			£5200
Cost of goods sold, replacement cost basis			4500
1. Distributable income			£ 700
Realized holding gains			500[a]
2. Realized income			£1200
Unrealized holding gains			150[b]
3. Economic income			£1350

[a] Realized holding gain during a period is replacement cost of goods sold less historical cost of goods sold; for 1976 the realized holding gain is £500 = £4500 – £4000.
[b] The total unrealized holding gain at any time is replacement cost of stock on hand at that time less historical cost of that stock. The unrealized holding gain during a period is the unrealized holding gain at the end of the period less the unrealized holding gain at the beginning of the period. The unrealized holding gain prior to 1976 is £200 = £1100 – £900. The unrealized holding gain during 1976 = £(1550 – 1200) – £(1100 – 900) = £350 – £200 = £150.

Source: A Falkenstein and R. L. Weil, Replacement cost accounting, *Financial Analysts Journal* 33 (January–February, 1977), p. 49.

Realized income is distributable income plus holding gains that have been realized during the period. The realized holding gain is the replacement value of goods sold less their historical costs. The sum of the distributable income and the realized holding gain is the realized income. This is the same as the conventional measure of income which is based on the realization principle. Replacement cost data make it possible to separate distributable income and realized holding gains.

The sum of realized income plus unrealized holding gains has been called *economic income*. This view holds that an increase in the value of assets is economic income whether or not the asset has been sold. The economic measure of income has been defined as the income that can be consumed during the period leaving the person as well off at the end of the period as at the beginning. This leads to an emphasis on the physical capacity of the firm. Thus a company may be said to be as well off at the end of the period as at the beginning only if it has sufficient physical assets to carry on the same level of business activity. Under this view, holding gains, whether or not realized, are tied up in the net assets required to conduct the operations of the firm at the current physical levels of activity. Thus it might be more appropriate to label the third measure of income 'realized plus unrealized income unadjusted for general purchasing power changes.'

In a study of the effects of using a system of current replacement cost accounting[9] analysts from the Phillips and Drew firm of stockbrokers applied the Sandilands system of replacement cost accounting to 28 out of the 30 member firms of the Financial Times Ordinary Index for 1976. They calculated that, on average, reported earnings under the Sandilands method of adjustment would be 85 per cent lower than the conventional reported figures for these companies for 1976. In addition, forecasts for 1977 suggested that 11 of the 28 companies would not have sufficient earnings to cover their historic dividends.

Therefore the use of a current replacement method in calculating distributable income can result in substantial changes in income as well as in financial position. When economic changes are so large that current values of assets differ greatly from their historical values, it is argued that major distortions will result if these changes are not taken into account in accounting procedures and practices.

---

9. M. Gibbs, K. Percy and R. Saville, Inflation accounting: Sandilands – the effect on dividends: *Accountancy* (August 1976), pp. 62–66.

CURRENT PURCHASING POWER ACCOUNTING

Many accountants would argue that current cost accounting is not a system of accounting for inflation. Rather it is a means of adjusting accounts for changes in the value of specific assets held by a business irrespective of the general rate of inflation. It is argued instead that a system of accounting for inflation should be concerned with making adjustments for changes in the general purchasing power of money from one time period to another. This has resulted in the proposals for Current Purchasing Power Accounting (CPP) as outlined in the Provisional Statement of Standard Accounting Practice No. 7 in May 1974.

CPP would seek to adjust the current value of non-monetary items by a general price index. The historic cost basis of accounting is retained but adjusted by a price index. CPP adjusts original cost data to compensate for changes in the purchasing power of the pound and capital consumption expenses, and the value of goods sold from stocks are adjusted accordingly. A new entry would be introduced to financial reports; net holding gains on monetary items. Operationally, monetary and non-monetary items must be separated in financial statements and a price index must be selected. Monetary items are assets, liabilities or capital, the amounts of which are fixed by contract or statute in terms of numbers of pounds regardless of changes in the purchasing power of the pound.

Non-monetary items are all items which are not monetary items, with the exception of the total equity interest which is neither a monetary nor a non-monetary item.[10]

Table 2A–2 *Financial Ratios for Selected UK Quoted Companies 1971–2.*

	Earnings per share			Dividend cover		
Industry classification and company	Historic cost	CPP	Percentage change	Historic cost	CPP	Percentage change
Electrical:						
GEC	7.9	0.2	−97	2.2	0.1	−95
Heavy engineering:						
Simon Engineering	5.9	3.4	−42	0.8	0.5	−38
Banks:						
Lloyds	49.0	30.9	−37	3.1	1.9	−39
Food retailing:						
Unigate	5.8	4.5	−23	1.9	1.5	−21
Breweries:						
Allied Breweries	5.3	6.6	+25	1.6	1.9	+19
Insurance:						
Commercial Union	12.6	32.5	+158	1.5	3.9	+160
Property:						
Land securities	5.2	26.6	+414	1.1	5.4	+391

Source: R. S. Cutler and C. A. Westwick, The impact of inflation accounting on the stock market, *Accountancy* (March 1973), pp. 15–24.

Table 2A–2 shows the effects of adjustment for CPP accounting on selected financial ratios for a number of UK quoted companies for 1971–2. The ratios indicate the wide disparity in the effects of the adjustments on firms in different industry groupings. 'What stands out from the above figures is the sharp division between manufacturing companies, whose earnings are generally reduced by CPP accounting principles, and the service companies whose earnings are generally increased.'[11] The broad significance of the two major forms of adjustments can be indicated by the results outlined above. Both CPP adjustments and replacement cost accounting have a major effect on accounts prepared on a conventional basis. The effect, however, differs tremendously according to the industry classification or firm which is under examination. The effects of inflation cannot then be said to affect all firms in the same way and thus be ignored. Rather, the published accounts of companies can be seen to contain serious weaknesses when based on the historic cost convention and can be dangerously misleading to external analysts. A reworking of financial ratio analysis based on an agreed system of 'current value accounting' is therefore an important requirement for internal or external analysts.

---

10. Accounting Standards Steering Committee, Accounting for changes in the purchasing power of money. ibid., para 29.
11. R. S. Cutler and C. A. Westwick, 'The impact of inflation accounting on the stock market, *Accountancy* (March 1973), pp. 15–24.

LIMITATIONS OF FINANCIAL STATEMENT ANALYSIS

For a number of reasons, therefore, we cannot place absolute reliance upon the results of financial ratio analysis. In general, 'window dressing' practices that will improve profitability in the short run may be utilized. Such practices include the postponement of the maintenance of fixed assets, which will decrease costs and increase profitability in the short run, but which will impact the firm severely when machine breakdowns occur and production processes are interrupted. A policy of delaying the purchase of more modern equipment will decrease capital outlays and reduce depreciation expenditures in the short run. However, failure to keep pace with competitors who are installing the most modern and efficient low-cost machinery will result in a cost disadvantage at some point in time.

In addition, we have seen how changing price levels and changes in the current values of assets can produce distortions in accounting measures of performance and financial position. It is desirable, therefore, to have made available the kind of additional information that has been outlined in the various statements.

Nevertheless, even with the additional supplementary information, we do not take the position that financial ratio analysis is the complete answer to evaluating the performance of a firm. When financial ratio analysis indicates that the patterns of a firm depart from industry norms, this is not an absolutely certain indication that something is wrong with the firm. Departures from industry norms provide a basis for raising questions and further investigation and analysis. Additional information and discussions may establish sound explanations for the differences between the pattern for the individual firm and industry composite ratios. Or the differences may reveal forms of mismanagement calling for correction.

Conversely, conformity to industry average ratios does not establish with certainty that the firm is performing normally and is managed well. In the short run many tricks can be used to make the firm 'look good' in relation to industry standards. The analyst must develop first-hand knowledge of the operations of the firm and of its management to provide a check on the financial ratios. In addition, the analyst must develop a sense, a touch, a smell, and a feel of what is going on in the firm. Sometimes it is this sixth sense kind of business judgement that uncovers weaknesses in the firm. The analyst should not be anaesthetized by financial ratios that appear to conform with normality.

Thus financial ratios are a useful part of an investigative and analytical process. They are not the complete answer to questions about the performance of firms.

Chapter 3

Profit Planning

The preceding chapter described how ratios are used in financial analysis and showed how the basic ratios are related to one another. A major area of financial management involves a continuous review of these ratios to ensure that no aspects of the firm's existing operations are getting out of control – this key element of the system of financial controls designed to maximize operating efficiency is discussed in Chapter 4. Still other tools are available to aid the financial manager in the planning and control process. Two of these – (a) break-even analysis, which is especially useful when considering factory expansion and new product decisions, and (b) the sources and applications of funds statement, which is an important aid in seeing how the firm has obtained funds and how these funds have been used – are discussed in this chapter.

BREAK-EVEN ANALYSIS

Break-even analysis is an analytical technique for studying the relations among fixed costs, variable costs, and profits. If a firm's costs were all variable, the problem of break-even volume would seldom arise; by having some variable and some fixed costs, the firm must suffer losses until a given volume has been reached.

Break-even analysis is a formal profit-planning approach based on established relations between costs and revenues. It is a device for determining the point at which sales will just cover total costs. If the firm is to avoid losses, its sales must cover all costs – those that vary directly with production and those that do not change as production levels change. Costs that fall into each of those categories are outlined in Table 3–1.

The nature of break-even analysis is depicted in Figure 3–1, the basic break-even chart. The chart is on a unit basis, with volume produced shown on the horizontal axis and costs and income measured on the vertical axis. Fixed costs of £40 000 are represented by a horizontal line; they are the same (fixed) regardless of the number of units produced. Variable costs are assumed to be £1.20 a unit. Total costs rise by £1.20, the amount of the variable costs, for each additional unit produced. Production is assumed to be sold at £2 a unit, so the total income is pictured as a straight line, which must also increase with production. The slope (or the rate of ascent) of the total-income line is steeper than that of

Table 3–1 *Fixed and Variable Costs.*

Fixed costs[a]	Direct or variable costs
Depreciation on plant and equipment	Factory labour
Rentals	Materials
Interest charges on debt	Sales commissions
Salaries of research staff	
Salaries of executive staff	
General office expenses	

[a] Some of these costs — for example, salaries and office expenses — could be varied to some degree; however, firms are reluctant to reduce these expenditures in response to temporary fluctuations in sales. Such costs are often called *semi-variable* costs.

the total-cost line. This must be true, because the firm is gaining £2.00 of revenue for every £1.20 paid out for labour and materials, the variable costs.

Up to the break-even point, found at the intersection of the total-income and total-cost lines, the firm suffers losses. After that point, the firm begins to make profits. Figure 3–1 indicates a break-even point at a sales and cost level of £100 000 and a production level of 50 000 units.

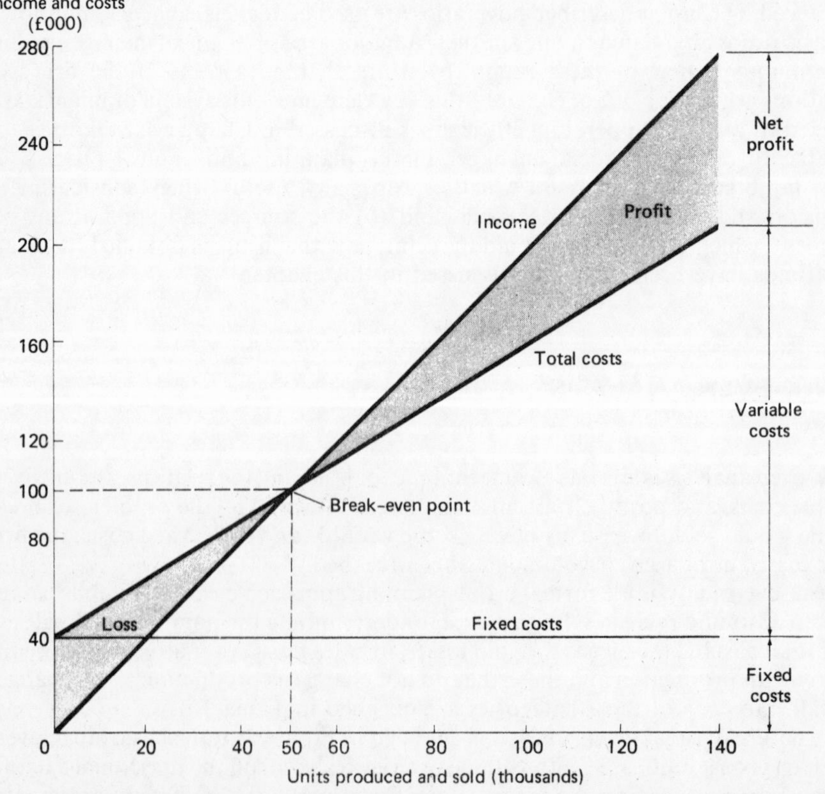

Figure 3–1 *Break-even Chart.*

More exact calculations of the break-even point can be carried out algebraically or by trial and error. In section A of Table 3–2, profit and loss relations are shown for various levels of sales; in section B the algebraic calculations are carried out.

Table 3–2 *Relations among Units Sold, Total Variable Costs, Fixed Costs, Total Costs and Total Income.*

A. Trial-and-error calculations

Units sold	Total variable costs	Fixed costs	Total costs	Sales	Net profit (loss)
20 000	£ 24 000	£40 000	£ 64 000	£ 40 000	£ (24 000)
40 000	48 000	40 000	88 000	80 000	(8 000)
50 000	60 000	40 000	100 000	100 000	—
60 000	72 000	40 000	112 000	120 000	8 000
80 000	96 000	40 000	136 000	160 000	24 000
100 000	120 000	40 000	160 000	200 000	40 000
120 000	144 000	40 000	184 000	240 000	56 000
140 000	168 000	40 000	208 000	280 000	72 000

B. Algebraic solution to break-even point

1. The break-even quantity is defined as that volume of output at which revenue is just equal to total costs (fixed costs plus variable costs).
2. Let:

   P = sales price per unit
   Q = quantity produced and sold
   F = fixed costs
   V = variable costs per unit.

3. Then:

$$P \cdot Q = F + V \cdot Q$$
$$P \cdot Q - V \cdot Q = F$$
$$Q(P - V) = F$$
$$Q = \frac{F}{P - V} \text{ at break-even } Q.$$

4. Illustration:

$$Q = \frac{£40\,000}{£2.00 - £1.20}$$
$$= 50\,000 \text{ units.}$$

Non-linear break-even analysis

In break-even analysis, linear (straight-line) relationships are generally assumed. Although introducing non-linear relationships complicates matters slightly, it is easy enough to extend the analysis in this manner. For example, it is reasonable to think that increased sales can be obtained only if sales prices are reduced. Similarly, empirical studies suggest that the average variable cost per unit falls over some range of output and then begins to rise. These assumptions are illustrated in Figure 3–2. There we see a loss region when sales are low, then a profit region (and a maximum profit), and finally another loss region at very high output levels.

Although non-linear break-even analysis is intellectually appealing, linear analysis is probably more appropriate for the uses to which it is put. Break-even charts allow focus to be placed on the key elements: sales, fixed costs, and variable costs. Even though linear break-even charts are drawn extending from *nil* output to very high output levels, no one who uses them would ordinarily be interested in or even consider the high and low extremes. In other words, users of break-even charts are really interested only in a 'relevant range'; within this range linear functions are for the most part reasonably accurate.

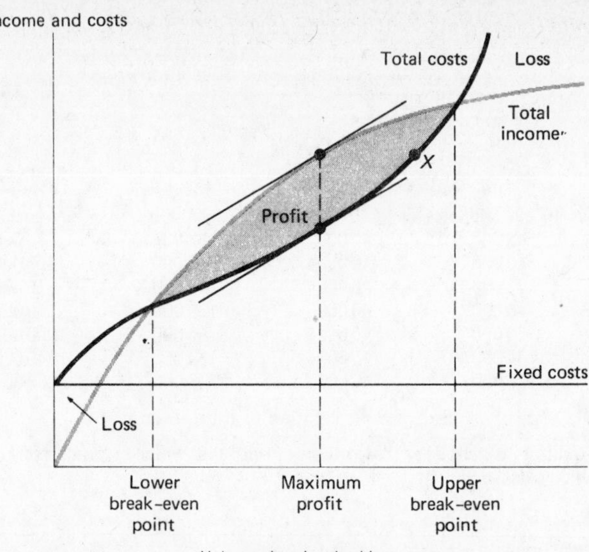

Note: The angle of a line from the origin to a point on the total-income line measures price (that is, total income units sold = price), and a line from the origin to the total-costs curve measures cost per unit. It can be seen that the angle of the line to the income curve declines as we move towards higher sales, which means that price reductions are necessary to obtain higher unit sales volume. Unit costs (total costs/units produced) declines to point *X*, the tangency point of a line from the origin to the total-costs curve, then begins to rise.

The slopes of the total-costs and total-income lines measure marginal cost (MC) and marginal revenue (MR), respectively. At the point where the slopes of the two total curves are equal, MR = MC, and profits are at a maximum.

Figure 3–2 *Non-linear Break-even Chart.*

An example of break-even analysis: new product decision

Break-even analysis can be used in three separate but related ways:

1. To analyse a programme to modernize and automate, where the firm would be operating in a more mechanized, automated manner and substituting fixed costs for variable costs. This topic is covered later in this chapter under the section on operating gearing.
2. To study the effects of a general expansion in the level of operations. This topic is covered in the section entitled 'Break-even point based on total sales revenue'.
3. In new product decisions: how large must the sales volume on a new product be if the firm is to break even on the proposed project? This topic is illustrated in this section.

The textbook publishing business provides a good example of the effective use of break-even analysis for new product decisions. To illustrate, consider the hypothetical example of the analysis of the production costs of a college textbook as described in Table 3–3. The costs and revenues are depicted in Figure 3–3.

The fixed costs can be estimated quite accurately; the variable costs, most of which are set by contracts, can also be estimated precisely (and they are linear). The sales price is variable, but competition keeps prices within a sufficiently narrow range to make a linear total-revenue curve reasonable. Applying the formula, we find the break-even sales volume to be 7767 copies.

Publishers know the size of the total market for a given book, the competition, and so forth. With these data as a base, they can estimate the possibility that sales of a given book will reach or exceed the break-even point. If the estimate is that they will not, the

Table 3–3 *Hypothetical Cost and Revenue Figures for a Textbook.*

Fixed costs		
Copy editing	£ 3 000	
Art work	1 000	
Type setting	36 000	
Total fixed costs	£ 40 000	
Variable costs per copy		
Printing and binding		£ 1.10
Bookshop discounts		2.00
Salesmen's commissions		.25
Author's royalties		1.00
General and administrative costs		.50
Total variable costs per copy		£ 4.85
Sales price per copy		£ 10.00

publisher may consider cutting production costs by spending less on art work and editing, using a lower grade of paper, negotiating with the author on royalty rates, and so on. In this particular business – and for new product decisions in many others – linear break-even analysis has proved itself to be a useful tool.

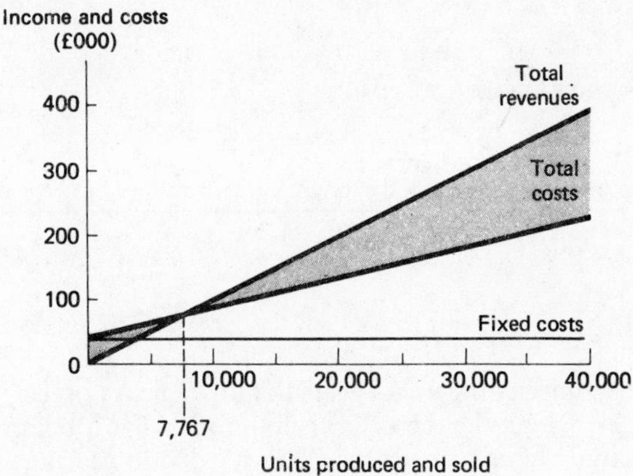

Figure 3–3 *Break-even Chart for a Hypothetical Textbook.*

Break-even point based on total sales revenue

Calculating break-even points on the basis of sales revenue instead of on units of output is frequently useful. The main advantage of this method, which is illustrated in Table 3–4, is that it enables one to determine a general break-even point for a firm that sells many products at varying prices. Furthermore, the procedure requires a minimum of data. Only three values are needed: sales, fixed costs and variable costs. Sales and total-cost data are readily available from annual reports of companies and from government statistics. Total costs must then be segregated into fixed and variable components. The major fixed charges (rent, interest, depreciation, and general and administrative expenses) may be taken from the income statement. Finally, variable costs are calculated by deducting fixed costs from total costs.

Table 3–4 *Calculation of Break-even Point Based on Total Sales Revenue.*

$$\text{Break-even point (sales volume)} = \frac{\text{total fixed costs}}{1 - \dfrac{\text{total variable costs}}{\text{total sales volume}}} = \frac{FC}{1 - \dfrac{VC}{S}}$$

Procedure

Take any sales level and use the related data to determine the break-even point. For example, assume that 20 000 units were actually produced and sold, and use the data related to that output in Table 3–2:

$$\text{Break-even point} = \frac{£40\,000}{1 - \dfrac{£24\,000}{£40\,000}} = \frac{£40\,000}{0.4} = £100\,000.$$

Rationale

1. At the break-even point, sales (S_B) are equal to fixed cost (FC) plus variable cost (VC):
   $S_B = FC + VC.$ (3–1)
2. Because both the sales price and the variable cost per unit are assumed to be constant in break-even analysis, the ratio VC/S for *any* level of sales is also constant and may be found from the annual income statement.
3. Since variable cost is a constant percentage of sales, equation 3–1 can be rewritten as:

$$S_B = FC + \frac{VC}{S}(S_B)$$

$$S_B\left(1 - \frac{VC}{S}\right) = FC$$

$$S_B = \frac{FC}{1 - \dfrac{VC}{S}} \text{ at break-even } S.$$

4. When more than one product is involved, the 'product mix' is assumed to be constant.

Operating gearing[1]

To a physicist, gearing implies the use of gears to move a heavy object with a small force. In business terminology, a high degree of gearing implies that a relatively small change in sales results in a large change in profits. We can divide gearing into two categories: (a) *financial gearing*, discussed briefly in Chapter 2 (and much more extensively in Chapter 18), and (b) *operating gearing*, the subject of this section.

The significance of the degree of operating gearing is clearly illustrated by Figure 3–4. Three firms, A, B and C, with differing degrees of gearing are contrasted. Firm A has a relatively small amount of fixed charges – it does not have much automated equipment, so its depreciation cost is low. Note, however, that A's variable-cost line has a relatively steep slope, denoting that its variable costs per unit are higher than those of the other firms. Firm B is considered to have a normal amount of fixed costs in its operations. It uses automated equipment (with which one operator can turn out a few or many units at the same labour cost) to about the same extent as the average firm in the industry. Firm B breaks even at a higher level of operations than does firm A. At a production level of 40 000 units, B is losing £8000 but A breaks even.

On the other hand, firm C has the highest fixed costs. It is highly automated, using expensive, high-speed machines that require very little labour per unit produced. With

1. The term 'leverage' is used instead of the word 'gearing' in many textbooks. Although the word 'gearing' is used in this chapter both words may be used interchangeably throughout the textbook.

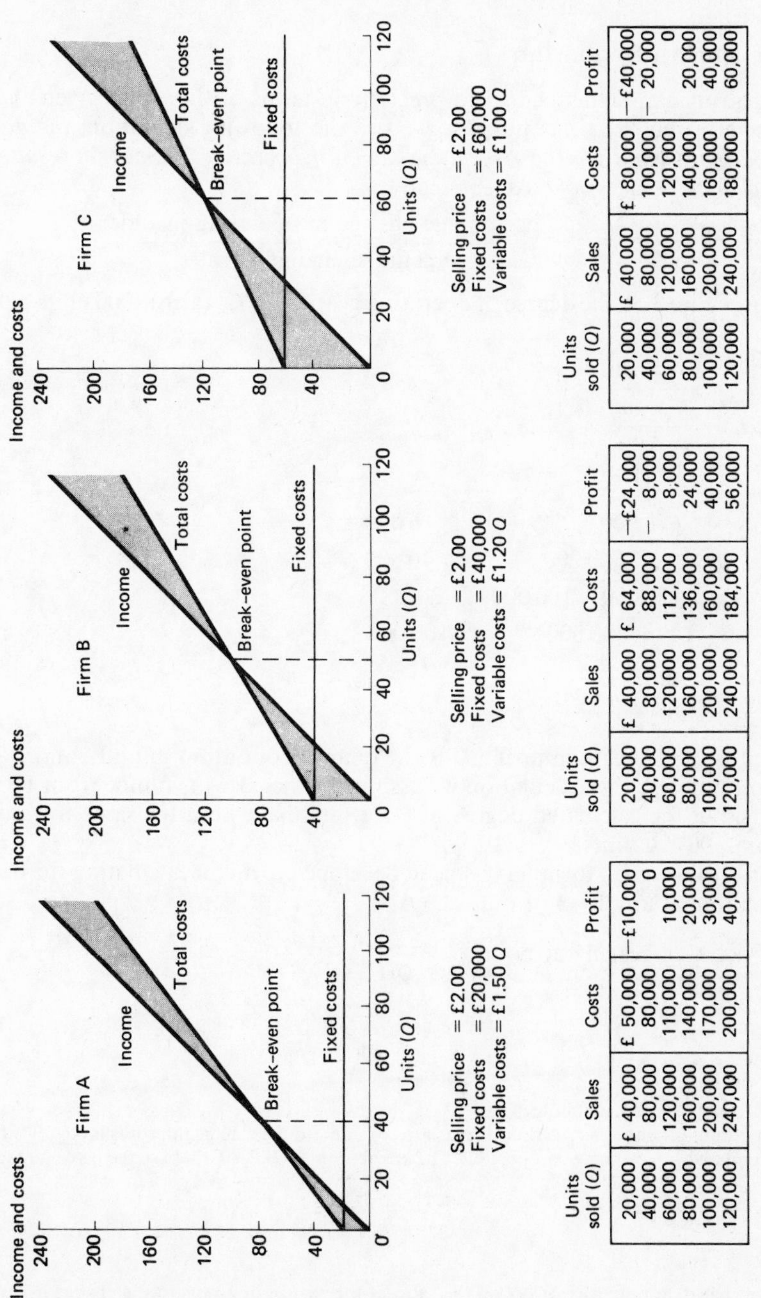

Firm A

Selling price = £2.00
Fixed costs = £20,000
Variable costs = £1.50 Q

Units sold (Q)	Sales	Costs	Profit
20,000	£ 40,000	£ 50,000	−£10,000
40,000	80,000	80,000	0
60,000	120,000	110,000	10,000
80,000	160,000	140,000	20,000
100,000	200,000	170,000	30,000
120,000	240,000	200,000	40,000

Firm B

Selling price = £2.00
Fixed costs = £40,000
Variable costs = £1.20 Q

Units sold (Q)	Sales	Costs	Profit
20,000	£ 40,000	£ 64,000	−£24,000
40,000	80,000	88,000	− 8,000
60,000	120,000	112,000	8,000
80,000	160,000	136,000	24,000
100,000	200,000	160,000	40,000
120,000	240,000	184,000	56,000

Firm C

Selling price = £2.00
Fixed costs = £60,000
Variable costs = £1.00 Q

Units sold (Q)	Sales	Costs	Profit
20,000	£ 40,000	£ 80,000	−£40,000
40,000	80,000	100,000	− 20,000
60,000	120,000	120,000	0
80,000	160,000	140,000	20,000
100,000	200,000	160,000	40,000
120,000	240,000	180,000	60,000

Figure 3–4 *Operating Gearing.*

such an operation, its variable costs rise slowly. Because of the high overhead resulting from charges associated with the expensive machinery, firm C's break-even point is higher than that for either firm A or firm B. Once firm C reaches its break-even point, however, its profits rise faster than do those of the other firms.

Degree of operating gearing

Operating gearing can be defined more precisely in terms of the way a given change in volume affects profits. For this purpose we use the following definition: *the degree of operating gearing is defined as the percentage change in operating income that results from a percentage change in units sold.* Algebraically:

$$\text{Degree of operating gearing} = \frac{\text{percentage change in operating income}}{\text{percentage change in sales}}.$$

For firm B in Figure 3–4, the degree of operating gearing (OL_B) at 100 000 units of output is:

$$\text{Degree of } OL_B = \frac{\dfrac{\Delta \text{ profit}}{\text{profit}}}{\dfrac{\Delta Q}{Q}}$$

$$= \frac{\dfrac{£56\,000 - £40\,000}{£40\,000}}{\dfrac{120\,000 - 100\,000}{100\,000}} = \frac{\dfrac{£16\,000}{£40\,000}}{\dfrac{20\,000}{100\,000}}$$

$$= \frac{40\%}{20\%} = \boxed{2.0}\,.$$

Here Δ profit is the increase in profit, Q is the quantity of output in units, and ΔQ is the increase in output. For this calculation we assume an increase in volume from 100 000 to 120 000 units, but the calculated degree of OL would have been the same for any other increase from 100 000 units.

For linear break-even, a formula has been developed to aid in calculating the degree of operating gearing at any level of output, Q:

$$\text{Degree of operating gearing at point } Q = \frac{Q(P-V)}{Q(P-V)-F} \qquad (3\text{–}2)^2$$

$$= \frac{S-VC}{S-VC-F} \qquad (3\text{–}2a)$$

2. Equation 3–2 is developed as follows:
The change in output is defined as ΔQ. Fixed costs are constant, so the change in profits is $\Delta Q(P-V)$, where P = price per unit and V = variable cost per unit. The initial profit is $Q(P-V)-F$, so the percentage change in profit is:

$$\frac{\Delta Q(P-V)}{Q(P-V)-F}$$

The percentage change in output is $\Delta Q/Q$, so the ratio of the change in profits to the change in output is:

$$\frac{\dfrac{\Delta Q(P-V)}{Q(P-V)-F}}{\dfrac{\Delta Q}{Q}} = \frac{\Delta Q(P-V)}{Q(P-V)-F}\cdot\frac{Q}{\Delta Q} = \frac{Q(P-V)}{Q(P-V)-F}$$

Here P is the price per unit, V is the variable cost per unit, F is fixed costs, S is total sales, and VC is total variable costs. Equation 3–2 expresses the relationship in terms of units, while equation 3–2a expresses it in terms of total sales revenue figures. Using the equations, we find firm B's degree of operating gearing at 100 000 units of output to be:

$$OL_B \text{ at } 100\,000 \text{ units} = \frac{100\,000(£2.00 - £1.20)}{100\,000(£2.00 - £1.20) - £40\,000}$$

$$= \frac{£200\,000 - £120\,000}{£200\,000 - £120\,000 - £40\,000}$$

$$= \frac{£80\,000}{£40\,000} = \boxed{2.0}\,.$$

The two methods must, of course, give consistent answers.

Equation 3–2 can also be applied to firms A and C. When this is done, we find A's degree of operating gearing at 100 000 units to be 1.67 and that of C to be 2.5. Thus, for a 100 per cent increase in volume, firm C, the company with the most operating gearing will experience a profit increase of 250 per cent; for the same 100 per cent volume gain, firm A, the one with the least gearing, will have only a 167 per cent profit gain.

In summary, the calculation of the degree of operating gearing shows algebraically the same pattern that Figure 3–4 shows graphically – that the profits of firm C, the company with the most operating gearing are most sensitive to changes in sales volume, while those of firm A, which has only a small amount of operating gearing are relatively insensitive to volume changes. Firm B, with an intermediate degree of gearing, lies between the two extremes.[3]

Cash break-even analysis

Some of the firm's fixed costs are non-cash outlays, and for a period some of its sales revenues may be outstanding. The cash break-even chart for firm B, constructed on the assumption that £30 000 of the fixed costs from the previous illustration are depreciation charges and, therefore, a non-cash outlay, is shown in Figure 3–5.[4] Because fixed cash outlays are only £10 000, the cash break-even point is at 12 500 units rather than 50 000 units, which is the profit break-even point.

Cash break-even analysis does not fully represent cash flows; for this a cash budget is required. But cash break-even analysis is useful because it provides a picture of the flow of funds from operations. A firm could incur a level of fixed costs that would result in losses during periods of poor business but large profits during upswings. If cash outlays are small, even during periods of losses the firm might still be operating above the cash break-even point. Thus, the risks of insolvency, in the sense of inability to meet cash obligations, would be small. This allows a firm to reach out for higher profits through automation and operating gearing.

Limitations of break-even analysis

Break-even analysis is useful in studying the relations among volume, prices and costs; it is

---

3. The degree of operating gearing is a form of *elasticity concept* and, thus, is akin to the familiar price elasticity developed in economics. Since operating gearing is an elasticity, it varies depending upon the particular part of the break-even graph that is being considered. For example, in terms of our illustrative firms the degree of operating gearing is greatest close to the break-even point, where a very small change in volume can produce a very large percentage increase in profits simply because the base profits are close to nil near the break-even point.
4. The nature of depreciation as a non-cash charge is explained later in this chapter.

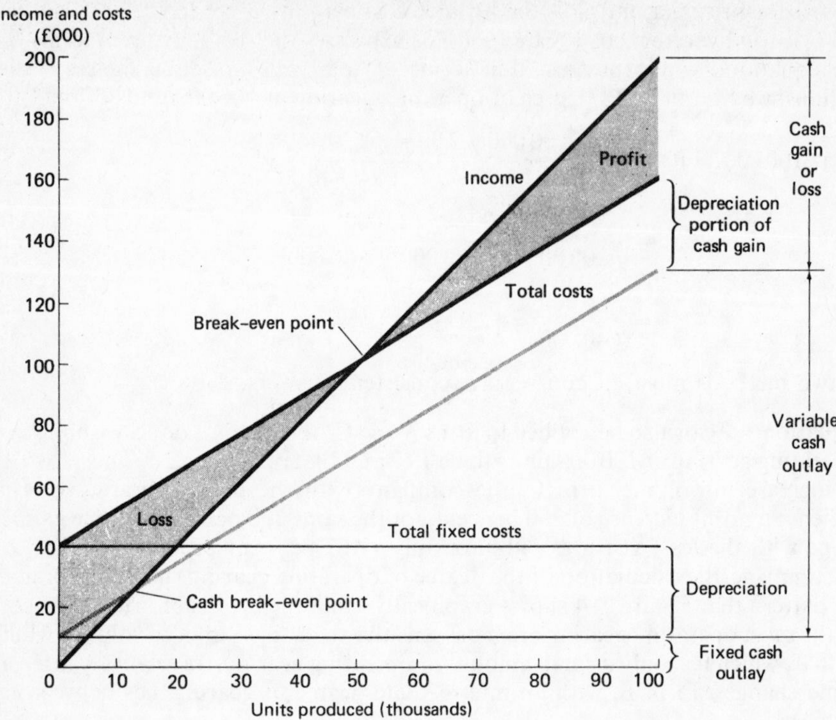

Figure 3–5 *Cash Break-even Analysis.*

thus helpful in pricing, cost control and decisions about alternative expansion programmes. It has limitations, however, as a guide to managerial actions.

Linear break-even analysis is especially weak in what it implies about the sales possibilities for the firm. Any linear break-even chart is based on a constant sales price. Therefore, in order to study profit possibilities under different prices a whole series of charts is necessary, one chart for each price. Alternatively, non-linear break-even analysis can be used.

With regard to costs, break-even analysis is also deficient; the relations indicated by the chart do not hold at all outputs. As sales increase, existing plant and equipment are worked to capacity; both this situation and the use of additional workers and overtime pay cause variable costs to rise sharply. Additional equipment and plant are required, thus increasing fixed costs. Finally, over a period the products sold by the firm change in quality and quantity. Such changes in product mix influence the level and slope of the cost function. Linear break-even analysis is useful as a first step in developing the basic data required for pricing and for financial decisions, but more detailed analysis, perhaps including non-linear analysis, is required before final judgements can be made.

SOURCES AND APPLICATIONS OF FUNDS STATEMENT[5]

When a firm requests a loan, the bank manager will doubtless pose these three questions:

5. Preparation of statements of sources and applications of funds for publication is considered in 'Statement of standard accounting practice', No. 10, entitled *Statements of Sources and Applications of Funds,* issued by the Accounting Standards Committee in July 1975.

What has the firm done with the money it had? What will it do with the new funds? How will it repay the loan? The sources and applications statement helps provide answers to these questions as well as to questions that other interested parties may have about the firm. This information may indicate that the firm is making progress or that problems are arising.

Depreciation as a source of funds

Before going on to construct a sources and applications of funds statement, it is useful to pause and consider why, in financial analysis, we consider depreciation to be a source of funds. First, what is depreciation? In effect, it is an annual charge against income which reflects the cost of the capital equipment used in the production process. For example, suppose a machine with an expected useful life of 10 years and a 0 expected salvage value was purchased in 1970 for £100 000. This £100 000 cost must be charged against production during those 10 years; otherwise, profits will be overstated. If the machine is depreciated by the straight-line method, the annual charge is £10 000. This amount is deducted from sales revenues, along with such other costs as labour and raw materials, to determine net profit. *However, depreciation is not a cash outlay; funds were expended back in 1970, so the depreciation charged against revenues in 1974 is not a cash outlay, as are labour or charges for raw materials.*

To illustrate the significance of depreciation in cash flow analysis, let us consider the Dallas Fertilizer and Chemical Company, which has the following income statement for 1978:

Sales	£300 000 000
Costs excluding depreciation	£270 000 000
Depreciation	10 000 000
Profit before tax	£ 20 000 000
Corporation tax	8 000 000
Profit after tax	£ 12 000 000

Assuming that sales are for cash and that all costs except depreciation are paid during 1978, how much cash was available from operations to pay dividends, redeem debt, or make investments in fixed or current assets or both? The answer is £22 million, the sum of profit after tax plus depreciation. The sales are all for cash, so the firm took in £300 million in cash money. Its costs other than depreciation were £270 million, and these were paid in cash, leaving £30 million. Depreciation *is not* a cash charge – the firm does not pay out the £10 million of depreciation expenses – so £30 million of cash money is still left after depreciation. Taxes, on the other hand, are paid in cash, so £8 million for corporation tax must be deducted from the £30 million gross operating cash flow, leaving a net cash flow from operations of £22 million. This £22 million is, of course, exactly equal to profit after tax plus depreciation: £12 million plus £10 million equals £22 million.

This example shows the rationale behind the statement that depreciation is a source of funds. However, we should note that without sales revenues, depreciation would *not* be a source of funds. If a strike closes the factory, the £300 million of sales revenues would vanish; cash flows from depreciation would evaporate.[6] Nevertheless, most firms do not suffer shutdowns for long periods, so normally a firm's depreciation does indeed constitute a source of funds as we use the term.

---

6. This potential problem was brought to our attention in connection with a project involving a financial plan for Communications Satellite Corporation of America. Comsat has very healthy projected cash flows that would seem able to support a substantial amount of debt. However, Comsat's revenues are derived almost entirely from three satellites (over the North Atlantic, Pacific and Indian Oceans), and if these satellites failed it would take months to replace them. Thus, when we recognized the degree of uncertainty about these cash flows, we adjusted downwards our estimates of how much debt Comsat could safely carry.

Sources and applications analysis

Several steps are involved in constructing a sources and applications statement. First, the changes in balance sheet items from one year to the next must be tabulated and then classified as either a source or a use of funds, according to the following pattern:

Source of funds: (a) decrease in asset item or (b) increase in liability item
Application of funds: (a) increase in asset item or (b) decrease in liability item.

Table 3–5 gives Dallas Chemical's comparative balance sheets for 1977 and 1978, and also net changes in each item classified as to source or application.

Table 3–5 *Dallas Fertilizer and Chemical Company, Comparative Balance Sheets and Sources and Applications of Funds (£millions).*

	31 Dec. 1977	31 Dec. 1978	Sources	Applications
	£	£	£	£
Gross fixed assets	150	180		30
Less: Accumulated depreciation[a]	40	50	10	
	110	130		
Stocks	25	30		5
Trade debtors	15	20		5
Quoted investments	25	15	10	
Cash	10	5	5	
	£185	£200		
Ordinary shares	50	50		
Retained earnings	30	40	10	
Preference shares	10	10	–	
Long-term debenture	60	70	10	
Bank loan	15	10		5
Creditors and accruals	20	20		
	£185	£200		

[a] The accumulated depreciation is actually a 'Liability' account (a contra-asset) that appears on the right side of the balance sheet. Note that it is deducted, not added, when totalling the column.

The next step in constructing a sources and applications statement involves (a) making adjustments to reflect net profit and dividends and (b) isolating changes in working capital (current assets and current liabilities). These changes are reflected in the sources and applications statement shown in Table 3–6. Net profit in 1978 amounted to £12 million, and dividends of £2 million were paid. The £12 million is treated as a source, the £2 million as an application. The £10 million retained earnings shown in Table 3–5 is deleted from Table 3–6 to avoid double counting. Notice that Dallas Chemical had no net change in working capital; the increases were exactly equal to the decreases. This was merely a coincidence; ordinarily there will be some change in net working capital.

What does this statement of sources and applications of funds tell the financial manager? It tells him that factory capacity was expanded and that fixed assets amounting to £30 million were acquired. Stocks and trade debtors also increased as sales increased. The firm needed funds to meet working capital and fixed assets demands.

Previously, Dallas had been financing its growth through bank loans. In the present period of growth, management decided to obtain some financing from permanent sources

Table 3–6 *Dallas Fertilizer and Chemical Company, Statement of Sources and Applications of Funds, 1978 (£millions).*

	Amount	Per cent
Sources		
Net profit from operations	£12	25.5
Add: depreciation	10	21.3
	22	46.8
Issue of debentures	10	21.3
Sale of quoted investments	10	21.3
Reduction in cash	5	10.6
Total sources of funds	£47	100.0
Applications		
Purchase of fixed assets	30	63.9
Payment of dividends	2	4.3
Increase in stocks	5	10.6
Increase in debtors	5	10.6
Reduction in bank loan	5	10.6
Total applications of funds	£47	100.0

(long-term debt). It obtained enough long-term debt not only to finance some of the asset growth but also to pay back some of its bank loans and to reduce trade creditors. In addition to the long-term debt, funds were obtained from earnings and from depreciation charges. Moreover, the firm had been accumulating quoted investments in anticipation of this expansion programme, and some were sold to pay for new buildings and equipment. Finally, cash had been accumulated in excess of the firm's needs and was also utilized. In summary, this example illustrates how the sources and applications of funds statement can provide both a fairly complete picture of recent operations and a good perspective on the flow of funds within the company.

Pro forma sources and applications of funds

A *pro forma*, or projected, sources and applications of funds statement can also be constructed to show how a firm plans to acquire and employ funds during some future period. In the next chapter we will discuss financial forecasting, which involves the determination of future sales, the level of assets necessary to generate these sales, and the manner in which these assets will be financed. Given the projected balance sheet and supplementary projected data on earnings, dividends and depreciation, the financial manager can construct a pro forma sources and applications of funds statement to summarize his firm's projected operations over the planning horizon. Such a statement is obviously of much interest to lenders as well as to the firm's own management.

SUMMARY

This chapter analyses two important financial tools, *break-even analysis* and the *sources and applications of funds statement*, and the key concept of *operating gearing.*

Break-even analysis

Break-even analysis is a method of relating fixed costs, variable costs and total revenues to show the level of sales that must be attained if the firm is to operate at a profit. The analysis can be based on the number of units produced or on total sales revenue. It can also be used for the entire company or for a particular product or division. Further, with minor modifications, break-even analysis can be put on a cash basis instead of a profit basis. Ordinarily, break-even analysis is conducted on a linear, or straight-line, basis. However, this is not necessary; non-linear break-even analysis is feasible and at times desirable.

Operating gearing

Operating gearing is defined as the extent to which fixed costs are used in operations. The *degree of operating gearing*, defined as the percentage change in operating income that results from a specific percentage change in units sold, provides a precise measure of how much operating gearing a particular firm is employing. Break-even analysis provides a graphic view of the effects of changes in sales on profits; the degree of operating gearing presents the same picture in algebraic terms.

Sources and applications of funds statement

The sources and applications of funds statement indicates where cash came from and how it was used. When a firm wishes to borrow funds, one of the first questions posed by the bank manager is 'What has the firm done with the money it had?' This question is answered by the sources and applications of funds statement. The information it provides may indicate that the firm is making progress or that problems are arising. Sources and applications data may also be analysed on a *pro forma*, or projected, basis to show how a firm plans to acquire and employ funds during some future period.

QUESTIONS

3–1. What benefits can be derived from break-even analysis?

3–2. What is operating gearing? Explain how profits or losses can be magnified in a firm with a great deal of operating gearing as opposed to a firm without this characteristic.

3–3. What data are necessary to construct a break-even chart?

3–4. What is the general effect of each of the following changes on a firm's break-even point?
(a) An increase in selling price with no change in units sold.
(b) A change from the leasing of a machine for £5000 a year to the purchase of the machine for £100 000. The useful life of this machine will be 20 years, with no salvage value. Assume straight-line depreciation.
(c) A reduction in variable labour costs.

3–5. Why is depreciation considered to be a source of funds?

PROBLEMS

3–1. Mayer Company produces toasters, which it sells for £18. Fixed costs are £110 000 for up to 24 000 units of output. Variable cost is £10 per unit.
(a) What is the firm's gain or loss at sales of 12 000 units? of 18 000 units?
(b) What is the break-even point? Illustrate by means of a chart.

(c) What is Mayer's degree of operating gearing at sales of 12 000 and 18 000 units?
(d) What happens to the break-even point if selling price falls to £16?
What is the significance of the change to financial management? Illustrate by means of a chart.
(e) How does the break-even point change when the selling price falls to £16 but variable cost falls to £8 a unit? Illustrate by means of a chart.

3–2. For Martin Industries the following relations exist: each unit of output is sold for £75; for output up to 25 000 units the fixed costs are £240 000; variable costs are £35 a unit.
(a) What is the firm's gain or loss at sales of 5000 units? of 8000 units?
(b) What is the break-even point? Illustrate by means of a chart.
(c) What is Martin's degree of operating gearing at sales of 5000 and 8000 units?
(d) What happens to the break-even point if the selling price rises to £85? What is the significance of the change to financial management? Illustrate by means of a chart.
(e) What occurs to the break-even point if the selling price rises to £85 but variable costs rise to £45 a unit? Illustrate by means of a chart.

3–3. The Chio Tyre Company is currently considering two possible mutually exclusive plant modernizations. Under the first, newer and more efficient machinery would be added; this would tend to reduce labour costs and, because of much less waste, raw material usage. The other alternative would involve a more extensive changeover in the plant to an entirely new process for forming and curing rubber. The second procedure would involve a more extensive investment in both plant and equipment, but it would result in larger savings in labour and materials costs.

The current sales level is about 76 500 units a year at a price of £40 each, but volume has fluctuated from year to year with changes in general economic conditions. The firm's management is primarily concerned with the extent to which profitability will be affected by each alternative project in relation to risk. (For current purposes, riskiness may be considered to be a function of the probability of not reaching the break-even point.) A break-down of costs for the current sales volume is given below, together with estimates of what each item would be after each of the modernization proposals.

Estimated costs	Currently	Modernization I	Modernization II
Depreciation on plant and equipment	£513 000	£630 000	£787 500
Depreciation on building	288 000	360 000	468 000
Rates	36 000	45 000	63 000
Salary expense	639 000	693 000	778 500
Other fixed expenses	54 000	72 000	99 000
Factory labour	625 500	468 000	270 000
Raw materials	450 000	378 000	270 000
Variable selling expenses	72 000	72 000	72 000

(a) Determine the break-even point in units for the firm, assuming (a) no modernization is undertaken, (b) the first programme is undertaken, and (c) the second programme is undertaken.
(b) Compute the degree of operating gearing at the current volume (76 500 units) for each of the three possibilities.
(c) Compute profits for each alternative, assuming future sales of 76 500 units. Profits for each alternative at other sales levels have been calculated (to save you work) and are given below:

Unit sales	Profits
No modernization	
65 000	£ 95 000
90 000	720 000
100 000	970 000
Modernization I	
65 000	£ 20 000
90 000	720 000
100 000	1 000 000
Modernization II	
65 000	£(116 000)
90 000	684 000
100 000	1 004 000

(d) Rank the alternatives in terms of potential riskiness.
(e) How would the decision if and how to modernize be affected by the expectation of large fluctuations in future sales?
(f) (To be worked at the option of the tutor.) Suppose we have estimated the following probability distribution for sales:

Probability	Sales (in units)
0.1	65 000
0.3	76 500
0.3	90 000
0.3	100 000

Use this information to determine the expected values of the three alternative courses of action.
(g) Which project is best? What factors would influence your decision?

3–4. The consolidated balance sheets for the Norton Company at the beginning and end of 1978 are shown below.

Norton Company Balance Sheet Beginning and End of 1978 (£ millions).

	1 Jan	31 Dec.	Source	Application
Fixed assets	£225	£450	____	____
less: accumulated depreciation	78	123	____	____
	147	327	____	____
Stocks	159	225	____	____
Debtors	66	90	____	____
Quoted investments	33	0	____	____
Cash	45	21	____	____
	£450	£663		
Ordinary share capital	114	192	____	____
Retained earnings	201	285	____	____
Debenture capital	24	78	____	____
Trade creditors	45	54	____	____
Accrued expenses	21	45	____	____
Bank loan	45	9	____	____
	£450	£663		

The company bought £225 millions worth of fixed assets. The charge for current depreciation was £45 million. Earnings after tax were £114 million, and the company paid out £30 million in dividends.
(a) Fill in the amount of sources and applications in the appropriate column.
(b) Prepare a percentage statement of sources and applications of funds.
(c) Briefly summarize your findings.

3–5. Transistor Electronics is considering developing a new miniature calculator.
The quantity (Q) sold is a function of the price (P) where $Q = 2000 - 10P$
Fixed costs are £24 000 and variable cost per unit is £60.
(a) Graphically determine the break-even points for the calculator in units and pounds.
(b) What is the company's price at an output of 700 units?
(c) What is its profit at that output?
(d) What happens to the price and profits if the company sells 1000 units?

SELECTED REFERENCES

Accounting Standards Steering Committee. *Statements of Sources and Applications of Funds* (July 1975).
Dean, Joel. Methods and potentialities of break-even analysis. In *Studies in Cost Analysis*, D. Solomons, ed. London: Sweet and Maxwell, 1968.

Helfert, Erich A. *Techniques of Financial Analysis.* 3rd ed. Homewood, Ill.: Irwin, 1972, chap. 2.

Jaedicke, Robert K. and Robichek, Alexander A. Cost-volume-profit analysis under conditions of uncertainty. *Accounting Review* 39 (October 1964): 917–926.

Jaedicke, Robert K. and Sprouse, Robert T. *Accounting Flows: Income, Funds, and Cash.* Englewood Cliffs, N. J.: Prentice-Hall, 1965.

Kelvie, William E. and Sinclair, John M. New techniques for breakeven charts. *Financial Executive* 36 (June 1968): 31–43.

Morrison, Thomas A. and Kaczka, Eugene. A new application of calculus and risk analysis to cost-volume-profit changes. *Accounting Review* 44 (April 1969): 330–343.

Pearl, L. and Clinton, G. Break-even analysis. *Management Accounting* (October 1977): 388–391.

Raun, D. L. The limitations of profit graphs, break-even analysis, and budgets. *Accounting Review* 39 (October 1964): 927–945.

Reinhardt, U. E. Break-even analysis for Lockheed's Tri Star: an application of financial theory. *Journal of Finance* 28 (September 1973): 821–838.

Searby, Frederick W. Return to return on investment. *Harvard Business Review* 53 (March–April 1975): 113–119.

Soldofsky, R. M. Accountant's versus economist's concepts of break-even analysis. *N. A. A. Bulletin* (December 1959): 5–18.

Chapter 4

Financial Forecasting

The planning process is an integral part of the financial manager's job. As we will see in subsequent chapters, long-term debt and equity funds are raised infrequently and in large amounts, primarily because the cost per £1 raised by selling such securities decreases as the size of the issue increases. Because of these considerations, it is important that the firm has a working estimate of its total needs for funds for the next few years. It is therefore useful to examine methods of forecasting the firm's overall needs for funds, and this is the subject of the present chapter.

CASH FLOW CYCLE

We must recognize that firms need assets to make sales; if sales are to be increased, assets must also be expanded. Growing firms require new investments – immediate investment in current assets and, as full capacity is reached, investment in fixed assets as well. New investments must be financed, and new financing carries with it commitments and obligations to service the capital obtained.[1] A growing, profitable firm is likely to require additional cash for investments in debtors, stocks and fixed assets. Such a firm can, therefore, have a cash flow problem. The nature of this problem, as well as the cause and effect relationship between assets and sales, is illustrated in the following discussion, in which we trace the consequences of a series of transactions.

Effects on the balance sheet

1. Two partners invest a total of £50 000 to create the Glamour Galore Dress Company. The firm rents a factory, equipment and other fixed assets, cost £30 000. The resulting financial situation is shown by Balance Sheet 1.

---

1. 'Servicing' capital refers to the payment of interest and principal on debt and to dividends and retained earnings (the cost of equity capital) on ordinary shares.

Balance Sheet 1.

Liabilities		Assets	
	£		£
		Fixed assets	
Ordinary share capital	50 000	Plant and equipment	30 000
		Current assets	
		Cash	20 000
	£50 000		£50 000

2. Glamour Galore receives an order to manufacture 10 000 dresses. The receipt of an order in itself has no effect on the balance sheet, but in preparation for the manufacturing activity the firm buys £20 000 worth of cotton cloth on 30 day's credit terms. Without additional investment by the owners, total assets increase by £20 000, financed by the trade creditors, i.e. the supplier of the cotton cloth.

Balance Sheet 2.

Liabilities			Assets		
	£	£		£	£
Ordinary share capital		50 000	Fixed assets		
Current liabilities			Plant and equipment		30 000
Trade creditors	20 000		Current assets		
Accrued wages	10 000		Stocks:		
		30 000	Work in progress	40 000	
			Cash	10 000	
					50 000
		£80 000			£80 000

After the purchase, the firm spends £20 000 on labour for cutting the cloth to the required pattern. Of the £20 000 total labour cost, £10 000 is paid in cash and £10 000 is owed in the form of accrued wages. These two transactions are reflected in Balance Sheet 2, which shows that total assets increase to £80 000. Current assets are increased; net working capital – total current assets minus total current liabilities – remains constant. The current ratio declines to 1.67, and the debt ratio rises to 38 per cent. The financial position of the firm is weakening. If it should seek to borrow at this point, Glamour Galore could not use the work in progress as security because a lender could find little use for partially manufactured dresses.

3. In order to complete the dresses, the firm incurs additional labour costs of £20 000 and pays in cash. It is assumed that the firm desires to maintain a minimum cash balance of £5000. Since the initial cash balance is £10 000, Glamour Galore must borrow an additional £15 000 from its bank to meet the wage bill. The borrowing is reflected in the bank overdraft in Balance Sheet 3. Total assets rise to £95 000, with stock of finished goods £60 000. The current ratio drops to 1.4 and the debt ratio rises to 47 per cent. These ratios show a further weakening of the financial position.

Balance Sheet 3.

Liabilities	£	£	Assets	£	£
			Fixed assets		
Ordinary share capital		50 000	Plant and equipment		30 000
Current liabilities			Current assets		
Trade creditors	20 000		Stocks		
Accrued wages	10 000		Finished goods	60 000	
Bank overdraft	15 000		Cash	5 000	
		45 000			65 000
		£95 000			£95 000

4. Glamour Galore ships the dresses on the basis of the original order, invoicing the purchaser for £100 000 payable in 30 days. Accrued wages and suppliers now have to be paid, so Glamour Galore must borrow an additional £30 000 in order to maintain the £5000 minimum cash balance. These transactions are shown in Balance Sheet 4.

   Note that in Balance Sheet 4, stock of finished goods is replaced by trade debtors, with the mark-up reflected as retained earnings. This causes the debt ratio to drop to 33 per cent. Since the debtors are shown at selling price, current assets increase to £105 000 and the current ratio rises to 2.3. Compared with the conditions reflected in Balance Sheet 3, most of the financial ratios show improvement. However, the absolute amount of debt is large.

   Whether the firm's financial position is really improved depends upon the credit worthiness of the purchaser of the dresses. If the purchaser is a good credit risk, Glamour Galore may be able to borrow further on the basis of the trade debtors.

Balance Sheet 4.

Liabilities	£	£	Assets	£	£
Ordinary share capital		50 000	Fixed assets		
Retained earnings		40 000	Plant and equipment		30 000
		90 000	Current assets		
Current liabilities			Trade debtors	100 000	
Bank overdraft		45 000	Cash	5 000	
					105 000
		£135 000			£135 000

Balance Sheet 5.

Liabilities	£	Assets	£
Ordinary share capital	50 000	Fixed assets	
Retained earnings	40 000	Plant and equipment	30 000
		Current assets	
		Cash	60 000
	£90 000		£90 000

5. The firm receives payment from trade debtors, pays off the bank overdraft and is in the highly liquid position shown by Balance Sheet 5. If a new order for 10 000 dresses is received, it will have no effect on the balance sheet, but a cycle similar to the one we have been describing will begin.
6. The idea of the cash flow cycle can now be generalized. An order that requires the purchase of raw materials is placed with the firm. The purchase in turn generates a creditor. As labour is applied, work-in-progress stocks build up. To the extent that wages are not fully paid at the time labour is used, accrued wages will appear on the liability side of the balance sheet. As goods are completed, they move into finished goods stocks. The cash needed to pay for the labour to complete the goods may make it necessary for the firm to borrow.

   Finished goods stocks are sold, usually on credit, which gives rise to trade debtors. As the firm has not received cash, this point in the cycle represents the peak in financing requirements. If the firm did not borrow at the time finished goods stocks were at their maximum, it may do so as stocks are converted into debtors by credit sales. As debtors become cash, short-term obligations can be paid off.

FINANCING PATTERNS

The influence of sales on current asset levels has just been illustrated. Over the course of several cycles, the fluctuations in sales will be accompanied in most industries by a rising long-term trend. Figure 4–1 shows the consequences of such a pattern. Total permanent assets increase steadily in the form of current and fixed assets. Increases of this nature should be financed by long-term debt, by equity, or by 'spontaneous' increases in liabilities, such as accrued taxes and wages and trade creditors which naturally accompany increasing sales. However, temporary increases in assets can be covered by short-term liabilities. The distinction between temporary and permanent asset levels may be difficult to make in practice, but it is neither illusory nor unimportant. Short-term financing for the financing of long-term needs is dangerous. A profitable firm may become unable to meet its cash obligations if funds borrowed on a short-term basis have become tied up in permanent asset needs.

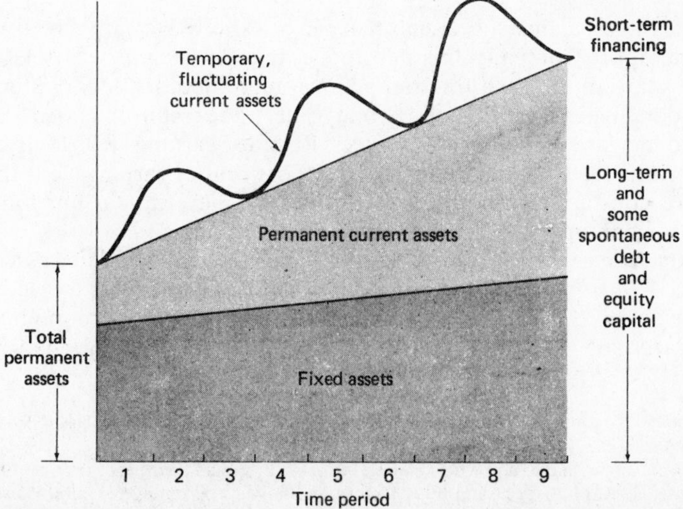

Figure 4–1 *Fluctuating versus Permanent Assets.*

PERCENTAGE-OF-SALES METHOD

It is apparent from the preceding discussion that *the most important variable that influences a firm's financing requirements is its projected monetary volume of sales. A good sales forecast is an essential foundation for forecasting financial requirements.* In spite of its importance, we shall not go into sales forecasting here; rather, we simply assume that a sales forecast has been made, then estimate financial requirements on the basis of this forecast.[2] The principal methods of forecasting financial requirements are described in this and the following sections.

The simplest approach to forecasting financial requirements expresses the firm's needs in terms of the percentage of annual sales invested in each individual balance sheet item. As an example, consider the Moore Company, whose balance sheet as of 31 December, 1978 is shown in Table 4–1. The company's sales are running at about £500 000 a year, which is its capacity limit; the profit margin after tax on sales is 4 per cent. During 1978, the company earned £20 000 after taxes and paid out £10 000 in dividends, and it plans to continue paying out half of net profits as dividends. How much additional financing will be needed if sales expand to £800 000 during 1979? The calculating procedure, using the percentage-of-sales method, is explained below.[3]

Table 4–1 *The Moore Company Balance Sheet, 31 December 1978.*

Liabilities		Assets	
	£		£
Ordinary share capital	100 000	Fixed assets (net)	150 000
Retained earnings	100 000	Stocks	100 000
Long-term loan	70 000	Debtors	85 000
Trade creditors	50 000	Cash	10 000
Accrued expenses	25 000		
	£345 000		£345 000

First, isolate those balance sheet items that can be expected to vary directly with sales. In the case of the Moore Company, this step applies to each category of assets; a higher level of sales necessitates more cash for transactions, more debtors, higher stock levels, and additional productive capacity. On the liability side, trade creditors as well as accruals may be expected to increase with increases in sales. Retained earnings will go up as long as the company is profitable and does not pay out 100 per cent of earnings, but the percentage increase is not constant. However, neither ordinary share capital nor long-term loans would increase spontaneously with an increase in sales.

The items that can be expected to vary directly with sales are tabulated as a percentage of sales in Table 4–2. For every £1.00 increase in sales, assets must increase by £0.69; this £0.69 must be financed in some manner. Trade creditors will increase spontaneously with sales, as will accruals; these two items will supply £0.15 of new funds for each £1.00

2. For a discussion of demand forecasting, see E. F. Brigham and J. L. Pappas, *Managerial Economics* (Hinsdale, Ill.: Dryden Press, 1972).

3. We recognize, of course, that as a practical matter, business firms plan their needs in terms of specific items of equipment, square feet of floor space, and other factors, and not as a percentage of sales. However, the outside analyst does not have access to this information; the manager, even though he has the information on specific items, needs to check his forecasts in aggregate terms. The percentage-of-sales method serves both these needs surprisingly well.

Table 4–2 *The Moore Company Balance Sheet Items Expressed as a Percentage of Sales, 31 December 1978.*

Liabilities		Assets	
Ordinary share capital	n.a.[a]	Fixed assets (net)	30.0
Retained earnings	n.a.[a]	Stocks	20.0
Long-term loan	n.a.[a]	Debtors	17.0
Trade creditors	10.0	Cash	2.0
Accrued expenses	5.0		
	15.0		69.0
Assets as percentage of sales			69.0
Less: spontaneous increase in liabilities			15.0
Percentage of each additional £1 of sales that must be financed			54.0

[a] Not applicable.

increase in sales. Subtracting the 15 per cent for spontaneously generated funds from the 69 per cent funds requirement leaves 54 per cent. Thus, for each £1.00 increase in sales, the Moore Company must obtain £0.54 of financing either from retained earnings or from external sources.

In the case at hand, sales are scheduled to increase from £500 000 to £800 000, or by £300 000. Applying the 54 per cent developed in the table to the expected increase in sales leads to the conclusion that £162 000 will be needed.

Some of that need will be met by retained earnings. Total sales during 1979 will be £800 000; if the company earns 4 per cent after taxes on this volume profits will amount to £32 000. Assuming that the 50 per cent dividend payout ratio is maintained, dividends will be £16 000 and £16 000 will be retained. Subtracting the retained earnings from the £162 000 that was needed leaves a figure of £146 000; this is the amount of funds that must be obtained through borrowing or by selling new ordinary shares.

This process may be expressed in equation form:

$$\text{External funds needed} = \frac{A}{TR}(\Delta TR) - \frac{B}{TR}(\Delta TR) - bm(TR_2) \qquad (4\text{–}1)$$

Here

$\frac{A}{TR}$ = assets that increase spontaneously with sales as a percentage of sales

$\frac{B}{TR}$ = those liabilities that increase spontaneously with sales as a percentage of sales

ΔTR = change in total revenue

m = profit margin on sales

TR_2 = *total sales projected for the year*

b = earnings retention ratio.

For the Moore Company, then,

$$\begin{aligned}\text{External funds needed} &= 0.69(300\,000) - 0.15(300\,000) - 0.04(800\,000)\,(0.5)\\ &= 0.54(300\,000) - 0.02(800\,000)\\ &= £146\,000.\end{aligned}$$

The £146 000 found by the formula method must, of course, equal the amount derived previously.

Notice what would have occurred if the Moore Company's sales forecast for 1979 had been only £515 000, or a 3 per cent increase. Applying the formula, we find the external funds requirements as follows:

$$\begin{aligned}\text{External funds needed} &= 0.54(15\,000) - 0.02(515\,000)\\ &= £8100 - £10\,300\\ &= (£2200).\end{aligned}$$

In this case, no external funds are required. In fact, the company will have £2200 in excess of its requirements; it should therefore plan to increase dividends, repay debt, or seek additional investment opportunities. The example shows not only that higher levels of sales bring about a need for funds but also that while small percentage increases can be financed through retained earnings, larger increases cause the firm to go into the market for outside capital. In other words, a certain level of growth can be financed from internal sources, but higher levels of growth require external financing.[4] Note that the increase in sales equals $(1+g)TR_1$ where g equals the growth rate in sales. The increase in sales can therefore be written:

$$\Delta TR = (1+g)TR_1 - TR_1 = TR_1(1+g-1) = gTR_1$$

Let us next take the expression for external funds needed, equation 4–1, and use it to derive the percentage of the increase in sales that will have to be financed externally (PEFR) as a function of the critical variables involved. In equation 4–1 let $(\frac{A}{TR} - \frac{B}{TR}) = I$, substitute for ΔTR and TR_2, and divide both sides by $\Delta TR(= gTR_1)$.

$$\text{PEFR} = I - \frac{m}{g}(1+g)b \qquad (4\text{–}2)$$

Using equation 4–2 we can now investigate the influences of factors such as an increased rate of inflation on the percentage of sales growth required to be financed externally. Assume that the relationships for a manufacturing company are:

$I = 0.5$, $m = 0.05$, and $b = 0.60$.

Let us further assume that the economy is growing at the rate of 6 to 7 per cent per annum. If the firm is in an industry that grows at the same rate as the economy as a whole and if the firm maintains its market share position in its industry, it will be growing at 6 to 7 per cent per annum as well. Let us see what the implications for external financing requirements would be. With a growth rate of 6 or 7 per cent the percentage of sales that would have to be financed externally would be as follows:

$$\begin{aligned}\text{at } 6\%\ \text{PEFR} &= 0.5 - \frac{0.05}{0.06}(1.06)(0.6)\\ &= 0.50 - 0.53 = -0.03 = -3\%\\ \text{at } 7\%\ \text{PEFR} &= 0.5 - \frac{0.05}{0.07}(1.07)(0.6)\\ &= 0.50 - 0.46 = 0.04 = 4\%\end{aligned}$$

Thus at a growth rate of 6 per cent the percentage of external financing to sales growth would be a negative 3 per cent. In other words, the firm would have excess funds with which it could increase dividends or increase its investment in liquid assets. With a growth

4. At this point, one might ask two questions: 'Shouldn't depreciation be considered as a source of funds, and won't this reduce the amount of external funds needed?' The answer to both questions is no. In the percentage-of-sales method, we are implicitly assuming that funds generated through depreciation (in the sources and applications of funds sense) must be used to replace the assets to which the depreciation is applicable. Accordingly, depreciation does not enter the calculations in this forecasting technique; it is netted out.

rate of 7 per cent the firm would have a moderate 4 per cent requirement of external financing as a percentage of sales increase.

Over recent years the inflation rate has been particularly high, often 10 per cent or more. Suppose we add sufficient percentage points per annum of an inflation rate to the previous 6 to 7 per cent growth rate to obtain a growth rate of 15 or 20 per cent for a firm. Then the external financing requirements will be as follows:

$$\text{at } 15\% \text{ PEFR} = 0.5 - \frac{0.05}{0.15}(1.15)(0.6)$$
$$= 0.50 - 0.23 = 0.27 = 27\%$$
$$\text{at } 20\% \text{ PEFR} = 0.5 - \frac{0.05}{0.20}(1.20)(0.6)$$
$$= 0.50 - 0.18 = 0.32 = 32\%$$

With a growth rate in sales of 15 per cent, external financing rises to 27 per cent of the firm's sales growth. If inflation caused the growth rate of the firm to rise to 20 per cent, then the external financing percentage rises to 32 per cent. The substantial increase in the growth rate of sales of firms measured in inflated currency in recent years indicates why external financing has become more important for firms. It explains also why the finance function in firms has taken on increased importance in recent years. There is simply more work to be done, particularly in requirements for using external financing sources to maintain the sales growth of a firm. Even though the firm were not growing in real terms, an inflation rate of 10 per cent, for example, would make it necessary for the firm to raise external financing of 17 per cent of its growth in sales of inflated currency even though the real growth of the firm was nil. This, again, underscores why financing has come to the fore as an important function in the firm.

The percentage-of-sales method of forecasting financial requirements is neither simple nor mechanical, although an explanation of the ideas requires simple illustrations. Experience in applying the technique in practice suggests the importance of understanding (a) the basic technology of the firm and (b) the logic of the relation between sales and assets for the particular firm in question. A great deal of experience and judgement is required to apply the technique in actual practice.

The percentage-of-sales method is most appropriately used for forecasting relatively short-term changes in financing needs. It is less useful for longer term forecasting for reasons that are best described in connection with the analysis of the regression method of financial forecasting discussed in the next sections.

SCATTER DIAGRAM OR LEAST SQUARES REGRESSION METHOD

An alternative method used for forecasting financial requirements is the *scatter diagram*, or *least squares regression* method. A scatter diagram is a graphic portrayal of joint relations. Proper use of the scatter diagram method requires practical but not necessarily statistical sophistication.

Table 4–3 and Figure 4–2 illustrate the use of the scatter diagram method and also demonstrate its superiority over the percentage-of-sales method for long-range forecasting. As in all financial forecasting, the sales forecast is the starting point. The financial manager is given the sales forecast, or he may participate in formulating it. Suppose he has data available to 1979 and is making a forecast of stock levels for 1984 as indicated in Table 4–3. If he is using the simple regression method, he draws a line through the points from 1974 to 1979, as shown in Figure 4–2. The line that fits the scatter of points in this example is a straight line. It is called the *line of best fit*, or the *least squares line*. Of course, all points

Table 4–33 *Relationship between Stock Levels and Sales.*

Year	Sales	Stock level	Stocks as a percentage of sales
1974	£ 50 000	£22 000	44
1975	100 000	24 000	24
1976	150 000	26 000	17
1977	200 000	28 000	14
1978	250 000	30 000	12
1979	300 000	32 000	11
.	.	.	.
.	.	.	.
.	.	.	.
1984 (estimated)	500 000	40 000	8

seldom fall exactly on the least squares line, and the line itself may be curved as well as linear.[5]

If the percentage-of-sales method had been used, some difficulties would have arisen immediately. Table 4–3 gives percentage of sales from 1974 to 1979. What relation should

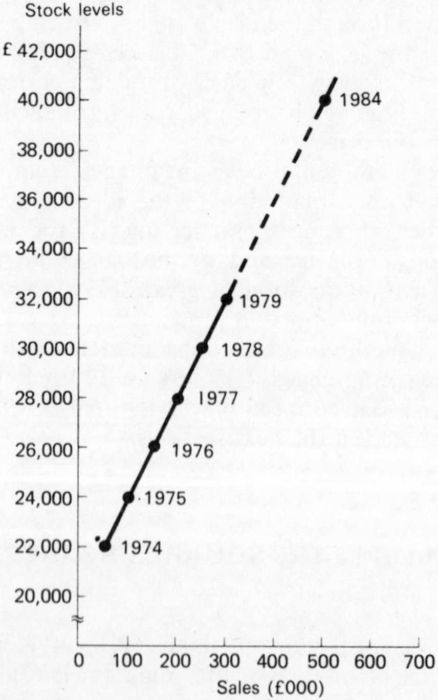

Figure 4–2 *Illustrative Relation between Sales and Stock Levels.*

5. In these illustrations, stock levels are used as the item to be forecast. Much theory suggests that stock levels increase as a square root of sales. This characteristic would tend to turn the least squares line between stock levels and sales slightly downwards. Also, improvements in stock control techniques would curve the line downwards. However, the increased diversity of types, models and styles tends to increase stock levels. Applications by the authors' students of the least squares method to hundreds of companies indicate that the linear straight-line relations frequently represent the line of best fit or, at worst, involve only a small error. If the line were in fact curved over, a curved line could be fitted to the data and used for forecasting purposes.

be used? The 44 per cent for 1974? The 11 per cent for 1979? Or some average of the relations? If the relation for 1979 had been used, a forecast of £55 000 for stock levels in 1984 would have been made, compared with £42 000 by the scatter diagram method. That forecast represents a large error.

The least squares method is thus seen to be superior for forecasting financial requirements, particularly for longer term forecasts. When a firm is likely to have a base stock, e.g. of finished goods or fixed assets, the ratio of the item to sales declines as sales increase. In such cases, the percentage-of-sales method results in large errors.[6]

MULTIPLE REGRESSION METHOD

A more sophisticated approach to forecasting a firm's assets calls for the use of *multiple regression analysis.* In simple regression, sales are assumed to be a function of only one variable; in multiple regression, sales are recognized to depend upon a number of variables. For example, in simple regression we might state that sales are strictly a function of GNP. With multiple regression, we might say that sales are dependent upon both GNP and a set of additional variables. For example, sales of ski equipment depend upon (a) the general level of prosperity as measured by GNP, personal disposal income, or other indicators of aggregate economic activity; (b) population increases; (c) number of lifts operating; (d) weather conditions; (e) advertising, and so forth.

We shall not go into detail on the use of multiple regression analysis at this time. However, most computer installations have regression packages incorporated into their systems, making it extremely easy to use multiple regression techniques. Multiple regression is widely used by at least the larger companies.

COMPARISON OF FORECASTING METHODS

Thus far we have considered three methods used in financial forecasting: (a) percentage of sales, (b) scatter diagram or least squares method, and (c) multiple regression. In this section we will summarize and compare those methods.

Percentage of sales

The percentage-of-sales method of financial forecasting assumes that certain balance sheet items vary directly with sales; that is, that the ratio of a given balance sheet item to sales remains constant. The postulated relationship is shown in Figure 4–3. *Notice that the percentage-of-sales method implicitly assumes a linear relationship that passes through the origin.* The slope of the line representing the relationship may vary, but the line always passes through the origin. Implicitly, the relationship is established by finding one point, or ratio, such as that designated as *X* in Figure 4–3, and then connecting this point with the origin. Then, for any projected level of sales, the forecasted level of the particular balance sheet item can be determined.

6. The widespread use of the percentage method makes for lax control. It would be easy to reduce stock levels below the £55 000 percentage-of-sales forecast level and still be inefficient because the correct target amount is closer to £40 000.

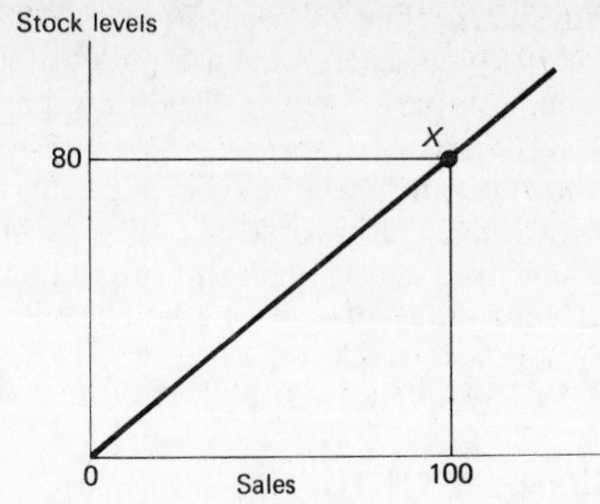

Figure 4–3 *Percentage-of-Sales.*

Scatter diagram, or least squares method

The scatter diagram method differs from the percentage-of-sales method principally in that it does not assume that the line of relationship passes through the origin. In its simplest form, the scatter diagram method calls for calculating the ratio between sales and the relevant balance sheet item at two points in time, extending a line through these two points, and using the line to describe the relationship between sales and the balance sheet item. The accuracy of the regression is improved if more points are plotted, and the least squares line can be fitted mathematically as well as drawn in by eye.

The scatter diagram method is illustrated in Figure 4–4, where the percentage-of-sales relationship is also shown for comparison. The error induced by the use of the percentage-of-sales method is represented by the gap between the two lines. At a sales level of 125, the percentage-of-sales method would call for a stock level of 100 versus a stock level of only 90 using a scatter diagram forecast. *Notice that the error is very small if sales continue to run at approximately the current level, but the gap widens and the error increases as sales deviate in either direction from current levels, as they probably would if a long-run forecast were being made.*

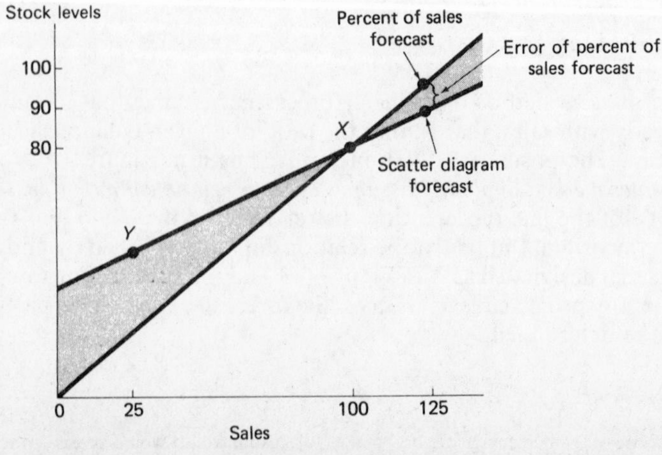

Figure 4–4 *Scatter Diagram, or Least Squares Method.*

Curvilinear simple regression

Linear scatter diagrams, or linear regressions, assume that the slope of the regression line is constant. Although this condition frequently exists, it is not a universal rule. Figure 4–5 illustrates the application of curvilinear simple regression to forecasting financial relationships. We have drawn this hypothetical illustration to show a flattening curve, which implies a decreasing relationship between sales and stock levels beyond point X, the current level of operations. In this case, the forecast of stock requirements at a sales level of 125 would be too high if the linear regression method was used (but too low if sales declined from 100 to 50).

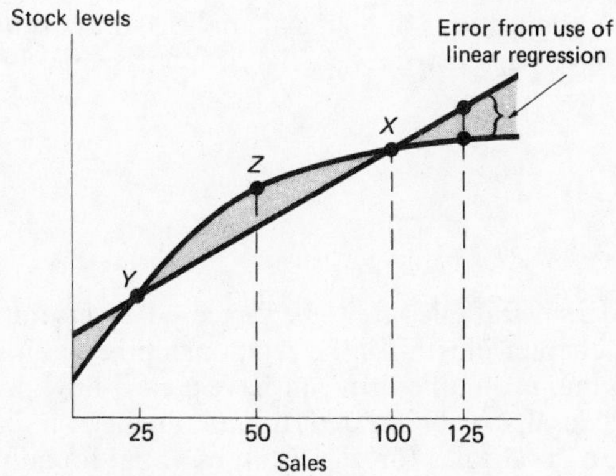

Figure 4–5 *Curvilinear Simple Regression.*

Multiple regression

In our illustrations to this point, we have been assuming that the observations fell exactly on the relationship line. This implies perfect correlation, something that, in fact, seldom occurs. In practice, the actual observations would be scattered about the regression line as shown in Figure 4–6. What causes the deviations from the regression line? One answer, if linear regression is used, is that the actual line of relationship might be curvilinear. But if curvilinear regression is used and deviations still occur, we must seek other explanations

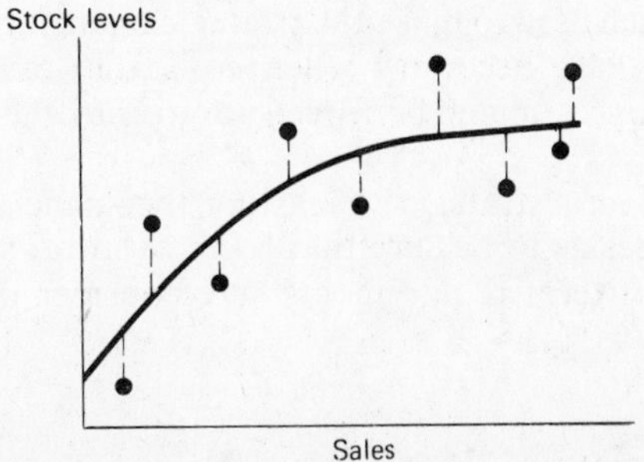

Figure 4–6 *Multiple Regression: Deviations in the Forecast.*

for the scatter around the regression line. The most obvious answer is that stock levels are determined by other factors in addition to sales. Stock levels are certainly influenced by work stoppages at the factories of suppliers. If a steel user anticipates a strike in the steel industry, he will stock up on steel products. Such precautionary buying would cause actual stock levels to be above the level forecast on the basis of sales projections. Then, assuming a strike does occur and continues for many months, stock levels will be run down and may end up well below the predicted level. Multiple regression techniques, which introduce additional variables (such as work stoppages) into the analysis, are employed to improve financial forecasting further.

The need to employ more complicated forecasting techniques varies from situation to situation. For example, the percentage-of-sales method may be perfectly adequate for making short-term forecasts where conditions are relatively stable, while curvilinear multiple regression may be deemed essential for longer term forecasts in more dynamic industries. As in all other applications of financial analysis, the cost of using more refined techniques must be balanced against the benefits of increased accuracy.

SUMMARY

Firms need assets to make sales; if sales are to be increased, assets must also be expanded. The first section of this chapter illustrates the relationship between sales and assets and shows how even a growing, profitable firm can have a cash-flow problem.

The most important causal variable in determining financial requirements is a firm's projected sales revenue; a good sales forecast is an essential foundation for forecasting financial requirements. The two principal methods used for making financial forecasts are (a) the percentage-of-sales method and (b) the least squares method. The first has the virtue of simplicity; the forecaster computes past relationships between asset and liability items and sales, assumes these same relationships will continue, and then applies the new sales forecast to get an estimate of the financial requirements.

However, since the percentage-of-sales method assumes that the balance-sheet-to-sales relationships will remain constant, it is only useful for relatively short-term forecasting. When longer range forecasts are being made, the least squares method is preferable because it allows for changing balance-sheet-to-sales relationships. Further, linear regression can be expanded to curvilinear regression, and simple regression to multiple regression. These more complex methods are useful in certain circumstances, but their increased accuracy must be balanced against the increased costs of using them.

The tools and techniques we have discussed in this chapter are generally used in the following manner: as a first step, one of the long-range forecasting techniques is used to make a long-term forecast of the firm's financial requirements over a three- to five-year period. This forecast is then used to make the strategic financing plans during the planning period. Long lead times are necessary when companies issue shares or debentures; otherwise financial managers might be forced to go into the market for funds during unfavourable periods.

In addition to the long-term strategic forecasting, the financial manager must also make accurate short-term forecasts to be sure that bank overdrafts will be available to meet seasonal and other short-term requirements. We consider this topic in the following chapter.

QUESTIONS

4–1. What should be the approximate point of intersection between the sales-to-asset regression line and the vertical axis (*Y*-axis intercept) for the following: stocks, trade debtors, fixed assets? State your answer in terms of positive, nil or negative intercept. Can you think of any items that might have a negative intercept?

4–2. How does forecasting financial requirements in advance of needs assist the financial manager to perform his responsibilities more effectively?

4–3. Explain how a downswing in the business cycle could either cause a cash shortage for a firm or have the opposite effect and generate excess cash.

4–4. Explain this statement: 'Current assets to a considerable extent represent permanent assets.'

4–5. What advantages might the multiple regression technique have over simple regression in forecasting sales? What might be some drawbacks in the actual use of this technique?

PROBLEMS

4–1. The Universal Supply Company is a wholesale steel distributor. It purchases steel in container lots from more than 20 producing mills and sells to several thousand steel users. The items carried include sheets, plates, wire products, bolts, windows, pipe and tubing.

The company owns two warehouses, each containing 15 000 square feet, and contemplates the erection of another warehouse of 20 000 square feet. The nature of the steel supply business requires that the company maintain large stock levels to take care of customer requirements in the event of mill strikes or other delays.

In examining patterns from 1972 to 1977, the company found a rather consistent relation between the following accounts as a percentage of sales.

Current assets	30 %
Net fixed assets	60 %
Trade creditors	5 %
Other current liabilities, including accruals and corporation tax payable but not bank overdrafts	5 %
Net profit after tax	3 %

The company's sales for 1978 were £3 million, and its balance sheet on 31 December 1978 was as follows:

Universal Supply Company Balance Sheet 31 December 1978.

Ordinary share capital	£ 550 000	Fixed assets	£1 800 000
Retained earnings	1 150 000		
Debenture capital	300 000	Current assets	900 000
Trade creditors	150 000		
Accrued expenses	150 000		
Bank overdraft	400 000		
	£2 700 000		£2 700 000

The company expects its sales to increase by £400 000 each year. If this is achieved what will its financial requirements be at the end of the five-year period? Assume that items not directly related to sales (for example, the bank overdraft) remain constant. Assume also that the company pays no dividend.

(a) Construct a *pro forma* balance sheet for the end of 1983, using 'additional financing needed' as the balancing item.

(b) What are the crucial assumptions made in your projection method?

4–2. One useful test, or guide, for evaluating a firm's financial structure in relation to its industry is by comparison with financial ratio averages for its industry. A new firm, or one contemplating entering a new industry, may use such industry averages as a guide to what its financial position is likely to approximate after the initial settling-down period.

The following data represent ratios for the publishing and printing industry for 1978:

Sales to shareholders' funds	2.3 times
Current liabilities to shareholders' funds	42%
Total debt to shareholders' funds	75%
Current ratio	2.9 times
Net sales to stock levels	4.7 times
Average collection period	64 days
Fixed assets to shareholders' funds	53.2%

(a) Complete the *pro forma* balance sheet below (round to the nearest thousand) assuming Creative Printers' 1978 sales are £3 200 000.
(b) What does the use of the financial ratio averages accomplish?
(c) What other factors will influence the financial structure of the firm?

Creative Printers Ltd, Pro Forma Sheet 31 December 1978.

	£		£
Share capital and retained earnings	———	Fixed assets	———
Long-term loans	———	Stocks	———
Current liabilities	———	Trade debtors	———
	———	Cash	———
	═══		═══

4–3. The 1978 sales of Electrosonics Ltd amounted to £12 million. Ordinary share capital and short-term loans are constant. The dividend payout ratio is 50 per cent. Retained earnings as shown on the 31 December 1977 balance sheet were £60 000. The percentage of sales in each balance sheet item that varies directly with sales are expected to be as follows:

Cash	4%
Trade debtors	10
Stocks	20
Net fixed assets	35
Trade creditors	12
Accrued expenses	6
Profit (after tax) on sales	3

(a) Complete the balance sheet given.

Electrosonics Ltd, Balance Sheet 31 December 1978

Ordinary share capital	£5 250 000	Fixed assets	
Retained earnings	———	Stocks	
Trade creditors	———	Debtors	
Accrued expenses	———	Cash	
Short-term loans	630 000		
	———		———
	═══		═══

(b) Now suppose that in 1979 sales increase by 10 per cent over 1978 sales. How much additional (external) capital will be required?
(c) Construct the year-end 1979 balance sheet. Assume that any required funds are borrowed as short-term loans.
(d) What would happen to capital requirements under each of the following conditions? Answer in words, without calculations.

1. The profit margin went (i) from 3 per cent to 6 per cent? (ii) from 3 per cent to 1 per cent? Set up an equation to illustrate your answer.
2. The dividend payout rate (i) was raised from 50 per cent to 80 per cent? (ii) was lowered from 50 per cent to 30 per cent? Set up an equation to illustrate your answer.
3. Inefficiencies caused trade debtors to rise to 45 days of sales.

4-4 Jones Ltd, a large drugs manufacturer, had the following balance sheet and profit and loss account for 1978. Also shown are average ratios for that sector of the economy (assumed).

Jones Ltd, Balance Sheet 31 December 1978.

	Jones Ltd	Industry average %
Fixed assets (net)	£143 300	31.5
Trade investments	16 200	4.0
Stocks	105 700	28.0
Debtors	125 100	22.8
Cash	186 700	12.5
Quoted investments	9 900	1.2
	£586 900	100.0
Share capital and retained earnings	312 200	51.1
Long-term loan	111 000	22.6
Short-term loan	77 700	8.0
Trade creditors	33 400	10.0
Accrued expenses	52 600	8.3
	£586 900	100.0

Jones Ltd, Profit and Loss Account for Year Ended 31 December 1978.

	Jones Ltd	Industry average %
Sales	£606 300	100.0
Cost of goods sold	228 000	60.2
Gross profit	378 300	39.8
Selling and administrative expenses	269 800	21.6
Operating profit	108 500	18.2
Less: interest expense	14 200	1.4
Net profit before tax	94 300	16.8
Less: corporation tax	30 600	8.4
Net profit after tax	£ 63 700	8.4

The industry ratio for sales to total assets is 1.5 times.

(a) Using the above information, prepare a balance sheet and income statement based on the industry averages and total sales of £606 300 (round figures to hundreds).

(b) For each item compute the percentage difference between actual and revised figures in the form (actual/revised) – 1.

(c) Comment on the difference between the actual and the revised accounts based on the industry averages.

4-5. A firm has the following relationships. The ratio of total assets to sales is 60 per cent. Liabilities that increase directly with sales amount to 15 per cent. The profit margin on sales after corporation tax is 5 per cent. The firm's dividend payout ratio is 40 per cent.

(a) If the firm's growth rate on sales is 10 per cent per annum, what percentage of the sales increase in any year must be financed externally?

(b) If the firm's growth rate on sales increases to 20 per cent per annum, what percentage of the sales increase in any year must be financed externally?

(c) How will your answer to part (a) change if the profit margin increased to 6 per cent?

(d) How will your answer to part (b) change if the firm's dividend payout ratio is reduced to 10 per cent?

(e) If the profit margin increased from 5 per cent to 6 per cent and the dividend payout ratio is 20 per cent, at what growth rate in sales would the external financing requirement percentage be exactly nil?

SELECTED REFERENCES

Ansoff, H. Igor. Planning as a practical management tool. *Financial Executive* 32 (June 1964): 34–37.

Chambers, John C., Mullick, Satinder K. and Smith, Donald D. How to choose the right forecasting technique. *Harvard Business Review* 49 (July–August 1971): 45–74.

Dev, Susan. Problems in interpreting prospectus profit forecasts. *Accounting and Business Research* (Spring 1973): 110–116.

Dev, Susan. Statements of company prospects. *Accounting and Business Research* (Autumn 1974): 270–285.

Dev, Susan and Webb, Michael. The accuracy of company profit forecasts. *Journal of Business Finance* 4, No. 3 (1972): 26–36.

Gentry, James A. and Pyhrr, Stephen A. Stimulating an EPS growth model. *Financial Management* 2 (Summer 1973): 68–75.

Gershefski, George W. Building a corporate financial model. *Harvard Business Review* (July–August 1969): 61–72.

Gordon, Myron J. and Shillinglaw, Gordon. *Accounting: A Management Approach*. 4th ed. Homewood, Ill.: Irwin, 1969, chap. 16.

Myers, Stewart C. and Pogue, Gerald A. A programming approach to corporate financial management. *Journal of Finance* 29 (May 1974): 579–99.

Pappas, James L. and Huber, George P. Probabilistic short-term financial planning. *Financial Management* 2 (Autumn 1973): 36–44.

Parker, George G. C. and Segura, Edilberto L. How to get a better forecast. *Harvard Business Review* 49 (March–April 1971): 99–109.

Smith, Gary and Brainard, William. The value of a priori information in estimating a financial model. *Journal of Finance* 31 (December 1976): 1299–1322.

Wagle, B. The use of models for environmental forecasting and corporate planning. *Operational Research Quarterly* 22, no. 3: 327–36.

Warren, James M. and Shelton, John P. A simultaneous equation approach to financial planning. *Journal of Finance* 26 (December 1971): 1123–1142.

Weston, J. Fred. Forecasting financial requirements. *Accounting Review* 33 (July 1958): 427–440.

Whittle, J. Problems of corporate forecasting. *Accountancy* (April 1978): 105–110.

Chapter 5

Financial Planning and Control: Budgeting

In the preceding chapter we first examined the relationship between assets and sales, then we considered several procedures the financial manager can use to forecast his requirements. In addition to his long-range forecasts, the financial manager is also concerned with short-term needs for funds. It is embarrassing for a company's accountant to 'run out of money'. Even though he may be able to negotiate a bank loan on short notice, his plight may cause the banker to question the soundness of the firm's management and, accordingly, to reduce the company's credit limit or raise the interest rate. Therefore, attention must be given to short-term budgeting, with special emphasis on cash forecasting or *cash budgeting*, as it is commonly called.

The cash budget is, however, only one part of the firm's overall budget system. The nature of the budget system, and especially the way it can be used for both planning and control purposes, is also discussed in this chapter.

BUDGETING

A budget is simply a financial plan. A household budget itemizes the family's sources of income and describes how this income will be spent: so much for food, housing, transport, entertainment, education, savings and so on. Similarly, the Chancellor's Budget indicates the government's income sources. By the same token, a firm's budget is a plan detailing how funds will be spent on labour, raw materials, capital goods and so on, and also how the funds for these expenditures will be obtained. Just as the Chancellor's Budget can be used as a device to ensure that the Ministries of Defence, Agriculture and others limit their expenditures to specified amounts, the corporate budget can also be used as a device for formulating the firm's plans and for exercising control over the various departments.

Budgeting is thus a management tool used for both *planning* and *control*. Depending on the nature of the business, detailed plans may be formulated for the next few months, the next year, the next five years, or even longer. A company engaged in, say, heavy construction is constantly extending bids that may or may not be accepted; it cannot, and indeed need not, plan as far ahead as the Central Electricity Generating Board which can base its projections on population growth, which is predictable for five- to ten-year periods, and it *must* plan asset acquisitions years ahead because of the long lead times involved in constructing nuclear power plants and the like.

NATURE OF THE BUDGETING PROCESS

Fundamentally, the budgeting process is a method of improving operations; it is a continuous effort to specify what should be done to get the job completed in the best possible way. Corporate budgeting should not be thought of as a device for limiting expenditures: the budgeting process is a tool for obtaining the most productive and profitable use of the company's resources. The budget requires a set of performance standards, or targets, that can be compared to actual results; this process is called 'controlling to plan'. It is a continuous monitoring procedure, reviewing and evaluating performance with reference to the previously established standards.

Establishing standards requires a realistic understanding of the activities carried on by the firm. Arbitrary standards, set without a basic understanding of the minimum costs as determined by the nature of the firm's operations, can do more harm than good. Budgets imposed in an arbitrary fashion may represent impossible targets at the one extreme or standards that are too lax at the other. If standards are unrealistically high, frustrations and resentment will develop. If standards are unduly lax, costs will be out of control, profits will suffer and morale will deteriorate. However, a set of budgets based on a clear understanding and careful analysis of operations can play an important, positive role for the firm.[1]

Budgets can provide valuable guides to both high-level executives and middle-management personnel. Well-formulated and effectively developed budgets make subordinates aware that top management has a realistic understanding of the nature of the operations in the business firm, and such a budget can be an important communication link between top management and the divisional personnel whom they guide.

Budgets also represent planning and control devices that enable management to anticipate change and adapt to it. Business operations in today's economic environment are complex and are subject to heavy competitive pressures. In such an environment many kinds of changes take place. The rate of growth of the economy as a whole fluctuates, and these fluctuations affect different industries in a number of different ways. If a firm plans ahead, the budget and control process can provide management with a better basis for understanding the firm's operations in relation to the general environment. This increased understanding leads to faster reactions to developing events, thus increasing the firm's ability to perform effectively.

The budgeting process, in summary, improves internal coordination. Decisions for each product at every stage – at the research, engineering, production, marketing, personnel and financial levels – all have an impact on the firm's profits. Planning and control is the

1. The authors are familiar with one case where an unrealistic budget ruined a major American company. Top management set impossible performance and growth goals for the various divisions. The divisions, in an effort to meet the sales and profit projections, expanded into high-risk product lines (especially property development ventures), employed questionable accounting practices that tended to overstate profits, and the like. Debt financing was emphasized to obtain a gearing effect on earnings. Things looked good for several years, but eventually the true situation became apparent. Top management brought in a team of consultants in an attempt to correct the problems, but it was too late – the firm was beyond help. The interesting point, to us, is that the consultants traced the firm's difficulties *directly* back to the unrealistic targets that were established by top management without adequate consultation with the division managers.

essence of profit planning, and the budget system provides an integrated picture of the firm's operations as a whole. Therefore, the budget system enables the manager of each division to see the relation of his part of the enterprise to the totality of the firm. For example, a production decision to alter the level of work-in-progress stocks, or a marketing decision to change the terms under which a particular product is sold, can be traced through the entire budget system to show its effects on the firm's overall profitability. The budgeting system is thus a most important financial tool.

Budget system

The overall nature of the budget process is outlined in Figure 5–1. Budgeting is a part of the total planning activity in the firm, so we must begin with a statement of corporate goals or objectives. The statement of goals (shown in the box at the top of the figure) determines the second section of the figure, the corporate long-range plan. Moving down the figure, we see that a segment of the corporate long-range plan includes a long-range sales forecast. This forecast requires a determination of the number and types of products that will be manufactured both at present and in the future years encompassed by the long-range plan: this is the product mix strategy.

Short-term forecasts and budgets are formulated within the framework of the long-range plan. For example, one might begin with a sales forecast covering six months or one year. The short-term sales forecast provides a basis for (and is dependent on) the broad

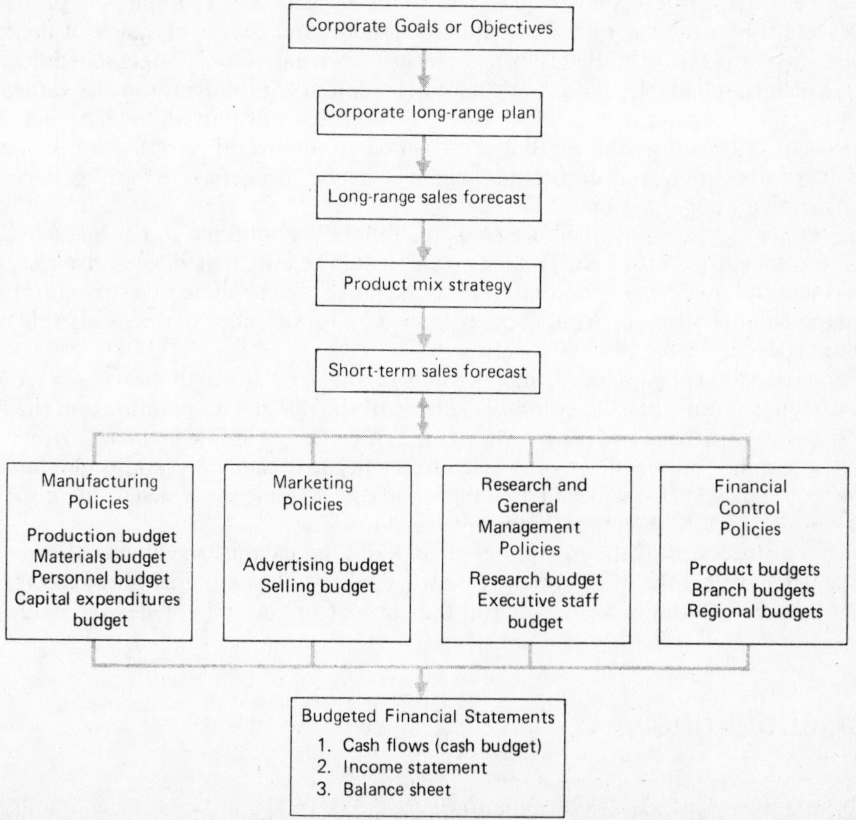

Figure 5-1 *Overall View of the Total Budgeting Process and Relations.*

range of policies indicated in the lower portion of Figure 5–1. *First*, there are manufacturing policies covering the choice of types of equipment, plant layout, and production-line arrangements. In addition, the kind of durability built into the products and their associated costs will be considered. *Second*, a broad set of marketing policies must be formulated. These relate to such items as the development of the firm's own sales organization versus the use of outside sales organizations; the number of salesmen, and the method by which they will be remunerated; the forms of, types of, and amounts spent on advertising; and other factors. *Third* are the research and general management policies. Research policies relate to relative emphasis on basic versus applied research and the product areas emphasized by both types of research. *Fourth* are financial policies, the subject of this chapter. The four major policy sets must be established simultaneously, as each affects the others. We shall concentrate on financial control policies, but it is important to realize the interdependencies between financial and other policies.

Financial control policies

Financial control policies include the organization and content of various kinds of financial control budgets. These include a budget for individual products and for every significant activity of the firm. In addition, budgets will be formulated to control operations at individual branch offices. Those budgets, in turn, are grouped and modified to control regional operations.

In a similar manner, policies established at the manufacturing, marketing, research and general management levels give rise to a series of budgets. For example, the production budget will reflect the use of materials, parts, labour, and overheads; each of the major elements in a production budget is likely to have its own individual budget schedule. There will be a materials budget, a labour or personnel requirements budget, and an overheads or long-run capital expenditures budget. After the product is produced, the next step in the process will call for a marketing budget. Related to the overall process are the general office and executive requirements, which will be reflected in the general and administrative budget system.

The results of projecting all those elements of cost are reflected in the budgeted (also called 'pro forma' or 'projected') income statement. The anticipated sales give rise to the various types of investments needed to produce the products; these investments, plus the beginning balance sheet, provide the necessary data for developing the assets side of the balance sheet.

Those assets must be financed, and a cash flow analysis – the cash budget – is required. The cash budget indicates the combined effects of the budgeted operations on the firm's cash flows. A positive net cash flow indicates that the firm has ample financing. However, if an increase in the volume of operations leads to a negative cash flow, additional financing will be required. And that will lead directly to choices of financing, which is the subject of a considerable portion of the remainder of the book.

Since the structures of the income statement and the balance sheet have already been covered in Chapter 2, the rest of this section will deal with the two remaining aspects of the budgeting process – the cash budget and the concept of variable, or flexible, budgets.

CASH BUDGETING

The cash budget indicates not only the total amount of financing that is required but its timing as well. This statement shows the amount of funds needed month by month, week by week, or even on a daily basis; it is one of the financial manager's most important tools.

Because a clear understanding of the nature of cash budgeting is important, the process is described by means of an example that makes the elements of the cash budget explicit.

Marvel Toy is a medium-sized toy manufacturer. Sales are highly seasonal. with the peak occurring in September when retailers stock up for the Christmas season. All sales are made on terms that allow a cash discount on payments made within 30 days; if the discount is not taken, the full amount must be paid in 60 days. However, Marvel, like most other companies, finds that some of its customers delay payment up to 90 days. Experience shows that on 20 per cent of the sales, payment is made within 30 days; on 70 per cent of the sales, payment is made during the second month after the sale; while on 10 per cent of the sales, payment is made during the third month.

Marvel's production is geared to future sales. Purchased materials and parts, which amount to 70 per cent of sales, are bought the month before the company expects to sell the finished product. Its own purchase terms permit Marvel to delay payment on its purchases for one month. In other words, if August sales are forecast at £30 000, then purchases during July will amount to £21 000, and this amount will actually be paid in August.

Wages and salaries, rent, and other cash expenses are given in Table 5–1. The company also has a tax payment of £8000 coming due in August. Its capital budgeting plans call for the purchase in July of a new machine tool costing £10 000, payment to be made in September. Assuming the company needs to keep a £5000 cash balance at all times and has £6000 on 1 July, what are Marvel's financial requirements for the period from July to December?

The cash requirements are worked out in the cash budget shown in Table 5–1. The top half of the table provides a worksheet for calculating receipts from sales and payments on purchases. The first line in the worksheet gives the sales forecast for the period from May to January; May and June sales are necessary to determine receipts for July and August. Next, cash receipts are given. The first line of this section shows that 20 per cent of the sales during any given month are collected that month. The second shows the receipts from the prior month's sales – 70 per cent of sales in the preceding month. The third line gives receipts from sales two months earlier – 10 per cent of sales in that month. The receipts are summed to find the total cash receipts from sales during each month under consideration.

With the worksheet completed, the cash budget itself can be considered. Receipts from debtors are given on the top line. Next, payments during each month are summarized. The difference between cash receipts and cash payments is the net cash gain or loss during the month; for July, there is a net cash loss of £4200. The initial cash on hand at the beginning of the month is added to the net cash gain or loss during the month to yield the cumulative cash that will be on hand if no financing is done; at the end of July, Marvel Toy will have cumulative cash equal to £1800. The desired cash balance, £5000, is subtracted from the cumulative cash balance to determine the amount of financing that the firm needs if it is to maintain the desired level of cash. At the end of July we see that Marvel will need £3200; thus, overdrafts outstanding will total £3200 at the end of July.

This same procedure is used in the following months. Sales will expand seasonally in August; with the increased sales will come increased payments for purchases, wages and other items. Moreover, the £8000 tax bill is due in August. Receipts from sales will go up too, but the firm will still be left with a £10 800 cash deficit during the month. The total financial requirements at the end of August will be £14 000–the £3200 needed at the end of July plus the £10 800 cash deficit for August. Thus, overdraft outstanding will total £14 000 at the end of August.

Sales peak in September, and the cash deficit during this month will amount to another £10 400. The total need for funds through September will increase to £24 400. Sales, purchases and payments for past purchases will fall markedly in October; receipts will be the highest of any month because they reflect the high September sales. As a result, Marvel Toy will enjoy a healthy £18 800 cash surplus during October. This surplus can be used to pay off borrowings, so the need for financing will decline by £18 800, to £5600.

Table 5-1 *Marvel Toy Company, Cash Budget.*

Worksheet	May	June	July	Aug.	Sept.	Oct.	Nov.	Dec.	Jan.
Sales (net of cash discounts)	£10 000	£10 000	£20 000	£30 000	£40 000	£20 000	£20 000	£10 000	£10 000
Receipts									
First month (20%)	£ 2000	£ 2000	£ 4000	£ 6000	£ 8000	£ 4000	£ 4000	£ 2000	£ 2000
Second month (70%)		7000	7000	14 000	21 000	28 000	14 000	14 000	7000
Third month (10%)			1000	1000	2000	3000	4000	2000	2000
Total	£ 2000	£ 9000	£12 000	£21 000	£31 000	£35 000	£22 000	£18 000	£11 000
Purchases (70% of next month's sales)	£ 7000	£14 000	£21 000	£28 000	£14 000	£14 000	£ 7000	£ 7000	
Payments (one month lag)		7000	14 000	21 000	28 000	14 000	14 000	7000	7000
Cash budget									
Receipts			£12 000	£21 000	£31 000	£35 000	£22 000	£18 000	£11 000
Payments									
Purchases			14 000	21 000	28 000	14 000	14 000	7000	
Wages and salaries			1500	2000	2500	1500	1500	1000	
Rent			500	500	500	500	500	500	
Other expenses			200	300	400	200	200	100	
Taxes			–	8000	–	–	–	–	
Payment on machine			–	–	10 000	–	–	–	
Total payments			£16 200	£31 800	£41 400	£16 200	£16 200	£ 8600	
Net cash gain (loss) during month			£ (4200)	£(10 800)	£(10 400)	£18 800	£ 5800	£ 9400	
Cash at start of month if no borrowing is done			6000	1800	(9000)	(19 400)	(600)	5200	
Cumulative cash (= cash at start plus gains or minus losses)			£ 1800	£ (9000)	£(19 400)	£ (600)	£ 5200	£14 600	
Less: desired level of cash			(5000)	(5000)	(5000)	(5000)	(5000)	(5000)	
Total overdrafts outstanding to maintain £5000 cash balance			£ 3200	£14 000	£24 400	£ 5600	–	–	
Surplus cash			–	–	–	–	£ 200	£ 9600	

Marvel will have another cash surplus in November, and this extra cash will permit the company to eliminate completely the need for financing. In fact, the company is expected to have £200 in surplus cash by the month's end, while another cash surplus in December will swell the extra cash to £9600. With such a large amount of unneeded funds, Marvel's accountant will doubtless want to make short-term investments or put the funds to use in some other way.[2]

VARIABLE OR FLEXIBLE BUDGETS

Budgets are planned allocations of a firm's resources, based on forecasts for the future. Two important elements influence actual performance. One is the impact of external influences over which the firm has little or no control – developments in the economy as a whole and competitive developments in the firm's own industry. The second element, which is controllable by the firm, is its level of efficiency at a given volume of sales. It is useful to separate the impact of these two elements, as this separation is necessary for evaluating individual performances.

The essence of the variable budget system is to introduce flexibility into budgets by recognizing that certain types of expenditures will vary at different levels of output. Thus, a firm might have an alternative level of outlay budgeted for different volumes of operation – high, low, medium. One of management's responsiblities is to determine which of the alternative budgets should be in effect for the planning period under consideration.

The regression method, which we described in the preceding chapter in connection with financial forecasting, may also be used to establish the basis for flexible budgeting. The use of the concept can be illustrated by a specific example. Suppose that a retail store, the Hubler Department Store, has had the experience indicated by the historical data set forth in Table 5–2. It is apparent from the data that the number of employees the firm needs is

Table 5–2 *Hubler Department Store, Relationship between Sales and Employees.*

Month	Sales (£ million)	Number of employees
January	4	42
February	5	51
March	6	60
April	7	75
May	10	102
June	8	83
July	5	55
August	9	92

dependent upon the sales revenue gained during a month. This is seen more easily from a scatter diagram such as that in Figure 5–2. The freehand regression line is sloped positively because the number of employees increases as the volume of sales increases. The independent variable, sales revenue, is called the *control variable*. Variations in the control variable cause changes in total expenses. The volume of sales can be forecast, and the number of employees can be read from the regression chart. The relations are expressed in

2. Types of investments for excess funds are discussed in Chapter 7.

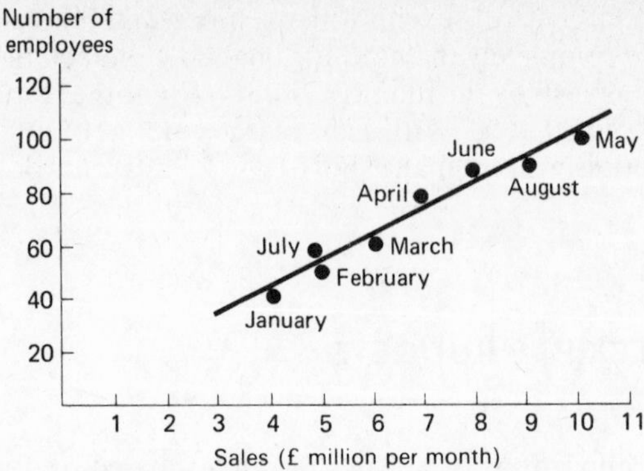

Figure 5–2 *Scatter Diagram and Regression Line: Hubler Department Store.*

tabular form in Table 5–3. Given the forecast of sales, standards are provided for the expected number of employees and the weekly wage bill.[3]

Table 5–3 *Hubler Department Store, Budget Allowance.*

Sales (£ million)	Number of employees	Weekly estimate (average wage £100)
6	62	6 200
7	72	7 200
8	82	8 200
9	92	9 200
10	102	10 200
11	112	11 200

PROBLEMS OF BUDGETING

Four major problems are encountered when using budget systems. First, budgetary programmes can grow to be so complete and so detailed that they become cumbersome, meaningless and unduly expensive. Overbudgeting is dangerous.

Second, budgetary goals may come to supersede corporate goals. A budget is a tool, not an end in itself. Corporate goals by definition supersede subsidiary plans of which budgets are a part. Moreover, budgets are based on future expectations that may not be realized. There is no acceptable reason for neglecting to alter budgets as circumstances change. This reasoning is the core of the argument in favour of more flexible budgets.

Third, budgets can tend to hide inefficiencies by continuing initial expenditures in succeeding periods without proper evaluation. Budgets growing from precedent usually

3. Note that regression analysis provides even more flexibility in budgeting than do the high, medium and low levels mentioned earlier. Also, it is possible to include *confidence levels* when using the regression methcd. For example, Table 5–3 shows that when volume is at £8 million, we expect to have 82 employees and a weekly wage bill of £8200. Although this relationship would probably not hold *exactly*, we might find that actual observations lie within 78 and 86 employees at this sales volume 95 per cent of the time. Thus, 95 per cent confidence levels would encompass the range 78 to 86. Similar ranges could be determined for other volumes; management might, as a matter of control policy, investigate whenever actual performances were outside this expected range.

contain undesirable expenditures. They should not be used as umbrellas under which slovenly, inefficient management can hide. Consequently, the budgetary process must contain provision for re-examination of standards and other bases of planning by which policies are translated into numerical terms.

Finally, case study evidence suggests that the use of budgets as a pressure device defeats their basic objectives. Budgets, if used as instruments of tyranny, cause resentment and frustrations, which in turn lead to inefficiency. In order to counteract this effect, it has been recommended that top management increase the participation of subordinates during the preparatory stages of the budgets.

USE OF FINANCIAL PLANS AND BUDGETS

Forecasts, or long-range plans, are necessary in all the firm's operations. The personnel department must have a good idea of the scale of future operations if it is to plan its hiring and training activities properly. The production department must be sure that the productive capacity is available to meet the projected product demand, and the finance department must be sure that funds are on hand to meet the firm's financial requirements.

The tools and techniques discussed in this and the preceding chapters are actually used in several separate, but related, ways. First, the percentage-of-sales method or, preferably, the regression method is used to make a long-range forecast of financial requirements over a projected three-to five-year period. This forecast is then used to draw up the strategic financing plans during the planning period. The company might, for example, plan to meet its financial requirements with retained earnings and short-term overdraft facility during, say, 1978 and 1979, a debenture issue in 1980, use retained earnings in 1981, and finally make an issue of ordinary shares in 1982. Fairly long lead times are necessary when companies issue shares or debentures; otherwise, they might be forced to go into the market during unfavourable periods.

In addition to the long-term strategic planning, the financial manager must also make accurate short-term forecasts to be sure that funds will be available to meet seasonal and other short-term requirements. He might, for example, have a meeting with his bank manager to discuss his company's need for funds during the coming year. Prior to the meeting, he would have his accountants prepare a detailed cash budget showing the need for money during each of the coming 12 months. The cash budget would show the maximum amount that would be needed during the year, how much would be needed during each month, and how cash surpluses would be generated at some point to enable the firm to repay the bank loan.

The financial manager would also have his firm's most recent, and its proforma, balance sheets and income statements. He would have calculated the key financial ratios to show both his actual and his projected financial positions to the banker. If the firm's financial position is sound and if its cash budget appears reasonable, the bank will commit itself to make the required funds available. Even if the bank decides that the company's request is unreasonable and denies the loan request, the financial manager will have time to seek other sources of funds. While it might not be pleasant to have to look elsewhere for money, it is much better to know ahead of time that the loan request will be refused.

DIVISIONAL CONTROL IN A DECENTRALIZED FIRM

In our discussion of the du Pont system of financial control in Chapter 2, we considered its use for the firm as a whole rather than for different divisions of a single firm. The du Pont system can, however, also be used to control the various parts of a multidivisional firm.

For organizational reasons, large firms are generally set up on a decentralized basis. For example, a firm such as General Electric in the USA establishes separate divisions for heavy appliances, light appliances, power transformers, fossil fuel generating equipment, nuclear generating equipment, and so on. Each division is defined as a *profit centre*. Each profit centre has its own investments – its fixed and current assets, together with a share of such general corporate assets as research labs and headquarters buildings – and each is expected to earn an appropriate return on its investment.

The corporate headquarters, or central staff, typically controls the various divisions by a form of the du Pont system. When it is used for divisional control, the procedure is frequently referred to as ROI (return on investment) control. If a particular division's ROI falls below a target figure, then the centralized corporate staff assists the division's own financial staff to trace back through the du Pont system to determine the cause of the substandard ROI. Each division manager is judged by his division's ROI, and he is rewarded or penalized accordingly. Therefore, division managers are motivated to keep their ROI up to the target level. These individual actions, in turn, should maintain the total firm's ROI at an appropriate level.

In addition to its use in managerial control, ROI can be used to allocate funds to the various divisions. The firm as a whole has financial resources – retained earnings, cash flow from depreciation, and the ability to obtain additional debt and equity funds from capital markets. Those funds can be allocated to different divisions on the basis of divisional ROIs, with divisions having high ROIs receiving more funds than those with low ROIs.[4]

A number of problems may arise if ROI control is used without proper safeguards. Since the divisional managers are rewarded on the basis of their ROI performance, if their morale is to be maintained it is absolutely essential that the divisional managers feel that their divisional ROI does indeed provide an accurate measure of relative performance. But ROI is dependent on a number of factors in addition to managerial competence. Some of them are listed below:

1. *Depreciation*. ROI is very sensitive to depreciation policy. If one division is writing off assets at a relatively rapid rate, its annual profits and, hence, its ROI will be reduced.
2 *Book value of assets*. If an older division is using assets that have been largely written off, both its current depreciation charges and its investment base will be low. This will make its ROI high in relation to newer divisions.
3. *Transfer pricing*. In most corporations some divisions sell to other divisions. In General Motors, for example, the Fisher Body Division sells to the Chevrolet Division; in such cases the price at which goods are transferred between divisions has a fundamental effect on divisional profits. If the transfer price of car bodies is set relatively high, then Fisher Body will have a relatively high ROI and Chevrolet a relatively low ROI.
4. *Time periods*. Many projects have long gestation periods – expenditures must be made for research and development, plant construction, market development and the like; such expenditures will add to the investment base without a commensurate increase in profits for several years. During this period, a division's ROI could be seriously reduced; without proper constraints, its divisional manager could be improperly penalized. Especially when we recognize the frequency of personnel transfers in larger corporations, we can see that the timing problem could possibly cause managers to refrain from making long-term investments that are in the best interests of the firm.
5. *Industry conditions*. If one division is operating in an industry where conditions are

4. The point of this procedure is to increase the total firm's ROI. To maximize the overall ROI, marginal ROI's between divisions should be equalized.

favourable and rates of return are high, whereas another is in an industry suffering from excessive competition, such environmental differences may cause the favoured division to look good and the other division to look bad, quite apart from any differences in their respective managers. The textile division of a major company, for example, could hardly be expected to show up as well as their petrochemical division in a period when the entire textile industry was suffering severe problems and petrochemical sales were booming. External conditions must be taken into account when appraising ROI performance.

Because of those problems, divisions' ROIs must be supplemented with other criteria when evaluating performance. For example, a division's growth rate in sales, profits and market share, as well as its ROI in comparison with other firms in its own industry, have all been used as a part of the overall control and evaluation procedure.

Although ROI control can be used with great success in British industry, the system cannot be used in a mechanical sense by inexperienced personnel. As with most other tools, it is a good one if used properly but a destructive one if misused.

EXTERNAL USES OF FINANCIAL FORECASTS AND BUDGETS

We have stressed the use of planning and budgeting for internal purposes, that is, to increase the efficiency of a firm's operations. With relatively minor modifications, those same tools and techniques can be used in both credit analysis and investment analysis. For example, external investment analysts can make a forecast of a given firm's sales and, through the income statement and balance sheet relationships, can prepare pro forma (projected) balance sheets and income statements. Credit analysts can make similar projections to aid in estimating the likely need for funds by their customers and the likelihood that borrowers can make prompt repayment.

This kind of analysis has actually been conducted on a large scale in recent years. Very complete financial data going back some 20 years on several thousand large American companies are now available on magnetic tapes (Standard and Poor's Compustat tapes). These tapes are being used by investment analysts in highly sophisticated ways. From what we have seen, analyses conducted in such a manner offer large potential benefits. The same tapes, frequently supplemented with additional data, are being used by the major lending institutions – banks and insurance companies – to forecast their customers' needs for funds and, thus, to plan their own financial requirements.

SUMMARY

A budget is a plan stated in terms of specific expenditures for specific purposes. It is used for both planning and control, its overall purpose being to improve internal operations, thereby reducing costs and raising profitability. A budgeting system starts with a set of performance standards, or targets. The targets constitute, in effect, the firm's financial plan. The budgeted figures are compared with actual results. This is the control phase of the budget system, and it is a crucial step in well-operated companies.

Although the entire budget system is of vital importance to corporate management, one aspect of the system is especially important to the financial manager – the cash budget. The cash budget is, in fact, the principal tool for making short-term financial forecasts. Cash budgets, if used properly, are highly accurate and can pinpoint the funds that will be needed, when they will be needed, and when cash flows will be sufficient to retire any loans that might be necessary.

A good budget system will recognize that some factors lie outside the firm's control. Especially important here is the state of the economy and its effects on sales, and *flexible budgets* will be set up as targets for the different departments assuming different levels of sales. Also, a good system will insure that those responsible for carrying out a plan are involved in its preparation; this procedure will help guard against the establishment of unrealistic targets and unobtainable goals.

As a firm becomes larger, it is necessary for it to decentralize operations to some extent, and decentralized operations require some centralized control over the various divisions. The principal tool used for such control is the return on investment (ROI) method. There are problems with ROI control. But if care is taken in its use, the method can be quite valuable to a decentralized firm.

QUESTIONS

5–1. What use might a confidence interval scheme have in flexible budgeting?

5–2. Why is a cash budget important even when there is plenty of cash in the bank?

5–3. What is the difference between the long-range financial forecasting concept (for example, the percentage-of-sales method) and the budgeting concept? How might they be used together?

5–4. Assume that a firm is making up its long-term financial budget. What period should this budget cover – one month, six months, one year, three years, five years, or some other period? Justify your answer.

5–5. Why is a detailed budget more important to a large, multidivisional firm than to a small, single-product firm?

5–6. Assume that your uncle is a major shareholder in a multidivisional firm that uses a naive ROI criterion for evaluating divisional managers and bases managers' salaries in large part on this evaluation. You can have the job of division manager in any division you choose. If you are a salary maximizer, what divisional characteristics would you seek? If, because of your 'good performance', you became managing director, what changes would you make?

PROBLEMS

5–1. The Simms Company is planning to request a line of credit from its bank.[5] The following sales forecasts have been made for 1979 and 1980:

May 1979	£150 000
June	150 000
July	300 000
August	450 000
September	600 000
October	300 000
November	300 000
December	75 000
January 1980	150 000

Estimates of receipts were obtained from the credit control department as follows: receipts within the month of sale, 5 per cent; receipts the month following the sale, 80 per cent; receipts the second month following the sale, 15 per cent. Payments for labour and raw materials are typically made during the month following the month in which these costs are incurred. Total labour and raw materials costs are estimated for each month as follows (payments are made the following month):

5. This problem is adapted from E. F. Brigham, R. L. Crum, T. J. Nantell, R. T. Aubey and R. H. Pettway, Cases in Managerial Finance (New York: Holt, Rinehart and Winston, second edition), Case 5.

May 1979	£ 75 000
June	75 000
July	105 000
August	735 000
September	255 000
October	195 000
November	135 000
December	75 000

General and administrative salaries will amount to approximately £22 500 a month; lease payments under long-term lease contracts will be £7500 a month; depreciation charges are £30 000 a month; miscellaneous expenses will be £2250 a month; corporation tax payments of £52 500 will be due in both September and December; and a progress payment of £150 000 on a new research laboratory must be paid in October. Cash on hand on 1 July will amount to £110 000, and a minimum cash balance of £75 000 should be maintained throughout the cash budget period.

(a) Prepare a monthly cash budget for the last six months of 1979.

(b) Prepare an estimate of required financing (or excess funds) for each month during the period, that is, the amount of money that the Simms Company will need to borrow (or will have available to invest) each month.

(c) Suppose receipts from sales come in uniformly during the month; that is, cash payments come in 1/30th each day, but all outflows are paid on the fifth of the month. Would this have an effect on the cash budget; that is, would the cash budget you have prepared be valid under these assumptions? If not, what could be done to make a valid estimation of financing requirements?

5–2. Gulf and Eastern Ltd is a diversified multinational company that produces a wide variety of goods and services, including chemicals, soaps, tobacco products, toys, plastics, pollution control equipment, canned food, sugar, motion pictures and computer software.[6] The company's major divisions were brought together in the early 1960s under a decentralized form of management; each division was evaluated in terms of its profitability, efficiency and return on investments. This decentralized organization persisted through most of the decade, during which Gulf and Eastern experienced a high average growth rate in total assets, earnings and share prices.

Towards the end of 1975, however, those trends were reversed. The organization was faced with declining earnings, unstable share prices and a generally uncertain future. This situation persisted into 1976, but during that year a new managing director, Lynn Thompson, was appointed by the board of directors. Thompson, who had served for a time on the financial staff of I.E. du Pont, used the du Pont system to evaluate the various divisions. All showed definite weaknesses.

Thompson reported to the board that a principal reason for the poor overall performance was a lack of control by central management over each division's activities. She was particularly disturbed by the consistently poor results of the company's budgeting procedures. Under the system, each division manager drew up a projected budget for the next quarter, along with estimated sales, revenue and profit; funds were then allocated to the divisions, basically in proportion to their budget requests. However, actual budgets seldom matched the projections; wide discrepancies occurred and this, of course, resulted in a highly inefficient use of capital.

In an attempt to correct the situation, Thompson asked the firm's chief accountant to draw up a plan to improve the budgeting, planning and control processes. When the plan was submitted, its basic provisions included the following:

1. To improve the quality of the divisional budgets, the divisional managers should be informed that the continuance of wide variances between their projected and actual budgets would result in dismissal.
2. A system should be instituted under which funds would be allocated to divisions on the basis of their average return on investment (ROI) during the last four quarters. Since funds were short, divisions with high ROIs would get most of the available money.
3. Only about one-half of each divisional manager's present compensation should be received as salary; the rest should be in the form of a bonus related to the division's average ROI for the quarter.
4. Each division should submit to the central office for approval all capital expenditure requests, production schedules and price changes. Thus, the company would be *re*centralized.

(a) (i) Is it reasonable to expect the new procedures to improve the accuracy of budget forecasts?
(ii) Should all divisions be expected to maintain the same degree of accuracy?
(iii) In what other ways might the budgets be made?

(b) (i) What problems would be associated with the use of the ROI criterion in allocating funds among the divisions?
(ii) What effect would the period used in computing ROI (that is, four quarters, one quarter, two years, and so on) have on the effectiveness of this method?

6. This problem is taken from *Cases in Managerial Finance*, second edition.

(iii) What problems might occur in evaluating the ROI in the crude rubber and motor car tyres divisions? between the sugar products and pollution control equipment divisions?

(c) What problems would be associated with rewarding each manager on the basis of his division's ROI?

(d) How well would Thompson's policy of recentralization work in a highly diversified corporation such as this, particularly in light of her chief accountant's three other proposals?

SELECTED REFERENCES

Argenti, John. Long term budgets can damage your company's health. *Accountancy* (May 1978): 105–107.

Bacon, Jeremy. *Managing the Budget Function*. Studies in Business Policy, Report No. 131. New York: National Industrial Conference Board, Inc., 1970.

Bromwich, M. Measurement of divisional performance: a comment and extension. *Accounting and Business Research* (Spring 1973): 123–132.

Buckley, A. and McKenna, E. Budgeting control and business behaviour. *Accounting and Business Research* (Spring 1972): 137–150.

Dearden, John. The case against ROI control. *Harvard Business Review* 47 (May–June 1969): 124–35.

Donaldson, A. A. and Golden, K. E. Budget modelling or financial simulation. *The Accountants Magazine* (Scotland) (December 1975): 414.

Flower, J. Measurement of divisional performance. *Accounting and Business Research* (Summer 1971): 205–214.

Hamermesh, Richard G. Responding to divisional profit crises. *Harvard Business Review* 55 (March–April 1977): 124–130.

Henning, Dale A. *Non-Financial Controls in Smaller Enterprises*. Seattle, Wash.: University of Washington, College of Business Administration, 1964.

Hunt, Pearson. Funds position: keystone in financial planning. *Harvard Business Review* 53 (May–June 1975): 106–115.

Judelson, David N. Financial controls that work. *Financial Executive* 45 (January 1977): 22–27.

Knight, W. D. and Weinwurn, E. H. *Managerial Budgeting*. New York: Macmillan, 1964.

Rappaport, Alfred. A capital budgeting approach to divisional planning and control. *Financial Executive* (October 1968): 47–63.

Shackleton, K. Management accounting and behavioural science. *Managerial Finance* (UK) 2, No. 3 (1976): 270.

Solomons, D. *Divisional Performance: Measurement and Control*. Irwin, 1976.

Appendix A to Chapter 5:

Illustrative Budget System

A complete budget system includes (a) a production budget, (b) a materials purchases budget, (c) a budgeted, or pro forma, income statement, (d) a budgeted, or pro forma, balance sheet, and (e) a capital expenditure budget. Since capital expenditures are related directly to problems of the firm's growth, they have been considered separately in Chapter 10.[1]

Tables 5A–1 to 5A–7 carry out a hypothetical budget system. In Tables 5A–2 to 5A–7 the lines are numbered consecutively from 1 to 54. This procedure has the advantage of making it easy to see the relations among the various budgets.

Table 5A–1 outlines the highly summarized cost accounting system. It is based on the standard costs of goods sold per unit. Standard costs include direct material, direct labour, and variable and fixed manufacturing expense. Standard costs are the costs of goods produced when the firm is operating at a high level of efficiency and when operations are near a level that may be regarded as 'normal'.[2]

Table 5A–1 *Standard Costs Based on Volume of 1000 Units per Month.*

	Per unit
Direct material: 2 pieces – £1 per piece	£2
Direct labour: 1 hour – £2 per hour	2
Variable manufacturing expense: £1 per unit	1
Fixed manufacturing expense: £1000 per month[a]	1
Cost of goods produced per unit	£6

[a] Includes £200 depreciation charges.

PRODUCTION BUDGET

The illustrative production budget (Table 5A–2) is based directly on the sales forecast and the estimated unit cost of production. It is assumed that the firm maintains its finished goods stock at 50 per cent of the following month's sales. In any month, the firm must produce the unit plus closing stock less the opening stock level.

1. Outlays for capital equipment do, of course, affect the cash budget, the income statement and the balance sheet.
2. The terminology in this chapter follows accounting usage, but anyone familiar with economics can readily translate it into economic terms. For instance, '£6 per unit at standard output' is 'average total (production) cost', 'marginal production cost' is £5 per unit, and so on.

This example illustrates the financial consequences of a rise in sales from a £10 000-per-month level to a new plateau of £12 000. As production rises in response to increased sales, the (standard) cost of goods produced also rises. But the standard cost of goods produced increases faster than actual costs increase because the unit cost of £6 includes fixed charges of £1 per unit. An increase of one unit of production actually raises total costs by only £5. The estimated total cost, however, increases by £6. Estimates of the cost of goods produced are made and then adjusted by the amount of under- or over-absorbed burden. Of course, the same result for calculating the adjusted cost of goods produced (Table 5A–2, line 9) is obtained by multiplying £5 by the number of units produced to get total variable costs, and adding £1000 in fixed costs to reach total adjusted cost of goods produced.

Table 5A–2 *Production Budget.*

Item	Monthly average 1977	Estimated 1978 first quarter: First month	Second month	Third month	Source of data
1. Sales at £10 per unit	£10 000	£10 000	£12 000	£12 000	Assumed
2. Unit sales	1 000	1 000	1 200	1 200	Line 1 divided by £10
3. Opening stock (units)	500	500	600	600	One half of current month's sales
4. Difference (units)	500	500	600	600	Line 2 minus line 3
5. Closing stock (units)	500	600	600	600	One half of next month's sales
6. Production in units	1 000	1 100	1 200	1 200	Line 4 plus line 5
7. Estimated cost of goods produced	£ 6 000	£ 6 600	£ 7 200	£ 7 200	Line 6 times £6
8. Burden absorption, under or (over)	0	(100)	(200)	(200)	Line 6 times £1 less £1000 fixed mfg expense
9. Adjusted cost of goods produced	£ 6 000	£ 6 500	£ 7 000	£ 7 000	Line 7 less line 8
9a. Adjusted cost per unit	£ 6	£ 5.91	£ 5.83	£ 5.83	Line 9 divided by line 6
10. Value of closing stock (finished goods)	£3 000	£ 3 545	£ 3 500	£ 3 500	Line 5 multiplied by line 9a (rounded)

The per unit adjusted costs of goods produced (£5.91 for the first month) is required to calculate the closing stock. The first-in, first-out method of stock valuation is employed. The calculation of the closing stock value is required for the worksheet (Table 5A–6) used in developing the budgeted balance sheet (Table 5A–7).

MATERIALS PURCHASES BUDGET

The level of operations indicated by the production budget in Table 5A–2 is based on sales forecast and stock requirements. The materials purchases budget (Table 5A–3) contains estimates of materials purchases that will be needed to carry out the production plans. Raw materials purchases depend in turn upon materials actually used in production, material costs (Table 5A–1), size of opening stocks and requirements for closing stocks.

The example in Table 5A–3 does not take into account economical ordering quantities (EOQs) as discussed in Chapter 7. EOQs are not integrated, primarily because they assume a uniform usage rate for raw materials, an assumption that is not met in the example. Also, the EOQ analysis assumes a constant minimum stock level, but the desired minimum stock level (Table 5A–3, line 13) shifts with production levels. In a practical situation, these assumptions might be approximated. EOQs can then be used to determine optimum purchase quantities, or more sophisticated operations research techniques may be used.

Table 5A–3 *Materials Purchases Budget.*

Item	Monthly average 1977	Estimated 1978 first quarter: First month	Second month	Third month	Source of data
11. Production in units	1 000	1 100	1 200	1 200	Line 6
12. Materials used (units)	2 000	2 200	2 400	2 400	Line 11 times 2
13. Raw materials, closing stock	2 200	2 400	2 400	2 400	Raw materials requirements next month
14. Total	4 200	4 600	4800	4800	Line 12 plus line 13
15. Raw materials, opening stock	2 000	2 200	2 400	2 400	Raw materials requirements this month
16. Raw materials purchases	£2 200	£2 400	£2 400	£2 400	(Line 14 less line 15) times £1

CASH BUDGET

The cash budget shown in Table 5A–4 is generated from information developed in the production and materials purchases budgets. In addition, estimates for other expense categories are required.[3] In Table 5A–4, only cash receipts from operations are considered in order to emphasize the logic of the budget system. No account is taken of receipts or expenditures for capital items. This is because of the emphasis in this illustration on budgeting consequences of short-term fluctuations in the sales volume of the firm, although in practical situations it is a simple matter to incorporate capital expenditures into the cash budget. However, the fact that capital expenditures are ignored does not diminish their impact on cash flows. Capital expenditures occur sporadically and in amounts that sometimes overwhelm operating transactions.

Period

The three-month period used in the cash budget, Table 5A–4, is not necessarily the length of time for which a firm will predict cash flows. Although this period has been chosen for the illustration, the firm is more likely to utilize a six-month or one-year period. Normally, a six-month forecast is prepared on a monthly basis. Briefly, the cash budget period will vary with the line of business, credit needs, the ability to forecast the firm's cash flows for the distant future, and requirements of suppliers of funds.

Illustrative cash budget

The cash flow for a given period is the difference between receipts and expenditures for that period. In Table 5A–4, for the 1977 monthly averages, cash from operations (£1200) is the difference between receipts from trade debtors (£10 000) and total disbursements (£8800). Note that receipts from debtors and payments to creditors depend upon sales and purchases from the preceding months rather than on current sales.

The significant figure for the manager is cash available (or needed). Cash from operations in the first month of 1978, plus the initial cash balance at the beginning of the month, total £6900. The financial manager has previously determined that only £5000 is needed to handle this level of sales. Consequently, the firm will have surplus cash of £1900 by the end of the month, and £3100 by the end of the third month. In the pro forma balance sheet (Table 5A–7), it is assumed that these cash surpluses are used to pay off the bank overdraft.

---

3. These are assumed to be paid in the months the expenses are incurred, in order to reduce the volume of explanatory information.

Table 5A–4 *Cash Budget.*

Item	Monthly average 1977	Estimated 1978 First month	Second month	Third month	Source of data
Receipts					
17. Trade debtors received	£10 000	£10 000	£10 000	£12 000	Sales of previous month
Disbursements					
18. Trade creditors paid	2 000	2 200	2 400	2 400	Raw materials purchases of previous month
19. Direct labour	2 000	2 200	2 400	2 400	Line 6 times £2
20. Indirect labour	700	700	700	700	Assumed
21. Variable manufacturing expenses	1 000	1 100	1 200	1 200	Line 6 times £1
22. Insurance and rates	100	100	100	100	Assumed
23. General and administrative expenses	2 500	2 500	2 500	2 500	Assumed
24. Selling expense	500	500	600	600	5% of line 1
25. Total disbursements	£ 8 800	£ 9 300	£ 9 900	£ 9 900	Sum of lines 18–24
26. Cash from operations	1 200	700	100	2 100	Line 17 less line 25
26a. Initial cash	5 000	6 200	6 900	7 000	Preceding month, line 26b
26b. Cumulative cash	6 200	6 900	7 000	9 100	Line 26 plus line 26a
27. Desired level of cash	5 000	5 000	6 000	6 000	50% of current month's sales; approx. 4.2% of annual sales
27a. Cash available (needed) cumulative	£ 1 200	£ 1 900	£ 1 000	£ 3 100	Line 26b less line 27

Use

As mentioned earlier in the chapter, the financial manager uses the cash budget to anticipate fluctuations in the level of cash. Normally, a growing firm will be faced with continuous cash drains. The cash budget tells the manager the magnitude of the outflow. If necessary, he can plan to arrange for additional funds. The cash budget is the primary document presented to a lender to indicate the need for funds and the feasibility of repayment.

In Table 5A–4 the opposite situation is illustrated. The firm will have excess cash of at least £1000 during each of the three months under consideration. The excess can be invested, or it can be used to reduce outstanding liabilities. In this example, the firm reduces the bank overdraft (Table 5A–7, line 48). Such a small amount as £1000 might be held as cash or on deposit account, but the alert financial manager will not allow substantial amounts of cash to remain idle.

BUDGETED INCOME STATEMENT

After a cash budget has been developed, two additional financial statements can be formulated: the budgeted income statement (Table 5A–5) and the budgeted balance sheet (Table 5A–7). They are prepared on an accrual rather than a cash basis. For example, the income statement accounts for depreciation charges. Expenses recognized on an accrual basis are included in total expenses (Table 5A–5, line 32); thus, calculated net profit is lowered. The only accrual item assumed in this exhibit is depreciation, and this is assumed to be £200 monthly. The pre-tax profit figure in the third month in the budgeted income statement (line 33) differs from line 26 in the cash budget only by the amount of depreciation.[4] This illustration makes clear the effect of non-cash expenses on the income statement.

4. This close correspondence holds only in a 'steady state', that is, when stocks and debtors are not being raised or lowered. Prior to the third month this condition does not hold.

Table 5A–5 *Budgeted Income Statement.*

Item	Monthly average 1977	Estimated 1978 first quarter: First month	Second month	Third month	Source of data
28. Sales	£10 000	£10 000	£12 000	£12 000	Line 1
29. Adjusted cost of sales	6 000	5 955	7 045	7 000	Line 54
30. Gross profit	£ 4 000	£4 045	£ 4 955	£ 5 000	Line 28 less line 29
31a. General and administrative expenses	2 500	2 500	2 500	2 500	Line 23
31b. Selling	500	500	600	600	5% of line 1
32. Total expenses	£ 3 000	£ 3 000	£ 3 100	£ 3 100	Line 31a plus 31b
33. Net profit before taxes	1 000	1 045	1 855	1 900	Line 30 less line 32
34. Corporation tax	500	522	927	950	50% of line 33
35. Net profit after taxes	£ 500	£ 522	£ 928	£ 950	Line 33 less line 34

The preparation of the budgeted income statement follows standard accounting procedures. The major calculation involved is adjusted cost of sales, explained in Table 5A–6.

The budgeted income statement shows the impact of future events on the firm's net profit. Comparison of future profit with that of past periods indicates the difficulties that will be encountered in maintaining or exceeding past performance. A forecast indicating low net profit should cause management to increase sales efforts as well as to make efforts to reduce costs. Anticipation and prevention of difficulties can be achieved by a sound budgeting system.

Table 5A–6 *Worksheet.*

Item	Monthly average 1977	Adjusted cost of sales, Estimated 1978 first quarter: First month	Second month	Third month	Source of data
50. Adjusted cost of goods produced	£6 000	£6 500	£ 7 000	7 000	Line 9
51. *Add*: Opening stock	3 000	3 000	3 545	3 500	Line 10 lagged one month
52. Sum	£9 000	£9 500	£10 545	£10 500	
53. *Less*: Closing stock	3 000	3 545	3 500	3 500	Line 10
54. Adjusted cost of goods sold[a]	£6 000	£5 955	£ 7 045	£ 7 000	Line 52 less line 53

[a] Note difference from line 9, adjusted cost of goods produced.

BUDGETED BALANCE SHEET

Lenders are interested in the projected balance sheet to see what the future financial position of the firm will be. Balance sheet projections discussed in the body of Chapter 5 were focused on year-to-year forecasts, and they assumed stable underlying relations. The budget technique deals with shorter term projections but is based on the same fundamental kinds of stable relations between the volume of sales and the associated asset requirements. Either method can be used and each can operate as a check on the other. The budgeted balance sheet presented in Table 5A–7, however, is the result of a more detailed and analytical forecast of future operations. It is the logical culmination of the budget system and provides a complete reconciliation among the initial balance sheet, the cash budget and the income statement.

The required information is readily available from past balance sheets or is contained in other elements of the budget system. For example, the initial balance for the bank overdraft is £3200. An increase in cash available (Table 5A–4, line 27a) is used to repay the bank overdraft; a decrease is met by additional borrowing from a commercial bank. Other new items, such as long-term debt and ordinary share capital (Table 5A–7, lines 45 and 42), are taken from previous balance sheets. The foregoing exhibit presents a simplified yet complete budget system. It contains all the elements found in a voluminous and complex actual budget system of a firm. If a person understands the logic and flow of this relatively simple budget system he can approach an actual budget with perspective, looking for the fundamental relationships involved. He can then apply the patterns to actual budget systems of any degree of complexity.

Table 5A–7 *Budgeted Balance Sheet.*

Item	Monthly average 1977	Estimated 1978 first quarter: First month	Second month	Third month	
36. Fixed assets (net)	£80 000	£79 800	£79 600	£79400	£80 000 less £200 per month depreciation.
Current assets:					
Stocks					
37. Raw materials	2 200	2 400	2 400	2 400	Line 13
38. Finished goods	3 000	3 545	3 500	3 500	Line 10
39. Debtors	10 000	10 000	12 000	12 000	Sales of current month
40. Cash	5 000	5 000	6 000	6 000	Line 27
41. Total assets	£100 200	£100 745	£103 500	£103 300	
42. Ordinary share capital £50 000	£50 000	£50 000	£50 000	£50 000	Assumed
43. Retained earnings £20 000	20 500	21 023	21 950	22 900	Assumed line 35 plus £20 000
44.	70 500	71 023	71 950	72 900	
45. Long-term loan	25 000	25 000	25 000	25 000	Assumed
46. Corporation tax payable	500	1 022	1 950	2 900	Line 34, accumulated
47. Trade creditors	2 200	2 400	2 400	2 400	Raw material purchases that month
48. Bank overdraft £3200	2 000	1 300	2 200	100	£3200 less line 27a
49. Total claims	£100 200	£100 745	£103 500	£103 300	

PROBLEMS

A5–1. Examine carefully the budget system set forth in the appendix, then answer the following questions:

(a) What advantages can you see to having a budget system such as the one described? Would such a system be more valuable (assuming a whole series of budgets where necessary) for a firm with 10 employees or for one with 10 000 employees?

(b) What would happen to the system if the sales forecast was far off the mark? How could variable sales be incorporated into the system?

(c) Would a budget system such as this one be more useful for a firm whose sales were highly predictable or one whose sales were not very predictable?

(d) How might a firm's budget system be computerized? Would such computerization be more useful for a firm with predictable or unpredictable sales?

(e) Would such a budget system be more valuable for planning or for control purposes?

PART 2

WORKING CAPITAL MANAGEMENT

In Part 1, we analysed the firm's operations in an overall, aggregate manner. Now we must examine the various aspects of the firm's financial picture in more detail. In Part 2, we focus on the bottom half of the balance sheet, studying current assets, current liabilities, and the interrelationship between these two sets of accounts. This type of analysis is commonly called *working capital management*.

In Chapter 6, we examine some general principles of overall working capital management. Then, in Chapter 7, we consider the determinants of current assets: cash, marketable securities, trade debtors and stocks. Finally, in Chapter 8, we discuss current liabilities, considering in some detail the principal sources and forms of short-term funds.

Chapter 6

Working Capital Policy

Working capital refers to a firm's investment in short-term assets – cash, short-term securities, trade debtors and stocks. *Net working capital* is defined as current assets minus current liabilities. *Working capital management* refers to all aspects of the administration of both current assets and current liabilities.

No new theories or basic principles are involved in working capital management; rather, this phase of financial management simply requires the application of valuation concepts developed throughout the text. Current asset holdings should be expanded to the point where marginal returns on increases in such assets are just equal to the cost of capital required to finance these increases, while current liabilities should be used in place of long-term debt whenever their use lowers the average cost of capital.

IMPORTANCE OF WORKING CAPITAL MANAGEMENT

Working capital management includes a number of aspects that make it an important topic for study, and we will now consider some of them.

Time devoted to working capital management

Surveys indicate that the largest portion of a financial manager's time is devoted to the day-by-day internal operations of the firm; this may be appropriately subsumed under the heading 'working capital management'. Since so much time is spent on working capital decisions, it is appropriate that the subject be covered carefully in managerial finance courses.

Investment in current assets

Characteristically, current assets represent more than half the total assets of a business firm. Because they represent a large investment and because this investment tends to be relatively volatile, current assets are worthy of the financial manager's careful attention.

Importance for small firms

Working capital management is particularly important for small firms. A small firm may minimize its investments in fixed assets by renting or leasing plant and equipment, but there is no way it can avoid an investment in cash, debtors and stocks. Therefore, current assets are particularly significant for the financial manager of a small firm. Further, because a small firm has relatively limited access to the long-term capital markets, it must necessarily rely heavily on trade credit and short-term bank loans, both of which affect net working capital by increasing current liabilities.

Relationship between sales growth and current assets

The relationship between sales growth and the need to finance current assets is close and direct. For example, if the firm's average collection period is 40 days and if its credit sales are £1000 a day, it will have an investment of £40 000 in trade debtors. If sales rise to £2000 a day, the investment in trade debtors will rise to £80 000. Sales increases produce similar immediate needs for additional stocks and, perhaps, for cash balances. All such needs must be financed, and since they arise so quickly it is imperative that the financial manager keep himself aware of developments in the working capital segment of the firm. Of course, continued sales increases will require additional long-term assets which must also be financed. However, fixed asset investments, while critically important to the firm in a strategic, long-term sense, do not generally have the same urgency as do current asset investments.

ORIGINAL CONCEPT OF WORKING CAPITAL

The term 'working capital' originated at a time when most industries were closely related to agriculture. Processors would buy crops in the autumn, process them, sell the finished product, and end up just before the next harvest with relatively low stocks. Bank overdraft loans with maximum maturities of one year were used to finance both the purchase and the processing costs, and these overdrafts were redeemed with the proceeds from the sale of the finished products.

The situation is depicted in Figure 6–1. There fixed assets are shown to be growing steadily over time, while current assets jump at harvest season, then decline during the

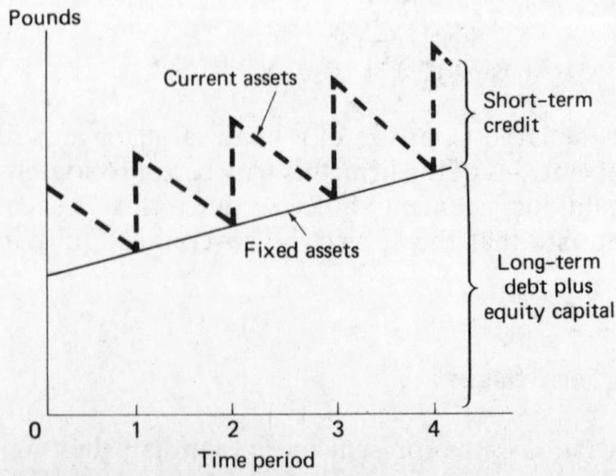

Figure 6–1 *Fixed and Current Assets and their Financing.*

year, ending at nil just before the next crop is harvested. Short-term credit is used to finance current assets, and fixed assets are financed with long-term funds. Thus, the top segment of the graph deals with working capital.

The figure represents, of course, an idealized situation – current assets build up gradually as crops are purchased and processed, stocks are drawn less regularly, and closing stock balances do not decline to nil. Nevertheless, the example does illustrate the general nature of the production and financing process, and working capital management consists of decisions relating to the top section of the graph; managing current assets and arranging the short-term credit used to finance them.

EXTENDING THE WORKING CAPITAL CONCEPT

As the economy became less oriented towards agriculture, the production and financing cycles of 'typical' business changed. Although seasonal patterns still existed, and business cycles also caused asset requirements to fluctuate, it became apparent that current assets rarely, if ever, dropped to nil. This realization led to the development of the idea of 'permanent current assets', shown in Figure 6–2. As the figure is drawn, it maintains the traditional notion that permanent assets should be financed with long-term capital, while temporary assets should be financed with short-term credit.

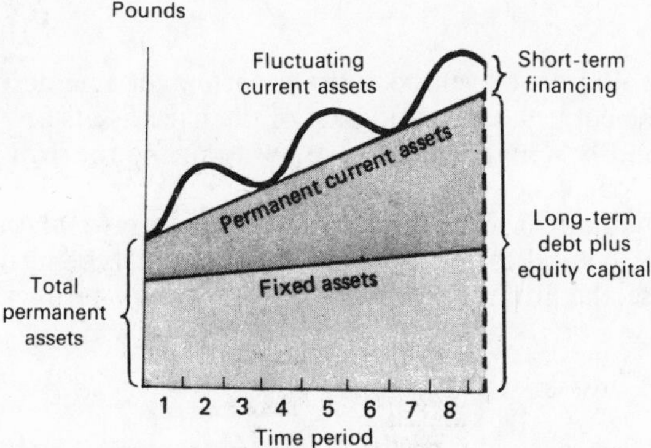

Figure 6–2 *Fluctuating versus Permanent Assets.*

The pattern shown in Figures 6–1 and 6–2 was considered to be desirable because it minimizes the risk that the firm may be unable to pay off its maturing obligations. To illustrate, suppose a firm borrows on a one-year basis and uses the funds obtained to build and equip a plant. Cash flows from the plant (profits plus depreciation) are not sufficient to pay off the loan at the end of the year, so the loan has to be renewed. If for some reason the lender refuses to renew the loan, then the firm has problems. Had the plant been financed with long-term debt, however, cash flows would have been sufficient to retire the loan and the problem of renewal would not have arisen. Thus, if a firm finances long-term assets with permanent capital and short-term assets with temporary capital, its financial risk is lower than it would be if long-term assets were financed with short-term debt.

At the limit, a firm can attempt to match the maturity structure of its assets and liabilities exactly. A machine expected to last for five years could be financed by a five-year loan; a 20-year building could be financed by a 20-year mortgage debenture; stock expected to be sold in 20 days could be financed by a 20-day bank loan; and so forth. Actually, of course, uncertainty about the lives of assets prevents this exact maturity matching. We will examine this point in the following sections.

Figure 6–2 shows the situation for a firm that attempts to match asset and liability maturities exactly. Such a policy could be followed, but firms may follow other maturity-matching policies if they desire. Figure 6–3, for example, illustrates the situation for a firm that finances all its fixed assets with long-term capital but part of its permanent current assets with short-term credit.[1]

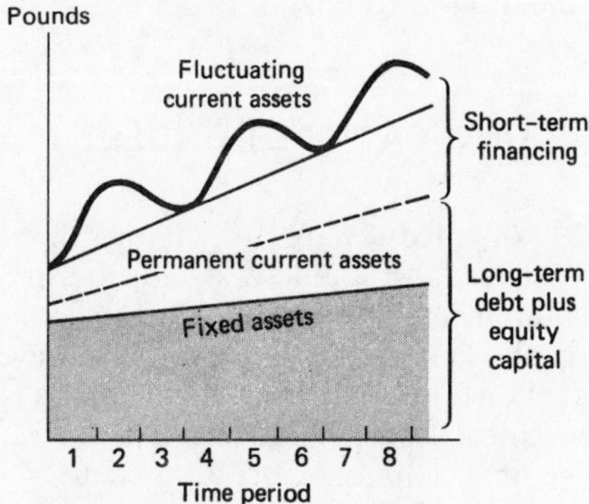

Figure 6–3 *Fluctuating versus Permanent Assets.*

The dashed line could have even been drawn *below* the line designating fixed assets, indicating that all the current assets and part of the fixed assets are financed with short-term credit; this would be a highly aggressive position, and the firm would be very much subject to potential loan renewal problems.

Alternatively, as in Figure 6–4, the dashed line could be drawn *above* the line designating permanent current assets, indicating that permanent capital is being used to meet seasonal demands. In this case, the firm uses a small amount of short-term credit to meet its peak

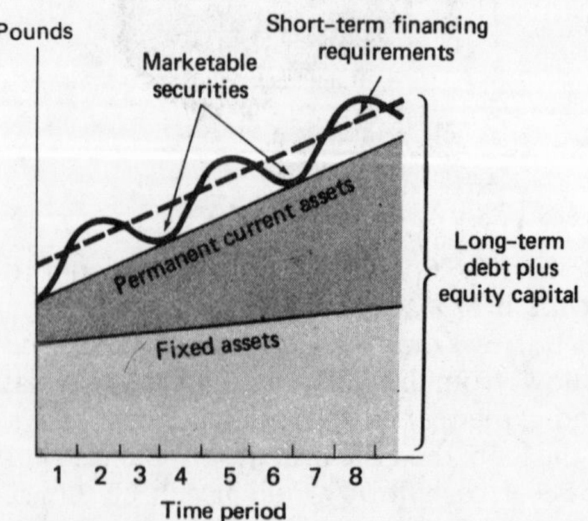

Figure 6–4 *Fluctuating versus Permanent Assets and Liabilities.*

1. Firms generally have some short-term credit in the form of 'spontaneous' funds – accounts payable and accruals (see Chapter 4). Used within limits, these constitute 'free' capital, so virtually all firms employ at least some short-term credit at all times. We could modify the graphs to take this into account, but nothing is lost by simply abstracting from spontaneous funds, as we do.

seasonal requirements, but it also meets a part of its seasonal needs by 'storing liquidity' in the form of marketable securities during the off-season. The humps above the dashed line represent short-term financing; the troughs below the dashed line represent short-term security holdings.

LONG-TERM VERSUS SHORT-TERM DEBT

Since the war, British Government economic policy has relied on the 'credit squeeze' as one method of controlling short-term liquidity within the economy. This policy has led to firms experiencing difficulty in renewing their short-term debt. In these circumstances it might be expected that firms would dispense with short-term debt and rely entirely on long-term debt. Why not just use long-term funds? There are three reasons for the use of short-term debt: flexibility, cost and risk.

Flexibility

If the need for funds is seasonal or cyclical, the firm may not want to commit itself to long-term debt. Examples of such firms are seed merchants or ice-cream manufacturers. Accordingly, if a firm expects its need for funds to diminish in the near future, or if it thinks that there is a good chance that such a reduction will occur, it may choose short-term debt for the flexibility it provides.

Additionally, in a period of high interest rates or at a time when it is believed that interest rates are likely to fall in the near future, the financial management of a company may consider that it is useful to obtain short-term finance rather than issue long-term debentures. Thus if a debenture loan can only be raised at 12 per cent in the London market in January but it is expected that long-term interest rates will have fallen to about 8 per cent by October it may pay a firm to obtain short-term loans to cover its borrowing requirements between January and October and then to issue a long-term debenture at 8 per cent in October.

Cost

The cost aspect of the maturity decision involves the term structure of interest rates or the relationship between yield and term to maturity. These relationships are usually plotted on a yield curve (illustrated in Figure 6–5). Although interest rates vary from time to time we can note here short-term rates are normally lower than long-term rates. Interest rates on loans to companies are usually higher than interest rates on British government stock of comparable maturity. In January 1978, for example, the rate of interest on 91 days Treasury Bills was 6 per cent and the yield on 25 year Government stock (Treasury 8 per cent 2002–6) was 10.66 per cent. We might expect, therefore, that a medium sized company wishing to borrow in the market could borrow on the following terms:

Loan maturity	Interest rate (%)
91 days	$6\frac{1}{2}$
6 months	$7\frac{1}{2}$
1 year	$8\frac{1}{2}$
3 years	9
10 years	10
25 years	$11\frac{1}{2}$

It may be expected that the shape of a company's yield curve will be similar to the yield curve operating within the gilt-edged market.

While the yield curve presented in Figure 6–5 is a fairly typical one with short-term rates considerably lower than long-term rates, there are times when the yield curve is downward sloping; for example, in December 1973 the Treasury Bill rate was higher than the yield on Consols. At such times, which almost always occur when both long- and short-term interest rates are high and when investors in the market expect short-term interest rates to fall, short-term money costs more than long-term debt. Normally, however, as short-term rates have generally been lower than long-term rates a firm's capital will probably be less costly if it borrows short-term money rather than long-term.

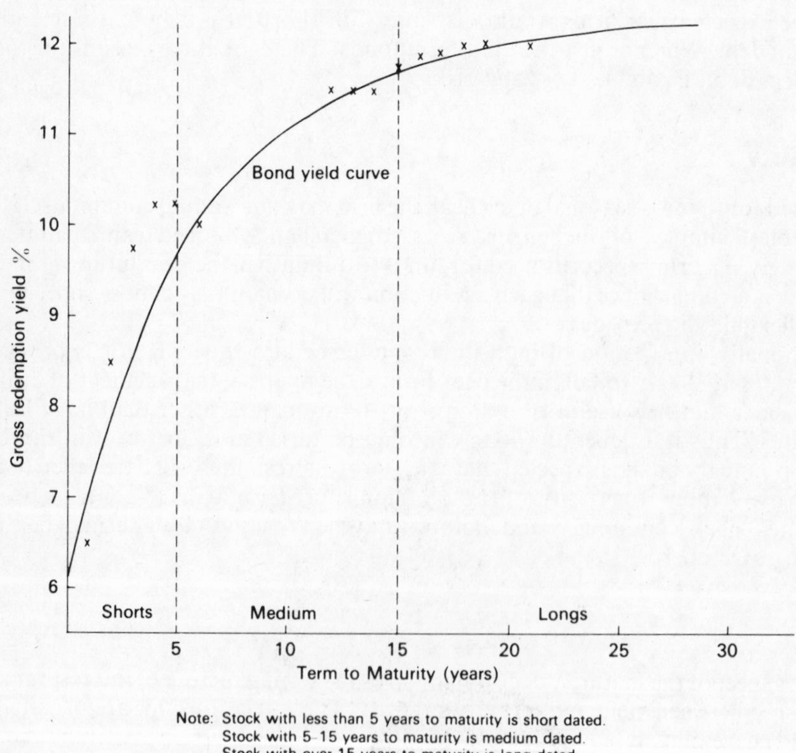

Figure 6–5 *Bond Yield Curve 3 February 1978.*

Risk

Even though short-term debt is generally less expensive than long-term debt, the use of short-term debt subjects the firm to greater risks than does long-term debt. This risk effect occurs for two reasons:

1. Long-term interest rates are generally more stable over time than short-term interest rates. If a firm borrows on a short-term basis its interest rate payments will fluctuate widely (between 5 March 1976 and 8 October 1976 the minimum lending rate rose from 9 to 15 per cent).
2. If a firm borrows heavily on a short-term basis it may find that it has difficulty in repaying the loan and thus develops liquidity problems or it may find that the lender is unwilling to extend the loan. This is particularly the case when banks are required to

operate a credit squeeze. As a result the firm may be forced into bankruptcy. We elaborate on these risk factors in the following sections.

Interest rate fluctuations

Figure 6–6 shows the pattern of long-term and short-term interest rates in the period since 1971. The long-term rate is represented by the yield on Consols and the short-term rate is represented by the Treasury Bill rate. Interest rates payable by companies will be slightly higher than these rates but they can be expected to have moved in a similar manner.

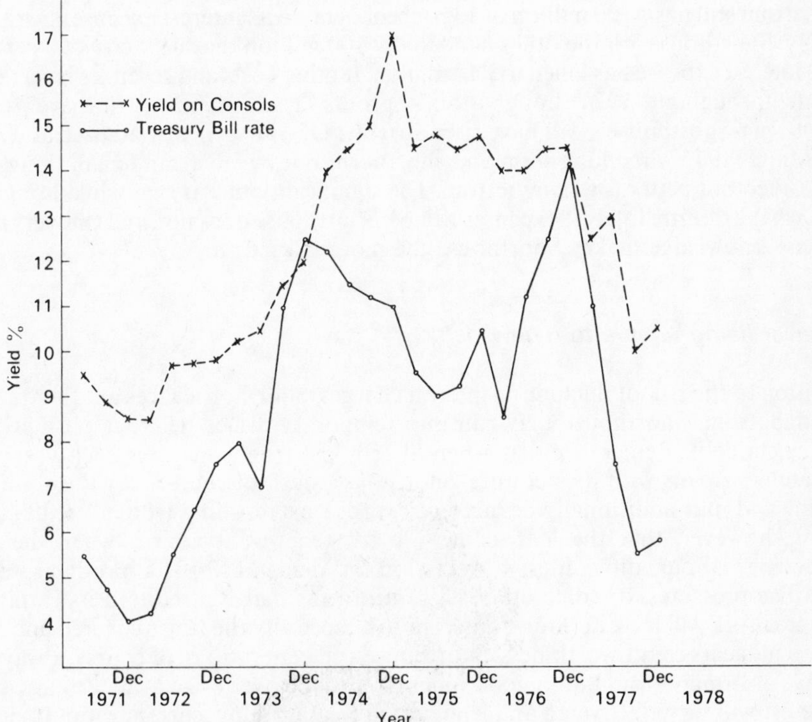

Figure 6–6 *Long- and Short-term Interest Rates.*

Several points should be noted about the graph. *First*, both long-term and short-term rates rose to reach a peak in October 1976 and both have subsequently fallen rather sharply. *Second*, short-term rates are generally more volatile than long-term rates. *Third*, only in November and December 1973 was the Treasury Bill rate higher than the yield on Consols. Long-term trends suggest that the yield curve will generally slope upwards: whenever the long-term rate in Figure 6–6 is above the short-term rate the yield curve in Figure 6–5 must be upward sloping.

Impact of a rise in rates on interest expenses

During November and December 1973 the shape of the yield curve was flat, indicating that short-term and long-term rates were the same. This can be seen in Figure 6–6 which shows that the long-term and short-term rates were about 12 per cent. Now suppose that in November 1973 we were considering two firms, each with £100 million in debt. Shorthouse Ltd has only short-term debt: Longbottom Ltd has only long-term debt. Both are stable mature companies, the total assets of each remain relatively constant from year to year and the debt of each remains at the £100 million level.

Shorthouse Ltd must 'turn over' its debt every year, borrowing at about 1 per cent above the Treasury Bill rate. Similarly, Longbottom Ltd will be able to borrow at about 1 per cent above the long-term rate (yield on Consols). For simplicity we assume that the Longbottom debt will not mature for 20 years so that its interest rate is fixed at 13 per cent for the next 20 years regardless of what happens to either long-term or short-term rates in the intervening years.

Now consider the interest expense of the two firms one year later, in December 1974. Longbottom still has £100 million of 13 per cent debt, so its interest expense is £13 million annually. Shorthouse, on the other hand, has £100 million that now costs 10 per cent so that its interest expense has fallen to £10 million. If other costs and revenues have remained constant throughout 1974 Longbottom's profits after interest will have remained constant, but Shorthouse's will have risen sharply. Of course, if we had used as a starting point March 1977 when long-term and short-term rates were again equal, things would have worked out better for Longbottom. The significant point is that while Longbottom knows what its future interest expenses will be, Shorthouse does not, and this very absence of precise knowledge makes Shorthouse the more risky firm.

Danger of being unable to renew debt

In addition to the risk of fluctuating interest charges, Shorthouse faces another risk vis-à-vis Longbottom: Shorthouse may run into temporary difficulties that prevent it from renewing its debt. Remember that when Shorthouse's debt matures each year it must negotiate new loans with its creditors. Shorthouse must, of course, pay the going short-term rate and may additionally be faced with problems resulting from a 'credit squeeze'. Suppose, however, that the loan comes up for renewal at a time when the firm is experiencing labour difficulties, a recession in demand for its products, extreme competitive pressures, or some other set of problems that has reduced its earnings.

The creditors will look at Shorthouse's ratios, especially the times covered and current ratios, to judge its credit worthiness. Shorthouse's current ratio is, of course, always lower than that of Longbottom but in good times this will be overlooked – if earnings are high the interest will be well covered and lenders will tolerate a low current ratio. If, however, earnings decline, creditors will re-evaluate the credit worthiness of Shorthouse. At the very least, because of the perceived increased riskiness of the company, creditors will raise the interest rate charged: at the extreme they will refuse to renew the loan. If the loan is not renewed the firm will be forced to sell assets cheaply, borrow from other sources at exorbitant interest rates or at the worst go into liquidation.

Example of the risk-return trade-off

Thus far we have seen that short-term debt is typically less costly than long-term debt, but that using short-term debt entails greater risk than does using long-term debt. Thus, we are faced with a trade-off between risk and rate of return. Although we are not prepared to resolve the conflict between risk and rate of return at this point in the book, a further example will help to clarify the issues involved.

Table 6–1 illustrates the nature of the trade-off. Here, we assume that the firm has £100 million of assets, one-half held as fixed assets and the other half as current assets, and that it will earn 15 per cent before interest and taxes on these assets. The debt ratio has been set at 50 per cent, but the policy issue of whether to use short-term debt, costing 6 per cent, or long-term debt, costing 8 per cent, has not been determined. Working through the relationships, we see that a defensive policy of using no short-term credit results in a rate of return on equity of 11 per cent, while the more aggressive policy of using only short-term credit boosts the rate of return to 12 per cent.

Table 6–1 *Effect of Maturity Structure of Debt on Return on Equity (Millions of Pounds).*

	Defensive	Average	Aggressive
Current assets	£ 50.00	£ 50.00	£ 50.00
Fixed assets	50.00	50.00	50.00
Total assets	£100.00	£100.00	£100.00
Short-term credit (6 %)	–	25.00	50.00
Long-term debt (8 %)	50.00	25.00	–
Current ratio	∞	2:1	1:1
Earnings before interest and taxes (EBIT)	15.00	15.00	15.00
Less interest	4.00	3.50	3.00
Taxable income	£ 11.00	£ 11.50	£ 12.00
Less taxes at 50 %	5.50	5.75	6.00
Earnings on ordinary shares	£ 5.50	£ 5.75	£ 6.00
Rate of return on ordinary shares (%)	11.0	11.5	12.0

What occurs when uncertainty is introduced into this example? We noted earlier that a firm that makes extensive use of short-term credit may find its earnings fluctuating widely. Suppose, for example, that interest rates rise significantly – a rise from 6 per cent to 10 per cent is not at all unrealistic. This rise would not affect the firm using the defensive policy, but it would increase the interest expense under the average policy to £4.5 million and under the aggressive policy to £5 million. The rates of return on equity for the three policies would consequently be 11 per cent, 10.5 per cent and 10 per cent, respectively – a reversal in relative ranking by rate of return. Of course, a decline in interest rates would have the opposite effect on the rates of return, but it should be clear that the variability of the return under an aggressive policy is more than that under defensive policy.

Fluctuations in earnings before interest and taxes (EBIT) can pose even more severe problems; If EBIT declines, lenders may simply refuse to renew short-term debt or agree to renew it only at very high rates of interest. To illustrate this, suppose the EBIT of £15 million in Table 6–1 declines to only £5 million. Since the firm's ability to repay has diminished, creditors would certainly be reluctant to lend to it. This would cause creditors to require a higher return on their investment and, thus, raise the interest expense, which would, of course, jeopardize the firm's future even more and, at the same time, compound the effects of the declining EBIT on shareholder returns.

It is possible for the general level of interest rates to rise at the same time a firm's EBIT is falling, and the compound effects could cause the situation to deteriorate so much that the aggressive firm could not renew its credit at any interest rate. The result is bankruptcy.

Notice that if the firm follows a conservative policy of using all long-term debt, it need not worry about short-term, *temporary* changes either in the term structure of interest rates or in its own EBIT. Its only concern is with its long-run performance, and its conservative financial structure may permit it to survive in the short run to enjoy better times in the long run.

Extending the example

These concepts can be incorporated into our example.[3] A firm has assets of £100 million and is considering the three financial structures, or policies, shown in Table 6–1. Management makes estimates of the future level of riskless interest rates (the Treasury bill rate) and the level of EBIT for the coming year. Management knows that the firm's earnings for next year will be the prime determinant of the risk premium that will be added to the riskless rate.[4]

Probability distribution for riskless rates and EBIT are given in Table 6–2. Assuming that the two probability distributions are independent of each other, we can determine the expected interest rate for the next year by the technique shown in Table 6–3. Column 1 gives the possible riskless rates of return. Column 2 gives the possible risk premiums. Column 3 combines the riskless rates of interest with the risk premiums to give the possible rates of interest the firm may face. Column 4 gives the joint probabilities – the probability of the simultaneous occurrence of each possible riskless rate and risk premium. Column 5 gives the products of each joint probability multiplied by its associated interest rate; the sum of column 5 is the expected interest rate, or 10.8 per cent.

Table 6–2 *Probability Distributions for Riskless Rates and EBIT.*

Treasury Bill rate one year hence

(i)	Probability
3%	0.2
5	0.3
7	0.3
9	0.2

EBIT for next year and associated risk premiums expected on next year's renewal of short-term credit

EBIT	Risk premium	Probability
(5.00) million	25.0%	0.15
5.00	5.0	0.20
15.00	2.0	0.30
25.00	1.2	0.20
35.00	1.0	0.15

Since the expected value of the firm's short-term rate exceeds the long-term rate, 8 per cent, the firm should probably use long-term rather than short-term financing. More important, however, is the fact that there is a 15 per cent probability that the interest rate will be 28 per cent or higher. Because total debt is £50 million, a 28 per cent rate of interest would require an EBIT of £14 million to break even. But at the time when this high rate is applied EBIT would be *minus* £5 million, so the firm would run a loss before taxes of £19 million. This loss would reduce equity and increase the debt ratio, making the situation

3. This illustration uses the concept of a probability distribution, a topic discussed at some length in Chapter 11. A probability is the chance of an event occurring, or the odds on the occurrence of the event. The sum of the probabilities must equal 1.0, or 100 per cent. The statistical aspects of this section may be omitted without loss of continuity if the statistical concepts are totally new.

4. As we see in detail later in the book, the higher the risk associated with a given loan, the higher the interest rate lenders require on the loan. The difference between the British government stock rate and the rate the firm must pay is defined as the *risk premium*. Obviously, the risk premium for I.C.I. is lower than that for a smaller, less seasoned borrower.

even more tense the next time the loan comes up for renewal. Good times might be just around the corner, but the aggressive firm, if its EBIT is subject to wide swings, may not survive until then.

Our example is unrealistic in that few firms will be able actually to generate the data needed to construct a table like Table 6–3. However, the events described are certainly *not* unrealistic, and the example does illustrate that the maturity structure of a firm's debt affects its overall risk. The example also shows that the risk tolerance of the firm with respect to the maturity composition of its liabilities depends to a large extent on the amount of risk already present in the firm owing to industry business risk, operating gearing and overall financial gearing. It is important to keep the overall risk level of the firm within reasonable limits. Thus, a firm with high business risk should probably not use a very aggressive policy in its financial structure and especially not in its maturity structure, but a firm in a stable industry might use such a policy to advantage. Of course, the firm's asset maturity structure has a bearing on its ability to employ short-term debt, and we cover this topic in the next section.

RELATIONSHIP OF CURRENT ASSETS TO FIXED ASSETS

In the chapters that deal with capital budgeting, we will see that capital budgeting decisions involve estimating the stream of benefits expected from a given project and then

Table 6–3 *Firm's Expected Interest Rate One Year Hence.*

i (1)	Risk premium (2)	Interest rate to firm (3) = (1) + (2)	Joint probability[a] (4)	Product (5) = (3) × (4)
3%	1.0%	4.0%	0.030	0.120%
	1.2	4.2	0.040	0.168
	2.0	5.0	0.060	0.300
	5.0	8.0	0.040	0.320
	25.0	28.0	0.030	0.840
5%	1.0	6.0	0.045	0.270
	1.2	6.2	0.060	0.372
	2.0	7.0	0.090	0.630
	5.0	10.0	0.060	0.600
	25.0	30.0	0.045	1.350
7%	1.0	8.0	0.045	0.360
	1.2	8.2	0.060	0.492
	2.0	9.0	0.090	0.810
	5.0	12.0	0.060	0.720
	25.0	32.0	0.045	1.440
9%	1.0	10.0	0.030	0.300
	1.2	10.2	0.040	0.408
	2.0	11.0	0.060	0.660
	5.0	14.0	0.040	0.560
	25.0	34.0	0.030	0.102
			1.000	
				Expected interest rate = 10.822%

[a] Joint probabilities are developed by multiplying the probabilities contained in Table 6–2 by each other. For example, the joint probability at the top of column 4 is the product 0.2 × 0.15 = 0.03; the second is the product 0.2 × 0.20 = 0.04; and so on. The expected value, or most likely interest rate, is found by multiplying the possible interest rates shown in column 3 by the joint probabilities given in column 4, then adding these products.

discounting these expected cash flows back to the present to find the present value of the project. Although current asset investment analysis is similar to fixed asset analysis in the sense that it also requires estimates of the effects of such investments on profits, it is different in two key respects. *First*, increasing the firm's current assets – especially cash and marketable securities – while holding constant expected production and sales reduces the riskiness of the firm, but it also reduces the overall return on assets. *Second*, although both fixed and current asset holdings are functions of *expected* sales, only current assets can be adjusted to *actual* sales in the short-run; hence, adjustments to short-run fluctuations in demand lie in the domain of working capital management.

Some of these ideas are illustrated in Figure 6–7, which shows the short-run relationship between the firm's current assets and output. The firm's fixed assets are assumed to be £50 million, and they cannot be altered in response to short-run fluctuations in output. Three possible current asset policies are depicted. CA_1 represents a defensive policy: relatively large balances of cash and marketable securities are maintained, large 'safety stocks'[5] are kept on hand, and the firm maximizes sales by adopting a credit policy that causes a high level of debtors. Policy CA_2 is somewhat less defensive than CA_1, while CA_3 represents a risky, aggressive policy.

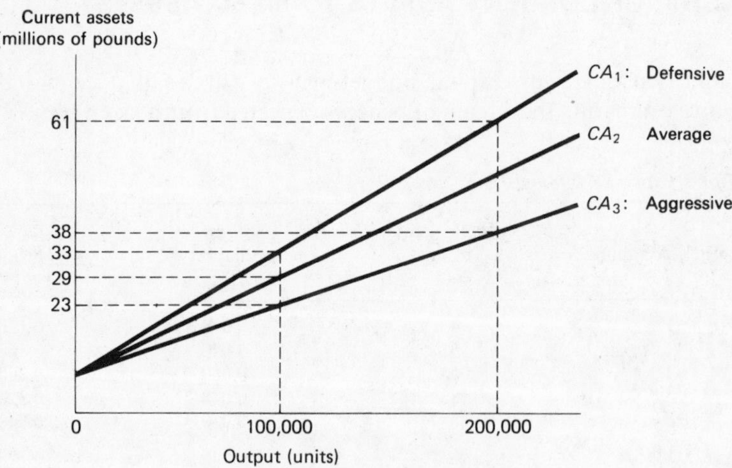

Figure 6–7 *Relationship between Current Assets and Output.*

Current asset holdings are highest at any output level under policy CA_1, lowest under CA_3. For example, at an output of 100 000 units, CA_1 calls for £33 million of current assets versus only £23 million for CA_3. If demand strengthens and short-run plans call for production to increase from 100 000 to 200 000 units, current asset holdings will likewise increase. Under policy CA_1, current assets rise to £61 million; under CA_3, the increase is to only £38 million. As we shall see in the following section, the more aggressive policy will lead to a higher expected rate of return; it also entails greater risk.

Risk-return trade-off for current asset holdings

If it could forecast perfectly, a firm would hold *exactly* enough cash to make disbursements as required, *exactly* enough stocks to meet production and sales

---

5. The concept of inventory safety stocks is discussed in Appendix A to Chapter 7.

requirements, *exactly* the trade debtors called for by an optimal credit policy, and no marketable securities unless the interest returns on such assets exceeded the cost of capital, which is an unlikely occurrence. The current asset holdings under the perfect foresight case would be the theoretical minimum for a profit-maximizing firm. Any larger holdings would, in the sense of the du Pont chart we described in Chapter 2, increase the firm's assets without a proportionate increase in its returns, thus lowering its rate of return on investment. Any smaller holdings would mean the inability to pay bills on time, lost sales and production stoppages because of stock shortages, and lost sales because of an overly restrictive credit policy.

When uncertainty is introduced into the picture, current asset management involves (a) determination of the minimum required balances of each type of asset and (b) addition of a safety stock to account for the fact that forecasters are imperfect. If a firm follows policy CA_1 in Figure 6–7, it is adding relatively large safety stocks; if it follows CA_3, its safety stocks are minimal. Policy CA_3, in general, produces the highest expected returns on investment, but it also involves the greatest risk; that is, following this policy may actually result in the *lowest* rate of return.

The effect of the three alternative policies on expected profitability is illustrated in Table 6–4. Under the defensive policy, CA_1, the rate of return on assets before interest and taxes is 13.5 per cent; the return rises to 15 per cent for an average policy and to 17 per cent for the risky, aggressive policy, CA_3. However, we know that CA_3 is the most risky policy, since lost sales, lost customer goodwill, and bad credit ratings caused by poor liquidity ratios could combine to bring the actual realized rate of return well below the anticipated 17 per cent.

Table 6–4 *Effects of Alternative Current Asset Policies on Rates of Return and Asset Turnover.*

	Defensive (CA_1)	Average (CA_2)	Risky (CA_3)
Sales			
Units	200 000	200 000	200 000
£s	£100 000 000	£100 000 000	£100 000 000
EBIT	£ 15 000 000	£ 15 000 000	£ 15 000 000
Current assets	£ 61 000 000	£ 50 000 000	£ 38 000 000
Fixed assets	50 000 000	50 000 000	50 000 000
Total assets	£111 000 000	£100 000 000	£ 88 000 000
Rate of return on assets (EBIT/assets)	13.5%	15.0%	17.0%

In the real world, things are considerably more complex than this simple example suggests. For one thing, different types of current assets affect both risk and returns differently. Increased holdings of cash do more to improve the firm's risk posture than a similar increase in debtors or stocks; idle cash penalizes earnings more severely than does the same investment in marketable securities. Generalizations are difficult when we consider trade debtors and stocks, because it is difficult to measure either the earnings penalty or the risk reduction that results from increasing the balances of these items beyond their theoretical minimums. In subsequent chapters, we consider determining the optimal balances of each type of current asset, where *optimal* is defined to include the theoretical minimum plus an optimal safety stock. First, however, we must complete our generalized discussion of working capital policy by combining current asset and current liability management.

WORKING CAPITAL POLICY: COMBINING CURRENT ASSET AND CURRENT LIABILITY MANAGEMENT

Table 6–5 illustrates the effect of working capital policy on expected returns and on risk as measured by the current ratio. A defensive policy calling for no short-term debt and large holdings of current assets results in a 9.6 per cent expected after-tax return on equity and a very high current ratio. The actual return would probably be quite close to 9.6 per cent. An aggressive policy, with minimal holdings of current assets and short-term rather than long-term debt, raises the expected return to 14 per cent. But the current ratio under this policy is only 0.86, a dangerously low level for most industries. Simultaneously, the increasing risks associated with the aggressive policy might adversely affect stock market opinion about the company; therefore, even if working capital policy pushes rates of return up, the net effect still might be to lower share prices.

Can we resolve this risk-return trade-off to determine *precisely* the firm's optimal working capital policy, that is, the working capital policy that will maximize the value of existing ordinary shares? In theory, the answer is yes, but in practice, it is no. Determining the optimal policy would require detailed information on a complex set of variables, information that is unobtainable today. Progress is being made in the development of computer simulation models designed to help determine the effects of alternative financial policy choices, including working capital decisions, but no one using such models would

Table 6-5 *Effects of Working Capital on the Rate of Return on Common Equity.*

	Defensive	Average	Aggressive
	Long-term debt large investment in current assets	Average use of short-term debt; average investment in current assets	All short-term debt; minimal investment in current assets
	(CA'_1)	(CA_2)	(CA_3)
Fixed assets	50 000 000	50 000 000	50 000 000
Current assets	£ 61 000 000	£ 50 000 000	£ 38 000 000
Total assets	£111 000 000	£100 000 000	£ 88 000 000
Share capital and reserves	£ 55 500 000	£ 50 000 000	£ 44 000 000
Long-term debts (8 %)	55 500 000	25 000 000	–
Current liabilities (6 %)	–	25 000 000	44 000 000
Total liabilities and net worth	£111 000 000	£100 000 000	£ 88 000 000
Sales in pounds (£s)	£100 000 000	£100 000 000	£100 000 000
EBIT	£ 15 000 000	£ 15 000 000	15 000 000
Less: interest	4 440 000	3 500 000	2 640 000
Taxable income	£ 10 560 000	£ 11 500 000	£ 12 360 000
Corporation tax (50 %)	5 280 000	5 750 000	6 180 000
Earnings on equity	£ 5 280 000	£ 5 750 000	£ 6 180 000
Rate of return on equity	9.6 %	11.5 %	14.0 %
Current ratio	[a]	2:1	0.86

[a] Under policy CA_1, the current ratio is shown to be infinitely high. Actually, the firm would doubtless have some spontaneous credit, but the current ratio would still be quite high.

suggest that they can actually reach *optimal* solutions. We can, however, establish guidelines, or ranges of values, for each type of current asset, and we do have ways of examining the various types of short-term financing and their effects on the cost of capital. Because such information, used with good judgement, can be most helpful to the financial manager, we will consider these topics in the remaining chapters of Part 2.

SUMMARY

Working capital refers to a firm's investment in short-term assets—cash, short-term securities, trade debtors and stocks. *Gross working capital* is defined as the firm's total current assets; *net working capital* is current assets minus current liabilities. *Working capital management* involves all aspects of the administration of both current assets and current liabilities.

Working capital policy is concerned with two sets of relationships among balance sheet items. First is the policy question of the level of total current assets to be held. Current assets vary with sales, but the ratio of current assets to sales is a policy matter. If the firm elects to operate aggressively, it will hold relatively small stocks of current assets. This will reduce the required level of investment and increase the expected rate of return on investment. However, an aggressive policy also increases the likelihood of running out of cash or stocks or of losing sales because of an excessively tough credit policy.

The second policy question concerns the relationship between types of assets and the way these assets are financed. One policy calls for matching asset and liability maturities, financing short-term assets with short-term debt, and long-term assets with long-term debt or equity. This is unsound because current assets are permanent investments as sales grow. If this policy is followed, the maturity structure of the debt is determined by the level of fixed versus current assets. Since short-term debt is frequently less expensive than long-term debt, the expected rate of return may be higher if short-term debt is used. However, large amounts of short-term credit increase the risks (a) of having to renew this debt at higher interest rates and (b) of not being able to renew the debt at all if the firm experiences difficulties.

Both aspects of working capital policy involve risk/return trade-offs. In the following chapter, we examine methods used to determine the optimal levels of each type of current asset. Then, in Chapter 8, we examine alternative sources and forms of short-term credit.

QUESTIONS

6–1. How does the seasonal nature of a firm's sales influence the decision about the amount of short-term credit in the financial structure?

6–2. 'Merely increasing the level of current asset holdings does not necessarily reduce the riskiness of the firm. Rather, the composition of the current assets, whether highly liquid or highly illiquid, is the important factor to consider.' What is your reaction to this statement?

6–3. What is the advantage of matching the maturities of assets and liabilities?

6–4. There have been times when the term structure of interest rates has been such that short-term rates were higher than long-term rates. Does this necessarily imply that the best financial policy for a firm would be to use all long-term debt and no short-term debt? Explain your answer.

6–5. Assuming a firm's volume of business remained constant, would you expect it to have higher cash balances during a tight-money period or an easy-money period? Does this situation have any ramifications for government monetary policy?

PROBLEMS

6–1. The Morgan Tile Corporation is attempting to determine an optimal level of current assets for the coming year. Management expects sales to increase to approximately £1.2 million as a result of asset expansion presently being undertaken. Fixed assets total £500 000, and the firm wishes to maintain a 60 per cent debt ratio. Morgan's interest cost is currently 8 per cent on both short-term debt and the longer term debt, which the firm uses in its permanent structure. Three alternatives regarding the projected current asset level are available to the firm: (1) an aggressive policy requiring current assets of only 45 per cent of projected sales; (2) an average policy of 50 per cent of sales as current assets; and (3) a defensive policy under which the current asset level would be 60 per cent of sales. The firm expects to generate earnings before interest and taxes at a rate of 12 per cent on total sales.

(a) What is the expected return on equity under each alternative current asset level? (Assume a 50 per cent tax rate.)
(b) In this problem, we have assumed that (1) level of expected sales is independent of current asset policy and (2) interest rates are independent of this policy. Are these valid assumptions?
(c) How would the overall riskiness of the firm vary under each policy? Discuss specifically such questions as the effect of current asset management on demand, expenses, fixed charge coverage, risk of insolvency and so on.

6–2. The Wilson Cane Company is attempting to project its financial requirements for the next 10-year period. The firm is a relative newcomer to the industry, having been in business only three years. Initially, the firm was totally unknown and found financing, particularly of a permanent nature, quite difficult to obtain. As a result, Cane was literally 'forced' to structure the left-hand side of its balance sheet as follows:

Share capital and reserves	£440 000
Bank overdraft	240 000
Trade creditors	200 000
	£880 000

In the three years the firm has been very successful, increasing its total capitalization by £120 000 of retained earnings. It is now in a position where it could obtain a long-term loan for ten years from an insurance company at a rate of 10 per cent in place of all or any of its present short-term borrowings. Alternatively, it could renew its existing £240 000 loan, or any part thereof, on a one-year loan from the bank at a rate of 8 per cent.

George Groves, the finance director, is considering three possible financing plans: (1) to renew the one-year loan with the bank; (2) to borrow £240 000 from the insurance company; and (3) to borrow £120 000 from each. Groves has estimated short-term riskless rates, the premiums that Cane might have to pay over the riskless rate for three possible 'states of the economy', and the probability of each possibility. The *average* rates that the firm would likely pay over the next ten years on its short-term borrowings are shown below.

State of economy	Cane EBIT[a]	Riskless rate	Cane risk premium	Joint probability
Good	£300 000	3%	2%	0.125
Good	300 000	5%	2	0.125
Average	160 000	5%	4	0.250
Average	160 000	7%	4	0.250
Bad	20 000	7%	10	0.125
Bad	20 000	9%	10	0.125

[a] Earnings before interest and taxes.

(a) Assuming a 50 per cent tax rate, compute expected profits under each of Groves three alternative financing plans. (Ignore possible growth effects. The expected EBIT is £160 000 under each plan.)
(b) On the basis of Groves' estimates, what is the worst profit that could result under each alternative? the best? (Assume no loss carry-back provision in the tax law.) Interpret your results and recommend a financing plan for Cane.

(c) Is there anything to prevent Cane from refinancing its short-term debt with the insurance company, thus converting it to long-term debt, at some future date if and when the short-term rate to the firm becomes unreasonably high?
(d) In both this problem and the example in the chapter, some very high interest rates were averaged into the computation of an expected short-term interest rate. If such rates would 'ruin' a firm, can you see any problem with using them in this computation?

6–3. Three companies (Aggressive, Between and Defensive) have different working capital management policies as implied by their names. For example, Aggressive employs only minimal current assets and finances almost entirely with current liabilities and equity. This tight ship approach has a dual effect. It keeps total assets lower, which would tend to increase return on assets. But for reasons such as stock-outs total sales are reduced, and since raw material stocks are ordered more frequently and in smaller quantities variable cost is increased. Condensed balance sheets for the three companies are presented below.

Balance Sheets.

	Aggressive	Between	Defensive
Fixed assets	£200 000	£200 000	£200 000
Current assets	150 000	200 000	300 000
Total assets	£350 000	£400 000	£500 000
Share capital and reserves	£150 000	£200 000	£250 000
Long-term debt (10%)	–	100 000	200 000
Current liabilities (8%)	200 000	100 000	50 000
Total claims on assets	£350 000	£400 000	£500 000
Current ratio	0.75:1	2:1	6:1

The cost of goods sold functions for the three firms are as follows:

	Cost of goods sold = Fixed costs + Variable costs
Aggressive	Cost of goods sold = £200 000 + 0.7(sales)
Between	Cost of goods sold = £250 000 + 0.6(sales)
Defensive	Cost of goods sold = £300 000 + 0.6(sales)

A company with normal net working capital, such as Between, will sell £1 000 000 in a year when economic growth is average. If the economy is weak, sales for Between would be reduced by £100 000; if strong, sales for Between would increase £100 000. In any given economic condition, Aggressive will sell £100 000 less than Between, and Defensive will sell £100 000 more. This is because of the working capital differences.
(a) Complete the income statements that follow for strong, average and weak economies.
(b) Compare the rates of return (EBIT/assets and return on equity). Which company is best in a strong economy? an average economy? a weak economy?
(c) What are the considerations for management of working capital that are indicated by this problem?

SELECTED REFERENCES

Bean, Virginia L. and Griffith, Reynolds. Risk and return in working capital management. *Mississippi Valley Journal of Business and Economics* 1 (Fall 1966): 28–48.
Beranek, William. *Working Capital Management*. Belmont, Calif: Wadsworth, 1968.
Brew, J. M. Gilt-edged yield curves. *Investment Analyst* (December 1966): 3–23.
Burman, J. P. Yield curves for gilt-edged stocks. *Bank of England Quarterly Bulletin* (September 1973): 315–326.
Carr, J. L., Halpern, P. J. and McCallum, J. S. Correcting the yield curve: a reinterpretation of the duration problem. *Journal of Finance* 29, no. 4 (September 1974): 1287–1294.
Chervany, Norman L. A simulation analysis of causal relationships within the cash flow process. *Journal of Financial and Quantitative Analysis* 5 (December 1970): 445–468.

Cossaboom, Roger A. Let's reassess the profitability-liquidity tradeoff. *Financial Executive* 39 (May 1971): 46–51.
Fisher, D. Expectations, the term structure of interest rates and recent British experience. *Economica* (August 1966): 319–329.
Ford, J. L. and Stark, T. S. *Long- and Short-term Interest Rates.* Oxford: 1967.
Glautier, M. W. E. Towards a reformulation of the theory of working capital. *Journal of Business Finance* 3 (Spring 1971): 37–42.
Grant, J. A. G. Meiselman on the structure of interest rates. *Econometrica* (February 1964): 51–71.
Knight, W. D. Working capital management: satisficing versus optimization. *Financial Management* 1 (Spring 1972): 33–40.
Merville, L. J. and Tavis, L. A. Optimal working capital policies: a chance-constrained programming approach. *Journal of Financial and Quantitative Analysis* 8 (January 1973): 47–60.
Pettway, Richard H. and Walker, Ernest W. Asset mix, capital structure, and the cost of capital. *Southern Journal of Business* (April 1968): 34–43.
Shackle, G. L. S. The nature of interest rates. *Oxford Economic Papers*, new series (January 1949): 99–120.
Smith, Keith V. *Management of Working Capital: A Reader*. New York: West, 1974.
Smith, Keith V. State of the art of working capital management. *Financial Management* 2 (Autumn 1973): 50–55.
Stancill, James McN. *The Management of Working Capital.* Scranton, Pa.: Intext Educational Publishers, 1971.
Tinsley, P. A. Capital structure, precautionary balances, and valuation of the firm: the problem of financial risk. *Journal of Financial and Quantitative Analysis* 5 (March 1970): 33–62.
Van Horne, James C. A risk-return analysis of a firm's working-capital position. *Engineering Economist* 14 (Winter 1969): 71–89.
Walker, Ernest W. Towards a theory of working capital. *Engineering Economist* 9 (January–February 1964): 21–35.
Walter, James E. Determination of technical solvency. *Journal of Business* 30 (January 1959): 30–43.
Yield curves and representative yields on British government securities. *Bank of England Quarterly Bulletin* (March 1967): 52–56.

Appendix A to Chapter 6:

Term Structure of Interest Rates

The term structure of interest rates describes the relationship between interest rates and loan maturity. When measuring the term structure, we generally use yields on British government securities. The term structure on other instruments, however, varies similarly. Figure 6A–1 shows the term structure of rates on 1 December 1973 and 1 December 1977. In the lower curve, for 1977 we see a pattern of rising yields – the shorter the maturity the

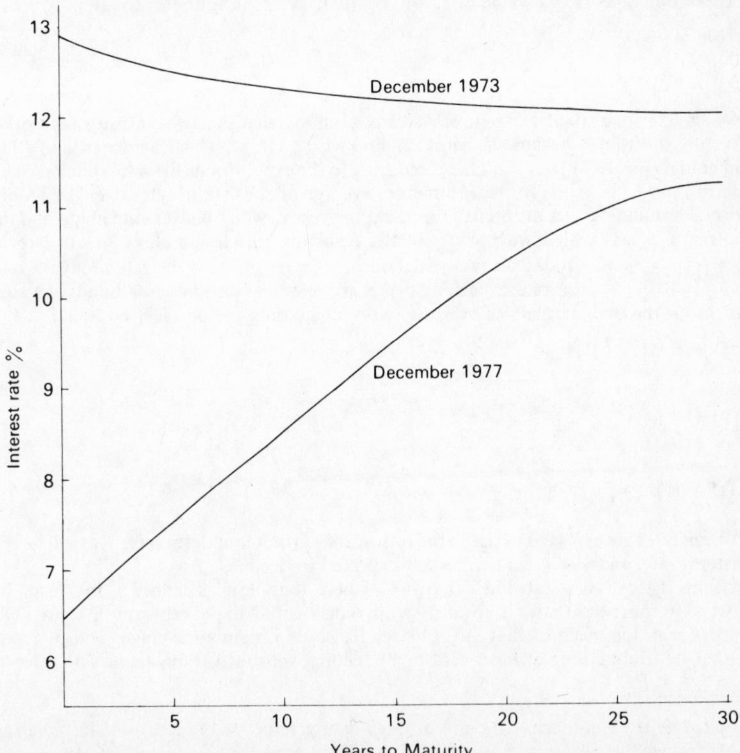

Figure 6A–1 *Term Structure of Rates on British Government Stocks December 1973 and December 1977.*

lower the rate of interest. This rising yield structure has been typical for most years since 1930 (see Chapter 6, Figure 6–6). The higher curve for 1973 shows a yield curve that declines as the term to maturity increases.

In addition to illustrating the changing term structure of interest rates Figure 6A–1 also reveals a shift in the 'level of rates'.

Between 1973 and 1977 the interest rate on all government securities – long term and short term – decreased. Such movements represent changes in the general level of interest rates.[1]

THEORETICAL EXPLANATION FOR THE TERM STRUCTURE OF INTEREST RATES

Three theories have been advanced to explain the term structure of interest rates: *the expectations theory, the liquidity preference theory* and *the market segmentation theory.* We will consider each in turn.

Expectations theory

The expectations theory asserts that in equilibrium the long-term rate is a geometric average of today's short-term rate and expected short-term rates in the future. To illustrate, let us consider an investor whose planning horizon is two years. Let r be the short-term interest rate and R be the long-term interest rate. Suppose he has £100 and is considering two alternative investment strategies: (a) purchasing a two-year bond with a yield of 9 per cent per year, or (b) purchasing a one-year bond that yields 8 per cent, then reinvesting the £108 he will have at the end of the year in another one-year bond. If he chooses strategy a, at the end of two years he will have[2]

Ending value = £100 (1.09) (1.09) = £118.81

If he follows strategy b, his value at the end of two years will depend upon the yield on the one-year bond during the second year, r_2:

Ending value = £100 (1.08) $(1+r_2)$ = £108 $(1+r_2)$.

Under the expectations theory, the value of r_2 will be 10.01 per cent, found as follows:

$$\begin{aligned} £118.81 &= £108\ (1+r_2) \\ 1+r_2 &= 1.1001 \\ r_2 &= 0.1001 = 10.01\,\% \end{aligned}$$

Suppose r_2 was greater than 10.01 per cent, say 10.5 per cent. In that case, our investor (and others) would be better off investing short-term, because he would end up with £119.34, which is greater than £118.81. Just the reverse would hold if $r_2 < 10.01$ per cent. Thus, according to the expectations theory, capital market competition forces long-term rates to be equal to the (geometric) average of short-term rates over the holding period.

In more formal terminology, let the prefix t represent the year in which a given rate holds, and the postscript t represent the maturity associated with a given rate. Applying this terminology to our previous example, ${}_tR_{t+1} = {}_1R_2 = 9\,\%$ = the rate today on two-year bonds; ${}_tr_t = {}_1r_1 = 8\,\%$ = the rate today on one-year bonds; and ${}_{t+1}r_t = {}_2r_1 = 10.01\,\%$ = the rate expected to prevail next year on one-year bonds. In equilibrium, the expected returns on the two alternatives over the two-year holding period must be equal:

$$(1+{}_tR_2)^2 = (1+{}_tr_1)(1+{}_{t+1}r_1),$$

or

$$(1+{}_tR_2) = [(1+{}_tr_1)(1+{}_{t+1}r_1)]^{1/2}.$$

In general,

$$(1+{}_tR_N) = [(1+{}_tr_1)(1+{}_{t+1}r_1)\ldots(1+{}_{t+N-1}r_1)]^{1/N}.$$

Thus, if short-term rates are expected to rise in the future, the current long-term rate, ${}_tR_N$, will be higher than the current short-term rate, and vice versa if rates are expected to decline.

The expectations theory is illustrated in Table 6A–1, where 'long-term' is defined as five years. In situation A, the expected trend in short-term rates is upward – from 6 per cent to 10 per cent over five years. The long-term rate is thus 8 per cent, the mean of that series;[3] a lender could obtain an average yield of 8 per cent on his investment either by lending long at 8 per cent or by lending short at various increasing rates.

---

1. In addition to the level and term structure of rates on a given class of securities – in this case government securities – there is also the pattern of relationships among different classes of securities. In general, movements in the term structure and level of rates are similar for most classes of securities.
2. Compound interest is discussed in more detail in Chapter 9.
3. The arithmetic mean is used for ease of exposition.

Table 6A–1 *Hypothetical Relationship between Short-term and Long-term Interest Rates.*

	Situation A expect rising rates			Situation B expect falling rates		
Year	Long-term[a] (5-year bond)	Short-term (1-year bond)	Intermediate-term (3-year bond)[b]	Long-term[a] (5-year bond)	Short-term (1-year bond)	Intermediate-term (3-year bond)[b]
1	8	6	7	8	10	9
2		7			9	
3		8			8	
4		9			7	
5		10			6	

[a] The long-term rate should be a geometrical average of short-term rates rather than the arithmetical average that we have used. This refinement is ignored here.
[b] Intermediate terms in this example could be anything between one and five years; for example, two-year bonds, three-year bonds or four-year bonds. Depending on the definition of intermediate term, different rates would emerge.

The situation is reversed in B. There the trend in short-term rates is expected to be downwards. Again, however, the mean of the short-term rates is 8 per cent, so 8 per cent is the effective long-term rate.

The term structure of rates in year 1 under situations A and B is graphed in Figure 6A–2. With expectations of rising rates, the yield curve is upward sloping. With expectations of falling rates, the yield curve slopes downwards.

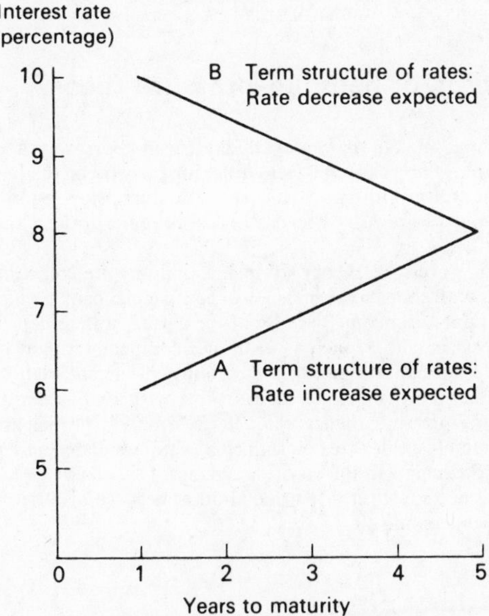

Figure 6A–2 *Term Structure of Rates under Two Hypothetical Situations.*

Liquidity preference theory

The future is inherently uncertain, and when uncertainty is considered, the pure expectations theory must be modified. To illustrate, let us consider a situation where short-term rates are expected to remain unchanged in the future. In this case, the pure expectations theory predicts that short- and long-term bonds sell at equal yields. The liquidity preference theory, on the other hand, holds that long-term bonds must yield more than short-term bonds for two reasons. *First*, in a world of uncertainty, investors will, in general, prefer to hold short-term securities because they are more liquid in the sense that they can be converted to cash without danger of loss of principal. (Short-term bond *prices* are less volatile than long-term bond prices; see Figure 17–1.) Investors will, therefore, accept lower yields on short-term securities. *Second*, borrowers react in exactly the opposite way from investors – business borrowers generally prefer long-term debt because, as we saw in Chapter 6, short-term debt subjects a firm to greater dangers of having to refund debt under adverse conditions. Accordingly, firms are willing to pay a higher rate, other things held constant, for long-term than for short-term funds.

We see, then, that pressures on both the supply and demand sides – caused by liquidity preferences of both lenders and borrowers – will tend to make the yield curve slope upward. Figure 6A–3 illustrates this effect.

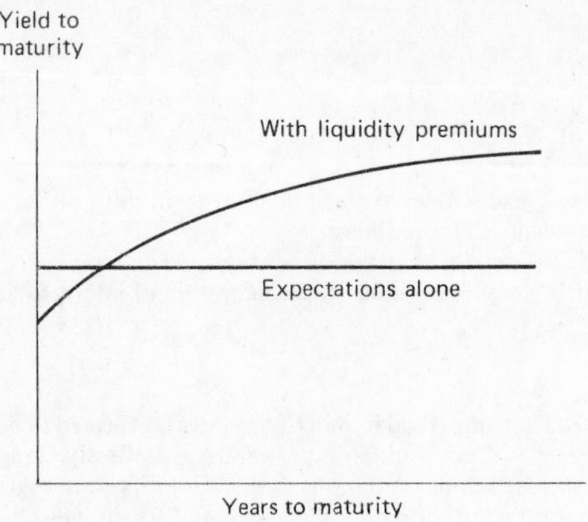

Figure 6A–3 *Term Structure with Liquidity Preference.*

Market segmentation, or hedging-pressure theory

The expectations theory assumes that, in the aggregate, lenders and borrowers are indifferent between long- and short-term investments except for any expected yield differentials between the types of securities.[4] The liquidity preference theory states that an upward bias exists – the yield curve slopes upward to a greater extent than is justified by expectations about future rates because investors prefer to lend short while borrowers prefer to borrow long.

The institutional, or hedging-pressure, theory admits the liquidity preference argument as a good description of the behaviour of investors with short horizons, such as commercial banks, which regard certainty of principal as more important than certainty of income because of the nature of their deposit liabilities. However, certain other investors with long-term liabilities, such as insurance companies, might prefer to buy long-term bonds because, given the nature of their liabilities, they find certainty of income highly desirable. On the other hand, borrowers typically relate the maturity of their debt to the maturity of their assets – recall the discussion in Chapter 6. Thus, the hedging-pressure theory characterizes market participants as having strong maturity preferences, then argues that interest rates are determined by supply and demand in each segmented market, with each maturity constituting a segment. In the strictest version of this theory, expectations play no role – bonds with different maturities are not substitutes for one another because of different demand preferences or the 'preferred habitat' of both lenders and borrowers.

EMPIRICAL EVIDENCE

Empirical studies suggest that there is some validity to each of these theories. Specifically, the recent work indicates that if lenders and borrowers have no reason for expecting a change in the general level of interest rates, the yield curve will be upward sloping because of liquidity preferences. (Under the expectations theory, the term structure of interest rates would be flat if there were no expectations of a change in the level of short-term rates.) However, it is a fact that during periods of extremely high interest rates, the yield curve is downward sloping; this proves that the expectations theory also operates. At still other times, when supply and demand conditions in

4. In discussing the term structure of interest rates, we are holding constant the risk of default. This is done by using government securities, which presumably have no default risk.

particular maturity sectors change, the term structure seems to be modified, thus confirming the market segmentation theory. In summary, each theory has an element of truth, and each must be employed to help explain the term structure of rates.

REFERENCES

A list of fairly up-to-date references can be found in C. Goodhart, *Money, Information, and Uncertainty* (London: Macmillan, 1975), chap. 4.

Chapter 7

Current Asset Management

In the preceding chapter we viewed working capital management in a general, overall sense. Now we focus our attention on the firm's investment in specific current assets, examining cash, marketable securities, trade debtors and stocks. Information published by the Department of Trade for 1976 shows that current assets represented approximately 64 per cent of manufacturing companies' assets, so current asset management is clearly an important subject.

CASH MANAGEMENT

Controlling the investment in current assets begins with cash management. Cash consists of the firm's holdings of current and deposit accounts, with current accounts being by far the more important for most firms.

Why hold cash?

Businesses or individuals have three primary motives for holding cash: (a) the transactions motive, (b) the precautionary motive and (c) the speculative motive.

Transactions motive

The transactions motive for holding cash is to enable the firm to conduct its ordinary business, that is, making purchases and sales. In some lines of business, such as the Gas Board, where invoicing may be staggered throughout the month, cash inflows can be scheduled and synchronized closely with the need for the outflow of cash. Hence, we expect the cash-to-sales ratio and cash-to-total-assets ratio for such firms to be relatively low. In retail trade, by contrast, sales are more random, and a number of transactions may actually be conducted by physical currency. As a consequence, retail trade requires a higher ratio of cash to sales and of cash to total assets.

The seasonality of a business may give rise to a need for cash for the purchase of stocks. For example, raw materials may be available only during a harvest season and may be perishable, as in the food-processing business. Or sales may be seasonal, as are department store sales around Christmas holidays, giving rise to an increase in needs for cash.

Precautionary motive

The precautionary motive relates primarily to the predictability of cash inflows and outflows. If the predictability is high, less cash must be held against an emergency or any other contingency. Another factor that strongly influences the precautionary motive for holding cash is the ability to borrow additional cash on short notice when circumstances necessitate. Borrowing flexibility is primarily a matter of the strength of the firm's relations with banking institutions and other credit sources.

The precautionary motive for holding cash is actually satisfied in large part by holding near-money assets – short-term government securities and the like.

Speculative motive

The speculative motive for holding cash is to be ready for profit-making opportunities that may arise. By and large, business accumulations of cash for speculative purposes are not widely found. Holding cash is more common among individual investors. However, the cash and marketable securities account may rise to rather sizeable levels on a temporary basis as funds are accumulated to meet specific future needs.

Advantages of adequate cash: specific points

In addition to these general motives, sound working capital management requires maintenance of an ample amount of cash for several specific reasons. First, it is essential that the firm have sufficient cash to take trade discounts. The payment schedule for purchases is referred to as 'the term of the sale'. A commonly encountered invoicing procedure, or term of trade, allows a 2 per cent discount if the invoice is paid within ten days, with full payment required in 30 days in any event. Since the net amount is due in 30 days, failure to take the discount means paying this extra 2 per cent for using the money an additional 20 days. If one were to pay 2 per cent for every 20-day period over the year, there would be 18 such periods:

$$18 = \frac{360 \text{ days}}{20 \text{ days}}.$$

This represents an annual interest rate of 37 per cent.[1] Most firms have a cost of capital that is substantially lower than 37 per cent.

---

1. The following equation may be used for calculating the cost, on an annual basis, of not taking discounts:

$$\text{Cost} = \frac{\text{discount percentage}}{(100 - \text{discount percentage})} \times \frac{360}{(\text{final due date} - \text{discount period})}.$$

The denominator in the first term (100 – discount percentage) equals the funds made available by not taking the discount. To illustrate; the cost of not taking a discount when the terms are 2 per cent discount if paid within 10 days, otherwise full payment is required in 30 days

$$\text{Cost} = \frac{2}{98} \times \frac{360}{20} = 0.0204 \times 18 = 36.72\%.$$

Second, since the current and acid test ratios are key items in credit analysis, it is essential that the firm, in order to maintain its credit standing, meet the standards of the line of business in which it is engaged. A strong credit standing enables the firm to purchase goods from trade suppliers on favourable terms and to maintain its line of credit with banks and other sources of credit.

Third, ample cash is useful for taking advantage of favourable business opportunities that may come along from time to time. Finally, the firm should have sufficient liquidity to meet emergencies, such as strikes, fires or marketing campaigns of competitors.

Using the knowledge about the general nature of cash flows presented in Chapter 4, the financial manager may be able to improve the inflow – outflow pattern of cash. He can do so by better synchronization of flows and by reduction of float, as will be explained in the following sections.

Expediting collections and cheque clearing

Another important method of economizing on the amount of cash required is to hasten the process of clearing cheques. Cheques sent from customers in distant cities are subject to delays because of the time required for the cheque to travel in the post and time required for clearing through the banking system.

Even after a cheque has been received by a firm and deposited in its account, the funds cannot be spent until the cheque has cleared. The bank in which the cheque was deposited presents the cheque to the bank on which it was drawn. Only when this latter bank transfers funds to the bank of deposit are they available for use by the depositor. Cheques are generally cleared through the London Clearing Banks system. An 'out-of-town' (or country) clearing exists where cheques take three days to be cleared, or five if a weekend intervenes. However a 'same-day' clearance operates for cheques of at least £5000 presented through the 'town' clearing system. To qualify for the same-day clearing the cheque must be drawn on and paid into one of the town branches situated within the City of London, that is, within about ten minutes' walking distance of the Clearing House in Lombard Street. Of course, if the cheque is drawn on the bank of deposit, that bank merely transfers funds by book-keeping entries from one depositor to another.

Slowing payments

Just as expediting the collection process conserves cash, slowing down payments accomplishes the same thing by keeping cash on hand for longer periods. One obviously could simply delay payments, but this involves equally obvious difficulties. Firms have, in the past, devised rather ingenious methods for 'legitimately' lengthening the collection period on their own cheques. One such practice is to write cheques on an 'out-of-town' branch, thus ensuring three days before the company's own account is debited, while at the same time paying cheques into their bank account through a 'town' clearing branch.[2]

Notice that the calculated cost can be reduced by paying late. Thus if the illustrative firm pays in 60 days rather than the specified 30, the credit period becomes 60 – 10 = 50, and the calculated cost becomes

$$\text{Cost} = \frac{2}{98} \times \frac{360}{50} = 0.0204 \times 7.2 = 14.7\%.$$

In periods of excess capacity, some firms may be able to get away with late payments, but such firms may suffer a variety of problems associated with being a 'slow-payer' account.

2. P. Frazer, How to play the float, *Accountancy* (February 1977), p. 54.

Using float

Float is defined as the difference between the balance shown in a firm's (or individual's) cash book and the balance on the bank's books. Suppose a firm writes, on the average, cheques to the amount of £5000 each day. It takes about six days for these cheques to clear and be deducted from the firm's bank account. Thus, the firm's own cash book shows a balance £30 000 less than the bank's records. If the firm receives cheques for the amount of £5000 daily but loses only four days while these cheques are being presented and cleared, its own books have a balance that is, because of this factor, £20 000 larger than the bank's balance. Thus the firm's float – the difference between the £30 000 and the £20 000 – is £10 000.

If a firm's own collection and clearing process is more efficient than that of the recipients of its cheques – and this is generally true of larger, more efficient firms – then the firm could show a negative balance on its own records and a positive balance on the books of its bank. Some firms indicate that they *never* have true positive cash balances. One large manufacturer of construction equipment in the USA stated that, while its account according to its bank's records shows an average cash balance of about $2 million, its *actual* cash balance is *minus* $2 million; it has $4 million of float. Obviously, the firm must be able to forecast its positive and negative clearings accurately in order to make such heavy use of float.

Cost of cash management[3]

We have just described a number of procedures that may be used to hold down cash balance requirements. Implementing these procedures, however, is not a costless operation. How far should a firm go in making its cash operations more efficient? As a general rule, the firm should incur these expenses so long as their marginal returns exceed their marginal expenses.

For example, suppose that by more efficient handling of receipts and payments and increasing the accuracy of cash inflow and outflow forecasts, a firm can reduce its investment in cash by £1 million. Further, suppose that the firm borrows at the prime rate, 12 per cent. The steps taken have released £1 million, and the cost of capital required to carry this £1 million investment in cash is £120 000.[4] If the costs of the procedures necessary to release the £1 million are less than £120 000, the move is a good one; if the costs exceed £120 000, the greater efficiency is not worth the cost. It is clear that larger firms, with larger cash balances, can better afford to hire the personnel necessary to maintain tight control over their cash positions. Cash management is one element of business operations in which economies of scale are clearly present.

Very clearly, the value of careful cash management depends upon the costs of funds invested in cash, which in turn depend upon the current rate of interest. In the 1970s, with interest rates at historic highs, firms are devoting more care than ever to cash management.

---

3. We are abstracting from the security aspects of cash management; that is, the prevention of fraud and embezzlement. These topics are better covered in accounting than in finance courses.

4. The borrowing rate, 12 per cent, is used rather than the firm's average cost of capital, because cash is a less risky investment than the firm's average asset. Notice, also, that we are using before-tax figures here; the analysis could employ either before-tax or after-tax figures, so long as consistency is maintained.

DETERMINING THE MINIMUM CASH BALANCE

Thus far we have seen that cash is held primarily for transactions purposes; the other traditional motives for holding cash, the speculative and precautionary motives, are today met largely by reserve borrowing power and by holdings of short-term marketable securities. Some minimum cash balance – which may actually be negative if float is used effectively – is required for transactions, and an additional amount over and above this figure may be held as a safety stock. For many firms the total of transactions balances plus safety stock constitutes the minimum cash balance, the point at which the firm either borrows additional cash or sells part of its portfolio of marketable securities. For many other firms, however, banking relationships require still larger balances.

Minimum cash balance

The firm's minimum cash balance will be the sum of its transaction balances plus precautionary balances (that is, safety stocks). Banks in the UK do not, as a rule, require customers to hold compensating balances to provide income to offset service costs. Customers with credit balances do, however, receive an abatement in their charges for transmission activity.

Overdraft system

The use of bank overdrafts as a short-term source of finance is now a very common practice among companies in the UK. The overdraft facility enables a customer to draw cheques to an amount in excess of the balance held on current account, up to some maximum limit agreed in advance with the banker. Interest is charged on overdrawn balances at a rate which varies from 1 to 5 per cent in excess of the banks' own base rate, depending upon the credit rating of the individual customer.

Overdrafts, as a source of short-term finance, are in theory repayable on demand. It is not, however, the practice of the clearing banks to call in overdrafts arbitrarily. Indeed it is quite usual for some accounts to operate permanently in overdraft, but with the balance fluctuating on a daily basis.

Utilization of agreed overdraft facilities normally averages between 55 and 60[5] per cent, reflecting what is, in effect, a reserve supply of funds for customers.

Cash management models

Several types of mathematical models designed to help determine optimal cash balances have been developed lately. These models are interesting, and they are beginning to become practical. Examples of cash management models are presented in Appendix B to Chapter 7.

---

5. *Evidence on the Financing of Industry and Trade*, Vol. 5 (London: HMSO, 1978), p. 145.

MARKETABLE SECURITIES

Firms sometimes report sizeable amounts of short-term marketable securities such as Treasury bills or sterling certificates of deposit[6] among their current assets. Why might marketable securities be held? The two primary reasons – as a substitute for cash and as a temporary investment – are considered in this section.

Substitutes for cash

Some firms hold portfolios of marketable securities in lieu of larger cash balances, liquidating part of the portfolio to increase the cash account when cash outflows exceed inflows. Data are not available to indicate the extent of this practice, but our impression is that it is not common. Most firms prefer to let their banks maintain such liquid reserves, with the firms themselves borrowing to meet temporary cash shortages.

Temporary investment

In addition to using marketable securities as a buffer against cash shortages, firms also hold them on a strictly temporary basis. Firms engaged in seasonal operations, for example, frequently have surplus cash flows during part of the year, deficit cash flows during other months. (See Table 5–1 for an example.) Such firms may purchase marketable securities during their surplus periods, then liquidate them when cash deficits occur. Other firms, particularly in capital goods industries, where fluctuations are violent, attempt to accumulate cash or near-cash securities during a downswing in order to be ready to finance an upswing in business volume.

Firms also accumulate liquid assets to meet predictable financial requirements. For example, if a major modernization programme is planned for the near future, or if a debenture issue is approaching redemption, the marketable securities portfolio may be increased to provide the required funds. Furthermore, marketable securities holdings are frequently large immediately preceding annual corporation tax payment dates.

Firms may also accumulate resources as a protection against a number of contingencies. When they make uninsurable product warranties, companies must be ready to meet any claims that may arise. Firms in highly competitive industries must have resources to carry them through substantial shifts in the market structure. A firm in an industry in which new markets are emerging – for example, foreign markets – needs to have resources to meet developments; these funds may be on hand for fairly long periods.

Criteria used in selecting security portfolios

Different types of securities, varying in risk of default, marketability and length of maturity, are available. We will discuss some of the characteristics of these securities, and the criteria that are applied in choosing among them, here.

---

6. 'A sterling certificate of deposit is a document, issued by a UK office of a British or foreign bank, certifying that a sterling deposit has been made with that bank which is repayable to the bearer upon the surrender of the ticket at maturity'. The certificate of deposit is generally for a minimum amount of £50 000 and normally a maximum of £500 000 with a term to maturity of between three months and five years. See: *Bank of England Quarterly Bulletin*, Vol. 12, No. 4 (December 1972), p. 487.

Risk of default

The firm's liquidity portfolio is generally held for a specific, known need; if it should depreciate in value, the firm would be financially embarrassed. Further, most non-financial companies do not have investment departments specializing in appraising securities and determining the probability of their going into default. Accordingly, the marketable securities portfolio is generally confined to securities with a minimal risk of default. However, the lowest risk securities also provide the lowest returns, so safety is bought at the expense of yield.

Marketability

The security portfolio is usually held to provide liquid reserves or to meet known needs at a specific time. In either case, the firm must be able to sell its holdings and realize cash on short notice. Accordingly, the securities held in the portfolio must be readily marketable.

Maturity

We shall see in Chapter 17 that the price of a long-term bond fluctuates much more with changes in interest rates than does the price of a similar short-term security. Further, as we saw in the last chapter, interest rates fluctuate widely over time. These two factors combine to make long-term bonds riskier than short-term securities for a firm's marketable security portfolio. However, partly because of this risk differential, higher yields are more frequently available on long-term than on short-term securities, so again risk-return trade-offs must be recognized.

Given the motives most firms have for holding marketable security portfolios, it is generally not feasible for them to be exposed to a high degree of risk from interest rate fluctuations. Accordingly, firms generally confine their marketable securities portfolios to the shorter maturities. Only if the securities are expected to be held for a long period, and not be subject to forced liquidation on short notice, will long-term securities be held.

Investment alternatives

The main investment alternatives open to business firms are given in Table 7–1. Rates vary with the general level of interest rates. Returns are lower on the lower-risk government securities and are generally lower on shorter maturities.

Table 7–1 *Alternative Marketable Securities for Investment.*

	Approximate maturities	Approximate yield 10 May 1978 (%)
Treasury bills	3 months	$8\frac{3}{8}$
Eligible bills of exchange	3 months	$8\frac{9}{16}$
Fine trade bills	3 months	$9\frac{1}{4}$
Local authority bonds	1 year	$9\frac{1}{4}$
Sterling certificates of deposit	1 year	$9\frac{11}{16}$
$9\frac{1}{4}$% Exchequer 1982 (government bonds)	4 years	10.79

Depending on how long he or she anticipates holding the funds, the financial manager decides upon a suitable maturity pattern for the holdings. The numerous alternatives can be selected and balanced in such a way that the maturities and risks appropriate to the financial situation of the firm are obtained. Commercial bankers, merchant bankers and brokers provide the financial manager with detailed information on each of the forms of investments in the list. Because their characteristics change with shifts in financial market conditions, it would be misleading to attempt to give detailed descriptions of these investment outlets here. The financial manager must keep up to date on these characteristics and should follow the principle of making investment selections that offer maturities, yields and risks appropriate to the firm.

MANAGEMENT OF TRADE DEBTORS: CREDIT POLICY

The level of trade debtors is determined by (a) the volume of credit sales and (b) the average period between sales and receipts. The average collection period is partially dependent upon economic conditions – during a recession or period of extremely tight money, customers may be forced to delay payment – but it is also dependent upon a set of controllable factors, or *credit policy variables*. The major policy variables include (a) *credit standards*, or the maximum riskiness of acceptable credit accounts; (b) *credit period*, or the length of time for which credit is granted; (c) *discounts* given for early payment; and (d) the firm's *collection policy*. We first discuss each policy variable separately and in qualitative rather than quantitative terms; then we illustrate the interaction of these elements and discuss the actual establishment of a firm's credit policy.

Credit standards

If a firm makes credit sales to only the strongest of customers, it will never have bad debt losses, and it will not incur much in the way of expenses for a credit department. On the other hand, it will probably be losing sales, and the profit forgone on these lost sales could be far larger than the costs it has avoided. Determining the optimal credit standard involves equating the marginal costs of credit to the marginal profits on the increased sales.

Marginal costs include production and selling costs, but we may abstract from these at this point and consider only those costs associated with the 'quality' of the marginal accounts, or *credit quality costs*. These costs include (a) default, or bad debt losses; (b) higher investigation and collection costs; and (c) if less credit-worthy customers delay payment longer than stronger customers, higher costs of capital tied up in debtors.

Since credit costs and credit quality are correlated, it is important to be able to judge the quality of an account. First, how should we define 'quality'? Perhaps the best way is in terms of the probability of default. These probability estimates are, for the most part, subjective estimates, but credit rating is a well-established practice, and a good credit manager can make reasonably accurate judgements of the probability of default by different classes of customers.

To evaluate the credit risk, credit managers consider the five Cs of credit: character, capacity, capital, collateral, conditions. *Character* refers to the probability that a customer will *try* to honour his obligations. This factor is of considerable importance, because every credit transaction implies a *promise* to pay. Will the creditor make an honest effort to pay his debts, or is he likely to try to avoid paying them? Experienced credit men frequently insist that the moral factor is the most important issue in a credit evaluation.

Capacity is a subjective judgement of the ability of the customer. This is gauged by his past record, supplemented by physical observation of the customer's factory or shop and business methods. *Capital* is measured by the general financial position of the firm as indicated by a financial ratio analysis, with special emphasis on the tangible net worth of the enterprise. *Collateral* is represented by assets that the customer may offer as a pledge for security of the credit extended to him. Finally, *conditions* refer to the impact of general economic trends on the firm or to special developments in certain areas of the economy that may affect the customer's ability to meet his obligations.

The major source of external information is the work of the credit-reporting agencies, the best known of which is Dun & Bradstreet. Agencies such as the National Debt Recovery Agency are able to provide factual data that can be used by the credit manager in his credit analysis.

An individual firm can translate its credit information into risk classes, grouped according to the probability of loss associated with sales to a customer. The combination of rating and supplementary information might lead to the following groupings of loss experience:

Risk class number	Loss ratio (in percentages)
1	None
2	0–½
3	½–1
4	1–2
5	2–5
6	5–10
7	10–20
8	over 20

If the selling firm has a 20 per cent margin over the sum of direct operating costs and all delivery and selling costs, and if it is producing at less than full capacity, it may adopt the following credit policies. It may sell on customary credit terms to groups 1 to 5; sell to groups 6 and 7 under more stringent credit terms, such as cash on delivery; and require advance payments from group 8. As long as the bad debt loss ratios are less than 20 per cent, the additional sales are contributing something to overheads.

Statistical techniques, especially regression analysis and discriminant analysis,[7] have been used with some success in judging credit worthiness. These methods work best when individual credits are relatively small and a large number of borrowers are involved. Thus, they have worked best in retail credit, consumer loans, mortgage lending and the like. As the increase in credit cards and similar procedures builds up, as computers are used more frequently, and as credit records on individuals and small firms are developed, statistical techniques promise to become much more important than they are today.

Terms of credit

The terms of credit specify the period for which credit is extended and the discount, if any, given for early payment. For example, as we saw earlier, a firm's credit terms to all approved customers may be that a 2 per cent discount from the stated sales price is granted if payment is made within 10 days, and the entire amount is due 30 days from the invoice date if the discount is not taken. If the terms are stated as 'net within 60 days' this indicates

7. Discriminant analysis is similar to multiple regression analysis, except that it partitions a sample into two or more components on the basis of a set of characteristics. The sample, for example, might be loan applicants to a hire-purchase finance company. The components into which they are classified might be those likely to make prompt repayment and those likely to default. The characteristics might be such factors as whether the applicant owns his home, how long he has been with his employer, and so forth.

that no discount is offered and that the invoice is due and payable 60 days after the invoice date.

If sales are seasonal, a firm may use seasonal dating. Jensen Ltd, a bathing suit manufacturer, sells on terms of 2 per cent discount if payment is made within 10 days of invoice date, 1 May, otherwise net within 30 days. This means that the effective invoice date is 1 May, so the discount may be taken until 10 May, or the full amount must be paid on 30 May, regardless of when the sale was made. Jensen produces output throughout the year, but retail sales of bathing suits are concentrated in the spring and early summer. Because of its practice of offering seasonal datings, Jensen induces some customers to stock up early, saving Jensen storage costs and also 'nailing down sales'.

Credit period

Lengthening the credit period stimulates sales, but there is a cost to tying up funds in debtors. For example, if a firm changes its terms from net payment within 30 days to net within 60 days, the average debtors for the year might rise from £100 000 to £300 000, with the increase caused partly by the longer credit terms and partly by the larger volume of sales. If the cost of capital needed to finance the investment in receivables is 8 per cent, then the marginal cost of lengthening the credit period is £16 000 (= £200 000 × 8 per cent). If the incremental profit – sales price minus all direct production, selling and credit costs associated with the additional sales – exceeds £16 000, then the change in credit policy is profitable. Determining the optimal credit period involves locating that period where marginal profits on increased sales are exactly offset by the costs of carrying the higher amount of trade debtors.

Cash discounts

The effect of granting cash discounts may be analysed similarly to the credit period. For example, if a firm changes its terms from 'net within 30 days' to '2 per cent discount for payment within 10 days, otherwise net', it may well attract customers who want to take discounts, thereby increasing gross sales. Also, the average collection period will be shortened, as some old customers will pay more promptly to take advantage of the discount. Offsetting these benefits is the cost of the discounts taken. The optimal discount is established at the point where costs and benefits are exactly offsetting.

Collection policy

Collection policy refers to the procedures the firm follows to obtain payment of overdue accounts. For example, a letter may be sent to such customers when the account is 10 days overdue; a more severe letter, followed by a telephone call, may be used if payment is not received within 30 days; and the account may be turned over to a collection agency after 90 days.

The collection process can be expensive in terms of both out-of-pocket expenditures and lost goodwill, but at least some firmness is needed to prevent an undue lengthening in the collection period and to minimize outright losses. Again, a balance must be struck between the costs and benefits of different collection policies.

Trade debtors versus trade creditors

Whenever goods are sold on credit, two accounts are created – an asset item entitled a *trade debtor* appears on the books of the selling firm, and a liability item called a *trade creditor* appears on the books of the purchaser. At this point, we are analysing the transaction from the viewpoint of the seller, so we have concentrated on the type of variables under his control. In Chapter 8, we will examine the transaction from the viewpoint of the purchaser. There we will discuss trade creditors as a source of funds and consider the cost of these funds vis-à-vis funds obtained from other sources.

Establishing a credit policy: an illustration[8]

Rexford Drug and Chemical Company manufactures and distributes proprietary medicines and related items to retail chemists throughout the United Kingdom. At a recent board meeting, several directors voiced concern over the firm's rising bad debt losses and increasing investments in trade debtors. This group suggested to the finance director that he instruct his credit manager to tighten up the credit policy. Several other directors, including the marketing director, took exception to this suggestion, stating that a tougher credit policy would cause Rexford to lose profitable sales. This group emphasized that the gross profit margin on sales is 50 per cent, and stated that, if anything, credit terms should be relaxed. After a heated discussion, the meeting broke up; but before adjournment, the board instructed Jim Nantell, the finance director, to conduct a study of the firm's credit policy. Nantell directed his credit manager, Bob Carleton, to study the firm's policy and to report on the desirability of instituting changes.

Carleton decided to draw up two new credit policies as alternatives to the one currently in use. One could be described as an 'easy' credit policy, the other a 'tough' credit policy. The current policy is an 'average' policy in the sense that it closely corresponds to the practices of other drug supply firms.

The new plans require changes in all four credit variables. The 'easy' credit policy involves (a) extending credit to a more risky class of customers, (b) extending the allowable payment period, (c) raising the cash discount allowed for prompt payments, and (d) reducing the 'pressure' of the collection procedure on overdue accounts. The new terms will be 3 per cent discount on payments within 15 days, otherwise net within 45 days, instead of the current 2 per cent within 10 days, net within 30. Those changes are expected to increase sales, but they will also increase the losses on bad debts and the investment in trade debtors.

The 'tough' credit policy involves tightening credit standards; reducing credit terms to 1 per cent discount on payments within 10 days, otherwise net within 20 days; and increasing the collection efforts on overdue accounts. It will result in lower sales but also in lower bad debt losses and a smaller investment in trade debtors. Working with the sales manager, Carleton developed probability estimates of the *changes* in sales and in costs that could result from the two new policies. This information is represented in Table 7–2, where the expected change in profits under each plan is also computed.

Columns 1, 2 and 3 give alternative sales levels, profit margins and profits. Column 4 gives the estimated probability of each gross profit outcome; column 5 gives an estimate of the incremental costs, including production, general and administrative, and credit costs, associated with each sales change. Notice that these cost estimates are themselves subject to probability distributions. For example, if sales increase by £100 million, costs may increase by £50, £60 or £70 million; the conditional probability estimate of each cost outcome is given in column 6.

Depending on which sales and cost increases actually occur, net profit will increase or decrease by the amount given in column 7. The joint probabilities, which represent the

8. In part of this example we employ statistical concepts that may be unfamiliar to the reader. However the 'words' are more important than the 'numbers', so if the statistics are confusing just concentrate on the verbal sections.

Table 7–2 *Incremental Profits from Credit Policy Changes (£ millions).*

Increase in sales (1)	Profit margin (2)	Increase in gross profit (3) = (1) × (2)	Probability of sales change (4)	Increase (or decrease) in cost (5)	Conditional probability (6)	Increase (or decrease) in net profit (7) = (3)–(5)	Joint probability (8) = (4) × (6)	Product (9) = (7) × (8)
				Easy credit policy				
				£ 50	0.30	–	0.06	–
£ 100	0.50	£ 50	0.20	60	0.40	£(10)	0.08	£(.80)
				70	0.30	(20)	0.06	(1.20)
				80	0.30	20	0.18	3.60
200	0.50	100	0.60	90	0.40	10	0.24	2.40
				100	0.30	–	0.18	–
				120	0.30	30	0.06	1.80
300	0.50	150	0.20	130	0.40	20	0.08	1.60
				140	0.30	10	0.06	0.60
			1.00				1.00	
						Expected increase in profit =		£ 8.00
				Tough credit policy				
				£(20)	0.20	£(5)	0.05	£(0.25)
£(50)	0.50	£(25)	0.25	(30)	0.60	5	0.15	0.75
				(40)	0.20	15	0.05	0.75
				(50)	0.20	(25)	0.10	(2.50)
(150)	0.50	(75)	0.50	(60)	0.60	(15)	0.30	(4.50)
				(70)	0.20	(5)	0.10	(0.50)
				(90)	0.20	(35)	0.05	(1.75)
(250)	0.50	(125)	0.25	(100)	0.60	(25)	0.15	(3.75)
				(110)	0.20	(15)	0.05	(0.75)
			1.00				1.00	
						Expected increase in profit =		£(12.5)

products of the probabilities in columns 4 and 6, give the probability of each net profit increase, and these joint probabilities are used to derive the expected profits under each proposed credit policy change. Since the easier credit policy produces positive incremental profits, this policy is superior to the present policy and much superior to that of tightening credit.

Two points should be noted. First, this kind of analysis requires that some very difficult judgements be made – estimating the changes in sales and costs associated with changes in credit policies is, to say the least, a highly uncertain business. Second, even if the sales and cost estimates are reasonably accurate, there is no assurance that some other credit policy would not be even better. For instance, an easy credit policy that involved a different mix of the four policy variables might be superior to the one examined in Table 7–2.

For both these reasons, firms usually 'iterate' slowly toward optimal credit policies. One or two credit variables are changed slightly, the effect of the changes is observed, and a decision is made to change these variables even more or to retract the changes. Further, different credit policies are appropriate at different times, depending on economic conditions. We see, then, that credit policy is not a static, once-for-all-time decision. Rather, it should be fluid, dynamic and ever changing in an effort to reach a continually moving optimal target.

STOCKS

Manufacturing firms generally have three kinds of stocks: (a) raw materials, (b) work in progress, and (c) finished goods. The levels of *raw material* stock are influenced by anticipated production, seasonality of production, reliability of sources of supply and efficiency of scheduling purchases and production operations.

Work-in-progress is strongly influenced by the length of the production period, which is the time between placing raw material in production and completing the finished product. Stock turnover can be increased by decreasing the production period. One means of accomplishing this is perfecting engineering techniques to speed up the manufacturing process. Another means of reducing work in progress is to buy items rather than make them.

The level of *finished goods stock* is a matter of coordinating production and sales. The financial manager can stimulate sales by changing credit terms or by allowing credit to marginal risks. Whether the goods remain on the books as stocks or as debtors, the financial manager has to finance them. Many times, firms find it desirable to make the sale and thus take one step nearer to realizing cash. The potential profits can outweigh the additional collection risk.

Our primary focus in this section is control of investment in stocks. *Stock models* have been developed as an aid in this task and have proved extremely useful in minimizing stock requirements. As our examination of the du Pont system in Chapter 2 showed, any procedure that can reduce the investment required to generate a given sales volume may have a beneficial effect on the firm's rate of return and hence on the value of the firm.

DETERMINANTS OF THE SIZE OF STOCKS

Although wide variations occur, stock-to-sales ratios are generally concentrated in the 15-to-25 per cent range, and stock-to-total assets ratios are concentrated in the 20-to-35 per cent range.

The major determinants of investment in stocks are the following: (a) level of sales, (b) length and technical nature of the production processes and (c) durability versus perishability, or style factor, in the end product. Stock levels in the tobacco industry, for example, are high because of the long curing process. Similarly, in the machinery-manufacturing industries, stock levels are large because of the long work-in-progress period. However, stock ratios are low in coal mining and in oil and gas production because no raw materials are used and the goods in progress are small in relation to sales. Because of the seasonality of the raw materials, average stocks are large in the food processing industry.

With respect to durability and style factors, large stocks are found in the hardware and the precious-metals industries because durability is great and the style factor is small. Stock ratios are low in baking because of the perishability of the final product. Stock levels are low in printing because the items are manufactured to order and require negligible finished goods stocks.

Within limits set by the economics of a firm's industry, there exists a potential for improvement in stock control from the use of computers and operations research. Although the techniques are far too diverse and complicated for a complete treatment in this text, the financial manager should be prepared to make use of the contributions of specialists who have developed effective procedures for minimizing the investment in stocks.[9]

Illustrative of the techniques at the practical level is the stock control system of the US firm Harris Electronics, which works like this: tabulator cards are inserted in each package of five electronic tubes leaving Harris's warehouse. As the merchandise is sold, the distributor collects the cards and files his replacement order without doing paper work. He simply sends in the cards, which are identified by account number, type of merchandise and price of the units he orders.

Western Union Telegraph Co. equipment accepts the punched cards and transmits information on them to the warehouse, where it is duplicated on other punched cards. A typical order of 5000 tubes of varying types can be received in about 17 minutes, assembled in about 90 minutes, and delivered to Boston's Logan Airport in an additional 45 minutes. Orders from 3000 miles away can be delivered within 24 hours, a saving of 13 days in some cases.

Information on the order also goes into a computer which keeps on file stock-on-hand data for each item. When an order draws the stock down below the *order point*, this triggers action in the production department – additional units of the item are then manufactured for stock. In the next section, we examine both the optimal order point and the number of units that should be manufactured, which is called the *economic ordering quantity* (EOQ).

GENERALITY OF STOCK CONTROL PROBLEM

Managing assets of all kinds is basically a stock control problem – the same method of analysis applies to cash and fixed assets as applies to stocks themselves. First, a basic stock must be on hand to balance inflows and outflows of the items, with the size of the stock depending upon the patterns of flows, whether regular or irregular. Second, because the unexpected may always occur, it is necessary to have safety stocks on hand. They represent the little extra to avoid the costs of not having enough to meet current needs. Third, additional amounts may be required to meet future growth needs. These are anticipation stocks. Related to anticipation stocks is the recognition that there are optimum purchase

9. The basic stock model is developed in Appendix A to this chapter.

sizes, defined as *economic ordering quantities.* In borrowing money, in buying raw materials for production, or in purchasing plants and equipment, it is cheaper to buy more than just enough to meet immediate needs.

With the foregoing as a basic foundation, we can develop the theoretical basis for determining the optimal investment in stocks, which is illustrated in Figure 7–1. Some costs rise with larger stocks – among these are warehousing costs, interest on funds tied up in stocks, insurance, obsolescence and so forth. Other costs decline with larger stock levels – these include the loss of profits resulting from sales lost because of running out of stock, costs of production interruptions caused by inadequate stocks, possible purchase discounts and so on.

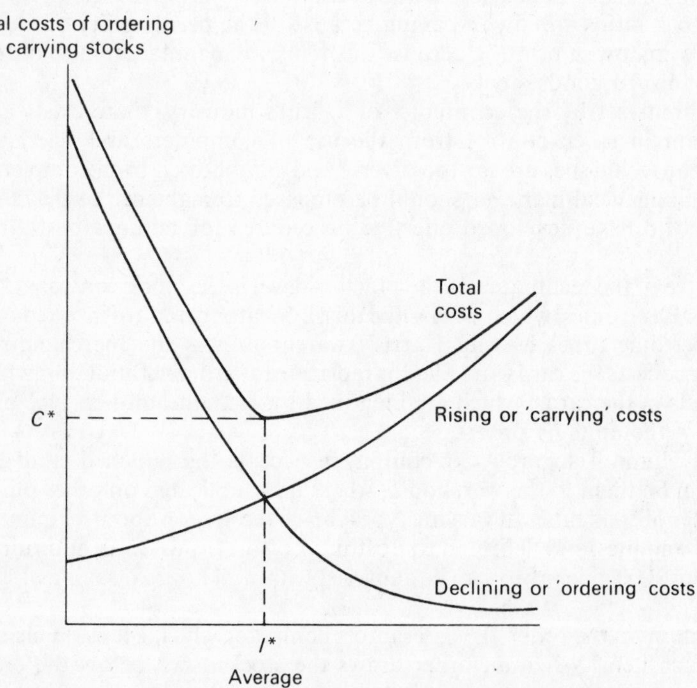

Figure 7–1 *Determination of Optimum Investment in Stocks.*

The costs that decline with higher stock levels are designated by the declining curve in Figure 7–1; those that rise with larger stocks are designated by the rising curve. The total costs curve is the total of the rising and declining curves, and it represents the total cost of ordering and holding stocks. At the point where the absolute value of the slope of the rising curve is equal to the absolute value of the slope of the declining curve (that is, where *marginal* rising costs are equal to *marginal* declining costs), the total costs curve is at a minimum. This represents the optimum size of investment in stocks.

STOCK CONTROL DECISION MODELS

The generalized statements in the preceding section can be made much more specific. In fact, it is usually possible to specify the curves shown in Figure 7–1, at least to a reasonable approximation, and actually to find the minimum point on the total cost curve. Since entire courses (in operations research programmes) are devoted to stock control techniques, and since a number of books have been written on the subject, we obviously cannot deal with stock decision models in a very complete fashion. The model we illustrate, however, is probably more widely used – even by quite sophisticated firms – than any other, and it can be readily expanded to encompass any refinements one cares to make.[10]

The costs of holding stocks – the cost of capital tied up, storage costs, insurance, depreciation and so on – rise as the size of stock holdings increases. Conversely, the cost of ordering stocks – the cost of placing orders, shipping and handling, quantity discounts lost and so on – falls as the average stock level increases. The total cost of stocks is the summation of these rising and declining costs, or the total costs curve in Figure 7–1. It has been shown that, under reasonable assumptions, the minimum point on the total costs curve can be found by an equation called the EOQ formula:

$$EOQ = \sqrt{\frac{2FU}{CP}}.$$

Here

EOQ = the economic ordering quantity, or the optimum quantity to be ordered each time an order is placed.
F = fixed costs of placing and receiving an order.
U = annual usage in units.
C = carrying cost expressed as a percentage of stock value.
P = purchase price per unit of stock.

For any level of usage, dividing U by EOQ indicates the number of orders that must be placed each year. The average stock on hand – the average balance sheet stock figure – will be

$$\text{Average stock level} = \frac{EOQ}{2}.$$

The derivation of the EOQ model assumes (a) that usage is at a constant rate and (b) that delivery lead times are constant. In fact, usage is likely to vary considerably for most firms – demand may be unexpectedly strong for any number of reasons; if it is, the firm will run out of stock and will suffer sales losses or production stoppages. Similarly, delivery lead times will vary depending on weather, strikes, demand in the suppliers' industries and so on. Because of these factors, firms add *safety stocks* to their stock levels, and the average stock becomes

$$\text{Average stock} = \frac{EOQ}{2} + \text{safety stock}.$$

The size of the safety stock will be relatively high if uncertainties about usage rates and delivery times are great, low if these factors do not vary greatly. Similarly, the safety stock will be larger if the costs of running out of stock are great. For example, if customer ill will would cause a permanent loss of business or if an elaborate production process would have to stop if an item were out of stock, then large safety stocks will be carried.[11]

---

10. In the text we simply illustrate the use of the EOQ stock model; for an explanation of its development see Appendix A to this chapter.

11. Formal methods have been developed to assist in striking a balance between the costs of carrying larger safety stocks and the cost of stock-outs (stock shortages). A discussion of these models, which goes beyond the scope of this book, can be found in most production textbooks.

USE OF EOQ MODEL: AN ILLUSTRATION

Let us assume that the following values are determined to be appropriate for a particular firm:

U = usage = 100 units.
C = carrying cost = 20 per cent of stock value.
P = purchase price = £1 per unit.
F = fixed cost of ordering = £10.

Substituting these values into the formula, we obtain

$$EOQ = \sqrt{\frac{2FU}{CP}}$$

$$= \sqrt{\frac{2 \times 10 \times 100}{0.2 \times 1}} = \sqrt{\frac{2000}{0.2}} = \sqrt{10\,000}$$

$$= 100 \text{ units.}$$

If the desired safety stock is 10 units, then the average stocks (A) will be

$$A = \frac{EOQ}{2} + \text{safety stock}$$

$$= \frac{100}{2} + 10$$

$$= 60 \text{ units.}$$

Since the cost of purchasing or manufacturing stock is £1 a unit, the average stock value will be £60 for this item.

CASH MANAGEMENT AS A STOCK CONTROL PROBLEM

In our cash budgeting discussion in Chapter 5, we indicated that firms generally have 'minimum desired cash balances'. Then, in discussing cash management, we considered the various factors that influence cash holdings. We did not, however, attempt to specify optimum cash balances. Optimum cash balances can be found by the use of stock-type models such as those we discussed just above – examples of such models are given in Appendix B to this chapter. Cash management, together with stock controls, is perhaps the area of financial management where mathematical tools have proved most useful.

Sophisticated cash management models recognize the uncertainty inherent in forecasting both cash inflows and cash outflows. Inflows are represented, in effect, by the 'orders' in our stock control model; they come principally from (a) receipts, (b) borrowing (c) sale of securities. The primary 'carrying cost' of cash is the opportunity cost of having funds tied up in non-earning assets (or in low-yielding near-cash items); the principal 'ordering costs' are brokerage costs associated with borrowing funds or converting marketable securities into cash.

SUMMARY

In this chapter we focused attention on four types of current assets – cash, marketable securities, trade debtors and stocks. First, we examined the motives for holding cash and ways of minimizing the investment in cash. With this background, we considered the minimum cash balances a firm is likely to hold.

Marketable securities are held as a substitute for 'cash safety stocks' and as temporary investments while the firm is awaiting permanent investment of funds. 'Safety stocks' are almost always held in low-risk, short-maturity securities; temporary investments are held in securities whose maturity depends upon the length of time before the funds are permanently employed.

The investment in trade debtors is dependent (a) upon sales and (b) upon the firm's credit policy. The credit policy, in turn, involves four controllable variables: credit standards, the length of the credit period, cash discounts and the collection policy. The significant aspect of credit policy is its effect on sales: an easy credit policy will stimulate sales but involves costs of capital tied up in debtors, bad debts, discounts and higher collection costs. The optimal credit policy is one in which these costs are just offset by the profits on sales generated by the credit policy change.

Stocks – raw materials, work in progress and finished goods – are necessary in most businesses. Rather elaborate systems for controlling the level of stocks have been designed. These systems frequently use computers for keeping records of all the items in stock; a stock control model that considers anticipated sales, ordering costs and carrying costs can be used to determine EOQs for each item.

The basic stock control model recognizes that certain costs (carrying costs) rise as average stock levels increase but that certain other costs (ordering costs and stock-out costs) fall as average stock levels rise. These two sets of costs make up the total cost of ordering and carrying stocks, and the EOQ model is designed to locate an optimal order size that will minimize total costs of stock control.

QUESTIONS

7–1. How can better methods of communication reduce the necessity for firms to hold large cash balances?

7–2. 'The highly developed financial system of the United Kingdom, with its myriad of different near-cash assets, has greatly reduced cash balance requirements by reducing the need for transactions balances.' Discuss this statement.

7–3. Would you expect a firm with a high growth rate to hold more or less precautionary and speculative cash balances than a firm with a low growth rate? Explain.

7–4. Many firms that find themselves with temporary surplus cash invest these funds in Treasury bills. Since Treasury bills frequently have the lowest yield of any investment security, why are they chosen as investments?

7–5. Assume that a firm sells on terms of net payment within 30 days and that its accounts are, on the average, 30 days overdue. What will its investment in debtors be if its annual credit sales are approximately £720 000?

7–6. 'It is difficult to judge the performance of many of our employees but not that of the credit manager. If he's performing perfectly, credit losses are nil; and the higher our losses (as a percentage of sales), the worse his performance.' Evaluate this statement.

7–7. Explain how a firm may reduce its investment in stock by having its supplier hold raw materials stocks and its customers hold finished goods stocks. What are the limitations of such a policy?

7–8. What factors are likely to reduce the holdings of stocks in relation to sales in the future? What factors will tend to increase the ratio? What, in your judgement, is the net effect?

7–9. What are the probable effects of the following on stock levels?

(a) Manufacture of a part formerly purchased from an outside supplier.
(b) Greater use of air freight.
(c) Increase, from 7 to 17, in the number of styles produced.
(d) Your firm receives large price reductions from a manufacturer of bathing suits if they are purchased in December and January.

7–10. Stock control models are designed to facilitate the minimization of the cost of obtaining and carrying stocks. Describe the basic nature of the fundamental stock control model, discussing specifically the nature of increasing costs, decreasing costs and total costs. Illustrate your discussion with a graph.

PROBLEMS

7–1. Gulf Distributors makes all sales on a credit basis. Once each year a routine credit evaluation is made on all its customers. The evaluation procedure allows customers to be ranked in categories from 1 to 5, in order of increasing risk. Results of the ranking are as follows:

Category	Percentage bad debts	Average collection period	Credit decision	Annual sales lost due to credit restrictions
1	None	10 days	Unlimited credit	£None
2	1.0	12	Unlimited credit	None
3	3.0	20	Limited credit	400 000
4	9.0	60	Limited credit	200 000
5	16.0	90	No credit	800 000

(a) Using this credit rule, gross profit has averaged 10 per cent of sales during the past five years. The opportunity cost of investment in debtors is 12 per cent. What would you estimate to be the effect on net profits of extending full credit to each of categories 3, 4 and 5?
(b) The implicit assumption in part (a) is that all costs leading to gross profit are variable. Recalculate your answers assuming that variable costs equal 85 per cent of sales (excluding bad debts and cost of debtors).

7–2. A firm issues cheques for the amount of £100 000 each day and deducts them from its own records at the close of business on the day they are written. On average, the bank receives and clears (that is, deducts from the firm's bank balance) the cheques the evening of the fourth day after they are written; for example, a cheque written on Monday will be cleared on Friday afternoon. The firm has a policy of maintaining a minimum safety stock balance of £75 000.
(a) Assuming that the firm makes deposits in the late afternoon (and the bank includes the deposit in that day's transactions), how much must the firm deposit each day to maintain a sufficient balance?
(b) How many days of float does the firm carry?
(c) What ending daily balance should the firm try to maintain at the bank and on its own records?
(d) Would it make a difference if the safety stock balance requirement called for an average rather than a minimum of £75 000?
(e) What would the firm's average balance on the bank's records and on its own records show if the minimum rather than the average balance is required?

7–3. The Hallaman Distributing Company has mounted an extended sales campaign. In order to move its goods, it has lowered its credit standards somewhat. As a consequence, its average collection period has increased from 20 days to the present level of 50 days under the new credit policies. Credit terms are 2 per cent discount on payments within 10 days, otherwise net in 30 days. Gross sales collected over time were as follows, before the sales campaign and during the sales campaign.

Payment by	Percent of gross before sale	Sales collected during sale
Cash sales	30%	5%
0–10 days (average 5)	20%	10%
11–30 days (average 20)	20%	10%
31–90 days (average 50)	30%	55%
over 90 days (average 100)	0%	20%

As a result of the sales campaign, annual sales increased from £2 million to £2.5 million. Profit before credit costs is 8 per cent. The cost of capital for debtors is 12 per cent. Cash sales are recorded at gross, and the credit discount is given.
(a) Calculate the gross profit before and during the sale, and determine the change in gross profit.
(b) Compute the change in discount costs.
(c) Compute the increased cost of carrying additional debtors outstanding.
(d) Compute the change in pre-tax profits. (Round to the nearest 100.)

7–4. The following relations for stock purchase and storage costs have been established for the Milton Processing Company.

1. Orders must be placed in multiples of 100 units.
2. Requirements for the year are 400 000. (Use 50 weeks in a year for calculations.)
3. The purchase price per unit is £5.
4. Carrying cost is 20 per cent of the purchase price of goods.
5. Cost per order placed is £25.
6. Desired safety stock is 10 000 units (on hand initially).
7. Two weeks are required for delivery.

(a) What is the economic order quantity? (Round to the 100s.)
(b) What is the optimal number of orders to be placed?
(c) At what stock level should a reorder be made?
(d) If annual unit sales double, what is the percentage increase in the EOQ? What is the elasticity of EOQ with respect to sales (% change in EOQ/% change in sales)?
(e) If the cost per order placed doubles, what is the percentage increase in EOQ? What is the elasticity of EOQ with respect to cost per order?
(f) If carrying cost declines by 50%, compute the elasticity of EOQ with respect to the change in carrying cost.
(g) If purchase price declines 50%, compute the elasticity of EOQ with respect to the change in purchase price.

SELECTED REFERENCES

Archer, Stephen H. A model for the determination of firm cash balances. *Journal of Financial and Quantitative Analysis* 1 (March 1966): 1–11.

Baumol, William J. The transactions demand for cash: an inventory theoretic approach. *Quarterly Journal of Economics* 65 (November 1952): 545–556.

Benishay, Haskel. A stochastic model of credit sales debt. *Journal of the American Statistical Association* 61 (December 1966): 1010–1028.

Benishay, Haskel. Managerial controls of accounts receivable: a deterministic approach. *Journal of Accounting Research* 3 (Spring 1965): 114–133.

Beranek, William. *Analysis for Financial Decisions.* Homewood, Ill.: Irwin, 1963, chap. 10.

Brosky, John J. *The Implicit Cost of Trade Credit and Theory of Optimal Terms of Sale.* New York: Credit Research Foundation, 1969.

Brown, Robert G. *Decision Rules for Inventory Management.* New York: Holt, Rinehart and Winston, 1967.

Calman, Robert F. *Linear Programming and Cash Management/CASH ALPHA.* Cambridge, Mass.: M.I.T., 1968.

Chen, Andrew H. Y., Jen, Frank C. and Zoints, Stanley. Portfolio models with stochastic cash demands. *Management Science* 19 (November 1972): 319–332.

Churchill, M. and Ward, B. How BMW computerized cash planning. *Accountancy* (UK), (June 1976): 26–29.

Clements, A. W. Cash management in I.C.I. *Managerial Finance* (UK) (1975), Vol. 1, No. 1, p. 5.

Creer, C. C. The optimal credit acceptance policy. *Journal of Finance and Quantitative Analysis* (December 1967). *Evidence on the Financing of Industry and Trade.* London: HMSO, March 1978, Vol. 5.

Firth, M. Management of working capital.

Frazer, P. How to play the float. *Accountancy* (UK) (February 1977): 54.

Friedland, Seymour. *The Economics of Corporate Finance.* Englewood Cliffs, N.J.: Prentice-Hall, 1966, chap. 4.

Goodhart, C. A. E. *Money, Information, and Uncertainty.* London: Macmillan, 1975, chap. 2.

Greer, Carl C. The optimal credit acceptance policy. *Journal of Financial and Quantitative Analysis* 2 (December 1967): 399–415.

Hutson, T. G. & Butterworth, J. Management of trade credit. Epping: Gower Press, 1974.

King, Alfred M. *Increasing the Productivity of Company Cash.* Englewood Cliffs, N.J.: Prentice-Hall, 1969, chaps. 4 and 5.

Kirkman, P. The management of trade debtors. *Accountancy* (UK) (April, 1974): 42–52.

La Londe, B. J. and Lambot, O. M. Calculating inventory carrying costs. *International Journal of Physical Distribution* (1977), No. 4, p. 195.

Lane, Sylvia. Submarginal credit risk classification. *Journal of Financial and Quantitative Analysis* 7 (January 1972): 1379–1385.

Lawson, G. H. and Stark, A. W. The concept of profit for fund raising. *Accountancy and Business Research* (Winter 1975): 21–41. (UK)

Long, Michael S. Credit screening system selection. *Journal of Financial and Quantitative Analysis* 11 (June 1976): 313–328.

Mehta, Dileep. The formulation of credit policy models. *Management Science* 15 (October 1968): 30–50.

Mehta, Dileep. Optimal credit policy selection: a dynamic approach. *Journal of Financial and Quantitative Analysis* 5 (December 1970).

Miller, Merton H. and Orr, Daniel. A model of the demand for money by firms. *Quarterly Journal of Economics* 80 (August 1966): 413–435.

Miller, Merton H. and Orr, Daniel. The demand for money by firms: extension of analytic results. *Journal of Finance* 23 (December 1968): 735–759.

Oh, John S. Opportunity cost in the evaluation of investment in accounts receivable. *Financial Management* 5 (Summer 1976): 32–36.

Parker, L. BACS – electronic funds transfer. *Accountancy* (September 1977): 122–124.

Rands, C. A., Vause, R. and Pemberton, K. G. Using computers in small company cash management. *Accounting and Business Research* (Autumn 1974): 251–262.

Savey, B. J. Numerical points systems in credit screening. *Managerial Finance* (UK) (1976), Vol. 2, No. 3, p. 180.

Schwartz, Robert A. An economic model of trade credit. *Journal of Financial and Quantitative Analysis* 9 (September 1974): 643–657.

Searby, Frederick W. Cash management: helping meet the capital crisis. In *The Treasurer's Handbook*, J. Fred Weston and Maurice B. Goudzwaard, eds. Homewood, Ill.: Dow Jones-Irwin, 1976, pp. 440–456.

Sprenkle, Case M. The uselessness of transactions demand models. *Journal of Finance* 24 (December 1969): 835–848.

Wagner, Harvey M. *Principles of Operations Research – with Applications to Managerial Decisions.* Englewood Cliffs, N. J.: Prentice-Hall, 1969, chaps. 9 and 19, and app. 2.

Wrightsman, Dwayne. Optimal credit terms for accounts receivable. *Quarterly Review of Economics and Business* 9 (Summer 1969): 59–66.

Appendix A to Chapter 7:

The Basic Stock Control Model

As we noted in Chapter 7, mathematical models have been applied to stock management with perhaps better results than in any other sphere of business management. In this appendix, we will see how the basic stock control model – the EOQ model – is developed.

The notation used in Chapter 7 and extended in this appendix is as follows:

A = average stock level
C = carrying cost expressed as a percentage of stock sales
EOQ = economic order quantity
F = fixed costs of placing and receiving an order
K = total holding costs
N = number of orders placed per year
P = purchase price per unit of stock
Q = order quantity
R = total ordering costs
T = total stock costs
U = annual usage in units
V = variable cost per unit of ordering, shipping and receiving

This notation is independent of notation used elsewhere in the book.

NATURE OF THE PROBLEM

Recalling Figure 7–1, we find (a) that some costs associated with stocks decline as stock levels increase, (b) that other costs rise and (c) that the total stock-related cost curve has a minimum point. The purpose of the basic stock control model is to locate this minimum and the economic order quantity (EOQ) which will lead to minimum costs. We will assume that the Norgaard Company expects to achieve a sales volume of 1000 widgets during 1978 and that Norgaard is quite confident of hitting this target. Further, these sales are expected to be evenly distributed over the year, so stock levels will decline smoothly and gradually. Widgets are purchased for £10 each. No stock is on hand at the beginning of the year, and none will be held at year's end.

Under these circumstances, the Norgaard Company could place one order for Q = 1000 units at the start of the year. If it did, the average stock for the year, A, would be equal to

$$A = \frac{Q}{2} = \frac{U}{2} = \frac{1000}{2} = 500 \text{ units.} \qquad (7A\text{–}1)$$

Since widgets cost £10 each, the average investment in stocks is £5000.

Alternatively, Norgaard could place two orders for 500 each, in which case average stocks would be

$$A = \frac{500}{2} = 250,$$

or four orders of 250 each for an average stock of 125, and so on. Investment in stocks declines correspondingly.

We can see that average stocks are a function of the number of orders placed per year, N. Specifically, when the number of orders placed is incorporated into the calculation, equation 7A–1 becomes

$$A = \frac{U/2}{N}. \tag{7A–1a}$$

By ordering more frequently (increasing N), Norgaard can reduce its average stock further and further.

How far should stock reductions be carried? Smaller stocks involve lower *holding costs* – cost of capital tied up in stocks, storage costs, insurance and so on – but, since smaller average stocks imply more frequent orders, they involve higher *ordering costs.*

CLASSIFICATION OF COSTS

The first step in the process of building a stock control model is to specify those costs that rise and those that decline with higher levels of stocks. Table 7A–1 gives a listing of some typical costs that are associated with carrying stocks. In the table, we have broken costs down into three categories: those associated with holding stocks, those associated with running short of stocks and those associated with ordering and receiving stocks.

Table 7A–1 *Costs Associated with Stocks.*

Holding costs
1. Cost of capital tied up
2. Storage costs
3. Insurance
4. Rates
5. Depreciation and obsolescence

Costs of running short
1. Loss of sales
2. Loss of customer goodwill
3. Disruption of production schedules

Shipping, receiving and ordering costs
1. Cost of placing order, including production setup costs
2. Shipping and handling costs
3. Quantity discounts lost

Although they may well be the most important element, we shall disregard the second category of costs – the costs of running short – at this point. These costs will be considered at a later stage, when we add 'safety stocks' to the stock control model. Further, we shall disregard quantity discounts, although it is easy enough to adjust the basic model to include discounts.[1] The costs that remain for consideration at this stage, then, are carrying costs and ordering costs.

Holding costs

Holding costs generally rise in direct proportion to the average amount of stock held and this is the case with the Norgaard Company. For example, Norgaard's cost of capital is 10 per cent, and depreciation is estimated to amount to 5 per cent per year. Lumping together these and Norgaard's other costs of holding stock produces a total cost of 25 per cent of the investment in stocks. Defining the percentage cost as C, we can, in general, find the

1. See John F. Magee and Harlan C. Meal, Inventory management and standards, *The Treasurer's Handbook*, J. Fred Weston and Maurice B. Goudzwaard, eds. (Homewood, Ill.: Dow Jones-Irwin, 1976).

total holding costs as the percentage holding cost (C) times the price per unit, (P) times the average number of units (A):

$$K = \text{total holding costs} \quad = (C)(P)(A). \qquad (7A\text{–}2)$$

If Norgaard elects to order only once a year, average stocks will be 1000/2 = 500 units; the cost of carrying the stock will be 0.25 × £10 × 500 = £1250. If the company orders twice a year and, hence, has average stocks that are half as large, total carrying costs will decline to £625, and so on.

Shipping, Receiving and Ordering Costs

Although holding costs are entirely variable and rise in direct proportion to the average size of stocks, ordering costs consist of both a fixed and a variable component. For example, the cost of *placing* an order – inter-office memos, long distance telephone calls, setting up a production run and so on – are fixed costs per order, so the total cost of placing orders may simply be the cost of placing an order times the number of orders placed. Shipping and receiving costs, on the other hand, generally involve a fixed charge plus a variable charge per unit.[2]

We can lump together all fixed costs of placing and receiving an order and define them as F. Norgaard's total fixed cost *per order*, for example, is £100. The company's per unit variable cost of ordering, shipping and receiving, which we define as V, depends upon the number of units ordered, and it amounts to £1 *per unit ordered.*

Combining the fixed and variable components of ordering costs, we obtain the following equation for R, the total cost of placing and receiving orders:

$$R = (F)(N) + (V)(U), \qquad (7A\text{–}3)$$

where F = fixed costs per order; N = number of orders placed; V = variable cost per unit ordered; and U = total number of units ordered during the year, which in this case equals the total sales in units.

Equation 7A–1a may be rewritten as $N = U/2A$, then substituted into equation 7A–3 as follows:

$$R = F\left(\frac{U}{2A}\right) + (V)(U). \qquad (7A\text{–}4)$$

To illustrate, if F = £100, U = 1000, A = 250, and V = £1, then R, the total ordering costs, is

$$R = £100(2) + £1(1000) = £1200.$$

Total stock costs

Stock holding costs (K) as defined in equation 7A–2, and ordering costs (R) as defined in equation 7A–4 may be combined to find total stock costs (T) as follows:

$$\begin{aligned} T &= K + R \\ &= (C)(P)(A) + F\left(\frac{U}{2A}\right) + (V)(U). \end{aligned} \qquad (7A\text{–}5)$$

Recognizing that $A = Q/2$, or one-half the size of each order quantity, Q, equation 7A–5 may be rewritten as:

$$\begin{aligned} T &= CP\left(\frac{Q}{2}\right) + F\left(\frac{U}{Q}\right) + (V)(U) \\ &= CP\left(\frac{Q}{2}\right) + \frac{F(U)}{Q} + (V)(U). \end{aligned} \qquad (7A\text{–}6)$$

The next step is to locate an optimal order quantity, or the value of Q that minimizes T. We find this optimal quantity, or the EOQ, by differentiating equation 7A–6 with respect to Q, setting the derivative equal to nil, and obtaining[3]

---

2. The fixed-versus-variable components in ordering costs can be confusing, so some elaboration on this point might be useful. First, *in toto*, ordering costs are considered to be a variable cost – if the firm does not place any orders, it does not incur any ordering costs. However, some of the costs of each order are fixed and some are variable. It is this fact – that a component of a *variable* cost is *fixed* – that occasionally causes confusion.

3. Proof: differentiate equation 7A–6 with respect to Q and set equal to zero, then solve for Q:

$$\frac{\partial T}{\partial Q} = \frac{CP}{2} - \frac{FU}{Q^2} = 0$$

$$EOQ = \sqrt{\frac{2FU}{CP}}$$

In the Norgaard case, we find the EOQ to be

$$EOQ = \sqrt{\frac{2(£100)(1000)}{(0.25)(£10)}}$$
$$= \sqrt{\frac{200\,000}{2.5}}$$
$$= \sqrt{80\,000}$$
$$\approx 280 \text{ units.} \qquad (7A\text{–}7)$$

If this quantity is ordered four times a year ($1000/280 \approx 4$), or every three months, total costs of ordering and carrying inventories, calculated from equation 7A – 6, will be:

$$T = CP\left(\frac{Q}{2}\right) + \frac{FU}{Q} + VU$$
$$= £2.50(140) + \frac{(£100)(1000)}{280} + £1(1000)$$
$$= £350 + £357 + £1000$$
$$= £1707.$$

That is the lowest possible cost of ordering and holding the required amount of stocks.

Equation 7A – 7 gives us the optimum, or cost minimizing, order quantity for given levels of usage (U), stock holding cost (C), and fixed order costs (F). Knowing the EOQ and continuing our assumption of nil opening and closing stock levels, we find the optimal average stock level as[4]

$$A = \frac{EOQ}{2} = \frac{280}{2} = 140.$$

Norgaard will thus have an average investment in stocks of 140 units at £10 each, or £1400.

RELATIONSHIP BETWEEN SALES AND STOCKS

Intuitively, we would suppose that the higher the ordering or processing costs, the less frequently orders should be placed. However, the higher the holding costs of stock, the more frequently stocks should be ordered. These two features are incorporated in the formula. Notice also that if Norgaard's sales had been estimated at 2000 units, the EOQ would have been 400, while the average stock level would have been 200 units instead of the 140 called for with sales of 1000 units. Thus, a doubling of sales leads to less than a doubling of stocks. That is, in fact, a general rule: the EOQ increases with the *square root* of sales, so any increase in sales calls for a less-than-proportionate increase in stocks. The financial manager should keep this in mind when he is establishing standards for stock control.

$$\frac{CP}{2} = \frac{FU}{Q^2}$$

$$Q^2 = \frac{2FU}{CP}$$

$$Q = \sqrt{\frac{2FU}{CP}}$$

4. If we maintain a 'safety stock' to guard against shipping delays, unexpectedly heavy demand and so on, then average stocks will be higher by this amount, and stock costs will be higher by CP times this amount. The nature of safety stocks will be considered later in this appendix.

EXTENDING THE EOQ MODEL TO INCLUDE 'SAFETY STOCKS'

The EOQ model, as we have developed it thus far, assumes that sales can be forecast perfectly and that usage is evenly distributed over the year. Further, the model assumes that orders are placed and received with no delays whatever.

The implications of these assumptions are graphed in Figure 7A–1. The Thompson Company, with a demand of 1000 units per year and an EOQ of 28, places 36 orders each year, or one every 10 days. With a nil opening and closing stock level, the maximum stock is 28 units and the average is 14 units. The slope of the line in Figure 7A–1 measures the daily rate of usage; in this case, 2.8 units of stock are used each day. The usage line is shown as a step function in the first period, then smoothed in subsequent periods for convenience.

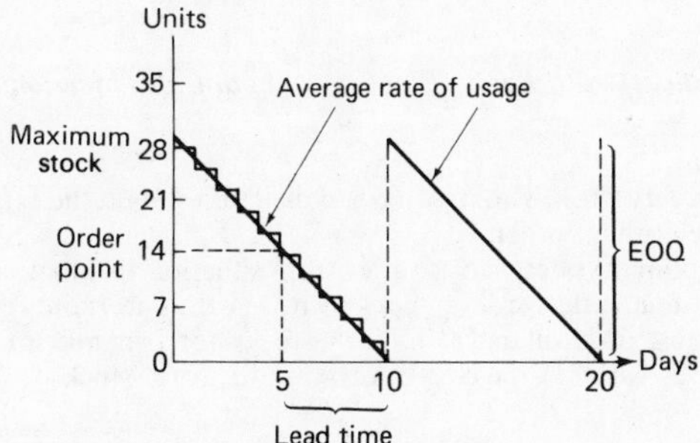

Figure 7A–1 *Demand Forecast with Certainty.*

Order point

We can relax the assumption of instantaneous order and delivery. Let us assume Thompson requires five days to place an order and take delivery. The company, then, must have a five-day stock, or 14 units on hand when it places an order (lead time × daily usage = 5 × 2.8 = 14). The stock that is required to be on hand at time of order is defined as the *order point*; when stock levels dip to this point, a new order is placed. If Thompson's stock control process is automated, the computer will generate an order when the stock on hand falls to 14 units.[5]

Safety stock

To this point we have assumed that usage (demand) is known with certainty and is uniform throughout time, and that the order lead time never varies. Either or both of these assumptions could be incorrect, so it is necessary to modify the EOQ model to allow for this possibility. This modification generally takes the form of adding a *safety stock* to average stocks.

The safety stock concept is illustrated in Figure 7A–2. First, note that the slope of the usage line measures expected daily usage. The company expects a usage of 2.8 units each day, but let us assume a maximum conceivable usage of twice this amount, or 5.6 units each day. It initially orders 42 units, the EOQ of 28 plus a safety stock of 14 units. Subsequently, it reorders the EOQ, 28 units, whenever the stock level falls to 28 units, the safety stock of 14 units plus the 14 units expected to be used while awaiting delivery of the order. Notice that Thompson could, over the five-day delivery period, sell 5.6 units a day ($^{28}/_{5}$ days = 5.6 units/day), or double its normal expected sales. This maximum rate of usage is shown by the steeper line in Figure 7A–2. The event that makes possible this higher maximum rate of usage, of course, is the introduction of a *safety stock* of 14 units.

The safety stock is also useful to guard against delays in receiving orders. The expected delivery time is five

5. We should note that if a new order must be placed before a subsequent order is received – that is, if the normal delivery lead time is longer than the time between orders – then what might be called a 'goods-in-transit' stock builds up. This complicates matters somewhat, but the simplest solution to the problem is to deduct goods in transit when calculating the order point. In other words, the order point would be calculated as

Order point = lead time × daily usage – goods in transit.

This situation arises in the problem at the end of this appendix.

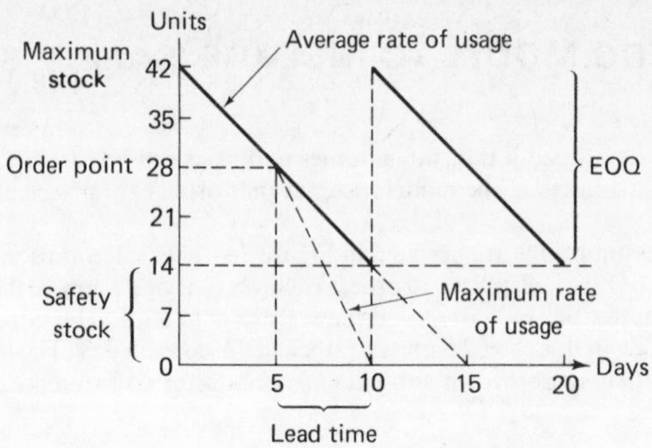

Figure 7A–2 *Demand Forecast with Safety Stock to Account for Uncertainty.*

days; however, with a 14-unit safety stock, Thompson could maintain sales at the expected rate for an additional five days if shipping delays held up an order.

The actual calculation of optimum safety stock varies from situation to situation, but it depends upon the following four factors. The optimum safety stock increases with (a) the uncertainty of demand forecasts, (b) the costs in terms of lost sales and lost goodwill that result from stock shortages, and (c) the probability of delays in receiving shipments; it decreases with (d) the cost of carrying the extra stocks.[6]

PROBLEM

7A–1. Jenjo Sales Company is a retail distributor of living room furniture. As a small firm, with sales under £1 000 000 a year, it has estimated that its cost of capital is a high 16 per cent. The firm employs 20 salesmen who average two orders a week. From this information the proprietor, John Morris, has estimated his sales volume for the coming year to be 2000 units. There is some seasonal variation – sales decrease before Christmas, Easter and Spring Bank Holiday, as consumers divert their income to purchase of gifts, clothes and holidays – which Morris ignores in his preliminary stock planning for the coming year.

In preparing his plans, Morris reviews the following data: average cost per living room ensemble is £150; depreciation and obsolescence on stocks is estimated at $\frac{1}{2}$ of 1 per cent a *month*; fire, theft and fully-comprehensive insurance coverage costs $\frac{1}{2}$ of 1 per cent a *year*; the current rates average is 1 per cent a *year*. Each living room set requires 20 square feet of storage space, and warehousing is available at 12 pence per square foot *per month*.

Morris' cost accountant has provided data revealing that shipping, receiving and ordering costs are as follows: inter-office memos £4 an order; airmail letter £2 per order (requires four weeks for delivery) or long distance telephone call £7 per order (requires two weeks for delivery). All other shipping, receiving and handling costs amount to £3 per unit ordered. (Note: this quantity does *not* enter the EOQ calculations.) The desired safety stock is one week's requirements. (Use 50 weeks in a year for your calculations.)

(a) Specify values for each element of stock cost:
 (i) holding costs per unit
 (ii) fixed ordering costs per unit
(b) What is the economic order quantity for each method of ordering?
(c) What is the optimal number of orders to be placed for each method of ordering? (Use 50 weeks per year.)
(d) Assuming airmail orders, at what stock level should a reorder be made? (See footnote 5 above before

6. For a more detailed discussion of safety stocks, see Magee and Meal, Inventory management and standards. If we knew (a) the probability distribution of usage rates and (b) the probability distribution of order lead times, we could determine joint probabilities of stock-outs with various safety stock levels. With a safety stock of 14 units, for example, the probability of a stock-out for the Thompson Company might be 5 per cent. If the safety stock is reduced to 10 units, stock-out probability might rise to 15 per cent, while this probability might be reduced to 1 per cent with a safety stock of 20 units. If we had additional information on the precise cost of a stock-out, we could compare this with the cost of holding larger safety stocks. The optimum safety stock is determined at the point where the marginal stock-out cost is equal to the marginal stock holding cost.

working this part of the problem. Also, note that seven orders, or $3\frac{1}{2}$ weeks of usage, will be in transit at the order point, one order having just been delivered.)

(e) What is the total cost of ordering and holding stocks under each of the two methods? Use the equation $T = CPA + FN + VU$.

(f) Why is V omitted from the EOQ solution formula?

(g) When should telephone orders be placed with two-week delivery rather than airmail orders for four-week delivery? (Use 50 weeks in a year for calculations.)

SELECTED REFERENCES

Beranek, William. Financial implications of lot-size inventory models. *Management Science* 13 (April 1967): 401–408.

Buchan, Joseph and Koenigsberg, Ernest. *Scientific Inventory Management.* Englewood Cliffs, N.J.: Prentice-Hall, 1963.

Friedland, Seymour. *The Economics of Corporate Finance.* Englewood Cliffs, N.J.: Prentice-Hall, 1966, chap. 3.

Hadley, G. and Whitin, T. M. *Analysis of Inventory Systems.* Englewood Cliffs, N.J.: Prentice-Hall, 1963.

Jagetia, L. C. Inventory control is simple as ABC. *Management Accounting* (UK) (September 1976): 305.

Magee, John F. Guides to inventory policy, I. *Harvard Business Review* (January–February 1956): 34; 49–60.

Magee, John F. Guides to inventory policy, II. *Harvard Business Review* (March–April 1956): 49–60.

Magee, John F. Guides to inventory policy, III. *Harvard Business Review* (May–June 1956): 103–116 and 57–70.

Magee, John F. and Meal, Harlan C. Inventory management and standards. In *The Treasurer's Handbook*, J. Fred Weston and Maurice B. Goudzwaard, eds. Homewood, Ill.: Dow Jones-Irwin, 1976, pp. 496–542.

Snyder, Arthur. Principles of inventory management. *Financial Executive* 32 (April 1964).

Starr, Martin K. and Miller, David W. *Inventory Control: Theory and Practice.* Englewood Cliffs, N.J.: Prentice-Hall, 1962.

Vienott, Arthur F. Jr. The status of mathematical inventory theory. *Management Science* 12 (July 1966): 745–777.

Wagner, Harvey M. *Principles of Operations Research–with Applications to Managerial Decisions.* Englewood Cliffs, N.J.: Prentice-Hall, 1969, chaps. 9 and 19, and app. 2.

Appendix B to Chapter 7:

Cash Management Models[1]

Stock-type models have been constructed to aid the financial manager in determining his firm's optimum cash balances. Four such models – those developed by Baumol, Miller and Orr, Beranek, and White and Norman are presented in this appendix.

BAUMOL MODEL

The classic article on cash management by William J. Baumol[2] applies the EOQ model to the cash management problem. Although Baumol's article emphasized the macroeconomic implications for monetary theory, he recognized the implications for business finance and set the stage for further work in this area. In essence, Baumol recognized the fundamental similarities of stocks and cash from a financial viewpoint. In the case of stocks, there are ordering and stock-out costs that make it expensive to keep stocks at a nil level by placing orders for immediate requirements only. But there are also costs involved with *holding* and an optimal policy balances off the opposing costs of ordering and holding stock.

With cash and securities the situation is very similar. There are order costs in the form of clerical work and brokerage fees when making transfers between the cash account and an investment portfolio. On the other side of the coin, there are holding costs consisting of interest forgone when large cash balances are held to avoid the costs of making transfers. Further, there are also costs associated with running out of cash, just as there are in the case of stocks. As with stocks, there is an optimal cash balance that minimizes these costs.

In its most operational form, the Baumol model assumes that a firm's cash balances behave, over time, in a sawtooth manner, as shown in Figure 7B–1. Receipts come in at periodic intervals, such as time 0, 1, 2, 3 and so forth; payments occur continuously throughout the periods. Since the model assumes certainty, the firm can adopt an optimal policy that calls for investing £I in a short-term investment portfolio at the beginning of each period, then withdrawing £C from the portfolio and placing it in the cash account at regular intervals during the period. The model must, of course, take into account both the costs of investment transactions and the costs of holding cash balances.

The decision variables facing the financial manager for a single period can be illustrated in Figure 7B–2. At the beginning of the period, he has an amount of cash equal to T. A portion of the initial cash, $R = T - I$, is retained in the form of cash, and the balance, I, is invested in a portfolio of short-term liquid assets that earns a rate of return, i. The retained cash, R, is sufficient to meet payments during the period from t_0 to t_1. At time t_1, an additional £C will be transferred from the investment portfolio to the cash account to cover payments for the

1. We would like to acknowledge the assistance of Richard A. Samuelson in the preparation of this appendix.
2. William J. Baumol, The transactions demand for cash: an inventory theoretic approach, *Quarterly Journal of Economics* 66 (November 1952), pp. 545–556.

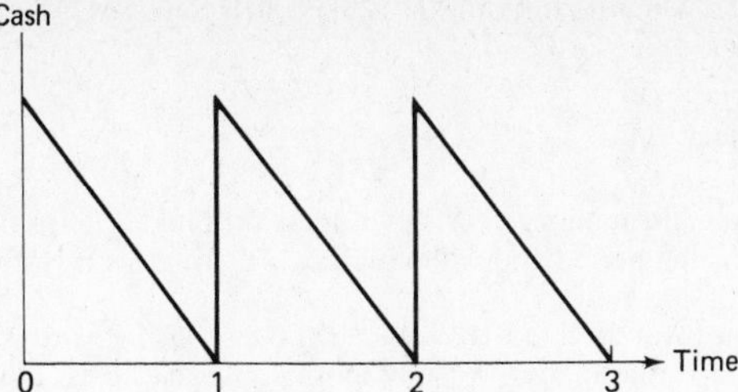

Figure 7B–1 *Baumol's Pattern of Receipts and Payments.*

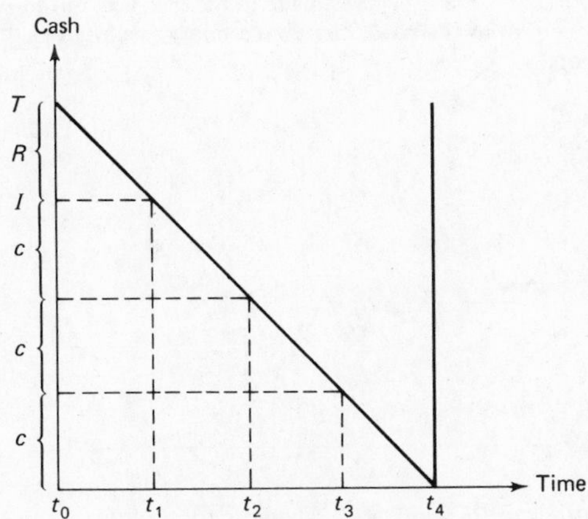

Figure 7B–2 *Baumol's Transfers from Securities to Cash.*

period from t_1 to t_2; C will again be withdrawn at time t_2 and t_3. At t_4, receipts of £T again flow into the cash account, and the same process is repeated during the following period.

If the disbursements are assumed to be continuous, then $R = £(T-I)$ withheld from the initial cash receipt will serve to meet payments during $(T-I)/T$, a fraction of the period between receipts. Further, since the average cash holding for that time will be $(T-I)/2$, the interest cost (opportunity cost) of withholding that money will be

$$\left(\frac{T-I}{2}\right)i\left(\frac{T-I}{T}\right),$$

where i is the interest rate on invested funds. A brokerage fee is required to invest the £I invested, and this fee is equal to $b_d + k_d I$, where b_d and k_d are fixed and variable costs, respectively, of making deposits (investments).

The cost of obtaining cash for the remainder of the period is found, similarly, to be

$$\left(\frac{C}{2}\right)i\left(\frac{I}{T}\right)+(b_w+k_w C)\frac{I}{C}.$$

The first term is the interest (opportunity) cost of holding the average amount $C/2$ of cash over the sub-period, and the second term is the brokerage cost of making withdrawals from the investment account.

Combining these component costs, the total cost function is given by

$$Z=\left(\frac{T-I}{2}\right)i\left(\frac{T-I}{T}\right)+b_d+k_d I+\left(\frac{C}{2}\right)i\left(\frac{I}{T}\right)+(b_w+k_w C)\frac{I}{C}. \tag{7B–1}$$

The optimal value for C is found by differentiating equation 7B–1 with respect to C and setting the derivative equal to nil. This gives

$$C=\sqrt{\frac{2b_w T}{i}}. \tag{7B–2}$$

R, the optimum cash balance to withhold from the initial receipt, is found by differentiating equation 7B–1 with respect to I, obtaining

$$R = T - I = C + T\left(\frac{k_w + k_d}{i}\right). \tag{7B–3}$$

The financial manager, in order to minimize costs, will then withhold £R from the initial receipts to cover payments for the beginning of the period and will withdraw £C from his investment portfolio I/C times per period.

While the Baumol model captures the essential elements of the problem, its restrictive assumptions about the behaviour of cash inflows and outflows are probably more applicable to an individual's situation than to a business firm's. For the firm, inflows are likely to be less lumpy, and outflows are likely to be less smooth. Instead, the behaviour of cash balances might resemble the pattern of Figure 7B–3. Daily changes in the cash balance may be up or down, following an irregular and somewhat unpredictable pattern. When the balance drifts upwards for some length of time, a point is reached at which the financial officer orders a transfer of cash to the investment portfolio, and the cash balance is returned to some lower level. When disbursements exceed receipts for some period of time, investments are sold and a transfer is made to the cash account to restore the cash balance to a higher level. If this particular behaviour is typical, then the certainty assumptions of the Baumol model are too restrictive to make it operational.

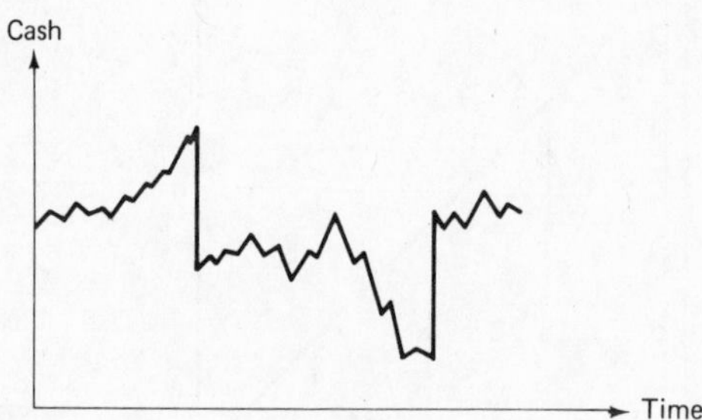

Figure 7B–3 *Realistic Pattern of Receipts and Payments for a Firm.*

MILLER-ORR MODEL

Merton Miller and Daniel Orr[3] expanded the Baumol model by incorporating a stochastic generating process for periodic changes in cash balances so that the cash pattern resembles that shown in Figure 7B–3. In contrast to the completely deterministic assumptions of the Baumol model, Miller and Orr assume that net cash flows behave as if they were generated by a 'stationary random walk'. This means that changes in the cash balance over a given period are random, in both size and direction, and form a normal distribution as the number of periods observed increases. The model allows for a priori knowledge, however, that changes at a certain time have a greater probability of being either positive or negative.

The Miller-Orr model is designed to determine the time and size of transfers between an investment account and the cash account according to a decision process illustrated in Figure 7B–4. Changes in cash balances are allowed to go up until they reach some level h at time t_1; they are then reduced to level z, the 'return point', by investing £$(h-z)$ in the investment portfolio. Next, the cash balance wanders aimlessly until it reaches the minimum balance point, r, at t_2, at which time enough earning assets are sold to return the cash balance to its return point, z. The model is based on a cost function similar to Baumol's, and it includes elements for the cost of making transfers to and from cash for the opportunity cost of holding cash. The upper limit, h, which cash balances should not be allowed to surpass, and the return point, z, to which the balance is returned after every transfer either to or from the cash account, are computed so as to minimize the cost function. The lower limit is assumed to be given, and it could be the minimum balance required by the banks in which the cash is deposited.

The cost function for the Miller-Orr model can be stated as $E(c) = bE(N)/T + iE(M)$, where $E(N)$ = the expected number of transfers between cash and the investment portfolio during the planning period; b = the cost per transfer; T is the number of days in the planning period; $E(M)$ = the expected average daily balance; and i = the daily rate of interest earned on the investments. The objective is to minimize $E(c)$ by choice of the variables h and z, the upper control limit and the return point, respectively.

The solution as derived by Miller and Orr becomes

3. Merton H. Miller and Daniel Orr, A model for the demand for money by firms, *Quarterly Journal of Economics* 80 (August 1966), pp. 413–435.

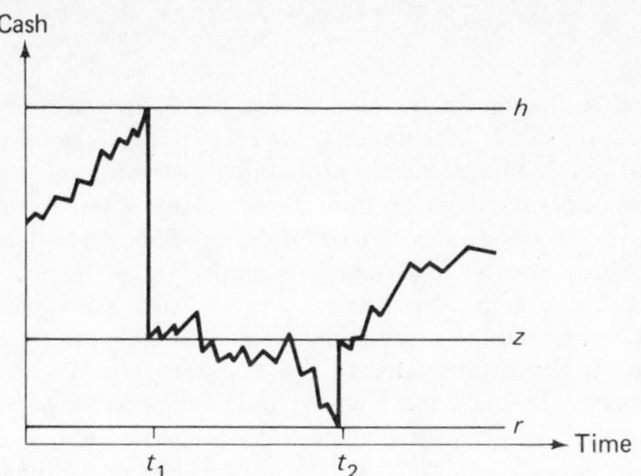

Figure 7B–4 *Miller-Orr Cash Management Model.*

$$z^* = \left(\frac{3b\sigma^2}{4i}\right)^{1/3} \qquad (7B\text{–}4)$$

$$h^* = 3x^*$$

for the special case where p (the probability that cash balances will increase) equals 0.5, and q (the probability that cash balances will decrease) equals 0.5. The variance of the daily changes in the cash balance is represented by σ^2. As would be expected, a higher transfer cost, b, or variance, σ^2, would imply a greater spread between the upper and lower control limits. In the special case where $p = q = 1/2$, the upper control limit will always be three times greater than the return point.

Miller and Orr tested their model by applying it to nine months of data on the daily cash balances and purchases and sales of short-term investments of a large industrial company. When the decisions of the model were compared to those actually made by the accountant of the company, the model was found to produce an average daily cash balance that was about 40 per cent *lower* (£160 000 for the model and £275 000 for the accountant). Looking at it from another side, the model would have been able to match the £275 000 average daily balance with only 80 transactions as compared to the accountant's 112 actual transactions.

As with most stock control models, its performance depends not only on how well the conditional predictions (in this case the expected number of transfers and the expected average cash balance) conform to actuality, but also on how well the parameters are estimated. In this model, b, the transfer cost, is sometimes difficult to estimate. In the study made by Miller and Orr, the order costs included such components as '(a) making two or more long-distance phone calls plus 15 minutes to a half-hour of the assistant accountant's time, (b) typing up and carefully checking an authorization letter with four copies, (c) carrying the original of the letter to be signed by the accountant and (d) carrying the copies to the controller's office where special accounts are opened, the entries are posted and further checks of the arithmetic are made.'[4] These clerical procedures were thought to be in the magnitude of £20 to £50 per order. In the application of their model, however, Miller and Orr did not rely on their estimate for order costs; instead they tested the model using a series of 'assumed' order costs until the model used the same number of transactions as did the accountant. They could then determine the order cost implied by the accountant's own action. The results were then used to evaluate the accountant's performance in managing the cash balances and, as such, provided valuable information to the accountant.

The accountant found, for example, that his action in purchasing securities was often inconsistent. Too often he made small-lot purchases well below the minimum of $h - z$ computed by the model, while at other times he allowed cash balances to drift to as much as double the upper control limit before making a purchase. If it did no more than give the accountant some perspective about his buying and selling activities the model was used successfully.[5]

4. Merton H. Miller and Daniel Orr, *An Application of Control Limit Models to the Management of Corporate Cash Balances*, Proceedings of the Conference on Financial Research and Its Implications for Management, ed. Alexander A. Robichek (New York: Wiley, 1967).
5. For a cash planning approach related to credit decisions by the use of a financial simulation model, see Bernell K. Stone, 'Cash planning and credit-line determination with a financial statement simulator: a cash report on short-term financial planning,' *Journal of Financial and Quantitative Analysis* 8 (November 1973), pp. 711–730.

BERANEK MODEL

William Beranek has devoted a chapter in his text, *Analysis for Financial Decisions*,[6] to the problem of determining the optimal allocation of available funds between the cash balance and marketable securities. His approach differs from Baumol's in that he includes a probability distribution for expected cash flows and a cost function for the loss of cash discounts and deterioration of credit rating when the firm is caught short of cash. The decision variable in Beranek's model is the allocation of funds between cash and investments at the beginning of the period. Withdrawals from investment are assumed possible only at the end of each planning period.

According to Beranek, it is more helpful for the analysis of cash management problems to regard cash *disbursements* as being directly controllable by management and relatively lumpy, and to regard *receipts* as being uncontrollable and continuous. In the certainty case this pattern of cash balance behaviour would be the reverse of the sawtooth pattern assumed by Baumol, and it would look similar to the pattern illustrated in Figure 7B–5. To rationalize this approach one can argue that institutional customs and arrangements might cause cash outflows to be concentrated at periodic intervals. Wages and salaries are ordinarily paid weekly or monthly, credit terms for merchandise purchases may allow payment on the tenth and final days of the month, and other significant outflows such as tax and dividend payments will be concentrated at regular intervals. In so far as cash outflows are controllable and recur in a cyclical manner, the financial manager can predict his needs for cash over a planning period and can invest a portion of the funds that are not expected to be needed during this period.

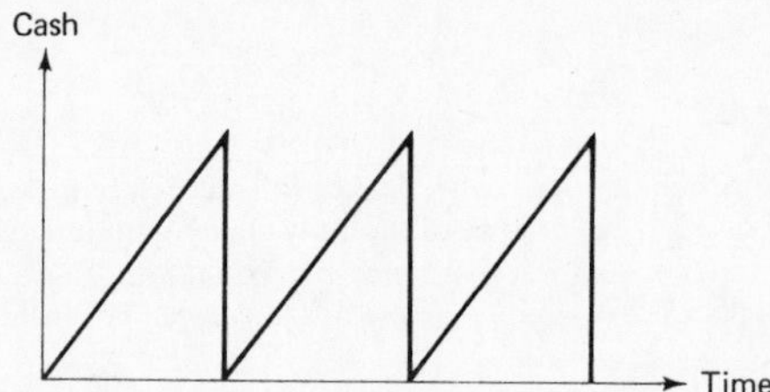

Figure 7B–5 *Beranek's Pattern of Receipts and Payments.*

In Beranek's model, the financial manager is regarded as having total resources of £k available at the beginning of a planning period. He expects his net cash drain (receipts less disbursements) at the end of the period to be £y (either positive or negative), with a probability distribution $g(y)$. His objective of maximizing returns by investment in securities is constrained by transactions costs and the risk of being short of cash when funds are needed for expenditures. 'Short costs' are regarded by Beranek as consisting of cash discounts forgone and the deterioration of the firm's credit rating when it is unable to meet payments in time. It might be more realistic, however, to think of 'short costs' as the cost of borrowing on a line of credit, since the company would undoubtedly prefer short-term borrowing to forgoing cash discounts or allowing its credit rating to deteriorate.

Given the probability distribution of net cash flows, the costs of running short of cash, and the opportunity cost of holding cash balances, Beranek develops a cost function and differentiates it to find the optimal initial cash balance, or the amount of cash that should be on hand at the start of the period. His solution calls for setting the cash balance at a level such that, if this critical level is set, the cumulative probability of running short of cash is equal to the ratio d/a, where d = net return on the investment portfolio and a = incremental cost of being short £1 of cash. Stated in words, this means that the financial manager should continue shifting resources from the opening cash balance to securities until the expectation that the ending cash balance will be below the critical minimum is equal to the ratio of the incremental net return per £1 of investment to the incremental short cost per £1.

WHITE AND NORMAN MODEL

D. J. White and J. M. Norman[7] developed a model for a UK insurance company similar in spirit to the Beranek model. Investment decisions are assumed to be considered periodically, and cash inflows from premiums and outflows for claims and expenses are assumed to fluctuate randomly according to some known distribution. In

6. William Beranek, *Analysis for Financial Decisions* (Homewood, Ill.: Irwin, 1963), pp. 345–387.
7. D. J. White and J. M. Norman, 'Control of cash reserves,' *Operational Research Quarterly* 16, no. 3 (September 1965).

addition, another cash outflow for 'call-offs' by the stockbrokers is assumed to have an independent distribution function. A penalty rate on overdrafts (borrowings), analogous to Beranek's short-cost function, is also included in the model, while transactions costs are ignored (or implicitly considered in the net rate of return on investments). The opening cash balance that maximizes expected wealth at the end of the period is the relevant decision variable. The optimal solution is a function of Beranek's d, the incremental return per £1 of investment, and the interest rate on overdrafts.

A COMPARISON OF THE MODELS

The models described in this appendix differ primarily in the emphasis given to various costs affecting their solutions. The Baumol and Miller-Orr models give critical emphasis to the costs arising from transfers between the cash account and the investment portfolio. They ignore the alternative of borrowing and concentrate on the liquidation of investments to meet the needs for cash outflows. The Beranek and White-Norman models, on the other hand, give critical emphasis to the costs arising from the shortage of cash (the cost of borrowing, from one viewpoint), while transactions costs are only indirectly considered. The latter models ignore the alternatives of liquidating investments to meet cash needs. A model that directly incorporates both the possibility of borrowing and the possibility of holding a portfolio of liquid assets would be desirable, since it is not clear that liquidation of investments would always be preferable to borrowing or vice versa.

Of all the models, the Miller-Orr version appears to be the easiest to implement, if for no other reason than that its decision rules are so simple. Decision models are more likely to be used when their application is easily understood by management. In addition, the Miller-Orr decision model's planning period covers a longer period of time, so it would not have to be revised as often as the Beranek and White-Norman models. In the Beranek and White-Norman versions, information must be fed into the model and a decision derived each time a transfer between cash and securities is being considered. While this must be counted as a disadvantage of these models, it could result in better decisions by making the models more responsive to conditions existing at the time decisions are made.

The Miller-Orr model has an element of flexibility, however, that should not be overlooked. Expectations that cash balances are more likely to either increase or decrease over a given period can be incorporated into the calculation of the optimal values for the decision variables. Thus, if a business is subject to seasonal trends, the optimal control limits can be adjusted for each season by using different values for p and q, the probabilities that cash will increase and decrease, respectively.

The Miller-Orr model is built on the assumption that cash balances behave as if they were generated by a random walk. To the extent that this assumption is erroneous, the model would be of little use to management. If the timing of cash outflows (and perhaps even cash inflows) can be controlled significantly by management, then a model of the Beranek or White-Norman type may be more suitable. In this case, management should not have too much difficulty in forming the subjective probability distributions that are needed for these models. In reality, it would probably be true that cash flows are partly random and partly controllable, so the applicability of any of the models can be determined only by testing them with actual data.

It should be remembered that decision models of the type discussed in this appendix are not intended to be applied blindly. There are, of course, difficulties in estimating parameters and probabilities, as has been pointed out. But even more important, there is often information available to the financial manager that is not directly incorporated into the model. Thus a model, acting ignorantly and unaware of other relevant information, might provide completely erroneous advice. On the other hand, despite their restrictive assumptions and errors, decision models often perform very well if they capture the essential elements in a decision problem. They should not, however, be used as the final answer to any particular decision; rather, cash management models should be used as a guide to intelligent decision-making, tempered with the manager's own good judgement.

SELECTED REFERENCES

Archer, Stephen H. A model for the determination of firm cash balance. *Journal of Financial and Quantitative Analysis* 1 (March 1966): 1–11.

Baumol, William J. The transactions demand for cash: an inventory theoretic approach. *Quarterly Journal of Economics* 65 (November 1952): 545–556.

Budin, Morris and Van Handel, Robert J. A rule-of-thumb theory of cash holdings by firm. *Journal of Financial and Quantitative Analysis* 10 (March 1975): 85–108.

Calman, Robert F. *Linear Programming and Cash Management/CASH ALPHA*. Cambridge, Mass,: M.I.T., 1968.

Constantinides, George M. Stochastic cash management with fixed and proportional transaction costs. *Management Science* 22 (August 1976): 1320–1331.

Daellenbach, Hans G. Are cash management optimization models worthwhile? *Journal of Financial and Quantitative Analysis* 9 (September 1974): 607–626.

Eppen, Gary D. and Fama, Eugene F. Cash balance and simple dynamic portfolio problems with proportional costs. *International Economic Review* 10 (June 1969): 110–133.

Miller, Merton H. and Orr, Daniel. A model of the demand for money by firms. *Quarterly Journal of Economics* 80 (August 1966): 413–435.

Orgler, Yair E. *Cash Management*. Belmont, Calif.: Wadsworth Publishing Co., 1970.

Sethi, Suresh P. and Thompson, Gerald L. Application of mathematical control theory to finance: modeling simple dynamic cash balance problems. *Journal of Financial and Quantitative Analysis* 5 (December 1970): 381–394.

Chapter 8

Major Sources and Forms of Short-term Financing

In Chapter 6 we discussed the maturity structure of the firm's debt and showed how this structure can affect both risk and expected returns. However, a variety of short-term sources of finance are available to the firm, and the financial manager must know the advantages and disadvantages of each. Accordingly, in the present chapter we take up the main forms of short-term finance, considering both the characteristics and the sources of this credit.

Short-term finance is defined as finance originally scheduled for repayment within one year. We discuss the three major sources of funds with short maturities in this chapter. Ranked in descending order by volume of credit supplied to business, the main sources of short-term financing are (a) trade credit between firms, (b) loans from commercial banks and (c) bills of exchange.

TRADE CREDIT[1]

In the ordinary course of events, a firm buys its supplies and materials on credit from other firms, recording the debt as trade creditors. Trade credit is the largest single category of short-term finance, and it represents about 60 per cent of the current liabilities of non-financial companies. This percentage is somewhat larger for small firms; because small companies may not qualify for financing from other sources, they rely rather heavily on trade credit.

Trade credit is a 'spontaneous' source of financing in that it arises from ordinary business transactions. For example, suppose a firm makes average purchases of £2000 a day on 30 days' credit. On the average it will owe 30 times £2000 or £60 000 to its suppliers.

1. In Chapter 7 we discussed trade credit from the point of view of minimizing investment in current assets. In the present chapter we look at 'the other side of the coin', viewing trade credit as a source of financing rather than as a use of financing. In Chapter 7, the use of trade credit by our customers resulted in an asset investment called trade debtors. In the present chapter, the use of trade credit gives rise to short-term obligations, generally called trade creditors.

If its sales and, consequently, its purchases, double trade creditors will also double to £120 000. The firm will have spontaneously generated an additional £60 000 of financing. Similarly, if the terms of credit are extended from 30 to 40 days, trade creditors will expand from £60 000 to £80 000; thus, lengthening the credit period, as well as expanding sales and purchases, generates additional financing.

Credit terms

The terms of sales, or *credit terms*, describe the payment obligation of the buyer. In the following discussion we outline the four main factors that influence the length of credit terms.

Economic nature of product

Commodities with high sales turnover are sold on relatively short credit terms; the buyer resells the product rapidly, generating cash that enables him to pay the supplier. Groceries have a high turnover, but perishability also plays a role. The credit extended for fresh fruits and vegetables might run from five to ten days, whereas the credit extended on tinned fruits and vegetables would more likely be 15 to 30 days. Terms for items that have a slow retail turnover, such as jewellery, may run six months or longer.

Seller circumstances

Financially weak sellers must require cash or exceptionally short credit terms. For example, farmers sell livestock to meatpacking companies on a cash basis. In many industries, variations in credit terms can be used as a sales promotion device. Although the use of credit as a selling device could endanger sound credit management, the practice does occur, especially when the seller's industry has excess capacity. Also, a large seller could use his position to impose relatively short credit terms, a situation which is often exacerbated during a period of credit squeeze.

Buyer circumstances

In general, financially sound retailers who sell on credit may, in turn, receive slightly longer terms. Some classes of retailers regarded as selling in particularly risky areas (such as clothing) receive extended credit terms, but they are offered large discounts to encourage early payment.

Cash discounts

A cash discount is a reduction in price based on payment within a specified period. The costs of not taking cash discounts often exceed the rate of interest at which the buyer can borrow, so it is important that a firm be cautious in its use of trade credit as a source of financing – it could be quite expensive. If the firm borrows and takes the cash discount, the period during which trade creditors remain on the books is reduced. The effective length of credit is thus influenced by the size of discounts offered.

CONCEPT OF 'NET CREDIT'

Trade credit has double-edged significance for the firm. It is a source of credit for financing purchases, and it is a use of funds to the extent that the firm finances credit sales to customers. For example, if, on the average, a firm sells £3000 of goods a day with an average collection period of 40 days, at any balance sheet date it will have trade debtors of approximately £120 000.

If the same firm buys £2000 worth of materials a day and the balance is outstanding for 20 days, trade creditors will average £40 000. *The firm is extending net credit of £80 000, the difference between trade debtors and trade creditors.*

Large firms and well-financed firms of all sizes tend to be net suppliers of trade credit; small firms and under-capitalized firms of all sizes tend to be net users of trade credit. It is impossible to generalize about whether it is better to be a net supplier or a net user of trade credit – the choice depends upon the firm's own circumstances and conditions, and the various costs and benefits of receiving and using trade credit must be analysed as described here and in Chapter 6.

Advantages of trade credit as a source of financing

Trade credit, a customary part of doing business in most industries, is convenient and informal. A firm that does not qualify for credit from a financial institution may receive trade credit because previous experience has familiarized the seller with the credit-worthiness of his customer. As the seller knows the merchandising practices of the industry, he is usually in a good position to judge the capacity of his customer and the risk of selling to him on credit. The amount of trade credit fluctuates with the buyer's purchases, subject to any credit limits that may be operative.

Whether trade credit costs more or less than other forms of financing is a moot question. Sometimes trade credit can be surprisingly expensive to the buyer. The user often does not have any alternative forms of financing available, and the costs to the buyer may be commensurate with the risks to the seller. But in some instances trade credit is used simply because the user does not realize how expensive it is. In such circumstances, careful financial analysis may lead to the substitution of alternative forms of financing for trade credit.

At the other extreme, trade credit may represent a virtual subsidy or sales promotion device offered by the seller. The authors know, for example, of cases where manufacturers quite literally supplied *all* the financing for new firms by selling on credit terms substantially longer than those of the new company. In one instance a manufacturer, eager to obtain a dealership in a particular area, made a loan to the new company to cover operating expenses during the initial phases and geared the payment of trade creditors to cash receipts. Even in such instances, however, the buying firm must be careful that it is not really paying a hidden financing cost in the form of higher product prices than could be obtained elsewhere. Extending credit involves a cost to the selling firm, and this firm may well be raising its own prices to offset the 'free' credit it extends.

SHORT-TERM FINANCING BY COMMERCIAL BANKS

Commercial bank lending is second in importance to trade credit as a form of short-term financing. Banks occupy a pivotal position in the short-term and intermediate-term money markets. Their influence is greater than the amounts they lend would suggest because they provide non-spontaneous funds. As the financing needs of a firm increase it asks the bank to provide additional funds. If the request is denied the alternative could be to slow down the rate of growth or cut back operations.

Characteristics of loans from commercial banks

In the following sections the main characteristics of lending patterns of commercial banks are briefly described.

Forms of loans

A single *loan* obtained from a bank by a business firm is not different in principle from a loan obtained by an individual. In fact it is often difficult to distinguish a bank loan to a small business from a personal loan. Repayment of bank loans is usually made in instalments throughout the life of the loan.

A bank *overdraft* is a formal or an informal understanding between the bank and the borrower concerning the maximum amount by which the borrower may overdraw his account. For example, a bank manager may indicate an overdraft limit of £50 000 to a particular firm. Although the firm may borrow up to and including this limit, interest is only charged on the total amount outstanding at the end of each day's business. A small commitment fee is usually paid by the firm to compensate the bank for the administrative costs of the overdraft facility.

Maturity

Commercial banks concentrate on the short-term lending market. If, however, overdrafts are continually renewed this means that in practice banks are providing long- or medium-term finance.

Security

If a potential borrower is a questionable credit risk, or if his financing needs exceed the amount that the bank manager considers to be prudent on an unsecured basis, some form of security is required. The most widely used form of company security required by a bank tends to be the floating charge, which is, generally speaking, the least restrictive on the borrower.

Size of customers

Although the range of services offered by banks to their customers has increased in recent years the small firm in Britain is still at a disadvantage compared with its counterpart in Europe or the United States. Only 10 per cent of total assets of British companies are financed by the banking system. Small firms are at a disadvantage compared with larger firms because the larger firm often has alternative sources of funds whereas the smaller firm is restricted mainly to bank finance.

Cost

Most loans from commercial banks have recently cost from 7 to 13 per cent, with the effective rate varying from 3 to 5 per cent over the London Inter-bank Offered Rate (LIBOR), depending upon the characteristics of the firm and the level of interest rates in the economy. For nationalized industries or 'blue chip' companies the rate of interest on bank loans is a little lower than that charged to most companies. On the other hand a small firm with below-average financial ratios may have to provide collateral security and pay 1 per cent or so more than normal firms.

Repayment of bank loans

Commercial banks attempt to prevent firms from using bank loans as a source of permanent financing. In order to ensure that this does not occur banks will tend to review overdraft facilities at regular intervals. Despite this arrangement it is still the case that many British firms have a permanent overdraft facility and see the overdraft as a 'natural' part of their financing requirements. As mentioned in Chapter 7, it is not the practice of banks arbitrarily to call in overdrafts from customers conducting their business in a proper manner.

Interest payments

Determination of the effective or true rate of interest on a loan depends on the stated rate of interest and the method of charging interest by the lender. If the interest is paid at the maturity of the loan, the stated rate of interest is the effective rate of interest. For example on a £10 000 loan for one year at 7 per cent the interest is £700.
Loan interest paid at maturity:

$$\frac{\text{interest}}{\text{borrowed amount}} = \frac{£700}{£10\,000} = 7\%$$

Discounted interest

If the bank deducts the interest in advance (discounts the loan) the effective rate of interest is increased. On the £10 000 loan for one year at 7 per cent, the discount is £700 and the borrower obtains the use of only £9300. The effective rate of interest is 7.5 per cent.
Discounted loan:

$$\frac{\text{interest}}{\text{borrowed amount} - \text{interest}} = \frac{£700}{£9300} = 7.5\%$$

Instalment loan

If the loan is paid in 12 monthly instalments but the interest is calculated on the original balance then the effective rate of interest is even higher. The borrower has the full amount of the money only during the first month and by the last month he has already repaid eleven-twelfths of the loan. Thus, our hypothetical borrower pays £700 for the use of about half of the amount he receives. The amount received is £10 000 or £9300, depending on the method of charging interest, but the *average* amount outstanding during the year is only £5000 or £4650. If interest is paid at maturity the approximate effective rate on an instalment loan is calculated as follows:

$$\text{Interest rate on original amount of instalment loan} = \frac{£700}{£5000} = 14\%$$

Under the discounting method the effective cost of the instalment loan would be approximately 15 per cent.

$$\text{Interest rate on discounted instalment loan} = \frac{£700}{£4650} = 15.05\%$$

The point to note here is that interest is paid on the original amount of the loan, not on the amount actually outstanding (the declining balance), and this causes the effective interest rate to be approximately double the stated rate.

Choice of bank

Banks differ in their assessment of the riskiness of individual customers. The effect of this would be that different banks, or even different branches of the same bank, would charge different rates of interest on the same loan. Banks also differ in respect of the charges made for the services provided. If a customer has a large number of payments into and out of his bank account the service charge may be much greater than the interest charge on overdrafts.

BILLS OF EXCHANGE

Bills of exchange are issued mainly by large firms and sold primarily to the discount houses. A bill is defined in Section 3 of the Bills of Exchange Act 1882 as 'an unconditional order in writing addressed by one person to another, signed by the person giving it, requiring the person to whom it is addressed to pay on demand, or at a fixed or determinable future time, a sum certain in money to or to the order of a specified person or bearer'.

This form of financing, which was considered by the Radcliffe Committee in 1959 to have 'irreversibly shrunk', has been growing rapidly in recent years. Although several factors have contributed to this resurgence the most dominant factor has been the existence of credit squeezes which have led business firms faced with shrinking availability of bank finance to resort to other means of short-term finance.

Maturity and cost

Normally bills of exchange are drawn for a period of three months (91 days) but in recent years one- and two-month bills have become more common. The normal maximum term to maturity is six months.

Rates of interest charged on bills of exchange vary. Those charged on eligible bank bills[2] are lower than those charged on fine trade bills. The normal rate will be slightly higher

---

2. An eligible bank bill is a bill which is accepted as collateral against loans made by the Bank of England to the discount houses. It is regarded as eligible if it has been accepted by one of the London Accepting Houses or by a member of the Clearing Banks. Some overseas banks may also endorse bills which then become eligible paper.

than the Treasury bill rate for that week in the case of eligible bills and higher still in the case of fine trade bills.

Use

Bills of exchange may be sold to the London discount houses who may rediscount them if they wish. The existence of a ready, well-established market in bills is a great advantage to British firms. The market, which was originally concerned mainly with bills which were used to finance external trade, has increasingly handled bills which are issued to finance internal trade in recent years.

Appraisal of use

The market in bills of exchange has several advantages:

1. Because it is a well-established market, and the risks of default are minimal, a considerable number of British companies use this market as a method of provision of short-term finance.
2. It provides funds at a relatively low rate of interest.
3. The borrower avoids the inconvenience and expense of having to make financing arrangements with a number of financial institutions.

A basic limitation of the discount market is that funds are limited to those funds available to the discount houses (the major suppliers of funds). A further problem is that the market is impersonal; bills of exchange can be rediscounted many times before they reach maturity. The relationship between a customer and his bank manager, on the other hand, is of a more personal nature; banks are often willing to provide funds which enable firms to weather temporary storms.

USE OF SECURITY IN SHORT-TERM FINANCING

Given a choice, it is ordinarily better to borrow on an unsecured basis, as the book-keeping costs of secured loans are often high. However, it frequently happens that a potential borrower's credit rating is not sufficiently strong to justify the loan. If the loan can be secured by the borrower's putting up some form of collateral to be claimed by the lender in the event of default, then the lender may extend credit to an otherwise unacceptable firm. Similarly, a firm that could borrow on an unsecured basis may elect to use security if it finds that this will induce lenders to quote a lower interest rate.

Several different kinds of collateral can be employed – marketable securities, land or buildings, equipment, stocks, and trade debtors. Marketable securities make excellent collateral, but few firms hold such portfolios. Similarly, real property (land and buildings) and equipment are good forms of collateral, but they are generally used as security for long-term loans.

FINANCING OF TRADE DEBTORS

The financing of trade debtors may involve either the assignment of debts (invoice discounting) or the selling of debts (factoring). Invoice discounting is characterized by the fact that the lender not only has a lien on the debts but also has recourse to the borrower (seller); if the person or firm that bought the goods does not pay, the selling firm must take the loss. In other words, the risk of default on the trade debtors pledged remains with the borrower. Also the buyer of the goods is not ordinarily notified about the pledging of the debts. Factoring, on the other hand, is normally undertaken 'without recourse'. That is, the factor must bear the loss in the event that the person or firm which bought the goods does not pay. The financial institutions which lend on the security of trade debtors are generally subsidiary companies of banks, such as Credit Factoring International Ltd, which is a wholly owned subsidiary of the National Westminster Bank.

Factoring, or selling trade debtors, involves the purchase of trade debtors by the lender normally without recourse to the borrower (seller). The buyer of the goods is notified of the transfer and makes payment directly to the lender. Since the factoring firm assumes the risk of default on bad debts, it must do the credit checking. Accordingly, factors provide not only money but also a credit department for the borrower. Incidentally, the same financial institutions that make loans against pledged debtors often serve as factors. Thus, depending on the circumstances and the wishes of the borrower, a financial institution will provide either form of debt financing.

Procedure for invoice discounting

The financing of trade debtors is initiated by a legally binding agreement between the seller of the goods and the financing institution. The agreement sets forth in detail the procedures to be followed and the legal obligations of both parties. Once the working relationship has been established, the seller periodically remits copy invoices to the invoice discounting company. Thus, the client has the option on which debts it wishes to sell to the finance company, subject to the latter's prior approval. Invoices of companies that do not meet the lender's credit standards are not accepted for pledging. The financial institution seeks to protect itself at every phase of the operation. Selection of sound invoices is the essential first step in safeguarding the financial institution. If the buyer of the goods does not pay the invoice, the lender still has recourse against the seller of the goods. However, if many buyers default, the seller may be unable to meet his obligation to the financial institution.

Additional protection is afforded the lender in that the loan will generally be for less than 100 per cent of the invoiced debts; for example, the lender may advance the selling firm 75 per cent of the amount of the invoiced debts, with the balance paid on the average date of customers' settlement after deducting the finance company's charge plus the value of any bad debts unrecovered.

Procedure for factoring trade debtors

The procedure for factoring is somewhat different from that for invoicing. The factoring company will make an appraisal of the credit-worthiness of each customer of the seller and set a credit limit for each of these customers. Once a sale has been made the invoice will be stamped to notify the buyer to make payment direct to the factor. Provided the credit limit has not been exceeded by the sale, the factor will then become liable for any bad debts arising subsequently. The factor performs three functions in carrying out the normal procedure as outlined above: (a) credit checking, (b) lending and (c) risk bearing. The seller can select various combinations of these functions by changing provisions in the factoring agreement. For example, a small or a medium-sized firm can avoid establishing a credit department. The factor's service might well be less costly than a department that may have excess capacity for the firm's credit volume. At the same time, if the firm uses part of the time of a non-credit specialist to perform credit checking, lack of education, training and experience may result in excessive losses. The seller may utilize the factor to perform the credit-checking and risk-taking functions but not the lending function. The following procedure is carried out on receipt of a £10 000 order. The factor checks and approves the invoices. The goods are shipped on terms of net payment within 30 days. Payment is made to the factor, who remits to the seller. But assume that the factor has received only £5000 by the end of the credit period. He must remit £10 000 to the seller (less his fee, of course). If the remaining £5000 is never paid, the factor sustains a £5000 loss.

Now consider the more typical situation in which the factor performs a lending function by making payment in advance of collection. The goods are shipped and, even though payment is not due for 30 days, the factor immediately makes funds available to the seller. Suppose £10 000 of goods are shipped; the factoring commission for credit checking is $2\frac{1}{2}$ per cent of the invoice price, or £250, and the interest expense is computed at a 9 per cent annual rate on the invoice balance, or £75.[3] The seller's accounting entry is as follows:

Cash	£9175	
Interest expense	75	
Factoring commission	250	
Reserve due from factor on collection of account	500	
Trade debtors		£10 000

The £500 'due from factor on collection of account' in the entry is a reserve established by the factor to cover disputes between sellers and buyers on damaged goods, goods returned by the buyers to the seller, and failure to make outright sale of goods. The amount is paid to the seller firm when the factor collects on the account.

Factoring is normally a continuous process instead of the single cycle described above. The seller of the goods receives orders. He transmits the purchase orders to the factor for approval. On approval, the goods are shipped. The factor advances the money to the seller. The buyers pay the factor when payment is due, and the factor periodically remits any excess reserve to the seller of the goods. Once a routine is established, a continuous circular flow of goods and funds takes place between the seller, the buyers of the goods and the factor. Thus, once the factoring agreement is in force, funds from this source are spontaneous.

Cost of trade debtors

Invoice discounting and factoring services are convenient and advantageous, but they can be costly. An interest charge is made on funds advanced by invoice discounts at a rate of 3 to 6 per cent above bank rate or Finance Houses Association base rate. The cost of factoring includes interest of 1 to 4 per cent above bank rate on the unpaid balance of funds advanced, together with a service charge of 1 to $2\frac{1}{2}$ per cent of the gross annual turnover.

---

3. Since the interest is for only one month, we take one-twelfth of the stated rate, 9 per cent, and multiply this by the £10 000 invoice price:

$\frac{1}{12} \times 0.09 \times £10\,000 = £75$

Note that the effective rate of interest is really above 9 per cent because a discounting procedure is used and the borrower does not get the full £10 000 in many instances. However, the factoring contract calls for interest to be computed on the invoice price less the factoring commission and the reserve account.

Evaluation of debtors financing

It cannot be said categorically that trade debtors financing is always either a good or a poor method of raising funds for an individual business. Among the advantages is, first, the flexibility of this source of financing. As the firm's sales expand and more financing is needed, a larger volume of invoices is generated automatically. Because the money value of invoices varies directly with sales, the amount of readily available financing increases. Second, debtors or invoices provide security for a loan that a firm might otherwise be unable to obtain. Third, factoring provides the services of a credit department that might otherwise be available to the firm only under much more expensive conditions.

Financing of trade debtors also has disadvantages. Firstly, when invoices are numerous and relatively small in value the administrative costs involved may render this method of financing inconvenient and expensive. Lenders are aware of this, however, and normally require average invoice values to be over £100. Secondly, the firm is using a highly liquid asset as security. For a long time, finance of trade debtors was frowned upon by most trade creditors. In fact, such financing was regarded as confession of a firm's unsound financial position. It is no longer regarded in this light, and many sound firms engage in invoice discounting or factoring. However, the traditional attitude causes some trade creditors to refuse to sell on credit to a firm that is factoring or invoice discounting on the grounds that his practice removes one of the most liquid of the firm's assets and, accordingly, weakens the position of other creditors. Because of this attitude a firm may wish to use a form of confidential invoice factoring, allowing it to act as agents for the factor in receiving payment from debtors who are not themselves informed of the existence of the factoring arrangement.

Future use of financing trade debtors

We might make a prediction at this point: in the future, trade debtors financing will increase in relative importance. Computer technology is rapidly advancing towards the point where credit records of individuals and firms can be kept in computer memory units. Systems have been devised so that a retailer can have on hand a unit that, when an individual's magnetic credit card is inserted into a box, gives a signal that his credit is 'good' and that a finance company is willing to 'buy' the debt created when the shop completes the sale. The cost of handling invoices will be greatly reduced over present-day costs because the new systems will be so highly automated. This will make it possible to use trade debtor financing for very small sales, and it will reduce the cost of all debtor financing. The net result will be a marked expansion of trade debtor financing.

SUMMARY

Short-term credit is defined as debt originally scheduled for repayment within one year. This chapter has discussed the three major sources of short-term credit – trade credit between firms, loans from commercial banks, and bills of exchange – as well as methods of securing this credit.

Trade credit

Trade credit, represented by creditors' accounts, is the largest single category of short-term credit and is especially important for smaller firms. Trade credit is a spontaneous source of financing in that it arises from ordinary business transactions; as sales increase, so does the supply of financing from trade creditors.

Bank credit

Bank credit occupies a pivotal position in the short-term money market. Banks provide the marginal credit that allows firms to expand more rapidly than is possible through retained earnings and trade credit; to be denied bank credit often means that a firm must slow its rate of growth.

Bank interest rates are quoted in three ways: regular compound interest, discount interest, and instalment interest. Regular interest needs no adjustment – it is 'correct' as stated. Discount interest requires a small upward adjustment to make it comparable to regular compound interest rates. Instalment interest rates require a large adjustment, and frequently the true interest rate is double the quoted rate for an instalment loan.

Bills of exchange

Bank loans are personal in the sense that the financial manager meets with the banker, discusses the terms of the loan with him, and reaches an agreement that requires direct and personal negotiation. Bills of exchange, however, although they are physically quite similar to a bank loan, are sold in a broad, impersonal market.

Only the very strongest firms are able to use the discount market – very large firms are often able to have their bills of exchange endorsed by merchant banks who are not members of the Accepting Houses Association. Small firms are unlikely to obtain acceptance from an accepting house and they often find it difficult to obtain endorsement from other merchant banks even though the rate of interest on a fine trade bill is higher than that paid on a bill eligible for use as collateral at the Bank of England. In any case, the higher cost of financing by means of a fine trade bill often acts as a deterrent to smaller firms.

Use of security in short-term financing

The most common form of collateral used for short-term credit is trade debtors. Trade debtors financing can be done either by pledging the debts or by selling them outright, which is frequently called factoring. When the debts are pledged, the borrower retains the risk that the person or firm who owes the debt will not pay; in factoring, this risk is typically passed on to the lender. Because the factor takes the risk of default, he will investigate the purchaser's credit; therefore, the factor can perform three services – a lending function, a risk-bearing function and a credit-checking function. When debts are pledged, the lender typically performs only the first of these three functions. The most common form of security required by a bank tends to be a floating charge on all the assets of the business.

QUESTIONS

8–1. It is inevitable that firms will obtain a certain amount of their financing in the form of trade credit which is, to some extent, a free source of funds. What are some other factors that lead firms to use trade credit?

8–2. Why do many firms prefer bank loans to the provision of finance by means of bills of exchange?

8–3. Trade credit has an explicit interest rate cost if discounts are available but not taken. There are also some intangible costs associated with the failure to take discounts. Discuss.

8–4. A large manufacturing firm that had been selling its products on a 30 day credit basis changed its credit terms to a 90 day basis. What changes might be anticipated on the balance sheets of the manufacturer and its customers?

8–5. The availability of bank credit is more important to small firms than to large ones. Why is this so?

8–6. Indicate whether each of the following changes would raise or lower the cost of a firm's trade credit, and why this occurs:
(a) The firm eases up on its credit standards in order to increase sales.
(b) The firm institutes a policy of refusing to make credit sales if the amount of the purchase (invoice) is below £100. Previously, about 40 per cent of all invoices were below £100.
(c) The firm agrees to give recourse to the finance company for all defaults.
(d) The firm, which already has a recourse arrangement, is merged into a larger, stronger company.

8–7. 'A firm that factors its trade debtors will look better in a ratio analysis than one that employs invoice discounting.' Discuss.

8–8. Name the industries, together with your reasons for doing so, that might be expected to use each of the following forms of credit:
(a) bills of exchange
(b) factoring
(c) discounting
(d) bank loan
(e) none of these

PROBLEMS

8–1. What is the equivalent annual interest rate that would be lost if a firm failed to take the cash discount under each of the following terms?
(a) 1% discount within 15 days, otherwise net within 30.
(b) 2% discount within 10 days, otherwise net within 60.
(c) 3% discount within 10 days, otherwise net within 60.
(d) 2% discount within 10 days, otherwise net within 40.
(e) 1% discount within 10 days, otherwise net within 40.

8–2. *Shelby Saw Company Balance Sheet.*

Total shareholders' funds	£900 000	Land and buildings	£700 000
Mortgage debenture	600 000	Plant and machinery	500 000
Short-term loan	500 000	Stocks	1 400 000
Trade creditors	600 000	Trade debtors	300 000
Accruals	400 000	Cash	100 000
	£3 000 000		£3 000 000

The Shelby Saw Company had sales of £4 million last year and earned a 3 per cent after-tax return on total assets. Although it purchases on 30 days' credit, creditors represent 60 days' purchases. The managing director is seeking to increase bank borrowings to enable the company to become up to date in meeting its trade obligations (that is, reduce to 30 days).
(a) How much bank financing is needed to eliminate overdue creditors?
(b) As a bank manager would you make the loan? Why?

8–3. The Shandow Insulation Company has been growing rapidly, but because of insufficient working capital it has now become slow in paying bills. Of its total debtors £96 000 is overdue. This threatens its relationship with its main supplier of powders used in the manufacture of various kinds of insulation materials for aircraft and missiles. Over 75 per cent of its sales are to six large defence contractors. The company's balance sheet, sales and net profits for the past year are shown below:
(a) If the same ratio of sales to total assets continues, and if sales increase to £2 304 000, how much non-spontaneous financing, including retained earnings, will be required?
(b) Could Shandow Insulation obtain much more funds by use of unsecured loan? Explain.
(c) Would financing debtors be a possibility for the company? Explain.
(d) Assuming the five facts listed below, on average what is the total amount of debtors outstanding at any given time when sales are £1 920 000? How much cash does the firm actually receive by factoring the average amount of debtors? What is the average duration of advances, on the basis of 360 days a year?

Shandow Insulation Company Balance Sheet.

Ordinary share capital	£96 000	Plant and equipment	£211 200
Reserves	96 000	Stocks	
Mortgage debenture	288 000	Raw materials	38 400
Short-term loan	192 000	Work in progress	192 000
[a] Trade creditors	240 000	Finished goods	57 600
[a] Accruals	48 000	Debtors	432 000
		Cash	28 800
Total claims	£960 000	Total assets	£960 000
Sales	£1 920 000		
Profit after tax	96 000		

[a] Increase spontaneously with increases in sales.

What is the total annual cost of the financing? What is the effective annual financing charge (percentage) paid on the money received?

1. Debtors turn over six times a year (sales/debtors = 6).
2. All sales are made on credit.
3. The factor requires an 8 per cent reserve for returns on disputed items.
4. The factor also requires a 2 per cent commission on average debtors outstanding, payable at the time the debtor is purchased, to cover the costs of credit checking.
5. There is a 6 per cent annual interest charge based on debtors less any reserve requirements and commissions. This payment is made at the beginning of the period and is deducted from the advance.

8–4. The Morton Plastics Company manufactures plastic toys. It buys raw materials, manufacturers the toys in the spring and summer and ships them to department stores and toy shops by late summer or early autumn. The company factors its trade debtors. If it did not, in October 1978 Morton's balance sheet would have appeared as follows:

Morton Company Pro Forma Balance Sheet, 31 *October* 1978

Ordinary share capital	£400 000	Fixed assets	£800 000
Reserves	160 000	Stocks	800 000
Mortgage debenture	200 000	Debtors	1 200 000
Short-term loan	800 000	Cash	40 000
Trade creditors	1 200 000		
Accruals	80 000		
Total claims	£2 840 000	Total assets	£2 840 000

Morton provides advanced dating on its sales; thus its debtors are not due for payment until 31 January 1979. Also, the company would have been overdue on some £800 000 of its trade creditors if the above situation actually existed. Morton has an agreement with a finance company to factor the debtors for the period from 31 October to 31 January of each selling season. The factoring company charges a flat commission of 2 per cent plus 6 per cent a year interest on the outstanding balance; it deducts a reserve of 8 per cent for returned and damaged materials. Interest and commission are paid in advance. No interest is charged on the reserved funds or on the commission.

(a) Show the balance sheet of Morton on 31 October 1978, giving effect to the purchase of all the debtors by the factoring company and the use of the funds to pay trade creditors.

(b) If £1.2 million is the average level of outstanding debtors and if they turn over four times a year (hence the commission is paid four times a year), what are the total costs of financing and the effective annual interest rate?

SELECTED REFERENCES

Chambers, P. and Oates, D. Stop sleeping on cash. *International Management* (UK) (November 1975): 22.

Faulkner, Sir Eric. Banks' failing industry – true or false? *Accountancy* (UK) (June 1976): 30–32.

Holden, James Milnes. The law and practice of banking. Pitman, 1978, vol. 1.

Kirby, D. Finance through factoring. *Managerial Finance* (UK) (1976), Vol. 2, No. 3, p. 211.

Kirkman, P. Trade credit in the U.K. – a matter of growing urgency. *Accountancy* (UK) (November 1975): 72–76.
Sten, M. When to discount bills of exchange. *Accountancy* (UK) (October 1977): 60–64.
Sten, M. The costs and rewards of payment of discounts. *Accountancy* (UK) (November 1977): 74–78.
Wooller, J. Factors and invoice discounters. *Accountancy* (UK) (July 1976): 82–86.
Wooller, J. Benefits of confidential factoring. *Accountancy* (UK) (June 1977): 104–106.

PART 3

DECISIONS INVOLVING LONG-TERM ASSETS

In Part 2, we dealt with the bottom portion of the firm's balance sheet – the current assets and liabilities. Now, in Part 3, we move up to the upper right side of the statement, focusing on the decisions involved in fixed asset acquisitions.

In Chapter 9 we discuss the concepts of compound interest and the time value of money, important subjects in all long-term financial decisions. Capital budgeting – the planning of expenditures whose returns will extend beyond one year – is covered in Chapter 10. Uncertainty about both the costs and the returns associated with a project is introduced in Chapter 11; since projects differ in riskiness, that chapter develops methods of analysis which can be used to incorporate risk into the decision-making process.

Chapter 9

The Interest Factor in Financial Decisions

Investing in fixed assets should, logically, be taken up at this point. However, the long-term nature of fixed investments makes it necessary to consider first the theory of compound interest – the 'maths of finance'. Compound interest is essential to an understanding of capital budgeting, the topic of the following chapter, and interest rate theory is also an integral part of several other topics taken up later in the text. Financial structure decisions, lease versus purchase decisions, debenture redemption operations, security valuation techniques, and the whole question of the cost of capital are some other subjects that cannot be understood without a knowledge of compound interest.

Many people are afraid of the subject of compound interest and simply avoid it. It is certainly true that many successful businessmen – even some bankers – know essentially nothing of the subject. However, as technology advances, as more and more engineers become involved in general management, and as modern business administration courses turn out more and more highly qualified graduates, this 'success in spite of yourself' pattern will become more and more difficult to achieve. Furthermore, a fear of compound interest relationships is quite unfounded – the subject matter is simply not that difficult. Almost all problems involving compound interest can be handled satisfactorily with only a few basic formulas.

COMPOUND VALUE

A person deposits £1000 in a building society account that pays 4 per cent interest compounded annually. How much will he have at the end of one year?

To treat the matter systematically, let us define the following terms:

P_0 = principal, or beginning amount at time 0.

i = interest rate.

$P_0 i$ = total amount of interest earned.

V_t = value at the end of t periods.

When t equals 1, V_t may be calculated as follows:

$$V_1 = P_0 + P_0 i$$
$$= P_0(1+i). \qquad (9\text{–}1)$$

Equation 9–1 shows that the ending amount (V_1) is equal to the beginning amount (P_0) times the factor $(1+i)$. In the example, where $P_0 = £1000$, $i = 4$ per cent, and t is one year, V_t is determined as follows:

$$V_1 = £1000\,(1.0 + 0.04) = £1000\,(1.04) = £1040.$$

Multiple periods

If the person leaves the £1000 on deposit for five years, to what amount will it have grown at the end of that period? Equation 9–1 can be used to construct Table 9–1, which indicates the answer. Note that V_2, the balance at the end of the second year, is found as follows:

$$V_2 = V_1(1+i) = P_0(1+i)(1+i) = P_0(1+i)^2.$$

Similarly, V_3, the balance after three years, is found as

$$V_3 = V_2(1+i) = P_0(1+i)^3.$$

In general, V_t, the compound amount at the end of any year t, is found as

$$V_t = P_0(1+i)^t. \qquad (9\text{–}2)$$

Table 9–1 *Compound Interest Calculations.*

Period	Beginning amount	× $(1+i)$	= Ending amount (V_t)
1	£1000	1.04	£1040
2	1040	1.04	1082
3	1082	1.04	1125
4	1125	1.04	1170
5	1170	1.04	1217

Equation 9–2 is the fundamental equation of compound interest. Note that Equation 9–1 is simply a special case of equation 9–2, where $t = 1$.

While it is necessary to understand the derivatlon of equation 9–2 in order to understand much of the material in the remainder of this chapter (as well as material to be covered in subsequent chapters), the concept can be applied quite readily in a mechanical sense. Tables have been constructed for values of $(1+i)^t$ for wide ranges of i and t. Table 9–2 is illustrative, while Table D–1, in Appendix D at the end of the book, is a more complete table.

Letting $CVIF$ (= compound value interest factor) = $(1+i)^t$, equation 9–2 may be written as $V_t = P_0(CVIF)$. It is necessary only to go to an appropriate interest table to find the proper interest factor. For example, the correct interest factor for the illustration given in Table 9–1 can be found in Table 9–2. Look down the Period column to 5, then across this row to the appropriate number in the 4 per cent column to find the interest factor, 1.217. Then, using this interest factor, we find the compound value of the £1000 after five years as

$$V_5 = P_0(CVIF) = £1000\,(1.217) = £1217.$$

Notice that this is precisely the same figure that was obtained by the long method in Table 9–1.

Table 9–2 *Compound Value of £1 (CVIF).*

Period	1%	2%	3%	4%	5%	6%	7%	8%	9%	10%
1	1.010	1.020	1.030	1.040	1.050	1.060	1.070	1.080	1.090	1.100
2	1.020	1.040	1.061	1.082	1.102	1.124	1.145	1.166	1.188	1.210
3	1.030	1.061	1.093	1.125	1.158	1.191	1.225	1.260	1.295	1.331
4	1.041	1.082	1.126	1.170	1.216	1.262	1.311	1.360	1.412	1.464
5	1.051	1.104	1.159	1.217	1.276	1.338	1.403	1.469	1.539	1.611
6	1.062	1.126	1.194	1.265	1.340	1.419	1.501	1.587	1.677	1.772
7	1.072	1.149	1.230	1.316	1.407	1.504	1.606	1.714	1.828	1.949
8	1.083	1.172	1.267	1.369	1.477	1.594	1.718	1.851	1.993	2.144
9	1.094	1.195	1.305	1.423	1.551	1.689	1.838	1.999	2.172	2.358
10	1.105	1.219	1.344	1.480	1.629	1.791	1.967	2.159	2.367	2.594
11	1.116	1.243	1.384	1.539	1.710	1.898	2.105	2.332	2.580	2.853
12	1.127	1.268	1.426	1.601	1.796	2.012	2.252	2.518	2.813	3.138
13	1.138	1.294	1.469	1.665	1.886	2.133	2.410	2.720	3.066	3.452
14	1.149	1.319	1.513	1.732	1.980	2.261	2.579	2.937	3.342	3.797
15	1.161	1.346	1.558	1.801	2.079	2.397	2.759	3.172	3.642	4.177

Graphic view of the compounding process: growth

Figure 9–1 shows how the interest factors for compounding increase, or grow, as the compounding period increases. Curves could be drawn for any interest rate, including fractional rates; we have plotted curves for 0 per cent, 5 per cent and 10 per cent. The curves in the graph were plotted from data taken from Table 9–2.

Figure 9–1 shows how £1 (or any other sum) grows over time at various rates of interest. The higher the rate of interest, the faster the rate of growth. The interest rate is, in fact, the growth rate: if a sum is deposited and earns 5 per cent, then the funds on deposit grow at the rate of 5 per cent per year.

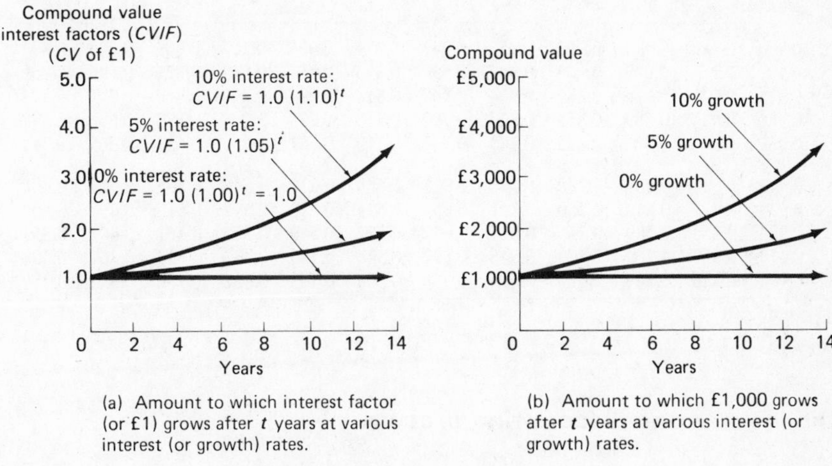

(a) Amount to which interest factor (or £1) grows after *t* years at various interest (or growth) rates.

(b) Amount to which £1,000 grows after *t* years at various interest (or growth) rates.

Figure 9–1 *Relationship between Compound Value Interest Factors, Interest Rates, and Time.*

PRESENT VALUE

Suppose you are offered the alternative of either £1217 at the end of five years or £X today. There is no question but that the £1217 will be paid in full (perhaps the payer is the

Treasury); having no current need for the money, you would deposit it in a building society account paying a 4 per cent interest. (Four per cent is defined to be your 'opportunity costs'.) How small must X be to induce you to accept the promise of £1217 five years hence?

Table 9–1 shows that the initial amount of £1000 growing at 4 per cent a year yields £1217 at the end of five years. Thus, you should be indifferent in your choice between £1000 today and £1217 at the end of five years. The £1000 is defined as the *present value* of £1217 due in five years when the applicable interest rate is 4 per cent. It should be noted that the subscript zero in the term P_0 indicates the present. Hence present value quantities may be identified by either P_0 or PV.

Finding present values (or *discounting*, as it is commonly called) is simply the reverse of compounding, and equation 9–2 can readily be transformed into a present value formula.

$$\text{Present value} = P_0 = \frac{V_t}{(1+i)^t} = V_t\left[\frac{1}{(1+i)^t}\right]. \qquad (9\text{–}3)$$

Tables have been constructed for the term in brackets for various values of i and t; Table 9–3 is an example. A more complete table, Table D–2, is found in Appendix D at the end of the book. For the illustrative case being considered, look down the 4 per cent column in Table 9–3 to the fifth row. The figure shown there, 0.822, is the present value interest factor ($PVIF$) used to determine the present value of £1217 payable in five years, discounted at 4 per cent.

$$\begin{aligned} P_0 &= V_5(PVIF) \\ &= £1217\,(0.822) \\ &= £1000. \end{aligned}$$

Table 9–3 *Present Values of £1 (PVIF).*

Period	1%	2%	3%	4%	5%	6%	7%	8%	9%	10%	12%	14%	15%
1	0.990	0.980	0.971	0.962	0.952	0.943	0.935	0.926	0.917	0.909	0.893	0.877	0.870
2	0.980	0.961	0.943	0.925	0.907	0.890	0.873	0.857	0.842	0.826	0.797	0.769	0.756
3	0.971	0.942	0.915	0.889	0.864	0.840	0.816	0.794	0.772	0.751	0.712	0.675	0.658
4	0.961	0.924	0.889	0.855	0.823	0.792	0.763	0.735	0.708	0.683	0.636	0.592	0.572
5	0.951	0.906	0.863	0.822	0.784	0.747	0.713	0.681	0.650	0.621	0.567	0.519	0.497
6	0.942	0.888	0.838	0.790	0.746	0.705	0.666	0.630	0.596	0.564	0.507	0.456	0.432
7	0.933	0.871	0.813	0.760	0.711	0.665	0.623	0.583	0.547	0.513	0.452	0.400	0.376
8	0.923	0.853	0.789	0.731	0.677	0.627	0.582	0.540	0.502	0.467	0.404	0.351	0.327
9	0.914	0.837	0.766	0.703	0.645	0.592	0.544	0.500	0.460	0.424	0.361	0.308	0.284
10	0.905	0.820	0.744	0.676	0.614	0.558	0.508	0.463	0.422	0.386	0.322	0.270	0.247

Graphic view of the discounting process

Figure 9–2 shows how the interest factors for discounting decrease as the discounting period increases. The curves in the figure were plotted from data taken from Table 9–3; they show that the present value of a sum to be received at some future date decreases (a) as the payment date is extended further into the future and (b) as the discount rate increases. If relatively high discount rates apply, funds due in the future are worth very little today; even at relatively low discount rates, funds due in the distant future are not worth much today. For example, £1000 due in ten years is worth £247 today if the discount rate is 15 per cent, but it is worth £614 today at a 5 per cent discount rate. Similarly, £1000 due in ten

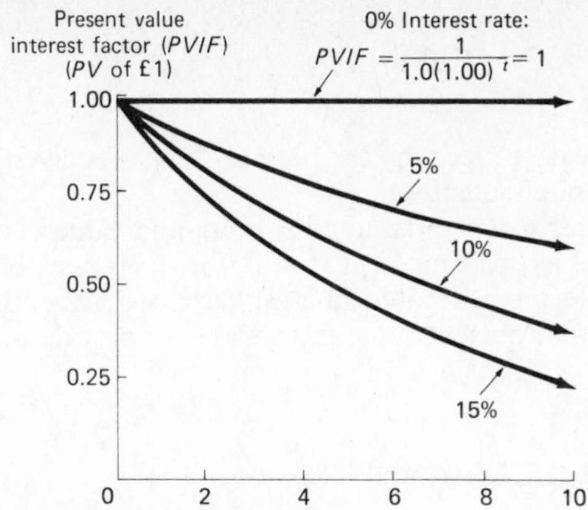

Figure 9–2 *Relationship between Present Value Interest Factors, Interest Rates, and Time.*

years at 10 per cent is worth £386 today, but at the same discount rate £1000 due in five years is worth £621 today.[1]

COMPOUND VALUE VERSUS PRESENT VALUE

Because a thorough understanding of compound value concepts is vital in order to follow the remainder of both this chapter and the book, and because compound interest gives many students trouble, it will be useful to examine in more detail the relationship between compounding and discounting.

Notice that equation 9–2, the basic equation for compounding, was developed from the logical sequence set forth in Table 9–1: the equation merely presents in mathematical form the steps outlined in the table. The present value interest factor ($PVIF_{i,t}$) in equation 9–3, the basic equation for discounting or finding present values, was found as the *reciprocal* of the compound value interest factor ($CVIF_{i,t}$) for the same i, t combination:

$$PVIF_{i,t} = \frac{1}{CVIF_{i,t}}.$$

For example, the *compound value* interest factor for 4 per cent over five years is seen in Table 9–2 to be 1.217. The *present value* interest factor for 4 per cent over five years must be the reciprocal of 1.217:

$$PVIF_{4\%,\,5\,\text{years}} = \frac{1}{1.217} = 0.822.$$

The $PVIF$ found in this manner must, of course, correspond with the $PVIF$ shown in Table 9–3.

The reciprocal nature of the relationship between present value and compound value permits us to find present values in two ways – by multiplying or by dividing. Thus, the present value of £1000 due in five years and discounted at 4 per cent may be found as

$$P_0 = PV = V_t(PVIF_{i,t}) = V_t\left[\frac{1}{1+i}\right]^t = £1000\ (0.822) = £822,$$

1. Note that Figure 9–2 is *not* a mirror image of Figure 9–1. The curves in Figure 9–1 approach ∞ as t increases; in Figure 9–2, the curves approach zero, not $-\infty$, as t increases.

or

$$P_0 = PV = \frac{V_t}{CVIF_{i,t}} = \frac{V_t}{(1+i)^t} = \frac{£1000}{1.217} = £822.$$

In the second form, it is easy to see why the present value of a given future amount (V_t) declines as the discount rate increases.

To conclude this comparison of present and compound values, compare Figures 9–1 and 9–2. Notice that the vertical intercept is at 1.0 in each case, but compound value interest factors rise while present value interest factors decline. The reason for this divergence is, of course, that present value factors are reciprocals of compound factors.

COMPOUND VALUE OF AN ANNUITY

An annuity is defined as a series of payments of a fixed amount for a specified number of years. Each payment occurs at the end of the year.[2] For example, a promise to pay £1000 a year for three years is a three-year annuity. If you were to receive such an annuity and were to deposit each annual payment in a savings account paying 4 per cent interest, how much would you have at the end of three years? The answer is shown graphically in Figure 9–3. The first payment is made at the end of year 1, the second at the end of year 2 and the third at the end of year 3. The last payment is not compounded at all; the next to the last is compounded for one year; the second from the last for two years; and so on back to the first, which is compounded for $t-1$ years. When the compound values of each of the payments are added, their total is the sum of the annuity. In the example, this total is £3122.

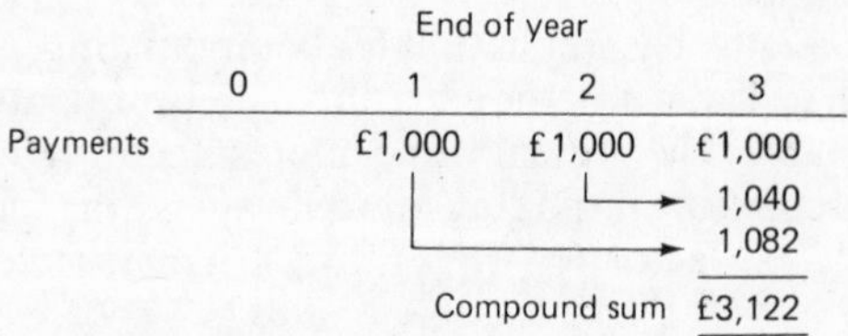

Figure 9–3 *Graphic Illustration of an Annuity: Compound Sum.*

Expressed algebraically, with S_t defined as the compound sum, a as the periodic receipt, t as the length of the annuity and $CVIF_a$ as the compound value interest factor for an annuity, the formula for S_t is

$$\begin{aligned} S_t &= a(1+i)^{t-1} + a(1+i)^{t-2} + \ldots + a(1+i)^1 + a(1+i)^0 \\ &= a[(1+i)^{t-1} + (1+i)^{t-2} + \ldots + (1+i)^1 + (1+i)^0] \\ &= a[CVIF_a]. \end{aligned}$$

The expression in brackets, $CVIF_a$, has been given values for various combinations of t and i. An illustrative set of these annuity interest factors is given in Table 9–4; a more complete set may be found in Table D–3 in Appendix D. To find the answer to the three-year, £1000 annuity problem, simply refer to Table 9–4, look down the 4 per cent column to the row for the third year, and multiply the factor 3.122 by £1000. The answer is the same as the one derived by the long method illustrated in Figure 9–3:

2. Had the payment been made at the beginning of the period, each receipt would simply have been shifted back one year. The annuity would have been called an *annuity due*; the one in the present discussion, where payments are made at the end of each period, is called a *regular annuity* or, sometimes, a *deferred annuity*.

Table 9–4 *Sum of an Annuity of £1 for t years ($CVIF_a$).*

Period	1%	2%	3%	4%	5%	6%	7%	8%
1	1.000	1.000	1.000	1.000	1.000	1.000	1.000	1.000
2	2.010	2.020	2.030	2.040	2.050	2.060	2.070	2.080
3	3.030	3.060	3.091	3.122	3.152	3.184	3.215	3.246
4	4.060	4.122	4.184	4.246	4.310	4.375	4.440	4.506
5	5.101	5.204	5.309	5.416	5.526	5.637	5.751	5.867
6	6.152	6.308	6.468	6.633	6.802	6.975	7.153	7.336
7	7.214	7.434	7.662	7.898	8.142	8.394	8.654	8.923
8	8.286	8.583	8.892	9.214	9.549	9.897	10.260	10.637
9	9.369	9.755	10.159	10.583	11.027	11.491	11.978	12.488
10	10.462	10.950	11.464	12.006	12.578	13.181	13.816	14.487

$$S_t = a \times CVIF_a$$
$$S_3 = £1000 \times 3.122 = £3122. \quad (9–4)$$

Notice that $CVIF_a$ for the sum of an annuity is always *larger* than the number of years the annuity runs.

PRESENT VALUE OF AN ANNUITY

Suppose you were offered the following alternatives: a three-year annuity of £1000 a year or a lump-sum payment today. You have no need for the money during the next three years, so if you accept the annuity you would simply deposit the receipts in a savings account paying 4 per cent interest. How large must the lump-sum payment be to make it equivalent to the annuity? The graphic illustration shown in Figure 9–4 will help explain the problem.

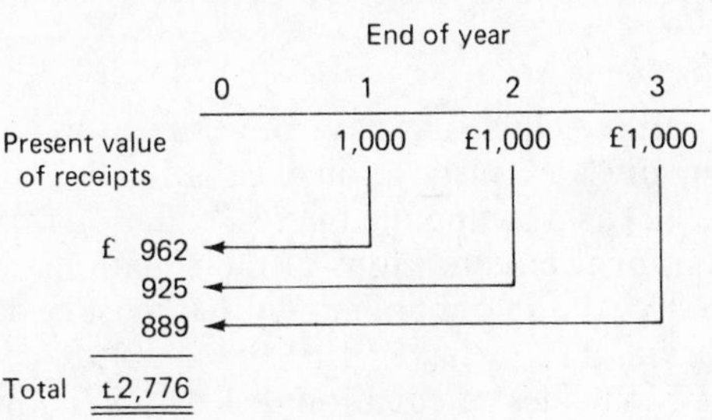

Figure 9–4 *Graphic Illustration of an Annuity: Present Value.*

The present value of the first receipt is $a[1/(1+i)]$; the second is $a[1/(1+i)]^2$; and so on. Defining the present value of an annuity of t years as PV_{at} and with $PVIF_a$ defined as the present value interest factor for an annuity, we may write the following equation:

$$PV_{at} = a\left[\frac{1}{1+i}\right]^1 + a\left[\frac{1}{1+i}\right]^2 + \ldots + a\left[\frac{1}{1+i}\right]^t$$
$$= a\left[\frac{1}{(1+i)} + \frac{1}{(1+i)^2} + \ldots + \frac{1}{(1+i)^t}\right]$$
$$= a[PVIF_a]. \quad (9–5)$$

Table 9–5 *Present Value of an Annuity of £1.*

Period	1%	2%	3%	4%	5%	6%	7%	8%	9%	10%
1	0.990	0.980	0.971	0.962	0.952	0.943	0.935	0.926	0.917	0.909
2	1.970	1.942	1.913	1.886	1.859	1.833	1.808	1.783	1.759	1.736
3	2.941	2.884	2.829	2.775	2.723	2.673	2.624	2.577	2.531	2.487
4	3.902	3.808	3.717	3.630	3.546	3.465	3.387	3.312	3.240	3.170
5	4.853	4.713	4.580	4.452	4.329	4.212	4.100	3.993	3.890	3.791
6	5.795	5.601	5.417	5.242	5.076	4.917	4.766	4.623	4.486	4.355
7	6.728	6.472	6.230	6.002	5.786	5.582	5.389	5.206	5.033	4.868
8	7.652	7.325	7.020	6.733	6.463	6.210	6.971	5.747	5.535	5.335
9	8.566	8.162	7.786	7.435	7.108	6.802	6.515	6.247	5.985	5.759
10	9.471	8.983	8.530	8.111	7.722	7.360	7.024	6.710	6.418	6.145

Again, tables have been worked out for the $PVIF_a$, the term in the brackets. Table 9–5 is illustrative; a more complete table is found in Table D–4 in Appendix D. From Table 9–5, the $PVIF_a$ for a three-year, 4 per cent annuity is found to be 2.775. Multiplying this factor by the £1000 annual receipt gives £2775, the present value of the annuity. This figure departs from the long-method answer shown in Figure 9–4 only by a rounding difference:

$$\begin{aligned} PV_{at} &= a \times PVIF_a \\ PV_{a3} &= £1000 \times 2.775 \\ &= £2775. \end{aligned} \qquad (9\text{–}6)$$

Notice that $PVIF_a$ for the *present value* of an annuity is always *less* than the number of years the annuity runs, whereas $CVIF_a$ for the *sum* of an annuity is *larger* than the number of years.

ANNUAL PAYMENTS FOR ACCUMULATION OF A FUTURE SUM

Thus far in the chapter all the equations have been based on equation 9–2. The present value equation merely involves a transposition of equation 9–2, and the annuity equations merely take the sum of the basic compound interest equation for different values of t. We now examine some additional modifications of the equations.

Suppose we want to know the amount of money that must be deposited at 5 per cent for each of the next five years in order to have £10 000 available to pay off a debt at the end of the fifth year. Dividing both sides of equation 9–4 by $CVIF_a$, we obtain

$$a = \frac{S_t}{CVIF_a}.$$

Looking up the sum of an annuity interest factor for five years at 5 per cent in Table 9–4 and dividing that figure into £10 000 we find

$$a = \frac{£10\,000}{5.526} = £1810.$$

Thus, if £1810 is deposited each year in an account paying 5 per cent interest, at the end of five years the account will have accumulated £10 000. We will employ this procedure in later chapters when we discuss sinking funds set up to provide for debenture redemption.

ANNUAL RECEIPTS FROM AN ANNUITY

Suppose that on 1 September 1978 you receive an inheritance of £7000. The money is to be used for your education and is to be spent during the academic years beginning September 1979, 1980 and 1981. If you place the money in a bank account paying 5 per cent annual interest and make three equal withdrawals at each of the specified dates, how large can each withdrawal be to leave you with exactly a nil balance after the last one has been made?

The solution requires application of the present value of an annuity formula, equation 9–6. Here, however, we know that the present value of the annuity is £7000, and the problem is to find the three equal annual payments when the interest rate is 5 per cent. This calls for dividing both sides of equation 9–6 by $PVIF_a$ to make equation 9–7.

$$PV_{at} = a \times PVIF_a \tag{9–6}$$

$$a = \frac{PV_{at}}{PVIF_a}. \tag{9–7}$$

The interest factor ($PVIF_a$) is found in Table 9–5 to be 2.723; substituting this value into equation 9–7, we find the three equal annual withdrawals to be £2571 a year:

$$a = \frac{£7000}{2.723} = £2570.69$$

This particular kind of calculation is used frequently in setting up insurance and pension plan benefit schedules; it is also used to find the periodic payments necessary to redeem a loan within a specified period. For example, if you want to redeem a £7000 bank loan, bearing interest at 5 per cent on the unpaid balance, in three equal annual instalments, the amount of each payment is £2570.69. In this case, you are the borrower, and the bank is 'buying' an annuity with a present value of £7000.

DETERMINING INTEREST RATES

In many instances the present values and cash flows associated with a payment stream are known, but the interest rate involved is not known. Suppose a bank offers to lend you £1000 today if you sign a note agreeing to pay the bank £1469 at the end of five years. What rate of interest would you be paying on the loan? To answer the question we must use equation 9–2:

$$V_t = P_0(1+i)^t = P_0(CVIF). \tag{9–2}$$

Simply solve for $CVIF$, then look up this value of $CVIF$ in Table 9–2 (or D–1) under the row for the fifth year:

$$CVIF = \frac{V_5}{P_0} = \frac{£1469}{£1000} = 1.469.$$

Looking across the row for the fifth year, we find the value 1.469 in the 8 per cent column; therefore, the interest rate on the loan is 8 per cent.

Precisely the same approach is taken to determine the interest rate implicit in an annuity. For example, suppose a bank will lend you £2577 if you sign a note in which you agree to pay the bank £1000 at the end of the next three years. What interest rate is the bank charging you? To answer the question, solve equation 9–6 for $PVIF_a$, then look up $PVIF_a$ in Table 9–5 (or D–4):

$$PV_{at} = a \times PVIF_a$$

$$PVIF_a = \frac{PV_{a3}}{a} = \frac{£2577}{£1000} = 2.577. \quad (9\text{–}6)$$

Looking across the third-year row, we find the factor 2.577 under the 8 per cent column; therefore the bank is lending you money at 8 per cent.

LINEAR INTERPOLATION

The tables give values for even interest rates, e.g., 8 per cent, 9 per cent, and so on. Suppose you need to find the present value of £1000 due in 10 years, discounted at $8\frac{1}{4}$ per cent. The appropriate $PVIF$ is not in the tables, but a very close approximation to the correct factor can be estimated by the method of *linear interpolation*. The $PVIF$ for 8 per cent, 10 years, is 0.463; that for 9 per cent is 0.422. The difference is 0.041. Since $8\frac{1}{4}$ is 25 per cent of the way between 8 and 9, we can subtract 25 per cent of 0.041 from 0.463 and obtain 0.453 as the $PVIF$ for $8\frac{1}{4}$ per cent due in 10 years. Thus, if the appropriate discount rate is $8\frac{1}{4}$ per cent, £1000 due in 10 years is worth £453 today.

In general, the formula used for interpolation is as follows:

$$IF \text{ for intermediate interest rate} = \left(\frac{i - i_L}{i_H - i_L}\right)(IF_H - IF_L) + IF_L.$$

Here i = the interest rate in question, i_L is the interest rate in the table just lower than i, i_H is the interest rate in the table just higher than i, and IF_H and IF_L are the interest factors for i_H and i_L, respectively. Using the equation with the preceding example, we have

$$PVIF \text{ for } 8\tfrac{1}{4}\% \text{ due in 10 years} = \left(\frac{8.25 - 8}{9 - 8}\right)(0.422 - 0.463) + 0.463$$

$$= \left(\frac{0.25}{1}\right)(-0.041) + 0.463 = 0.453,$$

which is the $PVIF$ found above. The equation can be used for each type of factor expression $PVIF$, $CVIF$, $PVIF_a$ or $CVIF_a$.

Interpolation can also be used to determine interest rates, given interest factors. For example, suppose an investment that costs £163 500 promises to yield £50 000 per year for 4 years, and you want to know the rate of return on the investment. You use equation 9–6 to find the $PVIF_a$:

$$PVIF_a = \frac{£163\,500}{£\ 50\,000} = 3.27.$$

Looking this value up in Table 9–5, period 4, you see that it lies between 8 and 9 per cent. Applying the interpolation formula, but solving for i, we have

$$PVIF_a \text{ for } i\% = 3.27 = \left(\frac{i - 8}{9 - 8}\right)(3.240 - 3.312) + 3.312$$

$$\begin{aligned} 3.27 &= (i - 8)(-0.072) + 3.312 \\ -0.042 &= -0.072i + 0.576 \\ 0.072i &= 0.618 \\ i &= 8.58\% \end{aligned}$$

PRESENT VALUE OF AN UNEVEN SERIES OF RECEIPTS

Recall that the definition of an annuity includes the words *fixed amount* – in other words, annuities deal with constant, or level, payments or receipts. Although many financial decisions do involve constant payments, many important decisions are concerned with uneven flows of cash. In particular, the kinds of fixed asset investments dealt with in the following chapter very frequently involve uneven flows. Consequently it is necessary to expand our analysis to deal with varying payment streams. Since most of the applications call for present values, not compound sums or other figures, this section is restricted to the present value (PV).

To illustrate the calculating procedure, suppose someone offers to sell you a series of payments consisting of £300 after one year, £100 after two years, and £200 after three years. How much would you be willing to pay for the series, assuming the appropriate discount rate (interest rate) is 4 per cent? To determine the purchase price, simply compute the present value of the series; the calculations are worked out in Table 9–6. The receipts for each year are shown in the second column; the discount factors (from Table 9–3) are given in the third column; and the product of these two columns, the present value of each individual receipt, is given in the last column. When the individual present values in the last column are added, the sum is the present value of the investment, £558.90. Under the assumptions of the example, you should be willing to pay this amount for the investment.

Table 9–6 *Calculating the Present Value of an Uneven Series of Payments.*

Period	Receipt ×	Interest factor ($PVIF$) =	Present value (PV or P_0)
1	£300	0.962	£288.60
2	100	0.925	92.50
3	200	0.889	177.80
		PV of investment	£558.90

Had the series of payments been somewhat different – say £300 at the end of the first year, £200 at the end of the second year, then eight annual payments of £100 each – we would probably want to use a different procedure for finding the investment's present value. We could, of course, set up a calculating table such as Table 9–6, but because most of the payments are part of an annuity we can use a short cut. The calculating procedure is shown in Table 9–7, and the logic of the table is depicted in Figure 9–5.

Section 1 of Table 9–7 deals with the £300 and the £200 received at the end of the first and second years respectively; their present values are found to be £288.60 and £185. Section 2 deals with the eight £100 payments. In part (a), the value of a £100, eight-year, 4 per cent annuity is found to be £673.30. However, the first receipt under the annuity comes at the end of the third year, so it is worth less than £673.30 today. Specifically, it is worth

Table 9–7 *Calculating Procedure for an Uneven Series of Payments that Includes an Annuity.*

1. PV of £300 due in 1 year = £300(0.962) =	£ 288.60
PV of £200 due in 2 years = £200(0.925) =	185.00
2. PV of eight-year annuity with £100 receipts	
(a) PV at beginning of year 3: £100(6.733) = £673.30	
(b) PV of £673.30 = £673.30(0.925) =	622.80
3. PV of total series =	£1096.40

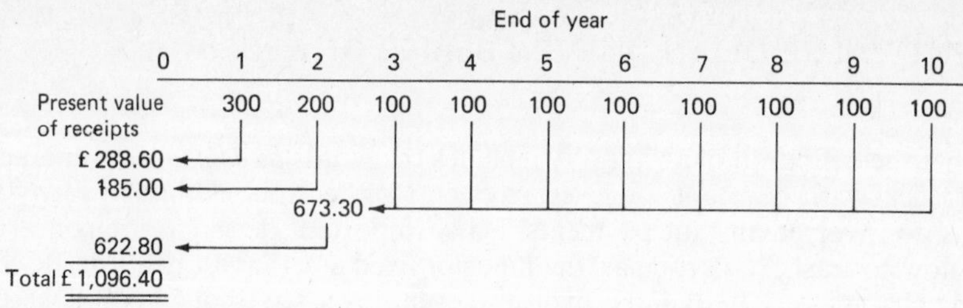

Figure 9–5 *Graphic Illustration of Present Value Calculations for an Uneven Series of Payments that Includes an Annuity.*

the present value of £673.30, discounted back two years at 4 per cent, or £622.80; this calculation is shown in part (b) of section 2.[3] When the present values of the first two payments are added to the present value of the annuity component, the sum is the present value of the entire investment, or £1096.40.

SEMI-ANNUAL AND OTHER COMPOUNDING PERIODS[4]

In all the examples used thus far, it has been assumed that returns were received once a year, or annually. For example, in the first section of the chapter, dealing with compound values, it was assumed that funds were placed on deposit in a building society account and grew by 4 per cent a year. However, suppose the advertised rate had been 4 per cent compounded *semi-annually*. What would this have meant? Consider the following example.

You deposit £1000 in a bank deposit account and receive a return of 4 per cent compounded semi-annually. How much will you have at the end of one year? Semi-annual compounding means that interest is actually paid each six months, a fact taken into account in the tabular calculations in Table 9–8. Here, the annual interest rate is divided by 2, but twice as many compounding periods are used, because interest is paid twice a year. Comparing the amount on hand at the end of the second six-month period, £1040.40, with what would have been on hand under annual compounding, £1040, shows that semi-annual compounding is better from the standpoint of the saver. *This result occurs, of course, because he earns interest on interest more frequently.*

Table 9–8 *Compound Interest Calculations with Semi-annual Compounding.*

Period	Beginning amount (P_0)	$\times (1+i)$	=	Ending amount (P_t)
1	£1000.00	(1.02)		£1020.00
2	1020.00	(1.02)		1040.40

General formulas can be developed for use when compounding periods are more frequent than once a year. To demonstrate this, equation 9–2 is modified as follows:

$$V_t = P_0(1+i)^t. \tag{9–2}$$

3. The present value of the annuity portion, £622.80, could also have been found by subtracting the $PVIF_a$ for a two-year annuity from the $PVIF_a$ for a ten-year annuity, then multiplying the result by £100.
4. This section can be omitted without loss of continuity.

$$V_t = P_0\left(1+\frac{i}{q}\right)^{qt}. \tag{9–8}$$

Here, q is the number of times per year compounding occurs. When banks compute daily interest the value of q is set at 365, and equation 9–8 is applied.

The interest tables can be used when compounding occurs more than once a year. Simply divide the nominal, or stated, interest rate by the number of times compounding occurs, and multiply the years by the number of compounding periods per year. For example, to find the amount to which £1000 will grow after five years if semi-annual compounding is applied to a stated 4 per cent interest rate, divide 4 per cent by 2 and multiply the five years by 2. Then look in Table 9–2 (or Table D–1 in Appendix D) under the 2 per cent column and in the row for the tenth period. You find an interest factor of 1.219. Multiplying this by the initial £1000 gives a value of £1219, the amount to which £1000 will grow in five years at 4 per cent compounded semi-annually. This compares with £1217 for annual compounding.

The same procedure is applied in all the cases covered – compounding, discounting, single payments and annuities. To illustrate semi-annual compounding in finding the present value of an annuity, for example, consider the case described in the earlier section, Present Value of an Annuity: £1000 a year for three years, discounted at 4 per cent. With annual compounding (or discounting) the interest factor is 2.775, and the present value of the annuity is £2775. For semi-annual compounding look under the 2 per cent column and in the year-6 row of Table 9–5, to find an interest factor of 5.601. This is now multiplied by half of £1000, or the £500 received each six months, to get the present value of the annuity, £2800. The payments come a little more rapidly – the first £500 is paid after only six months (similarly with other payments), so the annuity is a little more valuable if payments are received semi-annually rather than annually.

By letting q approach infinity, equation 9–8 can be modified to the special case of *continuous compounding.* Continuous compounding is extremely useful in theoretical finance, and it also has practical applications. Continuous compounding is discussed in the appendix to this chapter.

A SPECIAL CASE OF SEMI-ANNUAL COMPOUNDING: DEBENTURE VALUES[5]

Most debentures pay interest semi-annually, so semi-annual compounding procedures are appropriate for determining debenture values. To illustrate, suppose a particular debenture pays interest in the amount of £30 each six months, or £60 a year. The debenture will mature in 10 years, paying £1000 (the 'principal') at that time. Thus, if you buy the debenture you will receive an annuity of £30 each six months, or 20 payments in total, plus £1000 at the end of 10 years (or 20 six-month periods). What is the debenture worth, assuming that the appropriate market discount (or interest) rate is (A) 6 per cent; (B) higher than 6 per cent, say 8 per cent, and (C) lower than 6 per cent, say 4 per cent?

Part A

Step 1. You are buying an annuity plus a lump sum of £1000. Find the PV of the interest payments:

1. Use $i/q = 6\%/2 = 3\%$ as the 'interest rate'.

5. This section may be omitted without loss of continuity. The topic is also covered in Chapter 17.

2. Look up the $PVIF_a$ in Table D–4 (Appendix D at the end of the book) for 20 periods at 3 per cent, which is 14.877.
3. Find the PV of the stream of interest payments:
   PV of the interest = £30 ($PVIF_a$)
   = £30(14.877) = £446.

Step 2. Find the PV of the £1000 maturity value:

1. Use $i/q = 6\%/2 = 3\%$ as the 'interest rate'.
2. Look up the $PVIF$ in Table D–2 for 20 periods at 3 per cent, which is 0.554.
3. Find the PV of that value at maturity:
   PV of the maturity value = £1000 ($PVIF$)
   = £1000 (0.554) = £554.

Step 3. Combine the two component PVs to determine the value of the debenture:
Debenture value = £446 + £554 = £1000.

Part B

Repeating the process, we have

Step 1. $8\%/2 = 4\%$ = the 'interest rate'.
$PVIF_a$ from Table D–4 = 13.59.
$PVIF$ from Table D–2 = 0.456.

Step 2. Debenture value = £30(13.59) + £1000(0.456)
= £408 + £456
= £864.

Notice that the debenture is worth less when the going rate of interest for investments of similar risk is 8 per cent than when it is 6 per cent. At a price of £864, this debenture provides an annual rate of return of 8 per cent; at a price of £1000, it provides an annual return of 6 per cent. If 6 per cent is the coupon rate on a debenture of a given degree of risk, then whenever interest rates in the economy rise to the point where debentures of this degree of risk have an 8 per cent return, the price of our debenture will decline to £864, at which price it will yield the competitive rate of return, 8 per cent.

Part C

Using the same process produces the following results:

Step 1. 4 per cent/2 = 2 per cent = the 'interest rate'.
$PVIF_a$ from Table D–4 = 16.351.
$PVIF$ from Table D–2 = 0.673.

Step 2. Debenture value = £30(16.351) + £1000(0.673)
= £491 + £673 = £1164.

The debenture is worth *more* than £1000 when the going rate of interest is less than 6 per cent, because then it offers a yield higher than the going rate. Its price rises to £1164, where it provides a 4 per cent annual rate of return. This calculation illustrates the fact that when interest rates in the economy decline, the prices of outstanding debentures rise.

APPROPRIATE COMPOUNDING OR DISCOUNTING RATES

Throughout the chapter, assumed compounding or discounting rates have been used in the examples. Although we will cover the subject in depth later in the book, it is useful at this point to give some idea of what the appropriate interest rate for a particular investment might be.[6]

The starting point is, of course, the general level of interest rates in the economy as a whole. This level is set by the interaction of supply-and-demand forces, with demand for funds coming largely from businesses, individual borrowers and the government when it is running a deficit. Funds are supplied by individual and corporate savers and, under the control of the Treasury and the Bank of England, by the creation of money by banks. Depending on the relative levels of supply and demand, the basic pattern of interest rates is determined.

There is no one rate of interest in the economy – rather, there is, at any given time, an array of different rates. The lowest rates are found on the safest investments, the highest rates on the most risky ones. Usually, there is less risk on investments that mature in the near future than on longer term investments, so higher rates are usually associated with long-term investments. There are other factors that affect interest rate differentials (also called 'yield' differentials), but a discussion of these factors is best deferred until later in the book.

A person faced with the kinds of decisions considered in this chapter must accept the existing set of interest rates found in the economy. If he has money to invest, he can invest in short-term government securities and incur no risk whatever. However, he will generally have to accept a relatively low yield on his investment. If he is willing to assume a little more risk, he can invest in company debentures and get a higher fixed rate of return. If he is willing to accept still more risk, he can move into ordinary shares to obtain variable (and hopefully higher) returns (dividends plus capital gains) on his investment. Other alternatives include bank and building society deposits, local government stocks, property and land held for speculation, and so on.

Risk premiums

With only a limited amount of money to invest, one must pick and choose among investments; the final selection involves a trade-off between risk and returns. Suppose, for example, that you are indifferent between a five-year government stock yielding 7 per cent a year, a five-year debenture yielding 9 per cent, and an ordinary share on which you can expect a 12 per cent return. Given this situation, you can take the government stock as a riskless security, and you attach a 2 per cent risk premium to the debenture and a 5 per cent risk premium to the ordinary share. Risk premiums, then, are the added returns that risky investments must command over less risky ones if there is to be a demand for risky assets. The concept of the risk premium is discussed in more detail in Chapter 11 and also in the chapters dealing with the cost of capital.

Opportunity costs

Although there are many potential investments available in the economy at any given time, a particular individual actively considers only a limited number of them. After making

6. For convenience, in this chapter we speak of 'interest rates', which implies that only debt is involved. In later chapters this concept is broadened considerably, and the term 'rate of return' is used in lieu of 'interest rate'.

adjustments for risk differentials, he ranks the various alternatives from the most attractive to the least. Then, presumably, our investor puts his available funds in the most attractive investment. If he is offered a new investment, he must compare it with the best of the existing alternatives. If he takes the new investment, he must give up the opportunity of investing in the best of his old alternatives. *The yield on the best of the alternatives is defined as the opportunity cost of investing in the new alternative.* For example, suppose you have funds invested in a bank deposit account that pays 6 per cent. Now suppose that someone offers you another investment of equal risk. To make the new investment, you must withdraw funds from the bank deposit account; therefore *6 per cent is defined as the opportunity cost of the new investment.* You could determine the interest rate on the new investment (using equation 9–2 or procedures described in the next chapter); if the new investment yields more than 6 per cent, make the switch. The interest rates used in the examples throughout this chapter were all determined as opportunity costs available to the person in the example. This concept is also used in the following chapter, where we consider business decisions on investments in fixed assets, or the *capital budgeting decision.*

SUMMARY

A knowledge of compound interest and present value techniques is essential to an understanding of many important aspects of finance: capital budgeting, financial structure, security valuation and many other topics. The basic principles of compound interest, together with the most important formulas used in practice, were described in this chapter.

Compound value

Compound value (V_t), or compound amount, is defined as the sum to which a beginning amount of principal (P_o) will grow over t years when interest is earned at the rate of i per cent a year. The equation for finding compound values is

$$V_t = P_0(1+i)^t.$$

Tables giving the compound value of £1 for a large number of different years and interest rates have been prepared. The compound value of £1 is called the compound value interest factor (VIF); illustrative values are given in Table 9–2, and a more complete set of interest factors is given in Appendix Table D–1.

Present value (PV)

The present value of a future payment (PV) is the amount that, if we had it now and invested it at the specified interest rate (i), would equal the future payment (V_t) on the date the future payment is due. For example, if you were to receive £217 after five years and decide that 4 per cent is the appropriate interest rate (it is called *discount rate* when computing present values), then you could find the present value of the £1217 to be £1000 by applying the following equation:

$$PV = V_t\left[\frac{1}{(1+i)^t}\right] = £1217[0.822] = £1000.$$

The term in brackets is called the present value interest factor ($PVIF$), and values for it have been worked out in Table 9–3 and Appendix Table D–2.

Compound value of an annuity

An annuity is defined as a series of payments of a fixed amount (a) for a specified number of years. The compound value of an annuity is the total amount one would have at the end of the annuity period if each payment is invested at a certain interest rate and is held to the end of the annuity period. For example, suppose we have a three-year, £1000 annuity invested at 4 per cent. There are formulas for annuities, but tables are available for the relevant interest factors. The $CVIF_a$ for the compound value of a three-year annuity at 4 per cent is 3.122, and it can be used to find the present value of the illustrative annuity:

$$\text{Compound value} = CVIF_a \times \text{annual receipt} = 3.122 \times £1000 = £3122.$$

Thus, £3122 is the compound value of the annuity.

Present value of an annuity

The present value of an annuity is the lump sum one would need to have on hand today in order to be able to withdraw equal amounts (a) each year and end up with a balance exactly equal to nil at the end of the annuity period. For example, if you wish to withdraw £1000 a year for three years, you could deposit £2775 today in a bank account paying 4 per cent interest, withdraw the £1000 in each of the next three years, and end up with a nil balance. Thus, £2775 is the present value of an annuity of £1000 a year for three years when the appropriate discount rate is 4 per cent. Again, tables are available for finding the present value of annuities. To use them, one simply looks up the interest factor ($PVIF_a$) for the appropriate number of years and interest rate, then multiplies the $PVIF_a$ by the annual receipt.

$$PV \text{ of annuity} = PVIF_a \times \text{annual receipt} = 2.775 \times £1000 = £2775.$$

Relation of interest factors to one another

All interest factors given in the tables are for £1; for example, 2.775 is the $PVIF_a$ for finding the present value of a three-year annuity. It must be multiplied by the annual receipt, £1000 in the example, to find the actual value of the annuity. Students – and even financial managers – sometimes make careless mistakes when looking up interest factors, using the wrong table for the purpose. This can be avoided if one recognizes the following sets of relations.

1. *Compound value, single payment.* The $CVIF$ for the compound value of a single payment, with the normal interest rates and holding periods generally found, is *always* greater than 1.0 but seldom larger than about 3.0.
2. *Present value, single payment.* The $PVIF$ for the present value of a single payment is *always* less than 1.0; for example, 0.822 is the $PVIF$ for 4 per cent held for five years. $CVIF$ is larger than 1.0; the $PVIF$ is less than 1.0.
3. *Compound value of an annuity.* The $CVIF_a$ for the compound value of an annuity is always greater than the number of years the annuity has to run. For example, the $CVIF_a$ for a three-year annuity will be greater than 3.0, while the $CVIF_a$ for a 10-year annuity will be greater than 10.0. Just how much greater depends on the interest rate – at low rates the interest factor is slightly greater than N; at high rates it is very much greater.
4. *Present value of an annuity.* The $PVIF_a$ for the present value of an annuity is always less than the number of years it has to run. For example, the $PVIF_a$ for the present value of a three-year annuity is less than 3.0; at high rates it is very much less than 3.0.

Other uses of the basic equations

The four basic interest formulas can be used in combination to find such things as the present value of an uneven series of receipts. The formulas can also be transformed to find (a) the annual payments necessary to accumulate a future sum, (b) the annual receipts from a specified annuity, (c) the periodic payments necessary to amortise a loan and (d) the interest rate implicit in a loan contract.

Appropriate interest rate

The appropriate interest rate to be used is critical when working with compound interest problems. The true nature of the interest rates to be used when working with business problems can be understood only after the chapters dealing with the cost of capital have been examined; this chapter concluded with a brief discussion of some of the factors that determine the appropriate rate of interest for a particular problem – the risk of the investment and the investor's opportunity cost of money.

QUESTIONS

9–1. What kinds of financial decisions require explicit consideration of the interest factor?

9–2. Compound interest relations are important for decisions other than financial ones. Why are they important to marketing managers?

9–3. Would you rather have an account in a building society that pays 5 per cent interest compounded semi-annually or 5 per cent interest compounded daily? Why?

9–4. For a given interest rate and a given number of years, is the interest factor for the sum of an annuity greater or less than the interest factor for the present value of the annuity?

9–5. Suppose you are examining two investments, A and B. Both have the same maturity, but A pays a 6 per cent return and B yields 5 per cent. Which investment is probably riskier? How do you know it is riskier?

PROBLEMS

9–1. Which amount is worth more at 9 per cent: £1000 today or £2000 after 8 years?

9–2. At a growth rate of 7 per cent, how long does it take a sum to double?

9–3. (a) What amount would be paid for a £1000, 10-year debenture that pays £40 interest semi-annually (£80 a year) and is sold to yield 10 per cent, compounded semi-annually?
(b) What would be paid if the debenture is sold to yield 8 per cent?
(c) What would be paid if semi-annual interest payments are £50 and the debenture is sold to yield 6 per cent?

9–4. On 31 December Diane Baker buys a building for £80 000, paying 20 per cent down and the balance in 15 equal annual instalments that are to include principal plus 8 per cent compound interest on the declining balance. What are the equal instalments?

9–5. The Family Company is establishing a sinking fund to redeem a £900 000 debenture that matures on 31 December 1988. The company plans to put a fixed amount into the fund each year for 10-years. The first payment will be made on 31 December 1978, the last on 31 December 1988. The company anticipates that the fund will earn 9 per cent a year. What annual contributions must be made to accumulate the £900 000 as of 31 December 1988?

9–6. You have just purchased a newly issued £1000 five-year Plug Company debenture for £1000. This pays £60 in interest payments semi-annually (£120 a year); call this debenture A. You are also negotiating the purchase of a £1000 six-year Plug Company debenture which returns £30 in semi-annual interest payments and has six years remaining before it matures; call this debenture B.

(a) What is the 'going rate of return' on debentures of the risk and maturity of Plug Company's debentures?

(b) What should you be willing to pay for debenture B?

(c) How would your answer for the value of debenture B change if debenture A had paid £40 in semi-annual interest instead of £60, but still sold for £1000? The second debenture still pays £30 semi-annually and £1000 at the end of six years.

9–7. You need £129 200 at the end of 17 years. You know that the best you can do is to make equal payments into a bank account on which you can earn 5 per cent interest compounded annually.

(a) What amount must you plan to pay annually to achieve your objective? The first payment is to be made at the end of the first year.

(b) Instead of making annual payments, you decide to make one lump-sum payment today. To achieve your objective of £129 200 at the end of the 17-year period, what should this sum be? You can still earn 5 per cent interest compounded annually on your account.

9–8. You can buy an annuity at a price of £13 420. If you purchase the annuity, you will receive 10 annual payments of £2000, the first payment to be made one year from today. What rate of return, or yield, does the annuity offer?

9–9. You can buy a debenture for £1000 that will pay no interest during its 8-year life but will have a value of £1851 when it matures. What rate of interest will you earn if you buy the debenture and hold it to maturity?

9–10. A bank agrees to lend you £1000 today in return for your promise to pay the bank £1838 nine years from today. What rate of interest is the bank charging you?

9–11. If earnings in 1979 are £2.66 a share, while seven years earlier, in 1972, they were £1, what has been the rate of growth in earnings?

9–12. The Randolf Company's sales last year were £1 million.

(a) Assuming that sales grow 18 per cent a year, calculate sales for each of the next six years.

(b) Plot the sales projections.

(c) If your graph is correct, your projected sales curve is non-linear. If it had been linear, would this have indicated a constant, increasing, or decreasing percentage growth rate?

9–13. You are considering two investment opportunities, A and B. A is expected to pay £400 a year for the first 10 years, £600 a year for the next 15 years, and nothing thereafter. B is expected to pay £1000 a year for 10 years, and nothing thereafter. You find that alternative investments of similar risk yield 8 per cent and 14 per cent for A and B respectively.

(a) Find the present value of each investment. Show calculations.

(b) Which is the more risky investment? Why?

(c) Assume that your rich uncle will give you your choice of investments without cost to you, and that (i) you must hold the investment for its entire life (cannot sell it) or (ii) you are free to sell it at its going market price. Which investment would you prefer under each of the two conditions?

9–14. The Bronson Company's ordinary shares paid a dividend of £1 last year. Dividends are expected to grow at a rate of 18 per cent for each of the next six years.

(a) Calculate the expected dividend for each of the next six years.

(b) Assuming that the first of these six dividends will be paid one year from now, what is the present value of the six dividends? Given the riskiness of the dividend stream, 18 per cent is the appropriate discount rate.

(c) Assume that the price of the shares will be £27 six years from now. What is the present value of this 'terminal value'? Use an 18 per cent discount rate.

(d) Assume that you will buy the share, receive the six dividends, then sell the share; how much should you be willing to pay for it?

(e) Do not do any calculations for this question, but explain in words what would happen to the price of this share (i) if the discount rate declined because the riskiness of the share declined or (ii) if the growth rate of the dividend stream increased.

9–15. The Programmatics Consulting Company is considering the purchase of a new computer that will provide the following net cash flow (or profit) stream:

Year	
1	£10 000
2	20 000
3	30 000
4	40 000
5	50 000

(a) What is the present value of the profit stream, using a 12 per cent discount rate?
(b) If the computer costs £100 000, should Programmatics purchase it?

9–16. The Martan Company pays £480 000 for a machine that provides savings of £50 000 per year for 20 years. What is the return on the investment in the machine?

9–17. The Gorton Company invests £60 000 in a new item of equipment. The savings from the equipment during the five years of its economic life are:

Year	
1	£10 000
2	10 000
3	10 000
4	24 150
5	24 150

(a) At what discount rate is it profitable for the company to make the purchase?
(b) What changes would simplify the analysis?

9–18. The Brinkner Company has a cost of capital of 12 per cent. It invests in a machine which provides savings of £18 000 per year for six years. What is the maximum that can be paid for the machine if it is to earn the required 12 per cent cost of capital?

9–19. You are considering the economic value of an MBA. Assuming that you can and do enrol immediately, expenses are £4000 per year and forgone income £6000 per year for the required two years; your expected yearly income for the following 18 years is increased by £3713.
(a) What is the return on investment earned? (Hint: it is worth more than 10 per cent.)
(b) What are some of the major complicating factors ignored?

Appendix A To Chapter 9:

Continuous Compounding and Discounting

CONTINUOUS COMPOUNDING

In Chapter 9 we implicitly assumed that growth occurs at discrete intervals – annually, semi-annually, and so forth. For some purposes it is better to assume instantaneous or *continuous*, growth. The relationship between discrete and continuous compounding is illustrated in Figure 9A–1. Figure 9A–1(a) shows the annual compounding case, where interest is added once a year; in Figure 9A–1(b) compounding occurs twice a year; in Figure 9A–1(c) interest is earned continuously.

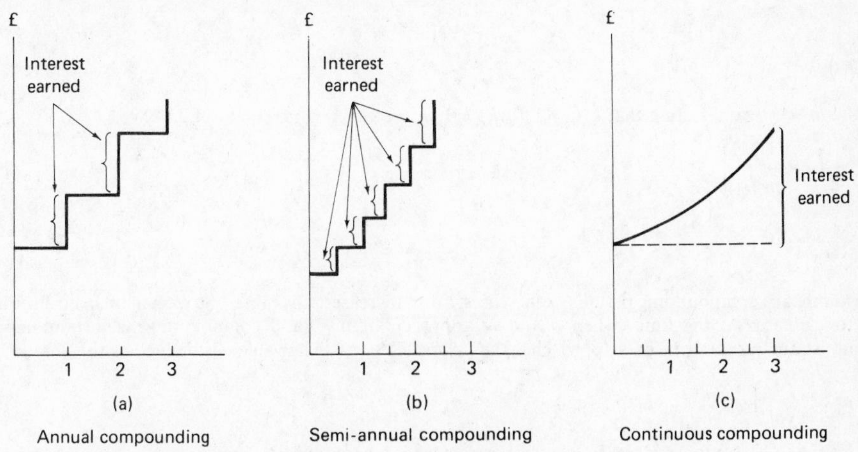

Figure 9A–1 *Annual, Semi-annual, and Continuous Compounding.*

In Chapter 9, equation 9–8 was developed to allow for any number of compounding periods per year:

$$V_t = P_0\left(1 + \frac{i}{q}\right)^{qt} \tag{9–8}$$

Equation 9–8, in turn, can be modified to allow for continuous compounding. The steps in this modification are developed below. In the literature of finance, where continuous compounding is employed, t is used for years (time). Recognize further that i is an interest rate, discount rate, or growth rate and is also denoted by k, which is used in the following material.

Step 1

First, assume that k, the interest or growth rate, is 100 per cent (k = 100 per cent = 1.0); that is, assume that with annual compounding the initial principal (P_0) will double each year:

$$\begin{aligned} V_t &= P_0(1+k)^t \\ &= P_0(1+1)^t \\ &= P_0(2)^t. \end{aligned}$$

Step 2

Now suppose that $P_0 = 1$ and that k remains at 100 per cent, but compounding occurs q times per year. The value after one year will be

$$V_1 = \left(1 + \frac{1}{q}\right)^q \tag{9A–1}$$

If $q = 1$, $V = 2$; if $q = 2$, $V = 2.25$; if $q = 3$, $V = 2.37$. Thus, V increases as q is increased.

Step 3

Returning to equation 9–8, the general case of compound growth (but using the new notation), we can develop an equation for the special case of continuous compounding. Starting with

$$V_t = P_0\left(1 + \frac{k}{q}\right)^{qt} \tag{9–8}$$

and noting that, since we can multiply qt by k/k, we can set $qt = (q/k)(kt)$ and rewrite equation 9–8 as

$$V_t = P_0\left[\left(1 + \frac{k}{q}\right)^{(q/k)}\right]^{(kt)} \tag{9A–2}$$

Step 4

Defining $m = q/k$ and noting that $k/q = 1/(q/k) = 1/m$, we can rewrite equation 9A–2 as

$$V_t = P_0\left[\left(1 + \frac{1}{m}\right)^{m}\right]^{kt} \tag{9A–3}$$

Step 5

As the number of compounding periods, q, increases, k also increases; this causes the term in brackets in equation 9A–3 to increase. At the limit, when q and m approach infinity (and compounding is instantaneous, or continuous), the term in brackets approaches the value 2.718 · · · . The value e is defined as this limiting case:

$$e = \lim_{m\infty}\left(1 + \frac{1}{m}\right)^m = 2.718 \cdots . \tag{9A–4}$$

Thus, we may substitute e for the bracketed term, rewriting equation 9A–3 as

$$V_t = P_0 e^{kt} \tag{9A–5}$$

for the case of continuous compounding (or continuous growth).

Step 6

Interest factors (IF) can be developed for continuous compounding; developing the factors requires the use of natural, or Napierian, logarithms.[1] First, letting $P_0 = 1$, we can rewrite equation 9A–5 as

$$V_1 = e^{kt}. \tag{9A–6}$$

Setting equation 9A–6 in log form and noting that *ln* denotes the log to the base *e*, we obtain

$$ln\ V_t = kt\ ln\ e. \tag{9A–7}$$

Since *e* is defined as the base of the system of natural logarithms, *ln e* must equal 1.0 (that is, $e^1 = e$, so $ln\ e = 1.0$). Therefore,

$$ln\ V_t = kt. \tag{9A–8}$$

One simply looks up the product *kt* in a table of natural logarithms and obtains the value V_t as the antilog. For example, if t = five years and k = 10 per cent, the product is 0.50. Looking up this value in Table 9A–1, a table of

Table 9A–1 *Natural Logarithms of Numbers between 1.0 and 4.99.*

N	0	1	2	3	4	5	6	7	8	9
1.0	0.00000	.00995	.01980	.02956	.03922	.04879	.05827	.06766	.07696	.08618
.1	.09531	.10436	.11333	.12222	.13103	.13976	.14842	.15700	.16551	.17395
.2	.18232	.19062	.19885	.20701	.21511	.22314	.23111	.23902	.24686	.25464
.3	.26236	.27003	.27763	.28518	.29267	.30010	.30748	.31481	.32208	.32930
.4	.33647	.34359	.35066	.35767	.36464	.37156	.37844	.38526	.39204	.39878
.5	.40547	.41211	.41871	.42527	.43178	.43825	.44469	.45108	.45742	.46373
.6	.47000	.47623	.48243	.48858	.49470	.50078	.50682	.51282	.51879	.52473
.7	.53063	.53649	.54232	.54812	.55389	.55962	.56531	.57098	.57661	.58222
.8	.58779	.59333	.59884	.60432	.60977	.61519	.62058	.62594	.63127	.63658
.9	.64185	.64710	.65233	.65752	.66269	.66783	.67294	.67803	.68310	.68813
2.0	0.69315	.69813	.70310	.70804	.71295	.71784	.72271	.72755	.73237	.73716
.1	.74194	.74669	.75142	.75612	.76081	.76547	.77011	.77473	.77932	.78390
.2	.78846	.79299	.79751	.80200	.80648	.81093	.81536	.81978	.82418	.82855
.3	.83291	.83725	.84157	.84587	.85015	.85442	.85866	.86289	.86710	.87129
.4	.87547	.87963	.88377	.88789	.89200	.89609	.90016	.90422	.90826	.91228
.5	.91629	.92028	.92426	.92822	.93216	.93609	.94001	.94391	.94779	.95166
.6	.95551	.95935	.96317	.96698	.97078	.97456	.97833	.98208	.98582	.98954
.7	.99325	.99695	.00063[a]	.00430[a]	.00796[a]	.01160[a]	.01523[a]	.01885[a]	.02245[a]	.02604[a]
.8	1.02962	.03318	.03674	.04028	.04380	.04732	.05082	.05431	.05779	.06126
.9	.06471	.06815	.07158	.07500	.07841	.08181	.08519	.08856	.09192	.09527
3.0	1.09861	.10194	.10526	.10856	.11186	.11514	.11841	.12168	.12493	.12817
.1	.13140	.13462	.13783	.14103	.14422	.14740	.15057	.15373	.15688	.16002
.2	.16315	.16627	.16938	.17248	.17557	.17865	.18173	.18479	.18784	.19089
.3	.19392	.19695	.19996	.20297	.20597	.20896	.21194	.21491	.21788	.22083
.4	.22378	.22671	.22964	.23256	.23547	.23837	.24127	.24415	.24703	.24990
.5	.25276	.25562	.25846	.26130	.26413	.26695	.26976	.27257	.27536	.27815
.6	.28093	.28371	.28647	.28923	.29198	.29473	.29746	.30019	.30291	.30563
.7	.30833	.31103	.31372	.31641	.31909	.32176	.32442	.32708	.32972	.33237
.8	.33500	.33763	.34025	.34286	.34547	.34807	.35067	.35325	.35584	.35841
.9	.36098	.36354	.36609	.36864	.37118	.37372	.37624	.37877	.38128	.38379
4.0	1.38629	.38879	.39128	.39377	.39624	.39872	.40118	.40364	.40610	.40854
.1	.41099	.41342	.41585	.41828	.42070	.42311	.42552	.42792	.43031	.43270
.2	.43508	.43746	.43984	.44220	.44456	.44692	.44927	.45161	.45395	.45629
.3	.45862	.46094	.46326	.46557	.46787	.47018	.47247	.47476	.47705	.47933
.4	.48160	.48387	.48614	.48840	.49065	.49290	.49515	.49739	.49962	.50185
.5	.50408	.50630	.50851	.51072	.51293	.51513	.51732	.51951	.52170	.52388
.6	.52606	.52823	.53039	.53256	.53471	.53687	.53902	.54116	.54330	.54543
.7	.54756	.54969	.55181	.55393	.55604	.55814	.56025	.56235	.56444	.56653
.8	.56862	.57070	.57277	.57485	.57691	.57898	.58104	.58309	.58515	.58719
.9	.58924	.59127	.59331	.59534	.59737	.59939	.60141	.60342	.60543	.60744

[a] Add 1.0 to indicated figure.

1. Recall that the logarithm of a number is the power, or exponent, to which a specified base must be raised to equal the number; that is, the log (base 10) of 100 is 2 because $(10)^2 = 100$. In the system of natural logs the base is $e \approx 2.718$.

natural logs, we find 0.5 to lie between 0.49470 and 0.50078, whose antilogs are 1.64 and 1.65 respectively. Interpolating, we find the antilog of 0.5 to be 1.648. Thus, 1.648 is the interest factor for a 10 per cent growth rate compounded continuously for five years; £1 growing continuously at this compound rate would equal £1.648 after five years.

Since continuous compounding is not commonly applied in practice, we have not provided a table of continuous interest factors. It should be noted, however, that the £1.648 obtained for five years of *continuous* compounding compares closely with £1.629, the figure for semi-annual compounding, and with the £1.611 obtained with annual compounding. Thus, continuous compounding does not produce values materially different from semi-annual or annual compounding. As was pointed out earlier, the importance of continuous compounding is its convenience in theoretical work where calculus must be employed.

CONTINUOUS DISCOUNTING

Equation 9A–5 can be transformed into equation 9A–9 and used to determine present values under continuous compounding. Using k as the discount rate (again, this is the standard notation: k is used as the discount rate, and g as the growth rate for compounding), we obtain

$$PV = \frac{V_t}{e^{kt}} = V_t e^{-kt}. \qquad (9A\text{–}9)$$

Thus, if £1648 is due in five years and if the appropriate continuous discount rate k is 10 per cent, the present value of this future payment is

$$PV = \frac{£1648}{1.648} = £1000.$$

CONTINUOUS COMPOUNDING AND DISCOUNTING FOR ANNUITIES

The treatment of continuous compounding for single values is more complex than that for discrete compounding, but it still involves nothing more than algebra. For continuously compounding and discounting *streams* of payments ('annuities'), however, elementary integral calculus must be employed. The procedures involved are outlined below.

Step 1

First, observe Figure 9A–2(a). An amount a is received at the end of each year. The amount received grows at the

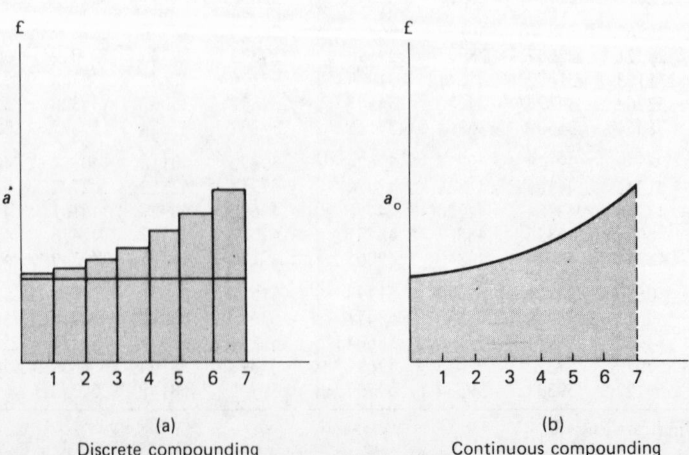

Figure 9A–2 *Sum of an 'Annuity' under Discrete and Continuous Compounding.*

rate g; thus the accumulated sum of the receipts at the end of any year N is

$$S_t = a(1+g)^0 + a(1+g)^1 + a(1+g)^2 + \dots a(1+g)^{t-1}$$
$$= a + a(1+g)^1 + a(1+g)^2 + \dots a(1+g)^{t-1}$$
$$= \sum_{t=1}^{N} a(1+g)^{t-1}.$$

The accumulated sum of the receipts, S_t, is equal to the sum of the rectangles in Figure 9A–2(a); this is the area under the discontinuous curve formed by the tops of the rectangles.

Step 2

Exactly the same principle is involved in finding the accumulated sum of the continuous equivalent of an annuity, or a stream of receipts received continuously. The accumulated sum is again represented by the area under a curve, but now the curve is continuous as in Figure 9A–2(b). In the discrete case, the area under the curve was obtained by adding the rectangles; in the continuous case, the area must be found by the process of integration.

Note that the stream of receipts, or the value of a_t, is found by taking the initial receipt, a_0 (*not* a_1), and letting it grow at the continuous rate g.

$$a_t = a_0 e^{gt}. \tag{9A–10}$$

Equation 9A–10 defines the curve, and the area under the curve (S_t) is represented by the integral

$$S_t = \int_{t=0}^{N} a_0 e^{gt} dt = a_0 \int_{t=0}^{N} e^{gt} dt. \tag{9A–11}$$

Step 3

Given a discrete series of receipts such as those shown in Figure 9A–2(a) and a discount rate, k, we find their PV as

$$PV = \sum_{t=1}^{N} a_t (1+k)^{-t}.$$

If the receipts accrue continuously, as do those in Figure 9A–2(b), we must find the present value of the stream of payments by calculus. First, note that by equation 9A–9 we find the PV of the instantaneous receipt for period t as

$$PV = a_t e^{-kt} dt. \tag{9A–9}$$

The present value of the entire stream of receipts is given as the integral

$$PV = \int_{t=0}^{N} a_t e^{-kt} dt. \tag{9A–12}$$

Step 4

Although the primary equations (9A–11 and 9A–12) developed thus far in this section are seldom used individually, one of the most important theoretical formulations in the field of finance – the Gordon model – is developed by combining them. The Gordon model is discussed at some length in Chapter 17, but we can facilitate that discussion by showing at this point how these equations can be combined.

First, note that $a_t = a_0 e^{gt}$ from equation 9A–10. Next, substitute this value into equation 9A–12, obtaining

$$PV = \int_{t=0}^{N} a_0 e^{gt} e^{-kt} dt. \tag{9A–13}$$

Now remove the constant term, a_0, from within the integral and combine the exponents of the e term, obtaining

$$PV = a_0 \int_{t=0}^{N} e^{gt-kt} dt$$
$$= a_0 \int_{t=0}^{N} e^{-(k-g)t} dt. \tag{9A–14}$$

Therefore, the integration of equation 9A–14 yields an indefinite integral of the form

$$PV = \frac{a_0 e^{-(k-g)t}}{k-g}$$

that, when evaluated at $t = \infty$, is equal to 0 and when evaluated at $t = 0$, is equal to

$$\frac{a_0}{k-g}.$$

Subtracting the lower bound from the upper (which is 0) yields:

$$PV = 0 - \left[-\frac{a_0}{k-g} \right]$$

$$= \frac{a_0}{k-g}. \qquad \text{(9A–15)}$$

Equation 9A—15 is thus the present value of a continuous stream of receipts growing at a rate g and discounted at a rate k. The basic Gordon model, which is essentially equation 9A–15, is widely used in finance, but its further development is deferred to Chapter 17.

Chapter 10

Capital Budgeting Techniques

Capital budgeting involves the entire process of planning expenditures whose returns are expected to extend beyond one year. The choice of one year is arbitrary, of course, but it is a convenient cut-off point for distinguishing between kinds of expenditures. Obvious examples of capital outlays are expenditures for land, buildings and equipment, and for permanent additions to working capital associated with factory expansion. An advertising or promotion campaign, or a programme of research and development, is also likely to have an impact beyond one year, so they too can be classified as capital budgeting expenditures.

Capital budgeting is important for the future well-being of the firm; it is also a complex, conceptually difficult topic. As we shall see later in this chapter, the optimum capital budget – the level of investment that maximizes the present value of the firm – is simultaneously determined by the interaction of supply and demand forces under conditions of uncertainty. Supply forces refer to the supply of capital to the firm, or its *cost of capital schedule.* Demand forces relate to the investment opportunities open to the firm, as measured by the *stream of revenues* that will result from an investment decision. *Uncertainty* enters the decision because it is impossible to know exactly either the cost of capital or the stream of revenues that will be derived from a project.

To facilitate an exposition of the investment decision process, we have broken the topic down into its major components. In this chapter, we consider the capital budgeting process and the techniques generally employed by reasonably sophisticated business firms. Here our focus is on the time factor, and the compound interest concepts covered in the preceding chapter are used extensively. Uncertainty is explicitly and formally considered in Chapter 11, and the cost of capital concept is developed and related to capital budgeting in Chapters 17 to 19, after a discussion of the sources and forms of long-term capital in Chapters 12 to 16.

SIGNIFICANCE OF CAPITAL BUDGETING

A number of factors combine to make capital budgeting perhaps the most importan decision with which financial management is involved. Further, all departments of firm – production, marketing, and so on – are vitally affected by the capital budgetin decisions, so all executives, no matter what their primary responsibility, must be aware o how capital budgeting decisions are made. These points are discussed in this section.

Long-term effects

First and foremost, the fact that the results continue over an extended period means tha the decision maker loses some of his flexibility. He must make a commitment into th future. For example, the purchase of an asset with an economic life of 10 years requires long period of waiting before the final results of the action can be known. The decisio maker must commit funds for this period and, thus, he becomes a hostage of future event

Asset expansion is fundamentally related to expected future sales. A decision to buy o to construct a fixed asset that is expected to last five years involves an implicit five-yea sales forecast. Indeed, the economic life of a purchased asset represents an implici forecast for the duration of the economic life of the asset. Hence, failure to forecas accurately will result in over-investment or under-investment in fixed assets.

An erroneous forecast of asset requirements can result in serious consequences. If th firm has invested too much in assets, it will incur unnecessarily heavy expenses. If it has no spent enough on fixed assets, two serious problems may arise. First, the firm's equipmen may not be sufficiently modern to enable it to produce competitively. Second, if it ha inadequate capacity, it may lose a portion of its share of the market to rival firms. To regai lost customers typically requires heavy selling expenses, price reduction, produc improvements, and so forth.

Timing the availability of capital assets

Another problem is to phase properly the availability of capital assets in order to hav them come 'on stream' at the correct time. For example, the managing director of decorative tile company gave the authors an illustration of the importance of capita budgeting. His firm tried to operate near capacity most of the time. For about four year there had been intermittent spurts in the demand for its product; when these spurt occurred, the firm had to turn away orders. After a sharp increase in demand, the firr would add capacity by renting an additional building, then purchasing and installing th appropriate equipment. It would take six to eight months to have the additional capacit ready. At this point the company frequently found that there was no demand for it increased output – other firms had already expanded their operations and had taken a increased share of the market, with the result that demand for this firm had levelled off. I the firm had properly forecast demand and had planned its increase in capacity six month or one year in advance, it would have been able to maintain its market – indeed, to obtain larger share of the market.

Quality of capital assets

Good capital budgeting will also improve the timing of asset acquisitions and the qualit of assets purchased. This situation follows from the nature of capital goods and the producers. Capital goods are not ordered by firms until they see that sales are beginning to press on capacity. Such occasions occur simultaneously for many firms. When the heavy orders come in, the producers of capital goods go from a situation of idle capacity to one where they cannot meet all the orders that have been placed. Consequently, large backlogs accumulate. Since the production of capital goods involves a relatively long work-in-progress period, a year or more of waiting may be involved before the additional capital goods are available. This factor has obvious implications for purchasing agents and factory managers.

Raising funds

Another reason for the importance of capital budgeting is that asset expansion typically involves substantial expenditures. Before a firm spends a large amount of money, it must make the proper plans – large amounts of funds are not available automatically. A firm contemplating a major capital expenditure programme may need to arrange its financing several years in advance to be sure of having the funds required for the expansion.

Ability to compete

Finally, it has been said with a great deal of truth that many firms fail, not because they have too much capital equipment but because they have too little. While the conservative approach of having a small amount of capital equipment may be appropriate at times, such an approach may also be fatal if a firm's competitors install modern, automated equipment that permits them to produce a better product and sell it at a lower price. The same thing also holds true for nations: if United Kingdom firms fail to modernize but those of other nations do, then the UK will not be able to compete in world markets. Thus, an understanding of business investment behaviour and of factors that motivate firms to undertake investment programmes is vital for cabinet ministers and others involved in governmental policy making.

A SIMPLIFIED VIEW OF CAPITAL BUDGETING

Capital budgeting is, in essence, an application of a classic proposition from the economic theory of the firm: namely, a firm should operate at the point where its marginal revenue is just equal to its marginal cost. When this rule is applied to the capital budgeting decision, marginal revenue is taken to be the percentage rate of return on investments, while marginal cost is the firm's marginal cost of capital.

A simplified version of the concept is depicted in Figure 10–1(a). Here the horizontal axis measures the total investment during a year, while the vertical axis shows both the percentage cost of capital and the rate of return on projects. The projects are denoted by boxes – project A, for example, calls for an outlay of £3 million and promises a 17 per cent rate of return; project B requires £1 million and yields about 16 per cent; and so on. The last investment, project G, simply involves buying 4 per cent Treasury stock, which may be purchased in unlimited quantities. In Figure 10–1(b) the concept is generalized to show smoothed investment opportunity schedules (*IRR*), and three alternative schedules are presented.[1]

1. The investment opportunity schedules measure the rate of return on each project. The rate of return on a project is generally called the *internal rate of return* (*IRR*). This is why we label the investment opportunity schedules *IRR*. The process of calculating the *IRR* is explained later in this chapter.

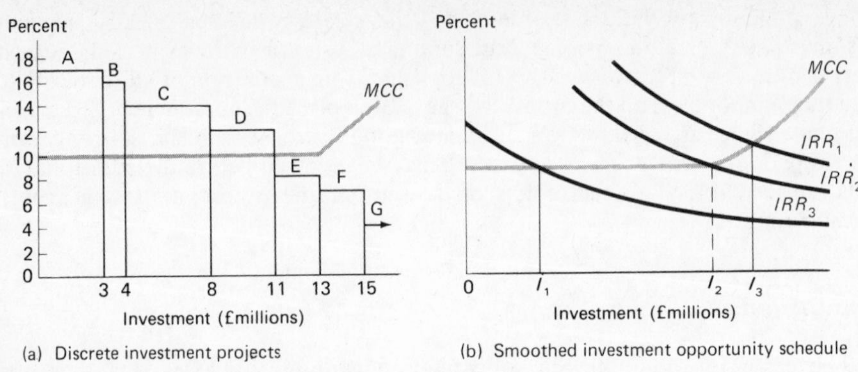

Figure 10–1 *Illustrative Capital Budgeting Decision Process.*

The curve *MCC* designates the marginal cost of capital, or the cost of each additional £1 acquired for purposes of making capital expenditures. As it is drawn in Figure 10–1(a), the marginal cost of capital is constant at 10 per cent until the firm has raised £13 million, after which the marginal cost of capital curve turns up.[2] To maximize profits, the firm should accept projects A through D, obtaining and investing £11 million, and reject E, F and G.

Notice that three alternative investment opportunity schedules are shown in Figure 10–1(b). IRR_1 designates relatively many good investment opportunities, while IRR_3 designates relatively few good projects. The three different curves could be interpreted as applying either to three different firms or to one firm at three different times. As long as the *IRR* curve cuts the *MCC* curve to the left of I_1 – for example, at I_2 – the marginal cost of capital is constant. To the right of I_2 – for example, at I_3 – the cost of capital is rising. Therefore if investment opportunities are such that the *IRR* curve cuts the *MCC* curve to the right of I_2, the *actual* marginal cost of capital (a single point) varies depending on the *IRR* curve. In this chapter we generally *assume* that the *IRR* curve cuts the *MCC* curve to the left of I_2, thus permitting us to assume that the cost of capital is constant. This assumption is relaxed in Chapter 19, where we show how the *MCC* varies with the amount of funds raised during a given year.

APPLICATION OF THE CONCEPT

At the applied level, the capital budgeting process is much more complex than the preceding example suggests. Projects do not just appear; a continuing stream of good investment opportunities results from hard thinking, careful planning and, often, large outlays for research and development. Moreover, some very difficult measurement problems are involved: the sales and costs associated with particular projects must be estimated, frequently for many years into the future, in the face of great uncertainty. Finally, some difficult conceptual and empirical problems arise over the methods of calculating rates of return and the cost of capital.

Businessmen are required to take action, however, even in the face of the kinds of problems described; this requirement has led to the development of procedures that assist in making optimal investment decisions. One of these procedures, forecasting, was discussed in Chapter 4; uncertainty is discussed in formal terms in the Chapter 11; and the important subject of the cost of capital is deferred to Chapter 19. The essentials of the other elements of capital budgeting are taken up in the remainder of this chapter.

2. The reasons for assuming this particular shape for the marginal cost of capital curve are explained in Chapter 19.

Investment proposals

Aside from the actual generation of ideas, the first step in the capital budgeting process is to assemble a list of the proposed new investments, together with the data necessary to appraise them. Although practices vary from firm to firm, proposals dealing with asset acquisitions are frequently grouped according to the following four categories:

1. Replacements.
2. Expansion: additional capacity in existing product lines.
3. Expansion: new product lines.
4. Other (for example, pollution control equipment).

These groupings are somewhat arbitrary, and it is frequently difficult to decide the appropriate category for a particular investment. In spite of such problems, the scheme is used quite widely and, as we shall see, with good reason.

Ordinarily, replacement decisions are the simplest to make. Assets wear out or become obsolete, and they must be replaced if production efficiency is to be maintained. The firm has a very good idea of the cost savings to be obtained by replacing an old asset, and it knows the consequences of non-replacement. All in all, the outcomes of most replacement decisions can be predicted with a high degree of confidence.

An example of the second investment classification is a proposal for adding more machines of the type already in use, or the opening of another branch in a nation-wide chain of food stores. Expansion investments are frequently incorporated in replacement decisions. To illustrate, an old, inefficient machine may be replaced by a larger and more efficient one.

A degree of uncertainty – sometimes extremely high – is clearly involved in expansion, but the firm at least has the advantage of examining past production and sales experience with similar machines or stores. When it considers an investment of the third kind, expansion into new product lines, little if any experience data are available on which to base decisions. To illustrate, when Union Carbide decided to develop the laser for commercial application, it had very little idea of either the development costs or the specific applications to which lasers could be put. Under such circumstances, any estimates must at best be treated as very crude approximations.

The 'other' category is a catchall and includes intangibles; an example is a proposal to boost employee morale and productivity by installing a music system. Mandatory pollution control devices, which must be undertaken even though they produce no revenues, are another example of the 'other' category. Major strategic decisions such as plans for overseas expansion, or mergers, might also be included here, but more frequently they are treated separately from the regular capital budget.

ADMINISTRATIVE DETAILS

The remaining aspects of capital budgeting involve administrative matters. Approvals are typically required at higher levels within the organization as we move away from replacement decisions and as the sums involved increase. One of the most important functions of the board of directors is to approve the major outlays in a capital budgeting programme. Such decisions are crucial for the future well-being of the firm.

The planning horizon for capital budgeting programmes varies with the nature of the industry. When sales can be forecast with a high degree of reliability for 10 to 20 years, the planning period is likely to be correspondingly long; the gas board is an example of such an industry. Also, when the product-technology developments in the industry require an eight-to-ten-year cycle to develop a new major product, as in certain segments of the aerospace industry, a correspondingly long planning period is necessary.

After a capital budget has been adopted, payments must be scheduled. Characteristically, the finance department is responsible for scheduling payments and for acquiring funds to meet payment schedule requirements. The finance department is also primarily responsible for cooperating with the members of operating divisions to compile systematic records on the uses of funds and the uses of equipment purchased in capital budgeting programmes. Effective capital budgeting programmes require such information as the basis for periodic review and evaluation of capital expenditure decisions – the feedback and control phase of capital budgeting, often called the 'post audit'.

The foregoing represents a brief overview of the administrative aspects of capital budgeting; the analytical problems involved are considered next.

CAPITAL BUDGETING ANALYSIS: CHOOSING AMONG ALTERNATIVE PROPOSALS

In most firms there are more proposals for projects than the firm is able or willing to finance. Some proposals are good, others are poor, and methods must be developed for distinguishing between the good and the poor. Essentially, the end product is a ranking of the proposals and a cut-off point for determining how far down the ranked list to go.

In part, proposals are eliminated because they are *mutually exclusive*. Mutually exclusive proposals are alternative methods of doing the same job. If one piece of equipment is chosen to do the job, the others will not be required. Thus, if there is a need to improve the materials handling system in a chemical plant, the job may be done either by conveyer belts or by fork-lift trucks. The selection of one method of doing the job makes it unnecessary to use the others. They are mutually exclusive items.

Independent items are pieces of capital equipment that are being considered for different kinds of projects or tasks that need to be accomplished. For example, in addition to the materials handling system, the chemical firm may need equipment to package the end product. The work would require a packaging machine, and the purchase of equipment for this purpose would be independent of the equipment purchased for materials handling.

To distinguish among the many items that compete for the allocation of the firm's capital funds, a ranking procedure must be developed. This procedure requires, first, calculating the estimated benefits from the use of equipment and, second, translating the estimated benefits into a measure of the advantage of the purchase of the equipment. Thus, an estimate of benefits is required, and a method for converting the benefits into a ranking measure must be developed.

IMPORTANCE OF GOOD DATA

Most discussions of measuring the cash flows associated with capital projects are relatively brief, but it is important to emphasize *that in the entire capital budgeting procedure, probably nothing is of greater importance than a reliable estimate of the cost savings or revenue increases that will be achieved from the prospective outlay of capital funds.* The increased output and sales revenue resulting from expansion programmes are obvious benefits. Cost reduction benefits include changes in quality and quantity of direct labour; in amount and cost of scrap and rework time; in fuel costs; and in maintenance expenses, time in which machinery is inactive during working hours, safety, flexibility, and so on. So many variables are involved that it is obviously impossible to make neat generalizations. However, this should not minimize the crucial importance of the required analysis of the benefits derived from capital expenditures. Each capital equipment expenditure must be examined in detail for possible additional costs and savings.

All the subsequent procedures for ranking projects are no better than the data input – the old saying, 'garbage in, garbage out', is certainly applicable to capital budgeting analysis. Thus, the data assembly process is not a routine clerical task to be performed on a mechanical basis. It requires continuous monitoring and evaluation of estimates by those competent to make such evaluations – engineers, accountants, economists, cost analysts and other qualified persons.

After costs and benefits have been estimated, they are utilized for ranking alternative investment proposals. How this ranking is accomplished is our next topic.

RANKING INVESTMENT PROPOSALS

The point of capital budgeting – indeed, the point of all financial analysis – is to make decisions that will maximize the value of the firm's share capital. The capital budgeting process is designed to answer two questions: (a) Which of several mutually exclusive investments should be selected? (b) How many projects, in total, should be accepted?

Among the many methods used for ranking investment proposals, three are discussed here:[3]

1. *Payback method (or payback period):* number of years required to return the original investment.
2. *Net present value (NPV) method:* present value of future returns discounted at the appropriate cost of capital, minus the cost of the investment.
3. *Internal rate of return (IRR) method:* interest rate which equates the present value of future returns to the investment outlay.

Future returns are, in all cases, defined as the net income after taxes, plus depreciation, that result from a project. This is also equal to net operating income before deduction of payments to the financing sources but after the deduction of applicable taxes. Thus net operating income after taxes is before deduction of financial payments such as interest on debt and dividends to shareholders. The net operating income after taxes is divided by the value of the firm to obtain the after-tax cost of capital of the firm as a whole:

$$\begin{aligned}\text{Cost of capital} &= \text{Net income plus depreciation/value of the firm}\\ &= \text{Net operating income } (1-T) + T \text{ (depreciation)/value of the firm}\end{aligned}$$

Note that since interest costs are included in the net operating income, they are reflected in the measurement of the cost of capital for the firm. *In other words, returns are synonymous with net operating cash flows from investments.* Next, the nature and characteristics of the three methods are illustrated and explained. To make the explanations more meaningful, the same data are used to illustrate each procedure.

---

3. A number of 'average rate of return' methods have been discussed in the literature and used in practice. These methods are generally unsound and, with the widespread use of computers, completely unnecessary. We discussed them in earlier editions, but they are deleted from this edition. We also note that a 'benefit/cost' or 'profitability index' method is sometimes used; this method is taken up in Appendix A to this chapter.

Payback method

Assume that two projects are being considered by a firm. Each requires an investment of £1000. The firm's marginal cost of capital is 10 per cent.[4] The net cash flows (net operating income after tax plus depreciation) from investments A and B are shown in Table 10–1.

Table 10–1 *Net Cash Flows.*

Year	A	B
1	£500	£100
2	400	200
3	300	300
4	100	400
5		500
6		600

The *payback period* is the number of years it takes a firm to recover its original investment from net cash flows. Since the cost is £1000, the payback period is two and one-third years for project A and four years for project B. If the firm were employing a three-year payback period, project A would be accepted but project B would be rejected.

Although the payback period is very easy to calculate, it can lead to the wrong decisions. As the illustration demonstrates, it ignores income beyond the payback period. If the project is one maturing in later years, the use of the payback period can lead to the selection of less desirable investments. Projects with longer payback periods are characteristically those involved in long-range planning – developing a new product or tapping a new market. These are just the strategic decisions which determine a firm's fundamental position, but they also involve investments which do not yield their highest returns for a number of years. This means that the payback method may be biased against the very investments that are most important to a firm's long-run success.

Recognition of the longer period over which an investment is likely to yield savings points up another weakness in the use of the payback method for ranking investment proposals: its failure to take into account the time value of money. To illustrate, consider two assets, X and Y, each costing £300 and each having the following cash flows:

Year	X	Y
1	200	100
2	100	200
3	100	100

Each project has a two-year payback; hence, each would appear equally desirable. However, we know that a pound today is worth more than a pound next year, so project X, with its faster cash flow, is certainly more desirable.

The use of the payback period is sometimes defended on the grounds that returns beyond three or four years are fraught with such great uncertainty that it is best to disregard them altogether in a planning decision. However, this is clearly an unsound procedure. Some investments with the highest returns are those which may not come to fruition for eight to ten years. The new product cycle in industries involving advanced technologies may not have a pay-off for eight or nine years. Furthermore, even though returns that occur after three, four or five years may be highly uncertain, it is important to

4. A discussion of how the cost of capital is calculated is presented in Chapter 19. For now, the cost of capital should be considered as the firm's opportunity cost of making a particular investment; that is, if the firm does not make a particular investment, it 'saves' the cost of this investment, and if it can invest these funds in another project that provides a return of 10 per cent, then its 'opportunity cost' of making the first investment is 10 per cent.

make a judgement about the likelihood of their occurring. To ignore them is to assign a nil probability to these distant receipts. This can hardly produce the best results.

Another defence of the payback method is that a firm that is short of cash must necessarily give great emphasis to a quick return of its funds so that they may be put to use in other places or in meeting other needs. However, this does not relieve the payback method of its many shortcomings, and there are better methods for handling the cash shortage situation.[5]

A third reason for using payback is that, typically, projects with faster paybacks have more favourable short-run effects on earnings per share. Firms that use payback for this reason are sacrificing future growth for current accounting income, and in general such a practice will not maximize the value of the firm. The discounted cash flow techniques discussed in the next section, if used properly, automatically give consideration to the present earnings versus future growth trade-off and strike the balance that will maximize the firm's value.

Also, the payback method is sometimes used simply because it is so easy to apply. If a firm is making many small capital expenditure decisions, the costs of using more complex methods may outweigh the benefits of possibly 'better' choices among competing projects. Thus, many large companies with very sophisticated capital budgeting procedures use discounted cash flow techniques for larger projects, but they use payback on certain small, routine replacement decisions. When these sophisticated companies do use the payback method, however, they generally do so only after special studies have indicated that the payback method will provide sufficiently accurate answers for the decisions at hand.

Finally, many firms use payback in combination with one of the discounted cash flow procedures described below. The *NPV* or *IRR* method is used to appraise a project's profitability, while the payback is used to show how long the initial investment will be at risk; that is, payback is used as a risk indicator. Recent surveys have shown that when larger firms use payback in connection with major projects, it is almost always used in this manner.

Net present value method

As the flaws in the payback method were understood, people began to search for methods of evaluating projects that would recognize that a pound received immediately is preferable to a pound received at some future date. This recognition led to the development of *discounted cash flow* (*DCF*) *techniques* to take account of the time value of money. One such discounted cash flow technique is called the 'net present value method', or sometimes simply the 'present value method'. *To implement this approach, find the present value of the expected net cash flows of an investment, discounted at the cost of capital, and subtract from it the initial cost outlay of the project.*[6] If the net present value is positive, the project should be accepted; if negative, it should be rejected. If the two projects are mutually exclusive, the one with the higher net present value should be chosen.

The equation for the net present value (*NPV*) is[7]

---

5. We interpret a cash shortage to mean that the firm has a high opportunity cost for its funds and a high cost of capital. We would consider this high cost of capital in the internal rate of return method or the net present value method, thus taking account of the cash shortage.

6. If costs are spread over several years, this must be taken into account. Suppose, for example, that a firm bought land in 1975, erected a building in 1976, installed equipment in 1977, and started production in 1978. One could treat 1975 as the base year, comparing the present value of the costs as of 1975 to the present value of the benefit stream as of that same date.

7. The second equation is simply a shorthand expression in which sigma (Σ) signifies 'sum up' or add the present values of N profit terms. If $t = 1$, then $F_t = F_1$ and $1/(1+k)^t = 1/(1+k)^1$; if $t = 2$, then $F_t = F_2$ and $1/(1+k)^t = 1/(1+k)^2$; and so on until $t = N$, the last year the project provides any profits. The

$$NPV = \left[\frac{F_1}{(1+k)^1} + \frac{F_2}{(1+k)^2} + \ldots + \frac{F_N}{(1+k)^N}\right] - I \qquad (10\text{–}1)$$

$$= \sum_{t=1}^{N} \frac{F_t}{(1+k)^t} - I.$$

Here F_1, F_2 and so forth, represent the net cash flows; k is the marginal cost of capital; I is the initial cost of the project; and N is the project's expected life.

The net present values of projects A and B are calculated in Table 10–2. Project A has an *NPV* of £92, while B's *NPV* is £400. On this basis, both should be accepted if they are independent, but B should be the one chosen if they are mutually exclusive.

Table 10–2 *Calculating the Net Present Value* (NPV) *of Projects with £1000 Cost.*

	Project A			Project B		
Year	Net cash flow	*PVIF* (10%)	*PV* of cash flow	Net cash flow	*PVIF* (10%)	*PV* of cash flow
1	£500	0.91	£ 455	£100	0.91	£ 91
2	400	0.83	332	200	0.83	166
3	300	0.75	225	300	0.75	225
4	100	0.68	68	400	0.68	272
5	10	0.62	6	500	0.62	310
6	10	0.56	6	600	0.56	336
		PV of inflows	£1092			£1400
		Less: cost	− 1000			− 1000
		NPV	£ 92			£ 400

When a firm takes on a project with a positive *NPV*, the value of the firm increases by the amount of the *NPV*. In our example, the value of the firm increases by £400 if it takes on project B, but by only £92 if it takes on project A. Viewing the alternatives in this manner, it is easy to see why B is preferred to A, and it is also easy to see the logic of the *NPV* approach.

Internal rate of return method

The internal rate of return (*IRR*) is defined as the *interest rate that equates the present value of the expected future cash flows, or receipts, to the initial cost outlay.* The equation for calculating the internal rate of return is

$$\frac{F_1}{(1+r)^1} + \frac{F_2}{(1+r)^2} + \ldots + \frac{F_N}{(1+r)^N} - I = 0$$

$$\sum_{t=1}^{N} \frac{F_t}{(1+r)^t} - I = 0. \qquad (10\text{–}2)$$

Here we know the value of I and also the values of $F_1, F_2, \ldots, F_N$, but we do not know the value of r. Thus, we have an equation with one unknown, and we can solve for the value of r. Some value of r will cause the sum of the discounted receipts to equal the initial cost of

---

symbol $\sum_{t=1}^{N}$ simply says 'go through the following process: Let $t = 1$ and find the *PV* of F_1; then let $t = 2$ and find the *PV* of F_2. Continue until the *PV* of each individual profit has been found; then add the *PV*s of these individual profits to find the *PV* of the asset.'

the project, making the equation equal to nil, and that value of r is defined as the internal rate of return; that is, the solution value of r is the *IRR*.

Notice that the internal rate of return formula, equation 10–2, is simply the *NPV* formula, equation 10–1, solved for that particular value of k that causes the *NPV* to equal nil. In other words, the same basic equation is used for both methods, but in the *NPV* method the discount rate (k) is specified and the *NPV* is found, while in the *IRR* method the *NPV* is specified to equal nil and the value of r that forces the *NPV* to equal nil is found.

The internal rate of return may be found by trial and error. First, compute the present value of the cash flows from an investment, using an arbitrarily selected interest rate. (Since the cost of capital for most firms is in the range of 10 to 15 per cent, projects will hopefully promise a return of at least 10 per cent. Therefore, 10 per cent is a good starting point for most problems.) Then compare the present value so obtained with the investment's cost. If the present value is higher than the cost figure, try a higher interest rate and go through the procedure again. Conversely, if the present value is lower than the cost, lower the interest rate and repeat the process. Continue until the present value of the flows from the investment is approximately equal to its cost. *The interest rate that brings about this equality is defined as the internal rate of return.*[8]

Table 10–3 *Finding the Internal Rate of Return.*

	Cash flows (F_1 values)		
	Year	F_A	F_B
I = Investment = £1000	1: F_1 =	£500	£100
	2: F_2 =	400	200
	3: F_3 =	300	300
	4: F_4 =	100	400
	5: F_5 =	10	500
	6: F_6 =	10	600

	10 per cent			15 per cent			20 per cent		
		Present value			Present value			Present value	
Year	*PVIF*	A	B	*PVIF*	A	B	*PVIF*	A	B
1	0.91	£ 455	£ 91	0.87	£ 435	£ 87	0.83	£415	£ 83
2	0.83	332	166	0.76	304	152	0.69	276	138
3	0.75	225	225	0.66	198	198	0.58	174	174
4	0.68	68	272	0.57	57	228	0.48	48	192
5	0.62	6	310	0.50	5	250	0.40	4	200
6	0.56	6	336	0.43	4	258	0.33	3	198
Present value		£1092	£1400		£1003	£1173		£920	£985
Net present value = $PV - I$		£92	£400		(3)	£173		£(80)	£(15)

This calculation process is illustrated in Table 10–3 for projects A and B. First, the 10 per cent interest factors are obtained from Table D–2 at the end of the book. These factors are then multiplied by the cash flows for the corresponding years, and the present values of the

8. In order to reduce the number of trials required to find the internal rate of return, it is important to minimize the error at each iteration. One reasonable approach is to make as good a first approximation as possible, then to 'straddle' the internal rate of return by making fairly large changes in the interest rate early in the iterative process. In practice, if many projects are to be evaluated or if many years are involved, relatively inexpensive hand calculators can be used to solve for the internal rate of return.

annual cash flows are placed in the appropriate columns. For example, the *PVIF* of 0.91 is multiplied by £500, and the product, £455, is placed in the first row of column A.

The present values of the yearly cash flows are then summed to get the investment's total present value. Subtracting the cost of the project from this figure gives the net present value. As the net present values of both investments are positive at the 10 per cent rate, increase the rate to 15 per cent and try again. *At this point the net present value of investment A is approximately nil, which indicates that its internal rate of return is approximately 15 per cent. Continuing, B is found to have an internal rate of return of approximately 20 per cent.*[9]

What is so special about the particular discount rate that equates the cost of a project with the present value of its future cash flows? Suppose that the weighted cost of all of the funds obtained by the firm is 10 per cent. If the internal rate of return on a particular project is 10 per cent, the same as the cost of capital, the firm would be able to use the cash flow generated by the investment to repay the funds obtained, including the costs of the funds. If the internal rate of return exceeds 10 per cent, the value of the firm increases. If the internal rate of return is less than 10 per cent, taking on the project would cause a decline in the value of the firm. It is this 'break-even' characteristic that increases or decreases the value of the firm and makes the internal rate of return of particular significance.

Assuming that the firm uses a cost of capital of 10 per cent, the internal rate of return criterion states that, if the two projects are independent, both should be accepted – they both do better than 'break even'. If they are mutually exclusive, B ranks higher and should be accepted, while A should be rejected.

A more complete illustration of how the internal rate of return would be used in practice is given in Table 10–4. Assuming a 10 per cent cost of capital, the firm should accept projects 1 to 7, reject projects 8 to 10, and have a total capital budget of £10 million.

Table 10–4 *The Prospective-Projects Schedule.*

Nature of proposal	Amount of funds required	Cumulative total	*IRR*
1. Purchase of leased space	£2 000 000	£2 000 000	23 %
2. Mechanization of accounting system	1 200 000	3 200 000	19
3. Modernization of office building	1 500 000	4 700 000	17
4. Addition of power facilities	900 000	5 600 000	16
5. Purchase of subsidiary	3 600 000	9 200 000	13
6. Purchase of loading cranes	300 000	9 500 000	12
7. Purchase of fleet of tankers	500 000	10 000 000	11
			10 % cut-off
8. Installation of conveyor system	200 000	10 200 000	9
9. Construction of new factory	2 300 000	12 500 000	8
10. Purchase of executive aircraft	200 000	12 700 000	7

IRR for level cash flows

If the cash flows from a project are level, or equal in each year, then the project's internal rate of return can be found by a relatively simple process. In essence, such a project is an annuity: the firm makes an outlay, I, and receives a stream of cash flow benefits, F, for a given number of years. The *IRR* for the project is found by applying equation 9–6, discussed in Chapter 9.

To illustrate, suppose a project has a cost of £10 000 and is expected to produce cash

9. The *IRR* can also be estimated graphically. First, calculate the *NPV* at two or three discount rates as in Table 10–3. Next, plot these *NPV*s against the discount rates – see Figure 10–2 in the next section for an example. The horizontal axis intercept is the *IRR*; with graph paper and a sharp pencil, the *IRR* can be estimated to three decimal places.

flows of £1627 a year for 10 years. The cost of the project, £10 000, is the present value of an annuity of £1627 a year for 10 years, so applying equation 9–6 we obtain

$$\frac{\mathrm{I}}{\mathrm{F}} = \frac{£10\,000}{£1627} = 6.146 = PVIF_a.$$

Looking up $PVIF_a$ in Table D–4, across the 10-year row, we find it (approximately) under the 10 per cent column. Accordingly, 10 per cent is the *IRR* on the project. In other words, 10 per cent is the value of r that would force equation 10–2 to nil when F is constant at £1627 for 10 years and I is £10 000. This procedure works only if the project has constant annual cash flows; if it does not, the *IRR* must be found by trial and error or by using a calculator.

BASIC DIFFERENCES BETWEEN THE NPV AND IRR METHODS[10]

As noted above, the *NPV* method (a) accepts all independent projects whose *NPV* is greater than nil and (b) ranks mutually exclusive projects by their *NPV*s, selecting the project with the higher *NPV* according to equation 10–3:

$$NPV = \sum_{t=1}^{N} \frac{\mathrm{F}_t}{(1+k)^t} - \mathrm{I}. \qquad (10\text{–}3)$$

The *IRR* method, on the other hand, finds the value of r that forces equation 10–4 to equal nil:

$$NPV = \sum_{t=1}^{N} \frac{\mathrm{F}_t}{(1+r)^t} - \mathrm{I} = 0. \qquad (10\text{–}4)$$

The *IRR* method calls for accepting independent projects where r, the internal rate of return, is greater than k, the cost of capital, and for selecting among mutually exclusive projects depending on which has the higher *IRR*.

It is apparent that the only structural difference between the *NPV* and *IRR* methods lies in the discount rates used in the two equations – all the values in the equations are identical except for r and k. Further, we can see that if $r > k$, then $NPV > 0$.[11] *Accordingly, the two methods give the same accept–reject decisions for specific projects – if a project is acceptable under the* NPV *criterion, it is also acceptable if the* IRR *method is used.*

However, under certain conditions the *NPV* and *IRR* methods can *rank* projects differently, and if mutually exclusive projects are involved or if capital is limited, then rankings can be important. The conditions under which different rankings can occur are as follows:

1. The cost of one project is larger than that of the other.
2. The timing of the projects' cash flows differs. For example, the cash flows of one project may increase over time, while those of the other decrease, or the projects may have different expected lives.

---

10. This section is relatively technical and may be omitted on a first reading without loss of continuity.
11. This can be seen by noting that $NPV = 0$ only when $r = k$:

$$NPV = \sum_{t=1}^{N} \frac{\mathrm{F}_t}{(1+k)^t} - 1 = \sum_{t=1}^{N} \frac{\mathrm{F}_t}{(1+r)^t} - 1 = 0,$$

if and only if $r = k$. If $r > k$, then $NPV > 0$, and if $r < k$, then $NPV < 0$. We should also note that, under certain conditions, there may be more than one root to equation 10–4, hence multiple *IRR*s are found. See Appendix A to this chapter for a more detailed discussion of the multiple root problem.

The first point can be seen by considering two mutually exclusive projects, L and S, of greatly differing sizes. Project S calls for the investment of £1.00 and yields £1.50 at the end of one year. Its *IRR* is 50 per cent, and at a 10 per cent cost of capital its *NPV* is £0.36. Project L costs £1 million and yields £1.25 million at the end of the year. Its *IRR* is only 25 per cent, but its *NPV* at 10 per cent is £113 625. The two methods rank the projects differently: $IRR_s > IRR_L$, but $NPV_L > NPV_s$. This is, of course, an extreme case, but whenever projects differ in size, the *NPV* and the *IRR* can give different rankings.[12]

The effect of differential cash flows is somewhat more difficult to understand, but it can be illustrated by an example. Consider two projects, A and B, whose cash flows over their three-year lives are given below:

Cash Flow from Project.

Year	A	B
1	£1000	£ 100
2	500	600
3	100	1100

Project A's cash flows are higher in the early years, but B's cash flows increase over time and exceed those of A in later years. Each project costs £1200, and their *NPV*s, discounted at the specified rates, are shown below:

	NPV	
Discount rate	A	B
0%	£400	£600
5	300	400
10	200	200
15	100	50
20	50	(85)
25	(25)	(175)
30	(100)	(250)

At a nil discount rate, the *NPV* of each project is simply the sum of its receipts less its cost. Thus, the *NPV* of project A at 0 per cent is £1000 + £500 + £100 − £1200 = £400; that of project B is £100 + £600 + £1100 − £1200 = £600. As the discount rate rises from nil, the *NPV*s of the two projects fall from these values.

The *NPV*s are plotted against the appropriate discount rates in Figure 10–2, a graph defined as a *present value profile*. Notice that the vertical axis intercepts are the *NPV*s when the discount rate is nil, while the horizontal axis intercepts show each project's *IRR*. The internal rate of return is defined as that point where *NPV* is nil; therefore, A's *IRR* is 22 per cent, while B's is 17 per cent. Because its largest cash flows come late in the project's life, when the discounting effects of time are most significant, B's *NPV* falls rapidly as the discount rate rises. However, since A's cash flows come early, when the impact of higher discount rates is not so severe, its *NPV* falls less rapidly as interest rates increase.

Notice that if the cost of capital is below 10 per cent, B has the higher *NPV* but the lower *IRR*, while at a cost of capital above 10 per cent A has both the higher *NPV* and the higher *IRR*. We can generalize these results: *whenever the* NPV *profiles of two projects cross one another, a conflict will exist if the cost of capital is below the cross-over rate.* For our

12. Projects of different size *could* be ranked the same by the *NPV* and *IRR* methods; that is, different sizes do not necessarily mean different rankings.

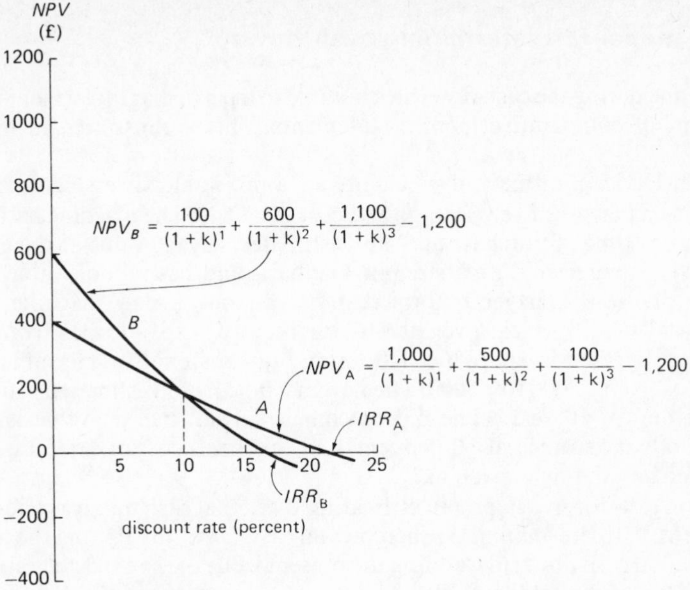

Figure 10–2 *Present Value Profile.*

illustrative projects, no conflict would exist if the firm's cost of capital exceeded 10 per cent, but the two methods would rank A and B differently if k is less than 10 per cent.

How should such conflicts be resolved; for example, when the *NPV* and *IRR* methods yield conflicting rankings, which of two mutually exclusive projects should be selected? Assuming that management is seeking to maximize the value of the firm, the correct decision is to select the project with the higher *NPV*. After all, the *NPVs* measure the projects' contributions to the value of the firm, so the one with the higher *NPV* must be contributing more to the firm's value. *This line of reasoning leads to the conclusion that firms should, in general, use the* NPV *method for evaluating capital investment proposals.*[13] Recognizing this point, sophisticated firms generally rely on the *NPV* method. These firms often calculate (by computer) both the *NPV* and the *IRR*, but they rely on the *NPV* when conflicts arise among mutually exclusive projects.

CAPITAL BUDGETING PROJECT EVALUATION

Thus far the problem of measuring cash flows – the benefits used in the present value calculations above – has not been dealt with directly. This matter will now be discussed, and a few simple examples given. The procedures developed here can be used both for expansion and for replacement decisions.

13. The question of *why* the conflict arises is an interesting one. Basically, it has to do with the reinvestment of cash flows – the *NPV* method implicitly assumes reinvestment at the marginal cost of capital (*MCC*), while the *IRR* method implicitly assumes reinvestment at the internal rate of return. For a value-maximizing firm, reinvestment at the *MCC* is the better assumption. The rationale is as follows: a value-maximizing firm will expand to the point where it accepts all projects yielding more than the *MCC* (these projects will have $NPV > 0$). How these projects are financed is irrelevant – the point is, they will be financed and accepted. Now consider the question of the cash flows from a particular project; if these cash flows are reinvested, at what rate will reinvestment occur? All projects that yield more than the cost of capital have already been accepted; thus, these cash flows can only be invested in physical assets yielding *less than* the *MCC*, or else be used in lieu of other capital with a cost of *MCC*. A rational firm will take the second alternative, so reinvested cash flows will save the firm the cost of capital. This means, in effect, that cash flows are reinvested to yield the cost of capital, which is the assumption implicit in the *NPV* method. For a detailed discussion, see Appendix A to this chapter.

Simplified model for determining cash flows[14]

One way of considering the cash flows attributable to a particular investment is to think of them in terms of comparative income statements. This is illustrated in the following example.

The Widget Division of the Culver Company, a profitable, diversified manufacturing firm, purchased a machine five years ago at a cost of £7500. The machine had an expected life of 15 years at time of purchase and a nil estimated salvage value at the end of the 15 years. It is being depreciated on a straight-line basis and has a book value of £5000 at present. The division manager reports that he can buy a new machine for £12 000 (including installation), which, over its 10-year life, will expand sales from £10 000 to £11 000 a year. Further, it will reduce labour and raw materials usage sufficiently to cut operating costs from £7000 to £5000. The new machine has an estimated salvage value of £2000 at the end of 10 years. The old machine's current market value is £1000. The marginal tax rate is assumed at 50 per cent, and the firm's cost of capital is 10 per cent. Should Culver buy the new machine?

The decision calls for five steps: (a) estimating the actual cash outlay attributable to the new investment, (b) determining the incremental cash flows, (c) finding the present value of the incremental cash flows, (d) adding the present value of the expected salvage value to the present value of the total cash flows, and (e) seeing whether the *NPV* is positive or whether the *IRR* exceeds the cost of capital. These steps are explained further in the following sections.

Estimated cash outlay

The net initial cash outlay consists of these items: (a) payment to the manufacturer, (b) tax effects, and (c) proceeds from the sale of the old machine.[15] Culver must make a £12 000 payment to the manufacturer of the machine but its next tax bill will be reduced because of capital allowances claimed on the new machine. Assuming that the firm had claimed 100 per cent capital allowances on the old machine, and that the initial allowance of 100 per cent is claimed on the new machine, then the tax saving will be: tax saving = (cost of new machine − sale proceeds of old machine) (tax rate) = £(12 000 − 1000) (0.5) = £5500.

To illustrate, suppose the Culver Company's taxable income in the year in which the new machine is to be purchased would have been £100 000 without the purchase of the new machine and consequent sale of the old machine. With a 50 per cent marginal tax rate, Culver would have had a corporation tax liability of £50 000. However, if it buys the new machine and sells the old one, the taxable profits will be reduced by the (net) capital allowances of £11 000 so that the taxable income becomes £89 000 with a corporation tax liability of £44 500. This means that the firm's cash outflow will be £5500 less because it has purchased the new machine.

In addition, there is to be a cash inflow of £1000 from the sale of the old machine. The

---

14. The procedure described in this section facilitates an understanding of the capital investment analysis process, but for repeated calculations the alternative worksheet illustrated in the next section is preferred.

15. A valid argument could be made for not including this item in the decision relating to the purchase of the new machine, provided it was intended to sell the old machine at that time whether or not the new machine was to be purchased. However, this is not the case in this situation and so we include the sale proceeds as a cash flow resulting from the decision to replace.

net result is that the purchase of the new machine involves an immediate net cash outlay[16] of £5500; this is its cost for capital budgeting purposes:

Invoice price of new machine	£12 000
Less: tax savings	− 5 500
Salvage of old machine	− 1 000
Net cash outflow (cost)	£ 5 500

If additional working capital is required as a result of a capital budgeting decision, as would generally be true for expansion-type investments (as opposed to cost-reducing replacement investments), this factor must be taken into account. The amount of *net* working capital (additional current assets required as a result of the expansion minus any spontaneous funds generated by the expansion) is estimated and added to the initial cash outlay. We assume that Culver will not need any additional working capital; hence this factor is ignored in this example.

Annual benefits

Column 1 in Table 10–5 shows the Widget Division's estimated income statement as it would be without the new machine; column 2 shows the statement as it will look if the new investment is made. (It is assumed that these figures are applicable for each of the next 10 years; if this is not the case, then cash flow estimates must be made for each year.) Column 3 shows the differences between the first two columns.

For capital budgeting analysis the cash flows that are discounted are the net after-tax operating cash flows. The data in Table 10–5 represent accounting income and must be adjusted in order (a) to be on a cash rather than accrual basis and (b) to exclude all payments to the sources of financing. In Table 10–5 depreciation is a non-cash charge; interest charges and dividends paid are cash flows to the financing sources.

The corporation tax liability has been calculated on 'income before taxes plus

Table 10–5 *Comparative Accounting Income Statement Framework for Considering Cash Flows.*

		(1) Without new Investment		(2) With new Investment		(3) (2) − (1) Difference
Sales		£10 000		£11 000		£1 000
Operating costs	£7 000		£5 000		(£2 000)	
Depreciation	500		1 000		500	
Interest charges	500		1 000		500	
Income before taxes		£ 2 000		£ 4 000		£2 000
Corporation tax (T)		1 250		2 500		1 250
Income after taxes		£ 750		£ 1 500		£ 750
Dividends paid		600		1 200		600
Additions to retained earnings		£ 150		£ 300		£ 150

depreciation', as depreciation is not an allowable deduction for the purpose of determining a firm's tax liability.[17]

16. The cash flow resulting from increased capital allowances has been assumed to benefit the firm immediately.
17. For an explanation of the treatment of depreciation and capital allowances in determining a firm's tax liability, see Appendix A at the end of the book.

Table 10–6 shows the operating cash flows without the new investment, with the new investment, and the difference or incremental flows.

Table 10–6 *Net Operating Cash Flow Statement.*

	(1) Without new Investment	(2) With new Investment	(3) (2) – (1) Difference or incremental flows
Sales ($P \cdot Q$)	£10 000	£11 000	£1 000
Operating cash costs (O)[a]	7 000	5 000	(2 000)
Net operating cash income (NOI)[a]	£ 3 000	£ 6 000	£3 000
Corporation tax (T)[b]	1 500	3 000	1 500
Net cash flow (F)	£ 1 500	£ 3 000	£1 500

[a] Does not include depreciation as a cash cost since this is a cash flow statement and depreciation is not a cash cost.
[b] Interest payments are not deducted in arriving at corporation tax liability in this illustration, their existence being a financing rather than an investing decision.

The incremental cash flows can also be calculated using the following equation. Let ΔSales be the change in sales, ΔO the change in operating costs, ΔNOI the change in operating cash income, ΔCap the change in annual capital allowances,[18] and T the marginal corporation tax rate. Then

$$\begin{aligned}\Delta \text{ cash flow} &= \text{change in after-tax operating cash income} \\ &\quad + \text{change in capital allowances tax benefit.} \\ \Delta\text{F} &= \Delta NOI(1-T) + T\Delta\text{Cap} \\ \Delta\text{F} &= (\Delta\text{Sales} - \Delta O)(1-T) + T\Delta\text{Cap} \\ \Delta\text{F} &= [(\text{Sales}_2 - \text{Sales}_1) - (O_2 - O_1)](1-T) \\ &\quad + T(\text{Cap}_2 - \text{Cap}_1) \qquad (10\text{–}5)\end{aligned}$$

For the Widget Division analysis:

$$\begin{aligned}\Delta\text{cash flow} &= [(£11\,000 - £10\,000) - (£5000 - £7000)](1-0.5) \\ &\quad + (0-0)(0.5) \\ &= [£1000 - (-£2000)](0.5) \\ \Delta\text{F} &= £1500 \qquad (10\text{–}6)\end{aligned}$$

This £1500 result checks out with the bottom line figure in the last column of Table 10–6. What happens if there is no change in sales? The equation is still valid, but ΔSales = 0. In this case, the problem is a simple replacement decision, with a new machine replacing an old one to reduce costs. The sales levels are the same with and without the investment and do not show up in the incremental column.

Finding the PV of the benefits. We have explained in detail how to measure the annual benefits. The next step is to determine the present value of the benefit stream. The interest factor for a 10-year, 10 per cent annuity is found to be 6.145 from Appendix Table D–4. This factor, when multiplied by the £1500 incremental cash flow, results in a present value of £9217.5.

18. In this illustration the increased annual capital allowances will be nil as a 100 per cent initial allowance was claimed.

Salvage Value

The new machine has an estimated salvage value of £2000; that is, Culver expects to be able to sell the machine for £2000 when it is retired in 10 years. The present value of an inflow of £2000 due in 10 years is £772, found as £2000 × 0.386. If additional working capital had been required and included in the initial cash outlay, this amount would be added to the salvage value of the machine because the working capital will be recovered if and when the project is abandoned.

As 100 per cent initial allowances will have been claimed on the new machine, a balancing charge of £2000 will arise on disposal, causing a tax liability of (0.5) × £2000 = £1000. The tax payable on the sale proceeds should not be due until year 11 and so the present value of this outflow will be £1000 × 0.350, or £350.

Determining the net present value

The project's net present value is found as the sum of the present values of the inflows, or benefits, less the outflows, or costs:

Inflows: *PV* of annual benefits	£9217.50
PV of salvage value, new machine	772.00
Less: net cash outflow, or cost	(5500.00)
PV of tax on salvage value, new machine	(350.00)
Net present value (*NPV*)	£4139.50

Since the *NPV* is positive, the project should be accepted.

Worksheet for determining cash flows

Table 10–7 summarizes the five-step capital budgeting decision process described above. Using the Culver Company investment problem as an example, we first calculate the total outflows for the proposed project by subtracting from the cost of the new machine the sum of the funds received from the sale of the old machine plus the tax savings resulting from the purchase of the new machine.

Next, we calculate the net annual benefits, then find the present value of this benefit stream, which is £9217.5.

We now find the present value of the expected salvage value of the new machine, £772. Also, the estimated tax payable on the salvage value is calculated at £350.

Finally, we sum up the *PV* of the inflows and then deduct the project cost to determine the *NPV*, £4139.5 in this example. Since the *NPV* is positive, the project should be accepted.[19]

19. Alternatively, the internal rate of return on the project could have been computed and found to be 25 per cent. Because this is substantially in excess of the 10 per cent cost of capital, the internal rate of return method also indicates that the investment should be undertaken. In this case, the r is found as follows:

PV of benefit stream + *PV* of salvage − *PV* of tax on salvage − cost = 0.

$$\sum_{t=1}^{10} \frac{£1500}{(1+r)^t} + \frac{£2000}{(1+r)^{10}} - \frac{£1000}{(1+r)^{11}} - £5500$$

£1500 (*IF* for *PV* of 10-year annuity) + £2000 (*PV* of £1 in 10 years) − £1000 (*PV* of £1 in 11 years) − £5500 = 0. Try *PVIF*s for 25%:

£1500 (3.571) + £2000 (0.107) − £1000 (0.086) − £5500 = £5356 + £214 − £86 − £5500 = £ − 16 which is very close to nil, indicating that the internal rate of return is approximately equal to 25 per cent.

Table 10–7 *Worksheet for Capital Budgeting Project Evaluation.*

1. Project cost or initial outflows required to undertake the project[a]		
Investment in new equipment		£12 000
Receipt from sale of old machine		(1 000)
Subtract the tax savings resulting from the purchase of the new machine: tax rate (T) times net cost of new machine		(5 500)
Total project cost		£5 500
2. Calculation of annual benefits[b]		
ΔSales		£ 1 000
Less: ΔO		(2 000)[c]
ΔCap		–
Δ Taxable income		£ 3 000
Less: Δ tax at 50%		1 500[d]
Δ After-tax profits		£ 1 500
Plus: Δ Cap		–
Δ Cash flow		£ 1 500
3. Present value of benefits		
Δ F + interest factor		
£1500 × 6.145 =		£ 9 217.5
4. Present value of expected salvage		
Expected salvage value × interest factor		
£2000 × 0.386 =		£ 772
5. Present value of tax on expected salvage		
£1000 × 0.350 =		£ 350
6. Net present value		
PV of inflows: annual benefits		£ 9 217.5
salvage		772.0
		£ 9 989.5
Less: project cost	£5500	
PV of tax on salvage	350	£ 5 850.0
NPV		£ 4 139.5

[a] If project costs are incurred over a number of years, then the present value of the project costs must be calculated.

[b] It should be noted that if the annual cash flows are not level, the annuity format cannot be used. This restriction might appear to present serious problems of practical applications in capital budgeting, but it really does not. Most companies have either computer facilities or time-sharing arrangements with computer service facilities that handle these non-annuity cases without difficulty.

[c] Refer to equation 10–6. We are subtracting the change in cost from the change in sales: $\Delta C = £5000 - £7000 = -£2000$. Therefore, Δ Sales $- \Delta C = £1000 - (-£2000) = £3000$.

[d] For simplicity we have assumed no delay in payment of tax liabilities. For actual dates of payment refer to Appendix A at the end of the book.

ALTERNATIVE CAPITAL BUDGETING WORKSHEET

Table 10–8 presents an alternative worksheet for evaluating capital projects. The top section shows net cash flows at the time of investment; since all these flows occur immediately, no discounting is required and the interest factor is 1.0. The lower section of the table shows future cash flows–benefits from increased sales and/or reduced costs, capital allowances, and salvage value. These flows do occur over time, so it is necessary to convert them to present values. The *NPV* as determined in the alternative format, £4139.5, agrees with the figure as calculated in Table 10–7.

Table 10–8 *Alternative Worksheet for Capital Budgeting Project Evaluation.*

	Amount before tax	Amount after tax[a]	Year event occurs	*PV* factor at 10%	*PV*
Outflows at time investment is made					
Investment in new equipment	£12 000	£12 000	0	1.0	£12 000
Salvage value of old	(1 000)	(1 000)	0	1.0	(1 000)
Tax effect of the net purchase[b]	(11 000)	(5 500)	0	1.0	(5 500)
Increased working capital (if necessary)	[c]	–	0	1.0	–
Total initial outflows (*PV* of costs)					£ 5 500
Inflows, or annual returns					
Benefits[d]	£ 3 000	£ 1 500	1–10	6.145	£ 9 217.5
Salvage value on new	2 000	2 000	10	0.386	£ 772.0
Balancing charge	(2 000)	(1 000)	11	0.350	(350.0)
Return of working capital (if necessary)	[c]	–	10	0.386	–
Total periodic inflows (*PV* of benefits)					£ 9 639.5

$NPV = PV$ of benefits less PV of cost = £9 639.5 – £5 500 = £4 139.5

[a] Amount after tax equals amount before tax times T or $(1 - T)$, where T = tax rate.
[b] Deductions (net capital allowances) are multiplied by T.
[c] Not applicable.
[d] Benefits are multiplied by $(1 - T)$.

CAPITAL RATIONING

Ordinarily, firms operate as illustrated in Figure 10–1; that is, they take on investments to the point where the marginal returns from investment are just equal to their estimated marginal cost of capital. For firms operating in this way, the decision process is as described above – they make those investments having positive net present values, reject those whose net present values are negative, and choose between mutually exclusive investments on the basis of the higher net present value. However, a firm will occasionally set an absolute limit on the size of its capital budget for any one year that is less than the level of investment it would undertake on the basis of the criteria described above.

The principal reason for such action is that some firms are reluctant to engage in external financing (borrowing or issuing shares). One management, recalling the plight of firms with substantial amounts of debt in the 1930s, may simply refuse to use debt. Another management, which has no objection to selling debt, may not want to sell equity capital for fear of losing some measure of voting control. Still others may refuse to use any form of outside financing, considering safety and control to be more important than additional profits. These are all cases of capital rationing, and they result in limiting the rate of expansion to a slower pace than would be dictated by 'purely rational profit-maximizing behaviour.'[20]

Project selection under capital rationing

How should projects be selected under conditions of capital rationing? First, note that under conditions of true capital rationing, the firm's value is not being maximized – if management was maximizing, then it would move to the point where the marginal project's *NPV* was nil, and capital rationing as defined would not exist. So, if a firm uses capital rationing, it has ruled out value maximization. The firm may, however, want to maximize value *subject to the constraint that the capital ceiling is not exceeded.* Following constrained maximization behaviour will, in general, result in a lower value than following unconstrained maximization, but some type of constrained maximization may produce reasonably satisfactory results. Linear programming is one method of constrained maximization that has been applied to capital rationing. To our knowledge, this method has not been widely applied, but much work is going on in the area, and linear programming may, in the future, prove useful in capital budgeting.[21]

If a financial manager does face capital rationing, and if he cannot get the constraint lifted, what should he do? His objective should be to select projects, subject to the capital rationing constraint, such that the sum of the projects' *NPV*s is maximized. Linear programming can be used, but there is really no practical alternative that will approximate the true maximum. Reasonably satisfactory results may be obtained by ranking projects by their internal rates of return and then, starting at the top of this list of projects, by taking investments of successively lower rank until the available funds have been exhausted. However, no investment with a negative *NPV* (or an internal rate of return below the cost of capital) should be undertaken.

A firm might, for example, have the investment opportunities shown in Table 10–9 and only £6 million available for investment. In this situation, the firm would probably accept projects 1 to 4 and project 6, ending with a capital budget of £5.9 million and a cumulative *NPV* of £2.6 million. Under no circumstances should it accept project 8, 9 or 10, as they all have internal rates of return of less than 10 per cent (and also net present values less than zero).

---

20. We should make three points here. First we *do not* necessarily consider a decision to hold back on expansion irrational. If the owner of a firm has what *he* considers to be plenty of income and wealth, then it might be quite rational for him to 'trim his sails', relax, and concentrate on enjoying what he has already earned rather than on earning still more. Such behaviour would not, however, be appropriate for a publicly owned firm.

The second point is that it is not correct to interpret as capital rationing a situation where the firm is willing to sell additional securities at the going market price but finds that it cannot because the market will simply not absorb more of its issues. Rather, such a situation indicates that the cost-of-capital curve is rising. If more acceptable investments are indicated than can be financed, then the cost of capital being used is too low and should be raised.

Third, firms sometimes set a limit on capital expenditures, not because of a shortage of funds, but because of limitations on other resources, especially managerial talent. A firm might, for example, feel that its personnel development programme is sufficient to handle an expansion of no more than 10 per cent a year, then set a limit on the capital budget to ensure that expansion is held to that rate. This is not *capital* rationing – rather, it involves a downward re-evaluation of project returns if growth exceeds some limit; that is expected rates of return are, after some point, a decreasing function of the level of expenditures.

21. For a further discussion of programming approaches to capital budgeting, see Appendix A to this chapter.

Table 10–9 *The Prospective-Projects Schedule.*

Nature of proposal	Project's cost	Cumulative total of costs	Internal rate of return	*PV* of benefits	Project's *NPV*
1. Purchase of leased space	£2 000 000	£ 2 000 000	23%	3 200 000	£1 200 000
2. Modernization of accounting system	1 200 000	3 200 000	19	1 740 000	540 000
3. Modernization of office building	1 500 000	4 700 000	17	2 070 000	570 000
4. Addition of power facilities	900 000	5 600 000	16	1 125 000	225 000
5. Purchase of subsidiary	3 600 000	9 200 000	13	4 248 000	648 000
6. Purchase of loading cranes	300 000	9 500 000	12	342 000	42 000
7. Purchase of fleet of tankers	500 000	10 000 000	11	540 000	40 000
cut-off					
8. Installation of conveyor system	200 000	10 200 000	9	186 000	(14 000)
9. Construction of new factory	2 300 000	12 500 000	8	2 093 000	(207 000)
10. Purchase of executive aircraft	200 000	12 700 000	7	128 000	(72 000)

COMPARING MUTUALLY EXCLUSIVE PROJECTS WITH DIFFERENT LIVES

To simplify the analysis, the previous capital budgeting examples assumed that alternative investments had equal lives. Suppose, however, that we must choose between two mutually exclusive investments that have different lives. For examplé, investment 1 has a life of five years while investment 2 has a life of seven years. An illustration would be a wooden bridge that would have a shorter life and lower initial cost than a steel bridge. Both provide about the same quantity of services per year, but the wooden bridge would require more maintenance and more frequent replacement. But since the lives of the two alternative investments are different, the net present value of the cash flows cannot be compared directly. The problem is pictured in Figure 10–3 for a five- and a seven-year alternative.

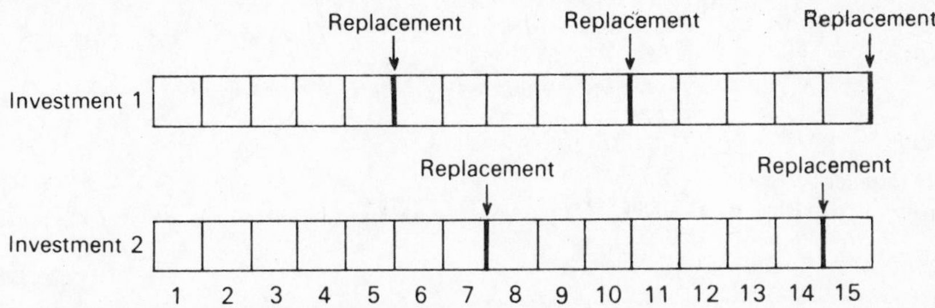

Figure 10–3.

A computationally easy and theoretically sound method for handling this different length of lives problem is to replace each alternative as it wears out and find the total net present value of each infinitely replaced alternative.[22] Then the net present value of each 'infinite' lived alternative can be compared. To find the net present value of each extended alternative (call it NPV_∞):

1. find the net present value NPV_N of the cash flows for each alternative for the original life and for the applicable cost of capital, k,

22. An alternative method is to equate lives by assuming a reinvestment rate for the shorter-lived project for the additional years required to equate lives.

2. divide NPV_N by the net present value factor for N years at rate k (this gives an equivalent level annuity amount a that will give the same present value NPV_N if invested at rate k for N years),
3. divide the annuity a by the applicable cost of capital k to obtain NPV_∞. (In Chapter 19 it will be shown that the present value of an amount received to infinity is the amount divided by the discount factor.)

(1) and (2) have the effect of normalizing, both by the amount of the investment and by the number of years duration that the cash flows from the investment are received. This makes it possible to compare directly the two streams of normalized annual cash flows.

The third step takes the level annual flows normalized by the amount of investment and discounts them to infinity. When the discount rates are different, we now have a NPV evaluation over infinite lives, so that again direct comparisons can appropriately be made.

The three steps above are summarized and expressed in symbols in equation 10–7.

$$NPV_\infty = \frac{[NPV_N/PVIF_a(N,k)]}{k} = \frac{a}{k} \tag{10–7}$$

where NPV_∞ is the present value of the 'infinite' lived alternative.
a is the equivalent level annuity.
N is the life of the original alternative.
k is the cost of capital.
NPV_N is the net present value of the cash flows for the original life N.
$PVIF_a(N,k)$ is the (net) present value factor for an annuity of £1 at rate k for N years.

The method is illustrated for the mutually exclusive projects 1 and 2 of Table 10–10.

Table 10–10.

Project	Initial cost (I)	Life (N)	Cost of capital (k)	Annual cash flow ($X[1-T]$)
1	£280	5 years	10%	£100
2	£350	7 years	12%	£105

For alternative 1,
$$NPV_N = PVIF_a(N, k)X(1-T) - I$$
$$= PVIF_a(5, 0.10)£100 - £280$$
$$= (3.7908)(£100) - £280 = £99.08,$$
$$a = \frac{NPV_N}{PVIF_a(N, k)} = \frac{£99.08}{3.7908} = £26.137,$$
and
$$NPV_\infty = \frac{£26.137}{0.10} = £261.37.$$

Similarly for alternative 2.
$$NPV_N = £105.00(4.5638) - £350 = £129.19,$$
$$a = \frac{£129.19}{4.5638} = £28.309,$$
and
$$NPV_\infty = \frac{£28.309}{0.12} = £235.91.$$

Thus alternative 1 is preferable. Note that comparison of the net present value for the original lives would have selected alternative 2 which has an NPV of £129.19 compared to the NPV of £99.08 for alternative 1.

Some methods for evaluating unequally lived mutually exclusive alternatives compare the annuities a in the above analysis. Since NPV_∞ is the quotient of a divided by k, this method can lead to the wrong choice if the risk classes of the alternatives differ so that the cost of capital, k, is different. In the above example a comparison of annuities would have selected alternative 2 of £28.31 versus £26.14 for alternative 1. In most replacement decisions, however, k will be the same and the two methods will give the same decision. The above method assumes that the projects can be repeated in perpetual replacement chains.

If this assumption is not appropriate, an alternative method is to assume a reinvestment rate for the project of shorter duration to equalize its life with the project of longer duration.

SUMMARY

Capital budgeting, which involves commitments for large outlays whose benefits (or drawbacks) extend well into the future, is of the greatest significance to a firm. Decisions in these areas will, therefore, have a major impact on the future well-being of the firm. This chapter focused on how capital budgeting decisions can be made more effective in contributing to the health and growth of a firm. The discussion stressed the development of systematic procedures and rules for preparing a list of investment proposals, for evaluating them and for selecting a cut-off point.

The chapter emphasized that one of the most crucial phases in the process of evaluating capital budget proposals is obtaining a dependable estimate of the benefits that will be obtained from undertaking the project. It cannot be overemphasized that the firm must allocate to competent and experienced personnel the making of these judgements.

Determining cash flows

The cash inflows from an investment are the incremental change in after-tax net operating cash income plus the incremental capital allowance tax benefit; the cash outflow is the cost of the investment less the salvage value received on an old machine plus any balancing charge (or less any balancing allowance) when the machine is sold.

Ranking investment proposals

Three commonly used procedures for ranking investment proposals were discussed in the chapter:

Payback is defined as the number of years required to return the original investment. Although the payback method is used frequently, it has serious conceptual weaknesses, because it ignores the facts (a) that some receipts come in beyond the payback period and (b) that £1 received today is more valuable than £1 received in the future.

Net present value is defined as the present value of future returns, discounted at the cost of capital, minus the cost of the investment. The *NPV* method overcomes the conceptual flaws noted in the use of the payback method.

Internal rate of return is defined as the interest rate that equates the present value of future returns to the investment outlay. The internal rate of return method, like the *NPV* method, meets the objections to the payback approach.

In most cases, the two discounted cash flow methods give identical answers to these questions: Which of two mutually exclusive projects should be selected? How large should the total capital budget be? However, under certain circumstances conflicts may arise. Such conflicts are caused by the fact that the *NPV* and *IRR* methods make different assumptions about the rate at which cash flows may be reinvested, or the opportunity cost of cash flows. In general, the assumption of the *NPV* method (that the opportunity cost is the cost of capital) is the correct one. Accordingly, our preference is for using the *NPV* method to make capital budgeting decisions.

QUESTIONS

10–1. A firm has £100 million available for capital expenditures. Suppose project A involves the purchase of £100 million of grain, shipping it overseas and selling it within a year at a profit of £20 million. The project has an *IRR* of 20 per cent, an *NPV* of 20 million, *and it will cause earnings per share (EPS) to rise within one year*. Project B calls for the use of the £100 million to develop a new process, acquire land, build a factory and begin processing. Project B, which is not postponable, has an *NPV* of £50 million and an *IRR* of 30 per cent, but the fact that some of the initial costs will be written off immediately, combined with the fact that no revenues will be generated for several years, means that accepting project B will *reduce* short-run *EPS*.

(a) Should the short-run effects on *EPS* influence the choice between the two projects?

(b) How might situations such as the one described here influence a firm's decision to use payback as a screening criterion?

10–2. Are there conditions under which a firm might be better off if it chooses a machine with a rapid payback rather than one with the largest rate of return?

10–3. Company X uses the payback method in evaluating investment proposals and is considering new equipment whose additional net after-tax earnings will be £150 a year. The equipment costs £500 and its expected life is 10 years. The company uses a three-year payback as its criterion. Should the equipment be purchased under the above assumptions? (Ignore the effect of capital allowances.)

10–4. What are the most critical problems that arise in calculating a rate of return for a prospective investment?

10–5. What other factors in addition to rate of return analysis should be considered in determining capital expenditures?

10–6. Would it be beneficial for a firm to review its past capital expenditures and capital budgeting procedures? Why?

10–7. Fiscal and monetary policies are tools used by the government to stimulate the economy. Explain, using the analytical devices developed in this chapter, how each of the following might be expected to stimulate the economy by encouraging investment.

(a) An increase in initial allowances (for example the 100 per cent first year allowance permitted in 1970 on plant and equipment).

(b) An easing of interest rates.

(c) An increase in public sector spending.

(d) A programme of investment grants.

PROBLEMS

(Where relevant, assume one year delay in payment of tax liabilities)

10–1. Sparkling Beverages Ltd is contemplating replacing one of its bottling machines with a newer and more efficient machine. The old machine has a book value of £500 000 and a remaining useful life of five years. The firm does not expect to realize any return from scrapping the old machine in five years, but if it is sold now to another firm in the industry, Sparkling Beverages would receive £300 000 for it. A first year allowance of 100 per cent was claimed by the company when the old machine was originally purchased.

The new machine has a purchase price of £1.1 million, an estimated useful life of five years, and an estimated salvage value of £100 000. The new machine is expected to economize on electric power usage, labour, and repair costs, and also to reduce defective bottles; in total, an annual saving of £200 000 will be realized if the new machine is installed. (Note: assume that the company has sufficient profits from other areas to be able fully to utilize a 100 per cent first year allowance.) The company has a 10 per cent cost of capital, and the tax rate is 50 per cent.

(a) What is the initial cash outlay required for the new machine?

(b) What are the cash flows in years 1 to 5?

(c) What is the cash flow from the salvage value in year 5?

(d) Should Sparkling Beverages purchase the new machine? Support your answer.

(e) In general, how would each of the following factors affect the investment decision, and how should each be treated?

1. The expected life of the existing machine decreases.
2. Capital rationing is imposed on the firm.
3. The cost of capital is not constant but is rising.
4. Improvements in the equipment to be purchased are expected to occur each year, and the result will be to increase the returns or expected savings from new machines over the savings expected with this year's model for every year in the foreseeable future.

10–2. The Feldwyn Company is using a machine whose original cost was £72 000. The machine is two years old and has a current market value of £16 000. The asset is being depreciated over a 12-year original life towards a nil estimated final salvage value. Depreciation is on a straight-line basis, and the tax rate is 50 per cent.

Management is contemplating the purchase of a replacement that costs £75 000 and has an estimated salvage value of £10 000. The new machine will have a greater capacity, and annual sales are expected to increase from £1 million to £1.01 million, or by £10 000. Operating efficiencies with the new machine will also produce expected savings of £10 000 a year. Depreciation is on a straight-line basis over a 10-year life, the cost of capital is 8 per cent, and a 50 per cent tax rate is applicable. The company's total depreciation costs are currently £120 000 and total annual operating costs are £800 000.

(a) Should the firm replace the asset?

(b) How would your decision be affected if a second new machine is available that costs £140 000, has a £20 000 estimated salvage value, and is expected to provide £25 000 in annual savings over its 10-year life? It also increases sales by £10 000 a year. (There are now three choices: (i) keep the old machine, (ii) replace it with a £75 000 machine, or (iii) replace it with a £140 000 machine.) Depreciation is still on a straight-line basis. For purposes of answering this question use both the *NPV*, which you must calculate, and the *IRR*, which you may assume to be 25 per cent for the £75 000 project and 17 per cent for the £140 000 project.

(c) Disregarding the changes in part (b) – that is, under the original assumption that one £75 000 replacement machine is available – how would your decision be affected if a new generation of equipment is expected to be on the market in about two years that will provide increased annual savings and have the same cost, asset life and salvage value?

(d) What factors in addition to the quantitative factors listed above are likely to require consideration in a practical situation?

(e) How would your decision be affected if the asset lives of the various alternatives were not the same?

10–3. The Crassner Company is considering the purchase of a new machine tool to replace an obsolete one. The machine being used for the operation has both a written-down (that is, for capital allowances) value and a market value of nil; it is in good working order and will last, physically, for at least an additional 15 years. The proposed machine will perform the operation so much more efficiently that Crassner engineers estimate that labour, material and other direct costs of the operation will be reduced by £4500 a year if it is installed. The proposed machine costs £24 000 delivered and installed, and its economic life is estimated to be 15 years with no salvage value. The company expects to earn 12 per cent on its investment after taxes (12 per cent is the firm's cost of capital). The tax rate is 50 per cent, and the firm uses straight-line depreciation.

(a) Should Crassner buy the new machine?

(b) Assume that the written-down value of the old machine had been £8000 and a written-down allowance of 25 per cent was being claimed. How does this information affect your answer?

(c) Rework part (a) assuming that relevant cost of capital is now 6 per cent. What is the significance of this? What can be said about part (b) under this assumption?

(d) In general, how would each of the following factors affect the investment decision, and how should each be treated?
1. The expected life of the existing machine decreases.
2. Capital rationing is imposed on the firm.
3. The cost of capital is not constant but is rising.
4. Improvements in the equipment to be purchased are expected to occur each year, and the result will be to increase the returns or expected savings from new machines over the saving expected with this year's model for every year in the foreseeable future.

10–4. Each of two mutually exclusive projects involves an investment of £120 000. Cash flows (after-tax profits plus depreciation) for the two projects have a different time pattern although the totals are approximately the same. Project M will yield high returns early with smaller returns in later years (this is a mining type of investment with the expenses of removing the ores lower at the entrance to the mines with easier access). Project O yields smaller returns in the earlier years and larger returns in the later years (this is an orchard type of investment since it takes a number of years for trees to mature and be fully bearing). The cash flows from the two investments are as follows:

Year	Project O	Project M
1	£10 000	£70 000
2	20 000	40 000
3	30 000	30 000
4	50 000	10 000
5	80 000	10 000

(a) Compute the present value of each project if the firm's cost of capital is nil per cent, 6 per cent, 10 per cent and 20 per cent.
(b) Compute the internal rate of return for each project.
(c) Graph the present values of the two projects, putting net present value (*NPV*) on the Y-axis and the cost of capital on the X-axis.
(d) Could you determine the *IRR* of the projects from your graph? Explain.
(e) Which project would you select, assuming no capital rationing and a constant cost of capital of (i) 8 per cent, (ii) 10 per cent, (iii) 12 per cent? Explain.
(f) If capital was severely rationed, which project would you select?

10–5. The Waterford Company is considering two mutually exclusive machine purchases. Machine A costs £6210 and will produce a return of £1750 per year. Machine B costs £5130 and will produce a return of £1375 per year. Both machines have a six-year life and no salvage value. Ignore tax.
(a) Compute the present value and net present value of each project if the firm's cost of capital is nil per cent, 6 per cent, 10 per cent and 20 per cent.
(b) Compute the internal rate of return for each project.
(c) Graph the present values of the two projects, putting net present value (*NPV*) on the Y-axis and the cost of capital on the X-axis.
(d) Could you determine the *IRR* of the projects from your graph? Explain.
(e) Treat the differential cost of machine A as an investment and its differential cash flows as the return from that investment. Calculate the internal rate of return on the £1080 investment.

10–6. The Harris Company is analysing two mutually exclusive machine purchases. One is an electric-powered materials handling unit that costs £10 000 and will produce a return of £3650 per year for five years. A gas-powered materials handling unit costs £7000 and produces a return of £2350 per year also for five years. If the firm's cost of capital is 12 per cent, which of the two machines should be purchased?

10–7. A firm is comparing the purchase of two mutually exclusive machine investments. Machine F involves an investment of £40 000, and would produce annual net cash flows after taxes of £12 000 for five years. Machine H would require an investment of £100 000 and would produce annual cash flows after taxes of £30 000 for seven years. Machine H is somewhat more risky and requires a cost of capital of 12 per cent, compared to 10 per cent for machine F. Which machine would have the greater net present value and should be selected?

SELECTED REFERENCES

Baumol, William J. and Quandt, Richard E. Investment and discount rates under capital rationing – a programming approach. *Economic Journal* 75 (June 1965): 317–329.
Beenhakker, Henri L. Sensitivity analysis of the present value of a project. *Engineering Economist* 20 (Winter 1975): 123–149.
Bernhard, Richard H. Mathematical programming models for capital budgeting – a survey, generalization, and critique. *Journal of Financial and Quantitative Analysis* IV (June 1969): 111–158.
Bierman, Harold, Jr and Smidt, Seymour. *The Capital Budgeting Decision*. 3rd ed. New York: Macmillan, 1971.
Bower, Richard S. and Jenks, Jeffrey M. Divisional screening rates. *Financial Management* 4 (Autumn 1975): 42–49.
Brigham, Eugene F. Hurdle rates for screening capital expenditure proposals. *Financial Management* 4 (Autumn 1975): 17–26.
Brigham, Eugene F. and Pettway, Richard H. Capital budgeting by utilities. *Financial Management* 2 (Autumn 1973): 11–22.
Bromwich, M. Inflation and the capital budgeting process. *Journal of Business Finance* 1 (Autumn 1969): 39–46.
Bromwich, M. Capital budgeting: a survey. *Journal of Business Finance* 2 (Autumn 1970): 3–26.
Bromwich, M. *The Economics of Capital Budgeting*. Harmondsworth: Penguin, 1976.
Carsberg, Bryan. *Analysis for Investment Decisions*. London: Accountancy Age Books, 1974.
Dean, Joel. *Capital Budgeting*. New York: Columbia University Press, 1951.
Donaldson, Gordon. Strategic hurdle rates for capital investment. *Harvard Business Review* 50 (March–April 1972): 50–58.
Elton, Edwin J. Capital rationing and external discount rates. *Journal of Finance* XXV (June 1970): 573–584.
Fogler, H. Russell. Ranking techniques and capital rationing. *Accounting Review* 47 (January 1972): 134–143.
Gordon, Myron J. and Shapiro, Eli. Capital equipment analysis: the required rate of profit. *Management Science* 3 (October 1956): 102–110.
Grinyer, J. R. Inflation and capital budgeting decisions: a comment. *Journal of Business Finance and Accounting* 1 (Spring 1974): 149–155.
Grinyer, J. R. Relevant criterion rates in capital budgeting. *Journal of Business Finance and Accounting* 1 (Autumn 1974): 357–374.

Hastie, Larry K. One businessman's view of capital budgeting. *Financial Management* 3 (Winter 1974): 36–44.
Hawkins, Clark A. and Adams, Richard A. A goal programming model for capital budgeting. *Financial Management* 3 (Spring 1974): 52–57.
Haynes, W. Warren and Solomon, Martin B. Jr. A misplaced emphasis in capital budgeting. *Quarterly Review of Economics and Business* (February 1962).
Horrigan, J. O. Benefit-cash ratios versus net present value: revisited. *Journal of Business Finance and Accounting* 1 (Summer 1974): 249–265.
Ignizio, James P. An approach to the capital budgeting problem with multiple objectives. *Engineering Economist* 21 (Summer 1976): 259–272.
Jean, William H. *Capital Budgeting.* Scranton, N.J.: International Textbook Company, 1969.
Jean, William H. On multiple rates of return. *Journal of Finance* XXIII, no. 1 (March 1968): 187–192.
Jean, William H. Terminal value or present value in capital budgeting programs. *Journal of Financial and Quantitative Analysis* VI (January 1971): 649–652.
Jeynes, Paul H. The significance of reinvestment rate. *Engineering Economist* XI (Fall 1965): 1–9.
Johnson, Robert W. *Capital Budgeting.* Belmont, Calif.: Wadsworth, 1970.
Kerr, H. W. T. Handling working capital in discounted cash flow calculations. *Accounting and Business Research* (Summer 1971): 294–299.
King, P. Is the emphasis of capital budgeting theory misplaced? *Journal of Business Finance and Accounting* 2 (Spring 1975): 69–82.
Klammer, Thomas. Empirical evidence of the adoption of sophisticated capital budgeting techniques. *Journal of Business* 45 (July 1972): 387–397.
Lerner, Eugene M. and Rappaport, Alfred. Limit DCF in capital budgeting. *Harvard Business Review* 46 (July–August 1968): 133–139.
Lewellen, Wilbur G., Lanser, Howard P. and McConnell, John J. Payback substitutes for discounted cash flow. *Financial Management* 2 (Summer 1973): 17–23.
Lorie, James H. and Savage, Leonard J. Three problems in rationing capital. *Journal of Business* XXVIII (October 1955).
Lutz, Friederich and Lutz, Vera. *The Theory of the Investment of the Firm.* Princeton, N.J.: Princeton University Press, 1951.
Mao, James C. T. The internal rate of return as a ranking criterion. *Engineering Economist* XI (Winter 1966): 1–13.
Mao, James C. T. Survey of capital budgeting: theory and practice. *Journal of Finance* 25 (May 1970): 349–360.
Martin, John D. and Scott, David F. Jr. Debt capacity and the capital budgeting decision. *Financial Management* 5 (Summer 1976): 7–14.
Merrett, A. J. and Sykes, A. *The Finance and Analysis of Capital Projects.* 2nd ed. London: Longmans, 1973.
Merrett, A. J. and Sykes, Allen. *Capital Budgeting and Company Finance.* London: Longmans, 1966.
Merville, L. J. and Tavis, L. A. A generalized model for capital investment. *Journal of Finance* 28 (March 1973): 109–118.
Meyers, Stephen L. Avoiding depreciation influences on investment decisions. *Financial Management* 1 (Winter 1972): 17–24.
Murdick, Robert G. and Deming, Donald D. *The Management of Corporate Expenditures.* New York: McGraw-Hill, 1968.
Nelson, Charles R. Inflation and capital budgeting. *Journal of Finance* 31 (June 1976): 923–931.
Oakford, Robert V. *Capital Budgeting.* New York: Ronald Press, 1970.
Peters, Donald H. Coupon rate of return. *Financial Management* 1 (Winter 1972): 25–35.
Petry, Glenn H. Effective use of capital budgeting tools. *Business Horizons* 19 (October 1975): 57–65.
Petty, J. William, Scott, David F. Jr and Bird, Monroe M. The capital expenditure decision-making process of large corporations. *Engineering Economist* 20 (Spring 1975): 159–172.
Quirin, G. David. *The Capital Expenditure Decision.* Homewood, Ill.: Irwin, 1967.
Robichek, Alexander A., Ogilvie, Donald G. and Roach, John D. C. Capital budgeting: a pragmatic approach. *Financial Executive* 37 (April 1969): 26–38.
Robichek, Alexander A. and Van Horne, James C. Abandonment value and capital budgeting. *Journal of Finance* XXII (December 1967): 577–590.
Sarnat, Marshall and Levy, Haim. The relationship of rules of thumb to the internal rate of return: a restatement and generalization. *Journal of Finance* XXIV (June 1969): 479–489.
Scholefield, H. H., McBain, N. S. and Bagwell, J. The effects of inflation on investment appraisal. *Journal of Business Finance* 5 (Summer 1973): 39–48.
Schwab, Bernhard and Lusztig, Peter. A comparative analysis of the net present value and the benefit-cost ratios as measures of the economic desirability of investments. *Journal of Finance* XXIV (June 1969): 507–516.
Schwab, Bernhard and Lusztig, Peter. A note on abandonment value and capital budgeting. *Journal of Financial and Quantitative Analysis* V (September 1970): 377–380.
Shore, Barry. Replacement decisions under capital budgeting constraints. *Engineering Economist* 20 (Summer 1975): 243–256.
Solomon, Ezra. *The Management of Corporate Capital.* New York: The Free Press of Glencoe, 1959.
Solomon, Ezra. *The Theory of Financial Management.* New York: Columbia University Press, 1963.

Stephen, Frank. On deriving the internal rate of return from the accountant's rate of return. *Journal of Business Finance and Accounting* 3 (Summer 1976): 147–150.

Van Horne, James C. A note on biases in capital budgeting introduced by inflation. *Journal of Financial and Quantitative Analysis* VI (March 1971).

Vickers, Douglas. *The Theory of the Firm: Production, Capital and Finance.* New York: McGraw-Hill, 1968.

Weingartner, H. Martin. Capital budgeting of interrelated projects: survey and synthesis. *Management Science* XII (March 1966): 485–516.

Weingartner, H. Martin. The generalized rate of return. *Journal of Financial and Quantitative Analysis* 1 (September 1966): 1–29.

Weingartner, H. Martin. *Mathematical Programming and the Analysis of Capital Budgeting Problems.* Englewood Cliffs, N.J.: Prentice-Hall, 1963.

Weingartner, H. Martin. Some new views on the payback period and capital budgeting decisions. *Management Science* 15 (August 1969): 594–607.

Wilkes F. M. Inflation and the capital budgeting decision. *Journal of Business Finance* 4 (Autumn 1972): 46–53.

Williams, John Daniel and Rakich, Jonathan S. Investment evaluation in hospitals. *Financial Management* 2 Summer 1973): 30–35.

Wright, F. K. The relationship between present value and value to the owner. *Journal of Business Finance* 5 (Summer 1973): 19–25.

Appendix A to Chapter 10:

Further Analysis of Discounted Cash Flow Selection Criteria

As we indicated in Chapter 10, the *NPV* and *IRR* methods generally give the same 'answers' to the important questions in capital budgeting: (a) they usually agree on which of two mutually exclusive projects is 'better', and (b) they ordinarily agree on how large the total capital budget should be. We did, however, show that under certain conditions the two methods produce conflicting results and that such conflicts are caused by differences in the assumed reinvestment rate for cash flows implicit in the two methods. In this appendix, we extend the discussion by utilizing the 'terminal value' concept to illustrate reinvestment rates. We also define another selection method (the *PI* criterion), consider the problem of multiple internal rates of return, and discuss the use of mathematical programming as a tool to help solve the problem of capital rationing.

MORE ON CAPITAL RATIONING: NPV VERSUS IRR

If a firm's management seeks to maximize the value of its shares, then it should use the *NPV* method, choosing among mutually exclusive projects the one that has the highest *NPV*. However, a problem can arise if capital rationing is imposed, that is, if an arbitrary limit is placed on the amount of capital investment during a given year. Consider the situation shown in Figure 10A–1. With its cost of capital constant at k_1 and with its investment opportunities given by the *IRR* schedule, this firm should expand its capital budget to I_3, where the marginal cost of capital is equal to the marginal return on investment. Suppose, however, that a management decision limits the capital budget to I_1. Obviously, the firm's value will not be maximized, but how should it select the projects whose total costs will be I_1?

Notice that no real selection problem exists if all projects have the same time pattern of returns and if all competing projects are about the same size; in this case, the *NPV* and the *IRR* methods will give identical rankings. Neither method will maximize the value of the firm – that would occur only if investment were expanded out to I_3 – but the *NPV* and *IRR* methods will lead to identical capital budgeting decisions. However, if different projects have different time patterns or if competing projects differ in size, conflicts can arise. *The resolution of these conflicts requires a consideration of the rate of return at which cash flows generated by current investments can be reinvested.* This point is explained in the following section.

THE REINVESTMENT RATE ASSUMPTION

The *NPV* method assumes that the opportunity exists to reinvest the cash flows from a project at the cost of capital, while the *IRR* method assumes reinvestment at the *IRR*. To demonstrate this, consider the following steps.

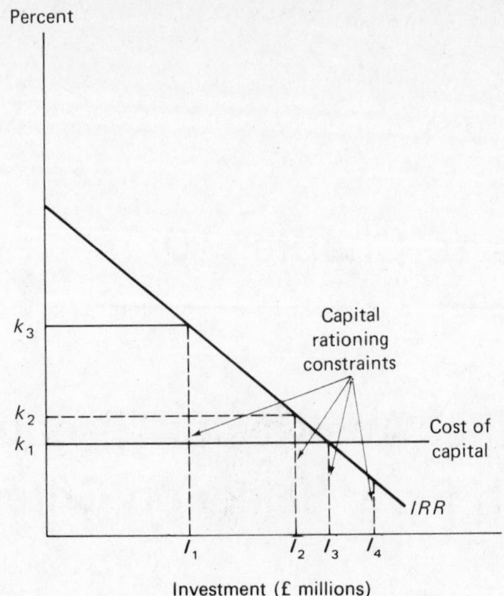

Figure 10A–1 *Illustration of Capital Rationing.*

Step 1

Notice that both the *NPV* and *IRR* methods employ present value interest factors (*PVIFs*) in the solution process; for example, to determine the *NPV*, multiply a series of cash flows by appropriate *PVIFs*, subtract the initial cost, and the result is the *NPV*. Essentially, this method involves using present value tables.

Step 2

Refer back to Chapter 9, Table 9–1 and equation 9–2; notice how present value tables are constructed. *The present value of any future sum is defined as the beginning amount which, when compounded at a specified and constant interest rate, will grow to equal the future amount over the stated time period.* From Table 9–1 we can see that the present value of £1217 due in five years, when discounted at 4 per cent, is £1000 *because £1000, when compounded at 4 per cent for five years, will grow to £1217.* Thus, compounding and discounting are reciprocal relationships, and *the very construction of PV tables implies a reinvestment process.*

Step 3

Since both the *NPV* and *IRR* methods involve the use of *IF* tables, and since the very construction of these tables involves an assumed reinvestment process, the concept of reinvestment underlies the two methods.

Step 4

The implicitly assumed reinvestment rate used in the NPV method is the cost of capital, *k*; that used in the *IRR* method is *r*, which is the *IRR* in the solution process.

Suppose the cash flows from a project are not reinvested but are used for current consumption. No reinvestment is involved, yet an *IRR* for the project could still be calculated – does this show that the reinvestment assumption is not *always* implied in the *IRR* calculation? The answer is no; reinvestment itself is not necessarily assumed, but the *opportunity* of reinvestment *is* assumed. Because that assumption is made in the very construction of the *PV* tables, we simply could not define or interpret the concept of *NPV* without it. Also, the calculation of the *IRR* involves finding the discount rate that makes $NPV = 0$, so the *IRR*, too, depends upon the reinvestment assumption.

TERMINAL VALUE

These concepts, and the impact of actual reinvestment rates on the choice of capital budgeting methods, can be made clear through the use of an example involving both *terminal value* (the value of an asset at a future time) and present value. First, note that the value of any asset, or a collection of assets such as a firm, can be estimated at any point in time. We are primarily interested in the value of the asset at the present time, or its present value, because this figure represents shareholders' wealth, which is what management seeks to maximize. However, the terminal value is useful for examining the difference between the NPV and the IRR.

Assume that a firm is set up with a total capital of £10 000. No additional funds can be brought into the firm, but cash flows from past investments can be reinvested in the business. Thus, the capital rationing constraint is £10 000 in year 1, while in later years it is the available cash flows from prior investments. Assume further that the investors who set up the firm have a 6 per cent cost of capital, so this is also the firm's cost of capital. Finally, the investors have mutually agreed to terminate the firm at the end of three years; accordingly, their welfare will be maximized by having the firm attain the highest possible terminal value.

The firm is considering two alternative projects, X and Y, whose salient features are given in Table 10A–1. Both projects cost £10 000, but X provides cash flows every year, while Y has no cash flows until year 3. Because of these timing differences, the IRR and NPV methods give conflicting rankings: $IRR_X = 23$ per cent $> IRR_Y = 18.2$ per cent, but $NPV_Y = £3860 > NPV_X = £3365$. Which of the two projects should be selected?

The best choice depends upon investment opportunities during years 2 and 3. Project Y has no intermediate cash flows, so its terminal value will be £16 500 regardless of reinvestment rates. However, the terminal values of project X range from £15 920 to £18 750, depending upon the reinvestment rate for cash flows during years 2 and 3. Notice that *the value of the firm today is the present value of the terminal value, discounted at the 6 per cent cost of capital.* The value of the firm today is £13 860 if project Y is chosen, but it will range from £13 370 to £15 750, depending upon reinvestment opportunities, if project X is selected.[1] At a reinvestment rate of 10 per cent, the two projects are approximately equal. If expected reinvestment rates exceed 10 per cent, the management should choose project X. If the expected reinvestment rate is less than 10 per cent, Y is preferable. Thus, 10 per cent corresponds to the cross-over point in Figure 10–2 of the text.

IRR AND NPV REDEFINED

We can use the terminal value concept to redefine both the NPV and the IRR in the following manner:

$$NPV^* = \frac{\text{Terminal value}}{(1+k)^N} - \text{cost}, \qquad \text{(10A–1)}$$

and

IRR^* = solution value of r in the equation

$$\frac{\text{Terminal value}}{(1+r)^N} - \text{cost} = 0. \qquad \text{(10A–2)}$$

In words, we can define NPV^* as the present value of the terminal value, discounted at the cost of capital, minus the cost, and IRR^* as the value of r that equates the PV of the terminal value to the cost of the project.

To calculate these modified NPVs and IRRs, we need to know the relevant terminal values, and in order to calculate terminal values, we need reinvestment rates. If the pattern of reinvestment rates is known, then we *should* calculate NPV^* and IRR^* – they are clearly more accurate measures of project profitability than the unmodified versions.

For example, for projects X and Y analysed in Table 10A–1, let us assume that the reinvestment rate and the cost of capital, k, are both 6 per cent. The present value of the terminal value of X is £13 370, which is less than the present value of the terminal value of Y (£13 860). The value of the IRR^* or the solution value of r in equation 10A–2 is 10.17 per cent for X, which is less than the 11.49 per cent for Y. Note that the NPV^* and the IRR^* give the same rankings. This will always be the case when the reinvestment rate and the cost of capital are equal. For the data in Table 10A–1 the IRR^* for project X would be greater than the IRR^* for project Y at reinvestment rates greater than 10 per cent. But the NPV^* will also be greater for X than for Y at reinvestment rates greater than 10 per cent.[2] The NPV^* and IRR^* may appear to give different rankings only if there is a failure to make the

1. At first glance, a conflict might seem to exist between equation 10–3, which states that the value of an asset or collection of assets (a firm) is the PV of a series of cash flows, and the statement that the value of the firm is the present value of its terminal value. In fact, no conflict exists because, in the second instance, the only cash flow *to the investors* is the terminal value.
2. A reliable estimate of the reinvestment rates is therefore of critical importance.

Table 10A–1 *Analysis of Projects X and Y.*

Alternative reinvestment rates (per cent)	Cost	*PV* of cash flows discounted at indicated rate	*NPV*	Receipts at end of			Terminal value at end of Year 3	Present value of terminal value discounted at 6%
				Year 1	Year 2	Year 3		
Project X	£10 000			£5 000	£5 000	£5 000		
6.0		£13 365	£3 365[a]				£15 920	£13 370[b]
10.0		12 435	2 435				16 550	13 902
18.2		10 900	900				17 900	15 036
20.0		10 530	530				18 200	15 288
23.0[c]		10 000	0				18 750	15 750
Project Y	£10 000			£ 0	£ 0	£16 500		
6.0		£13 860	£3 860[a]				£16 500	£13 860
10.0		12 391	2 391				16 500	13 860
18.2[c]		10 000	0				16 500	13 860
20.0		9 553	(447)				16 500	13 860
23.0		8 415	(1 585)				16 500	13 860

[a] *NPV* at the 6 per cent cost of capital.
[b] This value differs from the £13 365 shown in column 3 because of rounding.
[c] *IRR* = discount rate where *NPV* = 0.

proper adjustment for differences in project scale or size of the initial investment outlay – a critical requirement for the profitability index next discussed.

NPV VERSUS PROFITABILITY INDEX

The profitability index (*PI*), or the benefit/cost ratio as it is sometimes called, is defined as[3]

$$PI = \frac{PV \text{ benefits}}{\text{cost}} = \frac{\sum_{t=1}^{N} \frac{F_t}{(1+k)^t}}{\text{cost}}. \qquad (10A\text{–}4)$$

The *PI* shows the *relative* profitability of any project, or the *PV* of benefits per £1 of cost.

As was true in the *NPV* versus *IRR* comparison, the *NPV* and *PI* always make the same accept–reject decisions, but *NPV* and *PI* can give different project rankings, which presents problems when mutually exclusive projects are compared. Suppose, for example, that we are comparing project A, which calls for an investment of £1 million in a conveyor-belt system for handling goods in a storage warehouse, with project B, which calls for an expenditure of £300 000 to do the same thing by employing a fleet of fork-lift trucks. The conveyor-belt system has lower operating costs, so its cash flows are larger; the net present values are found to be £200 000 for A and £100 000 for B. Using the *NPV* criterion on the one hand, we would select project A. However, if we compute the ratio of the present value of the returns on each project to its cost, we find A's ratio to be 1.20 and B's ratio to be 1.33. Thus, on the other hand, using the *PI* for our ranking, we would select project B because it produces higher net returns for each £1 invested.

Given this conflict, which project should be accepted? Alternatively stated: is it better to use the net present value approach on an absolute basis (*NPV*) or on a relative basis (*PI*)? *Barring capital rationing, the* NPV *method is preferred.* The differential between the initial outlays of the two projects (£700 000) can be looked upon as an investment itself, project C; that is, project A can be broken down into two components, one identically equal to project B and one a residual project equal to the hypothetical project C. The hypothetical investment has a net present value equal to the differential between the *NPV* of the first two projects, or £100 000. This is shown below:

Project	Cost	NPV
A	£1 000 000	£200 000
B	– 300 000	– 100 000
C	£ 700 000	£100 000

Since the hypothetical project C has a positive net present value, it should be accepted. This amounts to accepting project A.

To put it another way, project A can be split into two components, one costing £300 000 and having a net present value of £100 000, the other costing £700 000 and having a net present value of £100 000. As each of the two components has a positive net present value, both should be accepted; but if project B is accepted, the effect is to reject the second component of project A, the hypothetical project C. As the *PI* method selects project B while the *NPV* method selects project A, we conclude that the *NPV* method is preferable.

Alternatively, we can make an adjustment to make the projects of equal scale or size. We can calculate the *NPV** based on terminal values by assuming an additional investment of £700 000 for project B earning at the firm's cost of capital. If the project cost of capital is 10 per cent, for example, the extra investment earns at a 10 per cent rate and is discounted at a 10 per cent rate. The present value of the inflows must therefore be £700 000. We have added £700 000 to both the gross present value and the investment cost, so the *NPV** of project B is £100 000, the same as its *NPV*. The *PI* method would now take into account the additional £700 000 investment and its present value of £700 000. The original *PV* of benefits was £400 000 (the cost of £300 000 plus the *NPV* of £100 000) to which is added the *PV* of £700 000, for total *PV* benefits equal to £1 100 000. Next we divide by the cost of £1 000 000 to obtain a *PI* of 1.1, which is less than the 1.2 *PI* calculated for project A. Thus when the *PI* is adjusted for differences in scale or size of investments, it will give the same rankings as the *NPV**.

An extreme example is often cited to argue for the superiority of the *PI* method. Suppose that project L costs

3. If costs are incurred in more than one year, they should be netted against cash inflows in the corresponding years; if costs exceed cash inflows in some years, the denominator must be the *PV* of the costs.

£1 million and has a net present value of £100000, while project S costs £100000 and has a net present value of £99 000. It may be argued that the benefits from project S are almost as great as for project L, but the amount of funds invested is much smaller. However, if we perform an *NPV** analysis by assuming an investment of an additional £900 000 in project S to make its cost equal with project L's, we find that the *NPV** of project S will be £1000 less than the *NPV** for project L. It may be argued that project S without the additional investment is less risky because of the smaller investment outlay. However, the operating flows of S are likely to be larger as a substitute for the larger investment outlay for L. For example, a decision to repair a machine will involve a smaller outlay than a replacement. But the repaired machine is likely to involve greater maintenance outlays in the future as compared with the replacement, and the actual size of the maintenance outlays is subject to uncertainty as well. While we have emphasized that, in finance, mechanical rules should not be substituted for judgement, the *NPV** generally provides the correct result, which should be set aside only for compelling reasons after all important facets of the evidence have been included in the analysis.

SHIFTING MCC OR IRR CURVES

If the *MCC* and *IRR* curves are expected to be reasonably stable over time, then the firm can form a judgement about the reinvestment rate, or opportunity cost of cash flows and, on the basis of this estimate, it can decide to use either the *NPV* or the *IRR* method. However, if either the *MCC* or the *IRR* curve shifts over time, as in Figure 10A–2, then a new problem arises: there is no simple way to prescribe decision rules for a firm faced with such a situation. Probably the most reasonable approach would involve computer simulation, wherein a number of assumptions about future investment opportunities and discount rates are fed into a computer and then present values of the firm are estimated under alternative courses of action. This involves capital budgeting under uncertainty, which is discussed in Chapter 11.

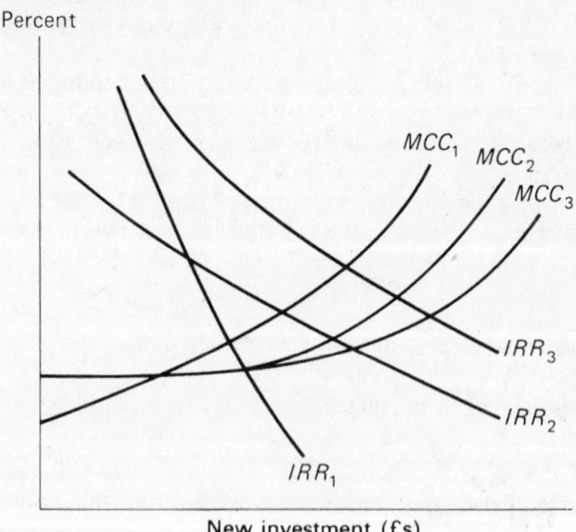

Figure 10A–2 *Shifting* MCC *and* IRR *Curves.*

MULTIPLE SOLUTION TO THE IRR

A totally different problem, unrelated to anything discussed thus far, can arise when the *IRR* is used to rank projects: under certain circumstances, several different values of *r* can be used to solve equation 10A–3:

$$I = \frac{F_1}{(1+r)^1} + \frac{F_2}{(1+r)^2} + \ldots + \frac{F_N}{(1+r)^N} \qquad (10A\text{–}3)$$

Notice that this equation is a polynomial of degree *N*. Therefore, there are *N* different roots, or solutions, to the equation. All except one of the roots either are imaginary numbers or are negative when investments are 'normal' – a normal investment being one that has one or more outflows (costs) followed by a series of inflows (receipts) – so in the normal case only one positive value of *r* appears. If, however, a project calls for a large outflow either sometime during or at the end of its life, then it is a 'non-normal' project, and the possibility of multiple real roots arises.

To illustrate this problem, suppose the project calls for an expenditure of £1600 for a pump that will enable the firm to recover £10 000 of oil from a field at the end of one year.[4] If the new pump is not installed, the firm will recover the same £10 000 of oil at the end of two years. Obviously, if the pump is installed and the oil is recovered at the end of year 1, there will be no oil at the end of year 2. Therefore, the project's cash flows are as follows:

Year end	0	1	2
Cash flow	−£1600	+£10 000	−£10 000

These values can be substituted into equation 10A–3 to derive the NPV for the investment:

$$NPV = £1600 + \frac{£10\,000}{(1+r)} - \frac{£10\,000}{(1+r)^2}.$$

$NPV = 0$ when $r = 25$ per cent *and* when $r = 400$ per cent, so the IRR of the investment is *both* 25 per cent and 400 per cent. This relationship is graphically depicted in Figure 10A–3. Note that no dilemma would arise if the NPV method were used – we would simply replace r with k in the equation above, find the NPV, and use this for ranking.

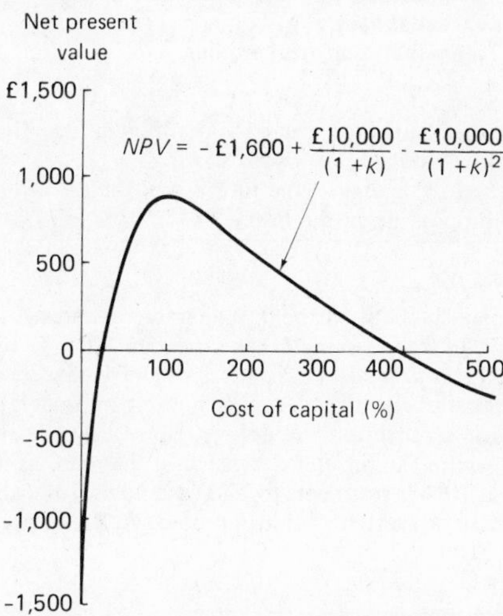

Figure 10A–3 *Net Present Value as a Function of Cost of Capital.*

A similar situation actually occurred when a major California bank *borrowed* funds from an insurance company, then used these funds (plus an initial investment of its own) to buy a number of jet engines, which it then leased to a major airline. The bank expected to receive positive net cash flows (lease payments minus interest on the insurance company loan) for a number of years, then several large negative cash flows as it repaid the insurance company loan, and finally, a large inflow from the sale of the engines when the lease expired.

The bank discovered two IRRs and wondered which was correct. It could not ignore the IRR and use the NPV method, as the lease was already on the books; meanwhile, both the bank's senior loan committee and the Federal Reserve Bank examiners wanted to know the return on the lease. The bank's solution called for compounding the cash flows – both positive and negative – at an assumed reinvestment rate of 9 per cent, its average return on loans, to arrive at a compounded terminal value for the operation. Then the interest rate that equated this terminal sum to the bank's initial cost was called the IRR^*, or the rate of return on the lease. This procedure satisfied not only the loan committee but also the bank examiners. Note, however, that the procedure would have been rejected if the bank had borrowed *all* the money to finance the investment. In fact, in most similar situations, the IRR becomes larger as the bank's 'investment' decreases, with the IRR approaching infinity as investment approaches nil.[5]

---

4. This example is drawn from J. H. Lorie and L. J. Savage, Three problems in capital rationing, *Journal of Business* (October 1955), pp. 236–237.

5. For additional insights into the multiple root problem, see James C. T. Mao, *Quantitative Analysis of Financial Decisions* (New York: Macmillan, 1969), chap. 6.

PROGRAMMING APPROACHES TO CAPITAL RATIONING

The problems encountered in capital budgeting that cause conflicts in making decisions are summarized in Table 10A–2. If none of the problems listed in the table apply, then the *NPV*, *IRR* and *PI* methods always provide identical answers to the critical capital budgeting question – What projects should be accepted in the capital budget? However, if any of the project characteristics shown in Part A of Table 10A–2 apply, then the three methods can give different rankings to mutually exclusive projects. If none of the firm characteristics in Part B of the table applies, these conflicts really present no problem, as all conflicts should be resolved in favour of the *NPV* method because it selects the set of projects that maximizes the firm's value.

Table 10A–2 *Conditions under which* NPV, IRR *and* PI *may Rank Conflicting Projects Differently.*

Part A: Project characteristics
1. The cash flow of one project increases over time, while that of the other decreases.
2. The projects have different expected lives.
3. The cost of one project is larger than that of the other.

Part B: Firm characteristics
4. Investment opportunities in the future are expected to be different from those of this year, and the direction of change (better or worse) is known.
5. The cost of capital is expected to change in the future, and the direction of change is known.
6. Capital rationing is being imposed upon the firm.

Very serious difficulties can arise when any of the firm characteristics exist, because then future investment opportunities cease to be constant. In that case, *neither the standard* NPV, IRR, *nor* PI *methods will necessarily select a set of projects that maximizes the firm's value*. However, the *NPV* concept can be expanded to take account of both firm and project characteristics through the programming approach outlined below.

The programming approach is, in essence, a methodology that seeks to determine the value of the 'modified *NPV*' (*NPV**) discussed above. Initially, consider a procedure that can, at least conceptually, improve our decision. Figure 10A–4 gives a matrix of investments in, and cash flows from, alternative projects. The values in the cells of the matrix are the net cash flows attributable to projects A, B, . . . over years 1, 2, . . . , *N*. The rows of

Years (t)

Projects (j)	1	2	3	4	5	6	7	8	9	10	11	12	13	14	15	...N
A	F_{a1}	F_{a2}	F_{a3}													
B	F_{b1}	F_{b2}	F_{b3}	F_{b4}												
C	F_{c1}	F_{c2}	F_{c3}	F_{c4}	F_{c5}	F_{c6}	F_{c7}									
D		F_{d2}	F_{d3}	F_{d4}	F_{d5}	→										
E		F_{e2}	F_{e3}	...												
F		F_{f2}	F_{f3}	...												
G		F_{g2}	F_{g3}	...												
H			F_{h3}	...												
I			F_{i3}	...												
J			F_{j3}	...												
K				F_{k4}												
L				F_{l4}												
M				F_{m4}												
N					F_{n5}	...										
O					F_{o5}	...										
P					F_{p5}	...										
⋮ ↓					⋮											↓

Figure 10A–4 *Matrix of Future Investment Opportunities.*

the matrix thus represent the investment opportunities available during the relevant time horizon, while the columns of the matrix represent the net cash flows from all projects during a given year. The cash flows in a particular cell can be either positive or negative; negative cash flow represents an investment, while a positive cash flow represents the benefits resulting from the investment.

Figure 10A–4 simply describes the investment opportunities open to the firm – the capital projects it can undertake. If no capital rationing is imposed, the firm will be able to take on all of the projects that have positive *NPVs*. If we make the further assumption that the cost of capital is constant, then the straightforward *NPV* method can be used to determine which of the available projects should be accepted.

Capital rationing

Suppose, however, that the firm is subject to capital rationing. Specifically, assume that it has an initial amount of money available for investment at the beginning of year 1. It can invest this amount but no more. Further, assume that the funds available for investment in future years must come from cash generated from these same investments. Therefore, the funds available for investment in year 2 will depend upon the profitability of the set of investments chosen in year 1; investment funds available in year 3 will depend upon cash throw-off from investments in years 1 and 2, and so forth.[6]

If the projects available for investment in year 2 are more profitable than those available in year 1 – that is, if they have higher internal rates of return – the firm should perhaps select investments in year 1 that will have fast paybacks. This will make funds available for the profitable investment opportunities in year 2. This is, however, only an approximation. Conceptually, the firm should select its investment in each year (subject to the capital rationing constraint) so as to maximize the net present value of future cash flows. These cash flows should, of course, be discounted at the firm's cost of capital. If the investment opportunities were infinitely divisible – for example, if they were securities such as stocks or shares that could be purchased in larger or smaller quantities – then the firm could use a technique known as *linear programming* to determine the optimal set of investment opportunities. If such opportunities are not infinitely divisible – and in capital budgeting they typically are not – then a more complex procedure known as *integer programming* must be used to find the optimal investment strategy.[7] Regardless of the computational process used to solve the problem, the firm should seek the set of investment opportunities that maximizes the *NPV* of the firm without exceeding the capital rationing constraint.

Changing cost of capital

Assuming that the cost of capital is constant, linear or integer programming offers a conceptual solution to the problem of capital budgeting under capital rationing. These methods do not, however, offer a solution to the general case of a changing cost of capital. For example, if the cost of capital is rising at the point where the *IRR* curve cuts the *MCC* curve, the wealth-maximizing set of projects – with regard both to the total budget and to the choices among competing projects – can be determined only by an iterative, or trial-and-error, process. With linear or integer programming, the cost of capital must be given as an input. If, however, the cost of capital *depends* upon the size of the capital budget, then the cost of capital obviously cannot be *assumed* when determining the capital budget. What is required is a dynamic programming model that, through an iterative process, simultaneously determines the capital budget and the marginal cost of capital. Such models are quite complex, but they do have practical applications in capital budgeting; these formal aspects may be pursued further in courses in management science or in operations research.

PROBLEMS

10A–1. Assume a firm is set up with total capital of £20 000. No additional funds can be brought into the firm, but cash flows can be reinvested in the business. Thus, the *capital rationing* constraint is £20 000 *in year* 1, and in later years it is the *available cash flows* resulting from this and its succeeding investments.

The investors who set up the firm have a 10 *per cent* cost of capital, and they have mutually agreed to terminate the firm at the end of *three* years. Therefore, the investor's welfare will be maximized by having

6. The concept could also be extended to include any specific amount of external funds during each year. In this case, the capital constraint would be the internally generated funds plus the allowed external funds.

7. H. Martin Weingartner, in *Mathematical Programming and the Analysis of Capital Budgeting Problems* (Englewood Cliffs, N. J.: Prentice-Hall, 1963), has shown how integer programming can be used in capital budgeting decisions.

the firm attain the highest possible *terminal value*. Two projects are available; each costs £20 000 and provides cash flows as follows:

Year	Project A	Project B
1	£10 000	£ 0
2	10 000	0
3	10 000	35 000

(a) Calculate *IRR** and *NPV** for each project. Assume cash flows from A are reinvested at 14 per cent.
(b) Which project should be accepted?
(c) Is there a reinvestment rate at which the firm should be indifferent between the two projects? If so, what is it?

10A–2. A tin mining firm is considering opening a strip mine, the cost of which is £4.4 million. Cash flows will be £27.7 million, all coming at the end of one year. The land must be returned to its natural state at a cost of £25 million, payable after two years. The *IRR* is found to be either 9.2 per cent or 420 per cent. Should the project be accepted (i) if $k = 8$ per cent, or (ii) if $k = 14$ per cent? Explain your reasoning.

SELECTED REFERENCES

Amey, L. R. Interdependencies in capital budgeting: a survey. *Journal of Business Finance* 4 (Autumn 1972): 70–86.

Bernhard, Richard H. Mathematical programming models for capital budgeting – a survey, generalization, and critique. *Journal of Financial and Quantitative Analysis* 4 (June 1969): 111–158.

Bhaskar, K. N. Linear programming and capital budgeting: a reappraisal. *Journal of Business Finance and Accounting* 3 (Autumn 1976): 29–40.

Burton, R. M. and Damon, W. W. On the existence of a cost of capital under pure capital rationing. *Journal of Finance* XXIX, No. 4 (September 1974): 1165–1173.

Findlay, M. Chapman III and Williams, Edward E. Capital allocation and the nature of ownership equities. *Financial Management* 1 (Summer 1972): 68–76.

Grinyer, J. R. An extension of Fisher's model. *Journal of Business Finance* 5 (Spring 1973): 13–23.

Hawkins, Clark A. and Adams, Richard A. A goal programming model for capital budgeting. *Financial Management* 3, No. 1 (Spring 1974): 52–57.

Hughes, J. S. and Lewellyn, W. J. Programming solutions to capital rationing problems. *Journal of Business Finance and Accounting* 1 (Spring 1974): 55–74.

Keane, S. M. Let's scrap IRR once for all. *Accountancy* (February 1974).

Lee, Sang M. and Lerro, A. J. Capital budgeting for multiple objectives. *Financial Management* 3, No. 1 (Spring 1974): 58–66.

Lorie, James H. and Savage, Leonard J. Three problems in rationing capital. *Journal of Business* 28 (October 1955): 227–239.

Ma, R. and Tydeman, J. Project selection criteria, wealth maximization and capital rationing. *Journal of Business Finance* 4 (Winter 1972): 34–43.

Myers, Stewart C. A note on linear programming and capital budgeting. *Journal of Finance* 27 (March 1972): 89–92.

Norström, C. J. A mathematical connection between the present value, the rate of return, and the scale of investment. *Journal of Business Finance* 4 (Summer 1972): 75–77.

Sarnat, Marshall and Levy, Haim. The relationship of rules of thumb to the Internal rate of return: a restatement and generalization. *Journal of Finance* 24 (June 1969): 479–489.

Sartoris, William L. and Spruill, M. Lynn. Goal programming and working capital management. *Financial Management* 3, No. 1 (Spring 1974): 67–74.

Schwab, Bernhard and Lusztig, Peter. A comparative analysis of the net present value and the benefit cost ratios as measures of the economic desirability of investments. *Journal of Finance* 24 (June 1969): 507–516.

Stephen, F. H. On deriving the internal rate of return from the accountant's rate of return. *Journal of Business Finance and Accounting* 3 (Summer 1976): 147–150.

Weingartner, H. Martin. *Mathematical Programming and the Analysis of Capital Budgeting Problems.* Englewood Cliffs, N.J.: Prentice-Hall, 1963.

Weingartner, H. Martin. Some new views on the payback period and capital budgeting decisions. *Management Science* 15 (August 1969): 594–607.

Weingartner, H. Martin. The excess present value index – a theoretical basis and critique. *Journal of Accounting Research* 1 (Autumn 1963): 213–224.

Chapter 11

Investment Decisions under Uncertainty

In order to develop the theory and methodology of capital budgeting in a systematic manner, the 'riskiness' of alternative projects was not treated explicitly in the preceding chapter. However, since investors and financial managers are generally risk averters, they should take into account whether one project is more risky than another when choosing between projects. Several approaches to risk analysis are discussed in this chapter.[1]

RISK IN FINANCIAL ANALYSIS

The riskiness of an asset is defined in terms of the likely variability of future returns from the asset. For example, if one buys a £1 million short-term government bond expected to yield 5 per cent, then the return on the investment, 5 per cent, can be estimated quite precisely, and the investment is defined as relatively risk free. However, if the £1 million is invested in the shares of a company just being organized to prospect for uranium in Central Africa, then the probable return cannot be estimated precisely. The rate of return on the £1 million investment could range from minus 100 per cent to some extremely large figure, and because of this high variability, the project is defined as relatively risky. Similarly, sales forecasts for different products of a single firm might exhibit differing degrees of riskiness. For example, Union Carbide might be quite sure that sales of its Eveready batteries will range between 50 and 60 million for the coming year, but be highly uncertain about how many units of a new laser measuring device will be sold during the year.

Risk, then, is associated with project variability – the more variable the expected future returns, the riskier the investment. However, we can define risk more precisely, and it is useful to do so. This more precise definition requires a step-by-step development, which constitutes the remainder of this section.

1. This chapter is long and introduces some important new concepts that will be applied in subsequent chapters as well.

Probability distributions

Any investment decision – or, for that matter, almost *any* kind of business decision – implies a forecast of future events that is either explicit or implicit. Ordinarily, the forecast of annual cash flow is a single figure, or *point estimate*, frequently called the 'most likely' or 'best' estimate. For example, one might forecast that the cash flows from a particular project will be £500 a year for three years.

How good is this point estimate; that is, how confident is the forecaster of his predicted return? Is he very certain, very uncertain, or somewhere in between? This degree of uncertainty can be defined and measured in terms of the forecaster's *probability distribution* – the probability estimates associated with each possible outcome. In its simplest form, a probability distribution could consist of just a few potential outcomes. For example, in forecasting cash flows, we could make an optimistic estimate, a pessimistic estimate, and a most likely estimate; or, alternatively, we could make high, low, and 'best guess' estimates. We might expect our high, or optimistic, estimate to be realized if the national economy booms, our pessimistic estimate to hold if the economy is depressed, and our best guess to occur if the economy runs at a normal level. These ranges are illustrated in Table 11–1. The figures in the table represent some improvement over our earlier best-guess estimate of £500, as additional information has been provided. However, some critical information is still missing: how likely is it that we will have a boom, a recession, or normal economic conditions? If we have estimates of the probabilities of these events, we can develop a weighted average cash flow estimate and a measure of our degree of confidence in this estimate. This point is explored in the next section.

Table 11–1 *Expected Cash Flows under Different Economic Conditions.*

State of the economy	Cash flows
Recession	£400
Normal	500
Boom	600

Risk comparisons

To illustrate how the probability distribution concept can be used to compare the riskiness of alternative investment projects, suppose we are considering two investment decisions each calling for an outlay of £1000 and each expected to produce a cash flow of £500 a year for three years. (The best-estimate cash flow is £500 a year for each project.) If the discount rate is 10 per cent, we can use the methods developed in the preceding chapter to estimate each project's net present value:

$$
\begin{aligned}
NPV &= £500 \times 2.487 - £1000 \\
&= £1243.50 - £1000 \\
&= £243.50 \text{ for each project.}
\end{aligned}
$$

The projects have the same expected returns; does this mean that they are equally desirable? To answer this question, we need to know whether the projects are also equally risky, since 'desirability' depends upon both returns and risk.

Let us suppose that project A calls for the replacement of an old machine used in normal operations by a more efficient one, and the benefits are labour and raw material savings that will result. Project B, on the other hand, calls for the purchase of an entirely new machine to produce a new product, the demand for which is highly uncertain. The replacement machine (project A) will be used more, hence savings will be greater, if demand for the product is high. Expected demand for the new product (project B) is also greatest when the economy is booming.

We stated above that the expected annual returns from each project are £500. Let us assume that these figures were developed in the following manner:

1. First, we estimate project returns under different states of the economy as in Table 11–2. Tables of this kind are typically referred to as *payoff matrices*.

Table 11–2 *Payoff Matrix for Projects A and B.*

State of the economy	Annual cash flows Project A	Project B
Recession	£400	£ 0
Normal	500	500
Boom	600	1000

2. Next, we estimate the likelihood of different states of the economy. Assume our economic forecasts indicate that, given current trends in economic indicators, the chances are two out of ten that recession will occur, six out of ten that the economy will be normal, and two out of ten that there will be a boom.
3. Redefining the word 'chance' as *probability*, we find that the probability of a recession is $2/10 = 0.2$, or 20 per cent; the probability of normal times is $6/10 = 0.6$, or 60 per cent; and the probability of a boom is $2/10 = 0.2$, or 20 per cent. Notice that the probabilities add up to 1.0, or 100 per cent: $0.2 + 0.6 + 0.2 = 1.0$ or 100 per cent.
4. Finally, in Table 11–3 we calculate weighted averages of the possible returns by multiplying each £1 return by its probability of occurrence. When column 4 of the table is summed, we obtain a weighted average of the outcomes for each alternative under various states of the economy; this weighted average is defined as the *expected value* of the cash flows from the project. It need not, of course, be equal to the project's outcome for a normal state of the economy, although this is the case for project A but not for project B.

Table 11–3 *Calculation of Expected Values.*

State of the economy (1)	Probability of this state occurring (2)	Outcome if this state occurs (3)	(2) × (3) (4)
Project A			
Recession	0.2	£ 400	£ 80
Normal	0.6	500	300
Boom	0.2	600	120
	1.0	Expected value	= £500
Project B			
Recession	0.2	£ 0	£ 0
Normal	0.6	500	300
Boom	0.2	1000	200
	1.0	Expected value	= £500

We can graph the results shown in Table 11–3 to obtain a picture of the variability of actual outcomes; this is shown in the bar charts in Figure 11–1. The height of each bar signifies the probability that a given outcome will occur. The range of probable outcomes

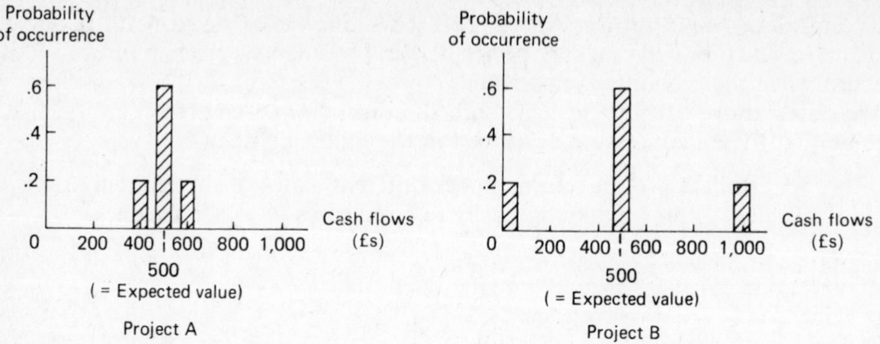

Figure 11–1 *Relationship between the State of the Economy and Project Returns.*

for project A is from £400 to £600, with an average or *expected value* of £500. The expected value for project B is also £500, but the range of possible outcomes is from £0 to £1000.

Continuous distributions

Thus far we have assumed that only three states of the economy can exist: recession, normal and boom. Actually, of course, the state of the economy could range from a deep depression, as in the early 1930s, to a fantastic boom; and there is an unlimited number of possibilities in between. Suppose we had the time and patience to assign a probability to each possible state of the economy (with the sum of the probabilities still equalling 1.0) and to assign a monetary outcome to each project for each state of the economy. We would have a table similar to Table 11–3 except that it would have many more entries for 'Probability' and 'Outcome if this state occurs'. These tables could be used to calculate expected values as shown above, and the probabilities and outcomes could be graphed as the continuous curves presented in Figure 11–2. Here we have changed the assumptions so that there is nil probability that project A will yield less than £400 or more than £600, and so that there is nil probability that project B will yield less than £0 or more than £1000.

Figure 11–2 is a graph of the *probability distributions* of returns on projects A and B. In general, the tighter the probability distribution, or, alternatively stated, the more peaked the distribution, the more likely it is that the actual outcome will be close to the expected value. Since project A has a relatively tight probability distribution, its *actual* profits are likely to be closer to the *expected* £500 than are those of project B.

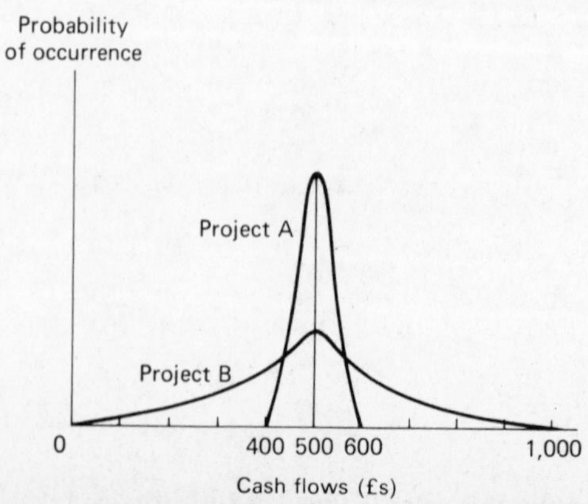

Figure 11–2 *Probability Distribution Showing Relationship between State of the Economy and Project Returns.*

Risk versus uncertainty

Sometimes a distinction is made between *risk* and *uncertainty*. When this distinction is made, risk is associated with those situations in which a probability distribution of the returns on a given project can be estimated; uncertainty is associated with those situations in which insufficient evidence is available even to estimate a probability distribution. We do not make this distinction; risk and uncertainty are used synonymously in this chapter.

We do, however, recognize that probability distributions of expected returns can themselves be estimated with greater or lesser precision. In some instances, the probability distribution can be estimated *objectively* with statistical techniques. For example, a large oil company may be able to estimate from past recovery data the probability distribution of recoverable oil reserves in a given field. When statistical procedures can be used, risk is said to be measured by *objective probability distributions*. There are, however, many situations in which statistical data cannot be used. For example, a company considering the introduction of a totally new product will have some idea about the required investment outlay, the demand for the product, the production costs, and so forth. These estimates will not, however, be determined by statistics; they will be determined subjectively and are defined as *subjective probability distributions*.

TRADITIONAL MEASURES OF RISK OF INDIVIDUAL PROJECTS

Risk is difficult to measure unambiguously. The traditional measures of risk have been applied to individual projects in isolation. Newer approaches have recognized that individual projects can be combined with other projects into groups of projects or portfolios. Viewing an individual project in its broader portfolio context changes the appropriate measure of risk to be applied. These relationships will be explained in the remainder of this chapter. We start with a discussion of the traditional measures of risk applied to individual projects so that the relationships between the different approaches can be seen.

The traditional measure of risk applied to individual projects is stated in terms of probability distributions such as those presented in Figure 11–2. The tighter the probability distribution of expected future returns, the smaller the risk of a given project. According to this traditional view, project A is less risky than project B because each of the possible returns for (A) is closer to the expected return than is true for (B).

Measuring risk: standard deviation

The traditional approach utilizes a measure of the tightness of the probability distribution of project returns. The measure of tightness it utilizes is the standard deviation, the symbol for which is σ, read 'sigma'. The tighter the probability distribution, the smaller the standard deviation. We can confirm this statement by the actual calculation of the standard deviation as presented in Table 11–4.

Column (1) lists the alternative states of the world as portrayed by alternative states of the economy. Column (2) lists the probability of each of the states. Column (3) lists the outcome if a particular state occurs. These are the possible returns from a given project under alternative states. Column (4) is the expected values obtained by multiplying the probability with the associated outcome. The sum of Column (4) is the expected value for the distribution of probable returns representing a weighted average of the various possible outcomes. We then proceed to calculate the variance and standard deviation of the probability distribution. In Column (5) we subtract the expected value from each

Table 11–4 *Calculation of Standard Deviations.*

State of the economy (1)	Probability of state occurring (2)	Outcome if state occurs (3)	Expected value (2) × (3) (4)	Deviation (5)	Squared deviation (6)	Variance (2) × (6) (7)
Project A						
Boom	0.2	600	120	100	10 000	2000
Normal	0.6	500	300	0	0	0
Recession	0.2	400	80	(100)	10 000	2000
		Expected value =	£500		Variance =	£4000
					Standard deviation (σ) =	£63.25
Project B						
Boom	0.2	1000	200	500	250 000	50 000
Normal	0.6	500	300	0	0	0
Recession	0.2	0	0	(500)	250 000	50 000
		Expected value =	£500		Variance =	£100 000
					Standard deviation (σ) =	£ 316.23

possible outcome to obtain a set of deviations about the expected value. In Column (6) we square each deviation. In Column (7) we multiply the squared deviation by the probability of occurrence for its related outcome and sum these products to obtain the variance of the probability distribution. The standard deviation is then obtained by taking the square root of the variance.

Using the procedures described, we observe in Table 11–4 that the standard deviation of project A is £63.25; that of project B is £316.23. By the standard deviation criterion, project B is 'riskier' since its standard deviation is much larger than the standard deviation for project A. Since the expected values of the net present values for returns from the two projects are equal at £500, project A would be preferred. It has the same expected value but a smaller variance and smaller standard deviation.

Measuring risk: the coefficient of variation

Certain problems can arise when the standard deviation is used as a measure of risk. To illustrate, consider Figure 11–3, which shows the probability distributions for investments C and D. Investment C has an expected return of £1000 and a standard deviation of £300.

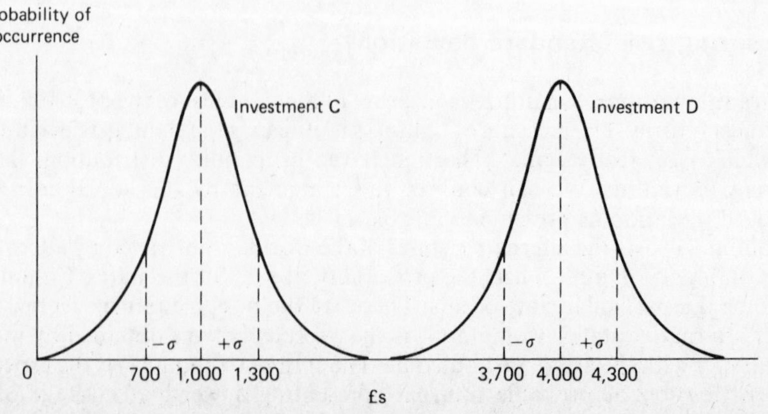

Figure 11–3 *Probability Distributions of Two Investments with Different Expected Returns.*

Investment D also has a standard deviation of £300, but its expected return is £4000. The likely percentage deviation from the mean of investment C is considerably higher than that from the mean of investment D, or, put another way, C has more risk *per £1 of return* than D. On this basis, it is reasonable to assign a higher degree of risk to investment C than to investment D even though they have identical standard deviations.

The standard procedure for handling this problem is to divide the standard deviation (σ_j) by the mean, or expected value of net cash flows ($\bar{F}_j$), to obtain the *coefficient of variation* (CV):

$$CV_j = \frac{\sigma_j}{\bar{F}_j}.$$

For investment C we divide the £300 standard deviation by the £1000 expected value or mean, obtaining 0.30 as the coefficient of variation. Similarly, for investment D we divide the standard deviation of £300 by the mean value £4000 to obtain 0.075. This is a much lower coefficient of variation than for investment C. Since investment D has a lower coefficient of variation, it has less risk per unit of return than investment C. For the higher expected return and a lower standardized measure of risk, investment D would be unambiguously preferred. Thus, if the standard deviation is to be used as a measure of risk for investments viewed in isolation, the normalization obtained by dividing through by the respective means to obtain the coefficient of variation should be performed.

Riskiness over time

We can also use Figure 11–2 to consider the riskiness of a stream of receipts over time. Visualize, for example, investment A as being the expected cash flow from a particular project during year 1, and investment B as being the expected cash flow from the *same* project in the tenth year. The expected return is the same for each of the two years, but the subjectively estimated standard deviation (hence the coefficient of variation) is larger for the more distant return. In this case, riskiness is *increasing over time*.

Figure 11–4 may help to clarify the concept of increasing riskiness over time. Figure 11–4(a) simply shows the probability distribution of expected cash flows in two years – years 1 and 10. The distribution is flatter in year 10, indicating that there is more uncertainty about expected cash flows in distant years. Figure 11–4(b) represents a three-

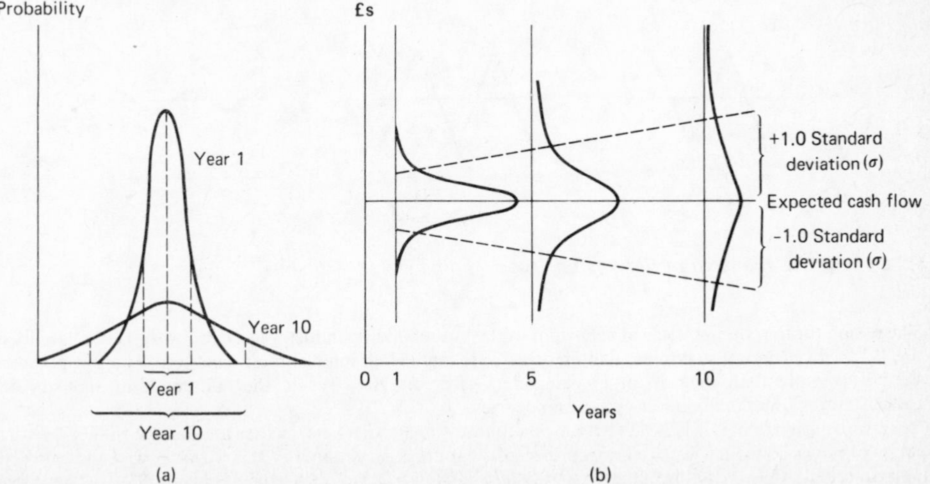

Figure 11–4 *Risk as a Function of Time.*

dimensional plot of the expected cash flows over time and their probability distributions. The probability distributions should be visualized as extending out from the page. The dashed lines show the standard deviations attached to the cash flows of each year; the fact that these lines diverge from the expected cash flow line indicates that riskiness is increasing over time. If risk was thought of as being constant over time – that is, if the cash flow in a distant year could be estimated equally as well as the cash flow of a close year – then the standard deviation would be constant and the boundary lines would not diverge from the expected cash flow line. The fact that the standard deviation is increasing over time, while the expected return is constant, would, of course, cause the coefficient of variation to increase similarly.

PORTFOLIO RISK

When considering the riskiness of a particular investment, it is frequently useful to consider the relationship between the investment in question and other existing assets or potential investment opportunities. To illustrate, a steel company may decide to diversify into housebuilding materials. It knows that when the economy is booming, the demand for steel is high and the returns from the steel mill are large. Housebuilding, on the other hand, tends to be counter-cyclical: when the economy as a whole is in a recession, the demand for construction materials is high.[2] Because of these divergent cyclical patterns, a diversified firm with investments in both steel and construction could expect to have a more stable pattern of revenues than would a firm engaged exclusively in either steel or housebuilding. In other words, the deviations of the returns on the *portfolio of assets*, σ, may be less than the sum of the deviations of the returns from the individual assets.[3]

This point is illustrated in Figure 11 – 5: 11–5(a) shows the rate of return variations for the steel plant, 11–5(b) shows the fluctuations for the housebuilding material division, and 11–5(c) shows the rate of return for the combined company. When the returns from steel are large, those from residential construction are small, and vice versa. As a consequence, the combined rate of return is relatively stable.

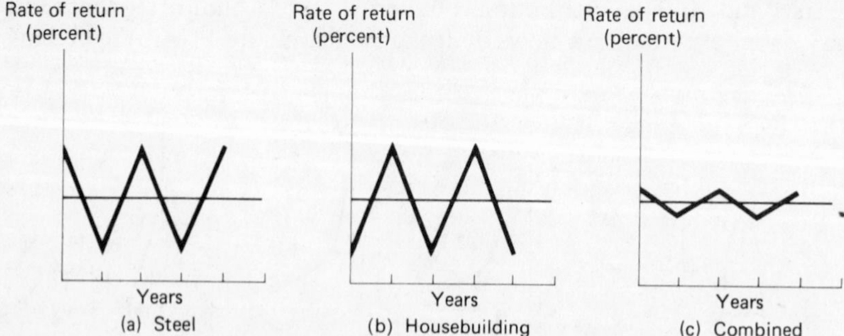

Figure 11–5 *Relationship of Returns on Two Hypothetical Investments.*

2. The reason for the counter-cyclical behaviour of the housebuilding industry has to do with the availability of credit. When the economy is booming, interest rates are high. High interest rates seem to discourage potential home buyers more than they do other demanders of credit. As a result, the housebuilding industry has historically shown marked counter-cyclical tendencies.

3. These conclusions obviously hold also for portfolios of financial assets – shares and bonds. In fact the basic concepts of portfolio theory were developed specifically for ordinary shares by Harry Markowitz and were first presented in his article, Portfolio Selection, *Journal of Finance* 7, No. 1 (March 1952), pp. 77–91. The logical extension of portfolio theory to capital budgeting calls for considering firms as having 'portfolios of tangible assets'.

If we calculate the correlation between rates of return on the steel and construction divisions, we find the correlation coefficient to be negative – whenever rates of return on the steel plant are high, those on the construction material plants are low. If any two projects, A and B, have a high degree of *negative correlation*, then taking on the two investments reduces the firm's overall risk. This risk reduction is defined as a *portfolio effect*.

On the other hand, if there had been a high *positive correlation* between projects A and B – that is, if returns on A were high at the same time as those on B were high – overall risk could not have been reduced significantly by diversification. If the correlation between A and B had been + 1.0, the risk reduction would have been nil, so no portfolio effects would have been obtained.

If the returns from the two projects were completely uncorrelated – that is, if the correlation coefficient between them was nil – then diversification would benefit the firm to at least some extent. The larger the number of uncorrelated, or independent, projects the firm takes on, the smaller will be the variation in its overall rate of return.[4] Uncorrelated projects are not as useful for reducing risk as are negatively correlated ones, but they are better than positively correlated projects.

Correlation coefficients range from + 1.0, indicating perfect positive correlations, to – 1.0, indicating perfect negative correlation. If the correlation coefficient is nil, then the projects are independent, or uncorrelated.

We can summarize the arguments on portfolio risk that have been presented thus far:

1. If *perfectly negatively correlated* projects are available in sufficient number, then diversification can completely eliminate risk. Perfect negative correlation is, however, almost never found in the real world.
2. If *uncorrelated* projects are available in sufficient number, then diversification can reduce risk significantly – to nil at the limit.
3. If all alternative projects are *perfectly positively correlated*, then diversification does not reduce risk at all.

In fact, most projects are *positively* correlated but not *perfectly* correlated. The degree of intercorrelation among projects depends upon economic factors, and these factors are usually amenable to analysis. Returns on investments in projects closely related to the firm's basic products and markets will ordinarily be highly correlated with returns on the remainder of the firm's assets, and such investments will not generally reduce the firm's risk. However, investments in other product lines and in other geographic markets may have a low degree of correlation with other components of the firm and may, therefore, reduce overall risk. Accordingly, if an asset's returns are not too closely related to the firm's other major assets (or, better still, are negatively correlated with other investments), this asset is more valuable to a risk-averting firm than is a similar asset whose returns are positively correlated with the bulk of the assets.

Expected return on a portfolio

A portfolio is defined as a combination of assets, and portfolio theory deals with the selection of optimal portfolios; that is, portfolios that provide the highest possible return for any specified degree of risk, or the lowest possible risk for any specified rate of return. Since portfolio theory has been developed most thoroughly for *financial assets* – shares and bonds – we shall, for the most part, restrict our discussion to these assets.[5] However,

4. The principle involved here is the so-called law of large numbers. As the number of independent projects is increased, the standard deviation of the returns on the portfolio of projects will decrease with the square root of the number of projects taken on.

5. Financial assets are highly divisible and available in large numbers, and a great deal of data is available on such assets. Capital assets such as plant and equipment, on the other hand, are 'lumpy', and the data needed to apply portfolio theory to such assets are not readily available.

extensions of financial asset portfolio theory to physical assets are readily made, and certainly the concepts are relevant in capital budgeting.

The rate of return on a portfolio is always a linear function – it is simply a weighted average of the returns of the individual securities in the portfolio. For example, if 50 per cent of the portfolio is invested in a security with a 6 per cent expected return (security L), and 50 per cent in one with a 10 per cent expected return (security M), the expected rate of return on the portfolio is

$$E(k_p) = w(6\%) + (1-w)(10\%)$$
$$= 0.5(6\%) + 0.5(10\%) = 8\%.$$

Here, $E(k_p)$ is the expected return on the portfolio, w is the percentage of the portfolio invested in L, and $(1-w)$ is the percentage invested in M. If all of the portfolio is invested in L, the expected return is 6 per cent. If all is invested in M, the expected return is 10 per cent. If the portfolio contains some of each, the expected portfolio return is a linear combination of the two securities' expected returns – for example, 8 per cent in our present case. Therefore, given the expected returns on the individual securities, the expected return on the portfolio depends upon the amount of funds invested in each security.

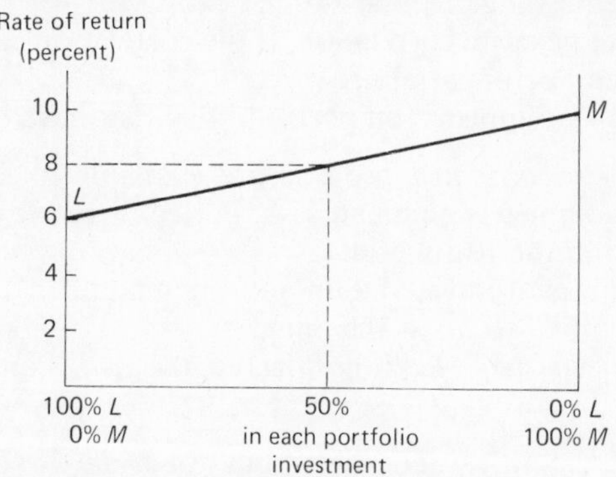

Figure 11–6 *Rates of Return on a Two-Asset Portfolio.*

Figure 11–6 illustrates the possible returns for our two-asset portfolio. Line LM represents all possible expected returns when securities L and M are combined in different proportions. Note that when 50 per cent of the portfolio is invested in each asset, the expected return on the portfolio is seen to be 8 per cent, just as we calculated above.

In general, the expected return on an n-asset portfolio is defined by equation 11–1a:

$$E(k_p) = \sum_{j=1}^{n} w_j k_j. \tag{11–1a}$$

Here w_j is the percentage of the portfolio invested in the jth asset, and k_j is the expected return on the jth asset. To illustrate, if the portfolio consists of five securities, whose individual returns are shown in the parentheses, then the expected return would be computed as follows:

$$E(k_p) = w_1 k_1 + w_2 k_2 + w_3 k_3 + w_4 k_4 + w_5 k_5$$
$$= 0.05(20\%) + 0.10(15\%) + 0.20(5\%) + 0.25(10\%) + 0.40(25\%) = 16\%.$$

Thus, the portfolio's expected return is a weighted average of the returns on each included asset, with the weights being the proportion of funds invested in each security. Of course, the sum of the weights is always equal to 1; for example,

$$\sum_{j=1}^{n} w_j = 0.05 + 0.10 + 0.20 + 0.25 + 0.40 = 1.$$

Riskiness of a portfolio

The riskiness of a portfolio is measured by the standard deviation of expected returns. Equation 11–2 is used to calculate any standard deviation:

$$\sigma_p = \sqrt{\sum_{s=1}^{n} (k_{ps} - \bar{k}_p)^2 P_s}. \qquad (11\text{–}2)$$

Here σ_p is the standard deviation of the portfolio's expected returns; k_{ps} is the expected portfolio return given the sth state of the economy; $\bar{k}_p$ is the mean value of the n possible returns; and P_s is the probability of occurrence of the sth state of the economy.[6] Figure 11–7 illustrates two possible distributions of expected portfolio returns for two portfolios. Portfolio X has more variability than portfolio Y; consequently, investors view portfolio X as being riskier than Y.

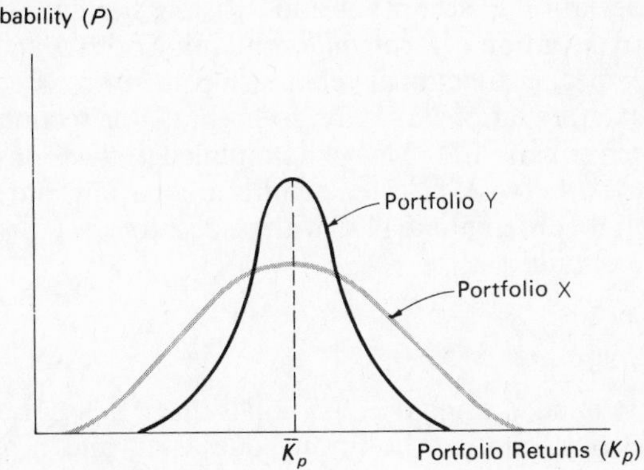

Figure 11–7 *Distributions of Portfolio Returns.*

A fundamental aspect of portfolio theory is the idea that the riskiness inherent in any single asset held in a portfolio is different from the riskiness of that asset held in isolation. As we shall see, it is possible for a given asset to be quite risky when held in isolation, but not very risky if held in a portfolio. The impact of a single asset on a portfolio's riskiness – which is the riskiness of the asset when it is held in a portfolio – is discussed later in this chapter.

Measuring the riskiness of a portfolio: the two-asset case

Equation 11–2 could be used to calculate the riskiness of a portfolio, but, under the assumption that the distributions of returns on the individual securities are normal, a complicated looking but operationally simple equation can be used to determine the risk of a two-asset portfolio:[7]

$$\sigma_p = \sqrt{w^2\sigma_A^2 + (1-w)^2\sigma_B^2 + 2w(1-w)Cov_{AB}}. \qquad (11\text{–}3)$$

6. Equation 11–2 is derived from the general definition of the standard deviation, and it may be interpreted similarly; that is, the actual returns earned on a portfolio should lie within $\pm 1\sigma_p$ approximately 68 per cent of the time.

7. Equation 11–3 is derived from 11–2 in the standard statistics books. Notice that if $w = 1$, all of the portfolio is invested in project A and equation 11–2 reduces to

$$\sigma_p = \sqrt{\sigma_1^2} = \sigma_4.$$

The portfolio contains but a single asset, so the risk of the portfolio and that of the asset are identical. It may also be noted that equations 11–2 and 11–3 can be expanded to include any number of assets by adding additional variance and covariance terms.

The *covariance* (*Cov*) between two securities depends upon (a) the *correlation* between the two securities, and (b) the *standard deviation* of each security's returns; it is calculated as follows:

$$Cov_{AB} = \rho_{AB}\sigma_A\sigma_B. \tag{11–4}$$

Here Cov_{AB} is the covariance between securities A and B; ρ_{AB} is the correlation coefficient between A and B; and σ_A and σ_B are the standard deviations of the securities' returns.

Substituting equation 11–4 for Cov_{AB} in 11–3, we may rewrite equation 11–3 as 11–5:

$$\sigma_p = \sqrt{w^2\sigma_A{}^2 + (1-w)^2\sigma_B{}^2 + 2w(1-w)\rho_{AB}\sigma_A\sigma_B}. \tag{11–5}$$

Here w is the percentage of the total portfolio value invested in security A; $(1-w)$ is the percentage of the portfolio invested in security B; σ_A is the standard deviation of security A; σ_B is the standard deviation of security B; Cov_{AB} is the covariance between securities A and B; and ρ_{AB} is the correlation coefficient between the securities. Stated another way, if σ_A is the standard deviation of security A and σ_B is the standard deviation of security B, then σ_p, the standard deviation of a *portfolio* containing both A and B, is a function of σ_A, σ_B, ρ_{AB} and w; the specific functional relationship is given as equation 11–3 or 11–5. Examples of the use of equation 11–5 are given in a later section.

If $\rho_{AB} = +1.0$, then equation 11–5 may be simplified to the following linear expression: $\sigma_p = w\sigma_A + (1-w)\sigma_B$; otherwise, 11–5 is a quadratic equation, and some value of w causes σ_p to be minimized. If we differentiate 11–5 with respect to w, set this derivative equal to nil, and solve for w, we obtain:

$$w_A = \frac{\sigma_B(\sigma_B - \rho_{AB}\sigma_A)}{\sigma_A{}^2 + \sigma_B{}^2 - 2\rho_{AB}\sigma_A\sigma_B}. \tag{11–6}$$

A usual condition assumed in using the equation is that $0 \leqq w \leqq 1.0$; that is, no more than 100 per cent of the portfolio can be in any one asset, and negative positions (short positions) cannot be maintained in any asset.

Two special cases of 11–6 are worthy to note. First, notice that when the returns of securities A and B are negatively correlated, that is, $\rho_{AB} = -1.0$, then substituting $\rho_{AB} = -1.0$ in equation 11–6 yields equation 11–6a:

$$w_A = \frac{\sigma_B}{\sigma_A + \sigma_B}. \qquad \text{(Use only if } \rho_{AB} = -1.0.\text{)} \tag{11–6a}$$

To illustrate the use of 11–6a, suppose the returns of securities A and B are perfectly negatively correlated, that is, $\rho_{AB} = -1.0$, $\sigma_A = 2.0$, and $\sigma_B = 4.0$. The riskiness of the portfolio (σ_p) consisting of securities A and B will be completely eliminated, or equal to nil, if and only if 67 per cent of the portfolio is invested in security A:

$$w_A = \frac{4}{2+4} = \frac{4}{6} = 0.67 = 67\%.$$

The second special case is when the returns of securities A and B are independent ($\rho_{AB} = 0$); now substituting $\rho_{AB} = 0$ in equation 11–6 yields equation 11–6b:

$$w_A = \frac{\sigma_B{}^2}{\sigma_A{}^2 + \sigma_B{}^2}. \qquad \text{(Use only if } \rho_{AB} = 0.\text{)} \tag{11–6b}$$

To illustrate the use of 11–6b, suppose $\rho_{AB} = 0$, $\sigma_A = 8$, and $\sigma_B = 6$. The riskiness of the portfolio (σ_p) is minimized if and only if the percentage of the portfolio invested in security A is equal to 36 per cent, computed as follows:

$$w_A = \frac{36}{64+36} = \frac{36}{100} = 0.36 = 36\%.$$

Measuring the riskiness of a portfolio: the *N*-asset case

An expanded form of equation 11–3 has been developed to compute the standard deviation of a portfolio consisting of any number of securities:

$$\sigma_p = \sqrt{\sum_{i=1}^{N} w_i^2\sigma_i^2 + 2\sum_{i=1}^{N-1}\sum_{j=i+1}^{N} w_i w_j \rho_{ij}\sigma_i\sigma_j}. \qquad (11\text{–}7)$$

Here w_i is the proportion of the individual's investment allocated to security i, w_j is the proportion of the individual's investment allocated to security j, ρ_{ij} is the correlation coefficient between security i and security j, and N is the number of securities contained in the portfolio.

Since equation 11–7 has N securities, there are N variance terms (that is, $w_i^2\sigma_i^2$) and $N^2 - N$ covariance terms (that is, $w_i w_j \rho_{ij}\sigma_i\sigma_j$). Since the covariance terms increase quadratically as the number of assets increases, the expanded equation becomes quite complex if N is large. For example, if N is 500, equation 11–7 will have 250 000 terms under the radical! The index model utilized by Sharpe reduces the computational requirements substantially.[8]

Portfolio opportunities

Suppose we are considering N assets, with N being any number greater than one. These assets can be combined into an almost limitless number of portfolios, and each possible portfolio will have an expected rate of return, $E(k_p)$, and risk, σ_p. The hypothetical set of all possible portfolios – defined as the *attainable set* – is graphed as the shaded area in Figure 11–8.

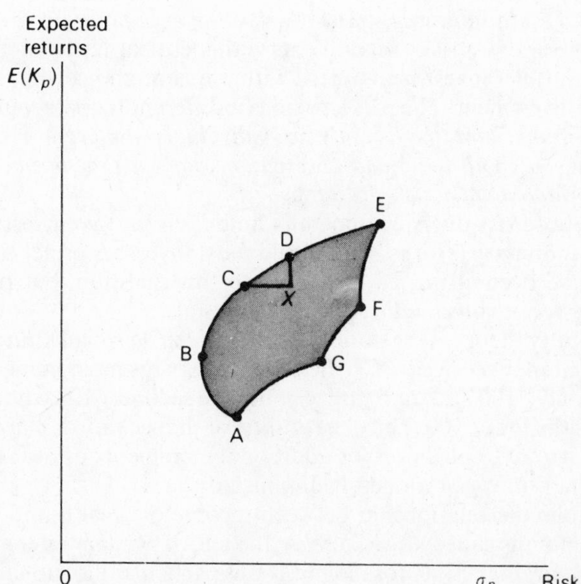

Figure 11–8 *The Efficient Set of Investments.*

8. W. F. Sharpe, *Portfolio Theory and Capital Markets* (New York: McGraw-Hill, 1970), chap. 7, Index Models.

Given the full set of potential portfolios that can be constructed from the available assets, which portfolio should *actually* be constructed? This choice involves two separate decisions: (a) determining the *efficient set of portfolios* and (b) choosing from the efficient set the single portfolio that is best for the individual investor. In the remainder of this section we discuss the concept of the efficient set of portfolios; then in the next section we consider choices among efficient portfolios.

An *efficient portfolio* is defined as a portfolio that provides the highest possible expected return for any degree of risk, or the lowest possible degree of risk for any expected return. In Figure 11–8 the boundary BCDE defines the *efficient set of portfolios.*[9] Portfolios to the left of the efficient set are not possible, because they lie outside the attainable set; that is, there is no set of k_i values that will yield a portfolio with an expected rate of return $E(k_p)$ and risk σ_p represented by a point to the left of BCDE. Portfolios to the right of the efficient set are inefficient, because some other portfolio could provide either a higher return with the same degree of risk or a lower risk for the same rate of return. To illustrate, consider point X. Portfolio C provides the same rate of return as does portfolio X, but C is less risky. At the same time, portfolio D is as risky as portfolio X, but D provides a higher expected rate of return. Points C and D (and other points on the boundary of the efficient set between C and D) are said to *dominate* point X.

UTILITY THEORY AND PORTFOLIO CHOICES

The assumption of risk aversion is basic to many decision models used in finance. Since this assumption is so important, it is appropriate to discuss why risk aversion generally holds.

In theory, we can identify three possible attitudes towards risk: a desire for risk, an aversion to risk, and an indifference to risk. A *risk seeker* is one who prefers risk; given a choice between more and less risky investments with identical expected monetary returns, he would prefer the riskier investment. Faced with the same choice, the *risk averter* would select the less risky investment. The person who is indifferent to risk would not care which investment he received. *There undoubtedly are individuals who prefer risk and others who are indifferent to it, but both logic and observation suggest that business managers and shareholders are predominantly risk averters.*

Why do you suppose risk aversion generally holds? Given two investments, each with the same expected monetary returns, why would most investors prefer the less risky one? Several theories have been advanced in answer to this question, but perhaps the most logically satisfying one involves *utility theory.*

At the heart of utility theory is the notion of *diminishing marginal utility for money.* If an individual with no money received £100, he could satisfy his most immediate needs. If he then received a second £100, he could utilize it, but the second £100 would not be quite as necessary to him as the first £100. Thus, the 'utility' of the second, or *marginal,* £100 is less than that of the first £100, and so on for additional increments of money. Therefore, we say that the marginal utility of money is diminishing.

Figure 11–9 graphs the relationship between income or wealth and its utility, where utility is measured in units called *utils.* Curve A, the one of primary interest, is for someone with a diminishing marginal utility for money. If this particular individual had £5000, then he would have 10 utils of 'happiness' or satisfaction. If he received an additional £2500, his utility would rise to 12 utils, *an increase of two units.* However, if he lost £2500, his utility would fall to six utils, *a loss of four units.*

---

9. A computational procedure for determining the efficient set of portfolios was developed by Harry Markowitz and first reported in his article, Portfolio selection, *Journal of Finance* 7, no. 1 (March 1952), pp. 77–91.

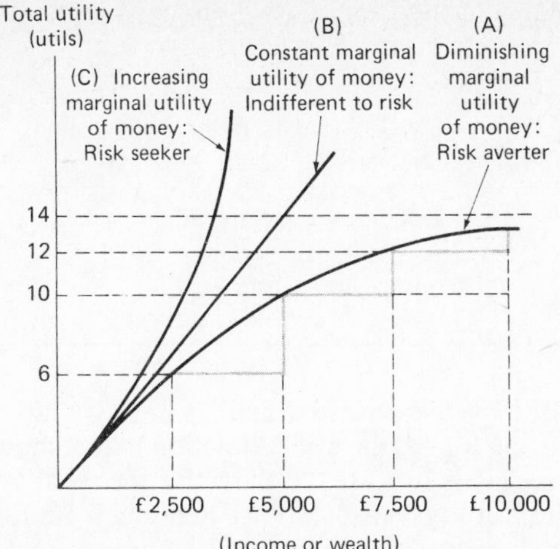

Figure 11–9 *Relationship between Money and its Utility.*

Most investors (as opposed to people who go to Las Vegas) appear to have a declining marginal utility for money, and this directly affects their attitudes towards risk. Our measures of risk estimate the likelihood that a given return will turn out to be above or below the expected return. Someone who has a constant marginal utility for money will value each £1 of 'extra' returns just as highly as each £1 of 'lost' returns. On the other hand, someone with a diminishing marginal utility for money will get more 'pain' from £1 lost than 'pleasure' from £1 gained. Because of his utility of money function, the second individual will be very much opposed to risk, and he will require a very high return on any investment that is subject to much risk. In curve A of Figure 11–9, for example, a gain of £2500 from a base of £5000 would bring 2 utils of additional satisfaction, but a £2500 loss would cause a 4-util satisfaction loss. Therefore, a person with this utility function and £5000 would be unwilling to make a bet with a 50–50 chance of winning or losing £2500. However, the risk-indifferent individual with curve B would be indifferent to the bet, and the risk lover would be eager to make it.

Diminishing marginal utility leads directly to risk aversion, and this risk aversion is reflected in the capitalization rate investors apply when determining the value of a firm. To make this clear, let us assume that government bonds are riskless securities and that such bonds currently offer a 5 per cent rate of return.[10] Thus, if someone bought a £5000 government bond and held it for one year, he would end up with £5250, a profit of £250. Suppose he had an alternative investment opportunity that called for the £5000 to be used to back a wildcat oil-drilling operation. If the drilling operation is successful, the investment will be worth £7500 at the end of the year. If it is unsuccessful, the investor can liquidate his holdings and recover £2500. There is a 60 per cent chance that oil will be discovered, and a 40 per cent chance of a 'dry hole'. If he has only £5000 to invest, should our investor choose the riskless government bond or the risky drilling operation?

Let us first calculate the expected monetary values of the two investments; this is done in Table 11–5. The calculation for the oil venture shows that the expected value of this venture, £5500, is higher than that of the bond. (Also, the expected return on the oil venture is 10 per cent [calculated as £500 expected profit/£5000 cost] versus 5 per cent for the bond.) Does this mean that our investor should put his money in the wildcat well? Not necessarily – it depends on his utility function. If his marginal utility for money is sharply diminishing, then the potential loss of utility that would result from a dry hole, or no oil,

10. We shall abstract from any risk of price declines in bond prices caused by increases in the level of interest rates. Thus, the risk with which we are concerned at this point is *default risk*, the risk that principal and interest payments will not be made as scheduled.

Table 11–5 *Expected Returns from Two Projects.*

States of nature	Drilling operation			Government bond		
	Probability (1)	Outcome (2)	(1) × (2) (3)	Probability (1)	Outcome (2)	(1) × (2) (3)
Oil	0.6	£7500	£4500	1.0	£5250	£5250
No oil	0.4	2500	1000			
		Expected value =	£5500			£5250

might not be fully offset by the potential gain in utility that would result from the development of a producing well. If the utility function that is shown in curve A of Figure 11–9 is applicable, this is exactly the case. To show this, we modify the expected monetary value calculation to reflect utility considerations. Reading from Figure 11–9, curve A, we see that this particular risk-averse investor would have approximately 12 utils if he invests in the wildcat venture and oil is found, 6 utils if he makes this investment and no oil is found, and 10.5 utils with certainty if he chooses the government bond. This information is used in Table 11–6 to calculate the *expected utility* for the oil investment. No calculation is needed for the government bond; we know its utility is 10.5 regardless of the outcome of the oil venture.

Table 11–6 *Expected Utility of Oil-drilling Project.*

States of nature	Probability (1)	Monetary outcome (2)	Associated utility (3)	(1) × (3) (4)
Oil	0.6	£7500	12.0	7.2
No oil	0.4	2500	6.0	2.4
			Expected utility =	9.6 utils

Since the *expected utility* from the wildcat venture is only 9.6 utils versus 10.5 from the government bond, we see that for this investor the government bond is the preferred investment. Thus, even though the *expected monetary value* for the oil venture is higher, *expected utility* is higher for the bond; risk considerations therefore lead us to choose the safer government bond.

Risk-return indifference curves

Given the efficient set of portfolio combinations, which specific portfolio should an investor choose? To determine the optimal portfolio for a particular investor, we must know his attitude towards risk, or his risk-return trade-off function.

An investor's risk-return preference function is based on the standard economic concept of indifference curves as illustrated in Figure 11–10. The curves labelled I_A and I_B represent the indifference curves of individuals A and B. Mr A is equally well satisfied with a riskless 4 per cent return, an expected 6 per cent return with risk of $\sigma_p = 4$ per cent, and so on. Mr B is indifferent between the riskless 4 per cent portfolio, a portfolio with an expected return of 6 per cent but with a risk of $\sigma_p = 2$ per cent, and so on.

Notice that B requires a higher expected rate of return to compensate him for a given increase in risk than does A; thus, B is more *risk averse* than A. For example, if $\sigma_p = 4$ per cent, Mr B requires a return of 10 per cent, while Mr A has a required return of only 6 per cent. In other words, Mr B requires a *risk premium* – defined as the difference between the

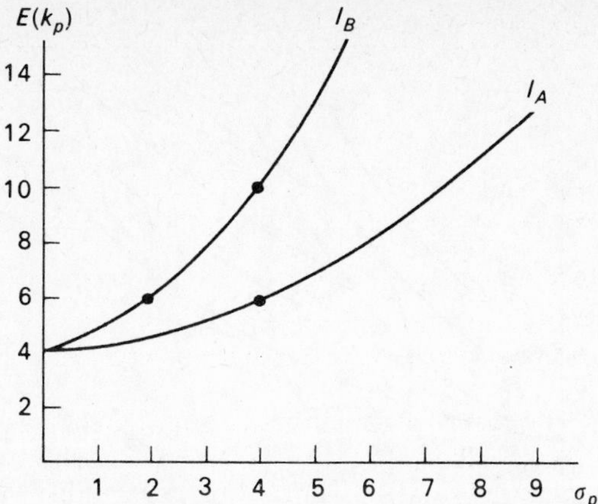

Figure 11–10 *Indifference Curves for Risk and Expected Rate of Return.*

riskless return (4 per cent) and the required return – of 6 percentage points to compensate for a risk $\sigma_p = 4$ per cent, while Mr A's risk premium for this degree of risk is only 2 percentage points.

An infinite number of utility curves could be drawn for each individual representing the risk-return trade-off for different levels of satisfaction (Figure 11–11). For a given level of σ_p, a greater $E(k_p)$ is received as the curves move farther out to the left. Each point on curve I_{A2} represents a higher level of satisfaction, or greater utility, than any point on I_{A1}, and I_{A3} represents more utility than I_{A2}. Also, different individuals are likely to have different sets of curves or different risk-return trade-offs. Since the curves of B start from the same point and have a greater slope in the risk-return plane than the curves of A, this indicates that investor B requires a higher return for the same amount of risk. Then similarly for investor B, as the curves move to the left this represents high levels of satisfaction.

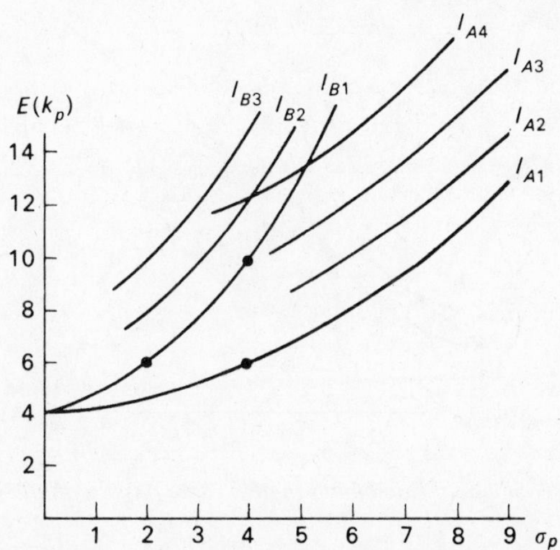

Figure 11–11 *Family of Indifference Curves for Individuals A and B.*

The optimal portfolio for an investor

We can now combine the efficient set of portfolios with indifference curves to determine an individual investor's optimal portfolio. In Figure 11–12 we see that the optimal portfolio is

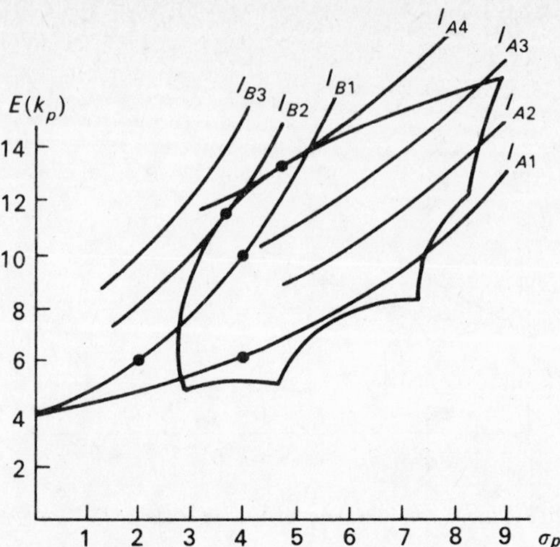

Figure 11–12 *Optimal Portfolio Selection.*

found at the tangency point between the efficient set of portfolios and an indifference curve – this tangency point marks the highest level of satisfaction the investor can attain. Mr A picks a combination of securities (a portfolio) that provides an expected return of about 13 per cent and has a risk of about $\sigma_p = 5$ per cent. Mr B, who is more risk averse than Mr A, picks a portfolio with a lower expected return (about 11 per cent) but a riskiness of only $\sigma_p = 3.7$ per cent.

To complete the analysis, we note that Mr A's portfolio contains a larger amount of the more risky securities, while our risk averter, Mr B, selects a portfolio more heavily weighted with low-risk securities.

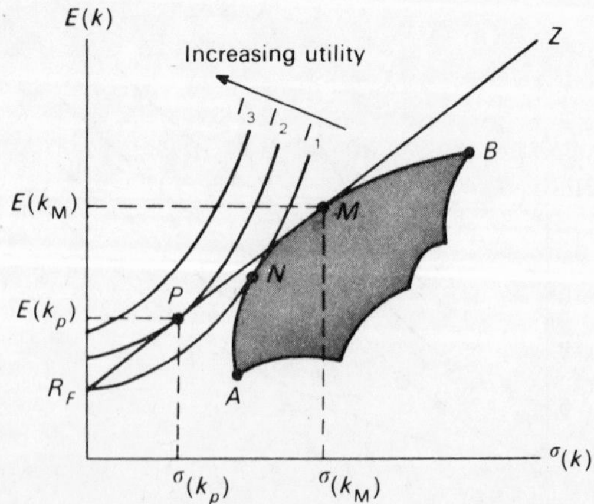

Figure 11–13 *Investor Equilibrium Combining the Risk-free Asset with the Market Portfolio.*

INVESTMENT DECISIONS UNDER UNCERTAINTY IN THE CAPM FRAMEWORK

In Figure 11–12 we graphed a set of portfolio opportunities provided by the market and illustrated a method for selecting the optimal portfolio. In Figure 11–13 the relationships are developed still further to convey the underlying logic of the capital asset pricing model (CAPM). Figure 11–13 shows a feasible set of portfolios of risky assets and a set of utility indifference curves (I_1, I_2, I_3), which represent the trade-off between risk and return for an investor. Point N, where the utility curve is tangent to the portfolio opportunities curve, $ANMB$, represents an equilibrium: it is the point where the investor obtains the highest return for a given amount of risk, σ_N, or the smallest risk while obtaining a given expected return, $E(k_N)$.[11]

However, the investor can do better than portfolio N – i.e., he can reach a higher indifference curve. In addition to the risky securities represented in the feasible set of portfolios, there is a risk-free asset that yields R_F; this is also shown in Figure 11–13. With the additional alternative of investing in the risk-free asset, the investor can create a new portfolio that combines the risk-free asset with a portfolio of risky assets. This enables him to achieve any combination of risk and return lying along a straight line connecting R_F and the point of tangency of the straight line at M on the portfolio opportunities curve. All portfolios on the line R_FMZ are preferred to the other risky portfolio opportunities on curve $ANMB$; the points on the line R_FMZ represent the highest attainable combinations of risk and return.

Given the new opportunity set R_FMZ, our investor will move to point P, where he will be on a higher risk-return indifference curve. Note that line R_FMZ dominates the opportunities that could have been achieved from the portfolio opportunities curve $ANMB$ alone. In general, if an investor can include both the risk-free security and a fraction of the risky portfolio, M, in his own portfolio, he will have the opportunity to move to a point such as P. In addition, if he can borrow as well as lend (lending is equivalent to buying risk-free securities) at the riskless rate R_F he can move out the line segment MZ, and he would do so if his utility indifference curve were tangent to R_FMZ in that section.

Under the conditions set forth in Figure 11–13, all investors would hold portfolios lying on the line R_FMZ; this implies that they would hold only efficient portfolios which are linear combinations of the risk-free security and the risky portfolio M. For the capital market to be in equilibrium, M must be a portfolio that contains every asset in exact proportion to that asset's fraction of the total market value of all assets; that is, if security j is w per cent of the total market value of all securities, w per cent of the market portfolio M will consist of security j. In effect, M represents 'the market'. Thus, in equilibrium, all investors will hold efficient portfolios with standard deviation-return combinations along the line R_FMZ. The particular location of a given individual on the line will be determined by the point at which his indifference curve is tangent to the line, and this in turn reflects his attitude towards risk, or his degree of risk aversion.

The line R_FMZ in Figure 11–13 (using the 'rise over run' concept) is given by equation 11–8:

$$E(k_p) = R_F + \frac{E(k_M) - R_F}{\sigma_{(k_M)}} \sigma_{(k_p)}. \tag{11–8}$$

Thus, the expected return on any portfolio is equal to the riskless rate plus a risk premium equal to $[E(k_M) - R_F]/\sigma(k_M)$ times the portfolio's standard deviation. Therefore, the capital market line for efficient portfolios bears a linear relationship between expected return and risk, and it may be rewritten as follows:

$$E(k_p) = R_F + \lambda^* \sigma_p. \tag{11–8a}$$

Here

$E(k_P)$ = expected return on an efficient portfolio
R_F = risk-free interest rate

11. To economize on notation we shall usually write σ_p for $\sigma_{(k_p)}$ and σ_m for $\sigma_{(k_M)}$, etc.

$$\lambda^* = \text{market price of risk; } \lambda^* = \frac{E(k_M) - R_F}{\sigma_M}$$

σ_P = standard deviation of returns on an efficient portfolio
$E(k_M)$ = expected return on the market portfolio
σ_M = standard deviation of returns on the market portfolio.

All efficient portfolios, including the market portfolio, lie on the capital market line (CML). Hence:

$$E(k_M) = R_F + \lambda^* \sigma_M. \tag{11–8b}$$

Both equations 11–8a and 11–8b state that the expected return on an efficient portfolio in equilibrium is equal to a risk-free return plus the market price of risk multiplied by the standard deviation of the portfolio returns. This relationship is shown in Figure 11–14. The *CML* is drawn as a straight line with an intercept at R_F, the risk-free return, and a slope equal to the market price of risk (λ^*), which is the market risk premium $[E(k_M) - R_F]$ divided by σ_M. Thus, the market price of risk, λ^*, is a normalized risk premium. The market price of risk reflects the attitudes of individuals in the aggregate (that is, all individuals) towards risk; thus, it reflects a composite of the utility functions of all individuals.

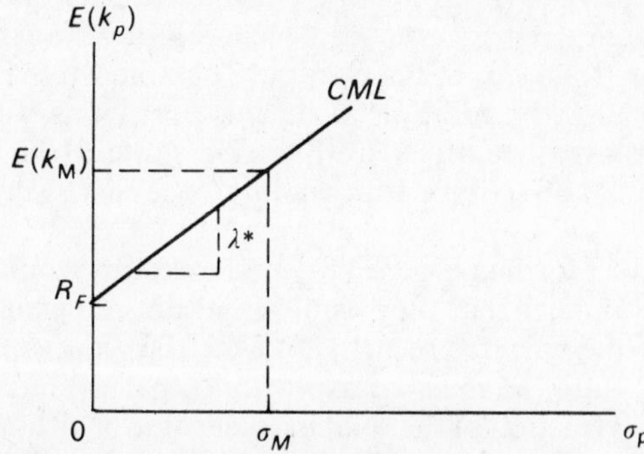

Figure 11–14 *Expected Return on an Efficient Portfolio.*

The security market line (SML)

Thus far we have developed the market model with respect to *portfolios.* Our next step is to relate the model to individual securities. First, note that the expected returns for an individual security or investment can be represented as points on the following *security market line:*[12]

$$E(k_j) = R_F + \lambda \, Cov(k_j, k_M). \tag{11–9}$$

Here:

λ = price of risk for securities = $[E(k_M) - R_F]/\sigma^2_M$

$Cov(k_j, k_M)$ = covariance of the returns of security j with returns on the market.

$E(k_j)$ = expected return on an individual securitity j.

Equation 11–9 for the security market line (*SML*) is depicted in Figure 11–15, which relates the covariance of the returns on the individual security to the expected return on the individual security.[13] The *SML* differs from the *CML* in two respects. First, for the

12. For a simple derivation, see Jensen, *Bell Journal* (1972).
13. The relationship between *SML* and *CML* can be shown as follows:

$$(SML)\text{: } E(k_j) = R_F + \frac{[E(k_M) - R_F]}{\sigma^2_M} Cov\,(k_j, k_M)$$

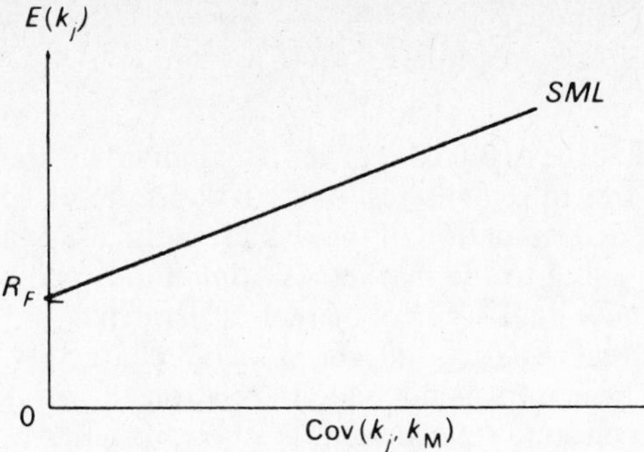

Figure 11–15 *The SML for Individual Securities.*

individual securities or individual firm, the risk measure is the covariance instead of the standard deviation. This is an important conceptual difference because it conveys the recognition that the risk of an individual security or firm is measured in terms of its contribution to the risk of the portfolio into which it is placed. Second, the price of risk is shown as the excess market return normalized by the *variance* of market returns in the denominator instead of the standard deviation. The effect is to change the dimensionality or scale of the security market line as compared with the capital market line.

BETA COEFFICIENTS

The final step in the development of the CAPM framework is to express risk in terms of the beta coefficient. Rearranging equation 11–9 by dividing the covariance of the individual securities by $\sigma^2{}_M$, we obtain equation 11–10, which is another version of the security market line with a different scaling:

$$E(k_j) = R_F + [E(k_M) - R_F]\beta_j. \qquad (11\text{–}10)$$

Here $\beta_j = Cov(k_j, k_M)/\sigma^2{}_M$; $E(k_j)$ is the expected return on an asset; and β_j is a measure of the volatility of the individual security's returns relative to market returns. In this form, we see that the individual security's risk premium is the market risk premium weighted by the relative risk or volatility of the individual security.

$Cov(k_j, k_M) = \rho(k_j, k_M)\sigma_j\sigma_M$,

where

$\rho(k_j, k_M)$ = correlation coefficient between the return of security j and the market portfolio
σ_j = standard deviation of the return of security j
σ_M = as defined before.

So,

$$E(k_j) = R_F + \frac{[E(k_M) - R_F]}{\sigma^2{}_M}\rho(k_j, k_M)\sigma_j\sigma_M$$

$$= R_F + \frac{[E(k_M) - R_F]}{\sigma_M}\rho(k_j, k_M)\sigma_j$$

If j is an efficient portfolio, $\rho(k_j, k_M) = 1$. Then SML reduces to CML.

$$E(k_j) = R_F + \frac{[E(k_M) - R_F]}{\sigma_M}\sigma_j$$

$$= R_F + \lambda^*\sigma_j.$$

REQUIRED RETURN ON AN INVESTMENT

Equation 11–10 states that the expected return on an individual security or real investment is represented by a risk-free rate of interest plus a risk premium. Earlier literature did not provide a theory for the determination of the risk premium. Capital market theory shows the risk premium to be equal to the market risk premium weighted by the index of the systematic risk of the individual security or real investment.

The β for an individual security reflects industry characteristics and management policies that determine how returns fluctuate in relation to variations in overall market returns. If the general economic environment is stable, if industry characteristics remain unchanged, and if management policies have continuity, the measure of β will be relatively stable when calculated for different time periods. However, if these conditions of stability do not exist; the value of β would vary.

The great advantage of equation 11–10 is that all its factors other than β are market-wide constants. If βs are stable, the measurement of expected returns is straightforward. For example, the returns on the market for long periods have been shown by the studies of Fisher and Lorie to be at the 9 to 11 per cent level.[14] The level of R_F has been characteristically at the 4 to 6 per cent level. Thus the expected return on an individual investment, using the lower of each of the two numbers and a β of 1.2, would be:

$$E(k_j) = 4\% + (9\% - 4\%)1.2 = 10\%. \qquad (11\text{–}10a)$$

The higher of each of the two figures gives an $E(k_j)$ of 12%:

$$E(k_j) = 6\% + (11\% - 6\%)1.2 = 12\% \qquad (11\text{–}10b)$$

Thus we have numerical measures of the amount of the risk premium that is added to the risk-free return to obtain a risk-adjusted discount rate. The risk-free rate and the market risk premium (the excess of the market return over the risk-free rate) are economy-wide measures. They vary for different time periods, but provide a basis for measurements that can be used in making judgemental decisions. In the numerical illustrations above, if a firm has a beta of 1.2, we would expect its required return according to the security market line to be between 10 and 12 per cent, depending upon general interest levels. This provides us with a relatively narrow boundary of returns within which managerial judgements may be exercised.

RISK ADJUSTED INVESTMENT HURDLE RATES

The capital asset pricing model permits the criteria for asset expansion decisions under uncertainty to be set out unambiguously and compactly. The basic relation expressed in equation 11–10 can also be used to formulate a criterion for capital budgeting decisions;[15] that is, the relation in equation 11–10 can be extended to apply to the expected return $E(k_j^0)$ on an individual project and its volatility measure, β_j^0, as set forth in equation 11–11.[16]

$$E(k_j^0) > R_F + [E(k_M) - R_F]\beta_j^0. \qquad (11\text{–}11)$$

14. L. Fisher and J. Lorie, Rates of return on investments in common stocks, *Journal of Business* 37 (January 1964), pp. 1–21. Fisher, Some new stock-market indexes, *Journal of Business* 39 (January 1966), pp. 191–218. In the UK the returns on shares have been very volatile in recent years. See S. J. Curry, A further look at equity capital, *Accountancy* (February 1976).

15. M. E. Rubinstein, A synthesis of corporate financial theory, *Journal of Finance* (March 1973), p. 167.

16. The superscript ^{0} indicates an individual investment project.

In inequality 11–11 the market constants remain the same. However, the variables for the individual firm now become variables for the individual project by addition of an appropriate superscript. Inequality 11–11 expresses the condition that must hold if the project is to be acceptable. The expected return on the new project must exceed the pure rate of interest plus the market risk premium weighted by β_j^o, the measure of the individual project's systematic risk.

The general relationships are illustrated in Figure 11–15. The criterion in graphical terms is to accept all projects that plot above the market line and reject all those that plot below the market line. Managers seek to find new projects such as A and B with returns in excess of the levels required by the risk-return market equilibrium relation illustrated in Figure 11–16. When such projects are added to the firm's operations, the expected returns on the firm's ordinary shares (their previous existing price) will be higher than required by the market line. These 'excess returns' induce a rise in price until the return on the shares $E(k_j)$ is at an equilibrium level represented by the security market line in Figure 11–16. These general concepts may now be illustrated more concretely in a numerical example.

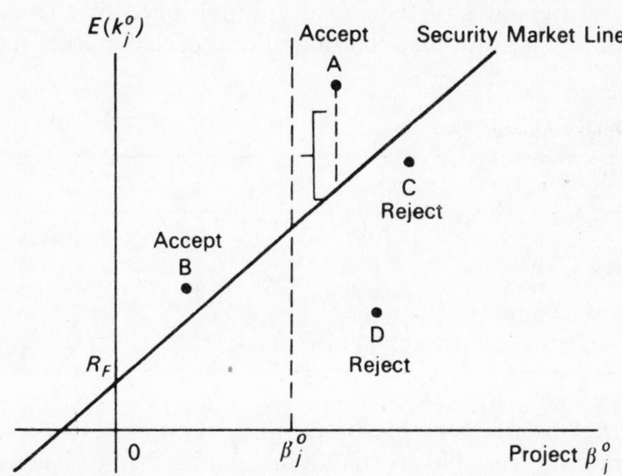

Figure 11–16 *Illustration of the Use of Investment Hurdle Rates.*

The Morton Company Case

In the case that follows, four states-of-the-world are considered with respect to future prospects for real growth in Gross National Product. State 1 represents a relatively serious recession, State 2 is a mild recession, State 3 is a mild recovery and State 4 is a strong recovery. The probabilities of these alternative future states-of-the-world are set forth in coloumn 2 of Table 11–7. Estimates of market returns and project rates of return are set forth in the remaining columns.

Table 11–7 *Summary of Information – Morton Case.*

(1) State of world (s)	(2) Subjective probability (P_s)	(3) Market return k_{Ms}	(4) Project rates of return	(5)	(6)	(7)
			Proj. #1	Proj. #2	Proj. #3	Proj. #4
1	0.1	−0.15	−0.30	−0.30	−0.09	−0.05
2	0.3	0.05	0.10	−0.10	0.01	0.05
3	0.4	0.15	0.30	0.30	0.05	0.10
4	0.2	0.20	0.40	0.40	0.08	0.15

The Morton Company is considering four projects in a capital expansion programme. The economics staff projected the future course of the market portfolio over the estimated life span of the projects under each of the four states-of-the-world (first three columns in Table 11–7); it recommended the use of a risk-free rate of return of 5 per cent. The finance department provided the estimates of project returns conditional on the state-of-the-world (columns 4 to 7 in Table 11–7). Each project involves an outlay of approximately £50 000.

Assuming that the projects are independent and that the firm can raise sufficient funds to finance all four projects, which projects would be accepted using the market price risk (MPR) criterion?

Solution procedure

In Table 11–8 the data provided by market relationships are utilized to calculate the expected return on the market along with its variance and standard deviation. The probabilities of the future states-of-the-world are multiplied by the associated market returns and their products are summed to obtain the expected market return $E(k_M)$ of 10 per cent.

Table 11–8 *Calculation of Market Parameters.*

s	P_s	k_M	$P_s k_M$	$(k_M - \bar{k}_M)$	$(k_M - \bar{k}_M)^2$	$P_s(k_M - \bar{k}_M)^2$
1	0.1	−0.15	−0.015	−0.25	0.0625	0.00625
2	0.3	0.05	0.015	0.05	0.0025	0.00075
3	0.4	0.15	0.060	0.05	0.0025	0.00100
4	0.2	0.20	0.040	0.10	0.0100	0.00200
			$\bar{k}_M = 0.10$		Var(k_M)	$= 0.01$

The expected market return $E(k_M)$ is used in calculating the variance and standard deviation of the market returns. This is shown in columns 4 to 6. The expected return is deducted from the return under each state, and deviations from $E(k_M)$ in column 4 are squared in column 5. In column 6 the squared deviations are multiplied by the probabilities of each expected future state (which appear in column 1). These products are summed to give the variance of the market return. The square root of the variance is its standard deviation.

A similar procedure is followed in Table 11–9 for calculating the expected return and the covariance for each of the four individual projects. The expected return is obtained by multiplying the probability of each state times the associated forecasted return. The deviations of the return under each state from the expected return are next calculated in column 5. The deviations of the market returns from their mean are repeated for convenience. In column 8, the deviations of project returns are multiplied by the deviations of the market returns and by the probability factors to determine the covariance for each of the four projects.

In Table 11–10, the beta for each project is calculated as the ratio of its covariance to the variance of the market return, and they are employed in Table 11–11 to estimate the required return on each project in terms of the market line relationship. The risk-free rate of return is assumed to be 5 per cent, with a market risk premium of 5 per cent.

Required returns as shown in column 2 of Table 11–11 are deducted from the estimated returns for each individual project to derive the 'excess returns'. These relations are depicted graphically in Figure 11–17. The MPR criterion accepts the projects with positive excess returns, which appear above the MPR line. It rejects those with negative excess returns (plotted below the MPR line).

Table 11–9 *Calculation of Expected Returns and Covariances for the Four Hypothetical Projects.*

s	P_s	k_j	$P_s k_j$	$(k_1-\bar{k}_1)(k_M-\bar{k}_M)$	$P_s(k_1-\bar{k}_1)(k_M-\bar{k}_M)$
1	0.1	−0.30	−0.03	(−0.50)(−0.25) = 0.125	0.0125
2	0.3	0.10	0.03	(−0.10)(−0.05) = 0.005	0.0015
3	0.4	0.30	0.12	(+0.10)(+0.05) = 0.005	0.002
4	0.2	0.40	0.08	(+0.20)(+0.10) = 0.020	0.0040
			$\bar{k}_1$ = 0.20		$\mathrm{Cov}(k_1, k_M)$ = 0.0200
1	0.1	−0.30	−0.03	(−0.44)(−0.25) = 0.110	0.0110
2	0.3	−0.10	−0.03	(−0.24)(−0.05) = 0.012	0.0036
3	0.4	0.30	0.12	(+0.16)(+0.05) = 0.008	0.0032
4	0.2	0.40	0.08	(+0.26)(+0.10) = 0.026	0.0052
			$\bar{k}_2$ = 0.14		$\mathrm{Cov}(k_2, k_M)$ = 0.0230
1	0.1	−0.09	−0.009	(−0.12)(−0.25) = 0.030	0.0030
2	0.3	0.01	0.003	(−0.02)(−0.05) = 0.001	0.0003
3	0.4	0.05	0.020	(+0.02)(+0.05) = 0.001	0.0004
4	0.2	0.08	0.016	(+0.05)(+0.10) = 0.005	0.0010
			$\bar{k}_3$ = 0.030		$\mathrm{Cov}(k_3, k_M)$ = 0.0047
1	0.1	−0.05	−0.005	(−0.13)(−0.25) = 0.0325	0.00325
2	0.3	0.05	0.015	(−0.03)(−0.05) = 0.0015	0.00045
3	0.4	0.10	0.04	(+0.02)(+0.05) = 0.0010	0.00040
4	0.2	0.15	0.03	(+0.07)(+0.10) = 0.0070	0.00140
			$\bar{k}_4$ = 0.08		$\mathrm{Cov}(k_4, k_M)$ = 0.00550

Table 11–10 *Calculation of the Betas.*

$\beta_1^0 = 0.0200/0.01 = 2.00$

$\beta_2^0 = 0.0230/0.01 = 2.30$

$\beta_3^0 = 0.0047/0.01 = 0.47$

$\beta_4^0 = 0.0055/0.01 = 0.55$

Table 11–11 *Calculation of Excess Returns.*

(1) Project number	(2) Measurement of required return	(3) Estimated return	(4) Excess return %
P1	$E(k_1) = 0.05 + 0.05(2.0) = 0.150$	0.200	5.00
P2	$E(k_2) = 0.05 + 0.05(2.3) = 0.165$	0.140	−2.50
P3	$E(k_3) = 0.05 + 0.05(0.47) = 0.0735$	0.030	−4.35
P4	$E(k_4) = 0.05 + 0.05(0.55) = 0.0775$	0.080	0.25

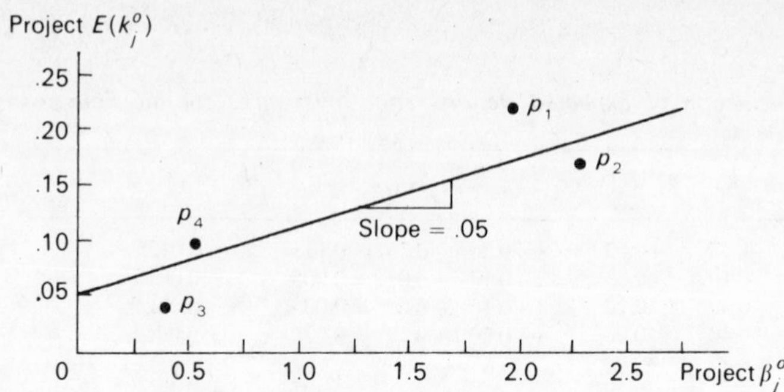

Figure 11–17 *Application of the CAPM Investment Criterion.*

RISK ADJUSTED DISCOUNT RATES VERSUS THE CERTAINTY EQUIVALENT METHOD

The capital asset pricing model as a market price of risk measure provides a risk-adjusted required rate of return for analysing risky projects. Recall that $E(k_j) = R_F + (k_M - R_F)\beta_j$ with the final term representing the risk adjustment added to the risk-free return, R_F. This is the discount rate that can then be utilized in the basic capital budgeting equation as shown in equation 11–12.

$$NPV_j^o = \sum_{t=0}^{n} \frac{F_t}{[1 + E(k_j)]^t} \qquad (11\text{–}12)$$

where

NPV^o = net present value of a project
F_t = project net cash flows
$E(k_j)$ = risk-adjusted discount factor.

Thus with no capital rationing, if the net present value of a project when discounted at the risk-adjusted required rate of return is greater than nil, then we should accept the project. This technique can be used to compare projects of all different risk classes. It is, therefore, superior to a net present value technique that uses only one discount rate for all projects even though the risk among projects is different. In concept, therefore, the risk-adjusted required rate of return is superior to a method in which only one discount rate is used for projects of different risks.

Project risk can be handled by making adjustments to the numerator of the present value equation (the certainty equivalent method) or to the denominator of the equation (the risk-adjusted discount rate method). The risk-adjusted discount rate method is the one most frequently used, probably because it is easier to estimate suitable discount rates than it is to derive certainty equivalent factors. However, Robichek and Myers[17] in 1966 advocated the certainty equivalent approach as being theoretically superior to the risk-adjusted discount rate method. Still, they, as well as H. Y. Chen, showed that if risk is perceived to be an increasing function of time, then using a risk-adjusted discount rate is a theoretically valid procedure.[18]

---

17. A. A. Robichek and S. C. Myers, Conceptual problems in the use of risk-adjusted discount rates, *Journal of Finance* 21 (December 1966), pp. 727–730.
18. H. Y. Chen, Valuation under uncertainty, *Journal of Financial and Quantitative Analysis* 2 (September 1967), pp. 313–326.

Robichek and Myers showed that risk-adjusted rates tend to lump together the pure rate of interest, a risk premium, and time (through the compounding process), while the certainty equivalent approach keeps risk and the pure rate of interest separate. This separation gives an advantage to certainty equivalents. However, financial managers are more familiar with the concept of risk-adjusted discounts, and it is easier to use market data to develop adjusted discount rates. We do feel, however, that the certainty equivalent method deserves further study and that it may eventually turn out to be the generally accepted method of taking risk into account in the capital budgeting process.

The use of the capital asset pricing model is sufficiently flexible so that if it is preferred to use a certainty equivalent formulation, the risk adjustment term can be deducted from the numerator and the risk-free rate employed as the discount factor. Begin with equation 11–9, presented earlier.

$$E(k_j) = R_F + \lambda Cov(k_j, k_M) \tag{11-9}$$

By definition: $k_j = \dfrac{E(X_j)}{V_j}$. So $\dfrac{E(X_j)}{V_j} = R_F + \lambda Cov\left(\dfrac{X_j}{V_j}, k_M\right)$ and

$$\frac{1}{V_j}[E(X_j) - \lambda Cov(X_j, k_M)] = R_F$$

$$V_j = \frac{E(X_j) - \lambda Cov(X_j, k_M)}{R_F} \tag{11-13}$$

For projects: $$V_j^o = \frac{E(X_j^o) - \lambda Cov(X_j^o, k_M)}{R_F} \tag{11-14a}$$

$$NPV_j^o = (V_j^o - \text{Cost}_j^o). \tag{11-14b}$$

Thus the use of the market price of risk criterion provides us with a very flexible tool for making an adjustment for risk in analysing investment projects of differing risks. To illustrate the application of the last two equations, we will use the data for project 4 in the Morton Company case discussed above. The required rate of return was:

$E(k_4^o) = R_F + [E(k_M) - R_F]\beta_4^o$. Inserting values:
$7.75\% = 5\% + [10\% - 5\%].55$.

The $E(k_4^o)$ value of 7.75 per cent represents a risk-adjusted required rate of return on the project based on the beta risk measure equal to 0.55. We can also express this equation with covariance, using the relationship:

$$\begin{aligned} Cov\ (k_4^o, k_M) &= \beta_4^o\ Var\ (k_M) \\ &= 0.55(0.01) \\ &= 0.0055. \end{aligned}$$

The returns from the project that we actually observe are the money returns indicated by the X_4^o values. Suppose that the cost of the project (Cost_4^o) or investment outlay is £1000. We can then calculate $Cov(X_4^o, k_M)$:

$Cov(k_4^o, k_M) = Cov\left(\dfrac{X_4^o}{\text{Cost}_4^o}, k_M\right) = \dfrac{1}{\text{Cost}_4^o} Cov(X_4^o, k_M)$. Hence,

$$\begin{aligned} Cov(X_4^o, k_M) &= \text{Cost}_4^o Cov(k_4^o, k_M) \\ &= 1000(0.0055) \\ &= 5.5. \end{aligned}$$

We now have the information to utilize equation (11–14a) for project 4:

$$V_4^o = \frac{E(X_4^o) - \lambda Cov(X_4^o, k_M)}{R_F}$$

$$= \frac{80 - 5(5.5)}{0.05} = \frac{80 - 27.5}{0.05}$$

$$V_4^0 = £1050.$$

Since the cost of project 4 is £1000 and its value is £1050, the net gain or the net present value for the investment in project 4 (NPV_4^0) is £50. Note that the risk adjustment factor is 27.5 or 0.344 times the expected money returns from the project.[19] This illustrates how the CAPM can provide a measure of the risk adjustment factor.

We recognize that the computations of beta for individual firms are sometimes not statistically significant and often not stable over time. Nevertheless, the methodology described provides a starting point. In addition, a risk adjustment factor taking other dimensions of risk into account as well as judgemental factors may be used in estimating a project's net present value.[20]

SUMMARY

Two facts of life in finance are (a) that investors are averse to risk and (b) that at least some risk is inherent in most business decisions. Given investor aversion to risk and differing degrees of risk in different financial alternatives, it is necessary to consider risk in financial analysis.

Our first task is to define what we mean by risk; our second task is to measure it. The concept of *probability* is a fundamental element in both the definition and the measurement of risk. A *probability distribution* shows the probability of occurrence of each possible outcome, assuming a given investment is undertaken. The mean, or weighted average, of the distribution is defined as the *expected value* of the investment. The *coefficient of variation* of the distribution or, sometimes, the *standard deviation*, both of which measure the extent to which actual outcomes are likely to vary from the expected value, are used as measures of risk.

Under most circumstances, more distant returns are considered to be more risky than near-term returns. Thus, the standard deviation and coefficient of variation for distant cash flows are likely to be higher than those for cash flows expected relatively soon, even when the cash flows are from the same project.

In appraising the riskiness of an individual capital investment, not only the variability of the expected returns of the project itself but also the correlation between expected returns on this project and the remainder of the firm's assets must be taken into account. This relationship is called the *portfolio effect* of the particular project. Favourable portfolio effects are strongest when a project is negatively correlated with the firm's other assets and weakest when positive correlation exists. Portfolio effects lie at the heart of the firm's efforts to diversify into product lines not closely related to the firm's main line of business.

The riskiness of a portfolio is measured by the standard deviation of expected returns. From any group of risky assets it is possible to develop an investment portfolio opportunity set in terms of risk and expected returns. Within the opportunity set there will be a smaller group of alternative portfolios that provide the maximum return for a given level of risk. This is the efficient set of portfolios. Given equal expected returns, a risk averse investor would choose the one that minimizes his risk.

The trade-off between risk and expected return is expressed graphically as indifference curves. For any individual there is a unique set of indifference curves that can be used to

19. The certainty equivalent adjustment factor (ϕ) would be $(1 - 0.344)$, which equals 0.656.
20. See Appendix E to this chapter for further material on making certainty equivalent adjustments.

determine the individual's optimum portfolio including the fraction that should be invested in risk-free assets. The availability of a risk-free asset enables the investor to combine the risk-free asset with a portfolio of risky assets. A straight line drawn from the return on the risk-free asset to a point through a point of tangency with the portfolio opportunities curve defines the risk-return relations for the market, and the line is the capital market line (CML). The highest utility level is achieved for the investor by the point of tangency of his indifference curve for risk and returns with the capital market line. If this point is to the left of the market portfolio tangency, the investor holds risk-free assets as well as risky assets, so he has both less risk and less return on his total portfolio. If the investor is less risk averse, his point of tangency with the CML is to the right of the market portfolio. He borrows to invest more in risky assets, so has more risk and higher expected returns.

The risk-return relationships for individual securities (imperfect portfolios) use the covariance of individual security returns with the market returns as the measure of risk. The relation between returns and the covariance for individual securities defines the security market line (SML).

Another way to describe the return-risk relationship is in terms of beta coefficients. β is simply the covariance standardized by the market variance. With risk expressed in this way, expected return can be stated as a β multiple of the market risk premium (expected return on the market less the risk-free rate) plus the risk-free rate. All factors except β are market-wide constants.

The capital asset pricing model provides a means for determining a market adjusted discount rate that is project specific and appropriate for determining the *NPV* of risky capital budgeting projects. The CAPM can be used with either the certainty equivalent or the risk adjusted discount rate formulation of the *NPV* equation.

QUESTIONS

11–1. Define the following terms:

(a) risk
(b) uncertainty
(c) probability distribution
(d) expected value
(e) standard deviation
(f) coefficient of variation
(g) portfolio effects
(h) market price of risk
(i) covariance
(j) coefficient of correlation
(k) variance
(l) beta
(m) risk-adjusted discount rate

11–2. The probability distribution of a less risky expected return is more peaked than that of a risky return. What shape would the probability distribution have (a) for completely certain returns and (b) for completely uncertain returns?

11–3. Project A has an expected return of £500 and a standard deviation of £100. Project B also has a standard deviation of £100 but an expected return of £300. Which project is the more risky? Why?

11–4. Assume that house building and industries related to it are countercyclical to the economy in general and to steel in particular. Does this negative correlation between steel and construction-related industries necessarily mean that a building firm, whose profitability tends to vary with construction levels, would be less risky if it diversified by acquiring a steel distributor?

11–5. 'The use of the security market line as a basis for determining risk-adjusted discount rates is all right in theory, but it cannot be applied in practice. Investors' reactions to risk cannot be measured precisely, so it is impossible to construct a set of risk-adjusted discount rates for different classes of investment.' Comment on this statement.

11–6. The risk-free rate is 6 per cent, the market price of risk is 4, and the covariance of the project return with the market return is 0.015. (a) If the variance of the market returns is 1 per cent, what is the beta of the project? (b) What is an estimate of the required risk adjusted return for the project?

11–7. The correlation of the project's return with the market is 0.6 and the standard deviation of the project's return is 0.3. The variance of the market return is 1 per cent, the market price of risk is 5, and the risk-free rate is 6 per cent. What is the covariance of the project returns with the market returns? Its beta? Its required risk-adjusted return?

11–8. For the project in question 11–7, the required investment outlay is £1800. The expected net cash flows after taxes are estimated at £600 for 5 years. Should the project be accepted?

PROBLEMS

11–1. The Jacobs Company is analysing two mutually exclusive investment projects. Each project costs £4500, and each has an expected life of three years. Annual net cash flows from each project begin one year after the initial investment is made and have the following probability distributions:

Probability	Cash flow
Project A: 0.2	£4 000
0.6	4 500
0.2	5 000
Project B: 0.2	£ 0
0.6	4 500
0.2	12 000

Jacobs has decided to evaluate the riskier projects at a 12 per cent rate and the less risky project at a 10 per cent rate.

(a) What is the expected value of the annual net cash flows from each project?
(b) What is the risk-adjusted *NPV* of each project?
(c) If it were known that project B was negatively correlated with other cash flows of the firm, while project A was positively correlated, how would this knowledge affect your decision?

11–2. Danly Ltd's marketing division is reviewing its advertising plans in conjunction with the firm's annual capital budget. Because of management's desire to retain a controlling equity position, each division has been given a budget limitation; £120 000 has been allocated to the marketing division, which is considering two mutually exclusive investments for promotion of new business for the firm's children's furniture.

The first is the continuation of the firm's direct mail advertising programme. Costs are 12 pence a mailing, enabling the firm to mail 1 000 000 pieces a year. Over many years, responses have averaged 1 per cent of pieces mailed – ranging from 0.8 to 1.2 per cent in 95 per cent of the years for which experience is available. Probability estimates for these response percentages are: 10 per cent chance for 0.8 per cent response, 70 per cent chance for 1 per cent response, and 20 per cent chance for 1.2 per cent response. One-third of these responses are converted to sales that average £125, with a £50 pre-tax profit margin after all costs except advertising. There are no substantial lagged effects for direct mail returns. However, there may be additional lagged benefits from the second alternative, a newspaper advertising campaign that the company is seriously considering.

The local sales representative of a national newspaper chain has proposed the following contract to the director of marketing: a four-column, four-inch advertisement (usual cost £210 a day) running 365 days in five major newspapers with an average circulation of 750 000 each (3 000 000 guaranteed minimum average circulation) for a total cost of £120 000. This represents an average daily cost of £329 versus a £1050 normal daily rate for the five papers. The newspaper chain also agrees to provide one hundred hours of free copywriting consulting time. Depending upon the effectiveness of the advertising copy, responses per day could be expected to range from 200 to only 20. Profits per response should be the same as with direct mail advertising. The marketing director has assigned the following subjective probabilities to the possible responses:

Daily responses	Probability
200	0.25
100	0.50
20	0.25

The applicable tax rate is 50 per cent.

(a) Construct a payoff matrix of profits and probabilities for each of the two marketing programmes, and determine the expected after-tax net profit under each plan.

(b) Construct a simple bar graph of the three possible profit outcomes for each plan. On the basis of the appearance of the two graphs, which plan seems to be the more risky?

(c) Calculate the risk (coefficient of variation of the profit distribution) associated with the direct mail campaign ($cv = 0.75$ for the newspaper advertising programme).

(d) Which project should the division accept? What other important factors should be considered?

11–3. During union negotiations this year, the Spitzer Company management realized that it must offer its employees greater retirement benefits. The company is considering offering either one of the following: plan A, an increase in the amount of the company's share of the annual contribution to the funded pension plan now in existence, or plan B, elimination of the existing pension plan and its replacement by a new plan calling for variable payback where the amount of the company's payment would depend upon the level of profits for the year.

The actual cost of the pension plan to Spitzer will depend upon many factors, such as age of employees, number of years they have been with the company and employees' current earnings. However, the prime causes of uncertainty for the new retirement offers are these: since employees are given options as to the extent to which they wish to participate in the pension plan, their individual decisions will determine the amount of the employer's contribution under plan A. This uncertainty will be resolved in the first year of the new plan. For plan B, the level of future profits is the big question; however, the success or failure of a new product line to be introduced in the last part of the coming year will greatly reduce this uncertainty.

Management wishes to make a two-year cost comparison for the two plans, and has therefore made the following cost and probability estimates:

Probability	Cost first year
Plan A: 0.1	£ 60 000
0.3	75 000
0.6	90 000
Plan B: 0.2	50 000
0.5	75 000
0.3	£100 000

In the second year for plan A, uncertainty is negligible, since all employees will have elected their participation in the programme. Management estimates the second-year cost of plan A to be £6000 greater than its first-year cost. For plan B, uncertainty about second-year profits will still exist, so estimates of costs are also still uncertain.

Given first-year cost	Probability	Second-year cost
£ 50 000	0.6	£ 50 000
50 000	0.4	75 000
75 000	0.5	85 000
75 000	0.5	100 000
100 000	0.4	110 000
100 000	0.6	130 000

(a) Construct a decision tree for management to use in evaluating the two plans. Assuming that all costs occur at the end of the year for which they apply and that an 8 per cent discount rate is appropriate, compute the PV of costs for each plan at each branch terminal of the tree. Next, find the expected PV costs of each project as a weighted average of these terminal PVs. (Note: the PVs of the two plans could be computed in a simpler manner, but information needed for the risk analysis would not be generated.)

(b) Which project is the more risky? (Do not calculate standard deviations.)

(c) Which plan should the firm offer to the union? What other factors might be relevant considerations of management?

11–4. Your firm is considering two mutually exclusive investment projects – project A at a cost of £110 000 and project B at a cost of £140 000. The planning division of your firm has estimated the following probability distribution of cash flows to be generated by each project in each of the next five years:

Project A		Project B	
Probability	Cash flow	Probability	Cash flow
0.2	£15 000	0.2	£10 000
0.6	30 000	0.6	40 000
0.2	35 000	0.2	60 000

(a) Which of those projects is the riskier? Why?
(b) Each project's risk is different from that of the firm as a whole. The firm's management adjusts for risk by means of the formula:

$k_j = R_F + 10cv$;

where

k_j = the required rate of return on the jth project;
R_F = the risk-free rate, and is equal to 6 per cent;
cv = coefficient of variation of the project's cash flows.

What are the required rates of return on projects A and B?
(c) Which of those projects, if either, should be accepted by your firm? Explain and support your answer. In calculating the *NPVs*, round the cost of capital figures calculated in part (b) to the nearest whole number.

11–5. The chief financial officer of Worldcorp seeks to determine the value and the required return for the Industrial Products Project (without taxes or gearing). He has gathered the following data.

Year (t)	Return on the market (k_{Mt})	Earnings before interest and taxes (X_{jt})
19 × 1	0.27	£ 25
19 × 2	0.12	5
19 × 3	(0.03)	(5)
19 × 4	0.12	15
19 × 5	(0.03)	(10)
19 × 6	0.27	30

The yield to maturity on Treasury bills is 0.066 and is expected to remain at this level in the forseeable future. For the ungeared project, compute (a) the value of the project and (b) the required rate of return on the project. (Assume five degrees of freedom for the covariance and variance calculations and six degrees for the means.)

11–6. You are given the following information for an investment project: P = £3 per unit; vc = £2 per unit; FC = £300. The risk-free rate is 5 per cent = R_F. (Use Var k_M = 0.01.)
Also:

P_s	k_M	Q
0.2	−0.05	0
0.5	0.10	600
0.3	0.20	1000

where: P = selling price per unit sold
vc = variable costs per unit sold
c = $(P - vc)$ = Contribution margin per unit
Q = units of output sold
FC = total fixed costs

(a) What is lambda or the market risk measure?
(b) What is the value of the investment project?
(c) What is the required return on the investment project?

11–7. Given the following facts (the investment cost of each project is equal):

S	P_s	k_{Ms}	Return to project 1	Return to project 2
1	0.1	−0.3	−0.4	−0.4
2	0.2	−0.1	−0.2	−0.2
3	0.3	0.1	0	0.6
4	0.4	0.3	0.7	0

Calculate:

(a) The three means, the variances, the standard deviations, and the covariance of project 1 with the market, covariance of project 2 with the market, covariance of project 1 with project 2, the correlation coefficients ρ_{1M}, ρ_{2M}, and the correlation coefficient of project 1 with project 2.

(b) If 1 and 2 were to be combined into a portfolio, what would be the weights of each project, w_1 and w_2 in the portfolio, to minimize the portfolio standard deviation?

Calculate the expected return on that portfolio and its standard deviation.

(c) $R_F = 0.04$. Calculate the security market line.

On a graph:

1. Plot the security market line.
2. Plot points for project 1 and for project 2.

(d) If you had to choose between the two projects, which would be selected?

SELECTED REFERENCES

Adler, Michael. On risk-adjusted capitalization rates and valuation by individuals. *Journal of Finance* 25 (September 1970): 819–836.

Baesel, Jerome B. On the assessment of risk: some further considerations. *Journal of Finance* 29 (December 1974): 1491–1494.

Baker, J. C. and Beardsley, L. J. Multinational companies' use of risk evaluation and profit measurement for capital budgeting decisions. *Journal of Business Finance* 5 (Spring 1973): 38–43.

Barron, M. J. Investment decisions under uncertainty. *Journal of Business Finance* 5 (Spring 1973): 3–9.

Bierman, Harold Jr and Hass, Jerome E. Capital budgeting under uncertainty: a reformulation. *Journal of Finance* 28 (March 1973): 119–130.

Bierman, Harold Jr and Hausman, Warren H. The resolution of investment uncertainty through time. *Management Science* 18 (August 1972): 654–662.

Blume, Marshall E. On the assessment of risk. *Journal of Finance* 26 (March 1971): 1–10.

Bogue, Marcus C. and Roll, Richard. Capital budgeting of risky projects with 'imperfect' markets for physical capital. *Journal of Finance* 29 (May 1974): 601–613.

Bonini, Charles P. Capital investment under uncertainty with abandonment options. *Journal of Financial and Quantitative Analysis* 12 (March 1977): 39–54.

Bromwich, Michael. Inflation and the capital budgeting process. *Journal of Business Finance* 1 (Autumn 1969).

Broyles, J. and Franks, J. Capital project appraisal: a modern approach. *Managerial Finance* 2, No. 2 (1976): 85–96.

Brumelle, Shelby L. and Schwab, Bernhard. Capital budgeting with uncertain future opportunities: a Markovian approach. *Journal of Financial and Quantitative Analysis* 7 (January 1973): 111–122.

Bussey, Lynn E. and Stevens, G. T. Jr. Formulating correlated cash flow streams. *The Engineering Economist* 18 (Fall 1972): 1–30.

Byrne, R., Charnes, A., Cooper, A. and Kortanek, K. Some new approaches to risk. *Accounting Review* 63 (January 1968): 18–37.

Chen, Houng-Yhi. Valuation under uncertainty. *Journal of Financial and Quantitative Analysis* 2 (September 1967): 313–325.

Cooley, Philip L., Roenfeldt, Rodney L. and It-Keong Chew. Capital budgeting procedures under inflation. *Financial Management* 4 (Winter 1975): 18–27.

Edelman, Franz and Greenberg, Joel S. Venture analysis: the assessment of uncertainty and risk. *Financial Executive* 37 (August 1969): 56–62.

Elton, Edwin J. and Gruber, Martin J. On the maximization of the geometric mean with lognormal return distribution. *Management Science* 21 (December 1974): 483–488.

Fairley, William B. and Jacoby, Henry D. Investment analysis using the probability distribution of the internal rate of return. *Management Science* 21 (August 1975): 1428–1437.

Gentry, James and Pike, John. An empirical study of the risk-return hypothesis using common stock portfolios of life insurance companies. *Journal of Financial and Quantitative Analysis* 5 (June 1970): 179–186.

Grayson, C. Jackson Jr. *Decisions Under Uncertainty: Drilling Decisions by Oil and Gas Operators.* Boston: Division of Research, Harvard Business School, 1960.

Greer, Willis R. Jr. Capital budgeting analysis with the timing of events uncertain. *Accounting Review* 45 (January 1970): 103–114.

Hayes, Robert H. Incorporating risk aversion into risk analysis. *Engineering Economist* 20 (Winter 1975): 99–121.

Hertz, David B. Investment policies that pay off. *Harvard Business Review* 46 (January–February 1968): 96–108.

Hertz, David B. Risk analysis in capital investment. *Harvard Business Review* 42 (January–February 1964): 95–106.

Hespos, Richard F. and Strassmann, Paul A. Stochastic decision trees for the analysis of investment decisions. *Management Science* 11 (August 1965): 244–259.

Hillier, Frederick S. The derivation of probabilistic information for the evaluation of risky investments. *Management Science* 9 (April 1963).

Hillier, Frederick S. and Heebink, David V. Evaluation of risky capital Investments. *California Management Review* 8 (Winter 1965): 71–80.

Hoskins, C. J. Distinctions between risk and uncertainty. *Journal of Business Finance* 5 (Spring 1973): 10–12.

Joy, O. Maurice. Abandonment values and abandonment decisions: a clarification. *Journal of Finance* 31 (September 1976): 1225–1228.

Keane, S. The investment discount rate – in defence of the market rate of interest. *Accounting and Business Research* 23 (Summer 1976): 228–236.

Keeley, Robert and Westerfield, Randolph. A problem in probability distribution techniques for capital budgeting. *Journal of Finance* 27 (June 1972): 703–709.

Kryzanowski, Lawrence, Lusztig, Peter and Schwab, Bernhard. Monte Carlo simulation and capital expenditure decisions – a case study. *Engineering Economist* 18 (Fall 1972): 31–48.

Latane, H. A. and Tuttle, Donald L. Decision theory and financial management. *Journal of Finance* 21, No. 2 (May 1966): 228–244.

Lerner, Eugene M. and Rappaport, Alfred. Limit DCF in capital budgeting. *Harvard Business Review* 46 (July–August 1968): 133–139.

Lessard, Donald R. and Bower, Richard S. An operational approach to risk screening. *Journal of Finance* 28 (May 1973): 321–338.

Lewellen, Wilbur G. and Long, Michael S. Simulation versus single-value estimates in capital expenditure analysis. *Decision Sciences* 3 (1973): 19–33.

Lintner, John. Security prices, risk and maximal gains from diversification. *Journal of Finance* 20 (December 1965): 587–616.

Lintner, John. The evaluation of risk assets and the selection of risky investments in stock portfolios and capital budgets. *Review of Economics and Statistics* 47 (February 1965): 13–37.

Litzenberger, Robert H. and Budd, Alan P. Corporate investment criteria and the valuation of risk assets. *Journal of Financial and Quantitative Analysis* 5 (December 1970): 395–420.

Litzenberger, Robert H. and Joy, O. M. Target rates of return and corporate asset and liability structure under uncertainty. *Journal of Financial and Quantitative Analysis* 6 (March 1971): 675–686.

Litzenberger, Robert H. and Joy, O. M. Decentralized capital budgeting decisions and shareholder wealth maximization. *Journal of Finance* 30 (June 1975): 993–1002.

Lockett, A. Geoffrey and Gear, Anthony E. Multistage capital budgeting under uncertainty. *Journal of Financial and Quantitative Analysis* 10 (March 1975): 21–36.

Lockett, A. Geoffrey and Tomkins, Cyril. The discount rate problem in capital rationing situations: comment. *Journal of Financial and Quantitative Analysis* 5 (June 1970): 245–260.

Magee, J. F. How to use decision trees in capital investment. *Harvard Business Review* 42 (September–October 1964): 79–96.

Maier, Steven F. and Vander Weide, James H. Capital budgeting in the decentralized firm. *Management Science* 23 (December 1976): 433–443.

Mao, James C. T. Survey of capital budgeting: theory and practice. *Journal of Finance* 25 (May 1970): 349–360.

Mao, James C. T. and Helliwell, John F. Investment decisions under uncertainty: theory and practice. *Journal of Finance* 24 (May 1969): 323–338.

Moag, Joseph S. and Lerner, Eugene M. Capital budgeting decisions under imperfect market conditions – a systems framework. *Journal of Finance* 24 (September 1969): 613–621.

Modigliani, Franco and Pogue, Gerald A. An introduction to risk and return. *Financial Analysts' Journal* 30 (March–April 1974): 68–80, and (May–June 1974): 69–88.

Myers, Stewart C. Procedures for capital budgeting under uncertainty. *Industrial Management Review* 9 (Spring 1968): 1–15.

Page, Alfred N., ed. *Utility Theory*. New York: Wiley, 1968.

Paine, Neil R. Uncertainty and capital budgeting. *Accounting Review* 39 (April 1964): 330–332.

Perrakis, Stylianos. Certainty equivalents and timing uncertainty. *Journal of Financial and Quantitative Analysis* 10 (March 1975): 109–118.

Peterson, D. E. and Laughhunn, D. J. Capital expenditure programming and some alternative approaches to risk. *Management Science* 17 (January 1971): 320–336.

Quirin, G. David. *The Capital Expenditure Decision*. Homewood, Ill.: Irwin, 1967.

Robichek, A. and Myers, S. *Optimal Financing Decisions*. Englewood Cliffs, N.J.: Prentice-Hall, 1965, chap. 5.

Robichek, A. and Myers, S. Risk-adjusted discount rates. *Journal of Finance* 21, No. 4 (December 1966): 727–730.

Robichek, A., Ogilvie, Donald G. and Roach, John D. C. Capital budgeting: a pragmatic approach. *Financial Executive* 37 (April 1969): 26–38.

Robichek, A. and Van Horne, James C. Abandonment value and capital budgeting. *Journal of Finance* 22 (December 1967), 577–589; Dyl, Edward A. and Long, Hugh W. Comment. *Journal of Finance* 24 (March 1969): 88–95; and Robichek, A. and Van Horne, James C. Reply. ibid., 96–97.

Robichek, Alexander A. Interpreting the results of risk analysis. *Journal of Finance* 30 (December 1975): 1384–1386.

Schwab, Bernhard and Schwab, Helmut. A method of investment evaluation for smaller companies. *Management Services* (July–August 1969): 43–53.

Schwendiman, Carl J. and Pinches, George E. An analysis of alternative measures of investment risk. *Journal of Finance* 30 (March 1975): 193–200.

Stapleton, Richard C. Portfolio analysis, stock valuation and capital budgeting rules for risky projects. *Journal of Finance* 26 (March 1971): 95–118.

Stevens, Bussey. A solution methodology for probabilistic capital budgeting problems using complex utility functions. *Engineering Economist* 21 (Winter 1976): 89–110.

Swalm, Ralph O. Utility theory – insights into risk taking. *Harvard Business Review* 44 (November–December 1966): 123–136.

Thompson, Howard E. Mathematical programming, the capital asset pricing model and capital budgeting of inter-related projects. *Journal of Finance* 31 (March 1976): 125–131.

Tuttle, Donald L. and Litzenberger, Robert H. Leverage, diversification and capital market effects on a risk-adjusted capital budgeting framework. *Journal of Finance* 23 (June 1968): 427–444.

U.S. Congress, Subcommittee on Economy in Government of the Joint Economic Committee. *Economic Analysis of Public Investment Decisions: Interest Rate Policy and Discounting Analysis.* Washington, D.C.: U.S. Government Printing Office, 1968.

Van Horne, James. Capital budgeting decisions involving combinations of risky investments. *Management Science* 13 (October 1966): 84–92.

Van Horne, James. The analysis of uncertainty resolution in capital budgeting for new products. *Management Science* 15 (April 1969): 376–386.

Van Horne, James. The variation of project life as a means for adjusting for risk. *The Engineering Economist* 21 (Spring 1976): 151–158.

Wallingford, B. A. A survey and comparison of portfolio selection models. *Journal of Financial and Quantitative Analysis* 3 (June 1967): 85–106.

Waters, Robert C. and Bullock, Richard L. Inflation and replacement decisions. *The Engineering Economist* 21 (Summer 1976): 249–257.

Weston, J. Fred. Investment decisions using the capital asset pricing model. *Financial Management* 2 (Spring 1973): 25–33.

Woods, Donald H. Improving estimates that involve uncertainty. *Harvard Business Review* 45 (July–August 1966): 91–98.

Young, Donovan and Contreras, Luis E. Expected present worths of cash flows under uncertain timing. *Engineering Economist* 20 (Summer 1975): 257–268.

Appendix A to Chapter 11:

Formal Analysis of Risk

In Chapter 11, we saw that probability distributions can be viewed in either of two ways: (a) as a series of *discrete values* represented by a bar chart, such as Figure 11–1, or (b) as a *continuous function* represented by a smooth curve, such as that in Figure 11–2. Actually, there is an important difference in the way these two graphs are interpreted: the probabilities associated with the outcomes in Figure 11–1 are given by the *height* of each bar, while in Figure 11–2 the probabilities must be found by calculating the *area* under the curve between points of interest. Suppose, for example, that we have the continuous probability distribution shown in Figure 11A–1. This is a normal curve with a mean of 20 and a standard deviation of 5; x could be pounds, percentage rates of return, or any other units. If we want to know the probability that an outcome will fall between 15 and 30, we must calculate the area beneath the curve between these points, or the shaded area in the diagram.

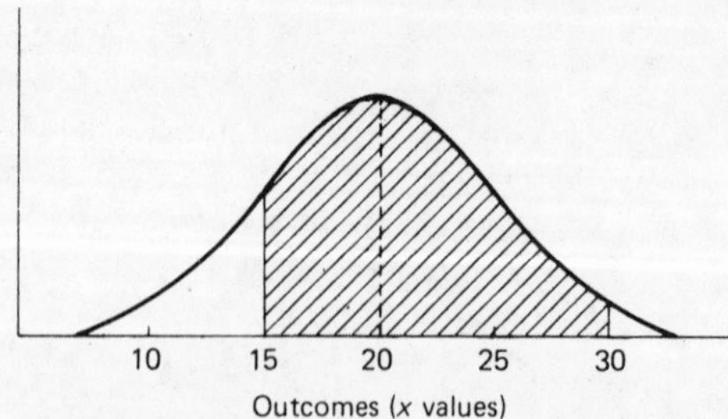

Figure 11A–1 *Continuous Probability Distribution.*

The area under the curve between 15 and 30 can be determined by integrating the curve over this interval, or, since the distribution is normal, by reference to statistical tables of the area under the normal curve such as Table 11A–1 or Appendix C to this book.[1] To use these tables, it is necessary only to know the mean and standard deviation of the distribution.[2]

---

1. The equation for the normal curve is tedious to integrate, thus making the use of tables much more convenient. The equation for the normal curve is

$$f(x) \quad \frac{1}{\sqrt{2\pi\sigma^2}} e^{-(x-\mu)^2/2\sigma^2},$$

where π and e are mathematical constants: μ (read mu) and σ denote the mean and standard deviation of the probability distribution, and x is any possible outcome.

2. The calculating procedure for means and standard deviations is illustrated in Chapter 11. Table 11–4.

Table 11A–1 *Area under the Normal Curve of Error.*

z	Area from the mean to the point of interest	Ordinate
0.0	0.0000	0.3989
0.5	0.1915	0.3521
1.0	0.3413	0.2420
1.5	0.4332	0.1295
2.0	0.4773	0.0540
2.5	0.4938	0.0175
3.0	0.4987	0.0044

z = number of standard deviations from the mean. Some area tables are set up to indicate the area to the left or right of the point of interest; in this book we indicate the area between the mean and the point of interest.

The distribution to be investigated must first be standardized by using the following formula:

$$z = \frac{x - \mu}{\sigma}, \tag{11A–1}$$

where z is the standardized variable, or the number of standard deviations from the mean;[3] x is the outcome of interest; and μ and σ are the mean and standard deviation of the distribution, respectively. For our example, where we are interested in the probability that an outcome will fall between 15 and 30, we first normalize these points of interest using equation 11A–1:

$$z_1 = \frac{15 - 20}{5} = -1.0; \; z_2 = \frac{30 - 20}{5} = 2.0.$$

The areas associated with these z values are found in Table 11A–1 to be 0.3413 and 0.4773.[4] This means that the probability is 0.3413 that the actual outcome will fall between 15 and 20, and 0.4773 that it will fall between 20 and 30. Summing these probabilities shows that the probability of an outcome falling between 15 and 30 is 0.8186, or 81.86 per cent.

Suppose we had been interested in determining the probability that the actual outcome would be greater than 15. Here we would first note that the probability is 0.3413 that the outcome will be between 15 and 20, then observe that the probability is 0.5000 of an outcome greater than the mean, 20. Thus, the probability is $0.3413 + 0.5000 = 0.8413$, or 84.13 per cent, that the outcome will exceed 15.

Some interesting properties of normal probability distributions can be seen by examining Table 11A–1 and Figure 11A–2, which is a graph of the normal curve. For any normal distribution, the probability of an outcome

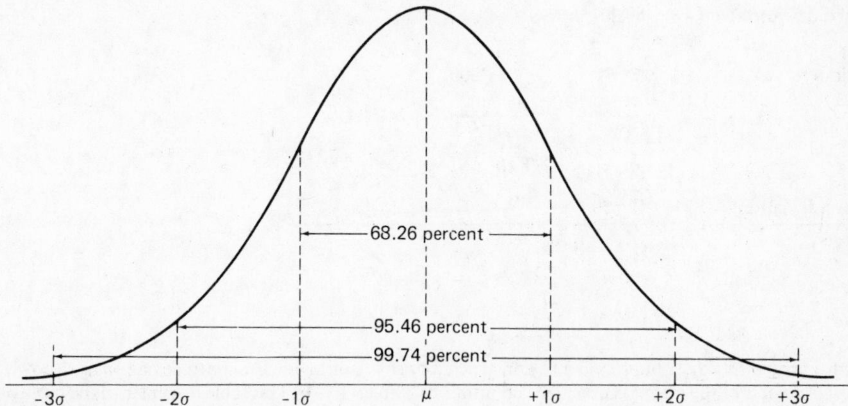

Figure 11A–2 *The Normal Curve.*

3. Note that if the point of interest is 1σ away from the mean, then $x - \mu = \sigma$, so $z = \sigma/\sigma = 1.0$. Thus, when $z = 1.0$, the point of interest is 1σ away from the mean; when $z = 2$ the value is 2σ, and so forth.

4. Note that the negative sign on z_1 is ignored, since the normal curve is symmetrical around the mean; the minus sign merely indicates that the point lies to the left of the mean.

falling within plus or minus one standard deviation from the mean is 0.6826, or 68.26 per cent: 0.3413 per cent × 2.0. If we take the range within two standard deviations of the mean, the probability of an occurrence within this range is 95.46 per cent, and 99.74 per cent of all outcomes will fall within three standard deviations of the mean. Although the distribution theoretically runs from minus infinity to plus infinity, the probability of occurrences beyond about three standard deviations is very near nil.

ILLUSTRATING THE USE OF PROBABILITY CONCEPTS

The concepts discussed both in the chapter and in the preceding section can be clarified by a numerical example. Consider three states of the economy: boom, normal and recession. Next, assume that we can attach a probability of occurrence to each state of the economy and, further, that we can estimate the money returns that will occur on each of two projects under each possible state. With this information, we construct Table 11A–2.

The expected values of projects A and B are calculated by equation 11A–2,

$$\bar{F}_j = \sum_{s=1}^{n} F_{js} P_s \tag{11A–2}$$

and the standard deviations of their respective returns are found by equation 11A–3,

$$\sigma_j = \sqrt{\sum_{s=1}^{n} (F_{js} - \bar{F}_j)^2 P_s}. \tag{11A–3}$$

On the assumption that the returns from projects A and B are normally distributed, knowing the mean and the standard deviation as calculated in Table 11A–2 permits us to graph probability distributions for projects A and B; these distributions are shown in Figure 11A–3.[5] The expected value of each project's cash flow is seen to be £500; however, the flatter graph of B indicates that this is the riskier project.

Table 11A–2 *Means and Standard Deviations of Projects A and B.*

State of the economy	Probability of its occurring P_s	Return F_{js}	$F_{js}P_s$
Project A			
Recession	0.2	£400	£ 80
Normal	0.6	500	300
Boom	0.2	600	120
	1.0	Expected value =	£500
Standard deviation = σ_A = £63.20.			
Project B			
Recession	0.2	£300	£ 60
Normal	0.6	500	300
Boom	0.2	700	140
	1.0	Expected value =	£500
Standard deviation = σ_B = £126.50.			

5. Normal probability distributions can be constructed once the mean and standard deviation are known, using a table of *ordinates* of the normal curve. (See column 3 of Table 11A–1.) This table is similar to the table of areas used above, except that the ordinate table gives relative *heights* of probability curve $f(x)$ at various z values rather than areas beneath the curve. Figure 11A–3 was constructed by plotting points at various z values according to the following formula:

$$f(x) = \frac{1}{\sigma} \times \text{(ordinate for } z \text{ value)},$$

where the ordinate value is read from a table of ordinates.

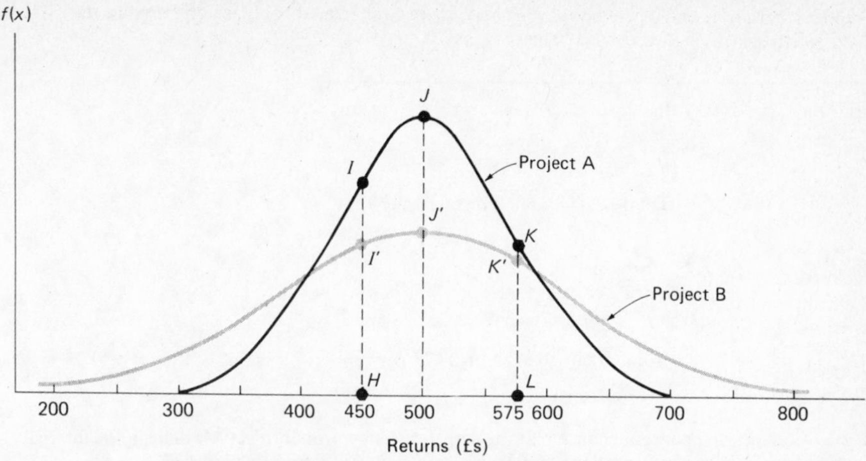

Figure 11A–3 *Probability Distributions for Projects A and B.*

Suppose we want to determine the probabilities that the actual returns of projects A and B will be in the interval £450 to £575. Using equation 11A–1 and Figure 11A–3, we can calculate the respective probability distributions. The first step is to calculate the z values of the interval limits for the two projects:

Project A

$$\text{lower } z_1 = \frac{£450 - £500}{£63.20} = -0.79.$$

$$\text{upper } z_2 = \frac{£575 - 500}{£63.20} = 1.19.$$

Project B

$$\text{lower } z_1 = \frac{£450 - £500}{£126.50} = -0.40.$$

$$\text{upper } z_2 = \frac{£575 - £500}{£126.50} = 0.59.$$

For example, the points corresponding to the mean and +1 standard deviation for projects A and B were calculated as follows:

	z	*Ordinate at z*	$1/\sigma$	$f(x)$
(1)	(2)	(3)	(4)	(5) = (3) × (4)
Project A				
mean = 500.00	0	0.3989	1/63.2	0.0063
$+1\sigma$ = 563.20	1	0.2420	1/63.2	0.0038
$+2\sigma$ = 626.40	2	0.0540	1/63.2	0.0008
Project B				
Mean = 500.00	0	0.3989	1/126.5	0.0032
$+1\sigma$ = 626.50	1	0.2420	1/126.5	0.0019
$+2\sigma$ = 753.00	2	0.0540	1/126.5	0.0004

Column 5 above gives the relative heights of the two distributions: Thus, if we decide (for pictorial convenience) to let the curve for project B be 3.2 inches high at the mean, then the curve should be 1.9 inches high at $\mu \pm 1\sigma$, and the curve for project A should be 6.3 inches at the mean and 3.8 inches at $\pm 1\sigma$. Other points in Figure 11A–3 were determined in like manner.

In Appendix C at the end of the book, which is a more complete table of z values, we find the areas under a normal curve for each of these four z values:

Project A	z Value	Area	
lower z:	−0.79	0.2852	
upper z:	1.19	0.3830	
	Total area =	0.6682	or 66.82 per cent
Project B	**z Value**	**Area**	
lower z:	−0.40	0.1554	
upper z:	0.59	0.2224	
	Total area =	0.3778	or 37.78 per cent

Thus, there is about a 67 per cent chance that the actual cash flow from project A will lie in the interval £450 to £575, and about a 38 per cent probability that B's cash flow will fall in this interval.

Now look back at Figure 11A–3 and observe the two areas that were just calculated. For project A, the area bounded by $HIJKL$ represents about 67 per cent of the area under A's curve. For project B, that area bounded by $HI'J'K'L$ includes about 38 per cent of the total area.

CUMULATIVE PROBABILITY

Suppose we ask these questions: What is the probability that the cash flows from project A will be at least £100? £150? £200? and so on. Obviously, there is a higher probability of their being at least £100 rather than £150, £150 rather than £200, and so on. In general, the most convenient way of expressing the answer to such 'at least' questions is through the use of *cumulative probability distributions*; these distributions for projects A and B are calculated in Table 11A–3 and plotted in Figure 11A–4.

Suppose projects A and B each cost £450; then, if each project returns at least £450, they will both break even. What is the probability of breaking even on each project? From Figure 11A–4 we see that the probability is 78 per cent that project A will break even, while the break-even probability is only 65 per cent for the riskier project B. However, there is virtually no chance that A will yield more than £650, while B has a 5 per cent chance of returning £700 or more.

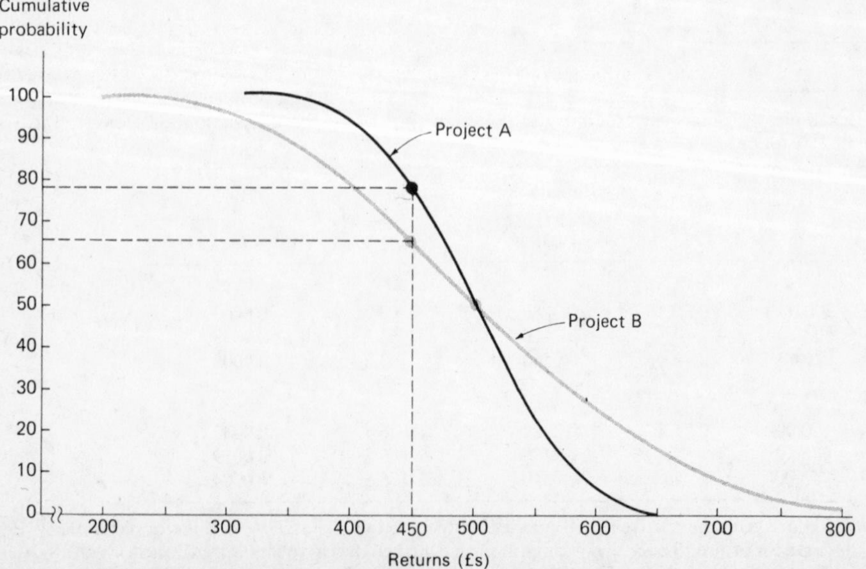

Figure 11A–4 *Cumulative Probability Distributions for Projects A and B.*

Table 11A–3 *Cumulative Probability Distribution for Projects A and B.*

Expected return	z Value	Cumulative probability
Project A		
£300	−3.16	0.9990[a]
400	−1.58	0.9429
450	−0.79	0.7855
500	0.00	0.5000[b]
575	1.19	0.1170[c]
600	1.58	0.0571
700	3.16	0.0001
Project B		
£200	−2.37	0.9911[a]
300	−1.58	0.9429
400	−0.79	0.7855
450	−0.39	0.6517
500	0.00	0.5000[b]
575	0.59	0.2776[c]
600	0.79	0.2148
700	1.58	0.0571
800	2.37	0.0089

[a] 0.5000 plus areas under left tail of the normal curve; for example, for project A, 0.5000 + 0.4990 = 0.9990 = 99.9 per cent for z = −3.16.
[b] The mean has a cumulative probability of 0.5000 = 50 per cent.
[c] 0.5000 less area under right tail of the normal curve; for example, for project A, 0.5000 − 0.1170 = 11.7 per cent for z = 1.19.

OTHER DISTRIBUTIONS

Thus far we have assumed that project returns fit a probability distribution that is approximately normal. Many distributions do fit this pattern, and normal distributions are relatively easy to work with. Therefore, much of the work done on risk measurement assumes a normal distribution. However, other distributions are certainly possible; Figure 11A–5 shows distributions skewed to the right and left, respectively. For two possible investments with equal expected returns, F, would an investor prefer a normal, left-skewed, or right-skewed

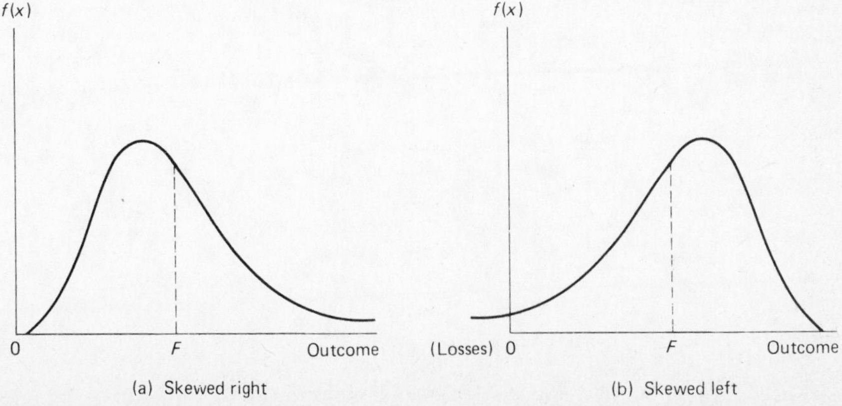

Figure 11A–5 *Skewed Distributions.*

distribution? A distribution skewed to the right, such as the one in Figure 11A–5(a), would probably be chosen because the odds on a very low return are small, while there is some chance of very high returns. For the left-skewed distributions, there is little likelihood of large gains but some possibility of losses.

SUMMARY

In this appendix we have reviewed some of the basics of probability theory and showed how it can be used in evaluating risky investments. More advanced concepts for multi-period cash flows, and for various return patterns, are presented in Appendices B, C, D, E and F.

PROBLEMS

11A–1. The sales of the Cleveland Company for next year have the following probability distribution:

Probability	Sales (millions)
0.1	£10
0.2	12
0.4	15
0.2	18
0.1	20

(a) On graph paper, plot sales on the horizontal axis and probability of sales on the vertical axis, using the points given above. Draw a smooth curve connecting your plotted points. What can you say about this curve?
(b) Compute the mean of the probability distribution.
(c) Compute the standard deviation of the probability distribution.
(d) Compute the coefficient of variation of the probability distribution.
(e) What is the probability that sales will exceed £16 million?
(f) What is the probability that sales will fall below £13 million?
(g) What is the probability that sales will be between £13 and £16 million?
(h) What is the probability that sales will exceed £17 million?

11A–2. Mutual of Portslade offers to sell your firm a £1 million one-year term insurance policy on your corporate jet for a premium of £7500. The probability that the plane will be lost or incur damages in that amount in any 12-month period is 0.001.
(a) What is the insurance company's expected gain from sale of the policy?
(b) What is the insurance company's expected gain or loss if the probability of a £1 million fire loss is 0.01? Would the insurance company still offer your firm the same policy for the same premium? Explain.

Appendix B to Chapter 11:

Evaluating Uncertain Cash Flows Over Time

In Appendix A to Chapter 11 we presented some of the statistical theory upon which risk analysis is based. In this appendix, somewhat more advanced theory is used to deal with the problem of uncertain returns over time. Our discussion is divided into two cases: (a) where expected returns are normally distributed and are independent from one period to another, and (b) where normality and intertemporal independence do not hold.

INDEPENDENT RETURNS OVER TIME

In Appendix A to Chapter 11 we calculated an investment's one-year expected return, and the standard deviation of that return, as follows:

Expected return for year t:

$$\bar{F}_t = \sum_{s=1}^{n} (F_{ts} P_{ts}). \tag{11B-1}$$

Variation of expected return for year t:

$$\sigma_1 = \left[\sum_{s=1}^{n} (F_{ts} - \bar{F}_t)^2 P_{ts} \right]^{1/2}. \tag{11B-2}$$

If the probability distribution P_{ts} is normally distributed, and if the cash flow in year t, F_t, is independent of the cash flow in year $(t-1)$, then we can find the present value of an uncertain stream of returns by use of equation 11B-3, and the standard deviation of this *PV* by use of equation 11B-4:

Expected present value of investment:

$$PV = \sum_{t=1}^{n} \left[\frac{\bar{F}_t}{(1+k)^t} \right]. \tag{11B-3}$$

Variation of expected present value of the investment:[1]

$$\sigma_{PV} = \left[\sum_{t=0}^{n} \frac{\sigma^2_t}{(1+k)^{2t}} \right]^{1/2}. \tag{11B-4}$$

Here

F_{ts} = cash flow return associated with the sth probability in year t

1. For a proof of equation 11B-4, see Frederick S. Hillier, The derivation of probabilistic information for the evaluation of risky investments. *Management Science* 9 (April 1963), pp. 443-457.

P_{ts} = probability of the sth return in year t
$\bar{F}_t$ = expected cash flow return from the investment in the tth year, an average weighted by probabilities
σ_t = standard deviation of the expected returns in the tth year
PV = present value of all expected returns over the n-year life of the investment
k = appropriate rate of discount for the future returns
σ_{PV} = standard deviation of the present value of expected returns.

Equation 11B–1 calculates the expected returns of an investment for a given year, t, as a weighted average, the items to be averaged being the possible outcomes and the weights being the probabilities associated with each possible outcome for the year. Equation 11B–2 calculates the standard deviation of the expected return in year t. Equation 11B–3 discounts the expected returns over each year of the project's life to find the present value of the project, and equation 11B–4 calculates the standard deviation of the expected PV of the project. The first two equations deal with the returns and risk for individual years, while the last two equations deal with returns and risk of the project as a whole.

Comparison of two investments with uncertain returns over future time periods

The application and significance of the basic formulas can best be conveyed by illustrative examples. The relevant data and calculations are set forth in Tables 11B–1 for project A and 11B–2 for project B. Project A's cash investment is £100. Returns are expected over three periods. There are five possible 'states-of-the-world'; that is, $s = 1 \ldots 5$, and the outcomes for each of these states are given in the columns headed F_{1s}, F_{2s}, F_{3s}. Note that the range of possible returns widens in the later periods. The associated probabilities are in the columns headed P_{1s}, P_{2s} and P_{3s}. It should be noted that in period 2 the probability distribution is somewhat flatter than in period 1, and that in period 3 the probability distribution is even more flat and is also skewed somewhat to the left, or towards the possibility of lower returns. Thus, the combination of a wider range of outcomes and flatter probability distribution for periods 2 and 3 indicates that greater uncertainty is associated with returns expected in the more distant future. This type of situation is shown in Figure 11–4, in the body of Chapter 11.

Table 11B–1 *Probable Returns from Risky Investment A.*

Investment A £100 (cash outflow in period 0)
(1) Calculation of expected returns

	Period 1			Period 2			Period 3		
State$_{(s)}$	F_{1s}	P_{1s}	$F_{1s}P_{1s}$	F_{2s}	P_{2s}	$F_{2s}P_{2s}$	F_{3s}	P_{3s}	$F_{3s}P_{3s}$
1	50	0.10	5	20	0.10	2	– 40	0.10	– 4
2	60	0.20	12	40	0.25	10	30	0.30	9
3	70	0.40	28	60	0.30	18	50	0.30	15
4	80	0.20	16	80	0.25	20	80	0.20	16
5	90	0.10	9	100	0.10	10	140	0.10	14

$\sum_{s=1}^{5} (F_{1s}P_{1s}) = \bar{F}_1 = 70$ $\qquad \bar{F}_2 = 60$ $\qquad \bar{F}_3 = 50$

(2) Calculation of standard deviation

State$_{(s)}$	$(F_{1s}-\bar{F}_1)^2$	P_{1s}	$(F_{1s}-\bar{F}_1)^2P_{1s}$	$(F_{2s}-\bar{F}_2)^2$	P_{2s}	$(F_{2s}-\bar{F}_2)^2P_{2s}$	$(F_{3s}-\bar{F}_3)^2$	P_{3s}	$(F_{3s}-\bar{F}_3)^2P_{3s}$
1	400	0.10	40	1600	0.10	160	8100	0.10	810
2	100	0.20	20	400	0.25	100	400	0.30	120
3	0	0.40	0	0	0.30	0	0	0.30	0
4	100	0.20	20	400	0.25	100	900	0.20	180
5	400	0.10	40	1600	0.10	160	8100	0.10	810

$\sum_{s=1}^{5} (F_{1s}-\bar{F}_1)^2 P_{1s} = 120 = \sigma_1^2$ $\qquad \sigma_2^2 = 520$ $\qquad \sigma_3^2 = 1920$

$\sigma_1 = \sqrt{120} = 10.95$ $\qquad \sigma_2 = \sqrt{520} = 22.80$ $\qquad \sigma_3 = \sqrt{1920} = 43.82$

$$(3)\ PV_A = \frac{70}{1.06} + \frac{60}{(1.06)^2} + \frac{50}{(1.06)^3} = \frac{70}{1.060} + \frac{60}{1.124} + \frac{50}{1.191} = £161.40$$

$$(4)\ \sigma_{PV} = \left[\frac{120}{(1.06)^2} + \frac{520}{(1.06)^4} + \frac{1920}{(1.06)^6}\right]^{1/2} = \left[\frac{120}{1.124} + \frac{520}{1.262} + \frac{1920}{1.419}\right]^{1/2}$$

$$= [106.76 + 412.04 + 1353.07]^{1/2} = [1871.87]^{1/2} = 43.25$$

Table 11B–2 *Probable Returns from Risky Investment B.*

Investment B = £100
Cash inflows

P_{ts}	F_{1s}	F_{2s}	F_{3s}
0.10	40	30	20
0.20	50	40	30
0.40	60	50	40
0.20	70	60	50
0.10	80	70	60
R_t	60	50	40

(2) $\sigma_t = [0.10(20)^2 + 0.20(10)^2 + 0.20(10)^2 + 0.10(20)^2]^{1/2} = [120]^{1/2} = £10.95$

(3) $PV_B = \frac{60}{1.060} + \frac{50}{1.124} + \frac{40}{1.191} = 56.60 + 44.48 + 33.58 = £134.66$

(4) $\sigma_{PV} = \left[\frac{120}{1.124} + \frac{120}{1.262} + \frac{120}{1.419}\right]^{1/2} = [106.76 + 95.08 + 84.57]^{1/2} = [286.40]^{1/2} = £16.91$

Given these data, the expected returns for project A for each period are calculated and found to be £70, £60 and £50, respectively. The standard deviation of each of these returns is then calculated, using equation 11B–2. Next, equation 11B–3 is used to calculate project A's expected present value, £161.40. Finally, equation 11B–4 is used to find the standard deviation of that present value, £43.25.

In Table 11B–2, similar calculations are performed for project B, which also involves an outlay of £100. To simplify the calculations, we assume that the indicated probabilities are the same for each of the three periods, but note that the expected returns drop with each successive year. Thus, the standard deviation of expected returns, $\sigma_t = £10.95$, is the same for each of the three periods, but the coefficient of variation, which is the standard deviation divided by the mean return, is lower for the earlier returns, because expected returns are declining. Thus, the riskiness of project B is also increasing over time. Equations 11B–3 and 11B–4 are again used to calculate the present value of the expected returns, £134.66, and the standard deviation of the expected value, £16.91.

Knowing the mean (PV) and the standard deviation (σ_{NPV}) as calculated in Tables 11B–1 and 11B–2, and assuming that the returns from projects A and B are normally distributed, we can construct probability distribution graphs for the two projects; these distributions are shown in Figure 11B–1. The expected PV of A is seen to be £161, while that of B is £134. However, the larger standard deviation and flatter graph of A indicate that A is the riskier project.

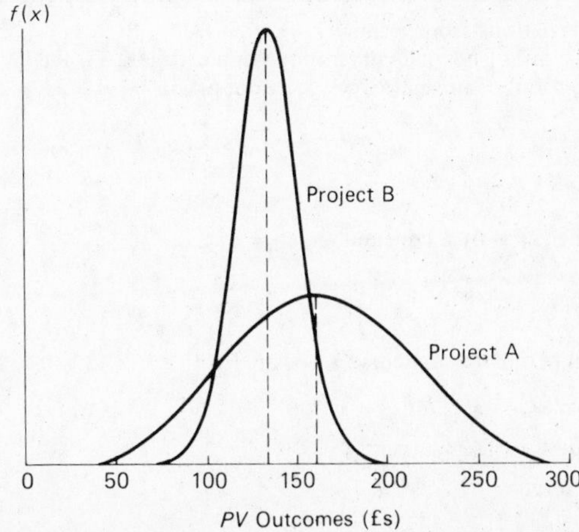

Figure 11B–1 *Probability Distributions of* PV *for Projects A and B.*

The decision maker must still choose between the riskier but probably more profitable project A and the less risky but probably less profitable project B. How is this choice made? Conceptually, the information on relative project riskiness could be used to establish risk-adjusted discount rates, which could then be used to calculate risk-adjusted NPVs, using the market price of risk theory described in Chapter 11. This would require the calculation of the systematic risk measures, covariance or beta, over multi-time periods.[2] Further discussion of the relationship between risk and the cost of capital will be deferred to Chapter 17.

CUMULATIVE PROBABILITY

A useful and practical way of expressing the distributions of projects A and B is in terms of cumulative probabilities (discussed in detail in Appendix A to Chapter 11). We know that projects A and B each have a cost of £100; what is the probability that the present value of the cash flows from each of these projects will be *at least* £100, that is, that the *NPV* will be nil or greater? Cumulative probabilities are used to answer this question.

Cumulative probabilities are developed from the data on the area under the normal curve given in Appendix C. In Table 11B–3, the data on projects A and B are combined with the information on the area under the normal curve. The various entries in columns 1 and 2 of this table represent possible outcomes for the *PV* of projects A and B. Since the investment outlay for each project is £100, this sum can be subtracted from the *PV* figures in columns 1 and 2 to obtain the *NPV* values in columns 3 and 4. The *z* values in column 5 simply denote the number of standard deviations each entry is from the mean, and column 6 gives the probability of realizing *PV*s and *NPV*s *at least* as large as those shown in columns 1 to 4. From Appendix C, we see that for the first line of Table 11B–3, the probability of an outcome's lying to the left of -3σ is 0.0013, or 0.13 per cent, so the probability of the outcome's lying to the right of -3σ; that is, the probability of NPV_A being at least (£68.35) or NPV_B being at least (£16.07) is 100.00 per cent: 0.13 per cent = 99.87 per cent ≈ 99.9 per cent. The other values in Table 11B–3 are developed similarly. Note that the last two rows of the table indicate that the probability of at least breaking even is 92.2 per cent for project A and 98.0 per cent for project B.

Table 11B–3 *Cumulative Probabilities of Expected Present Values of Investments A and B.*

Expected *PV* of at least		Expected *NPV* of at least		*z* value[a]	Cumulative probability
A	B	A	B		
(1)	(2)	(3)	(4)	(5)	(6)
£ 31.65	£ 83.93	(68.35)	(16.07)	−3z	99.9 %[b]
74.90	100.84	(25.10)	0.84	−2z	97.7
118.15	117.75	18.15	17.75	−1z	84.1
161.40	134.66	61.40	34.66	–	50.0
204.65	151.57	104.65	51.57	+1z	15.9[c]
247.90	168.48	147.90	68.48	2z	2.3
291.15	185.39	191.15	85.39	3z	0.1
£100.0		0.0		1.42	92.2 %[d]
	£100.0		0.0	2.05	98.0[e]

[a] z = number of standard deviations from mean *PV*.

[b] 0.5000 *plus* areas under *left* tail of normal curve; for example, 0.5000 + 0.4987 = 99.9 per cent for z = −3.

[c] 0.5000 *less* areas under *right* tail of normal curve; for example, 0.500–0.4773 = 2.3 per cent for z = 2.

[d] $NPV = PV - \text{Cost}$.

$$z = \frac{PV}{\sigma_{NPV}} \quad \text{where } NPV = 0.$$

Since the *PV* differs from the *NPV* by a constant, $\sigma_{NPV} = \sigma_{PV}$,

$$z = \frac{61.40}{43.25} = 1.42 \text{ for project A.}$$

The area under the right tail of the normal curve associated with z = 1.42 is 0.4222, so

Area = 0.5000 + 0.4222 = 0.9222,

and the probability of $NPV \geqq 0$ is 92.2 per cent.

[e] For project B,

$$z = \frac{34.66}{16.91} = 2.05 \text{ where } NPV = 0,$$

and the associated area = 0.5000 + 0.4798 = 0.9798, so the probability of $NPV \geqq 0$ is 98 per cent for project B.

2. See Marcus Bogue and Richard Roll, Capital budgeting of risky projects with 'Imperfect' markets for physical capital, *Journal of Finance* 29 (May 1974), 601–13.

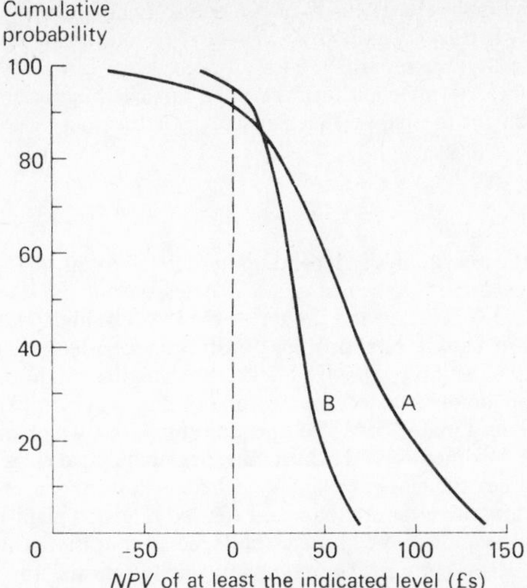

Figure 11B–2 *Cumulative Probability Analysis of* NPV *Values for Projects A and B.*

Figure 11B–2 shows these data on cumulative probabilities in graph form. Here it is easy to see that project B has only a small chance of not breaking even, but it also has virtually no chance of earning an *NPV* of more than about £60. Project A, on the other hand, has a higher probability of losing money, but it also has a fairly high probability of achieving an *NPV* of over £100.

It is clear that investment A has a higher expected return than investment B. However, disregarding portfolio effects, investment B is less risky. Selection between A and B would depend upon the decision maker's attitude towards risk, as well as upon how the two investments might fit in with the firm's other assets.

INTERDEPENDENT RETURNS OVER TIME: THE HILLIER AND HERTZ APPROACHES

The foregoing presentation represents a general method for dealing with risk when the returns of one period do not depend upon outcomes in other years; that is, when the returns are *independent* and when the expected returns for a given year are normally distributed. When these conditions of independence and normality do not hold, the calculations become more complicated. The models for which expected net cash flows between periods are correlated (the expected returns between time periods are dependent), and for which some of the returns of an investment are correlated and some are independent, have been treated by Frederick Hillier.[3] Mathematical techniques are also available for dealing with non-normal probability distributions. We shall not go into the technical methodology involved, but Hillier's approach has proved to be a useful way of dealing with uncertainty in at least some practical situations.

Another approach to capital budgeting under uncertainty is presented in an article by David Hertz.[4] He is particularly persuasive in indicating that, taking probabilities into account, the expected rate of return may be quite different from the conventional best-single-estimate approach. Hertz illustrates the use of the probability information in an approach that requires only a range of high and low values around expected values of such key variables as sales, profit margins, and so forth. Under his method, the decision maker is not required to assign probabilities to the variables; he must choose only (a) the expected value, (b) an upper estimate, and (c) a lower estimate. The Monte Carlo[5] method, which involves using a table of random numbers to generate the possible probabilities, is used to generate the required probability distributions.

The Monte Carlo method also permits assignment of values that reflect differing degrees of dependence between some events and some subsequent events. For example, the expected sales for the firm, as well as its

---

3. See Frederick S. Hillier, The derivation of probabilistic information for the evaluation of risk investments, *Management Science* 9 (April 1963), pp. 44–57, and Frederick S. Hillier and David V. Heebink, Evaluating risky capital investments, *California Management Review* 8 (Winter 1965), pp. 71–80.

4. David B. Hertz, Uncertainty and investment selection, in J. F. Weston and M. B. Goudzwaard, eds., *The Treasurer's Handbook* (Homewood, Ill.: Dow Jones-Irwin, 1976), chap. 18, pp. 376–420.

5. For a discussion of the nature of the Monte Carlo method and some applications, see C. McMillan and R. F. Gonzalez, *Systems Analysis* (Homewood, Ill.: Irwin, 1965), pp. 76–121.

selling prices, might be determined by the intensity of competition in conjunction with the total size of market demand and its growth rate. A further advantage of the Hertz technique is that, by separating the individual factors that determine profitability, the separate effects of each factor can be estimated and the sensitivity of profitability to each factor can be determined. If the effects of a particular factor on the final results are negligible, it is not necessary for management to analyse that particular factor in any great detail.

Sensitivity analysis

The *NPV* of a project will, in the final analysis, depend upon such factors as quantity of sales, sales prices, input costs and the like. If these values turn out to be favourable – that is, output and sales prices are high, and costs are low – then profits, the realized rate of return, and the actual *NPV* will be high, and conversely if poor results are experienced. Recognizing these causal relationships, businessmen often calculate projects' *NPVs* under alternative assumptions, then see just how sensitive *NPV* is to changing conditions. One example that recently came to the authors' attention involves a fertilizer company that was comparing two alternative types of phosphate plants. Fuel represents a major cost, and one plant uses coal, which may be obtained under a long-term, fixed-cost contract, while the other uses oil, which must be purchased at current market prices. Considering present and projected future prices, the oil-fired plant looks better – it has a considerably higher *NPV*. However, oil prices are volatile, and if prices rise by more than the expected rate, this plant will be unprofitable. The coal-fired plant, on the other hand, has a lower *NPV* under the expected conditions, but this *NPV* is not sensitive to changing conditions in the energy market. The company finally selected the coal-fired plant because the sensitivity analysis indicated it to be less risky.

Monte Carlo simulation analysis

Sensitivity analysis as practised by the fertilizer company described above is informal in the sense that no probabilities are attached to the likelihood of various outcomes. Monte Carlo *simulation analysis* represents a refinement that does employ probability estimates. In this section we first describe how *decision trees* can be used to attach probabilities to different outcomes, and then we illustrate how full-scale computer simulation can be employed to analyse major projects.

Decision trees

Most important decisions are not made once-and-for-all at one point in time. Rather, decisions are made in stages. For example, a petroleum firm considering the possibility of expanding into agricultural chemicals might take the following steps: (a) spend £100 000 for a survey of supply-demand conditions in the agricultural chemical industry; (b) if the survey results are favourable, spend £500 000 on a pilot plant to investigate production methods; and (c) depending on the costs estimated from the pilot study and the demand potential from the market study, either abandon the project, build a large plant, or build a small one. Thus, the final decision actually is made in stages, with subsequent decisions depending on the results of previous decisions.

The sequence of events can be mapped out like the branches of a tree, hence the name *decision tree*. As an example, consider Figure 11B–3. There it is assumed that the petroleum company has completed its industry supply–demand analysis and pilot plant study, and has determined that it should proceed to develop a full-scale production facility. The firm must decide whether to build a large plant or a small one. Demand expectations for the plant's products are 50 per cent for high demand, 30 per cent for medium demand, and 20 per cent for low demand. Depending upon demand, net cash flows (sales revenues minus operating costs, all discounted to the present) will range from £8.8 million to £1.4 million if a large plant is built, and from £2.6 million to £1.4 million if a small plant is built.

The initial costs of the large and small plant are shown in column 5; when these investment outlays are subtracted from the *PV* of cash flows, the result is the set of possible *NPVs* shown in column 6. One, but only one, of these *NPVs* will actually occur. Finally, we multiply column 6 by column 3 to obtain column 7, and the sums in column 7 give the expected *NPVs* of the large and small plants.

Because the expected *NPV* of the larger plant (£730 000) is larger than that of the small plant (£300 000), should the decision be to build the large plant? Perhaps, but not necessarily. Notice that the range of outcomes is greater if the large plant is built, with the actual *NPVs* (column 6 in Figure 11B–3 minus the investment cost) varying from £3.8 million to *minus* £3.6 million. However, a range of only £600 000 to minus £600 000 exists for the small plant. Since the required investments for the two plants are not the same, we must examine the coefficients of variation of the net present value possibilities in order to determine which alternative actually entails the greater risk. The coefficient of variation for the large plant's present value is 4.3, while that for the small plant is only 1.5.[6] Thus, risk is greater if the decision is to build the large plant.

6. Using equation 11–3 and the data on possible returns in Figure 11B–3 the standard deviation of returns for the larger plant is found to be £3.155 million, and that for the smaller one is £458 260. Dividing each of these standard deviations by the expected returns for their respective plant size gives the coefficients of variation.

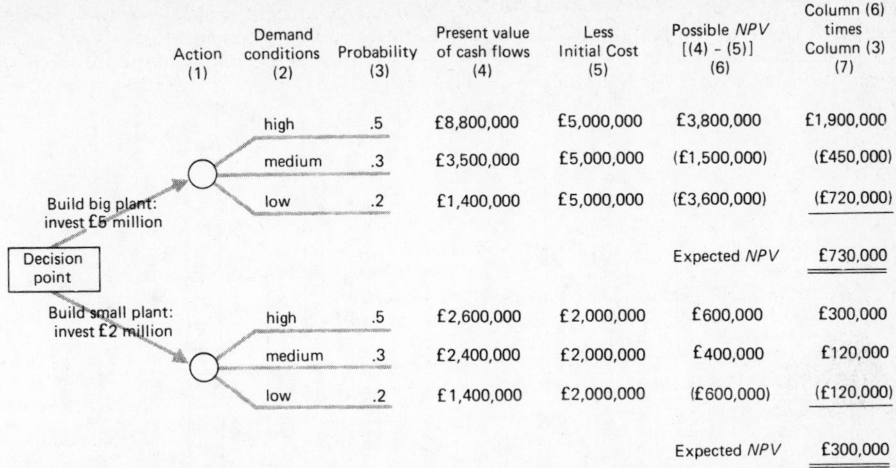

Action (1)	Demand conditions (2)	Probability (3)	Present value of cash flows (4)	Less Initial Cost (5)	Possible *NPV* [(4) - (5)] (6)	Column (6) times Column (3) (7)
Build big plant: invest £5 million	high	.5	£8,800,000	£5,000,000	£3,800,000	£1,900,000
	medium	.3	£3,500,000	£5,000,000	(£1,500,000)	(£450,000)
	low	.2	£1,400,000	£5,000,000	(£3,600,000)	(£720,000)
					Expected *NPV*	£730,000
Build small plant: invest £2 million	high	.5	£2,600,000	£2,000,000	£600,000	£300,000
	medium	.3	£2,400,000	£2,000,000	£400,000	£120,000
	low	.2	£1,400,000	£2,000,000	(£600,000)	(£120,000)
					Expected *NPV*	£300,000

Note: The figures in column 4 are the annual cash flows from operations–sales revenues minus cash operating costs–discounted at an appropriate rate. For reasons explained later in the chapter appendices, the riskless rate of interest is usually the appropriate discount rate. Variations of *NPV*s at the riskless rate are then analysed to provide insights into the appropriate risk-adjusted discount rate for each alternative, and these rates are used, together with expected cash flows, to determine a true expected *NPV* for the alternatives.

Figure 11B–3 *Illustrative Decision Tree.*

The decision maker could take account of the risk differentials in a variety of ways. He could assign utility values to the cash flows given in column 4 of Figure 11B–3, thus stating column 6 in terms of expected utility. He would then choose the plant size that provided the greatest utility. Alternatively, he could use the certainty equivalent or risk-adjusted discount rate methods in calculating the present values given in column 4. The plant that offered the larger risk-adjusted net present value would then be the optimal choice.

The decision tree illustrated in Figure 11B–3 is quite simple; in actual use, the trees are frequently far more complex and involve a number of sequential decision points. As an example of a more complex tree, consider Figure 11B–4. The boxes numbered 1, 2, and so on, are *decision points*, that is, instances when the firm must choose between alternatives, while the circles represent the possible actual outcomes, one of which will follow these decisions. At decision point 1, the firm has three choices: to invest £3 million in a large plant, to invest £1.3 million in a small plant, or to spend £100 000 on market research. If the large plant is built, the firm follows the upper branch, and its position has been fixed – it can only hope that demand will be high. If it builds the small plant, then it follows the lower branch. If demand is low, no further action is required. If demand is high, decision point 2 is reached, and the firm must either do nothing or else expand the plant at a cost of another £2.2 million. (Thus, if it obtains a large plant through expansion, the cost is £500 000 greater than if it had built the large plant in the first place.)

If the decision at point 1 is to pay £100 000 for more information, the firm moves to the centre branch. The research modifies the firm's information about potential demand. Initially, the probabilities were 70 per cent for high demand and 30 per cent for low demand. The research survey will show either favourable (positive) or unfavourable (negative) demand prospects: If they are positive, we assume that the probability for high final demand will be 87 per cent and that for low demand will be 13 per cent; if the research yields negative results, the odds on high final demand are only 35 per cent and those for low demand are 65 per cent. These results will, of course, influence the firm's decision whether to build a large or a small plant.

If the firm builds a large plant and demand is high, then sales and profits will be large. However, if it builds a large plant and demand is weak, sales will be low and losses, rather than profits, will be incurred. On the other hand, if it builds a small plant and demand is high, sales and profits will be lower than they could have been had a large plant been built, but the chances of losses in the event of low demand will be eliminated. Thus, the decision to build the large plant is riskier than the one to build the small plant. The decision to commission the research is, in effect, an expenditure to reduce the degree of uncertainty in the decision on which plant to build; the research provides additional information on the probability of high versus low demand, thus lowering the level of uncertainty.

The decision tree in Figure 11B–4 is incomplete in that no money outcomes (or utility values) are assigned to the various situations. If this step were taken, along the lines shown in the last two columns of Figure 11B–3, then expected values could be obtained for each of the alternative actions. These expected values could then be used to aid the decision maker in choosing among the alternatives.

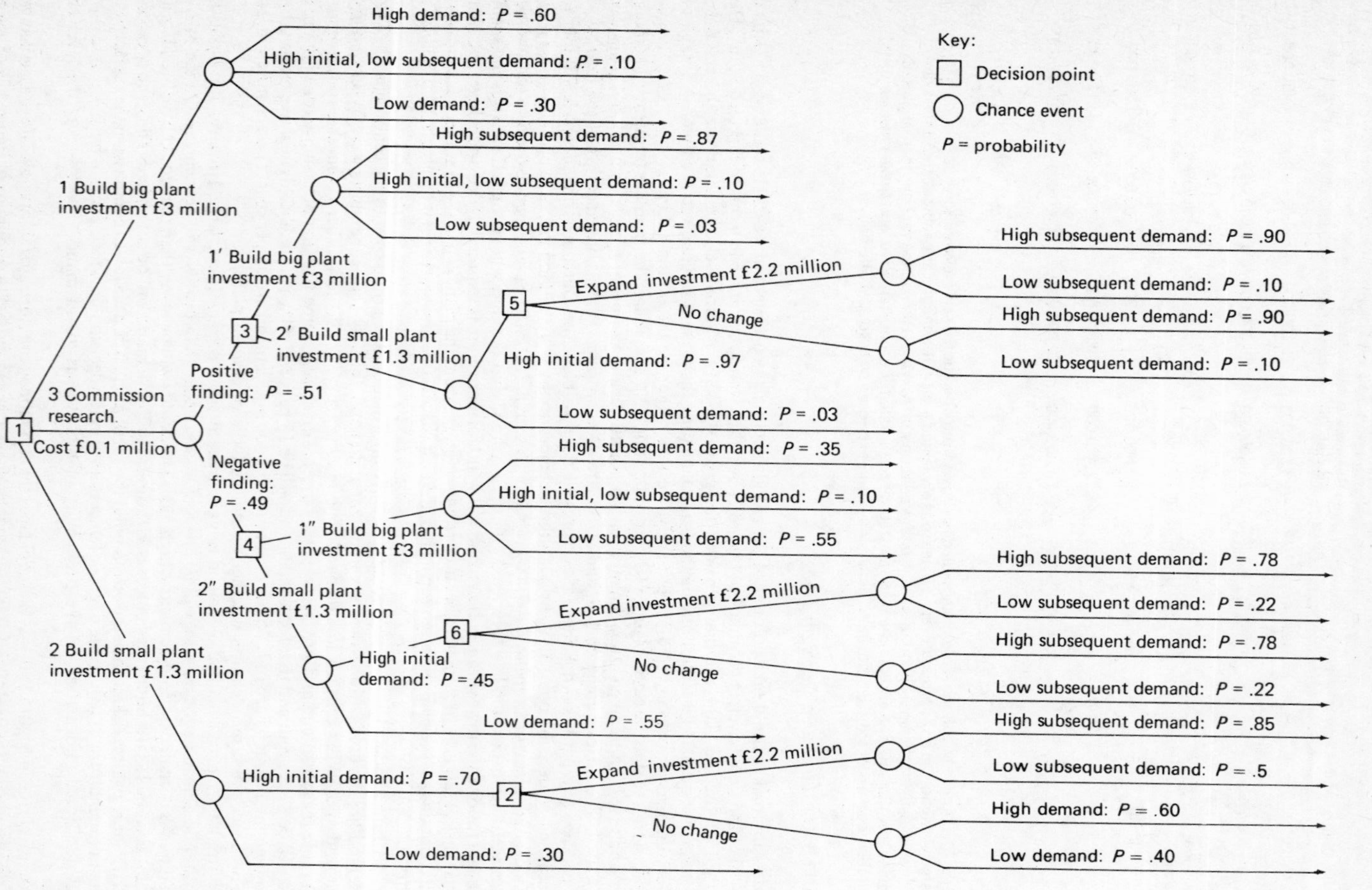

Figure 11B–4 *Decision Tree with Multiple Decision Points.*

Computer simulation

The concepts embodied in decision tree analysis can be extended to computer simulation. To illustrate the technique, let us consider a proposal to build a new textile factory. The cost of the factory is not known for certain, although it is expected to run to about £150 million. If no problems are encountered, the cost can be as low as £125 million, while an unfortunate series of events – strikes, unprojected increases in materials costs, technical problems, and the like – could result in the investment outlay running as high as £225 million.

Revenues from the new facility, which will operate for many years will depend on population growth and income in the region, competition, developments in synthetic fabrics research, and textile import quotas. Operating costs will depend on production efficiency, materials and labour cost trends, and the like. Since both sales revenues and operating costs are uncertain, annual profits are also uncertain.

Assuming that probability distributions can be assigned to each of the major cost and revenue determinants, a computer programme can be constructed to simulate what is likely to happen. In effect, the computer selects one value at random from each of the relevant distributions, combines it with other values selected from the other distributions, and produces an estimated profit and net present value or rate of return on investment.[7] This particular profit and rate of return occur, of course, only for the particular combination of values selected during this trial. The computer goes on to select other sets of values and to compute other profits and rates of return repeatedly, for perhaps several hundred trials. A count is kept of the number of times each rate of return is computed, and when the computer runs are completed, the frequency with which the various rates of return occurred can be plotted as a frequency distribution.

The procedure is illustrated in Figures 11B–5 and 11B–6.[8] Figure 11B–5 is a flowchart outlining the simulation procedure described above, while Figure 11B–6 illustrates the frequency distribution of rates of return generated by such a simulation for two alternative projects, X and Y, each with an expected cost of £20 million. The expected rate of return on investment X is 15 per cent, and that of investment Y is 20 per cent. However, these are only the *average* rates of return generated by the computer; simulated rates range from −10 per cent to +45 per cent for investment Y and from 5 to 25 per cent for investment X. The standard deviation generated for X is only 4 percentage points – 68 per cent of the computer runs had rates of return between 11 and 19 per cent – while that for Y is 12 percentage points. Clearly, then, investment Y is riskier than investment X.

The computer simulation has provided us with both an estimate of the expected returns on the two projects and an estimate of their relative risks. A decision about which alternative should be chosen can now be made, perhaps by using the risk-adjusted discount rate method or perhaps in a judgemental, informal manner by the decision maker.

However, computer simulation is not always feasible for risk analysis. The technique involves obtaining probability distributions about a number of variables – investment outlays, unit sales, product prices, input prices, asset lives, and so on – and a fair amount of programming and machine-time costs. Therefore, full-scale simulation is not generally worth while except for large and expensive projects, such as major factory expansions or new-product decisions. In those cases, however, when a firm is deciding whether to accept a major undertaking involving millions of pounds, computer simulation can provide valuable insights into the relative merits of alternative strategies.

PROBLEMS

11B–1. The financial accountant for the Atkins Manufacturing Company is analysing the potential of a £1500 investment in a new machine. His estimate of the cash-flow distribution for the three-year life of the machine is shown below:

Period 1		Period 2		Period 3	
Probability	Cash flow	Probability	Cash flow	Probability	Cash flow
0.10	£800	0.10	£800	0.20	£1200
0.20	600	0.30	700	0.50	900
0.40	400	0.40	600	0.20	600
0.30	200	0.20	500	0.10	300

Probability distributions are assumed to be independent. Treasury bills are yielding 5 per cent. To evaluate the investment, the accountant has asked you to make the following calculations:

(a) The expected net present value of the project.

(b) The standard deviation about the expected value.

---

7. If the variables are not independent, then conditional probabilities must be employed. For example, if demand is weak, then both sales in units and sales prices are likely to be low, and these interrelationships must be taken into account in the simulation.

8. Figure 11B–5 is adapted from Hertz, *Treasurer's Handbook*, Chapter 18.

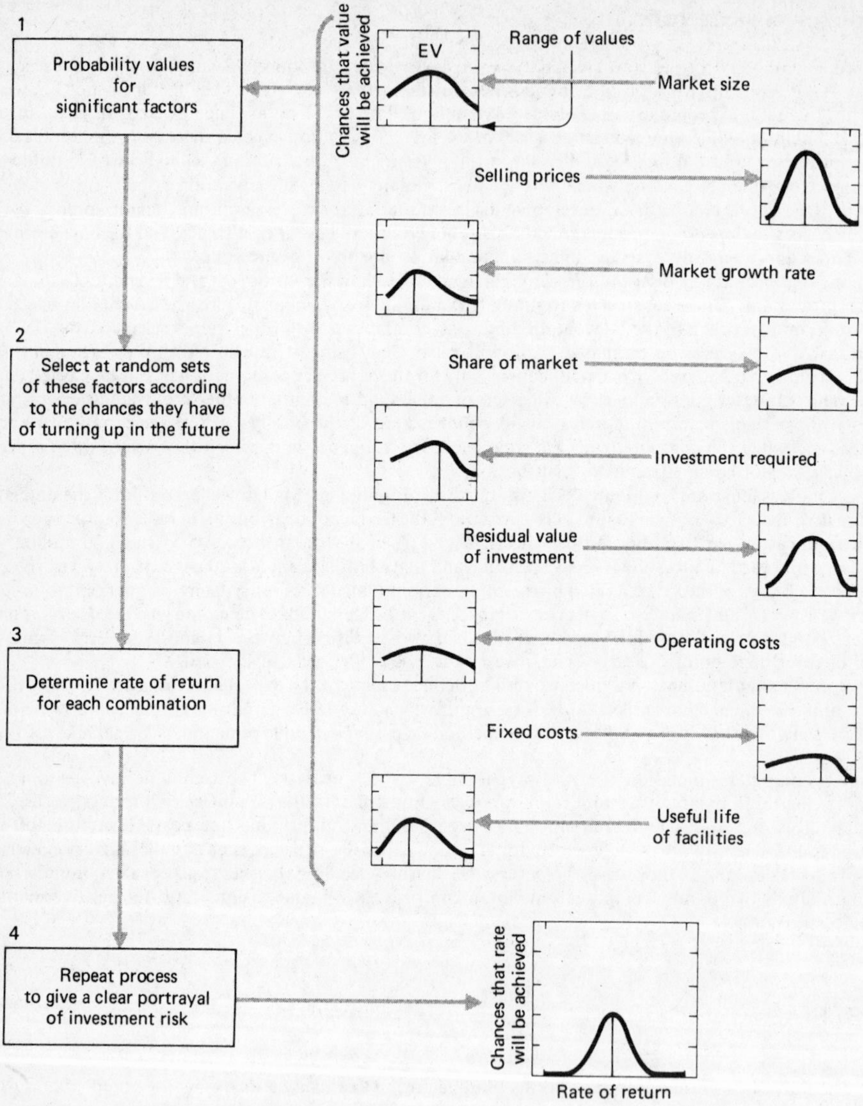

1
Probability values for significant factors
2
Select at random sets of these factors according to the chances they have of turning up in the future
3
Determine rate of return for each combination
4
Repeat process to give a clear portrayal of investment risk
Chances that value will be achieved
EV
Range of values
Market size
Selling prices
Market growth rate
Share of market
Investment required
Residual value of investment
Operating costs
Fixed costs
Useful life of facilities
Chances that rate will be achieved
Rate of return

Figure 11B-5 *Simulation for Investment Planning.*

Probability of occurrence
Investment X
Investment Y
−10
−5
0
5
10
15
20
25
30
35
40
45
Rate of return

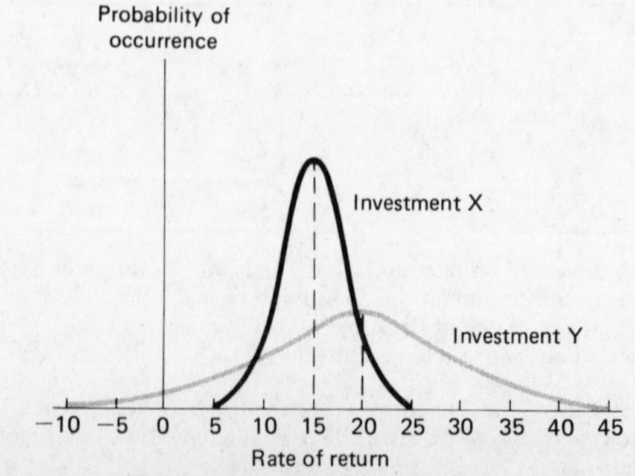

Figure 11B-6 *Expected Rates of Return on Investments X and Y.*

(c) The probability that the net present value will be nil or less (assume the distribution is normal and continuous).
(d) The probability that the net present value will be greater than nil.
(e) The probability that the net present value will at least equal the mean.
(f) The profitability index of the expected value.
(g) The probability that the profitability index will be (i) less than 1 or (ii) greater than 2.

11B–2. The Eastern Tool and Die Company is considering an investment in a project that requires an initial outlay of £3000 with an expected net cash flow generated over three periods as follows:

Period 1		Period 2		Period 3	
Probability	Cash flow	Probability	Cash flow	Probability	Cash flow
0.10	£ 800	0.10	£ 800	0.20	£ 800
0.20	1000	0.30	1000	0.50	1000
0.40	1500	0.40	1500	0.20	1500
0.30	2000	0.20	2000	0.10	2000

(a) What is the expected net present value of this project? (Assume that the probability distributions are independent and that Treasury bills are yielding 5 per cent.)
(b) Calculate the standard deviation about the expected value.
(c) Find the probability that the net present value will be nil or less. (Assume that the distribution is normal and continuous.) What is the probability that the *NPV* will be greater than nil?
(d) Calculate the profitability index of the expected value. What is the probability that the index will be (i) less than 1 and (ii) greater than 2?

11B–3. The Parker Company has the following probability distributions for net cash flows during the first year for a potential project:

Probability	Cash flow
0.50	£100
0.30	200
0.20	300

Performance of similar projects in the past has indicated that the net cash flow distributions are not independent. The level of demand and the related net cash flow returns experienced in period 1 influence the achievements in period 2 in the following way:

If year 1 = £100, the distribution for year 2 is:

0.70	£100
0.20	200
0.10	300

If year 1 = £200, the distribution for year 2 is:

0.10	£100
0.60	200
0.30	300

If year 1 = £300, the distribution for year 2 is:

0.10	£100
0.20	200
0.50	300
0.20	400

(a) If £200 is earned in year 1, what is the probability that the second year's earnings will be £200 or less?
(b) What is the probability that earnings for year 1 will be £100 and, for year 2, £200?
(c) What is the probability that the Parker Company will earn more than £300 on this project in the second year?
(d) If earnings for the first year are £300, what is the probability that £200 or more will be earned the second year?
(e) What is the probability that Parker will earn at least £600 over the life of the project?

Appendix C to Chapter 11:

Abandonment Value[1]

At some future time, usually because of some unforeseen problems, it may become more profitable to abandon a project, even though its economic life has not yet ended, than to continue its operation. Taking this possibility into consideration in the capital budgeting process may increase the project's expected net present value and reduce its standard deviation of returns. In this discussion we first show how to include *abandonment value* in the analysis when making accept – reject decisions, and then we look at criteria for actually abandoning a project after it has been accepted.

The analysis required for taking abandonment value into account in evaluating an investment project involves no principles beyond those already set forth. However, because it does represent an important aspect of the decision process, it is useful to have a decision model that includes abandonment value in its framework. The principles involved may best be conveyed through a specific example illustrating the role of abandonment value in evaluating projects under uncertainty.

Table 11C–1 *Expected Cash Flows.*

Year 1		Year 2	
Cash flow	Initial probability P(1)	Cash flow	Conditional probability P(2|1)
£200	(0.3)	£100	(0.3)
		200	(0.5)
		300	(0.2)
300	(0.4)	200	(0.3)
		300	(0.5)
		400	(0.2)
400	(0.3)	300	(0.3)
		400	(0.4)
		500	(0.3)

The Palmer Company has invested £300 in new machinery with expected cash flows over two years. This is shown in Table 11C–1. There are two sets of probabilities associated with the project: the initial probabilities should be interpreted as probabilities of particular cash flows from the first year only; the conditional probabilities are the probabilities of particular cash flows in the second year, given that a specific outcome has occurred in the first year. Thus, the results in the second year are *conditional* upon the results of the first year. If

1. For an early treatment of abandonment value, see Alexander A. Robichek and James C. Van Horne, Abandonment value and capital budgeting, *Journal of Finance* 22, No. 4 (December 1967), pp. 577–590.

Table 11C–2 *Calculation of Expected Net Present Value.*

Year 1			Year 2			Probability analysis				
Cash flow (1)	*PV* factor (2)	Present value (3) = (1 × 2)	Cash flow (4)	*PV* factor (5)	Present value (6) = (4 × 5)	Present value of total cash flow (7) = (3 + 6)	Initial probability (8)	Conditional probability (9)	Joint probability (10) = (8 × 9)	Expected value (11) = (7 × 10)
			£100	0.797	80	£259		0.3	0.09	£ 23
£200	0.893	179	200	0.797	159	338	0.3	0.5	0.15	51
			300	0.797	239	418		0.2	0.06	25
			200	0.797	159	427		0.3	0.12	51
300	0.893	268	300	0.797	239	507	0.4	0.5	0.20	101
			400	0.797	319	587		0.2	0.08	47
			300	0.797	239	596		0.3	0.09	54
400	0.893	357	400	0.797	319	676	0.3	0.4	0.12	81
			500	0.797	398	755		0.3	0.09	68
									1.00	£501

Expected net present value = £201
Expected present value = £501

high profits occur in the first year, chances are that the second year will also bring high profits. To obtain the probability that a particular first-year outcome and a particular second-year outcome will both occur, we must multiply the initial probability by the conditional probability to obtain what is termed the *joint probability*.

These concepts are applied to the data of Table 11C–1 to construct Table 11C–2. The project is not expected to have any returns after the second year. The firm's cost of capital is 12 per cent. To indicate the role of abandonment value, we first calculate the expected net present value of the investment and its expected standard deviation without considering abandonment value. This calculation is made in Table 11C–2, where we find the expected *NPV* to be £201.

Table 11C–3 *Calculation of Standard Deviation.*

NPV^a –	Exp. NPV =	Deviations	Squared deviations[a] ×	Joint probability =	Amount
(41)	201	(242)	58 564	0.09	5 271
38	201	(163)	26 569	0.15	3 985
118	201	(83)	6 889	0.06	413
127	201	(74)	5 476	0.12	657
207	201	6	36	0.20	7
286	201	85	7 225	0.08	578
296	201	95	9 025	0.09	812
375	201	174	30 276	0.12	3 633
455	201	254	64 516	0.09	5 806
				1.00	21 162

Expected standard deviation $= \sigma = (21\,162)^{1/2} = £145$

[a] Value from column 7, Table C11–2, minus £300 cost (some rounding differences).

Next, in Table 11C–3, we calculate the standard deviation of the future cash flows, finding $\sigma = £145$. The decision maker can expand this analysis to take abandonment value into account. Suppose the abandonment value of the project at the end of the first year is estimated to be £250. This is the amount that can be obtained by liquidating the project after the first year, and the £250 is independent of actual first-year results. If the project is abandoned after one year, then the £250 will replace any second-year returns. In other words, if the project is abandoned at the end of year 1, then year 1 returns will increase by £250 and year 2 returns will be nil. The present value of this estimated £250 abandonment value is, therefore, compared with the expected present values of the cash flows that would occur during the second year if abandonment did not take place. But to make the comparison valid, we must use the second year flows based on the conditional probabilities only, rather than the joint probabilities that were used in the preceding analysis. This calculation is shown in Table 11C–4.

We next compare the present value of the £250 abandonment value, £250 × 0.893 = £223, with the branch expected present values for each of the three possible cash flow patterns (branches) depicted above. If the £223 present value of abandonment exceeds one or more of the expected present values of the possible branches of

Table 11C–4 *Expected Present Values of Cash Flows during the Second Year.*

Cash flow	*PV* factor	*PV*	Conditional probability		Expected present value
£100	0.797	80	0.3		£ 24
200	0.797	159	0.5		80
300	0.797	239	0.2		48
				Branch total	£152
200	0.797	159	0.3		£ 48
300	0.797	239	0.5		120
400	0.797	319	0.2		64
				Branch total	£232
300	0.797	239	0.3		£ 72
400	0.797	319	0.4		128
500	0.797	398	0.3		119
				Branch total	£319

cash flows, taking abandonment value into account will improve the indicated returns from the project. This alternative calculation is presented in Table 11C–5 to show expected present values with abandonment taken into consideration, and the new calculation of the standard deviation is shown in Table 11C–6.

Table 11C–5 *Expected Net Present Value with Abandonment Value Included.*

Year 1 cash flow	×	*PV* Factor	=	*PV*	Year 2 cash flow	×	*PV* factor	=	*PV*	Present value of total cash flow	×	Joint proba-bility	=	Expected value
£450		0.893		£402	£ 0		0.797		£ 0	£402		0.30		£121
					200		0.797		159	427		0.12		51
300		0.893		268	300		0.797		239	507		0.20		101
					400		0.797		319	587		0.08		47
					300		0.797		239	596		0.09		54
400		0.893		357	400		0.797		319	676		0.12		81
					500		0.797		398	755		0.09		68
												1.00		

Expected present value = £523
Expected net present value = £223

Table 11C–6 *Calculation of Standard Deviation for Net Cash Flow with Abandonment Value Included.*

NPV_s –	Exp. NPV =	Deviation	Deviation^2 ×	Joint probability =	Amount
102	223	(121)	14 641	0.30	4 392
127	223	(96)	9 216	0.12	1 106
207	223	(16)	256	0.20	51
287	223	64	4 096	0.08	328
296	223	73	5 329	0.09	480
376	223	153	23 409	0.12	2 809
455	223	232	53 824	0.09	4 844
					14 010

Expected standard deviation = $(14\,010)^{1/2}$ = £118

We may now compare the results when abandonment value is taken into account with the results when it is not considered. Including abandonment value in the calculations increases the expected net present value from £201 to £223, or by about 10 per cent; and it reduces the expected standard deviation of returns from £145 to £118 and the coefficients of variation from 0.72 to 0.53. Thus, for this problem, abandonment value improves the attractiveness of the investment.

Abandonment value is important in another aspect of financial decision making: the re-evaluation of projects in succeeding years after they have been undertaken. The decision whether to continue the project or to abandon it sometime during its life depends upon which branch occurs during each time period. For example, suppose that during year 1 the cash flow actually obtained was £200. Then the three possibilities associated with year 2 are the three that were conditionally dependent upon a £200 outcome in year 1. The other six probabilities for year 2, which were considered in the initial evaluation, were conditional upon other first-year outcomes and, thus, are no longer relevant. A calculation (Table 11C–7) is then made of the second-year net cash flows, discounted back one year.

At the end of the first year the abandonment value is £250. This is compared with the expected present value of the second-year net cash flow series, discounted one year. This value is determined to be £171, so the abandonment value of £250 exceeds the net present value of returns for the second year. Therefore, the project should be abandoned at the end of the first year. Note that it is not necessary to compare the standard deviations, because with abandonment the standard deviation of returns is nil which is certainly lower than the standard deviation of any set of uncertain second-year cash flows.

In summary, it is sometimes advantageous to abandon a project even though the net present value of continued operation is positive. The basic reason is that the present value of abandonment after a shorter time may actually be greater than the present value of continued operation. For example, consider a truck with two years of remaining useful life. The present value of continued use is, say, £900, but the current market value of the truck is

Table 11C–7 *Calculation of Expected Net Cash Flow for Second Period when £200 was Earned during the First Year.*

Cash flow ×	*PV* factor =	*PV* ×	Probability factor	=	Discounted expected cash flow
£100	0.893	£ 89	0.3		£ 27
200	0.893	179	0.5		90
300	0.893	268	0.2		54
			Expected present value =		£171

£1000. Clearly, if the proceeds from the sale can be invested to earn at least the applicable cost of capital, the better decision would be to sell the truck.

FURTHER DEVELOPMENTS IN ABANDONMENT DECISION RULES[2]

The traditional abandonment decision rule is that the project should be abandoned in the first year that abandonment value exceeds the present value of remaining expected cash flows from continued operation. More recently it has become evident that this decision rule may not result in the optimal abandonment decision. Abandonment at a later date may result in an even greater net present value. Returning to our example of the truck, there is one option that has not been considered: that is, to operate the truck for another year with a present value of £500, and then abandon it, with the present value of abandonment in a year being £600. Thus, the present value of this alternative is £1100. The truck should be used for one year and then sold.

The optimal abandonment decision rule is to determine the combination of remaining operating cash flows and future abandonment that has the maximum expected net present value. This decision rule is, unfortunately, difficult to implement, especially when the project life is long and there are numerous opportunities for abandonment over time. If a piece of equipment can be used for 20 years or abandoned at the end of any year then 20 different net present value calculations would be required to determine the optimum pattern, resulting in maximum expected net present value.

It is argued that this approach is too cumbersome and that all that is required is to find that there is at least one pattern of cash flows that yields an expected net present value greater than the value of abandonment. Thus the rule becomes an accept – reject decision; continue to operate the project so long as expected present value of continued operation and abandonment at any later period is greater than the value of abandonment now. There is no need ever to determine the maximum expected net present value. Furthermore, since it is impossible to predict accurately future abandonment value, whatever the expected net present value is, it will surely be inaccurate.

The accept – reject decision has one shortcoming, however; it does not provide a means of selecting between mutually exclusive investments or of making capital rationing decisions. To return to our truck example a final time, we have shown that the present value is £1100, when the truck is operated for another year. Using the accept – reject rule we would continue to operate the truck. But suppose a truck could be leased for £1000 for one year and would produce cash flows worth £1200 at net present value. If only one truck is required (mutually exclusive choice decision) or the only source of the £1000 to lease the truck is the sale of the old truck (capital rationing) then the value to the firm is maximized if the truck is sold, and the new truck leased.

It is evident that both rules (the maximum net present value rule, and the accept – reject rule) have merit. Maximum net present value should be employed whenever capital rationing or mutually exclusive choices are involved. Accept – reject can be used to reduce the cumbersomeness of the problem whenever one decision is independent of all others. (Problem 11C–3 provides an opportunity to explore both of these approaches.)

PROBLEMS

* 11C–1. In its first year of operation at Delta Steel Company a new electric furnace employed in the scrap steel division produced a savings of £400 a month over the basic oxygen furnace. The scrap steel division at Delta Steel is quite old and inefficient. Before the new electric furnace was installed, management

2. See E. A. Dyl and H. W. Long, Abandonment value and capital budgeting: Comment, *Journal of Finance* (March 1969), pp. 88–95; Reply by A. A. Robichek and J. C. Van Horne, pp. 96–97; O. Maurice Joy, Abandonment values and abandonment decisions: a clarification, *Journal of Finance* (September 1976), pp. 1225–1228.

estimated that the company could save £4980 a year if the scrap-melting division was eliminated. Management must decide what action to take for the second year. The new furnace has no scrap value. The required rate of return for the firm is 6 per cent.

(a) If the savings in the second year are equal to those obtained in the first year, should the scrap division be abandoned?

(b) What decision would be reached if the cost analysis of savings per month with the electric furnace for the second year is:

Probability	Amount
0.05	£200
0.15	300
0.50	400
0.20	500
0.10	600

11C–2. A firm has invested £4000 in automated machinery with the probable net cash flows over two years as follows:

Year 1		Year 2	
Net cash flow	Initial probability P(1)	Net cash flow	Conditional probability P(2/1)
		£2500	(0.3)
£3000	(0.3)	3000	(0.5)
		3500	(0.2)
		£3000	(0.3)
£4000	(0.4)	4000	(0.5)
		5000	(0.2)
		£4000	(0.3)
£5000	(0.3)	5000	(0.4)
		6000	(0.3)

The firm's cost of capital is 12 per cent.

(a) Calculate the expected net present value of the investment and standard deviation without considering abandonment value.

(b) If the abandonment value at the end of year 1 is £2800, calculate the new expected net present value and standard deviation of the project.

(c) During period 1, the cash flow actually experienced was £3000. Should the project now be abandoned or should it be continued through period 2?

11C–3. The following investment decision is being considered by Citrus Farms. For £7000 the company can acquire ownership of 10 acres of 15-year-old orange trees and a 15-year lease on the land. The productive life of an orange tree is divided into stages as follows:

Stage	Age of trees	Expected annual profit from 10 acres
Peak	16–20 years	£1000
Adult	21–25 years	900
Mature	26–30 years	800

There is a market for decorative orange trees. Suppliers will buy trees and remove them according to a schedule based on age of the tree. Expected prices that could be obtained for the 10 acre-total are: £9000 at end of age 20, £12 000 at age 25, and £8000 at age 30.

(a) Citrus Farms has a 10 per cent cost of capital. What is the present value of each alternative? Since the land and anything on it will belong to the lessor in 15 years, assume that once the trees are harvested the land will not be replanted by Citrus.

(b) As an alternative to this investment, Citrus can use the £7000 to buy a new orange sorting machine. The machine would reduce sorting expense by £1300 a year for 15 years. Which investment would you make? Why? Assume all other investment opportunities for the next 15 years will earn the cost of capital.

(c) In the tenth year you discover that everyone else with 25-year-old trees has sold them. As a consequence, the price you can get for your trees is only £8000. Since so many trees have been sold for decoration, small orange crops are expected for the next five years. As a result, the price will be higher. Your acreage will yield £1200 a year. The selling price of your trees in another five years is expected to be still depressed to £6000. What should you do?

(d) What was the net present value of your actual investment over the 15-year period given the developments in part (c)?

(e) What would have been the outcome if you had sold the trees in year 10 for £8000?

Appendix D to Chapter 11:

Some Implications of Portfolio Theory; The Capital Asset Pricing Model

EFFECTS OF DIVERSIFICATION: SOME ILLUSTRATIONS WITH A TWO-ASSET PORTFOLIO

The concepts of portfolio diversification discussed in Chapter 11 are here further clarified by some additional illustrations. Assume that two investment securities, A and B, are available, and that we have a specific amount of money to invest in these securities. We can allocate our funds between the securities in any proportion. Security A has an expected rate of return $E(k_A) = 5$ per cent and a standard deviation of expected returns $\sigma_A = 4$ per cent; for security B, the expected return $E(k_B) = 8$ per cent and the standard deviation $\sigma_B = 10$ per cent.

Our ultimate task is to determine the optimal portfolio, that is, the optimal percentage of our available funds to invest in each security. Intermediate steps include (a) determining the attainable set of portfolios, (b) determining the efficient set from among the attainable set, and (c) selecting the best portfolio from the efficient set.

There is not yet sufficient information to select the best portfolio – we need data on the degree of correlation between the two securities' returns, ρ_{AB}, in order to construct the attainable and efficient portfolios. Let us assume three different degrees of correlation: $\rho_{AB} = +1.0$, $\rho_{AB} = 0$, and $\rho_{AB} = -1.0$, and then develop the portfolios' expected returns $E(k_P)$ and standard deviations of returns σ_P for each case.

To calculate $E(k_P)$ and σ_P, we use equations 11D–1 and 11D–2:

$$E(k_P) = w\,E(k_A) + (1-w)\,E(k_B), \tag{11D–1}$$

and

$$\sigma_p = \sqrt{w^2\sigma_A{}^2 + (1-w)^2\sigma_B{}^2 + 2w(1-w)\rho_{AB}\sigma_A\sigma_B}. \tag{11D–2}$$

We may now substitute in the given values for k_A and k_B, then solve equation 11D–1 for $E(k_P)$ at different values of w. For example, when w equals 0.75, then

$$E(k_P) = 0.75\ (5\%) + 0.25\ (8\%) = 5.75\%.$$

Similarly, we can substitute in the given values for σ_A, σ_B, and ρ_{AB}, then solve equation 11D–2 for σ_P at different values of w. For example, when $\rho_{AB} = 0$ and $w = 75$ per cent, then

$$\sigma_P = \sqrt{(0.5625)(16) + (0.0625)(100) + 2(0.75)(0.25)(0)(4)(10)}$$
$$= \sqrt{9 + 6.25} = \sqrt{15.25} = 3.9\%.$$

The equations can be solved for other values for w and for the three cases, $\rho_{AB} = +1.0$, 0, and -1.0; Table 11D–1 gives the solution values for $w = 100$ per cent, 75 per cent, 50 per cent, 25 per cent, and 0 per cent, and Figure 11D–1 gives plots of $E(k_P)$, σ_P, and the attainable set of portfolios for each case. In both the table and the graphs, note the following points:

Table 11D–1 $E(k_p)$ *and* σ_p *under Various Assumptions.*

Percentage of portfolio in security A (value of w)	Percentage of portfolio in security B (value of $1-w$)	$\rho_{AB} = +1.0$		$\rho_{AB} = 0$		$\rho_{AB} = -1.0$	
		$E(k_p)$	σ_p	$E(k_p)$	σ_p	$E(k_p)$	σ_p
100	0	5.00	4.0	5.00	4.0	5.00	4.0
75	25	5.75	5.5	5.75	3.9	5.75	0.5
50	50	6.50	7.0	6.50	5.1	6.50	3.0
25	75	7.25	8.5	7.25	7.6	7.25	6.5
0	100	8.00	10.0	8.00	10.0	8.00	10.0

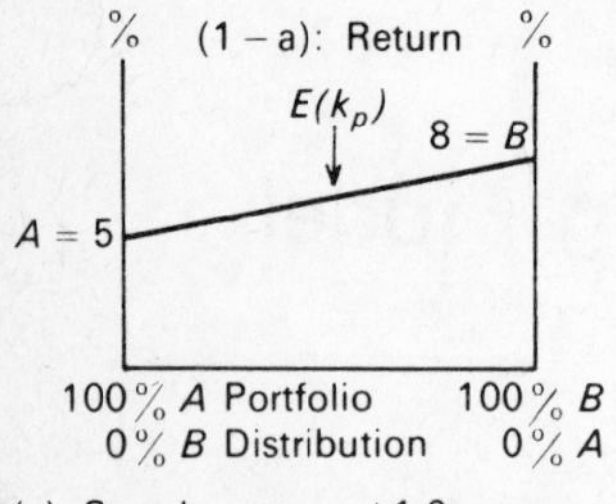

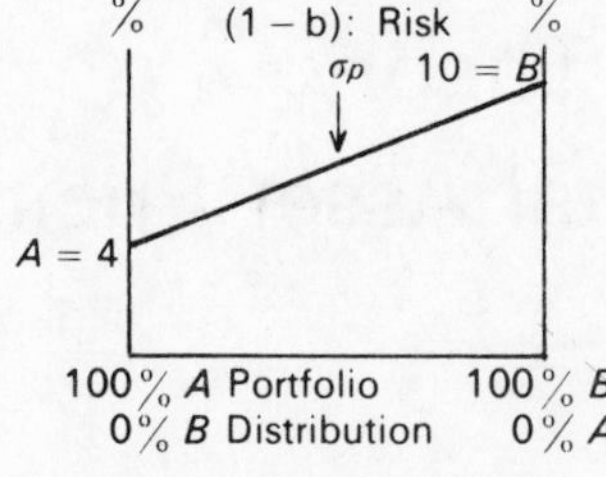

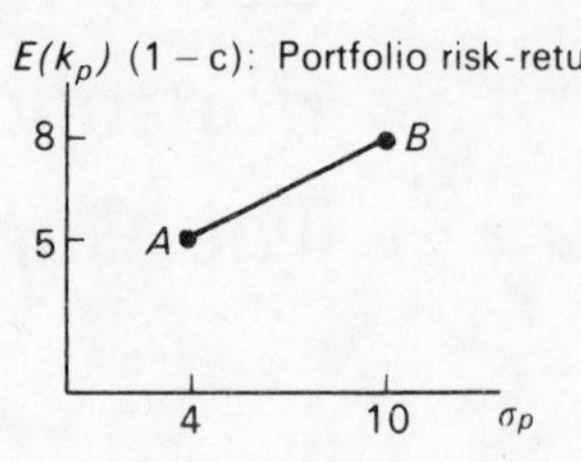

(a) Case I: $\rho_{AB} = +1.0$

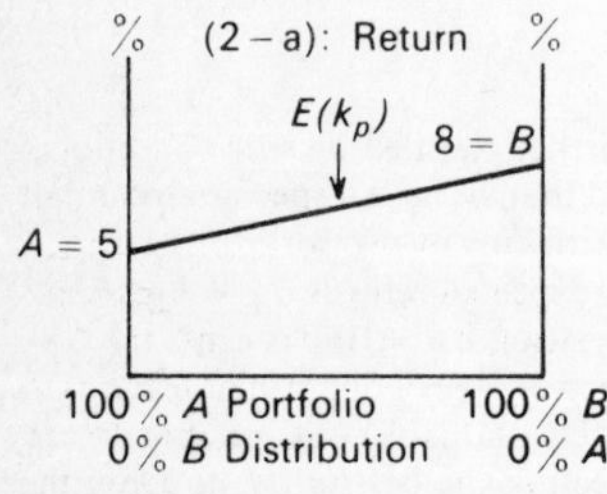

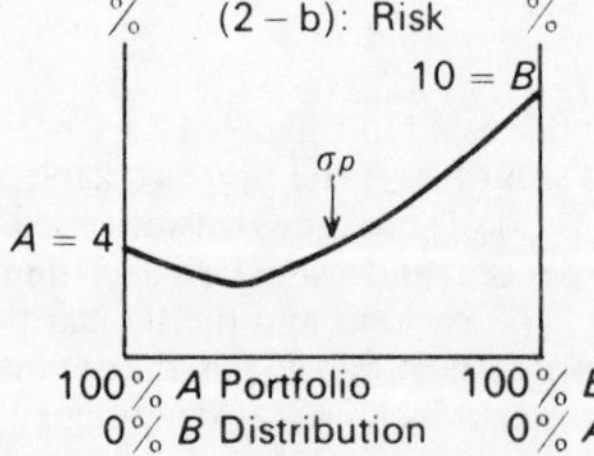

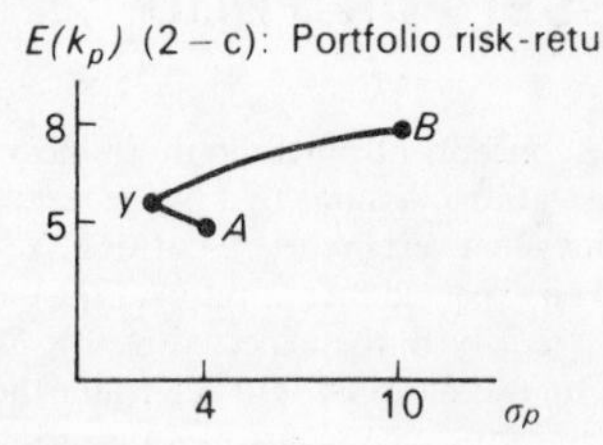

(b) Case II: $\rho_{AB} = 0$

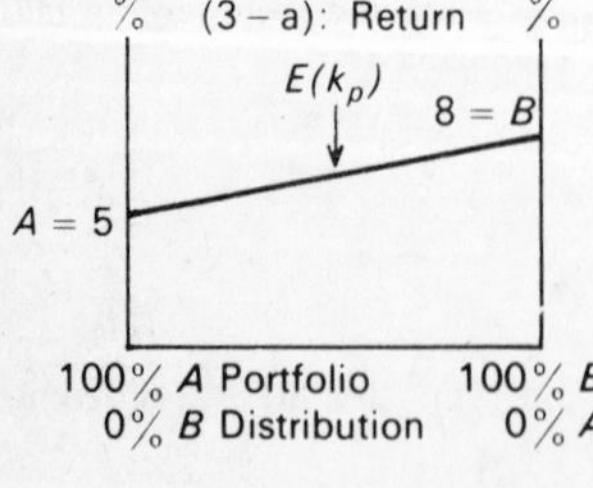

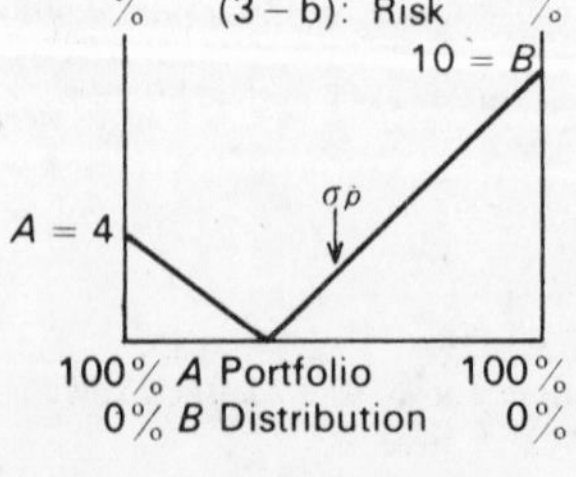

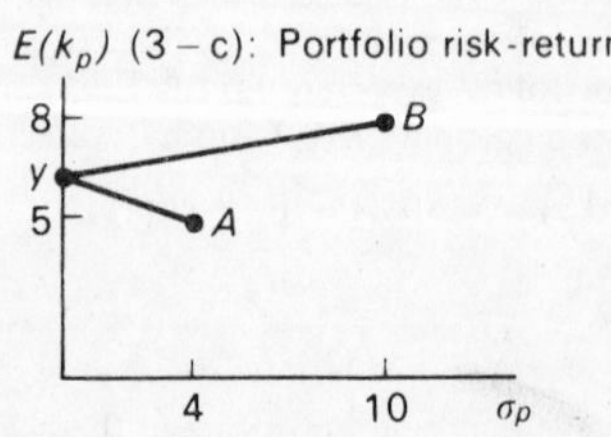

(c) Case III: $_{AB} = -1.0$

Figure 11D–1 *Illustrations of Portfolio Returns, Risk, and the Attainable Set of Portfolios.*

1. $E(k_P)$ is a linear function of w; and the graphs of $E(k_P)$ are identical in the three cases because $E(k_P)$ is independent of the correlation between securities A and B.
2. σ_P is linear in case I, where $\rho_{AB} = +1.0$; it is non-linear in case II; and case III of the figure shows that risk can be completely diversified away when $\rho_{AB} = -1.0$.[1]
3. Panels (1-c), (2-c), and (3-c) give the attainable set of portfolios consisting of securities A and B. With only two

1. The minimum points for Figure 11D–1(b) were found by using equation 11–6 in the chapter.

securities, the attainable set is a curve or line rather than an area. If more securities were added, then the shaded area shown in Figure 11–8 would develop.

4. That part of the attainable set from Y to B in cases II and III is efficient; that part from A to Y is inefficient. In case I, all parts of the attainable set are efficient.

Figure 11D–2 consolidates the attainable sets for the three cases to facilitate comparison. The most interesting aspect of the graph is the clear demonstration that the lower the value of ρ_{AB}, the better the portfolios that can be constructed. For any specified rate of return as shown on the horizontal axis, σ_p is lowest for $\rho_{AB} = -1$, and highest for $\rho_{AB} = +1$, while the rate of return that can be achieved at any specified degree of risk is highest for $\rho_{AB} = -1$, and lowest for $\rho_{AB} = +1$ (except for the point B at which all the curves converge, since the total investment is 100 per cent in B).

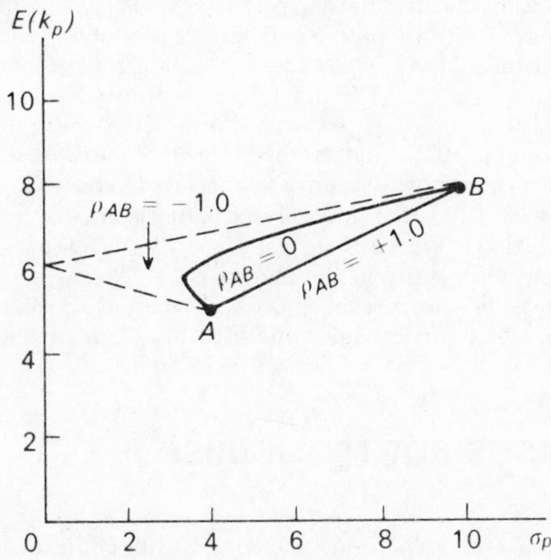

Figure 11D–2 *Attainable Sets of Portfolios for the Three Cases.*

Obviously, only one correlation coefficient can exist between securities A and B; assume that the actual ρ_{AB} is 0. It now remains to select the best portfolio (that is, the percentage of the total funds to be invested in each security). This decision depends upon the individual investor's risk aversion as represented by his risk-return indifference curves. In Figure 11D–3 we show the attainable set of portfolios for $\rho_{AB} = 0$ from Figure 11D–2 and

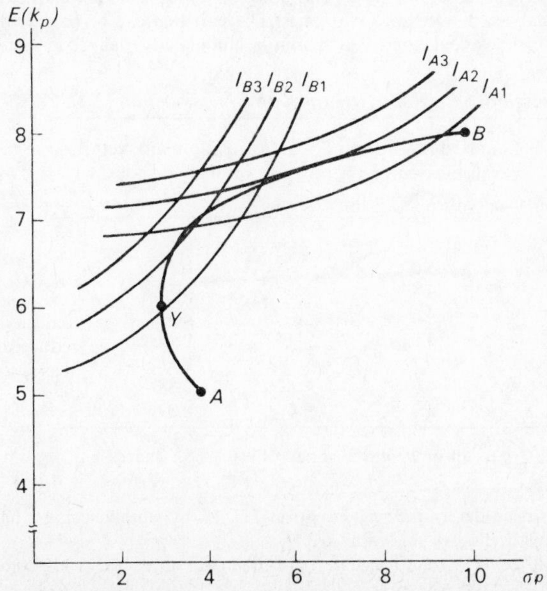

Figure 11D–3 *Selecting the Optimal Portfolio.*

the indifference curves for Mr A and Mr B taken from Figure 11–11 in Chapter 11. Given these possibilities, Mr A would choose a portfolio providing an expected rate of return of 7.2 per cent with $\sigma_p = 7.3$, while Mr B would choose a portfolio with $E(k_p) = 6.2$ and $\sigma_p = 4.2$. Mr A's portfolio would consist of 60 per cent security A and 40 per cent security B, while Mr B's portfolio would contain 27 per cent security A and 73 per cent security B.[2]

RELATIONSHIP BETWEEN CORRELATION AND EXPECTED RATES OF RETURN

If a security or other asset has returns that are less than perfectly correlated with the returns on other assets, then combining this new asset with other assets will produce favourable portfolio effects. Further, the lower the degree of correlation, the larger the portfolio effects. Now suppose you hold a portfolio of securities with an expected return $E(k_p) = 8$ per cent and $\sigma_p = 6$ per cent. You hear of a new security Z that has an expected return of 8 per cent, $\sigma_z = 6$ per cent, and the correlation of Z's returns with those on your present portfolio is -0.5.

If you sell off part of your present portfolio and use the proceeds to purchase security Z, your expected rate of return will remain at 8 per cent, but your portfolio's risk will decline, so you would make this shift. If others have favourable portfolio effects from security Z, they too will seek to buy it, and the collective action will tend to drive Z's price up and its expected yield down. We see, then, that a security's degree of correlation with other securities influences the rate of return on the security in the market-place. This aspect of portfolio theory is vitally important in analysing the riskiness of a firm's securities, hence its cost of capital. Accordingly, we shall return to portfolio theory in Chapter 19, where it is extended and used to obtain an index of a firm's risk.

SECURITY RISK VERSUS PORTFOLIO RISK

An empirical study by Wagner and Lau can be used to demonstrate the effects of diversification.[3] They divided a sample of 200 NYSE shares into six subgroups based on the Standard and Poor's quality ratings as of June 1960. Then they constructed portfolios from each of the subgroups, using 1 to 20 randomly selected securities and applying equal weights to each security. For the first subgroup (A + quality shares), Table 11D–2 can be used to summarize some effects of diversification. As the number of securities in the portfolio increases, the standard deviation of portfolio returns decreases, but at a decreasing rate, with further reductions in risk being relatively small after about 10 securities are included in the portfolio. More will be said about the third column of the table, correlation with the market, shortly.

These data indicate that even well-diversified portfolios possess some level of risk that cannot be diversified away. Indeed, this is exactly the case, and the general situation is illustrated graphically in Figure 11D–4. The risk of the portfolio, σ_p, has been divided into two parts. The part that can be reduced through diversification is defined as *unsystematic* risk, while the part that cannot be eliminated is defined as *systematic*, or market-related, risk.[4]

Table 11D–2 *Reduction in Portfolio Risk through Diversification.*

No. of securities in portfolio	Standard deviation of portfolio returns (σ_p) (% per month)	Correlation with return on market index[a]
1	7.0	0.54
2	5.0	0.63
3	4.8	0.75
4	4.6	0.77
5	4.6	0.79
10	4.2	0.85
15	4.0	0.88
20	3.9	0.89

[a] The 'market' here refers to an unweighted index of all *NYSE* shares.

2. These percentages can be determined by equation 11D–1, by simply seeing what percentage of the two securities is consistent with $E(k_p) = 7.2\%$ and 6.2%.
3. W. H. Wagner and S. C. Lau, The effect of diversification on risk, *Financial Analysts' Journal* (November–December 1971), pp. 48–53.
4. In the real world, it is extremely difficult to find stocks with nil or negative correlations; hence, some risk is inherent in any stock portfolio.

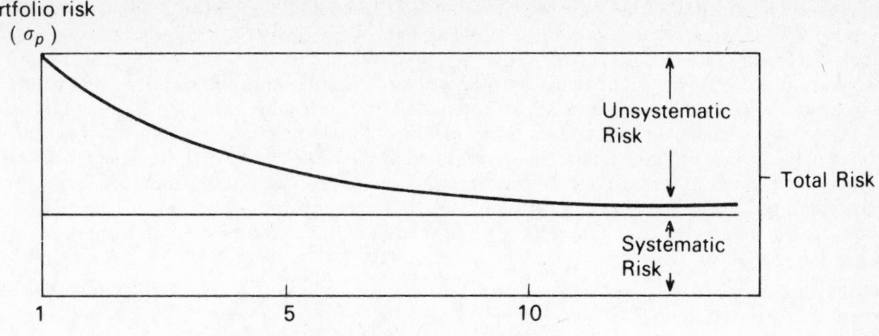

Figure 11D–4 *Reduction of Risk through Diversification.*

Now refer back to the third column of Table11D–2. Notice that as the number of securities in each portfolio increases, and as the standard deviation decreases, the correlation between the return on the portfolio and the return on the market index increases. Thus, a broadly diversified portfolio is highly correlated with the market, and its risk (a) is largely systematic and (b) arises because of general market movements.

We can summarize our analysis of risk to this point as follows:

1. The risk of a portfolio can be measured by the standard deviation of its rate of return, σ_p.
2. The risk of an individual security is its contribution to the portfolio's risk.
3. The standard deviation of a security's return, σ_i, is the relevant measure of risk for an undiversified investor who holds only security *j*.
4. A security's standard deviation reflects both unsystematic risk that can be eliminated by diversification and systematic or market-related risk; only the systematic component of security risk is relevant for the well-diversified investor, so only this element is reflected in the risk premium.
5. A security's systematic risk is measured by its volatility in relation to the general market. This factor is analysed next.

EFFICIENT VERSUS INEFFICIENT PORTFOLIOS

Professor Sharpe derived the following relationship between total risk and its components, unsystematic (diversifiable) and systematic risk:[5]

$$(\sigma_j^2) = (\sigma_j^s)^2 + (\sigma_j^u)^2 \tag{11D–3}$$

where σ_j = standard deviation of k_j
σ_j^s = security *j*'s systematic risk ($= b_j\sigma_M$)
σ_j^u = security *j*'s unsystematic risk.

These relationships apply to portfolios as well:

$$(\sigma_p)^2 = (\sigma_p^s)^2 + (\sigma_p^u)^2 \tag{11D–4}$$

where σ_p = standard deviation of rate of return on portfolio
σ_p^s = portfolio's systematic risk
σ_p^u = portfolio's unsystematic risk.

The relationship between systematic risk and volatility is the same for securities and portfolios. Thus,

$$\sigma_p^s = b_p\sigma_M \tag{11D–5}$$

Efficient portfolios have no unsystematic risk. Thus a portfolio with some unsystematic risk that has not been diversified away is inefficient. Individual securities are likely to include some unsystematic risk so they are inefficient portfolios.

Equation 11D–3 divides the variance of security j's return into two parts, (a) the systematic risk component, $(\sigma^s)^2$, which is $(b_j\sigma_M)^2$ – its beta coefficient and the variability of market returns, and (b) the unsystematic residual risk component, $(\sigma_j^u)^2$. The unsystematic component can be eliminated through diversification, but the systematic component can be reduced only by altering the firm's correlation with the 'market', that is, by attempting to change its beta coefficient through a change in investment or financial policy.

The logical conclusion of all this is that if investors think in portfolio terms then they should not worry about

---

5. William F. Sharpe, *Portfolio Theory and Capital Markets* (New York: McGraw-Hill, 1970), pp. 96–97.

the unsystematic risk because it can be diversified away. Thus, investors should consider only systematic risk, in equation 11D–3. Since the variance of the market is given, the determinant of relative riskiness among securities is the beta coefficient.

This type of analysis provides the foundations for the development of the capital asset pricing model (CAPM) summarized in the chapter. In this appendix we shall now set forth other aspects of the capital asset pricing model. The riskiness of a portfolio of assets as measured by its standard deviation of returns is generally less than the average of the risks of the individual assets as measured by their standard deviations. Since investors generally hold portfolios of securities, not just one security, it is reasonable to consider the riskiness of a security in terms of its contribution to the riskiness of the portfolio rather than in terms of its riskiness if held in isolation. *The significant contribution of the capital asset pricing model (CAPM) is that it provides a measure of the risk of a security in the portfolio sense.*

BASIC ASSUMPTIONS OF THE CAPM

Like all financial theories, several assumptions were made in the development of the CAPM; these were summarized by Jensen (1972, *Bell Journal*) as follows:

1. All investors are single-period expected utility of terminal wealth maximizers who choose among alternative portfolios on the basis of mean and variance (or standard deviation) of returns.
2. All investors can borrow or lend an unlimited amount at an exogenously given risk-free rate of interest, R_F, and there are no restrictions on short sales of any asset.
3. All investors have identical subjective estimates of the means, variances, and covariances of return among all assets, i.e., investors have homogeneous expectations.
4. All assets are perfectly divisible, perfectly liquid (that is, marketable at the going price), and there are no transactions costs.
5. There are no taxes.
6. All investors are price takers.
7. The quantities of all assets are given.

While these assumptions may appear to be severely limiting, they are similar to those made in the standard economic theory of the firm and in the basic models of Modigliani-Miller, Gordon, and others. Further, theoretical extensions in the literature that seek to relax the basic CAPM assumptions yield results that are generally consistent with the basic theory. Finally, the CAPM has been used in several rate cases and civil court cases in the USA, where its advocates have stood up quite well under intense and expert cross-examination.

THE TRADE-OFF BETWEEN RISK AND RETURN

Since investors as a group are averse to risk, the higher the risk of a security, the higher its required rate of return. Figure 11D–5 illustrates this concept. Here, the required rate of return is plotted on the vertical axis, and risk is shown on the horizontal axis. The line showing the relationship between risk and rate of return is defined as the *security market line* (SML). The intercept of the security market line, R_F, is the riskless rate of return, generally taken as the return on government stocks. Riskless securities have beta coefficients equal to nil; since returns on riskless securities are fixed and constant, they do not move at all with changes in the market. An 'average' security has a beta of 1.0, and such a security has a required rate of return, k_M, equal to the market average return. A relatively low-risk security might have a beta of 0.6 and a required rate of return equal to k_L, while a relatively high-risk security might have a beta of 1.4 and a required return equal to k_H.

Betas of portfolios

It should be noted that a portfolio made up of low beta securities will itself have a low beta, as the beta of any set of securities is a weighted average of the individual securities:

$$\beta_P = \sum_{i=1}^{n} w_i \beta_j. \qquad (11D\text{–}6)$$

Here β_P is the beta of the portfolio, which reflects how volatile the portfolio is in relation to the market index; w_i is the percentage of the portfolio invested in the ith security; and β_j is the beta coefficient of the jth security.

The beta coefficient of insurance companies' pension funds, and other large portfolios are presently being calculated and used to judge the riskiness of these portfolios, and funds are actually being constructed to provide investors with specified degrees of riskiness. It is too early to judge how well betas will work as a measure of long-

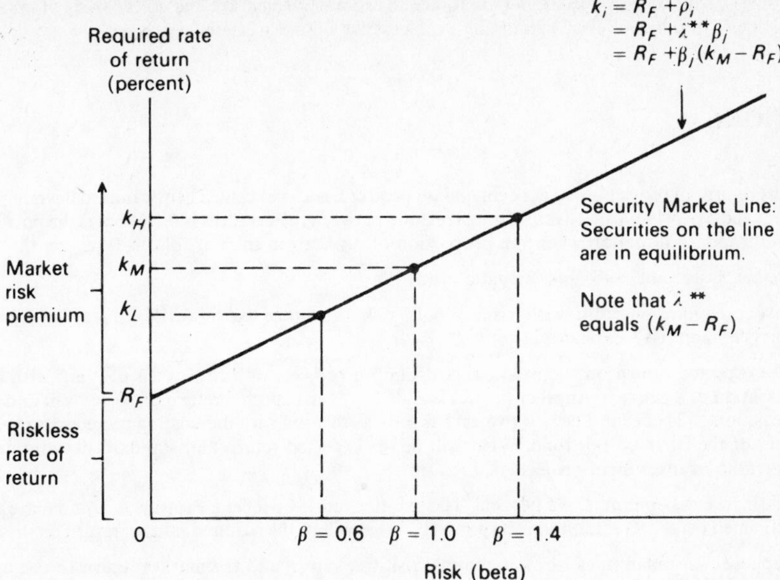

Figure 11D–5 *The Trade-off between Risk and Return: the Security Market Line (SML).*

term risk, but the financial community is actually using these concepts in security selection and portfolio construction.

COST OF CAPITAL DYNAMICS

The expected return on any security i is equal to the riskless rate of return plus a risk premium: $k_j = R_F + \rho_j$. Since the risk premium for the entire market is equal to $(k_M - R_F)$, we can develop the following equation for any individual security j:[6]

$$\bar{k}_j = R_F + \beta_j(\bar{k}_M - R_F). \qquad (11D\text{–}7)$$

Stated in words, the expected return on any security is equal to the sum of the riskless rate of return plus the product of the security's beta coefficient times the risk premium on the market as a whole. If beta is less than 1.0, then the security has a smaller than average risk premium, while if beta is larger than 1.0, the converse holds.

Interest rates change over time, and when they do, the change in R_F is reflected in the cost of equity both for the 'average' security k_M, and for any individual security, k_i. Such changes cause the capital market line in Figure 11D–5 to shift. The intercept term, R_F, goes up or down, while the slope of the line could increase, decrease, or remain constant.[7]

Risk premiums, which are reflected in the slope of the security market line, may also change over time. When investors are pessimistic and worried, the market line of Figure 11D–5 will tend to be steep, implying a high 'price of risk', whereas when investors are less risk averse, the price of risk declines and the market line is less steeply inclined.

Several careful studies confirm that rates of return rise with risk. However, the empirical tests do not show neat, stable relationships; rather, depending on the test period analysed and the methodology used, many security market lines could be generated. This instability is to be expected for two reasons: first, we would expect the market line to change over time as both interest rates and investors' outlooks change, so a stable market line over

---

6. Equation 11D–7 is developed as follows: first, the risk premium is a linear function of the security's beta coefficient – that is, $\rho_j = \lambda^{**}\beta_j$. Accordingly, $\bar{k}_j = R_F + \lambda^{**}\beta_j$. By definition, the market as a whole has a beta of 1.0 – the average security must move in proportion to the market and if this is so, then beta is 1.0. Therefore, this average or market risk premium must be equal to λ^{**} – that is, $\lambda^{**} = \rho_M$. Thus, $\bar{k}_j = R_F + \beta_j\rho_M$. But the market risk premium is equal to $(\bar{k}_M - R_F)$, so for any security we have the following equation:

$$k_j = R_F + \beta_j(\bar{k}_M - R_F)_j.$$

7. R. H. Litzenberger and A. P. Budd, Secular trends in risk premiums, *Journal of Finance* (September 1972), pp. 857–864.

time would be strange indeed. Second, we are forced to estimate the market line on the basis of imperfect data, and where errors in the data exist, estimating problems are bound to arise.[8]

QUESTIONS

11D–1. The return on project j is 80 per cent and on project k is 20 per cent. Their standard deviations are 2 per cent and 5 per cent respectively. The correlation between their returns is 0.1. What is the portfolio return and standard deviation when the proportion of project j in the portfolio is 0 per cent?

11D–2. Define 'systematic' and 'unsystematic' risk.

11D–3. Risk premiums increase with risk. Would risk premiums be more dependent on systematic or unsystematic risk? Explain.

11D–4. The expected return on the existing 'portfolio' of projects of a firm is 12 per cent with a standard deviation of 8 per cent. Another project is added with an expected return of 10 per cent and a standard deviation of 2 per cent. The new project has zero correlation with the existing projects and will be 10 per cent of the enlarged portfolio. What will be the expected return and standard deviation of the new portfolio of investment projects of the firm?

11D–5. The market risk premium is 5 per cent. The risk-free rate is 6 per cent. Projects A, B and C are added with estimated betas of 0.8, 1.2, and 2, respectively. What will be the required rates of return on these projects?

11D–6. Suppose that inflation causes the nominal risk-free return and the market return to rise by an equal amount. Will the market risk premium be affected?

PROBLEMS

11D–1. An investor plans to invest in security A, security B, or some combination of the two securities. The expected return for A is 9 per cent and $\sigma_A = 4$ per cent; the expected return for B is 10 per cent and $\sigma_B = 5$ per cent; $\rho_{AB} = 0.5$:
(a) Construct a table similar to Table 11D–1 giving $E(k_P)$ and σ_P for 100 per cent, 75 per cent, 50 per cent, 25 per cent, and 0 per cent investment in stock A.
(b) Use your calculated $E(k_P)$ and σ_P values to graph the attainable set of portfolios, and indicate which part of the attainable set is efficient.
(c) Using hypothetical indifference curves, show how an investor might choose a portfolio consisting of stocks A and B.

11D–2. You are planning to invest £100 000. Two securities, *i* and *j*, are available, and you can invest in either of them or in a portfolio with some of each. You estimate that the following probability distributions of returns are applicable:

Security *i*		Security *j*	
0.1	− 5 %	0.1	0 %
0.2	0	0.2	5
0.4	11.25	0.4	8.75
0.2	15	0.2	10
0.1	20	0.1	15

The expected returns are 9 per cent and 8 per cent for *i* and *j*, respectively; i.e., $E(k_i) = 9$ per cent and $E(k_j) = 8$ per cent. $\sigma_i = 7.56$ per cent and $\sigma_j = 3.75$ per cent.
(a) Assume $\rho_{ij} = -0.5$. What percentage of your portfolio should be invested in each security in order to minimize your investment risk?
(b) Calculate σ_P and $E(k_P)$ for portfolios consisting of 100 per cent *i* and 0 per cent *j*; 100 per cent *j* and 0 per cent *i*; and the minimum risk portfolio as calculated in (a). (Hint: Notice that some of these data are given above.)
(c) Graph the *feasible* set of portfolios, and identify the *efficient* section of the feasible set.

8. However, these problems are probably less severe in the capital asset pricing model than are the problems encountered using alternative approaches.

(d) Suppose your risk-return trade-off function, or indifference curve, is a linear family of lines with a slope of 0.15. Use this information, plus the graph constructed in (c), to locate (approximately) your optimal portfolio. Give the percentage of your funds invested in each security, and the optimal portfolio's σ_P and $E(k_P)$. [Hint: estimate σ_P and $E(k_P)$ graphically, then use the equation for $E(k_P)$ to determine w.]

(e) What is the probability that your optimal portfolio will, in fact, yield less than 4.15 per cent?

(f) Demonstrate *why* a graph of the efficient set such as the one you constructed in (c) above is always linear if portfolios are formed between a riskless security (a bond) and a risky asset (shares perhaps a portfolio of shares).

11D–3. You are planning to invest £200 000. Two securities, C and D, are available, and you can invest in either of them or in a portfolio with some of each. You estimate that the following probability distributions of returns are applicable:

Security C		Security D	
0.2	− 4	0.2	2
0.3	0	0.3	4
0.3	12	0.3	8
0.2	26	0.2	10

The expected returns are 8 per cent and 6 per cent for up–down and down–up, respectively; i.e., $E(k_C) = 8$ per cent and $E(k_D) = 6$ per cent. $\sigma_C = 10.84$ per cent and $\sigma_D = 2.97$ per cent.

(a) Assume $\rho_{CD} = 0.5$. What percentage of your portfolio should be invested in each security in order to minimize your investment risk?

(b) Calculate σ_P and $E(k_P)$ for portfolios consisting of 100 per cent C and 0 per cent D; 100 per cent D and 0 per cent C; and the minimum risk portfolio as calculated in (a). (Hint: notice that some of these data are given above.)

(c) Graph the *feasible* set of portfolios, and identify the *efficient* section of the feasible set.

(d) Suppose your risk-return trade-off function, or indifference curve is a linear family of lines with a slope of 0.25. Use this information, plus the graph constructed in (c), to locate (approximately) your optimal portfolio. Give the percentage of your funds invested in each security, and the optimal portfolio's σ_P and $E(k_P)$. [Hint: estimate σ_P and $E(k_P)$ graphically, then use the equation for $E(k_P)$ to determine w.]

(e) What is the probability that your optimal portfolio will, in fact, yield less than 1.15 per cent?

(f) Demonstrate *why* a graph of the efficient set such as the one you constructed in (c) above is always linear if portfolios are formed between a riskless security (a bond) and a risky asset (shares or perhaps a portfolio of shares).

SELECTED REFERENCES

Blume, Marshall E. Betas and their regression tendencies. *Journal of Finance* 30 (June 1975): 785–795.

Hagerman, Robert L. and Kim, E. Han. Capital asset pricing with price level changes. *Journal of Financial and Quantitative Analysis* 11 (September 1976): 381–392.

Hakansson, Nils H. and Miller, Bruce L. Compound-return mean-variance efficient portfolios never risk ruin. *Management Science* 22 (December 1975): 391–400.

Mayers, David. Nonmarketable assets, market segmentation, and the level of asset prices. *Journal of Financial and Quantitative Analysis* 11 (March 1976): 1–12.

Modigliani, Franco and Pogue, Gerald A. An introduction to risk and return. *Financial Analysts' Journal* 30 (March–April 1974): 68–80; (May–June 1974): 69–86.

Robichek, Alexander A. and Cohn, Richard A. The economic determinants of systematic risk. *Journal of Finance* 29 (May 1974): 439–447.

Thompson, Donald J. II. Sources of systematic risk in common stocks. *Journal of Business* 49 (April 1976): 173–188.

Appendix E to Chapter 11:

Certainty Equivalent Adjustments

Subjective certainty equivalent adjustments

In Chapter 11 we used the capital asset pricing model to show the precise relationship between a risk adjusted discount factor and a certainty equivalent discount factor. Because the parameters of the real world may be changing over time, some decision makers employ subjective risk adjustment factors similar to the procedures described in this section.

The *certainty equivalent* method follows directly from the concepts of utility theory presented in Chapter 11. Under the subjective certainty equivalent approach, the decision-maker must specify how much money is required with certainty to make him or her indifferent between this certain sum and the expected value of a risky sum. To illustrate, suppose a rich eccentric offered you the following two choices.

1. Flip a fair coin. If a head comes up, you receive £1 million, but if a tail comes up you get nothing. The expected value of the gamble is £500 000 (= 0.5 × £1 000 000 + 0.5 × 0).
2. You do not flip a coin; you simply pocket £300 000 cash.

If you find yourself indifferent between the two alternatives, then £300 000 is your certainty equivalent for the risky £500 000 expected return. In other words, the certain or riskless amount provides exactly the same utility as the risky alternative. Any certainty equivalent less than £500 000 indicates risk aversion.

The certainty equivalent concept is illustrated in Figure 11E–1. The curve shows a series of risk-return combinations to which the decision maker is indifferent. For example, point A represents an investment with a perceived degree of risk as measured by its beta value, β_A, and with an expected money return of £2000. The individual whose risk-return trade-off function, or indifference curve, is shown here is indifferent between a sure £1000, an expected £2000 with risk β_A, and an expected £3000 with risk β_B.

Given the risk-return indifference curve of investors in general, the firm could adjust the *NPV* equation as follows:

1. Substitute R_F for k in the denominator of the equation

$$NPV = \sum_{t=1}^{n} \frac{F_t}{(1+R_F)^t} - I,$$

where R_F is the discount rate applicable for riskless investments such as United States government bonds.

2. Divide the certainty equivalent of a risky return by the risky return to obtain a *certainty equivalent adjustment factor*;

$$\phi_A = \frac{\text{certain return}}{\text{risky return}} = \frac{£1000}{£2000} = 0.50 \text{ for } \beta_A$$

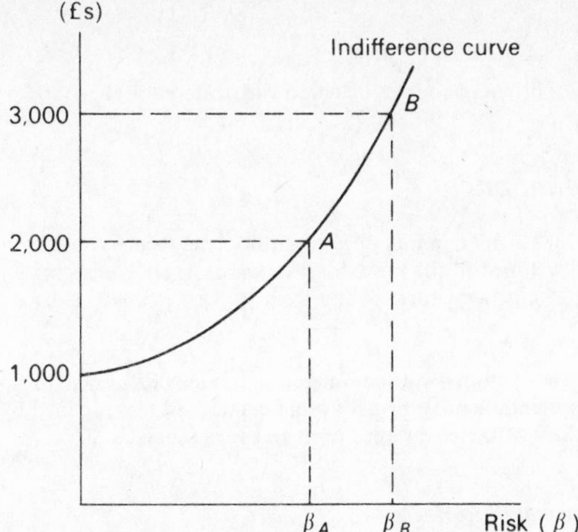

Figure 11E–1 *Certainty Equivalent Returns.*

and

$$\phi_B = \frac{£1000}{£3000} = 0.33 \text{ for } \beta_B.$$

3. Conceptually, ϕ values could be developed for all possible values of β. The range of ϕ would be from 1.0 for $\beta = 0$ to a value close to nil for large values of β, assuming risk aversion.[1]
4. The risk-aversion functions of all individuals could, conceptually, be averaged to form a 'market risk-aversion function'. An example of such a function is shown in Figure 11E–2.

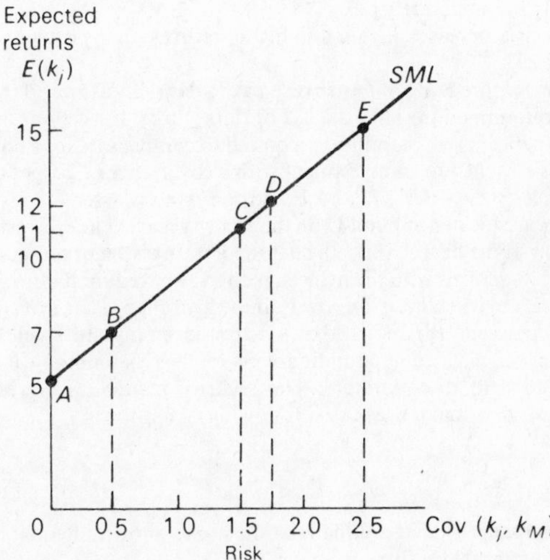

Figure 11E–2 *Illustrative Risk-Return Relationships.*

5. Given the market risk-aversion function and the degree of risk inherent in any risky return, the risky return could be replaced by its certainty equivalent:

   Certainty equivalent of $F_t = \phi_t F_t$.

---

1. Of course, different individuals may have different ϕ functions, depending on their degrees of risk aversion. Further, an individual's own α function might shift over time as personal situations, including wealth and family status, changed.

6. The basic NPV equation could then be converted to equation 11E–1, a model that explicitly accounts for risk:

$$NPV = \sum_{t=1}^{n} \frac{F_t}{(1+k)^t} - I = \sum_{t=1}^{n} \frac{\phi_t F_t}{(1+R_F)^t} - I \tag{11E–1}$$

In this form, the effects of different courses of action with different risk (β) and returns (F_t) can be appraised.

Risk-adjusted discount rates

An alternative procedure for taking risk into account utilizes the security market line discussed in Chapter 11, whose logic was further developed in the preceding Appendix 11D. The security market line provides a risk-return trade-off function. The general form of the security market line is shown in equation 11E–2.

$$E(k_j) = R_F + \lambda Cov(k_j, k_M) \tag{11E–2}$$

Suppose that we are given the economy-wide parameters of a value of R_F equal to 5 per cent and a λ of 4. The risk characteristics of the investment, security, firm, or other capital asset are defined by the value of the covariance term. Some illustrative values of the covariance term and the associated expected returns are shown in Table 11E–1.

Table 11E–1 *Returns Related to Risk.*

	Expressed as decimals		Expressed as percentages	
	$Cov(k_j, k_M)$	$E(k_j)$	$Cov(k_j, k_M)$	$E(k_j)$
A	0	0.05	0	5
B	0.005	0.07	0.5	7
C	0.015	0.11	1.5	11
D	0.0175	0.12	1.75	12
E	0.025	0.15	2.50	15

The relationships shown in Table 11E–1 can also be graphed as in Figure 11E–2. The security market line depicted in Figure 11E–2 is a risk-return trade-off function. The average investor is indifferent to a riskless asset with a certain 5 per cent return, a moderately risky asset with an 11 per cent return, or a very risky asset with a 15 per cent expected return. As risk increases, higher and higher returns on investment are required to compensate investors for the additional risk.

The difference between the required rate of return on a particular risky asset and the rate of return on a riskless asset is defined as the risk premium on the risky asset. For the security market line depicted in Figure 11E–2 the riskless rate is 5 per cent; a 2 per cent risk premium is required to compensate for a covariance of 0.5 per cent, and a 10 per cent risk premium is attached to an investment with a covariance of 2.5 per cent. The average investor is indifferent between risky investments B, C, D and E and the riskless asset A.

If a particular firm's shares are located at point D on the security market line, investors expect the rate of return on the shares to be 12 per cent. If the firm changes the nature of its investment projects so that it takes on projects that reduce the covariance of its returns with the market, then a lower required rate of return results; it may move down to point C on the security market line. Conversely, if the firm changes its investment programme so that its covariance moves up to 2.5 per cent, the return that is required by investors will be 15 per cent.

Because compounding over time has a compounding effect on the risk premium, it is sometimes desirable to be able to use a certainty equivalent discount rate. The security market line expression lends itself to this reformulation. To do this, we first make use of the following definition:

$$E(k_j) = \frac{E(X_j)}{V_j}$$

This enables us to rewrite the security market line relationship as shown in equation 11E–2a, which, after we rearrange terms, becomes equation 11E–2b.

$$\frac{E(X_j)}{V_j} = R_F + \lambda Cov\left(\frac{X_j}{V_j}, k_M\right) \tag{11E–2a}$$

$$\frac{1}{V_j}[E(X_j) - \lambda Cov(X_j, k_M)] = R_F$$

$$V_j = \frac{E(X_j) - \lambda Cov(X_j, k_M)}{R_F} \tag{11E–2b}$$

Equation 11E–2b makes an adjustment to the numerator representing the asset returns. This adjustment converts the returns to a certainty equivalent amount. When this is done, the risk-free rate of return can be used as a discount rate. To illustrate what is involved let us assume some values related to the previous example. Let: $X_j = £120$; $\lambda = 4$; $Cov(X_j, k_M) = 17.5$; $R_F = 0.05$.

These values can then be utilized in equation 11E–2b as shown in equation 11E–2b′:

$$V_j = \frac{120 - 4(17.5)}{0.05} = \frac{120 - 70}{0.05} = \frac{50}{0.05} = £1000 \quad (11E\text{–}2b')$$

Thus we see that the risky returns are £120. The risk adjustment is £70. Hence, the certainty equivalent returns are £50. When we discount the certainty equivalent returns at the risk-free rate of 5 per cent, we obtain a value for the asset of £1000. However, for a one-period model such as the CAPM reflected in the security market line, we will obtain the same results if we use risk-adjusted values both in the numerator and in the denominator. To illustrate, let us first recognize the relationship in equation 11E–3.

$$Cov\left(\frac{X_j}{V_j}, k_M\right) = Cov(k_j, k_M) \quad (11E\text{–}3)$$

Rearranging terms and inserting values known to this point we obtain:

$$Cov(X_j, k_M) = V_j\, Cov(k_j, k_M) \quad (11E\text{–}3a)$$

$$17.5 = 1000\, Cov(k_j, k_M) \quad (11E\text{–}3b)$$

$$Cov(k_j; k_M) = 17.5/1000 = 0.0175 \quad (11E\text{–}3c)$$

In developing the expression for the value of the asset in risk-adjusted terms, we express the security market line in the form of equation 11E–4:

$$\frac{E(X_j)}{V_j} = R_F + \lambda\, Cov(k_j, k_M) \quad (11E\text{–}4)$$

Solving for the value of the asset we obtain equation 11E–4a:

$$V_j = \frac{E(X_j)}{R_F + \lambda\, Cov(k_j, k_M)} \quad (11E\text{–}4a)$$

We can now use equation 11E–4a to obtain the value of the firm, using a risk-adjusted discount rate.

$$V_j = \frac{120}{0.05 + 4(0.0175)}$$

$$V_j = \frac{120}{0.05 + 0.07} = \frac{120}{0.12} = £1000$$

Thus we obtain the same value whether we use the certainty equivalent formulation and the risk-free return or the risk-adjusted values in both the numerator and the denominator.

Traditionally it has been customary to convert the risky return to a certainty equivalent return by applying a certainty equivalent factor, ϕ. In the informal approaches to the treatment of risk the value of ϕ was formulated on a judgemental basis. However, with the use of the security market line we were able to develop a data-based estimate of ϕ. Using the information from the example above we found that the certainty equivalent return was £50, while the risky return was £120. The ratio between the two was 0.4167. Hence, we can take equation 11E–2a and, instead of subtracting the risk adjustment factor, multiply by the certainty equivalent factor, ϕ, as shown in equation 11E–5:

$$V_j = \frac{\phi E(X_j)}{R_F} \quad (11E\text{–}5)$$

When we insert the appropriate values, we again obtain a value of the asset of £1000.

$$V_j = \frac{0.4167(120)}{0.05} = \frac{50}{0.05} = £1000$$

Thus the use of the security market line enables us to express valuation relationships in either the risk-adjusted form or in their certainty equivalent form.

Risk and the timing of returns

By its nature, the discount rate serves both to allow for the time value of money *and* to provide an allowance for the relative riskiness of a project's returns. In other words, both *time* and *risk* are accounted for by one adjustment process. Since time and risk are really separate variables, this combination value must be carefully chosen if it is to be appropriate for its intended purpose. It should be noted that the certainty equivalent method *does not* combine risk and time but, rather, keeps them separate, adjusting for risk in the numerator and for time in the denominator. As a result, it can be argued that certainty equivalents are superior to risk-adjusted discount rates. However, as was pointed out in Chapter 11, risk-adjusted discount rates are used by financial managers more frequently because of their greater convenience and familiarity.

If the risk-adjusted discount rate method is to be used, it is important to choose the values of these rates carefully. We will now consider the particular assumptions that are implicit in the choice of a constant risk-adjusted discount rate over time. Here the 'risk index' ϕ is calculated as the ratio of the present value interest factor for a risky cash flow divided by the present value interest factor of a riskless asset.[2]

$$\text{Index of risk} = \phi_t = \frac{PVIF_{\text{risky asset}}}{PVIF_{\text{riskless asset}}} = \frac{(1+\text{risky rate})^{-t}}{(1+\text{riskless rate})^{-t}}. \qquad (11E\text{–}6)$$

To illustrate, suppose we are calculating ϕ, the risk index, for a cash flow expected after 10 years when the riskless rate is 5 per cent and the risky rate is 10 per cent. The interest factors are found in Appendix Table D–2 to be 0.614 and 0.386 for the riskless and risky assets, respectively, so the certainty equivalent risk index is found as follows:

$$\text{Risk index} = \phi_{10} = \frac{0.386}{0.614} = 0.629.$$

Equation 11E–6 has some interesting implications that can be seen in Table 11E–2, which works out the ϕ values for a pair of interest rates over time, and in Figure 11E–3, where these values (and others) are plotted. Risk, as measured by ϕ_t, is an increasing function of both *time* and the *differential between the riskless and risky discount rates.* In other words, a given risk premium has a larger and larger impact on the risk index as the time horizon is lengthened. This phenomenon occurs, of course, because of the compounding effect.

Table 11E–2 *Calculation of Certainty Equivalents.*

Discount rate – Years	Riskless project 5%	Risky project 10%	*RI*
0	1.000	1.000	1.000
1	0.952	0.909	0.955
10	0.614	0.386	0.629
20	0.377	0.149	0.395
30	0.231	0.057	0.247

Note: The $RI = 1.0$ when $t = 0$ because

$$\frac{PVIF_{\text{risky rate}}}{PVIF_{\text{riskless rate}}} = \frac{(1+k)^0}{(1+R_F)^0} = \frac{1}{1} = 1.0$$

where R_F = riskless rate and k = risky rate.

This concept can be expressed analytically. Let the risk index for any year t, ϕ_t, be designated as

$$\phi_t = \frac{(1+R_F+\rho)^{-t}}{(1+R_F)^{-t}} = \frac{(1+R_F)^t}{(1+R_F+\rho)^t}$$

where R_F is the riskless rate and ρ is the risk premium. For a longer period of $t+1$ years, and holding constant ρ and R_F,

$$\phi_{t+1} = \frac{(1+R_F)^{t+1}}{(1+R_F+\rho)^{t+1}}$$

$$= \frac{(1+R_F)^t}{(1-R_F+\rho)^t} \cdot \frac{(1+R_F)}{(1+R_F+\rho)}$$

$$= \phi_t\left(\frac{1+R_F}{1+R_F+\rho}\right).$$

Therefore, $\phi_{t+1} < \phi_t$ provided $\rho > 0$. Since smaller values of ϕ are associated with higher risk, risk must be perceived to be *increasing* over time whenever the risk premium, ρ, is a constant. Further, note that the risk-adjusted discount rate, k, is equal to $R_F + \rho$. If R_F and ρ are both constants, then R_F is also a constant and

$$\phi_{t+1} = \phi_c\left(\frac{1+R_F}{1+k}\right).$$

2. This discussion parallels that of Robichek and Myers, Risk adjusted discount rates, *Journal of Finance* 21, No. 4 (December 1966), pp. 727–730.

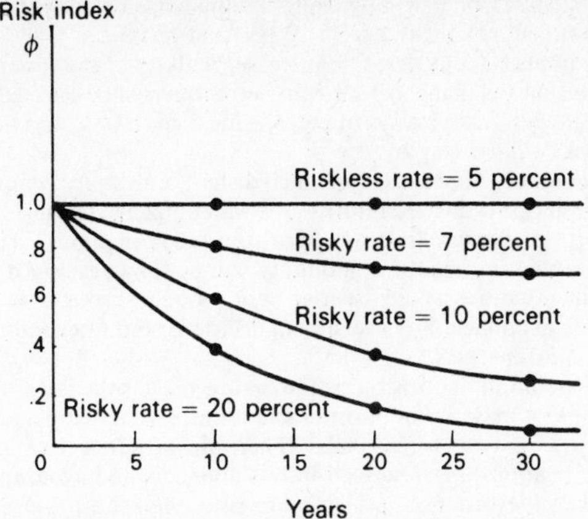

Notes: 1. The smaller the value of ϕ, the index of risk, the greater the perceived risk.
2. For a given riskless rate (for example, 5 per cent) and risky rate (for example, 10 per cent), the value of ϕ, declines over time; that is, with a constant risk premium (5 per cent = 10 per cent − 5 per cent), the declining curve indicates that perceived risk increases with time. Therefore, a constant risk premium (and risk-adjusted discount rate) implies that risk of an individual cash flow is perceived to be higher and higher the further into the future the cash flow is due.
3. At any given future point in time (other than $t = 0$), ϕ, the index of perceived risk, is lower the higher the risk premium. At the point 10 years for example, the ϕ for the 7 per cent risky rate, with a 2 per cent risk premium, is 0.826; it is 0.629 for the 10 per cent rate; and it is 0.403 for the 15 per cent rate.

Figure 11E–3 *Changes in Perceived Risk over Time.*

Therefore, a constant k implies that ϕ_t is declining and that risk is thought to be increasing over time.

The relationship between k, risk, and time is graphed in Figure 11E–4. If risk is thought to increase over time (in terms of Figure 11–4, the estimated coefficient of variation of returns is increasing), then the risk index should also increase over time. A constant value of k implies increasing risk; this condition is shown in Figure 11E–4(a). However, if the riskiness of returns is not higher for distant than for close-at-hand returns, then distant returns should be discounted at a *lower* k than close returns; this condition is shown in Figure 11E–4(b). Note again that the reason behind this result is the fact that the risk premium component of k is being compounded.

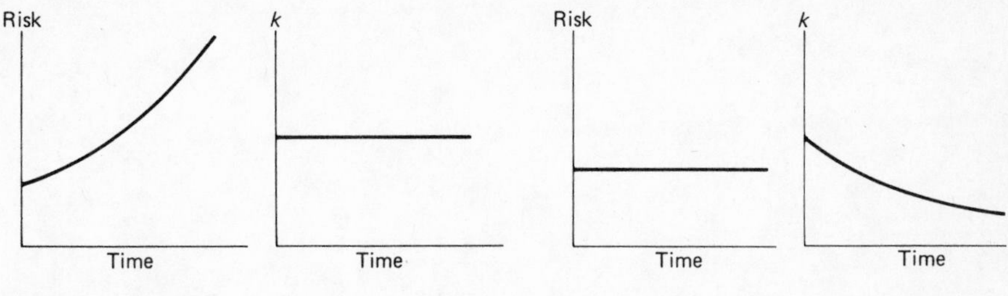

(a) Riskiness of distant returns greater than riskiness of early returns

(b) Riskiness of returns constant over time

Figure 11E–4 *Relationship between Risk and Time.*

IMPLICATIONS

A firm using the risk-adjusted discount rate approach for its capital budgeting decisions will have an overall rate that generally reflects its overall, market-determined riskiness. This rate will be used for 'average' projects. Lower rates will be used for less risky projects, and higher rates will be used for riskier projects. To facilitate the decision process, corporate headquarters may prescribe rates for different divisions and for different classes of investments (for example, replacement, expansion of existing lines, expansion into new lines). Then, investments of a given class within a given division are analysed in terms of the prescribed rate. For example, replacement decisions in the retailing division of an oil company might all be evaluated with an 8 per cent cost of capital, while exploration and production investments might require a 20 per cent return.

Notice what such a procedure implies about risk: risk increases with time, and it imposes a relatively severe burden on long-term projects. This means that short-payoff alternatives will be selected over those with longer payoffs when, for example, there are alternative ways of performing a given task, and that less capital-intensive methods of performing given tasks will be employed.

However, there is a substantial number of projects for which distant returns are *not* more difficult to estimate than near-term returns. For example, the estimated returns on a water pipeline serving a developing community maybe quite uncertain in the short run, because the rate of growth of the community is uncertain. However, the water company may be quite sure that in time the community will be fully developed and will utilize the full capacity of the pipeline. Similar situations could exist in many public projects – water projects, highway construction, schools, and so forth; in public utility investment decisions; and when industrial firms are building plants to serve specified geographical markets.

To the extent that this implicit assumption of rising risk over time reflects the facts, then a constant discount rate, k, may be appropriate. In the vast majority of business situations, risk actually is an increasing function of time, so a constant risk-adjusted discount rate is reasonable. There are, however, situations for which this is not true; one should be aware of the relationships described in this appendix and avoid the pitfall of unwittingly penalizing long-term projects when they are not, in fact, more risky than shorter-term projects.

Appendix F to Chapter 11:

Capital Budgeting Procedures Under Inflation[1]

The United Kingdom has experienced persistent inflation since the 1960s at levels exceeding the moderate price level changes of previous peacetime periods. What effects does this have on the results of capital budgeting analysis? We can analyse the impacts of inflation by using an illustrative example to clarify the new influences introduced.

Let us begin with the standard capital budgeting case in which inflation is absent. The expression for calculating the net present value of the investment is shown in equation 11F–1.

$$\overline{NPV} = \sum_{t=1}^{N} \frac{\overline{F}_t}{(1+k)^t} - I \qquad \text{(11F–1)}$$

The symbols used have the following meanings and values:

$\overline{NPV}$ = expected net present value of the project
$\overline{F}_t$ = expected net cash flows per year from the project = £12 500 (after tax)
k = cost of capital applicable to the risk of the project = 9 per cent
N = number of years the net cash flows are received = 5
I = required investment outlay for the project = £75 000.

With the data provided, we can utilize 11F–1 as follows:[2]

$$\begin{aligned}\overline{NPV_0} &= \frac{£50\,000}{(1.09)} + \frac{£12\,500}{(1.09)^2} + \frac{£12\,500}{(1.09)^3} + \frac{£12\,500}{(1.09)^4} + \frac{£12\,500}{(1.09)^5} - £75\,000 \\ &= £50\,000(0.917) + £12\,500(2.973) - £75\,000 \\ &= £45\,850 + £37\,163 - £75\,000 \\ &= £8013.\end{aligned}$$

We find that the project has an expected net present value of £8013, and under the simple conditions assumed, we would accept the project. Now let us consider the effects of inflation. Suppose that inflation at an annual rate of 6 per cent is expected to take place during the five years of the project. Since investment and security returns are based on expected future returns, the anticipated inflation rate will be reflected in the required rate of return on the project or the applicable cost of capital for the project. This relationship has long been recognized in financial economics and is known as the Fisher effect. In formal terms we have:

$$(1+k_j)(1+n) = (1+K_j) \qquad \text{(11F–2)}$$

---

1. For articles on this subject see J. C. Van Horne, A note on biases in capital budgeting introduced by inflation, *Journal of Financial and Quantitative Analysis* 6 (January 1971), pp. 653–658; and P. L. Cooley, R. L. Roenfeldt and It-Keong Chew, Capital budgeting procedures under inflation, *Financial Management* 4 (Winter 1975), pp. 18–27; also see their exchange with M. C. Findlay and A. W. Frankle in Financial Management (August 1976), pp. 83–90; see too C. A. Westwick, Investment appraisal and inflation, ICA Research Committee, Occasional Paper No. 7, and B. Carsberg and A. Hope, Business investment decisions under inflation, ICA.
2. Assuming 50 per cent rate of corporation tax and 100 per cent first year allowance. Also, for convenience, we have assumed no delay in payment of tax liability.

where k_j is the required rate of return in nominal terms and n is the anticipated annual inflation rate over the life of the project. For our example, equation 11F–2 would be:

$$(1+0.09)(1+0.06) = (1+0.09+0.06+0.0054).$$

If the cross product term 0.0054 is included in the addition, we would have 0.1554 as the required rate of return in nominal terms. However, since the cross product term is generally small and since both k_j, the required rate of return in real terms, and the anticipated inflation rate are estimates, it is customary practice to make a simple addition of the real rate and the inflation rate. The required nominal rate of return that would be used in the calculation would therefore be 15 per cent.

It is at this point that some biases in capital budgeting under inflationary conditions may be introduced. The market data utilized in the estimated current capital costs will include the premium for anticipated inflation. But while the market remembers to include an adjustment for inflation in the capitalization factor, in the capital budgeting analysis, the cash-flow estimates may fail to include an element to reflect future inflation. As a consequence, the analysis would appear as in the calculations below for $\overline{NPV}_1$.

$$\begin{aligned}\overline{NPV}_1 &= \frac{£50\,000}{(1.15)} + \frac{£12\,500}{(1.15)^2} + \frac{£12\,500}{(1.15)^3} + \frac{£12\,500}{(1.15)^4} + \frac{£12\,500}{(1.15)^5} - £75\,000 \\ &= £50\,000(0.870) + 12\,500(2.483) - £75\,000 \\ &= £43\,500 + £31\,038 - £75\,000 \\ &= £(462).\end{aligned}$$

It now appears that the project will have a negative net present value of almost £462. With a negative net present value, the project would be rejected. However, a sound analysis requires that the anticipated inflation rate also be taken into account in the cash flow estimates as well. Initially, for simplicity, let us assume that the same inflation rate of 6 per cent is applicable to the net cash flows. We take this step in setting forth the expression for $\overline{NPV}_2$ as follows:

$$\begin{aligned}\overline{NPV}_2 &= \frac{£50\,000(1.06)}{(1.09)(1.06)} + \frac{£12\,500(1.06)^2}{(1.09)^2(1.06)^2} + \frac{£12\,500(1.06)^3}{(1.09)^3(1.06)^3} + \frac{£12\,500(1.06)^4}{(1.09)^4(1.06)^4} + \frac{£12\,500(1.06)^5}{(1.09)^5(1.06)^5} - £75\,000 \\ &= \frac{£50\,000}{(1.09)} + \frac{£12\,500}{(1.09)^2} + \frac{£12\,500}{(1.09)^3} + \frac{£12\,500}{(1.09)^4} + \frac{£12\,500}{(1.09)^5} - £75\,000.\end{aligned}$$

Since the inflation factors are now in both the numerator and the denominator and are the same, they can be cancelled. The result for the calculation of $\overline{NPV}_2$ will therefore be the same as for $\overline{NPV}_0$, which was a positive £8013. Thus when anticipated inflation is properly reflected in both the cash flow estimates in the numerator and the required rate of return from market data in the denominator, the resulting $\overline{NPV}$ calculation will be both in real and nominal terms. This was noted by Professor Findlay as follows: 'Any properly measured, market-determined wealth concept is, simultaneously, *both nominal and real* . . . Hence, $\overline{NPV}$, or any other wealth measure, gives the amount for which one can "cash out" now (nominal) and also the amount of today's goods that can be consumed at today's prices (real).'[3] Thus if inflation is reflected in both the cash flow estimates and in the required rate of return, the resulting $\overline{NPV}$ estimate will be free of inflation bias.

To this point we have purposely kept the analysis simple to focus on the basic principles involved since controversy has erupted over the issues involved. In applying these concepts, the anticipated inflation might be expected to affect the required rate of return and the cash flow estimates differently. Indeed, the components of the net cash flows, the cash outflows and the cash inflows, may themselves be influenced by the anticipated inflation by different magnitudes. These complications will not, however, change the basic method of analysis, only the specifics of the calculations. The nature of the more complex case is indicated by equation 11F–3.

$$\overline{NPV}_0 = \sum_{t=1}^{N} \frac{[\overline{(\text{Inflows})}_t(1+n_i)^t - \overline{(\text{Outflows})}_t(1+n_0)^t](1-T) + \overline{(\text{Cap. All.})}_t(T)}{(1+K)^t} \qquad (11\text{F–}3)$$

The cash inflows may be subject to a rate of inflation that is different from the rate of inflation in the cash outflows. Both may differ from the anticipated rate of inflation reflected in the required rate of return in the denominator. Some illustrative data will demonstrate the application of 11F–3.

Table 11F–1 sets forth data for expected cash flows without inflation effects. The pattern is a constant £12 500 per annum with the exception of year 1 when the cash flow is £50 000 as in the original example. In Table 11F–2 the estimates of expected net cash flows include inflation effects. The cash inflows are subject to a 7 per cent inflation rate, while the cash outflows are subject to an 8 per cent inflation rate. The resulting expected net cash flows are shown in the bottom line of the table. The required rate of return of 15 per cent is assumed to reflect a 6 per cent inflation rate as before.

The calculation of the expected net present value ($\overline{NPV}_3$) is shown in Table 11F–3. Taking all the inflation influences into account, $\overline{NPV}_3$ is a positive £5587. The project would be accepted. In this example, the inflationary forces on the cash outflows were greater than for the cash inflows. Some have suggested that this

3. *Financial Management*, Autumn 1976, p. 85.

Table 11F-1 *Expected Net Cash Flows without Inflation Effects.*

	1	2	3	4	5
Expected cash inflows	£40 000	£50 000	£60 000	£70 000	£80 000
Expected cash outflows	15 000	25 000	35 000	45 000	55 000
	25 000	25 000	25 000	25 000	25 000
Times (1 – tax rate)	0.50	0.50	0.50	0.50	0.50
	12 500	12 500	12 500	12 500	12 500
Capital allowances (tax rate)[a]	37 500	–	–	–	–
Expected net cash flows ($\overline{F}_t$)	£50 000	£12 500	£12 500	£12 500	£12 500

[a] Assuming, for the sake of simplicity, that a 100 per cent first year allowance has been claimed and offset against total taxable income.

Table 11F-2 *Expected Net Cash Flows Including Inflation Effects.*

	1	2	3	4	5
Expected cash outflows (η = 7%)	£42 800	£57 250	£73 500	£91 770	£112 240
Expected cash outflows (η = 8%)	16 200	29 150	44 100	61 200	80 795
	26 600	28 100	29 400	30 570	31 445
Times (1 – tax rate)	0.50	0.50	0.50	0.50	0.50
	13 300	14 050	14 700	15 285	15 722
Capital allowances (tax rate)	37 500	–	–	–	–
Expected net cash flows ($\overline{F}_t$)	£50 800	£14 050	£14 700	£15 285	£15 722

Table 11F-3 *Calculation of* $\overline{NPV}_3$.

Year	Cash flow (1)	Discount factor (15%) (2)	Present value (1) × (2)
1	£50 800	.870	£44 196
2	14 050	.756	10 622
3	14 700	.658	9 212
4	15 285	.572	8 743
5	15 722	.497	7 814

$$\overline{NPV}_3 = £80\,587 - £75\,000$$
$$= £\ 5\,587$$

influence has been sufficiently widespread and that it accounts for the sluggish rate of capital investment in the United Kingdom since the early 1970s.

The situation that we illustrated was that failure to take inflation into account in the expected cash flows resulted in an erroneous capital budgeting analysis. Originally, no account was taken of the effects of inflation and the project provided a positive net present value of £8013. Secondly, the effect of inflation was accounted for by adjustment to the discount rate. This produced a negative net present value of £462 and would have led to rejection of the project. When, however, adjustment was made to the individual cash inflows and outflows we find that, despite the fact that the cash outflows grow at a higher rate than the cash inflows, the investment still has a positive net present value of £5587. We should, therefore, undertake the investment.

Making the inflation adjustment does not always necessarily result in a positive net present value for the project – it simply results in a more accurate estimate of the net benefits from the project, positive or negative.

PROBLEMS

11F–1. Your firm is considering an investment in a machine that produces bowling balls. The cost of the machine is £100 000 with nil expected salvage value. Annual production in units during the five-year life of the machine is expected to be: 5000; 8000; 12 000; 10 000; and 6000.

The price of bowling balls is expected to rise from £20 during year 1 at a rate of 2 per cent per year for the following four years. Production cash outflows are expected to grow at 10 per cent per year from the first-year production costs of £10 per unit.

The company claims 100 per cent first year allowance on the machine. The applicable tax rate is 50 per cent, and the applicable cost of capital is 15 per cent. Should the investment in the machine be made?

11F–2. You are given the following information about an investment of £40 000: it is expected to yield benefits over a five-year period. It is also expected that there will be annual cash inflows of £90 000 and annual cash outflows of £75 000, excluding taxes. The company claims 100 per cent first year allowance on the investment. The tax rate is 50 per cent, and the cost of capital is 0.08 per cent.

(a) Compute the net present value of the investment.

(b) On investigation you discover that no adjustments have been made for inflation or price level changes. Year 1 data are correct, but after that inflows are expected to increase at 4 per cent per year and outflows at 6 per cent per year. The general rate of inflation is expected to be about 6 per cent, causing the cost of capital to rise to 14 per cent. Re-evaluate the net present value of the project in the light of this information.

PART 4

SOURCES AND FORMS OF LONG-TERM FINANCING

In the introductory section; we analysed the firm in an overall, aggregate sense. Next, in Part 2, we considered the bottom half of the balance sheet, analysing current assets, current liabilities and the interactions between the two. Then, in Part 3, we moved to the upper right side of the balance sheet, examining the process by which firms decide on investments in fixed assets. Now, in Part 4, we move to the upper left side of the balance sheet, to consider the various types of long-term funds available to the firm when it seeks long-term external capital.

Chapter 12 presents an overview of the capital markets, explaining briefly certain institutional material without which no basic finance course is complete. Chapter 13 analyses the financial characteristics of ordinary shares, with particular reference to rights issues made by companies; Chapter 14 examines debentures and preference shares; Chapter 15 analyses term loans and leases; and Chapter 16 discusses the nature and use of warrants and convertibles. This institutional background is essential for an understanding of Part 5, Financial Structure and the Cost of Capital, where we take up the question of the optimal mix of financing.

Chapter 12

The Market for Long-term Securities

One fundamental basis for classifying securities markets is the distinction between *primary markets* in which securities are initially sold and *secondary markets* in which they are subsequently traded. Initial sales of securities are made either through the agency of issuing houses or by stockbrokers. The subsequent transactions in the securities take place in the market for old shares, the Stock Exchange. The operations of the securities markets provide a framework within which the new issue market can be better understood. Accordingly, we first develop the background provided by a study of the secondary markets and in particular the London Stock Exchange.

THE DEVELOPMENT OF THE UK STOCK EXCHANGE

Since the seventeenth century the Stock Exchange has provided a market in which the goods bought and sold are stocks and shares. Initially, transactions were facilitated by merchants and stockbrokers meeting together in coffee houses in the City of London. Stocks traded were mainly UK government stocks issued after the formation of the Bank of England in 1694. Some trading was carried out in the securities of trading companies such as the Hudson's Bay Company and the East India Company but the main impetus for the formation of the Stock Exchange came from the existence of the large quantities of government stock issued during the wars of the eighteenth century. Because the demand for shares did not always meet the supply of shares it became necessary for some intermediary to be willing to hold the surplus shares until a ready market developed. These intermediaries were the stockjobbers who were willing to buy shares for their own account if there were insufficient other buyers and to sell the shares when other buyers came into the market.

By the early nineteenth century the volume of trading was such that it was necessary to house the Stock Exchange in a purpose-built building. Membership was limited and rules were drawn up to regulate the activities of members.

STOCK MARKETING REPORTING

Securities that are traded on the UK Stock Exchange are known as *listed securities* and are distinguished from other securities known as *unlisted securities*. These unlisted securities are normally, although not always, the shares of private companies. In all cases the companies issuing these securities are those which do not have a quotation on the UK Stock Exchange.

Considerable information dealing with transactions among listed companies is available, and the very existence of this information reduces the uncertainty inherent in security investment. This reduction of uncertainty, of course, makes listed securities relatively attractive to investors and it lowers the cost of capital to firms.

1977/8					(pence gross)		
High	Low	Company	Price	Change	Div	Yield	P/E
122	77	AAH	110	−1	8.3	7.6	8.1
142	56	A B Electronic	97	−1	7.6	7.9	6.7
42	25	A C Cars	42	+4	1.4	3.4	7.8
86	39½	A G B Research	85	r	5.2n	6.1	8.9
228½	134	A P V Holdings	185		8.1	4.4	7.4
73	43	Aaronson Brothers	57	•	3.0	5.2	4.5
116	62	Acrow	112	•	3.6	3.2	12.7
98	52	Acrow 'A'	77	• −1	3.6	4.7	8.8
41	11	Adda International	33½	−1	0.8	2.3	
282	150	Adwest Group	237	−1	15.2	6.4	6.5

Source: *The Times*, 23 February 1978.
r = ex rights; n = forecast earnings; • = ex dividend.

Figure 12–1 *Stock Market Transactions.*

Figure 12–1 is a section of the 'stock market page' of *The Times*. Shares are listed alphabetically with the shares whose names consist of capital letters listed first. The terms are explained with reference to the information on Acrow. The two columns on the left show the highest and lowest prices at which the shares have been traded during 1977–8. Acrow prices have ranged from 116 pence to 62 pence. The figure just to the right of the company's name is the current market price of the shares. Next comes the change from the closing price on the previous day. Notice that Acrow's price is unchanged, although the same company's 'A' ordinary shares (which usually have no voting rights) have fallen by a penny. In the following column we have the gross dividend in pence based on the most recent payment. Next comes the dividend yield which is usually different from the gross dividend. In Acrow's case it is smaller because the shares are selling at a price slightly higher than their nominal value. Finally there is the price/earnings ratio or the current price of the shares divided by their earnings per share during the last year. (Price/earnings ratios are discussed at some length in Chapter 17.) A set of footnotes always accompanies the stock market quotes, giving additional information about specific issues.

THE DEALING PROCESS WITHIN THE UK STOCK EXCHANGE

In order to understand clearly the dealing process within the UK Stock Exchange it is necessary to be clear that the London system is quite different from the system operated in

Europe and that operated in the United States. The London system is known as a single-capacity system. Under a single-capacity system there is a division of labour between jobbers and brokers. In other countries the tasks of jobbers and brokers are carried out by the same individuals. The single-capacity system depends for its successful operation on this division of labour between the operators within the market.

Brokers

A member of the general public who wishes to buy or sell securities on the UK Stock Exchange must do so through the agency of a stockbroker, who will buy or sell the shares from a jobber. In return for his services the stockbroker will charge his client a commission. Brokers are also willing to give advice on investment policy to their clients, although the form of this advice is obviously more detailed in the case of large customers such as the institutional investors than it is for the small-scale private investors.

Jobbers and the jobbing mechanism

As has been mentioned previously the jobbing system developed in the eighteenth century because of an imbalance between the demand for shares and the supply of shares. Jobbers were willing to hold shares at times when other operators within the markets were anxious to sell their shares. As the number of jobbers was large competition was assured. It is this competition between jobbers which has led to the view that the Stock Exchange is one of the best examples that we have of a perfect market. Each jobber will hold a set of securities from within a particular section of the market and brokers who wish to deal in a particular security will go to the appropriate section of the market and bargain with the various jobbers in that section until they get the best deal for their clients. As mentioned earlier, the number of jobbers in the market has declined in recent years. In many sections of the market there will be only one jobber for a particular security or several jobbers will run a common book.

Jobbers determine the prices that they charge by 'the length of their book'. That is they will increase their prices if they find that they are short of a particular security, and if they are holding a large number of shares in one company they will lower the price of that security in order to encourage buyers. The jobbers make their profit partly from the jobbers' turn, which is the difference between the price at which they offer to sell shares and the price at which they are willing to buy, and partly from the capital gains which they are able to make when stock market prices are rising. Obviously, if share prices move downwards and jobbers hold large numbers of shares the jobbers are likely to make losses.

It will be useful at this point to consider an illustrative example. On 14 July 1978 Dunlop shares were quoted in the financial press at 83 pence per share. Assume that an investor decides that he would like to buy 1000 Dunlop shares. He contacts his stockbroker and asks him to buy 1000 Dunlop 'at best'; that is, the broker is to buy the Dunlop shares as cheaply as possible. When the broker arrives at the floor of the Stock Exchange he notes that there are three jobbers who are dealing in Dunlop shares. The three jobbers approached in connection with the Dunlop shares might give the following quotations:

First jobber	81–85
Second jobber	80–84
Third jobber	79–84

Out of this range of prices the best selling price is the 81 pence offered by the first jobber and the best buying price is the 84 pence offered by the second and third jobber. The broker will thus buy the 1000 Dunlop shares at 84 pence per share and pay £840 for them.

The broker and the jobber will note the deal in their notebooks and the transfer of shares and cash will take place subsequently.

The Stock Exchange account

The investor who has bought 1000 Dunlop shares will not have to pay for them until Settlement Day. All ordinary shares are bought 'on account'. Government stock such as Consols, on the other hand, is bought for cash and payment and transfer of certificates takes place on the day of the deal.

The Stock Exchange year is divided into 24 accounts. These accounts are of two weeks' duration except for the four which fall on the public holidays: Easter, Spring Bank Holiday, August Bank Holiday and Christmas. For these four accounts only the duration is three weeks. Each account begins on a Monday, except when that day is a public holiday, and ends on a Friday. All transactions which take place within an account must be settled on Settlement Day which is always on the Tuesday 11 days after the end of the account.

It is possible to buy and sell securities many times during the course of one account but the only payment which has to be made is for those transactions which are outstanding at the end of the account. This can encourage speculators who are able to buy shares at the beginning of an account and sell them at the end of the account taking a substantial gain for a relatively low outlay. Because these speculators need to pay only one lot of commission, the stamp duty that they pay will be reduced.

Investors known as 'bulls' buy shares at the beginning of the account in order to sell them later, when they hope that the price has risen. Investors known as 'bears' may sell shares which they do not possess at the beginning of the account in order to buy them back later when they hope that the price has fallen. This process is sometimes known as 'short selling'.

Account begins	Account ends	Contango Day	Settlement Day
Monday 1 March	Friday 12 March	Monday 15 March	Tuesday 23 March
Monday 15 March	Friday 26 March	Monday 29 March	Tuesday 6 April

Figure 12–2 *The Stock Exchange Account.*

The account in which the purchase of Dunlop shares took place (see Figure 12–2) ran from Monday 1 March to Friday 12 March. Payment for the shares will not take place until Tuesday 23 March, a date well into the next account.

There are certain circumstances under which the settlement does not take place on Settlement Day. These are:

1. On the last two days of an account it is possible to make deals for 'the new time'. Bargains struck in these two days need not be settled until the Settlement Day of the following account. Thus, if our investor had bought his 1000 Dunlop shares on either 11 March or 12 March he would not have to pay for them until Tuesday 6 April. On the last two days of an account jobbers tend to charge higher selling prices than during the rest of the account in order to recompense them for the delay in delivery and payment.
2. Dealings in certain new issues and all government stocks, together with stock issued by local authorities and other public boards, are for settlement on the next business day following the transaction.
3. If a purchaser wishes to delay payment for one account (that is, he wishes to pay for his

stock purchases two weeks later than is normal) he may do so provided only that he finds a seller who is willing to wait for the payment. Operations of this sort are initiated on the last day of the account and confirmed on the following Monday, which is known as Contango Day. The investor who wishes to delay payment will pay contango interest to the seller for the period between Settlement Days.

4. If there are more sellers than buyers in the market they may be anxious to pay a 'backwardation' charge to buyers in order that they can deliver the shares at a later date than the normal Settlement Day. This charge is the exact opposite of the contango rate of interest.

RECENT DEVELOPMENTS ON THE UK STOCK EXCHANGE

In recent years there have been several developments in the internal organization of the Stock Exchange. In March 1973 the various country exchanges, together with the Dublin Stock Exchange, decided voluntarily to amalgamate with the London Stock Exchange. Jobbing firms have been merged together with a resultant reduction in their numbers. Although the number of firms has been reduced there has been less than proportionate reduction in the number of dealers actually operating on the floor of the Stock Exchange and therefore much of the competition on which the jobbing system is based still remains. The Stock Exchange has introduced a visual price information service known as the Market Price Display Service which makes it possible for dealers on the trading floor to keep up to date with changes in share prices. The development of transistorized radios has made it easy for floor operators to keep in touch with their offices. The use of computers has transformed the settling mechanism and the new computerized procedure known as Talisman settles deals more quickly and efficiently than did the old system. The decline in significance of private investors and the growth in importance of institutional investors such as insurance companies, pension funds and investment trusts have affected the dealing mechanism. Institutional investors tend to be net buyers of securities and their assets are growing at such a rate (£1000 million per annum in the case of the insurance companies) that they are forced to find 'investment homes' for their funds and may thus bid up the price of securities.

In 1972 the Accepting Houses introduced a new dealing service known as Ariel as an alternative to the Stock Exchange. It aimed to bring together big buyers in order to reduce costs. For a short while it appeared that the Ariel system would threaten the traditional dealing system but it seems to have stabilized now with a very low percentage of the market.

BENEFITS PROVIDED BY SECURITY EXCHANGES

Organized security exchanges are said to provide important benefits to businesses in at least four ways:

1. Security exchanges facilitate the investment process by providing a market-place in which to conduct transactions efficiently and relatively inexpensively. Investors are thus assured that they will have a place in which to sell their securities, if they decide to do so. The increased liquidity thus provided by the exchanges makes investors willing to accept a lower rate of return on securities than they would otherwise require. This means that exchanges lower the cost of capital to businesses.

2. By providing a market, exchanges create an institution in which continuous transactions test the values of securities. The purchases and sales of securities record judgements on the values and prospects of companies and their securities. Companies whose prospects are judged favourably by the investment community will have a higher value, thus facilitating new financing and growth.
3. Security prices are relatively more stable because of the operation of the security exchanges. Organized markets improve liquidity by providing continuous markets which make for more frequent, but smaller, price changes. In the absence of organized markets, price changes would be less frequent but more violent.
4. The securities markets aid in the digestion of new security issues and facilitate their successful flotation.

THE LISTING REQUIREMENTS OF THE UK STOCK EXCHANGE

The UK Stock Exchange has certain requirements that firms must meet before their securities can be listed. Applications for a listing on the London Stock Exchange have to be accompanied by a prospectus drawn up according to the rules of the Stock Exchange. The nature of this prospectus will be considered in greater detail later in this chapter when the new issue market is discussed. Suffice it to say at this point that the requirements relate to size of company, number of years in business, earnings record, number of shares outstanding and the like.

The firm itself makes the decision to seek to list its securities on a stock exchange. Most firms will begin their lives as private companies whose shares are not quoted on any stock exchange. If they are a provincial firm they may initially seek a listing on the appropriate provincial exchange and later as the firm grows it may apply for a quotation on the UK Stock Exchange.[1]

The Stock Exchange Council requires that all companies seeking a listing on the UK Stock Exchange should adopt the terms of the Listing Agreement. A firm wishing to be listed should adopt the Listing Agreement by means of a vote of its Board of Directors. The Listing Agreement is intended to ensure that listed companies speedily disclose any new information regarding acquisitions, new operations abroad and changes in the character of the operations of the company which may lead to stock market price changes. The ultimate sanction of the Stock Exchange for a breach of the Listing Agreement is the suspension of dealing. For most firms the threat of a suspension is enough to ensure compliance with the rules.

Assuming a company qualifies, most people believe that a listing is beneficial both to it and to its shareholders. Listed companies receive a certain amount of free advertising and publicity, and their status as a listed company enhances their prestige and reputation. This probably has a beneficial effect on the sales of the products of the firm, and it is probably advantageous in terms of lowering the required rate of return on the ordinary shares. Investors respond favourably to increased information, increased liquidity and increased prestige; by providing investors with these services in the form of listing their companies' shares, financial managers lower their firms' cost of capital. It is much easier for a listed company to obtain new capital than it is for unquoted companies. Listing has some disadvantages. In recent years there have been signs of a trend in the opposite direction; that is, some companies have relinquished their listing. This has happened particularly as a result of the onerous listing requirements of the Stock Exchange and the greater risk of take-over faced by listed companies.

---

1. Since 1973 all the provincial stock exchanges have amalgamated with the UK Stock Exchange but firms quoted on, for instance, the Manchester exchange are not necessarily quoted in London, although they must still comply with the listing agreement.

THE MERCHANT BANKS

In the British economy, saving is done by one set of people whilst investing is done by another. ('Investing' is used here in the sense of actually putting money into plant, equipment and stocks, not in the sense of buying securities.) Thus, savings are made available to financial institutions who in turn channel the funds to firms who wish to use those funds to buy plant and equipment and to hold stocks.

One group of institutions performing this channelling role is the merchant banks. The term 'merchant bankers' is somewhat misleading in that merchant bankers are neither merchants nor bankers. That is, they do not invest their own funds permanently. What, then, is the nature of merchant banking?

The merchant banks operating in London are divided between the members of the London Accepting Houses Association (these are the oldest and longest-established institutions operating within this area and include such names as Rothschilds, Barings and Erlangers) and several other less-well-established merchant bankers. The merchant banks began life as merchants and began to operate in financial fields in the nineteenth century. In particular, they became the most significant acceptors of bills of exchange drawn on London. As British capital began to be exported overseas later in the century, the merchant banks became advisors to British companies operating abroad who wished to raise new capital on the London market. After the catastrophic loss of British investments abroad caused by the First World War and the Russian Revolution, the merchant banks began to be responsible for the issue of new capital in the domestic market.

Thus, the traditional role of the merchant banker has been the provision of advice regarding the issue of new securities by companies. Furthermore, the merchant banks have acted as middlemen in channelling the savings of individuals into the purchase of these new securities. In order to accomplish these objectives the merchant banks perform the functions of underwriting, marketing and pricing new issues.

Underwriting

Since the war most prospectus issues of shares have been *offers for sale*.[2] In all other methods of issuing securities the merchant bank or issuing house acts as the agent for the issue of shares. In the case of offers, the issuing house acts as the principal and buys the shares from the company before the issue is made. Irrespective of whether the issuing house is acting as the principal or merely the agent for a new issue of shares, it will be facing a business risk because it guarantees that the money will be raised. To cover itself it arranges with a number of other financial institutions, such as investment trusts or insurance companies, that they will underwrite the issue. These institutions are paid a fee (approximately $1\frac{1}{4}\%$) which is forthcoming even if the issue is fully subscribed. In addition, the institutions carrying out the underwriting facility will have the opportunity of obtaining some cheap shares. The underwriting commission is in any case a useful source of additional income for financial institutions such as investment trusts and insurance companies.

In periods of business uncertainty or depression (as, for instance, in the early 1970s) it is possible that a very large proportion of a new issue may be left with the underwriters.

2. The mechanics of offers for sale will be discussed later in this chapter.

Marketing new issues

The second function of merchant bankers is marketing new issues of securities. The merchant banker is a specialist who has a staff and dealer organization to distribute securities. He has an unrivalled knowledge of city institutions and a large number of contacts amongst them. Whenever it wished to make a new issue, each company would find it necessary to establish a marketing or selling organization. This would be a very expensive and inefficient method of selling new shares. The merchant banker has a permanent trained staff and dealer organization available to market new shares. In addition, the merchant bankers' reputation for selecting good companies and pricing securities fairly builds up a broad clientele over a period, further increasing the efficiency with which he can sell securities.

Pricing new issues

The issuing house has a considerable amount of discretion in the choice of security to be issued. In deciding between ordinary shares, debentures and preference shares it will take into account the problems of financial gearing and the likely impact on the cost of capital.[3]

Having decided how much new capital is required and the most suitable instrument by which that capital can be raised, the next task of the issuing house is to determine the price at which the shares are to be sold. The price at which a new issue of shares is offered to the market is determined to a large extent by the required rate of return that investors in that particular company expect from their investments. This is to a considerable degree a function of the opportunity cost of the investment; that is, the required rate of return currently enjoyed by investors from their investment in other firms in the same risk class as the firm seeking new capital. In order for the issue to be successful, the price must be attractive both to the underwriters and to the general public.

It is important for both the company and the issuing house that the issue should be a success. If the issue fails, that is if the shares are left with the underwriters because the issue was under-subscribed, the reputation of the issuing house will be sullied and a series of such failures could lead to a reduction in business in the future. From the point of view of the company, a failure could mean difficulties in coming to the market with future issues of capital and in the short run it would mean the embarrassment of a fall in the price of its existing shares. The success of the issue is therefore essential and it can best be assured by issuing the shares at a price slightly lower than the price at which the shares are expected to settle after the issue has been completed.

THE NEW ISSUE MARKET

After the issuing house has determined the price at which a new issue is to be made it becomes necessary to decide on the method by which the shares should be issued. Apart from rights issues which will be considered separately in Chapter 13 there are six different methods of issuing shares available to companies in Britain. These are the public issue by prospectus, the offer for sale, the private placing, the stock exchange introduction, the stock exchange placing and the tender method.

---

3. These factors will be discussed in more detail in Chapters 18 and 19.

Public issue by prospectus

This was the classic method by which British companies obtained new capital in the nineteenth and early twentieth century. It has now been to a large extent superseded by the offer for sale method which will be considered shortly in much more detail. By this method the *company*, through the agency of the issuing house, seeks to persuade the public to buy a large number of shares in the company in the shortest time possible. This is done by means of an advertisement in two London papers. The main difference between the public issue by prospectus method and the offer for sale is that in the former case the issuing house acts as the agent for the issue of shares whereas in the latter case it acts as the principal. Furthermore, vendor shares are prohibited in a public issue by prospectus.

Offer for sale

This method is used when a relatively large amount of capital is required. The shares are offered to the general public at a fixed price by the issuing house. The procedure of an offer can best be understood by considering an actual example. The example to be considered is the offer of shares in Eurotherm International by the issuing house Robert Fleming and Company on 18 May 1978. Eurotherm has been involved in the production of temperature controllers since 1965. By 1971 the company realized the need to diversify. Three subsidiary companies were created. These were Chessell Ltd, which produces potentiometric recorders, Shackleton Ltd, which produces controllers for electric motors, and Turnbull Ltd, which has developed a series of fully integrated measurement and control systems. The company hoped to be able to develop new products and market its existing products abroad. To do this it needed to obtain extra funds from the market. The directors decided to sell 2 850 390 shares with a book value of 10 pence at a price of £1 each.

Application for permission to publish the prospectus has to be made to the Committee on Quotations of the UK Stock Exchange. The rules regarding the composition of prospectuses are intended to ensure that investors are given enough information to enable them to make rational investment decisions. The information can now be summarized:

1. The prospectus must state the full names and addresses of all people concerned with the issue. In the case of Eurotherm these are the directors, the company secretary, the auditors, the solicitors, the bankers and the brokers.
2. Information is required concerning the capital structure and the voting rights of shareholders.
3. A summary of the company's articles of association is required.
4. A summary of the last five years' business of the company and a list of subsidiary companies must be made. For Eurotherm the creation of the subsidiary companies has been a significant part of its business in the past few years and thus a considerable amount of space is taken up with information concerning the activities of the subsidiary companies.
5. There must be a statement of trading and profit prospects.
6. The auditors of the company must produce a report setting out the profits and losses of the company during the previous five years.
7. Details of the shareholdings and salaries of each of the directors must be disclosed.
8. Contracts entered into during the past two years must be described. Eurotherm had been involved in the purchase of shares in a liquidated German company. As the Chessell Corporation was formed in 1977 it was necessary to mention the contract which led to its formation in the prospectus.

Once the prospectus has been published at least two days must elapse before a formal application for a quotation is made to the Stock Exchange Committee on Quotations. The application list for the shares will open on a date stated in the prospectus. In the case of Eurotherm this was Thursday 18 May 1978. Prior to this date the prospectus will have been placed in two London daily papers in order to appraise the public of the issue.

If the issue is a popular one, as was the case with Eurotherm which was over-subscribed 245 times, more than sufficient applications will have been received before the list is due to open. If over-subscription occurs, the issuing house has the problem of allotting the available securities among the applicants. In order that a ready market should exist when dealings in the securities commence it is necessary that as many applicants as possible get some shares. Thus, people who have applied for large holdings usually obtain only a small proportion of the shares they have applied for whilst a sizeable number of small applications is settled in full.

Private placing

This method is used by unquoted companies who require a small amount of funds and wish to keep the expenses of the issue as low as possible. Either the issuing house or a firm of stockbrokers will agree to buy a small number of the securities of the company in question with the intention of placing them with some institutional investors. It is usually the intention to have the shares quoted on the London Stock Exchange at some time in the future. Each issuing house will have a list of prospective institutional investors, such as insurance companies and pension funds, who are willing to accept such placings.

The main advantage of this method lies in its low cost. There is no need for the administrative costs of the allotment procedure which is necessary when making offers, nor is there any need for underwriting.

Stock Exchange introduction

This form of issue is different from all other methods of issue in that no extra capital is raised. The real function of an introduction is to make it possible for a firm to obtain a quotation on the UK Stock Exchange. After the introduction has been approved by the quotations subcommittee of the Stock Exchange and assurances have been given that there will eventually be a free market in the shares of the company, the introduction is advertised in two London daily papers. Sometimes the Stock Exchange requires existing shareholders in the firm to make some of their shares available to the jobbers to ensure that there will be a free market. There are several advantages of introductions from the point of view of the company:

1. It makes the shares of the company marketable. Quoted shares have a known price whereas shares in unquoted companies are difficult both to value and to sell privately.
2. Because the shares can readily be sold to the public the price of quoted shares tends to be higher than that of unquoted shares of the same quality.
3. One or more of the majority shareholders may wish to have a 'true' valuation of their holding in order that capital transfer tax can be levied at an appropriate rate in the event of their death. Many investors prefer to have this valuation made by the market rather than by the Inland Revenue.
4. An introduction is less expensive than other types of issue. Advertising costs are kept to a minimum, there is no need for underwriting and there is no need for an allocation procedure.

Stock Exchange placing

This method is an amalgam of the private placing and the stock exchange introduction. The company concerned will need both a quotation for its shares and a small amount of capital which is usually raised from selected institutional investors. Placings are permitted by the Stock Exchange only when there is unlikely to be a great public demand for the securities. Over the years the maximum amount that can be raised by a placing of equity shares has been increased. The present limit is £1 million.

Issues by tender

This method is sometimes used when the firm is not sure of the price at which to issue the shares. A minimum price is set on the shares and the public is invited to bid for shares. The method was used most frequently in the 1960s when share prices were rising.

Allotments are not made at the highest price but at the price which will just clear all the shares. Thus, if one million shares are on offer and if these shares can all be sold at a price of £2.50 per share, this will be the striking price (i.e. the price at which the shares are sold) even though some investors have made bids at prices greater than £2.50.

COSTS OF FLOTATION

The costs of selling new issues of securities is put into perspective in Tables 12–1 and 12–2.

Table 12–1 *Typical Costs of Issues to Raise £2 Million Ordinary Shares.*[a]

Item	Offers or prospectuses £	Placings £	Rights £
Capital duty at 1%	20 000	20 000	20 000
Advertising	25 000	–	–
Legal and accounting fees	35 000	8 000	8 000
Listing fee	2 400	1 200	1 200
Bankers' and registrars' fees	15 000	2 000	5 000
Printers:			
Extel card	2 000		–
Allotment letters	2 000	1 500	1 500
Share certificates	1 500	1 000	1 000
Offer for sale document	10 000	–	–
Circular	–	4 000	4 000
Underwriting commission at $1\frac{1}{4}$%	25 000	–	25 000
Broker's commission at $\frac{1}{4}$%	5 000	5 000	5 000
Issuing house $\frac{1}{2}$%	10 000	10 000	10 000
Total cost	152 900	52 700	80 700
Cost as percentage of proceeds of issue	7.6%	2.6%	4.0%

[a] Source: Committee to review the financing of financial institutions, *Evidence on the financing of Industry and Trade*, Vol. 3, London HMSO, 1978.

Two important generalizations can be drawn from this data:

1. The cost of flotation for ordinary shares is greater than for fixed interest stocks.
2. The cost of offers for sale as a percentage of gross proceeds is greater than the cost of placings.

What are the reasons for these relationships? The explanations are to be found in the amount of risk involved and in the problems of physical distribution. Fixed interest

Table 12–2 *Typical Costs of Issue to Raise £2 Million Fixed Interest Stock*[a].

Item	Placing £	Offer £
Advertising	1 700	12 500
Accountancy fees	4 700	5 000
Legal fees	10 000	15 000
Bankers' and registrars' fees	3 000	15 000
Listing fee	1 200	1 200
Printing:		
Extel card	2 500	2 000
Allotment letters	1 500	2 000
Stock certificates	1 000	1 500
Trust deed	2 500	2 500
Offer for sale document	–	10 000
Allotment commission at $\frac{1}{8}$%	–	2 500 max
Commitment commission	1 000	–
Market discount	1 500 max	
Underwriting commission at $1\frac{1}{4}$%	–	25 000
Broker's fee at $\frac{1}{4}$%	5 000	5 000
Issuing house $\frac{1}{2}$ to $\frac{3}{4}$%	15 000	15 000
Total cost of issue	50 600	114 200
Cost as percentage of proceeds of issue	2.5%	5.7%

[a] Source: Committee to review the financing of financial institutions, *Evidence on the Financing of Industry and Trade*, Vol. 3, London: HMSO, 1978.

securities are generally bought in large blocks by a relatively few institutional investors, whereas ordinary shares are bought by large numbers of individuals. This is one reason why the expenses of marketing ordinary shares are greater. Similarly, ordinary shares are more volatile than fixed interest securities, so underwriting risks are greater for ordinary shares than for fixed interest securities.

Costs tend to be greater as a percentage of total proceeds for small issues, such as placings, than for large issues, such as offers for sale. The explanation for this variation is easily found. In the first place, certain fixed expenses are associated with any issue of securities: the underwriting investigation, the legal fees and so forth. Since these expenses are relatively large and fixed, their percentage of the total cost of flotation runs high on small issues. Second, small issues are typically those of less-well-known firms, so underwriting expenses may be larger than usual because the danger of omitting vital information is greater.

Flotation costs are also influenced by whether or not the issue is a rights issue and, if it is, by the extent of the underpricing.[4] If there is substantial underpricing the issuing house bears little risk of inability to sell the shares. Furthermore, very little selling effort will be required in such a situation. These two factors combine to enable a company to float new securities to its own shareholders at a relatively low cost.

SUMMARY

Securities of large public companies are traded on the UK Stock Exchange. The UK Stock Exchange is unique in that it operates the single-capacity system. The opportunities for

4. Rights issues involve the sale of shares to existing shareholders only. This topic is discussed extensively in Chapter 13.

investors to buy shares on account lead to a greater volume of trade than might otherwise be the case.

Merchant banks provide middleman services to both buyers and sellers of securities. They help plan the issue, underwrite it and handle the job of selling the issue to potential investors. The cost of this service to a company is related to the amount of work that the merchant bank must do to place the issue. If investors are not satisfied with the performance of the issuing house they may go elsewhere.

Flotation costs are lower for debentures than for ordinary shares. Larger companies have lower flotation costs than smaller ones for each type of security and most companies can cut their flotation costs by making full use of rights issues as a method of issuing new securities. (Rights issues are discussed in Chapter 13.)

QUESTIONS

12–1. State the advantages to a firm that obtains a quotation on a major stock exchange.

12–2. Would you expect the cost of capital to a private company to be altered if it obtained a quotation on the UK Stock Exchange? Explain.

12–3. Evaluate the following statement: The existence of the Stock Exchange account can be seen either as a flexible process which encourages genuine investors by giving them some leeway before they have to pay for their shares or as a process which encourages speculation and gambling and is to be condemned.

12–4. Evaluate this statement: The fundamental purpose of the rules of the Stock Exchange governing new issues is to prevent investors, principally small ones, from sustaining losses on the purchase of shares.

12–5. Suppose two firms were each selling £10 million of ordinary shares. The firms are alike – that is, they are of the same size, in the same industry, have the same gearing and have other similarities – except that one is a public company and the other is an unquoted private company. Would their costs of flotation be the same? If different, state the probable relationships. If the issue were debentures would your answer be the same?

12–6. Define these terms: stockbroker, jobber, issuing house, and underwriting.

12–7. Before entering a formal agreement, issuing houses investigate quite carefully the companies whose securities they issue; this is especially true of the issues of firms going public for the first time. Since the issuing houses do not plan to hold the securities themselves but plan to sell them to others as soon as possible, why are they so concerned about making careful investigations?

12–8. Since new issues are priced in relation to existing shares, should there be a spread between the yields on the new and the existing issues? Discuss this matter separately for ordinary share issues and for debenture issues.

12–9. What issues are raised by the increasing purchase of equities by institutional investors?

12–10. Why, in your opinion, does the number of transactions by the Ariel system account for so small a percentage of total transactions on the UK Stock Exchange?

12–11. Do you believe that the jobbing system leads to a more efficient allocation of resources within the capital market?

12–12. Why are there so many methods of issuing shares on the UK Stock Exchange? Which method do you think would be most appropriate for (a) a long-established company requiring a large amount of new capital, and (b) a small company wishing to raise a small amount of capital and obtain a quotation on the Stock Exchange for the first time?

PROBLEMS

12–1. Macgregor Enterprises is planning to issue 5 million new £1 ordinary shares. In reaching the decision as to the method of issue, two alternatives were considered:

1. A rights issue. The flotation cost of this issue would be 4 per cent.

2. An offer for sale. The flotation cost of this issue would be 7 per cent.

Although the rights issue is cheaper, Macgregor chose to make an offer for sale. Why might this be so?

Discuss the influence of other factors in addition to direct costs that must be taken into account when choosing between the two alternatives. In your answer consider the following as well as other alternatives that might occur to you:

1. Risk.
2. Other internal benefits and costs.
3. Distribution.
4. The likely effect of the issue on share price.

12–2. Each of three companies is considering a new issue:
Bernard Bulldozers Ltd is a small company producing bulldozers which it leases to construction companies. The company has total assets of £3 million. It wishes to raise a further £500 000 and has decided upon a placing.

Atlas Aircraft has assets of £50 million and has decided to make a £5 million rights issue.
I.C.I. plans a £50 million rights issue.
(a) What will the likely costs of flotation be for each company?
(b) Why is there a difference in the percentage costs?

SELECTED REFERENCES

Bevan, J. Are the issuing houses getting it wrong? *Investors' Chronicle* (28 July 1978): 293.
Briston, R. J. *The Stock Exchange and Investment Analysis.* London: Allen and Unwin, 1975.
Dobbins, R. Institutional shareholders in the UK equity market. *Accounting and Business Research* (Winter 1974): 9–17.
Economist. The unchanging city (5 October 1976).
Larcier, R. The rise and fall of the P/E ratio. *Investment Analyst* (September 1977): 25–30.
Morgan, E. V. The Stock Exchange – its history and functions. *Elek* (1969).
Moyle, *The Pattern of Ordinary Share Ownership.* Cambridge University Press, 1971.
Naylor, G. *Guide to Shareholders' Rights.* London: Allen and Unwin, 1969.
Purdy, D. E. No par value shares. *Investment Analyst* (September 1974).
Stock Exchange Council. *Admission of Securities to Listing.* London: 1973.
Vernon, R. A., Middleton, M. and Harper, D. G. *Who Owns the Blue-Chips?* London: Gower Press, 1973.

Chapter 13

Ordinary Shares

Ordinary shares constitute the first source of funds to a new business. Accordingly, our discussion of the various forms of long-term financing will begin with ordinary shares.

APPORTIONMENT OF INCOME CONTROL AND RISK

The rights of ordinary shareholders are laid down in the Companies Acts of 1948 and 1967.

Collective rights

Certain collective rights are given to ordinary shareholders. Some of the more important rights allow shareholders:

1. To alter the company's objects. This requires a special resolution of the company and special resolutions must be passed by a majority of not less than three-quarters of the members who are entitled to vote and do so, either by proxy or in person. Such changes can be made only to a limited extent and must satisfy the relevant clauses of the Companies Act 1948.
2. To appoint and remove directors and to determine their duties.
3. To authorize the sale of fixed assets.
4. To enter into mergers.
5. To change the amount of authorized share capital.
6. To issue preference shares, debentures and other securities.

Specific rights

Holders of ordinary shares also have specific rights:

1. They have the right to vote in the manner prescribed in the Articles of Association.

2. They may sell their share certificates and thus transfer their ownership interest to other people.
3. They may attend the annual general meeting of the company and inspect the company accounts.
4. Although they will be the last to receive the assets of the company on liquidation they will share amongst themselves the residual assets of the company.

Apportionment of income

Two important positive considerations affect ordinary shareholders: income and control. The right to income carries risks of loss. Control also involves responsibility and liability. A sole proprietor has a 100 per cent right to income and control and to loss and responsibility. As soon as he incurs debt, however, he enters into contracts that place limitations on his complete freedom to control the firm and to apportion the firm's income.

In a partnership, these rights are apportioned among the partners in an agreed manner. In a company, more significant matters arise concerning the rights of the owners.

Apportionment of control

As a result of their voting rights, ordinary shareholders have legal control of the company. In practice, however, members of the board of directors, who often hold only a minority of the total shareholding, tend to control the company. Nevertheless, shareholders can reassert their control if they are dissatisfied with the policies of the company.[1]

As receivers of residual income, ordinary shareholders are frequently referred to as the ultimate entrepreneurs in the firm. They are the ultimate owners and they have the ultimate control. Presumably the firm is managed on behalf of its owners, the ordinary shareholders, but there has been much dispute about the actual situation. It has been suggested that companies are fictitious corporations with an identity separate from that of their owners and that the company exists to fulfil certain functions for shareholders as only one among many important groups such as workers, consumers and the economy as a whole. This view may have some validity but it should also be noted that often the managers of the firm are also large shareholders. There is an increasing trend towards the provision of shares as a form of bonus for managers. These actions are, of course, designed to increase the firm's earnings and share price and thus make the managers' personal goals more consistent with those of the shareholders.

Apportionment of risk

Because, on liquidation, ordinary shareholders' claims are last in the order of priority, the portion of capital they contribute provides a cushion for creditors if losses occur. The equity-to-total-assets ratio indicates the percentage by which assets may shrink in value on liquidation before creditors will incur losses.

For example, compare two companies, A and B, whose balance sheets are shown in Table 13–1. The ratio of equity to total assets in company A is 80 per cent. Total assets would therefore have to shrink by 80 per cent before creditors would lose money. By contrast, in company B the extent by which assets may shrink in value on liquidation before creditors lose money is only 40 per cent.

---

1. Shareholders often form 'ginger groups' to attend the annual general meeting with the intention of altering the composition of the board or altering the policies which the board has been pursuing.

Table 13–1 *Balance Sheets for Companies A and B.*

Company A	£	Company B	£
Debentures	20	Debentures	60
Ordinary shares	80	Ordinary shares	40
Total claims	100	Total claims	100
Total assets	100	Total assets	100

ORDINARY SHARE FINANCING

Before undertaking an analysis of ordinary share financing it is desirable to describe some of its additional important characteristics. These topics include:

1. The nature of the voting rights.
2. Pre-emptive rights.
3. Variations in the types of ordinary shares.

Voting rights

For each ordinary share owned, the holder has the right to cast one vote at the annual general meeting of the company or at such special meetings as may be called. This is not the case for owners of 'A' ordinary shares who do not possess voting rights although their shares are identical to other ordinary shares in other respects.

ORDINARY SHARES AS A SOURCE OF FUNDS

Thus far, the chapter has covered the main characteristics of ordinary shares. By way of a summary of the important aspects of ordinary shares we now appraise this type of financing from the standpoint of the issuer.

From the viewpoint of the issuer

Advantages

First, there are no fixed charges attached to ordinary shares. If a company generates enough earnings it will be able to pay a dividend but there is no legal obligation to pay dividends. Second, ordinary shares carry no fixed maturity date. Third, since ordinary shares provide a cushion against losses for creditors, the sale of ordinary shares rather than other securities increases the credit worthiness of the firm. Fourth, ordinary shares can often be sold more easily than debentures. Ordinary shares appeal to certain types of investors for two reasons:

1. They typically carry a higher expected return than do preference shares or debentures.

2. Traditionally they provide the investor with a better hedge against inflation than do preference shares or debentures. Normally, ordinary shares rise in value when the value of real assets rises during an inflationary period.

Fifth, returns from the sale of ordinary shares in the form of capital gains are subject to the capital gains tax rather than corporation tax. For investors whose marginal rate of tax is higher than the standard rate of tax there may be a lower effective tax rate on returns from ordinary shares than on returns from debentures.

Disadvantages

First, the sale of ordinary shares extends voting rights or control to the additional shareholders who are brought into the company. For this reason, amongst others, additional equity financing is often avoided by small and new firms. The owner-managers may be unwilling to share control of their company with outsiders. The institutional investors are not interested in very small shareholdings in companies.

Second, extra ordinary shares give more people the right to share with the existing owners in the company's profits. The issue of debentures may enable the firm to utilize funds at a fixed cost, whereas the issue of new ordinary shares gives equal rights to new shareholders to share in the net profits of the firm.

Third, as we saw in Chapter 12, the costs of underwriting and distributing new issues of ordinary shares are usually higher than those for underwriting and distributing preference shares or debentures.

Fourth, as we shall see in Chapter 19, if the firm has more equity or less debt than is called for in the optimum capital structure the average cost of capital will be higher than necessary.

Fifth, dividends payable to ordinary shareholders are not deductible as an expense for the purposes of corporation tax but debenture interest is deductible. The impact of this factor is reflected in the relative cost of equity capital vis-a-vis debt capital.

From a social viewpoint

Ordinary shares should also be considered from a social viewpoint. Firms financed by means of ordinary shares are less vulnerable to the consequences of declines in sales and earnings. If sales and earnings decline, ordinary share financing involves no fixed charges, the payment of which may force the firm into liquidation.

Another aspect of ordinary share financing may have less desirable consequences, however. Ordinary share prices fall in recessions, representing a rise in the cost of equity capital. The rising cost of equity raises the overall cost of capital which in turn reduces investment. This reduction further aggravates the recession. However, an expanding economy is accompanied by rising share prices and with rising share prices comes a drop in the cost of equity capital. This in turn stimulates investment which may add to the developing inflationary boom. In summary, a consideration of its effect on the cost of capital suggests that ordinary share financing may tend to amplify cyclical fluctuations.

RIGHTS ISSUES

A firm wishing to raise new equity capital has a choice of making the sale to its existing shareholders or to an entirely new set of investors. If a sale to existing shareholders is made this is known as a *rights issue.* Each existing shareholder is given an option to buy a certain number of the new shares. Each shareholder receives one right for each share he holds. The advantages and disadvantages of rights issues are described in the following section.

THEORETICAL RELATIONSHIPS

Several matters confront the financial manager who is considering a rights issue. The various considerations can be made clear by the use of the illustrative data on Delarue Enterprises Limited. The partial balance sheet and income statement for Delarue Enterprises are given in Table 13–2.

Table 13–2 *Delarue Enterprises, Financial Statements before Rights Issue.*

Partial balance sheet	£ million
50 000 000 £1 ordinary shares	50.0
Retained earnings	40.0
Total debt at 8%	60.0
Total assets £150 million. Total claims	150.0
Partial income statement	**£ million**
Total earnings	30.0
Interest	4.8
Taxable earnings	25.2
Taxation at 50%	12.6
Earnings available to ordinary shareholders	12.6
Earnings per share = 25.2 pence	

Delarue earns £12 600 000 after taxes and has 50 million shares outstanding, so earnings per share are 25.2 pence. The shares are selling for £2.50. The company wants to raise an additional £20 million through a rights issue. Having determined the amount that is to be raised by the rights issue it is necessary to determine the number of shares to be issued and to decide on their price. Although the firm could issue the new shares at the market price (£2.50) this is not the normal procedure. It is much more common in Britain for new shares issued by means of a rights issue to be issued at a price which is much lower than the existing market price.

If the ex-rights share price is based on a correct estimate of expected future earnings, and if the market correctly estimates the earnings from the new funds, the price at which the new shares are issued should cause no anxiety to the existing shareholders. The new issue should leave the existing shareholders at least as well off as they were before the rights issue even if they sell their rights rather than subscribe personally.

Value of a right

It is clearly worth something to be able to buy shares which are currently selling at £2.50 in the market for a price lower than that. To illustrate, we will continue with the example of Delarue Enterprises, assuming that it will raise the £20 million by selling 10 million new shares at £2 each. The market value of the old shares was £125 million (£2.50 per share times 50 million shares). When the firm sells the new shares it brings in an additional £20 million. At a first approximation we assume that the market value of the firm's ordinary shares increases by exactly this £20 million. In fact, the market value of all the ordinary shares will go up by more than £20 million if investors think that the company will be able to invest these funds at a yield substantially in excess of the cost of equity capital, but it will go up by less than £20 million if investors are doubtful of the company's ability to put the new funds to work profitably in the near future.

Under the assumption that market value exactly reflects the new funds brought in, the total market value of the ordinary shares after the new issue will be £145 million. Dividing this value by the new total number of shares outstanding, which is 60 million, we obtain a new market value of £2.42 per share. Therefore, we see that after the financing has been completed the price of the ordinary shares will have fallen from £2.50 to £2.42.

Since the rights gave the shareholders the privilege of buying for only £2 a share that will end up by being worth £2.42, thus saving 42 pence, 42 pence is the value of the right.

Timetable of rights

In order to understand the practical operation of a rights issue it will be useful to examine the timetable for an actual rights issue. In 1974 Commercial Union courageously made a rights issue in the trough of a severe depression in stock market prices. They issued 103 973 617 new ordinary shares at a price of 60 pence per share. Commercial Union's shares were standing at 85 pence at the time. Immediately after the news of the rights issue the price of Commercial Union's shares fell to 72 pence. The rights issue was announced on 24 September and an extraordinary general meeting of the company was held on 21 October. Dealings in the new ordinary shares began on 22 October and the latest time for acceptance was 11 November.

EFFECTS ON POSITION OF SHAREHOLDERS

A shareholder has the choice of exercising his rights or selling them. If he has sufficient funds and if he wants to buy more of the company's shares he will exercise the rights. If he does not have the money or does not want to buy any more shares he will sell his rights. In any case the shareholder will neither benefit nor lose by the rights issue. This statement can be made clear by considering the position of an individual Commercial Union shareholder.

Assume that the shareholder had eight Commercial Union shares before the rights issue. The eight shares each had a market value of 85 pence so the shareholder owned shares in Commercial Union to a total value of 8 × 85 pence = £6.80. If he exercises his rights he will be able to buy one new ordinary share for every two ordinary shares that he presently holds. The price of the new share is 60 pence per share so his new investment will be 4 × 60 pence = £2.40. His total investment is now £6.80 + £2.40 = £9.20. He now owns 12 Commercial Union shares which will have a theoretical ex-rights value of

$$(P_p N_o + P_N N_N)/N$$

where

P_p = pre-issue price
N_o = number of old shares
P_N = new issue price
N_N = number of new shares
N = total number of shares

that is

(85 × 8 + 60 × 4)/12 pence
= £9.20/12
= *76.67 pence*

The value of his shares is now 12 × 76.67 pence or £9.20, exactly what he has invested in the company.

Alternatively if he sold his four rights, which have a value which is simply the difference between the ex rights market price and the new issue price of the new shares he would have:

4 × (76.67 – 60) pence
= £0.67

He would now have his original eight shares plus £0.67 in cash. But his original eight shares now have a market price of 8 × 76.67 pence = £6.13. The £6.13 plus the £0.67 cash is the same as the original investment of £6.80 that he had in the company. From a purely mechanical or arithmetical standpoint the shareholder neither benefits nor gains from the sale of additional shares through rights. Of course, if he forgets to sell or exercise his rights or if brokerage costs of selling are excessive, then a shareholder can suffer a loss, but in general the issuing house makes special efforts to minimize brokerage costs, and adequate time is given to enable shareholders to take some action, so losses are minimal.

Effect on subsequent behaviour of market price

It is often said that rights issues will depress the price of the existing ordinary shares of a company. To the extent that the rights price is lower than the current market price the effect on the market price of the ordinary shares will be similar to that experienced when a company makes a bonus issue. That is, the new market price will probably be considerably lower than the original price.

The second point is whether, because of the rights issue, the actual new market price will be the same as the theoretical market price (in the case of Commercial Union this is 76.67 pence) or lower or higher. Again, empirical analysis of the movement in market prices indicates that generalization is not practical. What happens to the market price of the shares after the rights issue depends upon the future earnings prospects of the company.

ADVANTAGES OF THE USE OF RIGHTS ISSUES

We have seen that the pre-emptive right gives the shareholders the protection of preserving their share in the ownership and control of the company. Their earnings are also safeguarded. The firm also benefits. By offering new issues of securities to the existing shareholders, it increases the likelihood of a favourable reception for the new shares. By their ownership of ordinary shares in the company these investors have already indicated a favourable evaluation of the company. They may be receptive to the purchase of additional shares, particularly when the additional reasons indicated below are taken into account.

The flotation costs of rights issues are lower than those for offers for sale.[2] The stock exchange estimates that the average cost of rights issues is 4 per cent as compared with 7.6 per cent for offers for sale.

The company may obtain positive benefits from under-pricing. Since a rights issue is similar in some way to a bonus issue it will cause the market price of the shares to fall to a level lower than it would otherwise have been. But rights issues may increase the number of shareholders in a company by bringing the share price into a more attractive trading level.

Finally, the total effect of a rights issue may be to stimulate an enthusiastic response

2. See Table 12–1 in Chapter 12.

from shareholders and the investment market as a whole, with the result that opportunities for financing become more attractive to the firm. Thus, the company may be able to engage in ordinary share financing at lower costs and under more favourable terms.

SUMMARY

In this chapter the characteristics of ordinary share financing have been presented. The advantages and disadvantages of external equity financing, compared with the use of preference shares or debentures, have been described. The purpose of the descriptive background material has been to provide a basis for making sound decisions when ordinary share financing is being considered as a possible alternative.

The chapter also discussed the key decisions facing the financial manager when he considers a rights issue and indicated the major features bearing on such decisions. Rights issues may be used effectively by financial managers to increase the goodwill of shareholders. If the new financing associated with the rights represents a sound decision – one likely to result in improved earnings for the firm – a rise in share values will probably result. The use of rights will permit shareholders to preserve their positions or to improve them. However, if investors feel that the new financing is not well advised the rights issue may cause the price of the shares to decline by more than the value of the rights. Because the rights issue is directed to existing shareholders it may be possible to reduce the costs of floating the new issue.

The subsequent price behaviour of the ordinary shares after the rights issue will reflect the earnings and dividend prospects of the company, as well as the underlying developments in the securities markets. The fact that a rights issue has been made may be an indicator of prospective growth in the sales and earnings of the company. The effects of these developments on the market behaviour of the rights and the securities before, during and after the rights trading period will reflect the expectations of investors towards the outlook for the earnings and dividends of the firm.

QUESTIONS

13–1. By what percentage could total assets shrink in value on liquidation before creditors incur losses in each of the following cases:
   (a) Equity to total asset ratio, 50 per cent?
   (b) Debt to equity ratio, 50 per cent?
   (c) Debt to total asset ratio, 40 per cent?

13–2. Should the pre-emptive rights entitle shareholders to purchase convertible debentures before they are offered to outsiders?

13–3. It is frequently stated that the primary purpose of the pre-emptive right is to allow individuals to maintain their proportionate share of the ownership and control of a company. Just how important do you suppose this consideration is for the average shareholder of a firm whose shares are traded on the UK Stock Exchange? Is the pre-emptive right likely to be of more importance to shareholders of private companies?

13–4. How would the success of a rights offering be affected by a declining stock market?

13–5. What are some of the advantages and disadvantages of setting the subscription price on a rights issue substantially below the current market price of the shares?

PROBLEMS

13–1. The ordinary shares of Arlington Development Company are selling for £3.20 on the market. Shareholders are offered one new share at a subscription price of £2 for every three shares held. What is the value of each right?

13–2. United Appliance Company ordinary shares are priced at £4 on the market. Notice is given that shareholders may purchase one new share at a price of £2.75 for every four shares held. You hold 250 shares at the time of the notice.
(a) At approximately what market price will each right sell?
(b) Why will this be the approximate price?
(c) What effect will the issuance of rights have on the original market price?

13–3. Eileen has 600 shares of Fisher Industries. The market price per share is £8.10. The company now offers shareholders one new share to be purchased for £4.50 for every five shares held.
(a) Determine the value of each right.
(b) Assume that Eileen
(i) Uses half her rights and sells the others.
(ii) Sells all her rights at the theoretical market price. Prepare a statement showing the changes in her position, under the above assumptions.

13–4. As a shareholder of Younger Corporation, you are notified that for each seven shares you own you have the right to purchase one additional share at a price of £1.50. The current market price of Younger shares is £6.30 per share.
(a) Determine the value of each right.
(b) At the time of the issue your total assets consist of 490 shares of Younger stock and £1500 in cash. Prepare a statement to show total assets before the issue, and total assets after the issue if you exercise all of the rights.
(c) Prepare a statement to show total assets after the issue if you sell all of the rights.

13–5. The Northridge Company has the following balance sheet and income statement.

The Northridge company, Balance Sheet before Rights Issue.

	£	
1 000 000 ordinary shares	3 000 000	
Retained earnings	4 000 000	
Total debt (6%)	7 000 000	
Total claims	14 000 000	Total assets £14 000 000

Income statement

	£
Earnings	1 680 000
Interest	420 000
Earnings before tax	1 260 000
Corporation tax (50%)	630 000
Earnings available to ordinary shareholders	630 000
Earnings per share	63 pence
Dividend per share (56% payout)	35.3 pence
P/E ratio	15 times
Market price	£9.45

The Northridge Company plans to raise an additional £5 million through a rights issue. The additional funds will continue to earn 12 per cent. The price/earnings ratio is assumed to remain at 15 times, the dividend payout will continue to be 56 per cent, and the 50 per cent tax rate will remain in effect.
(a) Assuming subscription prices of £2.50, £5.0 and £8.0 a share:
(i) How many additional shares will have to be sold?
(ii) How many rights will be required to purchase one new share?
(iii) What will be the new earnings per share?
(iv) What will be the new market price per share?
(v) What will be the new dividend per share if the dividend payout ratio is maintained?

13–6. The Frost Crop Food Company is engaged principally in the business of growing, processing and marketing a variety of frozen vegetables and is a major company in this field. High-quality products are produced and marketed at premium prices.

During each of the past several years the company's sales have increased and the stocks have been financed from short-term sources. The board have discussed the idea of refinancing their bank loans with long-term debt or ordinary shares. An ordinary share issue of 310 000 shares sold at this time (present market price £7.20 a share) would yield £21 million after expenses. This same sum could be raised by selling 12-year debentures with an interest rate of 8 per cent and a sinking fund to redeem the debentures over their 12-year life. (See financial statements below.)

(a) Should Frost Crop Food refinance the short-term loans? Why?

(b) If the the bank loans should be refinanced, what factors should be considered in determining which form of financing to use? (This question should not be answered in terms of precise cost of capital calculated.)

Food Processing Industry Financial Ratios.

Current ratio	2.2 times
Sales to total assets	2.0 times
Sales to stock	5.6 times
Average collection period	22.0 days
Current debt/total assets	25–30%
Long-term debt/total assets	10–15%
Preferred/total assets	0.5%
Net worth/total assets	60–65%
Profits to sales	2.3%
Net profits to total assets	4.0%
Profits to net worth	8.4%
Expected growth rate of earnings and dividends	6.5%

Frost Crop Food Company, Balance Sheet 31 *March* 1978[a] *(in £millions).*

Ordinary share capital (20 000 000 ordinary shares)	£12	Fixed assets	£ 69
Reserves	63	Current assets	141
Preference share capital	9		
Debenture capital (5%)	63		
Short-term loan	36		
Trade creditors	12		
Accrued expenses	15		
Total claims on assets	£210	Total assets	£210

[a] The majority of harvesting activities do not begin until late April or May.

Frost Crop Food Company, Statement of Income Year Ended 31 *March (in £millions).*

	1975	1976	1977	1978
Net sales	£225.0	£234.6	£292.8	£347.1
Cost of goods sold	146.1	156.6	195.3	230.4
Gross profit	78.9	78.0	97.5	116.7
Other expenses	61.8	66.0	81.0	88.5
Operating income	17.1	12.0	16.5	28.2
Other income (net)	(3.3)	(4.2)	(5.7)	(9.3)
Earnings before tax	13.8	7.8	10.8	18.9
Corporation tax	7.2	3.3	5.4	9.6
Net profit	6.6	4.5	5.4	9.3
Preference dividend	0.3	0.3	0.3	0.3
Earnings available to ordinary shareholders	£ 6.3	£ 4.2	£ 5.1	£9.0
Earnings per share (pence)	31.5	21.0	25.5	45.0
Cash dividends per share (pence)	12.9	14.4	15.9	18.0
Price range for ordinary shares				
High	£6.60	£6.90	£6.60	£8.10
Low	£3.00	£4.20	£5.10	£6.30

SELECTED REFERENCES

Briston, R. J. and Greensted, C. S. Shareholder behaviour in the new issue market. *Accounting and Business Research* (Spring 1976): 125–134.

Darby, D. J. *The Financing of Industry and Trade.* London: Pitman, 1970.

Davis, E. W. and Yeomans, R. A. *Company Finance and the Capital Market.* Cambridge University Press, 1974.

Donaldson, Gordon. Financial goals: management vs. stockholders. *Harvard Business Review* 41 (May–June 1963): 116–129.

Finn, F. J. Stock splits: prior and subsequent price relationships. *Journal of Business Finance and Accounting* (Spring 1974): 93–108.

Firth, M. A. *A Study of the Incidence and Impact of Capitalisation Issues.* Institute of Chartered Accountants, 1974.

Furst, Richard W. Does listing increase the market price of common stocks? *Journal of Business* 43 (April 1970): 174–180.

Harding, P. A. Equity rights issues. *Investment Analyst* (September 1976): 5–15.

Ibbotson, R. R. Price performance of common stock new issues. *Journal of Financial Economics* 2 (September 1975): 235–272.

Keane, Simon M. The significance of the issue price in rights issues. *Journal of Business Finance* 4, no. 3 (1972): 40–45.

Lee, Steven James. Going private. *Financial Executive* 42 (December 1974): 10–15.

Logue, Dennis E. On the pricing of unseasoned equity issues: 1965–1969. *Journal of Financial and Quantitative Analysis* 8 (January 1973): 91–104.

Lowe, H. D. The classification of corporate stock equities. *Accounting Review* 36 (July 1961): 425–433.

McDonald, J. G. and Fisher, A. K. New issue stock price behavior. *Journal of Finance* 27 (March 1972): 97–102.

Midgeley, K. and Burns, R. G. *Business Finance and the Capital Market.* London: Macmillan, 1976.

Nelson, J. Russell. Price effects in rights offerings. *Journal of Finance* 20 (December 1965): 647–650.

Newbould, G. D. *Business Finance.* London: Harrap, 1970.

Skerratt, L. C. L. and Peasnell, K. V. Anti-dilution of earnings per share. *Accounting and Business Research* (Winter 1975): 57–62.

Stevenson, Harold W. *Common Stock Financing.* Ann Arbor, Mich.: University of Michigan, 1957.

Thompson, Howard E. A note on the value of rights in estimating the investor capitalization rate. *Journal of Finance* 28 (March 1973): 157–160.

Van Horne, James C. New listings and their price behavior. *Journal of Finance* 25 (September 1970): 783–794.

Weston, C. R. Adjustment to future dividend rates in the prediction of ex-rights prices. *Journal of Business Finance and Accounting* (Autumn 1974): 335–341.

Chapter 14

Loan Capital

Different classes of investors favour different classes of securities, and tastes change over time. By 'packaging' a company's securities it is possible at any given point of time to make them attractive to most potential investors. This will help to keep the cost of capital to a minimum. This chapter deals with the two most important types of long-term fixed income securities – debentures and preference shares.

INSTRUMENTS OF LONG-TERM DEBT FINANCING

For an understanding of long-term forms of financing we need some familiarity with technical terminology. The discussion of long-term debt therefore begins with an explanation of several important instruments and terms.

Mortgage debenture

This type of debenture is secured by means of a specific charge upon certain real assets of the company. A mortgage debenture is therefore secured by real property. Although creditors are assured of their security with this form of debenture the proposals for the disposal of the specific assets may be inflexible.

Debentures with a floating charge

These debentures are secured against all the assets of the company other than those assets which have been charged in the form of mortgage debentures. Although the legal security of these debentures is less than in the case of mortgage debentures the company does have greater flexibility in managing its assets. If a company defaults in the payment of interest the debenture holders have the right, with the consent of the court, to appoint a receiver to administer the assets until the interest has been paid or the default made good.

Unsecured debentures

These debentures, which are sometimes known as 'naked' debentures, have no security. The only security possessed by the debenture-holders is a note of indebtedness issued by the company. The holders of such debentures will, in the event of liquidation, be repaid after the holders of mortage debentures or debentures with a floating charge.

Trustees

Debentures are often issued in large denominations and then sold to institutional investors. In some cases, however, a large issue of debentures is made to the general public. To facilitate communication between the company and the numerous debenture-holders trustees are appointed. A trustee is expected to act on behalf of the debenture-holders. Although any authorized person can act as a trustee, the duties of trustees are normally carried out by a commercial bank.

The trustee has three main responsibilities:

1. He is responsible for ensuring that all legal documents concerning the issue of debentures are in order.
2. He maintains a watching brief over the operations of the company to make sure that the company does not act against the best interests of the debenture-holders.
3. He is responsible for taking appropriate action on behalf of the debenture-holders if the company defaults on payment of interest or principal.

CHARACTERISTICS OF LONG-TERM DEBT

From the viewpoint of the holder

Risk

Debt is favourable to the holder because it usually has a definite maturity, it gives him priority in terms of interest and it gives him priority in the event of liquidation.

Income

The debenture-holder enjoys a fixed return on his investment and his interest payments are not contingent on the level of earnings of the company. However, debenture-holders suffer during inflationary periods. A 20-year 6 per cent debenture pays six pence in interest each year on each £1 of debenture stock held. Under inflation the purchasing power of these six pence are eroded, causing a loss in real value to the debenture-holder.

Control

Debenture-holders usually do not have the right to vote. However, if the debentures go into default then the debenture-holders will, in effect, take control of the company. An overall appraisal of the characteristics of long-term debt indicates that for the investor it is good from the standpoint of risk, has limited advantages with regard to income and is weak with respect to control.

From the viewpoint of the issuer

Advantages

Companies issuing debentures have the following advantages:

1. The cost of debt is definitely limited. Debenture-holders do not participate in superior profits if earned.
2. Not only is the cost limited, but typically the expected yield is lower than the cost of equity capital.
3. There is no dilution of equity capital and the shareholders do not have to share their control when debt-financing is used.
4. The interest payment on debentures is deductible as a tax expense.

Disadvantages

The disadvantages to the company issuing debentures are as follows:

1. Debt is a fixed charge. There is greater risk if the earnings of the company fluctuate because the company may be unable to meet these fixed charges.
2. As we will see in Chapter 17 higher risks bring higher capitalization rates on equity earnings.[1] Thus, even though gearing is favourable and raises earnings per share, the higher capitalization rates attributable to gearing may drive down the market price of the ordinary shares.
3. Debentures usually have a fixed maturity date. Because of this fixed maturity date provision must be made for repayment of the debt.
4. Since long-term debt is a commitment for a long period it involves risk. The expectations and plans on which the debt was orginally issued may change. The debt may prove to be a burden, or it may prove to have been advantageous. For example, if income, employment, the price level and interest rates all fall greatly, the assumption of a large amount of long-term debt may prove to have been an unwise financial policy. Many companies experienced this sort of financial situation during the 1930s.
5. There is a limit to the extent to which funds can be raised through long-term debt. Generally accepted standards of financial policy dictate that the debt ratio shall not exceed certain limits. These standards of financial prudence set limits or controls on the extent to which funds may be raised through long-term debt. When debt gets beyond these limits its cost rises rapidly.

DECISIONS ON THE USE OF LONG-TERM DEBT

When several different methods of long-term financing are under consideration the following conditions favour the use of long-term debt:

---

1. Recognizing this fact, investors demand higher interest rates during inflationary periods. This point is discussed at length in Chapters 17 and 21.

1. If sales and earnings are relatively stable or a substantial increase in sales and earnings is expected. Increases in earnings will increase the earnings per share for ordinary shareholders, and the larger the amount of debt the larger will be the returns to ordinary shareholders.
2. A substantial rise in the price level is expected in the future, making it advantageous for the firm to incur debt that will be repaid in a depreciated currency.
3. The existing debt ratio is relatively low for the line of business.
4. Sales of ordinary shares would involve problems of maintaining the existing control pattern in the company. In the case of a family-controlled firm in particular, the creation of additional shareholders can lead to an alteration in the control mechanism.

Decisions about the use of debt may also be considered in terms of the average cost of capital curve as developed in Chapter 19. There we will see that firms have optimal capital structures or perhaps optimal ranges, and that the average cost of capital is higher than it need be if the firm uses a non-optimal amount of debt. All the factors listed above refer to the optimal debt ratio. Some cause the optimal ratio to increase others cause it to decrease.

Whenever the firm is contemplating raising new outside capital and is choosing between debt and equity it is implicitly making a judgement about its actual debt ratio in relation to the optimal ratio. For example, consider Figure 14–1 which shows the assumed shape of the Longstreet Company's average cost of capital schedule. If Longstreet is planning to raise external capital it must make a judgement about whether it is currently at point A or point B. If it decides that it is at A it should issue debt; if it believes that it is at B the decision should be to issue new ordinary shares. This subject is discussed further in Chapter 19.

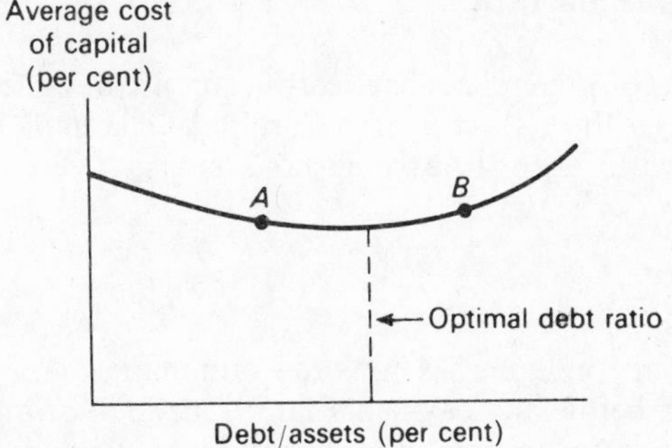

Figure 14–1 *The Longstreet Company's Average Cost of Capital Schedule.*

PREFERENCE SHARES

Preference shares have claims and rights before ordinary shares but after debentures. The preference is usually shown in a preferential position with regard to both earnings and assets.

Hybrid form

The hybrid nature of preference shares becomes apparent when we try to classify them in relation to debentures and ordinary shares. The priority features and the fixed dividend indicate a similarity to debentures. However, if the company does not earn enough to pay dividends to preference shareholders it can continue in existence without danger of liquidation. In this characteristic preference shares are similar to ordinary shares.

Debt and equity

In some types of analysis preference shares are treated similarly to debentures. For example, if the analysis is being made by a *potential shareholder* considering the earnings fluctuations induced by fixed-charge securities, preference shares would be treated like debentures. Suppose, however, that the analysis is being conducted by a *debenture-holder* studying the firm's vulnerability to failure brought on by declines in sales or in income. Since the dividend on preference shares is not a fixed charge in the sense that failure to pay it would represent a default of an obligation, preference shares represent a cushion; they provide an additional equity base. From the point of view of *shareholders*, preference shares are similar to debentures in that they provide gearing.[2]

CHARACTERISTICS OF PREFERENCE SHARES

Because the possible characteristics, rights and obligations of any specific security vary so widely, a point of diminishing returns is quickly reached in a descriptive discussion of different kinds of securities. As economic circumstances change new types of securities are manufactured. In recent years preference shares have been issued less and less and their place has been taken by convertible debentures.

Priority in assets and earnings

Many of the provisions of preference share certificates are designed to reduce risk to the purchaser in relation to the risk carried by ordinary shareholders. Preference shares usually have priority with regard to earnings and assets.

Cumulative dividends

Most dividends paid on preference shares are cumulative. All past preference share dividends must be paid before any payments can be made to ordinary shareholders. The cumulative feature is therefore a protective device. If the dividends on preference shares were not cumulative, then dividends on preference shares and ordinary shares could be passed by for a number of years. The company could then pay a large dividend to ordinary shareholders but only the stipulated payment to preference shareholders. Suppose a £1 preference share carried a 7 per cent dividend, and that the company did not pay dividends for several years so that it accumulated funds that would enable it to pay in total 50 pence in dividends. It could pay one seven-pence dividend to the preference shareholders and use the remaining 43 pence to pay ordinary shareholders a large dividend. Obviously, this device could be used to evade the responsibilities towards preference shareholders of the company. The cumulative feature prevents such evasion.[3]

Large arrears on preference share dividends would make it difficult to resume dividend payments on ordinary shares.[4] A compromise arrangement is often worked out. The arrears are wiped out by replacing preference shares with ordinary shares. Whether these provisions are worth anything depends on the future earnings prospects of the company.

The advantage to the company of substituting ordinary shares for dividends in arrears is

2. Accounts generally show preference shares as a part of the share capital along with ordinary shares.
3. Note, however, that compounding is absent in most cumulative plans. In other words, the arrears themselves earn no return.
4. This matter is dealt with in Chapter 23.

that the company balance sheet appears more presentable to investors and creditors. If earnings recover, dividends can be paid to the ordinary shareholders without any need to pay arrears to preference shareholders. As a result of this operation the original ordinary shareholders will, of course, have given up a portion of their ownership of the company; the equity will have been diluted.

EVALUATION OF PREFERENCE SHARES

From the viewpoint of the issuer

An important advantage of the issue of preference shares from the point of view of the company is that the obligation to pay a fixed rate of interest on the security is not binding in the same way as is the case with debentures. In addition, a firm with high earnings which wishes to expand can obtain higher earnings per share for the original ordinary shareholders if it issues preference shares rather than ordinary shares.

Advantages

By selling preference shares it is possible to avoid the dilution of equity capital which takes place when additional ordinary shares are issued. The issue of preference shares also permits a company to avoid sharing control through participation in voting. Because many preference shares are irredeemable they are more flexible than debentures.

Disadvantages

Characteristically, the yield on preference shares must be greater than that for debentures. Dividends paid to preference shareholders are not tax-deductible. This characteristic ensures that the true cost to a company of preference shares is far greater than the cost of debentures. As we shall see in Chapter 19 the after-tax cost of debt is approximately half the stated coupon for profitable firms. The cost of preference shares, however, is the full amount of the coupon dividend.

From the viewpoint of the investor

When a company is deciding which type of securities to issue it needs to consider the investor's point of view. It is frequently asserted that preference shares have so many disadvantages both to the issuer and to the investor that they should never be issued. Although the number of preference share issues in recent years has been low there have been some issues, usually as part of a package deal for a take-over bid.[5]

Advantages

Preference shares provide the following advantages to investors:

1. Preference shares provide a reasonably steady income.
2. Preference shareholders have preference over ordinary shareholders in liquidation

5. Mergers and take-overs are dealt with in Chapter 22.

circumstances; numerous examples can be cited where the preference shareholders have not incurred losses as great as those incurred by ordinary shareholders.

Disadvantages

Preference shares also have some disadvantages to investors:

1. Although the holders of preference shares bear a substantial proportion of ownership risk, their returns are limited.
2. Yields on preference shares are sometimes lower than those on debentures.
3. Holders of preference shares have no legally enforceable right to dividends.
4. Although most preference shares are cumulative, dividend arrears are often not paid in full.

DECISIONS REGARDING THE USE OF PREFERENCE SHARES

As a hybrid security, the use of preference shares is favoured by circumstances that fall between those favouring the use of ordinary shares and those favouring the use of debentures. When a firm's profit margin is high enough to more than cover the dividends payable to preference shareholders it will be advantageous to employ gearing. However, if the firm's sales and profits are subject to considerable fluctuations, the use of debentures may be unduly risky. Preference shares may offer a happy compromise. The use of preference shares will be particularly favoured if the firm already has a high debt ratio compared with other firms in the same industry.

Relative costs of alternative sources of financing are always important considerations. When the market price of ordinary shares is relatively low, the cost of ordinary share financing is relatively high; this is shown in Chapter 17. The costs of preference share financing follow interest rate levels more than ordinary share prices; in other words, when interest rates are low, the cost of preference shares is also likely to be low. When the costs of fixed-interest instruments such as preference shares are low and the costs of variable-dividend instruments such as ordinary shares are high, the use of preference shares is favoured.

Preference shares may also be the desired form of financing whenever the use of debt would involve excessive risk but issuing ordinary shares would result in problems of loss of control for the dominant ownership group within the company.

RATIONALE FOR DIFFERENT CLASSES OF SECURITIES

At this point the following questions are likely to come to mind. Why are there so many different forms of long-term securities? Why would anybody ever be willing to purchase debentures issued by risky companies? The answers to both questions may be made clear by reference to Figure 14–2. The now familiar trade-off function is drawn to show the risk and the expected returns for the various securities of the Longstreet Company.

Longstreet's mortgage debentures are slightly more risky than Treasury bills and sell at a slightly higher expected return. The debentures with a floating charge are yet more risky and have a still higher expected return. Unsecured debentures and preference shares are even riskier and have increasingly higher expected returns. Longstreet's ordinary shares,

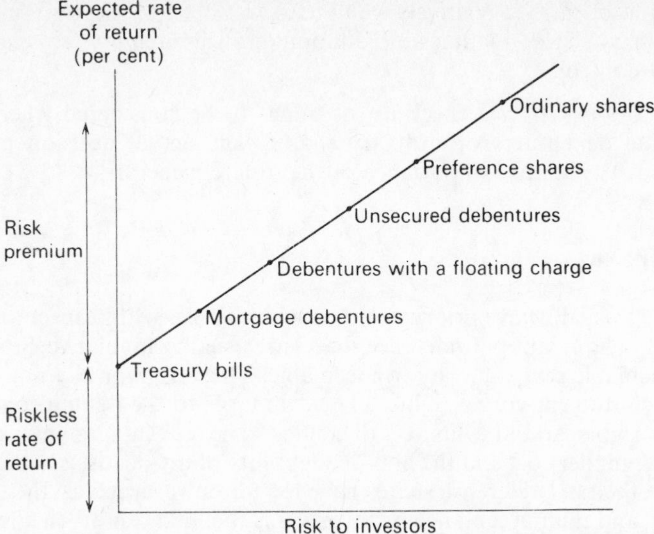

Figure 14–2 *The Longstreet Company. Risk and Expected Return on Different Classes of Securities.*

the riskiest security the firm issues, have the highest expected return of any of its instruments.

Why does Longstreet issue so many different classes of securities? Why not just issue one type of debenture plus ordinary shares? The answer lies in the fact that different investors have different risk-return trade-off preferences, so if its securities are to appeal to the broadest possible market, Longstreet must offer securities that appeal to as many investors as possible. Used wisely, a policy of selling differentiated securities can lower a firm's overall cost of capital below what it would be if it issued only one class of debentures and ordinary shares.

SUMMARY

Debentures

A *mortgage debenture* is secured by real property. *Debentures with a floating charge* are secured against all the assets of the company. If *unsecured debentures* are issued, *trustees* are appointed to act on behalf of the debenture-holders.

Secured long-term debt differs with respect to the priority of claims and the nature of the lien. These characteristics determine the amount of protection given to the debenture-holder by the terms of the security. Giving the investor more security will induce him to accept a lower yield but will restrict the future freedom of action of the issuing firm.

The characteristics of long-term debt determine the circumstances under which it will be used when alternative forms of financing are under analysis. The cost of debt is limited, but it is a fixed obligation. Debenture interest is an expense deductible for corporation tax purposes.

The nature of long-term debt encourages its use under the following circumstances:

1. Sales and earnings are relatively stable.
2. Profit margins are adequate to make gearing advantageous.
3. A rise in profits or the general price level is expected.

4. The existing debt ratio is relatively low.
5. Sales of ordinary shares might lead to dilution of owner's equity. This can also lead to problems of control.

This list of factors is simply a check list of things to be considered when deciding on whether to issue debentures or ordinary shares. The actual decision is based on a judgement about the relative importance of the different factors.

Preference shares

Preference shares usually have priority over ordinary shares with respect to earnings and claims on assets in liquidation. Preference shares are usually cumulative. Some preference shares are redeemable and some are irredeemable. They are typically non-participating and have only contingent voting rights. The advantages to the issuing company are the lack of voting rights and the limited dividends. The advantages may outweigh the disadvantages of higher cost and the non-deductibility of dividends as an expense for tax purposes. Nevertheless, preference shares have long been regarded as 'the orphan of the stock exchange' and their acceptance by investors is the final test of whether they can be sold on favourable terms.

Companies sell preference shares when they seek the advantage of financial gearing but fear the dangers of the fixed charges on debt in the face of potential fluctuations in income. If debt ratios are already high or if the costs of equity financing are relatively high, the case for using preference shares will be strengthened.

QUESTIONS

14–1. Where a company has the right to redeem debentures at will, do you think that individual shareholders should be able to demand repayments at any time they wish?

14–2. What are the relative advantages and disadvantages of issuing debentures during a recession versus during a period of prosperity?

14–3. A company's $4\frac{3}{4}$ per cent mortgage debentures due in 2020 are selling at 77 pence whilst the same company's ordinary debentures due for redemption in 2005 are selling for 93 pence. Why would the debentures with the lower coupon sell for a higher price? (Each has a par value of £1.)

14–4. When a firm sells debentures it must offer a package acceptable to potential buyers. Included in this package of terms are features such as the issue price, the term to maturity and the coupon interest rate. The package itself is determined through negotiations between the firm and the issuing house. What particular features would you, as company accountant, be especially interested in having, and which would you be most willing to give ground on, under each of the following conditions?
(a) You believe that the economy is near the peak of business cycle.
(b) Long-run forecasts indicate that your firm may have heavy cash inflows in relation to cash needs during the next five to ten years.
(c) Your current liabilities are presently low but you anticipate raising a considerable amount of funds through short-term borrowing in the near future.

14–5. Debentures are less attractive to investors during periods of inflation because a rise in the price level will reduce the purchasing power of the fixed interest payments and also of the principal. Discuss the advantages and disadvantages to the company of using a debenture whose interest payments and principal would increase in direct proportion to increases in the general price level (an inflation-proof debenture).

14–6. If corporation tax were abolished would this raise or lower the number of new preference shares issued?

14–7. Investors buying securities have some expected or required rate of return in mind. Which would you expect to be higher, the required rate of return (before tax) on preference shares or that on ordinary shares
(a) for individual investors and
(b) for institutional investors such as insurance companies?

14–8. For purposes of measuring a firm's gearing, should preference shares be classed as debt or as equity? Does it matter if the classification is being made:
(a) by the firm itself?
(b) by creditors?
(c) by equity investors?

14–9. When large issues of unsecured loan stock are made, trustees are sometimes appointed. Why is this? What are the responsibilities of trustees?

14–10. Why have there been so few issues of preference shares in recent years? Under what circumstances do you think that companies will once more be willing to issue preference shares?

14–11. Most preference shares issued since the Second World War have incorporated cumulative dividend payments into their terms of reference. Why should this be so? What would be the effect on shareholders if companies began to issue non-cumulative preference shares?

PROBLEMS

14–1. Longmount Ltd has a £600 000 long-term debenture issue outstanding. This debt has an additional 10 years to maturity and bears a coupon interest rate of 9 per cent. The firm now has the opportunity of refinancing the debt with 10-year debentures at a rate of 7 per cent. Further declines in the interest rate are not anticipated. The cost of redeeming the old debenture is £30 000 and the issue costs for the new debenture will be £20 000. If tax effects are ignored should the firm refund the debenture?

14–2. Cathode Electronics is planning a capital improvement programme to provide greater efficiency and versatility in its operations. It is estimated that by mid-1979 the company will need to raise £200 million. Cathode is a leading electronics producer with an excellent credit rating.

You are asked to set up a programme for obtaining the necessary funds. Using the following information, indicate the best form of financing. Some items you should include in your analysis are profit margins, relative costs, control of the company, cash flows, ratio analysis and implicit cost of capital. Cathode's ordinary shares are selling at 64 pence a share. The company could sell debt (25 years) at 8 per cent or preference shares at 8.5 per cent.

Electronics Industry Financial Ratios.

Current ratio (times)	2.1
Sales to total assets (times)	1.8
Coverage of fixed charges (times)	7.0
Average collection period (days)	42.0
Current debt/total assets (per cent)	20–25
Long-term debt/total assets (per cent)	10.0
Preference shares/total assets (per cent)	0–5
Net worth/total assets (per cent)	65–70
Profits to sales (per cent)	3.3
Profits to total assets (per cent)	6.0
Profits to net worth (per cent)	9.5
Expected growth rate in earnings and dividends	5.3

Cathode Electronics Company, Balance Sheet 31 December 1978 (in £ millions).

Land and buildings	£1140
Plant and equipment	140
Current assets	800
Total assets	£2080
Ordinary share capital (10p normal value)	320
Reserves	1260
Long-term loan ($5\frac{1}{2}\%$)	180
Current liabilities	320
Total claims on assets	£2080

Cathode Electronics Company, Income Statement for Years Ended 31 December 1976, 1977 and 1978 (in £millions).

	1976	1977	1978
Sales	£2440	£1820	£2160
Other income	20	20	20
Total	£2460	£1840	£2180
Cost and expenses	2113	1591	1910
Income before interest and taxes	£ 347	£ 249	£ 270
Interest on long-term debt	£ 7	£ 9	£ 10
Corporation tax	172	120	128
Net income	£ 168	£ 120	£ 132
Cash dividends	92	92	92

Shares outstanding (widely held) 320 000 000 for all three years

SELECTED REFERENCES

Brealey, R. A. A note on dividends and debt under the new taxation. *Journal of Business Finance* (Spring 1973).
Donaldson, G. *Corporate Debt Capacity*. Harvard University Press, 1961.
Fawthrop, R. A. and Terry B. Debt management and the use of leasing finance in UK corporate financing strategies, *Journal of Business Finance and Accounting* (Autumn 1975).
Franks, J. R. and Scholefield, H. H. *Corporate Financial Management*. London: Gower, 1977.
Investment Analyst (December 1974). British bond ratings.
Investment Analyst (September 1975). British bond ratings–a reply.
Keane, S. M. Some aspects of the cost of debt. *Accounting and Business Research* (Autumn 1975).
Lister, R. J. Corporate gearing – capacity and valuation. *Investment Analyst* (April 1976).
Millman, S. Sinking funds – UK corporate bonds. *Investment Analyst* (September 1976).
Samuels, J. M. and Wilkes, F. M. *Management of Company Finance*. London: Nelson 1975.

Chapter 15

Term Loans and Leases

Medium-term financing is defined as *debt originally scheduled for repayment in more than one year but in less than ten years.* Anything shorter is a current liability and falls in the class of short-term credit, while obligations due in ten or more years are thought of as long-term debt. This distinction is arbitrary, of course – we might just as well define intermediate-term credit as loans with maturities of one to five years. However, the one-to-ten year distinction is commonly used, so we shall follow it here.

The major forms of intermediate-term financing include (a) *term loans* and (b) *lease financing.*

TERM LOANS

A term loan is a business loan with a maturity of more than one year. Repayment arrangements are negotiable although the usual practice is for systematic repayments (often called amortization payments) over the life of the loan. The majority of loans made by the clearing banks are made without any security being taken. However, where it is felt that the capital resources of a borrower are not considered adequate in relation to the level of borrowing to warrant lending on a totally unsecured basis,[1] then security is taken, usually in the form of a fixed or floating charge over certain assets.

Until recently the opportunities for a firm to obtain medium-term finance were quite limited. Since the early 1970s, however, the position has improved considerably. With the ending of quantitative credit restrictions in 1971, the clearing banks have been able to provide much more of their funds in the form of medium-term loans, usually for periods of between five to seven years, although longer terms are becoming more common. In addition to the clearing banks, term loans are also provided by merchant banks, discount houses, and other financial institutions such as Finance Corporation for Industry Ltd. Some specific features of term loans are discussed in the following sections.

---

1. Evidence by the Committee of London Clearing Bankers to the Committee to Review the Functioning of Financial Institutions. Committee of London Clearing Bankers, London, 1978, para. 8.41.

Repayment schedule

Because the repayment, or amortization, schedule is a particularly important feature of almost all term loans, it is useful to describe how it is determined. The purpose of amortization, of course, is to have the loan repaid gradually over its life rather than fall due all at once. Amortization forces the borrower to repay the loan slowly, thus protecting both the lender and the borrower against the possibility that the borrower will not make adequate provisions for repayment during the life of the loan. This is especially important where the loan is for the purpose of purchasing a specific item of equipment; here the amortization schedule will be geared to the productive life of the equipment, and payments will be made from cash flows resulting from use of the equipment.

To illustrate how the amortization schedule is determined, let us assume that a firm borrows £1000 on a 10-year loan, that interest is computed at 8 per cent on the declining balance, and that the principal and interest are to be paid in 10 equal instalments. What is the amount of each of the 10 annual payments? To find this value we must use the present value concepts developed in Chapter 9.

First, notice that the lender advances £1000 and receives in turn a 10-year annuity of a pounds each year. In the section headed Annual Receipts from an Annuity in Chapter 9, we saw that these receipts could be calculated as

$$a = \frac{PV_{at}}{PVIF_a},$$

where a is the annual receipt, PV_{at} is the present value of the annuity, and $PVIF_a$ is the appropriate interest factor found either in Table 9–5 or in Appendix Table D–4. Substituting the £1000 for PV_{at} and the interest factor for a 10-year, 8 per cent annuity, or 6.710, for $PVIF_a$, we find

$$a = \frac{£1000}{6.710} = £149.$$

Therefore, if our firm makes 10 annual instalments of £149 each, it will have repaid the £1000 loan and provided the lender an 8 per cent return on his investment.

Table 15–1 breaks down the annual payments into interest and repayment components and, in the process, proves that level payments of £149 will, in fact, repay the £1000 loan and give the lender his 8 per cent return. This break-down is important for tax purposes, because the interest payments are deductible expenses to the borrower and taxable income to the lender.

Table 15–1 *Term-loan Schedule.*

Year	Total Payment	Interest[a]	Amortization Repayment	Remaining Balance
1	149	80	69	931
2	149	74	75	856
3	149	68	81	775
4	149	62	87	688
5	149	55	94	594
6	149	48	101	493
7	149	39	110	383
8	149	31	118	265
9	149	21	128	137
10	149	11	138	–

[a] Interest for the first year is 0.08 × £1000 = £80; for the second year, 0.08 × £931 = £74; and so on.

Characteristics of term loans

Maturity

For commercial banks, the term loan generally runs for a period of five to seven years, but with loans of up to 10 years' duration becoming more acceptable. For longer-term loans a company must approach a financial institution, such as Finance Corporation for Industry Ltd, which provides loans for periods of up to 15 years' length, or the insurance companies whose loans are usually for periods in excess of 20 years.

Security

As mentioned earlier, the majority of clearing bank loans are advanced without any security being taken. Such security that is taken is usually in the form of a floating charge over the total assets of a business, although fixed charges on specific assets are also possible. Banks are in general more concerned about the anticipated future cash flows of the borrowing company and its ability to meet repayment schedules than with imposing tight control on the company through adherence to various balance-sheet ratios.

Repayment provisions

Most term loans are repayable in equal instalments. In some cases, however, there may be a moratorium agreed on repayments during the early stages of a loan, particularly if there is a gestation period before the purpose for which the loan has been sought can produce benefits.

Cost of term loans

Another major aspect of term lending is its cost. As with other forms of lending, the interest rate on term loans varies with the size of the loan and the quality of the borrower. The interest rate on term loans will be related either to the bank's own base rate or to the London inter-bank offered rate (LIBOR), or else the loan may be made at a fixed rate. Very few loans are, in fact, made at fixed interest rates by commercial banks. Where the loan is made at a flexible rate, the margin charged will vary from 3 to 5 per cent over the base rate or LIBOR.

LEASE FINANCING

Firms are generally interested in *using* buildings and equipment, not in owning them per se. One way of obtaining the use of facilities and equipment is to buy them, but an alternative is to lease them. Prior to the 1960s, leasing was generally associated with real property – land and buildings – but today it is possible to lease virtually any kind of fixed asset.

Leasing business has grown rapidly in the UK, with the value of assets acquired through leasing increasing from around £60 million in 1967 to an estimated £600 million during 1977. At present, leasing accounts for approximately 7 per cent of new capital investment in the UK, with the volume of leasing expanding at a growth rate of around 7 per cent per annum.

A major factor contributing to the increased importance of equipment leasing has been the entry of the UK banks into this field following a change in Bank of England policy in 1972 towards the encouragement of price competition between UK banks. Subsidiaries of the major banks now dominate leasing business in the UK. Another important factor was the change in capital allowances for plant and equipment in 1971, with a 100 per cent first-year allowance being introduced.

In a number of respects, leasing is quite similar to borrowing. However, unlike debt or equity financing which, as a part of a general pool of financing sources, cannot be associated with specific assets, leasing is typically identified with particular assets. Leasing provides for the acquisition of assets and their 'complete financing' simultaneously.

A lease has an advantage compared to debt in that the lessor has a better position than a creditor if the user firm experiences financial difficulties. If the lessee does not meet his lease obligations, the lessor has a stronger legal right to take back the asset because the lessor still legally owns the asset. A creditor, even a secured creditor, encounters costs and delays in recovering assets that he has directly or indirectly financed. So the lessor has less risk than other financing sources used in acquiring assets. Hence the riskier the firm that is seeking financing, the greater the reason for the supplier of financing to formulate a leasing arrangement rather than a loan.

TYPES OF LEASES

Conceptually, as we show below, leasing is quite similar to borrowing, so leasing provides financial gearing. Leasing takes several different forms, the most important of which are sale and leaseback, operating leases, and straight financial leases. These three major types of leases are described below.

Sale and leaseback

Under a sale and leaseback arrangement, a firm owning land, buildings or equipment sells the property to a financial institution and simultaneously executes an agreement to lease the property back for a specified period under specific terms. If real property is involved, the financial institution is generally a life insurance company or pension fund; if the property consists of equipment and machinery, the financial institution could be an insurance company, a commercial bank or a specialized leasing company.

An illustration of a sale and leaseback arrangement is given by the sale of office buildings, in 1974, by the Commercial Union Assurance Company to a consortium of financial institutions, of which it was itself a member. Initially three other institutions bought a 36 per cent stake in the consortium for £30.9 million. This was followed later by the purchase of 44 per cent of the equity by the Abu Dhabi Investment board for £36 million, leaving Commercial Union's own share in the consortium at 20 per cent. Two-thirds of the office building were then leased back to Commercial Union for a 50-year period under an agreement which allowed for five-year rent reviews.

Note that the seller, or *lessee*, immediately receives the purchase price put up by the buyer, or *lessor*. At the same time, the seller-lessee retains the use of the property. This parallel is carried over to the lease payment schedule. Under a term loan arrangement, the financial institution would receive a series of equal payments just sufficient to amortize the loan and to provide the lender with a specified rate of return on his investment. The nature of the calculations was described above in the section on term loans. Under a sale and leaseback arrangement, the lease payments are set up in exactly the same manner – the payments are sufficient to return the full purchase price to the financial institution, in addition to providing it with a stated return on its investment.

Operating leases

Operating, or service, leases include both financing and maintenance services. IBM is one of the pioneers of the service lease contract; computers and office copying machines, together with motor vehicles and trucks, are the primary types of equipment involved in operating leases. These leases ordinarily call for the lessor to maintain and service the leased equipment, and the costs of this maintenance are built into the lease payments or contracted for separately.

Another important characteristic of the operating lease is the fact that it is frequently not fully amortized. In other words, the payments required under the lease contract are *not* sufficient to recover the full cost of the equipment. Obviously, however, the lease contract is written for considerably less than the expected life of the leased equipment, and the lessor expects to recover his cost either in subsequent renewal payments or on disposal of the leased equipment.

A final feature of the operating lease is that it frequently contains a cancellation clause giving the lessee the right to cancel the lease and return the equipment before the expiration of the basic lease agreement. This is an important consideration for the lessee, for it means that he can return the equipment if technological developments render it obsolete, or if he simply no longer needs it.

Financial leases

A strict financial lease is one that does *not* provide for maintenance services, is *not* cancellable, and *is* fully amortized (that is, the lessor receives rental payments equal to the full price of the leased equipment). The typical arrangement involves the following steps:

1. The firm that will use the equipment selects the specific items it requires and negotiates the price and delivery terms with the manufacturer or the distributor.
2. Next, the user firm arranges with a leasing company to buy the equipment from the manufacturer or the distributor, and the user firm simultaneously executes an agreement to lease the equipment from the financial institution. The terms call for full amortization of the financial institution's cost, plus a return of from 6 to 12 per cent a year on the unamortized balance. The lessee is generally given an option to renew the lease at a reduced rental on expiration of the basic lease, but he does not have the right to cancel the basic lease without completely paying off the financial institution.

Financial leases are almost the same as sale and leaseback arrangements, the main difference being that the leased equipment is new and the lessor buys it from a manufacturer or a distributor instead of from the user-lessee. A sale and leaseback may, then, be thought of as a special type of financial lease.

Inland Revenue requirements for a lease

The full amount of the annual lease payments is deductible for corporation tax purposes *provided the Inland Revenue agrees that a particular contract is a genuine lease and not simply an instalment loan called a lease.* This makes it important that a lease contract be written in a form acceptable to the Inland Revenue.

One particular aspect of the leasing agreement to which the Inland Revenue pay special attention is that relating to sale of the asset being leased. As the lessor is deemed to be the owner of the asset, then sale proceeds should be paid to him. However, rental payments are often calculated on the basis that the lessee will participate in the sale proceeds. In order to satisfy both the Inland Revenue and the lessee, leasing contracts normally stipulate a sharing of any sale proceeds between both lessor and lessee with the lessee typically receiving up to 95 per cent.

ACCOUNTING FOR LEASES

Under the requirements of the Companies Act 1967, companies are required to disclose, by way of note to their accounts, the amounts spent on the hire of plant and machinery, including leased assets. At present,[2] there is no Statement of Standard Accounting Practice dealing with the subject of accounting for leases, although an exposure draft is due to be placed before the Accounting Standards Committee within the next few months. In the USA, however, examination of the subject of accounting for leases is much more advanced, with a Statement of Financial Accounting Standards having been introduced in 1976. At the present time it appears likely that any future standard introduced in the UK will follow along the lines of the American standard which is outlined and discussed below.

In November 1976, the Financial Accounting Standards Board issued Statement of Financial Accounting Standards No. 13, *Accounting for Leases.* Like other FASB statements, the standards set forth must be followed by business firms if their financial statements are to receive certification by auditors. FASB No. 13 has implications both for the utilization of leases and for their accounting-financial treatment. Those elements of FASB No. 13 most relevant for financial analysis of leases will therefore be summarized.

For some types of leases, FASB No. 13 requires that the obligation be capitalized on the asset side with a related lease obligation on the liability side of the balance sheet. Since the treatment depends on the types of leases, the criteria for classification are first set forth. A lease is classified as a capital lease if it meets any one or more of four paragraph 7 criteria:

1. The lease transfers ownership of the property to the lessee by the end of the lease term.
2. The lease gives the lessee the option to purchase the property at a price sufficiently below the expected fair value of the property that the exercise of the option is highly probable.
3. The lease term is equal to 75 per cent or more of the estimated economic life of the property.
4. The present value of the minimum lease payments exceeds 90 per cent of the fair value of the property at the inception of the lease. The discount factor to be used in calculating the present value is the implicit rate used by the lessor or the lessee's incremental borrowing rate, whichever is lower. (Note that the use of the lower discount factor represents a higher present value factor and therefore a higher calculated present value for a given pattern of lease payments. It therefore increases the likelihood that the 90 per cent test will be met and that the lease will be classified as a capital lease.)

From the standpoint of the lessee, if a lease is not a capital lease, it is classified as an operating lease. From the standpoint of the lessor, four types of leases are defined: (a) sales-type leases, (b) direct financing leases, (c) geared leases and (d) operating leases representing all leases other than the first three types. A sales-type lease or a direct financing lease meets one or more of the four paragraph 7 criteria *and* both of two paragraph 8 criteria, which are: (a) Collectibility of the minimum lease payments is reasonably predictable: (b) no important uncertainties surround the amount of unreimbursable costs yet to be incurred by the lessor under the lease. Sales-type leases give rise to profit (or loss) to the lessor – the fair value of the leased property at the inception of the lease is greater (or less) than its cost of carrying amount. Sales-type leases normally arise

2. August, 1978.

when manufacturers or dealers use leasing in marketing their products. Direct financing leases are leases other than geared leases for which the cost of carrying amount is equal to the fair value of the leased property at the inception of the lease. Geared leases are direct financing leases in which substantial financing is provided by a long-term creditor on a non-recourse basis with respect to the general credit of the lessor.

Accounting by lessees

For operating leases, rentals shall be charged to expense over the lease term with disclosures of future rental obligations in total as well as by each of the following five years. For lessees, capital leases are to be capitalized and shown on the balance sheet both as a fixed asset and as a non-current obligation. Capitalization will represent the present value of the minimum lease payments less that portion of lease payments representing executory costs such as insurance, maintenance and rates to be paid by the lessor (including any profit return he includes in such charges). The discount factor would be as described in paragraph 7 (4), the lower of the implicit rate used by the lessor and the incremental borrowing rate of the lessee. The asset is to be amortized in a manner consistent with the lessee's normal depreciation policy for owned assets. During the lease term, each lease payment is to be allocated between a reduction of the obligation and the interest expense to produce a constant rate of interest on the remaining balance of the obligation.

Thus for capital leases, the balance sheet would include items as follows:

Company X, Balance Sheet.

Liabilities	31 December 1976	1977	Assets	31 December 1976	1977
Long term: Obligations under capital leases	XXX	XXX	Leased property under capital leases, less accumulated amortization	XXX	XXX
Current: Obligations under capital leases	XXX	XXX			

In addition to the balance sheet capitalization of capital leases, substantial additional footnote disclosures would be required for both capital and operating leases. These would include a description of leasing arrangements, an analysis of leased property under capital leases by major classes of property, a schedule by years of future minimum lease payments with executory and interest costs broken out for capital leases, and contingent rentals for operating leases.

FASB No. 13 sets forth requirements for capitalizing capital leases and for standardized disclosures for both capital leases and operating leases by lessees. Lease commitments will therefore not represent 'off-balance sheet' financing for capital assets, and standard disclosure requirements will make general the footnote reporting of information on operating leases. Hence, the argument that leasing represents a form of financing that lenders may not take into account in their analysis of the financial position of firms seeking financing will be even less valid in the future. We do not regard it as plausible that sophisticated lenders were fooled by off-balance sheet leasing obligations. However, the capitalization of capital leases and standard disclosure requirements for operating leases will make it easier for general users of financial reports to obtain additional information on the leasing obligations of firms. Hence, the requirements of FASB No. 13 are useful. We doubt whether the extent of use of leasing will be substantially altered since the particular circumstances that have provided a basis for the use of leasing in the past are not likely to be greatly affected by the increased disclosure requirements. However, one important factor to be considered if the UK standard should follow along these lines is the attitude of the Inland Revenue towards the granting of capital allowances. Any move by them to grant these allowances to lessee rather than to lessor would greatly reduce the attraction of leasing.

COST COMPARISON BETWEEN LEASE AND PURCHASE[3]

For an understanding of the possible advantages and disadvantages of lease financing, the cost of leasing must be compared with the cost of owning the equipment. To make the leasing versus owning cost comparison clear, we will first take the point of view of the lessor to understand the basic financial factors that are involved. Assume the following:

I = cost of an asset = £20 000
k = the cost of capital appropriate or the competitive risk-adjusted return of the project associated with the asset
= 10%
T = the lessor's corporate tax rate = 50%
N = the economic life of the asset
= 5 years
$Tcap$ = tax saving resulting from claiming 100% initial allowance
NPV_{LOR} = the net present value of the lease-rental income from the assets to the lessor.

With the above facts we can calculate the equilibrium lease rental rate in a competitive market of lessors. What we have posed is a standard capital budgeting problem question. What cash flow return from the use of an asset will earn the applicable cost of capital? The investment or cost of the capital budgeting project is $-I$. The return is composed of two elements. One is the cash inflow from the lease rental; the other is the tax shelter from capital allowances. The discount factor is the weighted cost of capital reflecting the appropriate debt gearing applicable to the kinds of equipment that are being leased. These factors represent the basic capital budgeting analysis discussed in Chapter 10. Consistent with the foregoing analysis, the equation to solve for the (uniform annual) lease rental rate, L_t, is equation 15–1.

$$NPV_{LOR} = -I + \sum_{t=1}^{N} \frac{L_t(1-T)}{(1+k)^t} + \frac{T\,Cap}{(1+k)} \qquad (15\text{–}1)$$

$$= -I + (PVIF_a)[L_t(1-T)] + (PVIF)(T\,Cap)$$

Given the above facts, and that relief for 100 per cent first year allowance is obtained at the end of year one, the solution to equation 15–1 is shown in equation 15–1a. The competitive market assumption constrains the net present value of the lessor in equation 15–1a to be nil. Hence the NPV of the lessor in equation 15–1 is set equal to nil. We then

3. These materials on the financial analysis of leasing reflect collaborative research by Fred Weston and Professor Larry Y. Dann, who provided valuable insights.

solve equation 15–1a for the competitive equilibrium rental rate.

$$0 = -20\,000 + \sum_{t=1}^{5} \frac{L_t(1-0.5)}{(1.1)^t} + \frac{0.5(20\,000)}{(1.1)} \tag{15–1a}$$

$$\begin{aligned} 3.791(0.5L_t) &= 20\,000 - 0.909(10\,000) = 10\,910 \\ 0.5L_t &= 10\,910/3.791 \\ L_t &= £5756 \end{aligned}$$

At an equilibrium rental (under the facts assumed) of £5756 the lessor companies earn their cost of capital of 10 per cent. Next we take the position of the user of the asset. The user faces the decision of whether to lease the asset or to own it. The new symbols and facts are:

NPV_o = the net present value to the user if the firm owns the assets.
NPV_L = the net present value to the user if the firm leases the assets.
F_t = the marginal product of the asset to a specific user firm or the cash flow benefits from the use of the capital assets (excluding depreciation effects) = £5756.
k = the cost of capital to the user firm reflecting the risk in use when the marginal value product of the machine varies systematically with the return on total wealth = 10%.

Let us first consider the results if the user is the owner of the equipment. The user's position is exactly the same as the lessor. The gearing position of the user and therefore the user's weighted average cost of capital would be the same as for the leasing company. The formula would be exactly the same as equation 15–1 except that the cash flows represent the marginal value of product of the equipment used, so that these benefits are indicated as F_t rather than L_t. The expression for determining the net present value of owning is set forth in equation 15–2:

$$\begin{aligned} NPV_0 &= \sum_{t=1}^{N} \frac{F_t(1-T)}{(1+k)^t} - I + \frac{T\,Cap}{(1+k)} \\ &= -I + (PVIF_a)[F_t(1-T)] + (PVIF)(T\,Cap) \end{aligned} \tag{15–2}$$

The first term represents the net cash flows from the use of the asset. These would be the same whether the asset is leased or owned. If the asset is owned, it would be purchased at the cost of the asset, which is I. The third term in equation 15–2 represents the benefits that the owner of the asset will have by virtue of tax shelter of the capital allowances. We can then use equation 15–2 to calculate the net present value of owning the asset. The calculation is shown in equation 15–2a:

$$\begin{aligned} NPV_0 &= -20\,000 + 3.791[(5756)(0.5)] + 0.909(10\,000) \\ &= -20\,000 + 10\,910 + 9090 \\ NPV_0 &= 0. \end{aligned} \tag{15–2a}$$

We next consider the user's alternative of leasing the equipment. The net present value of leasing is determined by taking the net present value of the net benefits from the use of the assets and calculating their present value over the life of the lease. From this is deducted the annual lease rental payments made by the lessee.[4] In formal terms this is expressed in

---

4. The actual pattern of payment on leases is different from the equal annual payment schedule assumed in the above analysis. Typically, monthly payments are required at the start to initiate the leasing contract. In fact, the payment patterns vary greatly depending on the requirements of the lessee and the circumstances of the lessor. The solution framework set forth in the text is sufficiently flexible to be used for whatever pattern of payments may be agreed upon in the leasing contract.

equation 15-3.

$$NPV_L = \sum_{t=1}^{N} \frac{F_t(1-T)}{(1+k)^t} - \sum_{t=1}^{N} \frac{L_t(1-T)}{(1+k)^t} \quad (15\text{-}3)$$

$$= (PVIF_a)[F_t(1-T) - L_t(1-T)].$$

Using the facts of the case as set forth above and assuming that F_t, the cash benefits from the use of the capital assets, is equal to £5756, equation 15-3 can be solved as shown in equation 15-3a:

$$NPV_L = 3.791[5756(1-T) - 5756(1-T)] \quad (15\text{-}3a)$$

$$= 0$$

This result is the same as for the position of the user as owner. It is also the same as the result for the lessor. These indifference results illustrate the principles set forth in recent articles by Miller and Upton and by Lewellen, Long, and McConnell.[5] The zero net present values reflect equilibrium in the equipment leasing market as well as in the equipment user's market.

However, it would not be unreasonable to have the particular uses to which users put the equipment represent some disequilibrium gains. For example, if the benefits from the use of the equipment by particular users with some special advantages were £6500 per year, the net present value of owning would be shown by equation 15-2b:

$$NPV_0 = -20{,}000 + 3.791[(6500)(0.5)] + 0.909[(20\,000)(0.5)] \quad (15\text{-}2b)$$

$$= -20\,000 + 12\,321 + 9090.$$

$$NPV_0 = £1411.$$

The net present value if the user leases the equipment is shown by equation 15-3b:

$$NPV_0 = 3.791[(6500)(0.5) - (5756)(0.5)] \quad (15\text{-}3b)$$

$$= 3.791(3250 - 2878)$$

$$= 3.791(372)$$

$$NPV_0 = £1411$$

Again, the indifference result between owning and leasing by the user is found. In the absence of some specified market imperfections, this indifference result between owning and leasing will result. A sound method of analysing leasing versus owning must obtain this indifference result, unless some specific market imperfections can be identified to account for differences. For example, it will require some differences in the applicable tax rates for the lessor versus user firm, or differences in the amount of tax subsidies available, or differences in transactions costs to cause differences in the costs of leasing versus owning for the user firm.

ADDITIONAL FACTORS THAT MAY AFFECT THE LEASING VERSUS OWNING DECISION

A number of other factors could influence the costs of leasing versus owning capital assets by the user firm. These include:

1. Different costs of capital for the lessor versus the user firm.

---

5. *Journal of Finance*, June 1976.

2. Financing costs higher in leasing.
3. Differences in maintenance costs.
4. The benefits of residual values to the owner of the assets.
5. The possibility of reducing obsolescence costs by the leasing firms.
6. The possibility of increased credit availability under leasing.
7. More favourable tax treatment such as more rapid write-off.
8. Possible differences in the ability to utilize tax reduction opportunities.

In connection with each of these factors various arguments are encountered with respect to the advantages and disadvantages of leasing. Many of the arguments carry with them a number of implicit assumptions, so that their applicability to real world conditions is subject to considerable qualifications. Each of the factors will be considered in turn.

Different costs of capital for the lessor versus the user firm

It can be argued that if the leasing company has a lower cost of capital than the user firm, the lower cost of capital will, in competitive markets, result in a lease-rental whose costs will be lower than the costs of owning by the user firm. This follows in a quite straightforward way from the type of financial analysis made in equations 15–1 to 15–3. But under what circumstances will the cost of capital be different for the leasing firm as compared with the user firm? We have to consider the basic risks involved in using capital assets. Miller and Upton have demonstrated that two broad types of risks are present.[6] One risk is that an asset's economic depreciation will vary in some systematic way with the level of the economy from the rate of depreciation expected when the lease rental rate is determined, that is, the risk that the agreed lease payments, which are based on expected depreciation, will be insufficient to cover the subsequent realized depreciation. This risk is borne by the owner, whether a leasing firm or a user-buyer.

Another risk is the risk associated with F_t, the (uncertain) future net cash flows to be derived from employing the capital services of the asset. This risk is borne by the leasing company if the lease contract is cancellable at any time with no penalty, by the user firm if the lease contract is non-cancellable over the life of the asset, and shared by them under any contractual arrangement between these two extremes. But competitive capital markets will ensure that the implicit discount rate in the leasing arrangement, as negotiated, will reflect the allocation of the risks under the particular sharing arrangement specified. Under the standard price equals marginal cost condition of competitive markets, it is the cost of capital of the project that is the relevant discount rate. Hence it is difficult to visualize why the risk in use of a capital asset will be different whether the asset is owned by a leasing company or by the user firm.

Another possibility is that the user firm may have a lower cost of capital than the leasing company. Miller and Upton evaluate this possibility as follows: 'It is true that such a company, looking only at the conventional formulas, might find it profitable to buy rather than rent. But it would find it even more profitable, under those circumstances, to enter the leasing business.'[7] This would eliminate any divergence.

Under competitive market conditions, it is not likely that the disequilibrium conditions implied by the different costs of capital will long persist. The supply of financial intermediaries of the leasing kind will either increase or decrease to restore equilibrium in the benefits from leasing versus owning an asset by a user firm.

---

6. M. H. Miller and C. W. Upton, Leasing, buying, and the cost of capital services, *Journal of Finance* 31 (June 1976), pp. 761–786.
7. Miller and Upton, Cost of capital services, p. 767.

Financing costs higher in leasing

A similar view is that leasing always involves higher implicit financing costs. This argument is also of doubtful validity. First, when the nature of the lessee as a credit risk is considered, there may be no difference. Second, it is difficult to separate the money costs of leasing from the other services that may be embodied in a leasing contract. If, because of its specialized operations, the leasing company can perform non-financial services such as maintenance of the equipment at a lower cost than the lessee or some other institution can perform them, then the effective cost of leasing may be lower than for funds obtained from borrowing or other sources. The efficiencies of performing specialized services may thus enable the leasing company to operate by charging a lower total cost than the lessee would have to pay for the package of money plus services on any other basis.

Differences in maintenance costs

Another argument frequently encountered is that leasing may be less expensive because no explicit maintenance costs are involved. But this is because the maintenance costs are included in the lease-rental rate. The key question is whether the maintenance can be performed at a lower cost when performed by the lessor as compared with having a separate maintenance contract with an independent firm which specializes in performing maintenance on capital assets of the type involved. Whether maintenance costs would be different if supplied by one type of specialist firm as compared with another type of specialist firm is a factual matter depending upon the industries and particular firms involved.

Residual values

One important point that must be mentioned in connection with leasing is that the lessor owns the property at the expiration of the lease. The value of the property at the end of the lease is called the *residual value*. Superficially, it would appear that where residual values are large, owning will be less expensive than leasing. However, even this apparently obvious advantage of owning is subject to substantial qualification. On leased equipment, the obsolescence factor may be so large that it is doubtful whether residual values will be of a great order of magnitude. If residual values appear favourable, competition between leasing companies and other financial sources, as well as competition among leasing companies themselves, will force leasing rates down to the point where the potentials of residual values are fully recognized in the leasing contract rates. Thus, the existence of residual values of equipment is not likely to result in materially lower costs of owning. However, in connection with decisions whether to lease or to own land, the obsolescence factor is not involved except to the extent of deterioration in areas with changing population or use patterns. In a period of optimistic expectations about land values, there may be a tendency to overestimate rates of increase in land values. As a consequence, the current purchase of land may involve a price so high that the probable rate of return on owned land may be relatively small. Under this condition, leasing may well represent a more economical way of obtaining the use of land than does owning. Conversely, if the probable increase in land values is not fully reflected in current prices, it will be advantageous to own the land.

Thus it is difficult to generalize about whether residual value considerations are likely to make the effective cost of leasing higher or lower than the cost of owning. The results depend on whether the individual firm has opportunities to take advantage of over-optimistic or over-pessimistic evaluations of future value changes by the market as a whole and whether the firm or market is correct on average.

Obsolescence costs

Another popular notion is that leasing costs will be lower because of the rapid obsolescence of some kinds of equipment. If the obsolescence rate on equipment is high, leasing costs must reflect such a rate. Thus, in general terms, it might be argued that neither residual values nor obsolescence rates can basically affect the cost of owning versus leasing.

In connection with leasing, however, it is possible that certain leasing companies may be well equipped to handle the obsolescence problem. For example, a manufacturer who is willing to undertake reconditioning of his own equipment, and who has his own sales organization and system of distributors, may be able to write favourable leases for his equipment. If the equipment becomes obsolete to one user, it may still be satisfactory for other users, after reconditioning, provided that the manufacturer can locate these other users. The position is similar in computer leasing.

This illustration indicates how a leasing company, by combining lending with other specialized services, may reduce the social costs of obsolescence and increase effective residual values. By such operations the total cost of obtaining the use of such equipment is reduced. Possibly other institutions that do not combine financing and other specialist functions, such as manufacturing, reconditioning, servicing and sales, may, in conjunction with financing institutions, perform the overall functions as efficiently and at as low cost as do integrated leasing companies. However, this is a factual matter depending upon the relative efficiency of the competing firms in different lines of business and different kinds of equipment.

Increased credit availability

Two possible situations may exist to give leasing an advantage to firms seeking the maximum degree of financial leverage. First, it is frequently stated that firms can obtain more money for longer terms under a lease arrangement than under a secured loan agreement for the purchase of a specific piece of equipment. Second, leasing may not have as much of an impact on future borrowing capacity as does borrowing to buy the equipment. This point is illustrated by the balance sheets of two hypothetical firms, A and B, in Table 15–2.

Table 15–2 *Balance Sheet Effects of Leasing.*

Before asset increase Firms A and B				After asset increase Firm A				Firm B			
Equity	£50			Equity	£50			Equity	£50		
Debt	50			Debt	150			Debt	50		
	£100	Total assets	£100		£200	Total assets	£200		£100	Total assets	£100

Initially, the balance sheets of both firms are identical, and they both have debt ratios of 50 per cent. Next, they each decide to acquire assets costing £100. Firm A borrows £100 to make the purchase, so an asset and a liability go on its balance sheet, and its debt ratio is increased to 75 per cent. Firm B leases the equipment. The lease may call for fixed charges as high as or even higher than the loan, and the obligations assumed under the lease can be equally or more dangerous to other creditors, but the fact that its reported debt ratio is lower may enable firm B to obtain additional credit from other lenders. The amount of the annual rentals is shown as a note to B's financial statements, so credit analysts are aware of it, but evidence suggests that many of them still give less weight to firm B's lease than to firm A's loan.

This illustration indicates quite clearly a weakness of the debt ratio – if two companies are being compared and if one leases a substantial amount of equipment, then the debt ratio as we calculate it does not accurately show their relative gearing positions.[8]

Rapid write off

Motor cars purchased by a leasing company now get the same 100 per cent first-year allowance as commercial vehicles. This contrasts with the purchase of motor cars by a non-leasing company which qualifies for capital allowances of 25 per cent per annum on the written down value, and then only on cars costing less than £5000. The benefits of the faster write-off to the leasing company will be passed on to customers in the form of lower rental charges.

Difference in ability to utilize tax relief

Many companies in recent years have found themselves in the position of having insufficient taxable profits to absorb 100 per cent first-year allowances now available for plant and equipment purchases. Finance companies and banks, on the other hand, normally have considerable income from other sources against which capital allowances may be offset. The introduction of a leasing agreement enables the lessor to obtain the benefit of the first-year allowances and pass them on to the lessee in the form of reduced rental charges.

SUMMARY

Medium-term financing is defined as any liability originally scheduled for repayment in more than one year but in less than 10 years. Anything shorter is a current liability, while obligations due in 10 or more years are thought of as long-term debt. The major forms of medium-term financing include (a) *term loans* and (b) *lease financing*.

Term loans

A term loan is a business loan with a maturity of more than one year but of less than ten years. There are exceptions to the rule, but ordinarily term loans are retired by systematic repayments (amortization payments) over the life of the loan. Normally, loans will be made on an unsecured basis, the lender being more concerned with the anticipated cash-flow position of the business and its ability to meet repayment schedules. Where security is required, however, this will normally take the form of a floating charge over the total assets of the business.

---

8. Two comments are appropriate here. First, financial analysts sometimes attempt to reconstruct the balance sheets of firms such as B by 'capitalizing the lease payments', that is, estimating the value of both the lease obligation and the leased assets and transforming B's balance sheet into one comparable to A's. Second, as we indicated in Chapter 2, lease charges are included in the fixed charge coverage ratio, and this ratio will be approximately equal for firms A and B, thus revealing the true state of affairs. Thus it is unlikely that lenders will be fooled into granting greater credit with a lease than with a conventional loan having terms similar to those of the lease.

The interest cost of term loans, like rates on other credits, varies with the size of the loan and the strength of the borrower. For small loans to small companies, rates may go up as high as 5 per cent over base rate; for large loans to large firms, the rate will be close to base rate. Since term loans run for long periods, during which interest rates can change radically, many loans have variable interest rates, with the rate set at a certain level over the base rate or LIBOR.

Lease financing

Leasing has long been used in connection with the acquisition of property by companies. In recent years, it has been extended to a wide variety of equipment.

Three different forms of lease financing were considered: (a) sale and leaseback, in which a firm owning land, buildings or equipment sells the property and simultaneously executes an agreement to lease the property for a specified period under specific terms; (b) operating leases or service leases, which include both financing and maintenance services, are often cancellable, and call for payments under the lease contract which may not fully recover the cost of the equipment; and (c) financial leases, which do not provide for maintenance services, are not cancellable, and do fully amortize the cost of the leased asset during the basic lease contract period.

To understand the possible advantages and disadvantages of lease financing, the cost of leasing an asset must be compared with the cost of owning the same asset. In the absence of major tax advantages, whether or not leasing is advantageous turns primarily on the firm's ability to acquire funds by other methods. A financial lease contract is very similar to a straight-debt arrangement and uses some of the firm's debt-carrying ability.

QUESTIONS

15–1. 'The type of equipment best suited for leasing has a long life in relation to the length of the lease, is a removable, standard product that could be used by many different firms, and is easily identifiable. In short, it is the kind of equipment that could be repossessed and sold readily. However, we would be quite happy to write a 10-year lease on paper towels for a firm such as Courtaulds Ltd.' Discuss the statement.

15–2. Leasing is often called a hedge against obsolescence. Under what conditions is this actually true?

15–3. Is leasing in any sense a hedge against inflation for the lessee? For the lessor?

15–4. One alleged advantage of leasing is that it keeps liabilities off the balance sheet, thus making it possible for a firm to obtain more leverage than it otherwise could. This raises the question of whether or not both the lease obligation and the asset involved should be capitalized and shown on the balance sheet. Discuss the pros and cons of capitalizing leases and the related assets.

15–5. A firm is seeking a term loan from a bank. Under what conditions would it want a fixed interest rate, and under what condition would it want the rate to fluctuate with the base rate?

PROBLEMS

15–1.(a) The Clarkton Company produces industrial machines. The machines have five-year lives. Clarkton sells the machines for £30 000. Alternatively, Clarkton offers a lease arrangement at a rental that, because of competitive factors, yields a return to Clarkton of 12 per cent, its cost of capital. What will their competitive lease rental rate be? (Assume 100 per cent first-year allowance, nil salvage value, and $T = 50\%$.)

(b) The Stockton Machine Shop, Inc., is contemplating the purchase of a machine exactly like those rented by Clarkton. The machines produce net benefits of £10 000 per year. They can also buy the machine for £30 000, or the machines can be rented from Clarkton at the competitive lease rental rate. Stockton's cost of capital is 12 per cent, and $T = 50\%$. Which alternative is preferred?

(c) If Clarkton's cost of capital is 9 per cent and competition exists among lessors, solve for the new equilibrium rental rate. Would Stockton's decision be altered?

15-2. The Scott Brothers Department Store is considering a sale and leaseback of its major property, consisting of land and a building, because it is 30 days overdue on payment of 80 per cent of its trade creditors. The recent balance sheet of Scott Brothers is shown below. Profits before taxes in 1977 were £36 000; after taxes, £20 000.

Annual depreciation charges are £40 000 on the building and £72 000 on the fixtures and equipment. The land and building could be sold for £2.8 million and leased back at an annual rental of £240 000.

Assume that annual allowances on the building for capital allowances are also £40 000 and that the marginal tax rate for the company is 50 per cent. Ignore any capital gains implications.

Scott Brothers Department Store, Balance Sheet 31 December 1977 (£000s).

Ordinary share capital	£1440	Land	£1152
Revenue reserves	720	Building	720
Short-term loan	1440	Fixtures and equipment	288
Trade creditors	1440	Stocks	1872
Accrued expenses	720	Debtors	1440
		Cash	288
	£5760		£5760

(a) Compare the current ratio before and after the sale and leaseback if the sale proceeds are used to repay the short-term loan and reduce trade creditors and accrued expenses.
(b) If the lease had been in effect during 1977, what would Scott Brothers' profit for 1977 have been, both before and after?
(c) What are the basic financial problems facing Scott Brothers? Will the sale and leaseback operation solve these problems?

SELECTED REFERENCES

Axelson, Kenneth S. Needed: a generally accepted method for measuring lease commitments. *Financial Executive* 39 (July 1971): 40–52.

Beechy, Thomas H. Quasi-debt analysis of financial leases. *Accounting Review* 44 (April 1969): 375–381.

Bloomfield, E. C. and Ma, R. The lease evaluation solution. *Accounting and Business Research* (Autumn 1974): 297–302.

Bower, Richard S. Issues in lease financing. *Financial Management* 2 (Winter 1973): 25–34.

Bower, Richard S., Herringer, Frank C. and Williamson, J. Peter, Lease evaluation. *Accounting Review* 41, No. 2 (April 1966): 257–265.

Bowles, G. N. Some thoughts on the lease evaluation solution. *Accounting and Business Research* (Spring 1977): 124–126.

Brigham, Eugene F. The impact of bank entry on market conditions in the equipment leasing industry. *National Banking Review* 2 (September 1964): 11–26.

Carty, J. Two vital aspects of accounting for leased assets. *Accountants Weekly* (15 October 1976): 15–16.

Chadder, P. What will be the impact of standards on leasing? *Accountants Weekly* (24 February 1978): 22–24.

Craig, M. The leasing answer. *Management Today* (June 1976): 34–40.

Craig, M. The Leasing Game. *Management Today* (January 1978): 27–36.

Fawthrop, R. A. and Terry, B. Debt management and the use of leasing finance in UK corporate financing strategies. *Journal of Business Finance and Accounting* (Autumn 1976): 295–314.

Fawthrop, R. A. and Terry, B. The evaluation of an integrated investment and lease-finance decision. *Journal of Business Finance and Accounting* (Autumn 1975): 79–111.

Ferrara, William L. Should investment and financing decisions be separated? *Accounting Review* 41 (January 1966): 106–114.

Ferrara, William L. and Wojdak, Joseph F. Valuation of long-term leases. *Financial Analysts' Journal* 25 (November–December 1969): 29–32.

Findlay, M. Chapman, III. Financial lease evaluation: survey and synthesis. Paper presented at the Eastern Finance Association Meetings, Storrs, Conn., April 12, 1973.

Findlay, M. Chapman, III. A sensitivity analysis of IRR leasing models. *Engineering Economist* 20 (Summer 1975): 231–241.

Gant, Donald R. Illusion in lease financing. *Harvard Business Review* 37 (March–April 1959): 121–142.
Gant, Donald R. A critical look at lease financing. *Controller* 29 (June 1961).
Gibson-Moore, D. Accounting for equipment leases. *Accountancy* (June 1974): 52–54.
Gordon, Myron J. A general solution to the buy or lease decision: a pedagogical note. *Journal of Finance* 29 (March 1974): 245–250.
Grinyer, J. R. The lease evaluation solution: a comment and alternative. *Accounting and Business Research* (Summer 1975): 231–235.
Hawkins, David F. Objectives, not rules for lease accounting. *Financial Executive* 38 (November 1970): 30–38.
Honig, Lawrence E. and Coley, Stephen C. An after-tax equivalent payment approach to conventional lease analysis. *Financial Management* 4 (Winter 1975): 18–27.
Johnson, Robert W. and Lewellen, Wilbur G. Analysis of the lease-or-buy decision. *Journal of Finance* 27 (September 1972): 815–823.
Keller, T. F. and Petersen, R. J. Optimal financial structure, cost of capital, and the lease-or-buy decision. *Journal of Business Finance and Accounting* (Autumn 1974): 405–415.
Knutson, Peter H. Leased equipment and divisional return on capital. *N.A.A. Bulletin* 44 (November 1962): 15–20.
Lester, T. The leasing question. *Management Today* (February 1972): 111–114.
Lewellen, Wilbur G., Long, Michael S. and McConnell, John J. Asset leasing in competitive capital markets. *Journal of Finance* 31 (June 1976): 787–798.
Maran, S. Equipment leasing in the UK. *The Accountant's Magazine* (April 1978): 143–148.
Middleton, K. A. The evaluation of leasing proposals. *Australian Accountant* (April, 1972).
Miller, Merton H. and Upton, Charles W. Leasing, buying, and the cost of capital services. *Journal of Finance* 31 (June 1976): 761–786.
Mitchell, G. B. After-tax cost of leasing. *Accounting Review* 45 (April 1970): 308–314.
Moyer, Charles R. Lease evaluation and the investment tax credit: A framework for analysis. *Financial Management* 4 (Summer 1975): 39–44.
Myers, John H. *Reporting of Leases in Financial Statements.* New York: American Institute of Certified Public Accountants, 1962.
Myers, Stewart C., Dill, David A. and Bautista, Alberto J. Valuation of financial lease contracts. *Journal of Finance* 31 (June 1976): 799 – 819.
Nantell, Timothy J. Equivalence of lease versus buy analyses. *Financial Management* 2 (Autumn 1973): 61–65.
Nelson, A. Thomas. Capitalized leases – the effect on financial ratios. *Journal of Accountancy* 116 (*July* 1963): 49–58.
Ofer, Aharon R. The evaluation of the lease versus purchase alternatives. *Financial Management* 5 (Summer 1976): 67–72.
Pizzey, A. V. Leases – their treatment in financial accounts. *Certified Accountant* (April 1978).
Roenfeldt, Rodney L. and Osteryoung, Jerome S. Analysis of financial leases. *Financial Management* 2 (Spring 1973): 74 – 87.
Sartoris, William L. and Paul, Ronda S. Lease evaluation – another capital budgeting decision. *Financial Management* 2 (Summer 1973): 46–52.
Schall, Lawrence D. The lease-or-buy and asset acquisition decisions. *Journal of Finance* 29, No. 4 (September 1974): 1203–1214.
Vancil, Richard F. Lease or borrow: new method of analysis. *Harvard Business Review* 39 (September–October 1961): 122–136.
Vancil, Richard F. Lease or borrow: steps in negotiation. *Harvard Business Review* 39 (November–December 1961): 238–259.
Vancil, Richard F. and Anthony, Robert N. The financial community looks at leasing. *Harvard Business Review* 37 (November–December 1959): 113–130.

Appendix A to Chapter 15:

Alternative Approaches to Leasing Decisions

Other points of view have been presented as applicable to formulating the appropriate framework for leasing decisions. Particularly, there has been considerable disagreement on the appropriate discount rate to be used in the analysis. In the presentation in the body of the chapter we have utilized the cost of capital applicable to the risk of the project.

COST OF DEBT AS THE DISCOUNT FACTOR

An alternative view is to use the after-tax cost of debt as the discount factor. The reasons given for using the cost of debt as the discount factor emphasize that leasing is a substitute for borrowing. If one form of borrowing is being compared with another form of borrowing, it is argued that the cost of debt can be used in comparing the costs. If this were true, the only elements that would be compared would be the interest costs and interest tax shields. But since other elements such as the costs of ownership to both the lessor and user-owner and other types of tax shields such as capital allowances enter into the analysis, the comparison involves more than one form of borrowing with another form of borrowing. Myers, Dill and Bautista describe the alternatives as follows:[1]

A firm that signs a lease contract really undertakes two simultaneous transactions:

Transaction 1A: Purchase the asset for cash.

Transaction 1B: Purchase the necessary cash by giving up the asset's depreciation tax shields, salvage value and investment tax credit, and by agreeing to make a stream of cash payments to the lessor.

The alternative is a second set of two transactions:

Transaction 2A: Purchase the asset for cash.

Transaction 2B: Purchase the necessary cash by selling whatever package of financing instruments is optimal when leasing is excluded.

We are concerned with how the market value of the firm changes if the lease is used as a substitute for 'normal' *financing. . . . To repeat, we define the value of the lease contract as the advantage of leasing vs. normal financing. (p.* 801.)

We agree that the comparison is between leasing and the normal mix of debt and equity financing since the lease provides for the acquisition of the asset as well as its financing. Although leasing is an alternative to debt financing, debt financing itself requires an equity base. Hence a weighted marginal cost of capital should be used

1. Stewart C. Myers, David A. Dill and Alberto J. Bautista, Valuation of financial lease contracts, *Journal of Finance* 31 (June 1976), pp. 799–820.

to discount the differential cash flows involved in leasing versus owning an asset. Nevertheless, a widely respected body of opinion would argue for using the after-tax cost of debt as the discount factor. This approach will be illustrated so that the reader will see the nature of its application.

We shall return to our previous illustration contained in the body of Chapter 15 to continue it with the use of the cost of debt as the discount factor. We had determined that the lease rental rate under competitive conditions in the leasing market would be £5756 per year. The cost of leasing can be determined by discounting the lease payments at the after-tax cost of debt. Let us assume that the cost of debt is 10 per cent. Assuming a uniform stream of payments as before, the present value of the cost of leasing can be expressed compactly.[2] We have:

$$\text{Present value of the cost of leasing} = \sum_{t=1}^{N} \frac{L_t(1-T)}{[1+k_b(1-T)]^t} \quad (15\text{A–1})$$

Equation 15A–1 consists of the lease payments less the tax shield on the lease payments. If the cost of debt, k_b, is 10 per cent, its after-tax cost is 5 per cent since the tax rate is 50 per cent. We can now insert the numerical values as shown in equation 15A–1a.

$$\text{Present value of the cost of leasing} = \sum_{t=1}^{5} \frac{5756(0.5)}{(1.05)^t} = 2878(4.330) = £12\,462 \quad (15\text{A–1a})$$

The conventional analysis of the cost of owning formulates it in a 'borrow-own' framework. It is assumed that the alternative to leasing is to borrow the full amount of the value of the asset, which is £20 000 in our example. Then a schedule of debt payments is made in order to determine the amount of the annual interest charges. The procedure is illustrated in Table 15A–1.

Table 15A–1 *Schedule of Debt Payments.*

End of year (1)	Balance of principal owed end of year (2)	Principal plus interest payments (3)	Annual interest 10% times (2) (4)	Reduction of principal (5)
1	£20 000	£5 276	£2 000	£3 276
2	16 724	5 276	1 672	3 604
3	13 120	5 276	1 312	3 964
4	9 156	5 276	916	4 360
5	4 796	5 276	480	4 796
Totals		£26 380	£6 380	£20 000

It is assumed that the loan of £20 000 is paid off in a level annual amount to cover annual interest charges plus amortization of the principal. The amount is an annuity that can be determined by use of the present value of an annuity formula as shown in equation 15A–2.

$$20\,000 = \sum_{t=1}^{N} \frac{a_t}{(1+k_b)^t} \quad (15\text{A–2})$$

$$a_t = \frac{£20\,000}{(PVIF_a)}$$

$$a_t = \frac{£20\,000}{3.791} = £5276$$

Solving equation 15A–2 for the level annual annuity we obtain £5276. This represents the principal plus interest payments set forth in column (3) of Table 15A–1. The sum of these five annual payments is shown to be £26 380.

---

2. We emphasize again that a wide variety of payment patterns may be encountered in leasing. One is to require the first payment or the first and last payments in advance. Or the pattern could start with high payments, scaling them down to lower ones. Or the payment schedule could start with low payments and increase them towards the end of the lease payment. Or a balloon payment might be required at some point. But since these are mechanical matters in the calculation, we shall assume the simplest pattern to focus on the central conceptual matters involved.

This represents repayment of the principal of £20 000 plus the sum of the annual interest payments. The interest payments for each year are determined by multiplying column (2), the balance of principal owed at the end of the year, by 10 per cent, the assumed cost of borrowing. The sum of the annual interest payments does, in fact, equal the total interest of £6380 obtained by deducting the principal of £20 000 from the total of the five annual payments shown in column (3).

A schedule of cash outflows for the borrow and own alternative is then developed to determine the present value of the after-tax cash flows. This is illustrated in Table 15A–2.

Table 15A–2 *Schedule of Cash Outflows: Borrow and Own.*

End of year	Loan payments	Annual interest	Capital allowances	Tax shield [(3)+(4)] × 0.5	Cash flows after tax (2) − (5)	Present value factor at 5%	Present value of cash flows
(1)	(2)	(3)	(4)	(5)	(6)	(7)	(8)
1	£5 276	£2 000	£20 000	£11 000	£(5 724)	0.952	£(5 449)
2	5 276	1 672	0	836	4 440	0.907	4 027
3	5 276	1 312	0	656	4 620	0.864	3 992
4	5 276	916	0	458	4 818	0.823	3 965
5	5 276	480	0	240	5 036	0.784	3 948
Totals	£26 380	£6 380	£20 000	£13 190	£13 190		£10 483

The analysis of cash outflows begins with a listing of the loan payments as shown in column (2). Next the annual interest payments from Table 15A–1 are listed in column (3). Assume that 100 per cent first-year allowance is claimed, on which tax relief is obtained at the end of the first year, as shown in column (4). The tax saving to the owner of the equipment is the sum of the annual interest plus capital allowances multiplied by the tax rate. The amounts of the annual tax shield are shown in column (5). Column (6) is cash flow after taxes obtained by deducting column (5) from column (2).

Since the cost of borrowing is 10 per cent, its after-tax cost with a 50 per cent tax rate is 5 per cent. The present value factors at 5 per cent are listed in column (7). They are multiplied by the after-tax cash flows to obtain column (8), the present value of after-tax cash flows.

The total of column (8) represents the present value of the after-tax cost of the borrow and own alternative. This amount is then compared with the £12 462 obtained as the present value of the cost of leasing in equation 15A–1a. The borrow and own alternative is shown to involve a cost that is lower than the cost of leasing by £1979.

The usual explanation for this difference is that under the borrow and own alternative the annual interest expenses are higher in the early years when the present value factors are higher. This provides a larger tax shield in the earlier years and is said to result in a lower cost under the borrow and own alternative.

However, this method of analysis is suspect because we have utilized the data from our example in the body of Chapter 15 in which the indifference result was found to obtain. There was no advantage to leasing versus owning consistent with competitive market equilibrium conditions. Since the use of the after-tax cost of debt as the discount factor produces something other than an indifference result, its underlying theoretical validity is suspect. In addition, as a practical matter the terms of the lease payments would not necessarily be an equal annual amount. The annual lease payments could readily be increased in the earlier years and decreased in the later years to result in the same present value of after-tax cost of leasing as for the borrow and own alternative.

Our framework is sufficiently broad and flexible to accommodate alternative choices of the discount rate to be employed in the valuation relationships. If one prefers to substitute the cost of debt for the weighted marginal cost of capital, this can be done. However, the symmetry between the position of the lessor and lessee which is generally agreed to be necessary for a correct analysis will not be possible to achieve if the cost of debt is used as the discount factor. Clearly, a 100 per cent debt ratio for the lessor firm would not be realistic, so a weighted cost to reflect some use of equity would be required. By symmetry, the use of the cost of debt alone is inappropriate for analysing the position of the lessee.

USE OF AN INTERNAL-RATE-RETURN ANALYSIS

A related second approach to analysing the cost of leasing versus alternative sources of financing utilizes the internal rate of return. In this approach the cost of leasing is the internal rate of return or discount rate that equates the present value of leasing payments, net of their tax shields plus the tax shields for capital allowances that would be obtained if the asset were purchased, with the cost of the asset. In this method the cost of leasing includes not only the after-tax lease payments but the capital allowances tax deductions that otherwise would have been obtained if the asset had been purchased.

The cost of the asset that is avoided by leasing is treated as a cash inflow, while the costs of leasing just described are treated as cash outflows. A column of cash flows after taxes is calculated. It begins with a positive figure, which is the cost of the asset avoided, and then moves to negative figures representing the costs of leasing. A rate of discount is then determined that equates the negative cash flows with the positive cash flows in the column. (This would be 10 per cent in our example.)

This discount rate is taken as a measure of the after-tax cost of lease financing. In the procedure, this after-tax cost of lease financing is then compared with the after-tax cost of debt financing. The after-tax cost of debt financing is 5 per cent in our example, so the 10 per cent after-tax cost of leasing would be considered more costly.

One of the advantages claimed for this approach is that it avoids the problem of having to determine a rate of discount. However, this claim is illusory. The internal rate of return approach to the leasing comparison is fundamentally no different from the use of the after-tax cost of debt method described in the previous section. The reason this is so is that when the discount rate, which is treated as the after-tax cost of lease financing, is compared with the after-tax cost of debt financing, this implies that the relevant measure for comparison is the after-tax cost of debt financing rather than the firm's cost of capital. Since leasing involves the acquisition of an asset as well as its financing and generally provides 'complete financing', which substitutes for a 'normal mix of financing', many authors agree that the appropriate discount factor to apply to lease payments is the firm's cost of capital. Hence the calculation of the discount factor called the after-tax cost of lease financing based on leasing payments could well be argued to be appropriately compared with the firm's cost of capital rather than with the firm's cost of debt. Hence, the internal rate of return analysis does not avoid the problem of selecting the appropriate rate of discount.

USE OF MULTIPLE DISCOUNT RATES

Still a third view is to vary the discount rate with the risk of the component cash flows. The counter-argument here is that the flows are part of one transaction whose risks are determined by the underlying risks of the cash flows which should not be broken into segments. Since this third view is also widely held, it is useful to summarize this approach.

The most complete statement of this alternative approach was provided by Professor Schall.[3] Schall emphasizes that the cost of capital applicable is the risk of the project rather than the cost of capital of the firm as a whole. Schall also argues that in analysing the leasing versus buy-own decision it is inappropriate always to require a one-to-one debt displacement between leasing and borrowing. He holds that the alternative to leasing should not be constrained to debt but may include a number of alternative combinations of financing.

Schall summarizes the comparison between leasing and purchasing in his formulations reproduced here as equations 15A–3 and 15A–4.

$$NPV_L = \sum_{t=1}^{N} \frac{(1-T)\bar{F}_t}{(1+k_X)^t} - \sum_{t=1}^{N} \frac{(1-T)\bar{L}_t}{(1+k_L)^t} \qquad (15A\text{–}3)$$

$$NPV_O = \sum_{t=1}^{N} \frac{\bar{G}_t}{(1+k_G)^t} + \sum_{t=1}^{N} \frac{Tk_b\bar{B}_t}{(1+k_R)^t} - I \qquad (15A\text{–}4)$$

$$= \sum_{t=1}^{N} \frac{(1-T)(\bar{F}_t - z_{mt}) + T\overline{Cap_t}}{(1+k_G)^t} + \sum_{t=1}^{N} \frac{Tk_bB_t}{(1+k_R)^t} - I + \frac{\bar{Z}_N}{(1+k_s)^{N'}}$$

where:

F_t = Cash revenues less cash expenses associated with the asset at time t if it is leased
L_t = Lease payment at time t
k = Discount rate used by investors in valuing a stream
k_bB_t = Interest paid on any new debt at time t issued to finance a purchase
T = Tax rate on ordinary firm income
z_{mt} = Cash costs at time t that are incurred under ownership of the asset but not if it is leased; for example, certain maintenance expenses, etc.
I = Cash purchase cost of the asset
Z_N = After tax salvage value of the asset at the end of the lease period
Cap_t = Capital allowances for period t allowed for tax purposes[4]
N = Economic life of the asset
G_t = Operating cash flow with purchase = $(1-T)(X_t - z_{mt}) + TCap_t$.

---

3. Lawrence B. Schall, The lease-or-buy and asset acquisition decisions, *Journal of Finance* 29 (September 1974), pp. 1203–1214.
4. Adapters' note: Schall's model, which originally considered depreciation deductions, has been modified slightly to relate to conditions in the UK.

Equation 15A–3, used by Schall to calculate the net present value of leasing, is exactly the same as our equation 15–4 in the text of Chapter 15 except that he applies different discount rates to the cash inflows as compared with the lease payments. In addition, he correctly indicates an uncertainty model since he places a bar above the F and L to convey that it is the expected cash flows and the expected lease payments that are discounted.

Schall's formulation reproduced here as equation 15A–4 is related to our equation 15–2. He introduces an additional term, z_{mt}, representing some costs incurred under ownership of the asset such as certain maintenance expenses. In our formulation we assume that a separate contract could be written for maintenance whether the asset is owned or leased. In addition, the term containing the Z covers an expected salvage value of the asset at the end of the lease period. This is presented on an after-tax basis. Finally, there is an expression for the present value of the tax shelter associated from interest payments on the debt utilized as a part of the financing of the asset purchased.[5]

Professor Schall explains how he would determine the different discount rates to be employed in the analysis. To estimate k_x in equation 15A–3 the firm would observe the returns and values of all equity firms that own similar assets. The k_G is somewhat different because maintenance costs and capital allowance flows are combined into the cash flow expression he refers to as G.[6] The k_R is a borrowing cost, and k_L is a cost related to 'leasing cash flows', indicated in his numerical example to be somewhat higher than k_R. The k_s is a higher discount factor than the others since the salvage value of the asset at the end of the life of the lease is judged to be more risky than the other cash flows.

The meaning of the Schall formulation can be conveyed by utilizing the specific example he provides to illustrate the application of his methodology.[7] The value of the items used in his example are summarized and their relationships indicated in Table 15A–3.

Table 15A–3 *Illustrative Data Utilized in Schall's Example of the Lease versus Purchase Analysis.*

		Lease analysis		Purchase analysis	
F_t	Earnings before interest, tax and lease payments		£700		£700
L_t	Lease payment or capital allowances, if purchase	600		300	
Z_{mt}	Maintenance expenses, etc., if purchase	–	600	100	400
$EBIT$	Earnings before interest and tax		100		300
k_bB	Interest paid on debt		–		72
	Profit before tax		100		228
T	Marginal tax rate (= 0.5); Tax		50		114
	Net Income		50		114
Z_N	After-tax salvage value of the asset at the end of the lease period = £50				
G_t	Operating cash flows with purchase = $(1-T)(F_t - Z_{mt}) + T\,Cap$ = £300 + £150 = £450				

Schall further assumes that the cost of the asset of £1500 is covered by borrowing £1200 and by utilizing equity funds of £300. He postulates in addition that only interest is payable annually on the debt so that, with a 6 per cent debt interest cost, the annual interest expense is £72. He makes no provision in his analysis for repayment of the debt, on the assumption that, if repaid, it could immediately be borrowed elsewhere. Nor does he explicitly take account of the cash outflows associated with the use of equity funds of £300. Their cost would appear to be encompassed in the discount factors he utilizes.

---

5. As will be shown in Appendix B to Chapter 19, when the discount factor used is the weighted cost of capital, the interest tax shelter is embodied in the discount factor. However, when the cost of *equity* capital is used to discount the net operating cash inflows, the interest tax shelter is shown as a separate term. The relationships appear as follows:

$$V = \frac{X(1-T)}{k} \quad \text{where } k \text{ is the weighted average cost of capital}$$

$$V = \frac{X(1-T)}{k_e} + \frac{Tk_bB}{k_b} \quad \text{where } k_e \text{ is the cost of equity capital}$$

Or $V = V_u + TB$. This is one of the relationships set forth by Modigliani and Miller in their 'tax correction' article in the *American Economic Review* of June 1963.

6. Note that Schall's approach implies that he could have treated each of the components of G as separate cash flows so that different discount rates could have been applied to each.

7. We have modified Schall's example slightly to simplify this presentation and to relate to the different tax laws in the UK.

The data are then used to evaluate the net present value from leasing as set forth in equation 15A–5. The k_x utilized by Schall appears to be the applicable cost of equity for firms that own assets similar to the asset under consideration here. The discount factor for G is somewhat lower because the G expression includes maintenance expenses and capital allowances representing cash flows that are somewhat less risky than the net operating income of the firm. The k_R is the cost of borrowing, assumed to be given at 6 per cent. Schall assumes that the cost of leasing, K_L, is somewhat higher and utilizes an 8 per cent cost of leasing. The cost of capital applied to the expected salvage value k_s is 10 per cent, which coincides with the 10 per cent he utilizes for K_G.[8]

The applicable values and discount factors are inserted in his formulation as shown in equation 15A–5. The result is that the net present value of leasing is £64.

$$NPV_L = \sum_{t=1}^{5} \frac{0.5(700)}{(1.12)^t} - \sum_{t=1}^{5} \frac{0.5(600)}{(1.08)^t} \tag{15A–5}$$

$$= \sum_{t=1}^{5} \frac{350}{(1.12)^t} - \sum_{t=1}^{5} \frac{300}{(1.08)^t}$$

$$= 350(3.605) - 300(3.993)$$

$$= 1262 - 1198$$

$$= £64.$$

Similarly, the analysis of the purchase decision is made in equation 15A–6. When evaluated, the net present value of purchasing is £389.[9]

$$NPV_0 = \sum_{t=1}^{5} \frac{0.5(700-100)+0.5(300)}{(1.10)^t} + \sum_{t=1}^{5} \frac{0.5(72)}{(1.06)^t} - £1500 + \frac{50}{(1.10)^5} \tag{15A–6}$$

$$= \sum_{t=1}^{5} \frac{450}{(1.10)^t} + \frac{36}{(1.06)^t} - 1500 + 50(0.621)$$

$$= 450(3.791) + 36(4.212) - 1500 + 31$$

$$= 1706 + 152 - 1500 + 31$$

$$= £389.$$

The conclusion reached is that purchase is preferred to leasing since the increase in the value of the firm resulting from the purchase is greater than the increase in the value of the firm resulting from leasing. In addition, purchasing meets the capital budgeting hurdle rate since the change in the value of the firm when the use of the asset is obtained by purchase (using the applicable project discount rate or rates) is a positive value.

THE VALUE ADDITIVITY PRINCIPLE IN LEASING ANALYSIS

The underlying model which Schall employs is the value additivity principle which holds that neither fragmenting cash flows nor recombining them will affect the resulting total values. This is the underlying model that he applies to his leasing analysis. From this stems his procedures under which each cash flow involved under either leasing or buying-owning must be discounted at its appropriate capitalization rate subject to the constraint that the value additivity principle holds. Otherwise, in his model of no transactions costs there would be profitable arbitrage opportunities. The discount rate employed is the discount rate for a stream that already exists in the market and is perfectly correlated with the cash flow stream under analysis. Or if the stream does not already exist, it can be created without cost.

Under the value additivity principle, in his numerical example one would have expected Schall to show that there was no net advantage to either leasing or purchasing. Yet in his original example there was an advantage to purchasing of the order of magnitude described here. Professor Schall's presentation would, therefore, seem to involve an internal inconsistency. If value additivity holds, there should be no advantage to either purchasing or leasing. Since his example portrayed an advantage to purchasing, he would be required to describe the

8. We are conveying the methodology applied by Professor Schall. As indicated, we do not necessarily agree with the assumptions employed in his approach to the lease versus purchase decision.

9. The £64 we obtain for the net present value of leasing is the same as the amount obtained by Professor Schall. However, Professor Schall obtained £425 for the net present value of the purchase alternative. This is because he used accelerated depreciation. In contrast, we used straight-line capital allowances so that the calculations could be made compactly using the conventional present value of annuity expressions. In fact, if 100 per cent capital allowances had been claimed in the first year and offset against other taxable income the net present value of the purchase alternative becomes £638.

imperfections such as monopolistic elements, transactions costs, or segmented markets to account for differences in the cost of leasing versus owning; then, the underlying model of his paper, the value additivity principle, no longer holds.

However, Schall's model can be modified to be consistent with his underlying value additivity principle model. Equation 15A–5′ reflects the requisite modification. The lease rental rate is changed so that there is now no advantage to leasing versus owning the asset.

$$NPV_L = \sum_{t=1}^{5} \frac{0.5(700)}{(1.12)^t} - \sum_{t=1}^{5} \frac{0.5(437.20)}{(1.08)^t} \tag{15A–5′}$$

$$= \sum_{t=1}^{5} \frac{350}{(1.12)^t} - \sum_{t=1}^{5} \frac{218.60}{(1.08)^t}$$

$$= 350(3.605) - 218.60(3.993)$$

$$= 1262 - 873$$

$$= £389.$$

The advantage of leasing is now as high as the advantage of owning. This is a result guaranteed by competitive market conditions and the value additivity principle upon which the Schall analysis is based.

Finally, Schall suggests that his method is applicable regardless of whether the lease provides for complete financing of the asset required or whether some combination of financing is utilized to acquire the use of the asset. If one believes that the cash flows associated with the financing of an asset that utilizes leasing as one of the sources of financing involves cash flows with segments of varying risk, the method set forth by Schall can be utilized. The methodology employed in our presentation of the approach to leasing is sufficiently general so that the particular discount rate the analyst prefers to use can be employed.

MULTIPLE DISCOUNTS WITH A BREAK-EVEN APPROACH

Closely related to the Schall approach is the formulation set forth by Professor Bower.[10] Bower sets forth a general formulation he suggests can be used to express any of the approaches to the leasing question in equation 15A–7.

$$NAL = I - \sum_{t=1}^{N} \frac{L_t}{(1+X_2)^t} + \sum_{t=1}^{N} \frac{TL_t}{(1+X_3)^t} - \sum_{t=1}^{N} \frac{TDep_t}{(1+X_4)^t} - \sum_{t=1}^{N} \frac{TI_t}{(1+X_5)^t} + \sum_{t=1}^{N} \frac{O_j(1-T)}{(1+X_6)^t} - \frac{V_N}{(1+X_7)^N} \tag{15A–7}$$

We have translated his symbols into those used in Chapter 15. Three additional symbols we have not used to this point: O_j represents maintenance costs of the equipment, I_t represents the interest component of the loan payment, V_n is the after-tax realized salvage value of the asset at the expiration of the lease period. Also, Dep_t represents a depreciation expense, which is an allowable deduction under American taxation laws.

Professor Bower observes that there is general agreement on the handling of the first term and the last two terms in the expression. The first term is the purchase price of the asset to be leased, representing the outlay that will be avoided if the asset is acquired through the lease. No discounting is involved. As Bower states, 'The last two terms include conventional project flows with risk characteristics and financing mix implications that fail to distinguish them from the flows usually considered in capital budgeting.' He observes that these two are typically discounted at the company's cost of capital. An alternative approach he describes is to adjust the flows to their certainty equivalence and then use a risk-free discount factor.[11]

In this key analysis framework Bower focuses on his decision format number 2. After some analysis he concludes that the cost of capital as the appropriate discount factor is applicable not only to the after-tax salvage and the after-tax operating savings but to the lease payments as well. The remaining areas of disagreement involve three factors each of which represents a tax shelter. He then applies a range of discount factors to determine the tax shelter discount factor, which makes the cost of leasing equal to the cost of purchasing. This is an after-tax interest rate, which can be converted into a before-tax borrowing rate based on the income tax rate of the firm. He then suggests that the executives of the firm can form their own judgement as to the appropriate pre-tax borrowing rate to apply and take into account as well 'the wide variety of other considerations that influence executives' actions.'

---

10. Richard S. Bower, Issues in lease financing, *Financial Management* 2 (Winter 1973), pp. 25–34.
11. Professor Schall correctly suggests that the appropriate cost of capital is that applicable to the project risk under analysis. This is also the weighted cost of capital that we have been employing.

But this leaves unsettled analytically the question of whether the applicable break-even discount factor is a cost of debt or whether it is the applicable cost of capital. Bower's approach can be used to demonstrate the generality of the indifference result employed in our general approach set forth in the body of Chapter 15. Bower's general equation is given in modified form in equation 15A–8. This differs from Bower's formulation in 15A–7 in using the cost of capital as the discount factor throughout and not listing the interest tax shelter separately since it is embedded in the weighted cost of capital employed.[12]

$$NAL = I - \sum_{t=1}^{N} \frac{L_t}{(1+k)^t} + \sum_{t=1}^{N} \frac{TL_t}{(1+k)^t} - \sum_{t=1}^{N} \frac{TDep}{(1+k)^t} + \sum_{t=1}^{N} \frac{O_j(1-T)}{(1+k)^t} - \frac{V_N}{(1+k)^N} \tag{15A–8}$$

To illustrate the application of equation 15A–8 assume the following additional information.

$I = 25{,}000$
$Z_N = 5{,}000$
$O_j = 2{,}000$

The additional factors that need to be taken into account can now be included in the solution process. Based on equation 15A–8 the net present value from the standpoint of the lessor is shown in 15A–9.

$$NPV_{LOR} = -I + \sum_{t=1}^{N} \frac{L_t(1-T) + TDep + O_j(1-T)}{(1+k)^t} - \frac{Z_N}{(1+k)^N}. \tag{15A–9}$$

Utilizing equation 15A–9 and the facts provided for this example, we obtain the formulation shown in equation 15A–9a.

$$\begin{aligned} NPV_{LOR} &= -20\,000 + 3.791[0.6L_t + 1600 + 1200] - 0.784(5000) \\ 3.791(0.6L_t) &= 20\,000 - 3.791[2800] + 3920 \\ 2.2746L_t &= 23\,920 - 10\,614.8 \\ 2.2746L_t &= 13\,305.2 \\ L_t &= £5850. \end{aligned} \tag{15A–9a}$$

For competitive conditions in the leasing industry in which the net present value is nil the equilibrium lease rental rate is £5850.

We can now turn to the analysis of the owning versus leasing decision. Again, we will assume that there is equilibrium in the market for the use of the equipment. The net present value of owning is shown by equation 15A–10.

$$NPV_0 = -I + \sum_{t=1}^{N} \frac{F_t(1-T) + TDep + O_j(1-T)}{(1+k)^t} - \frac{Z_N}{(1+k)^N} \tag{15A–10}$$

Again, the facts can be utilized to solve for the net present value of owning as shown in equation 15A–10a.

$$\begin{aligned} NPV_0 &= -20\,000 + 3.791[0.6(5850) + 1600 + 1200] - 0.784(5000) \\ &= -20\,000 + 3.791(6310) - 3920 \\ &= -23\,920 + 23\,921 \\ &\simeq 0. \end{aligned} \tag{15A–10a}$$

The solution is zero, indicating no net present value from owning. The firm simply earns its cost of capital. The analysis for leasing requires the use of equation 15A–11, which is similar to the original equation 15–3 utilized in the body of the chapter in analysing leasing except in relation to changes affecting UK taxation law. There are no new additional factors to be taken into consideration. All of the new elements affect the owning alternative only. Equation 15A–11 is utilized in equation 15A–11a.

$$NPL_L = \sum_{t=1}^{N} \frac{F_t(1-T) - L_t(1-T)}{(1+k)^t} \tag{15A–11}$$

$$\begin{aligned} NPV_L &= 3.791[0.6(5850) - 0.6(5850)] \\ &= 0. \end{aligned} \tag{15A–11a}$$

The net present value of leasing is shown to be nil. Thus the indifference result again obtains. We have illustrated equilibrium in both the market for leasing companies as well as the market for the use of the equipment. As

---

12. As we have observed, for an infinite time horizon the same result is produced whether the weighted cost of capital is used as the discount factor or alternatively all flows except the interest tax shelter are discounted at the firm's cost of equity and the interest tax shelter is discounted at the cost of debt. In the leasing analysis finite time periods are involved. However, it is customary to consider repetitions of the contracts to be equivalent to an infinite time horizon problem.

indicated in the body of the chapter, we could have illustrated net benefits over and above the firm's cost of capital in a market for the use of equipment. However, the indifference result would still have obtained whatever the size of the benefits. The size of the net present value would have been the same for owning as for leasing.

SUMMARY

We have illustrated that alternative approaches to leasing can be reformulated to obtain the necessary indifference result as the foundation for further analysis. Departures from the indifference result would require that the market frictions or market imperfections that produce an advantage to owning versus leasing be specified. If these frictions are appropriately specified, they can then be logically related to the quantitative differences in the analysis that may be found. Unless the analysis starts with the indifference result and is able to track clearly how a result other than the indifference result is produced, the comparison between the costs of leasing and the costs of owning may be unreliable. No matter how complicated or sophisticated the procedure is, it will yield a false security unless a clear relation to the indifference result can be tracked and set out clearly. A major source of advantages or disadvantages of leasing is the unequal tax positions of lessors and users of the assets.

PROBLEMS

15A–1. The Bradley Steel Company seeks to acquire the services of a rolling machine at the lowest possible cost. The choice is to either lease one at £17 142 annually or purchase one for £54 000. Their cost of capital is 14 per cent, and their tax rate is 40 per cent. The machine has an economic life of six years and no salvage value. The company uses straight-line depreciation. Which is the less costly method of financing?

15A–2. The Nelson Company is faced with the decision of whether it should purchase or lease a new fork-lift truck. The truck can be leased on an eight-year contract for £6280.50 a year, or it can be purchased for £24 000. The lease includes maintenance and service. The salvage value of the truck eight years hence is £2000. The company uses straight-line depreciation. If the truck is owned, service and maintenance charges (deductible costs) will be £500 per year. The company can borrow at 10 per cent and has a 40 per cent marginal tax rate and 12 per cent cost of capital.

(a) Analyse the lease versus purchase decision using the firm's cost of capital of 12 per cent as the discount factor.
(b) Make the analysis using the after-tax cost of debt as the discount factor.
(c) Compare your results.

Chapter 16

Warrants and Convertibles

Thus far in the discussion of long-term financing, we have examined the nature of ordinary shares, preference shares, various types of debt and leasing. We have also seen how offering ordinary shares by means of rights issues can facilitate low-cost share issues. In this chapter, we see how the financial manager, through the use of warrants and convertibles, can make his company's securities attractive to an even broader range of investors, thereby lowering his cost of capital. As we show in Chapter 21, 'Timing of Financial Policy', the use of warrants and convertibles has greatly increased in recent years.

Therefore, it is important to understand the characteristics of these two types of securities.

WARRANTS

A *warrant* is an option to buy a stated number of shares of stock at a specified price. For example, the Ladbroke Group have warrants outstanding that give the warrant holders the right to buy one ordinary share of the Ladbroke Group at a cash price of 171.2 pence for every warrant held. The warrants usually expire on a certain date – Ladbroke's warrants expire on 31 December 1987 – although some have perpetual lives.

Formula value of a warrant

Warrants have a calculated, or formula, value and an actual value, or price, that is determined in the market-place. The formula value is found by use of the following equation:

$$\text{Formula value} = \left(\begin{matrix}\text{market price of}\\ \text{ordinary shares}\end{matrix} - \begin{matrix}\text{option}\\ \text{price}\end{matrix}\right) \times \left(\begin{matrix}\text{number of shares each}\\ \text{warrant entitles owner}\\ \text{to purchase}\end{matrix}\right).$$

For example, a warrant may entitle the holder to purchase one ordinary share for £2.20. If the market price of the ordinary shares is £6.45, the formula price of the warrant may be obtained as follows:

(£6.45 – £2.20) × 1.0 = £4.25.

The formula gives a negative value when the shares are selling for less than the option price. For example, if our shares were selling for £2, the formula value of the warrants is minus 20 pence. This makes no sense, so we define the formula value to be nil when the shares are selling for less than the option price.

Actual price of a warrant

Generally, warrants sell above their formula values. When our shares were selling for £6.45, the warrants had a formula value of £4.25 but were selling at a price of £4.68. This represented a premium of 43 pence above the formula value.

Table 16–1 *Formula and Actual Values of Hypothetical Warrants at Different Market Prices.*

Value of warrant Share price	Formula price	Actual price	Premium
£0.00	£0.00	Not available	–
2.20	0.00	£0.90	£0.90
2.30	0.10	0.98	0.88
2.40	0.20	1.05	0.85
3.37	1.17	1.74	0.57
5.20	3.00	3.20	0.20
7.50	5.30	5.40	0.10
10.00	7.80	7.90	0.10
15.00	12.80	Not available	

A set of share prices, together with actual and formula warrant values, is given in Table 16–1 and plotted in Figure 16–1. At any share price below £2.20, the formula value of the warrant is nil; beyond £2.20, each 10 pence increase in the price of the shares brings with it

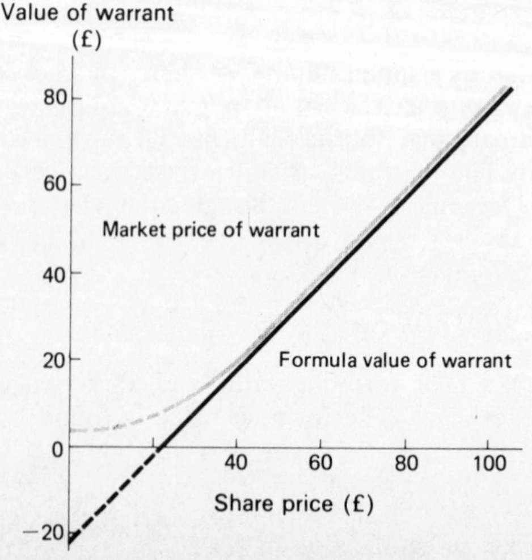

Figure 16–1 *Formula and Actual Values of Warrants at Different Stock Prices.*

a 10 pence increase in the formula value of the warrant. The actual market price of the warrants lies above the formula value at each price of the ordinary shares. Notice, however, that the premium of market price over formula value declines as the price of the ordinary shares increases. For example, when the ordinary shares sold for £2.20 and the warrants had a nil formula value, their actual price, and the premium, was 90 pence. As the price of the shares rises, the formula value of the warrants matches the increase penny for penny, but for a while the *market price* of the warrant climbs less rapidly and the premium declines. The premium is 90 pence when the shares sell for £2.20 a share, but it declines to 10 pence by the time the share price has risen to £7.50. Beyond this point the premium seems to be constant.

Why do you suppose this pattern exists? Why should the warrant ever sell for more than its formula value, and why does the premium decline as the share price increases? The answer lies in the speculative appeal of warrants – they enable a person to gain a high degree of personal gearing when buying securities. To illustrate, suppose our warrants always sold for exactly their formula value. Now suppose you are thinking of investing in the company's ordinary shares at a time when the share price is £2.50. If you buy a share and the price rises to £5 in a year, you have made a 100 per cent capital gain. However, had you bought the warrants at their formula value (30 pence when the share sells for £2.50), your capital gain would have been £2.50 on a 30 pence investment, or 833 per cent. At the same time, your total loss potential with the warrant is only 30 pence, while the potential loss from the purchase of the stock is £2.50. The huge capital gains potential, combined with the loss limitation, is clearly worth something – the exact amount it is worth to investors is the amount of the premium.[1]

But why does the premium decline as the share price rises? The answer is that both the gearing effect and the loss protection feature decline at high share prices. For example, if you are thinking of buying the shares at £7.50 a share, the formula value of the warrants is £5.30. If the stock price doubles to £15, the formula value of our warrants goes from £5.30 to £12.80. The percentage capital gain on the stock is still 100 per cent, but the percentage gain on the warrant declines from 833 per cent to 142 per cent. Moreover, notice that the loss potential on the warrant is much greater when the warrant is selling at high prices. These two factors, the declining gearing impact and the increasing danger of losses, explain why the premium diminishes as the price of the ordinary shares rises.

WARRANT VALUATION[2]

The formula defines the value of a warrant to be zero whenever the price of the share is below the option, or *exercise*, price. We know, however, that warrants frequently sell for a non-zero price even though the formula value is zero – for example, the Ladbroke Group shares mentioned earlier have in the past been quoted at a price below the subscription price of 171.2 pence. Why would someone pay a positive price for a warrant that permits him to buy shares for *more than* the current market price of the shares?

The answer to this question can be seen in Figure 16–2. The curve is the probability distribution of the 'average' investor regarding the future price of a share. The current market price, $p_M = 50$ pence, is at the mean of the distribution. Now suppose the exercise price is *less than* the current market price, say at $p_A = 40$ pence. In this case, assuming the warrant entitles the holder to buy one share, the warrant has a formula value of 10 pence.

---

1. However, a 30 pence decline in the stock price produces only a 12 per cent loss if the share is purchased, and a 100 per cent loss if you buy the warrant and it declines to its formula value.
2. This section is rather technical and may be omitted without loss of continuity.

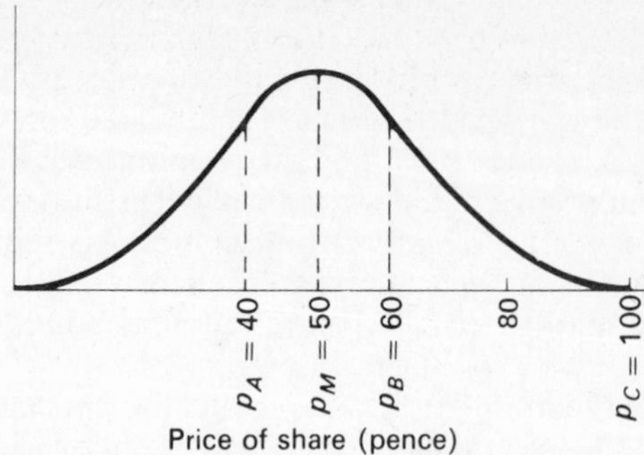

Figure 16–2 *Probability Distribution of Future Share Prices.*

But suppose the exercise price had been $p_B = 60$ pence or any higher price; now the formula value is zero.

Suppose you owned 100 of these warrants, saw that the exercise price was 60 pence, and calculated the formula value to be zero. Suppose you gave the warrants to your teacher, thinking they were worthless. A year later the price of the shares rises to 80 pence – after all, there was a reasonably good chance that it would reach this level. You now see that you gave away for nothing something that later turned out to be worth (80 – 60 pence) (100 warrants) = £20. This example shows why the price of a warrant may be greater than zero even though its formula value is zero.

Further inspection of Figure 16–2 suggests three generalizations: (a) Only if the exercise price is beyond the outer bound of the distribution (that is, there is a zero probability of the market price getting as high as the exercise price) will the warrant ever fall to a zero price. Further, *all* shareholders must share this view. (b) The flatter the distribution (that is, the higher the standard deviation), the higher the probability of an extremely high share price. It is these high share prices that give warrants value, so the larger the standard deviation, the higher the value of the warrant. (c) The life of the warrant is a consideration; if the warrant is due to expire in a few months, the share price will not be likely to reach an extreme value (that is, the shorter the time interval, the narrower the distribution of share prices), so the warrant will be less valuable than one that has a longer life.

Statistical models, including as independent variables the market price of the share, the exercise price, the expected growth rate of the share price, the variance of the share price, and the life of the warrant, have been developed to determine empirically the value of warrants. These models are discussed in the appendix to this chapter.

Use of warrants in financing

In the early 1970s warrants began to be used by investment trusts as a 'sweetener' when making new issues. They were used here to compensate subscribers to new issues for the fact that share prices usually fell to a discount in the initial dealings. Another reason for the growth in the use of warrants by investment trusts was the then high cost of debt financing, which had inhibited many trusts from increasing the gearing of their portfolios.

Additionally, small, rapidly growing firms may issue warrants as a further inducement to investors when making a debenture issue.

Giving warrants along with debentures enables investors to share in the company's growth, if it does, in fact, grow and prosper; therefore, investors are willing to accept a lower loan interest rate and less restrictive debenture provisions. A debenture with warrants has some characteristics of debt and some characteristics of equity. It is a hybrid security that provides the financial manager with an opportunity to expand his mix of securities, appealing to a broader group of investors and, thus, possibly lowering his firm's cost of capital.

Warrants can also bring in additional funds. The option price is generally set 15 to 20 per cent above the market price of the share at the time of the debenture issue. If the firm does grow and prosper, and if its share price rises above the option price at which shares may be purchased, warrant holders will surrender their warrants and buy shares at the stated price. There are several reasons for this. First, warrant holders will *surely* surrender warrants and buy shares if the warrants are about to expire with the market price of the share above the option price. Second, warrant holders will *voluntarily* surrender and buy as just mentioned if the company raises the dividend on the ordinary shares. No dividend is earned on the warrant, so it provides no current income. However, if the ordinary shares pay a high dividend, it provides an attractive dividend yield. This induces warrant holders to exercise their option to buy the shares. Third, warrants may have *stepped-up option prices*. For example, a company may have warrants outstanding with an option price of 25 pence until 31 December 1982, at which time the option price rises to 30 pence. If the price of the ordinary shares is over 25 pence just before December 1982, many warrant holders will exercise their option before the stepped-up price takes effect.

One desirable feature of warrants is that they generally bring in additional funds only if such funds are needed. If the company grows and prospers, causing the price of the shares to rise, the warrants are exercised and bring in needed funds. If the company is not successful and cannot profitably employ additional money, the price of its shares will probably not rise sufficiently to induce exercise of the options.

CONVERTIBLES

Convertible debentures are debentures that are exchangeable into ordinary shares at the option of the holder and under specified terms and conditions. The most important of the special features relates to how many shares a convertible holder receives if he converts. This feature is defined as the *conversion ratio*, which gives the number of shares the holder of the convertible receives when he surrenders his security on conversion. Related to the conversion ratio is the *conversion price*, or the effective price paid for the ordinary shares when conversion occurs. In effect, a convertible is similar to a debenture with an attached warrant.

The relationship between the conversion ratio and the conversion price is illustrated by a hypothetical company, Genoa Steamship Company convertible debentures, issued at their £100 nominal value in 1975. At any time prior to maturity on 1 July 1995, a debenture holder can turn in his debenture and receive in its place 20 ordinary shares; therefore, the conversion ratio is 20 shares for a £100 debenture. The debenture has a nominal value of £100, so the holder is giving up this amount when he converts. Dividing the £100 by the 20 shares received gives a conversion price of £5 a share:

$$\text{Conversion price} = \frac{\text{nominal value of debenture}}{\text{shares received}} = \frac{\pounds 100}{20} = \pounds 5.$$

The conversion price and the conversion ratio are established at the time the convertible debenture is sold. Generally, these values are fixed for the life of the debenture, although sometimes a stepped-up conversion price is used. Litton Industries' US convertible debentures, for example, were convertible into 12.5 shares until 1972, and they may be exchanged into 11.76 shares from 1972 until 1982 and into 11.11 shares from 1982 until they mature in 1987. The conversion price thus started at $80, rose to $85, then to $90. Litton's convertibles, like most, are redeemable at the option of the company.

Another factor that may cause a change in the conversion price and ratio is a standard feature of almost all convertibles – the clause protecting the convertible against dilution from scrip or bonus issues and the sale of ordinary shares at low prices (as in a rights issue). The typical provision states that no ordinary shares can be sold at a price below the conversion price and that the conversion price must be lowered (and the conversion ratio raised) by the percentage amount of any scrip issue. For example, if Genoa Steamship Company had a two-for-one scrip issue, the conversion ratio would automatically be adjusted to 40 and the conversion price lowered to £2.50. If this protection was not contained in the contract, a company could completely thwart conversion by the use of scrip issues. Warrants are similarly protected against dilution.

Like warrant option prices, the conversion price is characteristically set from 15 to 20 per cent above the prevailing market price of the ordinary shares at the time the convertible issue is sold. Exactly how the conversion price is established can best be understood after examining some of the reasons why firms use convertibles.

Advantages of convertibles

Convertibles offer advantages to companies as well as to individual investors. The most important of these advantages are discussed below.

As a 'sweetener' when selling debt. A company can sell debt with lower interest rates and less restrictive covenants by giving investors a chance to share in potential capital gains. Convertibles, like debentures with warrants, offer this possibility.

To sell ordinary shares at prices higher than those currently prevailing. Many companies actually want to sell ordinary shares, not debt, but feel that the price of the shares is temporarily depressed. Management may know, for example, that earnings are depressed because of a strike but that they will snap back during the next year and pull the price of the shares up with them. To sell shares now would require giving up more shares to raise a given amount of money than management thinks is necessary. However, setting the conversion price 15 to 20 per cent above the present market price of the shares will require giving up 15 to 20 per cent fewer shares when the debentures are converted than would be required if shares were sold directly.

Notice, however, that management is counting on the share price rising above the conversion price to make the debentures actually attractive in conversion. If the share price does not rise and conversion does not occur, then the company is saddled with debt.

How can the company be sure that conversion will occur when the price of the shares rises above the conversion price? Characteristically, convertibles have a provision that gives the issuing firm the opportunity of redeeming the convertible at a specified price. Suppose the conversion price is £5, the conversion ratio is 20, the market price of the ordinary shares has risen to £6, and the call price on the convertible debenture is £105. If the company redeems the debenture, debenture-holders can either convert into ordinary shares with a market value of £120 or allow the company to redeem the debenture for £105. Naturally, debenture-holders prefer £120 to £105, so conversion occurs. The call provision therefore gives the company a means of forcing conversion, provided that the market price of the share is greater than the conversion price.

Disadvantages of convertibles

From the standpoint of the issuer, convertibles have a possible disadvantage. Although the convertible debenture does give the issuer the opportunity to sell ordinary shares at a price

15 to 20 per cent higher than they could otherwise be sold, if there is a great increase in the ordinary share price the issuer may find that he would have been better off if he had waited and simply sold the ordinary shares. Further, if the company truly wants to raise equity capital and if the price of the shares declines after the debenture is issued, then it is stuck with debt.

ANALYSIS OF CONVERTIBLE DEBENTURES[3]

A convertible security is a hybrid, having some of the characteristics of ordinary shares and some characteristics of debentures or preference shares. Investors expect to earn an interest yield as well as a capital gains yield. Moreover, the company recognizes that it incurs an interest cost and a potential dilution of equity when it sells convertibles. In this section, we first develop a theoretical model to combine these two cost components and then discuss the conditions under which convertibles should be used.

Model of convertible debentures

Since an investor who purchases a convertible debenture expects to receive interest plus capital gains, his total expected return is the sum of these two parts. His expected interest return is dependent primarily upon the debenture's coupon interest rate and upon the price paid for the debenture, while the expected capital gains yield is dependent basically upon the relationship between the share price at the time of issue and the conversion price, and upon the expected growth rate in the price of the shares. We will now examine these two yield components.

Consider the graph in Figure 16–3, which we will examine in detail. In this analysis,

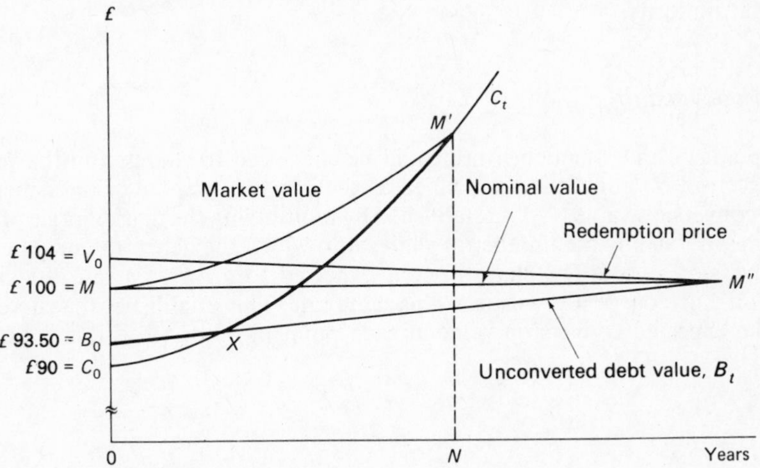

Figure 16–3 *Model of a Convertible Bond.*

3. This section is relatively technical, and it may be omitted on a first reading without loss of continuity.

think of the graph as showing the *ex ante*, or expected, relationships. We are now at year $t = 0$ and are projecting events into the future. The symbols used in Figure 16–3 and the remainder of this chapter are listed in Table 16–2.

Table 16–2 *Summary of Symbols Used in Chapter 16.*

B_t = value of unconverted debenture at time t
c = pounds of interest paid each year; £4 = 4 per cent of M
C_N = conversion value = $p_0(1+g)^N\#$
C_t = conversion value at time t
g = expected rate of growth of the share price
k_b = market rate of interest on equivalent risk, non-convertible debt issues
k_c = internal rate of return, or expected yield, on the convertible
M = price paid for the debenture
M' = market value of the convertible debenture when its conversion value becomes equal to its market value
M'' = maturity value
N = number of years debenture is expected to be held
$\#$ = conversion ratio, or number of shares received on conversion
p_c = conversion price $M/\#$
p_0 = current market price of the share
t = number of years since date of issue
t^* = number of years remaining until maturity = original term to maturity
T = marginal corporation tax rate
V_0 = original call price of an option

Redemption price and maturity value

Our hypothetical debenture is a new issue that can be purchased for M = £100, and this initial price is also the nominal (and maturity) value. The debenture is redeemable at the option of the company with a redemption price originating at V_0 = £104, somewhat above nominal value and declining linearly over the 20-year term to maturity to equal M'' = £100 at maturity.

Value in conversion

At any point in time, the debenture could be converted to shares, and the value of the shares received on conversion is defined as the *conversion value* of the debenture. The original conversion value (C_0) is established by multiplying the market price of the shares at the time of issue by the number of shares into which the debenture may be converted (the conversion ratio). The share price is expected to grow at a rate (g), causing the conversion value curve (C_t) to rise at this same rate. This establishes the curve C_t, which shows the expected conversion value at each point in time. All of this is expressed by equation 16–1:

$$C_t = p_0(1+g)^t\# \qquad (16\text{–}1)$$

where

C_t = conversion value at time t
p_0 = initial price of the ordinary shares = £4.50 per share
g = expected rate of growth of the share price = 4 per cent
$\#$ = conversion ratio, or number of shares received on conversion = 20.

The initial conversion value of the debenture, when $t = 0$, is simply £4.50 × 20, or £90. One year later it is expected to be £4.50 (1.04)(20) = £93.60; after two years it is expected to rise to £97.34 and so on. We see then that the expected conversion value curve C_t is a function of the expected growth in the price of the shares.

Debenture value

In addition to its value in conversion the debenture also has a straight debt value, B_t, which can be defined as the price at which the debenture would sell in any year t if it did not have the conversion option. At each point in time B_t is determined by the following equation:

$$B_t = \sum_{j=1}^{t^*} \frac{c}{(1+k_b)^j} + \frac{M''}{(1+k_b)^{t^*}}. \tag{16–2}$$

Here,

t = number of years since date of issue
t^* = number of years remaining until maturity = original term to maturity (20 years) minus t
j = time subscript from 1 to t^*
k_b = market rate of interest on equivalent risk, non-convertible debentures = $4\frac{1}{2}$ per cent. (Note that $k_b >$ coupon interest on the convertible.)
c = interest paid each year; £4 = 4 per cent of M
M'' = maturity value.

Equation 16–2 is used to calculate the debenture value B_t from each point t to the maturity date. To illustrate the use of the equation, we will calculate B_t at $t = 0$ and $t = 8$. First, note that $t = 0$ is the point in time when the debenture is issued, while $t = 8$ means the debenture is eight years old and has 12 years remaining to maturity. So, for B_0, the summation term refers to an annuity of £4 per year for $t^* = 20 - 0 = 20$ years, while for B_8, the summation represents a 12-year annuity; $t^* = 20 - 8 = 12$ years:

$$\begin{aligned} B_0 &= \sum_{j=1}^{20} \frac{£4.00}{(1.045)^j} + \frac{£100}{(1.045)^{20}} \\ &= £4.00(13.026) + £100(0.416) \\ &= £52.10 + £41.60 \\ &= \underline{£93.70} \end{aligned}$$

$$\begin{aligned} B_8 &= \sum_{j=1}^{12} \frac{£4.00}{(1.045)^j} + \frac{£100}{(1.045)^{12}} \\ &= £4.00(9.124) + £100(0.591) \\ &= £36.50 + £59.10 \\ &= £95.60 \end{aligned}$$

We see then that B_t rises over time and that $B_{20} = £100$.[4]

---

4. In equation 16–2, debenture values are calculated at the beginning of each period, just after the last interest payment has been made. Most debentures (convertible and non-convertible alike) are actually traded on the basis of a basic price, determined as in equation 16–2, plus interest accrued since the last payment date. Thus, if one were to buy this debenture a few days before the end of year 20, one would pay approximately £100 plus £4 accrued interest, and the invoice from the broker would indicate these two components.

Market value floor

The convertible will never sell below its value as a straight debenture – if it did, investors interested in buying debt instruments would see it as a bargain, start buying the debentures, and drive their value up to B_t. Similarly, the convertible could never sell below its conversion value – if it did, investors interested in the shares would buy the debentures, convert, and obtain shares at a bargain price, but drive the price of the convertible up to C_t in the process. Thus, the lines C_0C_t and B_0M'' in Figure 16–3 serve as floors below which the market price of the debenture cannot fall. The higher of these two floors dominates, with the thicker, discontinuous curve B_0XC_t forming the *effective market value floor*.

Expected market value

Ordinarily, convertibles sell at premiums over their debenture and conversion value floors. For our illustrative debenture, the expected market value is represented in Figure 16–3 by the curve MM', which lies above the effective floor (B_0XC_t) over most of the range but converges with B_0XC_t in year N. The rationale behind this price action is developed in the following two subsections.

Why the market value exceeds the B_0XC_t floor

The spread between MM' and B_0XC_t, which represents the premium marginal investors[5] are willing to pay for the conversion option, may be explained by several factors. First, since the convertible debenture may be converted into ordinary shares if the company prospers and the share price rises, it usually commands a premium over its value as a straight debenture (that is, the right of conversion has a positive value). Second, the convertible debenture usually commands a premium over its conversion value because, by holding convertibles, an investor is able to reduce his risk exposure. To illustrate, suppose someone buys the hypothetical debenture for £100. At the time, it is convertible into 20 shares with a market price of £4.50, giving a conversion value of £90. If the stock market turns sharply down and the share price falls to £2.25 per share, an investor would suffer a 50 per cent loss in value. Had he held a convertible debenture, its price would have fallen from £100 to the debenture value floor, B_0M'' in Figure 16–3, which is at least £93.70. Hence, holding the convertible entails less risk than holding ordinary shares; this also causes convertibles to sell at a premium above their conversion value.

Why the market value approaches the conversion value

The MM' curve in Figure 16–3 rises less rapidly than the C_0C_t curve, indicating that the market value approaches the conversion value as the conversion value increases. This is caused by three separate factors. First, and probably most important, the convertible debenture-holders realize that the debenture can be redeemed by the company; if it is in fact redeemed, they have the option of either surrendering the debenture at the redemption value or converting the debenture into ordinary shares. In the former case they receive the redemption value; in the latter they receive shares with a value designated by C_t. If the market price of the debenture is above both of these values, the holder of the debenture is in danger of a potential loss in wealth in the event of redemption. This fact

5. Marginal investors, often called 'the market', are defined as those just willing to hold the convertible at its going price. These investors are, in fact, the ones who actually determine the level of the convertible's price.

prevents wide spreads between MM' and B_0XC_t whenever the market value exceeds the redemption price.

The second factor driving MM' towards C_0C_t is related to the loss protection characteristic of convertibles. Barring changes in the interest rate on the firm's straight debentures, the potential loss on a convertible is equal to the spread between MM' and B_0M''. Since this spread increases at high conversion values, the loss potential also increases, causing the premium attributable to the loss protection to diminish.

The third factor causing the gap between MM' and C_0C_t to close has to do with the relationship between the yield on a convertible and that on the ordinary shares for which it may be exchanged. The yield on most ordinary shares consists of two components: a dividend yield and an expected capital gain yield. In the next section we will see that convertibles also have two yield components, one from interest payments and one from capital gains. After some point, the expected capital gain is the same for both instruments, but the current yield on the debenture declines vis-a-vis that on the ordinary shares because dividends on shares whose prices are rising are typically also rising, while interest payments are fixed. This causes the gap between MM' and C_0C_t to close and would eventually lead to a negative premium except for the fact that voluntary conversion occurs first.

Expected Rate of return on a convertible

The purchaser of a convertible generally expects the price of the shares to rise, the conversion value to rise with the share price, and the conversion to take place after some period of time, say N years. Thus, the purchaser expects first to receive a series of interest payments of c pence per year for N years and then to have shares with a value equal to $C_N = p_0(1+g)^N\#$. The expected rate of return on the convertible, k_c, is found by solving for k_c in the following equation:

$$M = \sum_{t=1}^{N} \frac{c}{(1+k_c)^t} + \frac{p_0(1+g)^N\#}{(1+k_c)^N}. \tag{16–3}$$

Here

M = maturity value, also equal to nominal value. Note also that M is the price paid for the debenture
c = interest in pence received per year
C_N = conversion value = $p_0(1+g)^N\#$
N = number of years debenture is expected to be held
k_c = internal rate of return, or expected yield, on the convertible.

The equation is purely definitional; it simply states that if an investor pays M pounds for a convertible debenture, holds it for N years, and receives a series of interest payments plus a terminal value, then he will receive a return on his investment equal to k_c.[6]

The *ex ante* yield on a convertible (k_c) is probabilistic – it is dependent upon a set of variables subject to probability distributions and hence must itself be a random variable. It is possible, however, to define each of the determinants of k_c in terms of its mean expected value; $E(g)$, for example, is the expected value of the growth rate in the share price over N years. For simplicity, $E(g)$ and other random variables are shortened to g, C_N and so on.

6. Three simplifications are made in this analysis. First, taxes are ignored. Second, the problem of re-investment rates is handled by assuming that all re-investment is made at the internal rate of return. Third, it is assumed that the debenture-holder does not hold shares after conversion; he exchanges for cash, as would be true of an institutional investor precluded from holding ordinary shares.

With the variables defined in this manner, it is possible to work sequentially through two equations to find the expected rate of return on a convertible debenture.

Remembering that debenture-holders are assumed to cash out in year N, presumably re-investing the terminal value received in some other security, we may establish the determinants of C_N; they are (a) the company's policy in regard to redeeming the debenture or (b) the investor's decision to hold the debenture until it is redeemed, to sell it, or to convert voluntarily.

Company's redemption policy

Companies issuing convertible debentures generally have policies regarding just how far up the C_0C_t curve they will allow a debenture to go before redeeming to force conversion. These policies range from redeeming as soon as they are 'sure' conversion will take place (this generally means a premium of about 20 per cent over the nominal value) to never redeeming at all. If the policy is never to redeem, however, the firm generally relies on the dividend–interest differential to cause voluntary conversion.

It is apparent that redemption policy has a very direct influence on the expected number of years a convertible will remain outstanding, hence on the value of C_N found by equation 16–3. Naturally, expectations about redemption policy influence the expected rate of return on a convertible debenture. Because of this, the issuing firm must take investor expectations into account. A policy that may be in the apparent short-run interest of the company may penalize the investor with such a low effective actual yield that the firm may have difficulties when it subsequently attempts to market additional securities. This point is illustrated in one of the problems at the end of the chapter.[7]

Investors' liquidity policy

Investors' liquidity policy is similar to a company's redemption policy in that it sets a limit on how far up the C_0C_t curve an investor is willing to ride. The decision is influenced by the interest–dividend relationship, by the investor's aversion to risk (recall that risk due to a share price decline increases as one moves up the C_0C_t curve), and by his willingness to hold securities providing low current yields. In general, it appears that investors are willing to ride higher up C_0C_t, given the dividend–interest relationship, than the firm is willing to let them ride; hence, company redemption policy generally supersedes investor liquidity policy.

Years the debenture is held

As we have seen, the path of the conversion value curve is traced out by equation 16–1:

$$C_t = p_0(1+g)^t \,\# \qquad (16\text{–}1)$$

Recognizing that $\# = M/p_c$, where p_c is defined as the initial conversion price of the shares,

---

7. We might also mention that some firms seek to encourage *voluntary conversion* rather than redeem to force conversion. One way of getting voluntary conversion is to include a provision for periodic stepped-up conversion prices; for example, Litton Industries' conversion price goes up every three years (so the number of shares received upon conversion goes down), and this stimulates voluntary conversion at the step-up date provided the conversion value of the debenture is above the straight-debt value. In addition, voluntary conversion occurs when the dividend yield on shares received on conversion exceeds the interest yield on the convertibles.

equation 16–1 may be rewritten:

$$C_t = \frac{p_0}{p_c}(1+g)^t M. \tag{16–4}$$

Setting equation 16–4 equal to the C_t defined by company policy (for example, £120 if a 20 per cent premium is used), we find

$$C_N = \frac{p_0}{p_c}(1+g)^N M = £120 \tag{16–5}$$

$$£120 = \frac{£4.50}{£5.00}(1.04)^N £100 = £90(1.04)$$

$$\frac{£120}{£90} = 1.333 = 1.04^N.$$

The 1.333 is the *CVIF* for the compound sum of £1 growing at 4 per cent for N years. Looking up this factor in the 4 per cent column of Table D–1, we find that the factor 1.333 lies between the seventh and eighth years, so $N \approx 7\frac{1}{2}$ years.

We may now substitute this value of N (rounded to eight years for simplicity), together with the other known data, into equation 16–3:

$$\text{M} = \sum_{t=1}^{N} \frac{C}{(1+k_c)^t} + \frac{p_0(1+g)^N \#}{(1+k_c)^N}$$

$$£100 = \sum_{t=1}^{8} \frac{c}{(1+k_c)^t} + \frac{£4.50(1.04)^8 20}{(1+k_c)^8}$$

$$= £4.00(PVIF_a) + £123.20(PVIF)$$

Using the interest factors for 6 per cent we find:

$$\begin{aligned}\text{PV} &= £4.00(6.210) + £123.20(0.627)\\ &= £24.80 + £77.20 = £102.00\end{aligned}$$

But £102 is greater than £100. Therefore, k_c is a little larger than 6 per cent. Using interest factors for 7 per cent we find:

$$\text{PV} = £23.90 + £71.70 = £95.60$$

which is less than £100.

Thus, k_c is between 6 and 7 per cent; interpolating, we find $k_c = 6.3$ per cent, so someone purchasing this convertible for £100 could expect to obtain a return of 6.3 per cent on his investment.[8]

Setting the terms of a convertible issue

As we know, investors have a risk-determined required rate of return for any security. They will not purchase a given security unless its terms are such that they can reasonably expect to earn at least their required rate of return. For our convertible issue, the expected rate of return is 6.3 per cent. If 6.3 per cent is also the required rate of return on securities with this degree of risk, then the debentures can be issued at a price of £100. If they are

8. We have not done so, but, conceptually, k_c could be split into two separate rates of return, one applicable to the expected interest payments and the other applicable to the conversion value in equation 16–3. If this was done, the rate used to discount interest payments would probably be the lower one, as interest payments are more certain than capital gains.

offered at that price, all the debentures will be sold. However, the price of the debentures after the flotation will remain in the vicinity of £100.

A company raising funds through convertibles will seek to set terms that will cause its debentures to just clear the market. What terms can the firm adjust, and what will happen if it sets these terms incorrectly? In fact, we can separate the key variables into two classes, those over which the firm has no direct control at the time the convertible is issued, and those over which the firm does have control.

Variables outside the firm's direct control:

1. p_0 = current market price of the shares
2. g = expected growth rate
3. the value of C_t at which investors expect the firm to redeem and force conversion. (However, if the debenture is made irredeemable for a period of years, this does have a bearing on C_t.)
4. the riskiness of the firm and its securities as seen by investors
5. k_b = interest rate on non-convertible debt.

Controllable variables:

1. M = nominal value = maturity value = issue price
2. p_c = conversion price = $M/\#$
3. c = coupon interest. (Note that c/M = initial interest yield on the debentures; c/M is generally $< k_b$, that is, the interest yield on convertibles is generally less than that on unconverted debentures of the same risk.)

Typically, M is set at £100. The value of M is really not very important, as a low value of M simply means the firm will have to issue more debentures, while a high M means that fewer, more valuable debentures will be issued.

Naturally, the firm would like to set c as low as possible, in order to hold down interest expense, and also to set p_c as high as possible (and # as low as possible) to minimize the number of shares it will have to issue upon conversion. Investors, on the other hand, want a high value for c and a low p_c. The company and its issuing house will seek to find a set of c and p_c values that will cause the issue to just clear the market; more generous terms would lead to a price run-up and unnecessarily penalize the firm, while insufficient terms would keep investors from buying the issue and prevent the firm from attracting the capital it needs.

The issuing firm can make trade-offs between p_c and c. Assume that the required rate of return on our illustrative debenture is 6.3 per cent and that all terms and conditions are as specified above. The debenture will sell at a price of £100. However, suppose the issuing firm wants conversion to occur earlier than eight years – perhaps it plans a major expansion programme and wants to issue ordinary debentures and, therefore, needs to have conversion occur to lower the debt ratio prior to the new issue. In that case, the firm would lower p_c by raising # above 20. That action, taken alone, would raise the value of the convertible above £100, but it could be offset by lowering c below £4. Thus, investors would be getting a lower interest yield but higher expected capital gains. If the changes were made precisely so as to keep equation 16–3 in balance, the package of expected interest plus expected capital gains could continue to equal 6.3 per cent. Exactly that kind of logic is used when firms set the terms on convertibles.

DECISIONS ON USE OF WARRANTS AND CONVERTIBLES

The Winchester Company, an electronic circuit and component manufacturer with assets of £12 million, illustrates a typical case where convertibles are useful.

Winchester's profits have been depressed as a result of its heavy expenditures on research and development for a new product. This situation has held down the growth rate of earnings and dividends; the price/earnings ratio is only 18 times, as compared with an industry average of 22. At the current 20 pence earnings per share and P/E of 18, the shares are selling for £3.60. The Winchester family owns 70 per cent of the 3 000 000 shares outstanding, or 2 100 000 shares. It would like to retain majority control but cannot buy more shares.

The heavy R & D expenditures have resulted in the development of a new type of printed circuit that management believes will be highly profitable. Five million pounds are needed to build and equip new production facilities, and profits will not start to flow into the company for some 18 months after construction on the new plant is started. Winchester's debt amounts to £5.4 million, or 45 per cent of assets, well above the 25 per cent assumed industry average. The company is restrained from selling additional debt unless the new debt is subordinate to that now outstanding.

Winchesters are informed by their financial advisers that subordinated debentures cannot be sold unless they are convertibles or have warrants attached. Convertibles or debentures with warrants can be sold with a 5 per cent coupon interest rate if the conversion price or warrant option price is set at 15 per cent above the present market price of £3.60 (that is, at £4.10 per share). Alternatively, they are willing to buy convertibles or debentures with warrants at a $5\frac{1}{2}$ per cent interest rate and a 20 per cent conversion premium or a conversion price of £4.35. If the company wants to sell ordinary shares directly it would receive a net value of £3.30 per share.

Which of the alternatives should Winchester choose? First, note that if ordinary shares are used, the company must sell 1 510 000 shares (£5 million divided by £3.30). Combined with the 900 000 shares held outside the family, this amounts to 2 410 000 shares versus the Winchester holdings of 2 100 000, so the family will lose majority control if ordinary shares are sold.

If the 5 per cent convertibles or debentures with warrants are used and the debentures are converted or the warrants are exercised, 1 220 000 new shares will be added. Combined with the old 900 000, the outside interest will then be 2 120 000, so again the Winchester family will lose majority control. However, if the $5\frac{1}{2}$ per cent convertibles or debentures with warrants are used, then after conversion or exercise only 1 150 000 new shares will be created. In this case the family will have 2 100 000 shares versus 2 050 000 for outsiders; absolute control will be maintained.

In addition to assuring control, using the convertibles or warrants also benefits earnings per share in the long run – the total number of shares is less because fewer new shares must be issued to get the £5 million, so earnings per share will be higher. Before conversion or exercise, however, the firm has a considerable amount of debt outstanding. Adding £5 million raises the total debt to £10.4 million against new total assets of £17 million, so the debt ratio will be over 61 per cent versus the 25 per cent assumed industry average. This could be dangerous. If delays are encountered in bringing the new plant into production, if demand does not meet expectations, if the company should experience a strike, if the economy should go into a recession – if any of these things occur – the company will be extremely vulnerable because of the high debt ratio.

In the present case, the decision was made to sell the $5\frac{1}{2}$ per cent convertible debentures. Two years later, earnings climbed to 30 pence a share, the P/E ratio to 20, and the price of the share to £6. Conversion occurred. After conversion, debt amounted to approximately £5.5 million against total assets of £17.5 million (some earnings had been retained), so the debt ratio was down to a more reasonable 31 per cent.

Convertibles were chosen rather than debentures with warrants for the following reason. If a firm has a high debt ratio and its short-term prospects are favourable, it can anticipate a rise in the price of its shares and thus be able to call the debentures and force conversion. Warrants, on the other hand, have a stated life, and even though the price of the firm's shares rises, the warrants may not be exercised until near their expiration date. If, subsequent to the favourable period (during which convertibles could have been called), the firm encounters less favourable developments and the price of its shares falls, the warrants may lose their value and may never be exercised. The heavy debt burden will then become aggravated. Therefore, the use of convertibles gives the firm greater control over the timing of future capital structure changes. This factor is of particular importance to the firm if its debt ratio is already high in relation to the risks of its line of business.

REPORTING EARNINGS IF CONVERTIBLES OR WARRANTS ARE OUTSTANDING

Before closing the chapter, we should note that firms with convertibles or warrants outstanding are required to report earnings per share in two ways: (a) *primary EPS*, which in essence is earnings available to ordinary shareholders divided by the number of shares actually outstanding, and (b) *fully diluted EPS*, which shows what EPS would be if all warrants had been exercised or convertibles converted prior to the reporting date. For firms with large amounts of option securities outstanding, there can be a substantial difference between the two EPS figures. The purpose of the provision is, of course, to give investors a more accurate picture of the firm's true profit position.[9]

SUMMARY

Both warrants and convertibles are forms of options used in financing business firms. The use of such long-term options is encouraged by an economic environment combining prospects of both boom or inflation and depression or deflation. The senior position of the securities protects against recessions. The option feature offers the opportunity for participation in rising share prices.

Both the convertibility privilege and warrants are used as 'sweeteners'. The option privileges they grant may make it possible for small companies to sell debt or preference shares that otherwise could not be sold. For large companies, the 'sweeteners' result in lower costs of the securities sold. In addition, the options provide for the future sale of the ordinary shares at prices higher than could be obtained at present. The options thereby permit the delayed sale of ordinary shares at more favourable prices.

The conversion of debentures by their holders does not ordinarily bring additional funds to the company. The exercise of warrants will provide such funds. The conversion of securities will result in reduced debt ratios. The exercise of warrants will strengthen the equity position but will still leave the debt or preference shares on the balance sheet. In comparing the use of convertibles to senior securities carrying warrants, a firm with a high debt ratio should choose convertibles. A firm with a moderate or low debt ratio may employ warrants.

In the past, larger and stronger firms tended to favour convertibles over debentures with warrants, so most warrants have been issued by smaller, weaker concerns.

---

9. For further analysis of the issues treated in this chapter, see E. F. Brigham, An analysis of convertible debentures: theory and some empirical evidence, *Journal of Finance* (March 1966).

QUESTIONS

16–1. Why do warrants typically sell at prices greater than their formula values?

16–2. Why do convertibles typically sell at prices greater than their formula values (the higher of the conversion value or straight-debt value)? Would you expect the percentage premium on a convertible debenture to be more or less than that on a warrant? (The percentage premium is defined as the market price minus the formula value, divided by the market price.)

16–3. What effect does the trend in share prices (subsequent to issue) have on a firm's ability to raise funds (a) through convertibles and (b) through warrants?

16–4. If a firm expects to have additional financial requirements in the future, would you recommend that it use convertibles or debentures with warrants? Why?

16–5. How does a firm's dividend policy affect each of the following?
(a) The value of long-term warrants.
(b) The likelihood that convertible debentures will be converted.
(c) The likelihood that warrants will be exercised.

16–6. Evaluate the following statement: 'Issuing convertible securities represents a means by which a firm can sell ordinary shares at a price above the existing market.'

PROBLEMS

16–1. The Garnet Lumber Company's capital consists of 24 000 ordinary shares and 8000 warrants, each good for buying three ordinary shares at £3. The warrants are protected against dilution. The company issues rights to buy one new share of common for £2.50 for every four shares. The shares are selling at £3.50. Compute:
(a) The theoretical value of the rights before the stock sells ex-rights.
(b) The new subscription price of the warrants after the rights issue.

16–2. The Ironhill Manufacturing Company was planning to finance an expansion in the summer of 1978. The principal executives of the company were agreed that an industrial company such as theirs should finance growth by means of ordinary shares rather than debt. However, they felt the price of the company's ordinary shares did not reflect its true worth, so they were desirous of selling a convertible security. They considered a convertible debenture but feared the burden of fixed interest charges if the ordinary shares did not rise in price to make conversion attractive. They decided on an issue of convertible preference shares.

The ordinary shares were currently selling at £4.80. Management projected earnings for 1979 at 36 pence a share and expected a future growth rate of 12 per cent a year. It was agreed by the company's financial advisers and the management that the ordinary shares would sell at 13.3 times earnings, the current price/earnings ratio.
(a) What conversion price should be set by the issuer?
(b) Should the preference shares include a redemption price provision? Why?

16–3. Quality Photocopy, Inc., has the following balance sheet:

Balance Sheet 1.

Ordinary share capital	£50 000	Fixed assets (net)	£125 000
Reserves	150 000	Current assets	125 000
Current liabilities	50 000		
Total claims	£250 000	Total assets	£250 000

(a) The firm earns 18 per cent on total assets before taxes (assume a 50 per cent tax rate). What are earnings per share? Two hundred and fifty thousand shares are outstanding.
(b) If the price/earnings ratio for the company's shares is 16 times, what is the market price of the company's shares?
(c) What is the book value of the company's shares?

In the following few years, sales are expected to double and the financing needs of the firm will double. The firm decides to sell debentures to meet these needs. It is undecided, however, whether to sell convertible debentures or debentures with warrants. The new balance sheet would appear as follows:

Balance Sheet 2.

Ordinary share capital	£50 000	Fixed assets (net)	£250 000
Reserves	200 000	Current assets	250 000
Debentures	150 000		
Current liabilities	100 000		
Total claims	£500 000	Total assets	£500 000

The convertible debentures would pay 7 per cent interest and would be convertible into 40 ordinary shares for each £100 debenture. The debentures with warrants would carry an 8 per cent coupon and entitle each holder of a £100 debenture to buy 25 ordinary shares at £5.

(d) Assume that convertible debentures are sold and all are later converted. Show the new balance sheet, disregarding any changes in retained earnings.

Balance Sheet 3.

Ordinary share capital	______	Fixed assets (net)	______
Reserves	______	Current assets	______
Debentures	______		
Current liabilities	______		
Total claims	______	Total assets	______

(e) Complete the firm's profit statement after the debentures have all been converted:

Profit Statement 1.

Net profit after all charges except debenture interest and before taxes (18% of total assets)	______
Debenture interest	______
Taxable income	______
Corporation tax, 50%	______
Net income after taxes	______
Earnings per share (net)	______

(f) Now instead of convertibles, assume that debentures with warrants were issued. Assume further that the warrants were all exercised. Show the new balance sheet figures.

Balance Sheet 4.

Ordinary share capital	______	Fixed assets (net)	______
Reserves	______	Current assets	______
Debentures	______		
Current liabilities	______		
Total claims	______	Total assets	______

(g) Complete the firm's income statement after the debenture warrants have all been exercised.

Income Statement 2.

Net income after all charges except debenture interest and before taxes	______
Debenture interest	______
Taxable income	______
Corporation tax	______
Net income after taxes	______
Earnings per share (net)	______

16–4. Printomat Ltd has grown rapidly during the past five years. Recently its bank has urged the company to consider increasing permanent financing. Its bank loan under a line of credit has risen to £175 000, at 7 per cent interest. Printomat has been 30 to 60 days late in paying trade creditors.

Discussions with merchant bankers have resulted in the suggestion to raise £350 000 at this time. The merchant bankers have assured the company that the following alternatives will be feasible (flotation costs will be ignored):

Alternative 1: Sell ordinary shares at £0.70.
Alternative 2: Sell convertible debentures at a 7 per cent coupon, convertible into ordinary shares at £0.80.
Alternative 3: Sell debentures at a 7 per cent coupon, each £100 debenture carrying 125 warrants to buy ordinary shares at £0.80.

Additional information is given below.

Printomat Ltd Balance Sheet.

Ordinary share capital (900 000 10 pence shares)	£90 000		
Reserves	45 000		
Current liabilities	315 000		
Total claims	£450 000	Total assets	£450 000

Printomat Ltd Income Statement.

Sales	£900 000
All costs except interest	810 000
Gross profit	£90 000
Interest	10 000
Profit before taxes	£80 000
Taxes at 50%	40 000
Profits after taxes	£40 000
Shares	900 000
Earnings per share (net)	4.4 pence
Price/earnings ratio	17 ×
Market price of shares	74.8 pence

Larry Anderson, the chairman, owns 70 per cent of the ordinary share capital of Printomat Ltd and wishes to maintain control of the company. Nine hundred thousand shares are outstanding.

(a) Show the new balance sheet under each alternative. For alternatives 2 and 3, show the balance sheet after conversion of the debentures or exercise of warrants. Assume that one-half the funds raised will be used to pay off the bank loan and one-half to increase total assets.
(b) Show Anderson's control position under each alternative, assuming that he does not purchase additional shares.
(c) What is the effect on net earnings per share of each alternative, if it is assumed that profits before interest and taxes will be 20 per cent of total assets?
(d) What will be the debt ratio under each alternative?
(e) Which of the three alternatives would you recommend to Anderson and why?

16–5. Continental Chemical Company is planning to raise £25 million by selling convertible debentures. Its shares are currently selling for £5 per share ($p_0 = £5$). The share price has grown in the past, and is expected to grow in the future, at the rate of 5 per cent per year. Continental's current dividend is 30 pence per share, so investors appear to have an expected (and required) rate of return of 11 per cent ($k = d/p_0 + g = £0.3/£5 + 5\%$) on investments as risky as the company's ordinary shares.

Continental recently sold non-convertible debentures that yield 7 per cent. Merchant bankers have informed the accountant that he can sell convertibles at a lower interest yield, offering him these two choices:

A. $p_c = £5.55$ ($\# = 18$)
$C = £6$ (6% coupon yield)
$M = £100$
25-year maturity

B. $p_c = £6.25$ ($\# = 16$)
$C = £6.50$ ($6\frac{1}{2}\%$ coupon yield)
$M = £100$
25-year maturity

In either case, the debentures are not recallable for two years; they are recallable thereafter at £100; investors do not expect the convertibles to be redeemed unless $C_t = £126.6$, but investors do expect them to be redeemed if $C_t = £126.6$.

(a) Determine the expected yield on debenture A; that on debenture B is 8.5%.
(b) Do the terms offered by the merchant bankers seem consistent?
Which debenture would an investor prefer? Which would Continental's financial accountant prefer?
(c) Suppose the company decided on debenture A, but wanted to step up the conversion price from £5.55 to £5.88 after 10 years. Should this stepped-up conversion price affect the expected yield on the debentures and the other terms on the debentures?
(d) Suppose, contrary to investors' expectations, Continental recalled the debentures after two years. What would the *ex-post* effective yield be on debenture A? Would this early recall affect the company's credibility in the financial markets?
(e) Sketch out a rough graph similar to Figure 16–3 for Continental. Use the graph to illustrate what would happen to the wealth position of an investor who bought Continental debentures the day before the announcement of the unexpected two-year redemption.
(f) Suppose the expected yield on the convertible had been less than that on straight debt (actually, it was higher). Would this appear logical? Explain.

16–6. The Seaboard Development Company plans to sell a 5 per cent coupon, 25-year convertible debenture on 1 January 1980 for £100. The debenture is redeemable at £105 in the first year, and the redemption price declines by £0.20 each year thereafter. The debenture may be converted into 14 shares that now (1 January 1979) sell for £6 per share. The share price is expected to increase at a rate of 4 per cent each year. Non-convertible debentures with the same degree of risk would yield 7 per cent. Investors expect Seaboard to redeem the convertibles if and when the conversion value exceeds the redemption price by 20 per cent.
(a) Make a graph model that represents investors' expectations for the debenture. Include as points on the graph B_0 and B_5; C_0, C_5 and C_{10}; and the redemption price at $t = 0$ and $t = 5$. Approximate the other points, and also the market price line.
(b) What rate of return do investors appear to be expecting on the debenture? Is this expected rate reasonable in view of the rate on Seaboard's straight (non-convertible) debentures? If not, what does this suggest about (i) probable success of the issue, (ii) the wisdom of the company's use of convertibles with the terms given above, and (iii) possible changes in the terms if your answer to (i) is that the debentures would probably not sell?

16–7. Inspiration Enterprises plans to issue a convertible debenture. The terms of the 10-year debenture have been tentatively set at 6 per cent interest with a 15 per cent conversion premium. However, if management will accept a 10 per cent premium, interest can be reduced to 4.5 per cent. Alternatively, for only three-fourths of one per cent more interest the conversion premium can be raised to 20 per cent.
(a) What would be the net present value of the decrease or increase in interest expense for one £100 debenture? Inspiration is in a 50 per cent tax bracket and the cost of capital is 12 per cent.
(b) The current share price is £2.50 per share. Determine the value of the differences from the 15 per cent conversion premium.
(c) Discuss the implications of parts (a) and (b).

16–8. The Piper Company plans to issue convertible debt with a 5 per cent coupon and £100 nominal value. The convertible will have a five-year life, but management hopes that future developments will make it advantageous to redeem the issue at an earlier date.
(a) Straight debt with equal risk, coupon, and maturity is selling with a market rate of interest of 8 per cent. Determine the straight debt value at time equals zero, and at the end of years one and two. Use these three points plus the maturity value to make a graph of the straight debt value of the convertible.
(b) At time zero the conversion value of the debenture is £79 since initial price of the ordinary shares is £7.90 and the conversion ratio is 10. The shares are expected to appreciate at a rate of 15.0 per cent per year. Draw the conversion value of the debenture (C_t) on the same graph.
(c) What is the minimum price the convertible can sell for at years zero, one, two and three, assuming the share value increases as predicted?
(d) Assume that the debenture is expected to be redeemed when the conversion value of the debenture reaches 120 per cent of nominal value, and that the debenture sells originally at nominal value. On the graph, locate the maturity conversion value (M') on C_t and draw a curve between the issue price (M) and M' with curvature similar to C_t.
(e) In what year is the debt expected to be redeemed?
(f) Assume the redemption price at year zero is £105, decreasing by £1 per year. Show the redemption price of debt on the same graph. What would the debt holders do if the debenture was redeemed at year one, two or three?
(g) What return on their investment is earned by purchasers of the convertible debenture at its issuance if the debenture is redeemed in three years?

SELECTED REFERENCES

Bacon, Peter W. and Winn, Edward L. Jr. The impact of forced conversion on stock prices. *Journal of Finance* 24 (December 1969): 871–874.

Baumol, William J., Malkiel, Burton G. and Quandt, Richard E. The valuation of convertible securities. *Quarterly Journal of Economics*, 80 (February 1966): 48–59.

Bird, A. P. Convertibles. *Investment Analyst* (September 1973): 14–32.

Bird, A. Some hypotheses on the valuation of stock warrants – a comment. *Journal of Business Finance and Accounting* (Summer 1975): 219–232.

Bird, A. P. The valuation of stock warrants: a reply. *Journal of Business Finance and Accounting* (Autumn 1975): 395–398.

Black, Fischer. Fact and fantasy in the use of options. *Financial Analysts' Journal* 31 (July–August 1975): 36–41.

Black, Fischer and Scholes, Myron. The valuation of option contracts and a test of market efficiency. *Journal of Finance* 27 (May 1972): 399–417.

Bond, F. M. Yields on convertible securities: 1969–1974. *Journal of Business Finance and Accounting* 3 (Summer 1976): 93–114.

Brigham, Eugene F. An analysis of convertible debentures: theory and some empirical evidence. *Journal of Finance* 21 (March 1966): 35–54.

Chen, Andrew H. Y. A model of warrant pricing in a dynamic market. *Journal of Finance* 25 (December 1970): 1041–1059.

Cretien, Paul D. Jr. Premiums on convertible bonds: comment. *Journal of Finance* 25 (September 1970): 917–922.

Cunningham, S. W. The predictability of British Stock Market prices. *Applied Statistics* (1973): 315–331.

Duvel, David Tell. Premiums on convertible bonds: comment. *Journal of Finance* 25 (September 1970): 923–927.

Frank, Werner G. and Kroncke, Charles. Classifying conversions of convertible debentures over four years. *Financial Management* 3 (Summer 1974): 33–42.

Frank, Werner G. and Weygandt, Jerry J. Convertible debt and earnings per share: pragmatism vs. good theory. *Accounting Review* 45 (April 1970): 280–289.

Frankle, A. W. and Hawkins, C. A. Beta coefficients for convertible bonds. *Journal of Finance* 30 (March 1975): 207–210.

Hayes, Samuel L. III. New interest in incentive financing. *Harvard Business Review* 44 (July–August 1966): 99–112.

Hettenhouse. G. W. and Puglisi, D. J. Investor experience with options. *Financial Analysts' Journal* 31 (July–August 1975): 53–58.

Horrigan, James O. Some hypotheses on the valuation of stock warrants. *Journal of Business Finance and Accounting* 1 (Summer 1974): 239–247.

Pilcher, C. James. *Raising Capital with Convertible Securities.* Ann Arbor, Mich.: Bureau of Business Research, University of Michigan, 1955.

Purdy, D. E. Accounting for convertible debt. *Journal of Business Finance and Accounting* (Spring 1977): 99–114.

Purdy, D. E. The rationale of convertible securities. *Investment Analyst* (May 1977): 24–33.

Reback, Robert. Risk and return in option trading. *Financial Analysts' Journal* 31 (July–August 1975): 42–52.

Rush, David F. and Melicher, Ronald W. An empirical examination of factors which influence warrant prices. *Journal of Finance* 29 (December 1974): 1449–1466.

Samuelson, Paul A. and Merton, Robert C. A complete model of warrant pricing that maximizes utility. *Industrial Management Review* 10 (Winter 1969): 17–46.

Schwartz, Eduardo S. The valuation of warrants: implementing a new approach. *Journal of Financial Economics* 4 (January 1977): 79–94.

Shelton, John P. The relation of the price of a warrant to the price of its associated stock. *Financial Analysts' Journal* 23 (May–June and July–August 1967): 143–151 and 88–99.

Skerrat, L. C. L. Convertibles: some further evidence. *Investment Analyst* (May 1974).

Skerrat, L. C. L. The price determination of convertible loan stock: a U.K. model. *Journal of Business Finance and Accounting* (Autumn 1974): 429–443.

Skerrat, L. C. L. The valuation of stock warrants: a comment on the Bird model. *Journal of Business Finance and Accounting* (Autumn 1975): 389–394.

Skerrat, L. C. L. The valuation of stock warrants: a rejoinder. *Journal of Business Finance and Accounting* (Summer 1976): 151–152.

Smith, C. W. Option pricing; a review. *Journal of Financial Economics* 3 (January–March 1976): 3–52.

Stone, Bernell K. Warrant financing. *Journal of Financial and Quantitative Analysis* 11 (March 1976): 143–154.

Walter, James E. and Que, Agustin V. The valuation of convertible bonds. *Journal of Finance* 28 (June 1973): 713–732.

Weil, Roman L. Jr, Segall, Joel E. and Green, David Jr. Premiums on convertible bonds. *Journal of Finance* 23 (June 1968): 445–464.

Weil, Roman L. Jr, Segall, Joel E. and Green, David Jr. A reply to premiums on convertible bonds: comment. *Journal of Finance* 25 (September 1970): 931–933.

Appendix A to Chapter 16:

The Option Pricing Model (OPM)

INTRODUCTION TO OPTIONS

Options are contracts that give their holder the right to buy (or sell) an asset at a predetermined price, called the striking or exercise price, for a given period of time. For example, on 5 October 1978, a call option on I.C.I. ordinary shares gave its holder the right to buy 1000 ordinary shares (deals in the London traded options market are in multiples of 1000 shares) at an exercise price of £3600 until April 1979. The price of I.C.I. shares at the closing of Stock Exchange business on 5 October was £3.97.

Therefore, 1000 I.C.I. shares had a market value of £3970. The call option sold for £580. This would be referred to as an 'in-the-money' option because the exercise price was less than the current market value of the shares. On the same day there were two in-the-money options available to investors with exercise prices of £3600 and £3900 and one out-of-the money option with an exercise price of £4200 (which is greater than the market valuation).

In recent years models for pricing options (OPM) have been derived which enable us to treat the variables discussed in Chapter 16 and in this appendix with numerical solutions.[1] These models are applicable to a wide range of option-type contracts, including warrants and convertibles discussed in Chapter 16.

The considerable increase in interest in options and option pricing has been associated with the development of new options markets and important new theoretical developments. In April 1973, organized trading in call options began on the Chicago Board Options Exchange (CBOE), followed by call option trading on the American Stock Exchange (AMEX options). The path-breaking paper by Fischer Black and Myron Scholes appeared at about the same time. In addition to deriving the general equilibrium option pricing equation as well as conducting empirical tests, Black and Scholes suggested other implications of option pricing that have significance for many other important aspects of business finance. A traded options market opened in London in April 1978 controlled by the Stock Exchange Council. This was preceded by a European options market based in Amsterdam.

Black and Scholes observed that option pricing principles can be used to value other complex contingent claim assets such as the equity of a geared firm. From this viewpoint, the shareholders of a firm have a call that gives them the right to buy back the firm from the debenture-holders by paying the face value of the debentures at maturity or exercising other alternatives for buying the debentures. Several important applications of the option pricing model were then made. As observed by Clifford Smith in his comprehensive review article,[2] 'the model is also applied by Merton (1974) to analyze the effects of risk on the value of corporate debt; by Galai and Masulis (1976) to examine the effect of mergers, acquisitions, scale expansions, and spin-offs on the relative values of the

1. F. Black and M. Scholes, The pricing of options and corporate liabilities, *Journal of Political Economy* 81 (May/June 1973), pp. 637–654; Black and Scholes, The valuation of option contracts and a test of market efficiency, *Journal of Finance* 27 (May 1972), pp. 399–417; R. C. Merton, Theory of rational option pricing, *Bell Journal* 4 (Spring 1973), pp. 141–183.

2. Clifford W. Smith, Jr, Option pricing; a review, *Journal of Financial Economics* 3 (January/March 1976), pp. 3–51.

debt and equity claims of the firm; by Ingersoll (1976) to value the shares of dual purpose funds; and by Black (1976) to value commodity options, forward contracts, and future contracts' (p. 5).

Because of the large number of additional areas on which the option pricing models provide new insights, it is useful to develop an understanding of the basic ideas involved. First, some of the fundamental characteristics of the use of options will be developed. Second, some of the basic relationships will be developed in an intuitive way as a background for the presentation and application of the Black and Scholes option pricing model.

THE USE OF CALL OPTIONS

The underlying nature of options can be explained most concretely by comparing four alternative strategies with regard to gains or losses from fluctuations in the price of the shares. Consider 100 shares whose current price is £5. The results of four alternative investment positions are depicted in Figure 16A–1. If an investor buys the shares and holds them (has a long position in the shares), he gains or loses if the shares increase or decrease in price. For a £1 rise or fall in the share price, the investor gains or loses £1 per share or plus or minus 20 per cent. (Brokerage costs, taxes and other factors not central to the main issues under analysis here are not taken into consideration.) This is a simple relationship that is used as the yardstick for comparison with the other possible strategies.

Next we consider the alternative of buying a call that gives an option to buy the shares at £5 for six months. A rough indication of the price (a pricing formula is presented later) would be £30 for the call or 30 pence per share of the 100 shares under consideration. Assume that the share price rises to £6 near the end of the six-month period. The value of the call would be £1 since it enables a purchase of a share worth £6 for £5. (As will be shown in the option pricing formula, since we have assumed that this opportunity becomes available only just before the end of the sixth-month option period, very little premium will be added to the difference between the share value (S) and the exercise price of the call (X_0). The net gain will be the £1 less the price paid for the call of 30 pence, which equals 70 pence. If the share price declines by £1, the holder of the option would simply not exercise it. He would lose the 30 pence per share he had paid for the call. Treating the 30 pence as the investment, the buyer of the call either gains 233 per cent or loses 100 per cent.

A third position is that a call is sold without owning the shares (a naked call). The seller would receive the 30 pence (the brokers will hold the £30 and will require additional deposits if the share price declines in value). If the share increases in price to £6 just before the end of the expiration of the call option, the option will be worth £1. To supply the shares or to balance off his option position will cost the seller of the naked option £1, so he has lost 70 pence net. If the share price declines in value to £4, the option will have no value and the seller has gained 30 pence.

The percentage gain or loss cannot be meaningfully calculated since it will depend upon how the investment position of the seller of the naked option is defined. Should it be an estimate of some contingent liability which he has? Or shall we infer some estimate of his investment worth, which enables him to trade in naked options? Since there is no clear number for his investment position, we shall not attempt to measure his percentage gain or loss. We can observe that his upside gain is limited to the selling price of the option. However, there is no downside limit on his loss since the rising price of the shares will increase the price of the option he would have to buy to balance the options he has sold or increase without limit the price of the shares he would have to buy to satisfy the call he has sold. Obviously, he would not sell a naked call unless he judged that the probability of a decline in the price of the shares was very high.

The fourth and final position we consider is the sale of a covered call by an investor who already owns the 100 shares (the sale of a covered call). Since he already owns the shares, we may view the sale of the call as a sale of the shares at £5.30 if the price of the shares rises to £6 or a shift in his investment basis for the shares to £4.70 if the

Table 16A–1 *Results of Four Separate Investment Strategies Involving Options.*

	Gain (or loss) per share with change in share price			
	Share price increases by £1.		Share price decreases by £1.	
	Amount	%	Amount	%
1. Buy and hold[a]	£1.00	20	(£1.00)	(20)
2. Buy a call	£0.70	233	(£0.30)	(100)
3. Sell a naked call	(£0.70)	[b]	£0.30	[b]
4. Sell a covered call	£0.30	6	(£0.70)	(14)

[a] Or long in stock.
[b] Depends on the definition of the 'investment' made.

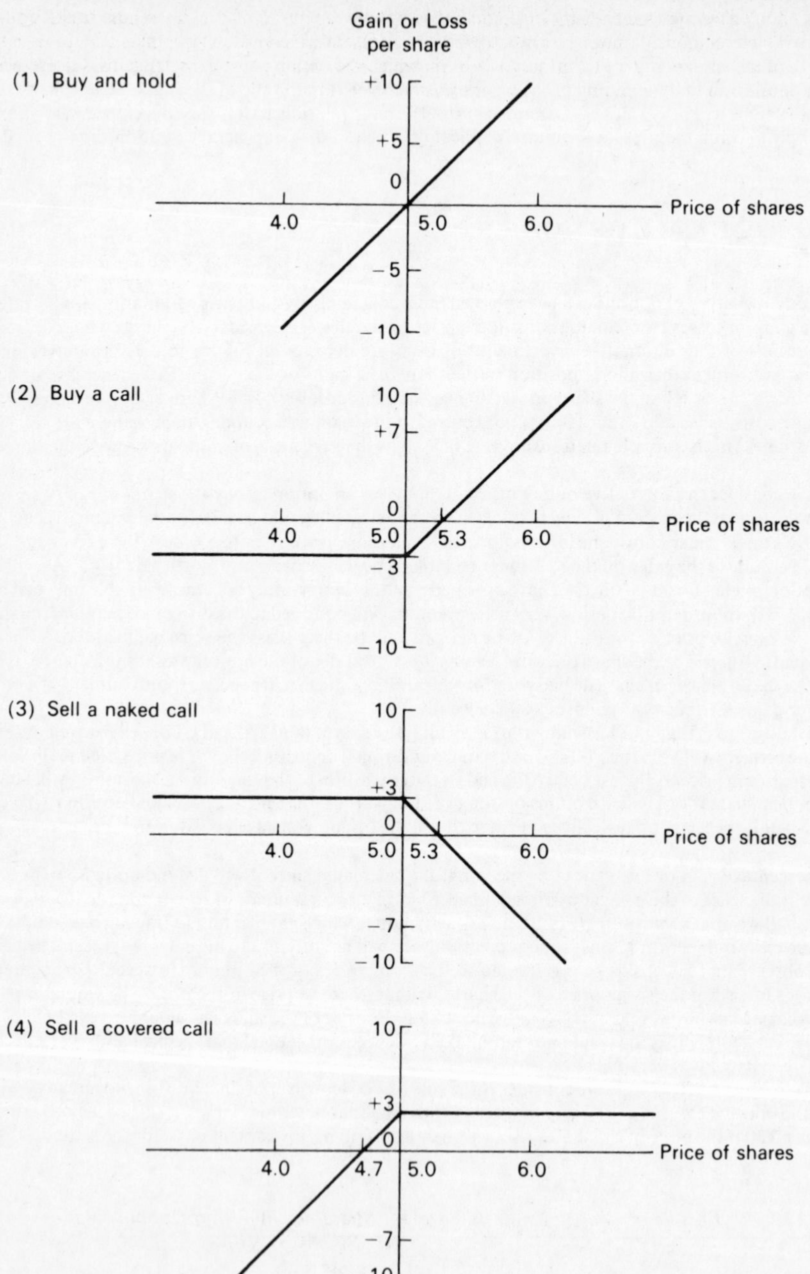

Figure 16A–1 *Results of Alternative Investment Positions.*

share price declines to £4. Thus a rise in the price of the shares to £6 represents a 6 per cent gain and a decline to £4 represents a 14 per cent loss.

Each of the four alternative strategies is depicted as a graph in Figure 16A–1. The results of the four strategies are summarized in Table 16A–1. Buying a call greatly magnifies the possible percentage gains and losses. Selling a naked call results in a pattern that is a mirror image of buying a call. Selling a covered call limits the upside percentage gain and reduces somewhat the downside percentage loss. Note that since the seller of a naked call is hurt most by a substantial rise in the price of the shares and the seller of a covered call is hurt most by a substantial decline in the price of the shares, divergent views of the price prospects of the shares may still result in the sale of calls on the shares. Thus transactions in calls may magnify gains or losses or dampen gains or losses, depending upon the position of the investor and the strategy that he elects to follow.

BASIC PRICE RELATIONS

With this background on the mechanics of option trading and its implications, we can begin the analysis of the determinants of option prices. An intuitive approach to option pricing is to consider the terminal call price under certainty.[3] Let C^* be the terminal call price, S^* be the terminal share price, and X_0 the exercise price of the option. The following relationship will obtain:

$$C^* = S^* - X_0$$

This is similar to the simple warrant formula. The call price will be equal to the difference between the share price and the exercise price, or nil if the exercise price is greater than the share price. Thus if the terminal share price just before the expiration of a call is £6 and the exercise price of the option is £5, the terminal call price, C^*, will be £1. In an equilibrium world of certainty, the return to all assets is equal to the rate, r. Hence the terminal values of the share price and option price may be written:

$$S_0{}^* = S_0 e^{rt} \quad \text{and} \quad C_0{}^* = C_0 e^{rt}$$

Substituting, we have

$$C_0 e^{rt^*} = e^{rt^*} S_0 - X_0$$
$$C_0 = e^{-rt^*}[e^{rt^*} S_0 - X_0]$$
$$C_0 = e^{-rt^*} e^{rt^*} S_0 - e^{-rt^*} X_0$$
$$C_0 = S_0 - e^{-rt^*} X_0$$

Thus the value of a call is equal to the share price less the exercise price discounted at r over the time of its remaining maturity period. This expression differs from the Black–Scholes pricing equation only in the multiplication of each of the terms on the right-hand side of the equation, S_0 and X_0, by probability factors. These probability terms reflect the uncertainty about the terminal share prices. With this background, we can now turn to the Black–Scholes option pricing model.

CALCULATIONS OF OPTIONS VALUES

In the Black–Scholes model, the derivation is based on the creation of a perfect hedge by simultaneously being long (short) in the underlying security and holding an opposite, short (long) position on a number of options. The return on a completely hedged position will then be equal to the risk-free return on the investment in order to eliminate arbitrage opportunities. A call option that can be exercised only at some future maturity date[4] can then be evaluated by the following expressions:

$$C_0 = S_0 N(\text{dist. } 1) - X_0 e^{-R_F t^*} N(\text{dist. } 2) \qquad (16A\text{–}1)$$

$$\text{dist. } 1 = \frac{ln(S_0/X_0) + [R_F + (\sigma^2/2)]t^*}{\sigma\sqrt{t^*}} \qquad (16A\text{–}2)$$

$$\text{dist. } 2 = \text{dist. } 1 - \sigma\sqrt{t^*} \qquad (16A\text{–}3)$$

where:

C_0 = the option price or value of the option
S_0 = current value of the underlying asset

---

3. Based on the presentation in Clifford W. Smith Jr, Option pricing.
4. This is called a 'European Option'. It is not unnatural to use a formula for the value of a European call option that can be exercised only at the maturity date of the option. Merton, in a purely probabilistic formulation for non-dividend paying shares, demonstrated that it is always advantageous to delay exercising a call option until the latest possible date, its maturity.

X_0 = the exercise or striking price of the option
$N(\cdot)$ = the standardized normal cumulative probability density function
R_F = the riskless interest rate
σ^2 = the instantaneous rate of variance of percentage returns
t^* = time to maturity or duration of the option.

The application of these expressions follows readily from the material we have previously set forth in Appendix A to Chapter 11.[5] For example, the $N(\cdot)$ expressions were treated in Table 11A–3 and the corresponding Figure 11A–4, both dealing with cumulative probability distributions. Some specific numerical examples will illustrate the application of equations 16A–1 to 16A–3.

Suppose we are valuing a warrant to purchase an ordinary share. The following facts could be directly observed or estimated from market data:

$S_0 = £1$
$X_0 = £1$
$t^* = 4$ years
$R_F = 6\%$
$\sigma^2 = 9\%$

The value of S could be read from the financial quotation page of a current newspaper. X_0 and t^*, the exercise price of a warrant and its maturity, respectively, are shown on the face of the warrant certificate. The risk-free rate can be estimated from the rates on three-month treasury bills. The rate of variance can be estimated by taking the daily prices of the shares for one year, from which a variance of prices could be calculated.[6] We can now proceed to make the calculations as shown in equations 16A–1a, 16A–2a and 16A–3a.

$$C_0 = 1\,N(\text{dist. }1) - 1e^{-0.06(4)}\,N(\text{dist. }2) \qquad \text{(16A–1a)}$$

$$\text{dist. }1 = \frac{ln(1/1) + [0.06 + (0.09/2)]4}{0.3(2)} \qquad \text{(16A–2a)}$$

$$= \frac{(0.105)4}{0.6} = 0.7$$

$$\text{dist. }2 = 0.7 - 0.3(2) = 0.1 \qquad \text{(16A–3a)}$$

$$C_0 = 1(0.758) - 1(0.787)(0.5398)$$
$$= 0.758 - 0.425$$
$$C_0 = 33.3 \text{ pence}$$

First, we calculate the value of the cumulative distribution function as shown in 16A–2a. It should be noted that the logarithm is the natural logarithm. The *ln* of 1/1 or 1, the first term in the numerator, is nil. The value of dist. 1 is found to be 0.7. We use Table C in the appendices at the end of the book and find the value of 0.7 in the *z* column. We find a value of 0.2580. This represents the shaded area in Figure 16A–2.

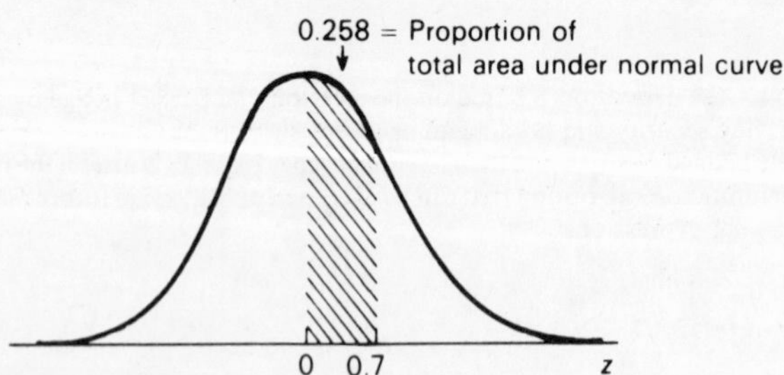

Figure 16A–2 *Graph of an Appendix Table C Value.*

---

5. Equations 16A–1 to 16A–3 can also be combined into one equation:

$$C_0 = S_0 \cdot N\left[\frac{In(S_0/X_0) + (r + \sigma^2/2)t^*}{\sigma\sqrt{t^*}}\right] - e^{rT} X_0 N\left[\frac{In(S_0/X_0) + (r - \sigma^2/2)t^*}{\sigma\sqrt{t^*}}\right]$$

6. The model presented here assumes no dividend payments, so that dividends would be ignored in calculating the variance of the percentage value changes. This is precisely correct for non-cash-dividend paying shares but only approximately correct for others.

Since the formula calls for the cumulative distribution, we add the total area under the left-hand tail of the distribution, which has a value of 0.5000 exactly. Thus the value of dist. 1 equals 0.758, which is used in 16A–1a. Because dist. 2 is related to dist. 1 by a simple relationship, we place 0.7 in 16A–2a to obtain a dist. 2 value of 0.1. In Table C we find a value of 0.0398 to which we add 0.5 to obtain 0.5398 to use in equation 16A–1a.

The evaluation of the $e^{-0.06(4)}$ term involves continuous compounding. In Appendix A to Chapter 9 we described how the Table 9A–1 of natural logarithms could be used to perform continuous compounding. Looking in Table 9A–1 for 0.24 and interpolating, we obtain 1.27125 for the future sum. We take the reciprocal to obtain the present value factor of 0.786628 or 0.787 used in 16A–1a.[7] Performing the remaining calculations, we obtain 33.3 pence for the option price.

Next let us assume that the current price of the shares is £2 rather than £1. We now utilize equations 16A–1b, 16A–2b and 16A–3b.

$$\text{dist. } 1 = \frac{ln(2/1)+0.42}{0.6} = \frac{0.693+0.42}{0.6} = 1.85 \qquad \text{(16A–2b)}$$

$$\text{dist. } 2 = 1.85 - 0.6 = 1.25 \qquad \text{(16A–3b)}$$

$$C_0 = 2\,N(\text{dist. } 1) - 1e^{-0.06(4)}\,N(\text{dist. } 2) \qquad \text{(16A–1b)}$$

$$C_0 = 2(0.968) - 1(0.787)(0.8940)$$

$$C_0 = £1.232$$

Proceeding as described before, we now obtain £1.232 as the value of the option. Thus we are enabled to derive the relationship for the predicted market value of the option as depicted in Figure 16–1. We will utilize another set of data to derive the values shown in Table 16A–2 to develop the lines shown in Figure 16A–3 for the indicated market price of a warrant as a function of the following key variables:

S_0 – the price of the shares varies from £1 to £4
t^* – duration of the warrant of 4 to 9 years
X_0 – exercise price of £2.

Table16A–2 *Relations between the Values of an Option for a Range of Values of Share Price and Option Maturity.*[a]

–1–	–2–	–3–	–4–	–5–	–6–	–7–	–8–
t^a	£V	% Change	N(dist. 1)	N(dist. 2)	C_0	% Change	Ratio, percentage change in option price to percentage change in share price
4	0.2		0.0000[b]	0.0000[b]	£0.00[b]		
4	1.0		0.3246	0.1457	0.09		
4	2.0	100	0.7580	0.5398	0.67	617	6.2
4	3.0	50	0.9155	0.8085	1.47	121	2.4
4	4.0	33	0.9677	0.8940	2.46	67	2.0
4	6.0	50	0.9943	0.9732	4.44	80	1.6
9	1.0		0.6103	0.2676	£0.30		
9	2.0	100	0.8531	0.5590	1.05	354	3.5
9	3.0	50	0.9332	0.7257	1.95	85	1.7
9	4.0	33	0.9656	0.8212	2.91	49	1.5
9	6.0	50	0.9884	0.9147	4.86	67	1.3

[a]For $C_0 = £2$, $R_F = 0.06$ and $\sigma^2 = 0.09$.
[b]These values approach zero.

7. We could obtain an approximate result by using Table C–2 for the present value factors with annual compounding.

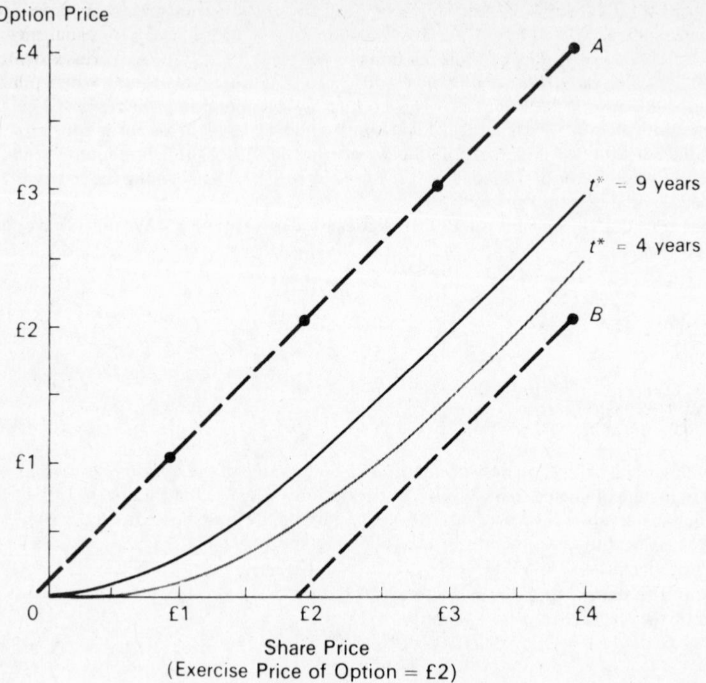

Figure 16A–3 *The Relation between Option Value and Share Price for a Given Exercise Price of the Option.*

FACTORS INFLUENCING OPTIONS VALUES

A number of relationships can be observed from the patterns in Table 16A–2 and Figure 16A–3. The higher the price of the shares, the greater the value of the option for fixed values of the other variables. The longer the maturity of the option, the higher its value. Line A represents the maximum value of the option, since it cannot be worth more than the shares. Line B represents the minimum value of the option, corresponding to the formula value of the warrant given in Figure 16–1 of Chapter 16. Its value cannot be negative and will be no less than the formula value of an option given on the first page of Chapter 16.

The longer the maturity of the option, the closer it moves towards line A, its maximum value. Conversely, the shorter the maturity of a warrant the closer it moves towards its minimum value, line B. In Chapter 16 in Figure 16–1, the market price of the TPA warrants is shown to be close to the formula value of a warrant that corresponds to line B of Figure 16A–3. Hence it is likely that the remaining maturity of the TPA warrants must be relatively short.

When the share price is substantially higher than the exercise price, the option will have a high value and is almost certain to be exercised. The value of the option we have been computing can also be approximated by calculating the current price of a debenture with a face value equal to the exercise price of the option and a maturity equal to the maturity of the option.[8] This current price is deducted from the current market price of the shares to give the value of the option. For example, for a current market price of £6 and an option maturity of four years,

$$C_0 = 6 - 2e^{-0.24} = 6 - 2(0.7866) = 6 - 1.573 = £4.43.$$

This result for the value of the option is the same as the result of £4.43 we obtained using the option pricing model (OPM). The option has a high value and is likely to be exercised. On the other hand, if the share price is considerably less than the exercise price of the option, such as the 20 pence value in Table 16A–2, the option will have no value and will be likely to expire without being exercised.

---

8. For an explanation see Black and Scholes, The pricing of options, p. 638.

We observe also that the curves depicting the value of an option as the share price varies are concave from above and lie below the 45° line drawn from the origin (line A). For an option of given maturity, any percentage change in the share price will result in a larger percentage change in the option value. This is demonstrated by the percentage change columns in Table 16A–2 and by the final column of Table 16A–2, which presents the ratio of the percentage change in the option price to the percentage change in the share price. For the longer maturity, the volatility of the option price is reduced somewhat. Also, at higher share prices for a given maturity, the volatility of the option prices relative to the share price changes is reduced.

Thus the use of the option pricing models enables us to observe some fundamental patterns in the relationships between share prices and the related option values. These relationships depend upon the level of share prices, the duration and exercise price of the option, the risk-free interest rate, and the variance of the percentage returns on the share values.

THE PRICING OF CORPORATE SECURITIES

The option pricing model also provides us with additional insights into the nature of debt and equity in a firm.[9] Since the debt has a maturity, the equity of a firm can be regarded as a European call option on the total value of the firm. The shareholders of the firm have an option to buy back the firm from the debenture-holders at an exercise price equal to the face value of the debentures at time N, the maturity date of the debentures. If the value of the firm, V_N, is above the face value of the debentures, the equity will have a positive value. If the value of the firm is below the face value of the debentures, the value of the equity is nil, but it cannot become negative because of the limited liability nature of the equity. The limited liability feature of corporate equity helps explain why the corporate form has facilitated raising large amounts of equity funds. The shareholders have protection against a decline in the firm's value below C_0 (the face value of the debentures, the option exercise price) and have a right to the differential in the firm's value above C_0.

The OPM enables us to price out the value of the equity, given the value of the debt, or C_0, the option exercise price. It also enables us to analyse the effect of the riskiness of the firm's investment or production programmes (the firm's degree of operating gearing) on the interests and positions of the shareholders in relationship to the creditors. A numerical example will illustrate the ideas involved.

Let us begin by pricing the value of the equity. Assume the following: The current value of the firm, V_0, is £3 000 000; the face value of the debt, C_0, is £1 000 000, and has a remaining maturity of four years. The variance of the percentage returns on the value of the firm (σ^2) is 0.01 and R_F is equal to 5 per cent. By using the OPM we can calculate the indicated market value of the firm's equity, S_0. First we calculate the two distribution functions:

$$\text{dist. } 1 = \frac{ln3 + (0.05 + 0.005)4}{0.1(2)} = \frac{1.0986 + 0.22}{0.2} = \frac{1.3186}{0.2} = 6.593$$

$N(\text{dist. } 1) \cong 1$
dist. 2 = 6.593 − 0.2 = 6.393
$N(\text{dist. } 2) \cong 1$

Second, we calculate the value of the ordinary shares:

$$S_0 = £3\,000\,000(1) - 1\,000\,000(1)e^{-0 \cdot 2} = £3\,000\,000 - £818\,731$$
$$S_0 = £2\,181\,000$$

Given that the value of the firm is £3 000 000 and the calculated value of the ordinary shares is £2 181 000, the indicated market value of the debt is £818 731. We can now investigate the effects of the firm's changing the riskiness of its investment programme. Assume that the firm takes on more risky investments so that the variance rises to a 0.16 level. We can now recalculate the values of the equity and debt under the assumption that the value of the firm remains at £3 000 000. We begin with the distribution functions:

$$\text{dist. } 1 = \frac{(1.0986) + (0.05 + 0.08)4}{0.4(2)} = \frac{1.0986 + 0.52}{0.8} = \frac{1.6186}{0.8} = 2.0233$$

$N(\text{dist. } 1) = 0.9785$
dist. 2 = 2.0233 − 0.8 = 1.2233
$N(\text{dist. } 2) = 0.8894$
We can next calculate the value of the equity in the firm by the OPM.

$$S_0 = £3\,000\,000\,(0.9785) - £1\,000\,000\,(0.8894)\,(0.81873)$$
$$= £2\,936\,500 - £728\,200$$
$$S_0 = £2\,208\,300$$

9. R. C. Merton, On the pricing of corporate debt: the risk structure of interest rates, *Journal of Finance* 29 (May 1974), pp. 449–470; D. D. Galai and R. W. Masulis, The option pricing model and the risk factor of stock, *Journal of Financial Economics* 3 (1976), pp. 53–81.

The market value of the debt therefore drops to £791 700. Hence, increasing the riskiness of the firm's production operations increases the value of the equity and reduces the value of the debt. Thus the OPM indicates some inherent divergence of interests between the shareholders and the creditors of the firm. Since the shareholders possess voting control of the firm, they may take actions that may be adverse to the interests of the creditors. It is for such reasons that various 'me first' rules are written into the debenture trust deeds representing restrictions on what the firm (through actions of the controlling group, the shareholders and its designated managerial group) may or may not do.[10] This is for the purpose of protecting the position of the creditors of the firm.

The OPM thus enables us to quantify a number of relations for which we formerly were unable to obtain solutions without making *ad hoc* assumptions about critical variables. In contrast, the OPM model provides a logical and internally consistent framework for valuing options and pricing out corporate securities. In addition, all of the elements of the OPM model are measurable by market-place data. Thus the OPM provides us with new insights on how to value options and new insights on the relative positions of the equity holders and the creditors of the firm. The OPM has been put to considerable practical uses by investment analysts during recent years. In addition, it opens up new interesting theoretical paths, many of which remain to be explored fully, especially in the areas of further large-scale empirical testing of a number of aspects of the options pricing model.

PROBLEMS

16A–1. The ordinary shares of Atom Sporting Goods, Inc., sell for £3 per share. Warrants to purchase the shares at a price of £2 are also available. The warrants have four years to maturity. The instantaneous variance of returns on the ordinary shares is 4 per cent. The risk-free rate is 5 per cent.
(a) Using the option pricing model, determine the value of a warrant.
(b) What would be the value of the warrant if the maturity were nine years? Why does the value of the warrant change with the change in maturity?

16A–2. Cold Water Land Development Company is currently valued at £10 000 000. Seventy-five per cent of current value is the face value of debt, all of which is redeemable in four years. Because land sales is a volatile business, the variance of percentage returns is 64 per cent. The risk-free rate is 6 per cent.
(a) Determine the market value of the equity.
(b) Determine the market value of the debt.
(c) Should the ordinary shareholders exercise their option to acquire the firm from its creditors? Explain.

16A–3. Great Plains Distributing Company is currently valued at £10 000 000. Ten per cent of current value is the face value of debt, all of which is redeemable in four years. The variance of percentage returns is 64 per cent. The risk-free rate is 6 per cent.
(a) Determine the value of the equity.
(b) Determine the value of the debt.
(c) Should the shareholders exercise their option to acquire the firm from its creditors? Explain.

SELECTED REFERENCES

Bird, A. and Henfrey, A. The Chicago Board Options Exchange. *Investment Analyst* (December 1975): 6–23.

Black, F. The pricing of commodity contracts. *Journal of Financial Economics* 3 (January–March 1976): 167–179.

Cox, J. C. and Ross, S. A. The valuation of options for alternative stochastic processes. *Journal of Financial Economics* 3 (January–March 1976): 145–166.

Cox, J. C. and Ross, S. A. A survey of some new results in financial option pricing policy. *Journal of Finance* 31 (May 1976): 383–402.

Fox, A. F. Put call parity theory and the London share option market. Paper presented to the Association of University Teachers in Accountancy Conference, 1977.

Galai, D. and Masulis, R. W. The option pricing model and the risk factor of stock. *Journal of Financial Economics* 3 (January–March 1976): 53–82.

Hughes, W. R. A decision theory approach to valuing call options. *Investment Analyst* (December 1977): 25–29.

---

10. Cf. E. F. Fama and M. H. Miller, *The Theory of Finance* (New York: Holt, Rinehart and Winston, 1972), pp. 150–170.

Ingersoll, J. E. A theoretical and empirical investigation of the dual purpose funds: an application of contingent-claims analysis. *Journal of Financial Economics* 3 (January–March 1976): 83–124.

Latane, Henry A. and Rendleman, Richard J. Jr. Standard deviations of stock price ratios implied in option prices. *Journal of Finance* 31 (May 1976): 369–381.

Leabo, Dick A. and Rogalski, Richard J. Warrant price movements and the efficient market model. *Journal of Finance* 30 (March 1975): 163–177.

Merton, Robert C. On the pricing of corporate debt: the risk structure of interest rates. *Journal of Finance* 29 (May 1974): 449–470.

Merton, Robert C. Option pricing when underlying stock returns are discontinuous. *Journal of Financial Economics* 3 (January–March 1976): 125–144.

Rubinstein, M. E. The valuation of uncertain income streams and the pricing of options. *Bell Journal of Economics* 7 (Autumn 1976): 407–425.

Scholes, Myron. Taxes and the pricing of options. *Journal of Finance* 31 (May 1976): 319–332.

PART 5

FINANCIAL STRUCTURE AND THE COST OF CAPITAL

In Part 4 we examined the major sources and forms of long-term external capital, considering the market for long-term securities and the principal types of securities – ordinary shares, preference shares, debentures, leases, warrants and convertible loan stock. We compared the advantages and disadvantages of these different instruments and considered some of the factors that financial managers keep in mind as they decide which form of financing to use at a specific time. Now, in Part 5, we examine the long-term financing decision in a somewhat different manner, searching for the *optimal* financial structure, or the financial structure that simultaneously minimizes the firm's cost of capital and maximizes the market value of its ordinary shares. As we shall see, financing decisions and investment decisions are interdependent – the optimal financing plan and the optimal level of investment must be determined simultaneously – so Part 5 also serves the important function of integrating the theory of capital budgeting and the theory of capital structure.

Part 5 contains four chapters: first, Chapter 17, Valuation and Rates of Return, examines the way risk and return interact to determine value; next, Chapter 18, Financial Structure and the Use of Gearing highlights the manner in which debt not only generally increases expected earnings, but also increases the firm's risk position; Chapter 19, The Cost of Capital, draws on the two preceding chapters to establish the firm's optimal capital structure as well as its cost of capital; and finally, in Chapter 20, Dividend Policy and Internal Financing, we analyse the decision of whether to pay out earnings in the form of dividends or to retain earnings for re-investment in the business, and we show the interrelationship between capital budgeting and the cost of capital.

Chapter 17

Valuation and Rates of Return[1]

One of the financial manager's principal goals is to maximize the value of his shareholders' wealth; accordingly, an understanding of the way the market values securities is essential to sound financial management. Also, the rate of return concepts developed in this chapter are used extensively in Chapters 18 and 19, where we analyse the optimal capital structure and show how to calculate a marginal cost of capital for use in capital budgeting.

DEFINITIONS OF VALUE

While it may be difficult to ascribe monetary returns to certain kinds of assets – works of art, for instance – the fundamental characteristic of business assets is that they give rise to income flows. Sometimes these flows are easy to determine and measure – the interest return on a debenture is an example. At other times, the cash flows attributable to the asset must be estimated, as was done in Chapters 10 and 11 in the evaluation of projects. Regardless of the difficulties of measuring income flows, it is the prospective income from business assets that gives them value.

Liquidating value versus going-concern value

Several different definitions of 'value' exist in the literature and are used in practice, with different ones being appropriate at different times. The first distinction that must be made is that between liquidating value and going-concern value. *Liquidating value* is defined as

1. This chapter is relatively long and difficult, but quite important. Students should allow for this in their preparation schedules.

the amount that could be realized if an asset or a group of assets (the entire assets of a firm, for example) are sold separately from the organization that has been using them. If the owner of a machine shop decides to retire, he might auction off his stock and equipment, collect his debts, then sell his land and buildings to a grocery wholesaler for use as a warehouse. The sum of the proceeds from each category of assets would be the liquidating value of the assets. If his debts are subtracted from this amount, the difference would represent the liquidating value of his ownership in the business.

On the other hand, if the firm is sold as an operating business to a company or to another individual, the purchaser would pay an amount equal to the *going-concern value* of the company. If the going-concern value exceeds the liquidating value, the difference represents the value of the organization as distinct from the value of the assets.[2]

Book value versus market value

We must also distinguish between *book value* or the accounting value at which an asset is carried, and *market value*, the price at which the asset can be sold. If the asset in question is a firm, it actually has two market values – a liquidating value and a going-concern value. Only the higher of the two is generally referred to as the market value.

For shares, an item of primary concern in this chapter, book value per share is the owners' equity – ordinary shares and accumulated retained earnings – divided by shares outstanding. Most British companies have market values which are greater than their book values. For example, in August 1974 the market price of Commercial Union's 25 pence ordinary shares was 106 pence. Since market value is dependent upon earnings, while book value reflects historical cost, it is not surprising to find deviations between book and market values in a dynamic, uncertain world.

Market value versus 'fair' or 'reasonable' value

The concept of a fair or reasonable value (sometimes called the 'intrinsic' value) is widespread in the literature on stock market investments. Although the market value of a security is known at any given time, the security's fair value as viewed by different investors could differ. Graham, Dodd and Cottle, in a leading investments text, define fair value as 'that value which is justified by the facts; e.g., assets, earnings, dividends . . . The computed [fair] value is likely to change at least from year to year, as the factors governing that value are modified.'[3]

Although Graham, Dodd and Cottle develop this concept for security valuation, the idea is applicable to all business assets. What it involves, basically, is estimating the future net cash flows attributable to an asset; determining an appropriate capitalization, or discount, rate; and then finding the present value of the cash flows. This, of course, is exactly what was done in Chapters 9, 10 and 11, where the concept of reasonable value was developed for application in finding the present value of investment opportunities.

The procedure for determining an asset's value is known as the *capitalization-of-income method of valuation.* This is simply a fancy name for the present value of a stream of earnings, discussed at length in Chapter 9. *In going through the present chapter, keep in mind that value, or the price of securities, is exactly analogous to the present value of assets*

---

2. Accountants have termed this difference 'goodwill', but 'organization value' would be a more appropriate description.

3. B. Graham, D. L. Dodd and S. Cottle, *Security Analysis* (New York: McGraw-Hill, 1961), p. 28.

as determined in Chapters 10 and 11. From this point on, whenever the word 'value' is used, we mean the *present value* found by capitalizing expected future cash flows.

THE REQUIRED RATE OF RETURN

The first step in using the capitalization of income procedure is to establish the proper capitalization rate, or discount rate, for the security. *This rate is defined as the required rate of return, and it is the minimum rate of return necessary to induce investors to buy or hold the security.* For any given risky security, j, the expected rate of return, k_j, is equal to the riskless rate of interest, R_F, plus a risk premium, ρ_j (read 'rho' of security):[4]

$$\bar{k}_j = R_F + \rho_j = R_F + (\bar{k}_M - R_F)\beta_j \qquad (17\text{–}1)$$

Equation 17–1 is the security market line (SML), which specifies the relationship between risk and the expected rate of return.[5] One advantage of the use of the SML is that the components of risk can be identified and estimated from readily available published data. The risk premium is composed of two parts: the risk premium on the market as a whole and a risk measure for the individual security. The risk premium for the market as a whole is the amount by which the return on a broad market index such as the *Financial Times* all-share index exceeds a risk-free return measured by the current yield on British government securities, which are free of default risk. The return on the market may be referred to as $\bar{k}_M$ so that the risk premium on the market is: $(\bar{k}_M - R_F)$.

$$\text{Market risk premium} = (\bar{k}_M - R_F) \qquad (17\text{–}1a)$$

It can be demonstrated that the securities market pays a premium only for that part of the risk of a security that cannot be eliminated by diversification. Risk that cannot be diversified away is called systematic risk and is measured by the covariance of the returns on the individual security with the returns on the market portfolio. The systematic risk of a security, when normalized by the variance of the market returns, is referred to as the 'beta' of the security. We have:

$$\beta_j = \frac{Cov(k_j, k_M)}{Var(k_M)}$$

where:

β_j = the risk of an individual security j

$Cov(k_j, k_M)$ = the covariance of the returns on the individual security with the returns on the market

$Var(k_M)$ = the variance of the returns on the market

To illustrate the application of these concepts, we shall use some realistic magnitudes for each of the terms involved. The return on the market $(\bar{k}_M)$ has ranged from 9 per cent to 13 per cent; the variance of the returns on the market $[Var(k_M)]$ is about 1 per cent; the risk-free rate (R_F) has ranged from about 5 per cent to 7 per cent. Using the mid-point of the

---

4. In Appendix 11E the application of the capital asset pricing model (CAPM) to analysing investment decisions under uncertainty was set forth. Here the application of the CAPM to the determination of the required rate of return on different types of securities and therefore to valuation questions is set forth.

5. Although not necessary to our use and application of the SML concepts, the interested reader can find a formal development of the SML relationships in Appendix E to Chapter 11. These SML relationships are now standard in finance literature and in general use among stockbrokers and investment analysts. The terms are now used in advertisements and discussions in the financial press such as the *Investors Chronicle* and *Financial Times*.

ranges of values for the market returns for the risk-free rate we have:

$$(\bar{k}_M - R_F) = (0.11 - 0.06) = 0.05 = 5\% \qquad (17\text{–}1b)$$

The risk premium, ρ_j, is the product of the market risk premium times the risk of the individual security, β_j, which varies somewhat above and below 1.[6] Hence for a β_j of 1.2 the value of the risk premium, ρ_j, on the individual security j is:

$$\rho_j = (\bar{k}_M - R_F)\beta_j = (0.11 - 0.06)1.2 = 0.06 = 6\%.$$

This indicates that 6 per cent would be added to the risk-free return, R_F, to obtain an expected return of 12 per cent on an individual security j. Note that the two measures, the risk-free return, R_F, and the market risk premium, $(\bar{k}_M - R_F)$, are economy-wide parameters. Thus we can use them with the beta of any security to obtain its expected return. This can be demonstrated by the use of the graph of the SML.

Figure 17–1 presents a graph of the SML. The expected rate of return is shown on the vertical axis, while risk, measured here as the beta of the security, is shown on the horizontal axis. Since a riskless asset, by definition, has no risk, R_F lies on the vertical axis. As risk increases, the expected rate of return also increases. A relatively low-risk security, such as that of firm A, might have a risk index of $\beta_A = 0.4$ and an expected rate of return of $\bar{k}_A = 8$ per cent. A more risky security, such as that of firm B, might have a risk index of $\beta_B = 1.4$ and an expected rate of return of $\bar{k}_B = 13$ per cent.

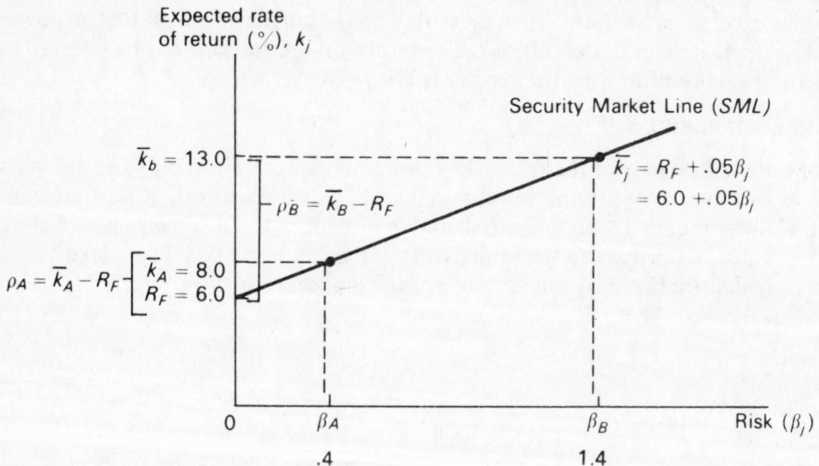

Figure 17–1 *The Relationship between Risk and the Expected Rate of Return: the Security Market Line (SML).*

In the illustrative case, the slope of the SML is 0.05, indicating that the expected rate of return rises by one per cent for each 0.2 increase in the security's beta. The beta is 0.4 for firm A, so the risk premium on that security is 2 per cent ($0.05 \times 0.4 = 2$ per cent), while the beta on security B is 1.4, making its risk premium 7 per cent ($0.05 \times 1.4 = 7$ per cent). When these two risk premiums are added to the riskless rate, R_F, we obtain the expected rates of return:

$$\bar{k}_A = 6\% + 2\% = 8\%.$$
$$\bar{k}_B = 6\% + 7\% = 13\%.$$

---

6. The covariance of the market returns with the market returns is its variance, so the beta of the market is $Var(k_M)/(Var(k_M))$, which equals 1. Normal values of the betas of individual securities would be from about 0.5 to 1.5.

Notice that the graph can also be used to analyse the securities of a single firm. Since a company's debentures have a smaller standard deviation of expected returns than its ordinary shares, $\bar{k}_A$ might be the expected rate of return on the firm's debentures, while $\bar{k}_B$ might refer to its ordinary shares. The company's preference shares and convertibles would lie on the SML between $\bar{k}_A$ and $\bar{k}_B$.

Shifts in the SML: changing interest rates

We noted in Chapter 6 that interest rates shift markedly over time, and when such shifts occur the SML can also be expected to shift. Figure 17–2 illustrates the effects of an increase in the riskless rate from 6 per cent to 8 per cent, with the increase perhaps resulting

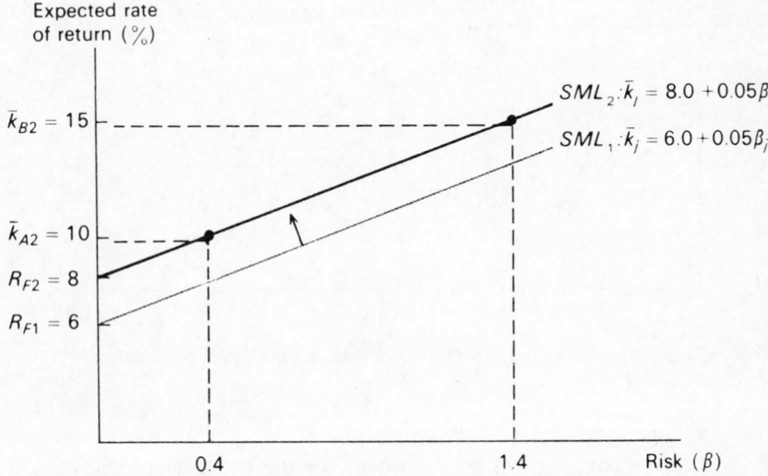

Figure 17–2 *The Effect of Rising Interest Rates on the Expected Rate of Return.*

from an increase in the rate of inflation. If it is assumed that $\bar{k}_M$ also increases by 2 percentage points as R_F increases by 2 percentage points, the slope of the SML remains constant, but the intercept shifts upward:

Original SML equation: $\bar{k}_j = 6.0\% + 0.05\beta_j$
Revised SML equation: $\bar{k}_j = 8.0\% + 0.05\beta_j$

This results in increases in the expected rates of return for firms A and B, with $\bar{k}_A$ rising from 8 to 10 per cent and $\bar{k}_B$ from 13 to 15 per cent.

Shifts in the SML: investor psychology

The slope of the SML depends upon investors' attitudes towards risk. When investors are gloomy and pessimistic, they are highly averse to risk, and at such times the SML has a relatively steep slope. Conversely, when investors on the whole are optimistic and have a bright outlook, the slope of the SML is not so steep. When investors' attitudes change, the SML shifts. Figure 17–3 illustrates a change in attitudes towards increased pessimism, or an increase in risk aversion. The slope of the SML increases from 0.05 to 0.07 as shown:[7]

---

7. R_F may also change when the slope of the SML curve shifts owing to the changed relationship between returns on risky and riskless assets.

Original SML equation: $\bar{k}_j = 6\% + 0.05\beta_j$

Revised SML equation: $\bar{k}_j = 6\% + 0.07\beta_j$

This results in increases in the expected rates of return for firms A and B, with $\bar{k}_A$ rising from 8 to 8.8 per cent and $\bar{k}_B$ from 13 to 15.8 per cent.

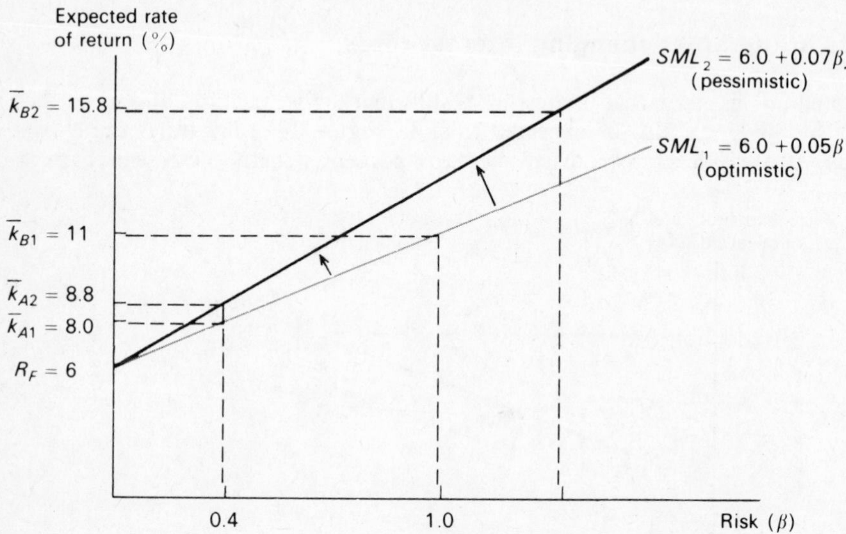

Figure 17–3 *The Effect of Changing Investor Attitudes on the Expected Rate of Return.*

Since the SML is a market-wide relationship, the 'expected' return on a security is 'required' for market equilibrium relationships. In the subsequent section on ordinary share valuation, the return on equity *required* by equilibrium relationships will be designated as k_s^* in contrast to k_s, a return *expected* from individual security earnings and price relationships.

VALUATION OF DEBENTURES

The rate of return concepts developed above may now be used to explain the process of security valuation. In this section we consider the valuation of debentures; in the two following sections we go on to study preference shares and ordinary shares. Debenture values are relatively easy to determine. The expected cash flows are the annual interest payments plus the principal amount due when the debenture reaches maturity. A problem regarding the valuation of debentures is the risk of default arising as a result of company difficulties. Different companies have varying degrees of risk attached to them so that, for example, the risk attached to debentures issued by I.C.I. is much less than that attached to debenture issues of smaller, less well-established firms. The actual calculating procedures employed in the valuation of debentures are illustrated in the following examples.

Perpetual bonds

Analysis of perpetual bonds is easier if we consider irredeemable government stocks. One of the most famous irredeemable government stocks is $2\frac{1}{2}$ per cent Consols. These were issued in 1814 in order to consolidate the many issues of government stock that had been made during the course of the Napoleonic wars. Like all government stocks, $2\frac{1}{2}$ per cent Consols are issued at a nominal price of £100. The coupon rate of $2\frac{1}{2}$ per cent signifies that £2.50 will be paid in interest each year in perpetuity. What would the stock be worth under current market conditions?

First, note that the value v_b of any perpetuity is computed as follows:[8]

$$v_b = \frac{c}{(1+k_b)^1} + \frac{c}{(1+k_b)^2} + \dots$$
$$= \frac{c}{k_b}. \qquad (17\text{–}2)$$

Here c is the constant annual interest (in the case of Consols, £2.50) and k_b is the yield or required rate of return on the stock. (In this chapter we use k_b, k_{ps} and k_s to designate the required rates of return on debt, preference shares and equity, respectively.) Equation 17–2 is an infinite series and the value of the Consols is the discounted sum of the infinite series.

We know that the annual interest payment on Consols is £2.50; therefore, the only other thing we need to know is the yield on other government stock of similar risk (i.e., the yield on other irredeemable government stocks). Suppose we find that other irredeemable government stocks are paying 4 per cent in current market conditions. Then the value of the Consol is determined as follows:

$$v_b = \frac{c}{k_b} = \frac{£2.50}{0.04} = £62.50$$

If the going rate of interest rises to 5 per cent the value of the Consols falls to £50 (£2.50/0.05 = £50). If interest rates continue rising, when the yield is 6 per cent the value of Consols will be only £41.67. Values of this perpetual bond for a range of interest rates are given in the following tabulation:

Current market interest rate	Current market value
0.02%	£125.00
0.03	83.33
0.04	62.50
0.05	50.00
0.06	41.67
0.07	35.71
0.08	31.25

8. A perpetuity is a bond that never matures; it pays interest indefinitely. Equation 17–2 is simply the present value of an infinite series; its proof is demonstrated below. Rewrite equation 17–2 as follows:

$$v_b = c\left[\frac{1}{(1+k_b)^1} + \frac{1}{(1+k_b)^2} + \dots + \frac{1}{(1+k_b)^N}\right]. \qquad (1)$$

Multiply both sides of equation (1) by $(1+k_b)$:

$$v_b(1+k_b) = c\left[1 + \frac{1}{(1+k_b)^1} + \frac{1}{(1+k_b)^2} + \dots + \frac{1}{(1+k_b)^{N-1}}\right] \qquad (2)$$

Subtract equation 1 from equation 2, obtaining:

$$v_b(1+k_b-1) = c\left[1 - \frac{1}{(1+k_b)^N}\right]. \qquad (3)$$

As $N \to \infty$, $\frac{1}{(1+k_b)^N} \to 0$, so equation 3 approaches

$$v_b k_b = c,$$

and

$$v_b = \frac{c}{k_b}. \qquad (17\text{–}2)$$

Short-term bond

Now suppose the British government issues stock with the same risk of default as the Consols but with a three-year maturity. The new stock also pays £2.50 interest and has a maturity value of £100. What will be the value of this new stock at the time of issue if the going yield is 4 per cent? To find this value we must solve equation 17–3:

$$v_b = \frac{c_1}{(1+k_b)^1} + \frac{c_2}{(1+k_b)^2} + \frac{c_3+M}{(1+k_b)^3}. \quad (17\text{–}3)$$

Here M is the maturity value of the bond. The solution is given in the following tabulation.[9]

Year	Receipt	4% discount factors	Present value
1	£2.50	0.962	£ 2.405
2	£2.50	0.925	2.313
3	£2.50+£100	0.889	91.122
		Bond value	= £95.840

At the various rates of interest used in the perpetuity example this bond would have the following values:

Current market interest rate	Current market value
0.2%	£101.41
0.3	98.77
0.4	95.84
0.5	93.30
0.6	90.68
0.7	88.13
0.8	85.84

Interest-rate risk

Figure 17–4 shows how the values of the long-term bond (the Consol) and the short-term bond change in response to changes in the going market rate of interest. Note how much less sensitive the short-term bond is to changes in interest rates. At a $2\frac{1}{2}$ per cent interest rate, both the perpetuity and the short-term bonds are valued at £100. When rates rise to 8 per cent, the long-term bond falls to £31.25, while the short-term security falls only to £85.84. A similar situation occurs when rates fall below $2\frac{1}{2}$ per cent. *This differential responsiveness to changes in interest rates always holds true – the longer the maturity of a security, the greater its price change in response to a given change in interest rates.* Thus, even if the risk of default on two bonds is exactly the same, the value of the one with the longer maturity is exposed to more risk from a rise in interest rates. This greater interest rate risk explains why short-term bonds usually have lower yields, or rates of return, than long-term bonds. It also explains why companies are reluctant to hold their liquid reserves in the form of long-term debt instruments – these liquid reserves are held for pre-

9. If the bond has a longer maturity, 20 years for example, we would certainly want to calculate its present value by finding the present value of a 20-year annuity and then adding to that the present value of the £100 principal amount received at maturity. Special bond tables have been devised to simplify the calculation procedure. Note also that k_b will frequently differ for the long- and short-term bonds; as we saw in Chapter 6, unless the yield to maturity curve is flat, long- and short-term rates differ.

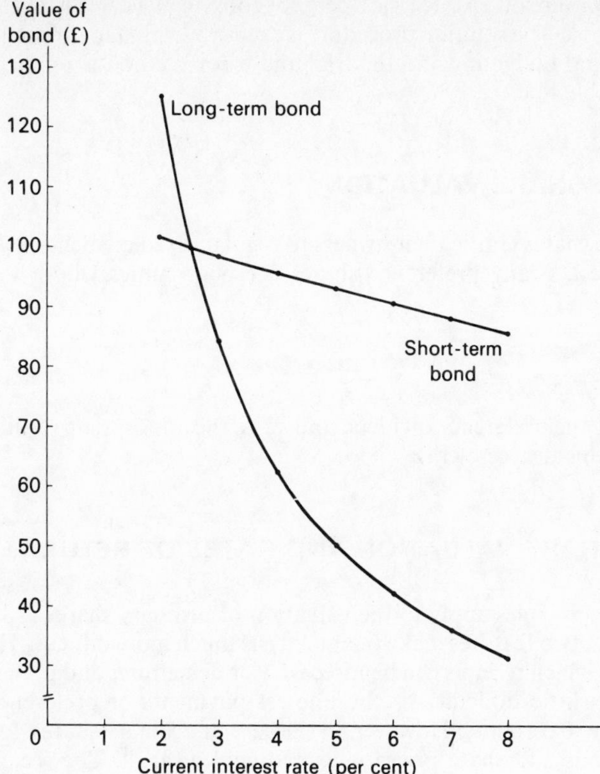

Figure 17–4 *Values of Long-term and Short-term Bonds, 2.5 Per Cent Coupon Rate, at Different Market Interest Rates.*

cautionary purposes, and a company would be unwilling to sacrifice safety for a little higher yield on a long-term bond.

Yield to maturity

The rate of return that is expected if a bond is held to its maturity date is defined as the *yield to maturity*. Suppose a perpetuity has a stated par value of £100, has a 5 per cent coupon rate (that is, pays 5 per cent, or £5 annually, on this stated value), and is currently selling for £62.50. We can solve equation 17–2 for k_b to find the yield on the bond:

$$k_b = \frac{c}{v_b} = \frac{£5}{£62.50} = 8\% = \text{yield on a perpetuity.}$$

If the bond sells for £125, the formula will show that the yield is 4 per cent.

For the three year bond paying £2.50 interest, if the price of the bond is £85.84 the yield to maturity is found by solving equation 17–3; the solution *PVIF* is the one for 8 per cent:

$$\begin{aligned} £85.84 &= £2.50(PVIF) + £2.50(PVIF) \\ &\quad + £102.50(PVIF) \\ &= £2.50(0.926) + £2.50(0.857) \\ &\quad + £102.50(0.794) \\ &= £2.315 + £2.142 + £81.385 \\ &= £85.84 \text{ when } PVIF = 8\,\% \end{aligned}$$

The interest factors are taken from the 8 per cent column of Table D–2 in the appendices at the end of this book. The solution procedure is exactly like that for finding the internal rate of return in capital budgeting and the trial-and-error method is required unless special tables are available.[10]

PREFERENCE SHARE VALUATION

Most preference shares entitle their owners to regular, fixed dividend payments similar to debenture interest. Many preference shares are perpetuities whose value is found as follows:

$$v_{ps} = \frac{d_{ps}}{k_{ps}} \tag{17–4}$$

In this case d_{ps} is the preference dividend and k_{ps} is the appropriate capitalization rate for investments of this degree of risk.

ORDINARY SHARE VALUATION AND RATES OF RETURN

While the same principles apply to the valuation of ordinary shares as to debentures or preference shares, two features make their analysis much more difficult. First is the degree of certainty with which receipts can be forecast. For debentures and preference shares this forecast presents little difficulty as the interest payments or preference dividends are known with relative certainty. However, in the case of ordinary shares, forecasting future earnings, dividends and share prices is exceedingly difficult. The second complicating feature is that, unlike interest and preference dividends, earnings and dividends on ordinary shares are generally expected to grow, not to remain constant. Thus, while standard annuity formulae can be applied, more difficult conceptual schemes must also be used.

Estimating the value of a stock: the single period case

The price today of a share, p_0, depends upon (a) the cash flows investors expect to receive if they buy the share and (b) the riskiness of these expected cash flows. The expected cash flows consist of two elements: (a) the dividend expected in each year t, defined as d_t, and (b) the price investors expect to receive when they sell the share at the end of year n, defined as p_n, which includes the return of the original investment plus a capital gain (or minus a capital loss): if investors expect to hold the share for one year, and if the share price is expected to grow at the rate g, the valuation equation is

$$p_0 = \frac{\text{expected dividend} + \text{expected price (both at end of year 1)}}{1.0 + \text{required rate of return}}$$

$$= \frac{d_1 + p_1}{(1 + k_s)} = \frac{d_1 + p_0(1 + g)}{(1 + k_s)}, \tag{17–5}$$

10. We first tried the *PVIF*s for 6 per cent, found that the equation did not 'work', then raised the *PVIF* to 8 per cent, where the equation did 'work'. This indicated that 8 per cent was the yield to maturity on the bond. In practice, specialized interest tables called *bond tables*, generated by a computer, are available to facilitate determining the yield to maturity on bonds with different maturities, with different stated interest rates, and selling for various discounts below or premiums above their maturity values.

which can be simplified to yield equation 17–6.[11]

$$p_0 = \frac{d_1}{k_s - g} \tag{17–6}$$

Equations 17–5 and 17–6 represent the present value of the expected dividends and the year-end share price, discounted at the required rate of return. Solving equation 17–6 gives the 'expected' or 'intrinsic' price for the share. To illustrate, suppose you are thinking of buying some Universal Rubber shares. If you buy the shares you will hold them for one year. You note that Universal Rubber earned £0.343 per share last year, and paid a dividend of £0.19. Earnings and dividends have been rising at about 5 per cent a year, on the average, over the last 10 to 15 years, and you expect this growth to continue. Further, if earnings and dividends grow at the expected rate, you think the share price will likewise grow by 5 per cent.

The next step is to determine the required rate of return on Universal Rubber shares. The current rate of interest on British government stocks, R_F, is 6 per cent, but Universal Rubber is clearly more risky than government securities: competitors could erode the company's market; labour problems could disrupt operations; an economic recession could cause sales to fall below the break-even point; car sales could decline, pulling down Universal Rubber's own sales and profits; and so on. Further, even if sales, earnings and dividends meet projections, the share price could still fall as a result of a generally weak market.

Given all these risk factors, you conclude that a 6 per cent risk premium is justified, so your required rate of return on Universal Rubber's shares, k_s, is calculated as follows:

$k_s^* = R_F + \rho = 6\% + 6\% = 12\%$.

Next, you estimate the dividend for the coming year, d_1, as follows:

$d_1 = d_0(1+g) = £0.19(1.05) = £0.20$.

Now we have the necessary information to estimate the fair value of the shares by the use of equation 17–6:

$$p_0 = \frac{d_1}{k_s^* - g} \tag{17–6}$$

$$= \frac{£0.20}{0.12 - 0.05} = £2.86$$

To you, £2.86 represents a reasonable price for Universal Rubber's shares. If the actual market price is less, you will buy them; if the actual price is higher, you will not buy them, or you will sell if you own them.[12]

---

11. $p_0 = \dfrac{d_1 + p_0(1+g)}{(1+k_s)}$

$p_0(1+k_s) = d_1 + p_0(1+g)$
$p_0(1+k_s-1-g) = d_1$
$p_0(k_s - g) = d_1$

$$p_0 = \frac{d_1}{k_s - g} \tag{17–6}$$

Notice that this equation is developed for a one-year holding period. In a later section, we will show that it is also valid for longer periods, provided the expected growth rate is constant.

12. Notice the similarity between this process and the *NPV* method of capital budgeting described in Chapter 10. In the earlier chapter, we (a) estimated a cost of capital for the firm, which compares with estimating k_s, our required rate of return, (b) discounted expected future cash flows, which are analogous to dividends plus the future stock price, (c) found the present value of future cash flows, which corresponds to the 'fair value' of the

Estimating the rate of return on a share

In the preceding section we calculated the 'expected price' of Universal Rubber's shares to a given investor. Let us now change the procedure somewhat, and calculate the rate of return the investor can expect if he purchases the shares at the current market price. The expected rate of return, which we define as $\bar{k}_s$, is analogous to the internal rate of return on a capital project: $\bar{k}_s$ is the discount rate that equates the present value of the expected dividends (d_1) and final share price (p_1) to the present share price (p_0):

$$p_0 = \frac{d_1 + p_1}{(1+\bar{k}_s)} = \frac{d_1 + p_0(1+g)}{(1+\bar{k}_s)}.$$

Suppose Universal Rubber is selling for £4 per share. We can calculate $\bar{k}_s$ as follows:

$$£4 = \frac{£0.2 + £4(1.05)}{(1+\bar{k}s)} = \frac{£0.2 + £4.2}{(1+\bar{k}s)}$$

$$£4(1+\bar{k}s) = £4.4$$
$$1+\bar{k}s = 1.10$$
$$\bar{k}s = 0.10 \text{ or } 10\%$$

Thus, if you expect to receive a £0.2 dividend and a year-end price of £4.2, then your expected rate of return on the investment is 10 per cent.

Notice that the expected rate of return, $\bar{k}_s$, consists of two components, an expected dividend yield and an expected capital gains yield:

$$\bar{k}_s = \frac{\text{expected dividend}}{\text{present price}} + \frac{\text{expected increase in price}}{\text{present price}}$$

$$= \frac{d_1}{p_0} + g. \tag{17–6a}$$

For a Universal Rubber share bought at a price of £4

$$\bar{k}_s = \frac{£0.2}{£4} + \frac{£0.2}{£4} = 5\% + 5\% = 10\%$$

Given an expected rate of return of 10 per cent, should you make the purchase? This depends upon how the expected return compares with the required return. If $\bar{k}_s$ exceeds k_s^*, buy; if $\bar{k}_s$ is less than k_s^*, sell; and if $\bar{k}_s$ equals k_s^*, the share price is in equilibrium and you should be indifferent. In this case, your 12 per cent required rate of return for Universal Rubber exceeds the 10 per cent expected return, so you should not buy the shares.[13]

Market equilibrium: required versus expected returns

In the two preceding sections we calculated (a) expected and required rates of return and (b) 'expected' share prices. Further, we saw that buy/no-buy decisions can be based upon a

---

shares, (d) determined the initial outlay for the project, which compares with finding the actual price of the shares, and (e) accepted the project if the PV of future cash flows exceeded the initial cost of the project, which is similar to comparing the 'fair value' of the shares to their market price.

13. Notice the similarity between this process and the IRR method of capital budgeting. The expected rate of return, $\bar{k}_s$, corresponds to the IRR on a project, and the required rate of return, k_s^*, corresponds to cost-of-capital cut-off rate used in capital budgeting.

comparison of either k_s^* versus k_s or 'expected' share value versus actual market price. In this section, we first show that the two decision rules are entirely consistent, then illustrate the process by which stock market equilibrium is maintained.

Consider again the Universal Rubber example, when the following data are applicable:

Expected dividend at year end $= \bar{d}_1 = £0.2$.
Expected growth rate in share price $= \bar{g} = 5\%$.
Required rate of return $= k_s^* = 12\%$.

We calculated an 'expected' price of £2.86. We next found that the actual market price, as read from a newspaper or obtained from a stockbroker, is £4, and on the basis of that price we calculated a 10 per cent expected rate of return.

By either the rate of return or calculated price criteria, Universal Rubber's shares are overvalued:

Actual price $= £4 >$ 'expected' price $= £2.86$,

and

Required rate of return $(k_s^*) = 12\% >$ expected rate of return $(\bar{k}_s) = 10\%$.

You should not buy these shares at the £4 price, and if you own them you should sell.

Now let us assume that you are a 'typical' or 'representative' investor, so that your expectations and actions actually determine stock market prices. You and others will start selling Universal Rubber shares, and this selling pressure will cause the price to decline. The decline will continue until the price reaches £2.86, which you, the typical investor, feel is its intrinsic value. At this price, the expected rate of return will also equal the required rate of return:

$$\bar{k}_s = \frac{d_1}{p_0} + g = \frac{£0.2}{£2.86} + 5\% = 7\% + 5\% = 12\%$$

and

$$k_s^* = R_F + \rho = 6\% + 6\% = 12\%.$$

This situation will always hold – whenever the actual market price is equal to the 'fair' price as calculated by a 'typical' investor, required and expected returns will also be equal, and the market will be in equilibrium; that is, there will be no tendency for the share price to go up or down.

FACTORS LEADING TO CHANGES IN MARKET PRICES

Let us assume that Universal Rubber's shares are in equilibrium, selling at a price of £2.86. If all expectations are exactly met, over the next year the price will gradually rise to £3, or by 5 per cent. However, many different events could occur to cause a change in the equilibrium price of the share. To illustrate the forces at work, consider again the share price model, the set of inputs used to develop the price of £2.86, and a new set of assumed input variables:

	Variable value	
	Original	New
Riskless rate (R_F)	6%	5%
Risk aversion coefficient (λ^{**})	0.04	0.05
Index of share's risk (β)	1.5	1.2
Expected growth rate (g)	5%	6%

The first three variables influence k_s^*, which declines as a result of the new set of variables from 12 per cent to 11 per cent:

Original: $k_s^* = 6\% + (0.04)(1.5) = 12\%$.
New: $k_s^* = 5\% + (0.05)(1.2) = 11\%$.

Using these values, together with the new d and g values, we find that p_0 rises from £2.86 to £4.02:

$$\text{Original:} \quad p_0 = \frac{£0.19(1.05)}{0.12 - 0.05} = \frac{£0.2}{0.07} = £2.86$$

$$\text{New:} \quad p_0 = \frac{£0.19(1.06)}{0.11 - 0.06} = \frac{£0.201}{0.05} = £4.02$$

At the new price, the expected and required rate of return will be equal:

$$\bar{k}_s = \frac{£0.201}{£4.02} + 6\% = 11\% = k_s^*,$$

as found above.

Evidence suggests that securities adjust quite rapidly to disequilibrium situations. Consequently, equilibrium ordinarily exists for any given security, and in general the required and expected returns are equal. Share prices certainly change, sometimes violently and rapidly, but this simply reflects changing conditions and expectations. There are, of course, times when shares continue to react for several months to a favourable or unfavourable development, but this does not signify a long adjustment period; rather, it merely shows that as more information about the situation becomes available, the market adjusts to these new bits of information. Throughout the remainder of this book we will assume that security markets are in equilibrium, with $k^* = \bar{k}$. Hence, we shall generally use k (with the appropriate subscript) for the required return or applicable discount rate unless we are directly contrasting the required return, k^*, with the expected return, $\bar{k}$.

MULTIPERIOD SHARE VALUATION MODELS

Thus far, our discussion of share values and rates of return has focused on a single-period model, where we expect to hold the shares for one year, receive one dividend, and then sell the shares at the end of the year. In this section, we expand the analysis to deal with more realistic, but more complicated, multiperiod models.

Expected dividends as the basis for share values

According to generally accepted theory, share prices are determined as the present value of a stream of cash flows. In other words, the capitalization of income procedure applies to shares as well as to debentures, and other assets. What are the cash flows that companies provide to their shareholders? What flows do the markets in fact capitalize? Several different models have been formulated. At least four different categories of flows have been capitalized in alternative formulations: (a) the stream of dividends, (b) the stream of earnings, (c) the current earnings plus flows resulting from future investment opportunities, and (d) the discounting of cash flows as in capital budgeting models. Miller and Modigliani have demonstrated that these different approaches are equivalent and yield the same valuations.[14] Since multiperiod valuation models are inherently complicated, we shall illustrate the methodology involved by use of the least complicated form – the stream of dividends approach. In this formulation, a share may be regarded as being similar to an irredeemable debenture or preference share and its value may be established as the present value of its stream of dividends:

$$\begin{aligned}\text{Value of share} = p_0 &= PV \text{ of expected future dividends}\\ &= \frac{d_1}{(1+k_s)^1} + \frac{d_2}{(1+k_s)^2} + \ldots\\ &= \sum_{t=1}^{\infty} \frac{d_t}{(1+k_s)^t}. \qquad (17\text{–}7)\end{aligned}$$

Unlike debenture interest and dividends paid on preference shares, ordinary share dividends are not generally expected to remain constant in the future; hence we cannot work with the convenient annuity formulas. This fact, combined with the much greater uncertainty about ordinary share dividends, makes ordinary share valuation a more complex task than the valuation of debentures or preference shares.

Equation 17–7 is a quite general share valuation model in the sense that the time pattern of d_t can be anything; d_t can be rising, falling, constant, or it can even fluctuate randomly, and equation 17–7 will still hold. For many purposes, however, it is useful to estimate a particular time pattern for d_t and then develop a simplified (that is, easier to evaluate) version of the share valuation model expressed in equation 17–7. In the following sections, we consider the special cases of nil growth, constant growth, and 'supernormal' growth.

Share values with zero growth

Suppose the rate of growth is measured by the rate at which dividends are expected to increase. If future growth is expected to be nil, the value of the share reduces to the same formula as was developed for a perpetual bond:

$$\text{price} = \frac{\text{dividend}}{\text{capitalization rate}}$$

$$p_0 = \frac{d_1}{k_s}. \qquad (17\text{–}8)$$

Solving for k_s, we obtain

$$k_s = \frac{d_1}{p_0}, \qquad (17\text{–}8a)$$

which states that the required rate of return on a share that has no growth prospects is simply the dividend yield.

'Normal', or constant growth

Year after year, the earnings and dividends of most companies have been increasing. In general, this growth is expected to continue in the foreseeable future at about the same rate as GNP. On this basis, it is expected that an average, or 'normal', company will grow at a rate of from 3 to 5 per cent a year. Thus, if such a company's previous dividend, which has

14. See their 'Dividend policy, growth, and the valuation of shares', *Journal of Business* 34 (October 1961), pp. 411–433.

already been paid, was d_o, its dividend in any future year t may be forecast as $d_t = d_0(1+g)^t$, where g = the expected rate of growth. For example, if Universal Rubber just paid a dividend of £0.19 (that is, d_0 = £0.19), and investors expect a 5 per cent growth rate, the estimated dividend one year hence will be d_1 = (£0.19) (1.05) = £0.20; d_2 will be £0.21; and the estimated dividend five years hence will be

$$\begin{aligned} d_t &= d_0(1+g)^t \\ &= £0.19(1.05)^5 \\ &= £0.242 \end{aligned}$$

Using this method of estimating future dividends, the current price, p_0, is determined as follows:

$$\begin{aligned} p_0 &= \frac{d_1}{(1+k_s)^1} + \frac{d_2}{(1+k_s)^2} + \frac{d_3}{(1+k_s)^3} + \ldots \\ &= \frac{d_0(1+g)^1}{(1+k_s)^1} + \frac{d_0(1+g)^2}{(1+k_s)^2} + \frac{d_0(1+g)^3}{(1+k_s)^3} + \ldots \\ &= \sum_{t=1}^{\infty} \frac{d_0(1+g)^t}{(1+k_s)^t}. \end{aligned} \qquad (17\text{–}9)$$

If g is constant, equation 17–9 may be simplified as follows:[15]

$$p_0 = \frac{d_1}{k_s - g}. \qquad (17\text{–}10)$$

Notice that the constant growth model expressed in equation 17–10 is identical to the single-period model, equation 17–5, developed in an earlier section.

A necessary condition for the constant growth model is that k_s be greater than g; otherwise, equation 17–10 gives nonsense answers. If k_s equals g, the equation blows up, yielding an infinite price; if k_s is less than g, a *negative* price results. Since neither infinite nor negative stock prices make sense, it is clear that in equilibrium k_s must be greater than g.

---

15. The proof of equation 17–10 is as follows. Rewrite equation 17–9 as

$$p_0 = d_0\left[\frac{(1+g)}{(1+k_s)} + \frac{(1+g)^2}{(1+k_s)^2} + \frac{(1+g)^3}{(1+k_s)^3} + \ldots + \frac{(1+g)^N}{(1+k_s)^N}\right]. \qquad (1)$$

Multiply both sides of equation 1 by $(1+k_s)/(1+g)$:

$$\left[\frac{(1+k_s)}{(1+g)}\right]p_0 = d_0\left[1 + \frac{(1+g)}{(1+k_s)} + \frac{(1+g)^2}{(1+k_s)^2} + \ldots + \frac{(1+g)^{N-1}}{(1+k_s)^{N-1}}\right]. \qquad (2)$$

Subtract equation 1 from equation 2 to obtain

$$\left[\frac{(1+k_s)}{(1+g)} - 1\right]p_0 = d_0\left[1 - \frac{(1+g)^N}{(1+k_s)^N}\right].$$

$$\left[\frac{(1+k_s)-(1+g)}{(1+g)}\right]p_0 = d_0\left[1 - \frac{(1+g)^N}{(1+k_s)^N}\right]$$

Assuming $k_s > g$, as $N \to \infty$ the term in brackets on the right side of the equation $\to$ 1.0, leaving

$$\left[\frac{(1+k_s)-(1+g)}{(1+g)}\right]p_0 = d_0,$$

which simplifies to

$$(k_s - g)p_0 = d_0(1+g) = d_1$$

$$p_0 = \frac{d_1}{k_s - g}. \qquad (17\text{–}10)$$

Note that equation 17–10 is sufficiently general to encompass the no-growth case described above. If growth is nil, this is simply a special case, and equation 17–10 is equal to equation 17–8.[16]

'Supernormal' growth

Firms typically go through 'life cycles' during part of which their growth is much faster than that of the economy as a whole. Motor car manufacturers in the 1920s and computer and office equipment manufacturers in the 1960s are examples. Figure 17–5 illustrates such supernormal growth and compares it with normal growth, zero growth and negative growth.[17]

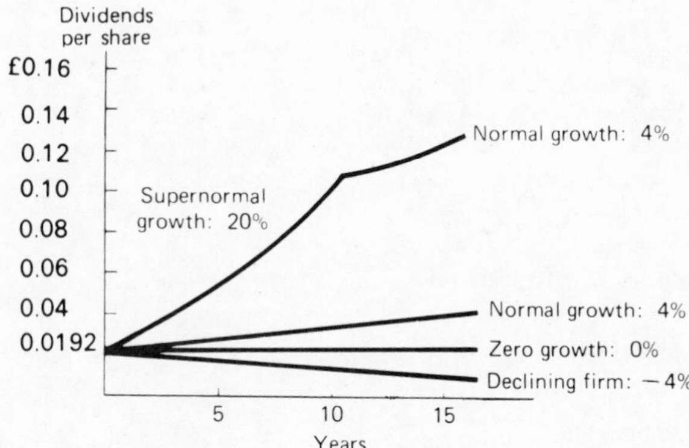

Figure 17–5 *Illustrative Dividend Growth Rates.*

The illustrative supernormal growth firm is expected to grow at a 20 per cent rate for 10 years, then to have its growth rate fall to 4 per cent, the norm for the economy. The value of a firm with such a growth pattern is determined by the following equation:

Present price = *PV* of dividends during supernormal growth period + Value of share price at end of supernormal growth period discounted back to present

$$p_0 = \sum_{t=1}^{N} \frac{d_0(1+g_s)^t}{(1+k_s)^t} + \left(\frac{d_{N+1}}{k_s - g_n}\right)\left(\frac{1}{(1+k_s)^N}\right). \qquad (17\text{–}11)$$

Here g_s is the supernormal growth rate, g_n is the normal growth rate, and N is the period of supernormal growth.

Working through an example will help make this clear. Consider a supernormal growth firm whose previous dividend was £0.0192 (that is, $d_0 = £0.0192$), with the dividend expected to increase by 20 per cent a year for 10 years and thereafter at 4 per cent a year indefinitely. If shareholders' required rate of return is 9 per cent after tax on an investment with this degree of risk, what is the value of the shares? On the basis of the calculations in Table 17–1, the value is found to be £1.3819, the present value of the dividends during the first 10 years plus the present value of the share at the end of the tenth year.

---

16. One technical point should at least be mentioned here. The logic underlying the analysis implicitly assumes that investors are indifferent to dividend yield or capital gains. Empirical work has not conclusively established whether this is true or not, but the question is discussed in Chapter 20.

17. A *negative* growth rate represents a declining company. A mining company whose profits are falling because of a declining ore body is an example.

Table 17–1 *Method of Calculating the Value of a Share with Supernormal Growth.*

Assumptions:

(a) Shareholders' capitalization rate is 9 per cent; i.e., $k_s = 9\%$.
(b) Growth rate is 20 per cent for 10 years, 4 per cent thereafter; i.e., $g_s = 20\%$, $g_n = 4\%$, and $N = 10$.
(c) Last year's dividend was 1.92 pence; i.e., $d_0 = 1.92$ pence.

Step 1. Find present value of dividends during rapid growth period:

End of year	Dividend $1.92(1.20)^t$	$PVIF = 1/(1.09)^t$	Present value
1	2.30 pence	0.917	2.11 pence
2	2.76	0.842	2.32
3	3.32	0.772	2.56
4	3.98	0.708	2.82
5	4.78	0.650	3.11
6	5.73	0.596	3.42
7	6.88	0.547	3.76
8	8.26	0.502	4.15
9	9.91	0.460	4.56
10	11.89	0.422	5.02

$$PV \text{ of first 10 years' dividends} = \sum_{t=1}^{10} \frac{d_0(1+g_s)^t}{(1+k_s)^t} = £0.3383$$

Step 2. Find present value of year 10 share price:
(a) Find value of shares at end of year 10:

$$p_{10} = \frac{d_{11}}{k_s - g_n} = \frac{£0.1189(1.04)}{0.05} = £2.4731$$

(b) Discount p_{10} back to present:

$$PV = p_{10}\left(\frac{1}{1+k_s}\right)^{10} = £2.4731\,(0.422) = £1.0436$$

Step 3. Sum to find total value of share today:

$$p_0 = £0.3383 + £1.0436 = £1.3819$$

Comparing companies with different expected growth rates

It is useful to summarize this section by comparing the four illustrative firms whose dividend trends were depicted in Figure 17–5. Using the valuation equations developed above, the conditions assumed in the preceding examples, and the additional assumptions that each firm had earnings per share during the preceding reporting period of £0.036 net of tax (that is, $EPS_0 = £0.036$) and paid out 53.3 per cent of its reported earnings (therefore net dividends per share last year, d_0, were £0.0192 for each company), we show prices, dividend yields, and price/earnings ratios (hereafter written P/E) in Table 17–2.

Investors require and expect a return of 9 per cent on each of the shares. For the declining firm, this return consists of a relatively high current dividend yield combined with a capital *loss* amounting to 4 per cent a year. For the no-growth firm, there is neither a capital gain nor a capital loss expectation, so the 9 per cent return must be obtained entirely from the dividend yield. The normal growth firm provides a relatively low current dividend yield, but a 4 per cent a year capital gain expectation Finally, the supernormal growth firm has the lowest current dividend yield but the highest capital gain expectation.

What is expected to happen to the prices of the four illustrative firms' shares over time? Three of the four cases are straightforward: The nil growth firm's price is expected to be constant (that is, $p_t = p_{t+1}$); the declining firm is expected to have a falling share price; and the constant growth firm's share price is expected to grow at a constant rate, 4 per cent. The

Table 17–2 *Prices, Dividend Yields and Price Earnings Ratios for 9 Per Cent Returns under Different Growth Assumptions.*

		Price (pence)	Current dividend yield (%)[b]	P/E ratio[a]
Declining firm:	$p_0 = \dfrac{d_1}{k_s - g} = \dfrac{1.84}{0.09-(-0.04)}$	14.15	13	3.9
No-growth firm:	$p_0 = \dfrac{d_1}{k_s} = \dfrac{1.92}{0.09}$	21.33	9	5.9
Normal growth firm:	$p_0 = \dfrac{d_1}{k_s - g} = \dfrac{2.00}{0.09-0.04}$	40.00	5	11.1
Supernormal growth firm:	p_0 = (see Table 17–1)	138.19	1.7	38.4

[a] It was assumed at the beginning of this example that each company is earning £0.036 initially. This £0.036, divided into the various prices, gives the indicated P/E ratios.

We might also note that as the supernormal growth rate declines towards the normal rate (or as the time when this decline will occur becomes more imminent), the high P/E ratio must approach the normal P/E ratio; that is, the P/E of 38.4 will decline year by year and equal 11.1, that of the normal growth company, in the tenth year. See A. A. Robichek and M. C. Pogue, A note on the behavior of expected price earnings ratios over time, *Journal of Finance* (June 1971).

Note also that d_1 differs for each firm, being calculated as follows:

$d_1 = \text{EPS}_0(1+g)(\text{payout}) = £0.036(1+g)(0.533)$.

[b] In the UK, the tax treatment of company profits is such that earnings can be treated on a 'nil', 'net' or 'full distribution' basis. To be consistent, the dividend yield shown is a net dividend yield. In published financial statistics, however, dividend yield may be calculated on a full distribution basis, e.g. to calculate dividend cover.

supernormal growth case is more complex, but what is expected can be seen from the data in Table 17–1.

It can readily be shown that[18]

$$\sum_{t=1}^{N} \frac{(1+g_s)^t}{(1+k_s)^t} = \frac{(1+g_s)[(1+h)^{10}-1]}{g_s - k_s} = \frac{(1+g_s)h}{(g_s-k_s)}\left[\frac{(1+h)^{10}-1}{h}\right]$$

---

18. Numerical calculation procedure for a summation expression.

$$\sum_{t=1}^{10} \frac{d_o(1+g_s)^t}{(1+k_s)^t} = d_o \sum_{t=1}^{10} \frac{(1+g_s)^t}{(1+k_s)^t}$$ Write out the summation expression:

$$\sum_{t=1}^{10}\left(\frac{1+g_s}{1+k_s}\right)^t = \left(\frac{1+g_s}{1+k_s}\right) + \left(\frac{1+g_s}{1+k_s}\right)^2 + \ldots + \left(\frac{1+g_s}{1+k_s}\right)^{10}$$ Factor $\left(\frac{1+g_s}{1+k_s}\right)$ from all terms.

$$= \left(\frac{1+g_s}{1+k_s}\right)\left[1 + \left(\frac{1+g_s}{1+k_s}\right) + \ldots + \left(\frac{1+g_s}{1+k_s}\right)^9\right]$$ Use the formula for the summation of a geometric progression over N periods and simplify.

$$S_N = \frac{r^N - 1}{r-1} = \frac{1+g_s}{1+k_s}\,\frac{\left[\left(\frac{1+g_s}{1+k_s}\right)^{10}-1\right]}{\left(\frac{1+g_s}{1+k_s}\right)-1} = \frac{(1+g_s)\left[\left(\frac{1+g_s}{1+k_s}\right)^{10}-1\right]}{(1+k_s)\dfrac{1+g_s-1-k_s}{(1+k_s)}} = \frac{(1+g_s)}{(g_s-k_s)}\left[\left(\frac{1+g_s}{1+k_s}\right)^{10}-1\right]$$

Let $\left(\frac{1+g_s}{1+k_s}\right) = (1+h)$. Then $S_N = \frac{(1+g_s)}{(g_s-k_s)}[(1+h)^{10}-1]$ Multiply by $\frac{h}{h}$

$$S_N = \left[\frac{(1+g_s)(h)}{(g_s-k_s)}\right]\left[\frac{[(1+h)^{10}-1]}{h}\right]$$ The second term is the sum of an annuity.

Thus $$\sum_{t=1}^{N}\frac{d_o(1+g_s)^t}{(1+k_s)^t} = d_o\left(\frac{1+g_s}{g_s-k_s}\right)[(1+h)^N-1] = d_o\frac{(1+g_s)(h)}{(g_s-k_s)}\left[\frac{(1+h)^{10}-1}{h}\right]$$

where $\frac{(1+g_s)}{(1+k_s)} = (1+h)$ for ease of expression.

The third term is expressed in the sum of an annuity form by multiplying the second term by h/h as shown above.

For the example in Table 17–1, we have:

$$1+h = \frac{(1+g_s)}{(1+k_s)} = \frac{1.20}{1.09} = 1.100917431 \qquad \frac{(1+g_s)}{(g_s-k_s)} = \frac{1.2}{0.11} = 10.909$$

$$(1+h)^{10} = (1.100917431)^{10} = 2.615456$$

$$(1+h)^{10} - 1 = 1.615456$$

$$\frac{(1+g_s)[(1+h)^{10}-1]}{(g_s-k_s)} = 10.909 \times 1.615456 = 17.623$$

$$d_0(17.623) = 1.92(17.623) = 33.836 \text{ pence.}$$

The *PV* of the first 10 years' dividends shown in Table 17–1 is 33.83 pence, approximately the same. Note that the present price, p_0, is £1.3819 and that the expected price in year 10, p_{10}, is £2.4731. This represents an average growth rate of 6 per cent.[19] We do not show, but we could, that the expected growth rate of the share price is higher than 6 per cent in the early part of the 10-year supernormal growth period and less than 6 per cent towards the end of the period, as investors perceive the approaching end of the supernormal period. From year 11 on, the company's share price and dividend are expected to grow at the 'normal' rate, 4 per cent.

The relationships among the P/E ratios, shown in the last column of Table 17–2, are similar to what one would intuitively expect – the higher the expected growth (all other things the same), the higher the P/E ratio.[20]

A GENERAL VALUATION FORMULATION

The most general valuation formula is the Modigliani – Miller temporary growth formula:

$$V(0) = \frac{X(0)(1+g)(1-T)}{k}\left\{1 + \frac{b(r-k)}{br-k}\left[\left(\frac{1+br}{1+k}\right)^N - 1\right]\right\}$$

Where: $V(0)$ = value of the firm in period 0
$X(0)$ = net operating income of the firm in period 0
T = effective corporation tax rate
g = growth rate in $X(t) = br$
b = ratio of $I(t)$ to $X(t)$
$I(t)$ = investment of the firm per year
r = internal profitability rate of the firm
k = applicable capitalization rate; k_u for an ungeared firm; k, the weighted cost of capital for a geared firm

For example, an investment has earned £5 million after corporation tax during the most recent year. Its internal profitability rate is expected to be 24 per cent per annum for the

19. Found from Table 17–1; £2.4731/£1.3819 = 1.79, and this is approximately the CVIF for a 6 per cent growth rate.

20. Differences in P/E ratios among firms can also arise from differences in the rates of return, k_s, which investors use in capitalizing the future dividend streams. If one company has a higher P/E than another, this could be caused by a higher g, a lower k, or a combination of these two factors.

next five years, after which it will drop to 12 per cent, which is the applicable cost of capital for an investment of its risk characteristics. The ratio of new investment to annual earnings is expected to be 0.8 for a long period of time. What is the appropriate value to be placed on this investment?

$$
\begin{aligned}
V(0) &= \frac{5(1.192)}{0.12}\left\{1+\frac{0.8(0.24-0.12)}{0.192-0.12}\left[\left(\frac{1.192}{1.12}\right)^5-1\right]\right\} \\
&= \frac{5.96}{0.12}\left\{1+\left[\frac{0.096}{0.072}(1.3655-1)\right]\right\} \\
&= 49.67\{1+0.4873\} \\
V(0) &= £73.87 \text{ million}
\end{aligned}
$$

Note that of the total value of £73.87 million, £49.67 million comes from capitalization of $X(1)(1-T)$ of £5.96 million at 12 per cent. The remaining £24.20 million reflects the addition to total value due to the supernormal ($r > k$) earning power for five years.

MARKETABILITY AND RATES OF RETURN

Throughout the chapter, whenever we discussed the required rate of return on securities, we concentrated on two factors, the riskless rate of interest and the risk inherent in the security in question. Before closing, however, we should also note that investors also value flexibility, or manoeuvrability. If an investor becomes disenchanted with a particular investment, or if he needs funds for consumption or other investments, it is highly desirable for him to be able to liquidate his holdings. Other things being equal, the higher the liquidity, or marketability, the lower an investment's required rate of return. Since investments in small firms are generally less liquid than those in large companies, we have another reason for expecting to find higher required returns among smaller companies.

SUMMARY

In the discussion of the capital budgeting process in Chapter 10, the discount rate used in the calculations was seen to be of vital importance. At that time, we simply assumed that the cost of capital – the discount rate used in the present value process – was known, and we used this assumed rate in the calculations. In this chapter, however, we began to lay the foundations for actually calculating the cost of capital.

Since the cost of capital is integrally related to investors' returns on capital, the basic principles underlying valuation theory were discussed, and a number of definitions of value were presented: (a) liquidating value versus going-concern value, (b) book value versus market value and (c) 'fair' value versus current market price. Market value is fundamentally dependent upon discounted cash flow concepts and procedures; it involves estimating future cash flows and discounting them back to the present at an appropriate rate of interest.

Rates of return on debentures and preference shares are simple to understand and to calculate, but ordinary share returns are more difficult. First, ordinary share returns consist (a) of dividends and (b) of capital gains, not a single type of payment as in the case of debentures and preference shares. This fact necessitates the development of a rate of return formula that considers both dividends and capital gains; the rate of return formula for ordinary shares is, therefore, a two-part equation:

Rate of return = dividend yield + capital gains yield.

The second complicating feature of ordinary shares is the degree of uncertainty involved. Debenture and preference share payments are relatively predictable, but forecasting dividends on ordinary shares and, even more, capital gains, is a highly uncertain business.

The expected rate of return for ordinary shares can be expressed as $\bar{k}_s = d_1/p_0 + g$ if the growth rate is a constant. p_0 is the price, d_1 is the dividend expected this year, and g refers to expected *future* growth.

Share values are determined as the present value of a stream of cash flows. Therefore, the time pattern of these expected cash flows is very important in valuation of shares. The earnings and dividends of most companies have been increasing at a rate of 3 to 5 per cent a year – this is considered a normal growth rate. Some companies may have prospects for no growth at all; others may anticipate a period of 'supernormal' growth before settling down to a normal growth rate; still others may grow in a random fashion.

The required rate of return on any security, k_j^*, is the minimum rate of return necessary to induce investors to buy or to hold the security. This rate of return is a function of the riskless rate of interest and the investment's risk characteristics:

$$\bar{k}_j = R_F + \rho_j = R_F + (\bar{k}_M - R_F)\beta_j$$

This equation, when shown graphically, is called the *security market line* (SML), from which the required return, k_j^*, is specified. Because investors generally dislike risk, the required rate of return is higher on riskier securities. Debentures as a class are less risky than preference shares, and preference shares, in turn, are less risky than ordinary shares. As a result, the required rate of return is lowest for debentures, next for preference shares and highest for ordinary shares. Within each of these security classes, there are variations among the issuing firms' risks; hence, required rates of return vary among firms.

In equilibrium, the expected rate of return ($\bar{k}$) and the required rate of return (k^*) for a firm j will be equal. If, however, some disturbance causes them to be different, the market price of the share (and thus its dividend yield) will quickly change to establish a new equilibrium where k_j^* and $\bar{k}_j$ are again equal.

The required rate of return also depends upon the marketability of a given security issue – the shares and debentures of larger, better-known firms are more marketable, hence the required rates of return on such securities are lower than those on smaller, less well-known firms. As we shall see in Chapter 19, the required rate of return is, in essence, a firm's cost of capital, so if small firms have relatively high required rates of return, they also have relatively high costs of capital.

QUESTIONS

17–1. Explain what is meant by the term 'yield to maturity' (a) for debentures and (b) for preference shares. Is it appropriate to talk of a yield to maturity on a debenture that has no specific maturity date?

17–2. Explain why bonds with longer maturities experience wider price movements from a given change in interest rates than do shorter maturity bonds. Preferably give your answer (a) in words (intuitively) and (b) mathematically.

17–3. Explain why ordinary shares that are not expected to grow are similar to preference shares. Use one of the equations developed in this chapter in your explanation.

17–4. Explain the importance in valuing ordinary shares (a) of current dividends, (b) of current market price, (c) of the expected future growth rate and (d) of the market capitalization rate.

17–5. Suppose a firm's articles explicitly preclude it from ever paying a dividend. Investors *know* that this restriction will never be removed. Earnings for 1974 were £0.10 a share, and they are expected to grow at a rate of 4 per cent for ever. If the required rate of return is 10 per cent, what is the firm's theoretical P/E ratio?

17–6. Describe the factors that determine the market rate of return on a particular share at a given point in time.

17–7. Explain how (a) interest rates and (b) investors' aversion to risk influence security prices.

17–8. The laws governing the payment of capital transfer tax state that for these purposes property shall be valued on the basis of 'fair market value'. Describe how the Inland Revenue might use the valuation principles discussed in this chapter to establish the value of (a) shares quoted on the London Stock Exchange and (b) unquoted shares.

PROBLEMS

17–1(a) Some British government irredeemable stocks are paying £4 per annum interest. Stock of this type is currently yielding 9 per cent. At what price should the stock sell?

(b) Assume that the required yield for stock of this type rises to 12 per cent. What will be the new price of the stock?

(c) Assume that the required yield drops to 10 per cent. What will be the new price?

(d) Now suppose that the British government issue some more bonds that pay £4 annual interest, mature in five years and pay £100 on maturity. What will be the value of these bonds when the going rate of interest is (i) 9 per cent, (ii) 12 per cent and (iii) 10 per cent?

(e) Why do irredeemable bonds fluctuate more when interest rates change than do short-term bonds?

17–2. What will be the 'yield to maturity' of a perpetual bond with a £100 par value, an 8 per cent coupon rate, and a current market price of (a) £80, (b) £100 and (c) £120? Assume interest is paid annually.

17–3(a) Assuming that a bond has four years remaining to maturity and that interest is paid annually, what will be the yield to maturity on the bond with a £100 maturity value, an 8 per cent coupon interest rate, and a current market price (i) of £82.50 or (ii) of £110.70? (Hint: try 14 per cent and 5 per cent for the two bonds but *show your work*.)

(b) Would you pay £82.50 for the bond described in part (a) if your required rate of return for securities in the same risk class is 10 per cent; that is, k_b = 10 per cent? Explain your answer.

17–4(a) The British government has issued some irredeemable bonds bearing a 9 per cent coupon. Bonds of this type yield 8 per cent. What is their price? Their nominal value is £100.

(b) Interest rate levels rise to the point where such bonds yield 12 per cent. What is their price now?

(c) Interest rate levels drop to 9 per cent. What is the new price?

(d) How would your answers to parts (a), (b) and (c) change if the bonds had a definite maturity date of 19 years?

17–5(a) Trans-Atlantic Aviation is currently earning £800 000 a year after taxes. A total of 4 500 000 shares are authorized, and 4 000 000 shares are outstanding. What are the company's earnings per share?

(b) Investors require a 16 per cent rate of return on shares in the same risk class as Trans-Atlantic ($k_e = 16\%$). At what price will the shares sell if the previous dividend was £0.10 (d_0 = £0.10), and investors expect dividends to grow at a constant compound annual rate of (i) *minus* 6 per cent, (ii) 0 per cent, (iii) 6 per cent and (iv) 12 per cent? (Hint: use $d_1 = d_0(1+g)$, not d_0, in the formula.)

(c) In part (b), what is the 'formula price' if the required rate of return is 16 per cent and the expected growth rate is (i) 16 per cent or (ii) 21 per cent? Are these reasonable results? Explain.

(d) At what price/earnings (P/E) ratio will the shares sell, assuming each of the growth expectations given in part (b)?

17–6 Kathy Kobb plans to invest in ordinary shares for a period of 12 years, after which she will sell out and retire. She feels that Ogden Mines is currently, but temporarily, undervalued by the market. Kobb expects Ogden Mines' current earnings and dividend to double in the next 12 years. Ogden Mines' last dividend was £0.20, and its shares are currently valued at £4.50 each.

(a) If Kobb requires a 10 per cent return on her investment, will Ogden Mines be a good buy for her?

(b) What is the maximum that Kobb could pay for Ogden Mines and still earn her required 10 per cent?

(c) What might be the cause of such a market undervaluation?

(d) Given Kobb's assumptions, what market capitalization rate for Ogden Mines does the current price imply?

17–7. In 1936 the Canadian government raised $55 million by issuing perpetual bonds at a 3 per cent annual rate of interest.[21] Unlike most bonds issued today, which have a specific maturity date, these perpetual bonds can remain outstanding for ever; they are, in fact, perpetuities.

At the time of issue, the Canadian government stated that cash redemption was *possible* at face value ($100) on or after September 1966; in other words, the bonds were callable at par after September 1966. Believing that the bonds would in fact be called, many investors in the early 1960s purchased these bonds with expectations of receiving $100 in 1966 for each perpetual bond they held. In 1963 the bonds sold for $55, but a rush of buyers drove the price to just below the $100 par value by 1966. Prices fell dramatically,

---

21. This case is based on an article that appeared in the *Wall Street Journal* on December 26, 1972.

however, when the Canadian government announced that these perpetual bonds were indeed perpetual and would *not* be paid off. A new 30-year supply of coupons was sent to each bondholder, and the bond's market price declined to $42 in December 1972.

Because of their severe losses, hundreds of Canadian bondholders have formed the Perpetual Bond Association to lobby for face value redemption of the bonds. Government officials in Ottawa insist that claims for face value payment are nonsense, that the bonds were clearly identified as perpetuals, and that they did not mature in 1966 or at any other time. One Ottawa official states, 'Our job is to protect the taxpayer. Why should we pay $55 million for less than $25 million worth of bonds?'

(a) Would it make sense for a business firm to issue bonds such as the Canadian bonds described above?
(b) If the British government today offered a five-year bond, a 50-year bond, a 'regular perpetuity', and a Canadian-type perpetuity, what do you think the relative order of interest rates would be; that is, rank the bonds from the one with the lowest to the one with the highest rate of interest. Explain your answer.
(c) (i) Suppose that because of pressure by the Perpetual Bond Association, you believe that the Canadian government will redeem this particular perpetual bond issue in five years. Which course of action is more advantageous to you: (1) to sell your bonds today at $42 or (2) to wait five years and have them redeemed? Similar risk bonds earn 8 per cent today, and are expected to remain at this level for the next five years.
(ii) If you have the opportunity to invest your money in bonds of similar risk, at what rate of return are you indifferent between selling your perpetuals today or having them redeemed in five years; that is, what is the expected yield to maturity on the Canadians?
(d) Show, mathematically, the perpetuities' value if they yield 7.15 per cent, pay $3 interest annually, and are considered as regular perpetuities. Show what would occur to the price of the bonds if the interest rate fell to 2 per cent.
(e) Are the Canadian bonds more likely to be valued as 'regular perpetuities' if the going rate of interest is above or below 3 per cent? Why?
(f) Do you think the Canadian government would have taken the same action with regard to retiring the bonds if the interest rate had fallen rather than risen between 1936 and 1966?
(g) Do you think the Canadian government was 'fair' or 'unfair' in its actions? Give pros and cons, and justify your reason for thinking that one outweighs the other.

17–8. In a 1972 study, it was determined that the following equation can be used to estimate the required rates of return on various types of long-term capital market securities (shares and debentures of various companies): $k_j^* = R_F + 0.04\beta_j$. Here k_j^* is the required rate of return on the jth security; R_F is the riskless rate of interest as measured by the yield on long-term British government bonds: and β_j is the beta of the jth security's rate of return during the past five years.
(a) What is the required rate of return, k_j^*, if the riskless rate of return is 6 per cent and the security in question has a beta of (i) 0.2, (ii) 0.5, (iii) 1.0 and (iv) 1.5? Graph your results.
(b) What is the required rate of return, k_j^*, using the betas given in part (a) but assuming the riskless rate (i) rises to 8 per cent or (ii) falls to 4 per cent? Graph these results.
(c) Suppose the required rate of return equation changes from $k_j^* = 6\% + 0.04\beta_j$ to $k_j^* = 6\% + 0.05\beta_j$. What does this imply about investors' risk aversion? Illustrate with a graph.
(d) Suppose the equation $k_j^* = 6\% + 0.04\beta_j$ is the appropriate one; that is, this is the equation for the security market line (SML). Further, suppose a particular share sells for £2, is expected to pay 10 pence dividend at the end of the current year, and has a beta of expected returns of 0.8; that is, $\beta_j = 0.8$. Information reaches investors that causes them to expect a future growth rate of 3 per cent, which is different from the former expected growth rate. β_j does not change. (i) What was the former growth rate, assuming the share was in equilibrium before the changed expectations as to growth? (ii) What will happen to the price of the share? That is, calculate the new equilibrium price, and explain the process by which this new equilibrium will be reached. The expected dividend for the current year is still 10 pence.

17–9. Because of ill health and old age, John Ashby contemplates the sale of his shoe shops. His business has the following balance sheet:

Liabilities		Assets	
Owner's capital employed	£28 000	Fixtures and equipment	£24 000
Short-term loan	2 000	Less: depreciation	10 000
		Net	14 000
Trade creditors	4 000	Stock	13 000
Accruals	1 000	Debtors	2 000
		Cash	6 000
	£35 000		£35 000

Annual before-tax earnings (after rent, interest, and salaries) for the preceding three years have averaged £8 000.

Ashby has set a price of £40 000, which includes all the assets of the business except cash; the buyer assumes all debts. The assets include a five-year lease on the building in which the store is located and the goodwill associated with the name of Ashby Shoes. Assume that both Ashby and the potential purchaser are in the 50 per cent tax bracket.

(a) Is the price of £40 000 a reasonable one? Explain.

(b) What other factors should be taken into account in arriving at a selling price?

(c) What is the significance, if any, of the five-year lease?

17–10. The Ellis Company is a small jewellery manufacturer. The company has been successful and has grown. Now, Ellis is planning to sell an issue of ordinary shares to the public for the first time, and it faces the problem of setting an appropriate price. The company feels that the proper procedure is to select firms similar to it with Stock Exchange quotations and to make relevant comparisons.

The company finds several jewellery manufacturers similar to it with respect to product mix, size, asset composition, and debt/equity proportions. Of these, Bonden and Seeger are most similar.

Relation	Bonden (pence)	Seeger (pence)	Ellis (total amounts) (£)
Earnings per share, 1978	5.00	8.00	1 500 000
Average, 1972–78	4.00	5.00	1 000 000
Price per share, 1978	48.00	65.00	–
Dividends per share, 1978	3.00	4.00	700 000
Average, 1972–78	2.50	3.25	500 000
Book value per share	45.00	70.00	12 000 000
Market-book ratio	107%	93%	–

(a) How would these relations be used in guiding Ellis in arriving at a market value for its stock?

(b) What price would you recommend if Ellis sells five million shares?

17–11. Grant and Temperley Ltd is expected to grow at a rate of about 18 per cent for the next four years, then at 12 per cent for another three years, and finally settle down to a growth rate of 6 per cent for the indefinite future. The company's ordinary shares currently pay a £0.06 dividend, but dividends are expected to increase in proportion to the growth of the firm.

(a) What values would you place on the shares if you require a 12 per cent return on your investment?

(b) How would your valuation be affected if you intend to hold the stock for only three years?

(c) What would you expect the trend (i) of market price, (ii) of price/earnings ratio and (iii) of dividend yield to be over the next 10 years (up, down or constant)?

17–12. An investor requires a 20 per cent return on the ordinary shares of the M Company. During its most recent complete year, the M Company shares earned £0.4 and paid £0.2 per share. Its earnings and dividends are expected to grow at a 32 per cent rate for five years, after which they are expected to grow at 8 per cent per year. At what value of the M Company shares would the investor earn his required 20 per cent return?

17–13. The Mason Company is contemplating the purchase of the Norton Company. During the most recent year, Norton had earnings of £2 million and paid dividends of £1 million. The earnings and dividends of Norton were expected to grow at an annual rate of 30 per cent for five years, after which they will grow at an 8 per cent rate per year. The required return on an investment with the risk characteristics of the Norton Company is 16 per cent.

What is the maximum that the Mason Company could pay for the Norton Company to earn at least a 16 per cent return on its investment?

SELECTED REFERENCES

Arditti, Fred D. Risk and the required return on equity. *Journal of Finance* (March 1967): 19–36.

Arditti, Fred D. A note on discounting the components of an income stream. *Journal of Finance* 29 (June 1974): 995–999.

Barnea, Amir and Logue, Dennis E. Evaluating the forecasts of a security analyst. *Financial Management* 2 (Summer 1973): 38–45.

Bauman, W. Scott. Investment returns and present values. *Financial Analysts' Journal* 25 (November–December 1969): 107–118.

Ben-Shahar, Haim and Sarnat, Marshall. Reinvestment and the rate of return on common stocks. *Journal of Finance* 21 (December 1966): 737–742.

Bower, Richard S. and Bower, Dorothy H. Risk and the valuation of common stock. *Journal of Political Economy*, 77 (May–June 1969): 349–362.

Brigham, Eugene F. and Pappas, James L. Duration of growth, changes in growth rates, and corporate share prices. *Financial Analysts' Journal* 24 (May–June 1966): 157–162.

Carr, J. L. Yield differentials and inflation 1960–1974. *Investment Analyst* (September 1975): 30–35.

Carr, J. L. , Halpern, P. J. and McCallum, J. S. Correcting the yield curve: a re-interpretation of the duration problem. *Journal of Finance* 29 (September 1974): 1287–1294.

Dickinson, J. P. and Kyuno, K. Inflation, corporate valuation and the reverse yield gap. *Investment Analyst* (December 1976): 31–33.

Draper, P. R. Industry influences on share price variability. *Journal of Business Finance and Accounting* 2 (Summer 1975): 169–186.

Edwards, Charles E. and Hilton, James G. High-low averages as an estimator of annual average stock prices. *Journal of Finance* 21 (March 1966): 112–115.

Elton, Edwin J. and Gruber, Martin J. Earnings estimates and the accuracy of expectational data. *Management Science* 18 (April 1972): 409–424.

Elton, Edwin J. and Gruber, Martin J. Valuation and asset selection under alternative investment opportunities. *Journal of Finance* 31 (May 1976): 525–539.

Fewings, David R. The impact of growth on the risk of common stocks. *Journal of Finance* 30 (May 1975): 525–531.

Fisher, Lawrence. Determinants of risk premiums on corporate bonds. *Journal of Political Economy* 67 (June 1959): 217–237.

Foster, Earl M. Price-earnings ratio and corporate growth. *Financial Analysts' Journal* (January–February 1970): 96–99.

Gentry, James A. and Pyhrr, Stephen A. Simulating an EPS growth model. *Financial Management* 2 (Summer 1973): 68–75.

Granger, Clive W. J. Some consequences of the valuation model when expectations are taken to be optimum forecasts. *Journal of Finance* 30 (March 1975): 135–145.

Haugen, Robert A. Expected growth, required return, and the variability of stock prices. *Journal of Financial and Quantitative Analysis* 5 (September 1970): 297–308.

Haugen, Robert A. and Heins, A. James. Risk and the rate of return on financial assets. *Journal of Financial and Quantitative Analysis* 10 (December 1975): 775–784.

Haugen, Robert A. and Wichern, Dean W. The elasticity of financial assets. *Journal of Finance* 29 (September 1974): 1229–1240.

Herzog, John P. Investor experience in corporate securities: a new technique for measurement. *Journal of Finance* 19 (March 1964): 46–62.

Holt, Charles C. The influence of growth duration on share prices. *Journal of Finance* 17 (September 1962): 465–475.

Lintner, John. Inflation and security returns. *Journal of Finance* 30 (May 1975): 259–280.

Logue, Dennis E. and Merville, Larry J. Financial policy and market expectations. *Financial Management* 1 (Summer 1972): 37–44.

Malkiel, Burton G. Equity yields, growth, and the structure of share prices. *American Economic Review* 53 (December 1963): 467–494.

Malkiel, Burton G. and Gragg, John G. Expectations and the structure of share prices. *American Economic Review* 40 (September 1970): 601–617.

Mao, James C. T. The valuation of growth stocks: the investment opportunities approach. *Journal of Finance* 21(March 1966): 95–102.

McDonald, J. G. Market measures of capital cost. *Journal of Business Finance* (Autumn 1970): 27–36.

McDonald, J. G. and Osborne, A. E. Forecasting the market return on common stocks. *Journal of Business Finance and Accounting* (Summer 1974): 217–237.

McDonald, John G. and Osborne Alfred E. Jr. Forecasting the market return on common stocks. *Journal of Business Finance and Accounting* 1 (Summer 1974): 217–237.

McEnally, Richard W. A note on the return behavior of high risk common stocks. *Journal of Finance* 29 (March 1974): 199–202.

Melicher, Ronald W. and Rush, David F. Systematic risk, financial data, and bond rating relationships in a regulated industry environment. *Journal of Finance* 29 (May 1974): 537–544.

Merret, A. J. and Sykes, A. *The Finance and Analysis of Capital Projects*. 2nd ed. London: Longman, 1973.

Merret, A. J. and Sykes, A. Return on equities and fixed interest securities 1919–1966. *District Bank Review*, No. 158 (1966): 29–44. Reprinted in *Modern Financial Management*, a book of readings edited by B. V. Carsberg and H. C. Edey. Harmondsworth: Penguin Books, 1969.

Ofer, Aharon R. Investors' expectations of earnings growth, their accuracy and effects on the structure of realized rates of return. *Journal of Finance* 30 (May 1975): 509–523.

Pringle, John J. Price/earnings ratios, earnings per share, and financial management. *Financial Management* 2 (Spring 1973): 34–40.

Ricketts, Donald E. and Barrett, Michael J. Corporate operating income forecasting ability. *Financial Management* 2 (Summer 1973): 53–62.

Robichek, Alexander A. and Pogue, Marcus C. A note on the behavior of expected price/earnings ratios over time. *Journal of Finance* 26 (June 1971): 731–736.

Soldofsky, Robert M. The history of bond tables and stock valuation models. *Journal of Finance* 21 (March 1966): 103–111.

Stone, B. K. The conformity of stock values based on discounted dividends to a fair-return process. *Bell Journal of Economics* 6 (Autumn 75): 698–702.

Thompson, Howard E. A note on the value of rights in estimating the investor capitalization rate. *Journal of Finance* 28 (March 1973): 157–160.

Van Horne, James C. and Glassmire, William F. Jr. The impact of unanticipated changes in inflation on the value of common stocks *Journal of Finance* 7 (December 1972): 1081–1092.

Walter, James E. Investment planning under variable price change. *Financial Management* 1 (Winter 1972): 36–50.

Warren, James M. An operational model for security analysis and valuation. *Journal of Financial and Quantitative Analysis* 9 (June 1974): 395–422.

Wendt, Paul F. Current growth stock valuation methods. *Financial Analysts' Journal* 33 (March–April 1965): 3–15.

Chapter 18

Financial Structure and the Use of Gearing

In the last chapter, we saw that each security has a required rate of return, k^*, and an expected rate of return, $\bar{k}$. The required rate of return is determined in part by the level of interest rates (the risk-free rate) in the economy, and in part by the riskiness of the individual security. The expected rate of return on debentures and preference shares is determined primarily by the interest or preference dividends, while the expected rate of return on ordinary shares depends upon earnings available for distribution as cash dividends and growth. Both risk and expected returns may be affected by financial gearing, as we see in this chapter.

BASIC DEFINITIONS

To avoid ambiguity in the use of key concepts, the meanings of frequently used expressions are given here. *Financial structure* refers to the way the firm's assets are financed: it is the entire left-hand side of the balance sheet. *Capital structure* is the permanent financing of the firm, represented primarily by long-term debt, preference shares and ordinary shares, but excluding all short-term credit. Thus, a firm's capital structure is only a part of its financial structure. *Equity* includes ordinary shares, capital surplus and accumulated retained earnings.

Our key concept for this chapter is *financial gearing*, or the *gearing factor*, defined as the ratio of total debt to total assets or the total value of the firm. For example, a firm having a total value of £100 million and a total debt of £50 million would have a gearing factor of 50 per cent.[1] Thus B/V = 50 per cent. The B/V ratio implies a debt to equity (B/S)

1. The present discussion will consider variations in financial gearing in the context of a debt-equity trade off. No distinction will be made between long- and short-term debt.

ratio. B/S is equal to B/V ÷ (1 – B/V). Thus if B/V = 0.5, then B/S = 1.

Finally, we should distinguish at the outset between business risk and financial risk. By *business risk* we mean the inherent uncertainty or variability of expected pretax returns on the firm's 'portfolio' of assets. This kind of risk was examined in Chapter 11, where it was defined in terms of the probability distribution of returns on the firm's assets. By *financial risk* we mean the additional risk that is induced by the use of financial gearing.

THEORY OF FINANCIAL GEARING

Perhaps the best way to understand the proper use of financial gearing is to analyse its impact on profitability and fluctuations in profitability under various gearing conditions.[2] As an example, consider four alternative financial structures for the Universal Machine Company, a manufacturer of equipment used by industrial firms. The alternative balance sheets are displayed in Table 18–1.

Table 18–1 *Four Alternative Financial Structures, Universal Machine Company (Based on Book Values) (£000).*

Structure 1: $B/S = 0\%$; $B/TA = 0\%$			
Ordinary shares (£1 nominal value)	£10 000		
Total debt	0		
Total claims	£10 000	Total assets	£10 000
Structure 2: $B/S = 25\%$; $B/TA = 20\%$			
Ordinary shares (£1 nominal value)	£ 8 000		
Total debt (10%)	2 000		
Total claims	£10 000	Total assets	£10 000
Structure 3: $B/S = 100\%$; $B/TA = 50\%$			
Ordinary shares (£1 nominal value)	£ 5 000		
Total debt (10%)	5 000		
Total claims	£10 000	Total assets	£10 000
Structure 4: $B/S = 400\%$; $B/TA = 80\%$			
Ordinary shares (£1 nominal value)	£ 2 000		
Total debt (10%)	8 000		
Total claims	£10 000	Total assets	£10 000

Structure 1 uses no debt and consequently has a gearing factor of zero. Structure 2 has a gearing factor of 20 per cent. Structure 3 has a gearing factor of 50 per cent, and structure 4 has a gearing factor of 80 per cent.

How do these different financial patterns affect shareholder returns? As can be seen from Table 18–2, the answer depends partly upon the level of sales of the firm and partly upon the probability assessments associated with the alternative potential sales levels of

2. We shall initially hold the level of investment constant, considering only different financial structures for a firm of the same size. Since firms also face decisions that require a choice between debt versus equity for financing an increase in investment, this second type of decision will next be analysed with the benefit of the perspective provided by the more general analysis of the financial structure decision in its pure form.

Table 18-2 *Shareholders' Returns and Earnings per Share under Various Gearing and Economic Conditions, Universal Machine Company (£000).*

Probability of indicated sales	0.1	0.3	0.4	0.2
Sales	£ 0	£6000	£10 000	£20 000
Fixed costs	2000	2000	2000	2000
Variable costs (40% of sales)	–	2400	4000	8000
Total costs (except interest)	£2000	£4400	£ 6000	£10000
Earnings before interest and taxes (*EBIT*)	£(2000)	£1600	£ 4000	£10000
Capital Structure 1:				
EBIT				
Less: interest				
Less: corporation tax[a]	(1000)	800	2000	5000
Net profit after taxes	£(1000)	£ 800	£ 2000	£ 5000
Earnings per share on 10 000 shares	−£0.10	£0.08	£0.20	£0.50
Return on equity	−10%	8%	20%	50%
Capital Structure 2:				
EBIT				
Less: interest (10% × 2000)	200	200	200	200
Earnings before taxes	(2200)	£1400	£ 3800	£ 9800
Less: corporation tax[a]	(1100)	700	1900	4900
Net profit after taxes	£(1100)	£ 700	£ 1900	£ 4900
Earnings per share on 8000 shares	−£0.138	£0.088	£0.238	£0.613
Return on equity	−13.8%	8.8%	23.8%	61.3%
Capital Structure 3:				
EBIT				
Less: interest (10% × 5000)	500	500	500	500
Earnings before taxes	(2500)	1100	3500	9500
Less: corporation tax[a]	(1250)	550	1750	4750
Net profit after taxes	£(1250)	£ 550	£ 1750	£ 4750
Earnings per share on 5000 shares	−£0.25	£0.11	£0.35	£0.95
Return on equity	−25%	11%	35%	95%
Capital Structure 4:				
EBIT				
Less: interest (10% × 8000)	800	800	800	800
Earnings before taxes (50%)[a]	(2800)	800	3200	9200
Less: corporation tax	(1400)	400	1600	4600
Net profit after taxes	£(1400)	£ 400	£ 1600	£ 4600
Earnings per share on 2000 shares	−£0.70	£0.20	£0.80	£2.30
Return on equity	−70%	20%	80%	230%

[a] The tax calculation assumes that losses are carried back and result in tax credits.

Universal. The probability distribution for future sales was constructed by Universal's marketing department in cooperation with representatives from the general staff group of top management based on their knowledge of present supply and demand conditions along with estimates for future economic conditions and sales. The alternative probable conditions range from very poor (zero sales due to the possibility of a strike resulting from some very difficult labour negotiations currently underway) to very good under an optimistic assessment of the future outlook. It is assumed that the firm has total assets of

£10 000 000.[3] The rate of interest on debt is 10 per cent and the assumed tax rate is 50 per cent. Variable costs are estimated to be 40 per cent of sales and fixed costs equal £2 000 000.

Table 18–2 lays out the pattern of the analysis. It begins by listing the probability of sales at levels indicated by the next line. The fixed costs as shown remain the same for each level of sales. The total amount of variable costs increases with the level of sales since variable costs are 40 per cent of sales. The fixed costs and variable costs are added to obtain total costs. Sales less total costs equals earnings before interest and taxes (*EBIT*). Based on the indicated level of earnings before interest and taxes for the four sales levels associated with probabilities ranging from 0.1 to 0.4, the effects of the four alternative capital structures are analysed.

Capital structure 1 is first considered. Since structure 1 employs no gearing, the interest expense is nil. *EBIT* divided by the 10 million ordinary shares gives earnings per share associated with each of the probability factors and with each of the alternative levels of sales. The rate of return on ordinary shares is *EBIT* minus taxes divided by shareholder's equity.

When debt is introduced into the capital structure, interest on the debt is deducted from the earnings before interest and taxes (*EBIT*) before the tax rate is applied and the net profit after tax is calculated. Then earnings per share on the indicated number of shares and the return on shareholders' equity is calculated as before. The capital structure with no debt is now compared with capital structure 3 with the 50 per cent gearing factor. For the capital structure with no debt, earnings per share range from a loss of £0.10 per share to a profit of £0.50 a share, a range of £0.60. Under the capital structure with a gearing factor of 50 per cent, the range in earnings per share is from a negative £0.25 to a positive £0.95. This is a range of £1.20, which is double the range in earnings per share with no gearing. Similarly the return on shareholders' equity for the ungeared firm has a range of 60 percentage points, while the return on shareholders' equity for the 50 per cent geared firm has a range of 120 percentage points.

Table 18–2 shows the two return relationships, earnings per share and return on shareholders' equity, associated with gearing. Under any given financial structure earnings per share and the return on shareholders' equity increase with improved sales levels. Also, these earnings are magnified as gearing is increased. Thus increased gearing increases the degree of fluctuations in earnings per share and in returns on equity for any given degree of fluctuation in sales and its related return on total assets. Gearing increases the returns to the owners of the firm if used successfully. But if gearing is unsuccessful, it may result in inability to pay fixed charge obligations and ultimately result in financial difficulties leading to financial reorganization or bankruptcy.[4]

In Table 18–3 a return-risk analysis of the four financial structure alternatives is performed. Applying the probability factors to each of the associated earnings per share results, the expected earnings per share are calculated for each financial structure and the associated variance and standard deviation for each financial structure are calculated as well. Then the standard deviation is divided by the expected earnings per share to obtain the coefficient of variation. These are all presented in Table 18–3 for each of the four alternative financial structures considered. Figure 18–1 provides a graph of the expected earnings per share as calculated in Table 18–3 in relation to the four alternative debt to equity and debt to total asset ratios. It will be seen that the expected earnings per share increase linearly with the debt to equity ratio and increase at an increasing rate when the gearing factor is measured by the debt to total asset ratio.

We now turn to a consideration of some alternative measures of the riskiness of the

---

3. The numbers are rounded for convenience and in most tables and calculations the analysis will be made in thousands of pounds, so that the last three zeros will be omitted explicitly.

4. See Chapter 23 for an explanation of the nature of financial reorganization and bankruptcy.

Table 18-3 *Return-Risk Analysis of the Four Financial Structure Alternatives.*

s		p_s	EPS	p_sEPS	$EPS-E(EPS)$	$[EPS-E(EPS)]^2$	$p_s[EPS-E(EPS)]^2$
Structure 1	1	0.1	−£0.10	−0.01	−0.294	8.6436×10^{-2}	8.644×10^{-3}
	2	0.3	£0.08	0.024	−0.114	1.2996×10^{-2}	3.899×10^{-3}
	3	0.4	£0.20	0.08	0.006	0.0036×10^{-2}	0.014×10^{-3}
	4	0.2	£0.50	0.10	0.306	9.3636×10^{-2}	18.727×10^{-3}
			$E(EPS)$	= £0.194			$\sigma^2 = 31.284\times10^{-3}$
							$\sigma = 17.687\times10^{-2}$
				$CV=\sigma/E(EPS)=0.912$			
Structure 2	1	0.1	−£0.138	−0.0138	−0.368	13.542×10^{-2}	13.542×10^{-3}
	2	0.3	£0.088	0.0264	−0.142	2.016×10^{-2}	6.049×10^{-3}
	3	0.4	£0.238	0.0952	0.008	0.006×10^{-2}	0.026×10^{-3}
	4	0.2	£0.613	0.1226	0.383	14.669×10^{-2}	29.338×10^{-3}
			$E(EPS)$	= £0.230			$\sigma^2 = 48.955\times10^{-3}$
							$\sigma = 22.126\times10^{-2}$
				$CV=0.962$			
Structure 3	1	0.1	−£0.25	−0.025	−0.588	34.574×10^{-2}	34.574×10^{-3}
	2	0.3	£0.11	0.033	−0.228	5.198×10^{-2}	17.155×10^{-3}
	3	0.4	£0.35	0.140	0.012	0.014×10^{-2}	0.058×10^{-3}
	4	0.2	£0.95	0.190	0.612	37.454×10^{-2}	74.909×10^{-3}
			$E(EPS)$	= £0.338			$\sigma^2 = 126.696\times10^{-3}$
							$\sigma = 35.594\times10^{-2}$
				$CV=1.05$			
Structure 4	1	0.1	−£0.70	−0.07	−1.47	216.1×10^{-2}	21.609×10^{-3}
	2	0.3	£0.20	0.06	−0.57	32.5×10^{-2}	9.747×10^{-3}
	3	0.4	£0.80	0.32	0.03	0.1×10^{-2}	0.036×10^{-3}
	4	0.2	£2.30	0.46	1.53	234.1×10^{-2}	46.818×10^{-3}
			$E(EPS)$	= £0.770			$\sigma^2 = 78.21\times10^{-3}$
							$\sigma = 88.44\times10^{-2}$
				$CV=1.15$			

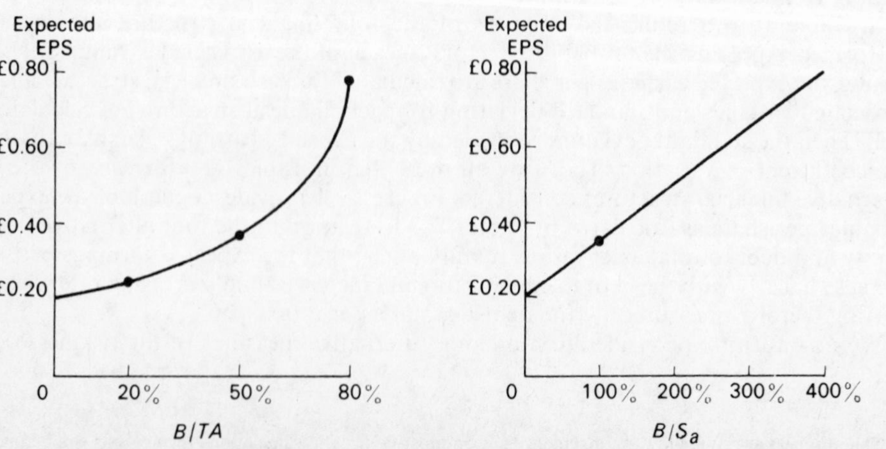

Figure 18–1 *Relationship between Return and Gearing.*

expected returns in relation to the alternative levels of sales and the alternative financial structures employed. We have noted how gearing increases the variability of earnings per share and the variability of returns to shareholders. For example, using no gearing, earnings per share range from a loss of £0.10 to a gain of £0.50. With a gearing of 80 per cent the range is from a loss of £0.70 to a gain of £2.30 per share.

There are three alternative measures of this variability in earnings induced by gearing, each of which in some sense is a measure of risk. These three alternative measures of risk are the standard deviation, the coefficient of variation and the beta coefficient. The standard deviation and coefficient of variation of expected earnings per share are calculated in Table 18–3. In each case the coefficient of variation is calculated by dividing the standard deviation by the average earnings per share. The coefficient of variation rises from 0.912 in structure 1 to 1.15 in structure 4. Clearly, both of these measures of risk rise with increased gearing.

The third measure of risk is the beta coefficient (β) for the various gearing factors illustrated. First, the market return parameters must be estimated. The basic estimates of the market return are shown for the four probability factors in Table 18–4. Applying the probability factors to the four alternative estimates of the return on the market, the expected or average return on the market is shown to be 10 per cent. When the expected return on the market is deducted from each of the four estimates of market returns, the deviations of the market returns from their mean are calculated as in column 5. In column 6 these deviations are squared. In column 7 the probability factors are applied, then the items are summed to obtain the variance of the market, which is approximately 1 per cent. The standard deviation of the market returns would, therefore, be 0.1.

Table 18–4 *Estimation of Market Parameters.*

(1)	(2)	(3)	(4)	(5)	(6)	(7)
s	p_s	k_M	$p_s k_M$	$[k_M - E(k_M)]$	$[k_M - E(k_M)]^2$	$p_s[k_M - E(k_M)]^2$
1	0.1	(0.15)	(0.015)	(0.25)	0.0625	0.00625
2	0.3	0.05	0.015	(0.05)	0.0025	0.00075
3	0.4	0.15	0.60	0.05	0.0025	0.00100
4	0.2	0.20	0.040	0.10	0.01	0.00200
		$E(k_M) =$	0.10		$Var\ k_M =$	0.01000
					$\sigma k_M \simeq$	0.10

With the use of the market parameters calculated in Table 18–4, we can utilize the procedures illustrated near the end of Chapter 11 to calculate the βs for each level of gearing of the Universal Machine Company, as shown in Table 18–5. The results in Table 18–5 are calculated as follows:

1. First obtain $E(X)$ and $Cov(X, k_u)$. Note that X is after taxes.

s	P_s	X	P_sX	$(X-\bar{X})(k_M-\bar{k}_M)P_s$	
1	0.1	−1000	− 100	$(-2940)(-0.25)0.1 =$	73.5
2	0.3	800	240	$(1140)(-0.05)0.3 =$	17.1
3	0.4	2000	800	$(60)(0.05)0.4 =$	1.2
4	0.2	5000	1000	$(3060)(0.10)0.2 =$	61.2
			$X = 1940$	$Cov(X, k_M) =$	153.0

Recall that $(k_M - \bar{k}_M)$ is in column (5) of Table 18–4.

$Cov(k_j, k_M) = Cov(X_j, k_M)/V_u = 153/23\,500 = 0.0065$

$\beta_j^* = Cov(k_j, k_M)/Var(k_M) = 0.0065/0.01 = 0.65$

2. Calculate beta for the gearing financial structures.

Financial structure (1)	TB (2)	V_L (3)	B (4)	B/V_L (4) − (3) (5)	S (3) − (4) (6)	B/S (4) − (6) (7)	$B/S(1-T)$ 0.5(7) (8)	$B/S(1-T)\beta^*$ 0.65(8) (9)	β_j 0.65 + (9) (10)
1	0	–	0	–	–	—	–	–	0.65
2	£1000	£24 500	£2000	8.16%	£22 500	8.89%	0.0444	0.0289	0.68
3	2500	26 000	5000	19.2	21 000	23.8	0.1190	0.0774	0.73
4	4000	27 500	8000	29.1	19 500	41.0	0.2051	0.1333	0.78

In Table 18–5 one risk measure, the beta coefficient, is exhibited in relationship to the gearing ratios of debt to the total market value of the firm and debt to the total market value of the equity. Since the gearing ratios are measured in market values in Table 18–5,

Table 18–5 *Calculation of the Beta Coefficients[a] for Four Alternative Gearing Ratios, Universal Machine Company (Based on Market Values).[b]*

Financial structure	B_j/V_j	B_j/S_j	B_j
1	0%	0%	0.65
2	8.16%	8.89%	0.68
3	19.2%	23.8%	0.73
4	29.1%	41.0%	0.78

[a] Recall that $\beta_j^* = Cov(k_j, k_M)/Var(k_M)$ where β_j^* is the beta for an ungeared firm, and, as will be developed in Chapter 19, $\beta_j = \beta_j^* + \beta_j^*(B_j/S_j)(1-T)$.

[b] First V_U is obtained by the method discussed in Chapter 11, which establishes that $V_U = \dfrac{E(X) - \lambda\, Cov(X, k_M)}{R_F}$. For this example, we have $V_U = \dfrac{1940 - 5(153)}{0.05} = £23\,500$. Second, we use the relation developed in Appendix B to Chapter 19, $V_L = V_U + TB$, where V_L is the value of the levered (geared) firm and V_U is the value of the ungeared firm. By definition, $S_j = V_j - B$.

as is required by the theoretical relationship between β and gearing, the gearing ratios at market values for the four financial structures are different from the gearing ratios measured at book values in Table 18–6.

Table 18–6 *Risk-Return Trade-off for Various Gearing Ratios, Universal Machine Company (Based on Book Values).*

Debt/assets	Debt/equity	Expected *EPS*	Standard deviation	Coefficient of variation
0%	0%	£0.194	£0.177	0.912
20%	25%	£0.230	£0.221	0.962
50%	100%	£0.338	£0.356	1.050
80%	400%	£0.770	£0.884	1.150

In Table 18–6 other risk-return trade-offs for various gearing ratios for Universal Machine Company are set forth. The table shows how the gearing ratio measured by both debt/assets and debt/equity influences expected earnings per share. In addition, two of the associated risk measures are exhibited. The risk measures are the standard deviation and the coefficient of variation. The gearing ratios are measured at book values.

These numerical relationships between gearing and the three risk measures are summarized in Figure 18–2. The relationship between risk as measured by the standard

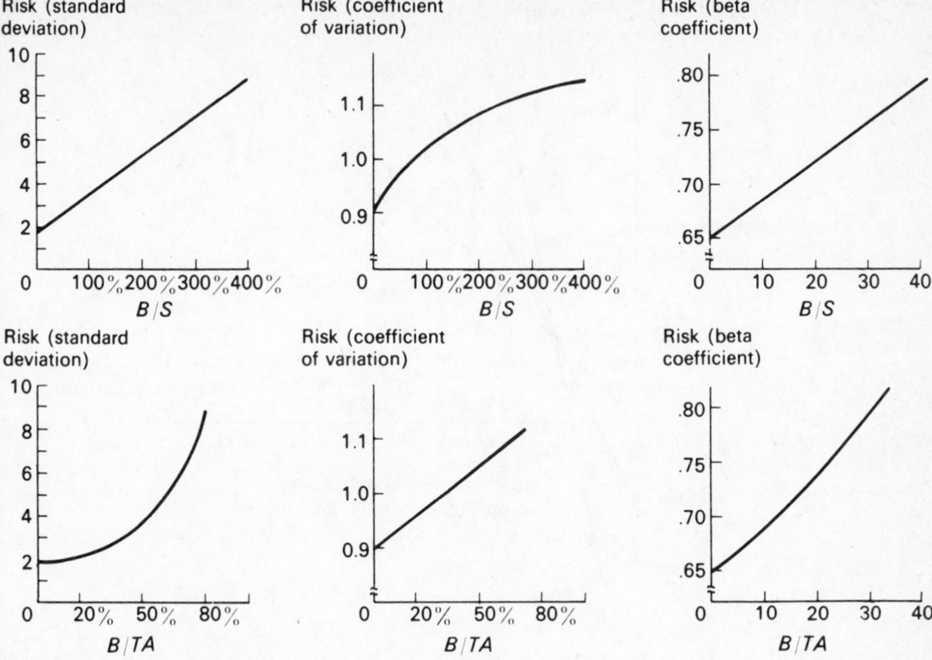

Figure 18–2 *Relationships between Risk and Gearing.*

deviation and the gearing ratio of debt/equity measured at book values, as well as risk as measured by the β coefficient and the debt/equity ratio measured at market values are both linear. Also, the relationship between the coefficient of variation and the debt/equity ratio measured at book value is curvilinear but curved down from above. The relationship when gearing is measured by debt/total assets is curvilinear upwards for the standard deviation and for the β coefficient. However, when risk is measured by the coefficient of variation in relation to the debt/total asset gearing ratio, a linear relationship obtains. The different shapes of the relationship stem from the basic underlying theory of the computations involved. But what is common to all the six portrayals of the relationship between risk and gearing is that to obtain the higher expected earnings, whether measured by earnings per share or return on shareholders' equity that go with increased gearing, the firm must incur more risk. As previously indicated, there is a positive relationship between return and risk and there is also a positive relationship between risk and the degree of gearing employed.

Another dimension of the return-gearing-risk relationship is exhibited by Figure 18–3. Figure 18–3 sets forth a relationship between rates of return on assets and rates of return on net worth under different gearing conditions. In the absence of gearing, the line of relationship begins at the origin and has a slope that is less steep than the slope of the relationship when gearing is employed. With gearing, the intercept of the line is negative, indicating that at low rates of return on total assets, the return on net worth is negative, representing a loss. The intersection of the three lines is at the 10 per cent rate of return on total assets, which is equal to the before-tax interest cost of debt. At this intersection point the return on net worth is 5 per cent. The 50 per cent tax rate reduces the 10 per cent return on total assets to a return of 5 per cent on net worth regardless of the degree of gearing. When returns on assets are higher than 10 per cent, debt-financed assets can cover interest cost and still leave something over for the shareholders. But the reverse holds if assets earn less than 10 per cent. Figure 18–3 illustrates a general proposition: whenever the return on assets exceeds the cost of debt, gearing is favourable, and the higher the gearing factor the higher the rate of return on ordinary shares.

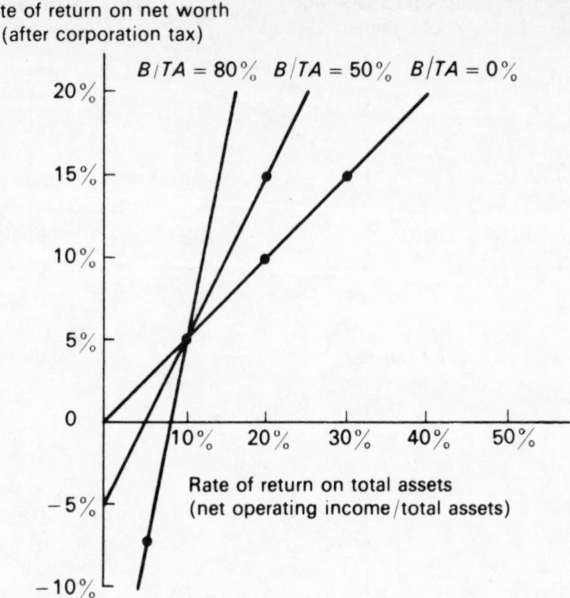

Figure 18–3 *Relationship between Rates of Return on Assets and Rates of Return on Net Worth under Different Gearing Conditions.*

ANALYSIS OF ALTERNATIVE METHODS OF FINANCING

Thus far in the analysis we have simply varied gearing, holding the total amount of investment by the firm constant. In real world decision making it is often necessary to perform an analysis in which alternative gearing structures are being considered along with financing which increases the amount of the investment of the firm and the size of total assets. This further aspect of combining the financing and gearing decisions will be developed by a continuation of the Universal Machine Company example. The latest balance sheet of the Universal Machine Company is set forth in Table 18–7. Universal Machine Company manufactures equipment used in industrial manufacturing. The major product is a lathe used to trim the rough edges off sheets of fabricated steel. The lathes sell for £100 000 each. As is typically the case for producers of durable capital assets, the company's sales fluctuate widely, far more than does the overall economy. For example, during nine of the preceding 25 years, sales of the Universal Machine Company have been below the break-even point, so losses have been relatively frequent.

Table 18–7 *Universal Machine Company, Balance Sheet 31 December 1977 (£000).*

Ordinary share capital (£1 nominal value)	£5 000	Equipment (net)	£4 100
		Fixtures (net)	3 000
		Stocks	1 400
Total liabilities having an average cost of 10%	5 000	Debtors	1 200
		Cash	300
Total claims on assets	£10 000	Total assets	£10 000

Although future sales are uncertain, current demand is high and expected to grow. Thus, if Universal is to continue its sales growth, it will have to increase capacity. A capacity increase involving £2 000 000 of new capital is under consideration. James Watson, the chief accountant, learns that he can raise £2 000 000 by selling debentures with a 10 per cent coupon. Alternatively, he can raise the additional funds by selling one million ordinary shares at a market price of £2 per share. Fixed costs after the planned expansion will be £2 000 000 a year. Variable costs excluding interest on the debt will be 40 per cent of sales.[5] The probability distribution for future sales possibilities is the same as was set forth in the previous section analysing the pure gearing decision for Universal.

Table 18–8 *Universal Machine Company, Profit Calculations at Various Sales Levels.*

Probability of indicated sales	0.1	0.3	0.4	0.2
Sales in units	0	60	100	200
	£000	£000	£000	£000
Sales	£ 0	£6000	£10 000	£20 000
Fixed costs	2000	2000	2 000	2 000
Variable costs (40% of sales)	0	2400	4 000	8 000
Total costs (except interest)	£2000	£4400	£6 000	£10 000
Earnings before interest and taxes (*EBIT*)	£(2000)	£1600	£4 000	£10 000
	Financing with debentures (B/A = 58.3%; B/S = 140%)			
Less: interest (10% × 7000)	700	700	700	700
Earnings before taxes	(2700)	900	3300	9300
Less: corporation tax	(1350)	450	1650	4650
Net profit after taxes	(1350)	450	1650	4650
EPS on 5000 shares[a]	−£0.27	£ 0.09	£ 0.33	£ 0.93
Expected *EPS* £0.318				
	Financing with ordinary shares (B/A = 41.7%; B/S_j = 71.4%)			
	£000	£000	£000	£000
Less: interest (10% × 5000)	500	500	500	500
Earnings before taxes	(2500)	1100	3500	9500
Less: corporation tax	(1250)	550	1750	4750
Net profit after taxes	(1250)	550	1750	4750
EPS on 6000 shares[a]	−£0.208	£0.092	£ 0.292	£ 0.791
Expected *EPS* £0.282				

[a] The *EPS* figures can be obtained using the following formula:

$$EPS = \frac{(\text{sales} - \text{fixed costs} - \text{variable costs} - \text{interest})\,(1 - \text{tax rate})}{\text{shares outstanding}}$$

For example, at sales = £10 million,

$$EPS_{\text{shares}} = \frac{(10-2-4-0.5)\,(0.5)}{6} = £0.292$$

$$EPS_{\text{debentures}} = \frac{(10-2-4-0.7)\,(0.5)}{5} = £0.33$$

5. The assumption that variable costs will be a constant percentage of sales over the entire range of output is not valid, but variable costs are relatively constant over the output range likely to occur.

Although Watson's recommendation will be given much weight, the final decision for the method of financing rests with the company's board of directors. Procedurally, the chief accountant will analyse the situation, evaluate all reasonable alternatives, come to a conclusion, and then present the alternatives with his recommendations to the board. For his own analysis, as well as for presentation to the board, Watson prepares the materials shown in Table 18–8.

In the top third of the table, earnings before interest and taxes (*EBIT*) are calculated for different levels of sales ranging from £0 to £20 million. The firm suffers an operating loss until sales are £3.3 million, but beyond that point it enjoys a rapid rise in gross profit.

The middle third of the table shows the financial results that will occur at the various sales levels if debentures are used. First, the £700 000 annual interest charges (£500 000 on existing debt plus £200 000 on the new debentures) are deducted from the earnings before interest and taxes. Next, taxes are taken out; notice that if the sales level is so low that losses are incurred, the firm receives a tax credit to be offset against taxable income of other relevant periods. Then, net profits after taxes are divided by the five million shares outstanding to obtain earnings per share (*EPS*).[6] The various *EPS* figures are multiplied by the corresponding probability estimates to obtain an expected *EPS* of £0.318. Finally, the coefficient of variation is calculated and used as a measure of the riskiness of the financing plan.

In the bottom third of the table, the financial results that will occur if the project is financed by means of ordinary shares are calculated. Net profit after interest and taxes is divided by six million – the original five million plus the new one million (£2 × one million = £2 million) – to find earnings per share. Expected EPS is computed in the same way as for the debt financing.

Figure 18–4 shows the probability distribution of earnings per share. Equity financing has the tighter, more peaked distribution. We know from Table 18–4 that it will also have a smaller coefficient of variation than debt financing. Hence, equity financing is less risky than debt financing. However, the expected earnings per share are lower for equity than for debt, so we are again faced with the kind of risk-return trade-off that characterizes most financial decisions.

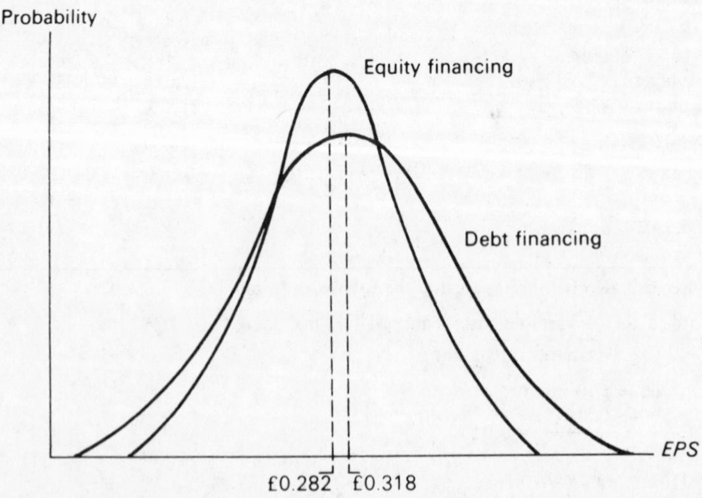

Figure 18–4 *Probability Curves for Equity and Debt Financing.*

6. The number of shares initially outstanding can be calculated by dividing the £5 million ordinary share figure given on the balance sheet by the £1 par value.

The nature of the trade-off can be made more specific. In Table 18–9 we present two measures of the gearing return and risk relationships. In Part A of the table the gearing ratio as measured by debt to total assets at book values is related to expected earnings per share and the coefficient of variation. In Part B the gearing as measured by debt to equity at market values is related to the expected return on equity and the beta measure of risk.

Table 18–9 *Gearing, Return, and Risk Relationships.*

	Gearing ratio *B/TA%*	Expected *EPS*	Coefficient of variation
Part A	0	0.194	0.912
	20	0.230	0.962
	50	0.338	1.05
	80	0.770	1.15
Part B	Gearing *B/S%*	Return on equity	Beta coefficient
	0	8.25	0.65
	8.16%	8.40	0.68
	19.2%	8.65	0.73
	29.1%	8.95	0.79

The nature of these relationships is depicted graphically in Figure 18–5. There is an upward curvilinear relationship between the coefficient of variation and earnings per share when the gearing ratio is measured by debt to total assets at book value. There is a linear relationship between beta and the return on equity when gearing is measured by the debt to equity ratio at market values.[7] But regardless of whether the relationship is linear or non-linear there is agreement that in order to obtain the higher expected earnings that go with increased gearing, the firm must accept more risk.

What choice should Watson recommend to the board? How much gearing should Universal Machine use? These questions cannot be answered at this point – we must defer answers until we have covered some additional concepts and examined the effects of gearing on the cost of both debt and equity capital.

BREAK-EVEN ANALYSIS

Another way of presenting the data on Universal's two financing methods is shown in Figure 18–6, a break-even chart similar to the charts used in Chapter 3. If sales fall to nil, the debt financing line would cut the Y axis at –£0.27, below the –£0.208 intercept of the equity financing line. The debt line has a steeper slope and rises faster, however, showing that earnings per share will go up faster with increases in sales if debt is used. The two lines cross at sales of £6.2 million. Below that sales volume the firm would be better off issuing ordinary shares; above that level, debt financing would produce higher earnings per share.[8]

---

7. These linearities result because we are implicitly employing the Modigliani–Miller model in a world with taxes but with no bankruptcy cost penalties. In Chapter 19 when we bring in bankruptcy cost penalties we indicate that there will be non-linearities in these relationships.

8. Since in this case the equation is linear, the break-even or indifference level of sales ($P \cdot Q$) can be found as follows:

$$EPS_S = \frac{(P\cdot Q - 0.2 - 0.4P\cdot Q - 0.5)(0.5)}{6} = \frac{(P\cdot Q - 0.2 - 0.4P\cdot Q - 0.7)(0.5)}{5} = EPS_B$$

$$P\cdot Q = £6.2 \text{ million}$$

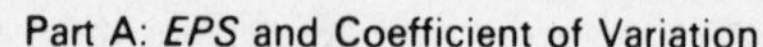

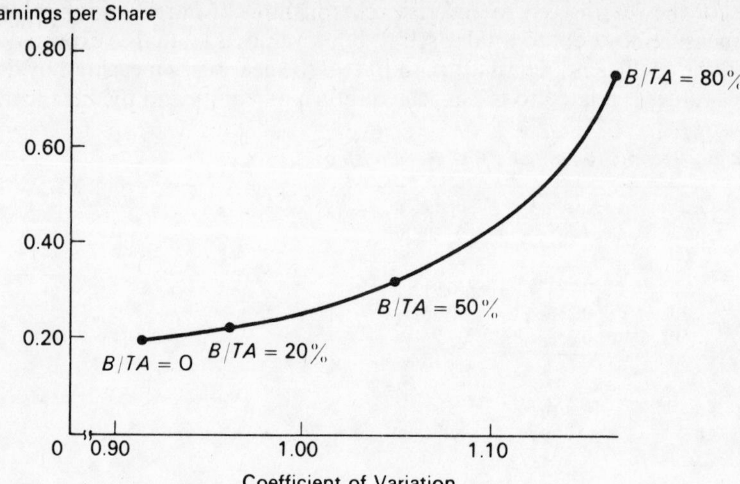

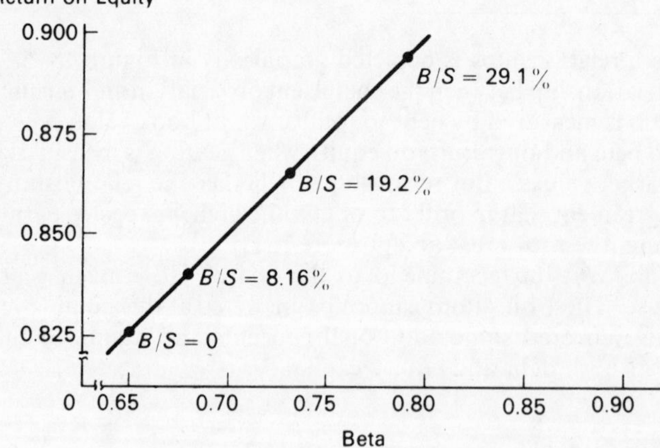

Figure 18–5 *Part A – EPS and Coefficient of Variation; Part B – Return on Equity and Beta.*

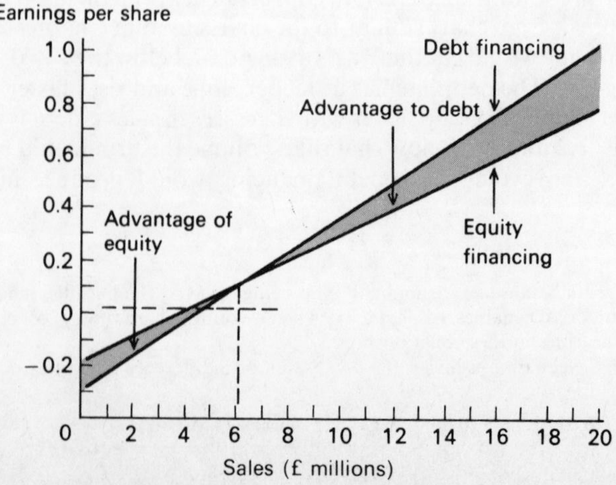

Figure 18–6 *Earnings per Share for Equity and Debt Financing.*

If Watson and his board of directors *know with certainty* that sales will never again fall below £6.2 million, the asset increase should be financed by means of debt. But they cannot know this for certain. They know that in previous years sales have in fact fallen below this critical level. Further, if any detrimental long-run events occur, future sales may again fall well below £6.2 million. If sales continue to expand, however, there would be higher earnings per share from using debt; no director would want to forgo these substantial advantages.

Watson's recommendation, and the decision of each director, will depend (a) upon each person's appraisal of the future and (b) upon his psychological attitude towards risk.[9] The pessimists, or risk averters, will prefer to employ equity financing, while the optimists, or those less sensitive to risk, will favour debt. This example, which is typical of many real-world situations, suggests that the major disagreements over the choice of forms of financing are likely to reflect uncertainty about the future levels of the firm's sales. Such uncertainty, in turn, reflects the characteristics of the firm's environment – general business conditions, industry trends and quality and aggressiveness of management.

RELATIONSHIP OF FINANCIAL GEARING TO OPERATING GEARING[10]

In Chapter 3 it was shown that a firm has some degree of control over its production processes; it can, within limits, use either a highly automated production process with high fixed costs but low variable costs or a less automated process with lower fixed costs but higher variable costs. If a firm uses a high degree of operating gearing, it was seen that its break-even point is at a relatively high sales level and that changes in the level of sales have a magnified (or 'geared') impact on profits. Notice that financial gearing has exactly the same kind of effect on profits: the higher the gearing factor, the higher the break-even sales volume and the greater the impact on profits from a given change in sales volume.

The *degree of operating gearing* was defined as the percentage change in operating profits associated with a given percentage change in sales volume, and equation 3–2 was developed for calculating operating gearing:

$$\text{Degree of operating gearing at point } Q = \frac{Q(P-vc)}{Q(P-vc)-FC} \qquad (3\text{–}2)$$

$$= \frac{P\cdot Q - VC}{P\cdot Q - VC - FC}. \qquad (3\text{–}2a)$$

Here Q is units of output, P is the average sales price per unit of output, vc is the variable cost per unit, and FC is total fixed costs, while PQ is sales in pounds and VC is total variable costs. Applying the formula to Universal Machine at a sales level of £10 000 (see Table 18–2 above) and assuming one machine sells for £100, we find its operating gearing to be

9. Theory suggests that the decision should be based upon shareholders' utility preferences, or the market risk-return trade-off function discussed in Chapter 11. In practice, it is difficult to obtain such information as *data*, so decisions such as this one are generally based upon the subjective judgement of the decision-maker. A knowledge of the theory, even if it cannot be applied directly, is extremely useful in making good decisions. Further, knowing the theory permits us to structure research programmes and data-collecting systems that will make direct application of the theory increasingly feasible in future years.

10. This section may be omitted without loss of continuity.

1.50, so a 100 per cent increase in volume produces a 150 per cent increase in profit:

$$\text{Degree of operating gearing} = \frac{100(£100 - £40)}{100(£100 - £40) - 2000}$$

$$= \frac{10\,000 - 4000}{10\,000 - 4000 - 2000}$$

$$= \frac{£6000}{£4000} = 1.50 \text{ or } 150\%$$

Operating gearing affects *earnings before interest and taxes* (*EBIT*), while financial gearing affects *earnings after interest and taxes*, the earnings available to ordinary shareholders. In terms of Table 18–4, operating gearing affects the top section of the table, financial gearing the lower sections. Thus, if Universal Machine had more operating gearing, its fixed costs would be higher than £2000, its variable cost ratio would be lower than 40 per cent of sales, and earnings before interest and taxes would vary with sales to a greater extent. Financial gearing takes over where operating gearing leaves off, further magnifying the effect on earnings per share of a change in the level of sales. For this reason, operating gearing is sometimes referred to as *first-stage gearing* and financial gearing as *second-stage gearing.*

Degree of financial gearing

The *degree of financial gearing* is defined as the percentage change in earnings available to ordinary shareholders that is associated with a given percentage change in earnings before interest and taxes (*EBIT*). An equation has been developed as an aid in calculating the degree of financial gearing for any given level of *EBIT* and interest charges (*iB*).[11]

$$\text{Degree of financial gearing} = \frac{EBIT}{EBIT - iB} \tag{18–1}$$

For Universal Machine at 100 units of output and an *EBIT* of £4000, the degree of financial gearing with debt financing is

---

11. The equation is developed as follows:

1. Notice that $EBIT = Q(P - vc) - FC$.

2. Earnings per share $(EPS) = \dfrac{(EBIT - iB)(1 - T)}{N}$, where *EBIT* is earnings before interest and taxes, *iB* is interest paid, *T* is the corporation tax rate, and *N* is the number of shares outstanding.

3. *iB* is a constant, so ΔEPS, the change in *EPS*, is

$$\Delta EPS = \frac{\Delta EBIT(1 - T)}{N}.$$

4. The percentage increase in *EPS* is the change in *EPS* over the original *EPS*, or

$$\frac{\dfrac{\Delta EBIT(1 - T)}{N}}{\dfrac{(EBIT - iB)(1 - T)}{N}} = \frac{\Delta EBIT}{EBIT - iB}.$$

5. The degree of financial gearing is the percentage change in *EPS* over the percentage change in *EBIT*, so

$$\text{Financial gearing} = \frac{\dfrac{\Delta EBIT}{EBIT - iB}}{\dfrac{\Delta EBIT}{EBIT}} = \frac{EBIT}{EBIT - iB}$$

$$\text{Financial gearing: debt} = \frac{£4000}{£4000 - £700} = 1.21$$

Therefore, a 100 per cent increase in *EBIT* would result in a 121 per cent increase in earnings per share. If equity financing is used, the degree of financial gearing may be calculated and found to be 1.14, so a 100 per cent increase in *EBIT* would produce a 114 per cent increase in *EPS*.

Combining operating and financial gearing

Operating gearing causes a change in sales volume to have a magnified effect on *EBIT*, and if financial gearing is superimposed on operating gearing, changes in *EBIT* will have a magnified effect on earnings per share. Therefore, if a firm uses a considerable amount of both operating gearing and financial gearing, even small changes in the level of sales will produce wide fluctuations in *EPS*.

Equation 3–2 for the degree of operating gearing can be combined with equation 18–1 for financial gearing to show the total gearing effect of a given change in sales on earnings per share.[12]

$$\text{Combined gearing effect} = \frac{Q(P - vc)}{Q(P - vc) - FC - iB} \qquad (18\text{–}2)$$

For Universal Machine at an output of 200 units (or £2 million of sales), the combined gearing effect, using debt financing, is

$$\begin{aligned}\text{Combined gearing effect} &= \frac{100(£100 - £40)}{100(£100 - £40) - £2000 - £700}\\ &= \frac{£6000}{£6000 - £2000 - £700}\\ &= 181.8 \text{ per cent}\end{aligned}$$

Therefore, a 100 per cent increase in sales from 100 units to 200 units would cause *EPS* to increase by 181.8 per cent, so the new *EPS* figure would be 1.818 times the original *EPS*:

$$\begin{aligned}EPS_{(200\text{ units})} &= EPS_{(100\text{ units})} + (\text{EPS}_{(100\text{ units})}) \times 1.81\\ &= EPS_{(100\text{ units})} \times (1 + 1.81)\\ &= £0.33 \times 2.818 = £0.93.\end{aligned}$$

These figures agree, of course, with those worked out in Table 18–8.

Financial and operating gearing can be employed in various combinations. In the

---

12. Equation 18–2 is developed as follows:

1. Recognize that $EBIT = Q(P - vc) - FC$, then rewrite equation 18–1 as

$$\frac{EBIT}{EBIT - iB} = \frac{Q(P - vc) - FC}{Q(P - vc) - FC - iB}. \qquad (18\text{–}1a)$$

2. The total gearing effect is equal to the degree of operating gearing times the degree of financial gearing of equation 3–2 times equation 18–1a:

Combined gearing effect = equation 3–2 × equation 18–1a

$$\begin{aligned}&= \frac{Q(P - vc)}{Q(P - vc) - FC} \cdot \frac{Q(P - vc) - FC}{Q(P - vc) - FC - iB} \qquad (18\text{–}2)\\ &= \frac{Q(P - vc)}{Q(P - vc) - FC - iB}.\end{aligned}$$

Universal Machine example, the combined gearing factor of 1.818 was obtained by using operating gearing of degree 1.50 and financial gearing of 1.21, but many other combinations of financial and operating gearing would have produced the same combined gearing factor. Within limits, firms can and do make trade-offs between financial and operating gearing.

The usefulness of the degree of gearing concept lies in the facts (a) that it enables us to specify the precise effect of a change in sales volume on earnings available to ordinary shareholders and (b) that it permits us to show the interrelationship between operating and financial gearing. The concept can be used to show a businessman, for example, that a decision to automate and to finance new equipment with debt will result in a situation wherein a 10 per cent decline in sales will produce a 50 per cent decline in earnings, whereas a different operating and financial gearing package will be such that a 10 per cent sales decline will cause earnings to decline by only 20 per cent. In our experience, having the alternatives stated in this manner gives the decision-maker a better · idea of the ramifications of his actions.[13]

VARIATIONS IN FINANCIAL STRUCTURE

As might be expected, wide variations in the use of financial gearing may be observed among industries and among the individual firms in each industry. Illustrative of these differences is the range of ratios of debt to total assets shown in Table 18–10. Among the

Table 18–10 *Variations in Financial Gearing in Selected Industry Groups.*

1976 Industry grouping	Debt (£)	Total assets (£)	B/TA
Food	2 848 027	6 087 368	0.47
Drink	1 424 545	4 154 948	0.34
Tobacco	1 401 140	2 818 960	0.50
Chemicals	4 222 012	9 295 336	0.45
Metal manufacture	1 131 452	2 216 777	0.51
Non-electrical engineering	2 027 519	4 133 575	0.49
Electrical engineering	2 819 712	6 312 764	0.45
Shipbuilding + marine engineering	12 387	29 991	0.41
Vehicles	2 048 968	3 107 896	0.66
Clothing + footwear	173 855	455 340	0.38
Bricks, pottery, glass, cement	1 002 135	2 827 176	0.35
Timber, furniture, etc.	164 925	397 790	0.41
Paper, printing, publishing	1 885 818	3 600 557	0.52
Other manufacturing	891 667	1 749 100	0.51
Mixed activities in manufacturing	365 140	816 232	0.45
Mixed activities in non-manufacturing	1 122 234	2 215 477	0.51
Construction	1 491 186	2 734 553	0.56
Transport + communication	133 889	330 070	0.41
Wholesale distribution	1 296 566	2 060 211	0.63
Retail distribution	1 889 588	5 408 810	0.35
Miscellaneous services	2 232 184	4 136 753	0.54
Property	2 369 601	4 072 457	0.58

Source: *Business Monitor M.3* (London: HMSO).

13. The concept is also useful for investors. If firms in an industry are classified as to their degrees of total gearing, an investor who is optimistic about prospects for the industry might favour those firms with high gearing, and vice versa if he expects industry sales to decline.

most highly geared industries are the various service industries (shown as mixed activities in non-manufacturing and miscellaneous services) which have gearing ratios greater than 50 per cent. This reflects that

1. Services include financial institutions which, as a group, have high liabilities.
2. There are many smaller firms in the service industries and smaller firms as a group are heavy users of debt.

Within the broad category 'manufacturing', wide variations are observed for individual industries. Table 18–11 presents an array of total debt to total assets ratios for selected manufacturing industries. The lowest ratio is that for soft drink companies in which cost pressures have been severe. Low debt ratios are also found in the consumer durable-goods industries, such as furniture. The highest debt ratios are found in consumer non-durable goods, such as food and tobacco, where demand is relatively insensitive to fluctuations in general business activity.

Table 18–11 *Financial Gearing in Selected Manufacturing Industries, 1976.*

Category	Total debt to total assets %
Soft drinks	34
Clothing and footwear	38
Furniture	41
Chemicals	45
Food	47
Tobacco	50

Source: *Business Monitor, M. 3* (London: HMSO).

FACTORS INFLUENCING FINANCIAL STRUCTURE

Thus far the discussion has touched on the factors that are generally considered when a firm formulates basic policies relating to its financial structure. The more important of these financial structure determinants are now listed and briefly discussed:

1. Growth rate of future sales.
2. Stability of future sales.
3. Competitive structure of the industry.
4. Asset structure of the firm.
5. Control position and attitudes towards risk of owners and management.
6. Lenders' attitudes towards the firm and the industry.

Growth rate of sales

The future growth rate of sales is a measure of the extent to which the earnings per share of a firm are likely to be magnified by gearing. If sales and earnings grow at a rate of 8 to 10 per cent a year, for example, financing by debt with limited fixed charges should magnify the returns to ordinary shareholders.[14] This can be seen from Figure 18–6 above.

14. Such a growth rate is also often associated with a high profit rate.

However, the ordinary shares of a firm whose sales and earnings are growing at a favourable rate command a high price; thus, it sometimes appears that equity financing is desirable. The firm must weigh the benefits of using gearing against the opportunity of broadening its equity base when it chooses between future financing alternatives. Such firms may be expected to have a moderate-to-high level of debt financing.

Sales stability

Sales stability and debt ratios are directly related. With greater stability in sales and earnings, a firm can incur the fixed charges of debt with less risk than it can when its sales and earnings are subject to periodic declines; in the latter instance it will have difficulty in meeting its obligations.

Competitive structure

Debt-servicing ability is dependent upon the profitability, as well as the volume, of sales. Hence, the stability of profit margins is as important as the stability of sales. The ease with which new firms may enter the industry and the ability of competing firms to expand capacity will influence profit margins. A growth industry promises higher profit margins, but such margins are likely to narrow if the industry is one in which the number of firms can be easily increased through additional entry.

Asset structure

Asset structure influences the sources of financing in several ways. Firms with long-lived fixed assets, especially when demand for their output is relatively assured, use long-term mortgage debt extensively. Firms whose assets are mostly debtors and stock whose value is dependent on the continued profitability of the individual firm – for example, those in wholesale and retail trade – rely less on long-term and more on short-term debt financing.

Management attitudes

The management attitudes that most directly influence the choice of financing are those concerning (a) control of the enterprise and (b) risk. Large companies whose shares are widely owned may choose additional sales of ordinary shares because they will have little influence on the control of the company. Also, because management represents a stewardship for the owners, it is often less willing to take the risk of heavy fixed charges.[15]

---

15. It would be inappropriate to delve too far into motivational theory in a finance book, but it is interesting to note that the managers of many larger, publicly-owned companies have a relatively small ownership position and derive most of their income from salaries. Some writers assert that in such cases managements do not strive for profits, especially if this effort involves using gearing with its inherent risk. Presumably, these managers feel that the risks of gearing for them, the ones who actually decide to use debt or equity, outweigh the potential gains from successful gearing. If sales are low, there is a chance of failure and the loss of their jobs, whereas if sales and profits are high, it is the shareholders, not management, who receive the benefits. Another way of looking at the situation is to say that most shareholders are more diversified than most managers – if the firm fails, a shareholder loses only that percentage of his net worth invested in the firm, but the manager loses 100 per cent of his job. While there is undoubtedly some merit to this argument, it should be pointed out that companies are increasingly using profit-based compensation schemes – bonus systems and share-option plans – to motivate management to seek profitability, and low gearing companies are subject to take-over bids (see Chapter 22).

In contrast, the owners of small firms may prefer to avoid issuing ordinary shares in order to be assured of continued control. Because they generally have confidence in the prospects of their companies and because they can see the large potential gains to themselves resulting from gearing, managers of such firms are often willing to incur high debt ratios.

The converse can, of course, also hold – the owner-manager of a small firm may be *more* defensive than the manager of a large company. If the net worth of the small firm is, say, £200 000, and if it all belongs to the owner-manager, he may well decide that he is already prosperous enough, and may elect not to risk using gearing in an effort to become still more wealthy.

Lender attitudes

Regardless of managements' analyses of the proper gearing factors for their firms, there is no question but that lenders' attitudes are frequently important – sometimes the most important – determinants of financial structures. In the majority of cases, the company discusses its financial structure with lenders and gives much weight to their advice. But when management is so confident of the future that it seeks to use gearing beyond norms for the industry, lenders may be unwilling to accept such debt increases. They will emphasize that excessive debt reduces the credit standing of the borrower and the credit rating of the securities previously issued.

SUMMARY

Financial gearing, which means using debt to boost rates of return on net worth over the returns available on assets, is the primary topic covered in this chapter. Whenever the return on assets exceeds the cost of debt, gearing is favourable and the return on equity is raised by using it. However, gearing is a two-edged sword, and if the returns on assets are less than the cost of debt, then gearing reduces the returns on equity. This reduction is greater the more gearing a firm employs. As a net result, gearing may be used to boost shareholder returns, but it is used at the risk of increasing losses if the firm's economic fortunes decline.

Probability data, whenever they are available, can be used to make the risk-return trade-off involved in the use of financial gearing more precise. The expected earnings per share (*EPS*) and coefficient of variation (*CV*) of these earnings may be calculated under alternative financial plans, and these *EPS* versus *CV* comparisons aid in making choices among plans.

Financial gearing is similar to operating gearing, a concept discussed in Chapter 3. As is true for operating gearing, financial gearing can be defined rigorously and measured in terms of the *degree of financial gearing*. In addition, the effects of financial and operating gearing may be combined, with the *combined gearing factor* showing the percentage changes in earnings per share that will result from a given percentage change in sales.

In the following chapter the concepts developed to this point in the book will be extended to the formal theory of the cost of capital. The way investors appraise the relative desirability of increased returns versus higher risks is seen to be a most important consideration – one that, in general, invalidates the theory that firms should strive for maximum earnings per share regardless of the risks involved.

QUESTIONS

18–1. How will each of the occurrences listed below affect a firm's financial structure, capital structure, and net worth?
(a) The firm retains earnings of £100 during the year.
(b) A preference share issue is refinanced by debentures.
(c) Debentures are sold for cash.
(d) An issue of convertible bonds is converted.

18–2. From an economic and social standpoint, is the use of financial gearing justifiable? Explain by listing some advantages and disadvantages.

18–3. Financial gearing and operating gearing are similar in one very important respect. What is this similarity and why is it important?

18–4. How does the use of financial gearing affect the break-even point?

18–5. Would you expect risk to increase (a) proportionately, (b) more than proportionately, or (c) less than proportionately, with added financial gearing? Give reasons for your answer.

18–6. What are some reasons for variations of debt ratios among the firms in a given industry?

18–7. Why is the following statement true? 'Other things being equal, firms with relatively stable sales are able to incur relatively high debt ratios.'

18–8. The use of financial ratios and industry averages in the financial planning and analysis of a firm should be approached with caution. Why?

18–9. Some economists believe that swings in business cycles will not be as wide in the future as they have been in the past. Assuming that they are correct in their analysis, what effect might this added stability have on the types of financing used by firms in Britain? Would your answer be true for all firms?

PROBLEMS

18–1. The Peterson Company plans to raise a net amount of £240 million for new equipment financing and working capital. Two alternatives are being considered. Ordinary shares may be sold at a market price of £4.2 a share to net £4, or debentures yielding 9 per cent may be issued with a 2 per cent flotation cost.

The balance sheet and income statement of the Peterson Company prior to financing are given below:

The Peterson Company, Balance Sheet 31 December 1978 (£m).

Ordinary share capital (£2 nominal value)	£ 50	Fixed assets (net)	£ 400
Reserves	300	Current assets	800
Debentures	250		
Short-term loan	250		
Trade creditors	150		
Accruals	200		
Total claims on assets	£1200	Total assets	£1200

The Peterson Company, Income Statement for Year Ended 31 December 1978 (£m).

Sales	£2200
Net income before taxes (10%)	220
Interest on debt	40
Net income subject to tax	180
Tax (50%)	90
Net income after tax	£ 90

Annual sales are expected to be distributed according to the following probabilities.

Annual sales	Probability
£1400	0.20
2000	0.30
2500	0.40
3200	0.10

(a) Assuming that net income before interest and taxes remains at 10 per cent of sales, calculate earnings per share under both the equity financing and the debt financing alternatives at each possible level of sales.
(b) Calculate expected earnings per share under both debt and equity financing.

18–2. British Battery Company produces one product, a long-life rechargeable battery for use in small calculators. Last year 50 000 batteries were sold at £20 each. British Battery's income statement is shown below.

British Battery Company, Income Statement for year ended 31 December 1978.

Sales		£1 000 000
Less: Variable cost	£400 000	
Fixed cost	200 000	
		600 000
EBIT		£ 400 000
Less: Interest		125 000
Net income before tax		£ 275 000
Less: Income tax ($T = 0.40$)		110 000
Net income		£ 165 000
EPS (one million shares)		0.165

(a) Calculate (i) the degree of operating gearing, (ii) the degree of financial gearing and (iii) the combined gearing effect for British Battery for the 1978 level of sales.
(b) British Battery is considering changing to a new production process for manufacturing the batteries. Highly automated and capital intensive, the new process will double fixed costs to £400 000 but will decrease variable costs to £4 a unit. If the new equipment is financed with debt, interest will increase by £70 000; if the equipment is financed by equity, total shares outstanding will increase by 200 000 shares. Assuming that sales remain constant, calculate for each financing method (i) earnings per share and (ii) the combined gearing if the new process is employed.
(c) Under what conditions would you expect British Battery to want to change its operations to the more automated plant?
(d) If sales are expected to increase, which alternative will have the greatest impact on *EPS*? Illustrate with an example.

18–3. The Hunter Company plans to expand assets by 50 per cent; to finance the expansion, it is choosing between a straight 7 per cent debt issue and ordinary shares. Its current balance sheet and income statement are show below.

Hunter Company, Balance Sheet 31 December 1980.

£1 ordinary shares	£350 000		
Reserves	210 000		
Debenture	140 000		
Total claims	£700 000	Total assets	£700 000

Hunter Company, Income Statement for Year Ended 31 December 1980.

Sales	£2 100 000	Earnings per share: $\frac{£105\,000}{350\,000} = £0.3$
Total costs (excluding interest)	1 881 600	
Net income before taxes	£ 218 400	Price/earnings ratio = 10 × [a]
Debt interest	8 400	
Income before taxes	£ 210 000	Market price: 10 × 0.3 = £3
Taxes at 50%	105 000	
Net income	£ 105 000	

[a] The price/earnings ratio is the market price per share divided by earnings per share. It represents the amount of money an investor is willing to pay for £1 of current earnings. The higher the riskiness of a share, the lower its P/E ratio, other things held constant. The concept of price/earnings ratio is discussed at some length in Chapter 17.

If the Hunter Company finances the £350 000 expansion with debt, the rate on the incremental debt will be 7 per cent and the price/earnings ratio of the ordinary share will be 8 times. If the expansion is financed by equity, the new shares can be sold at £2.50, the rate on debt will be 6 per cent and the price/earnings ratio of all the outstanding ordinary shares will remain at 10 times earnings.

(a) Assuming that net income before interest and taxes (*EBIT*) is 10 per cent of sales, calculate earnings per share at sales levels of £0, £700 000, £1 400 000, £2 100 000, £2 800 000, £3 500 000 and £4 200 000, when financing is with (i) equity and (ii) debt. Assume no fixed costs of production.

(b) Make a break-even chart for *EPS* and indicate the break-even point in sales (that is, where *EPS* using bonds = *EPS* using stock).

(c) Using the price/earnings ratio, calculate the market value per share for each sales level for both the debt and the equity financing.

(d) Make a break-even chart of market value per share for the company using data from part (c), and indicate the break-even point.

(e) If the firm follows the policy of seeking to maximize (i) *EPS* or (ii) market price per share, which form of financing should be used?

(f) Now assume that the following probability estimates of future sales have been made: 5 per cent chance of £0; 7.5 per cent chance of £700 000; 20 per cent chance of £1 400 000; 35 per cent chance of £2 100 000; 20 per cent chance of £2 800 000; 7.5 per cent chance of £3 500 000; and 5 per cent chance of £4 200 000. Calculate expected values for *EPS* and market price per share under each financing alternative.

(g) What other factors should be taken into account in choosing between the two forms of financing?

SELECTED REFERENCES

Altman Edward I. Corporate bankruptcy potential, stockholder returns, and share valuation. *Journal of Finance* 24 (December 1969):887–900.

Arditti, Fred D. Risk and the required return on equity. *Journal of Finance* 22 (March 1967): 19–36.

Bird, P. What is capital gearing? *Accounting and Business Research* (Spring 1973): 92–97.

Braun, M. E. Planning the debt mix: a linear programming approach. *Journal of Business Finance* (Summer 1973): 26–31.

Coates, J. H. and Woolley, P. K. Corporate gearing in the E.E.C. *Journal of Business Finance and Accounting* (Spring 1975): 1–18.

Donaldson, Gordon. *Corporate Debt Capacity.* Boston: Division of Research, Harvard Business School, 1961.

Donaldson, Gordon. New framework for corporate debt capacity. *Harvard Business Review* 40 (March–April 1962: 117–131.

Donaldson, Gordon. Strategy for financial emergencies. *Harvard Business Review* 47 (November–December 1969): 67–79.

Fox, R. B. Leverage in U. K. Companies 1967–1973. *Managerial Finance* 2, No. 3 (1976): 229–255.

Ghandhi J. K. S. On the measurement of leverage. *Journal of Finance* 21 (December 1966) 715–726.

Haslem, John A. Leverage effects on corporate earnings. *Arizona Review* 19 (March 1970): 7–11.

Hunt, Pearson. A proposal for precise definitions of 'trading on the equity' and 'leverage.' *Journal of Finance* 16 (September 1961): 377–386.

Keenan, M. and Maldonado, R. M. The redundancy of earnings leverage in a cost of capital decision framework. *Journal of Business Finance and Accounting* (Summer 1976): 43–56.

Krainer, Robert E. Interest rates, leverage, and investor rationality. *Journal of Financial and Quantitative Analysis* 12 (March 1977): 1–16.

Kraus, Alan and Litzenberger, Robert. A state-preference model of optimal financial leverage. *Journal of Finance* 28 (September 1973): 911–922.

Lev, Baruch and Pekelman, Dov. A multiperiod adjustment model for the firm's capital structure. *Journal of Finance* 30 (March 1975): 75–91.

Lister, R. J. Corporate gearing–capacity and valuation. *Investment Analyst* (April 1976): 31–34.

Lloyd-Davies, Peter R. Optimal financial policy in imperfect markets. *Journal of Financial and Quantitative Analysis* 10 (September 1975): 457–481.

Scott, David F. and Martin, John D. Industry influence on financial structure. *Financial Management* 4 (Spring 1975): 67–73.

Toy, Norman, Stonehill, Arthur, Remmers, Lee, Wright, Richard and Beekhuisen, Theo. A comparative international study of growth, profitability, and risk as determinants of corporate debt ratios in the manufacturing sector. *Journal of Financial and Quantitative Analysis* 9 (November 1974): 875–886.

Vickers, Douglas. Disequilibrium structures and financing decisions in the firm. *Journal of Business Finance and Accounting* 1 (Autumn 1974): 375–388.

Williams, Edward E. Cost of capital functions and the firm's optimal level of gearing. *Journal of Business Finance* 4, No. 2, 78–83.

Wippern, Ronald F. Financial structure and the value of the firm. *Journal of Finance* 21 (December 1966): 615–634.

Chapter 19

The Cost of Capital[1]

The cost of capital is a critically important topic. First, as we saw in Chapter 10, capital budgeting decisions have a major impact on the firm, and proper capital budgeting requires an estimate of the cost of capital. Second, in Chapter 18 we saw that financial structure can affect both the size and riskiness of the firm's earnings stream, hence the value of the firm. A knowledge of the cost of capital, and how it is influenced by financial gearing, is useful in making capital structure decisions. Finally, a number of other decisions, including those related to leasing, to repayment of debentures and to working capital policy, require estimates of the cost of capital.[2]

In this chapter, we first point out the necessity of using a weighted average cost of capital. Second, the cost of the individual components of the capital structure – debt, preference shares and equity – are considered: because investors perceive different classes of securities to have different degrees of risk, there are variations in the costs of different types of securities. Third, the individual component costs are brought together to form a weighted cost of capital. Fourth, the concepts developed in the earlier sections are illustrated with an example of the cost of capital calculation for an actual company. Finally, the interrelationship between the cost of capital and the investment opportunity schedule is developed, and the simultaneous determination of the marginal cost of capital and the marginal return on investment is discussed.

COMPOSITE, OR OVERALL, COST OF CAPITAL

Suppose a particular firm's cost of debt is estimated to be 8 per cent, its cost of equity is estimated to be 12 per cent, and the decision has been made to finance next year's projects by selling debt. The argument is sometimes advanced that the cost of these projects is 8 per cent, because debt will be used to finance them. However, this position contains a basic fallacy. To finance a particular set of projects with debt implies that the firm is also using

1. This chapter is relatively long and difficult; students should allow for this in their preparation schedules.
2. The cost of capital is also vitally important in the public sector. See C. V. Henderson, Notes on public investment criteria in the U.K., *Bulletin of the Oxford University Institute of Economics and Statistics*, 1965.

up some of its potential for obtaining new low-cost debt. As expansion occurs in subsequent years, at some point the firm will find it necessary to use additional equity financing or else the debt ratio will become too large.

To illustrate, suppose the firm has an 8 per cent cost of debt and a 12 per cent cost of equity. In the first year it borrows heavily, using up its debt capacity in the process, to finance projects yielding 9 per cent. In the second year it has projects available that yield 11 per cent, well above the return on first-year projects, but it cannot accept them because they would have to be financed with 12 per cent equity money. To avoid this problem, the firm should be viewed as an on-going concern, and its cost of capital should be calculated as a weighted average, or composite, of the various types of funds it uses: debt, preferred and equity.

BASIC DEFINITIONS

Both students and practitioners are often confused about how to calculate and use the cost of capital. To a large extent, this confusion results from imprecise, ambiguous definitions, but a careful study of the following definitions will eliminate such unnecessary difficulties.

Capital, or financial, components

Capital (or financial) components are the items on the left-hand side of the balance sheet: various types of debt, preference shares and ordinary shares. Any net increase in assets must be financed by an increase in one or more capital components.

Component costs

Capital is a necessary factor of production, and like any other factor, it has a cost. The cost of each component is defined as the *component cost* of that particular component. For example, if the firm can borrow money at 8 per cent, the component cost of debt is defined as 8 per cent.[3] Throughout most of this chapter, we concentrate on debt, preference shares, retained earnings and new issues of ordinary shares. These are the capital structure components, and their component costs are identified by the following symbols:

k_b = interest rate on firm's new debt
= component cost of debt, before tax.

$k_b(1-T)$ = component cost of debt after tax, where T = marginal tax rate; $k_b(1-T)$ is the debt cost used to calculate the marginal cost of capital.

k_{ps} = component cost of preference shares.

k_r = component cost of retained earnings.

k_e = component cost of new issues of ordinary shares. k_s was defined as the required rate of return on ordinary shares in Chapter 17. Here we distinguish between equity obtained from retained earnings and selling new shares, hence the distinction between k_e and k_r.

---

3. We will see that there is a before-tax cost of debt; 8 per cent is the before-tax component cost of debt. Also, the effects of debt on the cost of equity will be considered later.

k = an average or 'composite' cost of capital. If a firm raises £1 of capital to finance asset expansion, and if it is to keep its capital structure in balance (that is, if it is to keep the same percentage of debt, preference shares and equity) then it will raise part of the £1 as debt, part as preference shares and part as ordinary shares. k is also a marginal cost; there is a value of k for each £1 the firm raises during the year. k is, in effect, the marginal cost of capital used in Chapter 10 and the relationship between k and the amount of funds raised during the year is expressed as the *MCC* schedule in Figure 10–1.[4]

These definitions and concepts are explained in detail in the remainder of this chapter, where we seek to accomplish two goals: (a) to develop a marginal cost of capital schedule ($k = MCC$) that can be used in capital budgeting, and (b) to determine the mix of types of capital that will minimize the *MCC* schedule. If the firm finances so as to minimize its *MCC*, uses this *MCC* to calculate *NPV*s, and makes capital budgeting decisions on the basis of the *NPV* method, this will lead to a maximization of share prices.

BEFORE-TAX COMPONENT COST OF DEBT (k_b)

If a firm borrows £100 000 for one year at 6 per cent interest, the investors who purchase the debt receive, and the firm must pay them, a total of £6000 annual interest on their investment:

$$k_b = \text{before-tax cost of debt} = \frac{\text{interest}}{\text{principal}} = \frac{£6000}{£100\,000} = 6\%. \tag{19–1}$$

For now, assume that the firm pays no corporation tax; the effect of tax on the analysis of cost of capital is treated in a later section of the chapter. Under this assumption, the firm's interest cost is £6000, and its percentage cost of debt is 6 per cent. As a first approximation, *the component cost of debt is equal to the rate of return earned by investors, or the interest rate on debt.*[5] If the firm borrows and invests the borrowed funds to earn a return just equal to the interest rate, then the earnings available to ordinary shares remain unchanged.[6] This is demonstrated below.

The ABC Company has sales of £1 million, operating costs of £900 000, and no debt. Its income statement is shown in the Before column of Table 19–1. Then it borrows £100 000

---

4. k also reflects the riskiness of the firm's various assets as discussed in Chapter 11, Investment Decisions Under Uncertainty. If a firm uses risk-adjusted discount rates for different capital projects, the average of these rates, weighted by the sizes of the various investments, should equal k.

5. The cost of convertible debentures is slightly more complicated, but it can be calculated using the following formula:

$$M = \sum_{t=1}^{N} \frac{c}{(1+k_c)^t} + \frac{tv}{(1+k_c)^N}.$$

Here M is the price of the convertible debenture; c is the annual amount of interest; tv is the expected terminal value of the debenture in year N; N is the expected number of years that the debenture will be outstanding; and k_c is the required rate of return on the convertible. The risk to an investor holding a convertible is somewhat higher than that on a straight debenture, but somewhat less than that on ordinary shares. Accordingly, the cost of convertibles is generally between that on debentures and that on equity. This concept is discussed in detail in Chapter 16. We should also note that the after-tax cost of a convertible is found as k_c in the equation, but here c is multiplied by $(1-T)$, where T is the marginal tax rate.

6. Note that this definition is a *first approximation*, it is modified later to take account of the deductibility of interest payments for tax purposes. Note also that here the cost of debt is considered in isolation. The impact of debt on the cost of equity, as well as on future increments of debt, is treated when the weighted cost of a combination of debt and equity is derived. Finally, flotation costs, or the costs of selling the debt, are ignored. Flotation costs for debt issues are generally quite low; in fact, most debt is placed directly with insurance

at 6 per cent and invests the funds in assets whose use causes sales to rise by £7000 and operating costs to rise by £1000. Hence, profits before interest rise by £6000. The new situation is shown in the After column. Earnings are unchanged, as the investment just earns its component cost of capital.

Table 19-1 *Income Statement for the ABC Company.*

	Before	After
Sales	£1 000 000	£1 007 000
Operating costs	900 000	901 000
Earnings before interest	£ 100 000	£ 106 000
Interest	–	6 000
Earnings	£ 100 000	£ 100 000

Note that the cost of debt is applicable to *new* debt, not to the interest on any old, previously outstanding debt. In other words, we are interested in the cost of new debt, or the *marginal* cost of debt. The primary concern with the cost of capital is to use it in a decision-making process – the decision whether to obtain capital to make new investments; whether the firm borrowed at high or low rates in the past is irrelevant.[7]

PREFERENCE SHARES

Preference shares, described in detail in Chapter 14, are a hybrid between debentures and ordinary shares. Like debentures, preference shares bear a fixed rates of interest and in the event of liquidation the claims of preference shareholders take precedence over those of ordinary shareholders. Preference shares are thus somewhat less risky to the firm than debentures but more risky than ordinary shares. Just the reverse holds for investors. For an investor a preference share is riskier than a debenture but not as risky as an ordinary share. Thus, if an investor is willing to buy a particular firm's debentures at 6 per cent, he might, because of risk aversion, be unwilling to buy the same firm's preference shares at a yield of less than 9 per cent. Assuming the preference share is a perpetuity that sells at a price of £1 per share and pays an annual interest of 9 pence its yield is calculated as follows:

$$\text{Yield} = \frac{\text{preference dividend}}{\text{price}} = \frac{d_{ps}}{p_{ps}} = \frac{£0.09}{£1.00} = 9\% \qquad (19\text{–}2)$$

companies, pension funds and the like, and involves no flotation costs. If flotation costs are involved, the cost of debt can be approximated by the following equation:

$$k_b = \frac{c_t + \dfrac{M - p_b}{N}}{\dfrac{M + p_b}{2}}.$$

Here c_t is the periodic interest payment in pounds, M is the par or maturity value of the debenture, p_b is the debenture's issue price (hence $M - p_b$ is the premium or discount), and N is the life of the debenture. The equation is an approximation, as it does not consider compounding effects. However, the approximation is quite close; for example, with a 5 per cent, 25-year, £1000 par value debenture sold at £980, the formula gives $k_b = 5.13$ versus 5.15 as found from a debenture table.

7. The fact that the firm borrowed at high or low rates in the past is, of course, important in terms of the effect of the interest charges on current profits, but this past decision is not relevant for *current* decisions. For current financial decisions, only current interest rates are relevant.

Assuming the firm can sell additional preference shares at £1 per share the cost of preference share capital will be 9 per cent. In other words *as a first approximation the component cost of preference capital* (k_{ps}) *is equal to the return investors receive on the shares as calculated in equation 19–2.*

If the firm sells preference shares for less than their nominal value, p_{ps} in the denominator of equation 19–2 should be the net price received by the firm. Suppose, for example, the firm must incur a *flotation* cost of 4 pence per share so that the firm nets only 96 pence per share. The cost of the new preference shares to the firm is calculated as shown in equation 19–2a:

$$k_{ps} = \text{cost of preference shares} = \frac{d_{ps}}{p_{ps}} = \frac{£0.08}{£0.96} = 8.33\% \qquad (19\text{–}2a)$$

TAX ADJUSTMENT

As they stand, the definitions of the component costs of debt and preference shares are incompatible when we introduce taxes into the analysis, because interest payments are deductible expenses whereas preference dividends are not. The following example illustrates the point.

The ABC company can borrow £100 000 at 6 per cent or it can issue 100 000 6 per cent (net) £1 preference shares. Assuming a 50 per cent corporation tax rate and a 33½ per cent advanced corporation tax (ACT), its pre-investment position is given in the Before column of Table 19–2. At what rate of return must the company invest the proceeds from the new financing to keep the earnings available to ordinary shareholders from changing?

Table 19-2 *Tax Adjustment for Cost of Debt.*

		Invest in assets yielding		
			6%	12%
	Before	Debt	Preference	Preference
Earnings before interest and taxes (EBIT)	£100 000	£106 000	£106 000	£112 000
Interest	–	6 000	–	–
Earnings before tax (EBT)	£100 000	£100 000	£106 000	£112 000
Corporation Tax 50% (T)	(50 000)	(50 000)	(53 000)	(56 000)
Preference dividend	–	–	(6000)	(6000)
Available to ordinary shareholders	£ 50 000	£ 50 000	£ 47 000	£ 50 000

As can be seen from the tabulations in Table 19–2, if the funds are invested to yield 6 per cent before tax, earnings available to ordinary shareholders are constant if debt is used, but they decline if new preference shares are issued. To maintain the £50 000 net earnings requires that funds generated from the sale of preference shares be invested to yield 12 per cent before tax or 6 per cent after tax.[8]

Since shareholders are concerned with after-tax rather than before-tax earnings, only the cost of capital *after* corporation tax should be used. The cost of preference shares has been on an after-tax basis since the imputation system was introduced, but a simple adjustment is needed to arrive at the after-tax cost of debt. It is recognized that interest

8. The 12 per cent is found as follows: 6%/(1 – tax rate) = 6%/0.50 = 12.0%.

payments are tax deductible – the higher the firm's interest payments, the lower its tax bill. In effect, the government pays part of a firm's interest charges. Therefore, the cost of debt capital is calculated as follows:

$$k_b(1-T) = \text{after-tax cost of debt}$$
$$= (\text{before-tax cost}) \times (1.0 - \text{tax rate}). \qquad (19\text{–}3)$$

Whenever the weighted cost of capital (k) is calculated, $k_b(1-T)$ and not k_b is used.

Example

Before-tax cost of debt = 6 per cent
Corporation tax rate = 50 per cent

$k_b(1-T)$ = after-tax cost = (0.06)(1 – 0.50) = (0.06)(0.50) = 3 per cent.

COST OF RETAINED EARNINGS (k_r)[9]

The cost of preference shares is based on the return investors require if they are to purchase the preference shares; the cost of debt is based on the interest rate investors require on debt issues, adjusted for tax. The cost of equity obtained by retaining earnings can be defined similarly: *it is k_r, the rate of return shareholders require on the firm's ordinary shares.* (k_r is identical to k_s as developed in Chapter 17.)

As we saw in Chapter 17, the value of a share depends, ultimately, on the dividends paid on the shares:

$$p_0 = \frac{d_1}{(1+k_r)} + \frac{d_2}{(1+k_r)^2} + \ldots \qquad (19\text{–}4)$$

Here p_0 is the current price of the share; d_t is the dividend expected to be paid at the end of year t; and k_r is the required rate of return. If dividends are expected to grow at a constant rate, we saw in Chapter 17 that equation 19–4 reduces to

$$p_0 = \frac{d_1}{k_r - g}. \qquad (19\text{–}5)$$

In equilibrium, the expected and required rates of return must be equal, so we can solve for k_r to obtain the required rate of return on ordinary shares:

$$k_r = \frac{d_1}{p_0} + \text{expected } g. \qquad (19\text{–}6)$$

Example

To illustrate this calculation, consider Aubey Biscuits, a firm expected to earn £0.20 a share and to pay a £0.10 dividend during the coming year. The company's earnings,

---

9. The term 'retained earnings' can be interpreted to mean the balance sheet item 'retained earnings', consisting of all the earnings retained in the business throughout its history, or it can mean the income statement item 'additions to retained earnings'. This latter definition is used in the present chapter: '*Retained earnings' for our purpose here refers to that part of current earnings that is not paid out in dividends but, rather, is retained and re-invested in the business.*

'Equity' is defined in this chapter to *exclude* preference shares. Equity is the sum of ordinary shares, capital reserves and accumulated retained earnings.

dividends and share price have all been growing at about 5 per cent a year, and this growth rate is expected to continue indefinitely. The shares are in equilibrium and currently sell for £2 each. Using this information, we compute the required rate of return on the shares in equilibrium, using equation 19–6 as follows:

$$k_r = \frac{£0.10}{£2} + 5\% = 10\%.$$

The expected growth rate for the price of the shares is 5 per cent, which, on the £2 initial price, should lead to a £0.10 increase in the value of the shares, to £2.10. This price increase will be attained (barring changes in the general level of share prices) if Aubey invests the £0.10 of retained earnings to yield 10 per cent. However, if the £0.10 is invested to yield only 5 per cent, then earnings will grow by only 0.5 pence during the year, not by the expected 1.0 pence a share. The new earnings will be £0.205, a growth of only $2\frac{1}{2}$ per cent, rather than the expected £0.210, or 5 per cent increase. If investors believe that the firm will earn only 5 per cent on retained earnings in the future and attain only a $2\frac{1}{2}$ per cent growth rate, they will reappraise the value of the shares downwards according to equation 19–5 as follows:

$$p_0 = \frac{d_1}{k_r - g} = \frac{£0.10}{0.10 - 0.025} = \frac{£0.10}{0.075} = £1.33.$$

Note, however, that Aubey Biscuits will suffer this price decline *only if it invests equity funds – retained earnings – at less than its component cost of capital.*

If Aubey refrains from making new investments and pays all its earnings in dividends, it will cut its growth rate to nil. However, the price of the shares will not fall, because investors will still get the required 10 per cent rate of return on their shares:[10]

$$k_r = \frac{d_1}{p_0} + g = \frac{£0.2}{£2} + 0 = 10\%, \text{ or}$$

$$p_0 = \frac{£0.20}{0.10 - 0} = £2.$$

All the return would come in the form of dividends, but the actual rate of return would match the required 10 per cent.

The preceding example demonstrates a fundamentally important fact: *If a firm earns its required rate of return, k_r, then when it retains earnings and invests them in its operations, its current share price will not change as a result of this financing and investment. However, if it earns less than k_r the share price will fall; if it earns more, the share price will rise.*

COST OF EXTERNAL EQUITY (k_e)

The cost of *external* equity capital, k_e, is higher than the cost of retained earnings, k_r, because of flotation costs involved in selling new shares. Under the corporation tax system that existed before the introduction of the imputation tax system retained earnings also had a lower cost than externally raised equity capital because of the 'double taxation' of distributed profits.[11] This advantage has now largely disappeared and may in certain cases

10. This assumes that investors are indifferent to capital gains and dividends. Whether this assumption is correct or not will be considered in Chapter 20.

11. For a more comprehensive examination of the effects of ACT, see Appendix A, 'The Tax Environment', at the end of this book.

be reversed.[12] What rate of return must be earned on funds raised by selling shares to make the action worth while? To put it another way, what is the cost of new equity? The answer is found by applying the following formula:[13]

$$k_e = \frac{d_1}{p_0(1-f)} + g = \frac{d_1}{p_n} + g = \frac{\text{dividend yield}}{(1-\text{flotation percentage})} + \text{growth}. \qquad (19\text{–}7)$$

Here f is the percentage cost of selling the issue, so $p_0(1-f) = p_n$ is the net price received by the firm. For example, if $p_0 = £1$ and $f = 10$ per cent, then the firm receives £0.90 for each new share sold; hence $p_n = £0.90$. Notice that equation 19–7 is strictly applicable only if future growth is expected to be constant.

For Aubey Biscuits, the cost of new external equity is computed as follows:

$$k_e = \frac{£0.10}{£2(1-0.10)} + 5\% = 10.55\%.$$

Investors require a return of $k_r = 10$ per cent on Aubey's shares. However, because of flotation costs, Aubey must earn *more* than 10 per cent on equity-financed investments to provide this 10 per cent. Specifically, if Aubey Biscuits earns 10.55 per cent on investments financed by new equity issues, then earnings per share will not fall below previously expected earnings; its expected dividend can be maintained; the growth rate for earnings and dividends will be maintained; and as a result of all this, the price per share will not decline. If Aubey earns less than 10.55 per cent, then earnings, dividends and growth will fall below expectations, causing the price of the shares to decline. Since the cost of capital is *defined* as the rate of return that must be earned to prevent the price of the shares from falling, we see that the company's cost of external equity, k_e, is 10.55 per cent (see footnote 12).

---

12. The cost of external equity is sometimes defined as follows:

$$k_e = \frac{k_r}{1-f}$$

This equation is correct if the firm's expected growth rate is nil; see equation 19–7. In other cases it tends to overstate k_e.

13. The equation is derived as follows:

Step 1. The old shareholders expect the firm to pay a stream of dividends, d_t; this income stream will be derived from existing assets. New investors will likewise expect to receive the same stream of dividends, d_t. For new investors to obtain this stream *without impairing the d_t stream of the old investors*, the new funds obtained from the sale of shares must be invested at a return high enough to provide a dividend stream whose present value is equal to the price the firm receives:

$$p_n = \sum_{t=1}^{\infty} \frac{d_t}{(1+k_e)^t}. \qquad (19\text{–}8)$$

Here p_n is the net price to the firm; d_t is the dividend stream to new shareholders; and k_e is the cost of new external equity.

Step 2. If flotation costs are expressed as a percentage, f, of the gross price of the shares, p_0, we may express p_n as follows:

$$p_n = p_0(1-f).$$

Step 3. When growth is a constant, equation 19–8 reduces to

$$p_n = p_0(1-f) = \frac{d_1}{k_e - g}. \qquad (19\text{–}8a)$$

Step 4. Equation 19–8a may be solved for k_e.

$$k_e = \frac{d_1}{p_0(1-f)} + g. \qquad (19\text{–}7)$$

FINDING THE BASIC REQUIRED RATE OF RETURN ON ORDINARY SHARES

It is obvious by now that the basic rate of return investors require on a firm's equity, k_s as developed in Chapter 17, is a most important quantity. This required rate of return is the cost of retained earnings, and it forms the basis for the cost of capital obtained from new share issues. How is this all-important quantity estimated?

Although one *can* use very involved, highly complicated procedures for making this estimation, satisfactory estimates may be obtained in one of three ways:

1. Estimate the security market line (SML) as described in Chapter 17; estimate the relative riskiness of the firm in question; and then use these estimates to obtain the required rate of return on the firm's equity:[14]

   $$k_s = R_F + \rho.$$

   Under this procedure, the estimated cost of equity (k_s) will move up or down with changes in interest rates and with changes in 'investor psychology'.
2. An alternative procedure, the use of which is recommended in conjunction with the one described above, is to estimate the basic required rate of return as follows:
   (a) Assume that investors expect the past-realized rate of return on the shares to be earned in the future, so the expected return is equal to $\bar{k}_s$.
   (b) Assume that the shares are in equilibrium, with $k_s^* = \bar{k}_s$.
   (c) Under these assumptions, the required rate of return may be estimated as equal to the past realized rate of return:

   $$k_s^* = \bar{k}_s = \frac{d_1}{p_0} + \text{past growth rate.}$$

   Shareholder returns are derived from dividends and capital gains, and the total of the dividend yield plus the average growth rate over the past five to ten years may give an estimate of the total returns that shareholders expect in the future from a particular share.
3. For 'normal' companies in 'normal' times, past growth rates may be projected into the future, and the second method will give satisfactory results. *However, if the company's growth has been abnormally high or low, either because of its own unique situation or because of general economic conditions, then investors will not project the past growth rate into the future, so method 2 will not yield a good estimate of* k_s^*. In this case, g must be estimated in some other manner. Security analysts regularly make earnings growth forecasts, looking at such factors as projected sales, profit margins, competitive factors and the like. Someone making a cost of capital estimate can obtain such analysts' forecasts and use them as a proxy for the growth expectations of investors in general, combine g with the current dividend yield, and estimate $\bar{k}_s$ as

   $$k_s^* = \frac{d_1}{p_0} + \text{growth rate as projected by security analysts.}$$

   Again, note that this estimate of k_s^* is based upon the assumption that g is expected to remain constant in the future.

Based on our own experience in estimating equity capital costs, we recognize that both careful analysis and some very fine judgements are required in this process. It would be

14. See Appendix C to this chapter for illustrations of the use of the capital asset pricing model in calculating the cost of equity capital and the cost of capital for firms.

nice to pretend that these judgements are unnecessary and to specify an easy, precise way of determining the exact cost of equity capital. Unfortunately, this is not possible. Finance is, in large part, a matter of judgement, and we simply must face this fact.

EFFECT OF GEARING ON THE COST OF EQUITY

We have seen in earlier chapters that investors in general are averse to risk, and that risk aversion leads investors to require higher yields on riskier investments. In Chapter 18, we used the Universal Company case to demonstrate that for any given degree of business risk, the higher the debt ratio, the larger will be the measures of variability in earnings per share and return on equity.[15] Combining these results leads us to conclude that the more debt a given company employs, other things being equal, the higher its required rate of return on equity capital will be.

To illustrate this relationship consider Figure 19–1, which presents a probability distribution of *EBIT* for the Universal Machine Company.[16] The area under the curve in Figure 19–1 to the left of any level of fixed charges represents the probability of not covering these charges. The higher the level of debt, the larger the fixed charges and the

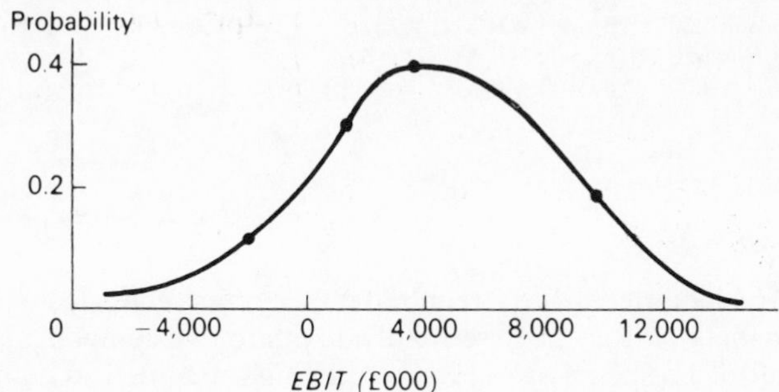

Figure 19–1 *Distribution of* EBIT *for Universal Machine Company.*

higher the probability of not being able to cover fixed charges. The inability to meet fixed charges may lead to reorganization or liquidation (see Chapter 23) with attendant costs of court proceedings. Even before such legal difficulties, the increasing risk of financial difficulties may result in the loss of key employees who find positions with firms whose financial outlook is safer, in the reduced availability of goods from key suppliers as well as in the reduced availability of financing.[17]

The fear of possible liquidation would cause the linear relationship between gearing and the related risks of equity and debt to become curvilinear upwards as well as to increase the required returns on equity and debt. In the present section we will analyse the effect on required returns on equity. The greater probability of not covering fixed charges, which also increases the probabilities of liquidation, will cause the relationship between gearing and the risk measures for Universal Machine to curve up more rapidly than discussed in Chapter 18 under the assumptions of no liquidation penalties. Accordingly, the

---

15. These relationships were worked out for Universal in Table 18–5.
16. This is based on the data in Table 18–2 from the previous chapter.
17. The possibilities that liquidation penalties may be substantial are developed in Appendix D to this chapter.

relationship between gearing, the indexes of risk and the required rates of return may be as set forth in Table 19–3.

Table 19–3 *Universal Machine Company: Gearing, Risk Indexes and the Required Rates of Return on Equity.*

Gearing (debt/equity) (B/S)	No liquidation penalties[a] ρ_1^*	ρ_2^*	With liquidation penalties[b] ρ_1	ρ_2	Required return on equity: No liquidation penalties[c]	With liquidation penalties[d]
0	6%	0%	6%	0%	12.00	12.00
0.25	6%	0.75%	6%	0.75%	12.75	12.75
0.43	6%	1.29%	6%	1.29%	13.29	13.29
0.67	6%	2.01%	6%	3.51%	14.00	15.51
1.00	6%	3.00%	6%	6.00%	15.00	18.00
1.50	6%	4.50%	6%	11.86%	16.50	23.86
4.00	6%	12.00%	6%	33.54%	24.00	45.54

[a] The columns are calculated as follows:
$\rho_1^* = \beta_U(k_M - R_F)$ $\rho_2^* = (B/S)(1-T)\rho_1^*$
[b] Calculations
$\rho_1 = \beta_U(k_M - R_F)$
For ρ_2 we have:
$B/S \geq 0.43$ $\rho_2 = (B/S)(1-T)\rho_1$
$B/S = 0.67$ $\rho_2 = (0.5 + B/S)(1-T)\rho_1$
$B/S = 1.00$ $\rho_2 = (1 + B/S)(1-T)\rho_1$
$B/S = 1.50$ $\rho_2 = (1 + B/S)^{1.5}(1-T)\rho_1$
$B/S = 4.00$ $\rho_2 = (1 + B/S)^{1.5}(1-T)\rho_1$
[c] Calculations
$6\% + \rho_1^* + \rho_2^*$
[d] Calculations
$6\% + \rho_1 + \rho_2$

In Chapter 17 we indicated that the required rate of return consisted of the riskless rate plus a risk premium: $k_s = R_F + \rho$. Here we divide ρ into two components, ρ_1 (read 'rho one'), a premium for business risk; and ρ_2, a premium required to compensate equity investors for the additional risk brought on by financial gearing. Expressed as an equation,

$$k_s = R_F + \rho_1 + \rho_2. \tag{19–9}$$

The riskless rate of return, R_F, is a function of general economic conditions and the actions of the authorities. The premium for business risk, ρ_1, is a function of the nature of the firm's industry, its degree of operating gearing, its diversification, and so on. Financial risk, ρ_2, depends upon the degree of financial gearing employed.[18]

In Table 19–3 we illustrate how the magnitudes of business and financial risk might be measured in relation to gearing and then indicate their plausible impact on the required rates of return on equity.[19] The calculations of ρ_1^* and ρ_2^* are based on the assumptions of no substantial liquidation costs. ρ_1^* is simply the beta for an ungeared firm and ρ_2^* is the (required return for an ungeared firm with a given beta times $[B/S][1-T]$).

18. ρ_2 increases at an increasing rate with gearing because liquidation, as opposed to simply lower earnings, becomes an increasing threat as the debt ratio rises, and liquidation may have high costs of its own (see Chapter 23). As we saw in Chapter 14, the specific terms of the firm's debt also affect its financial risk. Especially important here is the maturity structure of the debt. We might also note that some financial theorists argue that the relationship between ρ_2 and gearing is linear; see Appendix B to this chapter. Further, ρ_1 is always smaller for any firm whose asset returns are not perfectly correlated, or are negatively correlated, with most other firms, if negative correlation exists. ρ_1 could even be negative, as this firm's shares would be sought to reduce the overall risk in investors' portfolios. This covariance effect is discussed in Appendix C to this chapter.

19. Keep in mind that throughout this analysis we are holding constant the firm's assets and the *EBIT* on these assets. We wish to consider the effect of gearing on the cost of capital *holding other things constant.*

With liquidation costs, however, the indexes of financial risk are likely to increase at an increasing rate when gearing passes some critical point and become curvilinear upwards as measured in Table 19–3, which is also depicted as a graph in Figure 19–2. The required rate of return on equity is 12 per cent if the company uses no debt, but k_s^* increases after debt passes some critical level and is 23.86 per cent if the debt to value ratio is as high as 60 per cent.[20] With gearing beyond 60 per cent, it is likely that the required cost of equity is so high that the funds for all practical purposes are not available.

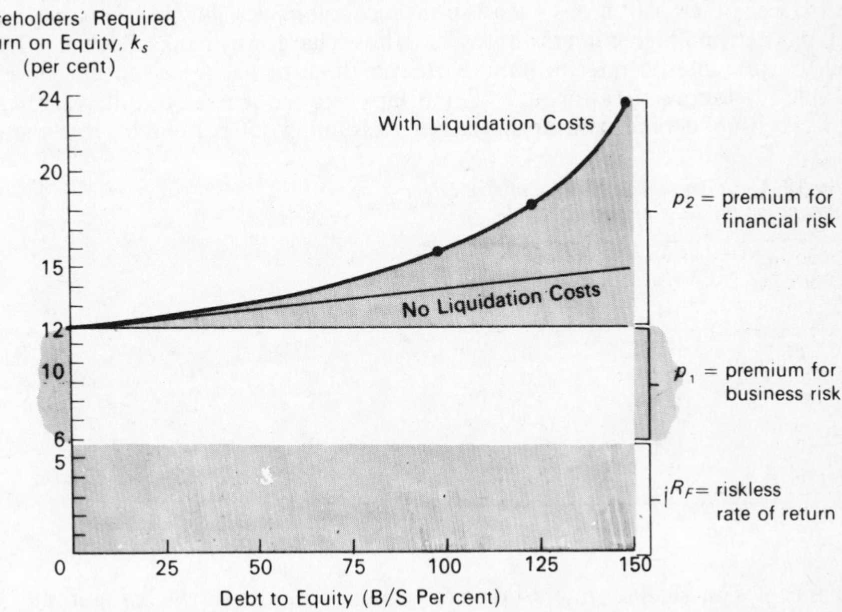

Figure 19–2 *Illustrative Relationship between the Cost of Equity and Financial Gearing.*

EFFECT OF GEARING ON THE COMPONENT COST OF DEBT

The component cost of debt is also affected by gearing: the higher the gearing ratio, the higher the cost of debt. Further, the cost of debt can be expected to rise at an increasing rate with gearing. To see why this is so, we can again consider the Universal Machine Company example. The probability distribution of earnings before interest and taxes (*EBIT*) is represented by Figure 19–1. The more debt the firm has, the higher the interest requirements; and the higher the interest charges, the greater the probability that earnings (*EBIT*) will not be sufficient to meet these charges.[21] Creditors will perceive this increasing

20. This corresponds to a debt-to-equity ratio of 150 per cent. In this example we assume that the risk-return trade-off function has been estimated, perhaps in a subjective manner, by the financial manager. The precise specification of such risk-return functions is one of the more controversial areas of finance, and having attempted to measure them empirically ourselves we can attest to the difficulties involved. However, even though the precise shape of the function is open to question, it is generally agreed (a) that the curve is upward sloping and (b) that some estimate, be it better or worse, is necessary if we are to obtain a cost of capital for use in capital budgeting. In this chapter our main concern is that the broad concepts be grasped.

21. Recall that the area under the curve in Figure 19–1 to the left of any level of fixed charges represents the probability of not covering these charges.

risk as the debt ratio rises, and they will begin charging a risk premium above the riskless rate, causing the firm's interest rate to rise. Since creditors are risk averters and are assumed to have a diminishing marginal utility for money, they will demand that interest rates be increased to compensate for the increased risk.

One other effect that may operate to raise interest rates at an increasing rate is the fact that a firm may need to use a variety of sources in order to borrow large amounts of funds in relation to its equity base. For example, a firm may be able to borrow from banks only up to some limit set by the authorities. In order to increase its borrowings, the firm would have to seek other institutions, such as insurance companies, finance companies and so on, that may demand higher interest rates than those charged by banks. Such an effect might tend to cause interest rates to jump whenever the firm was forced to find new lenders.

Table 19–4 shows the estimated relationships between gearing, the interest rate, and the after-tax cost of debt for Universal Machine. Assuming a 50 per cent tax rate, the after-tax

Table 19–4 *Universal Machine Company: Effect of Gearing on the Cost of Debt.*

Gearing (Debt/equity)	Interest rate (k_b)	After-tax cost of debt $k_b(1-T)$
0%	10%	5.0%
20	10	5.0
30	11	5.5
40	13	6.5
50	16	8.0
60	27	13.5

cost of debt is one-half the interest rate; these figures are also shown in Figure 19–3, where they are plotted against the debt ratio. In the example, Universal's cost of debt is constant until the debt ratio passes 20 per cent or £2 million; then it begins to climb.

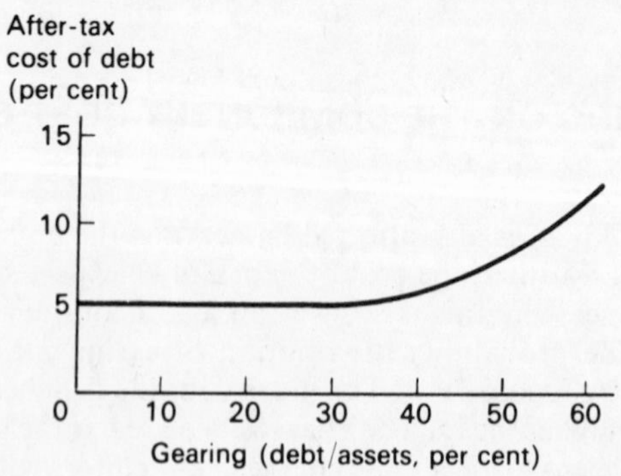

Figure 19–3 *Universal Machine Company: Weighted Average Cost of Capital.*

COMBINING DEBT AND EQUITY: WEIGHTED AVERAGE, OR COMPOSITE, COST OF CAPITAL

Debt and equity may now be combined to determine Universal Machine's average, or composite, cost of capital, and Table 19–5 shows the calculations used to determine the

Table 19–5 *Calculation of Points on Average Cost of Capital Curve (per cent), or the Composite Cost of Capital for Different Capital Structures.*

	Percentage of total (1)	Component costs (2)	Weighted, or composite, cost: $k = (1) \times (2) \div 100$ (3)[a]
Debt	0	5.0	0
Equity	100	12.0	12.0
	100		12.0
Debt	20	5.0	1.0
Equity	80	12.6	10.1
	100		11.1
Debt	30	5.5	1.7
Equity	70	12.9	9.0
	100		10.7
Debt	40	6.5	2.6
Equity	60	14.4	8.6
	100		11.2
Debt	50	8.0	4.0
Equity	50	17.0	8.5
	100		12.5
Debt	60	13.5	8.1
Equity	40	21.4	8.6
	100		16.7

[a] We divide by 100 to obtain percentage; figures rounded to nearest hundredth.

weighted average cost.[22] The average cost, together with the component cost of debt and equity, is plotted against the debt ratio in Figure 19–4. Here we see that the composite cost of capital is minimized when its debt ratio is approximately 35 per cent, so Universal's optimal capital structure calls for about 35 per cent debt, 65 per cent equity.

It is important to note that the average cost of capital curve is relatively flat over a fairly broad range: if Universal Machine's debt ratio is in the range of 20 to 40 per cent, the average cost of capital cannot be lowered very much by moving to the optimal point. This appears to be a fairly typical situation, as almost any 'reasonable' schedule for the component costs of debt and equity will produce a saucer-shaped average cost of capital schedule similar to that shown in Figure 19–4. This gives financial managers quite a degree of flexibility in planning their financing programmes, permitting them to sell debt one year, equity the next, in order to take advantage of capital market conditions and to avoid high flotation costs associated with small security issues.

Table 19–5 and Figure 19–4 are based on the assumption that the firm is planning to raise a given amount of new capital during the year. For a larger or smaller amount of new

---

22. A generalized equation can be used to calculate the weighted cost of capital:

$$k = \sum_{t=1}^{n} w_i k_i$$

where w_i is the weight of the ith type of capital and k_i is the cost of the ith component. If the firm had one class of debt, preference shares and equity, k would be found as

$$k = w_b k_b + w_{ps} k_{ps} + w_s k_s.$$

It would, of course, be possible to expand this equation to encompass long- and short-term debt, convertibles, 'free' capital, and the like.

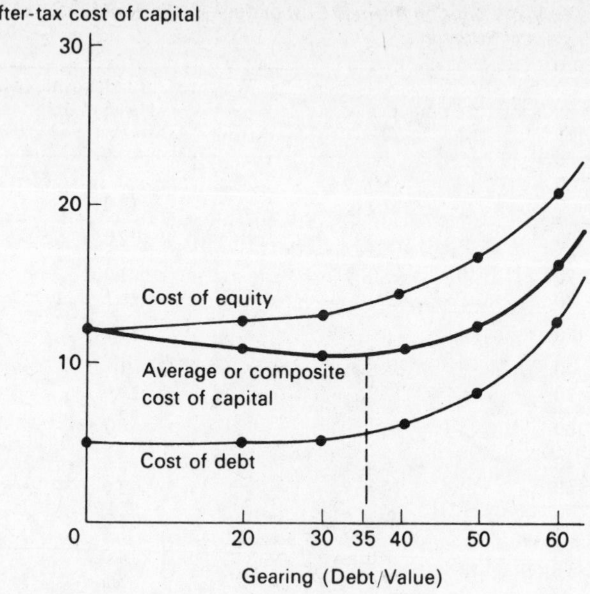

Figure 19–4 *Universal Machine Company: Cost of Capital Curves.*

capital, some other cost figures might be applicable; the optimal capital structure might call for a different debt ratio, and the minimum average cost of capital (k) might be higher or lower. This point is discussed in detail later in the chapter.

HIGH-RISK AND LOW-RISK FIRMS

Shown in Figure 19–5 are the cost of capital schedules for a firm in a risky industry (R) and for one in a stable industry (S). Firm R, the one on which Figure 19–4 was based, is

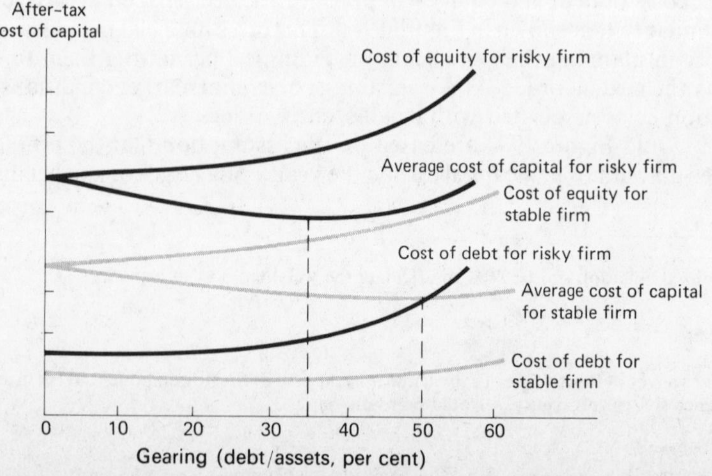

Figure 19–5 *Hypothetical Cost of Capital Schedules for High-risk (R) and Low-risk (S) Firms.*

Universal Machine; firm S is a relatively stable, safe company. We have already examined the interrelationships of the curves of Universal Machine – after declining for a while as additional low-cost debt is averaged in with equity, the average cost of capital for firm R begins to rise after debt has reached 35 per cent of total capital. Beyond this point, the fact that both debt and equity are becoming more expensive offsets the fact that the component cost of debt is less than that of ordinary equity.

While the same principles apply to the less risky firm, its cost functions are quite different from those of Universal Machine. In the first place, S's overall business risk is lower, giving rise to lower debt and equity costs at all debt levels. Further, its relative stability means that less risk is attached to any given percentage of debt; therefore, its costs of both debt and equity – and, consequently, its average cost of capital – turn up further to the right than do the corresponding curves for Universal Machine. The optimum debt ratio for the firm in the stable industry is 50 per cent as compared to only 30 to 35 per cent for Universal.

Determining the actual optimal capital structure for a specific firm requires both analysis and judgement, and it is up to a firm's financial manager to decide on the best capital structure for his company. Once this decision has been reached, the weighting system for the average cost of capital calculation is also determined. Unless otherwise noted, we will assume that management deems its present book value capital structure to be optimal, and we shall use this set of weights in our calculations.[23]

CALCULATING THE MARGINAL COST OF CAPITAL: AN ILLUSTRATION

The procedures discussed above are now applied to a theoretical company, the Maxwell Container Company, to illustrate the cost of capital calculation. Maxwell Container is a large firm, with assets of over £950 million and sales of over £1 billion. Sales and earnings are relatively stable, as food and drink companies make up the bulk of the firm's customers. Dividends have been paid since 1923, even during the depression of the 1930s. On the basis of an indicated dividend rate of £0.20 and a current price of £3.35 a share, the dividend yield is 6 per cent. Over the past 10 years, earnings, dividends and the price of the shares have grown at a rate of about 5 per cent; all indications suggest that this same rate of growth will be maintained in the foreseeable future.[24] Since internally generated funds provide sufficient equity, only the costs of internal equity, found in this case to be the 6 per cent dividend yield plus the 5 per cent growth rate, or a total of 11 per cent, need be considered.

The average interest rate on Maxwell Container's outstanding debt is 4.5 per cent, but much of this debt was issued in earlier years when interest rates were much lower than they are now. Current market yields on both long-term and short-term debt are about 8 per cent, and approximately this cost will be associated with new debt issues. After a 50 per cent corporation tax, the cost of debt is estimated to be 4 per cent. The preference shares pay a dividend of 3.75 per cent, but they were also issued when rates were low. On the basis of current market yields, the estimated cost of new preference shares is 7.5 per cent (net of tax).

The left-hand side of Maxwell Container's balance sheet is given in Table 19–6. A large portion (24 per cent) of the firm's funds are 'free' in the sense that no interest is charged for them – trade creditors and accruals are in this class. Some would argue that in the

23. The weights used to calculate the marginal cost of capital, k, should theoretically be based on market values.
24. Earnings per share for 1964 were £0.226 while *EPS* for 1974 were £0.365. Dividing £0.365 by £0.226 gives 1.62, which is the *CVIF* for 10 years at 5 per cent from Table D–1. Thus, *EPS* grew at a 5 per cent rate over the 10-year period from 1964 to 1974. Dividends grew similarly, and security analysts are projecting a continuation of these rates.

Table 19–6 *Maxwell Container Company, Left-hand Side of Balance Sheet (£millions).*

			non-free funds only	
Creditors and accruals	£186	19.4%		
Corporation tax payable	44	4.6		
Total 'free' current funds	£230	24.0%		
Owners' equity	£560	58.5%	£560	77%
Preference shares	7	0.8	7	1
Debenture capital	160	16.7	160	22
Non-free funds	727	76.0%	£727	100%
Total financing	£957	100.0%		

calculation of the overall cost of capital, this 'free' capital should be included. Under certain circumstances this procedure is valid; usually, however, only 'non-free' capital need be considered.[25] Of the target, or chosen long-term capital structure, 22 per cent is debt, 1 per cent is preference shares and 77 per cent is equity. This means, in effect, that each £1 of new capital is raised as £0.22 of debt, £0.01 of preference shares, and £0.77 as equity (retained earnings or new shares).

If management believes that some other capital structure is optimal, then other weights would be used; for purposes of illustration it is assumed that the existing structure has been determined to be the optimum. Further, let us assume that Maxwell Container plans to raise £20 million during the current year. To maintain the target capital structure, this £20 million must be raised as follows: £4.4 million as debt, £0.2 million as preference shares and £15.4 million as equity. Also, note that all equity is obtained in the form of retained earnings. On the basis of these weights and the previously determined costs of debt, equity and preference shares, the calculations shown in Table 19–7 indicate that

Table 19–7 *Maxwell Container Company, Illustrative Calculation of Average Cost of Capital: £20 millions New Capital.*

	Amount of capital (1)	Proportions (2)	Component costs (3)	Product (2) × (3) = (4)
Owners' equity	£15.4	77.0%	11.0	0.0847
Preference shares	0.2	2.0	7.5[a]	0.0008
Debentures	4.4	22.0	4.0	0.0088
	£20.0	100.0%		$k = 0.0943 = 9.4\%$

[a] Net of standard rate of tax.

25. The primary justification for ignoring 'free' capital is that, in the capital budgeting process, these spontaneously generated funds are netted out against the required investment outlay, then ignored in the cost of capital calculation. To illustrate, consider a retail firm thinking of opening a new shop. According to customary practices, the firm should (a) estimate the required outlay, (b) estimate the net receipts (additions to profits) from the new shop, (c) discount the estimated receipts at the cost of capital, and (d) accept the decision to open the new shop only if the net present value of the expected revenue stream exceeds the investment outlay. The estimated accruals, trade creditors, and other costless forms of credit are deducted from the investment to determine the 'required outlay' before making the calculation. Alternatively, 'free' capital could be costed in, and working capital associated with specific projects added in when determining the investment outlay. In most instances, the two procedures will result in similar decisions.

Maxwell Container's composite cost of new capital is 9.4 per cent. As long as Maxwell Container finances in the indicated manner and uses only retained earnings of equity, each pound of new funds should cost this amount.

Marginal cost of capital when new equity is used

In the preceding example of Maxwell Container, we assumed that the company would finance only with debt, preference shares and *internally generated equity*. On this basis we found the weighted average cost of new capital, or the marginal cost of capital, to be 9.4 per cent. What would have occurred, however, if the firm's need for funds had been so great that it was forced to sell new ordinary shares? The answer is that its marginal cost of new capital would have increased. To show why this is so, we shall extend the Maxwell Container example.

First, suppose that during 1975 Maxwell Container had total earnings of £59 million available for ordinary shareholders, paid £27 million in dividends, and retained £32 million. We know that to keep the capital structure in balance, the retained earnings should equal 77 per cent of the net addition to capital, the other 23 per cent being debt and preference shares. Therefore, the total amount of new capital that can be obtained on the basis of the retained earnings is

$$\text{Retained earnings} = (\text{per cent equity})(\text{new capital})$$

$$\text{New capital} = \frac{\text{retained earnings}}{\text{per cent equity}}$$

$$= \frac{£32 \text{ million}}{0.77} = £41.6 \text{ million.}$$

Next, we note that 1 per cent of the new capital, or about £400 000, should be preference shares and that 22 per cent, or £9.2 million, should be debt. In other words, Maxwell Container can raise a total of £41.6 million – £32 million from retained earnings, £9.2 million in the form of debt, and £400 000 in the form of preference shares – and still maintain its target capital structure in exact balance.

Table 19–8 *Calculation of Maxwell Container's Marginal Cost of Capital Using New Ordinary Shares.*

1. Find the cost of new equity:

$$\text{Cost of new equity} = \frac{\text{dividend yield}}{(1 - \text{flotation percentage})} + \text{growth}$$

$$k_e = \frac{0.06}{0.90} + 5\% = 11.7\%$$

2. Find the new weighted or composite cost of each £1 of new capital in excess of £41.6 million, using only new ordinary shares for the equity component:

	Proportion ×	component cost =	product
Equity (new)	77%	11.7[a]	0.0901
Preference shares	1	7.5[a]	0.0008
Debt	22	4.0	0.0088
	100%		$k =$ 0.0997
			≈ 10%

[a] Net of standard rate of tax.

If all financing up to £41.6 million is in the prescribed proportions, the composite cost of each pound of new capital *up to £41.6 million* is still 9.4 per cent, the previously computed weighted average cost of capital. In Table 19–7, we showed the calculation of the weighted average cost of raising £20 million; had we made the calculation for any other amount *up to £41.6 million*, the weighted average cost would have also been 9.4 per cent. Thus, each pound of new capital costs 9.4 per cent, so this is the marginal cost of capital.

As soon as the total of the required funds exceeds £41.6 million, however, Maxwell must begin relying on more expensive new equity. Therefore, beyond £41.6 million we must compute a new marginal cost of capital. Assuming Maxwell Container would incur a flotation cost on new equity issues equal to 10 per cent, we could compute the cost of capital for funds over £41.6 million as shown in Table 19–8.

According to Table 19–7, as long as Maxwell Container raises no more than £41.6 million, its weighted average and marginal cost of new or incremental capital is 9.4 per cent, but, as we have shown in Table 19–8, every £1 over £41.6 million has a cost of 10 per cent, so the marginal cost beyond £41.6 million is 10 per cent.

OTHER BREAKS IN THE *MCC* SCHEDULE

The *marginal cost of capital schedule* shows the relationship between the weighted average cost of each £1 raised (k) and the total amount of capital raised during the year, other things, such as the riskiness of the assets acquired, held constant. In the preceding section, we saw that Maxwell Container's *MCC* schedule increases at the point where its retained earnings are exhausted and it begins to use more expensive new ordinary shares.

Actually, any time any component cost rises, a similar break will occur. For example, if Maxwell could obtain only £10 million of debt at 8 per cent, with additional debt costing 9 per cent, then this rise in k_b would produce a higher $k_b(1-T)$, which in turn would lead to a higher k. Where would this break occur? Under the assumptions made thus far for Maxwell Container, it would occur at £45.5 million, found as:

$$\begin{array}{c}\text{break in } MCC\\ \text{schedule caused by}\\ \text{rising debt cost}\end{array} = \frac{\begin{array}{c}\text{amount of lower-cost}\\ \text{debt}\end{array}}{\begin{array}{c}\text{debt as percentage}\\ \text{of capital raised}\end{array}}$$

$$= \frac{£10}{0.22} = £45.5 \text{ million.}$$

Now suppose only an additional £5 million, over and above the first £10 million, can be borrowed at 9 per cent, after which the component cost of new debt rises to 10 per cent. A new break will occur, this one at £68.2 million:

$$\frac{\begin{array}{c}\text{amount of lower-cost}\\ \text{debt}\end{array}}{\text{debt/total capital}} = \frac{£10 + £5}{0.22} = £68.2 \text{ million.}$$

Similar breaks could be caused by increases in the cost of preference shares, higher ordinary shares' flotation costs as more shares are sold, and perhaps even a change in k_s, the basic required rate of return on the firm's ordinary equity as discussed in Chapter 17.[26]

---

26. It has been argued that, as a company sells more and more shares or other types of securities, it must attract investors who are less and less familiar with and impressed by the company, hence that the securities must be sold at lower prices and higher yields. This pressure could affect all securities, new and old. If the sale of additional shares (permanently) lowers the price of old shares, then this reduction in value must be assessed as a marginal cost of the new shares.

In general, breaks in the *MCC* schedule will occur whenever any component cost increases as a result of the volume of capital raised, and the breaking points can be calculated by use of equation 19–10:

$$\text{break in } MCC = \frac{\text{Total amount of lower-cost capital for a given component}}{\text{percentage of total capital represented by the component}} \tag{19–10}$$

If we determined that Maxwell Container would experience higher component costs for debt at £10 million and at £15 million, for preference shares at £5 million, and for ordinary shares at £32 million (when retained earnings are exhausted) and at £50 million, then equation 19–10 could be used to compute breaks in the company's *MCC* schedule:

Point where break occurs	Cause of break	k in interval before break
£41.5 million	(shift from k_r to k_e)	9.4%
45.5	(rising k_b)	10.0
64.9	(rising k_e)	10.6
68.2	(rising k_b)	11.2
500.0	(rising k_{ps})	11.6

It is necessary to calculate a different $MCC = k$ for the interval between each of the breaks in the *MCC* schedule. For example, we have already calculated the *MCC* from nil to £41.5 million as 9.4 per cent, and that from £41.5 to £45.5 million as 10 per cent. The values of k for each interval are shown above, and they are plotted as the step-function *MCC* schedule shown in Figure 19–6, panel (a).

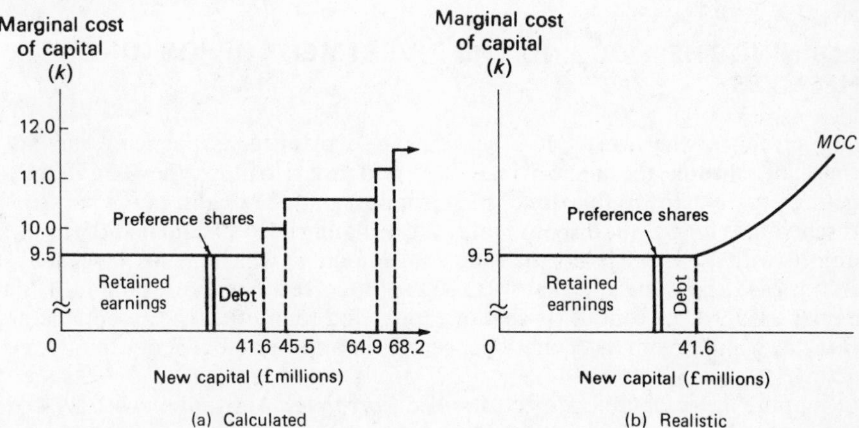

Figure 19–6 *Relationship between Marginal Cost and Amount of Funds Raised.*

This graph is highly idealized; in fact, the actual *MCC* curve looks much more like that shown in Figure 19–6(b). Here we see that the curve is flat until it reaches the vicinity of £41.6 million; it then turns up gradually and continues rising. It will go up gradually rather than suddenly because the firm will probably make small adjustments to its target debt ratio, its dividend payout ratio, the actual types of securities it uses, and so on. And the curve will continue to rise, because, as more and more of its securities are put on the market during a fairly short period, it will experience more and more difficulty in getting the market to absorb the new securities.

Ordinarily, a firm will calculate its *MCC* schedule as a step-function similar to the one shown in Figure 19–6(a), then 'smooth it out' by connecting the values of k shown in the middle of each interval. When one recognizes the types of estimates and approximations that go into the step-function curve, the smoothing process is less arbitrary than it might first appear to be.

In the earlier analysis associated with Figure 19–5, we were investigating the influence of the financing mix or financial structure on the firm's cost of capital. The financing mix was being varied, but not the total amount of capital raised. Since a marginal cost is the increment in cost as the total amount of financing is increased, when we vary the financing mix holding the total amount of financing constant, the relevant cost of capital is the weighted average cost of capital (WACC). We can say either that no marginal cost of capital is involved or that the marginal cost of capital is equal to the WACC. We use the symbol, k, as the WACC.

In the present analysis, Figure 19–6 portrays the effects of increasing the total amount of new financing, holding the financing mix fixed at the optimal proportions. We then calculate the weighted marginal cost of capital. In Figure 19–6 over the flat segment of the *MCC* curve, the average cost of capital is equal to the marginal cost of capital. When the marginal cost of capital begins to rise, the curve that is an average cost in relation to the *MCC* lies below the *MCC*. (If nine people all six feet tall come into a room in sequence, the average and marginal height will be six feet. If the tenth person entering is seven feet tall, the marginal height will be seven feet, but the average height will be 6.1 feet.) We exhibit only the *MCC* in Figure 19–6 because we are analysing the determination of the size of the total capital budget for a firm, and hence the *MCC* is relevant as the investment hurdle rate. But recall that we are holding the financing mix at its optimal proportions, so that the *MCC* for each amount of new financing is also the WACC for the optimal mix of financing that minimizes the level of the *MCC* curve. For these reasons, we again use k as the symbol for the cost of capital along the *MCC* curve.

COMBINING THE *MCC* AND THE INVESTMENT OPPORTUNITY SCHEDULES

Having developed the firm's *MCC* schedule, and planned its financing mix so as to minimize the schedule, the financial manager's next task is to utilize the *MCC* in the capital budgeting process. How is this done? First, suppose that the k value in the flat part of the *MCC* schedule is used as the discount rate for calculating the *NPV* and that the total cost of all projects with $NPV > 0$ is less than the total amount at which the *MCC* schedule turns up. In this case, the value of k that was used is the correct one. For example, if Maxwell Container used 9.4 per cent as its cost of capital and found that the acceptable projects totalled £41.6 million or less, then 9.4 per cent is the appropriate cost of capital for capital budgeting.[27]

But suppose the acceptable projects totalled *more than* £41.6 million with a 9.4 per cent discount rate. What do we do now? The most efficient procedure is given below:

Step 1

Calculate and plot the *MCC* schedule as shown in Figure 19–6.

---

27. We are, of course, abstracting from project risk; here we assume that the average riskiness of all projects undertaken is equal to the average riskiness of the firm's existing investments. Some projects may be more risky than average, hence call for a risk-adjusted cost of capital > 9.4 per cent, while others are less risky than average and call for a cost of capital < 9.4 per cent.

Step 2

Ask the operating personnel to estimate the total cost of acceptable projects at a range of discount rates, say 14 per cent, 13 per cent, 12 per cent, 11 per cent, 10 per cent and 9 per cent. There will, thus, be an estimate of the capital budget at a series of k values. For Maxwell Container, these values were estimated as follows:

k	Capital budget
14%	£20 million
13	30
12	40
11	50
10	60
9	70

Step 3

Plot the k, capital budget points, as determined in Step 2 on the same graph as the *MCC*; this plot is labelled *IRR* in Figure 19–7.[28]

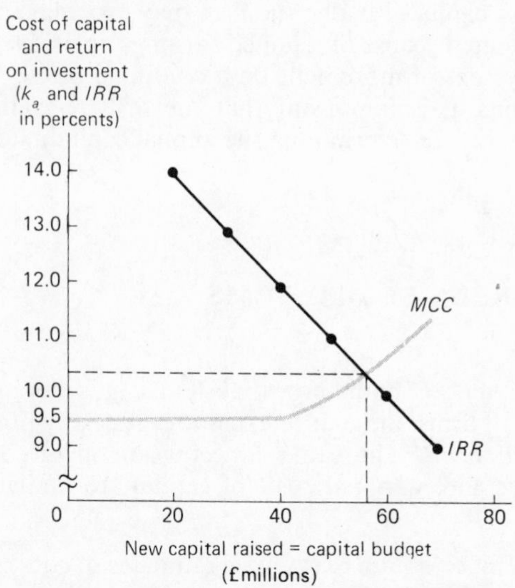

Figure 19–7 *Interfacing the* MCC *and* IRR *Curves to Determine the Total Capital Budget for a Given Time Period.*

---

28. To see why the k, capital budget line, is a type of *IRR* curve, consider the following:

1. The *NPV* of a project is nil if the project's *IRR* is equal to k.
2. Now suppose we determine that no projects have $NPV \geq 0$ at $k = 15\%$. This means that no projects have $IRR \geq 15\%$.
3. Next, suppose we determine that £20 million of projects have $NPV \geq 0$ at $k = 14\%$. This means that these projects all have $14\% \leq IRR \leq 15\%$.
4. If the projects were completely divisible, and if we examined very small changes in k, then we would have a continuous *IRR* curve. As it is, the curve labeled *IRR* in Figure 19–7 is an approximation. In any event, the example does illustrate how an *IRR* curve can be developed even though a company uses the *NPV* capital budgeting method.

Step 4

The correct *MCC* for use in capital budgeting – assuming both the *MCC* and *IRR* curves are developed correctly – is the value at the intersection of the two curves, 10.4 per cent. If this value of k is used to calculate *NPVs*, then projects totalling £56 million will have *NPVs* greater than nil. This is the capital budget that will maximize the value of the firm.

DYNAMIC CONSIDERATIONS

Conditions change over time; when they do, the firm must make adjustments. First, the firm's own individual situation may change. For example, as it grows and matures its business risk may decline; this may, in turn, lead to an optimal capital structure that includes more debt. Second, capital market conditions could undergo a pronounced, long-run change, making either debt or equity relatively favourable. This too could lead to a new optimal capital structure. Third, even though the long-run optimal structure remains unchanged, temporary shifts in the capital markets could suggest that the firm use either debt or equity, departing somewhat from the optimal capital structure, then adjust back to the long-run optimum in subsequent years. Fourth, the supply and demand for funds varies from time to time, causing shifts in the cost of both debt and equity, and, of course, in the marginal cost of capital. Finally, the firm may experience an almost unconscious change in capital structure because of retained earnings unless its growth rate is sufficient to call for the employment of more debt on a continual basis.

For all these reasons, it is important that the firm re-examine its cost of capital periodically, especially before determining the annual capital budget or engaging in new long-term financing.[29]

LARGE FIRMS VERSUS SMALL FIRMS

Before closing this chapter, we should note that significant differences in capital costs exist between large and small firms; these differences are especially pronounced in the case of privately owned small firms. The same concepts are involved, and the methods of calculating the average and marginal costs of capital are similar, but several points of difference arise:

1. It is especially difficult to obtain reasonable estimates of equity capital costs for small, privately-owned firms.
2. Tax considerations are generally quite important for privately-owned companies, as owner-managers may be in the top personal tax brackets. This factor can cause the effective after-tax cost of retained earnings to be appreciably lower than the after-tax cost of new outside equity.
3. Flotation costs for new security issues, especially new share issues, are much higher for small than for large firms (see Chapter 12).

---

29. Note that an exact calculation of a firm's need for funds cannot be made until the marginal cost of capital to be used in the capital budgeting process has been calculated. Thus, the marginal cost of capital and the amount of financing required for new projects should be simultaneously determined. This simultaneous determination is considered in Chapter 20, where dividend policy and internal financing decisions are discussed.

Points 2 and 3 both cause the marginal cost curves for small firms to rise rapidly once retained earnings are exhausted. These relationships have implications for the growth and development of large versus small firms; recognizing the plight of smaller companies, both the government and the financial institutions have set up a number of bodies to help them obtain finance.[30]

SUMMARY

In Chapter 17, the nature of the valuation process and the concept of expected rates of return were considered in some detail. The present chapter used these valuation concepts to develop an average cost of capital for the firm. First, the cost of the individual components of the capital structure – debt, preference shares and ordinary shares – were analysed. Next, these individual component costs were brought together to form an average, or composite, cost of capital. Finally, the conceptual ideas developed in the first two sections were illustrated with an example of the cost of capital for an actual company – Maxwell Container Company.

Cost of individual capital components

The *cost of debt*, $k_b(1-T)$, is defined as the interest rate that must be paid on new increments of debt capital multiplied by (1 – tax rate). The cost of preference capital to the company is the effective yield and this is found as the annual net dividend paid on preference shares divided by the net price the company receives when it sells new preference shares. In equation form the cost of preference shares is

$$\text{cost of preference shares} = k_{ps} = \frac{\text{net dividend paid on preference shares}}{\text{net price of preference shares}}$$

The *cost of equity capital* is defined as the minimum rate of return that must be earned on equity-financed investments to keep the value of the existing equity unchanged. This required rate of return is the rate of return that investors expect to receive on the company's ordinary shares – the dividend yield plus the capital gains yield. Sometimes, we assume that the investors expect to receive about the same rates of return in the future that they have received in the past; in this case, we can estimate the required rate of return on the basis of actual historical returns.

Equity capital comes from two sources, retained earnings and sale of new issues of ordinary shares. The basic required rate of return (k_r) is used for the cost of retained earnings. However, new shares have a higher cost because of the presence of flotation costs. The cost of new equity issues is computed as follows:

$$\text{Cost of new equity} = k_e = \frac{\text{dividend yield}}{(1-\text{flotation percentage})} + \text{growth.}$$

New ordinary shares are therefore usually more expensive than retained earnings.

Weighted average, or composite, cost of capital

The first step in calculating the weighted average cost of capital, k, is to determine the cost

30. See Chapter 25 for fuller details of financial help for smaller businesses.

of the individual capital components as described above. The next step is to establish the proper set of weights to be used in the averaging process. Unless we have reason to think otherwise, we generally assume that the present capital structure of the firm is at an optimum, where optimum is defined as the capital structure that will produce the minimum average cost of capital for raising a given amount of funds, or a minimum cost of incremental capital. The optimal capital structure varies from industry to industry, with more stable industries having optimal capital structures that call for the use of more debt than in the case of unstable industries.

Marginal cost

The marginal cost of capital schedule, defined as the cost of each additional £1 raised during the current year, is of interest for two reasons. First, the firm should finance in a manner that minimizes the *MCC* schedule, and therefore it must measure the *MCC*. Second, the *MCC* is the rate that should be used in the capital budgeting process – the firm should take on new capital projects only if their net present values are positive when evaluated at the marginal cost of capital.

The marginal cost of capital is constant over a range, then begins to rise. The rise is probably gradual, not abrupt, because firms make small adjustments in their target debt ratios, begin to use an assortment of securities, retain more of their earnings, and so on, as they reach the limit of internally generated equity funds.

QUESTIONS

19–1. Suppose that basic business risks to all firms in any given industry are similar.
(a) Would you expect all firms in each industry to have approximately the same cost of capital?
(b) How would the averages differ among industries?

19–2. Why are internally generated retained earnings generally less expensive than equity raised by selling shares? (Ignore personal tax implications.)

19–3. Describe how each of the following situations would affect the cost of capital to companies in general.
(a) The government solves the problem of business cycles (that is, cyclical stability is increased).
(b) The Bank of England takes action to lower interest rates.
(c) The cost of floating new share issues rises.

19–4. The firm's covariance is 0.014, the risk-free rate is 7 per cent, the market risk premium $(\bar{k}_M - R_F)$ is 5 per cent and the variance of the market returns is 1 per cent. With no liquidation costs, what is the cost of capital, k, for an ungeared firm? What is the beta of the firm?

19–5. Now assume that the information in 19–4 is all on an after-tax basis, the corporation tax rate is 50 per cent, and the firm has a debt to equity ratio of 50 per cent, with a debt cost of 10 per cent. What is the new beta of the firm? What is its required return on equity? What is the cost of capital for the geared firm?

19–6. An ungeared firm has a beta of 0.8. How much gearing can it employ if its corporation tax rate is 50 per cent and it aims to have a beta of 1.2?

19–7. The formula $k_r = (d_1/p_0) + g$, where d_1 = expected current dividend, p_0 = the current price of a share, and g = the past rate of growth in dividends, is sometimes used to estimate k_r, the cost of equity capital. Explain the implications of the formula.

19–8. What factors operate to cause the cost of debt to increase with financial gearing?

19–9. Explain the relationship between the required rate of return on equity (k_s^*) and the debt ratio.

19–10. How would the various component costs of capital, and the average cost of capital, be likely to change if a firm expands its operations into a new, more risky industry?

19–11. The shares of XYZ Company are currently selling at their low for the year, but management feels that the share price is only temporarily depressed because of investor pessimism. The firm's capital budget this year is so large that the use of new outside equity is contemplated. However, management does not want to sell new shares at the current low price and is therefore considering a departure from its 'optimal' capital structure by borrowing the funds it would otherwise have raised in the equity markets. Does this seem to be a wise move?

19–12. Explain the following statement: 'The marginal cost of capital is an average in some sense.'

PROBLEMS

19–1. On 1 January 1977, the total assets of the Rossiter Company were £60 million. By the end of the year total assets are expected to be £90 million. The firm's capital structure, shown below, is considered to be optimal. Assume there is no short-term debt.

Ordinary shares	£30 000 000
Preference shares (7% gross)	6 000 000
Debt (6% debentures)	24 000 000
	£60 000 000

New debentures will have an 8 per cent coupon rate and will be sold at par. Preference shares will have a 9 per cent gross dividend and will also be sold at par. Ordinary shares, currently selling at £3 a share, can be sold to net the company £2.70 a share. Shareholders' required rate of return is estimated to be 12 per cent, consisting of a dividend yield of 4 per cent and an expected growth of 8 per cent. Retained earnings are estimated to be £3 million (ignore depreciation). The marginal corporation tax rate is 50 per cent, and the standard rate of taxation is assumed to be 33 per cent.

(a) Assuming all asset expansion (gross expenditures for fixed assets plus related working capital) is included in the capital budget, what is the amount of the capital budget? (Ignore depreciation.)
(b) To maintain the present capital structure, how much of the capital budget must be financed by equity?
(c) How much of the new equity funds needed must be generated internally? externally?
(d) Calculate the cost of each of the equity components.
(e) At what level of capital expenditures will there be a break in the *MCC* schedule?
(f) Calculate the *MCC* (i) below and (ii) above the break in the schedule.
(g) Plot the *MCC* schedule. Also, draw in an *IRR* schedule that is consistent with the *MCC* schedule and the projected capital budget.

19–2. The Austen Company has the following capital structure as of 31 December 1978.

Ordinary shares (4 000 000)	£ 4 000 000
Retained earnings	12 000 000
	16 000 000
Preference shares ($8\frac{1}{2}$%)	4 000 000
Debentures (8%)	12 000 000
Total capitalization	£32 000 000

Earnings per share have grown steadily from 9 pence in 1967 to 20 pence estimated for 1978. The investment community, expecting this growth to continue, applies a price/earnings ratio of 18 to yield a current market price of £3.60. Austen's last annual net dividend was $12\frac{1}{2}$ pence and it expects the dividend to grow at the same rate as earnings. The addition to retained earnings for 1978 is projected at £4 million; these funds will be available during the next budget year. The corporation tax rate is 50 per cent, and the standard rate of income tax is 33 per cent.

Assuming that the capital structure relations set out above are maintained, new securities can be sold at the following costs:

Debentures: Up to and including £3 million of new debentures, 8 per cent yield to investor on all new debentures.
From £3.01 to £6 million of new debentures, $8\frac{1}{2}$ per cent yield to investor on this increment of debentures.
Over £6 million of new debentures, 10 per cent yield to investor on this increment of debentures.

Preference shares:[31] Up to and including £1 million of preference shares, $8\frac{1}{2}$ per cent yield to investor on all new preference shares.
From £1.01 to £2 million of preference shares, 9 per cent yield to investor on this increment of preference shares.
Over £2 million of preference shares, 10 per cent yield to investor on this increment of preference shares.

Ordinary shares: Up to £4 million of new external equity, £3.6 a share less £0.25 a share flotation cost.
Over £4 million of new external equity, £3.6 a share less £0.5 a share flotation cost on this increment of new equity.

(a) At what amounts of new capital will breaks occur in the *MCC*?
(b) Calculate the *MCC* in the interval between each of these breaks, then plot the *MCC* schedule.
(c) Discuss the breaking points in the marginal cost curve. What factors in the real world would tend to make the marginal cost curve smooth?
(d) Assume now that Austen has the following investment opportunities:
 (i) It can invest any amount up to £4 million at an 11 per cent rate of return.
 (ii) It can invest an additional £8 million at a 10.2 per cent rate of return.
 (iii) It can invest still another £12 million at a 9.3 per cent rate of return.
Thus, Austen's total potential capital budget is £24 million. Determine the size of the company's optimal capital budget for the year.

19-3. The following tabulation gives earnings-per-share figures for the Burnham Company during the preceding 10 years. The firm's ordinary shares, 140 000 shares outstanding, are now selling for £5 a share, and the expected net dividend for the current year is 50 per cent of the 1978 *EPS*. Investors expect past trends to continue.

Year	*EPS* (pence)
1969	20.0
1970	21.6
1971	23.3
1972	25.2
1973	27.2
1974	29.4
1975	31.8
1976	34.3
1977	37.0
1978	40.0

New preference shares paying a 50 pence net dividend could be sold to the public at a price of £5.25, which includes a 25 pence flotation cost (that is, the net price to Burnham is £5). The current interest rate on new debt is 8 per cent. The firm's marginal tax rate is 40 per cent, and standard rate of income tax is 33 per cent. The firm's capital structure, considered to be optimal, is as follows:

Ordinary shares	£ 7 000 000
Preference shares (7%)	500 000
Debentures (6%)	£2 500 000
	£10 000 000

(a) Calculate the after-tax cost (i) of new debt, (ii) of new preference shares and (iii) of equity, assuming new equity comes only from retained earnings. Calculate the cost of equity as $k_r = d_1/p_0 + g$.
(b) Find the marginal cost of capital, again assuming no new ordinary shares are sold.
(c) How much can be spent for capital investments before external equity must be sold? (Assume that retained earnings available for 1979 investment are 50 per cent of 1978 earnings.)
(d) What is the marginal cost of capital (cost of funds raised in excess of the amount calculated in part (c) if the firm can sell new ordinary shares at £5 a share to net £4.50 a share? The cost of debt and of preference shares is constant.
(e) In the problem, we assume that the capital structure is optimal. What would happen if the firm deviated from this capital structure? Use a graph to illustrate your answer.

31. All preference dividends are shown gross.

19-4. The New River Manufacturing Company has the following capital structure as of 31 December 1978:

Ordinary shares	£ 3 000 000
Retained earnings	9 000 000
	12 000 000
9% debentures	8 000 000
	£20 000 000

The company is planning its investment programme for the next year. It expects the following funds to be available as needed for capital investment:

Additional retained earnings of 10 per cent £1 million at a cost
External equity 0 to 2 million at 11.1 per cent
2.1 to 5 million at 12 per cent
5.1 to 8 million at 15 per cent
Debt financing 0 to 2 million at 9 per cent
2.1 to 4 million at 10 per cent
4.1 to 6 million at 11.5 per cent

The company pays corporation tax at 50 per cent and intends to maintain debt at 40 per cent of total assets.

(a) Assume the company has investment possibilities of £15 million and that the average return after tax is expected to be 11 per cent. Compute the weighted average cost of the £15 million of new capital required. Should the investments be made?

(b) Assume the investment can be broken up into three £5 million blocks, each yielding 11 per cent. Compute the marginal cost of capital for each increase of £5 million. What should be the total investment?

(c) Would your answer be any different if the expected return on the three blocks of investment were different – say 10 per cent on one, 11 per cent on another, and 12 per cent on a third? (Assume the investments are independent of one another.)

SELECTED REFERENCES

Adler, Michael. On the risk-return trade-off in the valuation of assets. *Journal of Financial and Quantitative Analysis* (December 1969): 493–512.

Adler, Michael. The cost of capital and valuation of a two country firm. *Journal of Finance* 29 (March 1974): 119–132.

Alberts, W. W. and Archer, S. H. Some evidence on the effect of company size on the cost of equity capital. *Journal of Financial and Quantitative Analysis* 8 (March 1973): 229–245.

Ang, James S. Weighted average versus true cost of capital. *Financial Management* 2 (Autumn 1973): 56–60.

Archer, Stephen H. and Faerber, LeRoy G. Firm size and the cost of equity capital. *Journal of Finance* 21 (March 1966): 69–84.

Arditti, Fred D. Risk and the required return on equity. *Journal of Finance* 22 (March 1967): 19–36.

Arditti, Fred D. The weighted average cost of capital: some questions on its definition, interpretation and use, *Journal of Finance* 28 (September 1973): 1001–1007.

Arditti, Fred D. and Tysseland, Milford S. Three ways to present the marginal cost of capital. *Financial Management* 2 (Summer 1973): 63–67.

Barges, Alexander. *The Effect of Capital Structure on the Cost of Capital.* Englewood Cliffs, N. J.: Prentice-Hall, 1963.

Baron, David P. Firm valuation, corporate taxes, and default risk. *Journal of Finance* 30 (December 1975): 1251–1264.

Baxter, Nevins D. Leverage, risk of ruin, and the cost of capital. *Journal of Finance* 22 (September 1967): 395–404.

Ben-Shahar, Haim. The capital structure and the cost of capital: a suggested exposition. *Journal of Finance* 23 (September 1968): 639–653.

Ben-Shahar, Haim and Ascher, Abraham. Capital budgeting and stock valuation: comment. *American Economic Review* 57 (March 1967): 209–214.

Beranek, William. *The Effects of Leverage on the Market Value of Common Stocks.* Madison, Wisc.: Bureau of Business Research and Service, University of Wisconsin, 1964.

Beranek, William. The cost of capital, capital budgeting, and the maximization of shareholder wealth. *Journal of Financial and Quantitative Analysis* 10 (March 1975): 1–20.

Beranek, William. A little more on the weighted average cost of capital. *Journal of Financial and Quantitative Analysis* 10 (December 1975): 892.

Beranek, William. The weighted average cost of capital and shareholder wealth maximization. *Journal of Financial and Quantitative Analysis* 12 (March 1977): 17–32.

Bierman, Harold, Jr. Risk and the addition of debt to the capital structure. *Journal of Financial and Quantitative Analysis* 3 (December 1968): 415–423.

Blume, Marshall E. On the assessment of risk. *Journal of Finance* 26 (March 1971): 1–10.

Blume, Marshall E. and Friend, Irwin. A new look at the capital-asset pricing model. *Journal of Finance* 28 (March 1973): 19–34.

Bodenhorn, Diran. A cash flow concept of profit. *Journal of Finance* 19 (March 1964): 16–31.

Boness, A. James. A pedagogic note on the cost of capital. *Journal of Finance* 19 (March 1964): 99–106.

Boot, John C. G. and Frankfurter, George M. The dynamics of corporate debt management, decision rules, and some empirical estimates. *Journal of Financial and Quantitative Analysis* 7 (September 1972): 1956–1966.

Bower, Richard S. and Bower, Dorothy H. Risk and valuation of common stock. *Journal of Political Economy* 77 (May–June 1969): 349–362.

Brearley, R. A. A note on dividends and debt under the new taxation. *Journal of Business Finance* (Spring 1973): 66–68.

Brennan, M. J. A new look at the weighted average cost of capital. *Journal of Business Finance* (Spring 1973): 24–30.

Brewer, D. E. and Michaelson, J. The cost of capital, corporation finance, and the theory of investment: comment. *American Economic Review* 55 (June 1965): 516–524.

Brigham, Eugene F. and Smith, Keith V. The cost of capital to the small firm. *Engineering Economist* 13 (Fall 1967): 1–26.

Chapman Findlay III, M. The weighted average cost of capital and finite flows. *Journal of Business Finance and Accounting* (Summer 1977): 217–227.

Crockett, Jean and Friend, Irwin. Capital budgeting and stock valuation: comment. *American Economic Review* 57 (March 1967): 214–220.

Davis, E. W. and Yeomans, K. A. Market discount on new issues of equity: the influence of firm size, method of issue and market volatility. *Journal of Business Finance and Accounting* 3 (Winter 1976): 27–42.

Dickinson, J. P. and Kyuno, K. Corporate valuation: a reconciliation of the Modigliani–Miller and traditionalist view. *Journal of Business Finance and Accounting* (Summer 1977): 217–227.

Donaldson, Gordon, *Corporate Debt Capacity*. Boston: Division of Research, Harvard Business School, 1961.

Donaldson, Gordon. New framework for corporate debt capacity. *Harvard Business Review* 40 (March–April 1962): 117–131.

Donaldson, Gordon. Strategy for financial emergencies. *Harvard Business Review* 47 (November–December 1969): 67–79.

Durand, David. Cost of debt and equity funds for business: trends and problems of measurement. Reprinted in Ezra Solomon, ed., *The Management of Corporate Capital* New York: Free Press, 1959, 91–116.

Elton, Edwin J. and Gruber, Martin J. The cost of retained earnings – implications of share repurchase. *Industrial Management Review* 9 (Spring 1968): 87–104.

Elton, Edwin J. and Gruber, Martin J. Valuation and the cost of capital for regulated industries. *Journal of Finance* 26 (June 1971): 661–670.

Ezzell, John R. and Porter, R. Burr. Flotation costs and the weighted average cost of capital. *Journal of Financial and Quantitative Analysis* 11 (September 1976): 403–414.

Fama, Eugene F. Risk, return, and equilibrium: some clarifying comments. *Journal of Finance* 23 (March 1968): 29–40.

Fama, Eugene F. and Miller, Merton H. *The Theory of Finance*. New York: Holt, Rinehart and Winston, 1972.

Fox, A. F. The cost of retained earnings – a comment. *Journal of Business Finance and Accounting* (Winter 1977): 463–468.

Glenn, David W. Super premium security prices and optimal corporate financing decisions. *Journal of Finance* 1 (May 1976): 507–524.

Gordon, Myron, *The Investment, Financing, and Valuation of the Corporation*. Homewood, Ill.: Irwin, 1962.

Gordon, Myron and Halpern, Paul J. Cost of capital for a division of a firm. *Journal of Finance* 29 (September 1974): 1153–1163.

Grinyer, J. R. The cost of equity capital. *Journal of Business Finance* (Winter 1972).

Grinyer, J. R. The cost of equity capital – a reply, *Journal of Business Finance and Accounting* (Autumn 1975): 383–387.

Grinyer, John R. The cost of equity, the C.A.P.M. and management objectives under uncertainty. *Journal of Business Finance and Accounting* 3 (Winter 1976): 101–121.

Groves, R. E. V. and Samuels, J. M. A note on the cost of retained earnings and deferred taxes in the U.K. *Journal of Business Finance and Accounting* 3 (Winter 1976): 143–150.

Hakansson, Nils H. On the dividend capitalization model under uncertainty. *Journal of Financial and Quantitative Analysis* 4 (March 1969): 65–87.

Haley, Charles W. A note on the cost of debt. *Journal of Financial and Quantitative Analysis* 1 (December 1966): 72–93.

Haley, Charles W. Taxes, the cost of capital, and the firm's investment decisions. *Journal of Finance* 26 (September 1971): 901–917.

Hamada, Robert S. Portfolio analysis, market equilibrium and corporation finance. *Journal of Finance* 24 (March 1969): 13–32.

Haugen, Robert A. and Kumar, Prem. The traditional approach to valuing levered-growth stocks: a clarification. *Journal of Financial and Quantitative Analysis* 9 (December 1974): 1031–1044.

Haugen, Robert A. and Pappas, James L. Equilibrium in the pricing of capital assets, risk-bearing debt instruments, and the question of optimal capital structure. *Journal of Financial and Quantitative Analysis* 6 (June 1971): 943–954.

Haugen, Robert A. and Wichern, Dean W. The intricate relationship between financial leverage and the stability of stock prices. *Journal of Finance* 30 (December 1975): 1283–1292.

Heins, A. James and Sprenkle, Case M. A comment on the Modigliani-Miller cost of capital thesis. *American Economic Review* 59 (September 1969): 590–592.

Henderson, Glenn V. Jr. On capitalization rates for riskless streams. *Journal of Finance* 31 (December 1976): 1491–1493.

Hensted, J. R. The cost of equity capital – a comment. *Journal of Business Finance and Accounting* (Autumn 1974): 445–448.

Higgins, Robert C. Growth, dividend policy and capital costs in the electric utility industry. *Journal of Finance* 29, no. 4 (September 1974): 1189–1201.

Hirshleifer, Jack. Investment decisions under uncertainty: applications of the state-preference approach. *Quarterly Journal of Economics* (May 1966): 252–277.

Hite, Gallen L. Leverage, output effects, and the M-M theorems. *Journal of Financial Economics* 4 (March 1977): 177–202.

Jensen, Michael C. Risk, the pricing of capital assets, and the evaluation of investment portfolios. *Journal of Business* 42 (April 1969): 167–247.

Jensen, Michael C. and Meckling, William H. Theory of the firm: managerial behaviour, agency costs and ownership structure. *Journal of Financial Economics* 3 (October 1976): 305–360.

Keane, S. M. The cost of capital and the relevance on nondiversifiable risk. *Journal of Business Finance and Accounting* (Spring 1974): 129–144.

Keane, S. M. Some aspects of the cost of debt. *Accounting and Business Research* (Autumn 1975): 298–304.

Keane, S. M. The tax deductibility of interest payments and the weighted average cost of capital. *Journal of Business Finance and Accounting* (Winter 1976). 53–61.

Keenan, Michael. Models of equity valuation: the great serm bubble. *Journal of Finance* 25 (May 1970): 243–273.

Keenan, Michael and Maldonado, Rita M. The redundancy of earnings leverage in a cost of capital decision framework. *Journal of Business Finance and Accounting* 3 (Summer 1976): 43–56.

Korsvold, P. E. K. The cost of raising new private debt capital and capital market efficiency. *Journal of Business Finance* (Summer 1971): 3–7.

Krouse, Clement G. Optimal financing and capital structure programs for the firm. *Journal of Finance* 27 (December 1972): 1057–1072.

Kumar, Prem. Growth of stocks and corporate capital structure theory. *Journal of Finance* 30 (May 1975): 532–547.

Lee, Wayne Y. and Barker, Henry H. Bankruptcy costs and the firm's optimal debt capacity: a positive theory of capital structure. *Southern Economic Journal* 43 (April 1977): 1453–1465.

Lerner, Eugene M. and Carleton, Willard T. Financing decisions of the firm. *Journal of Finance* 21 (May 1966): 202–214.

Lerner, Eugene M. and Carlton, Willard T. The integration of capital budgeting and stock valuation. *American Economic Review* 54 (September 1964): 683–702; Reply. *American Economic Review* 57 (March 1967): 220–222.

Lerner, Eugene M. and Carlton, Willard T. *A Theory of Financial Analysis.* New York: Harcourt, 1966.

Lewellen, Wilbur G. *The Cost of Capital.* Belmont, Calif.: Wadsworth, 1969, chaps. 3–4.

Lewellen, Wilbur G. A conceptual reappraisal of cost of capital. *Financial Management* 3 (Winter 1974): 63–70.

Lintner, John. The cost of capital and optimal financing of corporate growth. *Journal of Finance* 18 (May 1963): 292–310.

Lintner, John. Dividends, earnings, leverage, stock prices and the supply of capital to corporations. *Review of Economics and Statistics* 44 (August 1962): 243–269.

Lintner, John. Security prices, risk, and maximal gains from diversification. *Journal of Finance* 20 (December 1965): 587–616.

Lintner, John. The aggregation of investors' judgments and preferences in purely competitive security markets. *Journal of Financial and Quantitative Analysis* 4 (December 1969): 347–400.

Long, Michael S. and Racette, George A. Stochastic demand, output and the cost of capital. *Journal of Finance* 29 (May 1974): 499–506.

Machol, Robert E. and Lerner, Eugene M. Risk, ruin, and investment analysis. *Journal of Financial and Quantitative Analysis* 4 (December 1969): 473–492.

Malkiel, Burton G. Equity yields, growth, and the structure of share prices. *American Economic Review* 53 (December 1963): 467–494.

Mao, James C. T. The valuation of growth stocks: the investment opportunities approach. *Journal of Finance* 21 (March 1966): 95–102.

McDonald, John G. Market measures of capital cost. *Journal of Business Finance* (Autumn 1970): 27–36.

Melnyk, Lew Z. Cost of capital as a function of financial leverage. *Decision Sciences* (July – October 1970): 327–356.

Miller, M. H. and Modigliani, Franco. Cost of capital to electric utility industry. *American Economic Review* (June 1966): 333–391.

Modigliani, Franco and Miller, M. H. The cost of capital, corporation finance and the theory of investment. *American Economic Review* 48 (June 1958): 261–297.

Modigliani, Franco and Miller, M. H. The cost of capital, corporation finance and the theory of investment: reply. *American Economic Review* 49 (September 1958): 655–669; Taxes and the cost of capital: a correction. *American Economic Review* 53 (June 1963): 433–443; Reply. *American Economic Review* 55 (June 1965): 524–527.

Mossin, Jan. Security pricing and investment criteria in competitive markets. *American Economic Review* 59 (December 1969): 749–756.

Mumey, Glen A. *Theory of Financial Structure.* New York: Holt, Rinehart and Winston, 1969.

Myers, Stewart C. A time-state preference model of security valuation. *Journal of Financial and Quantitative Analysis* 3 (March 1968): 1–34.

Myers, Stewart C. Interactions of corporate financing and investment decisions – implications for capital budgeting. *Journal of Finance* 29 (March 1974): 1–25.

Myers, Stewart C. The application of finance theory to public utility rate cases. *Bell Journal of Economics and Management Science* 3 (Spring 1972): 58–97.

Nantell, Timothy J. and Carlson, C. Robert. The cost of capital as a weighted average. *Journal of Finance* 30 (December 1975): 1343–1355.

Petry, Glenn H. Empirical evidence on cost of capital weights. *Financial Management* 4 (Winter 1975): 58–65.

Pettit, R. Richardson and Westerfield, Randolph. Using the capital asset pricing model and the market model to predict security returns. *Journal of Financial and Quantitative Analysis* 9 (September 1974): 579–605.

Pfahl, John K., Crary, David T. and Howard, R. Hayden. The limits of leverage. *Financial Executive* (May 1970): 48–55.

Pfahl, John K. and Crary, David T. Leverage and the rate of return required by equity. *Investment Process.* Scranton, Pa.: The International Textbook Company, 1970, 175–191.

Pogue, G. A. An extension of the Markowitz portfolio selection model to include variable transactions costs, short sales, leverage policies and taxes. *Journal of Finance* 25 (December 1970): 1005–1027.

Porterfield, James T. S. *Investment Decisions and Capital Costs.* Englewood Cliffs, N. J.: Prentice-Hall, 1965.

Quirin, G. David. *The Capital Expenditure Decision.* Homewood, Ill.: Irwin, 1967, chaps. 5–6.

Reilly, Raymond R. and Wecker, William E. On the weighted average cost of capital. *Journal of Financial and Quantitative Analysis* 8 (January 1973): 123–126.

Resek, Robert W. Multidimensional risk and the Modigliani-Miller hypothesis. *Journal of Finance* 25 (March 1970): 47–52.

Robichek, Alexander A. Risk and the value of securities. *Journal of Financial and Quantitative Analysis* 4 (December 1969): 513–538.

Robichek, Alexander A., McDonald, J. G. and Higgins, R. C. Some estimates of the cost of capital to electric utilities, 1954–1957: comment. *American Economic Review* 57 (December 1967): 1278–1288.

Robichek, Alexander A. and McDonald, John G. The cost of capital concept: potential use and misuse. *Financial Executive* 33 (June 1965): 2–8.

Robichek, Alexander A. and Myers, Stewart C. *Optimal Financial Decisions.* Englewood Cliffs, N. J.: Prentice-Hall, 1965.

Rosenberg, Barr and Guy, James. Beta and investment fundamentals. *Financial Analysts' Journal* 32 (May–June 1976): 60–72.

Schwartz, Eli. Theory of the capital structure of the firm. *Journal of Finance* 14 (March 1959): 18–39.

Schwartz, Eli and Aronson, J. Richard. Some surrogate evidence in support of the concept of optimal capital structure. *Journal of Finance* 22 (March 1967): 10–18.

Scott, David F. Jr. Evidence on the importance of financial structure. *Financial Management* 1 (Summer 1972): 45–50.

Scott, J. H. A theory of optimal capital structure. *Bell Journal of Economics* 7 (Spring 1976): 33–54.

Scott, J. H. Bankruptcy, secured debt, and optimal capital structure. *Journal of Finance* 32 (March 1977): 1–19.

Sharpe, William F. A simplified model for portfolio analysis. *Management Science* 10 (January 1963): 277–293.

Sharpe, William F. Capital asset prices: a theory of market equilibrium. *Journal of Finance* 19 (September 1964): 425–442.

Sharpe, William F. *Portfolio Analysis and Capital Markets.* New York: McGraw-Hill, 1970.

Sharpe, William F. Security prices, risk, and maximal gains from diversification. *Journal of Finance* 21, no. 4 (December 1966): 743–744.

Sloane, William R. and Reisman, Arnold. Stock evaluation theory: classification, reconciliation, and general model. *Journal of Financial and Quantitative Analysis* 3 (June 1968): 171–204.

Soldofsky, Robert M. and Miller, Roger L. Risk-premium curves for different classes of long-term securities, 1950–1966. *Journal of Finance* (June 1969): 429–445.

Solomon, Ezra. Leverage and the cost of capital. *Journal of Finance* 18 (May 1963).
Solomon, Ezra. Measuring a company's cost of capital. *Journal of Business* 28 (October 1955): 240–252.
Solomon, Ezra. *The Theory of Financial Management*. New York: Columbia University Press, 1963.
Solomon, Ezra. *The Management of Corporate Capital*. New York: Free Press, 1959.
Stapleton, R. C. A note on default risk, leverage and the MM theorem. *Journal of Financial Economics* 2 (December 1975): 377–382.
Stiglitz, Joseph E. A re-examination of the Modigliani–Miller theorem. *American Economic Review* 59 (December 1969): 784–793.
Tinsley, P. A. Capital structure, precautionary balances, and valuation of the firm: the problem of financial risk. *Journal of Financial and Quantitative Analysis* 5 (March 1970): 33–62.
Tobin, James. Liquidity preference as behavior towards risk. *Review of Economic Studies* 25 (February 1958): 65–86.
Vandell, Robert F. and Pennell, Robert M. Tight-money financing. *Harvard Business Review* 49 (September–October 1971): 82–97.
Vickers, Douglas. Profitability and reinvestment rates: a note on the Gordon paradox. *Journal of Business* 39 (July 1966): 366–370.
Vickers, Douglas. The cost of capital and the structure of the firm. *Journal of Finance* 25 (March 1970): 35–46.
Weston, J. Fred. A test of cost of capital propositions. *Southern Economic Journal* 30 (October 1963): 105–212.
Weston, J. Fred. Investment decisions using the capital asset pricing model. *Financial Management* 1 (Spring 1973): 25–33.
Whitmore, G. A. Market demand curve for common stock and the maximization of market value. *Journal of Financial and Quantitative Analysis* 5 (March 1970): 105–114.
Wippern, Ronald F. Financial structure and the value of the firm. *Journal of Finance* 21 (December 1966): 615–634.
Woods, J. R. The cost of capital raised by way of a rights issue. *Investment Analyst* (September 1975): 20–29.
Zander, F. W. A. The cost of capital for debt-financed investments. *Journal of Business Finance and Accounting* (Autumn 1977): 277–283.

Appendix A to Chapter 19:

Some Unresolved Issues on the Cost of Capital

In this appendix we will show how some of the issues glossed over earlier can affect the cost of capital calculation. The purpose here is as much to raise questions as to answer them, yet the material has important practical implications. Moreover, anyone engaged in financial management must understand all the implications underlying the practical judgements that the financial manager will necessarily be forced to make.

COST OF RETAINED EARNINGS

Whenever a firm retains a portion of its net income rather than paying it out in dividends, there is an 'opportunity cost' to shareholders. If the firm in question has a required rate of return of 12 per cent on its shares (i.e. $k_s = 12\%$), presumably its shareholders could have invested the retained earnings, had they been paid out in dividends, in other firms of similar risk and received a 12 per cent return. This 12 per cent is, under certain assumptions, the cost of retained earnings. The two assumptions are:

1. that the shareholder pays no tax on his dividends;
2. that he incurs no brokerage costs when re-investing dividend receipts.[1]

To the extent that these assumptions are not met, the opportunity cost of retained earnings may be higher or lower than the cost of new ordinary shares. The following example illustrates the relative costs of retained earnings and new equity capital, under the imputation tax system:

Miles Ltd has net earnings of £1 million and all its shareholders are in the 45 per cent marginal tax bracket (T_m). Standard rate of income tax (T_s) is equal to 33 per cent. Management expect that under present economic conditions shareholders will require any investment to earn 12 per cent (k_s) after corporation tax.

If the earnings are all paid out as dividends, then the recipients will pay additional income tax of

$$£1\,000\,000\left[1-\frac{(1-T_m)}{(1-T_s)}\right] \tag{19A-1}$$

$$= £1\,000\,000\left[1-\frac{(0.55)}{(0.67)}\right]$$

$$= £179\,100$$

1. There is also the question of whether investors prefer to receive their rewards in the form of dividends or as capital gains. The question is considered in some detail in Chapter 20, but here it is assumed that investors are indifferent to differences between dividends and capital gains.

Net income available to ordinary shareholders becomes

£1 000 000 − £179 100 = £820 900

The shareholders will then re-invest the proceeds in the shares of similar firms which they anticipate will earn a return of 12 per cent. The brokerage costs to the shareholders will average 3 per cent of the investments (f).

What rate of return must be earned internally to provide the shareholders with incremental income equal to those they could earn externally?

1. Net income to ordinary shareholders = £820 900
2. Net investment after brokerage costs = £820 900(1 − 0.03)
   = £796 273
3. Earnings on new investment = £796 273(0.12)
   = £95 653
4. Internal rate of return (k_r) required to provide shareholders with incremental income of £95 653:
   £95 653 = £1 000 000 (k_r)
   k_r = 9.56%
5. If the firm is able to earn 9.56%, after corporation tax, on retained earnings, the shareholders will be as well off as they would be if all earnings were paid out and then re-invested to yield 12 per cent. Therefore, in the above case the opportunity cost of retained earnings is less than the shareholders' required rate of return.

The above example illustrates a situation where $T_m > T_s$.

Suppose we have a situation where the shareholders' marginal tax rate was less than the standard rate of income tax, i.e. $T_s > T_m$. If the shareholders' marginal tax rate was 20 per cent, for example, then net income to ordinary shareholders becomes

1. $£1\,000\,000 - £1\,000\,000\left(1 - \dfrac{0.80}{0.67}\right)$

   $= £1\,000\,000\left(\dfrac{0.80}{0.67}\right)$

   = £1 194 030

2. Net investment after brokerage costs

   = £1 194 030(1 − 0.03)
   = £1 158 209

3. Earnings on new investment

   = £1 158 209(0.12)
   = £138 985

4. The internal rate of return (k_r) becomes 13.90%.

   In this case, therefore, the opportunity cost of retained earnings will be higher than the shareholders' required rate of return and retained earnings will become more expensive than new equity capital.

The relative costs of retained earnings and new equity capital will be determined by the relationship between the standard rate of income tax (and thus the rate of advance corporation tax) and the shareholders' marginal rate of tax. The relationship will be given by the formula

$$k_r = k_s \frac{(1 - T_m)}{(1 - T_s)} \cdot (1 - f).$$

We have assumed in the above example that Miles Ltd has a 100 per cent dividend payout. Groves and Samuels[2] have pointed out that a full payout policy is optimal only when $T_m = T_s$. If we introduce the possibility that $T_m \neq T_s$, then, as has been shown by Alan Fox,[3] the optimal payout policy becomes a function of T_m, T_s and T_g (the personal capital gains tax rate). In addition, we are left with the problem of defining the effective tax rates of investors. However, as Fox points out, if there exist within the market investors with a nil effective tax rate, it is they who should determine market prices and shareholders' returns. With an effective marginal tax rate (T_m) of nil, 100 per cent payout again becomes optimal.

2. R. E. Groves and J. M. Samuels, A note on the cost of retained earnings and deferred taxes in the U.K. *Journal of Business Finance and Accounting* (Winter 1976), pp. 143–149.
3. A. F. Fox, The cost of retained earnings – a comment. *Journal of Business Finance and Accounting* (Winter 1977), pp. 463–468.

COST OF DEPRECIATION-GENERATED FUNDS

The very first increment of cash flow used to finance any year's capital budget is depreciation-generated funds. In their statements of sources and uses of funds, companies generally show depreciation charges to be one of the most important sources of funds, if not the most important. For capital budgeting purposes, should depreciation be considered 'free' capital; should it be ignored completely; or should a charge be assessed against it? The answer is that a charge should indeed be assessed against these funds, and that this cost is approximately equal to the average cost of capital before outside equity is used.

The reasoning here is that the firm could, if it so desired, distribute the depreciation-generated funds to its shareholders and creditors, the parties who financed the assets in the first place. For example, if £10 million of depreciation-generated funds were available, the firm could either re-invest them or distribute them. If they are to be distributed, the distribution must be to both debenture-holders and shareholders in proportion to their shares of the capital structure; otherwise the capital structure will change. Obviously, this distribution should take place if the funds cannot be invested to yield the cost of capital, but retention should occur if the internal rate of return exceeds the cost of capital. Since the cost of depreciation-generated funds is equal to the average cost of capital, depreciation does not enter the calculation of the average cost of capital.

Depreciation does, however, affect the cost of capital *schedule* in a very significant way. Consider Figure 19–6: here we see that the cost of capital schedule begins to rise once the total funds raised goes beyond £41.6 million. However, if depreciation were considered to be a source of funds available for capital budgeting purposes, then the flat part of the curve would be extended out by the amount of the depreciation. In the Maxwell Container example, if depreciation amounted to £20 million, then the cost of capital schedule would begin to rise at £61.6 million rather than at £41.6 million.

What difference does all this make, and should we be concerned with a cost of capital schedule that includes or excludes depreciation? If we are concerned with the effects of *net increases* in assets, then the schedule without depreciation is appropriate. However, if we are concerned with gross capital expenditures – including replacement as well as expansion investments – then the schedule that includes depreciation is the relevant one.

Appendix B to Chapter 19:

The Effect of Capital Structure on Valuation and the Cost of Capital

A firm's value is dependent upon its expected earnings stream and the rate used to discount this stream, or the cost of capital; therefore, if capital structure is to affect value, it must do so by operating either on expected earnings or on the cost of capital, or on both. Because interest is tax-deductible, gearing generally increases expected earnings, at least as long as the firm does not use so much gearing that liquidation seriously threatens its continued existence. The effect of gearing on the cost of capital is much less clear; indeed, this issue has been one of the major controversies in finance for the past 20 or so years, and perhaps more theoretical and empirical work has been done on this subject than on any other in the field. In this appendix we set forth the major theories on the relationship between gearing and the cost of capital.

THE NET INCOME (NI) AND NET OPERATING INCOME (NOI) APPROACHES

Economists have identified two basic market structures – pure competition and pure monopoly – and they can determine the optimal price–quantity solution for firms in either of these two positions. Most firms in the real world are in the grey area of oligopoly, which lies somewhere between the pure cases, but an understanding of the pure cases is helpful in understanding oligopoly and real-firm behaviour.

The situation is similar with respect to gearing – there are two extreme positions corresponding to pure competition and pure monopoly, and a middle ground actually occupied by most if not all firms. David Durand, in a key article,[1] identified the two extreme cases:

Net Income Approach (*NI*). Under the NI approach to valuation, the interest rate and the cost of equity are independent of the capital structure, but the weighted average or overall cost of capital declines, and the total value (value of equity plus value of debt) rises, with increased use of gearing.

Net Operating Income Approach (*NOI*). Under the NOI approach, the cost of equity increases, the weighted average cost of capital remains constant, and the total value of the firm also remains constant as gearing is changed.

Thus, if the NI approach is the correct one, gearing is an important variable, and debt policy decisions have a significant influence on the value of the firm. However, if the NOI approach is the correct one, then the firm's management need not be too concerned with financial structure, because it simply does not greatly matter.

1. See David Durand, Costs of debt and equity funds for business: trends and problems of measurement, reprinted in Ezra Solomon, ed., *The Management of Corporate Capital* (New York: Free Press, 1959), pp. 91–116.

Basic assumptions and definitions

In order to focus on the key elements of the controversy, we begin by making several simplifying assumptions:

1. Only two types of capital are employed, long-term debt and ordinary shares.
2. There is no corporation tax. This assumption is later relaxed.
3. The firm's total assets are given, but its capital structure can be changed by selling debt to repurchase shares, or shares to redeem debt.
4. All earnings are paid out as dividends.
5. All investors have the same subjective probability distributions of expected future operating earnings ($EBIT$) for a given firm; that is, investors have homogeneous expectations.
6. The operating earnings of the firm are not expected to grow; that is, the firm's expected $EBIT$ is the same in all future periods.
7. The firm's business risk is constant over time and is independent of its capital structure and financial risk.
8. The firm is expected to continue indefinitely.

In addition to these assumptions, we shall use the following basic definitions and symbols:

S = total market value of the shares (equity).
B = total market value of the debentures (debt).
V = total market value of the firm = $S+B$.
$EBIT$ = earnings before interest and taxes = net operating income (NOI).
IC = interest payments.

Our next task is to specify and define the key cost of capital and valuation relationships:

1 *Debt*

$$\text{Cost of debt capital} = k_b = \frac{IC}{B}.$$

$$\text{Value of debt} = B = \frac{IC}{k_b}.$$

2. *Equity, or ordinary shares*

$$\text{Cost of equity capital} = k_s = \frac{d_1}{p_0} + g.$$

Here d_1 is the next dividend, p_0 is the current price per share, and g is the expected growth rate. According to assumption 4 above, the percentage of earnings retained, or the retention rate (b), is nil; since $g = br$, where r is the rate of return on equity, $g = br = 0 \times r = 0$; in other words, the growth rate is nil. This is consistent with assumption 6 above. Note also that $d_1 = (1-b)(e_1)$, and with $b = 0$, $d_1 = (1)(e_1) = e_1$. Thus,

$$k_s = \frac{d_1}{p_0} + g = \frac{e_1}{p_0} + 0 = \frac{e_1}{p_0}.$$

This equation is on a per-share basis; multiplying both the numerator and denominator by the number of shares outstanding (n), we obtain

$$k_s = \frac{e_1(n)}{p_0(n)} = \frac{EBIT - IC}{S} = \frac{\text{Net income available to shareholders}}{\text{Total market value of shares}}.$$

Thus, k_s may be defined on either a per-share or a total basis.

The value of the shares, or equity, is equal to earnings divided by the cost of equity. On a per-share basis:

$$p_0 = \frac{e_1}{k_s},$$

or on a total firm basis:

$$S = \left(\frac{EBIT - IC}{k_s}\right) = p_0 n.$$

3. *Overall, or weighted average, cost of capital*

The overall, or weighted average, cost of capital is

$$\begin{aligned} k &= w_b k_b + w_s k_s \\ &= \left(\frac{B}{V}\right)k_b + \left(\frac{S}{V}\right)k_s \\ &= \left(\frac{B}{B+S}\right)k_b + \left(\frac{S}{B+S}\right)k_s. \end{aligned}$$

4. The total value of the firm is thus

$$V = B + S$$
$$= \frac{IC}{k_b} + \frac{(EBIT - IC)}{k_s}$$

These equations are not controversial – they are simply definitions that apply under either the NI or NOI approaches. However, there are major differences between the NI and NOI theories, as we shall see in the next sections.

The net income (NI) approach

The basic difference between NI and NOI relates to what happens to k_s as the firm's use of debt changes. Under NI, k_s is assumed to be fixed and constant regardless of the firm's degree of financial gearing, while under NOI, k_s is assumed to change. (Both theories assume that k_b, the interest rate on debt, is constant.) To illustrate the NI approach, assume that a firm has £4 million of debt at 7.5 per cent, an expected annual net operating earnings ($EBIT$) of £900 000, and an equity capitalization rate (k_s) of 10 per cent. With no corporation tax, the NI approach gives the value of the firm as follows:

Net operating earnings ($EBIT$)	£ 900 000
Interest on debt (£4 million × 7.5%)	−300 000
Available to ordinary shareholders	£ 600 000
Market value of equity = S = £600 000/0.10	£ 6 000 000
Market value of debt = B = £300 000/0.075	4 000 000
Total market value of firm = $V = S + B$	£10 000 000

Notice that the component costs of capital under the NI approach are

k_b = 7.5 per cent, given as constant, and
k_s = 10 per cent, given as constant,

so

$$k = 7.5\left(\frac{4\,000\,000}{10\,000\,000}\right) + 10\left(\frac{6\,000\,000}{10\,000\,000}\right)$$
$$= 7.5(0.4) + 10(0.6)$$
$$= 3\% + 6\% = 9\%.$$

Now we can examine the effect of a change in financing mix on the firm's cost of capital and market value. Suppose the firm increases its gearing by selling £1 million of debt. What effect will this change have on the value of the firm and its cost of capital? Under the NI approach, it is assumed that the component costs of debt and equity are held constant at 7.5 per cent and 10 per cent, respectively, so the new situation will be as follows:

Net operating earnings ($EBIT$)	£ 900 000
Less: interest on debt (£5 million × 7.5 per cent)	−375 000
Available to ordinary shareholders	£ 525 000
S = £525 000/0.10 =	£ 5 250 000
B = £375 000/0.075 =	5 000 000
$V = B + S$ =	£10 250 000

The overall, or average, cost of capital is calculated as follows:

$$k = 7.5\left(\frac{5\,000\,000}{10\,250\,000}\right) + 10\left(\frac{5\,250\,000}{10\,250\,000}\right)$$
$$= 7.5\left(\frac{5}{10.25}\right) + 10\left(\frac{5.25}{10.25}\right) = 8.78\%.$$

Thus, using additional gearing has caused the total value of the firm to rise and the average cost of capital to fall.

Table 19B–1 *Effect of Capital Structure on Value and Cost of Capital: NI(*EBIT = *£900 000; Other Funds in £millions).*

Gearing Ratio						
$\frac{B}{V}$	0%	30.77%	65.12%	80.00%	93.62%	100.00%
Value of debt (B)	0	£3.000	£ 7.000	£ 9.000	£11.000	£12.000
Value of equity (S)	£9.000	£6.750	£ 3.750	£ 2.250	£ 0.750	0
Total value (V)	£9.000	£9.750	£10.750	£11.250	£11.750	£12.000
k_b	7.5%	7.5%	7.5%	7.5%	7.5%	7.5%
k_s	10.0%	10.0%	10.0%	10.0%	10.0%	10.0%
k	10.0%	9.2308%	8.3720%	8.000%	7.6595%	7.500%

Table 19B–1 shows the firm's overall cost of capital and total market value at different degrees of financial gearing, while the cost of capital figures are plotted in Figure 19B–1. Notice, in the table, that the firm's value rises steadily as the debt ratio increases, and, in both the table and the figure, that the overall, or average, cost of capital declines continuously.

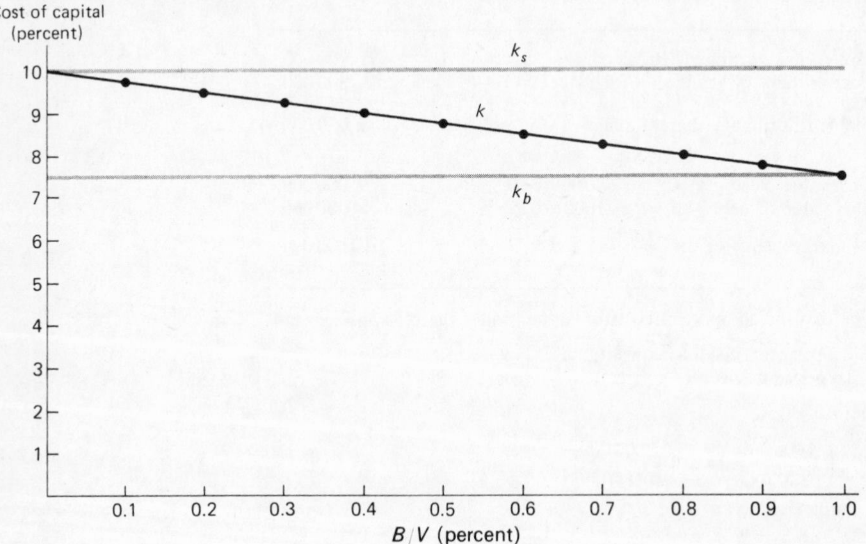

Figure 19B–1 *Cost of Capital under the NI Approach.*

The net operating income (NOI) approach

The second major approach, NOI, is closely identified with the works of Franco Modigliani and Merton Miller (MM), who strongly support NOI on the basis of their theoretical and empirical research.[2] In this section, we set forth the key features of the NOI approach, illustrate the cost of capital and valuation that result under NOI, and summarize Modigliani and Miller's theoretical arguments in support of NOI.

The major assumptions of the NOI approach (in addition to the set of assumptions common to both NI and NOI shown in the first section) are as follows:

1. In a world of no taxes, the total market value of the firm (V) is found by capitalizing net operating income

---

2. See F. Modigliani and M. H. Miller, The cost of capital, corporation finance and the theory of investment, *American Economic Review* 48 (June 1958), pp. 261–297, and The cost of capital, corporation finance and the theory of investment: reply, *American Economic Review* 49 (September 1958), pp. 655–669; Taxes and the cost of capital: a correction, *American Economic Review* 53 (June 1963), pp. 433–443; and Reply, *American Economic Review* 55 (June 1965), pp. 524–527.

($EBIT$ = NOI) at the overall cost of capital, k, which is a constant. Thus,

$$V = \frac{EBIT}{k}.$$

Since k is independent of financial mix, as is $EBIT$, V is also a constant and is independent of capital structure.

2. The value of the equity, or the total value of the shares (S), is found by subtracting the value of the debt (B) from V. Thus, $S = V - B$, which implies that S is a *residual* obtained by deducting the stated value of the debentures from the total value of the firm, *which was found by capitalizing* EBIT *or* NOI *at the constant overall cost of capital.*
3. The cost of equity was defined earlier as follows:

$$k_s = \frac{EBIT - IC}{S}.$$

As we shall see below, *this implies that k_s increases as gearing increases.*

4. The overall cost of capital is an average of the costs of debt and equity:

$$k = w_b k_b + w_s k_s = k_b\left(\frac{B}{V}\right) + k_s\left(\frac{S}{V}\right).$$

If the values of k and S are determined as shown above, then this value of k will equal the given and constant k for the firm. This point is also demonstrated in the examples given below.

We can use the data employed in the NI section to illustrate the NOI approach. Thus, the firm is assumed to have $EBIT$ = £900 000; a cost of debt (k_b) = 7.5%; an initial debt of £4 million; and an average cost of capital (k) = 10%. Under the NOI approach, the total value of the firm is calculated as follows:

Net operating income ($EBIT$)	£ 900 000
$V = B + S = EBIT/k$ = £900 000/0.10	£9 000 000
B = £4 000 000	−4 000 000
S = a residual =	£5 000 000

Given the value of the equity, we can now calculate the cost of equity capital as follows:

$$k_s = \frac{EBIT - IC}{S} = \frac{£900\,000 - 0.075(£4\,000\,000)}{£5\,000\,000}$$

$$= \frac{£600\,000}{£5\,000\,000} = 0.12 \text{ or } 12\%.$$

The weighted average cost of capital can now be calculated:

$$k = k_b\left(\frac{B}{V}\right) + k_s\left(\frac{S}{V}\right) = 7.5\%\left(\frac{4}{9}\right) + 12\%\left(\frac{5}{9}\right) = 3.33 + 6.67 = 10\%.$$

Thus, the average cost of capital is 10 per cent, just as the NOI theory says it should be.

If debt were increased to £5 million, the value of the firm would remain constant at £9 million, the value of the shares would drop to £4 million, and the cost of equity would rise to 13.12 per cent:

$$k_s = \frac{£900\,000 - 0.075(£5\,000\,000)}{£4\,000\,000} = \frac{£525\,000}{£4\,000\,000} = 13.12\%,$$

Table 19B-2 *Effect of Capital Structure on Value and Cost of Capital: NOI (*EBIT *= £900 000; Other Funds in £millions).*

$\frac{B}{V}$	0%	22.22%	44.44%	88.89%	100.00%
Debt (B)	0	£2.000	£4.000	£8.000	£9.000
Equity (S)	£9.000	£7.000	£5.000	£1.000	£ 0
Total value (V)	£9.000	£9.000	£9.000	£9.000	£9.000
k_b	7.5%	7.5%	7.5%	7.5%	7.5%
k_s	10.0%	10.71%	12.0%	30.0%	–
k	10.0%	10.0%	10.0%	10.0%	10.0%
$\frac{B}{S}$	0%	28.57%	80.00%	800.00%	–

and

$$k = 7.5\%\left(\frac{5}{9}\right) + 13.12\left(\frac{4}{9}\right) = 4.17 + 5.83 = 10\%.$$

Again, we see that the calculated average cost of capital is a constant.

Values for V, B, S, k and k_s at different debt ratios are shown in Table 19B-2, and a plot of the NOI cost of capital is shown in Figure 19B–2. The key features of these two exhibits are as follows:

1. Both the cost of debt (k_b) and the overall, or average, cost of capital (k) are constant.
2. The cost of equity (k_s) increases exponentially with gearing as measured by the ratio (B/V).[3]

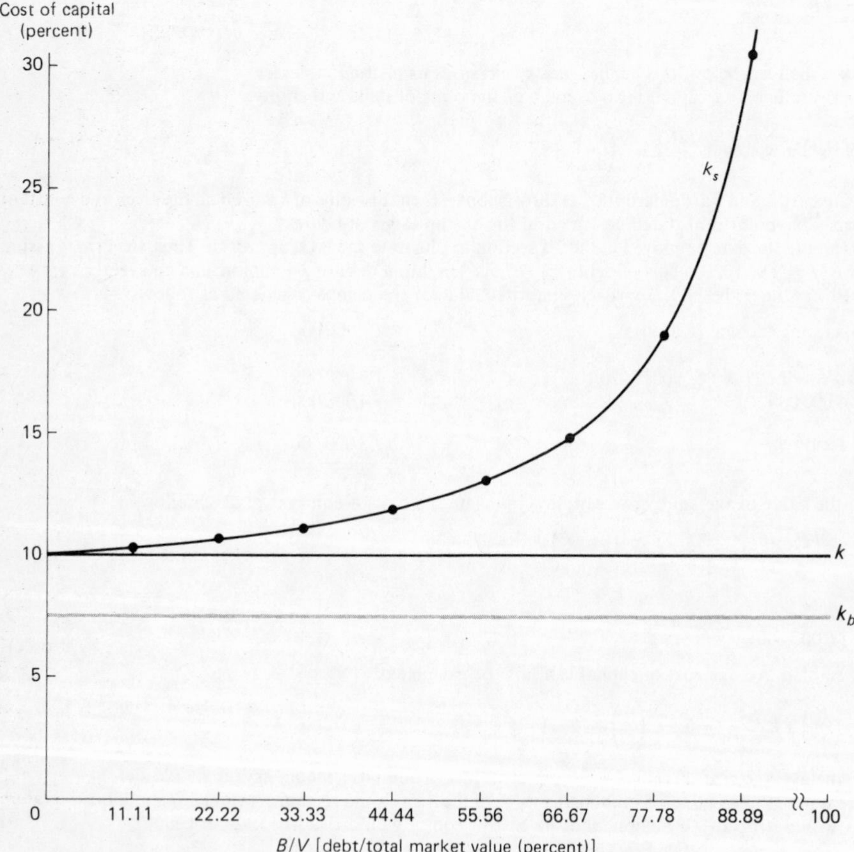

Figure 19B–2 *Cost of Capital under the NOI Approach, No Taxes.*

---

3. A firm's gearing can be measured (at market values) by either the debt-to-total-value ratio (B/V), or the debt/equity (B/S) ratio. Under the NOI–MM theory, the cost of equity is an exponential function of the B/V ratio (see Figure 19B–2) but a linear function of the B/S ratio. For a demonstration of this linear relationship, consider the following:

$$k = k_b(B/V) + k_s(S/V) \tag{19B-1}$$

or

$$k_s = \frac{k - k_b\left(\frac{B}{V}\right)}{\frac{S}{V}}. \tag{19B-2}$$

MODIGLIANI AND MILLER'S SUPPORT FOR NOI: THE ARBITRAGE ARGUMENT

Modigliani and Miller base their support of the NOI hypothesis on arbitrage, arguing that if two companies differ only in the way they are financed and in their total market value, investors will sell shares of the overvalued firm, buy those of the undervalued firm, and continue this process until the companies have the same market value. To illustrate the arbitrage argument, assume that two firms L (for levered [geared]) and U (for ungeared) are identical in all respects except financial structure. Firm L has £4 million of 7.5 per cent debt; firm U is all equity financed. Both firms have $EBIT$ = £900 000. In the initial situation, before arbitrage, both firms have an equity capitalization rate k_s = 10 per cent. Under these conditions, and assuming the NI approach is correct, the following situation will exist:

	Firm U	Firm L
Net operating income ($EBIT$)	£ 900 000	£ 900 000
Less interest on debt	0	−300 000
Available to ordinary shareholders	£ 900 000	£ 600 000
Value of equity (S)	£9 000 000	£ 6 000 000
Value of debt (B)	0	4 000 000
Total market value ($V = B + S$)	£9 000 000	£10 000 000

This is the NI solution, and MM argue that it cannot persist.

An investor in firm L can, according to MM, increase his total returns without increasing his financial risk. For example, suppose the investor owns 10 per cent of L's shares, so that his investment is £600 000. He can sell his shares in L, borrow an amount equal to 10 per cent of L's debt (£400 000), and then buy 10 per cent of U's shares for £900 000. Notice that the investor received £1 million from the sale of his shares plus borrowing, and spent £900 000 on U's shares so he has £100 000 in uncommitted funds.

Now consider the investor's income position:

Old income: 10% of L's £600 000 =		£60 000
New income: 10% of U's £900 000	£90 000	
Less 7.5% on £400 000 loan	−30 000	£60 000

Thus, his investment income is exactly the same as before, but he has £100 000 left over for investment elsewhere, so his total return will rise. Further, his risk, according to MM, is the same as before – he has simply substituted 'homemade' gearing for corporate gearing.

MM argue that this arbitrage process will occur, with sales of L's shares driving its price down and purchases of U's shares driving its price up, until the market values of the two firms are equal. When this equality is reached, the NOI conditions are fulfilled, and the value of the firms and their overall costs of capital are equal; that is, value

---

Now note that $V = B + S$, and that the equity ratio S/V may be rewritten as

$$\frac{S}{V} = 1 - \frac{B}{B+S}. \qquad (19B\text{–}3)$$

We may substitute (19B–2) and (19B–3) into (19B–1), then simplify as follows:

$$k_s = \frac{k - k_b \dfrac{B}{B+S}}{1 - \dfrac{B}{B+S}} = \frac{\dfrac{k(B+S) - k_b B}{B+S}}{\dfrac{B+S-B}{B+S}}$$

$$= \frac{kB + kS - k_b B}{S} = k + (k - k_b)\frac{B}{S}. \qquad (19B\text{–}4)$$

k and k_b are constants, so equation 19B–4 is of the form $y = a + bx$, which is linear. Equation 19B–4 states that the required rate of return on ordinary shares (k_s) is equal to the appropriate capitalization rate for a pure equity stream for that class (k) plus a premium for financial risk equal to the spread between that capitalization rate (k) and the yield on debt (k_b) times the debt–equity ratio (B/S). This expression for the cost of equity capital is referred to as MM's Proposition II.

and k are independent of capital structure. However, in reaching this conclusion, MM must make some important assumptions:

1. Their analysis implies that personal and company borrowing are perfect substitutes. In the case of company borrowings, the individual investing in the geared firm has only limited liability. If, however, he engages in arbitrage transactions, there is the possibility that he may lose not only his holdings in the ungeared firm but also his other assets.
2. In the analysis, transaction costs were assumed away, yet such costs may retard the arbitrage process.
3. Companies and individuals are assumed to borrow at the same rate. The cost of borrowing could be higher for the individual than for the firm.
4. At times, institutional restrictions may retard the arbitrage process. Institutional investors dominate stock markets today, yet some institutional investors are prohibited from engaging in 'homemade' gearing.

MM's critics argue that the assumptions of the MM model are invalid, and that, in the real world, firms' values and costs of capital are functions of financial gearing. We shall return to this debate later, after examining the situation when the assumption of no corporation tax is relaxed.

The Modigliani–Miller view with taxes

When taxes are introduced, MM's position changes: with corporation tax, they recognize that the geared firm commands a higher value because interest on debt is a deductible expense. Specifically, MM state that L's value exceeds that of U by an amount equal to L's debt multiplied by the tax rate:

$$V = V_U + BT.$$

Here V = value of firm L, V_U = value of firm U, B = amount of debt in L, and T = tax rate. Their proof goes as follows. Consider two firms that are identical in all respects except capital structure. Assume that firm U has no debt in its capital structure, while L employs debt, and that expected operating earnings, $EBIT = X$, are identical for each firm. Under these assumptions, the operating earnings after tax available to investors, X_U and X_L, for firms U and L respectively, are computed as follows:

$$X_U = X(1-T) \qquad (19B\text{–}5)$$

and

$$X_L = (X - k_b B)(1-T) + k_b B \qquad (19B\text{–}6)$$

where T = tax rate, k_b = interest rate on debt, and B = amount of debt. The first term to the right of the equal sign in equation 19B–6 is the income available to shareholders; the second term is that available to debenture-holders.

Since firm U does not employ debt, its value (V_U) may be determined by discounting its annual net income after corporation tax, $X(1-T)$, by its capitalization rate, k_U:

$$V_U = \frac{X(1-T)}{k_U}. \qquad (19B\text{–}7)$$

The geared firm's after-tax income, X_L, as set forth in equation 19B–6, can be re-stated as follows:

$$\begin{aligned} X_L &= (X - k_b B)(1-T) + k_b B \\ &= X - k_b B - XT + kB_bT + k_b B \\ &= X - XT + k_b BT \\ &= X(1-T) + k_b BT \end{aligned}$$

The first term in the final equation, $X(1-T)$, is equivalent to U's income, while the second part, $k_b BT$, represents the tax savings that occur because interest is deductible.

The value of the geared firm is found by capitalizing both parts of its after-tax earnings. MM argue that because L's 'regular' earnings stream is precisely as risky as is the income of firm U, it should be capitalized at the same rate (k_U). However, since the debt is assumed to be riskless, interest on the debt must be paid, and the tax saving represents a certain, riskless stream that should be discounted at the riskless rate (k_b). Thus, we obtain equation 19B–8:

$$V = \frac{X(1-T)}{k_U} + \frac{k_b BT}{k_b} = \frac{X(1-T)}{k_U} + BT. \qquad (19B\text{–}8)$$

However, since

$$V_U = \frac{X(1-T)}{k_U},$$

we may also express V as

$$V = V_U + BT,$$

which is what we set out to prove.

We may now illustrate the MM valuation and cost of capital hypotheses in a world with corporation tax.[4] Assume (a) that a firm starts in business with total capital of £5.4 million; (b) that this capital is used to purchase assets costing £5.4 million; (c) that the before-tax rate of return on these assets is 16.67 per cent, producing $EBIT = £900\,000$; (d) that the gearing-free equity capitalization rate is $k_s = 10$ per cent; and (e) that the corporation tax rate is 40 per cent. We may compute the value of the ungeared firm as follows:

$$V_U = \frac{X(1-T)}{k_U} = \frac{£900\,000(1-0.4)}{0.10} = £5\,400\,000.$$

As debt is added, the total market value of the firm rises by BT per unit of debt; for example, if £1 million of debt is used, then

$$V = V_U + BT = £5\,400\,000 + £400\,000 = £5\,800\,000.$$

Note also that if we divide $EBIT$ by V, the quotient is the before-tax rate of return on total market value, and this rate of return declines as debt is increased. Values of V and $EBIT/V$, together with several rates of return calculations which are explained below, are shown in Table 19B–3.

Table 19B–3 *Effect of Gearing on Valuation and the Cost of Capital: MM Assumptions in a World with Taxes (£millions).*

Debt (B)	Equity (S)	Total value (V)	B/S	$EBIT/V$	After-tax rate of return on equity: Book	After-tax rate of return on equity: Market (k_s)	Average cost of capital (k)
£0	£5.4	£5.4	0%	16.67%	10.00%	10.00%	10.00%
£2	£4.2	£6.2	47.6%	14.52%	13.23%	10.71%	8.72%
£4	£3.0	£7.0	133.0%	12.86%	17.14%	12.00%	7.77%
£6	£1.8	£7.8	333.3%	11.54%	n.a.	15.00%	6.92%
£8	£0.6	£8.6	1333.3%	10.47%	n.a.	30.00%	6.28%

n.a. = not applicable; implies debt greater than assets (£5 400 000), which would imply a negative accounting net worth, so the rate of return on book value of equity is not meaningful.

The book value and market value of equity, and the rates of return on these two values, will vary with gearing under the MM tax model. Total corporate assets are £5 400 000 by assumption, and we can establish other items as follows:

1. Net profit after interest and taxes = $(X - IC)(1-T)$.
2. Book value of equity = $£5\,400\,000 - B$.
3. Market value of equity = $V - B$.
4. Rate of return on book value of equity = $[(X-IC)(1-T)]/(£5\,400\,000 - B)$.
5. Rate of return on market value of equity = $k_s = [(X-IC)(1-T)]/(V-B)$ = the required rate of return on equity, or the cost of equity capital.
6. Overall cost of capital = $k = (B/V)(1-T)(k_b) + (S/V)(k_s)$.

Using these relationships, and values of V and B as shown in Table 19B–3, we can find the rates of return on book and market equity at different degrees of gearing:

Debt = £0:

$$\text{Rate of return on book value of equity} = \frac{(£900\,000 - £0)(0.6)}{£5\,400\,000 - £0} = 10.0\%.$$

$$\text{Rate of return on market value of equity} = k_s = \frac{£540\,000}{£5\,400\,000} = 10.0\%.$$

$$\text{Average cost of capital} = k = (0)(0.6)(7.5) + (1.00)(10.0) = 10.0\%.$$

---

4. First, it must be recognized that with the introduction of corporation tax, either (a) the values of business firms will be lower because of the decline in earnings, or (b) rates of return before taxes ($EBIT$/assets) will rise to offset the tax revenue; which condition holds depends upon the incidence of corporation tax, a long-standing question among economists. We simply note that something must change when taxes are imposed, although in our example we let the rate of return change.

Debt = £2 million:

$$\text{Rate of return on book value of equity} = \frac{(£900\,000 - £150\,000)(0.6)}{£5\,400\,000 - £2\,000\,000}$$

$$= \frac{£450\,000}{£3\,400\,000} = 13.23\%.$$

$$\text{Rate of return on market value of equity} = \frac{£450\,000}{£4\,200\,000} = 10.71\%.$$

Average cost of capital $= k = (0.32)(0.6)(7.5) + (0.68)(10.71) = 8.72\%$.

The cost-of-capital situation under the MM assumptions in a world with taxes is shown in Figure 19B–3. The materials in Figure 19B–3 and Table 19B–3 illustrate the following points:

1. The total value of the firm rises with gearing (Table 19B–3).
2. The rate of return on the book value of equity rises rapidly with gearing, but is meaningless for debt > £5.4 million (Table 19B–3).
3. The rate of return on the market value of equity, which is also the cost of equity capital, rises with gearing, but less rapidly than the rate of return on book values (Table 19B–3 and Figure 19B–3).
4. The after-tax cost of debt is constant (4.5 per cent in our example as shown in Figure 19B–3).
5. The overall, or average, cost of capital declines linearly as the debt ratio is increased. However, it would be difficult, if not impossible, for the firm to increase its market value debt ratio to or beyond the point where the book value debt ratio is 100 per cent, that is, beyond the point where $B = £5.4$ million (Table 19B–3 and Figure 19B–3).

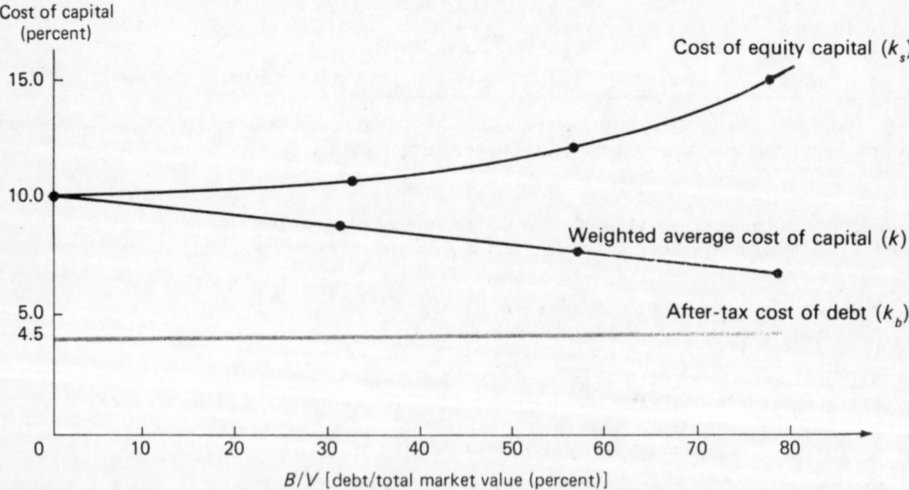

Figure 19B–3 *The Cost of Capital under the MM Assumptions, with Taxes.*

Thus, the MM model in a world with corporation tax leads to the conclusion that the value of a firm will be maximized, and its cost of capital minimized, if it uses only debt in its capital structure. Of course, firms do not engage in 100 per cent debt financing.

The Modigliani–Miller arbitrage process in a world with taxes

With corporation tax, both the NI and NOI approaches produce higher values for the geared than for the ungeared firms. However, the two theories differ with respect both to the size of this difference and to the manner in which it is generated. To illustrate, we shall use the same data as given previously. The tax rate is 40 per cent. Firm L has £4 million of 7.5 per cent debt; firm U is all equity financed; and both firms have $EBIT = £900\,000$. To begin, assume that both firms have an equity capitalization rate $k_s = 10$ per cent. Under these conditions, the NI approach establishes the value of firms U and L as follows:

	Firm U	Firm L
Net operating income (*EBIT*)	£ 900 000	£ 900 000
Less: interest on debt	– 0	– 300 000
Taxable income	£ 900 000	£ 600 000
Less: taxes at 40 per cent	– 360 000	– 240 000
Available to ordinary shareholders	£ 540 000	£ 360 000
Value of equity	£5 400 000	£3 600 000
Value of debt (B)	0	4 000 000
Total market value ($V = B + S$)	£5 400 000	£7 600 000

MM would argue that this NI solution represents a fundamental disequilibrium and therefore cannot persist. Using the MM equations developed above, we see that the equilibrium value of the geared firm is $V = V_u + BT = 5\,400\,000 + (4\,000\,000)\,(0.40) =$ £7 000 000, or £0.6 million less than the value calculated above. Firm L is thus overvalued, and, in a reasonably perfect market, a situation like this cannot exist – arbitrage will force the value of the firm back to equilibrium in accordance with the equation $V = V_u + BT$.

The arbitrage process with taxes works as follows. Assume an investor owns 5 per cent of L's shares (that is 0.05 × £3 600 000 = £180 000). His income from this investment is 0.10 × £180 000 = £18 000. Now this investor can obtain a higher income, without increasing his risk, by moving from L to U. He would reduce his percentage holdings in L's debt (5 per cent) times $(1 - T)$ – that is, 0.05(1 – 0.4) (£4 million) = £120 000. Finally, he would purchase 5 per cent of U's shares (0.05 × 5 400 000 = £270 000). The switch from L to U provides the investor with the following income and uncommitted funds:

Income = 0.10 × £270 000	£ 27 000
Less: cost of personal debt = 7.5 per cent × £120 000 borrowed capital	9 000
Net income from new investment	£ 18 000
Total funds: Original capital	£180 000
Borrowed funds	120 000
	£300 000
Total outlay	£270 000
Uncommitted funds	£ 30 000

Through arbitrage and the substitution of personal for company gearing, the investor can switch from the geared company into the ungeared one, earn the same total return (£18 000) on his net worth, be exposed to the same gearing as formerly (but on personal rather than company account), and have funds left over to invest elsewhere. According to MM, many investors would recognize this arbitrage opportunity, attempt to make the switch, and in the process drive the price of L's shares down to establish an equilibrium where the total market values of the two firms are consistent with the MM equation, that is, $V_U =$ £5.4 million, and $V = V_U \times BT =$ £5.4 million + £1.6 million = £7 million.

The weighted cost of capital again

A simple expression for the weighted cost of capital can also be developed from the above relationships. Recall that k_U is the after-tax cost of capital for an ungeared firm. With taxes, MM's proposition II is expressed by equation 19B–9:[5]

5. See footnote 3 for MM's proposition II without taxes.

$$k_s = k_U + (k_U - k_b)\frac{B(1-T)}{S} \tag{19B-9}$$

But the weighted cost of capital is:

$$k = k_b(1-T)\frac{B}{V_L} + k_s\frac{S}{V_L}$$

Substitute from equation 19B–9 for k_s.

$$k = k_b(1-T)\frac{B}{V_L} + \left[k_U + (k_U - k_b)\frac{B(1-T)}{S}\right]\frac{S}{V_L} \tag{19B-10}$$

We multiply through in equation 19B–10.

$$k = \frac{k_bB}{V_L} - \frac{k_bTB}{V_L} + \frac{k_US}{V_L} + \frac{k_UB}{V_L} - \frac{k_UTB}{V_L} - \frac{k_bB}{V_L} + \frac{k_b + B}{V_L}$$

The terms with opposite signs can be cancelled to obtain:

$$k = \frac{k_UB}{V_L} + \frac{k_US}{V_L} - \frac{k_UTB}{V_L} \tag{19B-11}$$

Since $B + S = V_L$, the first two terms on the right-hand side of equation 19B–11 equal k_U. We can factor k_U to obtain:

$$k = k_U\left(1 - \frac{TB}{V_L}\right) \tag{19B-12}$$

Equation 19B–12 states that the weighted cost of capital for a geared firm (in a world with corporation tax) is equal to the (after-tax) cost of capital for an ungeared firm times (one minus the firm's tax rate multiplied by its gearing ratio). Thus if:

$$k_U = 0.15$$
$$T = 0.5$$
$$B/V_L = 0.4$$

We can obtain k from equation 19B–12:

$$k = 0.15[1 - 0.5(0.4)]$$
$$k = 0.12.$$

THE EFFECT OF GEARING ON THE COST OF CAPITAL: A SUMMARY OF ALTERNATIVE POSITIONS

A review of the literature on the gearing question suggests that three alternative positions have, in the past, been advocated: the 'traditional' view, the MM view, and what can best be described as a compromise view. Figure 19B–4 gives representations in graph form of these three views. (No one has ever argued seriously that the NI approach holds.)

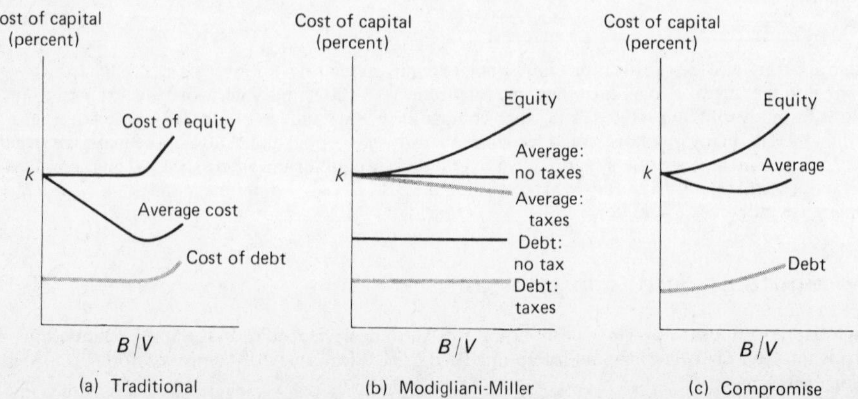

Figure 19B–4 *Alternative Views of the Relationship between the Use of Debt and the Cost of Capital.*

The traditional view

Prior to the appearance of the 1958 MM article, most writers dealing with the cost of capital seemed to advocate a position roughly consistent with that shown in panel (a) of Figure 19B–4. We say 'roughly' because, prior to MM's work, academic writers on the subject were not sufficiently rigorous to enable us to pin down their views. At any rate, most academicians who did express views on this subject seemed to agree with the net income approach up to a point – they seemed to feel that the cost of both debt and equity was independent of the debt ratio until some unspecified amount of debt was employed, after which the cost of equity and debt begin to rise rather sharply. As a result, the average or overall cost of capital in the traditional view declined rather sharply, then rose sharply beyond the optimum debt ratio.

Modigliani–Miller view

Panel (b) of Figure 19B–4 shows the MM view with and without corporation tax. This figure combines Figures 19B–2 and 19B–3 from Appendix B to Chapter 19 and reflects that related discussion.

Compromise view

Panel (c) of Figure 19B–4 shows what might be described as a compromise view of the relationship between debt and the cost of capital. Unlike the traditional view, which has the cost of debt and equity constant when relatively little debt is used, and the MM view, which is that the cost of equity rises at a rate that causes the average cost of capital to be constant (no taxes) or to decline linearly (with taxes), the compromise view holds that the cost of both debt and equity rises with the degree of financial gearing, with the result being a relatively shallow average cost of capital curve.

To summarize, the traditional view suggests that the average cost of capital declines rapidly with debt over a certain range and then begins to rise rapidly. The result is something approximating a V-shaped average cost of capital curve. The average cost of capital, according to MM, is constant in a world with no taxes, but declines continuously with increases in debt when corporation tax is considered. Thus, the MM model suggests that a firm that pays no corporation tax need not worry about its capital structure, while a firm that does pay tax should take on as much debt as it can get. Under the compromise view – which reflects our own feelings – the average cost of capital curve is saucer-shaped rather than V-shaped. There is an optimum capital structure, so it pays the financial manager to give careful consideration to his firm's capital structure. But the curve does not have a sharply defined minimum, so the firm is not penalized greatly by departing somewhat from the optimal debt structure. This permits flexibility in financial planning.

Neither theory nor empirical analysis has been able to specify precisely the optimal capital structure for an actual firm, or the precise cost of capital at any given capital structure – capital structure decisions are largely matters of informed judgement. However, *informed* judgement requires that some analysis of the type described in this book be undertaken, and an awareness of the theoretical considerations described here is very useful in such analyses.

PROBLEMS

19B–1. Companies U and L are identical in every respect except that U is ungeared while L has £10 million of 5 per cent debentures outstanding. Assume (i) that all of the MM assumptions are met, (ii) that the tax rate is 40 per cent, (iii) that *EBIT* is £2 million, and (iv) that the equity capitalization rate for company U is 10 per cent.
- (a) What value would MM estimate for each firm?
- (b) Suppose V_U = £8 million and V_L = £18 million. According to MM, do these represent equilibrium values? If not, explain the process by which equilibrium will be restored. No calculations are necessary.

19B–2. You are provided the following information: the firm's expected net operating income (X) is £400. Its value as an ungeared firm (V_U) is £2000. The tax rate is 40 per cent. The cost of debt is 8.7 per cent. The ratio of debt to equity for the geared firm, when it is geared is 1. Using the NOI approach.
- (a) Calculate the after-tax cost of equity capital for both the geared and ungeared firm.
- (b) Calculate the after-tax weighted average cost of capital for each.
- (c) Why is the cost of equity capital higher for the geared firm, but the weighted average cost of capital lower?

19B–3. Company A and Company B are in the same risk class, and are identical in every respect except that Company A is geared while Company B is not. Company A has £3 million in 5 per cent debentures outstanding. Both firms earn 10 per cent *before interest and taxes* on their £5 million of total assets. Assume perfect capital markets, rational investors, and so on, a tax rate of 60 per cent, and a capitalization rate of 10 per cent for an all-equity company.

(a) Compute the value of firms A and B using the net income (NI) approach.
(b) Compute the value of each firm using the net operating income (NOI) approach.
(c) Using the NOI approach, calculate the after-tax weighted average cost of capital, k, for firms A and B. Which of these two firms has an optimal capital structure according to the NOI approach? Why?
(d) According to the NOI approach, the values for firms A and B computed in part (a) above are not in equilibrium. If a situation like this exists, an investor in the overvalued firm can, through the arbitrage process, secure the same income at lower cost. Assuming that you own 1 per cent of A's shares, show the process which will give you the same amount of income but at less cost. At what point would this process stop?
(e) Company B (the wholly equity financed firm) wants to change its capital structure by introducing debt. Management believes that the cost of equity to the firm will take the form

$$k_s = R_F + \rho_1 + \rho_2$$

where

k_s = the cost of equity.
R_F = the after-tax riskless interest rate, currently at about 6 per cent.
ρ_1 = a premium demanded by the firm as a result of its particular business activity, currently estimated to be 4 per cent, and
ρ_2 = a premium demanded as a result of the firm's financial gearing.

Management believes that the premium, ρ_2, can be approximated by taking the firm's *debt–assets* ratio, squaring it, and multiplying by 0.10 to give the additional percentage points of premium required by the market. Management also feels that the firm's cost of debt is a function of the debt ratio, and estimates that this function is approximately equal to the following schedule:

Ratio Debt/assets	After-tax cost of debt
0%	0.05
20%	0.05
30%	0.06
40%	0.07
60%	0.12

Under these assumptions, is there an optimal capital structure for firm B? If so, what is this optimal debt–equity ratio?

19B–4. The cost of debt before taxes is 10 per cent. The cost of equity for a geared firm is 14 per cent. The debt to total value of the geared firm is 50 per cent. The corporation tax rate is 40 per cent.
(a) What is the cost of capital of the geared firm?
(b) What is the cost of capital of the firm if it were ungeared?

Appendix C to Chapter 19:

Using the CAPM to Estimate a Firm's Cost of Capital[1]

Three steps are required in using the capital asset pricing model (CAPM) to estimate a firm's cost of equity capital:

1. Estimate the market parameters in order to estimate the security market line.
2. Estimate the firm's beta coefficient.
3. Utilize the estimates to formulate a judgement of the firm's cost of equity capital.

Each of these steps will be covered, first explaining the formal methodology involved and then indicating the kinds of judgements required to arrive at a number or range of numbers for the firm's cost of equity capital.

ESTIMATING THE MARKET PARAMETERS

The key market parameters to estimate are the risk-free rate of return, the expected return on the market and the variance of the market return. With these we have estimates of the key market-determined variables of the security market line. For example, suppose that we estimated the risk-free return to be 5 per cent, the return on the market to be 10 per cent, and the variance of the market to be 1 per cent. The security market line could then be expressed as shown in equations 19C–1 and 19C–2:

$$\bar{k}_j = R_F + \lambda\, Cov\,(k_j, k_M) \text{ where } \lambda = \frac{k_M - R_F}{Var\,(k_M)} \tag{19C–1}$$

$$\bar{k}_j = R_F + (k_M - R_F)\beta_j \tag{19C–2}$$

When we fill in the illustrative market parameters we would obtain equations 19C–1a and 19C–2a:

$$\bar{k}_j = 0.05 + \frac{(0.10 - 0.05)}{0.01} Cov\,(k_j, k_M) \tag{19C–1a}$$

$$= 0.05 + 5\, Cov\,(k_j, k_M)$$

$$\bar{k}_j = 0.05 + 0.05(\beta_j) \text{ where } \beta_j = \frac{Cov\,(k_j, k_M)}{Var\,(k_M)} \tag{19C–2a}$$

1. Adaptors' note: Because research into this field has been concerned almost exclusively with American companies up to the present time, it has been decided to retain Weston and Brigham's original illustrations in this appendix. It is believed, however, that the principles expounded have a universal application.

Thus if we knew that the beta for the firm under analysis was 1.5, using equation 19C–2a we would have:

$\bar{k}_j = 0.05 + 0.05(1.5)$ $\bar{k}_j = 0.05 + 5(0.015)$ since $Cov(k_j, k_M) = \beta_j\, Var(k_M)$

$\bar{k}_j = 0.125$ $Cov(k_j, k_M) = 1.5(0.01) = 0.015$

Thus the cost of equity capital for the firm would be 12.5 per cent. This brief overview indicates the power of the CAPM approach. Once we have good estimates of the market parameters all we need to know is the systematic risk measure for the firm or project to obtain an estimate of the required return on that investment. Much empirical work has been performed on the estimates of the market parameters. Some of these represent formal scholarly studies analysing the empirical validity of the capital asset pricing model.[2] Other estimates of market parameters are available from various US financial firms and services such as Merrill Lynch, Pierce, Fenner and Smith, Wells Fargo Bank, and the Value Line. The sophisticated methodologies utilized include analysis over a number of periods typically using intervals of one month, but some services use intervals as short as one week or one day. The nature of the sophisticated procedures for estimating the market parameters can be conveyed by the data in Table 19C–1, which provides an approximation to the market parameters for the period 1960 to 1976. The percentage returns listed in column (5) are obtained by adding the dividend yield in column (4) plus the capital gain calculated in column (3) from the information on the Standard & Poor 500 share price index data listed in column (2). Taking the mean value of the data in column (5) we can obtain the mean market return over the period of approximately 8 per cent.

Table 19C–1 *Estimates of Market Parameters.*

Year	S&P 500 price index	% Change in price	Dividend yield	Percentage return	Return deviation	Market variance	Risk free return
(t)	P_t	$\frac{P_t}{P_{t-1}} - 1$	$\frac{d_t}{P_t}$	k_{Mt} (3+4)	$(k_{Mt} - \bar{k}_M)$ $(5 - \bar{k}_M)$	$(k_{Mt} - \bar{k}_M)^2$ (6^2)	R_F
(1)	(2)	(3)	(4)	(5)	(6)	(7)	(8)
1960	55.85						
1961	66.27	0.1866	0.0298	0.2164	0.1371	0.018796	0.03
1962	62.38	0.0587	0.0337	(0.0250)	(0.1043)	0.010878	0.03
1963	69.87	0.1201	0.0317	0.1518	0.0725	0.005256	0.03
1964	81.37	0.1646	0.0301	0.1947	0.1154	0.013317	0.04
1965	88.17	0.0836	0.0300	0.1136	0.0343	0.001176	0.04
1966	85.26	(0.0330)	0.0340	0.0010	(0.0783)	0.006131	0.04
1967	91.93	0.0782	0.0320	0.1102	0.0309	0.000955	0.05
1968	98.70	0.0736	0.0307	0.1043	0.0250	0.000625	0.05
1969	97.84	(0.0087)	0.0324	0.0237	(0.0556)	0.003091	0.07
1970	83.22	(0.1494)	0.0383	(0.1111)	(0.1904)	0.036252	0.06
1971	98.29	0.1811	0.0314	0.2125	0.1332	0.017742	0.05
1972	109.20	0.1110	0.0284	0.1394	0.0601	0.003612	0.05
1973	107.43	(0.0162)	0.0306	0.0144	(0.0649)	0.004212	0.07
1974	82.85	(0.2288)	0.0447	(0.1824)	(0.2617)	0.068487	0.08
1975	85.17	0.0280	0.0431	0.0711	(0.0082)	0.000067	0.06
1976	102.01	0.1977	0.0376	0.2353	0.1560	0.024336	0.06
				1.2699		0.214933	0.81
						$R_F = 0.81/16 = 0.051$	

$\bar{k}_M = 1.2699/16 = 0.079 \approx 0.080$ $\text{Var}(k_M) = 0.2149/15 = 0.0143$

Sources: *Economic Report of the President*, 1975, and individual issues of the *Federal Reserve Bulletin*.

---

2. F. Black, M. C. Jensen and M. Scholes, The capital asset pricing model: some empirical tests, in *Studies in the Theory of Capital Markets*, ed., M. C. Jenson (New York: Praeger, 1972); E. F. Fama and J. MacBeth, Risk, return and equilibrium: empirical tests, *Journal of Political Economy* 81 (May–June 1973), pp. 607–636; I. Friend and M. Blume, Measurement of portfolio performance under uncertainty, *American Economic Review* 60 (September 1970), pp. 561–575; N. Jacob,, The measurement of systematic risk for securities and portfolios: some empirical results, *Journal of Financial and Quantitative Analysis* 6 (March 1971), pp. 815–834; M. C. Jenson, ed., in *Studies in the Theory of Capital Markets*; M. H. Miller and M. Scholes, Rates of return in relation to risk: a re-examination of some recent findings, in *Studies in the Theory of Capital Markets*, pp. 47–78.

In column (6) the deviations from the market return are listed. In column (7) the deviations are squared, then summed and divided by 15 to obtain the 0.0143 estimate of market variance.[3]

The risk-free return is estimated by use of the six-month treasury bill rate. The average for the years indicated are listed in Column (8). These average annual values are summed and divided by 16 to obtain an estimate of the risk-free return for the time period covered of 5.1 per cent.

The estimates we have obtained reflect the characteristics of the market with the turbulence introduced by unsettled economic conditions following 1966. Other studies of market behaviour over more extended time periods and utilizing monthly intervals rather than annual time periods suggest a range of about 9 to 11 per cent for market returns. Thus our 8 per cent estimate, dominated by the weak market in recent years, is slightly low. Most previous studies of market parameters utilize at least 60 months of returns so have at least 60 observations as compared with the 16 observations in Table 19C–1. Of course, a larger number of observations will reduce the variance measured so that the longer-term studies suggest that 1 per cent is a good estimate of market variance on the average. Inspection of column (8) containing the risk-free return measures indicates a range of from 3 per cent to 8 per cent. Thus the higher values of R_F have predominated in the later years. Hence to make current estimates of the cost of equity or to make estimates for use in future periods, a range of 4 to 6 per cent as estimates of the risk-free return would be plausible. The somewhat unusual nature of the general economic conditions in recent years is suggested by a paradox observed in the results from Table 19C–1. The higher rate of inflation after 1966 is reflected in the rising levels of the risk-free return. The sharper market declines and relatively weaker recoveries in market returns indicate that stock market returns have not been able to capture the inflation premium fully.

Because of these shifts in the estimates of market parameters (their apparent underlying non-stationarities) our use of the CAPM is more as a normative model (normative indicates the way people ought to behave or a way of thinking rather than precise numbers). Thus in applying the market parameters we have an estimate of 4 to 6 per cent for the risk-free return, 8 to 11 per cent for the return on the market, and 1 per cent for the variance of the market. We can use these ranges in two ways: (a) we could apply the ranges to provide a sensitivity analysis of the range of possible estimates of the cost of equity capital for a firm or project; or (b) we could select from the range the single figures that would appear to be most appropriate for the time period for which the analysis is being

Table 19C–2 *Calculation of Beta for General Motors.*

Year (t)	GM price p_t	%Change in price $\frac{p_t}{p_{t-1}}-1$	Dividend yield $\frac{d_t}{p_t}$	Percent return k_{jt} (3+4)	Deviation of returns $(k_{jt}-\bar{k}_j)$ $(5-\bar{k}_M)$	Variance of returns $(k_{jt}-\bar{k}_j)^2$ (6^2)	Covariance with market $(k_{jt}-\bar{k}_j)(k_{Mt}-\bar{k}_M)$ (6 × 6 market)
(1)	(2)	(3)	(4)	(5)	(6)	(7)	(8)
1960	48						
1961	49	0.02	0.05	0.07	(0.029)	0.000841	(0.003976)
1962	52	0.06	0.06	0.12	0.021	0.000441	(0.002190)
1963	74	0.42	0.05	0.47	0.371	0.137641	0.026898
1964	90	0.22	0.05	0.27	0.171	0.029241	0.019733
1965	102	0.13	0.05	0.18	0.081	0.006561	0.002778
1966	87	(0.15)	0.05	(0.10)	(0.199)	0.039601	0.015582
1967	78	(0.10)	0.05	(0.05)	(0.149)	0.022201	(0.004604)
1968	81	0.04	0.05	0.09	(0.009)	0.000081	(0.000225)
1969	74	(0.09)	0.06	(0.03)	(0.069)	0.004761	0.003836
1970	70	(0.05)	0.05	0.00	(0.099)	0.009801	0.018850
1971	82	0.17	0.04	0.21	0.111	0.012321	0.014785
1972	78	(0.05)	0.06	0.01	(0.089)	0.007921	(0.005349)
1973	65	(0.17)	0.08	(0.09)	(0.189)	0.035721	0.012266
1974	42	(0.35)	0.08	(0.27)	(0.369)	0.136161	0.096567
1975	45	0.07	0.05	0.12	0.021	0.000961	(0.000172)
1976	68	0.51	0.07	0.58	0.481	0.231361	0.075036
				1.58		0.675616	0.269815

$\bar{k}_j = 1.58/16 = 0.099 \simeq 0.100$

$\mathrm{Var}(k_j) = 0.6756/15 = 0.0450$

$\mathrm{Cov}(k_j, k_M) = 0.2698/14 = 0.0193$

$$\beta_j = \frac{0.0193}{0.0143} = 1.35$$

$$\beta'_j = \frac{0.02}{0.01} = 2$$

3. We divide by 15 rather than 16 since one degree of freedom has been lost in that the calculation of the variance involves the use of the mean return on the market which has already been calculated.

Table 19C–3 *Calculation of Beta for Chrysler.*

Year	Chrysler price	% Change in price	Dividend yield	Percent return	Deviation of return	Variance of return	Covariance with market
(t)	P_t	$\frac{P_t}{P_t-1}-1$	$\frac{d_t}{P_t}$	k_{jt} (3+4)	$(k_{jt}-\bar{k}_j)$ $(5-k_M)$	$(k_{jt}-\bar{k}_j)^2$ (6^2)	$(k_{jt}-\bar{k}_j)(k_{Mt}-\bar{k}_M)$ (6 × 6 market)
(1)	(2)	(3)	(4)	(5)	(6)	(7)	(8)
1960	13						
1961	12	(0.08)	0.02	(0.06)	(0.184)	0.0339	(0.025226)
1962	14	0.17	0.02	0.19	0.066	0.0044	(0.006884)
1963	33	1.36	0.01	1.37	1.246	1.5525	0.090335
1964	51	0.55	0.02	0.57	0.446	0.1989	0.051468
1965	54	0.06	0.02	0.08	(0.044)	0.0019	(0.001509)
1966	45	(0.17)	0.04	(0.13)	(0.254)	0.0645	0.019888
1967	44	(0.02)	0.05	0.03	(0.094)	0.0088	(0.002905)
1968	60	0.36	0.03	0.39	0.266	0.0708	0.006650
1969	44	(0.27)	0.05	(0.22)	(0.344)	0.1185	0.019126
1970	25	(0.43)	0.02	(0.41)	(0.534)	0.2852	0.101674
1971	30	0.20	0.02	0.22	0.096	0.0092	0.012787
1972	35	0.17	0.03	0.20	0.076	0.0058	0.004568
1973	33	(0.06)	0.04	(0.02)	(0.144)	0.0207	0.009346
1974	14	(0.58)	0.10	(0.48)	(0.604)	0.3648	0.158067
1975	11	(0.21)	0	(0.21)	(0.334)	0.1116	0.002739
1976	16	0.45	0.02	0.47	0.346	0.1197	0.053976
				1.99		2.9712	0.494100

$k_j = 1.99/16 = 0.124$
$\text{Var}(k_j) = 2.9712/15 = 0.1981$
$\text{Cov}(k_j, k_M) = 0.4941/14 = 0.0353$

$$\beta_j = \frac{0.0353}{0.0143} = 2.47$$

$$\beta' = \frac{0.035}{0.01} = 3.5$$

made. To illustrate the methodology for calculating a cost of equity capital for individual firms, we shall use the estimates in equations 19C–1a and 19C–2a. These were: $k_M = 10\%$; $Var(k_M) = 1\%$; and $R_F = 5\%$. With these estimates of market parameters, we turn to their application to individual firms.

ESTIMATING THE BETA COEFFICIENT FOR INDIVIDUAL FIRMS

In Tables 19C–2 and 19C–3 we set forth the calculations of beta for General Motors Corporation and Chrysler Corporation. The first seven columns of these two tables exactly parallel the first seven columns of Table 19C–1 used to estimate the market parameters. Thus no furthur explanation is required. In column (8) we calculate the covariance of the returns for the individual companies with the market returns. Thus we use column (6) in Tables 19C–2 and 19C–3 along with column (6) representing the market deviations shown in Table 19C–1. The data in column (8) for General Motors and Chrysler are used to calculate the covariance of the two firms. The covariance for General Motors is approximately 2 per cent while the covariance for Chrysler is approximately 3.5 per cent. When we use our previous measure of the variance of the market obtained from the data in Table 19C–1 we obtain an estimate of beta of 1.35 for General Motors and an estimate of beta of 2.47 for Chrysler. We are now ready to apply these results in estimating the cost of equity for General Motors and Chrysler.

USE OF THE SECURITY MARKET LINE TO ESTIMATE THE COST OF EQUITY CAPITAL

The security market line we are using has been set forth in equations 19C–1a and 19C–2a. With the two estimates of beta for General Motors and for Chrysler, we obtain estimates of the cost of equity of 12 per cent for General

Motors and 17.35 per cent for Chrysler. The actual historical average returns of the two companies were on the low side of the range of their indicated costs of equity capital.

Our own judgement is that the relevant cost of equity capital for the two companies would be somewhat higher than the estimates we have produced. Our reasons are related to the underlying economic characteristics of the automobile industry currently and prospectively along with the respective position of each of the firms in the automobile industry. It is generally acknowledged that the automobile industry has become substantially more risky in recent years. The addition of safety devices and pollution controls has added substantially to the cost of automobiles. There are also increased risks whether the automobile manufacturers can meet the pollution control standards and petrol mileage standards that have been set by Congress for future years. The energy shortage may result in new and substantial excise taxes on larger automobiles which are said to be the more profitable line for companies such as General Motors and Chrysler. Thus we would add 1.25 per cent to make the estimate of the cost of equity 13 per cent for General Motors and add 1.65 per cent to make the estimate of the cost of equity 19 per cent for Chrysler. The estimate of the betas would rise to 1.6 for General Motors and 2.8 for Chrysler.

However, we are here only illustrating the methodology. Without substantial additional analysis we would not seek to defend any particular estimate of the costs of equity for General Motors and Chrysler. We believe, however, that the indicated ranges of 12 to 13 per cent for General Motors and 17 and 19 per cent for Chrysler are approximately correct. Other financial data would support our result that the cost of equity is greater for Chrysler, reflecting its much more volatile performance than General Motors. This suggests further analysis of the components of the beta measures for the two companies.

MEASURING BUSINESS AND FINANCIAL RISKS

The capital asset pricing model enables us to separate the components of business and financial risks. Proposition II of MM in their original (partial equilibrium) formulation can be expressed both without and with taxes:

$$\textit{No taxes}\ k_s = k_U + (k_U - k_b)\frac{B}{S}$$

$$\textit{With taxes}\ k_s = k_U + (k_U - k_b)\frac{B(1-T)}{S}$$

From a paper by Hamada,[4] the corresponding formulations in the CAPM framework are:

$$\textit{No taxes}\ \bar{k}_s = R_F + \lambda Cov(k_U, k_M)\left[1 + \frac{B}{S}\right]$$

$$\textit{With taxes}\ \bar{k}_s = R_F + \lambda Cov(k_U, k_M)\left[1 + \frac{B(1-T)}{S}\right]$$

Under both:

$$k_U = \frac{E(X)(1-T)}{V_U} \qquad k = \frac{E(X)(1-T)}{V_L}$$

Recall that: k_U = the cost of capital of an ungeared firm
k_s = the cost of equity capital of a geared firm
k = the weighted average cost of capital of a geared firm.

The CAPM formulations can also be expressed in the form that utilizes beta as the measure of risk as follows:

$$\bar{k} = R_F + [\bar{k}_M - R_F]\beta_U\left[1 + \frac{B(1-T)}{S}\right] \tag{19C–3}$$

where β_U is for an ungeared firm. When we multiply the terms we have the expression as shown in 19C–3a:

$$\bar{k}_s = R_F + [\bar{k}_M - R_F]\beta_U + [\bar{k}_M - R_F]\beta_U\frac{B(1-T)}{S} \tag{19C–3a}$$

The beta that we observe is thus composed of the elements as shown in equation 19C–4:

$$\beta_j = \beta_U\left[1 + \frac{B(1-T)}{S}\right] \tag{19C–4}$$

4. Robert S. Hamada, Portfolio analysis, market equilibrium and corporation finance, *Journal of Finance* 24 (March 1969), pp. 13–31.

We can thus separate the elements of business risk and financial risk as shown in equation 19C–4a.

$$\beta_j = \beta_U + \beta_U\left[\frac{B(1-T)}{S}\right] \tag{19C–4a}$$

Then solving 19C–4 for the business risk term from the observed data we have the relationship shown in equation 19C–4b:

$$\beta_U = \frac{\beta_j}{\left[1+\frac{B(1-T)}{S}\right]} \tag{19C–4b}$$

We may now apply these relationships using the data for General Motors and for Chrysler.

Based on an analysis of the capital structures of General Motors and Chrysler over a period of years, we have estimated the debt equity ratio of General Motors to be 0.25 and the debt equity ratio of Chrysler to be 1.0. We have utilized a tax rate of 0.5 for both companies. We can, therefore, proceed to calculate the beta measuring business risk for each company, utilizing the high values of beta, as shown in equation 19C–4c:

$$\text{General Motors: } \beta_U = \frac{1.6}{1+(0.25)(0.5)} = \frac{1.6}{1.125} = 1.4$$

$$\text{Chrysler: } \beta_U = \frac{2.8}{1+(1)(0.5)} = \frac{2.8}{1.5} = 1.9 \tag{19C–4c}$$

As shown, we obtain a β_U for General Motors of 1.4. The β_U for Chrysler is 1.9. This enables us now to set forth the relationships that show the components that make up the cost of equity capital for each company. This is shown in Table 19C–4.

Table 19C–4 *Components of the Firm's Cost of Equity Capital.*

	After-tax cost of equity capital		Risk free element		Premium for business risk		Premium for financial risk
	$\bar{k}_s$	=	R_F	+	$(\bar{k}_M - R_F)\beta_j^*$	+	$(\bar{k}_M - R_F)\beta_j^*\left[\frac{B(1-T)}{S}\right]$
GM			5%	+	4%(1.8)	+	4%(1.8)(0.25)(0.5)
	13%	≅	5%	+	7.2%	+	0.9%
Chrysler			5%	+	4%(2.3)	+	4%(2.3)(1)(0.5)
	19%	≅	5%	+	9.2%	+	4.6%

Differences due to rounding in calculation of β_j^*.

In Table 19C–4 we see that the risk-free element in the cost of equity capital for both General Motors and Chrysler is 5 per cent. This is a market parameter. The premium for business risk is the market risk premium multiplied times each firm's beta as an ungeared firm. This component is 7 per cent for General Motors, 2.5 percentage points lower than the 9.5 per cent for Chrysler. The third element in the cost of equity capital requirement for each firm is the premium for business risk multiplied by the gearing element. This adds slightly less than 1 per cent to the cost of equity for General Motors because of its low gearing ratio. Chrysler, which has a debt-to-equity ratio of 1, adds a premium for financial risk of 4.8 per cent. Thus the differential in the cost of equity capital for General Motors reflects its lower premium for business risk, and, more significantly, its lower premium for financial risk.

In this appendix we have illustrated the application of some of the central concepts of the capital asset pricing model. In actual use, much more sophisticated computations of each of the elements that we have used would be employed. However, one way of checking the results from the use of more complex methods is to make rough estimates utilizing the procedures here described.

ESTIMATE OF THE FIRM'S COST OF CAPITAL

We can now calculate the cost of capital for each of the two companies. We have estimated the market cost of debt as 8.2 per cent for General Motors and 9.4 per cent for Chrysler on the basis of the current yields to maturity of their outstanding debt, as well as their movements in recent years. Recall that we had already analysed their gearing ratios in separating the components of business and financial risk.

We utilize the standard expression for the cost of capital:

$$k = k_b(1-T)\frac{B}{V} + k_s\frac{S}{V}.$$

We can then calculate the cost of capital for each company:

General Motors

$$\begin{aligned} k &= 0.082(0.5)(0.2) + 0.13(0.8) \\ &= 0.0082 + 0.104 \\ &= 0.1182 \cong 12\% \end{aligned}$$

Chrysler

$$\begin{aligned} k &= 0.094(0.5)(0.5) + 0.19(0.5) \\ &= 0.0235 + 0.095 \\ &= 0.1185 \cong 12\% \end{aligned}$$

Although Chrysler has a higher cost of debt as well as a higher cost of equity, the weighted cost of capital for Chrysler is about equal to the 12 per cent cost of capital of General Motors. Since Chrysler uses a higher proportion of debt, it benefits to a higher degree from the tax advantages of debt.

PROBLEMS

19C–1. The following data have been developed for the Donovan Company, the manufacturer of an advanced line of adhesives.

State	Probability	Market return k_M	Return for the firm k_j
1	0.1	−0.15	−0.30
2	0.3	0.05	0.00
3	0.4	0.15	0.20
4	0.2	0.20	0.50

The risk-free rate is 6 per cent. Make calculations of the following:
(a) The market return.
(b) The variance of the market.
(c) The expected return for the Donovan Company.
(d) The covariance of the returns of the Donovan Company with the returns on the market.
(e) Write the equation of the security market line.
(f) What is the expected return for the Donovan Company?
(g) What is the required return for the Donovan Company?

19C–2. The following data have been developed for the Milliken Company.

Year	Return on the market	Company returns
1978	0.27	0.25
1977	0.12	0.05
1976	(0.03)	(0.05)
1975	0.12	0.15
1974	(0.03)	(0.10)
1973	0.27	0.30

The yield to maturity on Treasury bills is 0.066 and is expected to remain at this point for the foreseeable future. (Assume 5 degrees of freedom for the covariance and variance calculations and 6 degrees for the means.) Make calculations of the following:
(a) The market return.
(b) The variance of the market.
(c) The expected return for the Milliken Company.
(d) The covariance of the returns of the Milliken Company with the returns on the market.
(e) Write the equation of the security market line.
(f) What is the expected return for the Milliken Company?
(g) What is the required return for the Milliken Company?

19C–3. The chief financial officer of Worldcorp seeks to determine the value of the division and of the cost of capital for the Industrial Products Division (without any gearing). He has gathered the following data. (Ignore taxes.)

Year	Return on the market	Earnings before interest and taxes
19X1	0.27	£25
19X2	0.12	5
19X3	(0.03)	(5)
19X4	0.12	15
19X5	(0.03)	(10)
19X6	0.27	30

The yield to maturity on Treasury bills is 0.066 and is expected to remain at this level in the foreseeable future. For the ungeared division, compute (a) the value of the division and (b) the cost of capital. Assume 5 degrees of freedom for the covariance and variance calculations and 6 degrees for the means.

19C–4. The Myers Company has a total investment of £200 million in five divisions.

Division	Divisional investment	Divisional beta coefficient (estimated)
A	£60	0.5
B	50	2.0
C	30	4.0
D	40	1.0
E	20	3.0

Management believes that there is a systematic relationship between each division's return and market returns as described by the beta coefficients and these relationships are assumed to be stable over time.

The current risk-free rate is 5 per cent, while expected market returns have the following probability distribution for the next period:

Probability	Market return
0.1	6%
0.2	8
0.4	10
0.2	12
0.1	14

(a) What is the estimated equation for the security market line (SML)?
(b) Compute the expected return on the Myers Company for the next period.
(c) Suppose management receives a proposal for a new division. The investment needed to create the new division is £50 million; it will have an expected return of 15 per cent, and its estimated beta coefficient is 2.5. Should the new division be created? At what expected rate of return would management be indifferent to starting the new division?

19C–5. You are given the following data on market returns (k_M) and the returns on shares A and B.
(a) The risk-free rate of return is 6 per cent. Determine the market return and variance.
(b) For shares A and B determine the following:
expected return (k_i)
covariance with the market [$Cov(k_i, k_M)$]
beta (β_i)
required return (k_i^*)

Return	Returns by year 1973	1974	1975	1976	1977	1978
k_M	0.20	0.10	−0.05	0.15	0.30	−0.10
k_A	0.25	0.05	−0.15	0.15	0.55	−0.25
k_B	−0.20	0.30	0.70	−0.10	0.50	−0.60

variance of historic returns (σ_i^2)
(c) What percentage of the risk of shares A and B is systematic? Explain.
(d) Make a graph of the security market line and the returns of the two shares

(e) Assuming no changes in variance or covariance of returns what would you expect to happen to the prices of the two shares? Why?

(f) If both shares were priced on the SML which would have the higher yield? Which has the higher variance? Explain this apparent paradox.

SELECTED REFERENCES

Bierman, H. J. and Smidt, S. Application of the capital asset pricing model to multi-period investments. *Journal of Business Finance and Accounting* (Autumn 1975): 327–340.

Black, F. Capital market equilibrium with restricted borrowing. *Journal of Business* 45 (July 1972): 444–454.

Black, F., Jensen, M. C. and Scholes, M. The capital asset pricing model: some empirical tests. In *Studies in the Theory of Capital Markets*. Edited by M. C. Jensen. New York: Praeger, 1972.

Black, F. and Scholes, M. The pricing of options and corporate liabilities. *Journal of Political Economy* 81 (May–June 1973): 637–654.

Brennan, M. J. Capital market equilibrium with divergent borrowing and lending rates. *Journal of Financial and Quantitative Analysis* 6 (December 1971): 1197–1205.

Brennan, M. J. Investor taxes, market equilibrium and corporate finance. Ph.D. dissertation, M.I.T., June 1970.

Brigham, E. F. and Pappas, J. Rates of return on common stock. *Journal of Business* 42 (July 1969).

Choi, F. D. S. Financial disclosure in relation to a firm's capital costs. *Accounting and Business Research* (Autumn 1973): 282–292.

Douglas, George W. Risk in the equity markets: an empirical appraisal of market efficiency. *Yale Economic Essays* 9 (Spring 1969): 3–45.

Evans, J. L. and Archer, S. H. Diversification and the reduction of dispersion: an empirical analysis. *Journal of Finance* 23 (December 1968): 761–767.

Fama, E. F. Efficient capital markets: a review of theory and empirical work. *Journal of Finance* 25 (May 1970): 383–417.

Fama, E. F. Risk, return, and equilibrium. *Journal of Political Economy* 79 (January–February 1971): 30–55.

Fama, E. F. Risk, return, and equilibrium: some clarifying comments. *Journal of Finance* 23 (March 1968): 29–40.

Fama, E. F. and MacBeth, J. Risk, return and equilibrium: empirical tests. *Journal of Political Economy* 81 (May–June 1973): 607–636.

Fama, E. F. and Miller, M. H. *The Theory of Finance*. New York: Holt, Rinehart and Winston, 1972.

Fouse, W. L., Jahnke, W. W. and Rosenberg, B. Is beta phlogiston? *Investment Analyst* (December 1975): 44–54.

Friend, I., and Blume, M. Measurement of portfolio performance under uncertainty. *American Economic Review* 60 (September 1974): 1153–1163.

Friend, I., Landskroner, Yoram, and Losq, Etienne. The demand for risky assets under uncertain inflation. *Journal of Finance* 31 (December 1976): 1287–1297.

Gordan, Myron, J. and Halpern, Paul J. Cost of capital for a division of a firm. *Journal of Finance* 29, No. 4 (September 1974): 1153–1163.

Grinyer, J. The cost of equity, the capital asset pricing model, and management objectives under uncertainty. *Journal of Business Finance and Accounting* (Winter 1976): 101–121.

Hakansson, N. Capital growth and the mean-variance approach to portfolio selection. *Journal of Financial and Quantitative Analysis* 6 (January 1971): 517–558.

Hamada, R. S. Portfolio analysis, market equilibrium and corporation finance. *Journal of Finance* 24 (March 1969): 13–32.

Hamada, R. S. The effect of the firm's capital structure on the systematic risk of common stocks. *Journal of Finance* 27 (May 1972): 435–452.

Haugen, Robert A. and Pappas, James L. Equilibrium in the pricing of capital assets, risk-bearing debt instruments, and the question of optimal capital structure. *Journal of Financial and Quantitative Analysis* 6 (June 1971): 943–53. See also Imai, Yutaka and Rubinstein, Mark. Comment. *Journal of Financial and Quantitative Analysis* 7 (September 1972): 2001–2003; and Haugen and Pappas. Reply. ibid., 2005–2008.

Henfrey, A. Risk factors for individual securities in three European stock markets. *Investment Analyst* (May 1975): 26–32.

Hirshleifer, J. Efficient allocation of capital in an uncertain world. *American Economic Review* 54 (May 1964): 77–85.

Hirshleifer, J. *Investment, Interest and Capital*. Englewood Cliffs, N. J.: Prentice-Hall, 1970.

Hsia, C. C. Inflation risk and capital asset pricing. Typescript. Los Angeles. University of California, 1973.

Jacob, N. The measurement of systematic risk for securities and portfolios: some empirical results. *Journal of Financial and Quantitative Analysis* 6 (March 1971): 815–834.

Jensen, M. C. The foundations and current state of capital market theory. In *Studies in the Theory of Capital Markets*, M. C. Jensen, ed. New York: Praeger, 1972.

Jensen, M. C. The performance of mutual funds in the period 1945–1964. *Journal of Finance* 23 (May 1968): 389–416.

Jensen, M. C. Risk, the pricing of capital assets, and the evaluation of investment portfolios. *Journal of Business* 42 (April 1969): 167–247.

Jensen, M. C., ed. *Studies in the Theory of Capital Markets.* New York: Praeger, 1972.

Jensen, M. C., Capital markets: theory and evidence. *Bell Journal of Economics and Management Science* 3 (Autumn 1972).

Kraus, A. and Litzenberger, R. H. Skewness, preference and the valuation of risk assets. Stanford Calif.: Stanford University, 1972.

Kumar, Prem. Market equilibrium and corporation finance: some issues. *Journal of Finance* 29, no. 4 (September 1974): 1175–1188.

Latane, H. Criteria for choice among risky ventures. *Journal of Political Economy* 67 (April 1959): 144–155.

Lintner, J. The aggregation of investors' diverse judgment and preferences in purely competitive securities markets. *Journal of Financial and Quantitative Analysis* 4 (December 1969): 347–400.

Lintner, J. Security prices, risk, and maximal gains from diversification. *Journal of Finance* 20 (December 1965): 587–616.

Lintner, J. The valuation of risk assets and the selection of risky investments in stock portfolios and capital budgets. *Review of Economics and Statistics* 47 (February 1965): 13–37.

Litzenberger, R. H. and Budd, A. P. Secular trends in risk premiums. *Journal of Finance* 27 (September 1972): 857–864.

Litzenberger, Robert H. and Rao, C. U. Portfolio theory and industry cost-of-capital estimates. *Journal of Financial and Quantitative Analysis* 7 (March 1972): 1443–1462.

Long, J. B. Jr. Consumption-investment decisions and equilibrium in the securities market. In *Studies in the Theory of Capital Markets*, M. C. Jensen, ed. New York: Praeger, 1972.

Long, J. B. Jr. Stock prices, inflation, and the term structure of interest rates. Working Paper Series No. 7310 (April 1973), University of Rochester.

Markowitz, H. M. Portfolio selection. *Journal of Finance* 7 (March 1952): 77–91.

Markowitz, H. M. *Portfolio Selection: Efficient Diversification of Investments.* New York: Wiley, 1959.

Mayers, D. Non-marketable assets and capital market equilibrium under uncertainty. In *Studies in the Theory of Capital Markets*, M. C. Jensen, ed. New York: Praeger, 1972.

Mayers, D. Non-marketable assets and the determination of capital asset prices in the absence of a riskless asset. *Journal of Business* 46 (April 1973): 258–267.

Mossin, J. Equilibrium in a capital asset market. *Econometrica* 34 (October 1966): 768–783.

Mossin, J. Security pricing and investment criteria in competitive markets. *American Economic Review* 59 (December 1969): 749–756.

Myers, S. C. Procedures for capital budgeting under uncertainty. *Industrial Management Review* (Spring 1968).

Myers, S. C. and Pogue, G. A. *An Evaluation of the Risk of Comsat's Common Stock* (August 1973), submitted to the FCC in connection with Comsat's rate case (FCC Docket 16070).

Radner, R. Problems in the theory of markets under uncertainty. *American Economic Review* 60 (May 1970): 454–460.

Roll, R. Bias in fitting the Sharpe model to time series data. *Journal of Financial and Quantitative Analysis* 4 (September 1969): 271–289.

Roll, R. Investment diversification and bond maturity. *Journal of Finance* 26 (March 1971): 51–66.

Roll, R. Assets, money, and commodity price inflation under uncertainty: demand theory. Working Paper 48–71–2 (August 1972), Carnegie-Mellon University.

Rubinstein, M. E. A mean-variance synthesis of corporate financial theory. *Journal of Finance* 28 (March 1973): 167–181.

Schall, Lawrence D. Asset valuation, firm investment, and firm diversification, *Journal of Business* 45 (January 1972): 11–28.

Sharpe, W. F. A simplified model for portfolio analysis. *Management Science* 9 (January 1963): 277–293.

Sharpe, W. F. Capital asset prices: a theory of market equilibrium under conditions of risk. *Journal of Finance* 19 (September 1964): 425–442.

Sharpe, W. F. *Portfolio Theory and Capital Markets.* New York: McGraw-Hill, 1970.

Tobin, J. Liquidity preference as behavior toward risk. *Review of Economic Studies* 25 (February 1958): 65–85.

Treynor, J. L. How to rate management of investment funds. *Harvard Business Review* 43 (January–February 1965): 63–75.

Wagner, W. H. and Lau, S. C. The effect of diversification on risk. *Financial Analysts' Journal* (November–December): 48–53.

Weston, J. F. Investment decisions using the capital asset pricing model. *Financial Management* (Spring 1973): 25–33.

Appendix D to Chapter 19:

The State-Preference Model and Optimal Financial Gearing[1]

Three important recent developments in finance are the capital asset pricing model (CAPM), the options pricing model (OPM) and the state preference model (SPM). The capital asset pricing model has been discussed in Appendix D to Chapter 11. The option pricing model has been set forth in Appendix A to Chapter 16. We now utilize the state-preference model to provide a wrap-up of the discussion of financial gearing.

ALTERNATIVE FUTURE STATES-OF-THE-WORLD

The state-preference model provides a useful way of looking at the world and the nature of securities. One way of describing uncertainty about the future is to say that one of a set of alternative possible states-of-the-world will occur. Definition of a set of states provides a means of describing characteristics of securities, since any security can be regarded as a contract to pay an amount that depends on the state that actually occurs.

For example, the decision to invest in the securities of a capital goods manufacturer or of a capital goods manufacturer to issue securities under a favourable set of conditions will depend upon the potential future states of the economy. Will the economy be sufficiently strong so that the demand for capital goods will provide favourable demand factors for such a manufacturer? Similarly, in the production plans of a construction company or in contemplating investment in securities of a construction company, will the future state of the economy be sufficiently strong to stimulate consumer optimism, resulting in a high volume of demand for houses? Some of the main factors influencing the future states-of-the-world that will influence the sales of a firm or the prospects for investments in a firm are set forth in Table 19D–1

As a practical matter a person will explicitly consider only a small number of factors in making a decision. Hence, individual decision makers are likely to select those variables judged to be most critical for influencing the pay-off possibilities of securities in which a position or investment is contemplated. For practical reasons, therefore, alternative future states-of-the-world might be summarized into forecasts of alternative levels or rates of growth in the gross national product. Ultimately, a wide variety of the factors listed in Table 19D–1 is likely to be reflected in levels of gross national product. Furthermore, the rate of growth and the performance of most individual industries in the economy are greatly influenced with movements in gross national product. Thus alternative future states-of-the-world may be characterized in terms of four possibilities with respect to gross national product. These might be a strong rate of growth, a moderate rate of growth, a moderate decline, or a substantial decline.

While for practical problems we might limit the number of alternative future states-of-the-world, from another standpoint – that of personal portfolio construction – we would like to provide for all possible future

1. This section was written with the valuable counsel of Professor Harry DeAngelo.

Table 19D–1 *Central Factors Influencing Estimates of Future States-of-the World for Use in Forecasting the Sales of the Firm.*

A. Economy
  1. Growth rate of GNP – real terms
  2. Growth rate of GNP – inflation
  3. Growth rate of monetary base (availability)
  4. Long-term interest rates
  5. Short-term interest rates

B. Competition
  1. Prices of rivals' products
  2. New products by rivals
  3. Changes in products by rivals
  4. New advertising campaigns by rivals
  5. Salesman and other selling efforts by rivals
  6. Prices of products in industry-substitute products
  7. Quality of industry-substitute products

C. Cultural and political factors
  1. External factors and their influences on sales of our products
  2. Product liabilities

states-of-the-world. If we could always find a security that provided some pay-off under one of the many possible future states-of-the-world, we could hedge by combining a large number of securities so that regardless of the future state of the world that occurs, we would receive some pay-off. The actual securities we encounter in the real world are complex securities in the sense that their pay-offs are positive, but generally different, amounts under alternative states-of-the-world. If actual securities could provide some pay-off for every possible future state-of-the-world by appropriately combining long and short positions in securities, we could create a pure or primitive security.

THE CONCEPT OF A PURE SECURITY

A pure or primitive security is one that pays off £1 if one particular future state-of-the-world occurs and pays off nothing if any other state-of-the-world occurs. This seems like an abstract concept so let us develop the idea further by means of an example. We shall take the case of the Mistinback Company, which sells baskets of fruit. This particular company limits its sales to only two types of baskets. Basket 1 is composed of 10 bananas and 20 apples and sells for £8. Basket 2 is composed of 30 bananas and 10 apples and sells for £9. The question posed is: what is the price of one banana or one apple only?

Table 19D–2 *Pay-offs in Relation to Prices of Baskets of Fruit.*

	Bananas	Apples	Prices
Basket #1	10	20	£8
Basket #2	30	10	£9

The situation may be summarized by the following pay-offs set forth in Table 19D–2. To calculate the value of a banana or an apple, we set up two equations:

$$10\,V_B + 20\,V_A = £8$$
$$30\,V_B + 10\,V_A = £9$$

Solving simultaneously, we obtain

$$V_A = £0.30$$
$$V_B = £0.20$$

We may now apply this same analysis to securities. Any individual security is similar to a mixed basket of goods with regard to alternative future states-of-the-world. Recall that a pure security is a security that pays £1 if a specified state occurs and nothing if any other state occurs.[2]

2. Observe that this is a clear form of non-diversification. It represents putting all of one's financial resources into one state-basket.

We may proceed to determine the price of a pure security in a manner analogous to that employed for the fruit baskets. Consider security *j*, which pays £10 if state 1 occurs and £20 if state 2 occurs. The current price of security *j* is £8. Security *k* pays £30 if state 1 occurs and £10 if state 2 occurs. Its current price is £9. Note that state 1 might be a GNP growth during the year of 8 per cent in real terms, while state 2 might represent a growth in real national product of only 1 per cent. In Table 19D–3 the pay-off for the two securities is set forth. Here, F_{j1} is the

Table 19D–3 *Pay-off Table for Securities 1 and 2.*

	State 1		State 2
Security j	$p_{j1} = £10$	$p_{j2} = £20$	$p_j = £8$
Security k	$p_{k1} = £30$	$p_{k2} = £10$	$p_k = £9$

pay-off in state 1 to security *j*, F_{k1} is the pay-off in state 1 to security *k*, etc. The equations for determining the prices for the two pure securities related to the situation described are:

$$p_1 F_{j1} + p_2 F_{j2} = p_j$$
$$p_1 F_{k1} + p_2 F_{k2} = p_k$$

Proceeding analogously to the situation for the fruit baskets, we insert the value of security pay-offs into the two equations to obtain the price of pure security 1 as 20 pence and the price of pure security 2 as 30 pence.

$$10p_1 + 20p_2 = £8$$
$$30p_1 + 10p_2 = £9$$
$$p_1 = £0.20$$
$$p_2 = £0.30$$

It should be emphasized that the p_1 of £0.20 and the p_2 of £0.30 are not assigned to securities *j* and *k*.

In sum, securities *j* and *k* represent bundles of returns under alternative future states. Any actual security provides different pay-offs for different future states. But under appropriately defined conditions, from the prices of actual securities the prices of pure securities can be determined. The concept of a pure security is useful for analytical purposes as well as for providing a useful point of view in financial analysis as illustrated in the following section, which provides an application of the state-preference model to gearing decisions.

USE OF THE SPM TO DETERMINE THE OPTIMAL FINANCIAL GEARING

The state-preference model has been used to analyse the question of optimal financial gearing.[3] The ideas will be conveyed by a specific example. It is assumed that there are four possible states-of-the-world and that the capital markets are complete in that there exists at least one security for every possible state-of-the-world such that there is a full set of primitive securities.

The symbols that will be utilized are listed in Table 19D–4. The data that will be analysed in this example are summarized in Table 19D–5.

Table 19D–4 *Symbols Used in the SPM Analysis of Optimal Financial Gearing.*

p_s = the market price of the primitive security that represents a claim on one pound in state *s* and zero pounds in all other states.

X_s = the earnings before interest and taxes that the firm will achieve in state *s* (*EBIT*)

B = the nominal payment to debt, representing a promise to pay fixed amount B, irrespective of the state that occurs.

$S(B)$ = the market value of the firm's equity as a function of the amount of debt issued by the firm.

$V(B)$ = the market value of the firm as a function of the amount of debt issued.

f_s = the costs of failure in state *s*; $0 < f_s \leq X_s$

T = the corporation tax rate.

In Table 19D–5 we have ordered the states by the size of the *EBIT* that the firm will achieve under alternative states. Column (3) of the table lists the prices of primitive securities for each of the four states. In column (4) we list the failure or liquidation costs associated with the inability to meet debt obligations.

3. Alan Kraus and Robert Litzenburger, A state-preference model of optimal financial leverage, *Journal of Finance* 28 (September 1973), pp. 911–922.

Table 19D–5 *Data for SPM Analysis of Optimal Financial Gearing.*

(1) s	(2) X_s	(3) p_s	(4) f_s
1	100	0.30	100
2	500	0.50	400
3	1000	0.20	500
4	2000	0.10	1200

In this state-preference framework let us analyse the position of debt holders and equity holders. Table 19D–6 analyses the amounts received under alternative conditions. Under condition 1 the *EBIT* is equal to or exceeds the debt obligation. Under that condition debt holders will receive B and equity holders will receive the income remaining after deduction of B and of taxes. Under condition 2 the *EBIT* is positive, but less than the amount of the debt obligation, B. The debt holders will receive whatever *EBIT* remains after payment less the failure or liquidation costs. Equity holders will receive nothing. If the *EBIT* is negative, neither the debt holders nor equity holders receive anything. These relationships are quite logical and straightforward.

Table 19D–6 *Amounts Received under Alternative Conditions.*

Condition	(1) Amount of X_s in relation to B	(2) Debt holders receive	(3) Equity holders receive
1	$X_s \geq B$	B	$(X_s - B)(1 - T)$
2	$0 \leq X_s < B$	$(X_s - f_s)$	0
3	$X_s < 0$	0	0

The amounts received under alternative conditions as outlined in Table 19D–7 are multiplied by the prices of the primitive securities to obtain the value of debt holders' receipts and of equity holders' receipts as well as the value of the firm under alternative conditions. The value of debt holders' receipts is obtained by simply multiplying what the debt holders receive by p_s and similarly for the value of equity holders' receipts. The value of the firm is obtained by adding the value of the debt holders' receipts to the value of the equity holders' receipts.

Table 19D–7 *Formulas for the Value of the Firm under Alternative Conditions.*

Condition	(1) Amount of X_s in relation to B	(2) Debt holders receive	(3) Value of debt holders' receipts in state s	(4) Equity holders receive	(5) Value of equity holders' receipts in state s	(6) Value of the firm in state s
1	$X_s \geq B$	B	Bp_s	$(X_s - B)(1 - T)$	$(X_s - B)(1 - T)p_s$	$Bp_s + (X_s - B)(1 - T)p_s$
2	$0 < X_s < B$	$(X_s - f_s)$	$(X_s - f_s)p_s$	0	0	$(X_s - f_s)p_s$
3	$X_s < 0$	0	0	0	0	0

In Table 19D–8 we utilize the preceding information to calculate the value of the firm under alternative debt levels. On the left-hand side of the table we begin by specifying the amount of debt and the resulting relationships between X_s, the *EBIT* under alternative states, in relationship to the promised payment to debt. The subsequent lines on the left then set forth the applicable formulas for calculating the state contingent value of the firm depending upon the level of debt utilized. For example, when the firm is ungeared its value is equal to the sum of (*EBIT*) times (1 minus the tax rate) times (the price of the primitive security for each state). Using the illustrative data from Table 19D–5, we obtain the amounts on the right-hand column of Table 19D–8.

When debt is 100, *EBIT* is equal to or greater than debt for all states-of-the-world. The formula employed, therefore, is set forth in Table 19D–7 under condition 1 and shown in column (6). Again, the numbers from Table 19 D–5 are inserted to obtain a current market value of the firm, $V(100)$, of £385 for debt level 2 in Table 19D–8.

We shall discuss the pattern for debt of £1000 as illustrative of the remaining sections of Table 19D–8. When B is equal to £1000 the *EBIT* is less than the promised payment to debt for states 1 and 2 and equal to or greater than debt for states 3 and 4. As Table 19D–7 indicates, condition 2, therefore, obtains for states 1 and 2 while condition 1 obtains for states 3 and 4. The applicable formulas are, therefore, utilized to obtain a $V(1000)$ of £375, as shown in Table 19D–8.

An analysis of Table 19D–8 shows that the highest value of the firm is obtained when debt gearing of £500 is employed by the firm. For any other level of debt obligations the value of the firm is lower. This example illustrates that with taxes and liquidation costs there exists an optimal amount of gearing.[4]

Table 19D–8 *Calculations of the Value of the Firm under Alternative Debt Levels.*

Condition	State	Value of firm's state s pay-off	
1. $B = 0, X_s \geq B$ for all s	1	$100(0.5)0.3 =$	15
$V_s(0) = \sum_{s=1}^{4} X_s(1-T)p_s$	2	$500(0.5)0.5 =$	125
	3	$1000(0.5)0.2 =$	100
	4	$2000(0.5)0.1 =$	100
		$V(0) =$	£340
2. $B = 100, X_s \geq B$ for all s	1	$100(0.3)+(100-100)(0.5)0.3 =$	30
$V_s(100) = \sum_{s=1}^{4} Bp_s + \sum_{s=1}^{4} (X_s - B)(1-T)p_s$	2	$100(.5)+(500-100)(0.5)0.5 =$	150
	3	$100(0.2)+(1000-100)(0.5)0.2 =$	110
	4	$100(0.1)+(2000-100)(0.5)0.1 =$	95
		$V(100) =$	£385
3. $B = 500, X_s < B$ for $s = 1$	1	$(100-100)0.3 =$	0
$X_s > B$ for $s = 2,3,4$	2	$500(0.5)+(500-500)(0.5)0.5 =$	250
$V_s(500) = (X_s - f_s)p_s$ for $s = 1$	3	$500(0.2)+(1000-500)(0.5)0.2 =$	200
$V_s(500) = \sum_{s=2}^{4} Bp_s + \sum_{s=2}^{4} (X_s - B)(1-T)p_s$	4	$500(0.1)+(2000-500)(0.5)0.1 =$	75
		$V(500) =$	£525
4. $B = 1000, X_s < B$ for $s = 1,2$	1	$(100-100)(0.3) =$	0
$X_s \geq B$ for $s = 3,4$	2	$(500-400)(0.5)0.5 =$	25
$V_s(1000) = \sum_{s=1}^{2} (X_s - f_s)p_s$	3	$1000(0.2)+(1000-1000)(0.5)0.2 =$	200
$V_s(1000) = \sum_{s=3}^{4} Bp_s + \sum_{s=3}^{4} (X_s - B)(1-T)p_s$	4	$1000(0.1)+(2000-1000)(0.5)0.1 =$	150
		$V(1000) =$	£375
5. $B = 2000, X_s < B$ for $s = 1,2,3$	1	$(100-100)(0.3) =$	0
$X_s \geq B$ for $s = 4$	2	$(500-400)(0.5)0.5 =$	25
$V_s(2000) = \sum_{s=1}^{3} (X_s - f_s)p_s$	3	$(1000-500)(0.5)0.2 =$	50
$V_s(2000) = Bp_s + (X_s - B)(1-T)p_s$ for $s = 4$.	4	$2000(0.1)+(2000-2000)(0.5)0.1 =$	200
		$V(2000) =$	£275

4. Kraus and Litzenburger conclude with regard to their analysis as follows: 'Contrary to the traditional net income approach to valuation, if the firm's debt obligation exceeds its earnings in some states the firm's market value is *not* necessarily a concave (from below) function of its debt obligation' (p. 918). However, this result follows only from their formulation of the problem in discontinuous terms. The problem could equally well be formulated with continuous functions in such a way that the resulting value of the firm would be continuous and concave (from below) in B.

Implications for Gearing Decisions

Our use of the state-preference model has thereby enabled us to analyse some conditions under which an optimal capital gearing exists.[5] This result is, of course, not perfectly general since it was based on a specific illustration. Some more general relationships will now be set forth. First we need to introduce the concept of complete capital markets. Complete capital markets are those in which a security exists for every possible state-of-the-world so that it is possible to create a full set of primitive securities. In complete capital markets, in the absence of imperfections such as taxes, agency costs and liquidation costs, capital structure would not matter (the Modigliani – Miller propositions would obtain).

The gearing policy of a firm consists of repackaging the claims on its *EBIT*. The only reason why repackaging of claims on the firm's *EBIT* would have an effect on the value of the firm would be because the firm had thereby provided investors with a new set of market opportunities for forming portfolios or taking a position with regard to future states-of-the-world. But if the capital markets are already complete, the firm has added nothing by a repackaging of claims on *EBIT* since no new independent investment opportunities can be provided. All possible future states-of-the-world have already been covered by existing securities.

The proof of the Modigliani – Miller independence thesis does not depend on the assumption that the firm will always meet its debt obligations. For some debt levels the firm may not meet its debt obligations in some states-of-the-world and would be liquidated. If there are no liquidation penalties or liquidation costs (the situation in a perfect market), the *nature* of the claims on the firm's *EBIT* have been fundamentally unaltered. Thus the value of the firm remains unchanged.

Thus complete and perfect capital markets constitute sufficient conditions for the Modigliani – Miller propositions to hold. But as the foregoing example illustrated, the existence of corporation tax and liquidation penalties represents market imperfections under which the capital structure choice will affect the value of the firm. We conclude that Modigliani and Miller are correct under properly specified conditions.

Furthermore, it is the absence of complete and perfect capital markets that makes capital structure matter. It is not clear whether the actual number of securities approximates the condition of completeness of the capital markets. However, without question there are company taxes as well as agency and liquidation costs. The extent to which agency and liquidation affect capital structure significantly is an empirical matter.

The existence of market imperfections will cause the value of the firm to behave as generally depicted in Figure 19D–1. As the amount of debt in the financial structure increases, the present value of tax savings will initially cause the market value of the firm to rise as a linear function. The slope of the line will be equal to the corporation tax rate. However, at some point agency and liquidation costs will cause the market value of the firm to bend down from what it would be if the only imperfection were corporation tax.

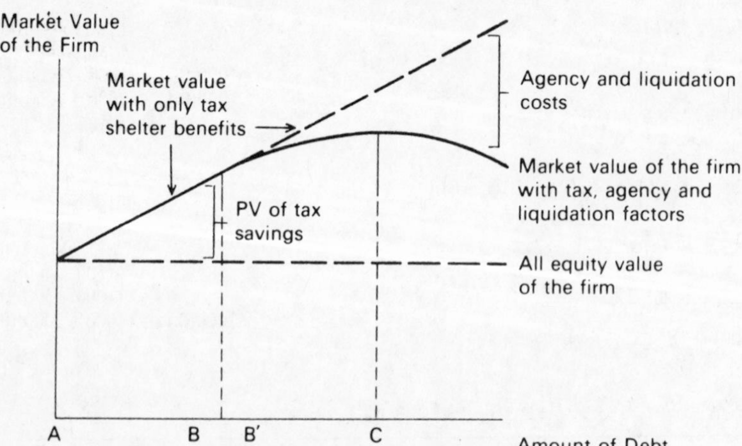

Figure 19D–1 *Influence of Debt on the Market Value of the Firm.*

THE NATURE OF AGENCY COSTS

The nature of agency costs has been indicated in Appendix A to Chapter 16 dealing with the options pricing model. It was shown that if the shareholders move the firm into a more risky production plan, the value of the

5. Problem 19D–4 illustrates that the production decisions and capital structure decisions of the firm can be interdependent given the presence of imperfections.

equity will rise in relation to the value of the debt. Thus there is a divergence of interest between shareholders and debt holders. In addition, if the managers of firms are paid on the basis of the size of the firm rather than its profitability rate, managers may seek to increase the size of the firm subject ot achieving some profit ratio which will avoid confrontation with the shareholders. Debenture-holders will be concerned if the inefficiencies and low profitability that may result from seeking size for its own sake potentially impair the coverage of fixed charges.

Because of the possible divergences of interests, the debenture contract will contain restrictions on the freedom of action of both the shareholders and the managers of the firm. These restrictions limit the freedom of action of the managers and shareholders and, therefore, represent some 'costs'. In addition, it is not possible to cover every possible contingency by contract restrictions.

In addition, 'liquidation costs' arise before actual formal legal procedures of liquidation take place. As the operating performance of the firm deteriorates in relation to its fixed contractual obligations, or as the amount of debt increases in relation to the firm's equity for a given level of operating performance, the financial markets may become increasingly reluctant to provide additional financing. Thus as conditions of this kind deteriorate, a number of costs will arise resulting from different degrees of financial inadequacy or failure on the part of the firm. These 'liquidation costs' that may be incurred successively include the following:

1. Financing under increasingly onerous terms, conditions and rates. These represent increased costs.
2. Loss of key employees. The prospects of the firm are unfavourable so that able employees and executives seek alternative employment.
3. The loss of suppliers of the most saleable types of goods. The suppliers may fear that they will not be paid or that this customer does not represent one who will achieve growth in sales in the future.
4. The loss of sales due to lack of confidence on the part of customers that the firm will be around to stand behind the product.
5. Lack of financing under any terms, conditions and rates to carry out favourable but risky investments. This is because the overall prospects of the firm are not favourable in relation to its existing obligations.
6. The need to liquidate fixed assets to meet working capital requirements. A forced reduction in the scale of operations.
7. Formal liquidation proceedings. Legal and administrative costs will be incurred. In addition, a receiver will be appointed to conduct the operation of the firm, which may involve a disruption of operations.

As a consequence of liquidation costs, the market value of the firm may begin to diverge from the straight line representing market value with only tax shelter benefits shown in Figure 19D–1. At some point, liquidation costs may become so large that the indicated market value of the firm actually begins to turn down, point C in Figure 19D–1. This point would represent the target gearing ratio at which the market value of the firm is maximized – the optimal financial structure.

PROBLEMS

19D–1. Security A pays £30 if state 1 occurs and £10 if state 2 occurs. Security B pay £20 if state 1 occurs and £40 if state 2 occurs. The price of security A is £5 and the price of security B is £10.
(a) Set up the pay-off table for securities A and B.
(b) Determine the prices of the two pure securities.

19D–2. The Sand Company is evaluating alternatives for financing its production. There are essentially three possible levels of production depending on which state-of-the-world occurs. Cost of failure and earnings before interest and taxes are different for each state. The company is considering use of debt in the amount of £0, £1000, £3000 or £6000, and would like to know which alternative will maximize the expected value of the firm, given the probabilities (or primitive security prices) associated with each state. The tax rate is 50 per cent.

State (s)	Planned production *EBIT* (X_s)	Price of primitive security (p_s)	Cost of failure (f_s)
1	2 000	0.30	500
2	4 000	0.50	1 500
3	8 000	0.20	4 000

19D–3. The Kendrick Company is evaluating three alternative production plans (X_s, Y_s and Z_s) as shown below. Cost of failure is the same for each plan. Prices of primitive securities for the four possible states are as indicated.

State (s)	Price of primitive security (p_s)	Cost of failure (f_s)	Planned production EBIT (X_s)	(Y_s)	(Z_s)
1	0.10	100	200	600	100
2	0.40	600	1200	1500	800
3	0.30	1500	3000	2800	3200
4	0.20	2000	3500	3000	3800

Assuming the production will be financed with funds including £3000 of debt, which of the three production plans would maximize the value of the firm? The tax rate is 50 per cent.

19D–4. Under production plan A the *EBIT* of the firm for alternative states-of-the-world is indicated by the X_s column. The price of the primitive pure securities in state s is p_s. The liquidation costs are f_s. Under production plan B, the *EBIT* of the firm is indicated by X'_s. Production plan B involves giving up 300 in state 3 to add 300 in state 2. Since the prices of pure securities and liquidation costs are given by the market, they remain unchanged under production plan B. The tax rate is 50 per cent.

s	X_s	p_s	f_s	X'_s
1	500	0.20	100	500
2	600	0.40	300	900
3	1400	0.30	500	1100
4	2000	0.10	800	2000

(a) What is the optimal financial gearing for production plan A by the criterion of maximizing the value of the firm?
(b) Is the optimal financial gearing changed by new production plan B?
(c) What implications do the results under A and B have for the interdependence between production plans and financial structure?

SELECTED REFERENCES

Arrow, K. J. The role of securities in the optimal allocation of risk-bearing. *Review of Economic Studies* 31 (April 1964): 91–96.

Hirshleifer, J. Investment decisions under uncertainty: application of the state-preference approach. *Quarterly Journal of Economics* 80 (May 1966): 262–277.

Kraus, Alan and Litzenberger, Robert. A state-preference model of optimal financial leverage. *Journal of Finance* 28 (September 1973): 911–922.

Myers, S. C. A time-state preference model of security valuation. *Journal of Financial and Quantitative Analysis* 3 (March 1968): 1–33.

Sharpe, W. F. *Portfolio Theory and Capital Markets*. New York: McGraw-Hill 1970. Chap. 10, State-preference theory.

Chapter 20

Dividend Policy and Internal Financing

Dividend policy determines the division of earnings between payments to shareholders and re-investment in the firm. Retained earnings are one of the most significant sources of funds for financing corporate growth, but dividends constitute the cash flows that accrue to shareholders. The factors that influence the allocation of earnings to dividends or retained earnings are the subject of this chapter.

FACTORS INFLUENCING DIVIDEND POLICY

What factors determine the extent to which a firm will pay out dividends instead of retain earnings? As a first step towards answering this question, we shall consider some of the factors that influence dividend policy.

Dividend rules

Although the legal rules regarding dividend policy are complicated, their essential nature can be stated briefly. The legal rules provide:

1. that dividends cannot be paid if this would result in a loss of solvency for the company;
2. that losses of fixed assets need not be made good before treating a revenue profit as available for dividend;
3. that losses of circulating assets in the current accounting period must be made good before a dividend can be paid;
4. that losses made in earlier accounting periods need not be made good before a dividend can be paid. Provided that there is a profit on the current year's trading dividends can be paid;
5. that undistributed profits of past years may be distributed in future years;
6. that in the treatment of capital gains, a realized capital gain may be distributed if the

articles so permit, after a general bona fide appraisal of all assets, and even an unrealized capital gain (Dimbula Valley [Ceylon] Tea Co. Ltd v. Laurie, 1961).

To summarize: dividends must be paid from earnings, either from the current year's earnings or from previous years' earnings, as reflected in the item 'retained earnings' in the balance sheet.

Since 1966, however, various governments have operated some form of dividend control as a part of the operation of a prices and incomes policy. These statutory regulations have meant that companies have not been able to pay as large a proportion of their earnings in the form of dividends as they may have wished in recent years.

Legal aspects are significant. They provide the framework within which dividend policies can be formulated. Within these boundaries, however, financial and economic factors have a major influence on policy.

Liquidity position

Profits held as retained earnings (which show up in the left-hand side of the balance sheet in the account labelled 'retained earnings') are generally invested in assets required for the conduct of the business. Retained earnings from preceding years are already invested in plant and equipment, stocks and other assets; they are not held as cash. This has been particularly true of UK companies in recent years, with high levels of the stock appreciation element in profits, and the need to allow for replacement of lost assets in addition to historic cost depreciation. Thus, although a firm has had a record of earnings, it may not be able to pay cash dividends because of its liquidity position. Indeed, a growing firm, even a very profitable one, typically has a pressing need for funds. In such a situation the firm may elect not to pay cash dividends.

Need to repay debt

When a firm has sold debt to finance expansion or to substitute for other forms of financing, it is faced with two alternatives; it can refund the debt at maturity by replacing it with another form of security, or it can make provision for paying off the debt. If the decision is to redeem the debt, this will generally require the retention of earnings.

Rate of asset expansion

The more rapid the rate at which the firm is growing, the greater will be its needs for financing asset expansion. The greater the future need for funds, the more likely the firm is to retain earnings rather than pay them out. If a firm seeks to raise funds externally, natural sources are the present shareholders who already know the company. But if earnings are paid out as dividends and are subjected to high personal income tax rates, only a portion of the earnings would be available for re-investment.

Profit rate

The rate of return on assets determines the relative attractiveness of paying out earnings in the form of dividends to shareholders who will use them elsewhere, compared with the productivity of their use in the present enterprise.

Stability of earnings

If earnings are relatively stable, a firm is better able to predict what its future earnings will be. A stable firm is therefore more likely to pay out a higher percentage of its earnings than is a firm with fluctuating earnings. The unstable firm is not certain that in subsequent years the hoped-for earnings will be realized, so it is more likely to retain a high proportion of earnings. A lower dividend will be easier to maintain if earnings should fall off in the future.

Access to the capital markets

A large, well-established firm with a record of profitability and some stability of earnings will have easy access to capital markets and other forms of external financing. The small, new, or venturesome firm, however, is riskier for potential investors. Its ability to raise equity or debt funds from capital markets is restricted, and it must retain more earnings to finance its operations. A well-established firm is thus likely to have a higher dividend payout rate than is a new or small firm, although a small firm's distribution policy may be dictated by close company regulations.

Control

Another important variable is the effect of alternative sources of financing on the control situation in the firm. Some companies, as a matter of policy, will expand only to the extent of their internal earnings. This policy is defended on the grounds that raising funds by selling additional ordinary shares dilutes the control of the dominant group in the company. At the same time, selling debt increases the risks of fluctuating earnings to the present owners of the company. Reliance on internal financing in order to maintain control reduces the dividend payout.

Tax position of shareholders

The tax position of the owners of the company greatly influences the desire for dividends. For example, a company with a small number of shareholders in high tax brackets is likely to pay a relatively low dividend. The owners of the company are interested in taking their income in the form of capital gains rather than as dividends, which are subject to higher personal income tax rates. However, the shareholders of a large company with many shareholders may be interested in a high dividend payout.

At times there is a conflict of interest in large companies between shareholders in high income tax brackets and those in low tax brackets. The former may prefer to see a low dividend payout and a high rate of earnings retention in the hope of an appreciation in the capital value of the company. The lower income shareholders may prefer a relatively high dividend payout rate. The dividend policy of such a firm may be a compromise between a low and a high payout – an intermediate payout ratio. If, however, one group dominates and sets, let us say, a low payout policy, those shareholders who seek income are likely to sell their shares over time and shift into higher yielding shares. *Thus, to at least some extent, a firm's payout policy determines its shareholder types, as well as vice versa.* This has been called the 'clientele influence' on dividend policy.

Tax on improperly accumulated earnings

In order to prevent a small group of shareholders from using a company as a means of avoiding high rates of personal income tax, tax regulations provide for an additional tax on unnecessary levels of retained earnings. This matter is dealt with more comprehensively in Appendix A, 'The Tax Environment', at the end of the book, but the basic idea is to tax the shareholders of those companies which have failed to pay adequate dividends as though the company had indeed paid out a greater amount in the form of dividends.

DIVIDEND POLICY DECISION

A fundamental relation observed in dividend policy is the widespread tendency of companies to pursue a relatively stable dividend policy. Profits of firms fluctuate considerably with changes in the level of business activity, although dividends are usually more stable than earnings.

Most companies seek to maintain a target dividend per share. However, dividends increase with a lag after earnings rise. Dividends are increased only after an increase in earnings appears clearly sustainable and relatively permanent. When dividends have been increased, strenuous efforts are made to maintain them at the new level. If earnings decline, the existing dividend will generally be maintained until it is clear that an earnings recovery will not take place.

Figure 20–1 illustrates these ideas by showing the earnings and dividends patterns for the Walter Watch Company over a 30-year period. Initially earnings are 20 pence and dividends 10 pence a share, providing a 50 per cent payout ratio. Earnings rise for four years, while dividends remain constant; thus, the payout ratio falls during this period. During 1955 and 1956, earnings fall substantially; however, the dividend is maintained and the payout rises above the 50 per cent target. During the period between 1956 and 1960, earnings experience a sustained rise. Dividends are held constant for a time, while management seeks to determine whether the earnings increase is permanent. By 1961, the earnings gains seem permanent, and dividends are raised in three steps to re-establish the 50 per cent target payout. During 1965 a strike causes earnings to fall below the regular dividend; expecting the earnings decline to be temporary, management maintains the dividend. Earnings fluctuate on a fairly high plateau from 1966 to 1972, during which time dividends remain constant. A new increase in earnings induces management to raise the dividend in 1973 to re-establish the 50 per cent payout ratio.

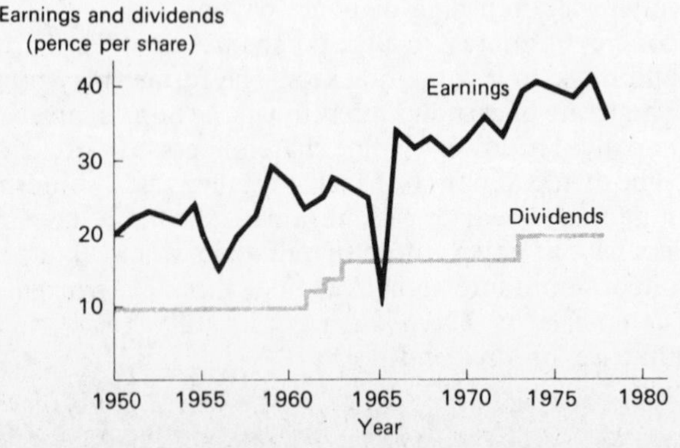

Figure 20–1 *Dividends and Earnings Patterns, Walter Watch Company.*

RATIONALE FOR STABLE DIVIDENDS

Walter Watch, like the great majority of firms, kept its dividend relatively stable but allowed its payout ratio to fluctuate. Why would it follow such a policy?

Consider the stable dividend policy from the standpoint of the shareholders as owners of a company. Their acquiescence with the general practice must imply that stable dividend policies lead to higher share prices on the average than do alternative dividend policies. Is this a fact? Does a stable dividend policy maximize equity values for a company? There has been no truly conclusive empirical study of dividend policy, so any answer to the question must be regarded as tentative. On logical grounds, however, there is reason to believe that a stable dividend policy will lead to higher share prices. First, investors might be expected to value more highly dividends they are more sure of receiving, since fluctuating dividends are riskier than stable dividends. Accordingly, the same average amount of dividends received under a fluctuating dividend policy is likely to have a higher discount factor applied to it than is applied to dividends under a stable dividend policy. In the terms used in Chapter 19, this means that a firm with a stable dividend would have a lower required rate of return – or cost of equity capital – than one whose dividends fluctuate.

Second, many shareholders live on income received in the form of dividends. Such shareholders would be greatly inconvenienced by fluctuating dividends, and they would be likely to pay a premium for a share with a relatively assured minimum dividend.

On the other hand, if a firm's investment opportunities fluctuate from year to year, should it not retain more earnings during some years in order to take advantage of these opportunities when they appear, then increase dividends when good internal investment opportunities are scarce? This line of reasoning would lead to the recommendation of a fluctuating payout for companies whose investment opportunities are unstable. However, the logic of the argument is diminished by recognizing that it is possible to maintain a reasonably stable dividend by using outside financing, including debt, to smooth out the differences between the funds needed for investment and the amount of money provided by retained earnings.

ALTERNATIVE DIVIDEND POLICIES

Before going on to consider dividend policy at a theoretical level, it is useful to summarize the three major types of dividend policies.

Stable dividend per share

Most firms pursue a policy of paying out a stable money sum per share each year. This is the policy that is implied when we say 'stable dividend policy'.

Constant payout ratio

A very few firms follow a policy of paying out a constant percentage of earnings. Earnings will surely fluctuate, so following this policy necessarily means that the amount of dividends will fluctuate. For reasons discussed in the preceding section, this policy is not likely to maximize the value of a firm's shares.

Low regular dividend plus extras

The low-regular-dividend-plus-extras policy is a compromise between the first two. It gives the firm flexibility, but it leaves investors somewhat uncertain about what their dividend income will be. But if a firm's earnings are quite volatile, this policy may well be its best choice.

The relative merits of these three policies can be evaluated better after a discussion of the residual theory of dividends, the topic covered in the next section.

RESIDUAL THEORY OF DIVIDENDS[1]

In the preceding chapters on capital budgeting and the cost of capital, we indicated that, generally, the cost of capital schedule and the investment opportunity schedule must be combined before the cost of capital can be established. In other words, the optimum capital budget, the marginal cost of capital and the marginal rate of return on investment are determined *simultaneously*. In this section we examine this simultaneous solution in the framework of what is called *the residual theory of dividends*. The theory draws on materials developed earlier in the book – capital budgeting and the cost of capital – and serves to provide a bridge between these key concepts.

The starting point in the theory is that investors prefer to have the firm retain and re-invest earnings rather than pay them out in dividends *if the return on re-invested earnings exceeds the rate of return the investor could, himself, obtain on other investments of comparable risk.* If the company can re-invest retained earnings at a 20 per cent rate of return, while the best rate the shareholder can obtain if the earnings are passed on to him in the form of dividends is 10 per cent, then the shareholder would prefer to have the firm retain the profits.

We saw in Chapter 19 that the cost of equity capital obtained from retained earnings is an *opportunity cost* that reflects rates of return open to equity investors. If a firm's shareholders could buy other shares of equal risk and obtain a 10 per cent dividend-plus-capital-gains yield, then 10 per cent is the firm's cost of retained earnings. As shown in Chapter 19, the cost of retained earnings is not necessarily cheaper than the cost of external equity capital since the introduction of the imputation system.

Most firms have an optimum debt ratio that calls for at least some debt, so new financing is done partly with debt and partly with equity. Debt has a different, and generally lower, cost than equity, so the two forms of capital must be combined to find the *weighted average cost of capital.* As long as the firm finances at the optimum point, using an optimum amount of debt and equity, and provided it uses only internally generated equity (retained earnings), its marginal cost of capital will be minimized.

Internally generated equity is available for financing a certain amount of new investment; beyond this amount, the firm must turn to more expensive new ordinary shares. At the point where new shares must be sold, the cost of equity and, consequently, the marginal cost of capital, rises.

These concepts, which were developed in Chapter 19, are illustrated in Figure 20–2. The firm has a marginal cost of capital of 10 per cent so long as retained earnings are available; the marginal cost of capital begins to rise when new shares must be sold.

Our hypothetical firm has £50 million of earnings and a 50 per cent optimum debt ratio.

---

1. 'Residual' implies *left over*. The residual theory of dividend policy implies that dividends are paid after internal investment opportunities have been exhausted.

It can make net investments (investments in addition to asset replacements financed from depreciation) up to £100 million: £50 million from retained earnings plus £50 million new debt supported by the retained earnings if it does not pay dividends. Therefore, its marginal cost of capital is constant at 10 per cent for up to £100 million of capital. Beyond £100 million, the marginal cost of capital begins rising as the firm begins to use more expensive new ordinary shares.

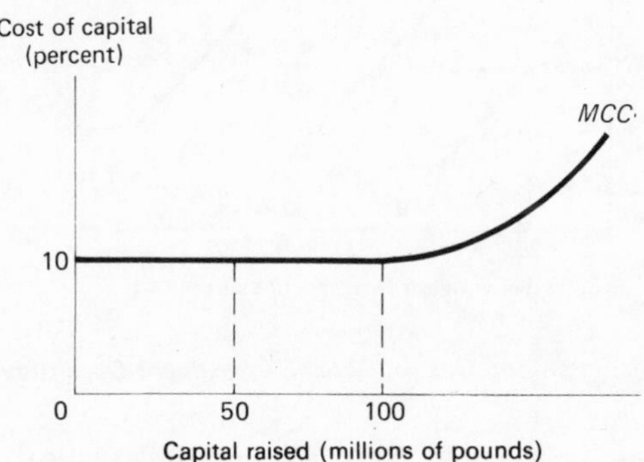

Figure 20–2 *The Marginal Cost of Capital.*

Next, suppose the firm's capital budgeting department draws up a list of investment opportunities, ranked in the order of each project's *IRR*, and plots them on a graph. The investment opportunity curves of three different years – one for a good year (IRR_1), one for a normal year (IRR_2), and one for a bad year (IRR_3) – are shown in Figure 20–3. IRR_1 shows that the firm can invest more money, and at higher rates of return, than it can when the investment opportunities are those given by IRR_2 and IRR_3.

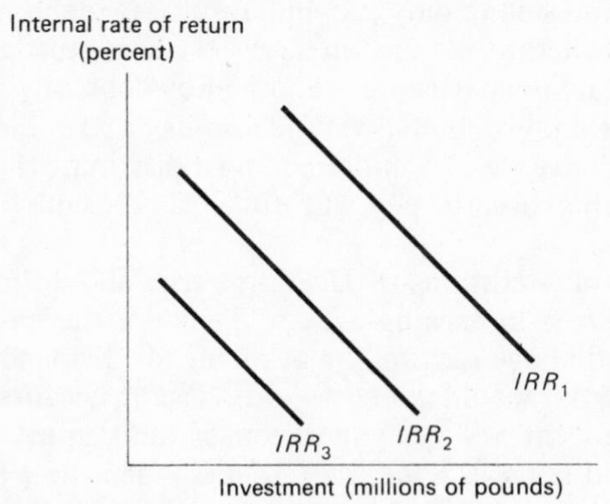

Figure 20–3 *Investment Opportunities.*

Now we combine the investment opportunity schedule with the cost of capital schedule; this is done in Figure 20–4. The point where the investment opportunity curve cuts the cost of capital curve defines the proper level of new investment. When investment opportunities are relatively poor, the optimum level of investment is £25 million; when opportunities are about normal, £75 million should be invested; and when opportunities are relatively good, the firm should make new investments in the amount of £125 million.

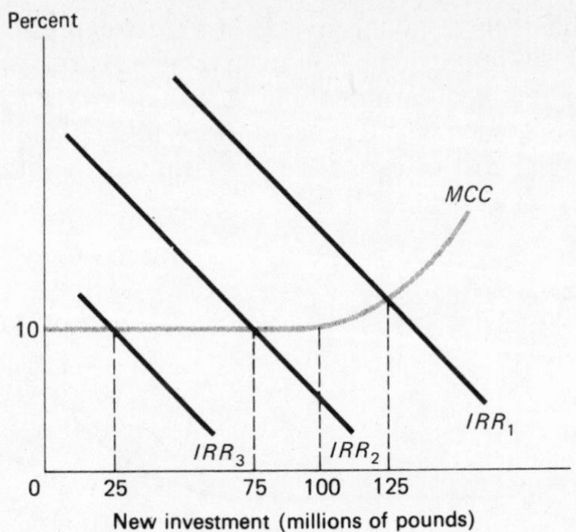

Figure 20–4 *Interrelationship among Cost of Capital, Investment Opportunities and New Investment.*

Consider the situation where IRR_1 is the appropriate schedule. Suppose the firm has £50 million in earnings and a 50 per cent target debt ratio, so it can finance £100 million, £50 million earnings plus £50 million debt, from retained earnings plus new debt *if it retains all its earnings.* If it pays part of the earnings in dividends, then it will have to begin using external equity capital (which could be more expensive than retained earnings, as explained in Chapter 19) sooner, so the cost of capital curve will rise sooner. This suggests that under the conditions of IRR_1, the firm should retain all its earnings and actually sell some new ordinary shares in order to take advantage of its investment opportunities. Its payout ratio would thus be nil.

Under the conditions of IRR_2, however, the firm should invest only £75 million. How should this investment be financed? First, notice that if it retains the full amount of its earnings, £50 million, it will need to sell only £25 million of new debt. However, by retaining £50 million and selling only £25 million of new debt, the firm will move away from its target capital structure. To stay on target, the firm must finance the required £75 million half by equity – retained earnings – and half by debt, or £37.5 million by retained earnings and £37.5 million by debt. Now if the firm has £50 million in total earnings and decides to retain and re-invest £37.5 million, it must distribute the £12.5 million residual to its shareholders. In this case, the payout ratio is 25 per cent (£12.5 million divided by £50 million).

Finally, under the bad conditions of IRR_3, the firm should invest only £25 million. Because it has £50 million in earnings, it could finance the entire £25 million out of retained earnings and still have £25 million available for dividends. Should this be done? Under the assumptions, this would not be a good decision, because it would move the firm away from its target debt ratio. To stay in the 50–50 debt/equity position, the firm must retain £12.5 million and sell £12.5 million of debt. When the £12.5 million of retained earnings is subtracted from the £50 million of earnings, the firm is left with a residual of £37.5, the amount that should be paid out in dividends. In this case the payout ratio is 75 per cent.

LONG-RUN VIEWPOINT

There seems to be a conflict between the residual theory and the statement made in an earlier section that firms should and do maintain reasonably stable cash dividends. How can this conflict be reconciled?

A firm may have a target capital structure without being at that target at all times. In other words, we would not recommend that a firm adjust its dividend each and every year – indeed, this is not necessary. Firms do have target debt ratios, but they also have a certain amount of flexibility – they can be moderately above or below the target debt position in any one year with no serious adverse consequences. This means that if an unusually large number of good investments is available in a particular year, the firm does not necessarily have to cut its dividend to take advantage of them – it can borrow somewhat more heavily than usual in that particular year without getting its debt ratio too far out of line. Obviously, however, this excessive reliance on debt could not continue for too many years without seriously affecting the debt ratio, necessitating either a sale of new shares or a cut in dividends and an attendant increase in the level of retained earnings.

HIGH AND LOW DIVIDEND PAYOUT INDUSTRIES

Some industries are experiencing rapid growth in the demand for their products, affording firms in these industries many good investment opportunities. Electronics, office equipment, entertainment and oil companies are examples of such industries in recent years. Other industries have experienced much slower growth, or perhaps even declines. Examples of such slow-growth industries are cigarette manufacturing and textiles. Still other industries are growing at about the same rate as the general economy – banking and machine tools are representative.

The theory suggests that firms in rapidly growing industries should generally have IRR curves that are relatively far out to the right on graphs such as Figure 20–4; for example, Ladbrokes and Plessey might have investment opportunities similar to IRR_1. The tobacco companies, on the other hand, could be expected to have investment schedules similar to IRR_3, while IRR_2 might be appropriate for Barclays Bank.

Each of these firms would, of course, experience shifts in investment opportunities from year to year, but the curves would *tend* to be in about the same part of the graph. In other words, firms such as Ladbrokes would *tend* to have more investment opportunities than money, so they would *tend* to have very low payout ratios. British American Tobacco, on the other hand, would *tend* to have more money than good investments, so we would expect to find British American Tobacco paying out a relatively high percentage of earnings in dividends. These companies do, in fact, conform with our expectations.

CONFLICTING THEORIES ON DIVIDENDS[2]

Two basic schools of thought on dividend policy have been expressed in the theoretical literature of finance. One school, associated with Myron Gordon and John Lintner, among others, holds that the capital gains expected to result from earnings retention are more risky than are dividend expectations. Accordingly, this school suggests that the earnings of a firm with a low-payout ratio will typically be capitalized at higher rates than the earnings of a high-payout firm, other things being equal.

The other school, associated with Merton Miller and Franco Modigliani, holds that

2. See the references at the end of this chapter for an extended discussion of the theory of dividend policy.

investors are basically indifferent to returns in the form of dividends or capital gains. If, when firms raise or lower their dividends, their share prices tend to rise or fall in like manner, does this prove that investors prefer dividends? Miller and Modigliani argue that it does not, that any effect a change in dividends has on the price of a firm's shares is related primarily to *information about expected future earnings conveyed by a change in dividends.* Recalling that boards of directors dislike cutting dividends, Miller and Modigliani argue that increases in cash dividends raise expectations about the level of future earnings – dividend increases have favourable *information content.* In terms of Figure 20–1, Miller and Modigliani would say that Walter Watch's dividend increases in 1961, 1962, 1963 and 1973 had information content about future earnings – these dividend increases signalled to shareholders that management expected the recent earnings increases to be permanent.

Dividends are probably subject to less uncertainty than capital gains, but dividends are taxed at a higher rate than capital gains. How do these two forces balance out? Some argue that the uncertainty factor dominates; others feel that the differential tax rate is the stronger force and causes investors to favour retention of earnings; still others – and we put ourselves in this group – argue that it is difficult to generalize. Depending on the tax status and the current income needs of its set of shareholders (both brokerage costs and capital gains taxes make it difficult for individual shareholders to switch their holdings), as well as the firm's internal investment opportunities, the optimum dividend policy will vary from firm to firm. We thus place heavy emphasis on the 'clientele effect'.

DIVIDEND PAYMENTS

Dividends are normally paid half yearly. For example, Findlay Ltd has paid annual dividends of 25 pence. In common financial language, we say that Findlay Ltd's *regular annual dividend* is 25 pence. The management of a company such as Findlay Ltd, sometimes by an explicit statement in the annual report and sometimes by implication, conveys to shareholders an expectation that the regular dividend will be maintained if at all possible. Further, management conveys its belief that earnings will be sufficient to maintain the dividend.

Under other conditions, a firm's cash flows and investment needs may be too volatile for it to set a very high regular dividend; on the average, however, it needs a high dividend payout to dispose of funds not necessary for re-investment. In such a case, the directors can set a relatively low regular dividend – low enough that it can be maintained even in low profit years or in years when a considerable amount of re-investment is needed – and supplement it with an extra dividend in years when excess funds are available.

SCRIP DIVIDENDS AND STOCK SPLITS

One of the significant aspects of dividend policy is that of *scrip dividends* and *stock splits.* A scrip dividend is paid in additional shares instead of in cash. This is essentially a transfer to the shareholder of a number of shares without the shareholder having to pay any extra cash for those shares. This operation preserves company liquidity since no cash leaves the company. Although the number of ordinary shares is increased there should be no fall in the share price provided that the company has sufficient profitable investment opportunities and that the number of new shares issued is not too great. Although shares are not as liquid as cash, they can be converted into cash by sales in the stock market at the going market price. Fluctuations in stock market prices may mean that shareholders suffer capital losses, but there is also the possibility that capital gains may be made.

A stock split, like a scrip dividend, increases the number of shares in a company without raising any new funds. A larger number of ordinary shares is issued. In a two-for-one split, each shareholder would receive two shares for each one previously held. Instead of an investor's holding one share with a par value of £1 he would own two shares with a par value of 50 pence each.

Stock splits are usually made in order to increase the marketability of a company's shares. If the marketability of a company's shares increases, the value of an investor's holding should also increase. Further, a stock split will mean that after the necessary dividend adjustment it is likely that a greater amount of dividend will be paid to the investor than was the case before the split. The increased dividends may lead to an increase in the value of the investor's holding. Since from a practical viewpoint there is little difference between a scrip dividend and a stock split, the issues outlined below are discussed in connection with both scrip dividends and stock splits.

Price effects

The results of a careful empirical study of the effects of scrip dividends are available and can be used as a basis for observations on the price effects of scrip dividends.[3] The findings of the study are presented in Table 20–1. When scrip dividends were associated with a cash dividend increase, the value of the company's shares six months after the ex dividend date had risen by 8 per cent. On the other hand, where scrip dividends were not accompanied by cash dividend increases, share values fell by 12 per cent during the subsequent six-month period.

Table 20–1 *Price Effects of Scrip Dividends.*

	Price at selected dates (in percentages)		
	Six months prior to ex dividend date	At ex dividend date	Six months after ex dividend date
Cash dividend increase	100	109	108
No cash dividend increase	100	99	88

These data seem to suggest that scrip dividends are seen for what they are – simply additional pieces of paper – and that they do not represent true income. When they are accompanied by higher earnings and cash dividends, investors bid up the value of the shares. However, when scrip dividends are not accompanied by increases in earnings and cash dividends, the dilution of earnings and dividends per share causes the price of the shares to drop. The fundamental determinant is underlying earnings and dividend trends.

Effects on extent of ownership

Table 20–2 shows the effect of scrip dividends on ordinary share ownership. Large scrip dividends resulted in the largest percentage increases in share ownership. The use of scrip

3. C. A. Barker, Evaluation of stock dividends, *Harvard Business Review* 36 (July–August 1958), pp. 99–114. Barker's study has been replicated several times in recent years, but his results are still valid – they have withstood the test of time.

Table 20-2 *Effect of Scrip Dividends on Share Ownership.*

	Percentage increase in shareholders, 1950–1953
Scrip dividend, 25% and over	30
Scrip dividend, 5–25%	17
All scrip dividends	25
No scrip dividends or stock splits	5

Source: C. Austin Barker, Evaluation of stock dividends, *Harvard Business Review* 36 (July–August 1958), pp. 99–144.

dividends increased shareholders by 25 per cent on the average. For companies and industries that did not offer stock splits or scrip dividends, the increase in ownership was only 5 per cent. Furthermore, the degree of increase in ownership increased with the size of the scrip dividend. This evidence suggests that scrip dividends increase share ownership. Regardless of the effect on the total market value of the firm, the use of scrip dividends and stock splits effectively increases share ownership by lowering the price at which shares are traded to a more popular range.

SUMMARY

Dividend policy determines the extent of internal financing by a firm. The firm decides whether to release earnings to shareholders or retain them within the firm for future expansion purposes. This decision has been constrained in recent years by the existence of controls over dividends imposed by the central government. Because dividend policy may affect the financial structure, the flow of funds, company liquidity, shares prices and investor satisfaction, it is clearly an important aspect of financial management.

In theory, once the firm's debt policy and cost of capital have been determined, dividend policy should automatically follow. Under our theoretical model, dividends are simply a residual after investment needs have been met; if this policy is followed and if investors are indifferent to receiving their investment returns in the form of dividends or of capital gains, shareholders are better off than they are under any other possible dividend policy. However, the financial manager simply does not have all the information assumed in the theory, and judgement must be exercised.

As a guide to financial managers responsible for dividend policy, the following check list summarizes the major economic and financial factors influencing dividend policy:

1. Rate of growth and profit level.
2. Stability of earnings.
3. Age and size of firm.
4. Cash position.
5. Need to repay debt.
6. Control.
7. Maintenance of a target dividend.
8. Tax position of shareholders.
9. Tax position of the company.

Of the factors listed, some lead to higher dividend payouts, some to lower payouts. It is not possible to provide a formula that can be used to establish the proper dividend payout for a given situation; this is a task requiring the exercise of judgement. The considerations summarized above provide a check list for guiding dividend decisions.

Empirical studies indicate a wide diversity of dividend payout ratios not only among industries but also among firms in the same industry. Studies also show that dividends are more stable than earnings. Firms are reluctant to raise dividends in years of good earnings, and they resist dividend cuts as earnings decline. In view of investors' observed preference for stable dividends and of the probability that a cut in dividends is likely to be interpreted as forecasting a decline in earnings, stable dividends make good sense.

Scrip dividends and splits

Neither scrip dividends nor stock splits alone exert a fundamental influence on prices. The fundamental determinant of the price of the company's shares is the company's earning power compared with the earning power of other companies. However, both stock splits and scrip dividends can be used as an effective instrument of financial policy. They are useful devices for reducing the price at which shares are traded, and studies indicate that scrip dividends and stock splits tend to broaden the ownership of a firm's shares.

QUESTIONS

20–1. As an investor, would you rather invest in a firm with a policy of maintaining (a) a constant payout ratio, (b) a constant dividend per share, or (c) a constant regular half-yearly dividend plus a year-end extra when earnings are sufficiently high or the company's investment needs are sufficiently low? Explain your answer.

20–2. How would each of the following changes probably affect aggregate payout ratios? Explain your answer.
(a) An increase in the income tax rate.
(b) A liberalization in depreciation policies for income tax purposes.
(c) A rise in interest rates.
(d) An increase in company profits.
(e) A decline in investment opportunities.

20–3. Discuss the pros and cons of having the directors formally announce what a firm's dividend policy will be in the future.

20–4. Most firms would like to have their shares selling at a high P/E ratio and also have a great variety of shareholders. Explain how scrip dividends or stock splits may be compatible with these aims.

20–5. What is the difference between a scrip dividend and a stock split? As a shareholder, would you prefer to see your company declare a 100 per cent scrip dividend or a two-for-one split?

20–6. 'The cost of retained earnings is less than the cost of new outside equity capital. Consequently, it is totally irrational for a firm to make a new issue of shares and to pay dividends during the same year.' Discuss this statement.

20–7. Would it ever be rational for a firm to borrow money in order to pay dividends? Explain.

20–8. 'Executive salaries have been shown to be more closely correlated to size of firm than to profitability. If a firm's board of directors is controlled by management instead of by outside directors, this might result in the firm's retaining more earnings than can be justified from the shareholders' point of view.' Discuss the statement, being sure (a) to use Figure 20–4 in your answer and (b) to explain the implied relationship between dividend policy and share prices.

PROBLEMS

20–1. The directors of Alexandra Motors Ltd have been comparing the growth of their market price with the growth of one of their competitors, Rexford Cars Ltd. Their findings are summarized below:

Alexandra Motors.

Year	*EPS* (pence)	Dividend (pence)	Payout (%)	Price (£)	*P/E*
1978	43	26	60	6.80	15.8
1977	39	23	60	6.00	15.6
1976	33	20	60	5.00	15.2
1975	31	18.5	60	4.20	13.6
1974	30.5	18	60	3.80	12.5
1973	26	16	60	3.10	11.7
1972	20	12	60	2.60	13.1
1971	29	17.5	60	3.10	10.6
1970	35	21	60	3.50	10.1
1969	29.5	18	60	3.00	10.2

Rexford Cars Ltd.

Year	*EPS* (pence)	Dividend (pence)	Payout (%)	Price (£)	*P/E*
1978	32.5	19.5	60	7.00	21.6
1977	27.5	18	65	5.60	20.4
1976	29.5	18	61	5.30	18.0
1975	29.5	17.5	59	4.80	16.4
1974	29	16.5	57	4.40	15.2
1973	28.5	16	55	4.10	14.3
1972	26	15	57	3.50	13.4
1971	15.5	15	97	2.00	12.9
1970	22.5	15	67	3.40	15.2
1969	22	15	68	3.00	13.7

Both companies are operating in the same markets and both are similarly organized (approximately the same degrees of operating and financial gearing). Alexandra Motors has been consistently earning more per share yet, for some reason, has not been valued at as high a *P/E* ratio as Rexford Cars. What factors would you point out as possible causes for this lower market valuation of Alexandra Motors?

20-2. New Life Tobacco Ltd has for many years enjoyed a moderate but stable growth in sales and earnings. However, cigarette consumption and, consequently, New Life sales have been falling off recently, partly because of a national awareness of the dangers of smoking to health. Anticipating further declines in tobacco sales for the future, New Life management hopes eventually to move almost entirely out of the tobacco business and, instead, develop a new diversified product line in growth-oriented industries.

New Life has been especially interested in the prospects for pollution-control devices – its research department having already done much work on problems of filtering smoke. Right now, the company estimates that an investment of £24 million is necessary to purchase new facilities and begin operations on these products, but the investment could return about 18 per cent within a short time. Other investment opportunities total £9.6 million and are expected to return about 12 per cent.

The company has been paying a 24 pence dividend on its 60 000 000 shares outstanding. The announced dividend policy has been to maintain a stable dividend, raising it only when it appears that earnings have reached a new, permanently higher level. The directors might, however, change this policy if reasons for doing so are compelling. Total earnings for the year are £22.8 million, ordinary shares are currently selling for £4.50, and the firm's current gearing ratio (*B/A*) is 45 per cent. Current costs of various forms of financing are:

New debentures	7%
New ordinary shares sold at £4.50 to yield the firm	£4.10
Investors required rate of return on equity	9%
Tax rate	50%

(a) Calculate the marginal cost of capital above and below the point of exhaustion of retained earnings for New Life.
(b) How large should New Life's capital budget be for the year?
(c) What is an appropriate dividend policy for New Life? How should the capital budget be financed?
(d) How might risk factors influence New Life's cost of capital, capital structure and dividend policy?

(e) What assumptions, if any, do your answers to the above make about investors' preference for dividends versus capital gain – that is, investors' preference regarding different d/p and g components of k?

20-3. Listed below are the essential financial data for the ordinary shares of International Metals Ltd, Precision Systems, and Amalgamated Fuel and Gas. International Metals is a leading producer of copper, zinc and lead, whose product demand is quite cyclical. Precision Systems is a computer manufacturer. Amalgamated Fuel and Gas is a user of waste products from the fuel industries.

What differences are revealed by the data on the dividend policies of the three firms? What explanations can be given for these differences? What is the relationship of dividend policy to the market price of the shares?

International Metals Ltd.

Year	*EPS* (pence)	Dividend (pence)	Price range (£)	Payout (%)	*P/E* ratio (range)
1978	46	11.5	4.60–1.90	25	10–4
1977	22.5	7	2.10–1.20	32	9–5
1976	10	7	2.10–1.10	70	18–10
1975	9	6.5	2.70–1.80	76	25–17
1974	20	6	2.40–1.50	29	11–7
1973	17	5.5	2.70–1.90	31	14–9
1972	9.5	4.5	2.50–1.30	48	20–10
1971	11	8	2.90–1.20	71	22–9
1970	22	7.5	3.70–2.60	34	12–8
1969	28	6.5	2.80–1.60	23	7–4

Precision Systems.

Year	*EPS* (pence)	Dividend (pence)	Price range (£)	Payout (%)	*P/E* ratio (range)
1978	11.5	0.5	4.60–3.20	5	40–28
1977	7	0.5	5.30–3.00	7	88–32
1976	6	0.5	5.50–2.00	8	115–85
1975	5	0.5	6.00–4.40	10	116–72
1974	5.5	0.5	6.50–4.10	9	68–35
1973	7	0.5	4.70–2.40	7	59–23
1972	5	0.5	2.70–1.10	11	37–18
1971	3.5	0.5	1.30–0.60	11	30–13
1970	2	Nil	0.70–0.30	–	21–11
1969	1	Nil	0.30–0.20	–	23–15

Amalgamated Fuel and Gas.

Year	*EPS* (pence)	Dividend (pence)	Price range (£)	Payout (%)	*P/E* ratio (range)
1978	21	13	3.40–3.10	63	16–14
1977	23	13	3.70–2.90	57	16–13
1976	21.5	12	3.10–2.30	57	14–11
1975	18.5	12	3.30–2.40	65	18–13
1974	18.5	12	2.40–2.20	64	13–12
1973	17.5	11.5	2.50–2.10	66	14–12
1972	18	11	2.40–1.70	62	13–10
1971	13	11	2.00–1.60	85	15–13
1970	16	10	2.20–1.90	65	14–12
1969	16	10	2.30–2.00	64	15–12

20–4. Listed below are pertinent financial data for the ordinary shares of United States Steel Corporation and Kellogg Company. US Steel is the largest domestic steel-maker, accounting for 23.4 per cent of the industry's steel products. Kellogg is the worlds' largest manufacturer of ready-to-eat breakfast cereals and accounts for about 42 per cent of the total domestic output.

What differences are revealed by the data on the dividend policies of the two firms? What explanations can be given for these differences? What is the relationship of dividend policy to the market price of the shares? What information content and legal listing differences are present?

United States Steel Corporation.

Year	Earnings ($)	Dividends ($)	Price range	Payout (%)	*P/E* ratio
1975	10.33	2.80	71–38	27	5.1
1974	11.72	2.20	48–35	19	5.3
1973	6.01	1.60	38–27	27	4.9
1972	2.90	1.60	35–27	55	5.2
1971	2.85	2.00	36–25	70	6.6
1970	2.72	2.40	39–28	88	7.1
1969	4.01	2.40	49–33	60	5.9
1968	4.69	2.40	45–38	51	5.7
1967	3.19	2.40	50–38	75	5.4
1966	4.60	2.00	56–35	43	4.4

Source: *Moody's Handbook of Common Stocks*, Spring 1976.

Kellogg Company.

Year	Earnings ($)	Dividends ($)	Price range	Payout (%)	*P/E* ratio
1975	1.40	0.73	11–8	52	13.3
1974	0.98	0.59	11–9	60	14.5
1973	0.89	0.55	12–9	62	17.2
1972	0.83	0.52	11–9	63	16.9
1971	0.76	0.50	12–9	66	16.7
1970	0.68	0.45	14–11	66	15.8
1969	0.62	0.40	17–11	65	16.8
1968	0.59	0.38	18–13	64	18.0
1967	0.57	0.33	18–10	58	17.7
1966	0.53	0.30	23–14	57	17.6

Source: *Moody's Handbook of Common Stocks*, Spring 1976.

SELECTED REFERENCES

Barker, C. A. Effective stock splits. *Harvard Business Review* 34 (January–February 1956): 101–106.

Barker, C. A. Stock splits in a Bull market. *Harvard Business Review* 35 (May–June 1957): 72–79.

Barker, C. A. Evaluation of stock dividends. *Harvard Business Review* 36 (July–August 1958): 99–114.

Barker, C. A. Price effects of stock dividend shares, at ex-dividend dates. *Journal of Finance* 14 (September 1959): 373–378.

Baumol, William J. On dividend policy and market imperfection. *Journal of Business* 36 (January 1963): 112–115.

Ben-Zion, Uri and Shalit, Sol S. Size, leverage, and dividend record as determinants of equity risk. *Journal of Finance* 30 (June 1975): 1015–1026.

Bierman, Harold Jr and West, Richard. The acquisition of common stock by the corporate issuer. *Journal of Finance* 21 (December 1966): 687–696.

Black, F. and Scholes, M. The effects of dividend yield and dividend policy on common stock prices and returns. *Journal of Financial Economics* 1 (May 1974): 1–22.

Brennan, Michael. A note on dividend irrelevance and the Gordon valuation model. *Journal of Finance* 26 (December 1971): 1115–1123.

Brigham, Eugene. The profitability of a firm's repurchase of its own common stock. *California Management Review* 7 (Winter 1964): 69–75.

Brigham, Eugene and Gordon, Myron J. Leverage, dividend policy, and the cost of capital. *Journal of Finance* 23 (March 1968): 85–104.

Brigham, Eugene and Gordon, Myron J. A reply to leverage, dividend policy and the cost of capital: a comment. *Journal of Finance* 25 (September 1970): 904–908.

Briston, R. J. and Tomkins, C. R. Dividend policy, shareholder satisfaction and the valuation of shares. *Journal of Business Finance* 2, No. 1 (Spring 1970).

Brittain, John A. *Corporate Dividend Policy*. Washington, D.C.: The Brookings Institution, 1966.

Davenport, Michael. Leverage, dividend policy and the cost of capital: a comment. *Journal of Finance* 25 (September 1970): 893–897.

Dobrovolsky, S. P. Economics of corporate internal and external financing. *Journal of Finance* 13 (March 1958): 35–47.

Ellis, Charles D. New framework for analysing capital structure. *Financial Executive* 37 (April 1969): 75–86.

Ellis, Charles D. Repurchase stock to revitalize equity. *Harvard Business Review* 43 (July–August 1965): 119–128.

Fama, E. F. The empirical relationships between the dividend and investment decisions of firms. *American Economic Review* 64 (June 1974): 304–318.

Fama, E. F. and Babiak, Harvey. Dividend policy: an empirical analysis. *Journal of the American Statistical Association* 63 (December 1968): 1132–1161.

Fama, E. F., Fisher, Lawrence, Jenson, Michael and Roll, Richard. The adjustment of stock prices to new information. *International Economic Review* 10 (February 1969): 1–21.

Friend, Irwin and Puckett, Marshall. Dividends and stock prices. *American Economic Review* 54 (September 1964): 656–682.

Gordon, Myron J. Dividends, earnings and stock prices. *Review of Economics and Statistics* 41 (May 1959): 99–105.

Gordon, Myron J. *The Investment, Financing and Valuation of the Corporation*. Homewood, Ill.: Irwin, 1962.

Gordon, Myron J. Optimal investment and financing policy. *Journal of Finance* 18 (May 1963).

Hausman, W. H., West, R. R. and Largay, J. A. Stock splits, price changes, and trading profits: a synthesis. *Journal of Business* 44 (January 1971): 69–77.

Higgins, Robert C. The corporate dividend-saving decision. *Journal of Financial and Quantitative Analysis* 7 (March 1972): 1527–1541.

Higgins, Robert C. Dividend policy and increasing discount rate: a clarification. *Journal of Financial and Quantitative Analysis* 7 (June 1972): 1757–1762.

Higgins, Robert C. Growth, dividend policy and capital costs in the electric utility industry. *Journal of Finance* 29 (September 1974): 1189–1201.

Johnson, Keith B. Stock splits and price changes. *Journal of Finance* 21 (December 1966): 675–686.

Lee, Cheng F. Functional form and the dividend effect in the electric utility industry. *Journal of Finance* 31 (December 1976): 1481–1486.

Lerner, Eugene M. and Carleton, Williard T. *A Theory of Financial Analysis*. New York: Harcourt Brace Jovanovich, 1966.

Lintner, John. Distribution of incomes of corporations among dividends, retained earnings, and taxes. *American Economic Review* 46 (May 1956): 97–113.

Lintner, John. Dividends, earnings, leverage, stock prices and the supply of capital to corporations. *Review of Economics and Statistics* 44 (August 1962): 243–269.

Lintner, John. Dividend policy and market valuations: a reply. *Journal of Business* 36 (January 1963): 116–119.

Lintner, John. Optimal dividends and corporate growth under uncertainty. *Quarterly Journal of Economics* 88 (February 1964): 49–95.

Mehta, Dileep R. The impact of outstanding convertible bonds on corporate dividend policy. *Journal of Finance* 31 (May 1976): 489–506.

Mendelson, Morris. Leverage, dividend policy and the cost of capital: a comment. *Journal of Finance* 25 (September 1970): 898–903.

Millar, James A. and Fielitz, Bruce D. Stock-split and stock-dividend decisions. *Financial Management* 2 (Winter 1973): 35–45.

Miller, Merton H. and Modigliani, Franco. Dividend policy, growth, and the valuation of shares. *Journal of Business* 34 (October 1961): 411–433.

Miller, Merton H. and Modigliani, Franco. Dividend policy and market valuation: a reply. *Journal of Business* 36 (January 1963): 116–119.

Miller, Merton H. and Modigliani, Franco. Some estimates of the cost of capital to the electric utility industry. *American Economic Review* 56 (June 1966): 333–391.

Pettit, R. Richardson. Dividend announcements, security performance, and capital market efficiency. *Journal of Finance* 27 (December 1972): 993–1007.

Pettit, R. Richardson. The impact of dividend and earnings announcements: a reconciliation. *Journal of Business* 49 (January 1976): 86–96.

Porterfield, James T. S. Dividends, dilution, and delusion. *Harvard Business Review* 37 (November–December 1959): 156–161.

Richards, P. H. Dividend controls – fact or fancy. *Investment Analyst* (April 1976): 24–30.

Robichek, Alexander A. and Myers, Stewart C. *Optimal Financing Decisions.* Englewood Cliffs, N.J.: Prentice-Hall, 1965, chap. 4.

Ryan, T. M. Dividend policy and market valuation in British industry. *Journal of Business Finance and Accounting* 1, No. 3 (Autumn 1974): 415–428.

Stapleton, Richard C. Portfolio analysis, stock valuation, and capital budgeting decision rules for risky projects. *Journal of Finance* 26 (March 1971): 95–118.

Walter, James E. Dividend policies and common stock prices. *Journal of Finance* 11 (March 1956): 29–41.

Walter, James E. *Dividend Policy and Enterprise Valuation.* Belmont, Calif.: Wadsworth Publishing Company, 1967.

Walter, James E. Dividend policy: its influence on the value of the enterprise. *Journal of Finance* 18 (May 1963): 280–291.

Watts, Ross. The information content of dividends. *Journal of Business* 46 (April 1973): 191–211.

West, Richard R. and Bierman, Harold, Jr. Corporate dividend policy and preemptive security issues. *Journal of Business* 42 (January 1968): 71–75.

West, Richard R. and Brouilette, Alan B. Reverse stock splits. *Financial Executive* 38 (January 1970): 12–17.

Weston, C. R. Adjustment to future dividend rates in the prediction of ex-rights prices. *Journal of Business Finance and Accounting* 1 (Autumn 1974): 335–342.

Whittington, G. The profitability of retained earnings. *Review of Economics and Statistics* 54 (May 1972): 152–160.

Woods, Donald H. and Brigham, Eugene F. Stockholder distribution decisions: share repurchase or dividends. *Journal of Financial and Quantitative Analysis* 1 (March 1966): 15–28.

Wrightsman, Dwayne and Horrigan, James O. Retention, risk of success, and the price of stock. *Journal of Finance* 30 (December 1975): 1357–1359.

Young, Allan. Financial, operating, and security market parameters of repurchasing. *Financial Analysts' Journal* 25 (July–August 1969): 123–128.

Young, Allan. The effects of share distribution on price action: *Financial Review*, Eastern Finance Association (1975).

PART 6

INTEGRATED TOPICS IN FINANCIAL MANAGEMENT

In the final five chapters we take up important but somewhat specialized topics, which draw on the concepts developed in earlier sections.

Chapter 21, 'Timing of Financial Policy', introduces dynamics into the decision process, showing how financial managers react to changing conditions in the capital markets. Chapter 22 deals with the growth of firms through mergers and holding companies, and the reasoning behind this development. Throughout the text, we have dealt with growing and successful firms; however, many firms face financial difficulties, and the causes and possible remedies to these difficulties are discussed in Chapter 23. Next, in Chapter 24, we discuss some of the financial aspects of multinational corporations, a topic of increasing importance in today's economy. Finally, in Chapter 25, we apply many of the topics covered throughout the book to the specific situation faced by a small firm; small business finance is an important and practical subject, but we also use the chapter to summarize and integrate many of the principles set forth throughout the book.

Chapter 21

Timing of Financial Policy

This chapter deals with the timing of financial policy. Although the topic has always been important, the new inflationary environment has caused timing to take on a greater significance than ever before. Since the early 1960s the British economy has experienced a series of 'credit squeezes' during which the costs of financing have risen substantially. Minimizing the need to raise capital during these 'squeezes' is important. In addition, a key question facing financial managers is whether financing costs will return to lower levels in the reasonably near future, or whether the continued upward trends in recent years will prevail. How this question is resolved will greatly influence the costs, amounts and types of capital raised by business firms.

In an inflationary environment changes in asset requirements are magnified by rising price levels. Financial managers must consider this when planning their requirements. Further, when analysing prospective returns from capital assets, financial managers must realize that the prices of similar capital assets will increase substantially in future years because of inflation. Finally, it is exceedingly difficult to raise the requisite amount of funds in an inflationary environment, and as a consequence the problem of planning to meet future maturing obligations is crucial.

SIGNIFICANCE TO FINANCIAL MANAGEMENT

Financial managers are faced with two problems when they encounter inflationary conditions. First, to quote Milton Friedman, 'People who borrow under conditions of sharp inflation are willing to pay any amount for money and people who lend ask high rates to protect themselves from loss of purchasing power'.[1] These actions on the part of borrowers and lenders lead inevitably to high interest rates. The existence of high interest rates gives additional problems to financial managers who are attempting to decide whether or not to borrow more money.

1. 'Is a money crunch on its way?' *Business Week* (29 September 1967), p. 36.

Second, financial managers have had to face another problem – fluctuating rates. This increased volatility is highlighted by a study of interest rate patterns in recent years. Interest rates have fluctuated very sharply over the past decade, rising steeply to reach a peak in December 1974 and then falling equally quickly to new low levels in 1977.

Financial managers are divided on the question of whether major fluctuations in money costs will continue to occur in the future. Nevertheless, experience suggests that this possibility should be taken into account in financial planning. Accordingly, in this chapter, we first analyse cyclical patterns in the costs of financing and then review the nature of monetary and fiscal policies, focusing particular attention on the implications of these policies for future patterns in the cost of external financing.

HISTORICAL PATTERNS IN THE COSTS OF FINANCING

Table 21–1 highlights changes in the costs of financing during the period 1974–7. One outstanding characteristic of interest rate behaviour is the wide magnitude of the changes in the price of money over the years. During the period 1932–51 the Bank Rate[2] remained constant at 2 per cent. The borrowing rate on three-month bills of exchange, which is the best indication of the cost of short-term money to large companies, was substantially lower than 2 per cent for most of this period. In more recent years this rate has been much higher than it was in the period of 'cheap money', reaching a peak of 14¼ per cent in October 1976. During the period 1974–7, yields on bills of exchange issued by British companies have fluctuated between 14.22 and 4.53 per cent; yields on company debentures have fluctuated, in a much less volatile manner, between 9.52 and 6.20 per cent.

The cost of equity capital is more difficult to measure than the cost of debt capital, but if we use the earnings yields on *The Times* Industrial Index as a proxy for the cost of equity we note that earnings yields have fluctuated from 29.73 to 9.78 per cent during the period 1974–7. We can see that the fluctuation in earnings yields during this period has been much greater than that of yields on company debentures, reflecting the uncertainties of the period and the high risk premiums ($k_s = k_g + \text{risk premium}$) that have had to be paid to induce investors to buy equities.

Table 21–1 *Selected Interest Rates (Per Cent).*

	1974		1975		1976		1977	
	High	Low	High	Low	High	Low	High	Low
Short term								
3-month Treasury bills	12.31	11.0	11.19	9.25	14.31	8.44	13.22	4.22
3-month bills of exchange (prime bank bills)	13.69	11.75	12.25	9.44	14.22	8.50	13.88	4.53
Long term								
3½% War loan	17.52	12.59	16.71	13.28	15.36	13.27	12.94	9.83
Company debentures (flat yield)[a]	9.52	8.01	9.25	7.84	7.81	7.15	7.36	6.20

Source: *The Times.*

[a] The gross redemption yield of UK company debentures is usually higher than the yield on government stocks with a similar period to maturity. Because the market in UK company debentures is relatively narrow, these figures are available only in a haphazard manner. It has therefore been decided to consider flat yields of UK company debentures rather than gross redemption yields.

---

2. Now known as the 'minimum lending rate'.

This brief review of fluctuations in short- and long-term interest rates is sufficient to demonstrate that the cost of capital is one of the most volatile inputs purchased by firms. Within relatively short time periods money costs have fluctuated by over 100 per cent.

INTEREST RATES AS AN INDEX OF AVAILABILITY OF FUNDS

While the cost variations associated with interest rate fluctuations are substantial, the greatest significance of interest rates is their role as an index of the availability of funds. A period of high interest rates reflects tight money which is in turn associated with pressure on the reserve asset ratios of the commercial banks. At such times interest rates rise, but there are conventional limits on interest rates.[3] Consequently, a larger quantity of funds is demanded by borrowers than banks are able to make available. Action by the 'authorities' to regulate the money supply may accentuate this problem.[4] Banks are thus forced to ration funds amongst prospective borrowers by continuing lines of credit to traditional customers but restricting loans to new borrowers.

Small firms characteristically have greater difficulty in obtaining finance during periods of 'credit squeeze', and even amongst large borrowers the bargaining position of lending institutions is stronger. It is a lenders' rather than a borrowers' market. Consequently, the conditions in all loan agreements are more restrictive when the demand for funds is high.

Interest rates are therefore of very great significance to financial managers as an index of the availability of funds. For small and medium-sized firms a period of rising interest rates may indicate increasing difficulty in obtaining any finance at all, or, if finance is obtained, it will be at a higher cost or under less favourable conditions.

A period of credit squeeze will particularly affect the capital goods industries, the construction industry and local authorities. Because the nature of their business necessitates long-term investments, the impact of high interest rates on these organizations is especially significant. For the construction industry, in particular, periods of credit squeeze often lead to an increase in company liquidation and bankruptcy.

COSTS OF DIFFERENT KINDS OF FINANCING OVER TIME

The preceding section showed that interest rates vary widely over time. In addition, the relative costs of debentures, preference shares and equity fluctuate. Data on these relative costs are presented in Figure 21–1, which shows that earnings yields on the shares composing *The Times* Industrial Index have fluctuated from 9.79 to 29.73 per cent during the period 1974–7. Yields on debentures have fluctuated to a much lesser extent. Furthermore, since both debentures and preference shares provide a stable fixed income to investors, they are close substitutes for each other.[5]

---

3. See B. G. Malkiel, *The Term Structure of Interest Rates*. New Jersey: Princeton, 1968.
4. The role of monetary policy is considered later in this chapter.
5. Nevertheless, debenture interest is, of course, tax deductible, unlike interest on preference shares.

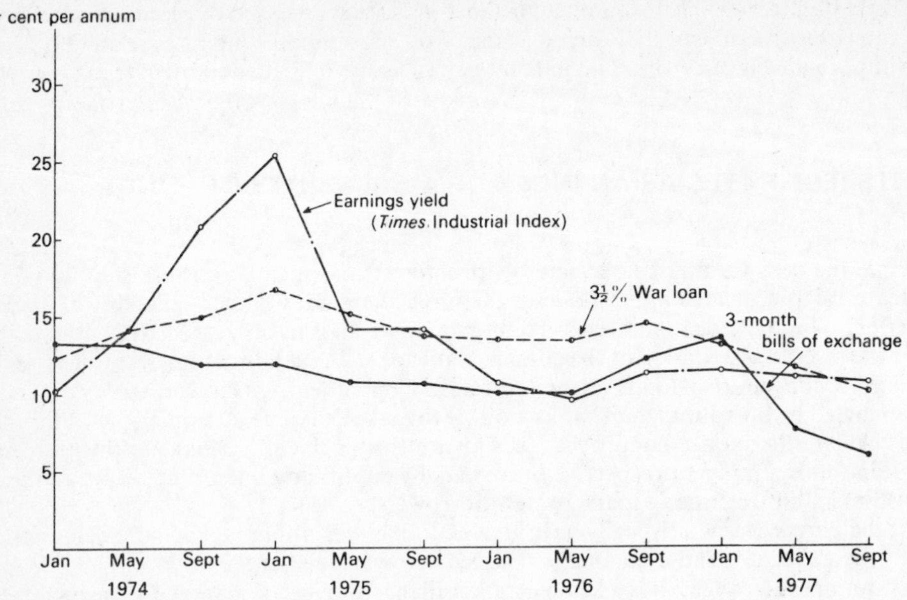

Figure 21–1 *Rates of Interest and Yields 1974–7.*

RELATIONSHIP BETWEEN LONG-TERM AND SHORT-TERM INTEREST RATES[6]

One of the important elements in the financial manager's timing decisions is an understanding of the relationship between long-term and short-term interest rates. Long-term interest rates are rates on securities with maturities in excess of 10 years. Short-term interest rates are those on securities with maturities of under one year.

Figure 21–1 shows the relationship between short-term rates, long-term rates and the earnings yield on representative securities between 1974 and 1977. Although long-term rates are normally higher than short-term rates, there are occasions when short-term rates rise above long-term rates. Such occasions are January 1974 and January 1977. This situation usually occurs when conditions in the money market are tight; that is, when there is a shortage of short-term funds. Under certain conditions there is greater risk to holding long-term securities than short-term securities. The longer the maturity of the security, the greater the danger that the issuer may not make an effective adaption to the changing environment and therefore may not be able to meet its obligations in 10, 15 or 20 years' time. Furthermore, the *prices* of long-term bonds are far more volatile than are those of short-term bonds when interest rates change; the reason for this is largely arithmetic and was discussed in Chapter 17.

The *expectations theory* states that long-term interest rates may in general be regarded as an average of expected future short-term interest rates. Thus the relationship between long and short rates will depend on what is expected to happen in the future to short-term interest rates. We can see in Figure 21–1 that when the short rate is higher than the long

---

6. The relationship between long-term and short-term interest rates – usually referred to as the 'term structure of interest rates' is developed in detail in the appendix to Chapter 6.

rate short rates can be expected to fall in the near future. This phenomenon is more clearly illustrated in Table 21–2.

In section A it is assumed that short-term interest rates will increase by 1 per cent each year, beginning at 2 per cent in year 1. The corresponding long-term interest rate in year 1 for a five-year period is approximately 4 per cent; that is, the average of the five short-term rates. Therefore, in year 1, the long-term rate is double the short-term rate.

Table 21–2 *Relationship between Short-term and Long-term Interest Rates.*

	A		B	
Year	5-year bond	Short-term rate(%)	5-year bond	Short-term rate(%)
1	4	2	4	6
2		3		5
3		4		4
4		5		3
5		6		2

Consider, however, the situation under section B. In a tight-money situation in year 1, short-term rates are 6 per cent, but they are expected to decline by 1 per cent each year. The average of these rates is the same as that in section A because the numbers are identical – their order is simply reversed. Now, however, the long-term rate of 6 per cent lies below the initial short-term rate of 4 per cent.

These examples do not prove the relationship between short- and long-term rates. They do, however, illustrate the pattern that would exist if the only factor operating was expected changes in interest rate movements, which themselves reflect a broad group of supply and demand factors. However, many other factors operate in the market. Some of these include differences in the risks of loss and failure amongst individual business firms, in the economic outlook for various industries, in the degree to which price-level changes affect various products and industries, and on the impact that changes in government legislation will have on different industries and different firms within a given industry.

CHARACTERISTIC PATTERNS IN THE COST OF MONEY

In Figure 21–2 we depict in a general way the typical pattern between GNP and interest rates in a developed economy. Short-term interest rates show the widest amplitude of swings. Since the long-term interest rates are *averages* of short-term rates, they are not as volatile as short-term rates; short-term rates move more quickly and fluctuate more than long-term rates. The cost of debenture interest tends to coincide with movements in general business conditions both at the peak and at the trough of the business cycle.

The cost of equity funds may best be approximated by expected equivalent yields – dividends plus capital gains. To understand the behaviour of equity yields, the behaviour of earnings, dividends and share prices must be analysed. Company earnings are extremely volatile – they lead the business cycle both on the upturn and on the downturn – and dividends follow earnings. Prices of ordinary shares often anticipate changes in company earnings. They are also influenced by money market conditions. Owing to the gradual tightening in money market conditions as expansion continues, yields on government stocks and debentures rise and money is attracted from the ordinary share market into the gilt-edged market. This causes the price of ordinary shares to turn

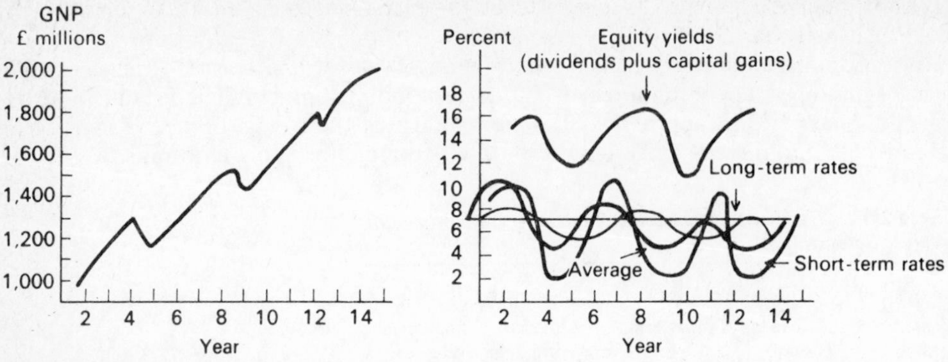

Figure 21–2 *Relation between Movements of Gross National Product and Interest Rates.*

down before company profits reach their peak. Because share prices fall, the cost of equity financing increases.[7] In other words, the cost of equity capital begins to rise in the later stages of the business cycle.

The relationships between the costs of various types of finance over time illustrated in Figure 21 – 2 represent generalizations that provide a frame of reference for the financial manager. The patterns are not intended as precise guidelines. A basic requirement for sound financial management is the ability to make judgements about future financial and economic conditions that will affect financial timing, and the forms and sources of finance that are used. The next section seeks to provide a foundation for evaluating trends in financial markets.

MONEY AND CAPITAL MARKET BEHAVIOUR

Fundamental to an understanding of the behaviour of the money and capital markets is an analysis of the role of the central bank, which in the United Kingdom is the Bank of England. The 'authorities' are the Bank of England and the Treasury acting in concert. They have a set of instruments with which to influence the operations of the commercial banks, whose lending activities in turn have an important influence on the cost and availability of funds.

The authorities traditionally sought to influence the aggregate demand within the economy by acting on the level of interest rates. In order to do this they were able to make use of two weapons:

1. Bank rate policy. By altering the rate of interest at which the Bank of England was willing to lend as lender of last resort to the Discount Houses, it was possible to cause an alteration in all other short-term interest rates.

---

7. Recall that in Chapter 17 we showed that, at least conceptually, share prices may be determined by the equation

$$p = \frac{d}{k_s - g}$$

where p = share price, d = dividend, k_s = required rate of return (or cost of equity capital) and g = expected growth rate. Since ordinary shares and fixed interest securities compete with one another for investors' funds, if monetary policy drives interest rates up k_s will likewise rise and p must fall.

2. Open market operations. By buying or selling securities in the open market the authorities could alter the price of government securities (or, more commonly, Treasury bills) and thus alter the rate of interest obtaining in the market.

Since the Second World War the authorities have supplemented their control of interest rates with attempts to control the money supply. At the time of the Radcliffe Report[8] there were two of these weapons:

1. Special deposits. These were introduced at the recommendation of the Radcliffe Committee and consisted of deposits that the Clearing Banks were requested to make with the Bank of England. This system was used throughout the 1960s and special deposits were repaid or called depending on whether or not the authorities wanted to increase or decrease the amount of money in circulation.
2. Directives. The Bank of England often asks the Clearing Banks to restrict their advances to customers.[9] This has an immediate impact on the creation of credit by the Clearing Banks and thus on the supply of money. During the 1960s, other financial institutions were eventually made subject to these lending directives.

In 1971 a new system, known as *competition and credit control*, was introduced. The authorities aimed to control the money supply through their ability to influence interest rates by their open market operations, supplemented by altering the level of special deposits. They also replaced liquidity ratios with a standard $12\frac{1}{2}$ per cent reserve asset ratio which applied to all banks.

In November 1973 the authorities sought to augment the controls at their disposal by the introduction of the supplementary *special deposits scheme* (known as the 'corset'). The arrangements now require that if any bank's average interest-bearing eligible liabilities (IBELS)[10] grow at a rate faster than that officially specified, that bank will incur a penalty in the form of calls to place non-interest-bearing supplementary deposits with the Bank of England. This form of control is particularly onerous to the banks since the day-to-day variations in overdraft levels are so great that, to be certain of being under the penalty ceiling, prudent management requires them to aim well below it.

FISCAL POLICY

The government's fiscal policy has a great impact on movements in interest rates. A deficit budget represents an attempt on the part of the government to stimulate the economy, and a surplus budget exerts a restraining influence on the economy. However, this generalization must be modified to reflect the way a deficit is financed and the way a surplus is used. If the authorities can sell more securities to the public than they buy from the public (whether by purchase before maturity or by redemption for cash upon maturity), they can so far finance the budget deficit. Net sales of securities allow the authorities to finance a budget deficit without adding to the credit base of the banking system.

---

8. *Report of the Committee into the Working of the Monetary System*, Cmnd 827, August 1959.
9. In early 1968, after the 1967 devaluation of the pound, the banks were asked to restrict the level of their advances to that which was operative at the time of devaluation – November 1967.
10. The interest-bearing part of the banks' eligible liabilities. The banks' eligible reserve assets as defined in the new competition and credit control regulations were balances with the Bank of England (other than special deposits), Treasury bills, tax reserve certificates, money at call and short notice, local authority bills and commercial bills of exchange eligible for rediscount at the Bank of England. Banks were required to maintain a minimum reserve asset ratio of at least $12\frac{1}{2}$ per cent of eligible liabilities. Eligible liabilities are sterling deposit liabilities of at least two years' original maturity plus resources obtained by switching foreign currencies into sterling, and include inter-bank transactions and sterling certificates of deposit.

Table 21–3 *Sources and Uses of Capital Funds of Industrial and Commercial Companies.*

	Sources of funds (£million)											
			Capital transfers				UK capital issues by listed companies[c]		Overseas[d]			
	Total	Undis-tributed income[a]	Invest ment grants	Other	Bank borrow-ing[b]	Other loans and mort-gages	Ordinary shares	Deben-tures and prefer-ence shares	Import credit and advance payments on exports	Capital issues overseas	Direct invest-ment in securities	Intra-company investment by overseas companies
1973	15 088	7 314	227	146	4 504	875	137	51	516	112	184	1 022
1974	15 017	7 519	137	227	4 411	245	118	−56	528	11	247	1 630
1975	12 511	8 169	96	346	418	385	1 014	202	350	10	107	1 414
1976	18 328	11 647	58	343	2 494	919	786	42	461	4	80	1 494
1977	18 475	11 547	32	283	3 081	152	723	−67	289	74	105	2 256

Uses of funds (£million)

					Acquisition of financial assets					Overseas[d]			
					Liquid assets								
	Total	Taxes on capital and other capital transfers	Gross domestic fixed capital formation	Increase in book value of stocks and work in progress	Bank deposits, notes and coin[e]	Other	British government securities[f]	Cash expenditure on acquiring subsidiaries and on trade investments	Other domestic assets[g]	Suppliers export credit and advance payments on imports	Intra-company investment by UK companies overseas[h]	Other identified assets	Unidentified items (residuals)
1973	15 088	26	4 826	3 809	2 426	68	39	1 420	−262	335	1 527	244	630
1974	15 017	31	6 048	6 119	92	−53	−39	678	96	518	1 431	−96	192
1975	12 511	42	6 961	2 240	1 478	286	92	531	−169	34	984	536	−504
1976	18 328	42	7 744	5 064	1 657	135	123	884	573	617	1 802	584	−897
1977	18 475	69	9 025	4 336	2 578	181	88	1 069	435	−48	1 405	680	−1 235

Source: Central Statistical Office.

[a] Before providing for depreciation, stock appreciation and additions to reserves.
[b] After addition of 40 per cent on the excess of debit over credit transit items.
[c] Including identified unlisted issues.
[d] Other than investments included in UK capital issues.
[e] After subtraction of 60 per cent of the excess of debit over credit transit items.
[f] Figures of large companies transactions from the Department of Industry.
[g] Including repayment of loans by public corporations, local authority, mortgages and N. Ireland central government debt.
[h] Other than cash expenditure on acquiring subsidiaries and on trade investment.

Ordinarily, when the authorities need to draw funds from the money market they have to compete with other potential users of funds; the result may be a rise in interest rates. However, the desire to hold down interest rates (and maintain high prices for government stocks) is often a factor in the policy of the authorities. The authorities may temporarily ease money conditions in order to reduce interest rates before selling securities in the market.

INTEREST RATE FORECASTS

Within this framework of general economic and financial patterns, short-term interest rate patterns and forecasts may be analysed through the statistics, showing the sources and uses of company finance, which are summarized in Table 21–3.[11] By projecting the sources and uses of company finance in different categories we can estimate the direction of the pressure on interest rates.

The table can be used in the following way: historical patterns can be established to show sources of funds in relation to the growth of the economy as a whole, as measured by GNP. When in any particular year the demand for funds grows faster than the supply in relation to historical patterns, interest rates are likely to rise. These extra funds are supplied by drawing on the commercial banking system which is the pivot in the financial mechanism. Whenever the demand for funds must be met by drawing on the commercial banking system to a greater-than-normal degree, interest rates rise.

Another significant statistic in the table is the fall in the supply of bank borrowing in 1975. Because of the operation of a 'credit squeeze' by the Bank of England in 1975, the ability of the commercial banks and other financial institutions to supply funds was curbed to relate to demand. Interest rates rose to a peak in early 1975 (see Figure 21–1).

Most longer-term predictions suggest that interest rates will remain much higher in the future than was the case in the 1940s and 1950s, with only moderate declines of short duration from time to time. The reasons for this suggestion are diverse, but a major factor reflects the efforts of governments throughout the world to achieve full employment and high growth rates. A world-wide capital shortage has resulted.

The table shows that as interest rates rose in recent years the form of finance used by British companies was changed to take these changed conditions into account:

1. Ordinary share issues which formed a low percentage of total sources from 1970–74 rose from a negative 0.1 per cent in 1974 to a positive 8 per cent in 1975, the year of the rights issue.[12]
2. The issue of debentures and preference shares fell during the 1970s, reflecting the higher rates that companies had to pay in order to secure new loans.
3. With increasing levels of inflation after 1967, the issues of convertible debentures increased substantially, representing approximately 40 per cent of gross external financing in 1969. In subsequent years, however, the use of convertibles moderated. The reduced attractiveness of convertibles may reflect the relatively weak stock market which existed during the early 1970s.
4. Convertible debenture issues began to grow again in 1975. It is clear that the increased uncertainties about the rate of inflation and the increased difficulties of forecasting

---

11. Such statistics can be obtained from either the February issue of the Midland Bank *Review*, which publishes a survey of recent developments in the new issue market, or from *Financial Statistics*, published by the Central Statistical Office.

12. See the Midland Bank's *Review*, February 1976, for a survey of new issues in 1975 and reasons for the increases in rights issues.

interest rate patterns in recent years have led to the greater use of hybrid forms of financing.

Thus the interaction of the higher rates of inflation since 1966 and fluctuating interest rate levels have produced changing patterns of financing policies in business firms. It is useful to analyse the relationship between price level changes and interest rate levels to understand likely implications for financing policy.

EFFECTS OF PRICE LEVEL CHANGES ON INTEREST RATES

The 'nominal' interest rate reflects expectations about future price behaviour. If prices are rising, and are expected to rise further, the expected rate of inflation is added to the interest rate that would have obtained in the absence of inflation to adjust for the decline in purchasing power represented by price increases. In these circumstances, the 'real' or inflation-adjusted rate of interest is often negative. If the 'real' rate of interest is negative, borrowers will be encouraged and lenders will be discouraged. The result of the interaction of borrowers and lenders will be an adjustment of the 'nominal' rate to a much higher level than that obtaining before the anticipated price rise.

Thus in periods of anticipated inflation the attempt to operate 'real' interest rates at a positive level on the part of market operators can lead to considerable increases in 'nominal' rates.

SUMMARY

Financial managers have at least some flexibility in their operations. Even though a firm may have a target debt/asset ratio, it can deviate from this target to some extent in a given year to take advantage of favourable conditions in either the money market or the stock market. Similarly, although it may have a target relationship between its long-term and short-term debt, it can vary this target if market conditions suggest that such action is appropriate.

Uncertainties about the future have increased in recent years, with a resultant increase in the importance of sound financial timing. Moreover, attempts to deal with the increasing uncertainty within the economy have given rise to new innovations in financing techniques and patterns. Some important changes in financing that have developed in response to changes in the economy, especially in the money and capital markets, are listed below:

1. Interest rates have fluctuated widely in the last decade. Generally speaking, long-term interest rates have fluctuated less than short-term interest rates. Bank borrowing has fallen off during periods of high interest rates (such as 1975) and companies have been forced to find alternative sources of finance.
2. Rights issues of ordinary shares have increased since 1975. A contributory factor to this increase has been the attempt to circumvent dividend control.[13]
3. An increased number of convertible debentures has been issued.
4. Small firms have found it more difficult to obtain finance from the large institutional investors.
5. The operation of the new credit policy of the Bank of England has proved more

13. Dividend control was discussed in Chapter 20.

onerous to the commercial banks than have previous policies, and this has made it more difficult for the banks to lend to industry.

6. Expectations of increased inflation have led market operators to increase interest rates to unusually high levels.

These developments indicate that trends in the money and capital markets are increasing in importance to financial managers. The changes have been so massive that not only has financial timing been involved but also innovations in forms of financing used have been stimulated. Thus financial policies of companies have been broadened and have taken on greater importance in the overall management of business firms.

QUESTIONS

21–1. 'It makes good sense for a firm to fund its short-term borrowings, because this relieves the possibility that it will be called upon to pay off debt at an awkward time. From the standpoint of cost, however, it is always cheaper to use short-term debt than long-term debt.' Discuss the statement.

21–2. Is the operation of a policy of severely curtailing growth of the money supply likely to lead to low economic growth? How would the operation of such a policy affect British companies?

21–3. Why do interest rates on different types of securities vary widely?

21–4. What does GNP represent? Why are its levels and growth significant to the financial manager?

21–5. When are short-term interest rates higher than long-term rates? What is indicated if short-term rates are high in relation to long-term rates for a prolonged period of time such as 20 years in a given country?

21–6. What is the likely effect of a sharp increase in the domestic price level on the level of interest rates prevailing in the London money and capital markets?

21–7. Why was there an increase in the use of convertible debentures as a means of financing during the late 1960s?

PROBLEMS

21–1. In mid-1958 the Towers Company made a reappraisal of its sales forecasts for the next one, two and five years. It was clear that the product development programme that had been under way for the previous five years was then coming to fruition. The directors of Towers were confident that a sales growth of 12 to 15 per cent a year (on a compound basis) for the next five years was strongly indicated unless general business declined.

The Towers Company had total assets of £10 million. It had a debt-to-total assets ratio of 29 per cent. Since it had been spending heavily on research and development during the past five years, its profits had been depressed and the company's share price had suffered.

The Towers Company learned that it could borrow on a short-term basis by issuing bills of exchange at 4 per cent and issue ordinary shares or raise long-term debt by the issue of debentures at $5\frac{1}{2}$ per cent. The company raised £2 million by means of a rights issue and obtained additional short-term finance by means of relatively cheap bills of exchange until early 1960, when it found that its growing financial requirements could not be met by short-term borrowing. Its need for financing was so great that it raised an additional £10 million by issuing a convertible debenture at 8 per cent (interest rates had risen during the previous two years). The price of its ordinary shares had quadrupled by mid-1959 but had dropped by 10 per cent in early 1960.

Evaluate the timing and the selection of forms of financing by the Towers Company.

21–2. In July 1975, as the economy in general was emerging from the 1973–4 downturn and Video Industries Ltd's business was resuming its strong growth in sales, Sam Lincoln, the Chief accountant, concluded that the firm would require more working capital financing during the year ending 30 June 1976. Below are the historical and the *pro forma* income statements and balance sheets of the Video Industries Ltd.

Video Industries Ltd, Income Statements for Years Ended 30 June 1975 and 1976 (in Thousands of Pounds).

	Pro forma 1975	1976
Sales, net	£20000	£28000
Cost of sales	16000	20000
Gross profit	4000	8000
Operating expenses	2000	3000
Operating profit	2000	5000
Other income, net	400	200
Profits before taxes	2400	5200
Taxes	1200	2600
Net profit after taxes	1200	2600
Dividends	200	400
To retained earnings	£1000	£2200

Video Industries Ltd, Balance Sheets 30 June 1975 and 1976 (in Thousands of Pounds).

	1975	Pro forma 1976
Owners' capital and liabilities:		
Ordinary shares (£1 nominal)	£2 000	£2 000
Retained earnings	2 000	4 200
	£4 000	£6 200
Additional financing needed	0	1600
	£4 000	£7 800
Deferred taxation	1 200	1 600
Accrued expenses	200	400
Creditors	600	1 000
Total claims on assets	£6 000	£10 800
Assets		
Fixed assets (net)	£2 000	£4 000
Stocks	2 000	3 200
Debtors	1 600	2 400
Cash	400	1 200
Total assets	£6 000	£10 800

How should the financing needs be met? Why? (Although the £1 600 000 *pro forma* financial requirements are shown in the long-term section of the balance sheet, they can be met with either long- or short-term funds.)

21–3. Drake Manufacturing Company has decided to undertake a two-part capital expansion programme, from which no benefits will accrue until both phases are completed. As chief accountant of Drake it is your responsibility to examine the various sources of funds available to the company to finance each phase. The first phase will cost £5 million and will be undertaken immediately. It is anticipated that the company will begin the second phase, which also has an estimated cost of £5 million, approximately one year from now. The estimate for the second phase includes an adjustment for the rate of inflation, which is expected to increase from the current rate of 6 per cent to approximately 9 per cent at the end of the coming year. Drake's ordinary shares are widely held and quoted on the London Stock Exchange. Drake's balance sheet, income statement and market information for the last fiscal year are given here:

Drake Manufacturing Company, Balance Sheet 31 December 1976 (£millions).

Ordinary shares (£1 nominal)		£21.5	Net property plant and equipment		£50.0
Share premium		13.0	Current assets:		
Retained earnings		22.1	Stocks	£20.0	
		£56.6	Debtors	10.0	
7% debenture		16.0	Cash	2.0	
		£72.6			£32.0
Current liabilities:					
Short-term loan	£2.0				
Creditors	5.0				
Accrued expenses	2.4				
		£9.4			
Total claims		£82.0	Total assets		£82.0

Drake Manufacturing Company, Income Statement for Year Ending 31 December 1976 (£millions).

Sales	£150.00	
Gross margin	60.00	
Operating expenses	39.00	
Operating income	21.00	
Interest	1.26	*EPS* = 45.9 pence
Pretax earnings	£ 19.74	*DPS* = 16 pence
Taxes (50 per cent)	9.87	*P/E* = 10 ×
Net income	£ 9.87	Market price = £4.59

After a thorough review of the situation, and discussions with several banks and underwriters, you conclude that the following options are open to Drake. (Note: in any given year, assume that only one source of funds may be used.)

(a) Use short-term debt to cover phases 1 and 2 of the construction programme, then refund this debt with any of the long-term methods noted in (b) below at the end of the construction period.

(b) Obtain long-term financing now for phase 1 of the construction programme, then obtain additional financing next year for phase 2. The long-term financing methods available are bank term loans, debentures and ordinary shares.

(c) Obtain long-term financing now to cover both phases of the expansion programme, using one of the methods outlined in (b) above, to raise £10 million.

A review of the latest issue of the *Financial Times* indicated that the following interest rates are now prevailing:

Bank loans	
LIBOR	6.75%
Long-term	9.25
Bills of exchange	
90–119 days	5.93%
4–6 months	6.27
Treasury bills	
3 months	4.93%
6 months	5.33
Company debentures	8.8%

Your analysis of the economy shows that economic activity began showing strong signs of improvement about two months ago, following a long period of sluggishness. You also notice that, according to today's *Financial Times*, the average *P/E* ratio for shares in the 30 Share Index is 13.1 compared to 8.6 less than one year ago.

You are concerned about the effect the additional financing will have on Drake's *EPS* and market price, as the benefits from the expansion will not begin to be realized for about three years. You also wish to maintain a strong, liquid balance sheet. The maximum acceptable ratio of long-term debt to total long-term capital is 33 per cent. Discussions with underwriters have indicated that a share issue could be sold at the current market price.

As chief accountant, you are requested to analyse the situation completely, and to support what you feel is the optimum financing plan and timing.

21–4. The objective of this assignment is to evaluate the timing decision associated with a recent issue of debentures.

(a) From a recent issue of the *Financial Times*, in the pages that describe new issues of shares and debentures sold to the public, identify a public issue of company debentures that were issued the preceding day. Record information identifying the issuer, the date of issue, the amount of the issue, its maturity, coupon rate, issue price, yield to maturity, any other stated terms of the issue, and the degree of success of the first day sales. Somewhere on the immediate surrounding pages will be a paragraph or a very short statement about the issue and the way the issue was received by the market.

(b) In the most recent monthly issue of the Bank of England *Quarterly Bulletin* (*BEQB*), locate in the index the item 'Interest Rates' and in that table under 'Company debentures' locate the column headed 'Total'. Record the yields under 'Total' for each of the last 15 months reported, and also the yield reported for each of the five years preceding the monthly data. Plot these data. Also, indicate the yield for your new issue as determined in part (a) above on this graph.

(c) Briefly explain what has happened to long-term corporate interest rates in general in the interim between the most recent *BEQB* data and the date of your new issue in part (a). Given the current state of the economy, what is the outlook for interest rates over the next six months to one year?

(d) Discuss the percentage interest cost incurred by the issuer of your debentures, and the timing of the new issue.

SELECTED REFERENCES

Dodds, J. C. and Ford, J. L. *The Term Structure of Interest Rates*. London: Robertson, 1974.

Freund, William C. The dynamic financial markets. *Financial Executive* 33 (May 1965): 11–26, 57–58.

Friedman, Milton. Factors affecting the level of interest rates. In *Savings and Residential Financing*. Chicago: U.S. Savings and Loan League, 1968, pp. 10–27.

Gibson, William E. Price expectations effects on interest rates. *Journal of Finance* 25 (March 1970): 19–34.

Grossman, Herschel I. The term structure of interest rates. *Journal of Finance* 22 (December 1967): 611–622.

Johnson, Ramon E. Term structures of corporate bond yields as a function of risk of default. *Journal of Finance* 22 (May 1967): 313–345.

Kessel, Reuben A. *Cyclical Behavior of the Term Structure of Interest Rates*. New York: National Bureau of Economic Research, 1965.

Malkiel, Burton G. *The Term Structure of Interest Rates*. Princeton, N.J.: Princeton University Press, 1969.

Mason, Sandra. *The Flow of Funds in Britain*. London: Elek, 1976.

Ritter, L. S. *Money and Economic Analysis*. 3rd ed. New York: Houghton Mifflin, 1967.

Robinson, Roland I. *Money and Capital Markets*. New York: McGraw-Hill, 1964.

Saunders, A. and Woodward, R. S. Monetary policy, exchange rate policy and the determination of U.K. interest rates 1972/6. *Investment Analyst* (December 1977): 15–20.

Tussing, A. Dale. Can monetary policy influence the availability of credit? *Journal of Finance* 21 (March 1966): 1–14.

Van Horne, James. Interest-rate expectations, the shape of the yield curve and monetary policy. *Review of Economics and Statistics* 48 (May 1966): 211–215.

Chapter 22

External Growth: Mergers and Holding Companies

Growth is vital to the well-being of a firm; without it, a business cannot attract able management because it cannot give recognition in promotions or offer challenging creative activity. Without able executives, the firm is likely to decline and die. Much of the material in the previous chapters dealing with analysis, planning and financing has a direct bearing on the financial manager's potential contribution to the growth of a firm. Because of the central importance of the growth requirement, the present chapter focuses on strategies for promoting growth.

Merger activity has played an important part in the growth of firms in the United Kingdom, and financial managers are required both to appraise the desirability of a prospective purchase and to participate directly in evaluating the respective companies involved in a merger.[1] Consequently, it is essential that the study of financial management provide the background necessary for effective participation in merger negotiations and decisions.

Financial managers – and intelligent laymen – also need to be aware of the broader significance of mergers. There have been three major periods of merger activity affecting UK industry. The first period occurred during the 1890s, the second during the period following the First World War up to 1930, and the third, and most prolonged, period began around 1952 and has continued to the present date, with peaks in the years 1967–9 and 1972–3. The dramatic change in the concentration of industry, resulting mainly from this merger activity, can be seen when we consider that the share in net output of the 100 largest firms in British manufacturing industry increased from around 15 per cent in 1900 to 50 per cent by 1975.[2] Regardless of the business objectives and motives of merger activity, its social, political and economic consequences must also be taken into account.

---

1. As we use the term, 'merger' means any combination that forms one economic unit from two or more previous ones. For legal purposes there are distinctions between the various ways these combinations can occur, but our emphasis is on fundamental business and financial aspects of mergers or acquisitions.
2. Hannah, L. and Kay, J. A., *Concentration in Modern Industry* (London: Macmillan, 1977), chap. 1, p. 1.

Table 22–1 *Acquired Companies with Net Worth of £20 million or More during 1970–77.*

Fiscal year	Acquiring company	Acquired company	Net worth (£millions)
1970–71	Reed Group	International Publishing Corp.	104.7
	Sears Holdings	British Shoe Corp.	70.7
	Trust Houses Group	Forte Holdings	60.2
	British American Tobacco Investments	Wiggins Teape	52.1
	Imperial Chemical Industries	Carrington Viyella Group	44.3
	Courage Barclay & Simonds	John Smith's Tadcaster Brewery	36.7
	Rio Tinto Zinc Corp.	R.T.Z. Pillar	35.5
	Grand Metropolitan Hotels	Mecca	30.1
1971–2	Watney Mann	International Distillers & Vintners	76.8
	Cavenham	Allied Suppliers	70.7
	Grand Metropolitan Hotels	Truman	39.5
	C. T. Bowring & Co.	Singer & Friedlander Holdings	24.1
	Trafalgar House Investments	Cunard Steam Ship Co.	23.2
	Sears Holdings	William Hill Organisation	23.1
	British Electric Traction	United Transport Co.	22.5
	Watney Mann	Samuel Webster & Sons	20.4
1972–3	Grand Metropolitan Hotels	Watney Mann	378.3
	Imperial Group	Courage	257.7
	Bowater Corporation	Ralli International	87.1
	British American Tobacco Co.	International Stores	63.5
	Consolidated Gold Fields	Amey Group	54.7
	Ocean Steam Ship Co.	Wm Cory & Son	53.2
	Burmah Oil Co.	Quinton Hazell (Holdings)	48.7
	Unigate	Scot Bowyers	41.7
	Rank Organisation	Butlins	38.2
	Guest, Keen & Nettlefolds	Firth Cleveland	27.2
	Richard Johnson & Nephew	Thos. Firth & John Brown	26.9
	United Drapery Stores	William Timpson	25.4
	Lewis & Peat	Guiness Mahon Holdings	23.3
	Acrow (Engineers)	Steel Group	22.4
	Matthews Wrightson Group	Matthews Wrightson Holdings	22.2
	Bowyers (Wiltshire)	Scot Meat Products	20.3
1973–4	Navcot Shipping (Holdings)	Shipping Industrial Holdings	90.4
	House of Fraser	Army & Navy Stores	40.3
	Champional International Corp.	A. W. (Securities)	40.0
	Rank Organisation	Oddenino's Property and Investment Co.	22.4
	Peninsular & Oriental Steam Navigation Co.	Bovis	21.8
1974–5	Town & City Properties	Sterling Guarantee Trust	27.3
	CSR	Australian Estates Co.	24.6
	American Tobacco International Corp.	Gallaher	23.3
1975–6	Inchcape & Co.	Anglo-Thai Corporation	28.2
	Magnet & Southerns	Magnet Joinery	28.0
	Magnet & Southerns	Southerns-Evans	22.8
1976–7	BAT Industries	British American Tobacco Co.	876.0
	Tate and Lyle	Manbré & Garton	47.9
	Wormald International Holdings (UK)	Mather & Platt	27.9
	EMI	Development Securities	22.9

Acquisitions of unquoted companies are not included. Also, alternative offers have been ignored and consideration has been calculated on the basic offer.
Source: *The Times, 1000 Leading Companies in Britain and Overseas.* Various years.

While the frenzied merger activity of the later 1960s and early 1970s has abated, mergers of major magnitude have continued to take place. It was reported that the number of acquisitions made by industrial and commercial companies rose during the second quarter of 1977 to the highest level since early 1974.[3] Table 22–1 provides information on the major mergers during the period 1970–77.

MERGERS VERSUS INTERNAL GROWTH

Many of the objectives of size and diversification may be achieved either through internal growth or by external growth through acquisitions and mergers. In the post-Second World War period, considerable diversification was achieved by many firms through external acquisition. Some financial reasons for utilizing external acquisition instead of internal growth to achieve diversification are discussed below.

Financing

Sometimes it is possible to finance an acquisition when it is not possible to finance internal growth. A large chemicals factory, for example, involves a large investment. Productive capacity may be acquired in a merger through an exchange of shares more cheaply than it can be obtained by buying the facilities themselves. Sellers may be more willing to accept the shares of the purchaser in payment for the facilities sold than would investors in a public offering. The use of shares reduces cash requirements for the acquisition of assets.

Market capitalization rates

While it is not strictly an operating factor, the fact that the earnings of larger economic units are frequently capitalized at lower rates and hence produce higher market values has stimulated many mergers. The securities of larger firms have better marketability; these firms are more able to diversify and thus reduce risks, and they are generally better known. All these factors lead to lower required rates of return and higher price/earnings ratios. As a result, it may be possible to consolidate firms and have the resulting market value greater than the sum of their individual values, even if there is no increase in aggregate earnings. To illustrate, three companies may each be earning £1 million and selling at 10 times earnings, for a total market value of (£1 million) (10) (3) equals £30 million. When these companies combine, the new company may obtain a stock exchange quotation or may take other actions to improve the price of its shares. If so, the price/earnings ratio may rise to 15, in which case the market value of the consolidated firm would be £45 million.[4]

Various studies have indicated a direct relationship between the index of share prices and the level of merger activity. It is interesting to note, however, that in 1973, while share prices were falling, merger activity remained at a high level.

Taxation

There can be little doubt that the high level of taxation has been a factor stimulating

---

3. *Trade and Industry*, 12 August, 1977.

4. The market capitalization rate is related to the cost of equity, as we discussed in Chapter 19. A lower capitalization rate results in a lower cost of capital. Therefore, the same actions that raise the market value of the equity also lower the firm's cost of new capital.

merger activity in the post-war period. This has been especially true in relation to acquisitions of small, successful firms. High levels of personal taxation (up to 83 per cent on earned income) can be avoided by disposing of the business and incurring a relatively moderate rate of tax of 30 per cent on capital gains. In addition, the burden of estate duty has, in the past, necessitated sale of businesses.

An important reason for the purchase of the Cunard Steam Ship Company by Trafalgar House Investments was the tax benefits accruing from accumulated tax losses of Cunard of over £6 million.

TERMS OF MERGERS

For every merger actually consummated, several other potentially attractive combinations fail during the negotiating stage. In some of these cases, negotiations are broken off when it is revealed that the companies' operations are not compatible. In others, tangible benefits would result, but the parties are unable to agree on the merger terms. Of these terms, the most important is the price to be paid by the acquiring firm for the firm acquired. Factors that influence this important aspect of a merger are now considered.

Effects on price and earnings

A merger carries potentialities for either favourable or adverse effects on earnings, on market prices of shares, or on both. Previous chapters have shown that investment decisions should be guided by the effects on market values, and these effects should in turn be determined by the effects on future earnings and dividends. These future events are difficult to forecast, however, so shareholders, as well as managers, attribute great importance to the immediate effects of a contemplated merger on earnings per share. Directors of companies will often state, 'I do not know how the merger will affect the market price of the shares of my company because so many forces influencing market prices are at work. But the effect on earnings per share can be seen directly.'

An example will illustrate the effects of a proposed merger on earnings per share and thus suggest the kinds of problems that are likely to arise. Assume the following facts for two companies:

	Company A	Company B
Total earnings	£20 000	£ 50 000
Number of ordinary shares	50 000	100 000
Earnings per share	£ 0.40	£ 0.50
Price/earnings ratio	15 ×	12 ×
Market price per share	£ 6.00	£ 6.00

Suppose the firms agree to merge, with B, the surviving firm, acquiring the shares of A by a one-for-one exchange of shares. The exchange ratio is determined by the respective market prices of the two companies. Assuming no increase in earnings, the effects on earnings per share are shown in the following tabulation:

	Shares of company B owned after merger	Earnings per share	
		Before merger	After merger
A's shareholders	50 000	£0.40	£0.467
B's shareholders	100 000	0.50	0.467
	150 000		

Since total earnings are £70 000 and a total of 150 000 shares will be outstanding after the merger has been completed, the new earnings per share will be £0.467. Earnings will increase by 6.7 pence for A's shareholders, but they will decline by 3.3 pence for B's.

The effects on market values are less certain. If the combined company sells at company A's price/earnings ratio of 15, the new market value per share of the new company will be £7. In this case, shareholders of both companies will have benefited. This result comes about because the combined earnings are now valued at a multiplier of 15, whereas prior to the merger one portion of the earnings was valued at a multiplier of 15 and another portion was valued at a multiplier of 12.

If, on the other hand, the earnings of the new company are valued at B's multiplier of 12, the indicated market value of the shares will be £5.6. The shareholders of each company will have suffered a £0.4 dilution in market value.

Because the effects on market value per share are less certain than those on earnings per share, the impact of earnings per share tends to be given great weight in merger negotiations. Because of this, the following analysis also emphasizes effects on earnings per share, while recognizing that maximizing market value is the valid rule of investment decisions.

If the merger takes place on the basis of earnings, neither earnings dilution nor earnings appreciation will take place, as shown below.

	Shares of company B owned after merger	Earnings per old share	
		Before merger	After merger
A's shareholders[a]	40 000	£0.4	£0.4
B's shareholders	100 000	0.5	0.5
	140 000		

[a] On the basis of earnings, the exchange ratio is 4:5; that is, company A's shareholders receive four shares of B for each five shares of A they own. Earnings per share of the merged company are £0.5. But, since A's shareholders now own only 80 per cent of the number of their old shares, their equivalent earnings per *old* share are the same £0.4. For example, suppose one of A's shareholders formerly held 100 shares. He will own only 80 shares of B after the merger, and his total earnings will be 80 × £0.5 = £40. Dividing his £40 total earnings by the number of shares he formerly owned, 100, gives the £0.4 per *old* share.

It is clear that the equivalent earnings per share after the merger are the same as before the merger. The effects on market values will depend upon whether the 15-times multiplier of A or the 12-times multiplier of B prevails.

Of the numerous factors affecting the valuation of the constituent companies in a merger, all must ultimately be reflected in the earnings per share, or market price, of the companies. Hence, all the effects on the earnings position or wealth position of shareholders are encompassed by the foregoing example. We will now consider both quantitative and qualitative factors that will influence the terms on which a merger is likely to take place.

Quantitative factors affecting terms of mergers

Five factors have received the greatest emphasis in arriving at merger terms:

1. Earnings and the growth rate of earnings.
2. Dividends.
3. Market values.
4. Book values.
5. Net current assets.

Analysis is typically based on the per share values of the foregoing factors. The relative importance of each factor and the circumstances under which each is likely to be the most influential determinant in arriving at terms will vary. The nature of these influences is described below.

Earnings and growth rates

Both expected earnings and capitalization rates as reflected in P/E ratios are important in determining the values that will be established in a merger. The analysis necessarily begins with historical data on the firms' earnings, whose past growth rates, future trends, and variability are important determinants of the earnings multiplier, or P/E ratio, that will prevail after the merger.

How future earnings growth rates affect the multiplier can be illustrated by extending the preceding example. First, we know that high P/E ratios are commonly associated with rapidly growing companies. Since company A has the higher P/E ratio, it is reasonable to assume that its earnings are expected to grow more rapidly than those of company B. Suppose A's expected growth rate is 10 per cent and B's is 5 per cent. Looking at the proposed merger from the point of view of company B and its shareholders, and assuming that the exchange ratio is based on present market prices, it can be seen that B will suffer a dilution in earnings when the merger occurs. However, B will be acquiring a firm with more favourable growth prospects; hence, its earnings after the merger should increase more rapidly than before. In this case, the new growth rate is assumed to be a weighted average of the growth rates of the individual firms, weighted by their respective total earnings before the merger. In the example, the new expected growth rate is 6.43 per cent.

With the new growth rate it is possible to determine just how long it will take company B's shareholders to regain the earnings dilution – that is, how long it will take earnings per share to revert back to their previous position before the merger. This can be determined graphically from Figure 22–1.[5] Without the merger, B would have initial earnings of £0.5 a

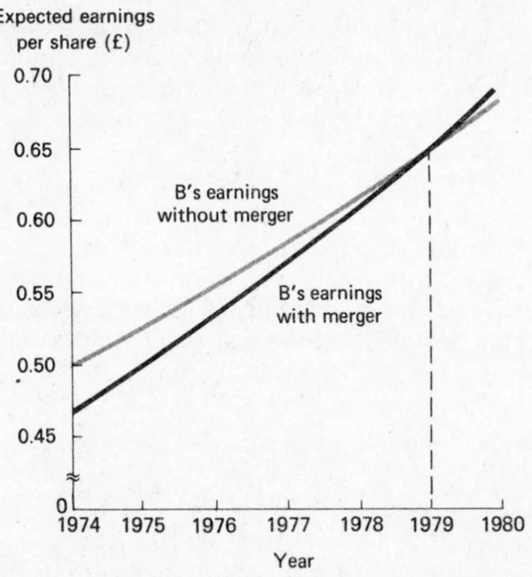

Figure 22–1 *Effect of Merger on Future Earnings.*

5. The calculation could also be made algebraically by solving for N in the following equation: $E_1(1+g_1)^N = E_2(1+g_2)^N$, *where* E_1 = earnings before the merger, E_2 = earnings after the merger, g_1 and g_2 are the growth rates before and after the merger, and N is the break-even number of years.

share, and these earnings would have grown at a rate of 5 per cent a year. With the merger, earnings drop to £0.467 a share, but the rate of growth increases to 6.43 per cent. Under these conditions, the earnings dilution is overcome after five years; from the fifth year on, B's earnings will be higher, assuming the merger is consummated.

This same relationship could be developed from the point of view of the faster growing firm. Here there would be an immediate earnings increase but a reduced rate of growth. Working through the analysis would show the number of years before the earnings accretion would be eroded.

It is apparent that the critical variables are (a) the respective rates of growth of the two firms; (b) their relative sizes, which determine the actual amount of the initial earnings per share dilution or accretion, as well as the new weighted average growth rate; (c) the firm's *P/E* ratios; and (d) the exchange ratio. These factors interact to produce the resulting pattern of earnings per share for the surviving company. It is possible to generalize the relationships somewhat; for our purposes, it is necessary simply to note that in the bargaining process the exchange ratio is the variable that must be manipulated in an effort to reach a mutually satisfactory earnings pattern.[6]

Dividends

Because they represent the actual income received by shareholders, dividends may influence the terms of merger. As the material in Chapter 20 suggests, however, dividends are likely to have little influence on the market price of companies with a record of high growth and high profitability.

It is interesting to note how often emphasis is placed on increases in proposed dividends of the target company, during takeovers which are being resisted. For example, in 1972, during the ultimately successful takeover bid by Grand Metropolitan Hotels Ltd for the ordinary share capital of Watney Mann Ltd there were exceptional increases in proposed dividends. In response to the initial offer by Grand Metropolitan, the directors of Watney Mann issued a statement in which they proposed a dividend rate for 1972 of 29 per cent as against a rate of only 21.5 per cent for 1971. When Grand Metropolitan Hotels increased their offer, the directors of Watney Mann countered with another statement showing a forecast dividend rate of 36. 25 per cent for 1973. Thus a dividend rate which had crept up from 17 to 21.5 per cent in the five years to 1971 was forecast to almost double over the next two years.

Market values

The price of a firm's shares reflects expectations about its future earnings and dividends, so current market values are expected to have a strong influence on the terms of a merger.

---

6. We should also mention at this point that certain companies, especially the 'conglomerates', are reported to have used mergers to produce a 'growth illusion' designed to increase the prices of their shares. When a high *P/E* ratio company buys a low *P/E* ratio company, the earnings per share of the acquiring firm rise *because* of the merger. Thus, mergers can produce growth in reported earnings for the acquiring firm. This growth by merger, in turn, can cause the acquiring firm to keep its high *P/E* ratio. With this ratio, the conglomerates can seek new low *P/E* merger candidates and thus continue to obtain growth through mergers. The chain is broken (a) if the rate of merger activity slows, or (b) if the *P/E* ratio of the acquiring firm falls.

Barclay Securities is an example of a conglomerate whose reported profits declined swiftly, leading to a fall in the share price and eventual 'takeover' by J. H. Vavasseur Ltd, another conglomerate. Trade union resistance, both to the sale of the Shepperton film studios of the newly-acquired British Lion Film Co. and to 'rationalization' plans in a toy company subsidiary, also prevented the management of Barclay Securities from implementing their previous 'asset-stripping' policies in order to finance new acquisitions. As a result of these factors the share price fell from a record high of 168 pence to only 86 pence prior to acquisition by Vavasseur.

However, the value placed on a firm in an acquisition is likely to exceed its current market price for a number of reasons. (a) If the company is in a depressed industry, its shareholders are likely to discount to too great an extent the dismal outlook for the company; this will result in a very low current market price. (b) The prospective purchaser may be interested in acquiring the company for the contribution that it may make to the acquiring company. Thus, the acquired company is worth more to an informed purchaser than it is in the general market. (c) Shareholders are offered more than current market prices for their shares as an inducement to sell. For these reasons, the offering price is usually in the range of 10 to 20 per cent above the market price before the merger announcement.

Book value per share

Book values are generally considered to be relatively unimportant in determining the value of a company, as they merely represent the historical investments that have been made in the company. These investments may have little relation to current values or prices. At times, however, especially when book values substantially exceed market values, they may well have an impact on merger terms. The book value is an index of the amount of physical facilities made available in the merger. Despite a past record of low earning power, it is always possible that, under effective management, a firm's assets may once again achieve normal earning power, in which case the market value of the company will rise. Because of the potential contribution of physical properties to improved future earnings, book values may have an influence on actual merger terms.

Net current assets per share

Net current assets (current assets minus current liabilities) per share are likely to have an influence on merger terms because they represent the amount of liquidity that may be obtained from a company in a merger. One of the factors leading to the rapid growth of the 'asset-stripping' conglomerates during the 1960s was their ability to purchase companies with the high levels of liquidity or with marketable assets which they would then convert to cash in order to provide funds to finance their next acquisition.

Relative importance of quantitative factors

Attempts have been made to determine statistically the relative weights assigned to each of the above factors in actual merger cases. These attempts have been singularly unsuccessful In one case, one factor seems to dominate; in another, some other determinant appears to be most important. This absence of consistent patterns among the quantitative factors suggests that qualitative forces are also at work, and we now turn our attention to these management factors.

Qualitative influences: synergy

Sometimes the most important influence on the terms of a merger is a business consideration not reflected at all in historical quantitative data. A soundly conceived merger is one in which the combination produces what may be called a *synergistic*, or 'two-plus-two-equals-five', effect. By the combination, more profits are generated than could be achieved by the sum of the individual firms operating separately.

For instance, in the case presented for the acquisition of Watney Mann Ltd by Grand

Metropolitan Hotels (mentioned above), it was suggested that each company complemented the other in an important way. Watney Mann was the third largest drinks company in Europe while the Grand Metropolitan Group controlled an extensive chain of hotels, restaurants and entertainment establishments through which Watney's products could be sold. Another example is the 1977 merger between Fison's Ltd and A. Gallenkamp which allowed the combined company to sell a more extensive range of scientific equipment products in a larger number of international markets. The two companies had in the past exported abroad, but to different markets and with different, though complementary, products.

The qualitative factors may also reflect other influences. The merger or acquisition may enable one company that lacks general management ability to obtain it from the other company. The reverse argument is also frequently made for conglomerates. Another factor may be the acquisition of a technically competent scientific or engineering staff if one of the companies has fallen behind in the technological race or, as in the case of the Bowater acquisition of Ralli in 1972, it may lead to a conservative firm's acquiring a dynamic management team. In such a situation, the company needing the technical competence possessed by the other firm may be willing to pay a substantial premium over previous levels of earnings, dividends, market values or book values of the acquired firm.

The purpose of the merger may be to develop a production capability a firm does not possess. Some firms are strong in producing custom-made items with high performance characteristics, yet these firms, on entering new markets, must make use of mass-production techniques. If the firm has had no such experience, this skill may have to be obtained by means of a merger. This has been particularly true of many of the acquisitions of the tobacco companies and also of the recent acquisition by Dixons Photographic of Weston Pharmaceuticals.

The foregoing are the kinds of qualitative considerations that may have an overriding influence on the actual terms of merger, and the values of these contributions are never easy to quantify. The all-encompassing question, of course, is how these factors will affect the contribution of each company to future earnings per share in the combined operation. The historical data and the qualitative considerations described, in addition to judgement and bargaining, combine to determine merger terms.

ILLUSTRATION OF AN ACTUAL TAKEOVER SITUATION

A good illustration of an actual takeover situation, and the manner in which it was resisted, is given by the offer made by Tate and Lyle Ltd in 1976 for the ordinary share capital of Manbré and Garton Ltd. At the time Tate and Lyle and Manbré were the largest and second largest British refiners of cane sugar, respectively. The offer was made against a background of a number of years' talks between the two companies and the government, aimed at rationalizing the cane sugar industry because of surplus capacity which had arisen mainly as a result of British entry into the EEC and cancellation of the old Commonwealth Sugar Agreement. The talks between the two companies had broken down because of disagreement as to which should bear the main burden of any plant closures.

Tate and Lyle Ltd initially made a bid approach to the directors of Manbré and Garton Ltd on 9 July 1976. This approach was rejected, however, and a Press announcement was made by the directors of Manbré and Garton to that effect on 15 July. On that day the ordinary shares of Manbré rose by 10 pence to 158 pence, after several previous days of speculative buying.

On 28 July 1976 Tate and Lyle Ltd launched their bid, offering for each share in Manbré either £1.70 in cash or £0.70 in cash plus £1 nominal 12 per cent convertible unsecured loan stock. The offer priced Manbré at around £44 million, but was rejected as totally unacceptable by the directors of Manbré and Garton Ltd.

The offer made by Tate and Lyle was also conditional upon a statement's being issued by the Office of Fair Trading, or by the Secretary of State for Prices and Consumer Protection that no referral of the offer would be made to the Monopolies and Mergers Commission.

Almost immediately after the offer was made, the directors of Manbré launched their opposition to it. A statement was issued to their shareholders pointing out, amongst other things, the closeness of the offer price of 170 pence per share to the market price of 150 pence per share immediately prior to the offer.[7] In addition, the directors announced that they were recommending a 62 per cent increase in dividends for the year. This increase was allowed, despite existing government dividend restrictions, because of the takeover bid by Tate and Lyle.

The directors of Manbré Ltd also pointed out, in a submission to the Office of Fair Trading, 'the serious monopoly implications of the takeover' in that, if Tate and Lyle's bid was essential, they would control over 50 per cent of the sugar, glucose, sweetener and starch markets in the United Kingdom. An attempt was thus being made by the directors of Manbré, and by a number of trade associations, to have the bid referred to the Monopolies and Mergers Commission, thus effectively killing it. Manbrés directors also offered to hold fresh talks with the directors of Tate and Lyle on the rationalization of the cane sugar refining industry, if the bid were indeed referred to the Monopolies Commission. In the event this offer was unnecessary as the Secretary of State for Prices and Consumer Protection decided, in early September, not to refer the offer to the Monopolies Commission.

On 21 September, as widely expected, Tate and Lyle increased the terms of their offer to £2 per share in Manbré, giving shareholders the option to receive, instead, £1 in cash plus £1 convertible unsecured loan stock. The revised offer followed the purchase by Tate and Lyle of 6.6 million shares in Manbré from institutional investors. These shares, comprising 27.5 per cent of the equity capital of Manbré, gave Tate and Lyle a total of 31 per cent of its share capital. In the meantime, the directors of Manbré announced that they were preparing a profits forecast for the coming year 'showing a material increase over the £10 million pre-tax forecast for the current year', together with a commensurate increase in dividends.

On 22 September, Tate and Lyle purchased a further 2.37 million shares, again chiefly from institutional investors. They also increased the coupon rate on the convertible loan stock from 12 to 13 per cent, 'in recognition of the fact that interest rates had risen since the bid was first announced'. Manbré followed this with a forecast pretax profit for 1977 of £13 million as against £10 million forecast for 1976, together with an increase in dividends from 15.4 pence to 20 pence gross. Despite this statement, Manbré's share price rose only 2 pence to the offer price of £2 while Tate and Lyle's shares rose 14 pence to £2.30.

Finally, on 23 September, victory was announced for Tate and Lyle after a further surge of institutional selling increased the total of shares held to 13.25 million, representing 55 per cent of the equity capital of Manbré and Garton Ltd. As a result the offer was declared unconditional.

The previous paragraphs merely describe the main events involved in the takeover. There were, in addition, many important factors which played their part in the unfolding of the events. For instance, government reluctance to refer the bid to the Monopolies Commission seems to have been based on a belief that the formation of a single sugar cane refining enterprise would be a useful way of rationalizing capacity within the

7. In fact, as the chairman of Tate and Lyle pointed out, the shares of Manbré had been quoted between 125 and 135 pence before any rumours of a potential bid had leaked out.

industry. In addition, much of the opposition to the bid by the directors of Manbré was explained by the fact that sugar accounted for only 30 per cent of their profits, and by their belief that Tate and Lyle had made the offer largely in order to break into the glucose and starch businesses, which were proving a very profitable area for Manbré.

Initial reluctance to sell, on the part of shareholders, could be explained by the fear that the bid might be referred to the Monopolies and Mergers Commission. There was also a well-founded belief that Tate and Lyle had become so heavily committed financially to the offer that they could not afford to let the bid lapse and that consequently the price was likely to be raised.

Finally, what seemed to have swayed a number of institutional investors to sell, apart from the higher price, was the latest upturn in the stock market which was producing a number of more attractive investment opportunities.

ACCOUNTING POLICIES IN MERGERS

After merger terms have been agreed upon, the financial manager must be familiar with the accounting principles for recording the financial results of the merger and for reflecting the initial effect on the earnings of the surviving firm. This section deals with these matters.

On 20 January 1971, the Accounting Standards Committee issued in Exposure Draft dealing with the accounting treatment of business amalgamations.[8] Traditional accounting methods treated amalgamations as the acquisition of one company by another regardless of the manner in which the acquisition had been financed. In recent years, however, it has become the practice to distinguish between amalgamations which represent substantial changes in the ownership and business of at least one of the companies involved, and those which represent a continuation of the former ownership and business of the acquiring companies.

An amalgamation where there is continuing ownership in a continuing business is considered a merger, which may be accounted for by using the American 'pooling of interests' method. A transfer to new ownership, on the other hand, is considered to be an acquisition and is accounted for by traditional accounting methods. Because of the requirement of continuation of ownership, a merger may be considered to have taken place only when the purchase consideration is in shares.

Four conditions must exist before a merger can be said to have taken place:

1. The substance of the main businesses of the constituent companies continues in the amalgamated undertaking.
2. The equity voting rights of the amalgamated undertaking to be held by the shareholders of any one of the constituent companies is not more than three times the equity voting rights to be held by the shareholders of any of the other constituent companies.
3. At lease 90 per cent in value of the offer is in the form of equity voting capital with rights identical with the equity voting rights of the offeree company or companies already in existence.
4. The offer is approved by the voting shareholders of the company making the offer and it is accepted by shareholders representing at least 90 per cent of the total equity capital of the company or companies receiving the offer.

---

8. Accounting Standards Committee, *Accounting for Acquisitions and Mergers, Exposure Draft*, No. 3 (London, 1971).

In contrast, an *acquisition* involves (a) new owners, (b) an appraisal of the acquired firm's physical assets and a re-statement of the balance sheet to reflect these new values, and (c) the possibility of an excess or deficiency of consideration given up vis-à-vis the book value of equity. Point (c) refers to the creation of goodwill. In an acquisition, the excess of the purchase price paid over the book value (re-stated to reflect the appraisal value of physical assets) is shown in the consolidated accounts as goodwill. Any deduction of goodwill from reserves must be shown in a note annexed to the annual accounts. Alternative treatments of goodwill involve either revaluation of the assets of the acquiring company or else the 'writing-off' of goodwill over a number of years in the profit and loss account of the new group of companies. In a pooling of interests, the combined total assets after the merger represent a simple sum of the asset contributions of the constituent companies.

Group accounts[9]

When one company – the holding company – exercises control over another company – the subsidiary company – the holding company is required by law to produce 'group accounts' at the end of its financial year, dealing with the consolidated results of the holding company and of the subsidiary, or subsidiaries, as the case may be.[10]

One company is defined as the subsidiary of another company if

1. that other either
   (a) is a member of it and controls the composition of its board of directors; or
   (b) holds more than half in nominal value of its equity share capital; or
2. the first-mentioned company is a subsidiary of any company which is that other's subsidiary.[11]

The results of subsidiaries may be excluded from group accounts if the company's directors are of the opinion that

1. it is impracticable, or would be of no real value to members of the company, in view of the insignificant amounts involved, or would involve expense or delay out of proportion to the value to members of the company; or
2. the result would be misleading, or harmful to the business of the company or any of its subsidiaries; or
3. the business of the holding company and that of its subsidiary are so different that they cannot reasonably be treated as a single undertaking.[12]

In fact, the vast majority of large and medium-sized public companies in the UK prepare group accounts.

Associated companies

It is possible for one company to hold less than 50 per cent of the equity capital of another company and yet exercise effective control over that second company. While the second company cannot be categorized as a subsidiary company, its relationship with the investing company is such that special accounting treatment is required, especially with regard to the profits of the second company. The Accounting Standards Committee have

---

9. The material in this section is technical and is generally covered in accounting courses. The reader may skip to the section on holding companies without loss of continuity.
10. Companies Act, 1948, Section 150(1).
11. Companies Act, 1948, Section 154(1).
12. Companies Act, 1948, Section 150(2)(b).

issued a statement[13] dealing with the treatment of those companies which are known as 'associated companies'. An 'associated company' is defined as one in which an investing company either has an interest of between 20 and 50 per cent of the equity voting rights, or else participates in the associated company by way of partnership or joint venture. The main information requirement is that the investing company's share of the associated company's profits or losses should be shown in the consolidated profit and loss account of the investing company, or ordinary profit and loss account if the investing company has no subsidiaries.

Financial treatment of an acquisition

The financial treatment of a purchase may best be explained by use of a hypothetical example. The Mammoth Company has just purchased the Petty Company under an arrangement known as an *acquisition*. The facts are as given in Table 22–2, which also shows the financial treatment. The illustration conforms to the general nature of an acquisition. Measured by total assets, the Mammoth Company is 20 times as large as Petty, while its total earnings are 15 times as large. Assume that the terms of the acquisition will be one share of Mammoth for two shares of Petty, based on the prevailing market value of their ordinary shares. Thus, in terms of Mammoth's shares, Mammoth is giving to Petty's shareholders £3 of market value and £0.7 of book value for each share of Petty.

Table 22–2 *Financial Treatment of an Acquisition.*

	Mammoth Company	Petty Company	Adjustments Debit	Adjustments Credit	Pro forma consolidated Balance sheet
Assets					
Net fixed assets	£100 000	£ 4 000			£104 000
Other assets	20 000	2 000			22 000
Current assets	80 000	4 000			84 000
Goodwill arising			£54 000		54 000
Total assets	£200 000	£10 000			£264 000
Liabilities and net worth					
Ordinary share capital	40 000	1 000	1 000	£4 000	44 000
Share premium account	20 000	–		£56 000	76 000
Revenue reserves	80 000	5 000	5 000		80 000
Long-term debt	20 000	–			20 000
Current liabilities	40 000	4 000			44 000
Total liabilities and net worth	£200 000	£10 000	£60 000	£60 000	£264 000
Explanation					
Nominal value per ordinary share	£0.40	£0.5			
No. of shares outstanding	100 000	20 000			
Book value per share	£1.40	£0.30			
Total earnings	£30 000	£2 000			
Earnings per share	£0.30	£0.10			
Price/earnings ratio	20 ×	30 ×			
Market value per share	£6	£3			

13. Accounting Standards Committee, Accounting for the results of associated companies, Statement of Standard Accounting Practice No. 1 (London, 1971).

Petty's market value is £3 a share, its book value is £0.3 a share, and the fair value of the equity is £6000.[14] The total market value of Mammoth paid for Petty is £60 000. The goodwill involved may be calculated as follows:

Value given by Mammoth	£60 000
Fair value of net worth of Petty purchased	6000
Goodwill	£54 000

The £54 000 goodwill represents a debit in the 'Adjustments' column and is carried to the pro forma balance sheet. The pro forma balance sheet is obtained by simply adding the balance sheets of the constituent companies, together with adjustments.

A total value of £60 000 has been given by Mammoth for a book value of £6000. This amount represents, in addition to the debt, a payment of £1000 for the ordinary share capital of Petty, £5000 for the retained earnings, and £54 000 goodwill. The corresponding credit is the 1000 shares of Mammoth given in the transaction at their nominal value of £0.4 a share, resulting in a credit of £4000, and the share premium account of Mammoth is increased by £56 000 (equals £60 000 paid minus £4000 increase in ordinary share capital). The net credit to the net worth account is £54 000, which balances the net debit to the asset accounts. When these adjustments are carried through to the *pro forma* consolidated balance sheet, total assets are increased from the uncombined total of £210 000 to a new total of £264 000. Total tangible assets, however, still remain £210 000.

The effects on earnings per share for shareholders in each company are shown below:

Total net earnings	£32 000
Total shares	110 000
Earnings per share	29.1 pence
For Petty shareholders	
New earnings per share[a]	14.55 pence
Pre-acquisition earnings per share	10.00 pence
Increase per share	4.55 pence
For Mammoth shareholders	
New earnings per share	29.1 pence
Pre-acquisition earnings per share	30.0 pence
Dilution per share	0.9 pence

[a] Petty shareholders, after the one-for-two exchange, have only one-half as many shares as they held before the amalgamation.

Total earnings represent the combined earnings of Mammoth and Petty. If the American treatment of amortization of goodwill had been adopted then an adjustment would be made to this figure. Under the American treatment, goodwill is written off over a maximum of 40 years. Thus an annual charge of £1350 would have been made (£54 000 divided by 40), reducing net earnings to £30 650.

There is, however, no obligation on the part of the directors of Mammoth Ltd to treat goodwill in this manner if it is their opinion that the value reflected in goodwill is permanent, and so no deduction has been made.

14. Where one company acquires the shares of another company, the shares should be recorded in the books of the acquiring company at cost, which will be the value of the consideration given. Where the consideration takes the form of an issue of shares, cost will be the 'fair value' of the shares issued, calculated by reference to the value of the underlying assets and liabilities at the date of acquisition.

The total shares are 110 000, because Mammoth has given one share for every two shares of Petty previously outstanding. The new earnings per share are therefore £0.291. The calculation of earnings accretion or dilution proceeds on the same principles as the calculations set forth earlier in the chapter. The results require two important comments, however.

It will be noted that although the earnings accretion per share for Petty is 4.55 pence, the earnings dilution per share for Mammoth is relatively small, only 0.9 pence a share. The explanation is that the size of Mammoth is large in relation to that of Petty. This example also illustrates a general principle – when a large company acquires a small one, it can afford to pay a high multiple of earnings per share of the smaller company. In the present example, the price/earnings ratio of Petty is 30, whereas that of Mammoth is 20. If the acquiring company is large in relation to the acquired firm, it can pay a substantial premium and yet suffer only small dilution in its earnings per share.

It is unrealistic, however, to assume that the same earnings on total assets will result after the merger. After all, the purpose of the merger is to achieve something that the two companies could not have achieved separately. When Tate and Lyle Ltd acquired Manbré and Garton Ltd, as explained earlier, it was acquiring the experience of Manbré and Garton in the lucrative starch and glucose markets. By means of this merger, Tate and Lyle Ltd was able to make an entry into these markets more rapidly than it could otherwise have done. As a result of this factor and of the expected rationalization of the sugar refining business, the post-acquisition earnings per share were expected to rise. In fact, several studies have shown that the expected gains from synergy, often quoted as a justification for a merger, frequently fail to materialize.

In the Mammoth–Petty illustration, the earnings rate on the tangible assets of Mammoth is 15 per cent and on the total assets of Petty is 20 per cent. Let us now assume that the return on total tangible assets of the combined companies rises to 20 per cent. The 20 per cent of tangible assets of £210 000 equals £42 000. With the same total shares of 110 000 outstanding, the new earnings per share will be 38.2 pence. Thus there will be an increase of 9.1 pence for the Petty shareholders and an increase of 8.2 pence for the Mammoth shareholders as well.

This illustrates another general principle – if the purchase of a small company adds to the earnings of the consolidated enterprise, earnings per share may increase for both participants in the merger. Even if the merger results in an initial dilution in earnings per share of the larger company, it may still be advantageous. The initial dilution in the earnings per share may be regarded as an investment that will have pay-off at some future date in terms of increased growth in earnings per share of the consolidated company.

Treatment of goodwill

Goodwill often arises on the acquisition of one company by another. Since, however, goodwill represents an intangible asset, its treatment is subject to the exercise of judgement. Currently, four methods are available for the treatment of goodwill in group accounts in the United Kingdom, as follows:

1. To retain the cost of goodwill as an asset indefinitely, unless some permanent loss in its value occurs. This particular treatment is possibly the least defensible in terms of good accounting practice.
2. To charge the cost of goodwill against group reserves in the first accounting period after acquisition. However, this treatment would seem to be an admission that there is no value attached to the goodwill.
3. To continue to include the cost of goodwill in the group balance sheet but only as a deduction against the total value of shareholders' equity. This treatment represents a variation of point 2 above.

4. To retain the cost of goodwill in the group balance sheet, but to amortize it over its estimated useful life, as with any other asset. This treatment tends to identify goodwill with the acquisition of future earnings potential by a company, and subsequently the expired portion of the cost is written off as the earnings are achieved. Where it is not possible to identify the useful life of the goodwill, then some arbitrary period must be used, such as the 40-year maximum period used in the US.

Financial treatment of pooling of interests

When a business combination is a *pooling of interests* rather than a purchase, the accounting treatment is simply to combine the balance sheets of the two companies. Goodwill will not ordinarily arise in the consolidation.

The financial treatment may be indicated by another example, which reflects the facts as they are set forth in Table 22–3. In order to focus on the critical issues, the balance sheets

Table 22–3 *Financial Treatment of Pooling of Interests.*

			Net adjustments to consolidated accounts		Consoldiated balance sheets and earnings if the exchange basis is	
	A	B	Debit	Credit	2/1	3/1
Fixed assets	£100 000	£100 000			£200 000	£200 000
Current assets	100 000	100 000			200 000	200 000
Total assets	£200 000	£200 000			£400 000	£400 000
Ordinary share capital	£ 60 000	£ 60 000	£30 000[a] 40 000[b]		£ 90 000	£ 80 000
Share premium account	50 000	50 000		£30 000[a] 40 000[b]	130 000	140 000
Reserves	10 000	10 000			20 000	20 000
Long-term debt	30 000	30 000			60 000	60 000
Current liabilities	50 000	50 000			100 000	100 000
Total claims on assets	£200 000	£200 000			£400 000	£400 000
			Ratios A/B			
Number of shares outstanding	120 000	120 000			180 000	160 000
Nominal value	£0.5	£0.5	1/1			
Book value	£1	£1	1/1			
Net earnings	£ 42 000	£ 21 000			£ 63 000	£ 63 000
Earnings per share	35 pence	17.5 pence	2/1		35 pence	39.4 pence
Price/earnings ratio	18	12				
Market value per share	£6.3	£2.1	3/1			
Dividends per share	17.5 pence	8.75 pence	2/1			
Net working capital per share	41.7 pence	41.7 pence	1/1			
Exchange ratio No. 1: earnings basis			2/1		Shareholders' new *EPS*	
					A	B
Equivalent earnings per share (new basis)					35 pence	17.5 pence
Exchange ratio No. 2: price basis			3/1			
Equivalent earnings per share (new basis)					39.4 pence	13.1 pence

[a] 2/1 ratio basis.
[b] 3/1 ratio basis.

are identical in every respect. However, a difference in the amount and rate of profit (after interest) of the two companies is indicated.

Book value per share is £1. The amount of profit after interest and taxes is £42 000 for company A and £21 000 for company B. Earnings per share are therefore 35 pence and 17.5, respectively. The price/earnings ratio is 18 for A and 12 for B, so the market price per share for A is £6.3 and for B £2.1. The net working capital per share is 41.7 pence in each instance. The dividends per share are 17.5 pence for A and 8.75 pence for B.

Now assume that the terms of the merger would reflect either (a) earnings or (b) market price per share. In both cases it is assumed that A is the acquiring and surviving firm. If A buys B on the basis of earnings, it exchanges 0.5 shares of A for 1 share of B. The total number of shares of A that will be outstanding after the acquisition is 180 000, of which 60 000 shares will be held by the old shareholders of B. The new earnings per share in the now larger A company will be the total earnings of £63 000 divided by 180 000, which equals 35 pence per share. Thus, the earnings per share for A remain unchanged. The old shareholders of B now hold 0.5 shares of A for each share of B held before the acquisition. Hence, their equivalent earnings per share from their present holdings of A shares are 17.5 pence, the same as before the acquisition. We see that the shareholders of neither A nor B have experienced earnings dilution or earnings accretion.

When the terms of exchange are based on market price per share, the terms of acquisition would be the exchange of $\frac{1}{3}$ share of A for 1 share of B. The number of A shares is increased by the 40 000 exchanged for the 120 000 shares of B. The combined earnings of £63 000 are divided by 160 000 shares to obtain an increase in A's earnings per share to 39.4 pence, which represents earnings accretion of 4.4 pence per share for the A shareholders. The old B shareholders now hold $\frac{1}{3}$ share of A for each 1 share of B held before the acquisition. Their equivalent earnings are now 39.4 pence divided by 3, or 13.1 pence, representing earnings dilution of 4.4 pence per share.

The adjustment to the ordinary share capital account in surviving company A's balance sheet reflects the fact that only 60 000 shares of A were used to buy 120 000 shares of B when the acquisition is made on the basis of earnings. The decrease of 60 000 shares times the nominal value of £0.5 requires a net debit of £30 000 to the ordinary share capital account of A (£60 000 + £60 000 − £30 000 = £90 000) with an offsetting increase of £30 000 in the share premium account of company A (£50 000 + £50 000 + £30 000 = £130 000). When the exchange is made on the basis of market values, only 40 000 shares of A are needed to acquire the 120 000 shares of B. Hence, the net decrease in the ordinary share capital account of A is £40 000, with an offsetting increase in the same amount in A's share premium.

The general principle is that when terms of merger are based on the market price per share and the price/earnings ratios of the two companies are different, earnings accretion and dilution will occur. The company with a higher price/earnings ratio will attain earnings accretion; the company with the lower price/earnings ratio will suffer earnings dilution. If the sizes of the companies are greatly different, the effect on the larger company wiil be relatively small, whether in earnings dilution or in earnings accretion. The effect on the smaller company will be large.

HOLDING COMPANIES

Around the year 1915, there emerged in the UK a growing number of companies formed for the sole purpose of owning the shares of other companies. One of the earliest of these companies, operating purely as the holding company of a number of subsidiaries, was United Dairies Ltd, formed in 1915. Government legislation in this area was confined mainly to the publication and form of accounts of such companies, although their activities were commented upon in the report of the Committee on Trusts, in 1919.

Many of the advantages and disadvantages of holding companies are no more than the advantages and disadvantages of large-scale operations already discussed in connection with mergers and consolidations. Whether a company is organized on a divisional basis or with the divisions kept as separate companies does not affect the basic reasons for conducting a large-scale, multiproduct, multiplant operation. However, the holding company form of large-scale operations has different advantages and disadvantages from those of completely integrated divisionalized operations.

Advantages of holding companies

Control with fractional ownership

Through a holding company operation, a firm may buy 5, 10 or 50 per cent of the shares of another company. Such fractional ownership may be sufficient to give the acquiring company effective working control or substantial influence over the operations of the company in which it has acquired share ownership. Sometimes holding company operations represent the initial stages of the transformation of an operating company into an investment company, particularly when the operating company is in a declining industry. When the sales of an industry begin to decline permanently and the firm begins to liquidate its operating assets, it may use these liquid funds to invest in industries having a more favourable growth potential.

One of the most spectacular illustrations of this is provided by the history of Slater Walker Securities Ltd. The company first came into existence in 1964 when Jim Slater and Peter Walker purchased H. Lotery Ltd, a clothing manufacturer with a declining level of profitability. The company name was changed and Slater-Walker began the first phase of its career as an industrial conglomerate, acquiring around 500 subsidiaries at its height. In the late 1960s this conglomerate was in turn dismantled and the company was converted into a banking and investment company.

Isolation of risks

Because the various operating companies in a holding company system are separate legal entities, the obligations of any one unit are separate from those of the other units. Catastrophic losses incurred by one unit of the holding company system are therefore not transmitted as claims on the assets of the other units.

Although this is the customary generalization of the nature of a holding company system, it is not completely valid. In extending credit to one of the units of a holding company system, an astute financial manager may require a guarantee or a claim on the assets of all the elements in a complete holding company system. To some degree, therefore, the assets in the various elements of a holding company are joined. The advantage remains to the extent that unanticipated catastrophes that may occur to one unit in a holding company system will not be transmitted to the other units.

Disadvantages of holding companies

Limited taxation relief

Where companies are members of the same group, dividends may be paid by a subsidiary to its parent company without deduction of ACT. Similarly, unrelieved ACT during an accounting period may be surrendered by a parent company to a subsidiary although it may not be carried back to earlier periods by the subsidiary. Where one member of a group incurs a trading loss during an accounting period, this may be offset against the profits of another member of the group during the same accounting period but cannot be offset against profits of previous periods, as is the case with single companies. In this last case a 'subsidiary' company is defined as one in which at least 75 per cent of the ordinary share capital is held by the parent company.

Ease of enforced dissolution

In the case of a holding company operation that becomes subject to an unfavourable report by the Monopolies Commission, it is in theory easier to order the dissolution of the group relationship. The Monopolies Commission has indeed considered the possibility of enforced structural change, for example in the case of Courtaulds Ltd's cellulosic fibre interests, but in this case as with others it was felt to be impractical to order the enforced dissolution of the company's interests.

Risks of excessive pyramiding

While pyramiding magnifies profits if operations are successful, as was seen in the financial gearing analysis, it also magnifies losses. The greater the degree of pyramiding, the greater the degree of risk involved for any fluctuations in sales or earnings of the company. This potential disadvantage of pyramiding operations through holding companies is discussed in the next section.

Gearing in holding companies

The problem of excessive gearing is worthy of further note, for the degree of gearing in certain past instances has been truly staggering. For example, in the US in the 1920s, Samuel Insull and his group controlled electric utility operating companies at the bottom of a holding company pyramid by a one-twentieth of 1 per cent investment. As a ratio, this represents 1/2000. In other words, \$1 of capital at the top holding company level controlled \$2000 of assets at the operating level. A similar situation existed in the railroad field. It has been stated that Robert R. Young, with an investment of \$254 000, obtained control of the Allegheny system, consisting of total operating assets of \$3 billion.

The nature of gearing in a holding company system and its advantages and disadvantages are illustrated by the hypothetical example developed in Table 22–4. Although, as in the previous example, this is a hypothetical case, it illustrates actual situations. Fifty-one per cent of the operating company's ordinary share capital is owned by holding company 1; in fact it is the only asset of holding company 1. Holding company 2 holds as its total assets slightly more than 51 per cent of the ordinary share capital of holding company 1. Consequently, £5000 of the ordinary share capital of holding company 2 controls £2 million of assets at the operating company level. Further gearing could have been postulated in this situation by setting up a fourth company to own ordinary share capital of holding company 2.

Table 22–5 shows the results of holding company gearing on returns to the shareholders of the ultimate holding company. In the first column, it is assumed that the operating company earns 15 per cent before tax on its £2 million of assets; in the second column it is assumed that the return on assets is 5 per cent. The operating and holding companies are those described in Table 22–4.

A return of 15 per cent on the operating assets of £2 million represents a total profit of £300 000, from which is deducted interest charges of £80 000 and a management fee of

Table 22-4 *Gearing in a Holding Company System.*

Operating company	£ 000		£ 000
Ordinary share capital	200	Total assets	2000
Retained earnings	800		
8% debentures	1000		
	£2000		£2000
Holding company 1	£ 000		£ 000
Ordinary share capital	30	Investment in operating company	102
Retained earnings	22		
8% debentures	50		
	£ 102		£ 102
Holding company 2	£ 000		£ 000
Ordinary share capital	5	Investment in holding company 1	16
Retained earnings	3		
8% debentures	8		
	£16		£16

£6000 charged by holding company 1. Corporation tax of 50 per cent is then applied to the remainder, leaving £107 000 available to ordinary shareholders. Assuming a £100 000 divided payout, holding company 1 receives £51 000 on the basis of its 51 per cent shareholding. Following the analysis through, the shareholders of holding company 2 receive earnings of £26 847, equivalent to a return of about 336 per cent on the book value of the share capital plus reserves.

On the other hand, if earnings in the operating company drop to 5 per cent of their total assets, the return to the shareholders of holding company 2 falls to around 22 per cent. Although this return sounds acceptable it must be remembered that it has been calculated on the book value of the owner's capital; the effect of such a fall in earnings would probably be a catastrophic fall in the market value of the shares of holding company 2.

REGULATION OF MERGERS

The City Code on Takeovers and Mergers[15]

Successive governments in the UK have refrained from introducing legislation to deal with the conduct of mergers and takeovers. Instead, regulation has been left largely in the hands of the City Working Party, a committee consisting of representatives of the major financial bodies operating in the City of London. The City Code on Mergers and Takeovers, first issued by this body in 1968 and subsequently revised, sets out both general principles and specific rules of conduct to be observed in merger and takeover transactions.

The general principles of the code are concerned with ensuring that all shareholders of an offeree company are treated in an equitable manner.

15. Copies of the City Code are obtainable from the Secretary to the Issuing Houses Association.

Table 22–5 *Results of Holding Company Gearing on Profits.*

	Earnings before tax	
Operating company	15%	5%
Earnings before tax	£300 000	£100 000
Management charge[a]	6 000	6 000
	£294 000	94 000
Debenture interest	80 000	80 000
	£214 000	14 000
Corporation tax[b]	107 000	7 000
Available to ordinary shareholders	107 000	7 000
Dividends paid	100 000	5 000
Holding company 1		
Management fees from operating company	£6 000	£6 000
Debenture interest	4 000	4 000
	2 000	2 000
Management charge	1 000	1 000
	1 000	1 000
Corporation tax	500	500
	500	500
Dividends received	51 000	2 550
Available to ordinary shareholders	51 500	3 050
Dividends paid	50 000	3 000
Holding company 2		
Management fees from holding company 1	£1 000	£1 000
Debenture interest	640	640
	360	360
Corporation tax	180	180
	180	180
Dividends received	26 667	1600
Available to ordinary shareholders	£26 847	£1 780
Percentage return on share capital plus reserves	335.6%	22.25%

[a] All management fees are assumed to be allowable tax deductions in this illustration. For regulations relating to group relief refer to sections 258 to 264 of the Income and Corporation Taxes Act, 1970.
[b] Corporation tax rate is assumed at 50 per cent.

The rules deal with such matters as the identity of the ultimate principal in an offer (Rule 2); any agreement which exists between the offeror and directors or shareholders, past or present, of the offeree company (Rule 13); intentions of the offeror with regard to continuation of business of the offeree company (Rule 15); and the ability of the offeror to meet the financial commitments of the offer (Rule 18).

Additional rules deal with situations where an individual, or group of individuals, obtains a substantial interest in a company, possibly with the intention of obtaining control through stealth (Rules 33 and 34), and also with the conduct of directors in implementing defensive tactics against a merger (Rule 38).

Although the City Code does not have the force of law behind it, its powers are considerable, with available penalties ranging from private reprimand to suspension of an offender from using the facilities of the securities markets, and, in certain cases, referral to the Department of Trade.

The Monopolies (and Mergers) Commission

In 1948, the Monopolies Commission was set up with the power to investigate and report monopoly situations referred to it by the then Board of Trade. A monopoly was stated to exist when one company produced at least one-third of the supply of particular goods. The 1965 Monopolies and Mergers Act widened the powers of the Monopolies Commission so that the Board of Trade were now able to refer to it prospective or actual mergers, provided either that the resulting company would have a monopoly or that the assets acquired were worth £5 million or more. Not only could a merger be held up until the Monopolies Commission had reported, but if it were found that a monopoly was against the public interest then various remedies could be implemented, including the forced division of an existing company.

The influence of the Monopolies Commission extends beyond the limited number of investigations in which it has been involved. It is argued that many potential merger situations have not gone ahead because they exhibited characteristics similar to one or other of the referred mergers. In addition, many merger proposals now contain a clause stating that if the proposal should be referred to the Monopolies Commission then the proposal would lapse.

The National Enterprise Board

That the National Enterprise Board should appear in a section devoted to the regulation of mergers reflects one of the contradictions of government in the UK. Frequent contradictions have appeared in the government attitude to mergers. Shortly after the 1965 Act was passed, the now defunct Industrial Reorganization Corporation was set up by government with the brief of sponsoring the rationalization of British industry. The role of the IRC now appears to have been taken over by the NEB. The National Enterprise Board was set up in November 1975 as a statutory public corporation with the following purposes:

1. To develop or assist the economy of the UK.
2. To promote industrial efficiency and international competitiveness.
3. To provide, maintain or safeguard productive employment.

In the pursuit of these purposes the NEB has become a holding company for a number of important industrial companies, including British Leyland, Alfred Herbet and Rolls-Royce. Minority interests are also held in several other companies, including ICL Ltd.

When the NEB invests in a company with the aim of ultimate acquisition it is required to act in accordance with the City Code on Takeovers and Mergers. Additionally, the NEB must consult the Director of Fair Trading before entering into arrangements for a merger which might qualify for investigation by the Monopolies Commission.

SUMMARY

Growth is vital to the well-being of a firm, for without it a business cannot attract able management because it cannot give recognition in promotions and challenging creative activity. Mergers have played an important part in the growth of firms, and since financial managers are required both to appraise the desirability of a prospective merger and to participate in evaluating the respective companies involved in the merger, the present chapter has been devoted to background materials on merger decisions.

Terms of mergers

The most important term that must be negotiated in a merger arrangement is the price the acquiring firm will pay for the acquired business. The most important *quantitative* factors influencing the terms of a merger are (a) current earnings, (b) current market prices, (c) book values, and (d) net working capital. *Qualitative* considerations may suggest that *synergistic*, or 'two-plus-two-equals-five', effects may be present to a sufficient extent to warrant paying more for the acquired firm than the quantitative factors would suggest.

Accounting policies and mergers

A merger may be treated as either an *acquisition* or a *pooling of interests*. In an *acquisition*, a larger firm generally takes over a smaller one and assumes all management control. The amount actually paid for the smaller firm is reflected in the acquiring firm's balance sheet; if more was paid for the acquired firm than the book value of its assets, goodwill is reflected in the consolidated financial statements. In a *pooling of interests*, the merged firms should be about the same size, both managements should carry on important functions after the merger, and ordinary shares rather than cash or debentures should be used in payment. The total assets of the surviving firm in a pooling are equal to the sum of the assets of the two independent companies, so no goodwill is required to be written off as a charge against earnings.

Holding companies

In mergers, one firm disappears. However, an alternative is for one firm to buy all or a majority of the ordinary share capital of another and to run the acquired firm as an operating subsidiary. When this occurs, the acquiring firm is said to be a *holding company*. A number of advantages arise when a holding company is formed.

1. It may be possible to control the acquired firm with a smaller investment than would be necessary in a merger.
2. Each firm in a holding company is a separate legal entity, and the obligations of any one unit are separate from the obligations of the other units.

There are also disadvantages to holding companies, some of which are listed below.

1. If the holding company does not own more than 75 per cent of the subsidiary's ordinary share capital, then it is unable to offset the trading losses of one subsidiary against the profits of another subsidiary for the same accounting period.
2. The gearing effects possible in holding companies can subject their shareholders to magnification of earnings fluctuations and related risks.
3. The Monopolies Commission can, in theory, much more readily recommend the break-up of a holding company situation than it can the dissolution of two completely merged firms.

Regulation of mergers

The City Code on Mergers and Takeovers is a code of practice drawn up, without the force of law, to regulate the conduct of merger negotiations. It is concerned with ensuring the equitable treatment of all the shareholders of an offeree company.

The Monopolies and Mergers Commission is a body set up by the government to investigate existing or potential merger situations which may be against the public interest.

The National Enterprise Board has been concerned with the implementation of several wide-ranging mergers on the authority of the government, particularly among smaller companies, as, for example, in the computer software industry. In this respect it has also become the holding company for a number of important subsidiaries, including British Leyland.

QUESTIONS

22–1. The number of mergers tends to fluctuate with business activity, rising when GNP rises and falling when GNP falls. Why does this relationship exist?

22–2. A large firm has certain advantages over a smaller one. What are some of the *financial* advantages of large size?

22–3. What are some of the potential benefits that can be expected by a firm that merges with a company in a different industry?

22–4. Distinguish between a holding company and an operating company. Give an example of each.

22–5. Which appears to be more risky, the use of debt in the holding company's capital structure or the use of debt in the operating company's? Why?

22–6. Is the public interest served by an increase in merger activity? Give arguments both pro and con.

22–7. Would the book value of a company's assets be considered the absolute minimum price to be paid for a firm? Why? Is there any value that would qualify as an absolute minimum?

22–8. Discuss the situation where one firm, Nationwide Motors, for example, calls off merger negotiations with another, Regional Data Labs, because the latter's share price is overvalued. What assumption concerning dilution is implicit in the above situation?

22–9. There are many methods by which a company can raise additional capital. Can a merger be considered a means of raising additional equity capital? Explain.

22–10. A particularly difficult problem regarding business combinations has been whether to treat the new company as an *acquisition* or as a *pooling of interests*.
(a) What criteria can be set down to differentiate between these two forms of business combinations?
(b) Would you as a shareholder in one of the firms prefer an acquisition or a pooling arrangement? Why?
(c) Which combination would you prefer if you were a high-ranking manager in one of the firms?

22–11. Question 22–10 discusses normal acquisition and pooling arrangements. Why is it important to make a distinction between these two combination forms?

22–12. Are the negotiations for merger agreements more difficult if the firms are in different industries or in the same industry? If they are about the same size or quite different in size? If the ages of the firms are about the same or if they are very different? Why?

22–13. How would the existence of long-term debt in a company's financial structure affect its valuation for merger purposes? Could the same be said for any debt account regardless of its maturity?

22–14. Discuss the relative advantages to a company of paying for an acquisition in cash or with shares.

22–15. Criticism has been levelled against the ability of the City institutions to regulate the conduct of merger and takeover situations through a voluntary code. Discuss the pros and cons of introducing statutory legislation to replace the City Code on Mergers and Takeovers.

PROBLEMS

22–1. You are given the following balance sheets.

Bala Services Company, Consolidated Balance Sheet.

Ordinary share capital	£1875	Land and buildings	£1875
Reserves	1500	Other assets	1125
Long-term loans	1125	Cash	1500
	£4500		£4500

White Lighting Company, Balance Sheet.

Share capital and reserves	£750	Land and buildings	£375
		Cash	375
	£750		£750

(a) The holding Company, Bala Services, buys the operating company, White Lighting, with available cash for £750. Show the new consolidated balance sheet for the group after the acquisition.
(b) Instead of buying White, Bala Services buys Conner Company with available cash of £1125. The balance sheet of Conner is as follows:

Conner Company, Balance Sheet.

Shareholders' funds	£1125	Land and buildings	£1125
Long-term loans	750	Cash	750
	£1875		£1875

Show the new consolidated balance sheet for the group after acquisition of Conner.
(c) What are the implications of your consolidated balance sheets for measuring the growth of firms resulting from acquisitions?

22–2. Octopus Ltd is a holding company owning the entire share capital of Bryant Ltd and Suther Ltd. The balance sheet of each subsidiary at 31 December 1977 is identical to the following one.

Balance Sheet, 31 December 1977.

Ordinary share capital	£5 000 000	Fixed assets (net)	£5 000 000
Reserves	1 250 000	Current assets	7 500 000
Preference shares (7%)	2 500 000		
Debentures (9%)	2 500 000		
Current liabilities	1 250 000		
Total claims on assets	£12 500 000		£12 500 000

Each operating company earns £1 375 000 annually before interest, taxes and the preference dividend. Assume a 50 per cent corporation tax rate.
(a) What is the annual rate of return on each company's net worth (ordinary share capital plus reserves)?
(b) Construct a consolidated balance sheet based on the following assumptions:
(i) The only asset of the holding company is the ordinary share capital of the subsidiaries (at nominal values).
(ii) The holding company has £1.2 million of 8% debentures and £2.8 million of 6% preference capital.
(c) What is the rate of return on the holding company's ordinary share capital, at nominal values?
(d) If ownership of 25 per cent of the holding company's ordinary shares gave effective control, what percentage would this be of the total operating assets?

22–3. You are given the following data on two companies:

	Company I	Company II	Adjustments	Consolidated balance sheet
Fixed assets	£34 000	£34 000		______
Current assets	56 000	56 000		______
Total assets	£90 000	£90 000		______
Ordinary share capital	£24 000	£24 000	______	______
Share premium	–	–	______	______
Reserves	16 000	16 000	______	______
Long-term loan (8%)	20 000	20 000	______	______
Current liabilities	30 000	30 000	______	______
Total claims on assets	£90 000	£90 000	______	______

			Ratios	
1. Number of ordinary shares	£24 000	£24 000		1.______
2. Book value per share	______	______	1.______	2.______
3. Profit before interest and tax[a]	£29 600	£13 600		3.______
4. Earnings per share	______	______	2.______	4.______
5. Price/earnings ratio	15	10		
6. Market price of shares	______	______	3.______	
7. Working capital per share	______	______	4.______	
8. Dividends per share (50% payout)	______	______	5.______	
9. Exchange ratio	______	______	6.______ (I/II)	
10. Equivalent earnings per old share	______	______		

[a] Assume a 50 per cent tax rate.

(a) In your judgement, what would be a reasonable basis for determining the terms at which shares in company I and in company II would be exchanged for shares in a new company III? What exchange ratio would you recommend and why?
(b) Use the relationship between the market prices of the two old companies for exchange of shares and, assuming each old share in I was exchanged for two share of II, fill in the blank spaces in the consolidated balance sheet, treating the problem as a pooling of interests situation.

22–4. The Vertical Company has just purchased the Horizontal Company through an exchange of shares based exactly on the indicated market prices of the two companies. Data on the two companies are given below. Assume that the purchase is treated as an acquisition.
(a) Fill in the blank spaces and complete the adjustments and pro forma balance sheet columns. Give an explanation for your adjustments.
(b) Calculate earnings dilution or accretion for both companies (i) on the assumption that total earnings are unchanged and (ii) on the assumption that the return on combined tangible assets rises to 20 per cent after interest and taxes.
(c) Comment upon your findings.

	Vertical	Horizontal	Adjustments Debit	Adjustments Credit	Pro forma balance sheet
Fixed assets	£400 000	£ 8 000			______
Other assets	150 000	5 000			______
Goodwill	–	–			______
Current assets	450 000	7 000			______
	£1 000 000	£20 000			______

	Vertical	Horizontal	Adjustments Debit	Adjustments Credit	Pro forma balance sheet
Ordinary share capital	£200 000	£2 000			________
Retained earnings	450 000	10 000			________
Capital surplus	–	–			________
Long-term loan	150 000	–			________
Current liabilities	200 000	8 000			________
	£1 000 000	£20 000			________
Nominal value per share	£1	£0.50			
Number of shares	________	________			
Total earnings available to ordinary shareholders	£125 000	£ 8 000			
Book value per share	________	________			
Earnings per share	________	________			
Price/earnings ratio	10 ×	25 ×			
Market value per share	________	________			

SELECTED REFERENCES

Aaronovitch, Sam and Sawyer, Malcolm C. *Big Business*. London: Macmillan Press, 1975.

Accounting Standards Committee, *Accounting for Acquisitions and Mergers*, Exposure Draft No. 3, London, 1971.

Accounting Standards Committee, *Accounting for the Results of Associated Companies*, Statement of Standard Accounting Practice, No. 1. London, 1971.

Allen, G. C. *Monopoly and Restrictive Practices*. London: Allen & Unwin, 1968.

Archer, S. Purchased goodwill – let's think again. *Accountancy* (January 1976): 42–43.

Barnes, P. A. The purely financial case for takeovers. *Management Accounting* (December 1976): 434.

Buckley, Adrian. Some guidelines for acquisitions. *Accounting and Business Research* 1 (Summer 1971): 215–232.

Buckley Adrian. A review of acquisition valuation models – a comment. *Journal of Business Finance and Accounting* 2 (Spring 1975): 147–152.

Cameron, D. Appraising companies for acquisition. *Long Range Planning* 10 (August 1977): 21–28.

Cohen, Manuel F. Takeover bids. *Financial Analysts' Journal* 26 (January–February 1970): 26–31.

Committee to Review the Functioning of Financial Institutions: *Evidence on the Financing of Industry and Trade*. London: HMSO, 1978, vol. 4.

Cunitz, Jonathan A. Valuing potential acquisitions. *Financial Executive* 39 (April 1971): 16–28.

Firth, Michael. *Share Prices and Mergers*. London: Saxon House, 1976.

Gerault, P. H. and Jackson, J. M. *The Control of Monopoly in the United Kingdom*. London: Longman, 1974.

Hannah, Leslie and Kay, J. A. *Concentration in Modern Industry*. London: Macmillan, 1977.

Haughen, Robert A. and Langetieg, Terence C. An empirical test for synergism in mergers. *Journal of Finance* 30 (June 1975): 1003–1014.

Heath, John, Jr. Valuation factors and techniques in mergers and acquisitions. *Financial Executive* 40 (April 1972): 34–44.

Hogarth, Thomas F. The profitability of corporate mergers. *Journal of Business* 44 (July 1970): 317–327.

Issuing Houses Association. *The City Code on Takeovers and Mergers*. London. Revised 1976.

Jewkes, John. *Delusions of Dominance*. London: The Institute of Economic Affairs, 1977.

Kelly, Eamon M. *The Profitability of Growth Through Mergers*. Pa.: Pennsylvania State University, 1967.

Kitchen, J. The accounts of British holding company groups: development and attitudes to disclosure in the early years. *Accounting and Business Research* 2 (Spring 1972): 114–136.

Kitching, John. Winning and losing with European acquisitions. *Harvard Business Review* 52 (March–April 1974): 124–136.

Kitching, John. Why acquisitions are abortive. *Management Today* (November 1974): 82–87.

Kuehn, Douglas. *Takeovers and the Theory of the Firm*. London: Macmillan Press, 1975.

Larson, Kermit D. and Gonedes, Nicholas J. Business combinations: an exchange-ratio determination model. *Accounting Review* 44 (October 1969): 720–728.

Lev, Baruch and Mandelker, Gershon. The microeconomic consequences of corporate mergers. *Journal of Business* 45 (January 1972): 85–104.

Lowellen, Wilbur G. A pure financial rationale for the conglomerate merger. *Journal of Finance* 26 (May 1971): 521–537.

Lorie, J. H. and Halpern, P. Conglomerates: the rhetoric and the evidence. *Journal of Law and Economics* 13 (April 1970): 149–166.

Mason, R. Hal and Goudzwaard, Maurice B. Performance of conglomerate firms: a portfolio approach. *Journal of Finance* 31 (March 1976): 39–48.

McLean, A. T. Accounting for business combinations and purchased intangibles. *Accountants Magazine* (November 1976): 427–428.

Melicher, Ronald W. and Rush, David F. Evidence on the acquisition-related performance of conglomerate firms. *Journal of Finance* 29 (March 1974): 141–149.

Mueller, Dennis C. A theory of conglomerate mergers. *Quarterly Journal of Economics* 83 (November 1969): 643–659.

Newbould, G. D. Stray, S. J. and Wilson, K. W. Shareholders' interests and acquisition activity. *Accounting and Business Research* (Summer 1976): 201–215.

Pendrill, D. Accounting for mergers. Why ED3 should be withdrawn. *Accountancy* (December 1975): 40–44.

Reilly, Frank K. What determines the ratio of exchange in corporate mergers? *Financial Analysts' Journal* 18 (November–December 1962): 47–50.

Rhys, D. G. Anatomy of a merger. *Accounting and Business Research* 2 (Winter 1972): 46–52.

Shad, John S. R. The financial realities of mergers. *Harvard Business Review* 47 (November – December 1969): 133–146.

Shick, Richard A. The analysis of mergers and acquisitions. *Journal of Finance* 27 (May 1972): 495–502.

Silberman, Irwin H. A note on merger valuation. *Journal of Finance* 23 (June 1968): 528–534.

Smalter, Donald J. and Lancey, Roderic C. P/E analysis in acquisition strategy. *Harvard Business Review* 44 (November–December 1966): 85–95.

Smith, Keith V. and Weston, J. Fred. Further evaluation of conglomerate performance. *Journal of Business Research* 5 (1977): 5–14.

Stacey, Nicholas. Cutting out the cant about mergers. *Accountancy* (June 1974): 46–50.

Stamp, Edward and Marley, Christopher. *Accounting Principles and the City Code: The Case for Reform.* London: Butterworths, 1970.

Stapleton, R. C. The acquisition decision as a capital budgeting problem. *Journal of Business Finance and Accounting* 2 (Summer 1975): 187–202.

Steward, I. C. Mergers and the institutional environment in the U.K. 1960–1970. *Accounting and Business Research* 6 (Winter 1976): 57–63.

Stotland, J. A. Planning acquisitions and mergers. *Long Range Planning* 9 (February 1976): 66–71.

Sutherland, Alistair. *The Monopolies Commission in Action.* Cambridge: Cambridge University Press, 1969.

Vancil, Richard F. and Lorange, Peter. Strategic planning in diversified companies. *Harvard Business Review* 53 (January–February 1975): 81–90.

Walsh, G. *Recent Trends in Monopoly in Great Britain.* Cambridge: Cambridge University Press, 1974.

Weston, J. Fred. *The Role of Mergers in the Growth of Large Firms.* Berkeley: University of California Press, 1953.

Weston, J. Fred, Smith, Keith V. and Shrieves, Ronald E. Conglomerate performance using the capital asset pricing model. *Review of Economics and Statistics* (November 1972): 357–363.

Weston, J. Fred and Mansinghka, Surendra K. Tests of the efficiency of conglomerate firms. *Journal of Finance* 26 (September 1971): 919–936.

Woods, Donald H. and Caverly, Thomas A. Development of a linear programming model for the analysis of merger/acquisition situations. *Journal of Financial and Quantitative Analysis* 4 (January 1970): 627–642.

Chapter 23

Failure, Reorganization and Liquidation

Thus far the text has dealt with issues associated mainly with the growing, successful enterprise. Not all business are so fortunate, however, so we must examine financial difficulties, their causes, and their possible remedies. This material is significant for the financial manager of successful, as well as potentially unsuccessful, firms. The successful firm's financial manager must know his firm's rights and remedies as a creditor and must participate effectively in efforts to collect from financially distressed debtors. Conversely, the financial manager of a less successful firm must know how to handle his own firm's affairs if financial difficulties arise. Such understanding may often mean the difference between loss of ownership of the firm and rehabilitation of the operation as a going enterprise.

Some dramatic business failures have occurred in recent years. Probably the most notable failure, although not the largest, was that of Rolls-Royce Ltd in February, 1971; a company which until that date had been the symbol of all that was best in British industry. Many famous business names which would otherwise have disappeared over the last decade are still in existence largely because of government intervention. Companies such as British Leyland, Ferranti and Alfred Herbert Ltd, as well as Rolls-Royce, now have the National Enterprise Board as their major or sole shareholder. Yet another major UK company, Burmah Oil, was saved from insolvency in 1975 after the Bank of England took the unprecedented step of guaranteeing the company's overseas borrowing of around £350 million. At the time, Burmah Oil was the 25th largest UK company, with total assets of around £1000 million and borrowing of almost £600 million.

In the early 1970s instabilities also involved the financial sector of the economy with the virtual collapse of the 'fringe banking sector'. The collapse of the property market sector in 1973 led to a run on many banks, leaving them insolvent. A special 'lifeboat' scheme, organized by the Bank of England and financed mainly by the clearing banks to the tune of £1200 million, saved many more companies from collapsing than would otherwise have happened. A few business failures have raised questions of improprieties in the management of the company involved. A recent illustration is that of Gray's Building Society, which appeared to be involved in the recording of non-existent investments.

THE FIRM'S LIFE CYCLE

The life cycle of an industry or firm is often depicted as an S-shaped curve, as shown in Figure 23–1. The figure represents a hypothetical life cycle of a firm, and although it is an over-simplification, it does provide a useful framework for analysis. The hypothesis represented by the four-stage life-cycle concept is based on a number of assumptions – competent management in the growth periods and insufficient management foresight prior to the decline phase. Obviously, one of management's primary goals is to prolong phase B and completely to forestall phase D; many firms are apparently successful in these endeavours. If an industry experiences the period of decline, financial readjustment problems will arise, affecting most firms in the industry. Furthermore, specific events may result in business failure – for example, a prolonged strike, a fire not adequately covered by insurance, or a bad decision on a new product.

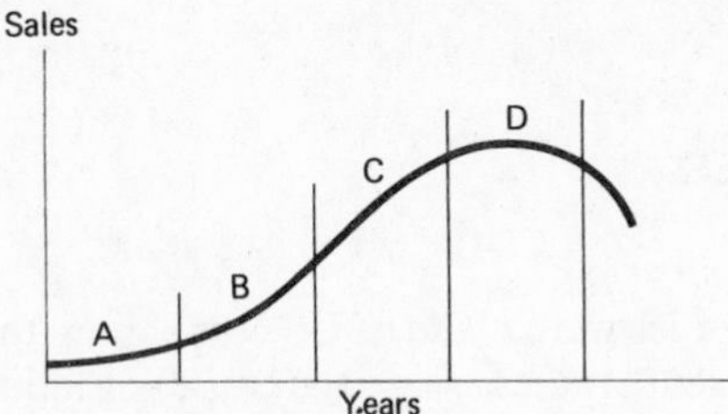

Figure 23–1 *Hypothetical Life Cycle of a Firm.*

FAILURE

Although failure can be defined in several ways according to various applications of the term, it does not necessarily result in the collapse and dissolution of a firm.

Economic failure

Failure in an economic sense usually signifies that a firm's revenues do not cover costs. Another definition of economic failure states that a firm has failed if the rate of earnings on the historical cost of investment is less than the firm's cost of capital. According to still another definition, a firm can be considered a failure if its actual returns have fallen below expected returns. There is no consensus on the definition of failure in an economic sense.[1]

Financial failure

Although financial failure is a less ambiguous term than the concept of economic failure, even here, two aspects are generally recognized:

---

1. In still another economic sense, a firm that goes into liquidation may not be a failure at all. To illustrate, suppose someone starts a business to *attempt* to develop a product that, if successful, will produce very large returns and, if unsuccessful, will result in a total loss of invested funds. The entrepreneur *knows* that he is taking a risk but thinks the potential gains are worth the chance of loss. If a loss in fact results, then the outcome simply occurred in the left tail of the distribution of returns.

Technical insolvency

A firm can be considered a failure if it is insolvent in the sense that it cannot meet its current obligations as they fall due, even though its total assets may exceed its total liabilities. This is defined as *technical insolvency*. Technical insolvency, while proving embarrassing to a company, is not in itself grounds for the winding-up of a company.

Legal insolvency

A company, unlike an individual, cannot be made bankrupt, but it can be put into liquidation – 'wound-up' – if the company is unable to pay its debts, taking into account both current and contingent liabilities, or if total liabilities exceed total assets.

It is an offence for the directors of a company to continue trading knowing that the company is insolvent.

When we use the word 'failure' hereafter we include both technical and legal insolvency.

CAUSES OF FAILURES

Although the following studies were made of US companies, the findings are also relevant to the UK situation. Different studies assign the causes of failure to different factors. The Dun & Bradstreet compilations assign these causes as follows:[2]

Cause of failure	Percentage of total
Neglect	2.0
Fraud	1.5
Disaster	0.9
Management incompetence	93.1
Unknown	2.5

A number of other studies of failures may be generalized into the following groups:[3]

Cause of failure	Percentage of total
Unfavourable industry trends (secular)	20
Management incompetence	60
Catastrophies	10
Miscellaneous	10

Both classifications include the effects of recessions and place the resulting failures in the category of managerial incompetence. This method is logical – managements should be prepared to operate in environments in which recessions occur and should frame their policies to cope with downturns as well as to benefit from business upswings. Also, managements must anticipate unfavourable industry trends.

Several financial remedies are available to management when it becomes aware of the imminence or occurrence of insolvency. These remedies are described in the remainder of this chapter.

---

2. *The Failure Record*, 1972 (New York: Dun & Bradstreet, Inc., 1973).
3. See studies referred to in A. S. Dewing, *The Financial Policy of Corporations* (New York: Ronald, 1953), vol. 2, chap. 28.

THE FAILURE RECORD

How widespread is business failure? Is it a rare phenomenon, or do failures occur fairly often? Table 23–1 shows that there has been a general upward movement in the number of company liquidations since 1967. This may be related partly to the general growth in the economy over the period and also to an increase in the use of corporate status by business firms. It is also interesting to note that there are twice as many companies in the course of liquidation during most of the years than are actually written off. It appears from this that the liquidation process takes about two years, largely due to companies' making use of section 353 of the Companies Act to obtain dissolution.

Table 23–1 *Record of Company Liquidations, 1967–76.*

Year	Companies on register	Dissolved or struck-off during year	In liquidation or course of removal at 31 December
1967	569 820	17 751	44 577
1968	553 282	37 244	57 924
1969	552 799	25 751	37 973
1970	559 497	23 750	40 840
1971	577 228	21 879	49 588
1972	603 935	27 898	61 357
1973	637 648	33 835	38 143
1974	657 859	22 574	59 480
1975	669 930	33 979	77 687
1976	690 897	35 539	69 214

Source: Department of Trade, *Companies in 1976*. London: HMSO, 1977.

Table 23–1 cannot itself be taken as a record of company failures in the UK since there are many other reasons for a company being dissolved, such as reversion to partnership status or merely completion of the specific task for which the company was formed.

A better indication of the number of companies failing in any one year is given by Table 23–2. Data in this table are compiled from the two categories of liquidation that could have resulted from a company's insolvency, namely compulsory liquidations and creditors' voluntary liquidations. It is interesting to note that the failure rate rose significantly in 1975–6 at a time when interest rates and the rate of inflation in the economy were at very

Table 23–2 *Rate of Company Liquidations in the United Kingdom.*

Year	Compulsory liquidations	Creditors' voluntary liquidations	Total	Average failure rate[a]
1967	1280	2435	3715	65
1968	1143	2157	3300	60
1969	1208	2474	3682	67
1970	1337	2549	3886	69
1971	1206	2455	3661	63
1972	1189	2042	3231	53
1973	1105	1568	2673	42
1974	1437	2438	3875	59
1975	2340	3262	5602	84
1976	2595	3573	6168	89

Source: *Trade and Industry* (4 August, 1978), p. 293. *Economic Trends* (March 1975), p. 116.
[a] Per 10 000 companies.

high levels. Provisional figures for 1977 indicate a slight fall in the number of failures, caused partly by the 1976 Insolvency Act which increased the minimum debt level required to support a creditor's petition.

Large firms are not immune to liquidation, but in recent years there has been a tendency for government intervention to be arranged to prevent the complete dissolution of manufacturing firms and consequent loss of jobs and productive capacity. One of the agencies for government intervention has been the National Enterprise Board which is described below. Apart from government intervention, other firms may absorb ailing firms, often at bargain prices, except in cases of fraud or excessive size on the part of the failing company.

The National Enterprise Board (NEB)

The NEB was set up in November 1975 as a statutory public company. Its main aims cover the development of, and the provision of assistance to, the UK economy and also include the safeguarding of productive employment. As a complementary function, the NEB is the holding company of a number of industrial companies acquired either through its own financial activities or else transferred to it by the government.

The actions of the NEB have prevented a number of well-known companies from disappearing completely from the industrial scene. Major shareholdings held by the NEB are shown in Table 23–3. In addition to these shareholdings, the NEB has made substantial loans to the companies listed in the table. One or two of the supporting schemes arranged by the government have been resisted by groups of shareholders. For example, the offer of 10 pence per share made to existing shareholders of British Leyland in 1975 was not considered sufficiently high by a small group of shareholders, although the company itself had contractual liabilities at the time in excess of £50 million, together with estimated redundancy payment liabilities of over £100 million, and specialized assets that were not readily marketable.

Table 23–3 *Major Shareholdings of the NEB.*

	Percentage of voting shares held
British Leyland Ltd	95.1
Ferranti Ltd	50.0
Herbert Ltd	100.0
Rolls-Royce Ltd	100.0
The Cambridge Instrument Co. Ltd	46.3

Source: Written evidence by the National Enterprise Board to the Committee to Review the Functioning of Financial Institutions. London: HMSO, 1978.

LIQUIDATION PROCEDURES

Liquidation of a business occurs when there is no hope of saving it or effecting a reorganization.

There are three main headings[4] under which a company may be 'wound-up', namely:

4. T. E. Cain, *Charlesworth and Cain, Company Law* (London: Stevens & Sons), 1977, 11th edition, p. 543.

1. by the court; or
2. voluntarily; or
3. subject to the supervision of the court.

In addition, there are two kinds of voluntary winding up: (a) by the creditors and (b) by the members of the company.

Winding up by the court

The Companies Act, 1948,[5] provides a number of grounds under which a petition may be presented for winding up by the court. For our purposes the most important ground is that of a company's inability to pay its debts. This is the ground on which a petition for compulsory winding up is usually presented.

A company is considered to be unable to pay its debts if one of the following conditions is met:

1. A creditor for more than £200 has served on the company, at its registered office, a signed demand for payment of the sum due and the company has not either paid, secured or compounded for the sum to the creditor's satisfaction within three weeks.
2. Execution issued on a judgement in favour of a creditor is returned unsatisfied in whole or in part.
3. It is proved to the satisfaction of the court that the company is unable to pay its debts, taking into account its contingent and prospective liabilities.[6]

Although a petition to the court for winding up may be made by the company itself or a member of the company, it is more common to find it presented by an unsecured creditor of the firm.

Presentation and hearing of the petition

The petition must be presented to the Registrar of the court who will then fix a date for the subsequent hearing. The petition must then be advertised to enable the creditors and members of the company either to support or oppose the petition at the hearing. Finally, the petition must be served on the company at its registered office.

If it is felt that the assets of the company are at risk, an application may also be made at this stage for the appointment of a provisional liquidator, who is normally the Official Receiver. If appointed, the provisional liquidator assumes most of the powers of the directors, including control over the assets of the company.

The hearng of the petition may be attended by any creditor or member of the company. The court may at this stage dismiss the petition, adjourn the hearing conditionally, or make any other order, including a winding-up order, that it thinks fit.

If a winding-up order is made, the consequences of the order back-date to an earlier date deemed to be the commencement of the winding up. This rule has the effect of making void any transfer of shares or property in the company since this date, whether made in good faith or not, unless the court orders otherwise. At this stage the Official Receiver becomes provisional liquidator and so acts until either he or another person is appointed liquidator. Within 14 days after the court has made the winding-up order, the company must submit a report to the Official Receiver listing assets and liabilities together with details relating to secured creditors.

---

5. Section 222, Companies Act, 1948.
6. Section 223, Companies Act, 1948, as amended by the Insolvency Act, 1976.

First meetings of creditors and members[7]

Separate meetings of both creditors and members are held to determine whether to appoint another liquidator in place of the Official Receiver and whether to appoint a committee of inspection to act with the liquidator. If the two meetings disagree over these matters, then the court decides on them. Before each meeting takes place the Official Receiver must send to the creditors and members a summary of the company's statement of affairs, together with an explanation of the reason for the company's failure.

Subsequent procedure

It is the duty of the liquidator on appointment to take control of all the assets of the company and draw up a list of members of the company, past or present, who may be expected to contribute to the company's debts. He must then convert these assets to cash as soon as possible and use the funds realized to pay off the creditors of the company, in order of priority. Any excess after payment of creditors will be distributed to members in proportion to their interest in the company.

During the liquidation process the liquidator must also investigate the past affairs of the company to determine whether any proceedings of a civil or criminal nature should be initiated against past officers of the company. No public examination of any officer can take place unless prima facie evidence of fraud has been placed before the Official Receiver. A recent case where an enquiry and public examination was effected is that of London and Counties Securities Group Ltd, which went into liquidation in 1973.

Completion of winding up and dissolution of the company

When the final payment has been made to the creditors of the company and any excess distributed to members, the liquidator may apply to the court for the company to be dissolved. Because of the expense involved in this later action, however, the normal procedure is to apply to the Registrar for dissolution of the company under section 353[8] of the Companies Act. The liquidator will then apply to the court for discharge or release from his duties. A further two years will then elapse before the Registrar strikes the company off the register.

Voluntary winding up

As mentioned earlier, voluntary winding up may take the form of either a members' or a creditors' voluntary winding up. As a members' voluntary winding up must be accompanied by a declaration of solvency, no further consideration of it is necessary to this chapter. Creditors' voluntary liquidations, on the other hand, require no declaration of solvency, and, as can be seen from Table 23–2, are more common than compulsory liquidations.

The company must initiate a creditors' voluntary liquidation, normally by passing an extraordinary resolution, in the case of insolvency, and also call a meeting of creditors. At this meeting a statement of the company's affairs must be presented, and a liquidator and committee of inspection appointed. The liquidation then proceeds in a similar manner to

---

7. In fact, the Companies Act refers to 'contributories', which is a term to include not only current members of the company but also people who have been members of the company within the past year.

8. Section 353 authorizes the Registrar of Companies to strike a company's name off the register if he believes that the company is not carrying on a business.

that of the winding up by the court, except where a compromise or scheme of arrangement (discussed later in the chapter) is entered into with the creditors.

Winding up subject to supervision of the court

A petition for winding up subject to the supervision of the court may be made by a creditor during a voluntary winding up. The effect of the order would be to cause certain actions of the liquidator to be subject to the sanction of the court. Petitions for winding up under supervision are rarely granted nowadays as the law offers, under other sections, ample protection to creditors who feel threatened.

Priority of claims in liquidation

The order of application of the assets of a company during winding up is as follows:

1. Costs and expenses incurred during the winding up, including the payment of the liquidator's fees.
2. Payment of preferential creditors including
   (a) Wages and salaries due to employees of the company within four months before the relevant date,[9] not exceeding £800 per person.
   (b) Accrued holiday remuneration of employees, including that arising through termination of employment, which occurs automatically on a winding-up order being made.
   (c) Any one year's assessment of tax.
   (d) Rates and value added tax which became payable within the 12 months preceding the relevant date.
3. General or unsecured creditors. Secured creditors should have obtained payment out of the proceeds of sale of the specific assets held by them as security; any unsatisfied balance ranks as an unsecured creditor.
4. Preference shareholders.
5. Ordinary shareholders.

To illustrate how this priority of claims works out let us trace the distribution of funds from the insolvent firm whose balance sheet is illustrated in Table 23–4. Assets total £90 million, and the claims on these assets are shown on the left-hand side of the balance sheet.

The short-term loan is secured by a floating charge on all the assets of the company but ranks in priority for repayment after the first mortgage charge. The first mortgage charge is a charge on the fixed assets of the business only.

Now assume that the assets of the firm are sold. The assets shown in the balance sheet in Table 23–4 are greatly overstated – they are in fact worth much less than the £90 million at which they are recorded. The following amounts are realized on liquidation:

Fixed assets	£ 5 000 000
Current assets	32 400 000
Total realized	£37 400 000

9. 'Relevant date' means date of appointment of a provisional liquidator in the case of compulsory winding up, or date of winding-up order if no provisional liquidator was appointed. In the case of a voluntary winding up, the relevant date is the date of passing the resolution for winding up.

Table 23–4 *Insolvent Company Balance Sheet*

Ordinary share capital	£26 000 000	Fixed assets	£10 000 000
Reserves	15 000 000		
	£41 000 000	Current assets	80 000 000
Preference share capital	2 000 000		
First mortgage debentures	7 000 000		
Unsecured debentures	8 000 000		
	£58 000 000		
Corporation tax payable	1 000 000		
	£59 000 000		
Short-term loan	10 000 000		
Trade creditors	20 000 000		
Accrued wages (1400 @ £500)	700 000		
Other accrued expenses	300 000		
Total claims on assets	£90 000 000	Total assets	£90 000 000

The order of priority of payment is shown by Table 23–5. Fees and expenses of liquidation are assumed to be £500 000. Next in priority are wages due to employees of £700 000 and the corporation tax assessment of £1 million. The first mortgage is then partly repaid out of the proceeds of the sale of the fixed assets, and the loan secured by the floating charge is repaid, i.e. £10 million. Total claims satisfied thus far equal £17.2 million, leaving £20.2 million available to the unsecured creditors.

The claims of the unsecured creditors total £30.3 million, including £2 million unsatisfied on the first mortgage debenture. As funds available are only £20.2 million each creditor will receive two-thirds of his claims. Since creditors cannot be satisfied in full there will be no payment to preference or ordinary shareholders. It will be noted that in this

Table 23–5 *Insolvent Company, Order of Priority of Claims.*

Distribution of proceeds on liquidation	
1. Proceeds of sale of assets	£37 400 000
2. Fees and expenses of liquidation	£ 500 000
3. Wages due to employees, earned within four months prior to liquidation	£ 700 000
4. Corporation tax assessment for previous year	£ 1 000 000
	£ 2 200 000
5. First mortgage paid out of sale of fixed assets charged	£ 5 000 000
6. Short-term loan repaid	£10 000 000
	£17 200 000
7. Available to unsecured creditors	£20 200 000

Claims of unsecured creditors	Claim	Amount received
Unsatisfied portion of first mortgage	£ 2 000 000	£ 1 333 333
Unsecured debenture	8 000 000	5 333 333
Trade creditors	20 000 000	13 333 334
Accrued expenses	300 000	200 000
	£30 300 000	£20 200 000

particular case the floating charge creditor is satisfied in full while the fixed charge creditor is not. In many cases the possession of a fixed charge by debenture-holders is also accompanied by a prior floating charge enabling them to be repaid in full before any of the unsecured creditors.

DEBENTURE-HOLDERS' ACTION

In addition to the normal remedies available to the creditors of a company to enforce payment of debts, debenture-holders, if their claim is secured by a fixed or floating charge on the assets of the company, have a further remedy available to them. If the company defaults in either payment of interest or repayment of principal, the debenture-holders may cause the appointment of a receiver to take possession of the assets charged and either sell them or else carry on the business of the company himself (or herself). The receiver so appointed is not in the same position as a liquidator as it is not the intention of the action to cause the company to be wound up, although it may be the ultimate consequence of the action. Instead, the receiver will withdraw from the business as soon as the legitimate claims of the debenture-holders have been satisfied, leaving the company to carry on as before, or at least as well as it can.

The action taken by the debenture-holders is not one that will be taken lightly. Default in payment of interest may be better remedied by arranging a compromise with the company to ensure continuation of the debenture-holders' source of income. Default in repayment of principal may be otherwise remedied by a scheme of arrangement, as described in the next section. A scheme of arrangement might be especially advisable if the security for the debenture-holders was in the form of a floating charge and it appeared unlikely that the sale of the assets would provide sufficient funds to satisfy the preferential creditors, who must be paid before this class of debenture-holders, and also allow for full repayment to the debenture-holders.

RECONSTRUCTION AND SCHEME OF ARRANGEMENT

In certain situations a company which has excellent future prospects may find itself unable to raise sufficient funds to realize these prospects because of the effect of adverse results in the past on the financial position of the company. Alternatively, a company which is in the course of being wound up may prove to have a higher value to the creditors and members if the business is continued in some modified form than if the business is dissolved. In both cases the law provides for the members and creditors of the company to make a compromise with each other and enter into a formal arrangement for the dissolution of the existing company and the transfer of the assets and liabilities to a new company specially set up for the purpose.

The essence of any such scheme is that the various groups of claimants on the existing company's asset must be prepared to modify their existing claims in order to secure better satisfaction of these revised claims in the future than could be obtained on the existing claims if the company were to be liquidated. In order to obtain approval for such a scheme it may be necessary to offer the ordinary shareholders a stake in the re-formed company although they might possibly have recovered nothing from their existing investment if the company had simply gone into liquidation. The next section deals with an illustration of a scheme of arrangement which shows how the various claims are modified.

Illustration of a scheme of arrangement

The Milldew Company has had two disastrous years' trading results which have not been helped by heavy expenditure on research and development. As can be seen from the company's balance sheet, illustrated in Table 23–6, losses over the last three years have completely eliminated the company's reserves, even allowing for the fact that £5 million of the research and development costs have not yet been written off.

Table 23–6 *Milldew Company, Balance Sheet 31 December 1974 (£millions).*

Land and buildings	£ 2.0
Plant and equipment	3.0
Patent rights	4.0
Research and development	5.0
Stocks	4.0
Trade debtors	1.0
	£19.0
Ordinary share capital £1 shares	£10.0
Reserves	(1.3)
Shareholders' funds	£ 8.7
12% mortgage debenture	8.0
Trade creditors and accruals[a]	2.0
Bank overdraft	0.3
Total claims on assets	£19.0

[a] 'Trade creditors and accruals' includes £500 000 preferential creditors.

Despite its recent poor performance the company has good prospects for the future. Milldew possesses valuable patent rights and the research and development programme has produced a number of very profitable projects. The company is finding it impossible, however, to generate sufficient funds to meet its current requirements for payment of creditors. In addition, the mortgage debenture, which was raised during a period of high interest rates, is shortly due for repayment. Meetings of shareholders and creditors have been presented with an alternative choice by the directors, namely that either the company must be dissolved, as it cannot continue in existence in its present state, or else a scheme of arrangement must be entered into. In support of the second alternative the directors produced the financial statements illustrated in Tables 23–7 and 23–8 which show both creditors and the debenture-holders (whose claims are secured by a fixed charge on the land and buildings) that there will be insufficient funds on a liquidation to meet their claims in full.

After viewing these statements, creditors, debenture-holders and shareholders agreed to proceed with a scheme of arrangement, details of which are as follows:

1. The preferential creditors are to be repaid in full.
2. Milldew Ltd is to be wound up and a new company, Phoenix Ltd, is to be formed.
3. Debenture-holders are to receive 3.5 ordinary shares at £1 each in the new company, together with £2 of 8 per cent convertible loan stock for every £8 of stock held in Milldew Ltd.
4. Ordinary creditors are to receive £1 of 8 per cent convertible loan stock plus 40 pence in cash for every £2 owed to them by Milldew Ltd. The bank overdraft will be taken over by the new company.

Table 23–7 *Estimated Realizable Value of Assets Held by the Company (£millions).*

	Book value	Estimated realizable value
Land and buildings	£2.0	£2.0
Plant and equipment	3.0	1.0
Patent rights	4.0	1.5
Stocks (mainly work-in-progress)	4.0	1.5
Trade debtors	1.0	1.0
	£14.0	£7.0

Note: Research and development, as an intangible asset, will have no realizable value on liquidation.

Table 23–8 *Estimated Short-fall to Creditors in the Event of a Liquidation (£millions).*

1. Sale of land and buildings	£2.0
Debenture-holders' claim	8.0
Short-fall in repayment	£(6.0)
2. Proceeds of sale of sundry assets (excluding land and buildings)	£5.0
Estimated liquidation expenses	0.6
	£4.4
Repayment of preferential creditors	0.5
Amount remaining for unsecured creditors	£3.9
3. Unsecured creditors:	
Trade creditors and accruals	£1.5
Bank overdraft	0.3
Short-fall in debenture-holders' claim	6.0
	£7.8
Short-fall in repayment to unsecured creditors	£3.9
Amount received: 50 pence in the £1	

5. Ordinary shareholders are to receive one £1 ordinary share in Phoenix Ltd for every five shares that they currently hold in Milldew Ltd.

Estimated costs of the scheme of arrangement are £300000. In order to help with the scheme of arrangement, an extension of the bank overdraft has been arranged in return for a prior floating charge on all the assets of the new company.

Table 23–9 shows how much the shareholders and each class of creditors will receive through the scheme of arrangement, as opposed to the proceeds of liquidation. As can be seen from the table each party to the scheme of arrangement will benefit more from this arrangement than they would have done in the event of a liquidation, provided that the company begins to earn sufficient profits. The ordinary shareholders lose overall control of the company to the debenture-holders but at least they will receive something out of the scheme, whereas they would have lost the whole of their investment in the case of a liquidation.

Table 23–9 *Amounts Received by Each Class from the Scheme of Arrangement (£millions).*

1. Debenture-holders:	
Ordinary share capital	£3.5
8% convertible loan stock	2.0
	£5.5
v. proceeds of liquidation:	
Receipts from sale of mortgage property	£2.0
Dividend on unsecured balance	3.0
	£5.0
2. Preferential creditors:	
Cash payment	£0.5
3. Unsecured creditors (excluding bank overdraft):	
Cash payment	£0.40
8% convertible loan stock	0.75
	£1.15
v. proceeds of liquidation:	
Dividend of 50 pence in the £1	£0.75
4. Ordinary shareholders:	
Ordinary share capital	£2.0
v. nothing in the event of a liquidation	

All the assets of Milldew Ltd are to be transferred to Phoenix Ltd and asset values in the new company's accounts are to be written down to the values shown in the balance sheet given in Table 23–10. Some of these values do not correspond to the estimated realizable values shown in Table 23–7 because of their higher value to the business when it is considered as a 'going concern'.

An example of a recent scheme of arrangement is provided by the case of British Leyland Motor Corporation Ltd. This was reconstructed under a scheme of arrangement in 1975 to form British Leyland Ltd. The result of this scheme of arrangement was different from many others, however, in that the government became the major

Table 23–10 *Phoenix Ltd Balance Sheet (£millions).*

Land and buildings	£2.00
Plant and equipment	2.00
Patents	1.50
Stocks	3.25
Trade debtors	1.00
Total assets	£9.75
Ordinary share capital	£5.50
8% convertible loan stock	2.75
Bank overdraft	1.50[a]
Claims on assets	£9.75

[a] Bank overdraft has increased from £300 000 due to payments to preferential creditors, unsecured creditors and administration expenses (£500 000 + £400 000 + £300 000).

shareholder in the new company, acquiring shares from the shareholders in the old company through a cash offer of 10 pence per share. Most of the long-term financing requirements of British Leyland are now secured from the government through the agency of the NEB.

EXTENSION

An extension represents a voluntary concession by the creditors of a company. Extension postpones the date of payment of overdue obligations. It has the aim of keeping the debtor in business and avoiding legal expenses. Although creditors suffer a temporary loss, the amount of debts finally recovered is often greater than if one of the formal procedures had been followed and the hope is that a stable customer will emerge. In some cases an extension might be arranged in order for the creditors to avoid the stigma of having caused a particular concern to be wound up.

At least three conditions are usually necessary to make an extension or a composition feasible:

1. The debtor is a good moral risk.
2. The debtor shows ability to make a recovery.
3. General business conditions are favourable to recovery.

SUMMARY

Problems associated with the decline and failure of a firm, and methods of rehabilitating or liquidating one that has failed, were the subjects treated in this chapter. The major cause of failure is incompetent management. Bad managers should, of course, be removed as promptly as possible; if failure has occurred, a number of remedies are open to the interested parties.

The first question to be answered is whether the firm is better off 'dead or alive' – whether it should be liquidated and sold off piecemeal or be rehabilitated. Assuming the decision is made that the firm should survive, it must be put through what is called a *reconstruction*. Legal procedures are always costly, especially in the case of a business failure. Therefore, if it is at all possible, both the debtor and the creditors are better off if matters can be handled on an informal basis rather than through the courts.

If voluntary settlement through extension is not possible then there are two formal remedies open to creditors, either (a) reconstruction through a scheme of arrangement or (b) liquidation. In order for a reconstruction to be a viable proposition there must be a compromise entered into with all classes of shareholders and creditors so that each group will see some advantage to itself from the reconstruction scheme. The reconstructed company must also have a good chance of surviving in the future, and not be in the position where its 'day of judgement' is merely being postponed.

In the event that a reconstruction proves impossible, the formal liquidation procedures should be entered into. There are three main headings under which a company may be wound up: (a) by the court; (b) voluntarily; and (c) subject to the supervision of the court. When a company is wound up due to its inability to pay its debts, winding up will normally be made by the court, although creditors' voluntary liquidation is also possible. In the event of liquidation, a liquidator will be appointed to ensure that the property of the company is applied to the benefit of the creditors in order of priority of their claims.

Finally, a further remedy is available to debenture-holders whose claims are secured by a fixed or floating charge. Rather than petition for the company to be wound up, the debenture-holders may seek the appointment of a receiver to take possession of the assets charged and to apply them to satisfy the debenture-holders' legitimate claims. This remedy is often conducted more rapidly than a liquidation and leaves the company with the opportunity to continue in business.

QUESTIONS

23–1. 'A certain number of business failures is a healthy sign. If there are no failures, this is an indication (a) that entrepreneurs are overly cautious, hence not as inventive and as willing to take risks as a healthy, growing economy requires, (b) that competition is not functioning to weed out inefficient producers, or (c) that both situations exist.' Discuss, giving pros and cons.

23–2. How can financial analysis be used to forecast the probability of a given firm's failure? Assuming that such analysis is properly applied, can it always predict failure?

23–3. Why do creditors often accept a plan for financial rehabilitation rather than demand dissolution of the business?

23–4. Would it be possible to form a profitable company by merging two companies, both of which are business failures? Explain.

23–5. Distinguish between a reconstruction and a liquidation.

23–6. Would it be a sound rule to liquidate whenever the liquidation value is above the value of the company as a going concern? Discuss.

23–7 Why do all liquidations usually result in losses for the creditors or the owners, or both? Would partial liquidation or liquidation over a period limit their losses? Explain.

23–8. Are liquidations likely to be more common for reconstruction, heavy engineering or other industrial companies? Why?

PROBLEMS

23–1. The balance sheet for the Motherwell Manufacturing Company for 1978 is shown below:

Motherwell Manufacturing Company, Balance Sheet 31 December 1978.

Ordinary share capital	£1 600 000	Net fixed assets	£1 000 000
Reserves	120 000	Research and development	1 000 000
8 % preference shares	500 000	Goodwill	800 000
10 % unsecured debentures	800 000	Investments (at current market value)	400 000
Current liabilities (including bank overdraft of £1 200 000)[a]	2 080 000	Current assets	1 900 000
Total claims	£5 100 000	Total assets	£5 100 000

[a] The bank overdraft is secured by a floating charge on all the assets of the company.

Profits over the last few years have been insufficient to pay a dividend to either class of shareholder, due mainly to a contraction in demand for the company's main product lines. The company has been developing a prototype solar engine for desert buggies, however, and has reached the stage where the product has become a viable proposition. Advance orders are already being accepted for the product but the company has run into a problem in obtaining sufficient capital to modernize its existing production facilities, £1.5 million being required urgently. Two institutional investors are willing to provide the necessary funds in return for a 50 per cent stake in the equity capital of the company. One condition of the provision of these funds is that there should be a complete reorganization of the capital structure of the company.

Outline a plan for reconstruction that would be acceptable to all the existing classes within Motherwell Ltd.

23–2. The Accurate Instrument Company produces precision instruments. The company's products are designed and manufactured according to specifications set out by its customers and are highly specialized.

Declines in sales and increases in development expenses in recent years resulted in a large deficit at the end of 1978.

Accurate Instrument Company, Balance Sheet 31 December 1978(£000).

Ordinary share capital	£150	Fixed assets	£375
Reserves (deficit)	(75)	Current assets	375
Shareholders' funds	£75		
Unsecured debentures	225		
Current liabilities	450		
Total claims	£750	Total assets	£750

Accurate Instrument Company, Sales and Profits, 1975–8(£000).

Year	Sales	Net profit after tax before fixed charges
1975	£2625	£262.5
1976	£2400	£225.0
1977	£1425	£(75.0)
1978	£1350	£(112.5)

Independent assessment led to the conclusion that the company would have a liquidation value of about £600 000. As an alternative to liquidation, the management concluded that a reorganization was possible with additional investment of £300 000. The management was confident of eventual success of the company and stated that the additional investment would restore earnings to £125 000 a year after taxes and before fixed charges. The price/earnings ratio of the reconstructed firm is estimated at eight times. The management is negotiating with a local investment group to obtain the additional investment of £300 000. If the funds are obtained, the holders of the long-term debentures would be given one-half of the ordinary shares in the reorganized firm in place of their present claims.

Should the creditors agree to the reorganization or should they force liquidation of the firm?

SELECTED REFERENCES

Altman, Edward I. *Corporate Bankruptcy in America.* Lexington, Mass.: Heath Lexington Books, 1971.

Altman, Edward I. Corporate bankruptcy potential, stockholder returns and share valuation. *Journal of Finance* 24 (December 1969): 887–900.

Altman, Edward I. Equity securities of bankrupt firms. *Financial Analysts' Journal* 25 (July–August 1969): 129–133.

Altman, Edward I. Financial ratios, discriminant analysis and the prediction of corporate bunkruptcy. *Journal of Finance* 23 (September 1968): 589–609.

Appleyard, A. R. and Yarrow, G. K. The relationship between take-over activity and share valuation. *Journal of Finance* 30 (December 1975): 1239–1249.

Argenti, J. Corporate collapse, the causes and symptoms. London: McGraw Hill 1976.

Argenti, J. Corporate planning and corporate collapse. *Long Range Planning* (UK) (December 1976): 12–17.

Argenti, J. Company failure – long range prediction is not enough. *Accountancy* (August 1977): 46–52.

Beaver, William H. Financial ratios as predictors of failure. *Empirical Research in Accounting: Selected Studies.* Supplement to *Journal of Accounting Research* (1966): 71–111.

Beaver, William H. Market prices, financial ratios, and the prediction of failure. *Journal of Accounting Research* 6 (Autumn 1968): 179–192.

Buckmaster, D. A., Copeland, R, M. and Dascher, P. E. The relative predictive ability of three accounting income models. *Accounting and Business Research* (Summer 1977): 177–186.

Cain, T. E. *Charlesworth & Cain. Company Law.* London: Stevens & Sons, 1977, 11th edition, chaps. 22–27.

Edmister, Robert O. An empirical test of financial ratio analysis for small business failure prediction. *Journal of Financial and Quantitative Analysis* 7 (March 1972): 1477–1493.

Fadel, H. & Parkinson, J. M. Liquidity evaluation by ratio analysis. *Accounting and Business Research* (Spring 1978): 101–108.

Gordon, Myron J. Towards a theory of financial distress. *Journal of Finance* 26 (May 1971): 347–356.

Johnson, Craig G. Ratio analysis and the prediction of firm failure. *Journal of Finance* 25 (December 1970): 1166–1168. See also Edward A. Altman, Reply. *ibid.*, pp. 1169–1172.

Lester, T. The secondary scandal. *Management Today* (October 1974): 64–69; 142–146.

Stapleton, R. C. Some aspects of the pure theory of corporate finance: bankruptcies and take-overs: comment. *Bell Journal of Economics* 6 (Autumn 1975): 708–710.

Stiglitz, J. E. Some aspects of the pure theory of corporate finance; bankruptcies and take-overs: reply. *Bell Journal of Economics* 6 (Autumn 1975): 711–714.

Täffler, R. J. and Tisshaw, H. Going, going, gone – four factors which predict. *Accountancy* (March 1977): 50–54.

Taffler, R. J. *The Correct Way to Use Published Financial Statement Data: The Assessment of Financial Viability Example.* Paper presented to the Annual Conference of the AUTA at Liverpool University, September 1977.

Van Horne, James C. Optimal initiation of bankruptcy proceedings. *Journal of Finance* 31 (June 1976): 897–910.

Walter, James E. Determination of technical insolvency. *Journal of Business* 30 (January 1957): 30–43.

Chapter 24

Multinational Business Finance[1]

Although the basic concepts underlying financial management in a multinational firm are essentially the same as those for a domestic company, a multinational firm's financial manager must make decisions within the framework of at least three separate economic and political environments: his own country's, the international economy, and that of at least one foreign country. This chapter shows how these different environmental influences affect the financial manager as he attempts to apply the concepts developed in previous chapters.

TREND TOWARDS INTERNATIONAL OPERATIONS

Table 24–1 is a list of the 50 largest industrial firms in the world ranked by sales. Although it is apparent that US firms, which account for eight of the first 12, dominate that list, it is equally important to note that of the total 50, there are only 23 US firms. In terms of total sales and total net income, US firms accounted for 45 per cent and 38 per cent respectively.

Many countries, particularly in Europe, have had foreign economic interests for centuries, but only recently has foreign commerce begun to represent a significant percentage of total United States economic activity. Before the Second World War, only a handful of American companies had important overseas investments. There were two or three international oil companies, a few mining groups, several banks and some manufacturers of automobiles, machinery and electrical equipment. Since 1945, however, American business has become much more world-oriented, and today over 10 000 US firms have significant foreign-based operations. The nature of international business has also changed: traditional 'foreign trade', with its emphasis on exporting goods

1. This chapter was written by Robert T. Aubey, Professor of Finance, The University of Wisconsin, and has been retained in its original form by the adapters because of the international nature of the contents.

Table 24–1 *The 50 Largest Industrial Companies in the World.*

Rank	Company	Headquarters	Sales ($000)	Net income ($000)
1	Exxon	New York	44 864 824	2 503 013
2	General Motors	Detroit	35 724 911	1 253 092
3	Royal Dutch/Shell Group	London/The Hague	32 105 096	2 110 927
4	Texaco	New York	24 507 454	830 583
5	Ford Motor	Dearborn, Mich.	24 009 100	322 700
6	Mobil Oil	New York	20 620 392	809 877
7	National Iranian Oil	Teheran	18 854 547	16 947 071
8	British Petroleum	London	17 285 854	369 202
9	Standard Oil of California	San Francisco	16 822 077	772 509
10	Unilever	London	15 015 994	322 108
11	International Business Machines	Armonk, N.Y.	14 436 541	1 989 877
12	Gulf Oil	Pittsburgh	14 268 000	700 000
13	General Electric	Fairfield, Conn.	13 399 100	580 800
14	Chrysler	Highland Park, Mich.	11 699 305	(259 535)
15	International Tel. & Tel.	New York	11 367 647	398 171
16	Philips' Gloeilampenfabrieken	Eindhoven (Netherlands)	10 746 485	152 190
17	Standard Oil (Ind.)	Chicago	9 955 248	786 987
18	Cie Française des Pétroles	Paris	9 145 778	168 472
19	Nippon Steel	Tokyo	8 796 902	111 935
20	August Thyssen-Hütte	Duisburg (Germany)	8 764 899	99 926
21	Hoechst	Frankfurt on Main	8 462 322	100 972
22	ENI	Rome	8 334 432	(134 869)
23	Daimler-Benz	Stuttgart	8 194 271	125 768
24	U.S. Steel	Pittsburgh	8 167 269	559 614
25	BASF	Ludwigshafen on Rhine	8 152 318	152 831
26	Shell Oil	Houston	8 143 445	514 827
27	Renault	Boulogne-Billancourt (France)	7 831 330	(128 702)
28	Siemens	Munich	7 759 909	201 275
29	Volkswagenwerk	Wolfsburg (Germany)	7 680 786	(63 971)
30	Atlantic Richfield	Los Angeles	7 307 854	350 395
31	Continental Oil	Stamford, Conn.	7 253 801	330 854
32	Bayer	Leverkusen (Germany)	7 223 302	128 229
33	E.I. du Pont de Nemours	Wilmington, Del.	7 221 500	271 800
34	Toyota Motor	Toyoda-City (Japan)	7 194 139	250 848
35	ELF-Aquitaine	Paris	7 165 390	199 875
36	Nestlé	Vevey (Switzerland)	7 080 160	309 365
37	ICI (Imperial Chemical Industries)	London	6 884 219	424 294
38	Petrobrás (Petróleo Brasileiro)	Rio de Janeiro	6 625 516	703 586
39	Western Electric	New York	6 590 116	107 308
40	British-American Tobacco	London	6 145 979	314 041
41	Proctor & Gamble	Cincinnati	6 081 675	333 862
42	Hitachi	Tokyo	5 916 135	94 084
43	Westinghouse Electric	Pittsburgh	5 862 747	165 224
44	Mitsubishi Heavy Industries	Tokyo	5 693 994	40 699
45	Union Carbide	New York	5 665 000	381 700
46	Tenneco	Houston	5 599 709	342 936
47	Nissan Motor	Tokyo	5 479 562	115 532
48	Goodyear Tire & Rubber	Akron, Ohio	5 452 473	161 613
49	Montedison	Milan	5 417 741	(183 912)
50	British Steel	London	5 340 183	171 867
	Totals		568 317 431	37 311 850

Source: *Fortune*, August 1976, p. 243.

Table 24–2 *US Firms Overseas: Patterns of Expansion (1961–72) (in Number of Activities).*

Type of Activity	1961	1962	1963	1964	1965	1966	1967	1968	1969	1970	1971	1972	1973	Total
New Establishments														
Manufacturing	382	445	516	507	426	398	363	371	524	469	311	368	396	5476
Non-manufacturing	178	139	202	254	259	190	182	202	348	275	193	242	264	2928
Subtotal	560	584	718	761	685	588	545	573	872	744	504	610	660	8404
Expansions														
Manufacturing	185	176	159	155	171	96	54	63	119	90	53	59	65	1445
Non-manufacturing	70	100	43	13	17	17	6	8	18	12	5	5	6	320
Subtotal	255	276	202	168	188	113	60	71	137	102	58	64	71	10169
Licensing Agreements	340	247	304	282	259	174	139	133	177	129	113	128	117	2542
Total	1155	1107	1224	1211	1132	875	744	777	1186	975	675	802	848	12711

Source: John B. Rhodes, U.S. new business activities abroad, *Columbia Journal of World Business*, vol. 9, no. 2, Summer 1974, p. 100.

manufactured in the United States, has declined dramatically in importance, being replaced by full-fledged overseas divisions with their own manufacturing plants.

When the emphasis was on export sales, foreign investments were minimal. Today, however, a great deal of investment is required to establish and support US overseas operations. In fact, direct foreign investment of US firms climbed sharply from $11.8 billion in 1950 to $133 billion by the end of 1975.[2] Table 24–2, which gives another indication of the growth of US private foreign investment, shows that during the period 1961–73 American firms established over 8404 new facilities overseas.

This rapid increase in foreign investments has had a tremendous impact on the operations of many American firms. Such companies are highly dependent upon their overseas operations because significant amounts of their total assets, sales and profits are accounted for by their foreign operating units. Table 24–3 gives the percentage of total earnings represented by foreign earnings for selected industries in 1972. Some of the firms whose data are included in the table – for example, IBM, Pfizer, Mobil, Foster Wheeler, International Systems & Controls, LRC International, Hoover, and F. W. Woolworth – obtained nearly half of their total earnings from their foreign operations.

Table 24–3 *Industry Comparison of Foreign Operations, Selected Industries, 1972.*

Industry	Number of companies	Total earnings	Foreign earnings to total earnings (per cent)	Foreign net assets to total net assets (per cent)
Chemicals	9	$ 926 109	36.8	30.3
Construction	11	467 653	19.8	25.5
Consumer goods	36	2 860 856	51.3	[a]
Electricals	16	870 113	32.1	35.8
Foodstuffs	15	708 504	21.6	22.4
Machinery	26	420 368	34.9	28.9
Metals	11	604 972	17.7	21.7
Office equipment	9	1 694 171	49.5	28.3
Petroleum	8	2 962 404	46.9	45.7
Pharmaceuticals	15	894 355	38.6	31.5

[a] Not available.
Source: *Business International*, 20 July 1973, p. 230.

Overseas expansion has not been limited to American firms; in fact, there is an increasing flow of foreign business investment into the United States.

According to an extensive survey undertaken by the US Department of Commerce, foreign direct investment in the United States reached $26.5 billion by the end of 1974.[3] This compares with $13.7 billion in 1971, $7.6 billion in 1962, and about $3 billion in 1950. The continuation of the growth of foreign investment in the United States is virtually assured with such recent ventures as Volkswagen's $400 million plant in Pennsylvania, Sweden's $100 million investment in Virginia to assemble Volvos, and Michelin's (France) $300 million tyre plant in South Carolina.

Although US direct private investment abroad is larger than that of all other countries combined, US firms face strong and increasing competition from foreign-based

---

2. 'Direct foreign investment' involves the ownership of 10 per cent or more of the stock of a foreign firm. Other investment is defined as 'portfolio investment', where neither control nor influence over the foreign firm is presumed to exist.
3. *International Letter*, Federal Reserve Bank of Chicago, No. 280, June 25, 1976. It is also reported that foreign portfolio investment in US stocks and bonds reached $67 billion by the end of 1974. Of that amount, $25 billion was in stock, and $16 billion in government bonds and notes. Government bonds and notes are held primarily by foreign official institutions as part of their international reserves. The total figure for 1975 is estimated at $86 billion.

multinational firms. A good example of this competition is the Dutch firm of Philips, which has plants in more than 40 countries and sales subsidiaries in 60 more, employs more than 360 000 people worldwide, and manufactures nearly one million different products.

CHANGING ORGANIZATION AND STRUCTURE OF MULTINATIONAL BUSINESS

Multinational corporations seldom use the word 'foreign': their involvement in overseas business is such that they now regard the world, rather than a single nation, as their area of operations.[4] The sheer size of many corporations' foreign direct investments has caused profound changes in their organizations and operating strategies. The way a firm can be affected by growing international interests is illustrated by the experience of Mid-State Manufacturing Company, Inc. Originally a manufacturer of food processing machinery, Mid-State, through domestic mergers and overseas investments, is now active in several separate lines of business.

In 1955 Mid-State, then a well-known company and highly respected for the quality of its food processing machinery, had its major plants and markets in the midwestern states. During that year, the firm received its first tentative orders from foreign countries. Although it could supply the products ordered, the firm had had no experience with the various regulations, means of transportation or special skills necessary to complete these transactions. Accordingly, it turned to specialized export brokers and international bankers for the required expertise.

As the volume of overseas orders increased, Mid-State created an export section within its sales department. Because most of the complexities of these export sales were handled by international intermediaries, the export section was basically an extension of the domestic sales department, and the scope of its activities was quite limited. This type of organization was adequate so long as Mid-State was satisfied simply to accept and fill orders as they were received.

In 1957, to acquaint himself with this overseas business and to investigate ways of expanding it, Edward Bronson, Mid-State's president, visited several Latin American countries to which substantial amounts of machinery had been shipped. He became convinced that because of growing industrialization in the region, Mid-State Manufacturing could easily increase its overseas business if it had a sales force in the field. Accordingly, Bronson authorized the recruitment and training of a foreign sales force. The venture proved to be highly productive; foreign sales increased at about twice the rate of domestic sales in 1958, 1959 and 1960.

During 1960, the firm's managers began to realize that, along with the advantages of the international market, there were complications. At first the problems were rather simple, consisting mainly of requests for small modifications in the machinery to meet local conditions. Such minor modifications were easily accomplished, but as the salesmen gained experience and expanded the territories they covered, the requested modifications became more complex. This forced the export section to expand its activities and to work more and more with Mid-State's engineering and production departments. At the same time, increasing foreign requests for credit required contacts between the export and finance departments. By 1961, even though foreign sales had increased to about 10 per cent of the companies total sales, it had become apparent that Mid-State's growth in foreign

4. There is no generally accepted definition of the term 'multinational corporation'. In the purest sense, the term should probably be applied to only a few large firms that have undisputed international ownership, operation and management. However, the term is commonly applied to any business that has significant operations in several different countries.

markets was not fulfilling its potential. Modifications of domestic machinery could not satisfy all the requests received, and the firm faced some problems servicing the modified machinery it sold.

Bronson decided to explore the feasibility of establishing a foreign production unit, so he again travelled to Latin America. The urgency of his investigation was emphasized by two events. First, a reliable source had reported that one of Mid-State's competitors was studying the possibility of building a plant in Venezuela. Second, in an effort to stimulate its own local industry, Peru, one of Mid-State's largest South American markets, was planning to impose a 50 per cent tariff on all imports of food processing machinery. These two events not only underlined the necessity of going ahead with plans for an overseas unit, but also gave a focus to these plans, for it was clear that those two market locations should be examined first.

Immediately upon his return to the United States, Bronson created a study group to inquire into the whole question of the international market and to recommend what actions the firm should take. The report of the international market study group, which was submitted in December 1961, recommended that a subsidiary for international operations be formed to meet the problems and challenges of the international market. Accordingly, in 1962, Mid-State International Corporation was established as a separate company, with its president reporting directly to Bronson.[5]

The proposed organization was put into effect in 1963, and it proved to be a reasonably satisfactory arrangement. By 1970, both the parent company and Mid-State International had grown substantially and had diversified into a number of related lines. Mid-State International, particularly, had found it advantageous to go into the food processing field. It then had units operating in 23 countries, and overseas sales accounted for about 35 per cent of total corporate sales.

During its overseas build-up, Mid-State International used several methods to establish itself in the various markets. In countries such as Honduras, where much of the processed food was imported, the company started from scratch and built its own plants. In countries where there were already previously esablished operations, or where the political conditions were highly uncertain, the company used a licensing arrangement through which Mid-State would supply a local manufacturing firm with financial and technical assistance, trademarks and general know-how. In countries such as Mexico and Japan, where host government regulations require at least some local ownership, the company went into joint ventures with local investors. Finally, in several European countries, Mid-State acquired local firms. Each time the firm went into a new market, it gained experience that made the next penetration easier.

Edward Bronson, who became chairman of the board in 1971, anticipated that overseas sales would eventually represent 50 per cent or more of Mid-State's total sales. Although Bronson realized that it had not yet happened, he looked forward to the time when the foreign and domestic operations would be completely integrated and the Mid-State Manufacturing Company would be a truly multinational firm. This line of thought evolved because of various difficulties encountered in the coordination of the activities of domestic and international operations. It was Mr Bronson's belief that if the company was to realize its full potential and to take advantage of world developments, reorganization towards the complete integration of domestic and foreign operations would be necessary. This idea was reinforced in June 1971, when he read in *Business Week* that Eaton Corporation was already in the process of developing this type of structure.[6] Bronson understood that because of the nationalistic government policies and legal requirements of many of the host countries, it would be several years before any company could make all its

---

5. For a more complete discussion of why companies go international and the various methods used to become established overseas, see Myles L. Mace, The President and international operations, *Harvard Business Review*, November–December 1966, p. 72.
6. *Business Week*, 12 June 1971, p. 87.

decisions concerning such things as transfer of funds, pricing policies and shifting of assets as a true multinational firm. However, to the extent possible, Bronson believed that Mid-State should view all operating units as interrelated parts of a single system.

EVALUATION OF FOREIGN INVESTMENT OPPORTUNITIES

Since 1972, when Mid-State achieved full integration of its domestic and international capital budgeting procedures, all investment proposals, domestic and foreign, have been required to go through an established screening process: each proposal is subjected to a cash flow analysis, which results in a net present value calculation, and all proposals compete for funds on their individual merits.

Although Mid-State uses the *NPV* method to evaluate projects, the firm's management realizes that there are some significant differences between domestic and international investments. These differences relate primarily to two factors: (a) the political and financial environments of the host countries, and (b) the fact that two cash flow analyses must be performed for each of the foreign investment proposals – one for the project itself, and one for cash flows from the foreign project to the parent. The effects of these two factors on the application of capital budgeting theory are discussed in this section.

THE SCREENING PROCESS

Analysis of the host country

In November 1975 Mr Bronson was approached by the government of Andovia, a West African republic, with a request that his company establish a cocoa processing plant there. Although this request was received as a direct result of one of Bronson's visits to Africa, it was immediately referred to Mid-State International for screening and analysis, as all foreign proposals are, regardless of their origin.

For administrative purposes, Mid-State International has separated the countries of the world into four areas: Europe, Africa and the Middle East, Latin America, and the Far East. The manager of each area group is responsible for the initial screening of all investment proposals for any country within his area. The primary function of this initial screening is to analyse the political environment of the proposed host country and to determine whether or not the economic environment would be receptive to the proposed project.

The initial screening of the cocoa processing plant proposal showed that Andovia was generally receptive to foreign direct investments. Further, according to the latest industrial policy statement of the Andovian government, food processing plants were to be given highest priority because they would reduce the nation's need for imports and thus save foreign exchange. The country had no plans to nationalize any business, and its constitution states that if nationalization becomes desirable in the public interest, adequate, prompt and effective compensation is guaranteed. At the time of the analysis, no foreign firm had ever been nationalized, although the electric utilities and railroads were nationalized shortly after the country gained its independence in 1948.

Andovia is one of the world's largest producers of cocoa, but virtually the entire crop of 2.5 million tons a year is exported unprocessed. For such products as chocolate, chocolate milk, Ovaltine and other beverages made of cocoa, the 62 million Andovians depended almost entirely on imports. Thus the country found itself in the position of first exporting the raw material and then importing the finished product. The government viewed the correction of this situation as an important economic task, making it likely that Mid-State International would experience very favourable tax treatment.

Analysis of the international environment

The favourable preliminary report on the project was sent to the office of Robert Harris, the president of Mid-State International, for the second screening stage. Here, the analysis shifts from sole concern with the host country environment to what may be called the 'international environment'. At this stage, the emphasis centres on such factors as whether the company has the experience to handle the project; whether the project conflicts with other proposals; whether the market could be better served in some other way; and how the project could be integrated into Mid-State's continuing efforts to manage and allocate working capital on a world-wide basis.

Since Mid-State International already had overseas units in the food processing industry, the Andovian proposal would benefit from the company's prior experience. Also, since the host government had indicated that it was willing to place an import tax on cocoa products once production was started, the market would enjoy a protected status. Finally, it was determined that although minor adjustments in some working capital allocations would be required, the anticipated export sales of the project were expected to provide an inflow of hard currency that would reduce the need for some hedging operations and thus reduce costs.

Financial analysis

The third stage of the screening process involves a standard financial analysis. Although foreign investment proposals are subject to a number of political and international constraints not associated with domestic investments, once these constraints have been considered, Mid-State's policy is that each project should undergo a financial cash flow evaluation to determine whether the project has a positive risk-adjusted *NPV*. There is, however, an important difference in the application of cash flow analysis to a foreign investment: for foreign investments, there must be two sets of cash flow analyses – one for the project itself and one for the parent company.

Factors affecting the cash flows

Demand forecast

As with any investment proposal, the first step in the analysis of the Andovian project was a forecast of demand. For Andovia, as is often the case for developing countries, there simply were no reliable figures on past cocoa consumption. There were, however, fairly good data on imports of cocoa products, and since almost no cocoa was then processed locally, these figures could be used to estimate past consumption. These past usage estimates were correlated with population, income and other factors, and, on the basis of population and income projections, were used to develop the estimated demand figures given in Table 24–4.

Duties and taxes

In arriving at the cash flow figures for a foreign investment, particular attention must be given to the fact that since the transactions to be analysed flow across national boundaries,

Table 24–4 *Estimated Demand for Cocoa Products.*

Year	Tons
1975	285 000
1976	291 000
1977	297 000
1978	304 000
1979	310 000
1980	316 000
1981	322 000
1982	328 000
1983	335 000
1984	342 000

a unique set of tax laws and customs duties may be applicable. In the case of Andovia, the government agreed that Mid-State could, under the Andovian Industrial Development Act of 1969, enjoy an income tax holiday for five years, and could also import, duty-free, any new production equipment and materials that could not be obtained from local sources. Used equipment could be imported under a relatively low duty of 10 per cent. After five years of production, Mid-State International would be subject to a 40 per cent income tax, plus a 'super-tax' of 25 per cent of all income over 15 per cent of equity capital. The super-tax, introduced in 1967 as part of Andovia's Social Reform Act, was originally scheduled to expire in 1977, but it appears that the tax will be extended. If this tax is ever eliminated or reduced, Mid-State's profit potential will, of course, increase.

Applicable exchange rates

Another unique feature of foreign investment analysis is that the transactions being examined frequently involve currency transfers, so foreign exchange rates and restrictions must be taken into account. When there is an official rate of exchange and that rate is stable, no problems are presented. However, if changes in the exchange rate are expected (through devaluation or revaluation), or if the exchange rate is allowed to 'float', the evaluation process is more complicated; it becomes necessary to forecast the rate of exchange that may be applicable to future transactions.[7] Although the Andovian

7. Prior to 15 August 1971, the United States operated under an international monetary system established towards the end of the Second World War at Bretton Woods, New Hampshire. At the Bretton Woods Conference, the participating nations agreed to adhere to an international monetary policy calling for fixed exchange rates between currencies. The dollar was based on gold, at $35 per ounce of gold, and all other currencies were stated in terms of their relationship to the dollar. For example, the British pound was stated to be worth $2.80. The US Treasury agreed to buy or sell gold to foreigners freely at the rate of $35 per ounce. President Nixon's action of August 1971, when he announced that the United States would no longer convert dollars to gold, ended the international monetary system formulated at Bretton Woods. The responsibility for deciding whether to let exchange rates 'float' – that is, find their own level in relation to other currencies in accordance with supply and demand forces – or to continue maintaining a stable relationship with other currencies was placed on the individual nations. For a time it appeared that fixed exchange rates would be permanently abolished, but they were reinstated in early 1972 when the United States devalued the dollar by raising the price of gold to $38 per ounce. It was hoped that this action would correct the overvaluation of the dollar and lead to a more stable balance of payment situation. This, however, did not happen; in February 1973, the dollar was again devalued by about 10 per cent when the official price of gold was raised to $42.20 per ounce.

As a result of the second dollar devaluation and the international monetary crisis that followed, all major European exchange markets were officially closed on 1 March 1973. On 11 March eight members of the European Economic Community agreed to maintain fixed exchange rates among themselves within $2\frac{1}{4}$ per cent margins – the so-called floating snake. These eight currencies would then be allowed to float as a bloc against the dollar. The Japanese yen, Swiss franc, British sterling and Italian lira each continued to float independently. Most of the smaller nations have continued to maintain fixed rates of exchange.

government allowed the pound to float for a few months after the dollar devaluation of February 1973, it soon became apparent that an equilibrium rate of exchange had been reached at about $2.80 to one Andovian pound. The Andovian government announced in June 1973 that this new rate would be established as the official rate. Mid-State International's screening report indicated that it was safe to assume that the current rate of exchange of $2.80 to one Andovian pound ($2.80:1) would be maintained for the foreseeable future.

Recognizing that many countries closely regulate who may purchase foreign exchange, the screening report also discussed exchange availability. In Andovia, the Central Bank is responsible for the administration of the exchange control regulations. Under those regulations, permission is required to purchase US dollars with Andovian pounds for payment of loan interest, management fees, royalties, home office administration expenses and most other billings for services rendered by an overseas supplier. Moreover, even if permission to purchase foreign exchange is given, Andovia is frequently so short of foreign exchange that it is simply not available. The screening report indicated that, because of the heavy burden that the armament programme has imposed on the country's exchange reserves, applications for permission are subject to considerable delay. Furthermore, the granting of permission does not ensure that the related exchange will be available. In general, the allocation of foreign exchange is administered by the country's commercial banks and each bank can allocate to its customers only such amounts as are made available to it by the Central Bank.

Re-investment and Restrictions on Repatriation of Profit

Andovian law restricts repatriation of profits to 70 per cent of the net income, as defined by law, during a given accounting period. Thus, regardless of the actual cash flows that might be generated during any period, there is a limit on the amount that can be transferred to the parent company. Since there was nothing to indicate that there would be any change in this law, it would have the effect of forcing Mid-State International to re-invest 30 per cent of net income each year in its Andovian operation.

To satisfy this required re-investment, Mid-State International's analysis suggested that the initial plant should be smaller than actual demand requirements. Then it could use the required retained earnings to expand in later years. Between the expansion required to meet current demand and the normal demand growth, it was anticipated that there would be no difficulty in profitably employing the required investment.

Analysis of cash flows

One of the major modifications that must be made when the capital budgeting process is applied to a foreign investment is that two sets of interrelated cash flows must be analysed. Mid-State invests funds to generate cash flows that can, ultimately, be paid out as dividends to its shareholders. For domestic investments, because no restrictions are placed on the use of funds, simple *NPV* analysis of cash flows is sufficient to evaluate the project. In the case of overseas projects, attention must be given to how and when cash flows can be made available to the parent company. As we have already seen, transfers of funds may be constrained either by direct restrictions or because the host country does not have foreign exchange available.

If the earnings in country A are restricted, while the earnings in country B's currency are freely convertible to dollars and are transferable either to the parent company or to other operating units, a rate of return of 25 per cent in country A may be less desirable than a 20 per cent return in country B. Although a multinational firm is certainly concerned with the profitability of each investment, it is equally concerned with the amount of earnings that are freely convertible and transferable. Thus, the multinational firm is ultimately concerned with the present value of the *net available inflows to the parent company.*

The general procedures for cash flow analysis are the same for a foreign investment as for a domestic investment. For the foreign investment, however, there are several inflow and outflow items that are not usually associated with domestic investment. The flow involved in Mid-State's proposed cocoa processing plant investment serves both to illustrate these items and to show the interrelations between cash flows from the project and cash flows to the parent company.

Project cash inflows

The major cash inflows shown in the top section of Table 24–5 are from sales in Andovia. These sales show a rapid increase during the first three years as the operation moves towards full production; after that, projected increases in sales are closely related to the growth in population.[8] It is also anticipated that once full production is reached, any surplus over local demand will be exported. Because all foreign exchange earnings must be turned over to the Central Bank, the export sales, like all the amounts in Table 24–5, are in Andovian pounds.

Project cash outflows

The lower portion of Table 24–5 shows the expected project outflows. The projected outflows for the first year – the construction period – consist primarily of expenditures for new and used assets and costs of preparing for operations. After the first year, the major expenditures are for raw materials, labour and other normal operating expenses as outlined in the table. Since Mid-State would be expanding the capacity of the processing plant, expenditures for fixed assets would continue, but at a much lower rate.

There are two expenses that are somewhat unusual. The first is a supervisory fee – Mid-State Manufacturing Company would supply the Andovian unit with certain supervisory personnel, for a fee. The second is local taxes – in accordance with Mid-State's agreement with the Andovian government, there would be no tax liability for the first five years of operations. After that, income taxes would be paid at the normal Andovian corporate tax rate.

The final row in Table 24–5 shows the net cash receipts for each year. Cash flows are negative for the first three years, but they rise rapidly thereafter.

Parent company cash flows

If this analysis were for a domestic investment, the yearly cash flow figures obtained in Table 24–5 would be discounted at the cost of capital to arrive at a net present value figure. For a foreign proposal, however, this is only the first stage; the multinational firm must be concerned with net inflows that will be available for dividends or employment elsewhere. Since net cash flows calculated in Table 24–5 might be restricted because of various laws and regulations, it is necessary to develop a second cash flow analysis to show the unencumbered net present values that would be available to the parent company.

Inflows to the parent company would come primarily from the project's net cash flows, the figures on the bottom line of Table 24–5. The parent company would also receive

---

8. The sales figures given in Table 24–5 are expected values derived from a probability distribution that incorporates the various elements of risk associated with the project.

Table 24–5 *Andovian Cocoa Processing Plant Proposal, 10-Year Cash Flow (Thousands of Andovian Pounds).*[a]

Year	1	2	3	4	5	6	7	8	9	10
Cash inflows										
Andovian sales		22 500	47 200	72 100	76 400	78 600	81 400	83 600	86 000	88 900
Export sales				500	500	500	500	500	500	500
Terminal value										200
Total inflows		22 500	47 200	72 600	76 900	79 100	81 900	84 100	86 500	89 600
Cash outflows										
New fixed assets	2 500	178	178	178	178	178	178	178	178	178
Used equipment	1 000									
Plant expansion		200	200							
Out-of-pocket set-up costs	400	200								
Raw material		20 700	41 400	62 000	62 400	62 800	63 000	63 200	63 400	63 600
Labour costs		379	782	1 258	1 332	1 408	1 479	1 553	1 724	1 775
Sales and administrative expense		2 500	5 000	7 500	7 700	7 800	8 200	8 400	8 600	8 800
Supervisory fee		43	57	89	89	89	89	89	89	89
Local taxes							2 890	3 605	4 220	5 075
Total outflows	3 900	24 200	47 617	71 025	71 699	72 275	75 836	77 025	78 211	79 517
Net cash receipts	– 3 900	– 1 700	– 417	1 575	5 201	6 825	6 064	7 075	8 289	10 083

[a] A token terminal value of 200 Andovian pounds is used for the project.

Table 24–6 *Cash Flows Associated with Andovian Proposal (Thousands of US Dollars).*

Year	1	2	3	4	5	6	7	8	9	10
Cash inflows										
Yearly inflows from project	−10 924	−4 641	−1 008	4 661	14 817	19 366	17 235	20 067	23 467	28 492
Terminal value										500
Total inflows	−10 924	−4 641	−1 008	4 661	14 817	19 366	17 235	20 067	23 467	28 992
Cash outflows										
US income tax[a]	−200	−100	−25	2 237	7 112	9 295	117			
US tax on supervisory fee		57	76	119	119	119	119	119	119	119
Div. withholding tax[b]		42	132	225	331	438	627	735	832	1 053
Export sales loss (after tax)				800	800	800	800	800	800	800
Total outflows	−200	−1	183	3 381	8 362	10 652	1 723	1 654	1 751	1 972
Net available inflows	−10 724	−4 640	−1 191	1 280	6 455	8 714	15 512	18 413	21 716	27 020
Discount factor (10%)	0.91	0.83	0.75	0.68	0.62	0.56	0.51	0.47	0.42	0.39
Present value	−9 759	−3 851	−893	870	4 002	4 880	7 911	8 654	9 121	10 538
Cumulative net present value[c]	−9 759	−13 610	−14 503	−13 633	−9 631	−4 751	3 160	11 814	20 935	31 473

[a] US income taxes decline in the seventh year and disappear thereafter because the firm is given a credit on US taxes for payments of Andovian taxes.
[b] Tax paid to Andovian government on dividends.
[c] If the project terminates after any given year, its *NPV* will be the figure in this last row under the year in question. For example, if the project operates as projected for 10 years, its *NPV* will be $31 473 000.

supervisory fees, so total potential repatriated cash flows, shown in dollars on the top line of Table 24–6, are the sum of these two items. Note that Table 24–6 is stated in United States dollars, whereas Table 24–5 was stated in Andovian pounds.[9] A terminal value for the project is expected in year 10; this figure, added to those in row one, constitutes the tenth year cash inflow.

Offsetting these inflows, however, are the several outflows shown in the lower section of Table 24–6, the first of which is for US income tax. There is a tax liability offset for the first three years, resulting from a US tax regulation that permits Mid-State to offset the losses of the foreign subsidiary against income from its other operations. After the initial loss period, parent company income results in a US tax liability. However, this liability may be reduced by the amount of taxes paid by the subsidiary in the host country. Since, under Andovian law, Mid-State would not be required to pay any taxes for the first five years of operation, this provision would not be effective until the sixth year of the project. Other US tax liabilities that would be incurred by the parent company are also shown in Table 24–6.

Recall that after the cocoa processing reaches full production, any surplus will be sold in the export market. Since any export sales made by the Andovian operations would be, to some extent, at the expense of Mid-State's other units serving those markets, the after-tax sales losses suffered by those units should be taken into account. This factor is shown as export sales losses (after tax) in Table 24–6.

Assuming that the project works out as planned, the *NPV* for the parent company is obtained by subtracting the present value of the required outflows from the present value of the anticipated inflows. As shown in Table 24–6, cash flows are discounted at the project's estimated cost of capital to arrive at a present value figure for each year;[10] the final amounts given in the table are cumulative net present values. We see that the project, from the parent company's standpoint, is in the black in the fourth year and has broken even on a discounted cash flow basis – that is, the *NPV* is nil – during the seventh year.

PROBLEMS FACED BY MULTINATIONAL FIRMS

Mid-State's board of directors must give final approval for all capital expenditures in excess of $1 million; since the Andovian project fell into this category, the board had to approve it before the project could be undertaken. Robert Harris, who is president of Mid-State International, and several members of his staff were requested to attend the board's budget meeting in order to answer any questions that might be raised.

During the discussion on the project, Everett Anderson, one of the board members, mentioned that he had just finished reading a survey of 166 international executives who had been asked to list the problems that concerned them most. The consequences of both foreign and domestic government actions, which most of those surveyed saw as beyond their control, were uppermost in their minds. Anderson, to demonstrate that this fear of foreign government action was certainly a legitimate concern, cited the nationalizations that had taken place in Peru and Chile, and the restrictions on foreign businesses being formulated by other South American countries. Specifically, Anderson wondered whether the Andovian government, although it presently had no intention of nationalizing any foreign firms, might not do so in the future if this was deemed to be in the Andovian public

9. The official rate of exchange established by the Andovian government was $2.8011:£1, and this is the rate used to calculate the cash inflow amounts used in Table 24–6.

10. A cost of capital of 10 per cent was used on the assumption that 10 per cent is the overall company cost of capital and that this project carries about the same risk as the average investment of the company. If the investment were considered to be more risky, then a higher discount rate should be used.

interest. He went on to say that if nationalization should occur, all of Mid-State's carefully developed cash flow analyses would be useless.

President Harris agreed that since nationalization appeared to be on the rise throughout the world, there was always some risk that a country might decide to nationalize foreign firms. He pointed out, however, that Andovia had recently emphasized its intention of adhering to international law and had promised to pay prompt and adequate compensation if it should ever nationalize a foreign firm. He added that, as long as Mid-State made a net contribution to the Andovian economy, the likelihood of nationalization was relatively small.

Harris explained his position, noting that in some cases host countries do have reasons for being unhappy with foreign businesses: when an industry is controlled from outside, the host country may pay quite a price. For one thing, if exhaustible natural resources such as minerals or oil are involved, the primary wealth of the host nation may be drained off without regard for the local economy. Further, the host country may lose tax revenue because the foreign corporation can report lower profits by manipulating transfer prices between subsidiaries. Also, when the parent company uses its financial network to pull money out of a country with balance of payment problems, or to move money into one struggling to reduce inflation, then the host government rightfully feels that it is losing control over its domestic economy. In addition, if a company uses its international flexibility to re-route a subsidiary's purchases through some other country, then it may cause a sudden drop in the host country's exports. Harris stated that, finally, a country's economy can be upset if a foreign company suddenly decides to pull out, as several had done in Europe because they had over-invested and wanted to consolidate their operations.

Here Bronson, the chairman of the board, entered the discussion to add that it was company policy to maintain good relations with its host governments, and the cocoa processing plant would make several major contributions towards that end. In the first place, according to Bronson, building a large plant and starting a new industry would benefit Andovia's economy in output, employment and expanded tax revenues. Second, since Mid-State would introduce more advanced equipment than was presently being used, local labour skills would be upgraded. Since Mid-State planned to train local administrators for almost all positions, management talent would be increased. Bronson held that of great importance was the fact that Mid-State would provide Andovian consumers with a better and cheaper product.

To summarize the discussion, Harris pointed out that the presence of foreign businesses could have both advantages and disadvantages for a host country. He felt that the issue was not which side was right or wrong but, rather, whether the two parties could work together to arrive at a mutually beneficial arrangement. He felt that the best way to counter nationalism was to demonstrate that the investment would make a net contribution to the host country's economy. Harris reminded the group that the Andovian government had been first to suggest the project. Since then, there had been several meetings with various Andovian government agencies, and Mid-State had agreed to consult with them on any decision that could adversely affect their country. Harris concluded that, although there was certainly no way to be sure that the situation would remain stable, at the present time nationalization did not appear to be a problem. Still, he did concede that in the analysis of the Andovian project, Mid-State had not given much weight to the possibility of nationalization when developing the estimated cash flows.[11]

Another board member, Jan Merriam, vice-president of Mid-State's New York bank, spoke up. He pointed out that many countries had recently experienced devaluation.

---

11. The values given in Tables 24–5 and 24–6 are expected values determined from probability distributions of cash flows. The probability of nationalization, and of the losses in this event, was given a low weight in the analysis.

Although the report on the Andovian project mentioned that the official position of the government was to maintain the present exchange, it also stated that foreign exchange had been in short supply recently. He said that it had been Merriam's experience that a short supply of foreign exchange often preceded devaluation, and he wanted to know if a full investigation of the Andovian situation had been made.

In reply, Harris explained that as a result of some unanticipated devaluations in the first year of foreign operations, Mid-State International had developed a devaluation monitoring procedure that, under normal circumstances, is applied on a monthly basis to each country in which the firm has operations. For potentially troublesome areas, the procedure is repeated more frequently either until the trouble has passed or until action has been taken to minimize the loss. The devaluation monitoring procedure consists, basically, of a constant examination of several items that are often indicators of currency weakness: inflation, balance of trade, balance of payments, deficits in the national budget, trends in interest rates, the international reserve position and foreign exchange quotations.

Harris assured the board members that Andovia had been subjected to the same examination as other countries. It had been determined that, while there was a shortage of foreign exchange and a trade deficit until recently, most of the problems could be attributed to the civil war of three years ago. Improvement had been made in the balance of trade, and for each of the last two years there had been a small net increase in Andovia's international reserve position. In addition, the rate of inflation had been rather low, at about 2 to 3 per cent, and the government had been successful in its efforts to hold down budget deficits. With the new petroleum tax decreed in 1970, and with the foreign exchange savings anticipated from import substitutions, it was most probable that the situation would continue to improve. Nevertheless, a close watch over the condition would be maintained.

Harris was also questioned about the steps that were taken when the devaluation monitoring procedure indicated that a given currency was vulnerable to devaluation. Before he could answer, Don March, manager of the research division and a new member of the board, asked a more fundamental question: how would an Andovian devaluation hurt Mid-State Manufacturing? Harris replied that there would be two effects. First, the cash flows (shown in Table 24–5) were stated in Andovian pounds. These pounds were converted to dollars at the currrent rate of 2.80 dollars to 1 pound. If the Andovian pound were devalued, fewer dollars could be obtained for each pound, so the dollar value of the Andovian project would be reduced. The second effect of devaluation follows directly from the first: recognizing that a foreign subsidiary is only a collection of 'projects', and that the value to the parent of all projects declines when a devaluation occurs, the accounting profession requires an immediate write-down to reflect the effect of the devaluation.

To illustrate the second effect, suppose that devaluation reduced the value of the Andovian pound in relation to the dollar by 50 per cent, causing the exchange rate to drop from \$2.80:£1 to\$1.40:£1. Further, assume that the Andovian company was financed entirely by Mid-State – that is, the Andovian subsidiary has no debt, only equity, and the equity is all owned by the parent company. Although the devaluation would have no effect on the balance sheet of the Andovian subsidiary, the parent company's consolidated balance sheet is stated in dollars, so that portion of consolidated assets represented by the subsidiary, as well as the consolidated net worth, would have to be reduced. The reduction in net worth is a loss and must be reported as a reduction of earnings by the parent. For example, if the subsidiary had assets with a value of 1 million pounds, or 2.8 million dollars, and a 50 per cent devaluation occurred, the parent would have to report a loss of \$1.4 million from devaluation during the year in which devaluation occurred. This could, of course, have a drastic effect on earnings per share if foreign operations were important and if the devaluation was a large one.

Harris hastened to explain that most subsidiaries are not 100 per cent equity financed – most buy supplies and materials locally and, hence, have trade creditors, and many also have long-term debt outstanding. In these cases, creditors bear part of the decline in asset value in the sense that although the liability in pounds is not reduced, the dollar value of the liability is reduced; this partly offsets the decline in asset dollar value. As a result, the parent company's write-down and loss are limited to its equity position. He went on to point out that, while this is *roughly* what happens, the accounting is actually considerably more complex.[12] He was about to explain these details when March stopped him, saying that he felt he now understood the general nature of the problem and doubted if he would be able to grasp the details. He did, however, wonder what could be done if devaluation appeared imminent.

Harris stated that in such cases the company attempted to accelerate funds flows to the parent, and to take on liabilities payable in local currencies, in order to minimize the danger of losses. In the Andovian case, not very much could be done along those lines, but since Harris felt there was little danger of devaluation, he thought the possibility of devaluation losses should not stand in the way of accepting the project.

At this point, Bronson noted that Mid-State had a $15 million reserve set up for devaluation losses. Thus, if such a loss occurred, it would be charged against the reserve, and current reported earnings would be penalized only if the write-off exceeded $15 million.

Jan Merriam, the banker on the board who had first brought up the topic of devaluation, re-entered the conversation, noting that it was the United States that had twice devalued the dollar with the result that the major trading nations were allowing their currencies to float. Merriam then quizzed Harris as to what action, if any, Mid-State was taking to prevent losses that could arise from changes in the floating rates. Harris readily admitted that the company had little experience in this field but that since March 1973, when the float was put into effect, the 'forward market' had been used several times to hedge certain international transactions. As an example, Harris described a recent contract to purchase machinery made in Germany for delivery six months hence for the equivalent of $200 000 in marks. To lock the dollar price of this machinery, the company had simply purchased a six-month forward contract for marks at a dollar price only slightly higher than the current dollar-to-mark exchange rate. Harris explained that, although there was a slight cost involved, the use of the forward market effectively reduced the risk involved with floating exchange rates.

Following this explanation, Merriam and several other directors began to discuss the current international monetary situation and how the trends might affect Mid-State's overseas operations. During this discussion one of the directors pointed out that the International Monetary Fund meeting in September 1973 had as its main topic international monetary reforms. Merriam noted that as a result of this meeting, it was clear that the direction of future reforms would be towards re-establishment of a modified fixed-rate system, one with a semi-automatic exchange procedure determined by some indicator such as a country's foreign exchange reserves or balance of payments surplus or deficit. Merriam cautioned, however, that it would take some time for the details to be worked out and that implementation of any such reforms would take even longer to analyse.

After these comments, Chairman Bronson moved that the board vote to approve the Andovian project. The motion was seconded, and the project received the board's unanimous approval.

---

12. A method for determining 'exposure' to devaluation is contained in *Hedging Foreign Exchange Risks*, Management Monograph No. 49, published by *Business International*.

FINANCING THE PROJECT

Once the project was approved, Bronson asked Harris to outline his financing plans. Since the board had to approve any external financing that involved issues in excess of $1 million, Bronson felt that time would be saved by clearing that point up immediately.

Harris outlined the following: plant construction and equipment costs for the project are estimated at $10 million, with another $7million required for working capital, or $17 million in total. The Andovian Industrial Development Bank will make a loan of $1.5 million, and two local commercial banks will jointly lend another $1.5 million. Mid-State will supply $5 million of new equipment for which it will accept an 8 per-cent note; the Andovian government agrees that the interest payment on the note will in no way affect the allowable remittance of earnings.[13] Mid-State will also be permitted to supply, as part of its investment, $3 million worth of used equipment. Since there is no effective capital market in Andovia, the remaining $6 million will have to come from other sources. In accordance with Mid-State's policy of further development of international sources of funds, Harris proposed that the final $6 million be raised in the Euro-currency market.

Although Euro-dollar[14] loans were currently available at about 9 per cent, well below their 1969–70 high of 11 per cent, Euro-bond rates were also very advantageous. Harris noted that one US company had just sold a German mark denominated Euro-bond issue with a yield of 7.26 per cent. He felt that the Andovian subsidiary could float an issue at about the same rate if it were denominated in German marks and guaranteed by the parent company. A Mid-State issue in the US would probably carry an $8\frac{1}{2}$ per cent rate. Thus, it was clear that Euro-bonds were less costly at the present time. Following a lengthy discussion of the capital restrictions prevailing in European countries and how they would effect a bond issue, the board approved a $3 million Euro-dollar loan to finance working capital and a Euro-bond issue of 7.3 million German marks (equivalent to $3 million) to finance the remaining requirements. Then, with the project approved and the financing settled, the board adjourned.

QUESTIONS

24–1. If it were known that Andovia's head of state was leaning toward a Cuban alliance, what effect might this have on the expected profitability of Mid-State's Andovian project?

24–2. Do you think that a discount rate of 10 per cent is appropriate for each year of the Andovian project's life? Why?

---

13. An intercompany loan has an advantage over an equity investment in that it is unaffected by remittance restrictions and will return the full principal at maturity. Therefore, this aspect of Harris' plan overcame the 30 per cent freeze on earnings imposed by the Andovian government. Of course, Andovia realized this too, and consequently restricted the extent of intercompany loan financing.

14. A 'Euro-dollar' is a US dollar deposited in a European bank, frequently a European branch of a US bank. If a US firm buys goods from a European firm, it pays in dollars, and these dollars can be placed in an interest-bearing account in a European bank. The bank can lend these dollars in the Euro-dollar market. Many US firms, attracted by the high interest rates paid on Euro-dollar deposits, shifted funds to Europe in the late 1960s. (US banks were restricted in the amount of interest they could pay on corporate time deposits or on certificates of deposit; this stimulated the flow of funds to Europe.) US firms (as well as many US banks) in need of funds, on the other hand, borrowed heavily in the Euro-dollar market when their traditional sources of funds in the US dried up in the monetary squeeze of the late 1960s. The Euro-dollar market is, currently, an alternative for both US firms with surplus cash seeking investments and US firms needing loans. The Euro-dollar market is a prime example of the internationalization of business and finance in recent years.

24–3. How does Mid-State take account of uncertainty in the Andovian project example? What alternatives might it consider?

24–4. What factors are responsible for the difference between the cash flow of Mid-State's Andovian subsidiary and the cash flow to the parent firm?

24–5. In what ways might it benefit the parent company *not* to own 100 per cent of the foreign subsidiary's Ordinary shares?

24–6. How useful is the Andovian 'tax holiday' to Mid-State?

24–7. If all markets were 'free', that is, if there were no trade restrictions such as import and export quotas and tariffs, would this tend to stimulate or retard the development of overseas subsidiaries vis-à-vis branches of a domestic firm?

24–8. In 1971, West Germany allowed its currency to 'float' upwards in value in relation to the United States dollar. By December 1971, its relative value had increased about 12 per cent. What effect would you expect this to have on US firms with large foreign investments in Germany?

PROBLEMS

24–1. The Overseas Manufacturing Company, a wholly owned subsidiary of a UK firm, operates in the country of Panagua. Panagua's balance of payments situation has deteriorated, and there has been talk of a possible devaluation. The latest balance sheet for the subsidiary is given below:

Overseas Manufacturing Company, Balance Sheet (in Pounds).

Ordinary share capital and retained earnings	£430 000	Fixed assets	£300 000
Long-term loan	200 000	Stocks	200 000
Trade creditors	100 000	Trade debtors	150 000
Accrued expenses	50 000	Quoted investments	100 000
Short-term loan	50 000	Cash	80 000
Total claims	£830 000	Total assets	£830 000

(a) Before devaluation, the assets and liabilities of Overseas are simply added to those of the parent and its other subsidiaries to develop the consolidated balance sheet. Now assume that Panagua devalues its currency by 20 per cent. What adjustments would have to be made to the sterling value of the accounts when the consolidated statement is made? (Note: the value of the long-term liability would not be reduced, since this is a monetary liability.) What effect would this have on the parent company's reported profits?

(b) Assume (i) that fixed assets are imported capital goods whose prices rise to offset the devaluation, and (ii) that 50 per cent of the stock items are imported components whose prices similarly rise to offset the devaluation. Under these conditions, would the adjustments made in part (a) be 'realistic'? If not, what do you feel would be a realistic value for the net write-down?

(c) If Panagua had revalued its currency upwards, or if the UK had devalued the pound by 20 per cent, what would have happened (i) immediately to the parent company's books, and (ii) to cash flows from the subsidiary to the parent over the next few years?

SELECTED REFERENCES

Albach, Horst. The development of the capital structure of German companies. *Journal of Business Finance and Accounting* 2 (Autumn 1975): 281–294.

Al-Dakheil, Abdulaziz and Wassink, Darwin. Oil and the international finance system. *Business Horizons* 20 (April 1977): 69–73.

Anderson, Gerald L. International project financing. *Financial Executive* 45 (May 1977): 40–45.

Baker, James C. and Bates, Thomas H. *Financing International Business Operations.* Scranton, Pa.: Intext Educational Publishers, 1971.

Bowditch, Richard L. and Burtle, James L. The corporate treasurer in a world of floating exchange rates. In *The Treasurer's Handbook*, J. Fred Weston and Maurice B. Goudzwaard, eds. Homewood, Illinois: Dow Jones-Irwin, 1976, pp. 84–112.

Davis, Steven I. How risky is international lending? *Harvard Business Review* 55 (January–February 1977): 135–143.

Denis, Jack, Jr. How to hedge foreign currency risk. *Financial Analysts' Journal* 32 (January–February 1976): 50–54.

Dufey, Gunter. Corporate finance and exchange rate variations. *Financial Management* 1 (Summer 1972): 51–57.

Eiteman, David K. and Stonehill, Arthur I. *Multinational Business Finance.* Menlo Park, Calif.: Addison-Wesley Publishing Company, 1973.

Folks, William R. Jr. Decision analysis for exchange risk management. *Financial Management* 1 (Winter 1972): 101–112

Folks, William R., J. and Stansell, Stanley R. The use of discriminant analysis in forecasting exchange rate movements. *Journal of International Business Studies* 6 (Spring 1975): 33–50.

Fouraker, L. and Stopford, J. Organization structure and the multinational strategy. *Administrative Science Quarterly* (June 1968).

Frank, Peter and Young, Allan. Stock price reaction of multinational firms to exchange realignments. *Financial Management* 1 (Winter 1972): 66–73.

Giddy, Ian H. An integrated theory of exchange rate equilibrium. *Journal of Financial and Quantitative Analysis* 11 (December 1976): 883–892.

Hackett, John T. New financial strategies for the MNC. *Business Horizons* 15 (April 1975): 13–20.

Hagemann, Helmut. Anticipate your long-term foreign exchange risks. *Harvard Business Review* 55 (March–April 1977): 81–88.

Hodgson, Ralphael W. and Uyterhoeven, Hugo. Analyzing foreign investment opportunities. *Harvard Business Review* (March–April 1962).

Imai, Yutaka. Exchange rate risk protection in international business. *Journal of Financial and Quantitative Analysis* 10 (September 1975): 447–456.

Jucker, James V. and de Faro, Clovis. The selection of international borrowing sources. *Journal of Financial and Quantitative Analysis* 10 (September 1975): 381–407.

Lessard, Donald R. World, national, and industry factors in equity returns. *Journal of Finance* 29 (May 1974): 379–391.

Lillich, Richard B. *The Protection of Foreign Investment.* Syracuse, N.Y.: Syracuse University Press, 1965.

Mueller, Gerhard G. *International Accounting.* New York: Macmillan, 1967.

Nehrt, Lee Charles. *The Political Climate for Private Foreign Investment.* New York: Praeger, 1970.

Ness, Walter L. Jr. A linear programming approach to financing the multinational corporation. *Financial Management* 1 (Winter 1972): 88–100.

Obersteiner, Erich. Should the foreign affiliate remit dividends or reinvest? *Financial Management* 2 (Spring 1973): 88–93.

Petty, J. William, II and Walker, Ernest W. Optimal transfer pricing for the multinational firm. *Financial Management* 1 (Winter 1972): 74–87.

Remmers, Lee, Stonehill, Arthur, Wright, Richard and Beekhuisen, Theo. Industry and size as debt ratio determinants in manufacturing internationally. *Financial Management* 3 (Summer 1974): 24–32.

Robbins, Sidney M. and Stobaugh, Robert B. Financing foreign affiliates. *Financial Management* 1(Winter 1972): 56–65.

Rodriguez, Rita M. FASB no. 8: what has it done to us? *Financial Analysts' Journal* 33 (March–April 1977): 40–47.

Rodriguez, Rita M. Management of foreign exchange risk in the U.S. multinationals. *Journal of Financial and Quantitative Analysis* 9 (November 1974): 849–857.

Rodriguez, Rita M. and Carter, E. Eugene. *International Financial Management.* Englewood Cliffs, New Jersey: Prentice-Hall, Inc., 1976.

Rolfe, Sidney E. and Damm, Walter, eds. *The Multinational Corporation in the World Economy.* New York: Praeger, 1970.

Shapiro, Alan C. Evaluating financing costs for multinational subsidiaries. *Journal of International Business Studies* 6 (Fall 1975): 25–32.

Shapiro, Alan C. Exchange rate changes, inflation, and the value of the multinational corporation. *Journal of Finance* 30 (May 1975): 485–502.

Shapiro, Alan C. International cash management – the determination of multicurrency cash balances. *Journal of Financial and Quantitative Analysis* 11 (December 1976): 893–900.

Shapiro, Alan C. and Rutenbert, David P. Managing exchange risks in a floating world. *Financial Management* 5 (Summer 1976): 48–58.

Smith, Don T. Financial variables in international business. *Harvard Business Review* (January – February 1966).

Solnik, B. H. The international pricing of risk: an empirical investigation of the world capital market structure. *Journal of Finance* 29 (May 1974): 365–378.

Stonehill, Arthur, Beekhuisen, Theo, Wright, Richard, Remmers, Lee, Toy, Norman, Pares, Antonio, Shapiro, Alan, Egan, Douglas and Bates, Thomas. Financial goals and debt ratio determinants: a survey of practice in five countries. *Financial Management* 4 (Autumn 1975): 27–41.

Teck, Alan. Control your exposure to foreign exchange. *Harvard Business Review* 52 (January–February 1974): 66–75.

Verroen, John. How ITT manages its foreign exchange. *Management Services* (January–February 1965).

Voupel, James W. and Curhan, Joan P. *The Making of Multinational Enterprise.* Boston: Harvard Business School, Division of Research, 1969.

Weston, J. Fred and Sorge, Bart W. *International Managerial Finance.* Homewood, Ill.: Irwin, 1972, pp. xv and 388.

Weston, J. Fred and Sorge, Bart W. *Guide to International Financial Management.* New York: McGraw-Hill Book Company, 1977.

Zenoff, David B. and Zwick, Jack. *International Finance Management.* Englewood Cliffs, N.J.: Prentice-Hall, 1969.

Appendix A to Chapter 24:

Export Finance

During the nineteenth century Britain developed a trading system that enabled her to obtain raw materials and primary products at relatively low prices in return for finished manufactured goods. Most of Britain's trade in the nineteenth century and the early part of the twentieth century was with other members of the Empire (later the Commonwealth). In the last 40 years Britain has found that:

1. the terms of trade (the prices at which exports are sold and imports are bought) have moved decisively against the developed nations and in favour of the underdeveloped nations. The quadrupling of the price of oil is only the most striking incidence of this development; sharp rises in the prices of coffee and sugar are other examples of this phenomenon;
2. there has been a movement away from traditional markets and towards new, untried, risky markets. In particular, trade with underdeveloped countries outside the Commonwealth has grown. The risk of non-payment in these markets is seen by many exporters to be greater than the risk which operated in Britain's traditional markets;
3. trade between developed countries has grown since the Second World War. The entry of Brtain into the European Economic Community in 1972 led to an acceleration of this trend. By 1975 almost half of Britain's total exports were made to countries in Western Europe (see Table 24A–1).

Table 24A–1[a] *The Changing Pattern of Britain's Exports.*

	1955	1975
Total UK exports (£m)	£3074	£19 922
Commonwealth	38.4 %	16.3 %
North America	11.4 %	11.7 %
Western Europe	32.2 %	49.1 %
Oil producers	4.4 %	11.4 %
Developing countries	29.9 %	14.7 %
UK exports as a percentage of total world exports	9 %	5 %

[a] Committee to Review the Functioning of Financial Institutions. *Evidence of the Financing of Industry and Trade*, vol. 3.

FINANCE FOR EXPORTS

The authorities have encouraged companies to export goods in many ways since the Second World War. In the immediate post-war period, when all applications to make new issues of capital had to be approved by the

Capital Issues Committee of the Treasury, issues made by firms who exported a high proportion of their finished goods were more favourably considered than were those made by firms selling mainly to the domestic market. Banks have been encouraged to make loans to firms requiring finance for exports, and often, when there has been a 'credit squeeze', banks have been required to restrict their lending to all customers except those requiring funds to finance their exporting activities. The use of bills of exchange[1] has increased in recent years for both domestic and overseas purposes. This expansion in the use of bill finance has been caused by the increasing use of controls over the lending practices of the banking system by the Bank of England, and by the expansion in world trade that has taken place since the Second World War.

The Export Credits Guarantees Department

The most significant institution in the field of export finance is the Export Credit Guarantees Department (ECGD) which was created by the government in 1919. Initially, the department simply provided insurance cover against a buyer's insolvency or default. ECGD provided insurance cover for 8 per cent of British exports in 1947 and now it is responsible for insuring 35 per cent of all British exports.

By means of unconditional guarantees to British banks, ECGD makes finance available to exporters who need to offer credit to overseas buyers. Whilst ECGD does not itself provide finance direct to exporters, it has played an increasingly significant role in the provision of finance through the clearing banks. Much of the finance provided by the clearing banks can be made available only because of the support of ECGD.

In recent years ECGD has developed a range of direct guarantees to banks providing export finance and these now extend over the whole field of export finance. If the credit period is less than two years and the financing instrument is either a promissory note or a bill of exchange, ECGD may give an unconditional guarantee to the exporter's bank that it will pay 100 per cent of any sum three months overdue. ECGD agrees a limit for the finance it will guarantee, based on its experience with the exporter and the exporter's general financial standing. To operate the scheme the exporter need only present the notes of bills to his bank after shipment of the goods, with the appropriate evidence (shipping documents or a buyers' certificate of performance) and a warranty that he has full insurance cover for the transaction from ECGD.

Much trade is financed without recourse to promissory notes or bills of exchange. Provided that the period for which credit is required is less than six months, ECGD will give a guarantee to the financing bank on lines similar to the bill guarantee. A limit for the finance guaranteed is agreed by ECGD.

Similar facilities are available for contracts requiring credit for two years or more. In this case, however, each contract is considered separately. A separate recourse agreement between ECGD and the exporter is made for each contract in order to safeguard ECGD in the event of its paying under the bank's guarantee amounts that would not have been paid under the exporter's policy.

For major projects exporters may arrange loans to buyers. These *buyer credit* guarantees are available to banks making such loans provided that the contracts are worth £1 million or more. Many exporters find that this method of financing is more appropriate for their business because progress payments can be made at intermediate stages of manufacture in the same way that such payments are made in building contracts. The buyer is normally expected to pay a deposit of 20 per cent of the contract price on signing the contract.

New facilities

In recent years ECGD has introduced new facilities to assist exporters involved in large overseas projects.

Performance bonds

If a contract is worth £1 million or more, ECGD is willing to give indemnity to a bank or other financial institution which wishes to issue such bonds. By February the department had issued 33 such guarantees involving contracts totalling £370 million.[2] This facility has been provided for two reasons:

1. Government buyers, in the Middle East in particular, have sought guarantees from suppliers.
2. As contract values have risen and company liquidity problems have become more common, the capacity of the United Kingdom market to issue the required bonds has been questioned.

---

1. The nature and operation of bill finance was discussed in Chapter 7.
2. Committee to Review the Functioning of Financial Institutions. *Evidence on the Financing of Industry and Trade*, vol. 3.

Cover against unfair calling of bonds

If a bond is issued *without* ECGD support and the exporter finds that the bond has been called (that is, the buyer does not consider the contract to have been adequately carried out and the bank or other financial institution insists on immediate repayment of the bond), unfairly, it seems ECGD will reimburse the exporter for 100 per cent of the value of the bond. It must be shown that the exporter was not in default in his performance of the contract and that any failure on his part was due to circumstances beyond his control.

Insolvency cover

If a member of a consortium operating overseas becomes insolvent, British members of that consortium may be subjected to heavy losses. ECGD is willing to insure main contractors in consortiums engaged in projects worth £20 million or more for up to 90 per cent of any losses caused by the insolvency of a sub-contractor or fellow consortium member.

Pre-shipment finance

If an exporter is having difficulty in raising finance for overseas capital projects valued at £1 million or more and involving a manufacturing period of at least one year, ECGD will consider issuing a pre-shipment finance guarantee. The total cost to the exporter is slightly more than that of normal overdraft finance. The department has issued seven guarantees in connection with contracts to a total of £380 million.[3]

These facilities have been introduced in order to deal with the special problems of exporters of large capital goods or those exporters who are involved in overseas projects which have a high value and a long manufacturing period.

QUESTIONS

24A–1. What have been the effects on the direction of British trade of the increase in the prices of primary products such as oil and coffee in recent years?

24A–2. What has been the effect on British trade of British membership of the European Economic Community?

24A–3. What is the purpose of ECGD direct guarantees to banks providing export finance?

24A–4. What do you understand by buyer credit guarantees?

24A–5. Why has ECGD found it necessary to introduce new facilities to assist exporters involved in large capital projects overseas?

SELECTED REFERENCES

British Overseas Trade Board. *Export Handbook*.

Committee to Review the Functioning of Financial Institutions. *Evidence on the Financing of Industry and Trade*, vol. 3.

---

3. Committee to Review the Functioning of Financial Institutions. *Evidence on the Financing of Industry and Trade*, vol. 3.

Chapter 25

Financial Management in the Small Firm[1]

Small firms are a key element of the United Kingdom economy. First, of the approximately 1.4 million firms in private industry and commerce in the UK, about one million are defined as 'small'. These 'small' firms employ almost five million people and produce around 16 per cent of gross national product. Thus, small businesses are quantitatively important. Second, and of perhaps even greater significance, small businesses often serve as the vehicle through which ideas for new products and services make their way to the consuming public. Many of the large electronics firms of the 1970s were new, small businesses in the 1950s. Third, the very existence of small businesses, and the fact that new ones are continually being started, serve to increase competition and to retard monopoly.

In some respects, there is no need to study small business finance as a separate topic – the same general principles apply to large and small firms alike. However, small firms face a somewhat different set of problems than larger businesses, and the goals of a small firm are likely to be oriented towards the aspirations of an individual entrepreneur rather than towards investors in general. Also, the characteristics of the money and capital markets create both problems and opportunities for small firms and specialized financial institutions exist to help small firms with their financing problems. For all these reasons, a chapter focusing directly on the small firm is useful in a book on financial management.

DEFINITION OF A 'SMALL FIRM'

It is impossible to provide a single definition which encompasses all those firms which might be considered 'small'. For instance, a small firm in the manufacturing industry is

1. The authors wish to acknowledge the assistance of D. A. Woolard and E. W. Jenks of the Small Business Administration in the preparation of this chapter.

defined as one employing fewer than 200 persons, whereas in the construction industry a firm employing 200 people would be considered one of the major firms in the industry. Any quantitative definition of 'smallness' would suffer from the same problem of lack of universal applicability. Different definitions have been produced for application to specific industries, however, such as the manufacturing industry mentioned above. Other definitions relate to size of turnover, as in retailing, or to number of vehicles owned, as in road haulage.

When undertaking their survey into financial facilities for small firms, the Economists Advisory Group found themselves unable to employ the definitions of 'smallness' adopted by the Bolton Committee and agreed instead to the industrial definitions based on net assets and turnover, as shown in Table 25–1.

Table 25–1 *Definition of 'Smallness' Adopted by the Economists Advisory Group.*

Industry classification	Maximum size Net assets £	Turnover £
Manufacturing industry	250 000	500 000
Retail distribution	20 000	50 000
Wholesaling	50 000	200 000
Construction	50 000	100 000
Mining and quarrying	50 000	100 000
Road transport	20 000	40 000
Motor trades (garages, etc.)	50 000	100 000
Hotels and catering etc.	50 000	100 000
Miscellaneous	20 000	50 000

Source: *Financial Facilities for Small Firms*: a study by the Economists Advisory Group. Committee of Inquiry into Small Firms. London: HMSO 1971, Research report No. 4.

ALTERNATIVE FORMS OF BUSINESS ORGANIZATION

From a technical and legal standpoint, there are three major forms of business organization: the sole proprietorship, the partnership, and the registered company.[2] In terms of numbers, about 56 per cent of business firms are operated as sole proprietorships, while the remainder are equally divided between partnerships and companies. In the remainder of this section we describe and compare the characteristics of these alternative forms of business organization.

Sole proprietorship

A proprietorship is a business owned by one individual. To go into business as a single proprietor is very simple – a person merely begins business operations.

The proprietorship has key advantages for small operations. It is easily and inexpensively formed. No formal charter for operations is required, and a proprietorship is subject to fewer government regulations than are limited companies. Further, it pays no corporate taxes, although all earnings of the firm are subject to personal income taxes, whether they are re-invested in the business or withdrawn.

2. Other less common forms of organizations include joint stock companies and co-operatives.

The proprietorship also has important limitations. Most significant is its inability to obtain large sums of capital. Further, the proprietor has unlimited personal liability for his business debts: the creditors may look to both his business assets and the proprietor's personal assets to satisfy their claims. Finally, the proprietorship is limited to the life of the individual who created it: it has no separate legal identity apart from the owner. For all of these reasons, the individual proprietorship is limited primarily to small business operations. However, businesses are frequently started as proprietorships and then converted to corporate status whenever their growth causes the disadvantages of the proprietorship form to outweigh its advantages.

Partnership

When two or more persons associate to conduct a business enterprise, a partnership is said to exist. A partnership may operate under different degrees of formality, ranging from an informal oral understanding up to a written partnership agreement. Like the proprietorship, the partnership has the advantages of ease and economy of formation, as well as freedom from certain governmental regulations, and partnership profits are taxed as personal income in proportion to the partners' claims whether they are distributed to them or not.

One of the advantages of the partnership over the proprietorship is that it makes possible a pooling of various types of resources. Some partners may contribute particular skills or contacts, while others may contribute funds. However, there are practical limits to the number of co-partners who can join in an enterprise without destructive conflict, so partnership agreements provide that a partner cannot transfer his share in the business unless all the partners agree to accept the new partner or partners.

If a new partner comes into the business, the old partnership ceases to exist and a new one is created. The withdrawal or death of any one of the partners also dissolves the partnership. To prevent disputes under such circumstances, the articles of the partnership agreement should include terms and conditions under which assets are to be distributed upon dissolution. Of course, dissolution of the partnership does not necessarily mean the end of the business – the remaining partners may simply buy the assets of the one who died or otherwise left the firm. To avoid financial pressures caused by the death of one of the partners, it is a common practice for each partner to carry life insurance naming the remaining partners as his beneficiaries. The proceeds of such a policy may then be used to buy out the investment of the deceased partner.

Several drawbacks stemming from the characteristics of the partnership limit its use. They include impermanence, difficulties of transferring ownership, and unlimited liability. partners, it is a common practice for each partner to carry life insurance naming the under partnership law, the partners are jointly and separately liable for business debts. This means that if any partner is unable to meet the claims on him resulting from the liquidation of the partnership, the remaining partners must take over the unsatisfied claims, drawing on their personal assets if necessary.[3]

Registered companies[4]

A company is regarded as a legal person separate and distinct from those other persons

---

3. However, it is possible to limit the liabilities of certain partners by establishing a *limited partnership*, wherein certain partners are designated *general partners* and others *limited partners*.
4. A registered company may be a company limited by shares, a company limited by guarantee, or an unlimited company. The vast majority of registered companies are companies limited by shares.

who are its shareholders and directors. This separateness of legal identity gives the company four major advantages over partnerships and proprietorships:

1. It has an unlimited life; it can continue in existence after its original owners and managers are dead.
2. It allows for separate corporate liability; the company contracts in its own name and the shareholders are not usually personally liable for the debts and contracts of the company.[5]
3. It permits easy transferability of ownership interest in the firm, as ownership interests can be divided into shares which can be transferred far more easily than partnership interests.
4. The liability of a member of a registered company to contribute to its own assets may be limited; in the case of a company limited by shares, to the amount unpaid on the shares.

While a proprietorship or a partnership can commence operations without much paper work, the registration of a company involves a complicated, but routinized, process. The following documents must be presented to the Register of Companies:

1. A memorandum of association. This document states the objects of the company, and, if it is a company limited by shares, the proposed amount of share capital and its division into shares of a fixed amount.
2. Articles of association. This is a document which regulates the affairs of members between themselves and covers such matters as the transfer of shares, the holding of meetings and the powers of directors.
3. A list of the proposed directors, plus particulars relating to other directorships held and their addresses.
4. A statement of the nominal share capital plus payment of the relevant stamp duty.
5. A declaration by the company solicitor that compliance has been made with the requirements of the Companies Act in respect of registration.
6. Notice of the address of the company's registered office.

The memorandum of association defines the powers of the company in relation to its external environment. It explains the purposes for which the company has been formed and states the capital available to perform these. Defining the objectives of the company is very important since companies may be liable to be wound up if, in the opinion of the court, their main purpose no longer exists. The articles of association is the document which regulates the internal rights of the members of the company. Major points dealt with in the articles include appointment and removal of directors, voting rights of shareholders, dividend rights, borrowing powers of the company, and audit of the accounts.

ECONOMIC ASPECTS OF FIRM SIZE

Average firm size varies from industry to industry; breweries, motor-car manufacturers and chemical firms tend to be large, while hotel businesses, restaurants and many types of retail firms tend to be small, although there are exceptions. As a result, breweries, motor-car manufacturers and chemical industries are relatively concentrated (oligopolistic), while even the largest hotel, restaurant, or retail operation has no more than a small percentage of its industry's sales.

---

5. In the case of small companies, the limited liability feature is often a fiction, as bank managers frequently require personal guarantees from the shareholders of small, weak businesses.

Why do these differences exist? Perhaps the most obvious reason relates to the extent of economies of scale in the industry: if the cost per unit produced and sold declines up to a high level of output, then firms will tend to be large. However, if costs in an industry decline only over a small range of outputs, then turn up, firms in the industry will tend to be small. Motor cars, beer and chemicals are produced more efficiently in large, integrated factories, and distribution costs are lowest if the firms can employ broad-based distribution systems and engage in nationwide advertising campaigns using national media. Certain types of retail shops or restaurants, on the other hand, are most efficiently operated as smaller, locally owned concerns.

Figure 25–1 depicts the long-run average cost curves in two industries, A and B. For various reasons, costs in industry A turn up at a relatively small output, so if firms are to be efficient they must produce in the vicinity of Q_A units of output.[6] Industry B, in contrast, is subject to economies of scale and declining costs over a much larger range of outputs, so the optimal size of firms in this industry is relatively large.

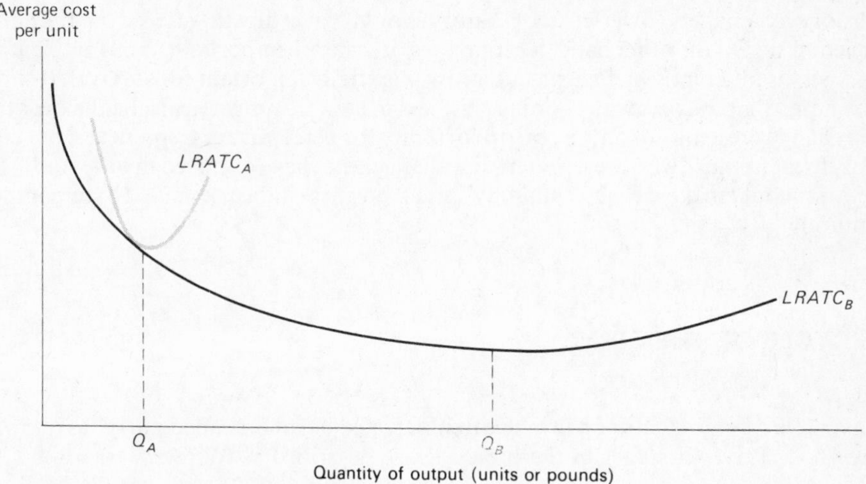

Figure 25–1 *Long-run Average Total Cost per Unit of Output.*

Firms in an industry may, however, be small simply because the industry is new and the firms have not yet had time to grow and reach their optimal size. In terms of Figure 25–1, $LRATC_A$ would represent a short-run cost curve on the long-run curve, not the long-run curve itself. Virtually all electronics firms were small businesses in the early years after the

6. It should be recognized that the optimal output for many businesses depends on the size of the market and the locations of potential customers. A retailer has a certain local market whose business is relatively easy to capture, but to gain additional customers means advertising over a wider area and offering both lower prices and extra services to offset the costs, including inconvenience, to customers coming to the shop. The same thing applies to manufacturers, although here the major cost factor is for the transportation to ship goods to distant markets. Economies of scale in production or distribution will lower unit costs, but transportation expenses rise, offsetting these factors to some degree.

In some instances multifactory and chainstore operations can be used to reduce the impact of transportation costs in time and money. However, in many businesses the need for close supervision precludes the possibility of branching, while in others branching is limited because of difficulty of transmitting data to top management, and top management decisions to field operations. These constraints are being lifted somewhat by computers, data transmission processes, better transportation systems and new management control processes, all of which are tending to make widely decentralized operations more feasible.

Second World War, when they were just getting started, even though many economies of scale were inherent in the industry. Today, there are several very large electronic firms, such as Philips Electronics, Plessey and Standard Telephones, which have expanded rapidly since the 1950s. The breweries industry went through a similar transition in the 1950s.

It is important to recognize that production methods can and do change, and as an industry's technology changes, so may average firm size. Franchised convenience-food service operators, such as McDonalds or Wimpey, have revolutionized the hamburger business, just as the supermarket chains did the grocery business some years earlier. As mentioned above, better transportation, communications and data processing systems are increasing the feasibility of some large-scale, geographically diversified operations. These factors have faciliated the development not only of various types of retail chains and franchise operators, but also of branch systems of financial institutions, such as banks and building societies.

The economies of their industries need to be understood by the managers of small firms. If the most efficient firm of its type is small, then it would be foolish to attempt a major expansion, as smaller, lower-cost operators would have drastic effects on the larger, inefficient firm. On the other hand, if economies of scale are important, then a small firm in the industry is inherently inefficient, and growth is vitally important for survival. It should also be noted that the best way of doing business in a given industry can change over time. Such a change presents not only a real opportunity for perceptive entrepreneurs, but also a serious threat to those who are less alert; the changes that have occurred in other industries in the past should make it clear that today's small business industries may not remain so in the future.[7]

LIFE CYCLE OF THE FIRM

The life cycle of an industry or firm is often depicted as an S-shaped curve, as shown in Figure 25–2. The four stages in the life cycle are described as follows:

1. *Experimentation period*: Sales and profits grow slowly following the introduction of a new product or firm.
2. *Exploitation period*: The firm enjoys rapid growth of sales, high profitability, and acceptance of the product.
3. *Maturity*: The rate of growth of sales begins to slow down; growth is dependent in large part upon replacement demand.
4. *Decline*: The firm faces the appearance of substitute products, technological and managerial obsolescence, and saturation of demand for its goods.

---

7. Some interesting philosophical issues are raised whenever conditions change so that a small business industry is consolidated, because an increase in concentration results. However, competition may actually increase, for small businesses tend to have local monopolies, and a local monopoly is just as much a monopoly as any other monopoly. Studies of the American banking industry, for example, suggest that competition is higher in areas where large branch banks exist than where smaller unit banks predominate. In other words, it appears that fewer, large, efficient and aggressive banks with plenty of branches provide better service at lower cost than do more numerous independent unit banks with their local monopolies. The same thing may also hold for various types of retailing in the United Kingdom.

We should also make a distinction between concentration resulting from changes that take advantage of new managerial developments to rationalize a small-business industry – for example, the development of supermarket chains in the grocery business – and concentration due to mergers among large firms. While we are not arguing for or against any particular change in industrial organization, we do want to point out some of the issues involved.

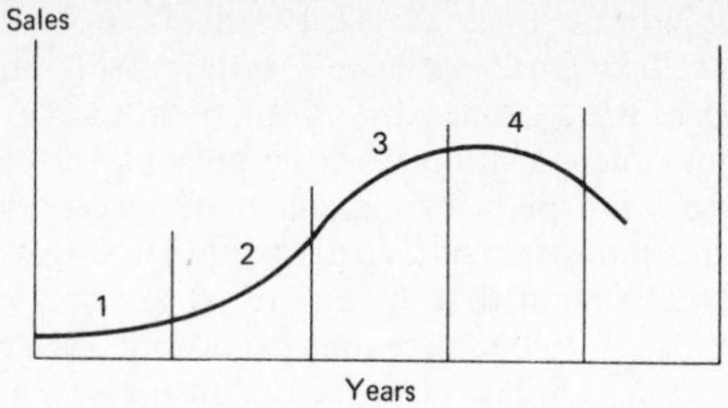

Figure 25–2 *Hypothetical Life Cycle of a Typical Firm.*

Although it is an over-simplification, Figure 25–2 provides a useful framework for analysis. The hypothesis represented by the four-stage life-cycle concept is based on a number of assumptions. It assumes competent management in the growth periods and insufficient management foresight prior to the decline phase. Obviously, one of management's primary goals is to prolong phase 2, completely forestalling phase 4; a great many firms are apparently successful in this endeavour.

The life cycle is substantially influenced by the form of organization a firm chooses – companies have potentially long lives, while sole traders obviously have finite lives. We shall discuss other aspects of the firm's life later, giving special attention to the financing forms employed at each stage.

SMALL FIRMS IN TRADITIONAL SMALL BUSINESS INDUSTRIES

As noted above, some firms are small because the nature of the industry dictates that small enterprises are more efficient than large ones, while other firms are small primarily because they are new companies – either new entrants to established industries or entrepreneurial enterprises in developing industries. Since these two types of small firms face fundamentally different situations, they have vastly different problems and opportunities. Accordingly, it is useful to treat the two classes separately. We first dicuss the small firm in the traditional small business industry, then consider the small firm with growth potential.

CHARACTERISTICS OF TRADITIONAL SMALL FIRMS

The industries or segments of industries in which small businesses predominate exhibit three common characteristics: (a) a localized market, (b) low capital requirements, and (c) relatively simple technology. Because these characteristics lead to heavy dependence on one man, problems often arise:

1. The key man may not possess the full range of managerial skills required: he may be a good salesman but be unable to handle his employees well; he may fail to keep adequate accounting records, financial control systems, and the like.
2. In a small business with one-man leadership, instead of formal, standardized controls, the control system tends to be informal, direct, and personal. If the business grows, the span of responsibilities may become excessive for the entrepreneur.
3. Because of the businessman's preoccupation with the pressing problems of day-to-day

operations, his planning for the future is often inadequate, so changes in the economic environment or competitive shifts can have severe impacts on his firm.

4. A relatively high degree of managerial training and breadth of experience are necessary, yet often lacking; in his preoccupation with the present, the characteristic small-firm entrepreneur simply does not plan for management succession. Dunn & Bradstreet data on business failures indicate that a larger proportion of failures is caused by the lack of experienced management than by any other factor.
5. When the key man wishes to retire there may be no-one suitably qualified to replace him. It may also be difficult to find a buyer for the business, at a reasonable price, if the owner wishes to liquidate his investment. Consequently, the business may have to be wound-up and the assets sold piecemeal.

Profitability of small firms

The problems of a small business may be illustrated by some representative numbers. Most small independent retailing shops have a turnover of less than £50 000 per annum, but let us assume that a particular shop is doing relatively well and has sales of £50 000 per annum. Assume that our shop has a net profit of 10 per cent on sales, after all expenses except wages. This would represent a total profit of only £5 000 for a year. The owners of a small shop typically work from 10 to 12 hours per day, six days a week. Making calculations on the conservative side, assuming a 10-hour day for a six-day week implies 60 hours' work a week. Assuming a 50-week working year, this gives us a total of 3000 hours worked during the year, yielding an hourly rate of around £1.67. If we consider the likelihood that two people work in the shop, the hourly rate would fall to 84 pence. This rate does not include a return on invested capital and is well below average hourly wage rates.

The owners may suffer even more problems. If we assume that the average net worth turnover ratio for this type of shop is 10 times a year, an optimistic figure, then on sales of £50 000 the owner would probably need about £5 000 of his or her own capital. Usually he does not have this much initial capital. As a consequence, the typical small firm incurs an inordinate amount of trade credit. It has a weak current ratio, it is slow in paying its suppliers, and, if it is inefficient, what little capital it has is quickly eroded. For reasons such as these, almost 60 per cent of all small firms are discontinued within their first five years of life: the infant mortality rate is high indeed among small businesses![8]

In the face of these discouraging statistics, why do people open their own businesses? The reasons vary. One is the hope that they will beat the statistics and will be successful – any community, large or small, has a group of very successful small businessmen who, while perhaps not millionaires, can afford expensive homes, yachts, and long holidays in the sun, or to give their children private education or support them through university. A second reason is the freedom of making one's own decisions, even if the price of this freedom is high. Third, a person may not regard the time he spends working in his own firm as drudgery; there is a wide variety of tasks to be performed in running a small enterprise, and the work can be both interesting and challenging.

Financing the traditional small firm

The typical small business, even the successful one, cannot look to the general capital markets for funds. If the firm owns any real property, it may be able to obtain a mortgage from a bank or other financial institutions. Equipment may perhaps be purchased under a

---

8. R. Brough, Business failures in Britain. *Business Ratios* (Summer 1970): 8–11.

conditional sales contract or be leased. After the business has survived a few years, bank financing may be available on a short- or medium-term basis, but not for permanent growth. Trade credit will, typically, represent the bulk of outside financing (that is, funds not supplied by the owner) available to the firm.

Financial ratio analysis must be of major and overriding importance to the small firm. Such analysis, on a regular basis, is essential to ascertain whether the firm is operating with the requisite managerial efficiency. Whereas a larger, stronger firm may have the financial strength to fall below its industry standards and still recover, the small firm has a smaller margin for error. Thus, anyone interested in a small firm is well advised to look at trends in its financial ratios, and to compare them with industry standards.

Working capital management is of overwhelming importance for most small firms. Because the amount of funds available is limited, liquidity is crucial. Trade credit appears to be an easy way of obtaining funds, yet even trade credit is obtained on terms that generally call for payment within 30 days. Since stocks typically represent a large percentage of total assets, a small firm's stock management policy must also be stressed. Large firms usually offer credit, so to meet competition small firms may also have to extend credit. The large firm is likely to have an established credit department, but how does the small firm evaluate credit risks? What volume of trade debtors can be built up without endangering both the solvency and the liquidity of the business? All of these are critical questions for the manager of a small business.

Current liability management is also important for the small firm. Although trade credit is relatively easy to obtain, it is often very costly. If discounts are available but not taken, the effective interest expense of such credit can be extremely high – as we know, not taking a 2 per cent discount for payment within 10 rather than 30 days implies a 36 per cent interest rate. Also, there is a temptation to be a perpetually slow payer, but this involves dangers: suppliers may refuse any credit whatever, or they may quote higher prices.

As the volume of operations becomes larger, the increased flow of funds through the firm may give the proprietor a false sense of affluence. He moves to a larger home with a large garden and swimming pool, and he buys the latest model car. Since his business is growing, he feels the firm can afford to take on more debt. What he may be doing is bleeding the business or, at least, removing retained earnings that are really needed to finance growth.

Many traditional small-business industries are today being conducted under franchise arrangement. Franchising represents a device whereby the training and experience required for a particular line of business is sold to the proprietor on a rental contract basis. Sometimes the franchise also includes a valuable trademark or calls for the supply of some key item. The franchiser may, through bulk buying, be able to sell supplies to the franchisee at lower costs than otherwise would be available. But, as many erstwhile franchise operators know, obtaining a franchise is not necessarily the road to riches – in many such arrangements, the owner of the franchised operation may be required to pay an excessive price for the trademark, specialty inputs and supplies, or managerial advice.

In summary, three areas of finance are of the utmost importance to firms in traditional small business industries. First, the proprietor of the traditional small business must rely on internal financing (retained earnings) to a greater extent than would the management of a larger firm. Second, to survive in the long run, he must be a somewhat better player of a relatively standardized game, in which financial ratio analysis can help him to excel. Third, working capital management is critical to the small entrepreneur; if he fails here, he will not remain solvent, and his firm will go out of business.

THE SMALL FIRM WITH GROWTH POTENTIAL

The second broad category of small business is the small firm with potential for substantial growth. Typically, such a firm has developed a new product or an innovative way of providing an old service: the electronics industry is a good example of the former, while franchised hamburgers and other food operations illustrate the latter. In this section, we discuss the financial aspects of such firms from inception until the business has matured enough to go public. The significant financial aspects of each stage of the firm's life cycle will be set out as a guide to the establishment and development of the new small business enterprise.

Stage 1: experimentation period

As indicated above and shown in Figure 25–2, the first stage of a firm's life cycle involves experimentation and simply getting itself firmly entrenched. During this period, management must lay the foundation for future growth, realizing that growth occurs either because the firm can increase its share of the market or because of industry expansion. Market share expansion is difficult due to the reaction of existing firms, and even if the industry is growing, management must recognize that every product and industry has a life cycle. Hence, supernormal growth, for whatever its cause, will continue for only a finite period.

Even though the prospects of growth in an industry are favourable, there will be fluctuations. In addition, managers must be aware of the sales-to-capacity situation in the industry. In America, for example, one of the most favourable growth industries in recent decades has been that of pleasure boats, which has generally grown at about the same rate as the growth in the population with incomes of over $12 000 per annum – 10 to 12 per cent per year. However, for a number of years capacity grew at a 20 per cent rate, so after a point individual firms experienced the problem of excess capacity in spite of the favourable growth.

Particularly in new industries, it is important that the firm identify the techniques needed to succeed in the line of business. When the motor-car industry was maturing, agency organizations and the availability of repair parts and service were the critical factors to the success of individual firms. In the computer industry, a back-up of software, of marketing, and of maintenance service personnel was vital. In the aerospace industry, the essentials were technological capability and cost control.

Like the owner of a firm in a traditional small business industry, a growth industry entrepreneur must have a knowledge not only of his product and industry, but also of the standard administrative tools essential for effective management in any line of business. Financial planning and control processes are especially important. Financial ratio analysis should be used to develop standards for determining the broad outlines of the balance sheet and the income statement, as well as for guidelines to help isolate developing problem areas.

It is especially important for a small firm that expects growth to plan for it. Initially, such planning will emphasize the expansion of existing operations; later in the firm's life cycle, it must consider possible movements into new product lines. A basic decision that must be made, whatever type of expansion occurs, is to choose between using more or less highly automated productive processes. Standard financial operating gearing, or break-even analysis, can be employed to measure how changing sales levels will affect the firm's risk and return characteristics. If its forecasts of future sales are optimistic, the firm may make larger investments in fixed assets and choose more highly automated productive processes. As a consequence, its fixed costs will be higher, but its variable costs will be lower. At high operating levels, its total costs per unit will be lower than those of a firm with a smaller ratio of fixed costs to total costs, putting the firm into a strong position in relation to its rivals. However, if volume should fall to low levels, a firm with high operating gearing will face greater risks of bankruptcy.

Stage 2: exploitation and rapid growth period

After the firm's inception, a successful firm with growth potential will enter stage 2 of its financial cycle. Here, the firm has achieved initial success – it is growing rapidly and it is reasonably profitable. Cash flows and working capital management have become increasingly important. Also, at this stage the firm will have an extraordinary need for additional outside financing; this is shown in Table 25–2, which compares rapid and moderate growth firms. The growth company (Firm 1) expands from £800 000 in sales to £1.2 million in one year; Firm 2 grows by the same amount, but over a four-year period. The percentages in parentheses following the asset–liability accounts indicate the assumed relationships between asset items and the spontaneous sources of funds, which we discussed in Chapter 4 in the section on the percentage of sales forecasting method. Note also that profits are assumed to be 6 per cent of sales during the year, and that all earnings are retained. Let us further assume that the bank overdraft is increased to cover the financing required – that is, the bank overdraft functions as the balancing item. If the firm grows by 50 per cent in one year, the bank overdraft almost doubles. However, if the firm grows from £800 000 to £1.2 million over a four-year period, then the overdraft not only does not increase at all, but it can actually be paid off. Hence, current liabilities decline from £200 000 to £148 000, while net worth increases from £200 000 to £452 000.

There is considerable doubt whether the growth firm could actually obtain short-term bank loans of the amount required. Such a large amount of short-term bank financing would cause its current ratio to drop to 1.1, and its debt ratio to rise to 54 per cent. This

Table 25–2 *Financial Effects of Different Rates of Growth (£000).*

	Firm 1		Firm 2				
	Year 1	Year 2	Year 1	Year 2	Year 3	Year 4	Year 5
Sales	£800	£1200	£800	£900	£1000	£1100	£1200
Fixed assets (20%)	160	240	160	180	200	220	240
Current assets (30%)	240	360	240	270	300	330	360
Total assets	£400	£ 600	£400	£450	£ 500	£ 550	£ 600
Ordinary share capital	100	100	100	100	100	100	100
Retained earnings[a]	100	172	100	154	214	280	352
Net worth	£200	£ 272	£200	£254	£ 314	£ 380	£ 452
Accounts payable (10%)	80	120	80	90	100	110	120
Accruals (3%)	24	36	24	27	30	33	36
Bank overdraft	96	172	96	79	56	27	(8)
Total claims	£400	£ 600	£400	£450	£ 500	£ 550	£ 600
Key ratios:							
Current ratio (times)	1.2	1.1	1.2	1.4	1.6	1.9	2.4
Debt ratio(%)	50	54	50	44	37	31	25
Sales to total assets (times)	2	2	2	2	2	2	2
Profit to net worth (%)	24.0	26.5	24.0	21.3	19.1	17.3	15.9

[a] Profit is 6 per cent of sales; retained earnings are equal to profit plus retained earnings from the previous year.

situation develops even with the very favourable 24 per cent rate of return on net worth. If the profit rate were lower, the firm's financing problem would be even more serious. When the firm uses four periods to achieve the same amount of growth, the financial ratios indicate a less risky situation. The current ratio never declines – it actually improves over the period. The debt ratio drops from 50 to 25 per cent, which is very low compared with the average for all manufacturing firms.

If the rapid growth firm continues to grow at the 50 per cent rate, the situation will further deteriorate, and it will become increasingly clear that the firm requires additional equity financing. The debt ratio will become much too high, yet the firm may well be reluctant to bring in additional outside equity money because the original owners are unwilling to share control. At this juncture, some financial pitfalls should be recognized and avoided. These are illustrated by the actual experiences of two individual small business owners who explained to the authors the difficulties they encountered. In one instance, the former owner of a firm described the problems that occurred after he obtained additional funds to support growth. He originally owned 100 per cent of his company, but the firm needed capital. When two potential suppliers of the necessary funds each requested 30 per cent ownership, the founder of the enterprise agreed, thinking that he would still have control with 40 per cent, the largest block of the ordinary share capital. However, the two new equity owners joined forces, interfered with the creative management of the company, and caused it to fail.

It is also an error to incur debt with an unrealistically short maturity. The former owner of another small firm borrowed for one- and two-year periods, but he failed to realize that if his firm continued to grow at a rapid rate, its needs for financing would increase, not decrease. Subsequently, he simply could not meet his maturing loan obligations. It was convenient to borrow funds that were critically needed for growth on a relatively short-term basis, but when he was unable to make payments as the loans matured, he was forced to give up the controlling share of the equity. Thus, failure to plan properly again caused the founder to lose control of his company.

Risks in the small business

Risk is encountered at every stage in a small firm's development. In previous chapters, we have seen that risk results from the impacts of economic conditions, labour problems, competitive pressures, and so on. All firms face such risks, but they are magnified in small businesses. In traditional small-firm industries, entry is easy, competitive pressures drive profit margins to low levels, and there is little margin for error in allowing for adverse developments or managerial mistakes.

For small growth firms, the problem is compounded still further. These firms are typically entering new areas about which little information is available. There may be great potential, but large risks are also involved, and for every glowing success story there are many instances of failure. Further, even after an innovative growth firm has been established, there are continued pressures because of the financial problems noted above. Also, its demonstrated success will stimulate imitators, so its projections must take into account the influx of new firms and the likelihood of a declining market share and increased competitive pressures. Furthermore, high profits may lead to excess capacity, causing problems for every firm in the industry. For all these reasons, the small, rapidly growing firm faces a precarious existence, even when the product-market opportunities upon which it was conceived are sound.

Venture capital financing

Small firms that have growth potential face greater risks than almost any other type of business, and their higher risks require special types of financing. This has led to the development of specialized venture capital financing sources. Some of these institutions, such as the National Research and Development Corporation, are government sponsored; others are privately owned, being financed by various financial institutions; for example, Industrial and Commercial Finance Corporation Ltd's subsidiary Technical Development Capital, which is financed jointly by the Bank of England and the UK clearing banks. Venture capital investments are often highly illiquid and cannot be easily realized until the new company has become firmly established. This requires investors to make a long-term commitment to a risky company which may not be able to produce an immediate pay-off. The major providers of venture capital will be examined in more detail later in this chapter.

When a new business makes an application for financial assistance from a venture capital firm, it receives a rigorous examination. Some companies use their own staffs for this investigation, while others depend on a board of advisers acting in a consultative capacity. A high percentage of applications is rejected, but if the application is approved, funds are provided. Venture capital companies generally take an equity position in the firms they finance, but they may also extend debt capital. However, when loans are made, they generally involve convertible debentures, or are tied in with the purchase of shares by the investment company.

Venture capital companies perform a continuing and active role in the enterprise. Typically, they do not insist on voting control, but they may have at least one member on the board of directors of the new enterprise. The matter of control has *not* been one of the crucial considerations in investment companies' decisions to invest – indeed, if the management of a small business is not sufficiently strong to make sound decisions, the venture capital firm is not likely to be interested in the first place. However, the investment company does want to maintain continuous contact, provide management counsel, and monitor the progress of its investment.

Stage 3: growth to maturity

Going public

With good management, the right economic conditions, and sufficient financing either from a venture capital company or from a government institution, the firm will move into Stage 3, the period of rapid growth. Here the increasing financing requirements will put pressure on the firm to raise capital from the new issues market. At this point, a full assessment of the critical step in a firm's life, that of 'going public', must be made.

Going public represents a fundamental change in life style in at least four respects: (a) The firm moves from informal, personal control to a system of formal controls, and the need for financial techniques such as ratio analysis and the du Pont system of financial planning and control greatly increases. (b) Information must be reported on a periodic basis to the outside investors, even though the founders may continue to have majority control. (c) The firm must have a breadth of management in all of the business functions if it is to operate its expanded business effectively. (d) The publicly owned firm typically draws on a board of directors to help formulate sound plans and policies; the board should include representatives of the public owners and other external interest groups to aid the management group in carrying out its broader responsibilities.

The valuation process is particularly important at the time the firm goes public: at what price will shares be sold to new outside investors? In analysing the investment value of the small and growing firm, some significant differences in capital costs between large and small firms should be noted:[9]

---

9. See Davis and Yeomans, *Company Finance and the Capital Markets*. Cambridge: Cambridge University Press, 1974.

1. It is especially difficult to obtain reasonable estimates of the cost of equity capital for small, privately owned firms.
2. Because of the risks involved, the required rate of return tends to be high for small firms. However, portfolio effects from a pooling of risks can reduce this factor somewhat.
3. Tax considerations are generally quite important for privately owned companies that are large enough to consider going public, as the owner-managers are probably in the top personal tax brackets.
4. Flotation costs for new security issues, especially new share issues, are much higher for small than for large firms. This factor, as well as (3) above, causes the marginal cost of capital curve for small firms to rise rapidly once retained earnings have been exhausted.

The timing of the decision to go public is also especially important, because small firms are more affected by variations in money market conditions than larger companies. During periods of tight money and high interest rates, financial institutions, especially commercial banks, find that the quantity of funds demanded exceeds the supply available at legally permissible and conventionally acceptable rates. One important method employed to ration credit is to raise credit standards. During tight money periods, both a stronger balance sheet record and a longer and more stable record of profitability may be required in order to qualify for bank credit. Since financial ratios for small and growing firms tend to be less strong, such firms bear the brunt of credit restraint. Obviously, the small firm that goes public and raises equity capital before a money squeeze is in a better position to ride it out. This firm has already raised some of its needed capital, and its equity cushion enables it to present a stronger picture to the banks, thus helping it to obtain additional capital in the form of debt.

There has been, even over the last 10 years, a dramatic slump in the number of companies going public. Since 1976 only a handful of companies have sought a Stock Exchange quotation, including the successful Eurotherm issue in 1978. There are several reasons for this slump, including recent introduction of capital transfer tax relief available only to unquoted companies, the slump in the equity market making companies vulnerable to takeover at bargain prices, and the increased domination of the stock markets by the large institutional investors who are not very interested in the smaller public quoted company. One other important reason for this decline is that the increased availability of financial help for small businesses through specialized institutions has almost eliminated the need of companies to go through the expensive and time-consuming procedure of obtaining a quotation in order to raise external long-term capital. In the next section we shall consider the major sources of financial help available to smaller firms in the UK. The financing patterns seen at the four stages of a firm's development are summarized in Table 25–3.

Table 25–3 *Financing Patterns at Four Stages of a Firm's Development.*

Stage	Financing Pattern
1. Formation	Personal savings, trade credit, bank overdrafts
2. Rapid growth	Internal financing, trade credit, term loans, specialized financial institutions
3. Growth to maturity	Going public, capital markets
4. Maturity and industry decline	Internal financing, diversification, mergers

FINANCIAL FACILITIES FOR SMALL FIRMS

Government reports

In 1931, the Macmillan committee identified a gap in the provision of finance to small firms over the range from £5000 to £200 000. As a result of the committee's report, a number of non-government controlled institutions, foremost of which was the Charterhouse group, began to provide financial help specifically to meet this gap.

By 1945 it had become apparent that further specialized financial help was necessary, not only to fill the gap, but also to aid in post-war reconstruction of the economy. As a result, the Industrial and Commercial Finance Corporation Limited (ICFC) was established. Since that time other specialized financial institutions have been established, and we have seen the Radcliffe Report in 1959 which considered, among other things, the financial problems of small firms, and the Bolton Report in 1971 which specifically examined problems of small firms, and we are currently awaiting the findings of the Wilson Committee which is considering the functioning of financial institutions and is concerned with the provision of financial help to smaller businesses.

As can be seen, there has been no lack of attention to this area. The Radcliffe Report concluded from its findings that the Macmillan gap had largely disappeared, mainly through the efforts of ICFC. This conclusion was largely supported by the Bolton Committee, although they identified an information gap: many small firms in need of external finance were either ignorant of the sources available to them, or else incapable of presenting a reasoned request for financial help to the institutions approached. From the evidence presented to the Wilson Committee it appears that this information gap still exists and that many providers of capital for small firms are finding that they have insufficient numbers of acceptable applicants for help. Some attempt has been made to reduce this information gap by the creation of a number of Small Firms Information Centres around the UK. In addition to these centres, set up by the Department of Trade, the government is also running a counselling scheme which makes available, at a reasonable fee, the advice of experienced businessmen who are either retired or semi-retired.

Specialized financial institutions

Industrial and Commercial Finance Corporation Ltd (ICFC)

ICFC was established in 1945 and is now a subsidiary of Finance for Industry (FFI), owned jointly by the major UK clearing banks and the Bank of England. It is not government controlled nor does it receive government sponsorship, being run on a specific profit-making basis. It has, since 1945, established itself as the major provider of long-term capital to the smaller business, having invested over £500 million in approximately 4500 companies. Financial aid is normally given by a long-term loan, repayable over 10 to 15 years, at a fixed rate of interest; terms can, however, be varied to suit the needs of individual applicants. ICFC will also be willing to take a minority equity stake in a company but will not normally press for a seat on the board, nor will it be willing to interfere in the day-to-day running of a client company's affairs.

The minimum amount that ICFC will lend is £5000 with a maximum limit of up to £2 million, although additional funds may be made available to existing clients. In addition to the financial help given to successful applicants, ICFC has been able to show many unsuccessful applicants that their financial needs could be satisfied by a more efficient organization of the internal affairs of the applicants' business, including, on many occasions, tighter control over working capital.

Estate Duties Investment Trust Ltd (EDITH)

Another subsidiary of FFI, which is managed by ICFC, EDITH purchases minority shareholdings in private or small public companies to enable shareholders to meet taxation and other liabilities without surrendering control of the company. Companies may also sell shares to EDITH rather than obtain a market quotation at an inopportune time, there being no obligation on the company ultimately to seek a quotation.

Charterhouse Development Capital

This company is a subsidiary of the Charterhouse Group and was one of the first companies set up specifically to fill the Macmillan gap. Minimum investment size is around £50 000 and help is normally provided by means of a minority equity investment. Charterhouse will also require a seat on the board, a requirement which makes them unpopular with many independently-minded businessmen.

Small Business Capital Fund

Founded in 1969 with financial backing from the Co-operative Insurance Society, its stated aim is to provide financial help for young or new companies which can demonstrate above-average growth potential. The minimum investment offered is also around £50 000 and will normally take the form of an equity stake in the applicant company, plus a loan on which interest may be 'rolled-over' for the early years of the investment.

Equity Capital for Industry (ECI)

This company was formed in 1976 with funds provided by City institutions. Help is normally provided by means of an equity stake, but as the minimum investment is around £250 000 ECI appears to be aiming at the top end of the small firm sector. ECI also offers underwriting facilities to its client companies with the intention of encouraging others to invest in them. This company is interested in those smaller quoted companies which are experiencing temporary financial difficulties, for example those companies unable to make a rights issue because of the low market value of their shares relative to nominal values.

Venture capital institutions

Although some of the institutions mentioned above provide equity capital to smaller businesses before a quotation is made, there are few providers of venture capital. The two institutions mainly concerned with the provision of risk capital are Technical Development Capital Ltd and the National Research Development Corporation.

Technical Development Capital Ltd (TDC)

TDC specializes in providing venture, or 'start-up', capital to newer companies. The venture capital area of finance is a high-risk area with a relatively high failure rate on such investments. TDC was formed initially to provide financial aid for the commercial development and exploitation of worthwhile technical innovations. Help is normally given to projects which are at the last stage of development, in which a viable product exists, for which capital is required to help in marketing. Because of the risk involved in this type of investment a minority equity stake is always required but this may be coupled to long-term loans secured by fixed and floating charges. TDC is also a subsidiary of ICFC which is itself a subsidiary of Finance for Industry.

National Research Development Corporation (NRDC)

NRDC was formed to promote the development and commercial exploitation of science-based inventions. Together with TDC it is the major provider of venture capital. NRDC is an independent public corporation, not a government department, and is financed, via the Secretary of State for Trade and Industry, with government loans. Since the corporation's commencement it has received around 30000 applications for financial help of which approximately one-third have been accepted. The type of project most likely to receive backing is one in which both risk and potential rewards are high. Preference is also given to those projects which have passed the development and prototype stages. Willingness of the corporation to bear risky projects is borne out by the high failure rate on accepted projects; only about 1000 projects are still going concerns. When a project does turn out to be successful, however, the rewards can be tremendous, as in the cases of the development of the hovercraft and the cephalosporin antibiotic. Returns are made by the NRDC either by taking an equity stake in the company, or by means of a levy on sales.

Other sources of financial help

Clearing banks

The clearing banks are the traditional source of external funds for small businesses. In the past, however, the official ceilings on lendings have tended to operate more to the disadvantage of the smaller firms than to the larger ones. Suspension of credit ceilings and greater emphasis on differentiation through interest rates have tended to increase the availability of bank loans to small businesses, although at a higher cost. The increased emphasis put by banks on term loans has also tended to benefit smaller businesses which might not otherwise have been able to obtain medium-term finance.

In addition to this there exists a number of other organizations, including that established by the British Rail Pension Fund to help in the provision of venture capital. Midland Montagu offer 'loan-plus-equity' packages of between £5000 and £250000. Additionally, several organizations formed in the last few years specifically to provide finance for small firms have been wound up because of lack of suitable applications for finance.

Government assistance

Apart from the National Research Development Corporation, the government offers help to small businesses through a number of agencies.

The Scottish and Welsh development agencies were established in 1975 to further the economic development of their respective countries. They provide loan and share capital and also offer loan guarantees on finance provided from other sources. Advisory services are also provided as well as factories and sites made available to businesses at attractive rents.

The Council for Small Industries in Rural Areas (COSIRA), financed by a development fund which is voted annually by Parliament, provides both local advice and professional and consultancy services, as well as financial help. Loans extending for periods from five to 20 years are given for amounts ranging from £250 to £300000. The facilities provided are available to small manufacturing and service firms employing fewer than 10 skilled workers and situated either within an English rural area or in towns of fewer than 10000 inhabitants.

Taxation relief

Reduced rates of tax are now available to companies, including small firms, which have taxable profits of less than £85 000. Corporation tax is levied at the reduced rate of 42 per cent on taxable profits of up to £50000, with marginal relief available to companies whose profits are between £50000 and £85000. Companies earning profits in excess of £85000 pay tax at the normal rate of 52 per cent.

For a further examination of this area, see Appendix A, 'The Tax Environment', at the end of this book.

The rules relating to the distribution of profits within close companies have been reduced, with companies earning less than £25000 exempt from the regulations and with abatement available on profits up to £75000.

FURTHER DEVELOPMENTS

Further developments in the provision of help to smaller business could include an extension of government-sponsored loan guarantee arrangements offered by a number of the government agencies. Suggestions made in the past for the establishment of an official secondary market in the securities of smaller businesses do not appear to have much support; the potential market is likely to be too narrow for unquoted securities, and the costs involved in trading too high to make such a market attractive to potential investors. Against these argument is the fact that an unofficial over-the-counter (OTC) market has existed in the UK since 1971, run by J. H. Nightingale, Investment Bankers.

SUMMARY

The key factors relating to small business financing are summarized briefly in Table 25–3, which sets forth the financing patterns at the firm's four stages of development. In its formative stage, the new, small firm must rely most heavily on personal savings, trade credit and bank overdrafts. During its period of rapid growth, internal financing will become an important source of meeting its financing requirements, although continued reliance will be placed on trade credit. At this stage, its record of accomplishment also makes it possible to obtain bank loans for medium-term financing. If it has the potential for really strong growth, the firm may also be able to attract equity from a venture capital company.

A particularly successful firm may reach the stage where going public becomes feasible – this leads to access to the broader capital markets, and it represents a true coming-of-age for the small firm. Even at this point, however, the firm must look ahead, analysing its products and their prospects. Because every product has a life cycle, the firm must be aware that without the development of new products, growth will cease, and eventually the firm will decline. Accordingly, as product maturity approaches, the firm must plan for the possibility of mergers, or other longer-term strategies. The best time to look ahead and plan for this is while the firm has energy, momentum and a high price – earnings ratio.

In our coverage of small business financing, the major emphasis has been on providing a framework for analysing financial needs and opportunities as the characteristics of the firm and its industry evolve. While this type of analysis cannot replace mature judgement, it can certainly aid such judgement and help the financial manager maximize his contribution to the successful development of a small business enterprise.

QUESTIONS

25–1. What are the advantages and disadvantages of the use of a sole proprietorship versus a partnership for conducting the operations of a small business firm?

25–2. Under what circumstances does it become advantageous for the small business to incorporate?

25–3. In what sense is the company a person?

25–4. Would it be practical for ICI to be organized as a partnership?

25–5. What influence does each of the following have on possible divergences between the goals and objectives of the managers who control a company and those of its shareholders?
(a) Profit sharing plans.
(b) Employee share option schemes.

25–6. Why is the John Lewis organization a partnership?

25–7. What are some sources of information on the past performance of a firm you are thinking of buying?

25–8. A friend of yours has just developed a new product and plans to start a business to produce it. One of his goals is to maintain absolute control but his own capital is limited. What are some of the ways he can reduce the amount of his initial outlay while still obtaining the use of an efficiently large plant?

25–9. Assume that you are starting a business of your own of the traditional small business type. Develop an outline of the kinds of decisions you will have to make in establishing and financing the small enterprise.

25–10. Why do many small businesses prefer not to approach the specialized institutions for financial help?

PROBLEMS

25–1. Susan Smith, discouraged by irrelevant arts courses, decided to leave university at the end of her second year. She plans to open the simplest of retail trade establishments, a grocery shop with an emphasis on health foods.

Susan had received an allowance from her parents for some years and was able to save a little over £1000. She could have saved more, but somehow she 'loaned some to friends', and from time to time she was tempted by some interesting new types of apparel. She also drove her car quite a bit, so petrol and repairs ate into what otherwise would have been even more savings.

After making some inquiries of her bus. ad. friends, Susan recognized that she must consider such things as location, potential flow of customer traffic, and present and potential competition. Also, she realized that she must analyse the alternatives of buying premises or renting a shop and buying or renting the equipment and fixtures she will need – counters, shelving, cash register and the like. The shop space she had in mind had not been occupied by a grocery before, so it lacked shelves and counters.

(a) Should Susan buy or rent the shop premises?
(b) How should Susan acquire the equipment and fixtures?
(c) What kinds of questions is she likely to face with regard to choice of product line?
(d) For planning purposes, assume sales per day of £100, £300 and £500, and a profit ratio of net income before taxes to sales of 4 per cent. What are her earnings per hour before taxes, assuming that she works 10 hours per day, seven days a week, for 50 weeks per year?
(e) With a sales to net worth ratio of 15 times, what investment on her part is indicated at each level of sales? Comment on how she may raise the funds if several years are required to reach each alternative level of sales, and also comment upon the implications of her taking withdrawals from the business.
(f) What additional questions must our heroine face if she sells on credit?
(g) What are the critical problems likely to be if sales start at £500 per day?

25–2. Fred Thatcher has been employed by the Universal Plastics Company, a Manchester firm, for several years. Because of his industrial engineering background, he has been used in the production department to help develop new plastic products to utilize more extensively the firm's available dies and presses. The product line of Universal Plastics is relatively limited.

While visiting friends in Aberdeen, Thatcher concluded that considerable opportunities for new plastics companies existed in the north-east of Scotland, and he decided on the spot to start his own firm. Initially, he would service the oil industry, but he thought the potential existed for later expansion into the oil industry generally as well as into a wide variety of products for the food and grocery industries, the school market, hospitals and department stores. Furthermore, he saw a great opportunity for the substitution of plastics products for wood containers.

Thatcher obtained the services of one of Universal Plastics' ablest salesmen, John Watson, by offering him the opportunity to become the sales manager and marketing director. Accordingly, in 1968 the Aberdeen Plastics Company was born. Thatcher received 90 per cent of the shares while Watson received 10 per cent.

By 1978, 10 years later, Thatcher, the chairman of Aberdeen Plastics, decided he had to give serious consideration to going public. To realize the firm's full growth potential seemed to require financing beyond what Aberdeen Plastics could achieve under its present form and method of operations. Through its commercial bank, Thatcher was brought into contact with a number of venture capital sources, as well as one or two issuing houses. They all asked for a report that would cover Aberdeen Plastics' background and present a five-year forecast of sales and earnings.

Thatcher had attended an MBA course at the University of the Highlands, where he had worked closely with Kent Smith of the finance faculty. Thatcher had a great deal of respect for Smith, so he asked him to help in the development of the report. Professor Smith utilized a wide range of tools encompassing most of the topics covered in a comprehensive book dealing with managerial finance; in fact, Smith was especially eager to work on the report so that he could later use it to indicate to his students how the tools and concepts of finance are utilized by a small firm in its growth and development process.

The first segment of the report contained a statement of Aberdeen Plastics' product concept. An excerpt from this statement is given below:

The products of Aberdeen Plastics consist primarily of the following items: modubox systems for industrial users, trays and cases for the school market, duro nesting boxes for the produce and food markets, duro tote boxes for hospitals, safety equipment for oil-riggers, display fixtures, instrument cases, instrument housings and other custom parts.

Most of the products and customers served by Aberdeen Plastics are growing rapidly. In addition, Aberdeen Plastics has a number of advantages that will enable the company to continue to increase its penetration of these markets. It has the rights and patents to various box design features and safety equipment and has product names which have been copyrighted. Even more important, Aberdeen Plastics continues to be the leader in the development of new ideas for materials handling systems. In the food and hospital industries, sanitation requirements are increasingly necessitating the substitution of the plastic products for wood containers.

The school market has been only scratched, and Aberdeen Plastics is beginning to supply the manufacturers of school equipment with its boxes and trays.

The advantages of Aberdeen Plastics' product line are continuing to lead to the substitution of its products for older materials. As a consequence, the replacement of older materials in industries whose total growth is low should result in tremendous further growth for Aberdeen Plastics.

Aberdeen Plastics has developed customer recognition and loyalty both by the quality of its products and by a 10-year programme of national advertising, including full-page advertisements in various trade journals. This advertising programme has strengthened the position of the company, as has its strong national distribution system, which utilizes 200 distributors.

Figure 1 shows actual and projected sales for Aberdeen Plastics. Sales have grown from about £300 000 during the first year of operations to £1.4 million in 1977, and to a forecasted level of over £5 million by 1983 [see the middle line of the range of future growth patterns shown in Figure 25P–1].

Figure 25 P–1 is based on Smith's analysis of Aberdeen Plastics' product lines and the prospective growth in each of its product areas. Because of Aberdeen Plastics' rapid growth rate, Smith used a semi-logarithmic chart.

Smith also developed some basic financial relations that he used as the foundation for pro forma balance sheets, income statements, and profitability relations as determined by the sales forecast. Table 25P–1 presents abbreviated income statements for each of the past five years, with each element of the income statement stated both in absolute terms and as a percentage of net sales. Table 25P–2 gives historical balance sheets for Aberdeen Plastics between 1973 and 1977. A related break-even chart is set forth in Figure 25P–2. The historical balance sheet and income statement (and break-even analysis) are used to construct the projected financial statements to make possible the analysis and valuation involved in the firm's going public. The following questions indicate the kind of analysis that is required for 'making the firm public'.

(a) From the data in Table 25P–1, plot a scatter diagram of the relation between each of the following items to sales: (i) cost of goods sold, (ii) selling expenses, and (iii) general and administrative

Table 25P-1 *Income Statement Accounting Years 1973–7 (£000).*

	1973		1974		1975		1976		1977	
	Amount	Per cent	Amount	Per cent	Amount	Per cent	Amount	Per cent	Amount	Per cent
1. Sales (net)	£403	100.0	£560	100.0	£853	100.0	£1169	100.0	£1407	100.0
2. Less: cost of goods sold	310	76.9	397	70.9	598	70.1	821	70.2	1000	71.1
3. Gross profit	£ 93	23.1	£163	29.1	£255	29.9	£ 348	29.8	£ 407	28.9
4. Selling expenses	54	13.4	92	16.4	120	14.1	187	16.0	205	14.6
5. Administrative and general expenses	38	9.4	51	9.1	105	12.3	113	9.7	118	8.4
6. Subtotal	£ 92	22.8	£143	25.5	£225	26.4	£ 300	25.7	£ 323	23.0
7. Profit from operations	1	0.2	20	3.6	30	3.5	48	4.1	85	5.9
8. Other income	9	2.2	4	0.7	6	0.7	3	0.3	–	–
9. Net income before Corporation tax	10	2.4	24	4.3	36	4.2	51	4.4	85	5.9
10. Corporation tax	1	0.2	8	1.4	13	1.5	21	1.8	39	2.8
11. Net income	£ 9	2.2	£ 16	2.9	£ 23	2.7	£ 30	2.6	£ 46	3.1

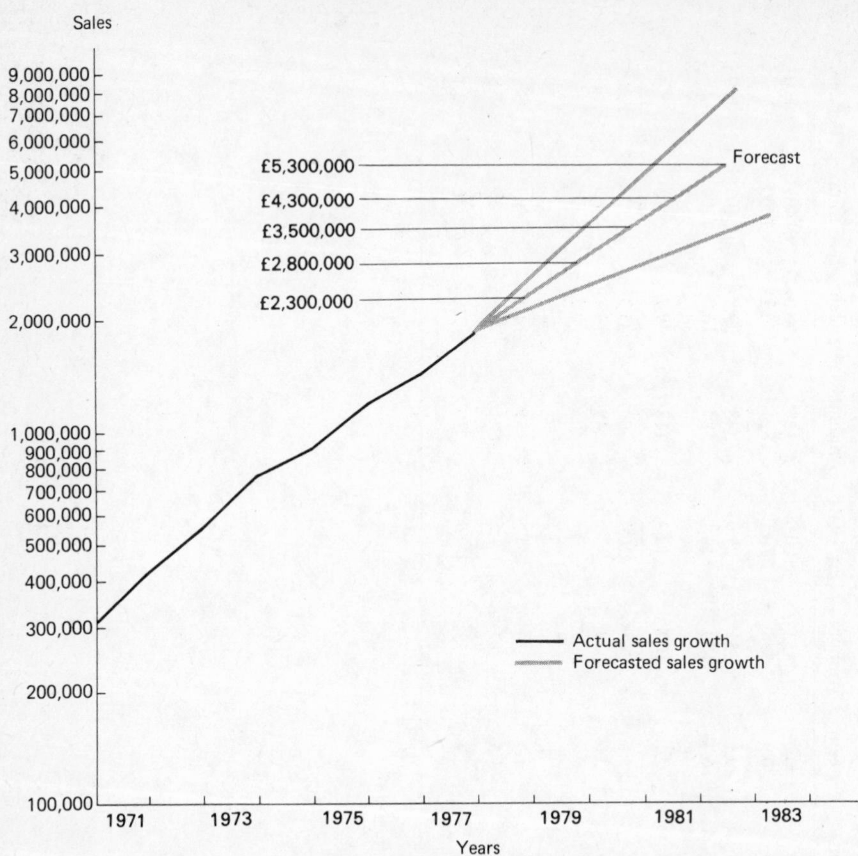

Figure 25P–1 *Sales Growth of Aberdeen Plastics – Actual 1973–7, Forecast 1978–83.*

Table 25P–2 *Aberdeen Plastics Ltd, Balance Sheet 1973–7.*

	1973 £000	1974 £000	1975 £000	1976 £000	1977 £000
Fixed assets	£ 46	£ 53	£ 72	£105	£130
Less: depreciation	27	36	42	55	74
	£ 19	£ 17	£ 30	£50	£ 56
Stocks	41	59	72	109	86
Trade debtors	44	69	86	102	165
Cash	8	1	8	15	35
Total assets	£112	£146	£196	£276	£342
Financed by:					
Ordinary share capital (50 pence nominal value)	£ 22	£ 22	£ 30	£ 30	£ 30
Reserves	3	19	32	62	108
	£ 25	£ 41	£ 62	£ 92	£138
Debentures	12	4	11	15	11
	£ 37	£ 45	£ 73	£107	£149
Trade creditors	43	61	81	100	122
Accrued expenses	13	24	30	45	68
Bank loan	19	16	12	24	3
Total claims on assets	£112	£146	£196	£276	£342

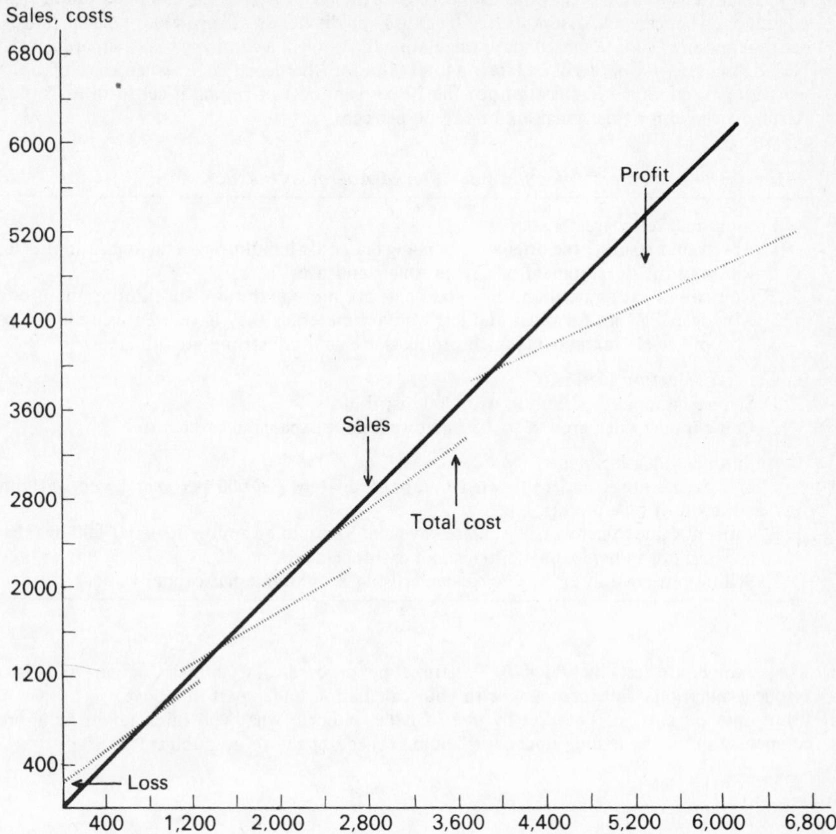

Figure 25P–2 *Aberdeen Plastics, Break-even Analysis (£000).*

expenses. Plot these in a chart, which we will label Figure 25P–3.

(b) Using the following equations: cost of goods sold = £24 000 + 0.69 (sales); selling expense = £90 000 + 0.08 (sales); general and administrative expenses = £20 000 + 0.0635 (sales); and corporate taxes = 0.5 (net income before tax), set forth a pro forma income statement forecast for Aberdeen Plastics to be Table 25P–4 for the years 1978 to 1983 with a percentage analysis as performed in Table 25P–1, on the relations that you observe.

(c) From the balance sheet data in Table 25P–2, plot scatter diagrams, in six parts of a chart which will be labelled Figure 25P–4, the relationship to sales of the following items: trade debtors, stocks, total fixed assets before depreciation, total assets, trade creditors, and total long-term liabilities. Fit regression lines where possible.

(d) Using the following equations: trade debtors = 0.12 (sales); total fixed assets before depreciation = 15 + 0.1 (assets); stocks = 2.8 + 0.086 (sales); trade creditors = 9.4 + 0.078 (sales); cash = 0.04 (sales); accruals = 0.08 (sales); and annual depreciation = 0.1 (gross fixed assets), make a forecast of the balance sheets for 1978 to 1983 to be labelled Table 25P–5. If more financing is needed, increase the bank loan as an adjusting item. If excess cash is available from operations, first pay off the bank loan and then create an additional asset account entitled 'cash available from operations' (marketable securities).

(e) Using the data from Table 25P–5, calculate financial ratios. Perform the financial ratio analysis for the years 1973 to 1977 and on a projected basis for 1978 and 1983 for the following ratios: (i) current ratio, (ii) average collection period, (iii) current liability/total assets, (iv) long-term debt/total assets, (v) total debt/total assets, (vi) net profits/sales, (vii) net profits/total assets, and (viii) net profits/net worth. Label this analysis Table 25P–6. From the ratios in your Table 25P–6, comment on the past financial position of Aberdeen Plastics and on the prospects for the forecasted years, 1978 and 1983.

(f) Comment on the pattern indicated by the break-even analysis set forth in Figure 25P–2.

(g) From the data in Table 25P–2, develop a sources and uses of funds statement for Aberdeen Plastics for the five-year period 1973 to 1977. Present your results in a table to be labelled Table 25P–7.

(h) The valuation is based on the projected net income figures in your Table 25P–4, assuming a dividend payout of 50 per cent and assuming that from 1984 on dividends will grow at a 'normal' rate of 10 per cent per annum. Using the method for calculating the value of a company with a supernormal growth period discussed in Chapter 17, set forth a total value for Aberdeen Plastics when a cost of capital of 20 per cent is used. Some justification for the 20 per cent cost of capital is set forth in Table 25P–3. Assume an investor's marginal tax rate of 30 per cent.

Table 25P–3 *Factors Affecting Valuation of Aberdeen Plastics.*

A. Product-market characteristics:
   1. Aberdeen Plastics is the originator of many materials-handling systems and continues to be the leader in the development of new products and uses.
   2. Companies in the food and hospital fields are more and more substituting the products of Aberdeen Plastics for older and less sanitary materials they have been using in the past.
   3. Five of the six markets in which products are sold are strong growth areas.

B. General valuation factors:
   1. Strong national distribution with 200 distributors.
   2. Can support sales growth to £5 million without expansion of factories.

C. Additional valuation items:
   1. Current earnings underestimated by approximately £30 000 per year based on immediate write-off of set-up costs.
   2. Current value of net worth estimated by Kent Smith to be approximately £1 000 000 based on appraisal of individual asset items and cash balances.
   3. Selling power built up by 10-year advertising programme has capital value.

(i) The issuing house actually sold 400 000 shares at net proceeds of £600 000. Compare and discuss this implied valuation of the company with your calculation under part (h) above.

(j) From data on costs of flotation by size of issue, indicate what you think might be appropriate compensation to the issuing house for helping this company to go public.

SELECTED REFERENCES

Archer S. H. and Faerber, L. G. Firm size and the cost of externally secured equity capital. *Journal of Finance* 21 (March 1966): 69–83.

Bates, J. *The Financing of Small Business.* London: Sweet and Maxwell, 1971, 2nd ed.

Bates, J. The activities of large and small companies. *Business Ratios* (1968).

Bank of England Quarterly Review. Competition and credit control. *Bank of England Quarterly Review* (June 1971): 189–193.

Bolton Report. *Report of the Committee of Inquiry on Small Firms.* London: HMSO, 1971, Cmnd. 4811.

Boswell, J. *The Rise and Decline of Small Firms.* London: Allen and Unwin 1973.

Brigham, E. F. and Smith, K. V. The cost of capital to the small firm. *Engineering Economist* (Fall 1967): 1–26.

Brough, R. Business failures in Britain. *Business Ratios* (Summer 1970): 8–11.

Buchele, R. B. *Business Policy in Growing Firms.*

Committee to Review the Functioning of Financial Institutions, *Progress Report on the Financing of Industry and Trade.* London: HMSO, 1977.

Committee to Review the Functioning of Financial Institutions. *Evidence on the Financing of Industry and Trade.* London: HMSO, 1977–8, vols. 1 to 6.

Committee to Review the Functioning of Financial Institutions. *Survey of Investment Attitudes and Financing of Medium-sized Companies.* London: HMSO, 1977, Research Report No. 1.

Davis, R. D. Small Business in the next decade. *Advanced Management Journal* 31 (January 1966): 5–8.

Davis, J. R. and Kelly, M. Small firms in the manufacturing sector. Committee of Inquiry on Small Firms. London: HMSO, 1971, Research Report No. 3.

Davis, E. W. & Yeomans, K. *Company Finance and the Capital Markets: a Study of the Effects of Firm Size.* University of Cambridge: C.U.P. (1974).

Economists Advisory Group, Financial facilities for small firms. Committee of Inquiry on Small Firms. London: HMSO, 1971, Research Report No. 4.

Economists Advisory Group. Problems of the small firm in raising external finance. The results of a sample survey. Committee of Inquiry on Small Firms. London: HMSO, 1971, Research Report No. 5.

Edmister, R. O. Financial ratios as discriminant predictors of small business failure [abstract]. *Journal of Finance* 27 (March 1972): 139–140.

Freeman, C. The role of small firms in innovation in the U.K. since 1945. Committee of Inquiry on Small Firms. London: HMSO, 1971, Research Report No. 4.

Gilmore, F. F. Formulating strategy in smaller companies. *Harvard Business Review* 49 (May 1971): 71–81.

Groves, R. E. & Harrison, R. Bank loans and small business financing in Britain. *Accounting and Business Research* (Summer 1974): 227–233.

Macmillan Report. *Report of the Committee on Finance and Industry*. London: HMSO, 1931, Cmnd. 3897.

McConkey, D. D. Will ecology kill small business? *Business Horizons* 15 (April 1972): 61–69.

Merrett Syriax Associates. Dynamics of small firms. Committee of Inquiry on Small Firms. London: HMSO, 1971, Research Report No. 12.

Phillips, W. Half-way house to a stock exchange quote: Britain's other share markets. *Investors Chronicle* (July 1977): 14–15.

Radcliffe Committee. *Report of the Committee on the Working of the Monetary System*. London: HMSO, 1959, Cmnd. 827.

Seebohm, Lord. Sources of finance for small and medium-sized businesses. *Accountant* (29 September 1977): 383–386.

Steiner, George. Approaches to long-range planning for small business. *California Management Review* 10 (Fall 1967): 3–16.

Travers, N. Venture capital. 'Focus on merchant banking'. *Accountancy* (November 1974): 52–59.

Various authors. Sources of funds. Special report. *Accountancy Age* (29 October 1976): I–XII.

Various authors. Small business finance. *Accountants' Weekly* (21 April 1978): 17–33.

Wheelright, S. C. Strategic planning in the small business. *Business Horizons* 14 (August 1971): 51–58.

White, L. T. Management assistance for small business. *Harvard Business Review* 43 (July 1965): 67–74.

Appendix A

The Tax Environment

In many respects the British government may be considered to be the most important shareholder in private industry in the United Kingdom. This is not literally true, because the government does not 'own' shares in the strict sense of the word, except in a limited number of cases through the NEB; it is, however, by far the largest recipient of business profits. Income from unincorporated businesses may be subject to tax rates ranging up to 83 per cent, while income of companies is taxed at rates varying from 42 to 52 per cent, or higher if one takes into account apportionment of income of close companies.

During the financial year 1977–8, UK government revenues on current account amounted to £57 609 million, almost 40 per cent of the GNP for that year. Taxes on income alone totalled £20 595 million.[1]

With such a large amount of funds being directed into government coffers it is hardly surprising that the methods used to raise the revenues should play an important part in financial decision-making. Lease or buy, size of dividend, source of new capital – all these decisions are influenced by taxation factors. This appendix summarizes some basic elements of the tax structure relating to financial decisions.

FISCAL POLICY

Central government uses both monetary and fiscal policy to influence the level of economic activity. Monetary policy, considered in Chapter 21, deals with actions to influence the availability and cost of credit. Fiscal policy is concerned with altering the level and composition of government receipts and expenditure to influence the level of economic activity. As direct taxes provide the major source of government revenue they are an important element of fiscal policy.

The basic tool of taxation legislation is the Finance Act which is normally introduced annually in April and passed by Parliament at the end of July. In addition, it has become the practice of Chancellors in recent years to introduce supplementary Finance Acts,

1. Central Statistical Office, *Financial Statistics.* London: HMSO (August 1978).

usually in the Autumn. Finance Acts are concerned with amendments to existing taxation legislation and also with imposing new rates of taxation and levels of relief.

Three principal methods have been employed to alter the level and effect of direct taxation on business and investors:

1. By changing tax rates.
2. By altering the rules relating to capital allowances.
3. By changing the system relating to the taxation of corporate profits.

Each of these points is discussed briefly in this section.

Changing tax rates

During periods of rapid and unsustainable economic expansion, especially when such expansion has inflationary consequences, the government may attempt to dampen the level of economic activity by increasing tax rates. When tax rates are raised, both personal disposable incomes and corporate profits after taxes are reduced. The reduction in personal disposable incomes reduces individuals' purchasing power and thereby decreases their demand for goods and services. The reduction in corporate after-tax profits reduces the profitability of new investments and, at the same time, reduces corporate funds available for investment. On the other hand, if the economy is depressed and requires some form of stimulation, tax rates can be reduced, providing both consumers and businesses with greater purchasing power and increasing the incentive of businesses to make investments in plant and equipment.

In 1975 when inflation was running at record high levels in the United Kingdom, the government increased the rate of personal tax from 33 to 35 per cent in order to reduce surplus purchasing power. Changes in the rate of corporation tax are relatively infrequent although changes in the rate of personal income tax and in the level of allowances given are becoming increasingly common. Indeed, since 1973–4, when the then system of income tax and surtax was replaced by a 'unified tax', there have been no fewer than five changes in the basic rate of income tax, as shown in Table A–1.

Table A–1 *Basic Rate of Income Tax.*

Income tax year	Basic rate %
1973/4	30
1974/5	33
1975/6	35
1976/7	35
1977/8	34
1978/9	33[a]

[a] In 1978/9 a new reduced rate of 25 per cent was introduced on the first £750 of disposable income.

Changing capital allowance

Companies rarely, if ever, pay tax on the profits disclosed in the published profit and loss account. Certain expenses deducted by businesses in preparation of their annual profit and loss accounts are not allowable deductions for tax purposes.

One major area in which taxation legislation may differ from accounting practice is in the treatment of capital expenditure; depreciation charged in the accounts is not allowed as a deduction from profits for tax purposes. Instead, taxation legislation determines the means by which capital allowances may be claimed on capital expenditure incurred by business on plant and machinery and other fixed assets.

Capital allowances are therefore standardized depreciation charges at rates specified in the current Finance Act. If rates are increased by any subsequent Finance Acts to permit more rapid write-off of capital expenditure, this will delay tax payments and, hopefully, stimulate capital investment.

In the case of plant and equipment acquired after 22 March 1972, for example, businesses may claim capital allowances by means of first-year allowance of 100 per cent.

A business may reduce the amount of first year allowance claimed to any figure it wishes and claim, in subsequent years, a writing-down allowance of 25 per cent on the written-down value. This practice may occur if a businessman wishes to benefit from taxation of profits at reduced rates over a number of years. In other words, if a company earned a level of profits just above £50 000 it may be to its advantage to seek to bring its taxable income below £50 000 over a number of years by claiming a writing-down allowance rather than to claim a first-year allowance to reduce taxable profits in the first year and then to pay tax at 52 per cent in later years. Against the advantage of paying tax at reduced rates over several years will be offset the opportunity cost of the tax that could have been avoided in the first year.

Conversely, the advantages of making early use of capital allowances stem from two factors:

1. Such use reduces taxation in the early years of an asset's life, thus increasing cash flows and releasing funds for further investment.
2. Faster cash flows increase the profitability, or rate of return, on an investment. This second point is made clear in Chapter 10, where capital budgeting is discussed.

Changes in the laws relating to capital allowances on plant and machinery are not as common as changes in tax rates, the last major change having occurred in 1972 with the introduction of 100 per cent initial allowances. Greater variation does, however, occur on the allowances given on other forms of capital expenditure such as industrial buildings and motor vehicles.

For information on up-to-date rates available on business assets, the current Finance Act should be consulted.

Changes in the corporate taxation system

Prior to 1965 there was no separate system of taxation for companies as opposed to unincorporated businesses. Both paid income tax, at the rates applicable to individuals, on their assessable profits. However, an additional tax, known as profits tax, was charged on companies with profits in excess of £12 000. Company dividends were paid net of the standard rate of income tax and the tax so deducted by companies was retained by them. Individual shareholders receiving the dividends were given credit for the income tax deducted but would either have to reclaim this tax or have to make an additional payment depending on their own marginal tax rate.

In the 1965 Finance Act there was a change in the system of taxing companies. Corporation tax, a single, distinct tax applicable to companies, was introduced. Dividends were again to be paid out of post-corporation tax profits but now the dividends to be paid were gross dividends on which the tax was to be deducted and then paid over to the Inland Revenue. Distributed profits were effectively subjected to levels of taxation, with the aim of encouraging retention of profits in order to stimulate further investment. One major effect of the new corporation tax system was to encourage firms to raise capital by loan stock, as interest payments were tax-deductible expenses, rather than by issues of ordinary shares.

By 1971 many analysts had abandoned the viewpoint that the encouragement of retained profits by companies was necessarily good for the economy. In fact, many believed that it may have led to a stagnation of investment in potential growth areas which had been deprived of the necessary funds due to re-investment policies of established firms. In addition, the United Kingdom was in the process of joining the European Economic Community and there was a desire to modify the system of company taxation to make it comparable to our EEC partners.

A new system of company taxation, known as an imputation system, was finally introduced in 1973. The basic feature of the new system was a single rate of corporate taxes to be charged on all profits of a company whether they were distributed or not. Dividends are now to be paid net of tax but with an imputed tax credit to the recipient. The company would itself hand over the tax on the dividends to the Inland Revenue but this would be considered to be an advance corporation tax (ACT) payment. There is still a tax advantage to companies wishing to raise new capital through debenture issues rather than issues of ordinary shares, but the advantage has now been reduced considerably.

Table A–2 illustrates the effect of different dividend policies on total tax liability under

Table A–2 *Effect of Different Dividend Payout Policies on Total Tax Liability under Corporation Tax Systems (a) before 1973, (b) after 1973.*

	Nil distribution	100% distribution
Pre-1973	£000	£000
Taxable profits	£100	£100
Corporation tax (at 40%)	40	40
	£60	£60
Dividends paid (gross)	–	60
Retained profits	£60	£ nil
Dividend received by shareholders	–	£36.75
Tax deducted and paid to Inland Revenue (at 38.75%)[a]	–	23.25
Gross equivalent of dividend	£ –	£60
Tax liability of company	£40	£40
Tax liability of shareholders[a]	–	23.25
Total tax liability	£40	£63.25
Post-1973	£000	£000
Taxable profits	£100	£100
Corporation tax (at 52%)	52	52
	£ 48	£48
Dividends paid (net)	–	48
Retained profits	£ 48	£nil
Dividend received by shareholders	–	£48
Imputed tax credit (at 33%)	–	23.6
Gross equivalent of dividend	£ –	£71.6
Total tax liability of company and shareholders	£52	£52

[a] Assuming all shareholders bear tax at the basic rate.

the systems in existence before and after 1973. As can be seen, before 1973 total tax liability of company and shareholders increased with the payment of a dividend – dividends being effectively taxed twice.

After 1973, in our illustration, the total tax liability of the firm remains at £52 000 even with 100 per cent dividend payout. In the case of 100 per cent dividend payout after 1973, the corporation tax liability has two elements:

Advance corporation tax of £48 000 × 33/67	=	£23 642
Mainstream corporation tax	=	28 358
		£52 000

Advance corporation tax is paid under a quarterly accounting system after adjustment for any ACT credits on dividends received from other UK companies. The ACT has normally been limited to the basic rate of income tax, which in our case is 33 per cent. Any surplus ACT may be carried back and offset against corporation tax paid in the previous two tax years or else carried forward to future accounting periods. The mainstream tax liability will become due for payment according to the rules explained later in this appendix. There is a minimum mainstream tax liability when a company has taxable profits currently standing at 19/52 of the corporation tax liability. In addition, ACT may be offset only against trading income of a particular period, not capital gains.

CORPORATE TAXATION

Tax rate

Companies pay corporation tax on the whole of their taxable income, whether it is distributed or not, at the rates fixed by the appropriate Finance Act. For the financial year to 31 March 1978, the rate of corporation tax is fixed at 52 per cent. There is also a 'small companies' rate of corporation tax of 42 per cent, applying to companies with profits of less than £50 000. Marginal relief is also available for companies with profits up to £85 000.

Because of the reduced rates of corporation tax payable on profits less than £85 000 it may pay a company to claim writing-down allowances on plant and machinery rather than first-year allowances, in order to bring itself into the range of the reduced rates of taxation for a number of years.

Corporate taxable income

Corporate taxable income consists of two components:

1. Profits from the sale of chargeable assets, i.e. corporate capital gains.
2. All other income.

Corporate capital gains

Until 1962 it was broadly the case that only income receipts were taxable and that only expenditure of a revenue nature could be taken into account when reducing tax liability. However, the distinction between capital and income was difficult to draw and taxpayers were encouraged to engage in elaborate schemes by which anticipated income might be converted into tax-free gains.

In 1962, capital gains tax was introduced for gains or losses on those chargeable assets disposed of within 12 months of acquisition. The scheme was extended by the Finance Act of 1965 to cover gains and losses on chargeable assets held for more than 12 months. Chargeable assets include all those assets which are not bought and sold in the ordinary course of a firm's business or which are not specifically exempt.

Unlike individuals, companies are not liable to capital gains tax but are liable, rather, to corporation tax on a proportion of any gain they make. The proportion at the moment stands at 15/26th, and with the corporation tax rate standing at 52 per cent this results in a net tax of 30 per cent on the capital gain. If a firm's capital gains were £13 000, for example, the tax payable would be computed as follows:

Proportion liable	: 15/26 × £13 000	= £7500
Corporation tax payable	: 52% × £7500	= £3900
		(i.e., 30% × £13 000)

Capital losses

Although there is no provision for deducting capital losses from ordinary income, they may be deducted from capital gains made in the same period. Any balance of losses must be carried forward against future capital gains, no provision being made for carrying losses back to previous periods.

Balancing charges and balancing allowances

Disposal of a business asset which has been subject to capital allowances will result in either a gain or a loss arising. If a gain has been made this may take the form of either a capital gain or an income gain for tax purposes.

An income gain, known as a balancing charge, arises where the business has written down the value of the asset, using capital allowances, to less than the sale value of the asset. For example, suppose equipment originally purchased for £10 000 has had £6000 capital allowances subsequently claimed on it. The equipment then has a written-down value of £4000(£10 000 – £6000).

If the firm sells the equipment for £7000 it will incur a balancing charge of £3000 (£7000 – £4000). This charge is classified as a revenue gain and as such will be added to business income and taxed accordingly.

The sale of a business asset will result in a capital gain where sale proceeds exceed the original cost. Thus if, in our example, the equipment had been sold for £12 000 a total profit of £8000 (£12 000 – £4000) would have been incurred. Of this amount, £6000 represents a balancing charge which would be taxed as business income, and the remaining £2000 (£12 000 – £10 000) would be classified as a capital gain for tax purposes and, as such, only 15/26th of the £2000 would be liable to corporation tax. The balancing charge can be seen, therefore, to be limited to the total capital allowances previously given.

Where the balancing charge arises on equipment that is being replaced, the business may elect to have it deducted from the cost of replacement before computing capital allowances on the replacement. Any excess of balancing charge over the cost of the replacement is added to business income for the year.

Finally, if the firm sells the equipment for less than £4000 it obtains a balancing allowance which is available for deduction from business income for the year.

Stock relief

One of the many effects of inflation on business investment programmes in the 1970s has been the increased proportion of funds tied up in stock-in-trade. This has led to deterioration in the liquidity positions of many business, making it increasingly difficult for them to provide funds to meet current tax obligations. As a result of this, government legislation was introduced in November 1974 to apply to accounting periods ending 31 March 1974, in order to allow businesses to reduce profits by the amount of any increase in stock-in-trade at the end of the accounting period as against stock-in-trade at the commencement. Since 1976, relief has been available on the basis that should the excess value of closing over opening stock-in-trade be greater than 15 per cent of trading profits (after deducting capital allowances) then such excess is treated as a further trading expense.

The following example illustrates how stock relief may be calculated. Assume a company having taxable profits for 1977 of £12 000, before deducting capital allowances of £4000, has increased its stock levels over the year as follows:

Opening stock	1 January 1977	£18 000
Closing stock	31 December 1977	£24 000
Stock increase		£ 6 000

Stock relief available will be reduced by 15 per cent of taxable profits after capital allowances (£12 000 – £4 000), i.e. £8 000 × 15% = £1200.

Thus total stock relief available is £6000 – 1200 = £4800

Profits subject to corporation tax become:

Net profit for year	£12000
Less: stock relief	£ 4800
	£ 7200
Less: capital allowances	£ 4000
Profits subject to tax	£ 3200

If there is a reduction in the closing stock-in-trade figure as compared with the opening figure then there will be a reclaiming of the difference by the Inland Revenue, provided that this difference is not greater than the total relief already given in earlier periods. The effect of stock relief has been to reduce the corporation tax liability for many large companies to the amount of unrelieved ACT in that year. In effect, the relief given was merely a deferment of the tax. Business do nonetheless receive help in this way with their liquidity problems.

In his Budget speech in 1978, however, the Chancellor announced that if a permanent system of inflation accounting was not introduced by 1979, the deferred tax built up through stock relief would be written off over a number of years.

Franked investment income (FII)

Franked investment income comprises dividends and other qualifying distributions received by one company resident in the United Kingdom from another. Such income is exempt from corporation tax in the hands of the receiving company as it has been paid out of profits which have already borne corporation tax. FII must, however, be included in company profits as a gross figure to determine the rate of corporation tax applicable.

Double taxation relief

Where a company receives income from abroad it is likely that overseas taxation will have been paid on that income. Where an agreement exists between the United Kingdom and the overseas country in which the tax has been paid, relief is given by means of a tax credit which is calculated on the overseas income at the lower of the United Kingdom and the overseas company tax rate.

For example, assume that a company receives income of £7000 from abroad which has borne overseas taxation at the rate of 30 per cent. Corporation tax payable on the income should be calculated as follows:

Overseas trading income (gross) £7000 × 100/70	= £10 000
Corporation tax: £10 000 × 52%	= £ 5 200
Less overseas tax credit £10 000 × 30%	= £ 3 000
Corporation tax payable	£ 2 200

Deductibility of interest and dividends

Interest payments made by a company are normally an allowable deduction from profits before calculation of corporation tax liability, but dividends paid on its share capital are not an allowable deduction. Thus if a firm, paying corporation tax at the marginal rate of 52 per cent, raises £100 000 and contracts to pay the supplier of this money 10 per cent gross, or £10 000 a year, the £10 000 is deductible if the £100 000 is raised by means of an issue of debt capital. It is not deductible if the £100 000 is raised through an issue of shares and the £10 000 is paid as dividends. The after-tax cost to the company of raising the £100 000 through a debt issue would be £10 000 (1 – 0.52) = £4800. The net cost to the company of raising the £100 000 through an issue of ordinary shares would be £10 000 (1 – 0.33) = £6700, as the company would receive a credit for the ACT deducted from the dividend at the basic rate of income tax.

There is still a differential treatment of dividends and interest payments, even after the introduction of the imputation system, which can have a major influence on the manner in which firms raise capital, as we show in Chapter 19.

Payment of corporation tax

The rules relating to the date on which companies must pay their corporation tax liabilities differ according to whether the company commenced trading before or after 1 April 1965.

For a company already trading on 1 April 1965, in general, the tax will be payable on 1 January following the end of the fiscal year in which the accounting period terminates; where the company commenced trading after 1 April 1965, the tax is liable for payment nine months after the end of its accounting period or 30 days after the issue of the assessment by the Inland Revenue, if later.

Thus if a company with an accounting year ended 30 June 1977 was already trading on 1 April 1965, corporation tax will not be paid on any profits until 1 January 1979; if the company began trading after 1 April 1965, the tax will become due for payment on 1 April 1978.

Advance corporation tax

Since 5 April 1973 companies have paid a single rate of tax on their profits whether these are distributed as dividends or not. Under the taxation system that existed before 1973 companies were discouraged from paying dividends, as not only would these dividends be paid out of post-tax profits but they would, in addition, be subject to a deduction of income tax at the standard rate.

Under the new system of company taxation, known as the imputation system, tax is still deducted when a distribution is made but this is now decreed to be an advance payment of corporation tax (ACT). Additionally, each shareholder receives a tax credit equal to the amount of tax deducted from the dividends paid by the company. Once the final corporation tax liability was determined for that company, this would be reduced by the ACT deducted from dividends paid during that accounting period. The net amount remaining, known as 'mainstream tax', would become due for payment on the dates explained by the rules above.

The following illustrates the situation as it now stands for payment of corporation tax. Suppose a company has trading profits for the year ended 31 December 1977 of £100 000. During the year dividends were paid, out of the previous year's profits, amounting to £33 500 (net). The tax liability is calculated as follows:

Trading profits for the year		£100 000
Corporation tax at 52%		£52 000
Less: advance corporation tax deducted on dividends paid:		16 500
Dividend (net)	£33 500	
ACT deducted at standard rate (33/67 × £33 500)	16 500	
Gross dividend	£50 000	
Mainstream tax now due		£35 500

Treatment of trading losses

Any ordinary trading loss may be offset against other profits of the company for the same accounting period. Any balance remaining may be dealt with by

1. carrying the unabsorbed loss back to be offset against the total profits of the three preceding periods and then carrying forward any remaining balance to be offset against the trading profits for future accounting periods; or
2. claiming the loss against surplus franked investment income of the same accounting period; or
3. carrying forward the unabsorbed loss immediately to be offset against profits from some trade for future accounting periods.

Companies operating within a group are able to surrender their losses for an accounting period to be offset against the total profits of other companies within the group for the same accounting period. For this purpose only, a subsidiary company is defined as one in which three-quarters of the ordinary share capital is owned, directly or indirectly, by another company. The right to offset group losses has at times made the purchase of otherwise unattractive companies a worthwhile buy.

Close companies and short-fall in distribution

Where distributions fall short of a prescribed standard, those companies defined as close companies[2] will be liable to income tax on the 'short-fall' as if it had been distributed. The income tax will be calculated by reference to the marginal rate of tax of each shareholder or 'participator'. This rule is designed to prevent non-distribution of profits by small companies with the sole purpose of enabling shareholders to avoid the payment of income tax on dividends received. If the company is able to convince the Inland Revenue that all profits are required for expansion, no short-fall provision will apply. These provisions do not apply to post-tax trading and property income below £25 000 and there is tapering relief between £25 000 and £75 000.

PERSONAL INCOME TAX

Of some 1.4 million firms in the United Kingdom, over 75 per cent are organized as sole proprietorships or as partnerships. The income of firms so organized is taxed as personal income to the owners or the partners. An account of this income is reported to the Inland Revenue and forms the basis for determining the individual's income tax liability. Thus, as a business tax, personal income tax may be as important as corporation tax. Indeed, income tax has the largest yield of any single tax in the United Kingdom.

Personal income tax structure

The tax rates applicable to the single individual are outlined in Table A–3. Generally, the income of a married woman is treated as that of her husband for tax purposes unless an election is made for separate assessment of husband and wife. An election for separate assessment would normally be made to enable each spouse's separate income to be taxed on a lower band than would otherwise be the case if they were combined.

It is not possible to compare the average tax rates for personal and corporate status and make a generalization about the relative tax advantages of each. Although Table A–3

Table A–3 *Tax Rates and Bands of Taxable Income.*[a]

Taxable income	Tax rate	Tax on band	Cumulative tax	Average tax rate at upper limit of each band	
				Personal	Corporate
£	%	£	£	%	%
0– 750	25	187.5	187.5	25	42
751– 8 000	33	2 392	2 580.0	32.3	42
8 001– 9 000	40	400.0	2 980.0	33.1	42
9 001–10 000	45	450.0	3 430.0	34.3	42
10 001–11 000	50	500.0	3930.0	35.7	42
11 001–12 500	55	825.0	4 755.0	38.0	42
12 501–14 000	60	900.0	5 655.0	40.4	42
14 001–16 000	65	1 300.0	6 955.0	43.5	42
16 001–18 500	70	1 750.0	8 705.0	47.1	42
18 501–24 000	75	4 125.0	12 830.0	53.5	42
Over 24 000	83	–	–	–	–

[a] There is no distinction between the tax rate applied to income received in the form of a salary or wage and that received as a share in a partnership or proprietorship income.

2. For a full definition of close companies status refer to The Taxes Act, 1970, section 282, as amended by the Finance Act, 1972. For our purposes, most unquoted companies would qualify as close companies.

shows that the average tax rate for a company is lower than that for an individual whose taxable income is above £14 000, the table does not show the effect of the receipt of income from a company on the individual's tax position. Any proprietorship or partnership contemplating a change to corporate status might be well advised to seek advice from a tax consultant first.

Individual capital gains and losses

As with companies, individuals are liable to tax on capital gains. There is no longer any distinction between short-term and long-term capital gains except that gains on disposal of Treasury stock purchased within the preceding 12 months will be liable to capital gains tax; gains on disposal of Treasury stock held for more than 12 months will be liable to no tax at all.

The tax on capital gains may be computed in either of two ways. The taxpayer may pay a flat rate of 30 per cent on the net gains, or he may elect to apply his marginal income tax rate on one-half of the chargeable gains when these do not exceed £5000; if the gains exceed £5000 the taxpayer will pay additionally the excess over £5000.

For example, a taxpayer with taxable income of £8000 and capital gains of £2200 would compute tax liability in two ways. He would either

1. apply the normal tax rates on £8000, plus 30 per cent on £2200, or
2. apply the normal tax rates on £8000 plus 50 per cent of £2200 = £9100.

The first method would produce a tax liability of £3550, the second a tax liability of £3445. The taxpayer would naturally elect the second method in this case.

In general, the first method of calculating tax liability would be beneficial only if the taxable income exceeds £12 500, the point at which the marginal tax rate reaches 60 per cent.

Capital losses may be set off against capital gains of the same year; any balance may be carried forward and deducted against future capital gains. There is no right to offset capital losses against ordinary income.

Investment income

Investment income received by a shareholder will be subject to a surcharge in addition to the normal income tax where this income exceeds £1700 (£2500 if the taxpayer is aged 65 years or more). The 1978–9 bands are shown in Table A–4. Personal allowances must be deducted against earned income first and then against investment income.

Table A–4 *Investment Income Surcharge 1978–9.*

Rate	Investment income	
	Aged 65 or over	Others
%	£	£
Nil	1–2500	1–1700
10	2501–3000	1701–2250
15	over 3000	over 2250

Personal allowances

The major personal allowances[3] which may be deducted from income before determining tax liability are as follows:

	£
Single, personal allowance	985
Married, personal allowance	1535
Wife's maximum earned income allowance	985
Age allowance – single person	1300
Age allowance – married couple	2075

Other reliefs

A few other items are also deductible from income before computing tax liability: covenants to charity, mortgage interest, and annual subscriptions to professional bodies and trade unions, among others.

SUMMARY

The appendix provides some basic background information on the tax environment within which business firms operate.

Company taxation

The UK corporation tax rate structure is relatively straightforward compared with the income tax rate structure. The tax rate is 52 per cent on income over £85 000 and 42 per cent on income below £50 000, with tapering relief on income falling between £50 000 and £85 000. Tax is due for payment nine months after the end of the accounting year in the case of companies which commenced trading after 1 April 1965; in the case of a company already trading on 1 April 1965 tax becomes due for payment on 1 January following the end of the tax year in which the accounting period terminates. Additionally, ACT is payable on distribution of dividends. Operating losses may be carried back for three years and forward for any number of years until absorbed. Capital losses may not be treated as a deduction from operating income, but may be used to offset capital gains arising either in that period or in future periods. Net capital gains are taxed at an effective rate of 30 per cent (as is also the case for individuals). Dividends received by one company operating in the UK from another also operating in the UK are not subject to corporation tax. Dividends paid are not treated as a tax-deductible expense, nor are distributed profits taxed at a higher rate than retained earnings. Companies categorized as close companies may, however, be subject to tax on 'notional distributions' if they have retained profits for the sole purpose of enabling shareholders to avoid paying income tax on dividends received. Interest received is taxable as ordinary income; interest paid is a deductible expense.

---

3. As these allowances tend to change very frequently, the current Finance Act should be consulted for the up-to-date position. In addition, information relating to the various other allowances available may be obtained from the same source.

Personal income tax

Unincorporated business income is taxed at the personal tax rates of the owners. Personal tax rates are progressive – the higher one's income, the higher the tax rate. Personal income tax rates begin at 25 per cent of taxable income and rise to 83 per cent. In addition, an investment income, surcharge exists on income received in excess of £1700 (£2500 if the recipient is over 65 years of age).

Capital gains are taxed at 30 per cent or at the marginal tax rate on one-half the gains, provided that they do not exceed £5000, whichever is the lower for the taxpayer. Capital losses can be used to offset capital gains, any balance being carried forward to be offset against capital gains of later years.

This material on the United Kingdom tax system is not designed to make a tax expert of the reader. It merely provides a few essentials for recognizing the tax aspects of business financial problems and for developing an awareness of the types of situations that should be taken to tax specialists. These basic facts are referred to frequently throughout the text, however, because of the important role taxes play in business financial decisions.

Appendix B

Depreciation Methods

The four principal methods of depreciation – straight line, sum-of-years'-digits, double declining balance and units of production – and their effects on a firm's profits are illustrated in this appendix. We will begin by assuming that a machine is purchased for £1100 and has an estimated useful life of ten years or ten thousand hours. It will have a scrap value of £100 after ten years of use or after ten thousand hours, whichever comes first. Table B–1 illustrates each of the four depreciation methods and compares the depreciation charges of each method over the ten-year period.

Table B–1 *Comparison of Depreciation Methods for a 10-year, £1100 Asset with a £100 Salvage Value.*

Depreciation methods Year	Straight line	Double declining balance	Sum-of-years'-digits	Units of production[a]
1	£ 100	£ 220	£ 182	£ 200
2	100	176	164	180
3	100	141	145	150
4	100	113	127	130
5	100	90	109	100
6	100	72	91	80
7	100	58	73	60
8	100	46	55	50
9	100	37	36	30
10	100	29	18	20
Total	£1000	£982	£1000	£1000

[a] The assumption is made that the machine is used the following number of hours: first year, 2000; second year, 1800; third year, 1500; fourth year, 1300; fifth year, 1000; sixth year, 800; seventh year, 600; eighth year, 500; ninth year, 300; tenth year, 200.

STRAIGHT LINE

With the straight line method, a uniform annual depreciation charge of £100 a year is provided. This figure is arrived at by simply dividing the economic life into the total cost of the machine minus the estimated salvage value:

$$\frac{(£1100 \text{ cost} - £100 \text{ salvage value})}{10 \text{ years}} = £100 \text{ a year depreciation charge.}$$

DOUBLE DECLINING BALANCE

The double declining balance (DDB) method of accelerated depreciation requires the application of a cost rate of depreciation each year to the undepreciated value of the asset at the close of the previous year. In this case, since the annual straight line rate is 10 per cent a year (£100 ÷ £1000), the double declining rate would be 20 per cent (2 × 10 per cent). This rate is applied to the full purchase price of the machine, not to the cost less salvage value. Therefore, depreciation under the DDB method is £220 during the first year (20 per cent × £1100). Depreciation amounts to £176 in the second year and is calcuated by applying the 20 per cent rate to the undepreciated value of the asset.

$$20\% \times (£1100 - £220) = £176,$$

and so on, as the undepreciated balance declines. Notice that under DDB the asset is not fully depreciated at the end of the tenth year. In our example the remaining depreciation would be taken in the tenth year.

SUM-OF-YEARS'-DIGITS

Under the sum-of-years'-digits method, the yearly depreciation allowance is determined as follows:

1. Calculate the sum of the years' digits; in our example, there is a total of 55 digits: 1 + 2 + 3 + 4 + 5 + 6 + 7 + 8 + 9 + 10 = 55. This figure can also be arrived at by means of the sum of an algebraic progression equation where N is the life of the asset:

$$\text{Sum} = N\left(\frac{N+1}{2}\right)$$
$$= 10\left(\frac{10+1}{2}\right) = 55$$

2. Divide the number of remaining years by the sum-of-years'-digits and multiply this fraction by the depreciable cost (total cost minus salvage value) of the asset:

Year 1: $\frac{10}{55}(£1000) = £182$ depreciation.

Year 2: $\frac{9}{55}(£1000) = £164$ depreciation.

Year 10: $\frac{1}{55}(£1000) = £18$ depreciation.

UNITS OF PRODUCTION

Under the units of production method, the expected useful life of 10 000 hours is divided into the depreciable cost (purchase price minus salvage value) to arrive at an hourly depreciation rate of ten pence. Since, in our example, the machine is run for 2000 hours in the first year, the depreciation in that year is £200; in the second year, £180; and so on. With this method, depreciation charges cannot be estimated precisely ahead of time; the firm must wait until the end of the year to determine what usage has been made of the machine and hence its depreciation.

EFFECT OF DEPRECIATION ON REPORTED PROFITS

The effect of the accelerated methods on a firm's reported profits is easily demonstrated. In the first year, should the firm choose to use the straight-line method, only £100 may be deducted from its earnings to arrive at the net profit for the year. However, using any one of the other three methods, the firm would have a much greater depreciation charge and, therefore, a lower net profit.

It should be remembered by students that the depreciation expense is not allowed in the calculation of taxable profits, but that capital allowances are granted by the Inland Revenue instead (see Appendix A, 'The Tax Environment').

Appendix C

The Normal Curve

Table C *Values of the Standard Normal Distribution Function.*

z	0.00	0.01	0.02	0.03	0.04	0.05	0.06	0.07	0.08	0.09
0.0	0.0000	0.0040	0.0080	0.0120	0.0160	0.0199	0.0239	0.0279	0.0319	0.0359
0.1	0.0398	0.0438	0.0478	0.0517	0.0557	0.0596	0.0636	0.0675	0.0714	0.0753
0.2	0.0793	0.0832	0.0871	0.0910	0.0948	0.0987	0.1026	0.1064	0.1103	0.1141
0.3	0.1179	0.1217	0.1255	0.1293	0.1331	0.1368	0.1406	0.1443	0.1480	0.1517
0.4	0.1554	0.1591	0.1628	0.1664	0.1700	0.1736	0.1772	0.1808	0.1844	0.1879
0.5	0.1915	0.1950	0.1985	0.2019	0.2054	0.2088	0.2123	0.2157	0.2190	0.2224
0.6	0.2257	0.2291	0.2324	0.2357	0.2389	0.2422	0.2454	0.2486	0.2517	0.2549
0.7	0.2580	0.2611	0.2642	0.2673	0.2704	0.2734	0.2764	0.2794	0.2823	0.2852
0.8	0.2881	0.2910	0.2939	0.2967	0.2995	0.3023	0.3051	0.3078	0.3106	0.3133
0.9	0.3159	0.3186	0.3212	0.3238	0.3264	0.3289	0.3315	0.3340	0.3365	0.3389
1.0	0.3413	0.3438	0.3461	0.3485	0.3508	0.3531	0.3554	0.3577	0.3599	0.3621
1.1	0.3643	0.3665	0.3686	0.3708	0.3729	0.3749	0.3770	0.3790	0.3810	0.3830
1.2	0.3849	0.3869	0.3888	0.3907	0.3925	0.3944	0.3962	0.3980	0.3997	0.4015
1.3	0.4032	0.4049	0.4066	0.4082	0.4099	0.4115	0.4131	0.4147	0.4162	0.4177
1.4	0.4192	0.4207	0.4222	0.4236	0.4251	0.4265	0.4279	0.4292	0.4306	0.4319
1.5	0.4332	0.4345	0.4357	0.4370	0.4382	0.4394	0.4406	0.4418	0.4429	0.4441
1.6	0.4452	0.4463	0.4474	0.4484	0.4495	0.4505	0.4515	0.4525	0.4535	0.4545
1.7	0.4554	0.4564	0.4573	0.4582	0.4591	0.4599	0.4608	0.4616	0.4625	0.4633
1.8	0.4641	0.4649	0.4656	0.4664	0.4671	0.4678	0.4686	0.4693	0.4699	0.4706
1.9	0.4713	0.4719	0.4726	0.4732	0.4738	0.4744	0.4750	0.4756	0.4761	0.4767
2.0	0.4772	0.4778	0.4783	0.4788	0.4793	0.4798	0.4803	0.4808	0.4812	0.4817
2.1	0.4821	0.4826	0.4830	0.4834	0.4838	0.4842	0.4846	0.4850	0.4854	0.4857
2.2	0.4861	0.4864	0.4868	0.4871	0.4875	0.4878	0.4881	0.4884	0.4887	0.4890
2.3	0.4893	0.4896	0.4898	0.4901	0.4904	0.4906	0.4909	0.4911	0.4913	0.4916
2.4	0.4918	0.4920	0.4922	0.4925	0.4927	0.4929	0.4931	0.4932	0.4934	0.4936
2.5	0.4938	0.4940	0.4941	0.4943	0.4945	0.4946	0.4948	0.4949	0.4951	0.4952
2.6	0.4953	0.4955	0.4956	0.4957	0.4959	0.4960	0.4961	0.4962	0.4963	0.4964
2.7	0.4965	0.4966	0.4967	0.4968	0.4969	0.4970	0.4971	0.4972	0.4973	0.4974
2.8	0.4974	0.4975	0.4976	0.4977	0.4977	0.4978	0.4979	0.4979	0.4980	0.4981
2.9	0.4981	0.4982	0.4982	0.4982	0.4984	0.4984	0.4985	0.4985	0.4986	0.4986
3.0	0.4987	0.4987	0.4987	0.4988	0.4988	0.4989	0.4989	0.4989	0.4990	0.4990

Appendix D

Interest Tables

Table D–1 *Compound Sum of £1 (CVIF)* $S = P(1+r)^N$

Period	1%	2%	3%	4%	5%	6%	7%
1	1.010	1.020	1.030	1.040	1.050	1.060	1.070
2	1.020	1.040	1.061	1.082	1.102	1.124	1.145
3	1.030	1.061	1.093	1.125	1.158	1.191	1.225
4	1.041	1.082	1.126	1.170	1.216	1.262	1.311
5	1.051	1.104	1.159	1.217	1.276	1.338	1.403
6	1.062	1.126	1.194	1.265	1.340	1.419	1.501
7	1.072	1.149	1.230	1.316	1.407	1.504	1.606
8	1.083	1.172	1.267	1.369	1.477	1.594	1.718
9	1.094	1.195	1.305	1.423	1.551	1.689	1.838
10	1.105	1.219	1.344	1.480	1.629	1.791	1.967
11	1.116	1.243	1.384	1.539	1.710	1.898	2.105
12	1.127	1.268	1.426	1.601	1.796	2.012	2.252
13	1.138	1.294	1.469	1.665	1.886	2.133	2.410
14	1.149	1.319	1.513	1.732	1.980	2.261	2.579
15	1.161	1.346	1.558	1.801	2.079	2.397	2.759
16	1.173	1.373	1.605	1.873	2.183	2.540	2.952
17	1.184	1.400	1.653	1.948	2.292	2.693	3.159
18	1.196	1.428	1.702	2.026	2.407	2.854	3.380
19	1.208	1.457	1.754	2.107	2.527	3.026	3.617
20	1.220	1.486	1.806	2.191	2.653	3.207	3.870
25	1.282	1.641	2.094	2.666	3.386	4.292	5.427
30	1.348	1.811	2.427	3.243	4.322	5.743	7.612

Period	8%	9%	10%	12%	14%	15%	16%
1	1.080	1.090	1.100	1.120	1.140	1.150	1.160
2	1.166	1.186	1.210	1.254	1.300	1.322	1.346
3	1.260	1.295	1.331	1.405	1.482	1.521	1.561
4	1.360	1.412	1.464	1.574	1.689	1.749	1.811
5	1.469	1.539	1.611	1.762	1.925	2.011	2.100
6	1.587	1.677	1.772	1.974	2.195	2.313	2.436

Table D–1 *Continued*

Period	8%	9%	10%	12%	14%	15%	16%
7	1.714	1.828	1.949	2.211	2.502	2.660	2.826
8	1.851	1.993	2.144	2.476	2.853	3.059	3.278
9	1.999	2.172	2.358	2.773	3.252	3.518	3.803
10	2.159	2.367	2.594	3.106	3.707	4.046	4.411
11	2.332	2.580	2.853	3.479	4.226	4.652	5.117
12	2.518	2.813	3.138	3.896	4.818	5.350	5.926
13	2.720	3.066	3.452	4.363	5.492	6.153	6.886
14	2.937	3.342	3.797	4.887	6.261	7.076	7.988
15	3.172	3.642	4.177	5.474	7.138	8.137	9.266
16	3.426	3.970	4.595	6.130	8.137	9.358	10.748
17	3.700	4.328	5.054	6.866	9.276	10.761	12.468
18	3.996	4.717	5.560	7.690	10.575	12.375	14.463
19	4.316	5.142	6.116	8.613	12.056	14.232	16.777
20	4.661	5.604	6.728	9.646	13.743	16.367	19.461
25	6.848	8.623	10.835	17.000	26.462	32.919	40.874
30	10.063	13.268	17.449	29.960	50.950	66.212	85.850

Period	18%	20%	24%	28%	32%	36%
1	1.180	1.200	1.240	1.280	1.320	1.360
2	1.392	1.440	1.538	1.638	1.742	1.850
3	1.643	1.728	1.907	2.067	2.300	2.515
4	1.939	2.074	2.364	2.684	3.036	3.421
5	2.288	2.488	2.932	3.436	4.007	4.653
6	2.700	2.986	3.635	4.398	5.290	6.328
7	3.185	3.583	4.508	5.629	6.983	8.605
8	3.759	4.300	5.590	7.206	9.217	11.703
9	4.435	5.160	6.931	9.223	12.166	15.917
10	5.234	6.192	8.594	11.806	16.060	21.647
11	6.176	7.430	10.657	15.112	21.199	29.439
12	7.288	8.916	13.215	19.343	27.983	40.037
13	8.599	10.699	16.386	24.759	36.937	54.451
14	10.147	12.839	20.319	31.961	48.757	74.053
15	11.974	15.407	25.196	40.565	64.359	100.712
16	14.129	18.488	31.243	51.923	84.954	136.970
17	16.672	22.186	38.741	66.461	112.140	186.280
18	19.673	26.623	48.039	85.071	148.020	253.340
19	23.214	31.948	59.568	108.890	195.390	344.540
20	27.393	38.338	73.864	139.380	257.920	468.570
25	62.669	95.396	216.542	478.900	1033.600	2180.100
30	143.371	237.376	634.820	1645.500	4142.100	10143.000

Period	40%	50%	60%	70%	80%	90%
1	1.400	1.500	1.600	1.700	1.800	1.900
2	1.960	2.250	2.560	2.890	3.240	3.610
3	2.744	3.375	4.096	4.913	5.832	6.859
4	3.842	5.062	6.544	8.352	10.498	13.032
5	5.378	7.594	10.486	14.199	18.896	24.761
6	7.530	11.391	16.777	24.138	34.012	47.046
7	10.541	17.066	26.844	41.034	61.222	89.387
8	14.758	25.629	42.950	69.758	110.200	169.836
9	20.661	38.443	68.720	118.588	198.359	322.688
10	28.925	57.665	109.951	201.599	357.047	613.107

Table D–1 *Continued*

Period	40%	50%	60%	70%	80%	90%
11	40.496	86.498	175.922	342.719	642.684	1164.902
12	56.694	129.746	281.475	582.622	1156.831	2213.314
13	79.372	194.619	450.360	990.457	2082.295	4205.297
14	111.120	291.929	720.576	1683.777	3748.131	7990.065
15	155.568	437.894	1152.921	2862.421	6746.636	15181.122
16	217.795	656.840	1844.700	4866.100	12144.000	28844.000
17	304.914	985.260	2951.500	8272.400	21859.000	54804.000
18	426.879	1477.900	4722.400	14063.000	39346.000	104130.000
19	597.630	2216.800	7555.800	23907.000	70824.000	197840.000
20	836.683	3325.300	12089.000	40642.000	127480.000	375900.000
25	4499.880	26251.000	126760.000	577060.000	2408900.000	9307600.000
30	24201.432	191750.000	1329200.000	8193500.000	45517000.000	230470000.000

Table D–2 *Present Value of £1 (PVIF)* $P = S(1+r)^{-N}$

Period	1%	2%	3%	4%	5%	6%	7%	8%	9%	10%	12%	14%	15%
1	0.990	0.980	0.971	0.962	0.952	0.943	0.935	0.926	0.917	0.909	0.893	0.877	0.870
2	0.980	0.961	0.943	0.925	0.907	0.890	0.873	0.857	0.842	0.826	0.797	0.769	0.756
3	0.971	0.942	0.915	0.889	0.864	0.840	0.816	0.794	0.772	0.751	0.712	0.675	0.658
4	0.961	0.924	0.889	0.855	0.823	0.792	0.763	0.735	0.708	0.683	0.636	0.592	0.572
5	0.951	0.906	0.863	0.822	0.784	0.747	0.713	0.681	0.650	0.621	0.567	0.519	0.497
6	0.942	0.888	0.838	0.790	0.746	0.705	0.666	0.630	0.596	0.564	0.507	0.456	0.432
7	0.933	0.871	0.813	0.760	0.711	0.665	0.623	0.583	0.547	0.513	0.452	0.400	0.376
8	0.923	0.853	0.789	0.731	0.677	0.627	0.582	0.540	0.502	0.467	0.404	0.351	0.327
9	0.914	0.837	0.766	0.703	0.645	0.592	0.544	0.500	0.460	0.424	0.361	0.308	0.284
10	0.905	0.820	0.744	0.676	0.614	0.558	0.508	0.463	0.422	0.386	0.322	0.270	0.247
11	0.896	0.804	0.722	0.650	0.585	0.527	0.475	0.429	0.388	0.350	0.287	0.237	0.215
12	0.887	0.788	0.701	0.625	0.557	0.497	0.444	0.397	0.356	0.319	0.257	0.208	0.187
13	0.879	0.773	0.681	0.601	0.530	0.469	0.415	0.368	0.326	0.290	0.229	0.182	0.163
14	0.870	0.758	0.661	0.577	0.505	0.442	0.388	0.340	0.299	0.263	0.205	0.160	0.141
15	0.861	0.743	0.642	0.555	0.481	0.417	0.362	0.315	0.275	0.239	0.183	0.140	0.123
16	0.853	0.728	0.623	0.534	0.458	0.394	0.339	0.292	0.252	0.218	0.163	0.123	0.107
17	0.844	0.714	0.605	0.513	0.436	0.371	0.317	0.270	0.231	0.198	0.146	0.108	0.093
18	0.836	0.700	0.587	0.494	0.416	0.350	0.296	0.250	0.212	0.180	0.130	0.095	0.081
19	0.828	0.686	0.570	0.475	0.396	0.331	0.276	0.232	0.194	0.164	0.116	0.083	0.070
20	0.820	0.673	0.554	0.456	0.377	0.312	0.258	0.215	0.178	0.149	0.104	0.073	0.061
25	0.780	0.610	0.478	0.375	0.295	0.233	0.184	0.146	0.116	0.092	0.059	0.038	0.030
30	0.742	0.552	0.412	0.308	0.231	0.174	0.131	0.099	0.075	0.057	0.033	0.020	0.015

Period	16%	18%	20%	24%	28%	32%	36%	40%	50%	60%	70%	80%	90%
1	0.862	0.847	0.833	0.806	0.781	0.758	0.735	0.714	0.667	0.625	0.588	0.556	0.526
2	0.743	0.718	0.694	0.650	0.610	0.574	0.541	0.510	0.444	0.391	0.346	0.309	0.277
3	0.641	0.609	0.579	0.524	0.477	0.435	0.398	0.364	0.296	0.244	0.204	0.171	0.146
4	0.552	0.516	0.482	0.423	0.373	0.329	0.292	0.260	0.198	0.153	0.120	0.095	0.077
5	0.476	0.437	0.402	0.341	0.291	0.250	0.215	0.186	0.132	0.095	0.070	0.053	0.040
6	0.410	0.370	0.335	0.275	0.227	0.189	0.158	0.133	0.088	0.060	0.041	0.029	0.021
7	0.354	0.314	0.279	0.222	0.178	0.143	0.116	0.095	0.059	0.037	0.024	0.016	0.011
8	0.305	0.266	0.233	0.179	0.139	0.108	0.085	0.068	0.039	0.023	0.014	0.009	0.006
9	0.263	0.226	0.194	0.144	0.108	0.082	0.063	0.048	0.026	0.015	0.008	0.005	0.003
10	0.227	0.191	0.162	0.116	0.085	0.062	0.046	0.035	0.017	0.009	0.005	0.003	0.002
11	0.195	0.162	0.135	0.094	0.066	0.047	0.034	0.025	0.012	0.006	0.003	0.002	0.001
12	0.168	0.137	0.112	0.076	0.052	0.036	0.025	0.018	0.008	0.004	0.002	0.001	0.001
13	0.145	0.116	0.093	0.061	0.040	0.027	0.018	0.013	0.005	0.002	0.001	0.001	0.000
14	0.125	0.099	0.078	0.049	0.032	0.021	0.014	0.009	0.003	0.001	0.001	0.000	0.000
15	0.108	0.084	0.065	0.040	0.025	0.016	0.010	0.006	0.002	0.001	0.000	0.000	0.000

Table D–2 *Continued*

Period	16%	18%	20%	24%	28%	32%	36%	40%	50%	60%	70%	80%	90%
16	0.093	0.071	0.054	0.032	0.019	0.012	0.007	0.005	0.002	0.001	0.000	0.000	
17	0.080	0.060	0.045	0.026	0.015	0.009	0.005	0.003	0.001	0.000	0.000		
18	0.089	0.051	0.038	0.021	0.012	0.007	0.004	0.002	0.001	0.000	0.000		
19	0.060	0.043	0.031	0.017	0.009	0.005	0.003	0.002	0.000	0.000			
20	0.051	0.037	0.026	0.014	0.007	0.004	0.002	0.001	0.000	0.000			
25	0.024	0.016	0.010	0.005	0.002	0.001	0.000	0.000					
30	0.012	0.007	0.004	0.002	0.001	0.000	0.000						

Table D–3 *Sum of an Annuity of £1 for N Periods* $(CVIF_a)\ S_{m/r} = £1\left[\dfrac{(1+r)^N - 1}{r}\right]$

Period	1%	2%	3%	4%	5%	6%
1	1.000	1.000	1.000	1.000	1.000	1.000
2	2.010	2.020	2.030	2.040	2.050	2.060
3	3.030	3.060	3.091	3.122	3.152	3.184
4	4.060	4.122	4.184	4.246	4.310	4.375
5	5.101	5.204	5.309	5.416	5.526	5.637
6	6.152	6.308	6.468	6.633	6.802	6.975
7	7.214	7.434	7.662	7.898	8.142	8.394
8	8.286	8.583	8.892	9.214	9.549	9.897
9	9.369	9.755	10.159	10.583	11.027	11.491
10	10.462	10.950	11.464	12.006	12.578	13.181
11	11.567	12.169	12.808	13.486	14.207	14.972
12	12.683	13.412	14.192	15.026	15.917	16.870
13	13.809	14.680	15.618	16.627	17.713	18.882
14	14.947	15.974	17.086	18.292	19.599	21.051
15	16.097	17.293	18.599	20.024	21.579	23.276
16	17.258	18.639	20.157	21.825	23.657	25.673
17	18.430	20.012	21.762	23.698	25.840	28.213
18	19.615	21.412	23.414	25.645	28.132	30.906
19	20.811	22.841	25.117	27.671	30.539	33.760
20	22.019	24.297	26.870	29.778	33.066	36.786
25	28.243	32.030	36.459	41.646	47.727	54.865
30	34.785	40.568	47.575	56.805	66.439	79.058

Period	7%	8%	9%	10%	12%	14%
1	1.000	1.000	1.000	1.000	1.000	1.000
2	2.070	2.080	2.090	2.100	2.120	2.140
3	3.215	3.246	3.278	3.310	3.374	3.440
4	4.440	4.506	4.573	4.641	4.770	4.921
5	5.751	5.867	5.985	6.105	6.353	6.610
6	7.153	7.336	7.523	7.716	8.115	8.536
7	8.654	8.923	9.200	9.487	10.089	10.730
8	10.260	10.637	11.028	11.436	12.300	13.233
9	11.978	12.488	13.021	13.579	14.776	16.085
10	13.816	14.487	15.193	15.937	17.549	19.337
11	15.784	16.645	17.560	18.531	20.655	23.044
12	17.888	18.977	20.141	21.384	24.133	27.271
13	20.141	21.495	22.953	24.523	28.029	32.089
14	22.550	24.215	26.019	27.975	32.393	37.581
15	25.129	27.152	29.361	31.772	37.280	43.842
16	27.888	30.324	33.003	35.950	42.753	50.980

Table D–3 *Continued*

Period	7%	8%	9%	10%	12%	14%
17	30.840	33.750	36.974	40.545	48.884	59.118
18	33.999	37.450	41.301	45.599	55.750	68.394
19	37.379	41.446	46.018	51.159	63.440	78.969
20	40.995	45.762	51.160	57.275	72.052	91.025
25	63.249	73.106	84.701	98.347	133.334	181.871
30	94.461	113.283	136.308	164.494	241.333	356.787

Period	16%	18%	20%	24%	28%	32%
1	1.000	1.000	1.000	1.000	1.000	1.000
2	2.160	2.180	2.200	2.240	2.280	2.320
3	3.506	3.572	3.640	3.778	3.918	4.062
4	5.066	5.215	5.368	5.684	6.016	6.392
5	6.877	7.154	7.442	8.048	8.700	9.398
6	8.977	9.442	9.930	10.980	12.136	13.406
7	11.414	12.142	12.916	14.615	16.534	18.696
8	14.240	15.327	16.499	19.123	22.163	25.678
9	17.518	19.086	20.799	24.712	29.369	34.895
10	21.321	23.521	25.959	31.643	38.592	47.062
11	25.733	28.755	32.150	40.238	50.399	63.122
12	30.850	34.931	39.580	50.985	65.510	84.320
13	36.786	42.219	48.497	64.110	84.853	112.303
14	43.672	50.818	59.196	80.496	109.612	149.240
15	51.660	60.965	72.035	100.815	141.303	197.997
16	60.925	72.939	87.442	126.011	181.870	262.36
17	71.673	87.068	105.931	157.253	233.790	347.31
18	84.141	103.740	128.117	195.994	300.250	459.45
19	98.603	123.414	154.740	244.033	385.320	607.47
20	115.380	146.628	186.688	303.601	494.210	802.86
25	249.214	342.603	471.981	898.092	1706.800	3226.80
30	530.312	790.948	1181.882	2640.916	5873.200	12941.00

Period	36%	40%	50%	60%	70%	80%
1	1.000	1.000	1.000	1.000	1.000	1.000
2	2.360	2.400	2.500	2.600	2.700	2.800
3	4.210	4.360	4.750	5.160	5.590	6.040
4	6.725	7.104	8.125	9.256	10.503	11.872
5	10.146	10.846	13.188	15.810	18.855	22.370
6	14.799	16.324	20.781	26.295	33.054	41.265
7	21.126	23.853	32.172	43.073	57.191	75.278
8	29.732	34.395	49.258	69.916	98.225	136.500
9	41.435	49.153	74.887	112.866	167.983	246.699
10	57.352	69.814	113.330	181.585	286.570	445.058
11	78.998	98.739	170.995	291.536	488.170	802.105
12	108.437	139.235	257.493	467.458	830.888	1444.788
13	148.475	195.929	387.239	748.933	1413.510	2601.619
14	202.926	275.300	581.859	1199.293	2403.968	4683.914
15	276.979	386.420	873.788	1919.869	4087.745	8432.045
16	377.690	541.990	1311.700	3072.800	6950.200	15179.000
17	514.660	759.780	1968.500	4917.500	11816.000	27323.000
18	700.940	1064.700	2953.800	7868.900	20089.000	49182.000
19	954.280	1491.600	4431.700	12591.000	34152.000	88528.000
20	1298.800	2089.200	6648.500	20147.000	58059.000	159350.000
25	6053.000	11247.000	50500.000	211270.000	824370.000	3011100.000
30	28172.000	60501.000	383500.000	2215400.000	11705000.000	56896000.000

Table D-4 *Present Value of an annuity of £1* $(PVIF_a)\ A_{n|r} = £\ 1\left[\frac{1-(1+r)^{-N}}{r}\right]$

Period	1%	2%	3%	4%	5%	6%	7%	8%	9%	10%
1	0.990	0.980	0.971	0.962	0.952	0.943	0.935	0.926	0.917	0.909
2	1.970	1.942	1.913	1.886	1.859	1.833	1.808	1.783	1.759	1.736
3	2.941	2.884	2.829	2.775	2.723	2.673	2.624	2.577	2.531	2.487
4	3.902	3.808	3.717	3.630	3.546	3.465	3.387	3.312	3.240	3.170
5	4.853	4.713	4.580	4.452	4.329	4.212	4.100	3.993	3.890	3.791
6	5.795	5.601	5.417	5.242	5.076	4.917	4.766	4.623	4.486	4.355
7	6.728	6.472	6.230	6.002	5.786	5.582	5.389	5.206	5.033	4.868
8	7.652	7.325	7.020	6.733	6.463	6.210	5.971	5.747	5.535	5.335
9	8.566	8.162	7.786	7.435	7.108	6.802	6.515	6.247	5.995	5.759
10	9.471	8.983	8.530	8.111	7.722	7.360	7.024	6.710	6.418	6.145
11	10.368	9.787	9.253	8.760	8.306	7.887	7.499	7.139	6.805	6.495
12	11.255	10.575	9.954	9.385	8.863	8.384	7.943	7.536	7.161	6.814
13	12.134	11.348	10.635	9.986	9.394	8.853	8.358	7.904	7.487	7.103
14	13.004	12.106	11.296	10.563	9.899	9.295	8.745	8.244	7.786	7.367
15	13.865	12.849	11.938	11.118	10.380	9.712	9.108	8.559	8.060	7.606
16	14.718	13.578	12.561	11.652	10.838	10.106	9.447	8.851	8.312	7.824
17	15.562	14.292	13.166	12.166	11.274	10.477	9.763	9.122	8.544	8.022
18	16.398	14.992	13.754	12.659	11.690	10.828	10.059	9.372	8.756	8.201
19	17.226	15.678	14.324	13.134	12.085	11.158	10.336	9.604	8.950	8.365
20	18.046	16.351	14.877	13.590	12.462	11.470	10.594	9.818	9.128	8.514
25	22.023	19.523	17.413	15.622	14.094	12.783	11.654	10.675	9.823	9.077
30	25.808	22.397	19.600	17.292	15.373	13.765	12.409	11.258	10.274	9.427

Period	12%	14%	16%	18%	20%	24%	28%	32%	36%
1	0.893	0.877	0.862	0.847	0.833	0.806	0.781	0.758	0.735
2	1.690	1.647	1.605	1.566	1.528	1.457	1.392	1.332	1.276
3	2.402	2.322	2.246	2.174	2.106	1.981	1.868	1.766	1.674
4	3.037	2.914	2.798	2.690	2.589	2.404	2.241	2.096	1.966
5	3.605	3.433	3.274	3.127	2.991	2.745	2.532	2.345	2.181
6	4.111	3.889	3.685	3.498	3.326	3.020	2.759	2.534	2.339
7	4.564	4.288	4.039	3.812	3.605	3.242	2.937	2.678	2.455
8	4.968	4.639	4.344	4.078	3.837	3.421	3.076	2.786	2.540
9	5.328	4.946	4.607	4.303	4.031	3.566	3.184	2.868	2.603
10	5.650	5.216	4.883	4.494	4.193	3.682	3.269	2.930	2.650
11	5.938	5.453	5.029	4.656	4.327	3.776	3.335	2.978	2.683
12	6.194	5.660	5.197	4.793	4.439	3.851	3.387	3.013	2.708
13	6.424	5.842	5.342	4.910	4.533	3.912	3.427	3.040	2.727
14	6.628	6.002	5.468	5.008	4.611	3.962	3.459	3.061	2.740
15	6.811	6.142	5.575	5.092	4.675	4.001	3.483	3.076	2.750
16	6.974	6.265	5.669	5.162	4.730	4.033	3.503	3.088	2.758
17	7.120	5.373	5.749	4.222	4.775	4.059	3.518	3.097	2.763
18	7.250	6.467	5.818	5.273	4.812	4.080	3.529	3.104	2.767
19	7.366	6.550	5.877	5.316	4.844	4.097	3.539	3.109	2.770
20	7.469	6.623	5.929	5.353	4.870	4.110	3.546	3.113	2.772
25	7.843	6.873	6.097	5.467	4.948	4.147	3.564	3.122	2.776
30	8.005	7.003	6.177	5.517	4.979	4.160	3.569	3.124	2.778

Appendix E

Answers to Selected End-of-Chapter Problems

We present here some partial answers to selected end-of-chapter problems. For the most part, the answers given are only the final answers (or answers at intermediate steps) to the more complex problems. Within limits, these answers will be useful to see if the student is 'on the right track' towards solving the problem. The primary limitation, which must be kept in mind, is that some questions may have more than one solution, depending upon which of several equally plausible assumptions are made in working the problem. Also, many of the problems involve some verbal discussion as well as numerical calculations. We have not presented any of this verbal material here.

2–2 (a) Debt/Assets = 30 per cent, stock turnover = 5, fixed asset turnover = 5.41, return on net worth = 7.14 per cent.

3–1 (a) (1) (£14 000); (b) 13 750 units; (c) (1) −6.86; (d) 18 333 units; (e) 13 750 units.

3–3 (a) (iii) 68 625 units; (b) (iii) 9.71; (c) (iii) £252 000; (f) (iii) 570.4.

3–4 (a) Total uses £351.

3–5 (b) £130; (c) £25 000; (d) P = £100, profits £16 000.

4–1 (a) Total assets £4 500 000, 5-year addition to retained earnings £630 000.

4–2 (a) Total assets £2 434 000.

4–3 (a) Total assets £8 280 000; (b) £414 000; (c) Total assets £9 108 000; (d) (3) External funds needed increase by £330 000.

4–5 (a) 12 per cent; (b) 27 per cent; (c) 5.4 per cent.

5–1 (a) Surplus cash: £85 250, £233 000, (£151 750), (£26 500), £91 250, £160 250.

6–1 (a) 11.3 per cent, 10.4 per cent, 8.8 per cent.

6–2 (a) Plan (1) £66 800, (2) £68 000, (3) £67 400; (b) Worst: (£25 600), (£4000), (£14 800), Best: £144 000, £138 000, £141 000.

7–1 (a) Net profit from extension (3) £25 610, (4) (£1600), (5) (£69 600); (b) (3) £45 733, (4) £8600, (5) (£28 400).

7–2 (a) £100 000; (b) four days; (c) £75 000, (£325 000); (e) £100 000, (£300 000).

7–3 (a) £160 000, £200 000, £40 000; (b) (£12 500); (c) £26 066; (d) £26 434.
7–4 (a) 4500 units; (b) 89 orders; (c) 26 000 units; (d) 6300, 40 per cent increase; (e) 40 per cent, 0.40; (f) −0.8; (g) −0.8.
8–1 (b) 14.69 per cent; (d) 24.49 per cent.
8–2 (a) £300 000.
8–3 (a) £134 400; (d) Effective annual interest charge, 19.5 per cent.
8–4 (b) £160 800, 15.12 per cent.
9–2 Ten years.
9–3 (a) £875.48; (b) £999.60.
9–4 £7477.51.
9–5 £59 237.81.
9–6 (b) £748.52; (c) £906.55.
9–7 (b) £56 369.98.
9–8 8 per cent.
9–9 8 per cent.
9–10 7 per cent.
9–11 15 per cent.
9–12 £1 180 000, £1 392 000, £1 643 000, £1 939 000, £2 288 000, £2 700 000.
9–13 (a) £5062, £5216.
9–14 (a) £1.18, £1.39, £1.64, £1.94, £2.29, £2.70; (b) £6.00; (c) £10; (d) £16.
9–15 (a) £100 020.
9–16 8.32 per cent.
9–17 (a) 8 per cent.
9–18 £73 998.
9–19 (a) 16 per cent.
10–1 (a) £800 000; (d) No. NPV = £(−22 200).
10–2 (a) Yes. NPV = £40 830; (b) (iii) NPV = £59 080.
10–3 (a) Yes. NPV = £2530; (b) NPV = £8907.
10–5 (b) A = 17.5 per cent, B = 15.5 per cent; e. 26 per cent.
10–6 Electric powered machine.
10–7 Machine H.
10A–1 (a) NPV^*_A = £5834.40, NPV^*_B = £6285.00, IRR_A = 19.9 per cent, IRR_B = 20.6 per cent; (c) 15.8 per cent.
11–1 (a) A £4500, B £5100; (b) A £6691.50, B £7750.20.
11–2 (a) Expected profit on mailings = £24 150, expected profit on advertising = £256 182; (c) 0.37.
11–4 (a) $E(F_A)$ = £28 000, σ_A = £6780, $CV_A = 0.242$; (b) $k_A = 8.42$ per cent; (c) NPV_A = £1804.
11–5 (a) 56; (b) 18 per cent.
11–7 (a) $E(k_M) = 0.10$, $\sigma_M = 0.2$, $E(k_1) = 0.20$, $\sigma_1 = 0.424$, $E(k_2) = 0.10$, $\sigma_2 = 0.349$, $Cov(k_1 k_M) = 0.080$, $Cov(k_2, k_M) = 0.024$, $Cov(k_1, k_2) = 0.004$; (b) w_1 = 40 per cent, w_2 = 60 per cent, $\sigma_p = 0.274$, $E(k_p) = 0.140$; (d) Project 1 is preferred.
11A–1 (b) £15 million; (c) £2.933 million; (d) 0.1955; (e) 36.7 per cent; (f) 24.8 per cent; (g) 38.5 per cent; (h) 24.8 per cent.
11A–2 (a) £6500; (b) (£2500).
11B–1 (a) NPV = £197; (b) $\sigma = 300$; (c) 25 per cent; (d) 75 per cent; (e) 50 per cent; (f) 1.13; (g) (i) 25 per cent, (ii) 0.00071 per cent.
11B–2 (a) NPV = £664; (b) $\sigma = 623$; (c) $P(NPV > 0)$ = 86 per cent; (d) (i) 14 per cent, (ii) 0.01 per cent.
11B–3 (a) 70 per cent; (b) 10 per cent; (c) 4 per cent; (d) 90 per cent; (e) 14 per cent.
11C–1 (a) NPV of abandonment value = £4696 exceeds NPV of expected savings of continued operation £4648.
11C–2 (a) NPV = £6716, $\sigma = 1420$; (b) NPV = £6762, $\sigma = 1359$; (c) Abandon.

11C–3 (a) *NPV* (sale after five years) = £2380, *NPV* (sale after ten years) = £3542, *NPV* (sale after 15 years) £1991; (d) £2097; (e) £1998.

11D–1 (a)

$E(k_p)$	σ_p
0.0900	0.0400
0.0925	0.0378
0.0950	0.0390
0.0975	0.0434
0.1000	0.0500

11D–2 (a) 28.12 per cent invested in i, 71.88 per cent in j; (d) Invest 55 per cent in i and 45 per cent in j; (e) 11.51 per cent.

11D–3 (a) 84.28 per cent invested in D, 15.72 per cent in C; (d) Invest 35 per cent in C and 65 per cent in D; (e) 7.78 per cent.

11F–1 *NPV* = £70 790 and project should be undertaken.

13–1 £0.90.

13–2 (a) £3.75.

13–3 (a) £3.

13–4 (a) £4.20.

13–5 (a) (i) 2 million; (ii) 1 million; (iii) 625 000; (b) (i) 0.5; (c) (ii) 46.5 pence; (d) (iii) £8.58.

13–6 (a) No; (b) No; (c) No; number required = 45 456; (d) 11.6 per cent; (e) 2.75 directors or 2 for sure.

15–1 (a) L_t = £9043; (b) No difference between owning and leasing.

15–2 (a) Before 1:1; After 2.5:1; (b) (£164 000).

16–1 (a) £0.20; (b) £2.80.

16–2 (a) A 5 per cent premium results in £5.04 conversion price.

16–3 (a) £0.09; (c) £0.80; (d) Total claims £500 000; (f) Total claims £687 500.

16–5 (a) 8.9 per cent.

16–6 (b) 6.8 per cent.

16–7 (a) £4.24 interest decrease; £2.12 interest increase.

16–8 (e) Year 3; (g) Approximately 11 per cent.

16A–1 (a) £1.39; (b) £1.76.

16A–2 (a) S = £6 824 500; (b) B = £3 175 500; (c) No.

16A–3 (a) S = £9 298 300; (b) B = £701 700; (c) No.

17–1 (a) £44.44; (b) £33.33; (d) (i) £80.56.

17–2 (a) 10 per cent; (b) 8 per cent; (c) 6.67 per cent.

17–3 (a) (i) £82.50.

17–4 (a) £112.50.

17–5 (a) £0.20; (d) 2.135.

17–6 (b) £5.30; (d) 10.7 per cent.

17–7 (c) (ii) 24 per cent; (d) $41.96, $150.

17–8 (a) (i) 6.8 per cent, (ii) 8 per cent; (b) (i) (1) 8.8 per cent, (2) 10 per cent, (ii) (1) 4.8 per cent, (2) 6 per cent; (d) (i) 4.2 per cent, (ii) £16.13.

17–11 (a) £1.805.

17–12 £4.24.

17–13 £31 million.

18–1 (b) Expected *EPS* = £0.31 (debt alternative); £0.29 (equity alternative).

18–2 (a) (i) 1.5; (ii) 2.18; (b) debt: (i) 12.3 pence; (ii) 3.9; equity: (i) 13.8 pence; (ii) 2.91.

18–3 (a) Sales (in £000)

	£0	£2100	£4200
EPS, debt:	−4.7 pence	25.3 pence	55.3 pence
EPS, equity:	−0.9 pence	20.6 pence	42.0 pence

(b) £941 500; (d) £2 370 670; (f) Debt: £2.02, equity = £2.06.

19–1 (a) £30 million; (b) £15 million; (c) £12 million externally; (d) $k_e = 12.4$ per cent, $k_r = 12$ per cent; (e) £6 million; (f) (i) 8.5 per cent, (ii) 8.7 per cent.

19–2 (a) £8 million, £16 million; (b) 9.47 per cent, 9.76 per cent, 10.33 per cent.

19–3 (a) (i) 4.8 per cent, (ii) 10 per cent, (iii) 12 per cent; (b) 10.10 per cent; (c) £400 000; (d) 12.44 per cent.

19–4 (a) 9.58 per cent; (b) 8.24 per cent, 9.20 per cent, 11.30 per cent.

19B–1 (a) £12 million, £16 million.

19B–2 (a) Non-geared 12 per cent, geared 14.4 per cent; (b) Non-geared 12 per cent, geared 9.6 per cent.

19B–3 (a) $V_A =$ £4.4 million, $V_B =$ £2 million (b) $V_A =$ £3.8 million, $V_B =$ £2 million; (c) $k = 5.26$ per cent for firm A, $k = 10$ per cent for firm B; (e) about 20 per cent debt.

19B–4 (a) 10 per cent; (b) 12.5 per cent.

19C–1 (a) 10 per cent; (b) 1 per cent; (c) 15 per cent; (d) 2.15 per cent; (e) 14.6 per cent; (f) 15 per cent; (g) 14.6 per cent.

19C–2 (a) 12 per cent; (b) 1.8 per cent; (c) 10 per cent; (d) 2.1 per cent; (e) 12.9 per cent; (f) 10 per cent; (g) 12.9 per cent.

19C–3 (a) $V_j = 56$; (b) 17.85 per cent.

19C–4 (a) 10 per cent; (b) 13.75 per cent; (c) No. The expected return of 15 per cent is *below* 17.5 per cent, the required rate of return.

19C–5 (a) $\bar{k}_M = 10$ per cent; $\sigma^2 = 0.023$; (b) $\beta_A = 1.87$, $k^*_A = 13.5$ per cent; $\beta_B = 0.78$, $k^*_B = 9.1$ per cent; (c) Percentage for Systematic A = 52 per cent, percentage for Systematic B = 8 per cent; (e) Price A declines, Price B rises.

19D–1 (b) $p_1 =$ £0.10, $p_2 =$ £0.20.

19D–2 Value is maximized at B = £3000.

19D–3 Production plan X.

19D–4 (a) B = £1400.

20–2 (a) 6.53 per cent (below), 6.82 per cent (above); (b) £33.6 million.

22–2 (a) 6.4 per cent; (c) (i) 9.73 per cent, (ii) 8.73 per cent; (g) 6 per cent.

22–4 (b) Horizontal £2.59, Vertical (£0.55); (c) Horizontal £5.04, Vertical £0.88.

25–1 (e) £2333, £7000, £11 667.

25–2 (b) Net after tax, 1972 = £81 000 or 4.5 per cent, 1975 = £222 000 or 6.4 per cent; (d) 1977 total assets = £2 245 000, cash available = £692 000; (e) 1977 current ratio = 1.54, $B/A = 38$ per cent, profit/net worth = 27 per cent; (g) Total sources, 1967–71 = £294 000; (h) £979 000; (i) £1.5 million with difference about £100 000.

Glossary

Abandonment Value The amount that can be realized by liquidating a project before its economic life has ended.

Accelerated Depreciation Depreciation methods that write off the cost of an asset at a faster rate than the write-off under the straight line method. The three principal methods of accelerated depreciation are: (1) sum-of-years'-digits, (2) double declining balance, and (3) units of production.

Accounting Standards Committee (ASC) A non-governmental body set up in the UK by the major accounting bodies to prepare statements of standard accounting practice.

Accruals Continually recurring short-term liabilities. Examples are accrued wages, accrued taxes, and accrued interest.

Acquisition The purchase of one company by another either for cash or other purchase consideration. Normally, in the case of an acquisition the shareholders of the acquiring company will have a dominant influence over the shareholders in the acquired company.

Ageing Schedule A report showing how long trade debtors have been outstanding. It gives the percentage of debtors not yet overdue and the percentage overdue by, for example, one month, two months, or other periods.

Amortize To liquidate on an instalment basis; an amortized loan is one in which the principal amount of the loan is repaid in instalments during the life of the loan.

Annuity A series of payments of a fixed amount for a specified number of years.

Arbitrage The process of selling overvalued and buying undervalued assets so as to bring about an equilibrium where all assets are properly valued. One who engages in arbitrage is called an arbitrager.

Associated Company A company in which an investing company owns between 20 and 50 per cent of the equity voting rights, or else participates in the associated company by way of a partnership or joint venture.

Bears Investors who sell shares in the anticipation that prices will fall in the near future. The term is also used to describe the state of the Stock Market itself when prices are falling.

Beta Coefficient Measures the extent to which the returns on a given security move with 'the stock market'.

Bill of Exchange An unconditional order in writing addressed by one person to another, signed by the person giving it, requiring the person to whom it is addressed to pay on demand, or at a fixed date in the future, a certain stated sum of money.

Book Value The accounting value of an asset. The book value of an ordinary share is equal to the net worth (ordinary share capital plus retained earnings) of the company divided by the number of shares outstanding.

Break-even Analysis An analytical technique for studying the relationship between fixed cost, variable cost and profits. A break-even *chart* graphically depicts the nature of break-even analysis. The break-even *point* represents the volume of sales at which total costs equal total revenues (that is, profits equal zero).

Bulls Investors who buy shares in anticipation that prices will rise in the near future and in order to realize a gain before payment for the securities is necessary. The term is also used to describe the state of the Stock Market itself when share prices are rising.

Business Risk The basic risk inherent in a firm's operations. Business risk plus financial risk resulting from the use of debt equals total corporate risk.

Call An option to buy (or 'call') a share at a specified price within a specified period.

Capital Allowances Statutory depreciation allowances granted against taxable profits. The rates given will differ according to the category of capital asset acquired. Currently plant and machinery acquisitions enable a business to claim a 100 per cent first year allowance.

Capital Asset An asset with a life of more than one year that is not bought and sold in the ordinary course of business.

Capital Budgeting The process of planning expenditures on assets whose returns are expected to extend beyond one year.

Capital Gains Profits on the sale of capital assets held for one year or more.

Capital Losses Losses on the sale of capital assets.

Capital Market Line A graphical representation of the relationship between risk and the required rate of return on an efficient portfolio.

Capital Markets Financial transactions involving instruments with maturities greater than one year.

Capital Rationing A situation where a constraint is placed on the total size of the capital investment during a particular period.

Capital Structure The permanent long-term financing of the firm represented by long-term debt, preference shares and net worth (net worth consists of capital, capital surplus and retained earnings). Capital structure is distinguished from *financial structure*, which includes short-term debt plus all reserve accounts.

Capitalization Rate A discount rate used to find the present value of a series of future cash receipts; sometimes called *discount rate*.

Carry-back; Carry-forwards For tax purposes losses that can be carried backwards or forwards to reduce business taxes.

Cash Budget A schedule showing cash flows (receipts, disbursements and net cash) for a firm over a specified period.

Cash Cycle (or Operating Cycle) The length of time between the purchase of raw materials and the collection of trade debtors generated in the sale of the final product.

Certainty Equivalents The amount of cash (or rate of return) that someone would require *with certainty* to make him indifferent between this certain sum (or *rate of return*) and a particular uncertain, risky sum (or rate of return).

Characteristic Line A linear least-squares regression line that shows the relationship between an individual security's return and returns on 'the market'. The slope of the characteristic line is the beta coefficient.

Coefficient of Variation Standard deviation divided by the mean: CV.

Collateral Assets that are used to secure a loan.

Commitment Fee The fee paid to a lender for a formal line of credit.

Composite Cost of Capital A weighted average of the component costs of debt, preference shares and ordinary shares. Also called the 'weighted average cost of capital', but it reflects the cost of each additional pound raised, not the average cost of all capital the firm has raised throughout its history (k).

Compound Interest An interest rate that is applicable when interest in succeeding periods is earned not only on the initial principal but also on the accumulated interest of prior periods. Compound interest is contrasted to *simple interest*, in which returns are not earned on interest received.

Compounding The arithmetic process of determining the final value of a payment or series of payments when compound interest is applied.

Continuous Compounding (Discounting) As opposed to discrete compounding, interest is added continuously rather than at discrete points in time.

Conversion Price The effective price paid for ordinary shares when they are obtained by converting either convertible preference shares or convertible debentures. For example, if a £100 debenture is convertible into 20 ordinary shares, the conversion price is £5 (£100/20).

Conversion Ratio or Conversion Rate The number of ordinary shares that may be obtained by converting a convertible debenture or a convertible preference share.

Convertibles Securities (generally debentures or preference shares) that are exchangeable at the option of the holder for ordinary shares of the issuing company.

Correlation Coefficient Measures the degree of relationship between two variables.

Cost of Capital The discount rate that should be used in the capital budgeting process.

Coupon Rate The stated rate of interest on a bond or debenture.

Covariance The correlation between two variables multiplied by the standard deviation of each variable: $\text{Cov} = r_{xy}\sigma_x\sigma_y$.

Covenant Detailed clauses contained in loan agreements. Covenants are designed to protect the lender and include such items as limits on total indebtedness, restrictions on dividends, minimum current ratio and similar provisions.

Cumulative Dividends A protective feature on preference shares that requires all past dividends on preference shares to be paid before any ordinary dividends are paid.

Current Purchasing Power (CPP) Accounting A proposal for adjusting the values of non-monetary items in financial statements to reflect changes in the general purchasing power of money. Adjustment would be made using a general price index.

Cut-off Point In the capital budgeting process, the minimum rate of return on acceptable investment opportunities.

Debenture A long-term debt instrument.

Debt Ratio Total debt divided by total assets.

Decision Tree A device for setting forth graphically the pattern of relationship between decisions and chance events.

Default The failure to fulfil a contract. Generally, default refers to the failure to pay interest or principal on debt obligations.

Degree of Gearing The percentage increase in profits resulting from a given percentage increase in sales. The degree of gearing may be calculated for financial gearing, operating gearing, or both combined.

Devaluation The process of reducing the value of a country's currency stated in terms of other currencies; e.g. the pound might be devalued from $2.30 for £1 to $2.00 for £1.

Discount Rate The interest rate used in the discounting process; sometimes called *capitalization rate*.

Discounted Cash Flow Techniques Methods of ranking investment proposals. Included are (1) internal rate of return method, (2) net present value method, and (3) profitability index or benefit/cost ratio.

Discounting The process of finding the present value of a series of future cash flows. Discounting is the reverse of compounding.

Dividend Yield The ratio of the current dividend to the current price of a share.

Du Pont System A system of analysis designed to show the relationship between return on investment, asset turnover and the profit margin.

EBIT Acronym for 'earnings before interest and taxes'.

Economical Ordering Quantity (EOQ) The optimum (least cost) quantity of merchandise which should be ordered.

EPS Acronym for 'earnings per share'.

Equity The net worth of a business, consisting of share capital, share premiums, retained earnings and, occasionally, certain specific reserves. Ordinary *equity* is that part of the total net worth belonging to the ordinary shareholders. *Total equity* would include preference shareholders.

Exchange Rate The rate at which one currency can be exchanged for another; e.g. $2.30 can be exchanged for £1.

Ex Dividend Date The date on which the right to the current dividend no longer accompanies a share. (For listed shares the ex dividend date is four working days prior to the date of record.)

Exercise Price The price that must be paid for a share when it is bought by exercising a warrant.

Expected Return The rate of return a firm expects to realize from an investment. The expected return is the mean value of the probability distribution of possible returns.

Ex Rights The date on which share purchase rights are no longer transferred to the purchaser of the shares.

Extension An informal method of reorganization in which the creditors voluntarily postpone the date of required payment on overdue obligations.

External Funds Funds acquired through borrowing or by selling new ordinary shares.

Factoring A method of financing trade debtors under which a firm sells its trade debtors (generally without recouse) to a financial institution (the 'factor').

Financial Gearing The ratio of total debt to total assets. There are other measures of financial gearing, especially ones that relate cash inflows to required cash outflows. In this book, the debt/total asset ratio is generally used to measure gearing.

Financial Intermediation Financial transactions which bring savings surplus units together with savings deficit units so that savings can be redistributed into their most productive uses.

Financial Lease A lease that does not provide for maintenance services, is not cancellable, and is fully amortized over the life of the lease.

Financial Markets Transactions in which the creation and transfer of financial assets and financial liabilities take place.

Financial Risk That portion of total corporate risk, over and above basic business risk, that results from using debt.

Financial Structure The entire left-hand side of the balance sheet – the way in which a firm is financed.

Fisher Effect The increase in the nominal interest rates over real (purchasing power adjusted) interest rates reflecting anticipated inflation.

Fixed Charges Cost that do not vary with the level of out put, especially fixed financial costs such as interest, lease payments and sinking fund payments.

Float The amount of funds tied up in cheques that have been written but are still in process and have not yet been collected.

Floating Exchange Rates Exchange rates may be fixed by government policy ('pegged') or allowed to 'float' up or down in accordance with supply and demand. When market forces are allowed to function, exchange rates are said to be floating.

Flotation Cost The cost of issuing new shares or debentures.

Funded Debt Long-term debt.

Funding The process of replacing short-term debt with long-term securities (shares or debentures).

Gearing Factor The ratio of debt to total assets.

Goodwill Intangible assets of a firm established by the excess of the price paid for the going concern over its book value.

Hire Purchase Sales Contract A method of financing new equipment by paying it off in instalments over a one-to-five-year period. The seller retains title to the equipment until payment has been completed.

Holding Company A company operated for the purpose of owning the ordinary shares of other companies.

Hurdle Rate In capital budgeting, the minimum acceptable rate of return on a project; if the expected rate of return is below the hurdle rate, the project is not accepted. The hurdle rate should be the marginal cost of capital.

Improper Accumulation Earnings retained by a business for the purpose of enabling shareholders to avoid personal income taxes.

Incremental Cash Flow Net cash flow attributable to an investment project.

Incremental Cost of Capital The average cost of the increment of capital raised during a given year.

Insolvency The inability to meet maturing debt obligations.

Interest Factor (IF) Numbers found in compound interest and annuity tables.

Internal Financing Funds made available for capital budgeting and working capital expansion through the normal operations of the firm; internal financing is approximately equal to retained earnings plus depreciation.

Internal Rate of Return (IRR) The rate of return on an asset investment. The internal rate of return is calculated by finding the discount rate that equates the present value of future cash flows to the cost of the investment.

Intrinsic Value That value which, in the mind of the analyst, is justified by the facts. It is often used to distinguish between the 'true value' of an asset (the intrinsic value) and the asset's current market price.

Invoice Discounting A term used in connection with financing of trade debtors. A firm sells its trade debtors to a financial institution under a recourse agreement; then if the debtors default, the selling firm must make good the loss.

Issuing House Underwrites and distributes new investment securities.

Lien A lender's claim on assets that are pledged for a loan.

Line of Credit An arrangement whereby a financial institute (bank or insurance company) commits itself to lend up to a specified maximum amount of funds during a specified period. Sometimes the interest rate on the loan is specified; at other times, it is not. Sometimes a commitment fee is imposed for obtaining the line of credit.

Liquidation A legal procedure for formally winding up a company. The winding-up may be voluntary, or made by the court, or subject to the supervision of the court.

Liquidity Refers to a firm's cash position and its ability to meet maturing obligations.

Listed Securities Securities traded on an organized security exchange.

Margin – Profit on Sales The *profit margin* is the percentage of profit after tax to sales.

Marginal Cost The cost of an additional unit. The marginal cost of capital is the cost of an additional unit of new funds.

Marginal Efficiency of Capital A schedule showing the internal rate of return on investment opportunities.

Marginal Revenue The additional gross revenue produced by selling one additional unit of output.

Merger Any combination that forms one company from two or more previously existing companies, in which the substance of the new business and its shareholders are substantially the same as in the previously existing companies.

Minimum Lending Rate The rate of interest at which the Bank of England is willing to lend as the lender of last resort to the discount houses.

Money Market Financial markets in which funds are borrowed or lent for short periods (i.e., less than one year). The money market is distinguished from the capital market, which is the market for long-term funds.

Mortgage A pledge of designated property as security for a loan.

Mortgage Debenture A long-term debt instrument secured by a mortgage on specific property.

Net Present Value (NPV) Method A method of ranking investment proposals. The NPV is equal to the present value of future returns, discounted at the marginal cost of capital, minus the present value of the cost of the investment.

Nominal Interest Rate The contracted or stated interest rate, undeflated for price level changes.

Normal Probability Distribution A symmetrical, bell-shaped probability function.

Objective Probability Distributions Probability distributions determined by statistical procedures.

Operating Gearing The extent to which fixed costs are used in a firm's operation. Break-even analysis is used to measure the extent to which operating gearing is employed.

Operating Income Income from the normal operations of a firm. Operating income specifically excludes income from the sale of capital assets.

Opportunity Cost The rate of return on the best *alternative* investment that is available. It is the highest return that will *not* be earned if the funds are invested in a particular project. For example, the opportunity cost of *not* investing in bond A yielding 8 per cent might be 7.99 per cent, which could be earned on bond B.

Options Contracts that give their holder the right to buy (or sell) an asset at a predetermined time for a given period of time.

Organized Security Exchanges Formal organizations having tangible, physical locations. Organized exchanges conduct an auction market in designated ('listed') investment securities. For example, the London Stock Exchange is an organized exchange.

Overdraft System A system where a depositor may write cheques in excess of his balance, with his bank automatically extending a loan to cover the shortage.

Par Value The nominal or face value of a debenture or government stock.

Payback Period The length of time required for the net revenues of an investment to return the cost of the investment.

Payout Ratio The percentage of earnings paid out in the form of dividends.

Perpetuity A stream of equal future payments expected to continue for ever.

Pooling of Interest An accounting method of combining the financial statements of firms that merge. Under the pooling-of-interest procedure, the assets of the merged firms are simply added to form the balance sheet of the surviving corporation. This method is different from the 'purchase' method, where goodwill is put on the balance sheet to reflect a premium (or discount) paid in excess of book value.

Portfolio Effect The extent to which the variation in returns on a combination of assets (a 'portfolio') is less than the sum of the variations of the individual assets.

Portfolio Theory Deals with the selection of optimal portfolios; i.e., portfolios that provide the highest possible return for any specified degree of risk.

Pre-emptive Right A provision that gives holders of ordinary shares the right to purchase on a pro rata basis new issues of ordinary shares.

Preference Shares Securities that have lower priority in claims on assets and income than debentures but a prior claim over ordinary shares. Preference dividends are not tax-deductible in the same way as interest paid to debenture-holders.

Present Value (PV) The value today of a future payment, or stream of payments, discounted at the appropriate discount rate.

Price/Earnings Ratio (P/E) The ratio of price to earnings. Faster growing or less risky firms typically have higher P/E ratios than either slower growing or riskier firms.

Pro Forma A projection. A *pro forma* financial statement is one that shows how the actual statement will look if certain specified assumptions are realized. *Pro forma* statements may be either future or past projections. An example of a backward *pro forma* statement occurs when two firms are planning to merge and shows what their consolidated financial statements would have looked like if they had been merged in preceding years.

Profit Centre A unit of a large, decentralized firm that has its own investments and for which a rate of return on investment can be calculated.

Profit Margin The ratio of profits after taxes to sales. Other definitions include the ratio of profit before taxes to sales.

Profitability Index (PI) The present value of future returns divided by the present value of the investment outlay.

Progressive Tax A tax that requires a higher percentage payment on higher incomes. The personal income tax in the United Kingdom, which is at a rate of 25 per cent on the lowest increments of income to 83 per cent on the highest increments, is progressive.

Prospectus A document issued for the purpose of describing a new security issue. The Stock Exchange Council examines prospectuses to insure that statements contained therein are not 'false and misleading'.

Proxy A document giving one person the authority or power to act for another. Typically, the authority in question is the power at the annual general meetings of companies.

Pure (or Primitive) Security A security that pays off £1 if one particular state of the world occurs and pays off nothing if any other state of the world occurs.

Put An option to sell a specific security at a specified price within a designated period.

Rate of Return The internal rate of return on an investment.

Reconstruction When a financially troubled firm goes through reconstruction its assets are restated to reflect their current market value, and its financial structure is restated to reflect any changes on the asset side of the statement. Under a reconstruction the firm continues in existence; this is contrasted to liquidation, where the firm is wound-up and ceases to exist.

Refunding Sale of new debt securities to replace an old debt issue.

Regression Analysis A statistical procedure for predicting the value of one variable (dependent variable) on the basis of knowledge about one or more other variables (independent variables).

Reinvestment Rate The rate of return at which cash flows from an investment are reinvested. The reinvestment rate may or may not be constant from year to year.

Replacement Cost Accounting This is the name given to a family of techniques which records the effect of specific price changes on costs and revenues. Profit on a transaction is defined as the difference between the selling price of an article and the cost of replacing the article at the date of sale.

Required Rate of Return The rate of return that shareholders expect to receive on ordinary share investments.

Residual Value The value of leased property at the end of the lease term.

Retained Earnings (or Reserves) That portion of earnings not paid out in dividends. The figure that appears on the balance sheet is the sum of the retained earnings for each year throughout the company's history.

Right A short-term option to buy a specified number of shares of a new issue of securities at a designated 'subscription' price.

Rights Issue A share issue offered to existing shareholders only.

Risk The probability that actual future returns will be below expected returns. Measured by standard deviation or coefficient of variation of expected returns.

Risk-adjusted Discount Rates The discount rate applicable for a particular risky (uncertain) stream of income: the riskless rate of interest plus a risk premium appropriate to the level of risk attached to the particular income stream.

Risk Premium The difference between the required rate of return on a particular risky asset and the rate of return on a riskless asset with the same expected life.

Risk-return Tradeoff Function (see *Security Market Line*).

Sale and Leaseback An operation whereby a firm sells land, buildings or equipment to a financial institution and simultaneously executes an agreement to lease the property back for a specified period under specific terms.

Salvage Value The value of a capital asset at the end of a specified period. It is the current market price of an asset being considered for replacement in a capital budgeting problem.

Scrip Issue An accounting action to increase the number of shares outstanding; for example, in a 3-for-1 issue, shares outstanding would be tripled and each shareholder would receive three new shares for each one formerly held. Scrip issues involve no transfer from reserves to ordinary share capital.

Securities, Junior Securities that have lower priority in claims on assets and income than other securities (*senior securities*). For example, preference shares are junior to debentures, but debentures are junior to mortgage bonds. Ordinary shares are the most junior of all corporate securities.

Securities, Senior Securities having claims on income and assets that rank higher than certain other securities (*junior securities*). For example, mortgage bonds are senior to debentures, but debentures are senior to ordinary shares.

Security Market Line A graphic representation of the relation between the required return on a security and the product of its risk times a normalized market measure of risk. Risk-return relationships for individual securities or investments.

Sensitivity Analysis Simulation analysis in which key variables are changed and the resulting change in the rate of return is observed. Typically, the rate of return will be more sensitive to changes in some variables than it will in others.

Service Lease A lease under which the lessor maintains and services the asset.

Short Selling Selling a security that is not owned by the seller at the time of the sale. The seller borrows the security from a brokerage firm and must at some point repay the brokerage firm by buying the security on the open market.

Simulation A technique whereby probable future events are simulated on a computer. Estimated rates of return and risk indexes can be generated.

Sinking Fund A required annual payment designed to amortize a debenture or a preference share issue. The sinking fund may be held in the form of cash or marketable securities, but more generally the money put into the sinking fund is used to retire each year some of the securities in question.

Standard Deviation A statistical term that measures the variability of a set of observations from the mean of the distribution (σ).

State Preference Model A framework in which decisions are based on probabilities of payoffs under alternative states of the world.

Statements of Standard Accounting Practice (SSAP) Methods of accounting approved by the major accounting bodies in the UK for application to all financial accounts. These statements do not possess the force of law.

Stock Dividend A dividend paid in additional shares rather than in cash. It involves a transfer from retained earnings to the capital account; therefore, stock dividends are limited by the amount of retained earnings.

Subjective Probability Distributions Probability distributions determined through subjective procedures without the use of statistics.

Subordinated Debenture A debenture having a claim on assets only after the senior debt has been paid off in the event of liquidation.

Subscription Price The price at which a security may be purchased in a rights offering.

Synergy A situation where 'the whole is greater than the sum of its parts'; in a synergistic merger, the post-merger earnings exceed the sum of the separate companies' pre-merger earnings.

Systematic Risk That part of a security's risk that cannot be eliminated by diversification.

Tangible Assets Physical assets as opposed to intangible assets such as goodwill and the stated value of patents.

Term Loan A loan generally obtained from a loan or an insurance company with a maturity greater than one year. Term loans are generally amortized.

Trade Credit Inter-firm debt arising through credit sales and recorded as trade creditors by the buyer and as trade debtors by the seller.

Trustee The representative of debenture-holders who acts in their interest and facilitates communication between them and the issuer. Typically these duties are handled by a department of a commercial bank.

Trustee Securities A list of securities in which mutual savings banks, pension funds, insurance companies and other fiduciary institutions are permitted to invest.

Underwriting The insurance function of bearing the risk of adverse price fluctuations during the period in which a new issue of shares is being distributed.

Underwriting Syndicate A syndicate of investment firms formed to spread the risk associated with the purchase and distribution of a new issue of securities. The larger the issue, the more firms typically are involved in the syndicate.

Unlisted Securities Securities that are not traded in the Stock Exchange.

Unsecured Debenture A long-term debt instrument that is not secured by a mortgage on specific property.

Unsystematic Risk That part of a security's risk associated with random events; unsystematic risk can be eliminated by proper diversification.

Utility Theory A body of theory dealing with the relationships among money income, utility (or 'happiness'), and the willingness to accept risks.

Value Additivity Principle Neither fragmenting cash flows or recombining them will affect the resulting values of the cash flows.

Warrant A long-term option to buy a stated number of ordinary shares at a specified price. The specified price is generally called the 'exercise price'.

Weighted Cost of Capital A weighted average of the component costs of debt, preference shares and ordinary equity. Also called the 'composite cost of capital'.

Working Capital Refers to a firm's investment in short-term assets – cash, short-term securities, trade debtors and stocks. *Gross working capital* is defined as a firm's total current assets. *Net working capital* is defined as current assets minus current liabilities. If the term 'working capital' is used without further qualification, it generally refers to gross working capital.

Yield The rate of return on an investment; the internal rate of return.

Index

Note: The page numbers of Figures and Tables are italicized